SYMPTOMS OF PSYCHOPATHOLOGY: A HANDBOOK

Keith was here.

Symptoms of PSYCHOPATHOLOGY

A Handbook

Edited by

CHARLES G. COSTELLO

Professor of Psychology
University of Calgary

JOHN WILEY & SONS, INC.

New York · London · Sydney · Toronto

10 9 8 7 6

Library of Congress Catalogue Card Number: 78–88309

SBN 471 17520 X

Photoset in Malta by St Paul's Press Ltd
Printed in the United States of America

Contributors

IHSAN AL-ISSA
Assistant Professor of Psychology
University of Calgary

G. P. BELTON
Instructor in Psychology
Medicine Hat Junior College

RALPH J. BERGER
Associate Professor of Psychology
Crown College
University of California

LANE K. CONN
Assistant Professor of Clinical Psychology
Department of Social Relations
Harvard University

M. A. COOTE
Director
Ramsey-Coote Instruments
Victoria, Australia

C. G. COSTELLO
Professor of Psychology
University of Calgary

A. H. CRISP
Professor of Psychiatry
St. George's Hospital Medical School
London

DONALD J. DALESSIO
Head
Division of Neurology
Scripps Clinic and Research Foundation

P. O. DAVIDSON
Associate Professor of Psychology
University of Calgary

J. A. EASTERBROOK
Professor and Head
Department of Psychology
University of New Brunswick

DAVID R. EVANS
Assistant Professor of Educational Psychology
University of Calgary

CYRIL M. FRANKS
Director
Psychology Service and Research Center
New Jersey Neuro-Psychiatric Institute

JAMES INGLIS
Professor of Psychology
Queen's University

BASIL JAMES
Senior Lecturer in Psychological Medicine
University of Otago

H. GWYNNE JONES
Professor of Psychology
University of Leeds

ANTHONY KALES
Director
UCLA Sleep Research and Treatment Facility
Associate Professor of Psychiatry
UCLA Medical Center

S. H. LOVIBOND
Professor of Applied Psychology
University of New South Wales

BARCLAY MARTIN
Professor of Psychology
University of Wisconsin

MARCIA D. MATHER
Senior Clinical Psychologist
Warley Hospital, Essex

JAMES N. McCLURE, JR.
Assistant Professor of Psychiatry
Director
Psychiatry Division
Student Health Service
Washington University

IVAN N. MENSH
Professor and Head
Division of Medical Psychology
School of Medicine
University of California

V. MEYER
Reader
Academic Department of Psychiatry
Middlesex Hospital, London

WILLIAM R. MORROW
Professor of Social Work
University of Missouri-Columbia

R. W. PAYNE
Chairman
Department of Behavioral Science
School of Medicine
Temple University

KENNETH PURCELL
Professor of Psychology and Chairman
Department of Psychology
University of Massachusetts

ROBERT L. SPRAGUE
Director of Research
Children's Research Center
Associate Professor of Psychology
University of Illinois

L. ALAN SROUFE
Assistant Professor of Child Psychology
Institute of Child Development
University of Minnesota

ERVIN STAUB
Assistant Professor of Clinical Psychology
Department of Social Relations
Harvard University

JOHN A. STERN
Professor of Psychology
Washington University

T. WECKOWICZ
Associate Professor of Psychiatry
University of Alberta

JONATHAN H. WEISS
Director
Behavior Science Division
Children's Asthma Research Institute and Hospital
Assistant Clinical Professor of Psychology
School of Medicine
University of Colorado

JOHN S. WERRY
Director
Institute for Juvenile Research
Associate Professor of Psychiatry
University of Illinois

AUBREY J. YATES
Professor of Psychology
University of Western Australia

Preface

Although this book is written by many people, it has one basic *raison d'être*: before we try to classify the symptoms of psychopathology and to establish syndromes, we must know much more about the symptoms themselves. This thesis is developed in Chapter 1.

Occasionally, it was not possible to escape completely the habitual tendency of both researchers and clinicians to classify. Most of the work on depression, for instance, was done within a classification system—particularly that of endogenous-versus-reactive depression. This work has been reviewed despite the doubts cast in Chapter 1 on the validity of such a distinction between the types of depressive illness. Depression is too serious a matter for authors to adhere rigidly to a single strategy. Furthermore, regardless of the status of the classifications of depressive conditions (since all of the patients studied were presumably depressed), the findings may possibly help us to understand depression as such—in other words, as a symptom.

Originally, chapters on autism, delusions, hallucinations, suicide, frigidity and impotence, eating problems, hypertension, skin disorders, loss of affect, and ulcers were planned but, for a variety of reasons, had to be omitted. It is hoped that, despite these exclusions, the final volume will meet its announced goal.

Now let me thank all of the people who helped in producing this book: the late Gordon Ierardi, of Wiley, who first discussed the content with me, Roger Holloway, Dorothy Baron, Deborah Herbert, of Wiley, and Brendan Maher, Wiley's consultant, who skillfully guided me through the labors of my first edited book. I am also grateful to the contributors, the secretarial staff of the Department of Psychology at the University of Calgary and, in particular, Mrs. Vi Biden. Finally, I must thank my wife Violet, who helped with the secretarial chores and accepted the burdens of a housewife and mother while I pursued (unfairly, it must be admitted) the more intellectually stimulating life of a psychologist.

Charles G. Costello

Calgary, Alberta, 1969

Contents

PART III

DISORDERS OF BEHAVIOR 261

PART IV

PSYCHOSOMATIC DISORDERS 595

SYMPTOMS OF PSYCHOPATHOLOGY: A HANDBOOK

Chapter 1

Classification and Psychopathology

C. G. COSTELLO

INTRODUCTION

We may agree that classification of the symptoms of psychopathology is required before much progress can be made with regard to the aetiology of psychopathologies of varying kinds. It is at least equally important, however, that the symptoms be defined and measured as precisely as possible before attempts are made to classify them. The establishment of syndromes of psychopathology is not likely to come from the too hasty attempts at classifying ill-defined symptoms. To attempt to classify, for instance, ill-defined symptoms such as "anxiety," "depression," "hostility," and "guilt feelings," does not appear to be a very promising pursuit. There is probably little disagreement about the poor definition of these symptoms, and we have evidence like that of Cattell (1957) who has reported a correlation of only 0.25 between experienced psychiatrists rating the symptom "anxiety" in 80 psychiatric patients.

The careful investigation of the symptoms themselves, especially when part of that investigation involves the experimental study of the covariation of the symptoms, would appear to be a far more promising approach than symptom classification at the present stage of the science of psychopathology.

The aim of this chapter is to justify the symptomatic approach that is taken in the rest of the book. This justification will be based on an attempted demonstration of the inadequacy of typical systems of classification. We emphasize that no arguments are presented against the *eventual* necessity of classification in psychopathology. The only argument presented is that *present* classification systems are inadequate, primarily because they are *premature*.

The first classification system considered is the traditional psychiatric classification system. It is not discussed in detail since this has been done many times before. Instead the main conclusions and observations that we can make as a result of previous reviews will be presented.

PSYCHIATRIC CLASSIFICATION

The psychiatric classification system appears to be inadequate because of the following reasons.

1. The classes have been formed by majority vote of psychiatric professional associations rather than by scientific investigation (Cameron, 1944).

2. Measures of agreement between diagnoses made independently by different psychiatrists are generally found to be very low [see, for example, reviews by Eysenck (1952), Kreitman (1961), and Zubin (1967)]. Zubin's review indicates that in the case of the kinds of functional psychosis the agreement may be as low as 26 percent; for the kinds of psychoneurosis as low as 60 percent; and for the kinds of characterological disorders, 8 percent. The agreement in relation to *broad* diagnostic categories such as organic, functional, etc., is higher

ranging from 46 to 84 percent. Such categories, however, are rarely of much theoretical or pragmatic value.

3. Psychiatric diagnoses do not show consistency over time (Kaelbling & Volpe, 1963). Zubin (1967) has indicated some consistency over time for organic psychosis. However, although it may be as high as 92 percent, as in epileptic psychosis, it may be as low as 29 percent, as in cerebrovascular psychosis. Consistency of diagnosis of the functional psychoses may go as low as 10 percent, as with involutional psychosis. For subcategories of psychoneurosis, it may drop to 0 percent, as with situational depression. For subcategories of characterological disorders it drops as low as 10 percent, as in the case of personality pattern disturbance.

Even when we consider broad diagnostic categories, we find that consistency figures are low. For organic psychosis the figure may be as low as 53 percent, for schizophrenia 37 percent, for psychoneurosis 24 percent, and for personality and characterological disorders 46 percent.

4. The distribution of diagnoses in samples drawn from the same population differ significantly. This significant difference in distribution may occur across different wards or different ward administrators in the same hospital—Zubin (1967), Pasamanick, Dinitz, and Lefton (1959), and Jenkins, Bemiss and Lorr (1953).

5. Considerable overlap of symptoms exists among the various diagnostic groups. Zigler and Phillips (1961) concluded on the basis of their review that "... membership in a particular diagnostic group conveys only minimal information about the symptomatology of the patient." Similar observations have been made by Freudenberg and Robertson (1956).

6. There is no good evidence for the concurrent validity of psychiatric diagnosis. This validity, of course, is assessed by matching the results of techniques such as the MMPI against clinical diagnosis (Zubin, 1967).

7. Diagnostic classification, to be of value, should indicate the best form of treatment that is to be used. There does not seem to be a consistent relationship between diagnosis and treatment. Kreitman and his colleagues (1961) found that the degree of agreement between two psychiatrists on the choice of therapy for functional psychosis was 77 percent, which may be considered as being fairly satisfactory. But for neurosis it was 54 percent, for organics 51 percent, and for other diagnoses 33 percent. Similar findings are reported by Bannister, Salmon, and Leiberman (1964).

8. Syndromes are ill-defined. Lorr, Klett and McNair (1963) have indicated that "The number of symptoms or other criteria required before a patient is properly allocated to a class is left unspecified. The weight to be assigned individual criteria for membership in a class or the method of combination is left to the clinician's judgment."

9. In some cases, despite the apparent use of many symptoms by diagnosticians, one or two particular symptoms may actually be used. Zubin (1967) reports a study by Katz in which the experimenter asked a group of diagnosticians to view the same video tape of an interview to indicate the presence of psychopathology on behavioral items and to make a diagnosis. Of the group of 35 diagnosticians, 21 labeled the patient psychotic and 14 labeled him neurotic. The patient's profiles from all 35 diagnosticians were quite alike, but the ones who perceived much apathy in the patient diagnosed the patient psychotic, and the ones who did not perceive the apathy diagnosed him as neurotic.

A continuation of reliance on psychiatric diagnostic categories of the traditional kind would appear to be quite unwarranted and might be a disservice to both the psychiatric discipline and the psychiatric patient. It seems unlikely that the improved training of psychiatrists in relation to the classification of symptoms will help matters very much. Ward and his colleagues (1962), by investigating the sources of disagreement in diagnosis, found that the inadequacy of the nosological system contributed far more (62.5 percent) to the disagreement than did the inconstant behavior of the psychiatrists (32.5 percent).

Because of the inadequacy of the traditional psychiatric classification system, a number of investigators have attempted to develop new systems by using multivariate statistical procedures as their tools. In the remainder of this chapter, we review some of these attempts. We suggest that, although the research in this area has been statistically sophisticated and potentially of great value, the data subjected to the statistical analyses have, for one reason or another, been inadequate. We deal first with Eysenck's system (1947, 1952, and 1961).

PSYCHOTICISM, NEUROTICISM AND EXTRAVERSION

Three assumptions underlie Eysenck's work in this area. They are assumptions that would probably be accepted by most of the present investigators who advocate the use of multivariate statistical procedures in the development of classification systems in psychopathology. These assumptions are:

1. The notion of *disease* is not a useful one in the field of functional psychiatric illnesses. Eysenck (1961) differentiates between the medical part of psychiatry, "... dealing with the effects of tumors, lesions, infections and physical conditions ..." and "the behavioural part dealing with disorders of behaviour acquired through the ordinary processes of learning." He suggests that "Most neurotic disorders will come under this heading, as well as possibly some or most of the schizophrenic and manic-depressive (functional) psychoses."
2. The major difference between the medical and the behavioral disorders lies in the absence in the latter of a single "cause," which is characteristic of the former.
3. Invariant conjunctions of symptoms in psychiatric illnesses is not to be expected. Relative conjunction is to be expected and should be investigated by the use of the probabilistic terms of modern statistical analysis.

As Eysenck points out, the present distinction between the medical part and the behavioral part of psychiatry probably is a result, to a certain extent, of the early stage of our knowledge concerning most, if not all, of the functional illnesses. Certainly many investigators, particularly biochemists, work in the hope of finding a *single primary cause* underlying many of the illnesses diagnosed as schizophrenic. The three assumptions are the kind that can lead to a semantic quarrel. They do not in themselves appear to lead to obviously correct or incorrect experimental work. Because of the early stage of our knowledge, a probabilistic approach to the data must be taken, whether or not the above assumptions in the end will be found to be correct. A further point should be made here. Probabilistic statistical theory may be used in connection with correlation coefficients. It may also be used in connection with predictions that are made, for instance, from factor scores. It cannot be used in connection with the procedures that are used in factor analysis itself, except for relatively minor aspects of this analysis, for example, the testing for the normality of a distribution of residual coefficients.[1]

Eysenck's aim has been to identify broad dimensions of personality that could accommodate the present traditional psychiatric diagnostic groups. By identifying broad dimensions of personality that encompass the psychiatric groupings, he has hoped that the placing of an individual in one of the traditional psychiatric groups can be replaced by assigning to the patient a reliable and valid set of scores that are based on the dimensions of personality. "*Continuity* is thus substituted for *discontinuity* and *measurement* for *discrete classification*." (Eysenck, 1961, p. 10).

Before we consider the dimensions themselves, we should say a word in general, at this point, about the discontinuity-continuity conflict that runs through much of the classification work that is being done. We wonder with Zubin (1967) if it is not a pseudoconflict dependent on the state of knowledge in the field of psychopathology. Certainly, no good evidence indicates that a classification system based on discontinuous groups is any better or any worse than classification systems based on continuous dimensions. Some investigators, for example, Lorr, Klett, and McNair (1963) have used continuous dimensions to provide scores that enable them to classify patients into discontinuous groups. Here, also, one can get involved in semantic

---

[1] I wish to express my thanks to E. S. Edgington who pointed out this distinction to me.

quarrels, and it is probably better to wait and to see what type of classification system will work best.

Eysenck (1961) has suggested that one of the main conclusions to which his evidence leads is that two independent factors in the psychiatric field are associated with the psychotic and the neurotic disorders, respectively. He has called these psychoticism (P-factor) and neuroticism (N-factor). He suggests further that the evidence indicates that both of these factors define continua that range all the way from extreme disorders to normality. There are no breaks or qualitative differences that would enable us to classify people into separate groups.

One of the first studies that identify a psychoticism factor and a neuroticism factor was the one by Trouton and Maxwell (1956). They used psychiatric ratings of patients in relation to 45 symptoms and traits. Unfortunately, data obtained by ratings do not have the degree of objectivity that one would desire, and the inter-rater agreement was not reported by Trouton and Maxwell. Even if there were a high degree of rater agreement, it might reflect nothing more, of course, than the fact that the raters agree with regard to preconceived notions concerning the symptoms that make up psychotic behavior and the symptoms that make up neurotic behavior. In other words, the result may reflect the preconceived notions of the raters more than it reflects the actual covariances that exist in the behavior of the patients themselves. This is a point that we shall come across a number of times in this chapter. Lorr, Klett, and McNair (1963) have also criticized the Trouton and Maxwell study on the grounds that the defining symptoms do not represent all the major diagnostic categories and, of course, in multivariate statistical procedures of this sort, the sampling of the symptoms to be analyzed is a major problem. They also note the fact that some symptoms are combined, for example, compulsive acts and/or obsessive thoughts. The reanalysis of the Trouton and Maxwell (1956) data by Lorr and O'Connor (1957) resulted in quite a different factorial solution.

Eysenck has admitted that the data analyzed in Trouton and Maxwell's (1956) study are not all that one would desire. In one of his own studies, Eysenck (1955) and a study by S. B. G. Eysenck (1956), the data analyzed were obtained from objective tests such as visual acuity and static ataxia. By using the method of canonical variate analysis, they both found that two dimensions were required to account for the differences in test performance between groups of normals, neurotics, and psychotics. They labeled the two dimensions, neuroticism and psychoticism. This research then supposedly demonstrates the existence of two independent factors, neuroticism and psychoticism.

Eysenck (1952) has used his method of criterion analysis in an attempt to demonstrate that the differences between normal and psychotic groups are *quantitative* rather than *qualitative*. In this experiment, 100 normal, 50 schizophrenic, and 50 manic-depressive subjects took part. A battery of objective tests were given to the subjects. Intercorrelation of the scores on the tests were calculated separately for the normal and the combined psychotic group. Factors were extracted from the two correlation matrices separately. A factor was found in the analysis of the matrix of correlations for the normal group, which Eysenck identified as psychoticism. A factor was found in the analysis of the matrix of correlations for the psychotic group, which was also identified as psychoticism. The factors obtained from the two groups correlated 0.871. Both sets of loadings (the set on the normal-group factor and the set on the psychotic-group factor) were proportional to a set of index values that denoted the adequacy of each test in separating the normal and psychotic group from each other. The column containing these index values, Eysenck called the "criterion column." The factor for the normal group correlated with the criterion column 0.899, and the one from the psychotic group correlated 0.954 with the criterion column.

There is no doubt that such extensions of the method of factor analysis are potentially valuable because the power of the method may be increased. Whether, in this instance, its use helps us with the problem of the continuity or discontinuity of the difference between normals and psychotics is another matter. It seems quite likely, for instance, that a number of tests of femininity could be found that would produce the same factor in both groups of men and of women, that these factors would be highly intercorrelated, and that they would also correlate highly with a set of index values that denote the adequacy of each test in separating the group of men from the group of women. Even if we were able to demonstrate this, it would do nothing to weaken the general observation that some of the important differences between men and women are of a discontinuous sort. Whether we would be interested in the continuous or discontinuous distinctions would depend on how we want to use the classification. An obstetrician is unlikely to have much use for continuous dimensions on which men and women can be placed.

Certainly, statistical procedures themselves cannot provide the answer to the question of continuity or discontinuity. The use of measures that give us continuous scores can be expected to result in continuous dimensions and there is no need to assume continuity of underlying processes from continuity of symptoms. We must also be cautious about conclusions that concern the number of dimensions required to account for differences between groups. We must ask if any two or, indeed, if any number of dimensions that are found in a particular study to account for the differences between two groups, necessarily, are related to the *important* differences between the two groups. It would not appear to be logically impossible that two groups differ essentially in relation to one important dimension, although they also differ in other less important ways in relation to other dimensions. How many dimensions we obtain will depend on what measurements we take, and the importance of the particular measurements taken cannot be decided by any statistical procedure alone.

Let us take, for instance, a group of men with a Ph.D. degree and a group of men with Grade 12 education. Probably the most important dimension that differentiates the two groups is the continuous one of intelligence. Other dimensions may be involved, but they will probably be closely related to one another and to intelligence, so that essentially we shall be dealing with one dimension. In other words, the dimensions are not independent. Now suppose that we obtain the following data from all the men.

1. Number of days absent from the office
2. Status in the company
3. Number of days absent due to illness
4. Distance of home from the office
5. Number of visits to the company's medical officer.

If we analyze this data, it is quite likely that we shall find that two clusters will form, one made up of variables 1, 2, and 4, and the other made up of variables 1, 3, and 5. In other words, to account for the differences between the two groups in relation to these particular measures, two dimensions are required. One that we could label "professional status" and the other that we could label "state of health." Of course, these two dimensions are not required and, indeed, would not be adequate to account for the *essential* difference between the members of the two groups.

We can argue that we have no reason to suspect that the kind of measures taken in the above two studies fall on unimportant rather than on important dimensions. This is true, of course, but it is also true that we just do not know whether the dimensions are important or not without doing further research. Once individuals have been labeled psychotic or neurotic, they can be expected to differ in many ways, and these differences may require more than one dimension. Once an individual has been labeled psychotic, he may receive different drugs, more physical forms of treatment, be kept in a mental hospital rather than attend an outpatient clinic, and so on. As a result, psychotics may differ very much from neurotics on measures such as those of perceptual and motor processes, but these differences may reflect more the attitude of society to individuals so labeled rather than the basic difference between psychosis and neurosis. Eysenck (1961) himself has argued that factor analytic studies usually provide data of only a *descriptive* sort and suggests that what is required is "a set of theories linking the major aspects of the descriptive system to *causal* theories." Eysenck's general personality theory will not be evaluated here. It can be stated, however, that there is no strong empirical evidence available to indicate that the classification system plus the theory has furthered our knowledge of the aetiology or prognosis of psychiatric illnesses.

A third dimension identified by Eysenck is the extraversion dimension, which is considered to be independent from the ones of psychoticism and neuroticism. Eysenck has presented evidence which, he suggests, indicates that the interaction between the extraversion and neuroticism factor is such that

> "A person who is high on neuroticism and high on extraversion will show a distinct tendency to be labelled 'hysteric' or 'psychopath' by an examining psychiatrist, while a person who is high on neuroticism and high on introversion will more likely be labelled 'anxiety state' or 'reactive depressive' " (Eysenck, 1961, p. 10).

The group of introverted neurotic symptoms was labeled dysthymia by Eysenck. A person high on neuroticism and intermediate with respect to extraversion-introversion is most likely, he suggested, to be labeled "mixed neurosis."

The dimension extraversion-introversion appears to be an important one in view of its constant appearance in the analysis of self-report and rating data (Peterson, 1965). But the evidence concerning its relationship with diagnostic categories is at best conflicting (Sigal, Star & Franks 1958; Crookes & Hutt, 1963; McGuire, Mowbray & Vallance, 1963). The fact that the relationship between scores on the extraversion dimension and diagnostic categories is not in line with Eysenck's original findings would not, of course, be too discomforting if scores on the extraversion dimension were shown to be related to such things as response to treatment. But there is no evidence to show that this is so.

A particular problem we face when trying to use scores on the neuroticism dimension, in relation to groupings of psychiatric illnesses, is the question of whether we are measuring a stable personality disposition or some changing state of the individual. Bartholomew and Marley (1959) and Knowles (1960) have reported high test-retest reliabilities for both the N and E scores within a neurotic sample but, without evidence that relates to change in clinical condition of the patients, we cannot properly evaluate the resistance of the scale scores to such change. We may also find a high test-retest correlation where the mean scores on test 2 are significantly different from those obtained on test 1. Wretmark, Åström, and Örlander (1961) found a significant decrease in the neuroticism scores on the Maudsley Personality Inventory following recovery in a group of patients who suffered from endogenous depression when retesting was done after two to six months. Similar findings are reported by Coppen and Metcalf (1965). Ingham (1966) also found that the degree of change in neuroticism and extraversion scores was related to degree of recovery from illness when followed up three years later. He concluded that

> "... variations in N and E means between neurotic and normal samples probably arise from causes associated with the occurrence of the neurotic illness itself. Such variations are unlikely to reflect stable personality differences related to predisposition to neurosis."

Levinson and Meyer (1965), in a study of the effects of leucotomy, found a patient's N score had changed most nine months after the operation for those who had improved most according to the psychiatric rating. Crookes and Hutt (1963), comparing the scores of manic-depressives-manic on the E and N scales with the scores of manic-depressives-depressed, concluded that the scores were measuring temporary conditions or symptoms rather than permanent personality characteristics.

There is also some controversy that concerns the independence of the neuroticism and extraversion dimensions. Although there is a fair amount of data indicating that within normal groups the two dimensions are not significantly correlated (for example, Farley 1967), within psychiatric patients, the intercorrelation can be quite high (Ingham, 1966; Levinson & Meyer, 1965; McGuire, Mowbray & Vallance, 1963; Sigal, Star & Franks, 1958; Jensen, 1958). The possibility that the two dimensions have different meanings within a normal group as compared with an abnormal group is also indicated by the findings of Franks, Holden, and Phillips (1961), which indicated that the relationship between self-report scores on each of the dimensions and ratings by others on the dimensions were significantly intercorrelated within a normal group, but that the intercorrelation of the self-report and rating scores was not significant within psychiatric groups.

Eysenck and Claridge (1962) have discussed this problem of the loss of independence of E and N scores when neurotic samples are being tested. They have suggested that this loss of independence may be the result of (1) the influence of response sets, (2) a genuine interaction between introversion and neuroticism, (3) a concentration on dysthymic symptoms in the construction of the N scale, and (4) the complex relationship between constitutional and behavioral differences between individuals. Thus, "... a *constitutional* extravert may turn out to be a behavioral introvert. . . ."

Another problem that casts doubt on the adequacy of the extraversion-introversion dimension in contributing to the most efficient classification of psychiatric illnesses concerns the question of the number of lower-order dimensions that underlie the present dimensions (Carrigan, 1960; Eysenck & Eysenck, 1963).

Eysenck's concern has been with broad dimensions that he hopes, will encompass groupings of psychiatric patients. Other workers have tried to delineate narrow dimensions. For instance, some investigators have attempted to delineate dimensions of psychotic illnesses instead of investigating a dimension of psychoticism as such. The next task is to review this work. We shall learn that the main criticism of the work to be reviewed in the next section is the lack of agreement between the various workers. Eysenck (1964) has noted that this is not true of his broad dimensions and refers to the work of Cattell and Vernon. It is indeed true that his dimensions do not appear to be open to this criticism. We have observed, however, that there are other problems with which his system has to contend.

SYNDROMES OF PSYCHOSIS

Table 1.1 presents some of the details of factor analytic studies of the symptoms of psychosis. Table 1.2 presents the factors that have been obtained in the 11 studies reviewed.

On the left side of Table 1.2 is listed the most common description of the factors that were obtained in these studies. Under each study an X is placed when a dimension in that study has been given the name indicated in the list of factors on the left of the table. When a dimension has been given a name that is not the *same* as the one under the main list of factors at the left of the table but that is very *similar*, the name of the similar dimension has been given. Table 1.2 gives then some idea of the degree of agreement between the studies in the identification of dimensions or syndromes of psychosis. We can observe that the number of dimensions any particular investigator presents, as accounting for variation among psychotics in their behavior, ranges from 4 to 21. Wittenborn (1963) identified 21 dimensions, or factors. Two of them "Manic" and "Excitement" have been brought together for the table, and two others have also been brought together, namely, "Compulsive behavior" and "Phobic reaction." Of course, it is well known that the number of dimensions, or factors, that can be obtained in factor analytic studies may indeed vary considerably. This variation depends on a number of differences in the procedures used. We do not intend to go into this matter at this time. Discussions of the matter would still leave us with the question of how many dimensions are required to best account for the differences in behavior of psychotic patients. What is best, of course, is at least to some degree that which leads to the greater prediction of individual patient's behavior in the future, including, for instance, the prediction of the effect of various kinds of treatment. It will also be noticed in Table 1.2 that not one of the factors has been obtained in all of the studies!

The procedures of the various investigations can be criticized on different grounds:

1. Lorr, Klett, and McNair (1963), for instance, criticized the development of the Wittenborn Scales and their use on the grounds that the time interval for the observations and the source of information are unspecified. Similar criticisms can be voiced particularly in relation to the comparability of the work of different investigators. For instance, in some investigations, ward and interview data are pooled. In other investigations only interview material or ward information is used.
2. Ratings are sometimes restricted to current behavior and sometimes include past behavior.
3. In some investigations some perhaps obvious variables have not been included. For instance, one cannot hope to find a syndrome such as aggressive-antisocial in

Table 1.1 Factor Analytic Studies of the Symptoms of Psychosis

Study	Sample	Type and Number of Measures	Data Source	Raters
Wittenborn & Holzberg (1951) Also Lorr (1957)	250 newly admitted male functional psychotics	51 scales	Interview and ward	Psychiatrists
Moore (1933) Also Degan (1952)	367 psychotics male, female, 2 hospitals	32 graphic ratings	Interview and ward observation and history	Psychiatrists, Physicians Nurses
Guertin (1952)	100 newly admitted schizophrenics, male and female	52 symptoms	Interview; mainly observation	Psychologists
Guertin & Krugman (1959)	100 male psychotics	76 items	Behavior ratings—ward, therapy, church	Therapists Chaplains
Lorr, Klett, McNair (1963)	566 psychotics 44 hospitals	78 scales	Interview	Psychiatrists Psychologists
Wittenborn (1963)	150 male psychotics	98 scales	Interview and ward	Psychiatrists and Nurses
Spitzer, Fleiss, Burdock, & Hardesty (1964)	2000 psychotic patients	248 items	Interview	Psychiatrists Psychologists
Cohen et al. (1966)	1274 male psychotics 12 hospitals	20 scales	Interview	
Vestre (1966)	240 Psychotics	85 items	Ward	Nursing Assistants

an investigation in the absence of a number of defining variables of that particular dimension in the correlation matrix.

4. The groups in the various studies differ in the degree of heterogenity.

Lorr, Klett, and McNair (1963) have criticized some attempts at classification within special groups and have suggested that the small correlation between traits or symptoms can be expected because of the homogeneity of the groups studied, and that this may affect the results of factor analysis. Restrictions in the range of subjects on one or more of the variables studied may result, they suggest, in the loss of one or more of the factors and also in the appearance of "incidental" factors of no psychological interest. Syndromes isolated in such studies, they suggest, may not be confirmable within broader, more heterogeneous populations. Arguments of this sort, unfortunately, can be endless. Eysenck (1963) has suggested that a second-order factor of psychoticism has not been found in the studies by Lorr and his colleagues because they have restricted their work to psychotics. Eysenck indicates that where there is no variance of first-order factor scores, there can be no correlation between them and, therefore, little opportunity for a second-order factor to emerge. Under these circumstances it is quite likely, he says, that group factors will emerge. Eysenck also mentions the continuity-discontinuity conflict in relation to the work of Lorr and his colleagues. He points out that his tests give scores on which there is continuity between normal, neurotic, and psychotic subjects, whereas Lorr used ratings on the majority of which a positive entry would suffice to classify the subject as grossly abnormal. Again, however, how important this countinuity-discontinuity problem is must remain suspect. As G. A. Foulds has suggested, the observations of investigators in this area have simply indicated that if we use a ruler for our measure, our answer will not be in pints. We still do not know, however, whether it is better to use a metric system, of the ruler kind, or a pint system in our approach to the data of psychopathology.

Eysenck (1963) has also criticized the work of Lorr and his colleagues on the grounds that most of the factors that have been isolated are not syndromes validated, but are symptoms shown to be rated reliably. He indicates that items making up a particular factor may be "reports voices telling him to do things," "reports voices threatening him," etc., and he suggests that these items are tautologous. Correlations between them have the status of reliability coefficients. Eysenck has made an important point but, unfortunately, we are still left in the dark about the syndromes of psychosis.

It is suggested that an important criticism that can be applied to all work in this area is that *the behaviors being measured are not being measured well enough*. We have observed that there is very little stability in the factors from one study to another. However, even, if we were to demonstrate that there was a stability in factor structure from one study to another, we wonder to what extent this would again only reflect on the agreement between the investigators in their preconceived notions about the illnesses that they are investigating. In other words, it would be a kind of consensual validation. Individual investigators do appear able to obtain stable factors which appear across their own studies. For instance, Cohen and his colleagues (1966) note "That the stability of the five factors withstood the cumulative effects of time, setting and rater differences and the diminishing variance is further testimony to their viability" (Cohen et al., 1966, p. 41). Lorr, Klett, and McNair (1963) have found a similar stability of their factors across their studies (see also Lorr & Klett, 1965). But this seems to give some weight to the suggestion that stability reflects only on the firmness with which the individual investigator holds on to his notions concerning the illnesses he is investigating.

The subjective element in all this work cannot be overemphasized. The studies of Raskin and his colleagues (1966) have indicated that although the report of reliabilities of the 10 Inpatient Multidimensional Psychiatric Scale (IMPS) factor scores obtained by the use of Lorr's scales were high, as differences between raters in age, years of psychiatric experience, and involvement in personal psychotherapy or psychoanalysis increased, there was a corresponding increase in interrater dissimilarity in IMPS ratings (Raskin & Sullivan, 1963; Raskin et al., 1966).

We not only have the problem of the preconceived notions of the raters concerning the illnesses of the patients they are rating, we also have the problem of the patients' notions regarding how they should behave and the interdependence between the social factors existing in a ward and the patients' symptom fluctuation (see, for instance, Kellam & Chassan, 1962). A similar problem is the effect of observers on the behavior of the observed. Littman, Moore, and Pierce-Jones (1957) have referred to this as the "girdle on girdle off phenomenon." When collecting observation data in the homes of volunteer families, they noticed that on the occasion of the first visit, all mothers were wearing silk stockings, girdles, and formal attire. After the observers had been around for a few weeks, the mothers slipped back to housecoats and slippers.

Some of the disturbing confusion in this area can be illustrated by a quote from a paper by Lorr (1957):

> "The fourth factor D [in his oblique rotation of Wittenborn and Holzberg's (1951) data] is essentially the same as Wittenborn's Anxiety. It is characterized by the following: unrealistic

Table 1.2 Factors Obtained in 11 Factor Analytic Studies of the Symptoms of Psychosis

Factors	Lorr et al. (1963)	Lorr (1957) Wittenborn, & Holzberg (1951) data	Wittenborn, & Holzberg (1951)	Guertin (1952)	Degan (1952)
Excitement	X	Manic excitement	Excited Manic vs. depressed		Manic hyper-excitability
Hostile belligerence	X	Hostile belligerence		Excitement hostility	Hyper-irritability
Paranoid projection	X		Paranoid condition	Persecutory suspicious	
Grandiose expansiveness	X				
Perceptual distortion	X	Paranoid schizophre-nia	Paranoid schizophre-nia		Hyper-projection
Anxious intropunitiveness	X	Anxious depressed	Anxious depressed	Guilt conflict	Depression
Retardation and apathy	X			Retardation and withdrawal	
Disorientation	X				
Motor disturbances	X				Catatonia
Conceptual disorganization	X	Conceptual disorganiz-ation		Personality disorganization	Schizophrenic dissociation
Resistive isolation					
Traumatic hysteria		Conversion hysteria	Conversion hysteria		X

Guertin & Krugman (1959)	Moore (1933)	Wittenborn (1963)	Spitzer, Fleiss Burdock, & Hardesty (1964)	Cohen et al. (1966)	Vestre (1966)
	Manic	Manic excitement	Agitation excitement		
Emotional controls		Spontaneous assaultiveness	Hostile belligerence	Paranoid hostility	Paranoid belligerence
	Paranoid irritability	Delusions of persecution			
		Ideas of grandeur	Grandiosity		
	Deluded and hallucinated		Suspicion persecution or hallucinations		
	Constitutional heredity depression	Anxiety	Depression anxiety	Depression anxiety	Agitated depression
	Retarded depression	Motoric passivity	Retardation emotional withdrawal	Unmotivated	
			Disorientation memory		
	Catatonic				
	Cognitive defect			Deteriorated thinking	Thinking disorganization
X		Obstructive disruptive resistance		Uncooperativeness	
		Hysterical conversions			

Table 1.2 (*continued*)

Factors	Lorr et al. (1963)	Lorr (1957) Wittenborn, & Holzberg (1951) data	Wittenborn & Holzberg (1951)	Guertin (1952)	Degan (1952)
Neurasthania					X
Deterioration					X
Catatonic excitement					
Confused withdrawal				X	
Obsessive phobic		Obsessive phobic	Obsessive phobic		
Interpersonal tensions					
Regressive agitation					
Reality concern					
Intellectual impairment					
Affective flatness					
Attention demanding					
Homosexual motivation					
Silliness					
Greediness					

Guertin & Krugman (1959)	Moore (1933)	Wittenborn (1963)	Spitzer, Fleiss Burdock, & Hardesty (1964)	Cohen et al. (1966)	Vestre (1966)
Deteriorated behavior		Incontinence	Inappropriate or bizarre behavior or appearance		
		Schizophrenic excitement			
		Social withdrawal	Social isolation		Withdrawal
		Compulsive behavior phobic reaction			
X					
X					
X					
		X			
		X			
		X			
		X			
		X			
		X			

Table 1.2 (*continued*)

Factors	Lorr et al. (1963)	Lorr (1957) Wittenborn, & Holzberg (1951) data	Wittenborn & Holzberg (1951)	Guertin (1952)	Degan (1952)
Suicidal					
Disordered form of speech					
Somatic concerns					
Sociopathic impulses or acts					
Impairment or restriction of daily routine					
Insight deficiency					

self-blame, feelings of impending doom, doubts he can be helped, suicidal thoughts or impulses, avoids people, difficulty in sleeping, overt activity slow or delayed, and anxiety affects task performance. Factor D seems identical with Degan's Depression Syndrome and Lorr, Jenkins, and O'Connor's Melancholy Agitation" (p. 443).

Now anxiety and depression may tend to coexist, but it does not appear justifiable to suggest that they are the same.

Another fault with most of this work is that the empirical validity in terms of the predictive validity of the dimensions have not been adequately enough investigated. Indeed, it may be that classifying symptoms, no matter how well-defined and described, without taking into account their course, will not be the best classification approach. In any case, at the present time the syndromes and types produced in work of this sort remain statistical phantoms until they can be shown to be valid in relation to prognosis, treatment responses, and etiology. Statistically based classification systems, if they are to replace the traditional psychiatric classification system, must be shown to have a greater predictive validity. Studies by Lasky and his colleagues (1962) and by Overall and his colleagues (1962, 1964) have demonstrated that despite the error variance resulting from the unreliability of psychiatric diagnoses, membership in the classes of "schizophrenic" or "depressed" patients has differential predictive value for responsiveness to certain drugs. But Galbrecht and Klett (1967) have reported on a study which encountered ". . . a regrettable lack of success in its efforts to predict the right drug for the right patient." The IMPS was used in an attempt to make the predictions.

CLASSIFICATION OF CHILDREN'S ILLNESSES

In Table 1.3 the factors obtained in six studies of the symptoms of psychiatric illness in children are presented. Once again, a plus sign under a particular study indicates that the factor in the list to the left of the table was obtained in that study. Where a factor in any particular study was obtained that appears similar to one of the factors in the list at the left, the name of the similar factor is given under the particular study.

Guertin & Krugman (1959)	Moore (1933)	Wittenborn (1963)	Spitzer, Fleiss Burdock, & Hardesty (1964)	Cohen et al. (1966)	Vestre (1966)
		X	Suicide self-mutilation		
			X		
			X		
			X		
			X		
			X		

The data here is little better than the data reviewed in the previous section. There is one factor that has been identified in four studies—antisocial aggressiveness or rebelliousness. It is interesting to notice that when the data from boys and girls were analyzed separately in the study by Collins and his colleagues (1962), differences in factorial structure were found.

The comments made about the studies in the previous section can also be made about the studies in this section. The data from the studies of children's psychiatric illnesses are presented primarily to indicate that, here too, the same kind of instability of the factors identified is found as in adult illnesses.

Patterson (1965) has suggested that classification systems based on ratings or parent's reports, as in the Illinois studies [represented here by Peterson (1961)], and the studies of Dreger and his associates (1964) may be working with a too restricted data domain. He advocates the use of extensive behavioral observations. We must agree that extreme and careful observation of children's symptoms of psychopathology will be required before successful classification systems can be developed.

ENDOGENOUS VERSUS REACTIVE DEPRESSION

The investigators of the syndromes of psychosis, although they have been interested in and have commented on the relationships between the dimensions they have identified and the traditional psychiatric classification, have not set out to confirm the validity of these traditional classifications. There are, however, some investigators whose primary purpose is indeed to confirm the validity of traditional classification systems. One group of investigators has attempted to provide data that will confirm the distinction in clinical psychiatry between endogenous depression and reactive depression. In Table 1.4 the results from six experimental studies are presented.

Unlike the tables presented in the section on the syndromes of psychosis, we do not have here a list of factors or dimensions, but instead a list of symptoms and features of the patient's illness. In the remainder of Table 1.4, under each study, the plus signs indicate which symptoms or features were found to be particularly indicative in terms of their factor loadings, or similar statistics, of endogenous as against reactive depression. Most of the studies provide similar

Table 1.3 Factors Obtained in Three Studies of the Symptoms of Psychiatric Illness in Children

	Dreger et al. (1964)	Collins et al. (1962) Boys	Collins et al. (1962) Girls	Himmelweit (1951)	Patterson (1964)	Hewitt & Jenkins (1946)	Peterson (1961)
Paranoid, aggressive isolated egocentricity	+						
Antisocial aggressiveness	+	Rebelliousness	Rebellious and rootless		+	+	
Intellectual and scholastic retardation	+		Dull Backwardness				
Psychoid type of desurgency	+						
Appreciative sociableness	+						
Hyperactivity	+				+		
Sadistic aggressiveness	+						
Disturbed sleep and dreams	+						
Anxiety	+	+	+		+		
Social immaturity	+				+		
Rootlessness		+					
Withdrawn					+		
Conduct problems							+
Personality problems							+

Table 1.3 (*continued*)

	Dreger et al. (1964)	Collins et al. (1962) Boys	Girls	Himmelweit (1951)	Patterson (1964)	Hewitt & Jenkins (1964)	Peterson (1961)
Socialized delinquency behavior						+	
Overinhibited behavior						+	
Neuroticism				+			
Extraversion				+			

data that show the symptoms and features indicative of reactive depression. We decided to present only the data for endogenous depression, since the same kind of comments can be made about both the data that relate to endogenous depression and the data that relate to reactive depression.

The main point that has been made by the investigators in this area is that when the data on the symptoms of groups of depressed patients are intercorrelated and factor analyzed, it is found that the symptoms do tend to group together in such a way that a bipolar factor of endogenous depression versus reactive depression can be identified. Unfortunately, however, such clustering of symptoms may, in this instance as in the other instances we have discussed above, simply reflect the preconceptions of the interviewers or raters. The tenuousness of the findings, on the other hand, is indicated by the dissimilarity, across the studies, in the particular symptoms that are given weight as a result of the statistical analyses—weight that is in relation to their ability to discriminate endogenous from reactive depressions. Notice in Table 1.4 that only in one instance—retardation—is a particular symptom selected in all of the studies.

Like the investigations of the syndromes of psychosis, some of the differences between the studies may result from matters such as differences in representation of depressive illnesses and also differences in the sampling of symptoms and features for use in the analysis. Again, however, it is likely that the main reason for the discrepancies in these studies is the poor state of our knowledge concerning these symptoms themselves. That this may be true has been indicated with respect to one particular symptom that is supposedly indicative of endogenous depression—namely, early morning awakening.

Although in Table 1.4 we are concerned only with the signs indicative of endogenous depression, in our discussion of disturbances of sleep, we shall also deal with the data that concerns reactive depression. A widely accepted feature that supposedly differentiates endogenous from reactive depression is that, whereas patients in the latter group have difficulty in getting off to sleep, the patients who are suffering from endogenous depression typically have the problem of waking up early. We observe from Table 1.4 that, in two of the six studies reviewed, early morning awakening appeared as a good indicator of endogenous depression. One of these studies is by Kiloh and Garside (1963). In their study they also reported that difficulty in getting off to sleep was one of the best indicators of reactive depression. However, in a later study from the same research unit (Carney, Roth, & Garside, 1965), early morning awakening, which had a factor loading in the Kiloh and Garside study of -0.692, now had a factor loading of only -0.227 on the bipolar factor endogenous versus reactive depression. The

Table 1.4 Symptoms and Features Found to be Indicative of Endogenous Depression in Six Experimental Studies

	Carney et al. (1965)	Kiloh & Garside (1963)	Rosenthal & Gudeman (1967)	Hamilton & White (1959)	Mendels & Cochrane (1968b)	Rosenthal & Klerman (1966)
Age 40 or above		+				
Anxiety						
Inadequacy						
Adequacy	+					
Previous attacks	+	+				
Duration 1 year or less		+				
Positive family history						
No adequate						
Psychogenesis	+					
Depth of depression		+				+
Depressed mood			+	+		
Quality of depression	+	+	+			
Depression worse in morning		+				
Guilt	+			+		+
Retardation	+	+	+	+	+	+
Agitation			+			+
Weight loss	+	+				+
Suicidal ideas			+			
Suicidal attempt				+		
Failure of concentration		+	+			

Table 1.4 (*continued*)

	Carney et al. (1965)	Kiloh & Garside (1963)	Rosenthal & Gudeman (1967)	Hamilton & White (1959)	Mendels & Cochrane (1968b)	Rosenthal & Klerman (1966)
Hypochondriasis						
Nihilistic delusions	+					
Early awakening		+	+	+		+
Loss of insight				+		
Middle insomnia			+			+
Global rating of illness						+
Delusional symptoms						+
Visceral symptoms			+			+
Loss of interest			+			+
Feelings of worthlessness			+			
Obsessive and compulsive symptoms			+			
Obsessional traits					+	

correlation of the symptom early morning awakening with the diagnosis of endogenous depression in the first study by Kiloh and Garside was 0.831, wheras in the later study by Carney and his colleagues it was only 0.271. Similarly, in the first study by Kiloh and Garside, difficulty in getting off to sleep had a factor loading on the endogenous-reactive factor of 0.237, whereas in the second study the loading was only 0.038. The correlation of the symptom difficulty in getting off to sleep with the diagnosis of reactive depression was 0.332 in the first study, and 0.356 in the second study. Mendels (1965) did not find an association between sleep pattern and the diagnosis of depressive illness.

Insufficient stability of the findings once again suggests an unreliability in the observations which may be partly the result of the subjective factors involved. When sleep patterns have been objectively recorded, either by nurses' observations [Costello & Smith (1963), Costello & Selby (1965), McGhie (1966)] or by motility records [Hinton (1963), Oswald & his colleagues (1963)] or by EEG and eye-movement recordings, Oswald and his colleagues (1963), endogenous and reactive depressions are not found to differ in their sleep patterns. Costello and Selby (1965) also found that in a standardized interview, aimed at obtaining a patient's own assessment of his sleep, there was no difference between endogenous and reactive depression in their patterns of sleep.

We do not suggest, of course that, because more objective data do not reveal a difference between endogenous and reactive depression in their sleep patterns, these two groups of depressive illnesses do not exist. We do suggest, however that, if there are two broad groups of depressive illnesses, little is known about the way in which they differ. We also suggest that a more objective investigation of some of the symptoms that supposedly differentiate endogenous and reactive depression, as with the sleep-pattern symptom, may be found not to discriminate between the two groups.

The main emphasis to be made is that more precise and objective symptom data must be obtained. Carney and his colleagues (1965) give this description of how their data were obtained: "Before the first treatment each patient was assessed for each item . . . by one of the authors in an interview of 45 minutes. In order to decide the presence or absence of some items it was found necessary to supplement the information from the interview with material from the case notes and the observations of the nursing staff" (p. 660–661). We suggest that data obtained in this way are not the best data to subject to analysis.

Carney and his colleagues (1965) have commented on the differences in results from the various studies. They note:

"Certain differences from the results recorded by Kiloh and Garside are perhaps worthy of comment. A significant negative correlation between anxiety and a diagnosis of endogenous depression was found in the present enquiry (–0.619) in contrast to the small negative correlation (–0.192) recorded in their studies. This is also reminiscent of the negative correlation between depressed mood and guilt on the one hand, and agitation and psychic anxiety on the other hand, in Hamilton's investigation (Hamilton, 1960). These observations may, at first sight, appear anomalous in that a state of anguished hand-wringing restlessness is widely thought to be a common feature in and even pathognomic of one form of endogenous depression. However, a much less specific form of anxiety with motor unrest is a common component of a neurotic form of depression which is one of the most common syndromes encountered in psychiatric practice. The two phenomena are not easily differentiated and failure to discriminate between them may have caused the discrepancy to which reference has been made. More detailed clinical analysis in definition may serve to eliminate disagreement of this kind in future studies" (Carney et al., 1965, p. 670).

Mendels and Cochrane (1968a) presented some of the findings from seven factor analytic studies in which the presence of an endogenous-reactive factor was claimed. They noted that a "... discussion of all factors found in all factor analytic studies of depression . . ." was beyond their review and concentrated on the "... so-called endogenous-reactive factor . . ." What may not be obvious to some readers of their paper is the fact that not all of the historical, personality, or symptom items of all of the studies have been presented, and it is not clear how the selection was made by the reviewers.

They note that 25 items were included in at least four of the seven studies, but they do not use this frequency of occurrence as the criterion for selection, since some of the items they listed occurred in only two of the seven studies.

This has resulted in the omission of what appear to be important items. For instance, the studies by Kiloh and Garside (K & G) (1963) and Carney, Roth, and Garside (C, R & G) (1965) suggest that the item "duration of illness—one year or less," when present is indicative of endogenous depression (factor loadings, .34 and .60, respectively), whereas Rosenthal and Klerman (R & K) (1966) found that a *long* duration of illness was indicative of endogenous depression (factor loading, .32). Three studies found the "quality of depression" to have a high loading on the factor of endogenous depression (K & G) loading .39; Rosenthal and Gudeman (R & G) (1967), loading .61; (C, R, & G), loading .42.

Other items and their loadings that occur in two or more studies are: (1) failure of concentration, (K & G), .26; (R & G), .55; (2) obsessive personality, (K & G), .20; Mendels and Cochrane (M & C) (1968b), loading .62; (3) obsessive and compulsive acts, (R & K), .28; (R & G), .61; (4) loss of libido, Hamilton and White (H & W) (1959), .47; (R & G), .39; (5) paranoid features, (K & G), .08; (R & K), .44; (R & G), .04; (M & C), .14; (C, R, & G), .45; (6) loss of insight, (H & W), .60; (M & C), .10.

It is true that, except in the case of duration of illness, obsessive personality, and paranoid features, there are no marked differences between the studies, but the relative weights (in terms of factor loadings) are quite variable across studies.

Mendels and Cochrane report the finding of Rosenthal and Klerman (1966) which was that, when they gave each of their patients factor scores in relation to the factors found in the various studies, the intercorrelations were quite high (they ranged from .60 to .90). However, since these comparisons were made on data obtained from one sample of patients and, it seems, in relation only to those items that the Rosenthal and Klerman study had in common with all the other studies, they do not establish strong evidence in relation to the consistency of the factor solutions. A more rigorous test would appear to be to intercorrelate the factors across the studies. When this was done by the writer the results that are given in Table 1.5 were obtained and, since they show only a range of 2 to 60 percent common variance between the factors, with 11 of the 15 comparisons showing less than 30 percent common variance, they do not provide particularly convincing evidence for the consistency of the endogenous pattern.

The degree of agreement between the studies also might appear greater than it really is as a result of the selection of items in the Mendels and Cochrane (1968a) review. They noted that eight items were in perfect agreement (that is, all of the studies were agreed in the direction and significance of an item's loading). This is, of course, only eight of 28 items selected by the reviewers (29 percent). But if we take all of the items that had a significant loading in at least one of the studies (52 items), the percentage of items for which there is perfect agreement, (15 percent) is even less impressive.

Mendels and Cochrane point out that the studies reviewed generally did not pay sufficient attention to the problem of rater bias. We have already suggested that this vitiates all of the conclusions from these kinds of studies. Mendels and Cochrane despite this problem believe that the "... impressive amount of agreement between the factor analytic studies ..." is noteworthy. It appears on the basis of these comments that the amount of agreement is far from impressive, and that the question of the endogenous-reactive distinction remains an open one.

In this section we have been concerned with symptoms that are associated with the classical distinction between endogenous and reactive depressions. We have not discussed the general problem of the optimum number of dimensions required to account for depressive illness. We might mention, however, that a fair number of studies by using factor analytic procedures have suggested that more than two dimensions or one bipolar dimension are needed (Hamilton, 1960; Grinker, Miller, Sabshin, Nunn

Table 1.5 Intercorrelation of Endogenous-Reactive Factors from Six Studies

	K & G	R & K	H & W	R & G	M & C	C, R & G
K & G		56	53	41	43	68
R & K			34	77	32	49
H & W				42	59	53
R & G					15	70
M & C						50
C, R, & G						

& Nunnally, 1961; Friedman, Cowit, Cohen & Granick, 1963; Cropley & Weckowicz, 1966).

PROCESS VERSUS REACTIVE SCHIZOPHRENIA

The studies that we have reviewed thus far have been concerned with the classification of symptoms of illness. The final group of investigations that we review have been concerned primarily with classification of the features indicative of premorbid adjustment in schizophrenic patients. Although the criticism of poor symptom measurement is not as applicable here as in the other areas of work reviewed, it is included in this chapter because of some important differences in the approach when it is compared with the other approaches.

We can immediately observe that one way in which the investigations in this area appear to be an improvement over the other investigations we have reviewed is that they are concerned with the classification system in relation to prognosis. They have not tried to establish dimensions in relation to a particular theoretical system as has Eysenck; they have not been content to identify dimensions that run through cross-sectional approaches to symptoms of illness as have Lorr, Wittenborn, and other investigators of the syndromes of psychosis; nor have they been content to try to confirm the existence of traditional psychiatric classifications. They have been concerned, instead, with the predictive value of the classification which is, of course, one of the important aspects of any classification system. It may very well be that if one forms one's classes from the start in relation to a criterion to be predicted, it will be of some practical value. However, this approach may lose out in terms of the generality of the results.

A number of instruments have been developed to assess the premorbid personality features and developmental aspects of schizophrenia that appear to have something to do with prognosis. They are the Elgin Prognostic Scale that was developed by Wittman (1944) and was revised by Becker (1956, 1959). A similar scale is the one developed by Kantor, Wallner, and Winder (1953). A third scale is the Phillips (1953) scale.

All of these scales contain items concerning the patient's history and presenting symptoms. But it is the first part of the Phillips Scale, in particular, that has been the subject of much investigation, and it consists of five items that pertain to premorbid history.

A useful study has been conducted recently on these three scales by Garfield and Sundland (1966). The scales were used with 65 female schizophrenic patients. One of the most striking findings in their study was that marital status predicted hospital stay as well as the scores on any of the three scales. The percentage of correct classification in relation to length of hospitalization is 71 percent for marital status, 71 percent for the Elgin Scale, and 58 percent for the Kantor and Phillips Scales. The findings of Garfield and Sundland (1966) are of particular importance since, as Higgins and Peterson (1966) have pointed out, there is no good evidence available of acceptable relationships between the many criteria used to distinguish between process and reactive schizophrenics, and no evidence at all of the relative efficacy of the criteria as predictors. We can observe that, although in relating the classification data to prognosis, workers in this area have introduced a positive feature into their studies, they have paid little attention to the kind of item analysis that would supply data on the relative efficacy of the various items used. A start on this problem has been made in the study by Nuttall and Solomon (1965). They factor-analyzed data from 291 male schizophrenic patients on 28 items drawn from the Becker revision of the Eligin Prognostic Scale and the Phillips Prognostic Rating Scales. Seven factors were obtained, four of which were of prognostic significance.

The work on process versus reactive schizophrenia has been included to indicate the manner in which classification systems may be related to important items such as prognosis. It appears that the work itself may be doing nothing more than classifying one particular group of patients—schizophrenic—into the ones who have had a generally premorbid adequately adjusted life as against the ones who had an inadequate adjustment to life. This is a distinction that can be meaningfully applied to nonschizophrenic diagnostic groups. As Higgins and Peterson (1966) have recently pointed out, a considerable amount of research on the distinction merely reports that process schizophrenics perform more poorly than reactive schizophrenics. All that these findings imply, of course, is that the process reactive continuum parallels, or even perhaps is, a severity of illness continuum. This particular approach to classification, therefore, despite incorporating the important feature of a relationship with a criterion to be predicted in the end, may be of limited value in our understanding of syndromes of psychopathology.

CONCLUSION

Probably some of the tables that have been presented in this chapter will be criticized on the grounds that they include both first-order and second-order factors. It will be argued that mixing factors at both levels, of course, will give the appearance of inconsistency. But we would be justified in presenting first-order and second-order factors separately only if investigators working with first-order factors differed in their aims from those who worked with second-order factors. This is not true, since they are all attempting to provide an optimum classification system for some range of psychopathology. To group the studies in relation to the levels of the factors produced would be to make the mistake of assigning too much importance to the *procedures* of factor analysis and too little to its *aims*.

In concluding this Chapter, we reaffirm that classification procedures themselves are not being criticized. Indeed, the development of statistically based classification procedures by workers such as Eysenck, Lorr, and Wittenborn represent an important contribution to the science of psychopathology. When our observations and measurements are more precise, these classification procedures will probably be put to good use. This, of course, is the main point of the chapter—that their present use is premature.

We hope that the development of multivariate procedures will continue. Of course, it is always necessary to avoid becoming enchanted by the procedures themselves. Peterson (1965) has shown how this happened in factor analytic research of verbally defined personality traits.

In this book, before the symptoms of psychopathology are presented in individual chapters, the influence of culture on those symptoms is discussed. It is well to remember not only that this book is primarily concerned with symptoms of psychopathology as they occur in the Western World but also that these symptoms as they occur in the West can be better understood by knowledge of the way in which Eastern cultures may modify them. Even in the Western Hemisphere, symptoms may change in terms of their frequency or nature across cultural subgroups.

REFERENCES

Bannister, D., Salmon, P., & Leiberman, D. M. Diagnosis—treatment relationship in psychiatry: a statistical analysis. *Brit. J. Psychiat.*, 1964, **110**, 726–732.

Bartholomew, A. A. & Marley, E. The temporal reliability of the Maudsley Personality Inventory. *J. ment. Sci.*, 1959, **105**, 238–240.

Becker, W. C. A genetic approach to the interpretation and evaluation of the process-reactive distinction in schizophrenia. *J. abnorm. soc. Psychol.*, 1956, **53**, 229–236.

Becker, W. C. The process-reactive distinction: a key to the problem of schizophrenia. *J. nerv. ment. Dis.*, 1959, **129**, 442–449.

Cameron, N. The functional psychosis. In J. V. Hunt (Ed.) *Personality and the behavior disorders*. New York: Ronald Press, 1944.

Carney, M. W. P., Roth, M., & Garside, R. F. The diagnosis of depressive syndromes and the prediction of ECT response. *Brit. J. Psychiat.*, 1965, **111**, 659–674.

Carrigan, P. Extraversion-introversion as a dimension of personality: a reappraisal. *Psychol. Bull.*, 1960, **57**, 329–360.

Cattell, R. B. The conceptual and test distinction of neuroticism and anxiety. *J. clin. Psychol.*, 1957, **13**, 221–233.

Cohen, J., Gurel, L., & Stumpf, J. C. Dimensions of psychiatric symptom ratings determined at thirteen timepoints from hospital admission. *J. consult. Psychol.*, 1966, **30**, 39–44.

Collins, L. F., Maxwell, A. E., & Cameron, K. A factor analysis of some child psychiatric clinic data. *J. ment. Sci.*, 1962, **108**, 274–285.

Coppen, A., & Metcalf, Maryse. Effect of a depressive illness on MPI scores. *Brit. J. Psychiat.* 1965, **111**, 236–239.

Costello, C. G., & Selby, M. M. Sleep patterns in reactive and endogenous depression. *Brit. J. Psychiat.*, 1965, **111**, 497–501.

Costello, C. G., & Smith, C. M. The relationships between personality, sleep and the effects of sedatives *Brit. J. Psychiat.*, 1963, **109**, 568–571.

Crookes, T. G., & Hutt, S. J. Scores of psychotic patients on the Maudsley Personality Inventory. *J. consult. Psychol.*, 1963, **27**, 243–247.

Cropley, A. J., & Weckowicz, T. E. The dimensionality of clinical depression. *Austr. J. Psychol.*, 1966, **18**, 18–25.

Degan, J. W. Dimensions of functional psychosis. *Psychometr. Monogr.*, 1952, **6**.

Dreger, R. M., Lewis, P. M., Rich, T. A., Miller, K. S., Reid, M. P., Overlade, D. C., Taffel, C. & Flemming, E. L. Behavioral Classification Project. *J. consult. Psychol.*, 1964, **28**, 1–13.

Eysenck, H. J. *Dimensions of personality.* London: Routledge & Kegan Paul, 1947.

Eysenck, H. J. *The structure of human personality.* London: Methuen & Co., 1951.

Eysenck, H. J. *Scientific study of personality.* London: Routledge & Kegan Paul, 1952.

Eysenck, H. J. Psychiatric diagnosis as a psychological and statistical problem. *Psychol. Rep.*, 1955, **1**, 3–17.

Eysenck, H. J. *Handbook of abnormal psychology.* New York: Basic Books, 1961.

Eysenck, H. J. Psychoticism or the psychotic syndromes? *J. consult. Psychol.*, 1963, **27**, 179–180.

Eysenck, H. J. Principles and methods of personality description, classification and diagnosis. *Brit. J. Psychol.*, 1964, **55**, 284–294.

Eysenck, H. J., & Claridge, G. The position of hysterics and dysthymics in a two-dimensional framework of personality description. *J. abnorm. soc. Psychol.*, 1962, **64**, 46–55.

Eysenck, S. B. G. Neurosis and psychosis: an experimental analysis. *J. ment. Sci.*, 1956, **102**, 517–529.

Eysenck, S. B. G., & Eysenck, H. J. On the dual nature of extraversion. *Brit. J. soc. clin. Psychol.*, 1963, **2**, 46–55.

Farley, F. H. On the independence of extraversion and neuroticism. *J. clin. psychol.*, 1967, **23**, 154–156.

Franks, C. M., Holden, E. A., & Phillips, M. Eysenck's "stratification" theory and the questionnaire method of measuring personality. *J. clin. Psychol.*, 1961, **17**, 248–253.

Freudenberg, R. K., & Robertson, J. P. Symptoms in relation to psychiatric diagnosis and treatment. *A.M.A. Arch. neurol. Psychiat.*, 1956, **76**, 14–72.

Friedman, A. S., Cowit, B., Cohen, H. W., & Granick, S. Syndromes and themes of psychotic depression. *Arch. gen. Psychiat.*, 1963, **9**, 504–509.

Galbrecht, C. R., & Klett C. J. Predicting response to phenothiazines: The right drug for the right patient. *Central neuropsychiat. res. lab.* Report No. 69. Perry Point, Maryland, 1967.

Garfield, S. L., & Sundland, D. M. Prognostic scales in schizophrenia. *J. consult. Psychol.*, 1966, **30**, 18–24.

Grinker, R. R., Miller, J., Sabshin, M., Nunn, R., & Nunnally, J. C. *The phenomena of depressions.* New York: Harper & Row, 1961.

Guertin, W. H. A factor analytic study of schizophrenic symptoms. *J. consult. Psychol.*, 1952, **16**, 308–312.

Guertin, W. H., Krugman, A. D. A factor analytically derived scale for rating activities of psychiatric patients. *J. clin. Psychol.*, 1959, **15**, 32–35.

Hamilton, M. A rating scale for depression. *J. neurol. neurosurg. and Psychiat.*, 1960, **23**, 56–62.

Hamilton, M., & White, J. M. Clinical syndromes in depressive states. *J. ment. Sci.*, 1959, **105**, 985–998.

Hewitt, L. E., & Jenkins, R. L. *Fundamental patterns of maladjustment: the dynamics of their origin.* Illinois: D. H. Green, 1946.

Higgins, Jerry, & Peterson, Judith C. Concept of process-reactive schizophrenia: A critique. *Psychol. Bull.*, 1966, **66**, 201–206.

Himmelweit, H. T. A factorial study of "children's behavior problems." Unpublished MS reported in Eysenck, H. J. *The structure of human personality.* London: Methuen & Co., 1951.

Hinton, J. M. Patterns of insomnia in depressive states. *J. neurol. neurosurg. Psychiat.*, 1963, **26**, 184–189.

Ingham, J. G. Changes in MPI scores in neurotic patients: A three-year follow-up. *Brit. J. Psychiat.*, 1966, **112**, 931–939.

Jenkins, R. L., Bemiss, E. L., Jr., & Lorr, M. Duration of hospitalization, readmission rate and stability of diagnosis in veterans hospitalized with neuropsychiatric diagnosis. *Psychiat. Quart.*, 1953, **27**, 59–72.

Jensen, A. R. The Maudsley Personality Inventory. *Acta Psychol.*, 1958, **14**, 314–325.

Kaelbling, R., & Volpe, P. Constancy of psychiatric diagnoses in readmissions. *Comprehensive Psychiat.*, 1963, **4**, 29–39.

Kantor, R. E., Wallner, J. M., & Winder, C. L. Process and reactive schizophrenia. *J. consult. Psychol.*, 1953, **17**, 157–162.

Kellam, S. G., & Chassan, J. B. Social context and symptom fluctuation. *Psychiat.*, 1962, **25**, 370–381.

Kiloh, L. G., & Garside, R. F. The independence of neurotic depression and endogenous depression. *Brit. J. Psychiat.*, 1963, **109**, 451–463.

Knowles, J. B. The temporal stability of MPI scores in normal and psychiatric populations. *J. consult. Psychol.*, 1960, **24**, 278.

Kreitman, N. The reliability of psychiatric diagnosis. *J. ment. Sci.*, 1961, **107**, 876–886.

Kreitman, N., Sainsbury, P., Morrissey, J., Towers, J., & Scrivener, J. The reliability of psychiatric assessment: An analysis. *J. ment. Sci.*, 1961, **107**, 887–908.

Lasky, J. J., Klett, C. J., Caffey, E. M., Jr., Bennett, J. L., Rosenblum, M. P., & Hollister, L. E. Drug treatment of schizophrenic patients. *Dis. nerv. Syst.*, 1962, **23**, 698–706.

Levinson, Freda, & Meyer, V. Personality changes in relation to psychiatric status following orbital cortex undercutting. *Brit. J. Psychiat.*, 1965, **111**, 207–218.

Littman, R. A., Moore, R. C., & Pierce-Jones, J. Social class differences in child rearing: a third community for comparison with Chicago and Newton. *Amer. soc. Rev.*, 1957, **22**, 694–712.

Lorr, M. The Wittenborn psychiatric syndromes: an oblique rotation. *J. consult. Psychol.*, 1957, **21**, 439–444.

Lorr, M., & Klett, C. J. Constancy of psychotic syndromes in men and women. *J. consult. Psychol.*, 1965, **29**, 309–313.

Lorr, M., Klett, C. J., & McNair, D. M. *Syndromes of psychosis.* New York: Pergamon Press, 1963.

Lorr, M., & O'Connor, J. P. The relation between neurosis and psychosis: a re-analysis. *J. ment. Sci.*, 1957, **103**, 375–380.

Mendels, J. Electroconvulsive therapy and depression. The prognostic significance of clinical factors. *Brit. J. Psychiat.*, 1965, **111**, 675–681.

Mendels, J., and Cochrane, C. The nosology of depression: The endogenous-reactive concepts. *Amer. J. Psychiat.*, 1968a (Supp), **124**, 1–11.

Mendels, J., and Cochrane, C. Depressive factors and the response to electroconvulsive therapy. Unpublished paper. 1968b.

Moore, T. V. The empirical determination of certain syndromes underlying praecox and manic depressive psychosis. *Amer. J. Psychiat.*, 1933, **9**, 719–738.

McGhie, A. The subjective assessment of sleep patterns in psychiatric illness. *Brit. J. Med. Psychol.*, 1966, **39**, 221–230.

McGuire, R. J., Mowbray, R. M., & Vallance, R. C. The Maudsley Personality Inventory used with psychiatric inpatients. *Brit. J. Psychol.*, 1963, **54**, 157–166.

Nuttall, R. L., & Solomon, L. F. Factorial structure and prognostic significance of premorbid adjustment in schizophrenia. *J. consult. Psychol.*, 1965, **29**, 362–372.

Oswald, I., Berger, R. J., Jaramillo, R. A., Keddie, K. M. G., Olley, P. C., & Plunkett, G. B. Melancholia and barbiturates: a controlled EEG, body and eye movement study of sleep. *Brit. J. Psychiat.*, 1963, **109**, 66–78.

Overall, J. E., Hollister, L. E., Meyer, F., Kimbell, I., & Shelton, J. Imipramine and thioridazine in depressed and schizophrenic patients. *J. Amer. med. Assoc.*, 1964, **189**, 605–608.

Overall, J. E., Hollister, L. E., Pakorny, A. D., Casey, J. F., & Katz, G. Drug therapy in depressions. *Clin. Pharmacol. Therapeut.*, 1962, **3**, 16–22.

Pasamanick, B., Dinitz, S., & Lefton, M. Psychiatric orientation and its relation to diagnosis and treatment in a mental hospital. *Amer. J. Psychiat.*, 1959, **116**, 127–132.

Patterson, G. R. An empirical approach to the classification of disturbed children. *J. clin. Psychol.*, 1964, **20**, 326–337.

Patterson, G. R. Some problems in the classification of deviant children. Paper presented to Peabody Symposium for Classification, 1965.

Peterson, D. Scope and generality of verbally defined personality factors. *Psychol. Rev.*, 1965, **72**, 48–59.

Peterson, D. R. Behavior problems of middle childhood. *J. consult. Psychol.*, 1961, **25**, 205–209.

Phillips, L. Case history data and prognosis in schizophrenia. *J. nerv. ment. Dis.*, 1953, **117**, 515–525.

Raskin, A., Schalterbrandt, Joy G., & Reatig, Natalie. Rater and patient characteristics associated with rater differences in psychiatric rating scales. *J. clin. Psychol.*, 1966, **22**, 417–423.

Raskin, A., & Sullivan, P. D. Factors associated with interrater discrepancies on a psychiatric rating scale. *J. consult. Psychol.*, 1963, **27**, 547.

Rosenthal, S. H. & Gudeman, J. E. The endogenous depressive pattern: An empirical investigation. *Arch. gen. Psychiat.*, 1967, **16**, 241–249.

Rosenthal, S. H. & Klerman, G. L. Content and consistency in the endogenous depressive pattern. *Brit. J. Psychiat,* 1966, **112**, 471–484.

Sigal, J. J., Star, K. H., & Franks, C. M. Hysterics and dysthymics as criterion groups in the study of introversion-extraversion. *J. abnorm. soc. Psychol.*, 1958, **57**, 143–148.

Spitzer, R. L., Fleiss, J. L., Burdock, E. I., & Hardesty, Anne S. The mental status schedule: rationale, reliability and validity *Comprehen. Psychiat.*, 1964, **5**, 384–395.

Trouton, D. S., & Maxwell, A. E. The relation between neurosis and psychosis. *J. ment. Sci.*, 1956, **102**, 1–21.

Vestre, Norris D. Validity data on the psychotic reaction profile. *J. consult. Psychol.*, 1966, **30**, 84–85.

Ward, C. H., Beck, A. T., Mendelson, M., Mock, J. E., & Erbaugh, J. K. The psychiatric nomenclature: reasons for diagnostic disagreement. *Arch. gen. Psychiat.*, 1962, **7**, 198–205.

Wittenborn, J. R. Distinctions within psychotic dimensions: a principal component analysis. *J. nerv. ment. Dis.*, 1963, **137**, 543–547.

Wittenborn, J. R., & Holzberg, J. D. The generality of psychiatric syndromes. *J. consult. Psychol.*, 1951, **15**, 372–380.

Wittman, P. Follow-up on Elgin Prognostic Scale results. *Illinois Psychiat. J.*, 1944, **4**, 56–59.

Wretmark, G., Åström, J., & Ölander, F. MPI—resultat vid endogen depression före och efter behandling. *Nord. Psykiat. T.*, 1961, **15**, 448–454.

Zigler, E., & Phillips, L. Psychiatric diagnosis: a critique. *J. abnorm. soc. Psychol.*, 1961, **63**, 607–618.

Zubin, J. Classification of the behavior disorders. *Ann. Rev. Psychol.*, 1967, **18**, 373–401. Ann. Rev. Inc. Palo Alto, California.

Chapter 2

Culture and Symptoms

IHSAN AL-ISSA

Underlying the recent interest in the cultural variations of symptomatology has been the question whether the present psychiatric classification system could be universally applied in the diagnosis of mental disorders. Since this system is based on symptoms of patients from a Western cultural background, it is possible that it would be inappropriate for use with patients from other than Western cultures. It is possible also that some cultures are more stressful than others, and cultural pressures and stresses may differentially dispose individuals toward mental illness. Thus, symptoms might be expected to occur with different frequencies or constellate into different patterns of syndromes in various cultures. This chapter deals mainly with the variations in symptoms of psychopathology in non-Western cultures. Furthermore, it is concerned with some of the major methodological problems involved in the field of the cross-cultural study of mental illness.

SCHIZOPHRENIA

If cultural and social factors[1] are important in the development of schizophrenia and other mental illnesses, variations in their incidence might be found in different cultures. In the early 1930's, it was claimed that schizophrenia, as known in the West, was nonexistent among certain culturally isolated Indians of the interior of Brazil (Lopez, 1932), the forest Bantu of Africa (Faris, cited by Opler, 1956), and among some culturally isolated groups in India (Dhunjiboy, 1930). In contrast to these studies is the more recent finding by Tooth (1950) that schizophrenia among Africans of the Gold Coast occurs in the familiar European pattern of simple, mixed, hebephrenic, catatonic schizophrenic, and paranoic. Other studies indicate that all types, except paranoid schizophrenia, may occur in a primitive society (Opler, 1956; Kline, 1963a, 1963b; Pfeiffer, 1966; Loudon, 1959). Loudon (1959) also found that simple and hebephrenic schizophrenia are the most familiar types among the Zulu Africans. The recent evidence from different surveys shows that schizophrenia may occur all over the world (Wittkower & Rin, 1965). Unfortunately, the reliability of all these observations must be in doubt because of the doubtful reliability of the psychiatric classification system even when used in the Western world.

Are the classical schizophrenic symptoms the same all over the world? Catatonic rigidity negativism and stereotype behavior seem to be more common in India than in other countries (Wittkower & Rin, 1965). Patients are quieter in Africa, with more features that suggest deterioration, such as blunting of affect or bizarreness of

[1]Sociocultural factors in the epidemiology of Schizophrenia have been extensively reviewed by Mishler and Scotch (1963).

behavior. African schizophrenia is claimed to be a "poor imitation of the European forms" (Gordon, 1934), showing less violence and aggression than in the West (Benedict & Jacks, 1954; Marinko 1966). The description of the African "schizophrenia" by Gordon and others makes one wonder whether it is true schizophrenia at all. By comparing Japanese and Filipino paranoid schizophrenics, Enright and Jaeckle (1963) found that ideas of reference, thinking disturbance, suspicion, and withdrawal are significantly more frequent among the former patients. However, Filipino patients showed significantly more delusions of persecution, and violence. Eaton and Weil (1955) also observed that unlike their counterpart in the West, the Hutterite schizophrenic does not show severe regression, excitement, or any extreme antisocial behavior.

Among the most extensive cross-cultural studies of schizophrenic symptomatology is the one conducted by Murphy et al. (1961). The researchers sent a questionnaire to psychiatrists who represented different cultures. Their findings show some definite associations between the frequency of symptoms and certain cultural backgrounds. Delusions of destructiveness and religious delusion are frequently reported only among Christians and Muslims. Delusional jealousy is most frequent among Asians regardless of religion; visual hallucinations are reported most often in Africa and the Near East. Urban and rural patients seem to differ in their symptoms. Although the presence of depersonalization is found most frequently among urban patients, delusions of grandeur seem to occur among the rural patients. One important finding by Murphy et al. (1961) is that symptoms such as social and emotional withdrawal, auditory hallucinations, general delusions, and flatness of affect appear to occur frequently in all their samples. Since these data were collected by questionnaire, it is not certain whether their results reflect variations in the sociocultural background of the respondents or variation in the symptoms of their patients.

Another cross-cultural study that compares symptomatology between Japanese and American schizophrenics was conducted by Schooler and Caudill (1964). They found significant differences between the two groups. The Americans, for instance, show greater disruption of reality testing and are more likely to show hallucinations and bizarre ideas. Physical assaultiveness is found more prevalent among the Japanese, since physical assaultiveness involves breaking a highly valued norm in the Japanese culture. Schooler and Caudill suggest that schizophrenic symptomatology seems to appear in the areas of functioning that are stressed most by the culture.

Although non-Western patients sometimes show the familiar Western symptoms, they may differ in their onset and duration. Consider, for instance, the transitory psychotic states reported by Collomb (1966) in the Senegal. These psychotic attacks appear to be sudden and without any preliminary symptoms. They are characterized by transitory delusions with hallucinations and ideas of reference. Unlike Western patients, the onset of their symptoms have a clear detectable relationship to the patient's everyday life. They seem to occur when the individual faces a difficulty or are used as a means of avoiding traumatic situation.

Similarly, cases of catatonia among the Eskimo seem to be a result of intense fears of the spirits. This interferes with their motility but does not affect their human relationships—for example, having a gay conversation with others (Opler, 1956).

It should be noted that even in the West there are subcultural differences in symptomatology. Thus, Opler (1959) reported that there is more hostility, acting out, elation, and bizarre mannerisms among Italian paranoid schizophrenics than among their Irish counterpart. The Italian picture seems to be similar to that in an Iraqi mental hospital (Bazzoui & Al-Issa, 1966). Opler (1959) also reported that although Irish patients had sin and guilt preoccupations concerning sexuality, Italians had no feelings of sin or guilt in this area.

In addition to the finding that there are cross-cultural or subcultural variations of symptomatology, manifestations of schizophrenia seem to change during certain periods of time within the same culture. Linz (1964) studied these changes during the last 100 years in Vienna. His data show that ideas of grandeur and aggressive behavior are less frequent in the

20th than in the 19th century. Although visual hallucinations decreased during the period of study, there was an increase in auditory hallucinations. (This result may be compared with the general finding that, although auditory hallucinations are more predominant among Western schizophrenics, visual hallucination are more present in illiterate non-Western patients.) Diethelm (1953) has also described several changes in the characteristic symptomatology of the schizophrenias with the passage of time. These studies give the impression that symptoms of Western patients in the past (for example, the Middle Ages) are somehow similar to the patients in primitive cultures at present. Since studies over a long period of time use case histories, it is again difficult to decide whether the results indicate the different background of the psychiatrists over these periods or whether they reflect true changes in symptomatology.

Interpretation of variation in symptomatology: The early findings that schizophrenia is nonexistent in some cultural groups suggested an explanation of the illness in terms of Western influence. Devereux (1934) for instance, developed a "sociological theory of schizophrenia," suggesting that the illness may be a result of the increasing cultural complexity. As a result of this complexity, individuals become disoriented and uncertain of their social roles. Later studies which showed that the incidence of "schizophrenia" is universal have cast doubt on this interpretation. Furthermore, the finding by Goldhamer and Marshall (1953) that the admission rates of functional psychoses (schizophrenia and affective psychoses) were just as high during the last half of the 19th century as they are during the present century is incompatible with this sociological theory of schizophrenia.

Variations in specific schizophrenic symptoms such as paranoid delusions have been mainly attributed to the non-Western peoples' lack of education or contact with modern "civilization." Similarly, the shallowness of affect and gross deterioration of the patients' habits in a primitive, illiterate culture may be the result of the poverty of their intellectual and cultural resources. Taking these interpretations as a starting point, Al-Issa (1967b) predicted that the frequency of certain conventional schizophrenic symptoms should differ in literate and illiterate patients in a non-Western culture. Among ten symptoms investigated, only formal thinking disorder and flatness of affect were significantly related to literacy, the illiterates showing greater evidence of these symptoms. It is interesting to note that contrary to prediction from cross-cultural studies, paranoid delusions were not significantly related to literacy. Thus, the clinical findings that paranoid delusions are very rare among illiterate patients are not supported by this study. It is suggested that paranoid delusions in an illiterate culture may tend to appear in action (assaulting or killing somebody) rather than in thought (for example, during the clinical interview, Al-Issa, 1967b).

However, literacy may affect the contents of the patients delusions. It affects, for instance, the tendency of urban Africans to develop ideas of influence of the European type such as grandiose delusions of identification with Christ and God or influences that involve electricity or the wireless (Tooth, 1950). These tendencies are not evident with rural illiterate Africans.

Differences in cultural values are also suggested to explain differences in the manifestation of schizophrenic symptoms. Although the quiet behavior of the Indian has been explained in terms of cultural control of anger and aggression, the opposite behavior of Italian and Iraqi patients was thought to be a result of cultural encouragement of aggression and the lack of strong feeling of guilt. The absence of extreme antisocial acts among the Hutterite patients was attributed to the good custodial care and the affectionate regard for the patient (Eaton & Weil, 1955).

MANIC DEPRESSIVE PSYCHOSIS

It is reported that manic-depressive psychosis occurs in non-Western cultures, but its depressive type is very rare and this type is believed to be confined to the Westernized part of the population (Carothers, 1948; Loudon, 1959). In a series of 558 patients, Carothers (1948) saw no case of depression other than a few involutional melancholics. He noted that in none of them was psychomotor retardation or ideas of sin and unworthiness in evidence. That non-Western depressive patients show no feeling of guilt, self-accusation, or ideas of unworthiness is reported by many authors (Eaton & Weil, 1955; Pfeiffer, 1966; Collomb, 1966; Bazzoui & Al-Issa, 1966). Suicide also seems to be rare among these patients (Loudon, 1959; Bazzoui & Al-Issa, 1966; Collomb, 1966). It is interesting to note that similar characteristics have been found in a study of Jewish depressive patients in East London (Fernando, 1966). As compared with non-Jewish depressives, they scored significantly less on an intropunitive scale and on two subscales of guilt and self-criticism. Their hostility tended to be directed toward the outside environment rather than toward the self. Similarly, Prange and Vitols (1962) have shown that the admission of depressive Negroes to hospitals and the incidence of suicide among them is lower than among whites. However, Ethiopian depressives appear to be more similar to Western patients than to their African neighbors. Depressive states are more common in Ethiopia, and the patients tend to express feelings of guilt and delusions of punishment. Suicide or an attempt at it appears to be a predominant symptom in depressive Ethiopians (Marinko & Pavicevic, 1966). Murphy et al. (1964) conducted an extensive cross-cultural study of depression. They found that a mood of depression and dejection, diurnal mood change, insomnia with early morning wakening, and a decrease of interest in social environment were almost universally recorded in depressive patients. They also found that self-neglect and semimutism was rare among Europeans in contrast to members of other cultures. There was a definite association between religion and feeling of guilt. Intensity of belief among Christians was positively related to the feeling of guilt and self-depreciation. Hindus, Muslims, and other religious groups did not show an association between intensity of belief and these symptoms. Although guilt feeling and suicidal ideas were uncommon among the Muslim sample, they show symptoms that are not usually included in the classical description of depression (for example, ideas of influence and possession). Symptoms such as religious preoccupation, loss of sexual interest, excitement, and theatrical grief appeared to occur significantly less among the Japanese than among other groups. On the other hand, despondency and thought retardation appeared to occur more frequently among the Japanese patients. Although the study of Murphy et al. (1964) draws our attention to the possible variations of symptomatology in depression, it may also indicate that these results could have been obtained because of the unreliability of the research instrument (for example, the questionnaire) used by the investigators or because of differences in the cultural background of the respondents.

Again, differences between Western and non-Western patients may be contrasted with changes in symptomatology in the West over a period of time. Linz (1964) has studied these changes in depressive symptoms during the last 50 years in Vienna. In his analysis of 167 cases of endogenous and senile depression, he found that feelings of guilt and suicidal ideas have decreased in frequency, especially during the last ten years. However, he also found that hypochondriacal complaints and anxiety have remained constant, although the content of anxiety has changed (in the past it was related to fear of God's wrath, and now it is related to the fear of death). These results may again reflect the orientation of psychiatrists during different periods of time.

Interpretation of variation in Depressive Symptoms: The rarity of depression or self-reproach in primitive societies has been attributed by Opler (1956) to the individual's tendency to minimize free will, and to shift responsibility to groups from personal levels, or to shift grief from isolated to group ritual. Tooth (1950), to explain the rare incidence of depression gave similar interpretations such as the cultural provision of institutionalized grief after death. Where depression occurs, as among the Hutterites, the absence of feelings of shame and guilt may be because of the belief that the illness is a spiritual or religious trial by God to test the sincerity of man's belief in him (Eaton & Weil, 1955). Suicide is also considered one of the most serious sins among the Hutterites (Eaton & Weil, 1955) and Muslims (Bazzoui & Al-Issa, 1966). Since the person who takes his own life is thought to be condemned to eternal hell, it is not surprising to find that suicide is rare among the Hutterites or Muslims.

Finally, the high incidence of the manic form of manic-depressive psychosis has been attributed to the misdiagnosis of states of excitement and confusion. Psychiatrists may confuse cases of mania with catatonic excitement or schizo-affective states. This is not surprising considering the inadequacies of the classification system. We perhaps should emphasize again that the work reviewed in this chapter might be suggestive concerning the cultural variations in symptomatology. It cannot give as much of a lead concerning the syndromes of psychopathology.

PSYCHONEUROSES

Although all the traditional psychoneurotic disorders appear to occur in non-Western cultures, they may take different form than their Western counterparts. Phobia, for instance, is reported to be widespread in West Africa (for example, in the Senegal), but it is not based on individual experience; certain phobias are widespread in the whole culture (Collomb, 1965). Cultural beliefs, rather than individual traumatic experience with the objects of fear, appear to be important in conditioning members of the community to fear certain objects. Thus, the American Indians studied by Hallowell (1938) were not afraid of dangerous animals such as wolves and bears, but of harmless animals like toads and frogs, and these fears were related to local beliefs. Sometimes, the similarity between the cultural background and the neurotic reaction makes the latter unnoticeable to the community. Hallowell (1934), for instance, described a case of zoophobia that was not recognized by the Berens River Indians because of their usual "abnormal" fear of animals.

Acute anxiety states of short duration appear to be more common in primitive than in advanced societies. They seem to occur as a result of disturbing events such as migrating to the city or passing through a place believed to be habituated by spirits. Severe anxiety may reach a panic state with incoherent thoughts, confusion, delusions, and hallucinations. This state was termed by Carothers (1953) as "frenzied anxiety." Similar cases have been reported from South China where male patients recovering from physical illness frequently develop acute anxiety concerning the shrinking of the penis. This anxiety is in line with the cultural belief that the penis is at such times in danger of disappearance (Carpenter, 1935). In the Trukese society, there is strong but largely unrealistic anxieties associated with the possibility of food deprivation (Gladwin & Sarason, 1959). It is obvious why anxieties associated with food deprivation are very rare in the West.

Among the Hutterites, neurotics react to most stressful situations with depressive rather than with anxiety symptoms and paranoid or obsessive tendencies as patients often do in the American culture. The rare incidence of free floating anxiety among the Hutterites was explained by Eaton and Weil (1955) as a result of the individual's close interpersonal relationship, and the great social and psychological support he receives from his family and the community.

Obsessive-Compulsive neuroses were rarely found in the studies of Kenya (Carothers, 1953), Nigeria (Tooth, 1950) or among the Hutterites (Eaton & Weil, 1955). One reason given for this rare incidence was that these cases are unrecognized because the symptoms resemble characteristics of the cultural background. Persons may seem compulsive in a loosely organized social system, but would be more normal in a rigid culture where life is very much regulated by tradition (Eaton & Weil, 1955).

Hysterical reactions seem to be more common among primitive peoples than in the West. Mass hysteria, which used to occur in Europe in the Middle Ages, can be found in Africa and Asia. In its dramatic form, hysteria is more common among the illiterate and less sophisticated member of the community (Bazzoui & Al-Issa, 1966; Rankin & Philip, 1963). It seems that neurotic problems find expression in somatic rather than psychological complaints, for example, patients experience vague pains and aches, strong painful sensations of heat, and functional visceral disorders. The observation of Bazzoui and Al-Issa (1966) is that the change from the traditional long flowing robe to Western men's clothes has brought about many tics whose origin can be traced to the expression of pressure discomfort. [Western clothes appear to represent an aspect of modernization in the Middle East (Badri & Dennis, 1964)].

These tics as well as other mannerisms are accepted in the culture, and they are neither noticeable by other observers nor do they become troublesome to the individual.

SEXUAL DEVIATION

Two observations are widely emphasized in cross-cultural studies of sexual behavior. One observation is that societies show striking contrasts in the amount of permissiveness regarding sexual behavior. The other observation is that some deviant sexual behavior in the West may be regarded as normal in other cultures.

In the sphere of extramarital sexual relations, societies show marked differences in the restrictions placed on such behavior. In his study of 118 preliterate societies from all over the world, Murdock (1949) found that only three societies seem to have a general taboo against all sexual intercourse outside marriage. However, Castairs (1964) observes that the communal interest in marital relations characteristic of primitive societies may become a major source of emotional tension, for example, the tension that a couple in Iraq experience on the wedding night when the extended family await impatiently the consummation of the marriage, and that hence brings about impotence.

Offering one's wife to sleep with an honored guest among the Himalayan tribes and the Eskimo (Castairs 1964), the encouragement of sex play among children, sexual intercourse among adolescents (Malinowski, 1932), and the acceptance of transvestites (Pfeiffer, 1966) are only some aspects of sexual behavior that deviate from the Western norms.

Tolerance of nudity appears to be related to attitudes toward sex among some primitive peoples. The Navaho people are contrasted to the Urubu Indians in their complete acceptance of nudity (Castairs 1964); and this is considered as a factor in the predominance of sexual conflicts and preoccupation with sex among members of the Urubu Indians.

That different attitudes toward sex may result in contrasted sexual behavior is demonstrated by Castairs (1956) in his study of the high caste Hindus and the Bhil tribes who live in the same area of northwest India. The high caste Hindus regard sex as degrading, and they tend to punish sex interest or activities of their children. The Bhil tribe, on the other hand, are more tolerant towards sex play or sex adventures. One consequence of these contrasted attitudes appears to be the widespread preoccupation with impotence among the Hindus. Impotence seems to be unknown among the Bhil population. Furthermore, homosexuality occurs much more frequently among the Hindus.

Homosexuality: There seems to be more cross-cultural studies of homosexuality than any other sexual deviation. In the study by Malinowski (1932) referred to previously, it was maintained that homosexuality was very rare among the Trobrianders and this was attributed to the freedom in heterosexual experience. In their study of 76 primitive societies, Ford and Beach (1952) concluded that homosexuality exists all over the world. They also found that in approximately two thirds of these societies, homosexuality is regarded as normal and acceptable; all male members are expected to practice paederasty as an essential preliminary activity to adult heterosexual life (for example, some groups in New Guinea and North Africa). In other societies, mutual masturbation is a recognized form of homosexual male activity. Kline (1963a) estimates that about 90 percent of the male population in Kuwait have some kind of homosexual relationships, and it seems to be almost universal among the lower classes. In Oman where the nomads are the most primitive, "marriage" between men is publicly celebrated.

The following North African picture of initiation reported by De Vos and Miner (1959) is applicable to other primitive parts of the Arab Middle East. At a certain age, young boys must leave the world of women and children (that is, female and young members of the family at home) and must join the exclusive society of men. Their strong need to belong to this male world is exploited by older adult males to induce them to homosexual practices. As the culture looks down on this passive sexual role (that is, a feminine role) these young boys soon assert their virility and, in their turn, they start playing the role of active homosexuals. Here, as well as in other cultures where homosexuality is an accepted practice (Mead, 1939), this behavior is not tolerated outside its prescribed cultural context.

ALCOHOLISM

The main finding in cross-cultural studies of alcoholism is that alcoholism as a problem tends to be associated with the attitudes of the society toward alcohol rather than with the amount of alcohol consumed by the individuals. Studies of American Indians by Mangin (1957), Hamer (1965), and Simmons (1959) show that although the majority of these groups are heavy drinkers (for example, the Potawatomi Indians), compulsive drinking is very rare. Alcohol drinking seems to bring about social participation, and it is not used for adjustment to personal problems. It is also not regarded as sinful, and the individual has little guilt connected with it. Similar interpretation was given to the low rate of alcoholism among Italians (Lolli et al., 1958) and Jewish groups (Glad, 1947). That the rate of alcoholism among Italians is one eighth the rate in the United States may be because of the integration of alcohol consumption into the Italian daily life, and this is viewed very positively. The integration of alcohol drinking with religion and family life was again given as the reason for the low rate of alcoholism among Jewish groups.

We must note that in a culture where the pattern of drinking is culturally prescribed and socially controlled, drinking may become a serious problem in the case of migration. This is shown in the following quotation from Fried (1959) that describes the Indian migrants in Peru.

> "If we accept Mangin's formulation that a strong sense of social solidarity enhanced by ritual and convivial drinking, and combined with lack of conflict, guilt, or ambivalance connected with the overt act of drinking itself, accounts for a lack of alcohol-related psychosis in the Sierras, then the extremely high rate among Lima Indians must represent a new kind of situation in which drinking behavior now out of cultural context has disastrous consequences" (Fried, 1959, p. 132).

In contrast with the above cultural groupings, the high rate of alcoholism among the Irish is explained in terms of the use of alcohol by the individual in adjusting to certain situations (Hyde & Chisholm, 1944; Bales, 1946).

Culture seems to be an important variable in determining the pattern of alcoholism. Gamma alcoholism, which involves a loss of control, is more prevalent in Anglo-Saxon countries in which whisky consumption predominates; delta alcoholism, which involves inability to abstain, is more prevalent in Latin countries in which wine consumption predominates.

The observations of this author in the Middle East indicates that public prohibition of alcohol consumption seems to reduce the incidence of alcoholism. This is true despite the fact that individuals tend to drink heavily in private when they are given the opportunity. Where Muslim laws severely punish alcohol drinking (in Kuwait and Saudi Arabia), individuals must be able to abstain from drinking for long periods of time when this is necessary. In his adaptation to this situation, the individual has to build up tolerance for this periodic abstinence (c.f. Horton, 1943). This observation may not be applicable to drug intake, which is not forbidden by the religious laws, or to Muslim countries undergoing cultural and social change with its concomitant relaxation of prohibition laws.

PSYCHOSOMATIC DISORDERS

The guiding assumption underlying the study of psychosomatic disorders appears to be that they are the result of tensions and anxieties in modern living; and they are expected to be less frequent in non-Western cultures. The general findings show that, although there are variations in their incidence, all psychosomatic disorders are prevalent in non-Western cultures (Loudon, 1959; Baasher, 1965; Pflanz & Lambert 1965; Collomb, 1965). Pflanz and Lambert for instance, found that, although coronary disease, peptic ulcer, and hypertension seem to occur less frequently in India than in Germany, all other "diseases of civilization" occurred as frequently as in Germany. Collomb (1965) found that vascular disorder, hypertension, gastrointestinal ulcers, bronchial asthma, skin diseases, and diabetes mellitus were as frequent in the Senegal as in Europe. Loudon (1959), on the other hand, found that duodenal ulcer, asthma, and psoriosis were rare among the African Bantu.

Rin et al. (1966) investigated the relationship between social class and the choice of systems in Taiwan. Their findings showed that the lower class tended to react more frequently in musculoskeletal and cardiovascular systems, while the upper class group tended to choose respiratory, skin and gastrointestinal systems. Similar studies concerned with culture specific factors in the development of certain psychosomatic disorders have been recently reviewed by Wittkower and Lipowski (1966). They are mainly speculative and involve the application of psychoanalytical theories to explain variations in the incidence of certain psychosomatic disorders.

CULTURE-BOUND SYNDROMES

Thus far, we have been concerned mainly with cultural variations in symptomatology familiar in the West. This section is devoted to atypical psychiatric symptomatology reported in non-Western cultures. One important objective of future research is to find out whether processes underlying these atypical psychiatric symptoms are similar to the ones underlying Western symptoms.

A number of acute psychotic-like reactions are reported in the literature. The Latah syndrome is characterized by the imitation of the reactions (echopraxia) or words (echolalia) of others and by a startle or fright reaction (Aberle, 1952). Latah appears to be similar to catatonic schizophrenia commonly seen in the West; it also has some features in common with the Gilles de la Tourette syndrome. Amok which refers to violent homicidal outburst with ideas of possession and persecution is more similar to the behaviors of paranoid schizophrenics. Similar states of excitement such as cannibalistic Windigo psychosis (Hallowell, 1938), frenzied anxiety (Carothers, 1953), or the running wild of Fuegian tribes (Cooper, 1934) appear to resemble acute catatonic or paranoid symptoms. However, the Greenland Eskimo piblokto, in which women run around naked, may be considered as resembling either mania or severe hysteria (Vallee, 1966). In general, there seems to be a high incidence among primitive people of acute excitement that is accompanied by homicidal tendencies. The above symptomatology may be contrasted with the low incidence of depression and suicide, which is referred to in a previous section of this chapter. However, more similar to depression is the susto syndrome, which is characterized by restlessness during sleep, listlessness, loss of appetite, and weight (Rubel, 1964). Since susto is usually precipitated by stressful situations, it is more similar to reactive depression.

Koro, which is described by Yap (1965), is more similar to obsessive-compulsive neuroses or anxiety neuroses. This syndrome consists mainly of anxiety concerning the shrinkage of the penis in the case of male patients and the vulval labia and the breasts in the case of female patients. Similar to Koro is a morbid fear of loss of energy and vitality, and it may take the form of fear of cold (frigophobia). In this case, the patient experiences extreme cold that is especially felt on the chest. The patient has to wear several layers of clothes even during the hot summer (Rin, 1965).

Atypical hysterical reaction is found in the New Guinea Highlands (Salisbury, 1966). This has a sudden onset when the patient is hit by a wave of coldness that is followed by complete or partial deafness. He loses muscular control, shivers, and tends to exhibit sudden violence. Again, these attacks seem to be a breakaway from facing frustrating social situations (Newman, 1964). The patient's abnormal behavior tends to be of short duration, lasting for a maximum of 48 hours, but sleep usually brings about recovery (Reay, 1965).

Opler (1956) has subsumed most of the above atypical syndromes under the rubric of schizo-affective disorders as known in the West. Opler (1956, p. 133) wrote:

> "The lack of delusional systematizations in a wide variety of mental disorders of nonliterate peoples: the 'running wild' of Fuegian tribes (Cooper, 1934), the Greenland Eskimo piblokto, (women running around naked) (Cooper, 1934), the 'Arctic hysteria' of Lapps, Eskimos, and northeast Siberian tribes (Cooper, 1934; Yap, 1951), and the similar forms of psychosis, Latah of Malaya and Imu of the Ainu tribes of Hokkaido (Yap, 1951; Aberle, 1952)

all point to atypical forms of schizophrenias varying from the Western standard. Like the 'frenzied anxieties' with hysterical elements of Carothers and Aubin, they remind us of schizo-affective disorders as discussed by Adolf Meyer, but more loosely organized, more episodic, and more bound to action modes of emotional expression than to fantasy."

These atypical syndromes appear to differ from the conventional Western syndromes in their description and in the behavioral problems they pose to the patients in a non-Western culture. In the light of this observation as well as our limited knowledge of processes that underlie psychiatric syndromes in the West, the identification of non-Western syndromes with Western ones seems to have very weak foundation.

FURTHER CULTURAL OBSERVATIONS

The incidence of mental illness among the aged appears to be lower in non-Western cultures than in the West. The integration of the aged within the extended family, and the high prestige they receive appear to obviate the development of symptoms of social withdrawal, deterioration, or other disturbed behavior that leads to institutionalization (Eaton & Weil, 1955; Marinko & Pavicevic, 1966). The rare incidence of presenile and senile psychosis has been generally attributed to the short span of life in primitive countries (Wittkower, 1966).

The reasons given for the high frequency of puerperal psychosis in some non-Western countries are (1) the great importance attached to fecundity, (2) the reality of the dangers of delivery, and (3) the high infantile mortality (Wittkower, 1966; Collomb, 1965; Dorzhadamba, 1965).

Sibling rank is shown to be related to mental breakdown. Murphy (1959) reported that the first born Chinese in Malaya shows a higher rate of mental breakdown. Similarly, the older person in a simple Chinese family shows more risk of breakdown than in an extended Chinese family where responsibilities are shared. Studies by Schooler (1961, 1964) show that the relationships between the incidence of schizophrenia and sibling rank or family size are dependent on many factors such as sex or class. In addition to these factors, it is possible that family size may be related to the amount of contact with the parents and, thus, may dispose certain siblings to mental breakdown (Fontana, 1966).

Migration is another factor that is given special attention in the incidence of mental illness. In a study by Malzberg and Lee (1956) it was found that the rates of first admission to mental hospitals in New York State were markedly higher for migrants than for nonmigrants, regardless of sex and color. It is also found that the rates of first admission for total psychoses were much higher for recent rather than for earlier migrants. From his study of mental illness among refugees in England, Murphy (1955) concluded that the rates of mental breakdown are highest when the local population is unfriendly and mixing is made difficult. Although the maintenance of emotional ties with their families in the homeland may lead to instability of adjustment in the new environment, the existence of an ethnic community seems to provide secure guidance and aid to the migrants (Fried, 1959). Fried described the reaction of new migrants as follows:

> "A useful preliminary hypothesis is that migrants will continue to respond to problem situations in the city with the psychological and cultural modes that they learned in childhood in their home communities as long as they do not have to face insurmountable problems. Previously effective patterns of behavior when applied out of context may be entirely dysfunctional. Because under distressing conditions his behavior patterns, attitudes, values and skills are not effective, the migrant has at least four possible alternatives: (1) he can try to master new skills and attitudes and develop new sets of social contacts; (2) he can so restrict, narrow, or distort his contacts with the alien environment that he can get along with what he already has . . .; (3) he can give up and go home, which thousands, in fact, do without waiting long enough to experience acute mental or physical breakdown leading to hospitalization; (4) he can escape into illness" (Fried, 1959, p. 132).

More relevant to the problem of mental illness among migrants is the study by Tyhurst (1951). She concluded from her study of 48 mentally ill and 70 normal migrants in the Montreal area that there are two distinct periods in the psychological reaction of these individuals following arrival:

1. There is an initial period that lasts about two months after arrival and that is characterized by a subjective sense of well being or the tendency toward increased psychomotor activity, which is a primitive way of getting rid of tension and anxiety as a result of the stresses and strains of migration. During this period, the imigrants also tend to limit their interest in the new environment to the fulfillment of their basic and immediate needs.

2. In this period an appreciation of the current social situation gradually occurs, and the individual becomes increasingly aware of the language difficulties and differences in values and customs. In this case, the migrants tend to reject both the present and the future and start to idealize the past. It is during this second period that the psychiatric reactions tend to become obvious and reach their peak about six months after arrival.

Although Tyhurst noticed an almost day to day variability in the patients' symptoms, she was able to distinguish three main trends that are typical of their symptoms: (1) suspiciousness and paranoid trends; (2) the presence of anxiety and depression; (3) somatic complaints. It seems clear from the present studies that problems of maladjustment and psychiatric disturbances are more prevalent among migrant groups. However, these studies raise the question of whether this is a result of migration as such or of selective factors where maladjusted individuals may tend to emigrate from their home country in the first place.

METHODOLOGY

In the cross-cultural study of mental illness, it is sometimes difficult to differentiate between unfamiliar but culturally acceptable forms of behavior and the manifestations of genuine mental disorder. Behavior that seems to indicate abnormal symptoms to a Westerner might well be in keeping with indigenous beliefs and practices. The West Indian society, for instance, supports the belief of possession by Christ and God as well as ghosts; and the patients' delusions may be similar to these beliefs, making diagnosis very difficult (Kiev, 1963). The confusion between normal and abnormal behavior in a non-Western culture is well illustrated by Yap (1951). He reported that

> "if a Hindu Fakir behaves much like a catatonic schizophrenic in Britain he need not be necessarily insane, since not only can he begin or stop his apparently catatonic behavior at will, but such behavior has a recognized place, and possesses some degree of social approbation, in his own culture" (p. 315).

Thus, if the Western diagnosis criterion is inappropriately applied to other cultures, the clinician may be able to observe "group psychoses and neuroses" (Opler, 1959) or group paranoid delusions (Bazzoui & Al-Issa, 1966). Consider, for instance, the observation by Gladwin and Sarason (1959) that the normal personality traits of individuals in Truk is similar to the traits of the inadequate personalities of psychopaths in the West. They are characterized by shallow emotions, limited goals or expectancies for the self, and diffuse hostility. However, it is difficult to believe that the whole Truk society consists of inadequate psychopaths.

The difficulty in the diagnosis of mental illness in non-Western culture may in part result from the wholesale application of Western criteria without the due attention being given to cultural factors or individual variations within the culture. For instance, it is suggested by some workers in the field of transcultural psychiatry that some symptoms cannot be accepted universally as signs of abnormality because of differences in the degree of their acceptability from one culture to the other, for example, hallucinations that involve religion are accepted in some cultures. Buss (1966) has pointed out that this suggestion may be applicable to deviations where social evaluations are important in distinguishing between normality and abnormality (for example, sexual deviations, nonconformity with the rules of society). Deviations that involve cognitive symptoms, which appear to be universal (c.f. Murphy et al., 1961), represent failure to adapt to the physical rather than to the social environment. These cognitive abnormalities involve the inability to perceive correctly the nature of the physical world and do not depend on social environment. Whether a person is hallucinating is relevant to physical stimuli and can be studied objectively, irrespective of the cultural background. Reality in the sense of recognizing the physical world is a universal issue, and the failure to be in contact with reality should be considered universally abnormal.

In addition to the attribution of abnormality to culturally accepted behavior, atypical mental syndrome may be confusing to a Western-trained psychiatrist. The diagnosis as well as the rating of specific symptoms is very much determined by the background and the outlook of the psychiatrist. The fact that the concept of mental illness (for example, schizophrenia) is very loosely defined in the West (Guertin, 1961) may add to the difficulty of diagnosis in non-Western culture. Furthermore, it is possible that in a culturally isolated environment, a patient may be able to achieve "superficial adjustment," and his illness is less likely to be detected (Eaton & Weil, 1955). Adjustment may be possible in a primitive culture because it makes less demands on the individual. These factors, therefore, will influence results obtained by using the method of clinical observations or the questionnaire method referred to in the sections on schizophrenia and depression.

Data obtained from clinical observations may be misleading because only certain cases come into the psychiatric clinic. Traditional treatment is usually attempted before the patient comes to the psychiatrist's notice. In Iraq the mental-hospital patients are admitted mainly by order from the religious court or when their symptoms are beyond the control of the family. That these conditions may affect clinical observations is suggested in a study by Vitols et al. (1963). Their finding that there are more hallucinations and delusions among Negro than among white schizophrenics was attributed to the Negroes' delay in coming to the hospital; thus, the predominance of these symptoms reflected only the degree of severity of illness among the Negro patients in the mental hospital. Similarly, the observation that Iraqi hospitalized schizophrenics are aggressive and noisy may not necessarily apply to patients kept at home. It is possible that selective factors play a part in bringing aggressive patients to the hospital. Furthermore, social isolation and material deprivation within the hospital framework seem to be conducive to noisiness and aggression (Bazzoui & Al-Issa, 1966).

As the samples of cross-cultural reports of symptomatology are confined to a limited group of the population, it is not surprising to find contradictory results in the literature, for example, the traditional withdrawn, mute, and negativistic picture of the Indian schizophrenic patient is contrasted with a recent report describing him as "aggressive and boisterous" (Sharadamba, 1966). In countries where the mental patient is tolerated and kept at home, statistics of the incidence of mental illness are not reliable [for example, the finding that the admission rate of psychotics in the south of Italy is one third of the rate in the United States was given this interpretation (Lemkaw & de Sanctis, 1950)]. Poorly organized hospitals and official records may contribute to the unreliability of data on mental patients.

Even in the West, the finding by Hollinghead and Redlich (1953) that neuro ses is concentrated at the higher class level and psychoses at the lower class level was interpreted in terms of the diagnosed or treated prevalence rather than the true prevalence of mental illness. The finding of Myers and Roberts (1959) that the working class have some delay in obtaining treatment may well affect the statistics of the prevalence of mental illness. In England, it was found that social and attitudinal factors rather than the clinical severity or diagnosis of the patient influence the referral to psychiatrists (Rawnsley & Loudon, 1962). Since the initial detection and referral of mental illness is usually in the hand of the layman (the patient himself, the family friends, or other agents in the community) it is not surprising that cultural and social factors tend to bias the prevalence of mental illness (Zubin & Kietzman, 1966).

We should also observe that data obtained through the use of clinical observations or official records may be contaminated by linguistic and semantic misunderstanding. If the investigator is not familiar with the local language, it is difficult for him to check on the reliability of his reports. Yap (1951) has observed that studies showing more catatonic than paranoid symptoms in non-Western cultures may be a result of linguistic misunderstanding, or that the patient is discouraged from expressing his thoughts. The role of language in the diagnosis and observation of psychiatric symptoms is expressed by Stengel (1961) as follows:

"... certain symptoms which to psychiatrists using one language appear very important do not exist for psychiatrists and patients using another language, because there are no words for them. Take the example of the symptom of Gedankenentzug, which many German psychiatrists regard as a basic schizophrenic symptom. You find no reference to it in British or American textbooks, and patients using the English language do not complain about this experience" (p. 59).

The linguistic problem is sometimes complicated by the unwillingness of the local population to cooperate. Moreover, it may be difficult to obtain information about their emotional or even their everyday life, for example, in Nigeria and Haiti (Wittkower & Bijou, 1963). Topics related to mental illness may be classified as shameful and "unspeakable."

From this discussion, the obvious solution to these methodological problems seems to be the use of standardized tools specific to different cultures for the assessment of symptomatology. Psychologists have been aware of this problem for some time, but their role in the studies reported in the previous sections has been very slight. Therefore, it is of interest to discuss the possible contribution of the psychologist to cross-cultural studies.

THE PSYCHOLOGICAL APPROACH

It is generally recognized that the conventional diagnostic tests are inapplicable in non-Western cultures. Since these tests were validated on selected Western population of a certain age, level of income, and education, it is not surprising that the application of these tests to non-Western patients is questionable. One solution to this problem by the psychologist is the use of the so-called culture fair tests such as the Cattell Culture Fair Test, the Porteus Maze, the Draw a Man Test, and the Rorschach. These tests are thought to require minimal verbal abilities and to have little dependence on past experience. It is assumed, therefore, that they are applicable to different cultures, but the validity of this assumption appears to be doubtful. Relevant to the discussion of cultural variations in the criterion for abnormality, is the finding that abnormal test responses as defined by Western criterion may be characteristic of a whole non-Western society. Take, for instance, the study by Bleuler and Bleuler (1935) which shows that the desert Moroccans give a much larger number of fine-detail responses on the Rorschach than do Europeans. The interpretation of these Moroccan subjects of very tiny and hardly observable details in an ink blot seems to be very bizarre, when judged by Western clinical standards. In the West, fine detail responses are regarded as an indication of compulsive tendency or mental disorganization. The Moroccan results may be partly attributed to the obsessional concern with detail in the ritual of the Muslim religion. Henry (1941) has suggested that the use of rare detail in the Rorschach records of a jungle people in South America is a function of their need to observe their surroundings in order to survive. Henry's observation also may be applicable to the Moroccan Bedouin's keen surveillance of the desert environment. In contrast to the Moroccan Bedouins, Cook (1942) found that the Samoans give whole responses to the entire blot, for example, an animal. Samoans also differ from Western subjects in giving more responses to the white space of the blots. According to Western criterion, the responses of the Samoans would indicate a high level of creativity and intelligence for the whole responses, or negativism and stubbornness for the white-space responses. Since it is difficult to assume that the whole Moroccan Bedouin community or the Samoans are abnormal, these results throw some doubt on the efficacy of the Rorschach as a diagnostic tool in the cross-cultural study of mental illness. There is also considerable evidence that it is not valid even in Western culture (Costello, 1966). Dennis (1960) has also recently shown that the Draw a Man Test is not suitable for diagnostic purposes. It is art tradition and experience rather than emotional state that determine the drawings of the human figure of the Syrian Bedouins. The analysis of the Goodenough scores of 40 groups from different cultures appears to support the hypothesis that variations in these scores is related to the amount of experience with representational art and the encouragement of members of these groups to engage in it (Dennis, 1966). Mensh and Henry (1953) observed that the findings from the projective testing of primitive peoples and the ones from non-Western cultures regularly show signs of psychopathology. The authors commented that:

> "It is difficult to understand why this should be so, unless we take the position that everybody is sick but the observer. One impression is that not only do such interpretations stem from preconceived notions of what is 'normal', but that something inherent in the instrument's past history in our culture compels us to see the responses of peoples from other cultures as psychopathological" (p. 469).

Abnormal perceptual processes as indicated by psychometric measures are also found to be prevalent among non-Western normal individuals. Shapiro (1960) found that illiterate Africans show more rotation of drawings than English brain-damaged patients. Other perceptual anomalies are concerned with the African underestimation of figure size or the passage of time (Schwitzgebel, 1962), or his performance on the Müller-Lyer Illusion Test (Biesheuval, 1952; Hudson, 1960; Jahoda, 1966). In the Müller-Lyer Illusion Test, it was found that the degree of rectangularity in the environment and the inability of the illiterate African to interpret two-dimensional representations of three-dimensional objects affect the subject's perception. Verhaegen and Laroche's (1958) African bush subjects, who perseverate with the wrong response on a Form Board Test, are reminiscent of the responses given by schizophrenic and brain-damaged subjects in the West. The authors, however, point out that their subjects' inability to differentiate between a cross and a five-point star is the result of their unfamiliarity with these forms. By using Indian and British students, Thouless (1933) found that Indians showed a greater tendency toward object constancy than his British subjects. It should be noted that experimental results show that Western schizophrenics tend to show underconstancy (Venables, 1964). However, paranoid schizophrenics show overconstancy, a result similar to that reported by Thouless concerning Indian students. Here again, non-Western subjects are found to respond in a similar way to abnormal subjects in the West.

In addition to perceptual anomalies observed in non-Western illiterate peoples, it is assumed that they are unable to form concepts. In the study of the abstract abilities of Western schizophrenic patients, it has been demonstrated that they are less able than normals in forming abstract concepts on nonverbal classification tests (Goldstein & Scheerer, 1941; Hanfmann & Kasanin, 1942) and on verbal tests that require the definition of words (Choderkoff & Mussen, 1952, Feifel, 1949; Flavell, 1956; Gerstein, 1949). (See Chapter 3.) Using the Draw a Man Test, Haward and Roland (1953) claimed that the Nigerian mental approach is characterized by a concreteness that is so rigid that it produced schizophrenic signs in the drawings. Similarly, Joseph and Murray (1951) also claimed that there is concreteness in the Rorschach responses of the Chamorros and Carolinians at Saipan. In general, the claim that non-Western peoples are characterized by concreteness of thinking is based either on little relevant evidence (Carothers, 1953; Haward & Roland, 1954) or it has disregarded factors that might be effective in determining the subject's level of abstraction. Jahoda (1956), for instance, found that literacy and familiarity with the test material (Goldstein Scheerer Cube Test) affect the African level of abstraction. By using some native material for classification (plant material and animal material), Price-Williams (1962) showed that in addition to literacy, motivation and interest may also be effective. By using a word definition test, Al-Issa (1967a) obtained similar results with four groups that consisted of literate schizophrenics, literate normals, illiterate schizophrenics, and illiterate normals. These results show that both literacy and schizophrenia affect the subjects' level of abstraction. Al-Issa (1967a) reported as follows:

> "... significant differences between literate and illiterate subjects may reflect a difference in the frequency of usage of abstract concepts in the written and spoken Arabic. Spoken Arabic which is the main source of information for the illiterates, makes less use of abstract

concepts, and this use is closely related to the practical situation and to the interest and motivation of the subjects. An illiterate may be aware of a complex system of family or tribe on the abstract level (his awareness that it is possible to live in different parts of Iraq, and yet belong to the same tribe) while at the same time giving . . . concrete or fictional definitions" (p. 42).

An interesting aspect of these results is that literate schizophrenics scored significantly higher than illiterate normals and illiterate schizophrenics. However, the relationship between the level of abstraction and literacy or schizophrenia does not hold true when the presence of specific psychiatric symptoms and the level of abstraction are investigated within a schizophrenic population (Al-Issa, 1966). The inapplicability of Western norms for the assessment of schizophrenics symptoms might have affected the relationship between verbal abstraction and symptomatology. These studies clearly point out that *under certain conditions*, normal and schizophrenic subjects equally may show either concrete or abstract thinking abilities.

The search for abnormal signs in apparently normal subjects (for example, illiterates) is also demonstrated by the study of Gallais et al. (1951). In their analysis of the EEG records of 100 normal subjects from Guinea, they found that about 58 percent of these records were abnormal. By comparing 66 Bantus and 72 whites in South Africa, Mundy-Castle et al. (1953) found no significant difference in the incidence of abnormal EEG between the two groups. Thus, it is concluded that there is no significant difference in the EEG patterns of normal Africans and whites. If future research demonstrates that different cultural groups (Western and non-Western subjects) show similar abnormal patterns of the EEG in the case of mental disturbance, it would be plausible to suggest that similar processes may be responsible for their deviant behavior.

The above EEG study is one of the few investigations that is in line with the "behavioral approach" suggested by Zubin and Kietzman (1966) for the cross-cultural study of mental illness. In contrast to the conventional measures used in cross-cultural studies, their approach is based on the measurement of the initial components of the patient's response in the various modalities and under controlled experimental conditions. For instance, the speed and accuracy of responses to specified types of stimuli may be measured and contrasted in patients and controls. Zubin and Kietzman (1966) attempted to arrange responses according to the differential influence of culture. Conceptual responses are regarded as the most amenable to cultural influences, although physiological responses are the least influenced, with psychomotor, perceptual, and sensory responses falling in between. Zubin (1966) described these influences as follows:

"Though no measures can be said to be completely culture-free, the way in which culture affects certain measures (as pupillary response to light stimuli) is indirect, unlike the direct way in which it influences primarily conceptual measures like vocabulary. The major way in which culture will tend to influence the culture-free or culture-fair tests is probably not in the function under measurement, but in the subject's approach to the testing situation, e.g., in the subject's understanding of the purpose of the test, in the degree of fear, in his motivation, attention and co-operation, etc. In other words, the influence of culture is specifically on those variables which also tend to contaminate comparisons of schizophrenics and normals even when they come from the same cultural background" (p. 66–67).

The findings of Robertson and Batcheldor (1956) are relevant to the "indirect" influences of culture in the test situation. They found that British subjects tended to stress accuracy at the expense of speed when compared with the American norms of the Wechsler Adult Intelligence Scale. However, these influences are controllable in the test situation, for instance, by emphasizing speed or accuracy in the instructions.

If the experimental culture-fair approach which is postulated by Zubin (1966) and Zubin and Kietzman (1966) is applied cross-culturally, similar patterns of responses (for example, psychophysiological) may be found in subjects from different cultures. This would suggest that, although there are cross-cultural differences in the manifestations of mental illness, similar processes may under-lie these illnesses. Similarly, the comparison of the responses of Western abnormal subjects with non-Western subjects who show the same response pattern but without behavioral pathology, may give us some indications of the types of interactions between different variables (sociocultural, perceptual, physiological) that led to mental illness in one group but not in the other. At the present stage of cross-cultural studies, the best contribution to the understanding of mental illness would be to establish normative data for normal and abnormal processes that are already known in the West. This data would then be used as a basis for the cross-cultural comparisons of mental illness.

REFERENCES

Aberle, D. F. Arctic hysteria and latah in Mongolia. *Trans. New York Acad. Sci.*, 1952, **14**, 291–297.

Al-Issa, I. Effects of literacy and schizophrenia on verbal abstraction in Iraq. *J. soc. Psychol.*, 1967a, **71**, 39–43.

Al-Issa, I. Literacy and symptomatology in chronic schizophrenia. *Brit. J. Soc. Psychiat.*, 1967 (b), **1**, 313–315.

Al-Issa, I. Word definition in chronic schizophrenia. *Psychol. Reports*, 1966, **19**, 934.

Baasher, T. A. Treatment and prevention of psychosomatic disorders: psychosomatic diseases in East Africa. *Amer. J. Psychiat.*, 1965, **121**, 1095–1102.

Badri, M. B., & Dennis, W. Human figure drawings in relation to modernization in Sudan. *J. Psychol.*, 1964, **58**, 421–425.

Bales, R. F. Cultural differences in the rate of alcoholism. *Quart. J. stud. Alc.*, 1946, **6**, 482–498.

Bazzoui, W., & Al-Issa, I. Psychiatry in Iraq. *Brit. J. Psychiat.*, 1966, **112**, 827–832.

Benedict, P. K., & Jacks, I. Mental illness in primitive societies. *Psychiatry*, 1954, **17**, 377–389.

Biesheuvel, S. The study of African ability. *Afr. Stud.*, 1952, **11**, 105–117.

Bleuler, M., & Bleuler, R. Rorschach ink-blot tests and social psychology. *Charact. and pers.*, 1935, **4**, 99–114.

Buss, A. H. *Psychopathology*. New York: John Wiley, 1966.

Carothers, J. C. *The African mind in health and disease*. Geneva: World Health Organization, 1953.

Carothers, J. C. A study of mental derangement in Africans and an attempt to explain its peculiarities more especially in relation to the African attitude to life. *Psychiatry*, 1948, **11**, 47–85.

Carpenter, E. S. Witchfear among the Aivilik Eskimos. *Amer. J. Psychiat.*, 1935, **110**, 194–199.

Carstairs, G. M. Cultural differences in sexual deviation in I. Rosen (Ed.) *The pathology and treatment of sexual deviation*. London: Oxford University press, 1964.

Carstairs, G. M. Hinjra and Jiryan: two derivatives of Hindu attitudes to sexuality. *Brit. J. med. Psychol.*, 1956, **29**, 128–138.

Choderkoff, B., & Mussen, P. Qualitative aspect of the vocabulary responses of normals and schizophrenics. *J. consult. Psychol.*, 1952, **16**, 43–48.

Collomb, H. Bouffeés Delirantes En psychiatrie Africaine (Transitory delusional states in African psychiatry) Mimeograph p. 87. Abstracted in *Transcultural psychiat. Res.*, 1966, **3**, 29–34.

Collomb, H. Assistance psychiatrique En Afrique: Expérience Sénégalaise, Psychopathologie Africaine, 1965, **1**, 11–84.

Cook, T. H. The application of the Rorschach test to a Samoan group. *Rorschach Res. Exch.*, 1942, **6**, 51–60.

Cooper, J. M. Mental disease situations in certain cultures. *J. Abnorm. Soc. Psychol.*, 1934, **29**, 10–17.

Costello, C. G. *Psychology for psychiatrists*. Oxford: Pergamon Press, 1966.
Dennis, W. Good-enough scores, art experience, and modernization. *J. soc. Psychol.*, 1966, **68**, 211–228.
Dennis, W. The human figure drawings of Bedouins. *J. soc. Psychol.*, 1960, **52**, 209–219.
Devereux, G. A sociological theory of schizophrenia. *Psychoanalytic Rev.*, 1934, **26**, 315–342.
DeVos, G., & Miner, H. Oasis and Casbah, a study in acculturative stress, in M. K. Opler (Ed.) *Culture and mental health*. New York: McMillan, 1959.
Dhunjiboy, J. Brief resumé of the types of insanity commonly met with in India *J. ment. Sci.*, 1930. **16**, 254–264.
Diethelm, O. Report of the Payne Whitney Psychiatric Clinic. New York Hospital 1953 (cited by Opler, 1956).
Dorzhadamba, S. The epidemiology of mental illness in the Mongolian People's Republic. *Transcult. Psychiat. Res. Rev.*, 1965, **2**, 19–22.
Eaton. J. W., & Weil, R. J. *Culture and mental disorders*. Glencoe, Illinois: The Free Press, 1955.
Enright, J. B., & Jaeckle, W. R. Psychiatric symptoms and diagnosis in two sub-cultures. *Internat. J. soc. Psychiat.*, 1963, **9**.
Faris, E. The nature of human nature, cited by M. K. Opler. *Culture, psychiatry and human values*. Springfield: Charles C. Thomas, 1956, p. 80.
Feifel, H. Qualitative differences in the vocabulary response of normals and abnormals. *Genet. psychol. Monogr.*, 1949, **39**, 151–204.
Fernando, S. J. M. Depressive illness in Jews and non-Jews. *Brit. J. Psychiat.*, 1966, **112**, 991–996.
Flavell, J. H. Abstract thinking and social behavior in schizophrenia. *J. abnorm. soc. Psychol.*, 1956, **52**, 208–211.
Fontana, A. F. Familial etiology of schizophrenia: Is a scientific methodology possible? *Psychol. Bull.*, 1966, **66**, 214–227.
Ford, C. S., & Beach, F. A. *Patterns of sexual behavior*. New York: Ace Books, 1952.
Fried, J. Acculturation and mental health among Indian migrants in Peru, in M. K. Opler (Ed.) *Culture and mental health*. New York: The MacMillan Co., 1959.
Gallais, P., Miletto, G., Corriol, J., & Bert, J. Introduction à l'étude d'EEG physiologique de Noir d'Afrique, deux mém. *Mêd. Trop.*, 1951, **11**, 128–146.
Gerstein, R. A. A suggested method of analyzing and extending the use of Bellevue-Wechsler vocabulary responses. *J. consult. Psychol.*, 1949, **13**, 366–374.
Glad, D. D. Attitudes and experiences of American Jewish and Americn Irish male youth as related to differences in adult rates of inebriety. *Quart. J. stud. Alc.*, 1947, **8**, 406–472.
Gladwin, T., & Sarason, S. B. Culture and individual personality integration in Truk in M. K. Opler (Ed.) *Culture and mental health*. New York: MacMillan, 1959.
Goldhamer, H., & Marshall, A. *Psychosis and civilization*. Glencoe, Illinois: The Free Press, 1953.
Goldstein, K., & Scheerer, M. Abstract and concrete behavior. An experimental study with special tests. *Psychol. Monogr.*, 1941, 53, No. 2.
Gordon, H. L. Psychiatry in Kenya Colony. *J. ment. Sci.*, 1934, **80**, 167.
Guertin, W. H. Medical and statistical — psychological models for research in schizophrenia. *Behav. Sci.*, 1961, **6**, 200–204.
Hallowell, A. I. Fear and anxiety as cultural and individual variables in a primitive society. *J. soc. Psychol.*, 1938, **9**, 25–47.
Hallowell, A. I. Culture and mental disorder. *J abnorm. soc. Psychol.*, 1934, **29**, 1–9.
Hamer, J. H. Acculturation stress and the functions of alcohol among the forest Potawatomi. *Quart. J. Stud. Alc.*, 1965, **62**, 285–302.
Hanfmann, E. & Kasanin, J. *Conceptual thinking in schizophrenia*. New York: Nervous and Mental Disease Monographs, 1942, No. 67.
Haward, L. C. R. & Roland, W. A. Some inter-cultural differences on the Draw-a-Man test: Goodenough scores. *Man*, 1954, **54**, 86–88.

Henry, J. Rorschach Technique in primitive cultures. *Amer.J. Orthopsychiatry,* 1941, **11**, 230–234.

Hollingshead, A. B. & Redlich, F. C. Social stratification and psychiatric disorder. *Amer. sociol. Rev.*, 1953, **18**, 163–167.

Horton, D. The function of alcohol in primitive societies: A cross-cultural study. *Quart. J. stud. Alc.*, 1943, **4**, 191–320.

Hudson, W. Pictorial depth perception in sub-cultural groups in Africa. *J. soc. Psychol.*, 1960, **52**, 183–208.

Hyde, R. W. & Chisholm, R. M. Studies in medical sociology III. The relation of mental disorder to race and nationality. *New England J. Med.*, 1944, **231**, 612–618.

Jahoda, G. Geometric illusions and environment: A study in Ghana. *Brit. J. Psychol.*, 1966, **57**, 193–199.

Jahoda, G. Assessment of abstract behavior in a non-Western culture. *J. abnorm. soc. Psychol.*, 1956, **53**, 237–243.

Joseph, A., & Murray, V. F. *Chamorros and Carolinians of Saipan: personality studies.* Cambridge: Harvard Univers. Press, 1951.

Kiev, A. Beliefs and delusions of West Indian Immigrants. *Brit. J. Psychiat.*, 1963, **109**, 356–363.

Kline, N. S. Psychiatry in Kuwait. *Brit. J. Psychiat.*, 1963a, **109**, 766–774.

Kline, N. S. Psychiatry in Indonesia. *Amer. J. Psychiat.*, 1963b, **119**, 809–815.

Lemkaw, P. V., & DeSanctis, S. A survey of Italian psychiatry. *Amer. J. Psychiat.*, 1950, **107**, 401–408.

Linz, H. L. *Verleichende Psychiatrie. Eine Studie Über die Beziehung von Kultur Sociologie und Psychopathologie*. Vienna: Wilhelm Mandrich Verlag, 1964.

Lolli, G., Serianni, E., Golder, G. M., & Luzzatto-Fegiz, P. *Alcohol in Italian culture. Food and wine in relation to sobriety among Italians and Italian Americans.* New Haven, Publications Division, Yale Centre of Alcohol Studies. Clencoe, Illinois: Free Press, 1958.

Lopez, C. Ethnographische Betrachtunger über schizophrenie, *Ztshr. Ges. Neurol. u. Psychiat.*, 1932, **142**, 706–711.

Loudon, J. B. Psychogenic disorder and social conflict among the Zulu, in M. K. Opler (Ed.) *Culture and Mental Health*. New York: MacMillan, 1959.

Malinowski, B. *The sexual life of Savages in North-Western Melanesia.* New York: Harcourt, 1932.

Malzberg, B., & Lee, E. S. *Migration and mental disease.* New York: Social Science Research Council, 1956.

Mangin, W. Drinking among Andean Indians. *Quart. J. stud. Alc.*, 1957, **18**, 55–66.

Marinko, B. P., Psychoses in Ethiopia. *Transcult. Psychiat. Res.,* 1966, **111**, 152–154.

Mead, M. *From the South Seas: Studies of adolescence and sex in primitive societies.* New York: W. M. Morrow and Co., 1939.

Mensh, I. N., & Henry, J. Direct observation and psychological tests in anthropological field work. *Amer. Anthropologist*, 1953 **55**, 461–480.

Mishler, E. G., & Scotch, N. A. Sociocultural factors in the epidemiology of schizophrenia. *Psychiatry*, 1963, **26**, 315–351.

Mundy-Castle, A. C., McKiever, B. L., & Prinsloo, T. A comparative study of the electroencephalograms of normal Africans and Europeans of Southern Africa. *E.E.G. Clin. Neurophysiol.*, 1953, **5**, 533–543.

Murdock, G. P. *Social structure*. New York: MacMillan, 1949.

Murphy, H. B. M. Culture and mental illness in Singapore, in M. K. Opler (Ed.) *Culture and mental health*. New York: MacMillan, 1959.

Murphy, H. B. M. Refugee psychoses in Great Britain: admission to mental hospitals. In H. B. M. Murphy (Ed.) *Flight and Resettlement*. Paris: Unesco, 1955.

Murphy, H. B. M., Wittkower, E. D., Fried, J., & Ellengerger, H. *A cross-cultural survey of schizophrenic symptomatology*. In proceedings of the Third World Congress of Psychiatry, 1961, **2**, 1309–1315.

Murphy, H. B., Wittkower, E. D., & Chance, N. A. Cross-cultural inquiry into the symptomatology of depression. *Transcult. Psychiat. Res. Rev.*, 1964, **1**, 5–18.

Myers, J. K., & Roberts, B. H. *Family and class dynamics in mental illness*. New York: John Wiley, 1959.

Newman, P. L. "Wild Man" behaviour in a New Guinea Highlands Community. *Amer. Anthrop.*, 1964, **66**, 1–19.

Opler, M. K. Cultural differences in mental disorders: An Italian and Irish contrast in the schizophrenias. In M. K. Opler (Ed.) *Culture and Mental Health*. New York: MacMillan, 1959.

Opler, M. K. *Culture psychiatry and human values*. Springfield: Charles C. Thomas, 1956.

Pfeiffer, W. M. Psychiatrische Besonderheiten in Indonesien (Psychiatric peculiarities in Indonesia). *Transcult. Psychiat. Res.*, 1966, **111**, 116–119 (English abstract).

Pflanz, M. & Lambelet, L. Zivilisationskrankheiten und psychosomatische probleme im Laendlichen Indien. *Munch. Med. Wchschr.*, 1965, **107**, 1493–1502.

Prange, A. J., & Vitols, M. M. Cultural aspects of the relatively low incidence of depression in Southern Negroes. *Internat. J. soc. Psychiat.*, 1962, **8**, 104–112.

Price-Williams, D. R. Abstract and concrete modes of classification in a primitive society. *Brit. J. educ. Psychology*, 1962, **32**, 50–61.

Rankin, A. M., & Philip, P. J. An epidemic of laughing in the Bukoba district of Tanganyka. *The Central African J. Medicine*, 1963, **9**, 167–170.

Rawnsley, K., & Loudon, J. B. Factors influencing the referral of patients to psychiatrists by general practitioners. *Brit. J. Prev. Soc. Med.*, 1962, **16**, 174–182.

Reay, M. Mushroom and collective hysteria. *Australian Territories*, 1965, **5**, 18–28 (cited by Salisbury, 1966).

Rin, H. A study of the aetiology of Koro in respect to the Chinese concept of illness. *Internat. J. soc. Psychiat.*, 1965, **11**, 7–13.

Rin, H., Chu, H. & Lin, T. Psychophysiological reactions of a rural and suburban population in Taiwan. *Transcult. Psychiat. Res.*, 1966, **111**, 98–101 (abstract).

Robertson, J. P. S., & Batcheldor, K. J. Cultural aspects of the Wechsler Adult Intelligence Scale in relation to British mental patients. *J. ment. Sci.*, 1956, **102**, 612–618.

Rubel, A. J. The epidemiology of a folk illness: Susto in Hispanic America. *Ethnology*, 1964, **3**, 268–283.

Salisbury, R. Possession on the New Guinea Highlands: Review of literature. *Transcult. Psychiat. Res.*, 1966, **111**, 103–108.

Schooler, C. Birth order and schizophrenia. *Arch. gen. Psychiat*, 1961, **4**, 117–123.

Schooler, C. Birth order and hospitalization for schizophrenia. *J. abnorm. soc. Psychol.*, 1964, **69**, 574–579.

Schooler, C., & Caudill, W. Symptomatology in Japanese and American schizophrenics. *Ethnology*, 1964, **3**, 172–178.

Sharadamba, R. Culture and mental disorder: a study in an Indian mental hospital. *Internat. J. soc. Psychiat.*, 1966, **12**, 139–148.

Schwitzgebel, R. The performance of Dutch and Zulu adults on selected perceptual tasks. *J. soc. Psychol.*, 1962, **57**, 73–77.

Shapiro, M. B. The rotation of drawings by illiterate Africans. *J. soc. Psychol.*, 1960, **52**, 17–30.

Simmons, O. G. Drinking patterns and interpersonal performance in a Peruvian Mestizo Community. *Quart. J. stud. Alc.*, 1959, **20**, 103–111.

Stengel, E. Problems of nosology and nomenclature in the mental disorders, in J. Zubin (Ed.) *Field studies in the Mental Disorders*. New York: Grune and Stratton, Inc., 1961.

Thouless, R. H. A racial difference in perception. *J. soc. Psychol.*, 1933, **4**, 330–339.

Tooth, G. Studies in mental illness in the Gold Coast. London: Her Majesty's Stationery Office. Colonial Research publication, 1950, **6**.

Tyhurst, L. Displacement and migration: A study in social psychiatry. *Amer. J. Psychiat.*, 1951, **107**, 561–568.

Vallee, F. G. Eskimo theories of mental illness in the Hudson Bay Region. *Anthropologica*, 1966, **8**, 53–83.

Venables, P. H. Input dysfunction in schizophrenia, in B. A. Maher (Ed.) Progress in experimental personality research. New York: Academic Press, 1964, Vol. I.

Verhaegen, P., & Laroche, J. L. Some methodological considerations concerning the study of aptitudes and elaboration of psychological tests for African natives. *J. soc. Psychol.*, 1958, **47**, 249–256.

Vitols, M. M., Water, H. G., & Keeler, M. H. Hallucinations and delusions in White and Negro schizophrenics. *Amer. J. Psychiat.*, 1963, **120**, 472–476.

Wittkower, E. D., & Bijou, L. Psychiatry in developing countries. *Amer. J. Psychiat.*, 1963, **120**, 218–221.

Wittkower, E. D. Perspectives of transcultural psychiatry, presented at the IV World Congress of Psychiatry Madrid, September 5–11, 1966.

Wittkower, E. D., & Rin, H. Transcultural psychiatry. *Arch. gen. Psychiat.*, 1965, **13**, 387–394.

Wittkower, E. D. & Lipowski, Z. J. Recent developments in psychosomatic medicine. *Psychosom. Med.*, 1966, **28**, 722–737.

Yap, P. M. Koro — a culture-bound depersonalization syndrome. *Brit. J. Psychiat.*, 1965, **111**, 43–50.

Yap, P. M. Mental diseases peculiar to certain cultures: A survey of comparative psychiatry. *J. Ment. Sci.*, 1951, **97**, 313–327.

Zubin, J. A cross-cultural approach to psychopathology and its implications for diagnostic classification, in L. D. Eron (Ed.) The Classification of Behavior Disorders. Chicago: Aldine publishing Co., 1966.

Zubin, J. & Kietzman, M. L. A cross cultural approach to classification in schizophrenia and other mental disorders, in P. H. Hoch and J. Zubin (Ed.) *Psychopathology of schizophrenia*. New York: Grune and Stratton, Inc., 1966.

Part I

Cognitive and Perceptual Disorders

Chapter 3

Disorders of Thinking

R. W. PAYNE[1]

INTRODUCTION

Frame of Reference

Thought disorder is regarded by most psychiatrists as a primary feature of some types of mental illness, such as schizophrenia, and an important secondary feature of others. Therefore, one approach to a discussion of disorders of thought, would be to organize it around the generally accepted psychiatric syndromes that make up the psychoses. This has not been done in the present chapter for several reasons. First of all, the detection of specific psychiatric signs and symptoms by talking to patients is an unreliable and uncertain affair. Patients tend to say different things to different people at different times, so that there is often very little agreement about whether or not a patient is, for example, deluded or retarded. Second, there is far from universal agreement about how psychiatric signs and symptoms do in fact cluster, or what particular term should be applied to a particular cluster. A number of studies have been carried out in which psychiatrists have employed standard rating scales to assess the symptoms of groups of mental patients. The ratings then are usually intercorrelated and the correlation matrix factor analyzed, in order to discover whether or not the symptoms cluster according to the anticipated psychiatric syndromes. These studies (Payne and Sloane, 1968) by and large have produced inconsistent results, some of which have accorded well with the anticipated syndromes, and some of which have not. Two criticisms can be made of these studies. The first is a purely statistical one. In the factor analyses carried out, no explicit mathematical definition of what constitutes a cluster has ever been agreed on, nor has any "null hypothesis" ever been specified that would enable the investigator unambiguously to rule out the existence of a postulated syndrome. Therefore, the same set of data could suggest different sets of clusters to different investigators applying different factor analytical techniques. The second point concerns the validity of the ratings themselves. However objectively the symptoms are described on the rating scales, if psychiatrists, or actually any raters with a knowledge of psychiatry, interview and rate the patients, their ratings are likely to be influenced by their preconceptions. Thus, for instance, if the rater knows that symptoms A and B are supposed to occur together, when he elicits A, he may be more likely to question the patient about B, more likely to encourage the patient to describe B and, given an ambiguous response, more likely to rate B as being present. Thus the statistical results may in part, or even largely, reflect only the psychiatric training of the raters. For these reasons then, the symptom rating studies that have been carried out cannot be regarded as conclusive. There is no evidence

[1] I am deeply indebted to Miss Carol Witham without whose help this chapter could not have been prepared.

for the existence of the various syndromes which have been suggested. A third point is that psychiatric classification is unreliable in the sense that psychiatrists, working independently, do not achieve very high levels of agreement, especially when they attempt to employ relatively specific and precise diagnostic categories.

The data that form the basis of the system of classification to be followed in this chapter, are derived from formal psychological tests or experiments. These data have the advantage of being relatively objective, "public," and reliable. Nevertheless, a classification based on test results also has serious disadvantages. The most important one is that, generally, the relation between a specific abnormality measured by psychological tests, and the peculiar behavior that brought the patient to the doctor in the first place, is usually not known. Thus we may have acquired objectivity and reliability in our classification, at the expense of immediate practical descriptive and predictive implications. Even so, in the long run, it appears likely that these stable data form a better basis, because practical implications are likely to be discovered to an increasing degree, and the stability of the data eventually will make predictions more accurate, and implications less ambiguous.

We restrict the present chapter to a discussion of thinking disturbances that have been acquired after birth. Thus, we shall not deal with the very large area of congenital mental deficiency, which includes both primary and secondary amentia. For each type of cognitive abnormality, the measures that most frequently have been used to define it are described briefly, and what is known of the causes, treatment and implications of the disorder is summarized

Thinking in Normal People

Before attempting to measure and explain thought disorder, we must outline the way in which normal thought processes take place. Unfortunately, although intelligence testing is one of the oldest branches of psychology, and much is known about how rote learning takes place, very little is yet known about the way in which human problem solving occurs. It is beyond the scope of the present chapter to discuss all the more recent experimental attempts to investigate some of the specific processes that are involved in problem solving, although obviously they will be important in the future to an understanding of pathological thinking. Only the techniques that have been used to throw light on clearly pathological behavior will be mentioned.

For want of a better frame of reference, in the present chapter we classify the different psychological tests and experiments that have been used to study mental patients on the basis of a rather simplistic, logical analysis of the processes likely to be involved in problem solving. For the present purpose, we regard the terms "thinking," "cognition," and "problem solving" as equivalent. Thinking is considered a purposeful activity designed to solve some problem, or to resolve some intellectual conflict. The individual processes incoming sensory data, in part by rearranging them, and in part by relating them to other data stored internally, and some definite answer (or response) occurs which terminates the sequence. We must also assume that, for any particular set of data presented in a particular context, there is a single "correct" response that would satisfy everyone if he were aware of it, and if he could comprehend the way in which it related to the initial elements of the problem.

The first process involved in this series of events is attention. An inability to attend will clearly be detrimental to thought, since not all the relevant perceptual material will be registered. This stage of problem solving is the subject of Chapter 4 and will not be discussed further here.

Given an adequate degree of attention, the individual perceives the various elements of the problem. If his perception is distorted or inaccurate, the subsequent manipulation will be affected. Thus, perceptual distortions are a possible cause of thought disorder, and will be discussed in the present chapter. "Perceptual set" refers to the range and type of stimuli that are apprehended. If this is too narrow or restrictive, essential data may be excluded, and thinking may be affected. If it is too broad or "overinclusive," thinking may be adversely affected in a different way. Both types of disorder of set will be discussed.

Once the relevant information has been perceived, it must be held in some kind of temporary store (the "immediate memory span"), while it is processed. Disorders either in the capacity of this short-term store, or in its ability to retain information, could adversely affect thinking. These disorders will be discussed in Chapter 4, and will not be dealt with here.

Essential items of information that exceed the storage capacity of the immediate memory span must presumably be memorized before further manipulation can proceed. Disorders in the ability to memorize material could also influence thinking, but again this will be dealt with in Chapter 2 and is not discussed further here.

The third stage in the process of problem solving can be called "conceptualization." Usually the perceived data must be organized or rearranged before they can be manipulated, and the problem solved. This process of conceptual organization often employs previously acquired concepts or categories (represented by language symbols). Occasionally, new concepts must be formulated before the data can be grouped in a way which allows for the successful solution of the problem. The inability to formulate such abstract general categories and to utilize them in classifying data, has been labeled "concreteness," and is held to be a common form of thought disorder. Indeed severely concrete individuals are apparently unable even to employ previously learned concepts to group items of information, because they seem to regard each individual item as unique, and they appear unable to abstract any common properties. Another possible consequence of concreteness may be an unusual use of words, because some of the normal abstract connotations of words are no longer understood. This could result in a failure on some occasions to comprehend all the relevant information for a particular problem.

A second disorder of conceptualization has been called "overinclusion." Individuals with this disorder appear to define categories (words) so broadly that they include items which for normal people are irrelevant or only distantly associated. This may produce overlapping of normally mutually exclusive categories, so that some items become ambiguous, falling under more than one category. Newly developed categories are apparently also unnecessarily extensive in the same way. Both concreteness and overinclusion can produce characteristic disorders of thinking, which we describe below.

Once information has been perceived and classified, different sorts of manipulation of the data are involved in different sorts of problems. Some problems involve purely deductive reasoning, some require induction, and some a combination of both. It is possible to conceive of abnormalities associated with each type of manipulation. There is also some evidence (Furneaux, 1961) that there are three relatively independent aspects of problem solving as a process, the speed with which it is carried out, the accuracy of the results and the persistence with which any individual pursues the manipulations involved in solving time-consuming problems. An abnormal degree of retardation can produce a characteristic type of thought disorder, and gross inaccuracy or lack of persistence both clearly affect thinking in different ways. One final characteristic of performance has been termed "rigidity." The successful solution of a problem may require most people to attempt a variety of different sequences of manipulation before a correct solution emerges. However, some people tend to persevere rigidly to a certain line of attack, and are relatively unable to perceive alternative approaches. This restriction of the range of possible solutions clearly affects thinking adversely, and this disorder seems to characterize some people.

The Measurement and Significance of General Intelligence

General intelligence is sometimes defined as that which intelligence tests measure in common. Although this begs the question of what defines an intelligence test, it does underline the often repeated observation that people who are good at solving one type of problem tend also to be good at solving other types, even when the content, the mode of presentation, the type of response, and the type of reasoning involved seem to be different.

Although different kinds of intelligence tests, as scored conventionally, tend to intercorrelate fairly highly and, thus, yield a strong general factor when factor analyzed, we cannot conclude from this that general intelligence is necessarily a unitary phenomenon. Furneaux (1961), working with a typical *g* test composed of Thurstone type letter series items (for example, complete the following series: A B B A B B –), found that the *g* score obtained from an untimed version of the test is a function of three relatively independent characteristics of performance—speed (of solving correct, but not incorrect or abandoned items), accuracy, and persistence. He found that these three characteristics can be measured very reliably, and he also found that there are some reasons for regarding them as being of more fundamental importance than a single *g* score. For example, there appears to be a linear relationship between log solution time and item difficulty level which has the same slope for all people. Furneaux points out that the same *g* score can be obtained in a number of different ways (by a slow, accurate worker, or a fast, inaccurate worker), so that measuring these characteristics separately is of more descriptive value, and is potentially of greater predictive value.

Furneaux's work suggests that we must therefore regard "IQ" scores as being ambiguous. If, for example, we demonstrate that two types of symptoms among the mentally ill both tend to be associated with a decline in general intelligence, we cannot necessarily conclude that the same "general" ability is being affected in both conditions. The reduced IQ scores might be the result of two quite different abnormalities in the two cases (for example, slowness in the first instance, and inaccuracy in the second).

GENERAL INTELLIGENCE AND INTELLECTUAL DETERIORATION

Intellectual Deterioration and Mental Illness

If intellectual impairment is an important feature of mental illness, we would expect that patients who are diagnosed as psychotic should have lower tested intelligence quotients on admission to the hospital than they had before they became ill. Studies that involve direct measurements of this kind are not easy because of the obvious difficulty of obtaining comparable preillness intelligence measures. Some investigators have been able to find schizophrenic patients who had been given IQ tests in high school prior to their illness, and have been able to retest them on the same measures (Rappaport & Webb, 1950). In most recent studies, newly admitted patients have been retested on selection tests that they had taken first when they were inducted into one of the armed services. These data are available for relatively large groups of schizophrenics retested on the Army Classification Battery (Lubin, Gieseking, & Williams, 1962; Kingsley & Struening, 1966) and the Canadian Army M test (Schwartzman & Douglas, 1962). These three groups of investigators all report a decrease of approximately one third of a standard deviation, or 6 IQ points from the pre-illness level. However, the normal controls were found to increase their scores over the same period by a similar amount, presumably because of practice. Thus the deterioration shown by the schizophrenics may amount to as much as two thirds of a standard deviation on average.

However, other studies have found no evidence for intellectual deterioration from the highest childhood level (Batman, Albee, & Lane, 1966; Albee, Lane, Corcoran, & Wernecke, 1963) or from Army induction level (Griffith, Estes, & Zerof, 1962). These three negative studies have in common the fact that the subjects were retested on tests different from the ones that they took first, so that differences would be harder to detect, because of the relative lack of correlation between the measures. Also, the patients in these studies were of nearly subnormal intelligence initially. For instance, Batman, Albee, and Lane's chronic schizophrenics had a mean IQ of 81.2 in childhood. It is possible to speculate that the dull who become psychotic deteriorate little intellectually. However, this finding may be, in part, an artifact of the kinds of tests used, which may not be sensitive enough to measure changes among the very dull, since they have too high a "floor."

There is clear evidence that not all people deteriorate to the same extent when they become ill. Not surprisingly, the nature of the illness is a very important factor. Kingsley and Struening (1966) found that nonparanoid schizophrenics had dropped an average of 15 score units, while paranoid schizophrenics had dropped only 3.7 units on average. The findings of Lubin, Gieseking, and Williams (1962) agree on this, but the difference is much less pronounced. It appears that psychiatrists tend to attach the label "paranoid schizophrenic" to those patients who are relatively undeteriorated intellectually. This hypothesis is supported by the data quoted by Payne (1961) on the intellectual levels of patients tested while ill. Payne found that schizophrenics with low functioning IQ's tended to be diagnosed as Catatonic, Hebephrenic, or Simple, while the ones who were diagnosed as "paranoid," or "mixed," or the ones not specified, had near average IQ's when ill.

Whether affective disorder or neurosis also produces a degree of general intellectual deterioration is not certain, as test-retest studies are lacking. However, data on the level of the functioning of these patients when ill, which is average (Payne, 1961), suggest that the general deterioration in these groups is not large. The only exception to this generalization derives from British army psychiatrists during World War II, who tended to label dull inductees as "neurotic" (Payne, 1961), probably because they were using criteria of neurosis different from the ones employed by psychiatrists in civilian life.

A second question is whether deterioration is progressive if the illness continues. Kraepelin believed that most schizophrenic patients continue to deteriorate intellectually. Even if this were true, however, we need not necessarily indict the "disease" process. Continued incarceration, with its relative sensory and social deprivation, could cause this result. In fact, sensory deprivation could well mask the intellectual improvement normally associated with clinical improvement among those patients who remain in the hospital.

Several direct test-retest studies have been reported which suggest that further intellectual deterioration does indeed take place among those who continue to be hospitalized as schizophrenic. Trapp and James (1937) retested 41 schizophrenics who had taken the Binet test within two weeks of admission. The retest interval varied from four months to 13 years. There was an average decline of 7.6 IQ points, and the data also suggested that the longer the patients had been ill, the greater was the decline (Payne, 1961). Schwartzman, Douglas, and Muir (1962) followed up 23 schizophrenics for ten years after they had first been tested in hospital, and found that the 10 who were still in hospital had continued to decline on the Canadian Army M test. However, the ones who had been released from hospital had improved significantly, almost to the level of their pre-morbid scores. Haywood and Moelis (1963) similarly found that "improved" schizophrenics had increased their IQ's 5 years after admission, while "unimproved" schizophrenics had decreased their IQ's, although all were still hospitalized.

Three other studies (Batman, Albee, & Lane, 1966; Hamlin & Ward, 1965; Smith, 1964) found no evidence for progressive deterioration after hospitalization in groups of schizophrenics, although not all were well controlled.

These studies on the whole suggest that, apart from the initially very dull, intellectual deterioration can continue during hospitalization among those regarded as schizophrenic and, at least, a part of this decline may be the result of some worsening disability and not just the effect of social and cultural isolation. However, it does not occur in all cases.

The final question is whether this intellectual deterioration is reversible. Kraepelin originally thought that dementia praecox was, like organic dementia, progressive and irreversible. However, the experimental evidence, on the whole, suggests that, when patients improve, their level of intelligence improves again. The findings of Schwartzman, Douglas, and Muir (1962) and Haywood and Moelis (1963), which support this conclusion, have already been described. Early studies by Davidson (1939) who used the Binet test, and Carp (1950) who used the Wechsler-Bellevue, found that IQ level went up as the patients improved clinically, although they tested no control group to assess the effects of practice.

The evidence suggests, therefore, that intellectual deterioration in patients diagnosed as schizophrenic is not completely irreversible, but tends to recover if the patient's other symptoms improve.

Indirect Measures of Deterioration

In many cases the clinical psychologist is

called on to decide whether a particular patient has deteriorated, without having any pre-illness intelligence level to use as a baseline. In these circumstances it is common practice to use one of the standard indirect measures of deterioration. Three of the most common, the Babcock-Levy test for the measurement of efficiency of mental functioning (Babcock & Levy, 1940), the Shipley-Hartford test of deterioration (Shipley, 1940) and the Hunt-Minnesota test for organic brain damage (Hunt, 1943) utilize a vocabulary test to provide a measure of pre-illness intellectual level. The rationale for this is that in normal people, vocabulary is very highly correlated with most tests of general intelligence. Furthermore, there is a great deal of indirect evidence (Payne, 1961) that vocabulary is the ability least affected by mental illness, since conventionally scored vocabulary tests show the smallest difference between mentally ill groups of all types, and normal people.

The Babcock-Levy test measures current functioning ability by a battery of tests of mental and motor speed, and rote learning ability. They were chosen because the evidence suggested that they are the abilities most seriously affected by mental illness of all kinds. Thus, in theory, the Babcock deterioration index might be expected to underestimate current general level of functioning, and to overestimate the extent of general deterioration. The Shipley-Hartford test measures present intellectual level by means of a conventional verbal *g* test of abstract reasoning. In principle, this would seem more reasonable. The Hunt-Minnesota test was not originally intended to be a test of deterioration, but a test of brain damage, so that the learning tests that are contrasted to vocabulary level were chosen because they are most affected by brain damage. A fourth common indirect measure is the Wechsler Bellevue Deterioration Index (Wechsler, 1944). This index measures present level by the subtests most affected by the normal aging process, and measures past level by the subtests least affected by age. The somewhat dubious assumption is that the deterioration produced by age and by mental illness is the same. A fifth test, not originally designed to measure deterioration at all, but very similar to the Shipley-Hartford Scale, is the combination of the Mill Hill Vocabulary Scale (Raven, 1948) and Raven's Progressive Matrices (Raven, 1950), a nonverbal test of general intelligence (Foulds & Dixon, 1962).

In all these tests, an estimate of previous IQ and an estimate of present IQ can be obtained, and the difference (expressed as an "index" or a "ratio") indicates the degree of deterioration.

Because normal people tend to keep adding to their vocabulary until about 30, and show no subsequent decline until about 50, whereas they begin to decline in abstract ability before 30, it is essential to standardize these scales very carefully over their entire age range. Unfortunately, the Babcock-Levy Scale utilized the Binet vocabulary test norms for very young adults, and the original standardization of the Shipley-Hartford was based almost entirely on normal people under twenty. As a result, when either test is given to middle-aged, normal people and the original norms are used, the score suggests a considerable degree of "deterioration," since no allowance has been made for normal changes with age (Payne, 1961; Lewinsohn, 1963). Only two of these scales are adequately standardized for age, the Wechsler Deterioration Index and the Mill Hill Vocabulary-Matrices combination (Foulds & Dixon, 1962). The latter is preferable because, as the correlation between the scales is available, it is possible to say, for any given discrepancy, how frequently it would have arisen in the standardization population, and, thus, to assess the statistical abnormality of the amount of indirectly assessed "deterioration" shown by a particular patient (Payne & Jones, 1957).

Quite apart from the problem of standardization, however, is the question of the validity of these measures. It has frequently been claimed that a conventional vocabulary test is not the best measure of premorbid intelligence, because some deterioration of vocabulary score does in fact occur in mental illness. There is a good deal of evidence, which has been reviewed by Payne (1961), that this is the case, and more recent studies confirm this (Hamlin & Jones, 1963) although the rate of deterioration of vocabulary among the chronically ill may be very slow (Moran, Gorham & Holzman, 1960). It would probably be better to use the Ammons Full Range Picture Vocabulary Test in future attempts to develop indirect measures of deterioration, since the evidence (Payne, 1961; Blatt, 1959) suggests that this vocabulary test is minimally affected by mental disorder; it involves recognition rather than recall, and requires the subject merely to point to the appropriate picture.

Although indirect techniques of assessing deterioration may yet prove valuable, it is necessary first to demonstrate their validity by showing a substantial correlation between an indirect measure of deterioration, and a direct measure of deterioration based on a test-retest follow-up study. Thus far, no studies of this kind appear to have been carried out. Studies in which the Wechsler and Shipley-Hartford indixes of deterioration have been related to clinical ratings of the amount of deterioration, have yielded insignificant results (Payne, 1961). However, one study (Dowis & Buchanan, 1961) by using the Matrices as a measure of present intellectual level, and by using the Wide Range Vocabulary Test as a measure of former level, obtained very promising results. Seventy-five inpatients were tested when they were judged to be as well as possible, and again when their pathology was judged to be at maximal level. It was found that the vocabulary score remained the same, whereas the Matrices dropped significantly during the pathological state. One can conclude that, at least this combination of tests, which is logically the most satisfactory, may yet prove useful.

Behavioral Abnormalities Associated with General Intellectual Deterioration

It has been noted that when young (adolescent) schizophrenic patients are compared with older (middle aged) patients, the young show a much lower level of tested intelligence (Pollack, 1960). This and other evidence suggests that, when schizophrenia is diagnosed in the young, an important diagnostic criterion is intellectual deterioration, whereas this is not the case in middle-aged individuals. In the young, schizophrenic deterioration may be mistaken for mental deficiency (Chapman & Pathman, 1959).

Payne (1961) reports that there is a tendency for schizophrenics with low levels of intellectual functioning while ill to be diagnosed as "Hebephrenic," "Catatonic," or "Simple." This suggests that there may be a tendency for these impaired patients to exhibit mood swings, and silly, bizarre or grotesque forms of behavior. Schizophrenic patients who are functioning at an average intellectual level or better, tend to be diagnosed as paranoid schizophrenic (Payne, 1961; Smith, 1964; Lubin, Gieseking & Williams, 1962). More or less systematized delusions of persecution are for some reason common among intellectually well-preserved patients. This suggests that their cognitive deficit may be relatively specific. Unfortunately, there appear to be very few objective studies of the specific symptomatology that is associated with different levels of intellectual functioning when ill.

Another common descriptive method of subdividing the very large and heterogeneous group diagnosed as "schizophrenics," is by the form of onset of the condition, as defined in terms of some standard scale such as the Elgin Scale (Wittman, 1941) or the Phillips (1953) Scale. When the onset of the illness is very gradual and of long standing, associated with increasing social withdrawal but reactive to no discernible trauma, the condition is labeled "process" schizophrenia. However, when the illness has a rapid onset, in persons who were formerly sociable and extraverted, and seems to be a response to some environmental trauma, the term "reactive" schizophrenia is used. There is now a good deal of evidence that "reactive" patients have a relatively good prognosis, whereas "process" schizophrenics tend to become chronic patients (Chapman, Day, & Burstein, 1961; Higgins, 1964). In spite of the popularity of this classification there appear to be no studies of the differences between these groups in general level of intellectual functioning when ill. Of course, it is possible that once the condition has developed, there are no marked differences in this respect.

Prognostic Significance of Low IQ Scores

There is now a considerable body of evidence that individuals who have a low (dull normal to borderline defective) tested IQ in their childhood, are more likely to develop a breakdown which will be diagnosed as "schizophrenic" when they are young adults, than are their peers of normal intelligence (Lane & Albee, 1964; Albee, Lane, & Reuter, 1964; Pollack, 1960). Furthermore, in a group of adult schizophrenics, the ones who recover tend to have had a higher childhood IQ than the ones who become chronic patients (Batman, Albee, & Lane, 1966). Similarly, chronic schizophrenics tend to have had a lower tested IQ on army induction than schizophrenics who recover (Schwartzman & Douglas, 1962). It is also the case that schizophrenics who have a higher tested IQ on their hospital admission, more frequently tend to recover than patients with a lower tested admission IQ, who tend more often to become chronic (Payne, 1961).

Possibly these findings are related to the process-reactive dimension. It may be the case that "process schizophrenia" starts to develop very slowly even in childhood, so that some amount of deterioration has occurred very early in life. It would seem that this type of patient has a poor prognosis (Phillips, 1963). A study by Heath, Albee, and Lane (1965) supports this view. Forty-six adult schizophrenics were given a standard Process-Reactive rating scale, and their childhood intelligence quotients on the Kuhlmann-Anderson Group Intelligence test were obtained. The process schizophrenics, as expected were significantly duller as children. The process schizophrenics as children had also been significantly duller than their own siblings, but the reactive schizophrenics as children were not significantly different from their siblings.

The Possibility of Manipulating General Intelligence in Psychosis

The studies thus far cited suggest that any procedure that improves the general clinical status of the patient is likely also to improve his general intellectual level. However, there are very few carefully controlled studies about the specific effects of certain types of treatment on general intelligence.

Graham (1940) investigated the effect of insulin shock therapy on performance on the Stanford Binet in 33 schizophrenics, but he found that the treatment produced no significant improvement. Carp (1950) by studying 42 schizophrenics, found a 4.7 point rise on the Wechsler IQ following insulin treatment, but the lack of a control group made it impossible to rule out the effects of practice. Thorpe and Baker (1958) in a similarly uncontrolled study of the effects of insulin in nine schizophrenics found a substantial improvement on the Matrices test score. However, the faulty design of these studies, which control neither for practice, nor for the well-known "placebo" effect of suggestion, make it impossible to draw any conclusions about the possible specific effect of insulin therapy on general intellectual performance.

Similarly, there is no clear evidence that electro-convulsive therapy improves performance on intelligence tests. Callagan (1952) found that ECT had no significant effect on improving the performance of 25 depressed patients on several Wechsler subtests. Thorpe and Baker (1958) on the other hand, found that nine schizophrenics given ECT improved in their performance of Raven's Matrices. Again, the inadequate design failed to assess either the placebo effect or the effect of practice.

Another treatment that it has been claimed has temporary beneficial effects on the general intellectual performance of schizophrenics, is sodium amytal. Layman (1940), testing 20 schizophrenics with the Binet, before, during, and after amytal found a significant improvement with the drug, and a significant decline again when the drug was withdrawn. Mainord (1953) in an exactly similar study, by using the Wechsler-Bellevue with 22 deteriorated schizophrenics, found a pre-amytal mean IQ of 84.5, a highly significant mean improvement to 100.6 under amytal, and a decline to a mean of 86.4 when the effects of the amytal had worn off. However, Senf, Huston, and Cohen (1955) by using 24 chronic schizophrenics tested with three Wechsler verbal tests, could not obtain a significant effect. Similarly, Ogilvie (1954) and Broadhurst (1957) could not obtain this amytal effect with the Nufferno Level test, although they report large practice effects over the three sessions among the acute undeteriorated schizophrenics that they tested, which in part may have obscured the influence of amytal. It is likely that the drug, for some reason, works with some patients but not with others, and it is conceivable that it works only with very deteriorated patients. None of the studies allow the effect of suggestion *per se* to be evaluated.

A more recent form of treatment is phenothiazine medication. A very carefully controlled double-blind study of the effects of nine weeks of Thorazine treatment, as contrasted to a placebo on the intellectual performance of 40 chronic schizophrenics is reported by Nickols (1958). He found that the drug produced a slight but statistically insignificant improvement on the performance of the Wechsler-Bellevue Test and the Arthur Point Stencil Design Test. The addition of a "total push" regime for a further 12 weeks to the drug/placebo treatment similarly had no statistically significant effect on test performance.

Intellectual Variability and Mental Illness

The data thus far discussed are all intelligence quotient scores obtained from an entire test session. Although, clearly, the tested IQ of some patients commonly declines, this fact tells us nothing about which particular intellectual process or processes are at fault. Obviously, different patients could get low IQ scores for different reasons.

Before turning to an assessment of specific intellectual processes, it is worth discussing briefly one descriptive hypothesis about the nature of intellectual deterioration in schizophrenia. It has frequently been maintained (Payne, 1961) that schizophrenics are characteristically very variable in their performance, and it is this trait which tends to bring down their average level of ability both individually and as a group. Thus, for some periods, a schizophrenic patient may perform normally, but he may then perform very badly, the fluctuations being unpredictable. Several measures of this supposed variability have been commonly used. The first, derived from the Binet test, is merely the difference between the "basal" mental age (at which all subtests are passed) and the "ceiling" mental age (at which no subtests are passed) (Payne, 1961). A very variable performance, it was thought, would increase this difference. Several ways of assessing the subtest scatter on the Wechsler-Bellevue Scale have been used, although the best is probably the one used by Monroe (1952) who calculated the standard deviation of the weighted subtest scores around their own mean, for each patient.

There is a considerable amount of evidence (Payne, 1961) that subtest scatter on the Binet and on the Wechsler, so measured, is increased in mental illness. However, this could be the result, either of an increased variability of performance *or* of a reduction of the subtest intercorrelations within the mentally ill. Payne (1961), in reviewing the literature, concluded that the reliability studies on the Wechsler and on the Binet do not in fact bear out the hypothesis that schizophrenics are more variable in their test performance. If anything, their scores are more consistent from one occasion to another, than are the scores of normal people both in subtest and Full Scale performance. More recent studies reviewed by Guertin, Rabin, Frank, and Ladd (1962) similarly find high coefficients of reliability among mental patients on the Wechsler Bellevue. Therefore, it seems that the increased subtest discrepancies shown by schizophrenics are the result of a reduction in the average subtest intercorrelation. Indeed, these changes in subtest intercorrelations have been found in schizophrenic groups (Payne, 1961; Berger, Bernstein, Klein, Cohen, & Lucas, 1963). The clear implication of these results is that, among psychotics, certain subtests are probably affected by a relatively specific type of thought disorder, which does not affect the performance of normal people on these tests, and which does not affect performance on other subtests. The intrusion of an additional, specific source of subtest variance for psychotic patients would increase the size of subtest discrepancies, and would reduce subtest intercorrelations in an abnormal population. In the following sections, several specific types of this kind of impairment are discussed; all of them could easily affect the performance of psychotics on specific Wechsler and Binet subtests.

DISORDERS OF PERCEPTION

Perceptual Distortion

Perceptual disorders are common among brain-damaged patients, and Kraepelin's original view that Dementia Praecox is an organic illness, has led some investigators to look for perceptual defects among schizophrenics. Some have even gone as far as to suggest that schizophrenia may be the result of a perceptual defect (Cooper, 1960). Groups of schizophrenics have been found to be significantly worse than normal at matching and at reproducing patterns (Payne, 1961; Chapman & McGhie, 1962; Schwartz, 1967) at estimating sizes (Cooper, 1960; Silverman, 1964), and at estimating distances (Blumenthal & Meltzoff, 1967), although not all studies report significant differences (Rutschmann, 1961). Weight discrimination thresholds have been found to be raised, and some studies suggest that the inability to judge weights may be a poor prognostic sign (Rosenbaum, Flenning, & Rosen, 1965).

Some studies report more specific perceptual anomalies. Salzinger (1957) found in a weight judgment experiment, that acute schizophrenics have a much more pronounced "anchor" effect than normals. They judge weights to be heavier after they have been given a very heavy weight to lift (but not to judge). Hoffer and Osmond (1963) in a very interesting study found that 25 schizophrenic patients were less accurate than normals in judging when an investigator was looking into their eyes. These authors speculate that such a disability might contribute to a common feeling among paranoid schizophrenic patients that people are watching them.

These studies do not necessarily indicate that the sensory input is at fault. The apparent defective acuity found in some sensory threshold experiments can be shown to be the result of a response bias (for example, adopting a more conservative attitude) (Clark, 1966; Clark, Brown, & Rutschmann, 1967) and other apparent sensory defects in part may be defects of judgment and interpretation.

One type of perceptual distortion, which has been studied often, is size constancy. As Silverman (1964) points out, judging the sizes of objects accurately at varying distances depends on observing distance cues carefully. Children tend to make their judgments in terms of the size of the retinal image. Therefore, distant objects are judged to be smaller than they really are, and objects that are near at hand are judged to be larger than they really are. Normal adults slightly overcompensate for this, and tend to underestimate the size of objects close at hand, and overestimate the size of distant objects. There is a considerable amount of evidence that paranoid schizophrenics show "overconstancy" to an abnormal degree. That is to say, they overestimate the size of distant objects even more than normal adults (Weckowitz & Blewett, 1959; Silverman, 1964a, 1964b, 1967, Davis, Cromwell, & Held, 1967). Silverman has suggested that this is because paranoid schizophrenics scan their environment more carefully and, therefore, observe distance cues more closely which, like normal adults, they slightly overestimate. Scanning behavior has been measured by filming eye movements during size-estimation experiments, and the evidence supports this hypothesis (Silverman, 1964a). Paranoid schizophrenic patients still indulge in an abnormal amount of scanning up to three years after they have been in the hospital (Silverman, 1967).

There is a marked tendency for paranoid symptomatology to occur among reactive rather than process schizophrenics (Claridge, 1967), and the evidence suggests that acute reactive schizophrenics as a group may demonstrate overconstancy (Davis, Cromwell, & Held, 1967; Silverman, 1964a). This excessive amount of scanning may well be a function of the high level of anxiety in these patients. Claridge (1967) used the sedation threshold and the duration of the afterimage produced by the Archimedes Spiral as measures of central nervous system arousal (a short afterimage suggests quick recovery from fatigue and high arousal). On these measures, reactive schizophrenics were found to have a higher level of arousal than process schizophrenics. This finding is consistent with the results obtained by Ward and Carlson (1966) by using GSR responsiveness.

On the other hand, "simple" or "hebephrenic" schizophrenics, like children, show underconstancy, their size judgments being based largely on the size of the retinal image (Weckowitz & Blewett, 1959; Silverman, 1964a). These nonparanoid schizophrenic patients tend also to be "process" schizophrenics, and to become chronic; hence, it is hardly surprising that the evidence suggests that acute "process" schizophrenics and chronic schizophrenics both show perceptual "underconstancy" (Weckowitz & Blewett, 1959; Silverman, 1964a, 1964b, 1967; Davis, Cromwell, & Held, 1967). Silverman (1964a), attributes this to an abnormal reduction in scanning. Following Berlyne, he suggests that the amount of scanning may be learned.

> "The excessive scanner has learned that his most effective means of escaping or avoiding anxiety is to be hyperalert to the presence of cues which often precede or co-occur with noxious events" (Silverman, 1964a).

The "minimal-scanner," on the other hand, he postulates, avoids anxiety by directing his attention away from the environment and on to internal processes. This, Silverman believes, could lead to hallucinations. Silverman does not explain how reactive schizophrenics learn one technique of reducing anxiety, while process schizophrenics learn another. However, the evidence suggests that reactive schizophrenics, in fact, do not succeed in reducing their anxiety in this way, since they are evidently in a chronically high state of arousal, and show autonomic signs of anxiety (Stern, Surphlis, & Koff, 1965) which empirically, nevertheless, seem to indicate a good prognosis.

Process schizophrenics, who scan very little and give other indications of being withdrawn from their environment, may be in an abnormally low drive state, at least, in the early stages of their illness. Claridge (1967), by using the measures already described, found evidence for this, which is consistent with other findings (Stern, Surphlis, & Koff, 1965) that a low level of autonomic responsiveness is a poor prognostic sign. However, the picture is far from clear, because Venables and his colleagues (Venables, 1960, 1963a, 1963b, 1963c, 1964, 1966a, 1966b, 1967; Venables & Wing, 1962), have produced a great deal of evidence that chronic nonparanoid schizophrenics are in an abnormally *high* state of cortical arousal. Furthermore, there is a marked correlation between the amount of withdrawal and arousal level, very withdrawn patients being most aroused. Such chronic patients apparently show underconstancy, so that the relation between arousal and scanning in chronic patients is not clear. One important point is that Venables and his colleagues have measured cortical arousal level by the two flash, or two click fusion thresholds. It is conceivable that these measures are not related to the ones used by Claridge and, possibly, it is inappropriate to talk about level of arousal as if it were a unitary phenomenon. In fact, arousal may be a complex of several independent cortical and subcortical events.

Although the evidence is not complete, it is likely that all types of perceptual disorders are confined to nonparanoid, process schizophrenics.

One factor in perceptual disorders among chronic patients may well be the effect of continued institutionalization. Silverman, Berg, and Kantor (1966) found that the ability to judge the size of circles is significantly worse in long-term prison inmates than in short-term prison inmates. They attribute this to the decrease in scanning acquired over the years as a way of avoiding "aversive inescapable surroundings."

The recent interest in psychotomimetic drugs has led to several attempts to produce the same type of perceptual disorders in normals as are found in schizophrenics. LSD 25 (Lysergic Acid Diethylamide) significantly impaired the size judgments of normal subjects in one study (Liebert, Werner, & Wapner, 1958), and the ability to judge size, to estimate eye level, and to judge the upright in another (Krus, Wapner, Freeman, & Casey, 1963). The theory that schizophrenics are resistant to the effect of this drug was also tested in both studies, and was found not to be true. Schizophrenics were poorer than the normal subjects without LSD, but their perception deteriorated to the same extent as the normals under the influence of the drug.

Another reputedly (psychotomimetic agent is Sernyl [1- (1-phenylcyclohexyl) piperidine monohydrochloride]–a sensory blocking agent, with anesthetic and sedative properties, that produces severe disturbances of the body image, affect, attention, and thinking. Depersonalization and repetitive motor behavior have also been observed clinically in normal people who have taken this drug. Rosenbaum, Cohen, Luby, Gottlieb, and Yelen (1959) found that the ability to discriminate weights in normals is considerably impaired by this drug.

Disorders of Perceptual "Set"

Perceptual Overinclusion or Distractibility

One of the earliest experimental observations made in psychiatry was that, as a group, schizophrenics have a slow and variable reaction time. This observation has been repeated many times, and the most generally accepted explanation of the phenomenon is the one put forward by Rodnick and Shakow (1940), that schizophrenics are unable to preserve a set to respond over a long period of time. Their performance instead depends on a series of minor "sets." If they react when set, they are quick, but if they are not set, they are slow. Put another way, their slowness and variability suggest that they cannot avoid becoming distracted from the task periodically. Normal subjects improve their reaction time when they are given a warning signal, and they respond fastest when there is a regular interval between the warning and the stimulus. Rodnick and Shakow (1940) demonstrated that, unlike normals, schizophrenics work faster with irregular warning intervals. It may be that it is more difficult to become habituated to these irregular warning signals which, in a sense, distract the attention of the schizophrenic back to the task in hand. Shakow and his associates and other workers have repeated this observation a number of times (Shakow, 1946, 1962, 1963; Zahn, Rosenthal, & Shakow, 1963; Shakow & McCormick, 1965; Tizard & Venables, 1955; Gzudner & Marshall, 1967).

Payne, Matussek, and George (1959) hypothesized that distractibility is associated with overinclusive thinking, both being the result of a failure of some central inhibitory process to screen out irrelevant information, either perceptions or thoughts. Payne and his associates (Payne & Hewlett, 1960; Payne, 1961; Payne, Caird, & Laverty, 1964) have suggested that overinclusion may be one factor in the development of paranoid delusions. Overinclusive individuals, they hypothesize, perceive aspects of the behavior of others that normal people are unaware of because they screen them out as being irrelevant. They also tend to make unwarranted generalizations, and both these characteristics could lead to the formation of delusions, which, indeed, could be defined as unwarranted generalizations. Payne and Caird (1967) carried out a study to investigate the relations between distractibility in a reaction-time experiment, overinclusive thinking, and paranoid delusions. Fifteen paranoid schizophrenics, 15 nonparanoid schizophrenics, and 15 nonschizophrenic psychiatric inpatients were given a simple and a multiple choice auditory reaction-time test in which the presence and number of distracting stimuli were varied. The test stimuli were tones delivered through earphones, and the distracting stimuli, which the patients were told to ignore, were similar tones delivered from a loud speaker. Overinclusive thinking was measured by the average number of words needed to explain the Benjamin Proverbs. As predicted, the reaction times of the paranoid patients were more affected by the distraction than the ones of the nonschizophrenics. The distractibility of the nonparanoid schizophrenics was intermediate. Also, as expected, overinclusive subjects were more distractible than nonoverinclusive subjects, there being highly significant correlations between the proverbs test word-count score and the reaction time under conditions of distraction.

Although these results appear plausible, they are unfortunately inconsistent with the body of work that has been done by others. McGhie, Chapman, and Lawson (1965a) studied distractibility in paranoid patients, depressed patients, schizophrenics, and controls. They found that simple (but not choice) visual and auditory reaction times were not significantly affected by distraction in the form of the sound of an irregular metronome rhythm, or a circle of randomly flashing white lights around the stimulus light in any of the subjects. However, they did find that distraction had a significant effect on more complex psychomotor performance that contained some degree of uncertainty.

The effect of distraction on a wide range of tasks has been investigated in several studies (McGhie, 1966; McGhie, Chapman, & Lawson, 1965a, 1965b; Chapman & McGhie, 1962; Cohen, Rosenbaum, Luby, & Gottlieb, 1962). For example, in one experiment (McGhie, Chapman, & Lawson, 1965a), the subjects were required to listen to digits read by a female voice, and to screen out those read by a male voice. The effect of auditory distraction on a visual task (reading letters, or digits) and visual distraction on an auditory task have also been studied. The results have been consistent in suggesting that as a group, schizophrenics are indeed significantly more distractible than nonschizophrenics and normals. However, it was the chronic and the hebephrenic schizophrenics who were distractible in these studies. The paranoid patients were not significantly different from normal. Although distractibility was related to symptomotology, it was not related to chronicity.

A slightly different group of perceptual tasks are the ones which require the subject to recognize or to abstract some picture from a distracting irrelevant background. A good example of this is the Gottschaldt Figures Test (Weckowitz & Blewett, 1959). Studies in which these tests of selective visual perception have been used (Chapman & McGhie, 1962; Weckowitz & Blewett, 1959; Krus, Wapner, Freeman, & Casey, 1963; Bemporad, 1967; Schwartz, 1967; Weckowitz, 1960; Snyder, Rosenthal, & Taylor, 1961) consistently suggest that schizophrenics as a group are significantly worse than normal controls. Again, however, when symptomatology has been reported, paranoid patients have been found to be normal in this respect. This type of perceptual distractibility seems to characterize hebephrenic or chronic patients.

Very similar studies present the patient auditorily with a word mixed with masking noise, or a picture masked by visual noise ("snow"), and systematically decrease the amount of noise until correct recognition occurs (Donovan & Webb, 1965; Stilson & Kopell, 1964 Stilson, Kopell, Vandenbergh, & Downs, 1966). Schizophrenics as a group appear to be poor at these recognition tasks, and "process" schizophrenics are worse than "reactive" schizophrenics.

A quite different approach to the same problem has been taken by Callaway and his associates (Callaway, Jones, & Layne, 1965; Jones, Blacker, & Callaway, 1966; Jones, Blacker, Callaway, & Layne, 1965). They have measured, by using an EEG, the cortical electrical response to both visual and auditory stimuli. These evoked cortical potentials vary in amplitude and in wave form. Normally, two identical stimuli produce identical cortical responses. However, the wave forms produced by two identical stimuli in schizophrenics tend to be quite dissimilar. This suggests that, in some way, schizophrenics are paying attention to small differences in nearly identical stimuli, or are being distracted by extraneous events that do not register in normal people. It has been found that this lack of consistency in cortical response characterizes schizophrenic patients while they are ill, and improves with clinical improvement. It is associated with disordered talk, disorganized delusions, and thought disorder as rated clinically. It does not characterize paranoid schizophrenics who are nearly normal in this respect. It is more severe in process than in reactive schizophrenics, and is more severe in chronic than in acute schizophrenics.

These studies on the whole are consistent in suggesting that distractibility in a variety of perceptual situations characterizes nonparanoid, "process," and chronic schizophrenics. Reactive schizophrenics, especially the ones who are paranoid, on the other hand, seem well able to focus their attention and to screen out irrelevant perceptual stimuli when required.

There appear to have been relatively few attempts to manipulate distractibility experimentally. Rosenbaum, Cohen, Luby, Gottlieb, and Yelen (1959), by using the Rodnick and Shakow reaction-time experiment as a measure of distractibility, found that neither LSD nor Sodium Amytal given to normal subjects could make them as slow as schizophrenics. However, the drug Sernyl did. On the other hand, if the subjects were given an electric shock until they reacted, normals, drugged with Sernyl, and schizophrenics produced normal reaction times. Undrugged normals were not affected by the shock. It is possible to speculate that the higher drive level induced by the shocks enhanced the ability of anesthetized normals and schizophrenics to focus their attention. If we accept Claridge's (1967) findings that "process" schizophrenics are abnormally lacking in drive, we can argue that distractibility is a function of low drive. There is some evidence that in states of high drive the attention is more narrowly focused (Easterbrook, 1959). There is also evidence that a number of stimulant drugs, which can be presumed to increase arousal level, lower the response to peripheral stimuli and thus focus the attention more narrowly (Callaway & Dembo, 1958; Callaway & Stone,

1960). This hypothesis was tested by Venables (1963a) who found that chronic schizophrenics in a high state of cortical arousal were best able to ignore distractions in a sorting test. Again in this study, paradoxically, the most aroused chronic schizophrenics were the most withdrawn, as they were consistently found to be in Venables (1966a) and other studies.

DISORDERS OF CONCEPTUALIZATION

Concreteness

Concreteness can be defined as the inability to formulate an abstract general principle from a group of particular items, or the inability to recognize that a group of objects with some common characteristics can be grouped together under some general category. In effect, it is the inability to carry out inductive reasoning. Since inductive reasoning is required in a large numer of intellectual tasks, it is not surprising to find that measures of concreteness have been found to be highly correlated with conventional measures of general intelligence (Payne & Hewlett, 1960; Payne, 1961; Shimkunas, Gynther, & Smith, 1966; Holtzman, Gorham, & Moran, 1964; Karson & Pool, 1957). Nevertheless, it is possible to conceive of someone whose deductive powers are intact, and who can perform satisfactorily on some tasks (for example, mechanical arithmetic) but not on others, which require inductive reasoning.

It has long been held that concreteness results from brain damage (Payne, 1961), and many authorities believe that schizophrenic patients resemble brain-damaged patients in this, as in several other respects. Nevertheless, in 1961, Payne, after reviewing the literature, was forced to conclude that there was no unambiguous evidence for this proposition. This was mainly because most of the studies carried out prior to that time were ambiguous, either because they failed to control for crucial variables such as pre-illness intelligence, or age, or because they made use of tests whose evaluation was essentially subjective. Since that time, however, in addition to the proliferation of ill-controlled studies, a number of more adequate experiments have made possible some more positive conclusions.

Since not all tests of "concreteness" appear to involve the same process, it is best to review the literature with respect to the different kinds of experimental situations employed.

The Interpretation of Proverbs

A proverb is a concrete illustration of a general principle, and the ability to interpret proverbs has been a popular method of assessing the ability to generalize for many years. Early proverbs tests, such as the Benjamin Proverbs (Payne, 1961) lacked a standardized scoring system. More recently, however, tests have been developed, such as Gorham's proverbs (Gorham, 1956a, 1956b, 1956c; Elmore & Gorham, 1957), with carefully standardized scoring criteria which, it has been demonstrated, can be applied reliably to the spontaneous interpretations of proverbs by patients. Proverb interpretation is obviously affected by educational background and word knowledge, so that a considerable amount of detailed normative data would be necessary if one were to use such a test clinically with an individual patient. Even the best standardized proverbs test thus far available does not, for example, supply norms that specify the mean "abstraction" scores (with standard deviations and ranges) which can be expected from normal people at different age levels and of different levels of educational background, without which interpreting a score from an individual patient would be impossible. Proverbs tests can, nevertheless, be used in group studies, provided that care is taken to match the groups to be compared on these variables.

Two types of response are usually scored from proverb interpretations, an "abstract" answer which correctly states the general principle illustrated by the proverb, and a "concrete" answer which does not make any generalization at all (for example, Rome was not built in a day. Abstract answer, "Great things come about slowly." Concrete answer, "It took years"). One disadvantage with the "clinical" form of the proverbs test is that a number of responses, sometimes called "autistic" or "idiosyncratic" are difficult to classify under either heading. This scoring problem is avoided by using a multiple choice version of the test.

Studies that use the clinical versions of the proverbs test have employed either Benjamin's (1946) original proverbs and scoring, the Benjamin proverbs scored according to Becker's (1955) system, Gorham's (1956a) test, or the Friedes proverbs test (Friedes, Fredenthal, Grisell, & Cohen, 1963). Most studies have found that process schizophrenic patients give more concrete answers, and fewer abstract answers than a matched group of normal people, or a matched group of reactive schizophrenics (Gregg & Frank, 1966; Johnson, 1966; Little, 1966), although the results have not always been statistically significant (Judson & Katahn, 1963). Reactive schizophrenics, on the other hand, appear relatively unimpaired. As we might expect, chronic schizophrenics are also concrete in their proverb interpretation (Gorham, 1956c; Lewinsohn & Riggs, 1962). Brain damaged patients, like process and chronic schizophrenics, are also concrete (Gregg & Frank, 1966). Studies that use multiple-choice forms of proverbs tests have produced similar results (Brattemo, 1962; Fogel, 1965).

The concreteness manifested by schizophrenic patients on the proverbs test while ill, improves significantly with clinical recovery (Schwartz, 1967b; Shimkunas, Gynther, & Smith, 1966). However, there is some evidence that the relatives (parents, siblings, and children) of schizophrenics are significantly more concrete on proverbs than normal people (Phillips, Jacobson, & Turner, 1965). Although this suggests a degree of pathology in the "well" members of these families, this study throws on light on the etiology of this particular disorder.

There has been at least one attempt to induce concrete thinking on the proverbs test in normals by the use of drugs (Cohen, Rosenbaum, Luby, & Gottlieb, 1962). Two drugs, LSD 25 and sodium amytal had no significant effect, but Sernyl produced a significant increase in concrete responses.

There has been some suggestion that, although concreteness on proverbs is a characteristic that chronic and process schizophrenics share with brain damaged patients, in part, it is emotionally determined. The hypothesis is that an emotional response to the material can induce concrete behavior. Lewinsohn and Riggs (1962), replicated a finding made by Lewis, Griffith, Riedel, and Simmons (1959) that acute schizophrenics have more difficulty interpreting "oral" proverbs than they do "anal," "phallic," or "neutral" ones. Chronic schizophrenics, on the other hand, were significantly more concrete, and were uninfluenced by the content. Normals similarly were uninfluenced by the content. By using a different approach to the problem, Feffer (1961) found that a group of concrete schizophrenics, as selected by the Gorham test, showed an avoidance reaction to affect-laden words in that they did not recognize them when they were presented tachistoscopically as background material. Abstract schizophrenics did not behave in this way. This result is ambiguous, as concrete, probably process schizophrenics might be expected to have less visual acuity. However, it is possible that concrete behavior can be exacerbated by emotional disturbance.

At least one approach has been made to improve the concrete behavior of schizophrenics in explaining proverbs. Hamlin, Haywood, and Folsom (1965), repeating a study by Blaufarb (1962), instead of using a single proverb to illustrate each principle, presented proverbs in groups of threes. Each set of three illustrated the same principle and, in this way, the subjects had more instances from which to generalize. Under these circumstances, schizophrenics with a mild degree of concreteness improved to a normal level. However, the severely ill, closed-ward schizophrenics remained concrete.

Because of its apparent relation to the process-reactive continuum, one would expect that concreteness on the proverbs test would be a bad prognostic indication in early psychosis. However, no follow-up studies to test this hypothesis appear to have been conducted.

The Use of Words

A second method of assessing concreteness is by studying how patients use words. Some words, in addition to having a concrete meaning, also symbolize an abstract principle and, therefore, can be used in at least two different senses. It has been claimed that concrete individuals no longer use words in their abstract sense and, in this respect, words have reduced meaning for them.

One way of assessing this is by the use of a test designed by Flavell (1956) and modified by Milgram (1959). The subject is presented with a stimulus word and two response words. He is asked to underline the response word which is closest in meaning to the stimulus word. One association is always more abstract than the other, so that a measure of concreteness can be obtained. The results of this test are very similar to the ones obtained with the proverbs. Schizophrenics as a group appear to be concrete, but not so concrete as brain damaged patients (Milgram, 1959), although schizophrenics in a state of remission are no longer concrete (Schwartz, 1967a).

A different technique is a word-meaning test designed by Chapman (1960), who was interested in measuring not only misinterpretations resulting from concreteness, but also figurative misinterpretations, or unusual abstract uses of words. This is a multiple-choice test, and two typical items are as follows:

David turned yellow when he faced the enemy.

This means:

A. David became cowardly (abstract correct)
B. David became hungry (figurative incorrect)
C. David's skin became discolored (concrete incorrect)

Miss Bailey's illness turned her yellow.

This means:

A. Miss Bailey became cowardly (abstract incorrect)
B. Miss Bailey became hungry (figurative incorrect)
C. Miss Bailey's skin became discolored (concrete correct)

Chapman (1960; Chapman, Burstein, Day, & Verdone, 1961) found that chronic schizophrenics made more errors of both types than normal adults. Brain damaged patients made more figurative errors than chronic schizophrenics, although chronic schizophrenics made more literal errors than brain damaged patients. Children were like chronic schizophrenics and unlike brain damaged patients, as they made concrete but not figurative errors.

One reason why chronic schizophrenics use words more concretely is suggested in another study by Chapman and Chapman (1965). These investigators first ranked the strength of the different meanings of each word of a group of words, as judged by the frequency with which the meaning was mentioned first by normals. They then asked normals and schizophrenics to rank the degree of similarity between pairs of words. They found that chronic schizophrenics in this task relied mainly on the strongest normal meaning response, ignoring subsidiary meanings. Thus, schizophrenics judged words to be identical in meaning if they had the same strongest meaning, but if not, they found them completely different in meaning, even though they shared a large number of subsidiary meanings. This reliance on only the strongest meaning in a hierarchy of possible meanings may well be the essence of verbal "concreteness." These findings are confirmed by a study by Faibish (1961) who found that a group of schizophrenics defined words with multiple meanings more poorly than normals, being able to give fewer of their meanings. Willner (1965) also found that chronic schizophrenics could give fewer unfamiliar meanings of words than brain damaged patients.

Chronic schizophrenics are not only restricted in their use of individual words, but they also appear to employ a reduced vocabulary. Hammer and Salzinger (1964) found their speech to be more stereotyped than normal, as judged by a lower "type-token" ratio, indicating a greater amount of word repetition in a given speech sample.

We could expect that these verbal disabilities would impair the ability of chronic schizophrenics to communicate with others, and there is evidence that this is true. Cohen and Camhi (1967) found that chronic schizophrenics were less able to provide useful verbal clues than normals, when speaking either to normals or to one another. However, they had no significant defect in understanding the speech of others. Two studies that used the Flavell test (Payne, 1961) suggest that concrete subjects are less sociable, probably because they find communication with others more difficult.

Another line of research on the same problem has been carried out by Salzinger and his colleagues (Salzinger, Portnoy, & Feldman, 1966). Salzinger has used the "Cloze" technique to assess the intelligibility of schizophrenic speech. Speech samples from chronic schizophrenics were typed out, and every fifth word was deleted. Normals were less able to guess the missing words in the schizophrenic speech samples than they were in normal speech samples.

At least one attempt has been made to induce concrete verbal behavior in normals by the use of LSD. Krus, Wapner, Freeman, and Casey (1963) were able to increase the number of concrete verbal responses on the Flavell (1956) word-definition test by giving LSD 25 to normal subjects.

In an attempt to see how far concrete verbal behavior in schizophrenics is reversible, True (1966), following a period of base-line measurement, positively reinforced abstract responses and negatively reinforced concrete responses in a word association task. He found that reactive schizophrenics could be made to respond normally, but the behavior of the initially more concrete process schizophrenics could not be significantly altered in this way.

The Use of Sorting Tests

Requiring patients to sort objects into groups in order to determine whether they are able to formulate and employ abstract categories has been used for many years in assessing concreteness. One of the most commonly used tests of this sort, the Goldstein-Scheerer (1941) Object Sorting Test, consists of a set of everyday objects such as a pipe, cigar, cutlery, matches, and so on. Another of Goldstein and Scheerer's sorting tests, the Color Form Test consists of a small set of plastic objects in three different shapes, squares, circles, and triangles, and four different colors, red, blue, green and yellow. Goldstein and Scheerer argued that concrete individuals would be unable to sort the objects into groups or, if they did, they would be unable to give an adequate account of the abstract principle which formed the basis of the grouping. However, they added a second criterion for what they regarded as a normal, abstract performance, namely, the ability, having produced one type of abstract sorting, to "shift" and re-sort the objects according to a quite different abstract principle. Clearly, people differ in respect to their "rigidity" in this situation, but it has never been demonstrated that concreteness and rigidity on these tests are the same phenomenon.

The difficulty with these tests as they were originally used is that, although a more or less standard administrative procedure was employed, no standard scoring system was laid down. Accordingly, earlier studies with these tests (Payne, 1961) are difficult to evaluate because of the subjective assessments involved. Rapaport (1946) has produced a standard technique for scoring concreteness on the Object Sorting Test, and Payne, Matussek, and George (1959) have produced a standard scoring procedure for both the Object Sorting Test and the Color Form Test.

Tutko and Spence (1962), by using the Rapaport version of the Goldstein Object Sorting Test found that acute "process" schizophrenics were concrete like a group of brain damaged patients, whereas a group of matched "reactive" schizophrenics were not significantly different from normal. Payne, Matussek, and George (1959) and Payne and Hewlett (1960), by using both sorting tests, found no significant differences between a group of acute schizophrenics and a group of normal controls. However, the process-reactive variable was not considered in either study, and it is not known how many, if any, "process" schizophrenics were included. Weckowitz and Blewett (1959) found that concreteness on these tests was associated with poor perceptual constancy among chronic schizophrenics. This suggests that concrete schizophrenics make use of a very constricted range of cues, both in perception and in concept formation.

Several sorting tests employ words or pictures instead of real objects, although the same principle is involved. Two-word "similarities" tests, like the one in the Wechsler-Bellevue Scale, are sorting tests in this sense, and Tolor (1964) has developed a special multiple-choice version of this test. Trunnell (1964, 1965) has developed a version in which subjects must say what three words have in common (for example, car, bicycle, and train), and Bernstein (1960) used a five-word test of the same sort. Schizophrenics as a group were inferior on these tests in some studies, but the process-reactive variable has not been investigated.

A slightly different technique has been employed by Feldman and Drasgow (1951; Drasgow & Feldman, 1957). This test consists of a set of cards, each of which depicts four objects in a row. For example, the first card pictures four lines; three are horizontal, and one vertical, and one of the horizontal lines is colored red. The subjects are asked to find three objects which can be grouped together for one reason (three horizontal lines), and then three objects which can be grouped together for a different reason (three black lines). Subjects must explain each grouping, and can score 0, 1, or 2 on each card, 2 indicating that both groupings were perceived. Payne, Matussek, and George (1959) and Schwartz (1967a) used a similar test with different items, and Bernstein (1960) developed a version of the test by using words instead of pictures. Nathan (1964) developed a multiple-choice test along similar lines, except that no "shift" was involved. Four pictures illustrate the concept and the subject must select the one of four sentences that best describes the concept. Studies that use these tests are inconclusive, some (Feldman & Drasgow, 1951; Bernstein, 1960) finding schizophrenics to be concrete, and some (Payne, Matussek, & George, 1959; Nathan, 1964) finding no evidence for this. Again, however, such variables as chronicity and the process-reactive dimension are usually not considered. Both studies that tested brain damaged patients found them to be concrete (Bernstein, 1960; Feldman, & Drasgow, 1951). Bernstein (1960) found evidence that schizophrenics are more concrete on tests of this kind when they are dealing with emotionally arousing material (pictures illustrating social interaction).

It seems probable that concreteness on sorting tests will be found to characterize only process and not reactive schizophrenics, as was the case with verbal tests, but at present no studies of this dimension are available.

Concept Attainment Experiments

A somewhat more elaborate extension of the sorting test is the concept-attainment technique developed by Heidbreder in experiments with normal subjects (Payne, 1961). This technique is exemplified by the Wisconsin Sorting Test (Payne, 1961), which consists of 64 cards. They must be sorted one at a time with one of four meaningless stimulus cards. The subject is not told the basis of the sorting, but each time he sorts a card he is told "right" or "wrong." When the subject has sorted ten cards correctly consecutively, the sorting principle is changed. The first principle is color, and the second "form," and so on. When the same criterion is reached for the second principle, the principle is changed again. The test requires five shifts in all. The test is over when all five principles have been attained, or when all 64 cards have been sorted without the criterion of ten correct consecutive sortings being achieved.

A more difficult version of the Heidbreder technique was used by Hall (1962). In this task, the subjects are first presented with six nonsense syllables (pran, ling, relk, moft, dilt and faud). Six pictures are then given, one at a time, and the subject is told which of these six names should be applied to each picture. A series of 90 more different pictures is then given. The pictures are in sets of 6 and, in each set of 6, each concept is illustrated once in a random order. The subjects are instructed to guess which name goes with each picture, and are given the correct answer following each guess, whether right or wrong. Concept attainment is said to have occurred when two successive correct anticipations have been made.

These concept-attainment tests differ from the sorting tests of concreteness in that trial and error learning is involved, correct responses being reinforced. It is not certain that these two different kinds of concept formation are related, and there appear to be no correlational studies.

In studies using concept-attainment tests, it has generally been found that acute schizophrenics are significantly worse than normals (Fey, 1951; Hall, 1962). Remitted schizophrenics, however, are no worse than nonschizophrenic psychiatric patients (Schwartz, 1967a). Curiously, in the only study of chronic schizophrenics in a task of this type (Snelbecker, Sherman, Rothstein & Downes, 1966) the schizophrenic patients did not make significantly more errors than normals. There appear to be no studies relating these measures either to the process-reactive dimension or to symptomatology, so that few conclusions can be drawn.

Conclusions

The evidence suggests that concreteness is a disability that process schizophrenics share with brain damaged patients. It seems likely that this disability contributes largely to these patients' low level of general intelligence, in view of the high correlation between IQ tests and tests of concreteness in psychiatric groups. Concreteness seems to be associated with the perceptual inaccuracies that are presumably caused by deficient "scanning," and may be related to insufficient sensory input and low drive. It causes difficulties in verbal communication, and is associated with social withdrawal. It characterizes, at least, some chronic schizophrenics and can be presumed to be a poor prognostic sign, although direct studies are not available.

Overinclusive Thinking

Definition

The term overinclusive thinking was introduced by Norman Cameron (1938), although this type of thought disorder was described earlier by other writers under different names. Overinclusion was defined as the inability to preserve conceptual boundaries. Ideas that are associated with, or distantly related to concepts become incorporated in them, so that they come to be regarded as essential parts of the concept. Cameron thought that this kind of thought disorder was characteristic of schizophrenic patients, and he first investigated it by using a sentence-completion test and the Vigotsky sorting test (Payne, 1961). He noted among other things that personal themes "interpenetrated" the thought processes of schizophrenic patients when carrying out these tasks, so that the "boundaries" of the task became overly extensive and ill-defined. Cameron's early experiments made use of an essentially subjective evaluation of the performance of patients on these tasks.

Payne, Matussek, and George (1959) suggested that overinclusive concept formation might be one aspect of a more general disability. They hypothesized that normal problem solving depends on the ability to "filter" out irrelevant perceptions and thoughts that might otherwise intrude into the thinking process. This type of internal filter mechanism, as described by Broadbent (1958), breaks down in the case of overinclusive individuals, who seem unable to develop the necessary cortical inhibition to suppress irrelevant thoughts and stimuli. They speculated further that this might be associated with a general inability to carry out discrimination learning, which is presumably the process whereby such mental "sets" or "filters" are developed. Payne, Matussek, and George found that a group of tests of overinclusive thinking differentiated significantly between acute schizophrenics and neurotics, as predicted.

Payne and Hewlett (1960) carried out a further study to test this hypothesis. They administered a number of the tests of overinclusive concept formation that are described below and several measures of the tendency to produce unusual responses, also attributed to overinclusive thinking, along with tests of intelligence, psychomotor retardation, and concreteness to matched groups of 20 normals, 20 neurotics, 20 depressives, and 20 schizophrenics. There was a tendency for all the tests of overinclusion to be correlated significantly. The entire battery of tests was factor analyzed, and a discriminant function analysis was carried out on the factor scores from the first three centroid factors, in order to define the rotated factor that maximized the discrimination between the depressives and the schizophrenics. As predicted, only the tests of overinclusive thinking had high loadings on this factor. It was also predicted that overinclusive individuals would be relatively unable to develop "Einstellung" rigidity on Luchins' water-jar test because the "set" which blinds normal people to certain types of solution is gradually acquired during the test because only certain types of solution are found to work (and are thus reinforced). It was thought that this kind of discrimination learning, which gradually inhibits certain types of responses, (possible solutions in this case) is defective in overinclusive subjects, either because, for some reason, they cannot develop the necessary cortical inhibition, or because they are defective at discrimination learning. The results from this test were as predicted.

There have been relatively few other studies of the intercorrelations between different measures of overinclusion. Payne and Hewlett (1960) did not include any tests of overinclusive perception, such as the ones described above. Watson (1967) found no significant correlation between two measures of stimulus generalization in a visual reaction-time experiment (assessing the ability to ignore irrelevant lights) and three tests of overinclusive thinking. Thus, there is no evidence that overinclusive perception and overinclusive thinking are the same phenomenon.

Several investigators have tried to repeat Payne and Hewlett's findings by using a number of the same tests of overinclusive thinking. Hawks (1964), by using three tests yielding four overinclusion scores with a group of 58 acutely ill patients who were suspected of having thought disorder, found that only two of the six intercorrelations were significantly greater than zero. Watson (1967), intercorrelating three tests used with 100 schizophrenics, found no significant correlations, and Phillips, Jacobson, and Turner (1965) found no significant correlation between two tests. Craig (1965) gave a large battery of tests of overinclusive thinking to 66 newly admitted patients, and factor analyzed them. He was able to extract three independent factors, although the initial correlation matrix is not reported.

Therefore, we must conclude that there is still no very clear evidence that overinclusive thinking is a unitary phenomenon. For this reason, the different kinds of tests that have been used to measure overinclusive thinking will be discussed separately.

Measures of Overinclusive Concept Formation

Moran's (1953) Definitions Test

Moran developed a word-usage test with a number of sections, two of which were specifically designed to measure overinclusive concept formation. In one section, the subjects are asked to give as many synonyms as possible for each of 25 words. Moran found that schizophrenics gave more, but less precise synonyms. In a second section, each of the same 25 stimulus words is printed on a page and is followed by five to eight response words, including neologisms. The subjects are asked to underline every response word that they regard as an essential part of the concept denoted by the stimulus word. Moran found, as expected, that schizophrenics did not underline significantly fewer correct responses, but they did underline significantly more of the distantly related words. Seth and Beloff (1959) found similar results in an attempt to repeat Moran's findings.

The Epstein Overinclusion Test

Epstein (1953) developed a very similar test, which consisted of 50 stimulus words, each followed by 6 response words, including the word "none." The results obtained from this test have recently been reviewed by Sturm (1965), who points out that acute schizophrenics have usually been found to be more overinclusive than normals, although in one study neurotics were also overinclusive, and in another, psychotic depressives were found to be overinclusive. No particular subgroup of schizophrenics is especially overinclusive on this test, there being no consistently reported differences between deteriorated schizophrenics, acute schizophrenics, chronic schizophrenics, process schizophrenics or reactive schizophrenics (Eliseo, 1963; Sturm, 1965). There is, however, no evidence that the Epstein test is significantly related to any other measures of overinclusive concept formation. Payne and Hewlett (1960) found it to be the only overinclusion test that had no loading on their overinclusion factor. Watson (1967) found it to be unrelated to a proverbs overinclusion score or a measure of concept breadth devised from the Goldstein Object Sorting Test, and Phillips, Jacobson, and Turner (1965) found it unrelated to the Payne Object Classification Test "Non-A" score.

One reason for these results is suggested by a study carried out by Desai (1960), who found that the overinclusion score on this test is a function of word knowledge—people with low vocabularies getting high overinclusion scores. In an effort to improve the test, Sturm (1965) revised it, but found no evidence that the revised overinclusion score differentiated between groups of process schizophrenics, reactive schizophrenics, brain damaged patients, and tubercular patients. It seems likely that overinclusive concept formation is better measured in different ways that are less affected by the vocabulary level of the patients.

The Zaslow (1950) Test

Zaslow developed a different technique for assessing overinclusive concept formation. It consists of 14 cards. Card 1 depicts an equilateral triangle, and card 14 a perfect circle. In the intervening cards the shape gradually changes from a triangle to a circle. In one part of the administration procedure the examiner places the cards in order and asks the subject to indicate where the circles and where the triangles end. Overinclusive subjects should include more cards in each concept. Zaslow (1950) found that the schizophrenics were significantly more overinclusive than surgical patients, but Kugelmass and Fondeur (1955) could not confirm these findings on much larger groups of schizophrenics and normals. They found, however, that the test-retest reliabilities of the scores derived from this test were so low as to be insignificant in some cases.

The Pettigrew (1958) Test

A slightly different method of assessing breadth of concepts was devised by Pettigrew who produced a 20 item multiple-choice test in which subjects are asked to estimate the extremes of a number of diverse categories, such as the length of whales and the annual rainfall in Washington, D.C. Overinclusive subjects are expected to produce very broad ranges. There is no evidence that schizophrenics as a group produce wider categories than do normal college students (Silverman, 1964b; Silverman, Berg, & Kantor, 1966), although college students produce significantly broader categories than do convicts. The relation between this and other tests of overinclusion has not been studied.

The Goldstein Object Sorting Test

This test is perhaps the most frequently used measure of breadth of concepts. McGaughran (1954) suggested that one way of scoring the object-sorting test was by measuring the number of objects that were sorted under each category. He referred to this as the "open-closed" dimension, a "closed" category containing few objects, and an "open" category indicating an extensive generalization. There has been a general tendency to identify the production of closed sortings on this test with concreteness. Studies that use this test suggest that paranoid schizophrenic patients use significantly more "open" sortings than do normals (McGaughran & Moran, 1956) or neurotics (Silverman & Silverman, 1962) and that brain damaged patients use significantly more "closed" (concrete) sortings (McGaughran & Moran, 1957; Leventhal, McGaughran, & Moran, 1959).

Tutko and Spence (1962) found evidence that process schizophrenics and brain damaged patients produced "closed" (concrete) sortings, whereas reactive schizophrenics produced "open" sortings, although Sturm (1964) was unable to repeat this finding, by testing the same three groups.

Weckowicz and Blewett (1959) found that schizophrenics who produced "closed" (concrete) sortings had a perceptual defect in the form of poor size constancy.

Lovibond (1954) has produced a somewhat more elaborate technique for rating overinclusive concept formation from the Object Sorting Test. He found that schizophrenics were more overinclusive than normal controls, and other investigators (McConaghy, 1959; Lidz, Wild, Schafer, Rosman, & Fleck, 1962; Rosman, Wild, Ricci, Fleck, & Lidz, 1964) have shown consistently that the parents of schizophrenic patients also tend to be significantly more overinclusive than normal on this same measure. Whether this indicates that overinclusive concept formation results from some genetically determined abnormality such as the inability to develop sufficient cortical inhibition, or whether it indicates that this type of concept formation is learned from one's family, we cannot say.

The Goldstein Object Sorting "Handing Over" Score

Payne, Matussek, and George (1959) suggested a different technique for assessing overinclusive concept formation on the Goldstein Object Sorting Test. During the initial "handing over" section of this test, subjects are asked to select all the objects that they think can be grouped together with an initial object (the "point of departure"). Payne et al. allowed the subjects to select the initial point of departure object, but repeated the experiment three more times using three standard objects as points of departure. The score was merely the average number of objects grouped together. This score differentiated acute schizophrenics from normal and psychiatric controls in two studies (Payne, Matussek, & George, 1959; Payne & Hewlett, 1960) and was one of the best measures of Payne and Hewlett's overinclusion factor. However, Hawks (1964) and Watson (1967) found this score to be insignificantly correlated with four of the other measures of overinclusive thinking used by Payne and Hewlett (1960).

The Proverbs Test

Payne, Matussek, and George (1959) suggested that, to an overinclusive individual, Benjamin's proverbs might illustrate a set of more extensive and elaborate generalizations than they do for normal people. Because of this, overinclusive subjects should use more words and take longer to explain the proverbs. The score is merely the average number of words used per proverb. However, care must be taken in specially instructing the subject to give a positive indication that he has completed his explanation before going on to the next proverb. It is also essential to tape-record the answer, and to count the words from the tape. Whenever studies have relied on longhand recording, relatively few words per proverb have been reported, and the significant differences vanish (Payne, Matussek, and George, 1959; Goldstein & Salzman, 1965), because it is almost impossible to record in longhand without condensation.

Payne and Hewlett (1960) and Payne, Caird, and Laverty (1964) found acute schizophrenics to be significantly more overinclusive than normals on this measure. Payne, Friedlander, Laverty, and Haden (1963) found that chronic schizophrenics on the other hand were not abnormally overinclusive. Payne and Hewlett (1960) found that this score was one of the best measures of their factor of overinclusion, although Watson (1967) found it unrelated to two other overinclusion measures, and Hawks (1964) found that it was correlated significantly only with a measure of the tendency to produce unusual responses on the Payne Object Classification Test. Clearly, this score must depend on a number of other nonpathological variables such as verbosity and extraversion (but not on IQ—Payne & Hewlett, 1960), so that, used by itself, this test must necessarily produce equivocal results.

The Shneidman (1948) Make-a-Picture-Story (MAPS) Test

In this test, subjects are asked to select as many figures as they like from a large group of cardboard cutout human figures in different positions and costumes. They must then place the figures on a background card (background cards depict different outdoor and indoor settings), and make up a story about each scene created. It has been found that, among other things, schizophrenics select an unusually large number of figures for each picture, and make up diffuse, overinclusive stories. It is not known how this test relates to other measures of overinclusive conceptualization.

Chapman's Sorting Test

Chapman and Taylor (1957) produced an entirely different technique for measuring overinclusive concepts. The test material consists of 30 words typed on index cards, which are equally divided into three categories. Two of these categories are very similar, but not overlapping (for example, alcoholic and nonalcoholic beverages), while the third is quite different (for example, insects). The subjects are asked to sort all the cards in one of the two similar categories into one box (for example, put all the cards which name an alcoholic beverage into this box), and place all the rest of the cards into a second box. Overinclusive subjects, it is predicted, will be unable to restrict their concept of "alcoholic beverages," and will incorporate some of the nonalcoholic beverages into it, thus, committing sorting errors of overinclusion. They are not expected to include cards from the dissimilar category (insects).

Chapman and Taylor (1957) found that chronic schizophrenics produced more errors of overinclusion than did a group of matched normals.

It is possible also to define errors of underinclusion on this test (rejecting correct cards). Chapman (1961) found that the broader the categories used, the more errors of overinclusion were made by chronic schizophrenics. He found also that brain damaged patients on this test made errors of underinclusion like children (Chapman, Burstein, Day, and Verdone, 1961), but unlike chronic schizophrenics and normals. Chapman and Knowles (1964) found that phenothiazine treatment in chronic schizophrenics significantly reduced errors of overinclusion, did not change errors of underinclusion, but did increase random errors on this test. The implication is that phenothiazine therapy may specifically improve overinclusive conceptualization, but at the expense of producing some generalized inefficiency.

The results using this test are consistent with the ones using other measures insofar as the performance of brain damaged patients is concerned. However, on other types of sorting tests, the acute (or reactive) but not the chronic schizophrenics tend to be overinclusive. Studies of the relation between Chapman's sorting tests and other tests of conceptual overinclusion are needed before this apparent contradiction can be resolved.

Miscellaneous Sorting Tests

A test very similar to Chapman's has been used by Hammer and Johnson (1965), who used cards with pictures. The category to be selected was illustrated by four different pictures (for example, four pictures of fruit), and the subject was also told what the category was. These four cards remained in front of the subject during the sorting, so that the correct category was constantly defined, and did not need to be held in mind. It was found that acute schizophrenics made significantly more errors of overinclusion than normals, whereas organics made significantly more errors of underinclusion.

Nickols (1964) asked chronic schizophrenics and controls to select from a group of differently shaped figures of different sizes, all those that seemed "to go with" a relatively amorphous multicolored stimulus card. Chronic schizophrenics unexpectedly did not select significantly more objects, and on this measure of overinclusion they were not abnormal.

Paranoid Delusions and Conceptual Overinclusion

Two quite different attempts have been made to relate paranoid delusions to the breadth of conceptual categories. Silverman (1964b) following Bruner and Cameron, has suggested that paranoid individuals progressively decrease the breadth of any conceptual category which is painful. If it is a broad category, a wide range of perceptual input will be subsumed under this category, and in one sense it will be frequently reinforced. However, in order to reduce the extent to which painful categories are employed, Silverman argues that they become increasingly restricted, so that in the end, many incoming data remain unclassified. This serves the purpose of reducing the anxiety level of the patient.

On the face of it, this explanation seems to deny some of the main clinical features of paranoia. Paranoid delusions do *not* succeed in reducing anxiety. Rather than failing to classify relevant stimuli under their false beliefs (underinclusion), paranoid patients appear to interpret a wide range of irrelevant input in the light of their delusional system, thereby increasing and not decreasing their level of discomfort. Silverman (1964b) nevertheless has produced some evidence that is consistent with his position. By using the Pettigrew (1958) test, he found that a group of paranoid schizophrenics employed significantly more underinclusive categories than a group of nonparanoid schizophrenics.

Payne, Caird, and Laverty (1964) on the other hand formulated exactly the opposite explanation. They suggest that, in one sense, a delusion is by definition an unwarranted generalization from the facts. Thus, a paranoid patient who hates one man, may incorporate all similar men into the hated category (for example, all foreigners or all Jews). They therefore predicted that paranoid delusions would be associated with conceptual overinclusion.

Payne, Caird, and Laverty (1964) tested their theory by using the Benjamin proverbs test. As predicted, they found that paranoid schizophrenics used more words per answer than did nonparanoid schizophrenics, a result which they attributed to overinclusive thinking. This finding, again using the proverbs word count, was repeated by Lloyd (1967). It was not confirmed by Goldstein and Salzman (1965), but these investigators, who found no significant differences between their groups, relied on longhand recording rather than tape recording, and report an unusually small word count in all their groups. To some extent this formulation is also supported by a study by Miller and Chapman (1968) who found that deluded schizophrenics show more "halo" effect in their ratings of independent dimensions, a tendency which could be associated with overinclusive conceptualization.

These strikingly discrepant theories and findings emphasize the need for better controls in such experiments. The results from a single test score such as the proverbs word count, or the Pettigrew test are necessarily ambiguous. It is also possible that each investigator, biased in favor of his own theory, unconsciously gave verbal reinforcement to those sorts of responses which supported his theory. It is, for example, relatively easy to encourage patients to talk or not to talk, and this could affect the proverb word count profoundly. It is also necessary to obtain a more objective criterion of paranoid delusional behavior, so that one study can more easily be compared with another. At present we must record a verdict of "not proven" for both theories.

The Prognostic Significance of Overinclusive Conceptualization

The studies discussed suggest that, on most tests, the reactive, acute schizophrenics, rather than the process or chronic schizophrenics, form overinclusive concepts. This suggests that this disability may be a relatively good prognostic sign. This hypothesis was tested by Payne (1968), who tested 114 admissions to a mental hospital, the majority (88) of whom were later diagnosed as psychotic, and 67 of whom were finally diagnosed as schizophrenic. The patients were given Payne and Friedlander's (1962) battery of overinclusion tests, two of which (Goldstein Object Sorting "Handing Over" Score, Proverbs word count) are measures of conceptual overinclusion, and one of which is a measure of unusual response tendencies (Payne Object Sorting Test Non-A score), from which a single overinclusion score was derived. The patients were followed up, on the average, for a three-year period, at which time their level of adjustment was rated on a 9 point scale. There was a statistically significant tendency ($r = +\cdot 329$) for patients who suffered from overinclusive conceptualization on admission to have a better than average prognosis.

The Stimulus Generalization Theory of Overinclusive Conceptualization

Payne (1961) suggested that overinclusive concept formation might be associated with an abnormal amount of stimulus generalization that, in turn, could be the result of an extremely high level of drive, as suggested by Mednick (1958). Mednick has measured stimulus generalization by means of a technique developed by Brown, Bilodeau, and Baron (1951). Subjects are seated in front of a row of lights, and required to lift their finger from a key as soon as possible whenever the center light goes on (none of the other lights function during this training period). In a second period, the instructions are the same, but the lights go on at random. The measure of stimulus generalization is the frequency with which the peripheral, irrelevant lights evoke a response.

One study using this technique is consistent with Payne's (1961) hypothesis. Kirschner (1964) found that, among a group of neurotics, schizophrenics, and organics, subjects judged to be concrete, as assessed by verbal and by sorting tests, show less stimulus generalization than the subjects judged to be abstract. Of course, this could be the result of a reduced field of scanning in concrete subjects, or even a constricted visual field, both of which are associated with brain damage.

The one direct test of the same hypothesis that has been carried out failed to support it. Watson (1967) gave Mednick's stimulus generalization test to 100 male schizophrenics, who were also given the Epstein overinclusion test, the Proverbs (total words) test, and the Goldstein Object Sorting "Handing Over" test. None of these measures correlated significantly with stimulus generalization. *Post hoc*, it is not surprising that this result was obtained. Presumably, subjects in a state of high drive in the Mednick experiment made errors because they could not discriminate between the lights. However, it is unlikely that such a failure of discrimination can explain the behavior of some schizophrenics on tests of overinclusive conceptualization. It is unlikely, for example, that conceptually overinclusive subjects group together a large number of the Goldstein Object Sorting Test objects simply because they cannot tell them apart. It must be concluded that no very convincing explanation of overinclusive concept formation can be offered at the moment. Of course, it is first necessary to demonstrate that the various tests of conceptual overinclusion, which have been described above, to some extent measure the same disability, before we seek a general explanation for this phenomenon.

Measures of Unusual Concepts or Responses

The Payne (1962) Object Classification Test

It has been pointed out for many years that schizophrenic responses in a variety of situations tend to be unusual. It is not immediately obvious that this tendency must be regarded as one aspect of overinclusive thinking. Payne, Matussek, and George (1959) related these two different phenomena because of their "defective filter" explanation of overinclusive thinking. They argued that unusual responses occur when overinclusive patients are unable to screen out or inhibit irrelevant perceptual material on the one hand, and irrelevant thoughts and associations on the other. As we have pointed out, however, the "defective filter" hypothesis has not been supported by subsequent experiments. There is no evidence that perceptual overinclusion (filtering) is in any way related to overinclusive conceptualization, and the two disabilities seem to occur in two quite different groups. "Process" and many chronic schizophrenics show defective perceptual filtering, whereas on most measures it appears to be "reactive," acute schizophrenics who form overinclusive concepts.

The object classification test was originally devised to measure concrete thinking and is derived from the Goldstein Sorting Tests. It consists of 12 small objects that are squares, circles, and triangles, that differ in size, thickness, and weight, and that are made of different materials, and are painted in colors of different hues and saturations. Subjects are asked to sort the objects in as many ways as they can think of. There are intended to be 10 "correct" ways to sort the objects and these are scored as "A" responses. Any other sorting which the subject is willing to explain is scored as a "non-A" response.

In the initial studies with the test (Payne, Matussek, & George, 1959; Payne & Hewlett, 1960; Payne, Friedlander, Laverty, & Haden, 1963), it was found that about 50 percent of acute schizophrenics produce an abnormally large number of "non-A" responses, but that neither normals, neurotics, nor depressives behave in this way. Non-A scores tend not to characterize chronic schizophrenic patients, who appear to be "concrete," instead, giving very few "A" responses. Although Payne, Ancevich, and Laverty (1963) found that remitted schizophrenics did not produce an abnormal number of non-A responses, Phillips, Jacobson, and Turner (1965) have found that an abnormal number of non-A responses are produced by the relatives of schizophrenic patients. Payne and Hewlett (1960) found that the non-A score was significantly correlated with tests of overinclusive concept formation, and that it had a high loading on their factor of "overinclusion," although Phillips, Jacobson, and Turner (1965) found it insignificantly correlated with the Epstein Overinclusion Test. At present, the evidence does not unequivocably support the view that overinclusive conceptualization, and unusual response production on this test are the result of the same disability.

Claridge (1967) has produced evidence that non-A responses are associated with a high level of arousal in acute psychotic patients. In one study, there was a significant relationship between "non-A" sortings and sedation threshold (but not with spiral aftereffect duration). In a second study, only certain types of non-A responses (those judged "overinclusive") were associated with high drive. Claridge's results suggest that high drive in acute schizophrenics may be associated with a constellation of characteristics, including the tendency to produce unusual responses on the Object Classification Test, the tendency to react quickly rather than slowly, the tendency to be "reactive" rather than "process," the tendency to be extraverted rather than introverted, the tendency to be paranoid, the tendency to be active rather than withdrawn, the tendency to have mood swings, and the tendency to have a good prognosis.

Unusual Responses on the Goldstein Object Sorting Test

McGaughran (1954) suggested that a second, independent dimension of sorting performance on the Goldstein test is the "public-private" classification, the term "public" referring to usual, and the term "private" referring to unusual responses. The results obtained suggest that chronic paranoid schizophrenics tend to produce more "private" responses than either normals or brain damaged patients (McGaughran & Moran, 1956, 1957; Leventhal, McGaughran, & Moran, 1959). Undifferentiated schizophrenics have also been reported to produce more unusual sortings than neurotics (Silverman & Silverman, 1962; Payne & Hewlett, 1960). The only failure to find such differences on this test was reported by Sturm (1964), who was unable to differentiate significantly between groups of brain damaged patients, tubercular patients, process schizophrenics, and reactive schizophrenics.

Unusual Responses on Other Sorting Tests

Payne and Hewlett (1960) used the Shaw sorting test with groups of acute schizophrenics, neurotics, depressives, and normals and found that the schizophrenics produced unusual responses on this test as well as on the Goldstein. Both tests had loadings on their "overinclusion" factor. Other investigators have found that on word-sorting tests, schizophrenics as a group produce more unusual sortings than do normals (McReynolds & Collins, 1961; Rashkis, 1947; Rashkis, Cushman, & Landis, 1946).

Unusual Responses to Proverbs

In addition to reporting "abstract" or "concrete" responses, several investigators have found responses to the proverbs test that could not be placed in either category. These responses are often labeled "autistic." Although some workers have suggested that these responses might be related to overinclusive thinking (Shimkunas, Gynther, & Smith, 1967), correlations with other measures of overinclusive concept formation have not been reported. There is some evidence (Brattemo, 1965) that these kinds of responses diminish among schizophrenics following phenothiazine treatment, although properly controlled studies are lacking.

Unusual Responses to Other Stimuli

One technique, which has often been used, is to present subjects with some barely recognizable perceptual material and ask them to say what it is. For example, White (1949) gave schizophrenics and normals very blurred carbon copies of words printed on cards and asked what they were. The schizophrenics more frequently gave responses which were not words, such as "teeth" or "spots."

Adams and Berg (1961) made use of fifty tape-recorded sounds that were relatively meaningless such as clicks, pure tones, chords, and so on, and asked subjects to rate how much they liked them. Schizophrenics produced more deviant ratings than normals. Another auditory technique is the "tautophone" (Shakow, Rosenzweig, & Hollander, 1966) which was originally called the "verbal summator" by Skinner. It consists of a recording of spoken vowel combinations that are, in fact, meaningless. The subjects are told that it is a record of a man who does not speak clearly, and are asked what he is saying. The evidence suggests that schizophrenics as a group tend to give more unusual interpretations than do normals.

A somewhat similar technique, which has been used for many years, is the word association test. No attempt will be made here to review the literature concerned with this test, but studies suggest that schizophrenics tend to make unusual associations (Payne & Hewlett, 1960).

High Drive and Unusual Responses

It is probable that there is a group of schizophrenic patients who consistently produce unusual responses in a variety of different situations. This hypothesis nevertheless needs to be confirmed for there appear to be no studies of the intercorrelations in psychiatric groups among the different measures of unusual response tendency which have been described. However, a wealth of clinical observation suggests that some schizophrenic patients consistently have unusual thoughts and unusual responses in normal situations. One of the most widely investigated explanations of this type of schizophrenic thought disorder is the one put forward by Mednick (1958).

Mednick argues that acutely disturbed schizophrenics are extremely anxious, and that this anxiety is evoked by a wide range of normal stimuli. This very high anxiety drive level has the effect of raising the response strengths of all the different competing responses to a particular stimulus (following Hull). A number of the less probable responses, whose response strengths are normally below the response threshold, become possible because their response strengths are now above the response threshold. By chance, occasionally, one of these very improbable responses occurs to a particular stimulus in the highly anxious person. When it does, Mednick argues, it receives an increment of reinforcement. This is because all the usual responses (thoughts or actions) have come to evoke anxiety. However, the unusual response does not. Accordingly, the acute schizophrenic gradually learns to produce unusual thoughts and behavior as a means of reducing his anxiety. The end result is the "affectless," "flat" schizophrenic who is not anxious, but whose most probable responses are all bizarre.

Mednick tested this theory by measuring a somewhat different theoretical consequence of high drive, stimulus generalization. We might argue that a more direct test of the hypothesis would have been to measure response generalization, since it is this and not stimulus generalization which presumably causes unusual responses to appear in the early schizophrenic.

Mednick and his associates have measured stimulus generalization in several ways. The reaction-time test that involves a row of peripheral distraction lights has already been described and, although Mednick (1955) found that a group of schizophrenics showed more generalization on this test than a group of normals or a group of brain damaged patients, this study is open to criticism on the grounds that variables such as the tendency to produce random errors and age were uncontrolled. It is also curious that the schizophrenics in this sample were chronic, and presumably no longer highly anxious. In a subsequent study, Gaines, Mednick, and Higgins (1963) made use of a different procedure. Subjects were trained to respond to a tone of 2.25 seconds duration, and then tested on tones of a different duration (2.50 seconds and 3 seconds) to determine how much generalization occurred. As expected, acute schizophrenics showed more stimulus generalization than normals, but chronics did not. In another study, Mednick (1966) investigated the generalization of a GSR response that had been conditioned to a specific tone and found that the children of schizophrenics showed more generalization than normal children. Buss and Daniell (1967) carried out a stimulus generalization experiment in which the stimuli were lines of different lengths. They found no difference in stimulus-generalization gradient between chronic schizophrenics and normals, as might be predicted, but no acute patients were tested for comparison.

In a different test of the theory, Higgins, Mednick, and Thompson (1966) found that process schizophrenics in a learning experiment retained remote associations better than reactive schizophrenics, a result thought to confirm the hypothesis.

Spence and Lair (1964) investigated another hypothetical effect of high drive on the rote learning of schizophrenics—associative interference—but found no support for Mednick's theory.

Although the experimental evidence is not conclusive, Mednick's theory has not yet been disproved, and it offers the best explanation for the development of unusual responses that thus far has been put forward.

Broen and Storms (1966; Broen, 1966) have suggested an elaboration of Mednick's theory. They believe that there is a "ceiling" to the possible strength of any response. When high drive increases the strength of a less probable competing response, if the dominant response is already at the ceiling, the difference between the strengths (probability of evocation) of the two responses will diminish, and the competing response will become *more likely* to occur than it was under a lower drive level. They also suggest that schizophrenics have a lower response strength ceiling than normal people, further exaggerating the effect. Thus, high drive not only makes more responses possible, because unlikely responses become suprathreshold, but it also alters the probability of evocation of all the responses in the response hierarchy, making the probabilities of all the alternatives more nearly the same. In this way, they explain the apparent frequency with which uncommon responses seem to occur in highly anxious early schizophrenics. Broen, Storms, and Goldberg (1963) produced evidence supporting this hypothesis. The drive level of two samples of psychiatric patients was increased by having them grip a hand dynamometer during a discrimination task that involved responding to different shades of gray. Under these conditions, the appropriate (strongest) responses occurred less frequently. Storms, Broen, and Levin (1967) also found that 40 acute schizophrenics gave more uncommon associations to words than normals, or neurotics. All subjects gave more uncommon associations to anxiety words than to neutral words. This tendency was exacerbated in the schizophrenic group by the stress of time pressure, but time pressure had the opposite effect on the neurotics. This result is held to support the view that the schizophrenic has a lower response strength ceiling than the neurotic or the normal, so that his response strength hierarchy is more susceptible to disruption by stress. However, why stress should have the opposite effect on neurotics is not clear.

Unusual Responses, High Drive and Paranoid Delusions

As we have mentioned above, the "over-inclusive conceptualization" theory of delusions has not been adequately substantiated. Mednick's hypothesis suggests a possible alternative explanation for the development of paranoid delusions. Occasionally, an improbable response to a situation might not only alleviate anxiety but also might receive more specific reinforcement. For instance, suppose, that an anxious person draws the improbable (and incorrect) conclusion that he is hated by an associate; he might also act on this conclusion by returning the believed aggression. Once he is aggressive himself, however, he is likely to evoke hostility in return, thus, reinforcing his initially unlikely hypothesis. Certainly, one characteristic of deluded patients is that they entertain possible interpretations of situations that do not occur to normal people. They are also usually willing to concede that their paranoid interpretation is only one of a number of possible alternative interpretations, which they can specify if required. It may not be the strength with which a delusional idea is held that characterizes the early paranoid patient, so much as the fact that it is held at all under the circumstances.

Claridge (1967) found that paranoid delusions were associated with a high level of drive in schizophrenia, a result which is consistent with this formulation.

Distractibility in Sorting Tests

A third type of experiment which has been carried out with sorting tests is different from the ones thus far discussed. Chapman (1956a) produced a test in which the subjects were required to sort cards into three boxes. Each box was labeled with a stimulus card which contained four pictures. Only the picture in the lower right-hand corner was relevant to the task, the other three being distractors. The response cards, which were to be sorted into one of the three boxes, also had four pictures. Again, only the picture in the lower-right hand corner was relevant. The subjects were asked to sort each response card into the box labeled with the stimulus card that pictured "something of the same kind." The cards depicted categories such as numbers, letters, clothing, etc. The variable that was manipulated was the number of relevant distractor items. For some categories the cards to be sorted had distractor items identical to the picture that defined one of the other (incorrect) categories. For some categories, the cards to be sorted had distractor items of the same kind as the card that defined one of the other (incorrect) categories. Some categories had no relevant distractors, in order to estimate the baseline error rate. Chapman (1956a) found that chronic schizophrenics made significantly more errors as a result of the distractions, than did a matched group of normals.

Chapman (1956b) also found that chronic schizophrenics were more often distracted by the identical distractor items, whereas normals were more often distracted by different items in the same category. This result was confirmed with a slightly different test by Downing, Ebert, and Shubrooks (1963b). Downing, Shubrooks and Ebert (1966) in another study confirmed that the closer the associational link between distractor and stimulus word, the more effective the distractor, at least among schizophrenic patients.

In a somewhat different sorting test, Chapman (1958) asked subjects to sort cards with a single word on each, into three boxes defined by a single stimulus word. Some of the words to be sorted had a connection with one stimulus word only, whereas some were of the same category as one of the stimulus words, but also had an association with one of the other stimulus words. This association, it was predicted, would lead to errors of distraction, and a group of chronic schizophrenics made more of these errors than a matched normal group. In a different type of verbal distractor experiment, Blumberg, and Giller (1965) tested chronic schizophrenics, acute schizophrenics, and nonschizophrenic patients with a test in which the subjects were asked to choose the synonym of a word from a group of words that also included an antonym, a homonym, and an irrelevant word. All subjects were distracted by the antonyms and homonyms, but the chronic schizophrenics were most seriously affected.

Feinberg and Mercer (1960) gave both types of Chapman distraction tests to groups of schizophrenics and brain damaged patients and found that the organic patients made more distraction errors than the schizophrenics.

Downing, Ebert, and Shubrooks (1963a) developed a form of Chapman's distractor test in which the items to be sorted were cards containing one relevant word and two distractor words. They tested 37 acute schizophrenics and retested them after six weeks of treatment with Chlorpromazine, Fluphenazine, Thioridazine, or placebo. Placebo and Chlorpromazine produced no significant improvement, but Fluphenazine and Thioridazine did. The authors note that neither of the drugs that were effective in cutting down distractibility are members of the "Chlorpromazine model" group, but their other dissimilarities make these results difficult to interpret.

These "'distraction" tests, in many respects, are like the measures of overinclusive perception, which have been discussed, although correlational studies are lacking. As on the tests of perceptual distractibility, the chronic schizophrenics rather than the acute schizophrenics seem most seriously affected. In this respect, the results are different from the ones found with tests of overinclusive concept formation. Again, one of the two drugs that improved performance on sorting distraction tests (Fluphenazine) is thought to be a stimulant, and it has been seen earlier that stimulant drugs may help focus the attention and reduce distractibility.

Personal Construct Theory

A different approach to the problem of schizophrenic thought disorder has been made by Bannister (1960). Bannister has described schizophrenic thought disorder in terms of Kelly's Personal Construct theory. A construct can be regarded as a kind of hypothesis whereby individuals learn to predict the behavior of others. It is a way of classifying one's experience. As Bannister (1960) writes:

> "To construe a business as profitable or a woman as affectionate is to predict future events in relation to the elements construed and predictions are inevitably validated or invalidated . . . (by subsequent events)."

Kelly has developed the Repertory Grid technique as a method of assessing the way in which constructs are employed. Subjects are asked to rate a number of people known to them (for example, mother, father, or close friend) on a number of different characteristics.

> ". . . if a subject nominates 40 people known personally to him, and categorizes each in turn as Moral (emergent pole) or Not Moral (implicit pole) and Honest or Not Honest, and we find that the 20 designated as Honest are also designated as Moral, and the 20 designated as Not Honest are designated as Not Moral, then we can infer a high positive relationship (which can be measured in terms of its binomial probability) between the concepts Honest and Moral."

These constellations of concept ratings of groups of people are personal constructs. Constructs are formed when people behave consistently with respect to a number of characteristics. Constructs break down when the experience of an individual invalidates such interrelationships. Bannister's view is that in the early environment of the schizophrenic, people behaved so inconsistently that normally related characteristics (for example, "friendly," "good") are no longer found to cohere. Thus, schizophrenics on this test show a weakening of the relationship between normally associated ratings.

In a series of experiments Bannister (1960, 1962) found evidence for such a weakening of the relations between these ratings in schizophrenic subjects. As a further test of this hypothesis, Bannister (1963, 1965) attempted to produce this type of "disassociative" thought disorder in normal subjects by asking them to rate ten photographs of people on a number of characteristics. This experiment was repeated on a number of days, but the subjects were told each day that their ratings were correct of some pictures, and of others that their ratings were incorrect. It was predicted that this consistent invalidation of the latter set of constructs (which hypothetically mimics the early experience of schizophrenics) would lead to a breakdown of the construct hierarchies (that is, characteristics which formerly cohered would no longer cohere). These experiments supported this hypothesis.

There is some evidence that loosening of constructs is associated with thought disorder as clinically rated (Bannister & Fransella, 1966), and as assessed by a variety of cognitive tests (Al-Issa & Robertson, 1964). There is also evidence that the loosening of constructs in schizophrenics applies more to constructs about people than it does to constructs about inanimate objects, as one might expect if it were associated with a disturbed family background (Bannister & Salmon, 1966; Salmon, Bramley & Presley, 1967).

It is not known how this kind of thought disorder is related to the measures already discussed, and at present there is no evidence relating it to any particular type of symptomatology or other developmental characteristic.

Conclusions

It is difficult to draw any definite conclusions from the rather heterogeneous set of results that have been described. This is mainly because little is known about the interrelations between the various measures. It would seem that conceptual overinclusion occurs in acute, rather than chronic schizophrenics, and that it characterizes reactive rather than process schizophrenics. The obverse, which is conceptual underinclusion, may be one aspect of concreteness, and it appears to characterize brain damaged patients and process schizophrenics. Overinclusive conceptualization appears to be a relatively good prognostic sign but it is not known what specific symptoms tend to be associated with it or what causes it, although there is a suggestion that it may respond to phenothiazine therapy.

Although it is conceivable that the tendency to produce unusual responses is related to conceptual overinclusion, there is no clear cut evidence one way or the other. It is a plausible hypothesis that this tendency is associated with an unusually high level of drive, and some evidence exists to support this. Again, this kind of thought disorder seems to characterize acute, reactive schizophrenics, rather than process schizophrenics, and it may well lead to the development of paranoid delusions. The prognosis of this disability is not known.

Distractibility in conceptual experiments may well be the same phenomenon as perceptual distractibility. It appears to be a characteristic of chronic, and probably process schizophrenics, and may be a correlate of an unusually low level of drive. It appears to be related to concreteness. Distractibility and the inability to focus one's attention may be improved by the administration of stimulant drugs.

DISORDERS OF MANIPULATION

Inductive and Deductive Reasoning

Most of the studies of the ability to perform inductive reasoning utilize "sorting" tests and have been discussed in the last section. Altogether there seems to be considerable evidence that process and chronic schizophrenics do especially poorly on tests that require inductive reasoning or the formation of an abstract generalization.

Tests of arithmetical or syllogistic problem-solving usually involved deductive reasoning. After many studies, Von Domarus (1946) attempted to clarify an error he found in the syllogistic reasoning of schizophrenics. He found that when a schizophrenic is given two premises with identical predicates, that is, A is B; some C are B, then he will conclude that some C are A, or more simply that the subjects are identical because the predicates are identical. Arieti (1959) attributes this error to an inability of the schizophrenic to abstract, and further explains this thought process as being a regression to a "lower level of rationality," or "Paleological" reasoning.

Williams (1964) assessed the investigations of Von Domarus and Arieti as inadequate on the basis of their assumption that a normal person would automatically apply the Aristotelian laws of logic without knowing them. In an investigation,

Williams administered a 96-item syllogistic test and a verbal IQ test to fifty hospitalized normal patients and fifty schizophrenic patients. He found no significant differences between the two groups in all cases except the ones that involved negative items. In this situation, schizophrenics made fewer errors than normals, which Williams attributes to the possibility that the negative items were uniformly more difficult. In conclusion, he states that

> "... schizophrenics and normals are least inclined to draw an affirmative inference on the basis of similar predicates, but are more inclined to draw affirmative inferences on the basis of similar subjects or in instances where a predicate term and a subject term are similar."

This is contrary to the expectation derived from the Von Domarus principle.

Gottesman and Chapman (1960) gave a multiple-choice syllogism test (Chapman & Chapman, 1959) to thirty schizophrenics and thirty normal controls, in which they also found results that were inconsistent with the predictions of the Von Domarus principle. Their results were similar to Williams' results in that the schizophrenics showed qualitatively and quantitatively similar error patterns to the normals.

In a study involving the interpretation and use of words in schizophrenia, Chapman and Chapman (1965) found support for the theory that chronic schizophrenics have a "steeper gradient of strength of meaning responses to words." In relating this investigation to the previous studies of syllogistic reasoning in schizophrenia, Chapman and Chapman conclude that the "error" found by Von Domarus and Arieti may simply be a result of having the predicate term refer to one of the strongest (but not necessarily relevant) meaning responses of both subject terms.

Therefore, we can conclude that the disturbance found by Von Domarus and Arieti is probably not an error in syllogistic reasoning, but rather an error in the definition of words associated with concreteness.

Speed

Speed of Problem Solving

Furneaux (1956a, 1956b) has demonstrated that on the Thurstone letter-series test of general intelligence, problem-solving speed is one of the major determinants of final score, whether a timed or untimed (as far as the subjects are aware) version of the test is used. In Furneaux's experiments, each test item was timed individually, and incorrect or abandoned items were not scored. Furneaux found that in normal people there is a linear relation between the logarithm of the solution time and the difficulty level of an item. Furthermore, the slope of this linear function is the same from one person to another, people differing only with respect to the origin. This suggests that speed may be a basic characteristic of an individual's problem solving, and that it represents the time taken to carry out a single operation of some "mental search" process. Difficulty refers to the number of these "searches" that a problem requires, and it increases exponentially with problem complexity.

There is some evidence (Payne, 1961) in normal people that speed may depend partly on the kind of reasoning involved, and on the content of the problem. It may also be that motor speed and perceptual speed are relatively independent of the speed of problem solving.

In view of Furneaux's findings, it is tempting to relate problem-solving speed to some fundamental characteristic of the nervous system. Payne (1961) has suggested that it may be a linear function of the level of cortical arousal, in view of the evidence that, even in a relatively homogenous student group, it is highly correlated with thyroid function.

Harriet Babcock has suggested that an extreme degree of intellectual slowness may be the primary cause of schizophrenic thought disorder (Payne, 1961). Shapiro and Nelson (1955) investigated this hypothesis by giving a large battery of Babcock and Levy's (1940) simple mental and motor speed tests and the Nufferno Speed and Level Test (Furneaux, 1956a, 1956b) to matched groups of 20 normals, 20 neurotics, 20 schizophrenics, 20 manic depressives, and 20 organics. It was found in this study that the neurotics were slightly slower than the normals, followed by the manic depressives and the schizophrenics, in that order. Slowest of all were the brain damaged patients. There was a good deal of overlap in score on all the speed tests, the schizophrenics being most heterogenous, suggesting that slowness is not very clearly associated with any particular psychiatric diagnostic category. The investigators found evidence that these tests were more highly intercorrelated in the abnormal population than they were in the normal group. This finding suggests the presence of some pathological variable that influences the performance of abnormal subjects on all the tests, which is not present in normal people. Shapiro and Nelson also found that two independent factors could account for most of the covariance of the test battery. They suggested that these two factors might correspond to motor and mental speed, but other interpretations of the data are possible.

Payne and Hewlett (1960), in an experiment described previously, gave tests of mental and motor speed, concreteness, intelligence, and overinclusive thinking to matched groups of 20 normals, 20 neurotics, 20 depressives, and 20 schizophrenics. They found mean differences similar to the ones reported by Shapiro and Nelson. In Payne and Hewlett's study, the neurotics were not significantly slower than the normals and, on the average, the schizophrenics and the depressives were equally retarded. The main difference was that the schizophrenic group was extremely heterogenous, with about one half of the subjects falling within the normal speed range. In their factor analysis, Payne and Hewlett obtained a single factor of speed, which they labeled "retardation." However, this result is not necessarily inconsistent with that of Shapiro and Nelson because the tests were different, the groups were different, and Payne and Hewlett extracted only three independent factors, leaving a good deal of their test covariance unanalyzed. (They were concerned only with the first three major sources of covariance for other theoretical reasons.)

These two studies are consistent with a number of other investigations that use some of the same tests, which have been reviewed by Payne (1961).

Payne has suggested that there may be two independent causes of intellectual slowness in abnormal patients, an hypothesis which could account for Shapiro and Nelson's finding of two independent factors. Some subjects are slow because they have an extremely low level of drive, and others are slow because they are distracted. Payne has suggested that the mild degree of slowness shown by neurotics on some tests might be the result of distraction that is caused by task interfering anxiety responses, especially when working under "stressed" conditions. Some data obtained from the Nufferno test are consistent with this prediction. Payne (1961) has also suggested that the moderate slowness found in many depressed patients could result from the distracting effect of their depressive thoughts.

If extreme slowness results from a very low level of drive, the finding that process schizophrenics are slower than reactive schizophrenics (Ward & Carlson, 1966), and that chronic schizophrenics are especially slow (Payne, 1961), could be explained. In an investigation of the autonomic responsivity in a matching task to variable rates of stimulus input among process and reactive schizophrenics, Ward and Carlson (1966) found that process schizophrenics consistently showed low autonomic responsivity and were unable to perform the task under speeded conditions. Harris and Metcalf (1956, 1959) found that extreme slowness occurs in patients who show flattening of affect, and incongruous affect—two characteristics of process and chronic schizophrenia. They also found that slowness characterized those patients independently judged by the psychiatrist to have a poor prognosis.

The only direct study of the prognostic implications of extreme retardation has been carried out by Payne (1968). As described above, Payne gave a battery of tests to a large group of newly admitted mental patients. The tests included three measures of overinclusiveness, as defined by Payne and Friedlander (1962) and three measures of retardation, as defined by Payne and Hewlett (1960). As predicted, it was found in a follow-up study that those patients who suffered from overinclusive thinking on admission tended to have a slightly better than average prognosis, while those suffering from retardation had a worse than average prognosis.

Means of Modification

Broadhurst (1958a, 1958b) has investigated the possibility of bringing the speed of mental functioning under experimental control. Matched groups of early schizophrenics and normal controls were given the Nufferno Speed tests under three different experimental conditions by using depressant drugs (sodium amytal), central stimulants (dexamphetamine sulphate), and practice. No significant effects were found under the drug conditions, and the slight change recorded was attributed to practice. However, it was found that there was a significant practice effect in both schizophrenics and normals, and under conditions in which measures of mental speed were taken, schizophrenic subjects responded to daily practice with greater improvement than normals. Although these results are significant, further investigation is necessary before concluding that the effect of practice has a long-term effect in the improvement of mental speed in schizophrenics.

Reaction Time

There is much evidence that schizophrenics are characterized by an extremely slow reaction time. Payne and Caird (1967) hypothesized that slow reaction time could be due either to overinclusion, which produces a variable slowness as a function of the number of external distractions, or retardation, which produces a consistent slowness that is not a function of the amount of distraction. They found that retarded schizophrenics, as defined by psychomotor tests, had slow reaction times, and that this characteristic could not be explained as being the result of distraction.

There have been various studies that measure the reaction time of normal and abnormal groups under varying conditions of stimulation (Tizard & Venables 1955, 1957). Venables and O'Connor (1959) found that a group of normal subjects had an auditory reaction time that was significantly faster than their visual reaction time. However, in a group of schizophrenics, matched for age, the reaction time to visual stimuli was faster than the reaction time to auditory stimuli.

In a later study, Venables (1966b) made a comparison of two-flash and two-click thresholds in schizophrenic and normal subjects and found a pattern of thresholds similar to that found by Venables and O'Connor for reaction time. If the two-click and two-flash thresholds measure cortical reactivity, it would appear that chronic schizophrenics are more defective in the auditory than in the visual center, but the reason for this is not clear.

It does not seem possible at present to formulate any very satisfactory hypothesis about the cause of the low level of cortical arousability that seems to be responsible for the retardation, including slowness in reaction time, shown by some schizophrenics.

Error

Giving a wrong answer in a cognitive test in the mistaken belief that it is right is the most important single determinant of the score on most intelligence tests. Nevertheless, very little is known about the causes of errors in problem solving, and the nature of the checking process whereby a possible solution is verified.

Furneaux (1961) has found that there is a very low correlation between error and speed in normal people, although his standard measure of accuracy is obtained from test items that are at a relatively low level of difficulty. It seems probable that errors can have many causes, including the inaccurate perception of the data of the problem, incorrect generalizations from the data as a result of conceptual difficulties, and misunderstanding of the data because of an idiosyncratic use of words. One factor is clearly the complexity of the problem. Complex problems require that more separate items of information be held in mind and be manipulated, and not surprisingly, individuals with a larger immediate memory span make fewer errors (Payne, 1961). One would expect slow thinkers to be handicapped because they must hold information in temporary store for longer periods of time, and the probability becomes greater that relevant information will be forgotten before the problem is solved.

Wadsworth, Wells, and Scott (1962) have demonstrated on a work task involving sequential operations, that as the complexity of a task increases, normals tend to show decrements in both speed and accuracy. However, in this particular study, schizophrenics maintained their level of speed with a considerable loss in accuracy as the complexity of the task increased. The significance of this investigation is not clear, however, because of the difficulty of assessing the effect that attention and distraction had on the two groups.

There is evidence that on such tests as the Porteus Mazes, "delinquent" children make an abnormally large number of "impulsive" errors which are the result of disobeying the instructions not to cross lines or enter blind alleys in tracing the mazes (Payne, 1961). There is also evidence that on the Nufferno speed and level tests, extraverts make more errors than introverts, but whether this represents the "carelessness" of insufficient checking, or some "cognitive" difference such as a smaller memory span, it is not possible to say.

Similarly, there is evidence that psychotic patients make more errors than normals on the Nufferno tests at any given difficulty level (Payne, 1961). This could be caused by any of the specific defects thus far discussed, and the implications of this result are not clear. There appear to be no studies of the relation between the tendency to make errors and specific symptomatology, nor is it known how accuracy responds to different sorts of treatment.

Persistence

Furneaux has demonstrated that persistence is another important determinant of the score on cognitive tests, and that it becomes increasingly important when the tests are given with no time limit. It is obvious that individuals abnormally lacking in persistence would obtain reduced scores on most cognitive tests.

Factorial studies in normals (Payne, 1961) suggest that there may be two fairly well-defined and relatively independent types of persistence, "ideational" and "physical." The former refers to the amount of time spent on very difficult or unsolvable intellectual problems, and the latter to the length of time people are prepared to submit to boring, fatiguing, or uncomfortable physical tasks.

Most of the work with abnormal subjects appears to refer to tests of physical persistence (Payne, 1961). These studies suggest that neurotics as a group may be less persistent than normals, and that extraverted neurotics are less persistent than introverted neurotics. The data on psychotics are inconsistent, but it appears that they are less persistent than neurotics on most physical tests.

Although there are only a few investigations of persistence on cognitive tests, Lynn and Gordon (1961) and Payne (1961) have demonstrated that introverts are more persistent than extraverts on the Raven's Matrices test. In both of these investigations, extraverted neurotics tended to do as well as or better than the introverted neurotics at the beginning of the test, but then became much worse at the end of the test. The reason for this is unclear, but it is possible that extraverts become more fatigued and tend to give up on the later problems.

Some evidence exists that ambulatory schizophrenics are significantly more persistent than hospitalized schizophrenics on cognitive tests (Blumenthal, Meltzoff, & Rosenberg, 1965). It is possible that hospitalized patients also become fatigued more quickly.

Rigidity

There is some evidence (Payne, 1961) that two relatively independent kinds of mental rigidity are relevant to problem solving. One, "adaptive rigidity," is the inability to change a set in order to meet the requirements imposed by changing problems. The other is the opposite of "spontaneous flexibility," or the ability to produce a diversity of ideas in a problem-solving situation. Only "adaptive rigidity" appears to have been studied in psychiatric subjects.

As we have described above, Payne and Hewlett (1960), by using a modification of the Luchins water-jar test of adaptive rigidity, found that acute schizophrenics were significantly less rigid than nonschizophrenic patients and normal controls. They related it to overinclusive thinking, and attributed it to the inability of overinclusive schizophrenics to build up a "filter" which blinds them to possible solutions to a problem. As we have seen, however, other predictions made from the "filter" theory of overinclusive thinking have not been supported, hence, the theoretical implications of this finding in acute schizophrenics are not clear.

All the other investigators of "adaptive rigidity" in schizophrenics have used different techniques and have investigated chronic rather than acute schizophrenics.

Weiss and Nordtvedt (1964), by using a

perceptual task, found that schizophrenics were more rigid than normals, in the sense that they developed a set in conditions in which normals did not. Kristofferson (1967) used a reaction-time task in which attention had to be switched from an auditory to a verbal stimulus. She found that the reaction times of schizophrenics were more affected by the switch than the reaction times of normal subjects, suggesting an abnormal degree of rigidity in this situation. In general, this finding is consistent with other similar studies reviewed by Kristofferson.

Although Goldstein suggested that rigidity was one aspect of concrete behavior, Payne (1961) concluded that there were no adequate studies of the relationship between these phenomena, and no further work appears to have been done in this area.

Payne (1961), reviewing the literature on perceptual tests of rigidity, concluded that normals tend to become more rigid when tested under stress, and suggested that "adaptive rigidity" could be associated with high drive because it facilitates the learning of a "set." However, there appear to be no studies of the relation between "adaptive rigidity" and neurotic behavior in psychiatric groups.

SUMMARY AND CONCLUSIONS

In spite of the inadequacies of the data, we can make one or two broad generalizations that account for many of the findings.

There appear to be three distinctly different psychiatric groups, all of which have thought disorder as a primary characteristic. There is a group of patients whose abnormality begins in childhood. They tend to be of low average to borderline defective intelligence, and to do poorly in school. The development of further symptoms takes place slowly but, by the time they reach adolescence or early adulthood, they typically require hospitalization, and have deteriorated even further intellectually. These patients suffer from two striking intellectual disabilities that probably account, to a large extent, for their low intelligence. They are concrete, or unable to make adequate inductive generalizations. They are also extremely slow in all their psychomotor activity. Both these characteristics carry with them a poor prognosis. In addition, they suffer from perceptual defects that may be a consequence of their failure to "scan" their environment carefully enough. They are also distractible. They are unable to confine their attention to relevant perceptions. At least some of these symptoms, for example, their slowness and distractibility, may result from the fact that they have a chronically low level of drive or cortical arousal. These patients tend not to develop paranoid delusions, and they are usually diagnosed as process schizophrenics, or simple schizophrenics. These patients share a number of characteristics with brain damaged people, and they may well be suffering from some organic disorder. There is some evidence that stimulant drugs may improve their performance. There is also evidence that a strong anesthetic and cortical depressant drug such as Sernyl can produce many of these symptoms in normal people.

There is a second group of patients whose illness appears to start much more dramatically, often in response to some environmental trauma or stress in late adolescence, early adulthood or, not infrequently, in early middle age. These patients characteristically have more or less organized paranoid delusions. They show little general intellectual deterioration and, even if they remain ill for many years, they remain well-preserved intellectually. They have no perceptual disabilities. In fact, they are unusually accurate perceptually, perhaps because they scan their environment more than is usual. They are better than average at concentrating and at focusing their attention, and are not distractible. They show no evidence of psychomotor retardation. Many of these characteristics can be explained by their apparently very high drive level, or level of cortical arousability. This high drive, usually experienced as tension or anxiety, appears to produce a good deal of "response generalization." That is to say, unusual ideas or behavior patterns, which remain subthreshold responses in normal people, appear to be evoked occasionally because of their very high drive level. This unusual response tendency may predispose them to develop delusions. The prognosis of this disorder is not known, although these patients tend to be regarded as reactive rather than process schizophrenics. For reasons which are unclear, when some of these patients become chronically ill, they learn to become more and more peculiar, and more and more withdrawn, perhaps because they find that it alleviates their high anxiety. Thus, as chronic patients, they still manifest a very high level of cortical arousal, are overresponsive ideationally to perceptual stimuli but, nevertheless, are socially withdrawn and inactive.

A third type of thought disorder also appears to develop quite suddenly. It consists of overinclusive conceptualization. A great deal of disparate material is all subsumed under the same conceptual label, so that thinking becomes very vague and imprecise. It is possible that this thought disorder is also accompanied by a heightened perceptual awareness, and a feeling that the world has somehow changed. Patients who develop this condition in some respects resemble normal people under the influence of psychotomimetic drugs such as LSD. They often tend to be excited and overactive and may have mood swings. The prognosis of this disorder is good, the condition tending to remit spontaneously. It is tempting to speculate that it is the result of a temporary toxic condition that some individuals are predisposed to develop. Some substance, such as adrenochrome, may ultimately be found responsible. This disorder could be classified as a reactive schizophrenia, and it is probably usually diagnosed psychiatrically as acute schizophrenia, or schizo-affective psychosis. There is some suggestion that phenothiazine drugs improve this condition.

REFERENCES

Adams, H. E., & Berg, I. A. Schizophrenia and deviant response sets produced by auditory and visual test content. *J. Psychol.*, 1961, **51**, 393–398.

Albee, G. W., Lane, Ellen S., Corcoran, Clare, & Wernecke, Ann. Childhood and intercurrent intellectual performance of adult schizophrenics. *J. consult. Psychol.*, 1963, **27**, 364–366.

Albee, G. W., Lane, Ellen A., & Reuter, Jeanette M. Childhood intelligence of the future schizophrenics and neighborhood peers. *J. Psychol.*, 1964, **58**, 141–144.

Al-Issa, I., & Robertson, J. P. S. Divergent thinking abilities in chronic schizophrenia. *J. clin. Psychol.*, 1964, **20**, 433–435.

Arieti, S. Schizophrenia: the manifest symptomatology, the psychodynamic and formal mechanisms. In S. Arieti (ed.) *American Handbook of Psychiatry, Vol. I.* New York: Basic Books, 1959, 455–484.

Babcock, Harriet, & Levy, Lydia. *Manual of Directions for the Revised Examination of the Measurement of Efficiency of Mental Functioning*. Chicago: Stoelting, 1940.

Bannister, D. Conceptual structure in thought-disordered schizophrenics. *J. ment. Sci.*, 1960, **106**, 1230–1249.

Bannister, D. The nature and measurement of schizophrenic thought disorder. *J. ment. Sci.*, 1962, **108**, 825–842.

Bannister, D. The genesis of schizophrenic thought disorder: A serial invalidation hypothesis. *Brit. J. Psychiat.*, 1963, **109**, 680–686.

Bannister, D. The genesis of schizophrenic thought disorder: Retest of the serial invalidation hypothesis. *Brit. J. Psychiat.*, 1965, **111**, 377–382.

Bannister, D., & Fransella, Fay. A grid test of schizophrenic thought disorder. *Brit. J. soc. clin. Psychol.*, 1966, **5**, 95–102.

Bannister, D. & Salmon, Phillida. Schizophrenic thought disorder: Specific or diffuse? *Brit. J. med. Psychol.*, 1966, **39**, 215–219.

Batman, R., Albee, G. W., & Lane, Ellen A. Intelligence test performance of chronic and recovered schizophrenics. *Proceedings of the 74th Annual Convention of the American Psychological Association.* Washington: American Psychological Association, 1966, 173–174.

Becker, W. C. The relation of severity of thinking disorder to the process-reactive concept of schizophrenia. Unpublished doctoral dissertation. Stanford University, 1955.

Bemporad, J. R. Perceptual disorders in schizophrenia. *Amer. J. Psychiat.*, 1967, **123**, 971–976.

Benjamin, J. D. A method for distinguishing and evaluating formal thinking disorders in schizophrenia. In. J. S. Kasanin (ed.), *Language and Thought in Schizophrenia.* Berkeley and Los Angeles: Univ. of Calif. Press, 1946.

Berger, L., Bernstein, A., Klein, E., Cohen, J., & Lucas, G. Effects of aging and pathology on the factoral structure of intelligence. *Newsletter for Research in Psychology*, 1963, **5**, 35–36.

Bernstein, L. The interaction of process and content on thought disorders of schizophrenic and brain-damaged patients. *J. gen. Psychol.*, 1960, **62**, 53–68.

Blatt, S. J. Recall and recognition vocabulary: Implications for intellectual deterioration. *Arch. gen. Psychiat.*, 1959, **1**, 473–476.

Blaufarb, H. A demonstration of verbal abstracting ability in chronic schizophrenics under enriched stimulus and instructional conditions. *J. consult. Psychol.*, 1962, **26**, 471–475.

Blumberg, S., & Giller, D. W. Some verbal aspects of primary-process thought: A partial replication. *J. pers. soc. Psychol.*, 1965, **1**, 517–520.

Blumenthal, R., & Meltzoff, J. Social schemas and perceptual accuracy in schizophrenia. *Brit. J. soc. clin. Psychol.*, 1967, **6**, 119–128.

Blumenthal, R., Meltzoff, J., & Rosenberg, S. Some determinants of persistence in chronic schizophrenic subjects. *J. abnorm. Psychol.* 1965, **70**, 246.

Brattemo, C. E. Interpretations of proverbs in schizophrenic patients: Further studies. *Acta Psychol.*, 1962, **20**, 254–263.

Brattemo, C. E. The effectiveness of a non-standardized categorization in differentiating schizophrenic patients of various levels of abstracting functioning. *Acta Psychol.*, 1965, **24**, 314–328.

Broadbent, D. E. *Perception and Communication.* London: Pergamon Press, 1958.

Broadhurst, Anne H. Some variables affecting speed of mental functioning in schizophrenics. Unpublished doctoral dissertation. University of London Library, 1957.

Broadhurst, Anne H. Experimental studies of the mental speed of schizophrenics: I. Effects of a stimulant and a depressant drug. *J. ment. Sci.*, 1958a, **104**, 1123–1129.

Broadhurst, Anne H. Experimental studies of the mental speed of schizophrenics: II. Effects of practice, *J. ment. Sci.*, 1958b, **104**, 1130–1135.

Broen, W. E. Response disorganization and breadth of observation in schizophrenia. *Psychol. Rev.*, 1966, **73**, 579–585.

Broen, W. E., & Storms, L. H. Lawful disorganization: the process underlying a schizophrenic syndrome. *Psychol. Rev.*, 1966, **73**, 265–279.

Broen, W. E., Storms, L. H., & Goldberg, D. H. Decreased discrimination as a function of increased drive. *J. abnorm. soc. Psychol.*, 1963, **67**, 266–273.

Brown, J. E., Bilodeau, E. A., & Baron, M. R. Bidirectional gradients in the strength of a generalized voluntary response to stimuli on a visual-spatial dimension. *J. exp. Psychol.*, 1951, **41**, 52–61.

Buss, A. H., & Daniell, Edna F. Stimulus generalization and schizophrenia. *J. abnorm. Psychol.*, 1967, **72**, 50.

Callagan, J. E. The effect of electroconvulsive therapy on the test performances of hospitalized depressed patients. Unpublished Ph.D. thesis, Univ. of London Library, 1952.

Callaway, E. III, & Dembo, D. Narrowed attention. *Arch. neurol. Psychiat.*, 1958, **79**, 74–90.

Callaway, E. III, Jones, R. T., & Layne, R. S. Evoked responses and segmental set of schizophrenia. *Arch. gen. Psychiat.*, 1965, **12**, 83–89.

Callaway, E. III, & Stone, G. Re-evaluating focus of attention. In L. Uhr, & J. G. Miller (eds.) *Drugs and Behavior*. New York: Wiley, 1960.

Cameron, N. Reasoning, regression and communication in schizophrenics. *Psychol. Monogr.*, 1938, **50**, 1–33.

Carp, A. Performance on the Wechsler-Bellevue scale and insulin shock therapy. *J. abnorm. soc. Psychol.*, 1950, **45**, 127–136.

Chapman, J., & McGhie, A. A comparative study of disordered attention in schizophrenia. *J. ment. Sci.*, 1962, **108**, 487–500.

Chapman, L. J. Distractibility in the conceptual performance of schizophrenics. *J. abnorm. soc. Psychol.*, 1956a, **53**, 286–291.

Chapman, L. J. The role of type of distractor in the "concrete" conceptual performance of schizophrenics. *J. Pers.*, 1956b, **25**, 130–141.

Chapman, L. J. Intrusion of associative responses into schizophrenic conceptual performance. *J. abnorm. soc. Psychol.*, 1958, **56**, 374–379.

Chapman, L. J. Confusion of figurative and literal usages of words by schizophrenics and brain damaged patients. *J. abnorm. soc. Psychol.*, 1960, **60**, 412–416.

Chapman, L. J. A reinterpretation of some pathological disturbances in conceptual breadth. *J. abnorm. soc. Psychol.*, 1961, **62**, 514–519.

Chapman, L. J., & Chapman, Jean P. Atmosphere effect re-examined. *J. exp. Psychol.*, 1959, **58**, 220–226.

Chapman, L. J., & Chapman, Jean P. Interpretation of words in schizophrenia. *J. pers. soc. Psychol.*, 1965, **1**, 135–146.

Chapman, L. J., Burstein, A. G., Day, Dorothy, & Verdone, P. Regression and disorders of thought. *J. abnorm. soc. Psychol.*, 1961, **63**, 540–545.

Chapman, L. J., Day, Dorothy, & Burstein, A. G. The process-reactive distinction and prognosis in schizophrenia. *J. nerv. ment. Dis.*, 1961, **133**, 383–391.

Chapman, L. J., & Knowles, R. R. The effects of phenothiazine on disordered thought in schizophrenia. *J. consult. Psychol.*, 1964, **28**, 165–169.

Chapman, L. J., & Pathman, J. H. Errors in the diagnosis of mental deficiency in schizophrenics. *J. consult. Psychol.*, 1959, **23**, 432–434.

Chapman, L. J., & Taylor, J. A. Breadth of deviate concepts used by schizophrenics. *J. abnorm. soc. Psychol.*, 1957, **54**, 118–123.

Claridge, G. S. *Personality and Arousal. A Psychophysiological Study of Psychiatric Disorder.* London: Pergamon, 1967.

Clark, W. C. The psyche in psychophysics: A sensory-decision theory analysis of the effect of instructions on flicker sensitivity and response bias. *Psychol. Bull.*, 1966, **65**, 358–366.

Clark, W. C. Brown, Jane, C. & Rutschmann, J. Flicker sensitivity and response bias in psychiatric patients and normal subjects. *J. abnorm. Psychol.*, 1967, **72**, 35–42.

Cohen, B. D., & Camhi, J. Schizophrenic performance in a word-communication task. *J. abnorm. Psychol.*, 1967, **72**, 240–246.

Cohen, B. D., Rosenbaum, G., Luby, E. D., & Gottlieb, J. S. Comparison of phencyclidine hydrochloride (Sernyl) with other drugs: Stimulation of schizophrenic performance with phencyclidine hydrochloride (Sernyl), lysergic acid diethylamide (LSD–25) and amobarbital (Amytal) sodium, II. Symbolic and sequential thinking. *Arch. gen. Psychiat.*, 1962, **6**, 395–401.

Cooper, Ruth. Objective measures of perception in schizophrenics and normals. *J. consult. Psychol.*, 1960, **24**, 209–214.

Craig, W. J. Objective measures of thinking integrated with psychiatric symptoms. *Psychol. Rep.*, 1965, **16**, 539–546.

Czudner, G., & Marshall, Marilyn. Simple reaction time in schizophrenic, retarded, and normal children under regular and irregular preparatory interval conditions. *Canad. J. Psychol.*, 1967, **21**, 369–380.

Davidson, M. Studies in the application of mental tests to psychotic patients. *Brit. J. med. Psychol.*, 1939, **18**, 44–52.

Davis, D., Cromwell, R. L., & Held, Joan. Size estimation in emotionally disturbed children and schizophrenic adults. *J. abnorm. Psychol.*, 1967, **72**, 395–401.

Desai, M. M. Intelligence and verbal knowledge in relation to Epstein's overinclusion test. *J. clin. Psychol.*, 1960, **16**, 417–419.

Donovan, M. J., & Webb, W. W. Meaning dimensions and male-female voice perception in schizophrenics with good and poor premorbid adjustment. *J. abnorm. Psychol.*, 1965, **70**, 426.

Dowis, J. L., & Buchanan, C. E. Some relationships between intellectual efficiency and the severity of psychiatric illness. *J. Psychol.*, 1961, **51**, 371–381.

Downing, R. W., Ebert, J. N., & Shubrooks, S. J. Effect of phenothiazines on the thinking of acute schizophrenics. *Percept. mot. Skills.*, 1963a, **17**, 511–520.

Downing, R. W., Ebert, J. N., & Shubrooks, S. J. Effects of three types of verbal distractors on thinking in acute schizophrenia. *Percept. mot. Skills.*, 1963b, **17**, 881–882.

Downing, R. W., Shubrooks, S. J., & Ebert, J. N. Intrusion of associative distractors into conceptual performance by acute schizophrenics; role of associative strength. *Percept. mot. Skills.*, 1966, **22**, 460–462.

Drasgow, J., & Feldman, M. J. Conceptual processes in schizophrenia revealed by the visual-verbal test. *Percept. mot. Skills.*, 1957, **7**, 251–264.

Easterbrook, J. A. The effect of emotion on cue utilization and the organization of behavior. *Psychol. Rev.*, 1959, **66**, 183–200.

Eliseo, T. S. Overinclusive thinking in process and reactive schizophrenics. *J. consult. Psychol.*, 1963, **27**, 447–449.

Elmore, C. M., & Gorham, D. R. Measuring the impairment of the abstracting function with the proverbs test. *J. clin. Psychol.*, 1957, **13**, 263–266.

Epstein, S. Overinclusive thinking in a schizophrenic and a control group. *J. consult. Psychol.*, 1953, **17**, 384–388.

Faibish, G. M. Schizophrenic response to words of multiple meaning. *J. Pers.*, 1961, **29**, 414–427.

Feffer, M. H. The influence of affective factors on conceptualization in schizophrenia. *J. abnorm. soc. Psychol.*, 1961, **63**, 588–596.

Feinberg, I., & Mercer, Margaret. Studies of thought disorder in schizophrenia. *Arch. gen. Psychiat.*, 1960, **2**, 504–511.

Feldman, M. J., & Drasgow, J. A visual-verbal test for schizophrenics. *Psychiatric Quarterly Supplement*, 1951, **25**, 55–64.

Fey, Elizabeth T. The performance of young schizophrenics and young normals on the Wisconsin card sorting test. *J. consult. Psychol.*, 1951, **15**, 311–319.

Flavell, J. H. Abstract thinking and social behavior in schizophrenia. *J. abnorm. soc. Psychol.*, 1956, **52**, 208–211.

Fogel, M. L. The proverbs test in the appraisal of cerebral disease. *J. gen. Psychol.*, 1965, **72**, 269–275.

Foulds, G. A., & Dixon, Penelope. The nature of intellectual deficit in schizophrenia and neurotics: I. A comparison of schizophrenics and neurotics. *Brit. J. soc. clin. Psychol.*, 1962, **1**, 7–19.

Freides, D., Fredenthal, B. J., Grisell, J. L., & Cohen, B. D. Changes in two dimensions of cognition during adolescence. *Child Develpm.*, 1963, **34**, 1047–1055.

Furneaux, W. D. Manual of Nufferno speed tests. London: *National Foundation of Educational Research*, 1956a.

Furneaux, W. D. Manual of Nufferno level tests. London: *National Foundation of Educational Research*, 1956b.

Furneaux, W. D. Intellectual abilities and problem solving behavior. In H. J. Eysenck (ed.) *Handbook of Abnormal Psychology*. London: Pitman, 1960, New York: Basic Books, 1961, 167–193.

Gaines, Julie A., Mednick, S. A., & Higgins, J. Stimulus generalization in acute and chronic schizophrenia. *Acta Psychiatrica Scandinavica*, 1963, **39**, 601–605.

Goldstein, K., & Scheerer, M. Abstract and concrete behavior, an experimental study with special tests. *Psychol. Monogr.*, 1941, **53**, No. 2.

Goldstein, R. H., & Salzman, L. F. Proverb word counts as a measure of overinclusiveness in delusional schizophrenics. *J. abnorm. Psychol.*, 1965, **70**, 244–245.

Gorham, D. R. A proverbs test for clinical and experimental use. *Psychol. Rep.*, 1956a, **2**, 1–12.

Gorham, D. R. Clinical manual for the proverbs test. *Psychol. Test Specialists.*, 1956b, 1–16.

Gorham, D. R. Use of the proverbs test for differentiating schizophrenics from normals. *J. consult. Psychol.*, 1956c, **20**, 435–440.

Gottesman, L., & Chapman, L. J. Syllogistic reasoning errors in schizophrenia. *J. consult. Psychol.*, 1960, **24**, 250–255.

Graham, Virginia T. Psychological studies of hypoglycemia theory. *J. Psychol.*, 1940, **10**, 327–358.

Gregg, A. H., & Frank, G. H. An analysis of conceptual thinking in process and reactive schizophrenics. *Proceedings of the 74th Annual Convention of the American Psychological Association.* Washington: American Psychological Association, 1966, 183–184.

Griffith, R. M., Estes, Betsy W., & Zerof S. A. Intellectual impairment in schizophrenia. *J. consult. Psychol.*, 1962, **26**, 336–339.

Guertin, W. H., Rabin, A. I., Frank, G. H., & Ladd, C. E. Research with the Wechsler Intelligence Scales for adults: 1955–1960. *Psychol. Bull.*, 1962, **59**, 1–26.

Hall, G. C. Conceptual attainment in schizophrenics and nonpsychotics as a function of task structure. *J. Psychol.*, 1962, **53**, 3–13.

Hamlin, R. M., Haywood, H. C., & Folsom, Angela, T. Effect of enriched input on schizophrenic abstraction. *J. abnorm. Psychol.*, 1965, **70**, 390–394.

Hamlin, R. M., & Jones, R. E. Vocabulary deficit in improved and unimproved schizophrenic subjects. *J. nerv. Ment. Dis.*, 1963, **136**, 360–364.

Hamlin, R. M., & Ward, W. D. Aging, hospitalization, and schizophrenic intelligence. *Proceedings of the 74th Annual Convention of the American Psychological Association.* Washington: American Psychological Association, 1965, 221–222.

Hammer, A. G., & Johnson, Laurel. Overinclusiveness in schizophrenia and organic psychosis. *Brit. J. soc. clin. Psychol.*, 1965, **4**, 47–51.

Hammer, Muriel, & Salzinger, K. Some formal characteristics of schizophrenic speech as a measure of social deviance. *Annals New York Academy Science*, 1964, **105**, 861–889.

Harris, A., & Metcalfe, Maryse. Inappropriate affect. *J. Neurol. Neurosurg. Psychiat.*, 1956, **19**, 313–318

Harris, A., & Metcalfe, Maryse. Slowness in schizophrenia. *J. Neurol. Neurosurg. Psychiat.*, 1959, **22**, 239–242.

Hawks, D. V. The clinical usefulness of some test of over-inclusive thinking in psychiatric patients. *Brit. J. soc. clin. Psychol.*, 1964, **3**, 186–195.

Haywood, H. C., & Moelis, I. Effect of symptom change on intellectual function in schizophrenia. *J. abnorm. soc. Psychol.*, 1963, **67**, 76–78.

Heath, Elaine B., Albee, G. W., & Lane, Ellen A. Predisorder intelligence of process and reactive schizophrenics and their siblings. *Proceedings of the 73rd Annual Convention of the American Psychological Association.* Washington: American Psychological Association, 1965, 223–224.

Higgins, J. The concept of process-reactive schizophrenia: criteria and related research. *J. nerv. Ment. Dis.*, 1964, **138**, 9–25.

Higgins, J., Mednick, S. A., & Thompson, R. E. Acquisition and retention of remote associates in process-reactive schizophrenia. *J. nerv. Ment. Dis.*, 1966, **142**, 418–423.

Hoffer, A., & Osmond, H. People are watching me. *Psychiat. Quart.*, 1963, **37**, 7–18.

Holtzman, W. H., Gortham, D. R., & Moran, L. J. A factor-analytic study of schizophrenic thought processes. *J. abnorm. soc. Psychol.*, 1964, **69**, 355–364.

Hunt, H. F. A practical clinical test for organic brain damage. *J. appl. Psychol.*, 1943, **27**, 375–386.

Johnson, M. H. Verbal abstracting ability and schizophrenia. *J. consult. Psychol.*, 1966, **30**, 275–277.

Jones, R. T., Blacker, K. H., & Callaway, E. Perceptual dysfunction in schizophrenia: clinical and auditory evoked response findings. *Amer. J. Psychol.*, 1966, **123**, 639–645.

Jones, R. T., Blacker, K. H., Callaway, E., & Layne, R. S. The auditory evoked response as a diagnostic and prognostic measure in schizophrenia. *Amer. J. Psychol.*, 1965, **122**, 33–41.

Judson, A. J., & Katahn, M. The relationship of autonomic responsiveness to process-reactive schizophrenia and abstract thinking. *Psychiat. Quart.*, 1963, **37**, 19–24.

Karson, S., & Pool, K. B. The abstract thinking abilities in mental patients. *J. clin. Psychol.*, 1957, **13**, 126–132.

Kingsley, L., & Struening, E. L. Changes in intellectual performance of acute and chronic schizophrenics. *Psychol. Rep.*, 1966, **18**, 791–800.

Kirschner, D. Differences in gradients of stimulus generalization as a function of "abstract" and "concrete" attitude., *J. consult. Psychol.*, 1964, **28**, 160–164.

Kristofferson, Marianne. Shifting attention between Modalities: A comparison of schizophrenics and normals. *J. abnorm. Psychol.*, 1967, **72**, 388–394.

Krus, D. M., Wapner, S., Freeman, H., & Casey, T. M. Differential behavior responsivity to LSD-25: Study in normal and schizophrenic adults. *Arch. gen. Psychiat.*, 1963, **8**, 557–563.

Kugelmass, S., & Fondeur, M. R. Zaslow's test of concept formation: reliability and validity. *J. consult. Psychol.*, 1955, **19**, 227–229.

Lane, Ellen A., & Albee, G. W. Early childhood intellectual differences between schizophrenic adults and their siblings. *J. abnorm. soc. Psychol.*, 1964, **68**, 193–195.

Layman, J. W. A quantitative study of certain changes in schizophrenic patients under the influence of sodium amytal. *J. gen. Psychol.*, 1940, **22**, 67–86.

Leventhal, D. B., McGaughran, L. S., & Moran, L. J. Multivariable analysis of the conceptual behavior of schizophrenic and brain-damaged patients. *J. abnorm. soc. Psychol.*, 1959, **58**, 84–90.

Lewinsohn, P. M. Use of the Shipley-Hartford Conceptual Quotient as a measure of intellectual impairment. *J. consult. Psychol.*, 1963, **27**, 444–447.

Lewinsohn, P. M., & Riggs, Ann. The effect of content upon the thinking of acute and chronic schizophrenics. *J. abnorm. soc. Psychol.*, 1962, **65**, 206–207.

Lewis, J. M. Griffith, E. C., Riedel, A. F., & Simmons, B. A. Studies in abstraction: schizophrenia and orality: preliminary results. *J. nerv. ment. Dis.*, 1959, **129**, 564–567.

Lidz, T., Wild, Cynthia, Schafer, Sarah, Rosman, Bernice, & Fleck, S. Thought disorders in the parents of schizophrenic patients: A study utilizing the object sorting test. *J. psychiat. Res.*, 1962, **1**, 193–200.

Liebert, R. S., Werner, H., & Wapner, S. Studies in the effect of LSD-25: Self- and object-size perception in schizophrenics and normal adults. *Arch. neurol. Psychiat.*, 1958, **79**, 580–584.

Little, L. K. Effects of the interpersonal interaction on abstract thinking performance in schizophrenics. *J. consult. Psychol.*, 1966, **30**, 158–164.

Lloyd. D. N. Overinclusive thinking and delusions in schizophrenic patients: A critique. *J. abnorm. Psychol.*, 1967, **72**, 451–453.

Lovibond, S. H. The object sorting test and conceptual thinking in schizophrenia. *Australian J. Psychol.*, 1954, **6**, 52–70.

Lubin, A., Gieseking, C. F., & Williams, H. L. Direct measurement of cognitive deficit in schizophrenia. *J. consult. Psychol.*, 1962, **26**, 139–143.

Lynn, R., & Gordon, I. E. The relation of neuroticism and extraversion to intelligence and educational attainment. *Brit. J. educ. Psychol.*, 1961, **31**, 194–203.

McConaghy, N. The use of an object sorting test in elucidating the hereditary factor in schizophrenia. *J. neur. Psychiat.*, 1959, **22**, 243–246.

McGaughran, L. S. Predicting language behavior from object sorting. *J. abnorm. soc. Psychol.*, 1954, **49**, 183–195.

McGaughran, L. S., & Moran, L. J. "Conceptual level" v. "Conceptual area" analysis of object-sorting behavior of schizophrenic and nonpsychiatric groups. *J. abnorm. soc. Psychol.*, 1956, **52**, 43–50.

McGaughran, L. S., & Moran, L. J. Differences between schizophrenic and brain-damaged groups in conceptual aspects of object sorting. *J. abnorm. soc. Psychol.*, 1957, **54**, 44–49.

McGhie, A. Psychological studies of schizophrenia. *Brit. J. med. Psychol.*, 1966, **39**, 281–288.

McGhie, A., Chapman, J., & Lawson, J. S. The effect of distraction on schizophrenic performance: I. Perception and immediate memory. *Brit. J. Psychiat.*, 1965a, **111**, 383–390.

McGhie, A., Chapman, J., & Lawson, J. S. The effect of distraction on schizophrenic performance: II. Psychomotor ability. *Brit. J. Psychiat.*, 1965b, **111**, 391–398.

McReynolds, P., & Collins, Beverly. Concept-forming behavior in schizophrenic and non-schizophrenic subjects. *J. Psychol.*, 1961, **52**, 369–378.

Mainord, W. A. Some effects of Sodium Amytal on deteriorated schizophrenics. *J. consult. Psychol.*, 1953, **17**, 54–57.

Mednick, S. A. Distortions in the gradient of stimulus generalization related to cortical brain damage and schizophrenia. *J. abnorm. soc. Psychol.*, 1955, **51**, 536–542.

Mednick, S. A. A learning theory approach to research in schizophrenia. *Psychol. Bull.*, 1958, **55**, 316–327.

Mednick, S. A. A longitudinal study of children with a high risk for schizophrenia. *Mental Hygiene*, 1966, **50**, 522–535.

Milgram, N. A. Preference for abstract versus concrete word meanings in schizophrenic and brain-damaged patients. *J. clin. Psychol.*, 1959, **15**, 207–212.

Miller, G. A., & Chapman, L. J. Response bias and schizophrenic beliefs. *J. abnorm. Psychol.*, 1968, **73**, 252–255.

Monroe, J. J. The effects of emotional adjustment and intelligence upon Bellevue scatter. *J. consult. Psychol.*, 1952, **16**, 110–114.

Moran, L. J. Vocabulary knowledge and usage among normal and schizophrenic subjects. *Psychol. Monogr.*, 1953, **67**, no. 20 (whole no. 370).

Moran, L. J., Gorham, D. R., & Holtzman, W. H. Vocabulary knowledge and useage of schizophrenic subjects: A six-year follow-up. *J. abnorm. soc. Psychol.*, 1960, **61**, 246–254.

Nathan, P. E. A comparative investigation of schizophrenic and normal conceptual performance. *J. nerv. ment. Dis.*, 1964, **138**, 443–451.

Nickols, J. E., Jr. A controlled exploratory investigation into the effects of thorazine upon mental test scores of chronic hospitalized schizophrenics. *Psychol. Rec.*, 1958, **8**, 67–76.

Nickols, J. Overinclusion under unstructured conditions. *J. clin. Psychol.*, 1964, **20**, 422–429.

Ogilvie, B. C. A study of intellectual slowness in schizophrenia. Unpublished doctoral dissertation. University of London Library, 1954.

Payne, R. W. Cognitive Abnormalities. In H. J. Eysenck (ed.) *Handbook of Abnormal Psychology*. London: Pitman, 1960, New York: Basic Books, 1961, 193–261.

Payne, R. W. An object classification test as a measure of overinclusive thinking in schizophrenic patients. *Brit. J. soc. clin. Psychol.*, 1962, **1**, 213–221.

Payne, R. W. The long-term prognostic implications of overinclusive thinking in mental patients: a follow-up study using objective tests. *Proceedings of the IV World Congress of Psychiatry, Madrid, 1966*. N.Y: Excerpta Medica Foundation, 1968, 2657–2666.

Payne, R. W., Ancevich, Singrida S., & Laverty, S. G. Overinclusive thinking in symptom-free schizophrenics. *Canad. Psychiat. Assoc. J.*, 1963, **8**, 225–234.

Payne, R. W., & Caird, W. K. Reaction time, distractibility and overinclusive thinking in psychotics. *J. abnorm. Psychol.*, 1967, **72**, 112–121.

Payne, R. W., Caird, W. K., & Laverty, S. G. Overinclusive thinking and delusions in schizophrenic patients. *J. abnorm. soc. Psychol.*, 1964, **68**, 562–566.

Payne, R. W., & Friedlander, D. A short battery of simple tests for measuring over-inclusive thinking. *J. ment. Sci.*, 1962, **108**, 362–367.

Payne, R. W., Friedlander, D., Laverty, S. G., & Haden, P. Overinclusive thought disorder in chronic schizophrenics and its response to "Proketazine." *Brit. J. Psychiat.*, 1963, **109**, 523–530.

Payne, R. W., & Hewlett, J. H. G. Thought disorder in psychotic patients. In H. J. Eysenck (ed.), *Experiments in Personality Volume II, Psychodiagnostics and Psychodynamics*. London: Routledge and Kegan Paul, 1960, 3–104.

Payne, R. W., & Jones, H. G. Statistics for the investigation of individual cases. *J. clin. Psychol.*, 1957, **13**, 115–121.

Payne, R. W., Mattussek, P., & George, E. I. An experimental study of schizophrenic thought disorder. *J. ment. Sci.*, 1959, **105**, 627–652.

Payne, R. W., & Sloane, R. B. Can schizophrenia be defined? *Dis. nerv. Syst.* 1968, **29** (No 5 Suppl.) 113–117.

Pettigrew, T. F. The measurement and correlates of category width as a cognitive variable. *J. Pers.*, 1958, **26**, 532–544.

Phillips, J. E., Jacobson, Naomi, & Turner, Wm. J. Conceptual thinking in schizophrenics and their relatives. *Brit. J. Psychiat.*, 1965, **478**, 823–839.

Phillips, L. Case history data and prognosis in schizophrenia. *J. nerv. ment. Dis.*, 1953, **117**, 515–525.

Pollack, M. Comparison of childhood adolescent and adult schizophrenics. *AMA Arch. gen. Psychiat.*, 1960, **2**, 652–660.

Rapaport, D. *Diagnostic Psychological Testing*. Chicago: The Year Book Publishers, 1946.

Rappaport, S R., & Webb, W. An attempt to study intellectual deterioration by premorbid and psychotic testing. *J. consult. Psychol.*, 1950, **14**, 95–98.

Rashkis, H. A. Three types of thinking disorder. *J. nerv. ment. Dis.*, 1947, **106**, 650–670.

Rashkis, H., Cushman, T. F., & Landis, C. A new method for studying disorders of conceptual thinking. *J. abnorm. soc. Psychol.*, 1946, **41**, 70–74.

Raven, J. C. *Guide to Using Progressive Matrices* (1938). London: H. K. Lewis, 1950.

Raven, J. C. *The Mill Hill Vocabulary Scale*. London: H. K. Lewis, 1948.

Rodnick, E. H., & Shakow, D. Set in the schizophrenic as measured by a composite reaction time index. *Amer. J. Psychiat.*, 1940, **97**, 214–225.

Rosenbaum, G., Cohen, B. D., Luby, E. D., Gottlieb, J. S., & Yelen, D. Comparison of Sernyl with other drugs: Stimulation of schizophrenic performance with Sernyl, LSD-25, and Amobarbital (Amytal) Sodium: I. Attention, motor function and proprioception. *Archives of gen. Psychiat.*, 1959, **1**, 651–656.

Rosenbaum, G., Flenning, F., & Rosen, H. Effects of weight intensity on discrimination thresholds of normals and schizophrenics. *J. abnorm. Psychol.*, 1965, **70**, 446–450.

Rosman, Bernice, Wild, C., Ricci, Judith, Fleck, S., & Lidz, T. Thought disorders in the parents of schizophrenic patients: A further study utilizing the object sorting test. *J. Psychiat. Res.*, 1964, **2**, 211–221.

Rutschmann, J. Oppel-Kundt illusion in normals and schizophrenic patients: an examination of the perceptual primitivization hypothesis. *Percept. mot. Skills*, 1961, **13**, 399–415.

Salmon, Phillida, Bramley, Judith, & Presly, A. S. The word-in-context test as a measure of conceptualization in schizophrenics with and without thought disorder. *Brit. J. Med. Psychol.*, 1967, **40**, 253–259.

Salzinger, K Shift in judgment of weights as a function of anchoring stimuli and instructions in early schizophrenics and normals. *J. abnorm. soc. Psychol.*, 1957, **55**, 43–49.

Salzinger, K., Portnoy, Stephanie, & Feldman, R. S. Verbal behavior in schizophrenics and some comments toward a theory of schizophrenia. In P. H. Hoch and J. Zubin (eds.) *Psychopathology of Schizophrenia*. New York: Grune and Stratton, 1966, 98–128.

Schwartz, S Cognitive deficit among remitted schizophrenics: The role of a Life-history variable. *J. abnorm. Psychol.*, 1967a, **72**, 54.

Schwartz, S. Daignosis, level of social adjustment, and cognitive deficits. *J. abnorm. Psychol.*, 1967b, **72**, 446–453.

Schwartzman, A. E., & Douglas, Virginia I. Intellectual loss in schizophrenia: Part I. *Canad. J. Psychol.*, 1962, **16**, 1–10.

Schwartzman, A. E., Douglas, Virginia I., & Muir, W. R. Intellectual loss in schizophrenia: Part II. *Canad. J. Psychol.*, 1962, **16**, 161–168.

Senf, Rita, Huston, P. E., & Cohen, B. D. Thinking deficit in schizophrenia and changes with amytal. *J. abnorm. soc. Psychol.*, 1955, **50**, 383–387.

Seth, G., & Beloff, H. Language impairment in a group of schizophrenics. *Brit. J. med. Psychol.*, 1959, **32**, 288–293.

Shakow, D. The nature of deterioration in schizophrenic conditions. *Ner. Ment. Dis. Monogr.*, 1946, **70**, 1–88.

Shakow, D. Segmental Set. *Arch. gen. Psychiat.*, 1962, **6**, 1–17.

Shakow, D. Psychological deficit in schizophrenia. *Behav. Sci.*, 1963, **8**, 275–305.

Shakow, D., & McCormick, M. Y. Mental set in schizophrenia studied in a discrimination reaction setting. *J. Pers. soc. Psychol.*, 1965, **1**, 88–95.

Shakow, D., Rosenzweig, S., & Hollander, L. Auditory apperceptive reactions to the tautophone by schizophrenic and normal subjects. *J. nerv. ment. Dis.*, 1966, **143**, 1–15.

Shapiro, M. B., & Nelson, E. H. An investigation of the nature of cognitive impairment in co-operative psychiatric patients. *Brit. J. med. Psychol.*, 1955, **28**, 239–256.

Shimkunas, A. M., Gynther, M. D., & Smith, Kathleen. Abstracting ability of schizophrenics before and during phenothiazine therapy. *Arch. gen. Psychiat.*, 1966, **14**, 79–83.

Shimkunas, A. M., Gynther, M. D., & Smith, Kathleen. Schizophrenic responses to the Proverbs Test: abstract, concrete, or autistic? *J. abnorm. Psychol.*, 1967, **72**, 128–133.

Shipley, W. C. A self-administering scale for measuring intellectual impairment and deterioration. *J. Psychol.*, 1940, **9**, 371–377.

Shneidman, E. S. Schizophrenia and the MAPS test: a study of certain formal psycho-social aspects of fantasy production in schizophrenia as revealed by performance on the Make-A-Picture-Story (MAPS) test. *Genet. Psychol. Monogr.*, 1948, **38**, 145–223.

Silverman, J. Perceptual control of stimulus intensity in paranoid and nonparanoid schizophrenia. *J. nerv. ment. Dis.*, 1964, **139**, 545–549.

Silverman, J. The problem of attention in research and theory in schizophrenia. *Psychol. Rev.*, 1964a, **71**, 352–379.

Silverman, J. Scanning-control mechanism and "cognitive filtering" in paranoid and nonparanoid schizophrenia. *J. consult. Psychol.*, 1964b, **28**, 385–393

Silverman, J. Variations in cognitive control and psychophysiological defense in the schizophrenias. *Psychosom. Med.*, 1967, **29**, 225–245.

Silverman, J., Berg, P. S. D., & Kantor, R. Some perceptual correlates of institutionalization. *J. nerv. ment. Dis.*, 1966, **141**, 651–657.

Silverman, L. H., & Silverman, Doris K. Ego impairment in schizophrenia as reflected in the object sorting test. *J. abnorm. soc. Psychol.*, 1962, **64**, 381–385.

Smith, A. Mental deterioration in chronic schizophrenia. *J. nerv. ment. Dis.*, 1964, **139**, 479–487.

Snelbecker, G. E., Sherman, L. J., Rothstein, E., & Downes, R. C. Schizophrenic and normal behavior on programmed inductive reasoning problems. *J. clinic. Psychol.*, 1966, **22**, 415–417.

Snyder, S., Rosenthal, D., & Taylor, I. A. Perceptual closure in schizophrenia. *J. abnorm. soc. Psychol.*, 1961, **63**, 131–136.

Spence, Janet T., & Lair, C. V. Associative interference in the verbal learning performance of schizophrenics and normals. *J. abnorm. soc. Psychol.*, 1964, **68**, 204–209.

Stern, J. A., Surphlis, W., & Koff, E. Electrodermal responsiveness as related to psychiatric diagnosis and prognosis. *Psychophysiology*, 1965, **2**, 51–61.

Stilson, D. W., & Kopell, B. S. The recognition of visual signals in the presence of visual noise by psychiatric patients. *J. nerv. ment. Dis.*, 1964, **139**, 209–221.

Stilson, D. W., Kopell, B. S., Vandenbergh, R., & Downs, Marion P. Perceptual recognition in the presence of noise by psychiatric patients. *J. nerv. ment. Dis.*, 1966, **142**, 235–247.

Storms, L. H., Broen, W. E., Jr., & Levin, I. P. Verbal associative stability and commonality as a function of stress in schizophrenics, neurotics, and normals. *J. consult. Psychol.*, 1967, **31**, 181–187.

Sturm, E. I. "Conceptual area" among pathological groups: a failure to replicate. *J. abnorm. soc. Psychol.*, 1964, **69**, 216–223.

Sturm, E. I. Overinclusion and concreteness among pathological groups. *J. consult. Psychol.* 1965, **29**, 9–18.

Thorpe, J. G., & Baker, A. A. The effects of physical treatment on some psychological functions. *J. ment. Sci.*, 1958, **104**, 865–869.

Tizard, J., & Venables, P. H. Reaction time responses by schizophrenics, mental defectives and normal adults. *Amer. J. Psychiat.*, 1955, **112**, 803–807.

Tizard, J., & Venables, P. H. The influence of extraneous stimulation on the reaction time of schizophrenics. *Brit. J. Psychol.*, 1957, **48**, 299–305.

Tolor, A. Abstract ability in organics and schizophrenics. *J. projective Tech. Pers. Assessment*, 1964, **28**, 357–362.

Trapp, C. E. & James, Edith, B. Comparative intelligence ratings in the four types of dementia praecox. *J. nerv. ment. Dis.*, 1937, **86**, 399–404.

True, J. E. Learning of abstract responses by process and reactive schizophrenic patients. *Psychol. Rep.*, 1966, **18**, 51–55.

Trunnell, T. L. Thought disturbance in schizophrenia. *Archives gen. Psychiat.*, 1964, **11**, 126–136.

Trunnell, T. L. Thought disturbance in schizophrenia: Replication study utilizing Piaget's theories. *Archives gen. Psychiat.*, 1965, **13**, 9–18.

Tutko, T. A., & Spence, Janet T. The performance of process and reactive schizophrenics and brain injured subjects on a conceptual task. *J. abnorm. soc. Psychol.*, 1962, **65**, 387–394.

Venables, P. H. The effect of auditory and visual stimulation on the skin potential response of schizophrenics. *Brain*, 1960, **83**, 77–92.

Venables, P. H. Selectivity of attention, withdrawal and cortical activation. *Archives gen. Psychiat.*, 1963a, **9**, 92–96.

Venables, P. H. The relationship between level of skin potential and fusion of paired light flashes in schizophrenic and normal subjects. *J. Psychiat. Res.*, 1963b, **1**, 279–287.

Venables, P. H. Changes due to noise in the threshold of fusion of paired light flashes in schizophrenics and normals. *Brit. J. soc. clin. Psychol.*, 1963c, **2**, 94–99.

Venables, P. H. Performance and level of activation in schizophrenics and normals. *Brit. J. Psychol.*, 1964, **55**, 207–218.

Venables, P. H. Psychophysiological aspects of schizophrenia. *Brit. J. med. Psychol.*, 1966a, **39**, 289–297.

Venables, P. H. A comparison of two-flash and two-click thresholds in schizophrenic and normal subjects. *Quart. J. exp. Psychol.*, 1966b, **18**, 371–373.

Venables, P. H. The relation of two-flash and two-click thresholds to withdrawal in paranoid and nonparanoid schizophrenics. *Brit. J. soc. clin. Psychol.*, 1967, **6**, 60–62.

Venables, P. H., & O'Connor, N. Reaction times to auditory and visual stimulation in schizophrenic and normal subjects. *Quart. J. exp. Psychol.*, 1959, **11**, 175–179.

Venables, P. H., & Wing, J. K. Level of arousal and the subclassification of schizophrenia. *Archives gen. Psychiat.*, 1962, **7**, 114–119.

Von Domarus, E. The specific laws of logic in schizophrenia. In J. S. Kasanin (Editor). *Language and Thought in Schizophrenia* Berkeley: University of California Press, 1946, 104–114.

Wadsworth, W. V., Wells, B. W. P., & Scott, R. F. A comparative study of chronic schizophrenic and normal subjects on a work task involving sequential operations. *J. ment. Sci.*, 1962, **108**, 309–316.

Ward, W. D., & Carlson, W. A. Autonomic responsivity to variable input rates among schizophrenics classified on the process-reactive dimension. *J. abnorm. Psychol.*, 1966, **71**, 10–16.

Watson, C. G. Interrelationships of six overinclusion measures. *J. consult. Psychol.*, 1967, **31**, 517–520.

Wechsler, D. *The Measurement of Adult Intelligence*. Baltimore: Williams & Wilkins, 1944.

Weckowitz, T. E. Perception of hidden pictures by schizophrenic patients. *Arch. gen. Psychiat.*, 1960, **2**, 521–527.

Weckowitz, T. E., & Blewett, D. B. Size constancy and abstract thinking in schizophrenic patients. *J. ment. Sci.*, 1959, **105**, 909–934.

Weiss, R. L., & Nordtvedt, Emilia I. Programmed stimulus input and the development of a perceptual set in schizophrenic and normal subjects. *Psychonomic Sci.*, 1964, **1**, 195–196.

White, Mary A. A study of schizophrenic language. *J. abnorm. soc. Psychol.*, 1949, **44**, 61–74.

Williams, E. B. Deductive reasoning in schizophrenia. *J. abnorm. Psychol.*, 1964, **69**, 47–61.

Willner, A. Impairment of knowledge of unusual meanings of familiar words in brain damage and schizophrenia. *J. abnorm. Psychol*, 1965, **70**, 405.

Wittman, M. P. A scale for measuring prognosis in schizophrenic patients. *Elgin State Hospital Papers*, 1941, **4**, 20–33.

Zahn, T. P., Rosenthal, D., & Shakow, D. Effects of irregular preparatory intervals on reaction time in schizophrenia. *J. abnorm. soc. Psychol.*, 1963, **67**, 44–52.

Zaslow, R. W. A new approach to the problem of conceptual thinking in schizophrenia. *J. consult. Psychol.*, 1950, **14**, 335–339.

Chapter 4

Memory Disorder[1]

JAMES INGLIS

When the clinician speaks of "memory disorder," he is more often than not referring to an inadequate performance or product rather than to the breakdown of any clearly defined process. More than half a century ago Hull (1917) had already pointed out that the notion of "memory," as it is commonly used, is too imprecise in meaning for the psychologist's purpose. It directs attention towards a single aspect of output—usually the reproduction of previously learned material—when, in fact, it is known that the accuracy of this output may depend on the integrity of a whole prior sequence of events involved in learning. It has long been recognized that this sequence involves at least the three phases broadly labeled registration, retention, and retrieval. The disturbance of any of these stages might lead to the impairment of the product usually called "memory."

Finer, and more useful, subdivisions have been suggested. Welford (1958) has distinguished several critical stages in learning. They comprise perception of the data that are to be stored, the short-term storage of the material once it has been perceived, the development of a more durable trace subsequent to the short-term holding process, the endurance of this more permanent trace, the retrieval, through recall or recognition of the stored material, and finally the use of the data once recovered.

It is evident that if they are, indeed, several stages of a sequence, with "memory" their loosely defined product, then a breakdown at any one point in such a system could disrupt the whole later succession of the learning chain and the defective output might then be labeled "memory disorder."

The aim of this chapter is to make a conspectus of some of those conditions in which a cardinal element is that defect of output commonly labeled "memory disorder." An attempt will be made to show how psychology can contribute to the description and to the understanding of this defect as conceived in terms of the processes of learning. More extended reviews of the range of this disorder are to be found in volumes edited by Richter (1966) and by Whitty and Zangwill (1966).

To reduce the scope of this consideration to fit within present limits, discussion of defects of learning in animals will be omitted. Childhood learning defects will not be considered. For reviews of the former the reader is referred to Brazier (1964) and Kimble (1965), and for the latter to Ellis (1963) and Kessler (1966).

Only incidental note will be taken of the studies of the amnesias that are often regarded as "functional" disorders of remembering. It has been argued elsewhere (Inglis, 1961) that this form of amnesia, or

[1]This chapter was prepared while the author was in receipt of a United States Public Health Service Grant No. HD 02250 from the National Institute of Child Health and Human Development. This aid is most gratefully acknowledged. The author is also very deeply indebted to Carol Tansey Green for invaluable editorial assistance.

what might be called "motivated forgetting," can be understood in terms of the more or less efficient ways in which an individual may deal with stress by initiating, or failing to initiate, avoidance reactions to his own anxiety producing, covert, symbolic responses. This behavioral approach maintains that the elimination of anxiety-mediating self-produced stimuli involves active *avoidance* behavior; that is to say, the experimental paradigm is "shock-escape-avoidance" activity. In man, unlike the lower animals, the anxiety producing stimuli are not always external and the behavior initiated for the reduction of anxiety may be much less overt and may, in fact, consist in the suppression or avoidance of certain *symbolic* activities. It will be seen in some of the material to be reviewed here that this kind of anxiety avoidance may even constitute a part of the kind of "memory disorder" induced by grosser means, such as concussion and electroconvulsive treatment.

Before attention is directed to any empirical findings, one major difficulty encountered in research in learning disorder must also be mentioned; the need for a satisfactory taxonomy of learning. Although it seems self-evident that most human behavior is learned behavior, when we try to assess learning, at least, in normal subjects, there often seems to be a surprising lack of agreement between our different measures. For example, it has been found that there may be very low correlations between different kinds of conditioning (for example, eyeblink in response to a puff of air, finger withdrawal in response to shock) in the same individual. If it is true that these observations of normal behavior do not cohere in any very systematic way, we must then surely beware of those studies that purport to describe "learning disorder" on the basis of performance on any single test.

It must be pointed out, however, that even if it is difficult to demonstrate any general form of "learning ability" in the test performance of normal persons, it may still be an important factor in abnormal behavior. Let us suppose, for example, that performance on test *X* requires, for its efficient execution, a critical amount of ability *y*; it might nevertheless be the case that any increase in *y* over this crucial threshold value would have little or no effect on performance on *X* whereas different levels of *y below* the threshold might covary with efficiency of performance. It may be that such a low modicum of learning ability is required in most psychological tests that all normal people reach and exceed this minimum level; other sources of variance then account for individual differences in performance. In the abnormal, or "memory disordered," however, some essential aspect of learning ability may fall below this threshold value and, hence, become an important determinant of test performance. Whatever the merit of this argument, we must certainly still be cautious in the interpretation of specific results on particular tests.

We intend to determine what a number of conditions characterized by memory disorder can tell us about the likely defects in the processes of learning that may underlie the appearance of this disorder. For convenience of exposition, these conditions are here divided into two kinds—the ones due to pathology and the ones due to intervention.

1. *Effects of pathology*. Under this heading we review some clinical states in which disorders of learning appear in man without deliberate human intervention. These conditions include the concussive effects of head injury, Korsakoff's syndrome, and senile dementia.

2. *Effects of intervention*. Under this heading we include conditions that result from means deliberately applied for other reasons, such as electroconvulsive treatment and neurosurgery.

It is unfortunate that the main emphasis of this chapter must weigh on the impairment of function rather than on its improvement. It is, however, possible to maintain (Inglis, 1966) that to induce *any* alteration in a condition is to begin the specification of powerful independent variables that are the necessary prerequisites of change and, hence, of prevention and cure.

EFFECTS OF PATHOLOGY

Head Injury and Concussion

The effects to be considered under this heading are, in fact, the results of accident rather than of disease. They are included in this section because (with the trivial exception of prizefighters) they are seldom intentionally induced in human subjects.

Because the effects of closed head injuries are usually adventitious and often transient, most information has come from keen clinical observation rather than from systematic test or formal experiment. Much of the literature has already been excellently summarized in monographs by Courville (1953) and by Russell (1959).

Concussion may be regarded as a state that involves, in an acute and transitory way, important kinds of dysfunction that are often found to be chronic and even permanent in other conditions characterized by memory disorder.

A definition put forward by Trotter (1924) still seems quite adequately to define the condition; the term concussion is, he said, used

"... to indicate an essentially transient state due to head injury, which is of instantaneous onset, manifests widespread symptoms of a purely paralytic kind, does not as such comprise any evidence of structural cerebral injury, and is always followed by amnesia for the actual moment of the accident" (1924, p. 935).

Some of the phrases used in this definition require further elucidation.

The kind of head injury which is most likely to induce the state of concussion has been studied experimentally in animals. Denny-Brown and Russell (1941) have thus found, by using a kind of pendulum striker, that a powerful factor in the production of concussion is a sudden acceleration or deceleration of the head.

"... when the head is allowed to take up velocity suddenly as a result of the impact, a certain critical speed of the striking body is required to produce concussion as judged by the loss of the corneal reflex. If concussion be regarded as a nervous reaction, the *threshold* for its elicitation is therefore very sharp, and lies between 25 and 28 feet per second, for a blunt striking force of a mass greater than that of the head" (1941, p. 111).

They further note that

"... in using the lighter pendulum (which does not crush the fixed skull) ... *if the animal's head is prevented from moving at the moment of injury, concussion could not be produced* even with the maximum velocity obtainable with this pendulum (28.7 feet per. sec.), whereas, if even slight movement of the head were allowed (e.g., 3mm.) concussion occurs ... We shall refer to this type as *acceleration concussion* (including both positive and negative acceleration, or deceleration) to distinguish it from the results obtained by crushing injury" (1941, p. 114).

Crushing injuries to the head have been studied both clinically and experimentally. Russell and Schiller (1949) showed that, although severe injuries of this kind may often be fatal, in surviving patients concussion may be very slight or absent. Even when the skull has been fractured and cranial nerves injured by this kind of trauma, the patient may remain conscious throughout.

A further physical characteristic of injuries that produce concussion has been cited by Holbourn (1943) who has maintained that rotational acceleration forces are the main cause of the critical brain injuries that produce concussion. From his experiments with skull-and-brain models he concluded that shear-strains on the nervous tissues are of particular importance. As this review of memory disorder is developed, another of his conclusions may well come to be of significance, in that he found some areas of the brain more liable to injury than others when the head is subjected to concussive blows. One prominent feature he found was a large amount of shear-strain in the anterior part of the temporal lobe, and a comparative absence of shear-strain in the cerebellum. The importance of the shearing of nerve fibres as a cause of brain damage as a result of head injury has been confirmed in pathological studies by Strich (1961).

Another part of Trotter's definition states that concussion involves widespread symptoms of a purely paralytic kind. Williams and Denny-Brown (1941), among others have maintained that concussion may indeed have a temporary "silencing" effect on the electroencephalogram. This point of view has been disputed by Walker, Kollros, and Case (1945) who quote evidence to suggest that

"... the physiological basis of concussion consists of the traumatic discharge of the polarized cell membranes of the central nervous system by the shaking up or commotion of the brain and that the subsequent course of events is that which would be expected when large masses of nerve cells discharge, such as is seen in the spontaneous or electrically induced convulsive seizures. The concussive syndrome is then to be looked upon as an excitatory rather than paralytic state, the latter being merely the normal physiologic sequel of the primary intense stimulation" (1945, pp. 459–460).

Most authorities seem to agree with Trotter that no very gross structural cerebral injury need underlie concussion, but that the amnestic phenomena are crucial. It is these latter that are of most significance for this chapter.

The sequence of events in concussion and the range of its effects on remembering can be shown in Figure 4.1.

At the time of the head injury the patient is "knocked out." The duration of this unconsciousness has been cited as one index of the severity of injury (Pilcher & Angelucci, 1942). A period of impaired consciousness, also of variable length, may follow before complete recovery and full consciousness is restored. Russell (1959) distinguishes the following stages of recovery.

"1. Return of simple reflex activity.
2. Return of restless and purposeless movement.
3. Movements more purposeful, but no speech or understanding.
4. Restless movements and the return of a few words or phrases—often explosive.
5. Return of uninhibited speech and action, but disorientated and amnesic for current events, and may confabulate about injury.
6. Return of orientation, social decorum and behavior. The limits of traumatic amnesia become established. In general the capacity for rational thought only returns when this last stage is reached" (1959, p. 51).

On recovery of full consciousness the patient shows a variety of phenomena which may help to reveal some of the processes underlying normal learning and also the learning dysfunctions that manifest as "memory disorder."

The patient is, of course, understandably amnesic for the period, after trauma, during

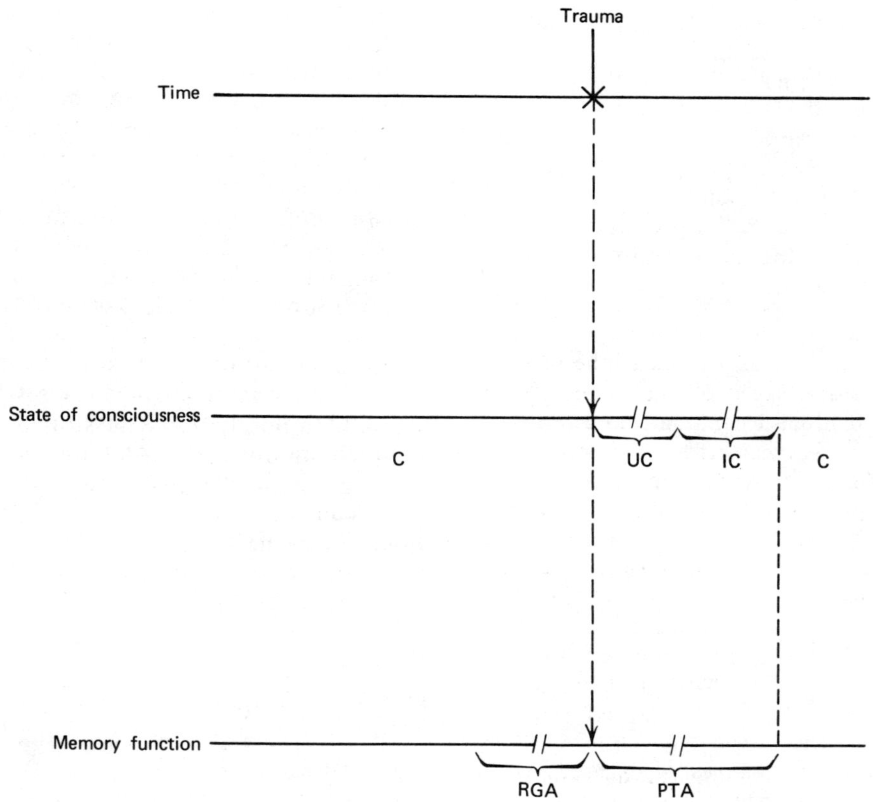

Figure 4.1 Diagrammatic representation of relations between trauma, consciousness, post-traumatic and retrograde amnesia. C, consciousness. IC, impaired consciousness. UC, unconsciousness. RGA, retrograde amnesia. PTA, post-traumatic amnesia.

which he is completely unconscious; evidently we cannot assimilate or retain information of which we are completely unaware. The period of post-traumatic amnesia (PTA), however, extends beyond the period of total and partial unconsciousness, into the period of impaired consciousness. This roughly corresponds to the fifth stage defined by Russell (1959) above. The activity of the patient, at this stage, however, need not seem quite purposeless to the observer. Gillespie (1936) has suggested that in violent sports, such as boxing, purposeful action may be taken during this phase of which the combatant has little or no later recollection.

In terms of the simplest linear scheme of the different phases of learning, the cerebral commotion that follows on head injury can evidently interfere with some of the processes that lie between "perception" and the "evolution of a durable trace" (Welford, 1958). If this stage involves a change from an activity trace to a structural trace (Hebb, 1949) or an alteration in stability through a process of consolidation (Glickman, 1961; Deutsch, 1962) then concussion disrupts this phase. We shall observe that this part of the learning process is one that is probably particularly vulnerable to disruption.

In this impaired condition the organism lives precariously, so to speak, at the tenuous interface between those events that have just been and those that are just becoming. Lacking the shaping influence of the immediate past, no useful anticipation can be made of the immediate future. This absence of storage capacity may itself produce the symptoms of disorientation and confusion characteristic of concussion.

Russell (1959) has noted

> "The return of orientation with the resumption of mental activity coincides with the return of the capacity to remember from one moment to the next. The patient 'wakes up' to appreciate his environment. his period of post-traumatic amnesia (PTA) is ended. He will probably remember indefinitely the time or date at which he recovered memory and thus the duration of the PTA can often be given with accuracy long after the injury. It is for this reason that the duration of PTA is now widely used as a useful indication of the severity of head injury as far as the general concussive effect is concerned" (1959, p. 53).

However, it is not only the incoming events *after* the injury that are vulnerable. Events that took place *before* the injury may also be expunged, with a lesser degree of permanence. Furthermore, the nearer the incidents are to the moment of trauma the more likely they are to be forgotten. The severer the injury the further back the amnesia is likely at first to extend. This phenomenon has been labeled retrograde amnesia or RGA.

It seems possible that the same mechanism may underlie both the PTA and part of the RGA. If consolidation be regarded as continuous rather than as a process of quite limited duration, then the recall of events before head injury is also liable to be disrupted. On this view, any learning trace involves both a structural and an activity component. The activity function preponderates in recent learning, whereas structural factors preponderate in what has been more remotely learned. It may be supposed that concussive injury that causes no gross brain damage interferes mainly with the activity component, which is maximal just before, at, and just after the injury. The period of PTA, then, is the result of the interruption of activity that had, as yet, produced no structural change. The interval of RGA, however, represents a period in which, before trauma, both activity and increased structural organization had played a mutually supportive part. Thus, whereas the period of PTA usually remains constant after recovery, RGA often progressively "shrinks" up to the time of the accident. Whatever the length of PTA, the eventual duration of RGA is usually of less than half an hour, which in man may therefore represent the critical period for maximum consolidation from activity to structure. The relation between the two has been examined by Russell and Nathan (1946), with the results shown in Table 4.1.

The progressive decrease of RGA may take place at variable rate. As Russell (1959) has noted:

> "In these cases of slow shrinking RA, the PTA terminates long before the RA shrinks to its final duration. While the RA extends over many months or years the patient may, to careful testing, be slightly confused, but he has often recovered sufficiently to have continuous memory and to behave in a rational way.

Table 4.1 Duration of PTA and RGA Compared in 1029 Cases of "Accidental" Head Injury (Gunshot Wounds Excluded)

	Duration of PTA						
Duration of RGA	Nil	< 1 Hour	1–24 Hours	1–7 Days	> 7 Days	No Record	Total
Nil	99	23	9	2	0	0	133
Under 30 minutes	—	178	274	174	80	1	707
Over 30 minutes	—	3	16	41	73	0	133
No record	—	4	14	14	15	9	56
Total	99	208	313	231	168	10	1,029

Source. Russell and Nathan, 1946.

During this period of shrinking amnesia the patient is unable to recall an important group of memories which, as later recovery shows, were well registered. The recovery occurs not in order of importance but in order of time. Long-past memories are the first to return, and the temporary blocking of relatively recent memory may be so marked that several years of recent life may be entirely eliminated. For a limited time, the patient may relive his childhood, a state of affairs reminiscent of the case of senile dementia.

During recovery, the RA shrinks at a varying rate to a point where memory of subsequent events ceases abruptly. This usually leaves the duration of RA clearly indicated, but this can only be estimated accurately after full recovery of consciousness" (1959, pp. 70–71).

Lengthy RGA suggests that concussion may also impair the retrieval phase of the learning process.

It has also been noted (Russell, 1959; Williams & Zangwill, 1952) that the progressive shrinkage of RGA need not always proceed uniformly or completely from the more remote to the more recent past.

It has sometimes been suggested, usually on the basis of single case studies, that the apparent failures of learning in these forms of traumatic amnesia, are really failures of recall of the kind referred to above as "motivated forgetting." Gillespie (1936) and Syz (1937) cite cases in which some aspects of recall after head injury were improved under hypnosis. Russell and Nathan (1946) have reported on the effects of sodium thiopentone on 40 cases and found both RGA and PTA unchanged in 28 cases with slight improvement in the remaining 12.

Two kinds of effect may here interact. Trauma produces "cerebral commotion," which disrupts learning, especially the stage of consolidation. Injury may also produce anxiety, which the mediation-avoidance hypothesis (Inglis, 1961) suggests can be reduced in some cases by symbolic suppression. A subsequent reduction in anxiety might then permit increased recall without the anxiety being the whole, or even the major cause of the observed amnesia. This contention parallels an argument already put forward by McGaugh (1965) and by Chorover (1965) who state that electroconvulsive shock (ECS) may have both amnestic and aversive effects. They claim that these effects have often been confounded in the experimental work on ECS in animals. The two effects may also both influence recall after head injury in man.

A number of studies have tried to make a more formal analysis of the behavioral effects of head injury. By the very accidental nature of the disorders of concussion, however, few of these investigations have managed to examine anything but the remote aftereffects of this injury. Given severe enough trauma these studies must then concern themselves with the whole range of the variable effects of human brain-damage (Meyer, 1961; Piercy, 1964) which widens their scope beyond the limits of concern of this chapter. Thus, only a very brief and general account of the conclusions derived will be presented.

When batteries of tests that involve different kinds of mental activity have been given to patients with head injury, to hospital patients without head injury, and to normal controls, it has generally been concluded that the acquisition of new data through learning lags in relative improvement behind other behavior in the head injured. One early study was done by Conkey (1938). Williams (1953), through a visual "prompting" test, reports not only poorer initial acquisition of data for her amnesic group, but also suggests a defect at the retrieval stage of learning or an inaccessibility of memory. She maintains that it is the *speed* with which accessibility diminishes that accounts for the prime difference between normals and amnesics.

Of interest in the further development of this chapter are the conclusions of Ruesch and his associates (Ruesch & Moore, 1943; Ruesch, 1944; Moore & Ruesch, 1944; Ruesch & Bowman, 1945; Ruesch, Harris, & Bowman, 1945) who found that the older and more alcoholic patients showed longer periods of confused consciousness after head injury. It is likely, in fact, that the direct effects of age and some of the indirect effects of chronic drinking on learning ability may themselves resemble the effects of head injury, since both seem to hinder the acquisition of new material.

Lynn, Levine, and Hewson (1945) also objectively studied the effects of closed head injury. They reported that the post-concussive patient is slow in his rate of new learning and in forming new associations, as compared to both normal and neurotic subjects.

The experimental study of traumatic concussion in man is almost impossible. It is too difficult to test a group that is homogeneous in terms of such critical variables as age, severity of injury, and length of time since injury. This can mean that while control is being exercised over one possibly relevant set of variables, other equally important sources of variance may be left uncontrolled so that the phenomena we desire to study are swamped.

If, then, we may conceive that the adequate memory of an event depends at least on its adequate perception, brief registration (activity trace), long-term retention (structural trace), and retrieval, the weight of the evidence suggests that the second of these stages, or perhaps the transition phase from the second stage to the third, is one particularly vulnerable to disruption by head injury. Since the consolidation from ephemeral to longer-term recording is not instantaneous, the data being recorded just before *and* just after trauma are particularly liable to disturbance and so may result in both retrograde amnesia (RGA) and post-traumatic amnesia (PTA).

If the damage is severe enough or is of a particular kind, then the patient may never completely recover the ability briefly to hold new information or pass it into long-term storage, and may therefore have to function entirely in terms of old learning.

At the descriptive level, at least, this is the kind of impairment that appears to characterize part of the condition known as Korsakoff's syndrome, which we now discuss.

Korsakoff's Syndrome

An excellent review of the polyglot literature on the disorders of behavior involved in Korsakoff's syndrome has been provided by Talland (1965).

This condition was described by S. S. Korsakoff in 1889 in a paper since made available in English by Victor and Yakovlev (1955). In its classical form the syndrome includes both behavioral and neurological symptoms, these being principally a marked memory loss and a polyneuritis (which involves inflammation of peripheral nerve trunks with consequent pain, anaesthesias, and paralyses). Korsakoff is said (Talland, 1965) to have recognized that these two aspects of the disorder could occur independently.

Although the condition may often appear as a sequel to chronic alcoholism, it arises in these cases from the nutritional defects that may accompany the abuse of alcohol rather than from any direct effects of the alcohol itself. The underlying neural damage mainly results from a lack of or a failure adequately to metabolize one constituent of the vitamin B complex, vitamin B_1 or thiamine. Impaired gastrointestinal absorption in chronic alcoholism may also be a factor, as it is in more severe form in gastric cancer which has, in some cases, been found to produce this syndrome.

Brierley (1966a) has concluded, concerning the principal sites of crucial brain lesions, that, those of

"... the brain stem and cerebellum are unrelated to amnesia, while at least some of those (structures) within the diencephalon can, if damaged, result in retrograde and anterograde amnesia" (1966a, p. 158).

Adams, Collins, and Victor (1962) specify these regions as certain thalamic nuclei, the mammillary bodies, and often the terminal portions of each fornix. According to Remy (1942), Delay and Brion (1954), and Gruner (1956), Korsakoff's psychosis can exist on the basis of damage confined almost entirely to the mammillary bodies.

It is of interest that Brierley (1966a) has also concluded that

"... some impairment of memory for recent events, and frequently some period of retrograde amnesia, are symptoms of damage within two topographically separate but interconnected regions of the brain. These are the mammillary bodies, together with certain thalamic nuclei in the diencephalon and the hippocampal formations within the temporal lobe" (1966a, p. 151).

In other words, particular importance in the genesis of learning disorder has to be accorded to damage to parts of that complex of structures lying within and mesial to the region of the temporal lobes. This conclusion may well tie back in with the observations adduced by Holbourn (1943) that the temporal lobes are physically also the most vulnerable structures in concussive brain injuries which, as we have seen, produce transient "memory" disturbances.

It is difficult to make further summary of what is already summarized so well by Talland (1965) in his book on *Deranged Memory*, and in his two papers (1964; 1967) that reviewed his work on the psychopathology of the amnesic syndrome, but a brief account must be attempted here since his was the major behavioral research effort in this area for at least a decade.

The criteria for the selection of Korsakoff patients for these studies were the ones enunciated by Adams (1959); diagnosis depended mainly on

"... the demonstration of an impairment of memory for recent events (those occurring before the illness began) and an inability to form memories of present experiences, i.e., to learn or memorize even though the mind is alert and attentive and capable of perceiving with reasonable accuracy and of thinking clearly about simple everyday problems. In fact, the very essence is the discrepancy between an alert, wide-awake state of mind and the memory and learning defect" (1959, pp. 76–77).

An additional diagnostic criterion, Talland (1965) says, was a record, or residual signs, of the neurological abnormalities characteristic of Wernicke's (1881) disease. The latter condition is exemplified, according to Victor and Adams (1953), by the patient who

"... is unable to focus his attention on any one topic and may suspend a conversation to turn over and sleep. What questions he deigns to answer betray disorientation in time and place, misidentification of those around him, and an inability to grasp the meaning of his illness or immediate situation. In addition many of his remarks are irrational, nor do these show any consistence from moment to moment. If one persists in questioning the patient, it is obvious that impairment of retentive memory especially for recent events is probably the outstanding feature of the general mental disorganization" (1953, p. 555).

Of a series of 80 patients with Wernicke's encephalopathy studied by Victor and Adams (1953), 62 were eventually left with Korsakoff's syndrome. Conversely of a series of 45 Korsakoff patients, 42 showed evidence of Wernicke's disease on admission to hospital.

Some elements of the simple sequential chain of the learning process modified from Welford's (1958) analysis may be used here as a means of structuring a brief account of Talland's studies of these patients.

Perception and Awareness

If any response or output function is to be studied, it is first necessary to ensure that the organism can both apprehend and comprehend pertinent input. Therefore, it is essential to inquire if patients in the chronic phase of Korsakoff's syndrome can perceive and discriminate the kind of material that they might be required to learn, and also to find out if they maintain a sufficient general level of cognitive ability to grasp relevant instructions. At least four papers (Talland,

1958a; 1958b; 1960a; Talland and Miller, 1959) have reported on the comparative perceptual capacities of patients and control subjects.

Talland (1958a) compared perceptual task performance of 24 chronic Korsakoff patients (mean age = 53.3; sd = 9.3; mean IQ = 103.4; sd = 8.9) and two control groups. The first control group comprised 24 alcoholic outpatients without memory disorder (mean age = 48.3; sd = 10.4; mean IQ = 114.0; sd = 12.8) and the second was composed of 8 neurological inpatients who had no record of alcoholism or memory disorder (mean age = 49.0; sd = 8.7; mean IQ = 103.5; sd = 9.8). The test material was classified under four main headings: (a) span of perception, (b) integration of fragments into completed wholes, (c) comparison and discrimination, and (d) perceptual set. Some differences were found between Korsakoff patients and controls in category (c); however, the main differences were found in category (d), perceptual set, which included the four subtests (i) concentration, (ii) ability to detect embedded figures, (iii) reversible perspective using the Necker cube phenomenon, and (iv) shape and size constancy.

In addition to the evidence from these tests, Talland and Miller (1959) have reported that the Korsakoff patients also performed more poorly on auditory tests involving perceptual set, in which, for example, discrimination was required of particular classes of words from recorded lists. If only a single set were provided these patients were less impaired than with a set to distinguish, for example, two classes of material. These patients, however, gave evidence of trying to use the sets given; they did not, in other words, merely make random selection from the stimuli provided. This suggested that the principle of selection was not qualitatively different, as it might be if the patients simply misperceived all stimuli, but it was, as Talland and Miller (1959) say, narrowly limited.

Other kinds of phenomena, including the perception of apparent movement (Talland, 1958b) and the development of perception of ambiguous figures (Talland, 1960a) also showed the Korsakoff patients to be different from the controls.

Despite the fact that some differences were found, Talland (1965) concluded that

"... Korsakoff patients are not subject to severe perceptual anomalies ... They recognize objects for what they are and can follow them in movement; they understand causal connections in commonplace occurences; things and events appear to them in their normal connectedness" (1965, p. 170).

If the Korsakoff patient's simplest apprehension of input is not so disrupted as to explain all other deficit, neither is that kind of comprehension which depends on prior early learning and socialization. Talland (1965) noted that the mean IQ of 22 Korsakoff patients, adjusted for age on the Wechsler-Bellevue (1944) was 103 (sd = 9.3) which is, of course, within the average range for the normal standardization population.

Victor, Talland, and Adams (1959) have reported in some detail on the cognitive testing and retesting of two groups of these patients, one in a more acute, the other in a more chronic phase of the disorder. The same patients were also tested on the Wechsler Memory Scale (1945). Not surprisingly, improvement was found on repeated testing, and the less disturbed, chronic cases performed better than the more acutely ill patients. Only two mean IQ scores, however, fell below the limit of "lower average"—these were mean IQ's of 89.1 and 89.7 on the Performance Scale for the chronic patients on the first and second occasions of testing; otherwise, the range of means was from 90.8 to 102.2. The Memory Quotients (MQ's) were predictably lower, ranging from 73.7 to 88.1.

Talland (1959a) has shown that Korsakoff patients may reveal defects on tests of concept attainment, particularly in the development of sequential concepts. Talland (1965) concluded that

"The greatest defect in the Korsakoff patients' concept attainment was directly related to their amnesic derangement, namely, their virtual inability to form concepts in the temporal dimension" (1965, p. 199).

These careful studies of perception and cognition suggest that whatever defects may appear in the learning process, they cannot be blamed entirely on poor acuity or simple stupidity in these patients. Indeed, it may be the case that part of the perceptual and intellectual defects found were themselves based on impairments of some aspects of learning ability.

Registration and Acquisition in Learning

On the basis of observations already cited on the transient effects of concussion, the earliest stages of the learning process might also be expected to be vulnerable in the more chronic disorders of learning. Talland's evidence related to these stages are considered next.

Among the original writers on the disorder it is said to have been Bonhöffer (1901) who placed greatest stress on the part that might be played by impairment of registration. Even if this stage should prove to be defective, there is no logical reason to suppose that it must be the only one damaged in the progression of the learning chain, although later parts of the sequence could hardly function efficiently if earlier parts were damaged.

A variety of measures have conventionally been used as indices of registration and acquisition. A few of those dealt with by Talland will be considered here.

Span of Prehension

Talland (1958a) was able to confirm observations previously made by Wechsler (1917) and by Zangwill (1943) that Korsakoff patients do *not* show impairment, as compared to control patients, in the length of span of digits that they can reproduce correctly after hearing a series but once. This test is apparently not even affected in cases of the very serious kind of learning disturbance usually diagnosed as senile dementia (Inglis, 1957). Either this test does not involve storage, or it calls on a kind of storage that is unaffected in conditions characterized by the grossest symptoms of "memory disorder." It is evidently most unwise to employ this test, in the way that it is often still used clinically, as an index of "immediate memory." Perhaps this mistake could be rectified if the test were again described in Jacobs' (1887) original terms as the span of prehension.

Talland (1965) found, however, that the patients did perform worse than their controls on the "running digit span test" in which subjects are required to repeat the last five items heard, after a longer list has been read. He argued that this test calls on a kind of storage mechanism that "holds" material while yet further data are being processed. This is very like the mechanism which the present author, by using Broadbent's (1958) model, has found also to be impaired in memory-disordered elderly patients.

Acquisition of New Learning

Among the indices of acquisition commonly used in learning experiments may be included the number of times new material must be presented before being learned to a particular criterion of mastery, or the amount of material which is acquired in a set period or in a given number of trials. Talland (1965) has provided a range of data from which these measures may be derived for Korsakoff patients and controls.

(i) Lists of nonsense syllables and of meaningful words. For this experiment (Talland, 1960b) Korsakoff patients and controls were required to learn as many words as possible from two printed lists of ten three-letter words (one list of nonsense syllables, the other of real words) within a 3-minute inspection period. The relevant results for "acquisition" thus measured are shown at the point of zero seconds of the graph in Figure 4.2. It can be seen from this figure that the Korsakoff and control patients are already significantly different on immediate testing. They were also poorer in learning in a nonverbal situation provided

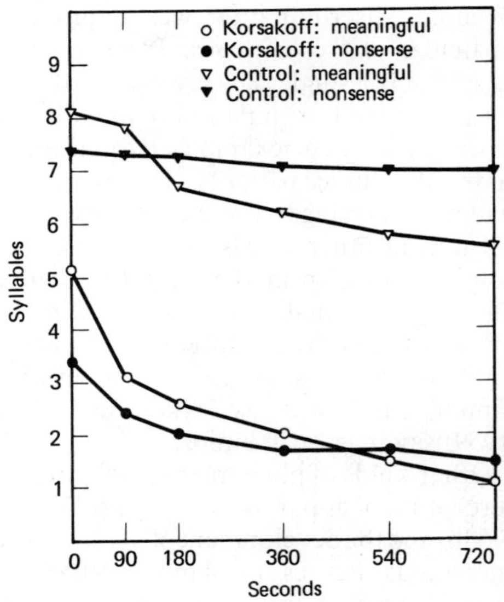

Figure 4.2 Recall of meaningful and nonsense material by Korsakoff patients and control subjects. (From Talland, 1960b.)

by the Rey-Davis Performance test (Zangwill, 1946).

(ii) Learning paired-associates and narrative material. In the Victor, Talland and Adams (1959) study already mentioned above, it was found that the Korsakoff patients performed poorly on the Wechsler (1945) Memory Scale. Much of their impairment was found on two of the subtests involving new learning.

In the paired-associate item of this test the subjects are required to learn as many as possible of 6 "easy" pairs (for example, baby-cries) and 4 "hard" pairs of words (for example, crush-dark) in three learning trials. Talland (1965) found that only acquisition scores on these last items significantly differentiated Korsakoff from control patients.

Another discriminating subtest on the Memory Scale was the one requiring recall, after a single repetition, of a short passage of narrative prose; the score being the number of defined "items" recalled. A more extensive study of this kind of material has been reported by Talland and Ekdahl (1959). The Korsakoff patients were tested for spontaneous recall or reproduction, and for assisted recall or recognition; control subjects were tested for recall alone. Comparative scores for these groups for immediate recall can be seen at the zero hour point on Figure 4.3. The mean score for the control group is 9.12, for the Korsakoff patients the corresponding score is only 5.82.

These examples suffice to show that among the other impairments suffered by the Korsakoff patients is a malfunction of the registration part of the learning process, so far as this can be estimated from the indices employed.

Talland and Ekdahl (1959) also tested the notion put forward by Betlheim and Hartmann (1951) that the apparent registration defect may actually be because of a form of repression practiced by these patients. No evidence was found for this contention. Zangwill (1967) on the other hand, has given a detailed historical description of a notorious case, long believed to be one of pure registration defect, in which social circumstances (life and wife) may have acted so as to perpetuate for decades, by positive reinforcement, the appearance of a disorder which, in its original form, was probably organically based.

Retention And Forgetting

Korsakoff (1889) himself believed that, in the disorder that bears his name, the phase of learning most affected is that of recall. Recall itself, however, is a complex process. It is the convention to regard the reproduction or the relearning of learned material after some delay as an index of retention. Some of the complexities of this inference

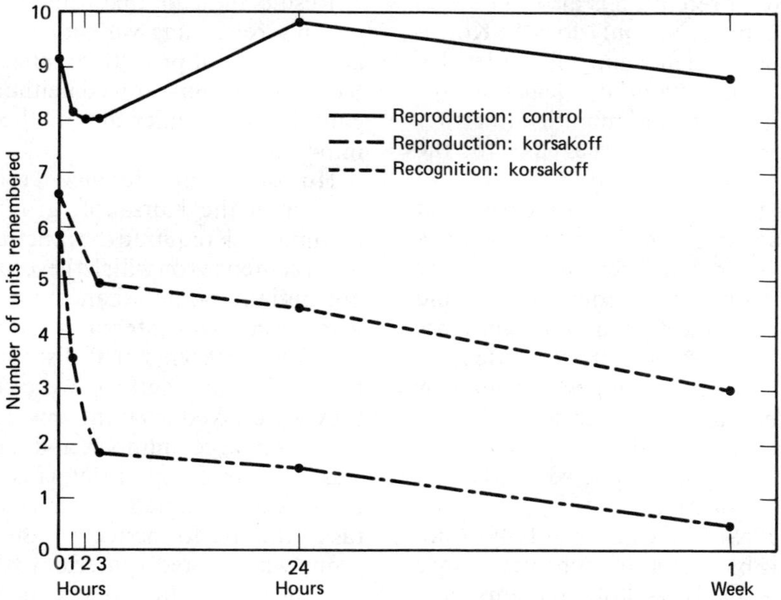

Figure 4.3 Retention curves for narrative material by Korsakoff patients and control subjects. (From Talland, 1965.)

have been well recognized by Talland (1964), who has pointed out that

> "When delayed recall is successful, by implication registration and retention too are intact: when recall fails or is only partly accurate, there is no immediate way of telling whether the defect has occurred in that process or previously in retention. Indirect measures are often applied, e.g., if recall fails but not recognition, or if relearning is achieved more rapidly than original learning, the inference is made that there was some retention. 'Some retention', however, may not be the same as retention adequate for recall; success in recognition or saving in relearning do not prove that recall failed in spite of intact retention. It does happen though, quite commonly, and not only with amnesic patients, that some memory inaccessible on one occasion becomes available subsequently. Recall can fail even though sufficient information has been retained for its efficient function; the source of the failure must then be sought in some interfering effect of the momentary situation" (1964, pp. 446–447).

Talland used some of the learning material already described to examine delayed accomplishment, or retention. His results may be considered under the same headings.

(i) Lists of nonsense syllables and of meaningful words. The progressive decrease in accurate recall over time that is often used as a measure of retention is also to be seen in Figure 4.2 above. Not only does the Korsakoff group start off at a much lower level of acquisition, this material "leaks away" faster during the first few minutes after it has been registered than is the case for the control group.

As seems to be true for most learning, at least two factors might help to produce a diminution of recall over time; they are trace-decay (or spontaneous fading) and interference (or the effect of other activity), both of which have been held to affect retention even in normal subjects: when new learning effects older learning deleteriously, the interference is said to be retroactive; when old learning affects newer, this effect is said to be proactive.

Talland (1959b) has experimentally examined the possible effects of such interference on learning in Korsakoff patients and controls. The learning task used has already been described above and involved the learning and relearning of printed lists of words (nonsense and meaningful) within three-minute inspection periods. The effect of interference on retention was mainly estimated by the amount of initial learning saved when the subjects were required to relearn.

Parallel lists (A or B) of either meaningful or nonsense syllables were used. Talland (1959b) has described the general procedure as follows:

> "S's were first tested for retroactive interference, alternately beginning their work with list A or B, the other being used for the intermediate task. An S whose first test used the lists in order A-B-A would on the following occasion be given list B for learning and relearning, and on the last test (for proactive interference) he would again start with B and have A for learning and relearning. Intervals between two tests were two weeks or longer. The parallel tests with nonsense syllables and with meaningful words were conducted within one session" (1959b, p. 11).

The scores obtained were the number of words or syllables correctly recalled; the mean scores for the alternate lists (A and B) proved not to be significantly different. Meaningful words produced better scores than nonsense syllables. The control group's scores, of course, were consistently higher than the scores made by the Korsakoff group.

Results indicate that whereas the control group's relearning was impaired by retroactive (but not proactive) interference, the Korsakoff group showed neither significant gain *nor* loss under any of the conditions imposed.

However, interference effects were greater in the Korsakoff group when the learning task required the repetition of a ten-word sentence (on which these patients were not initially poorer than the controls) and when recall was interrupted, for example, by a brief interview that disrupted their set to recall. Similar effects were shown when they were asked to count upwards from one to a given target number, and their progress was interrupted by a brief pause. When this break was occupied by another (drawing) task, the performance of the Korsakoff group was markedly inferior to the controls.

Concerning the effects of interference in general on the learning of these patients, Talland has concluded that

"It undoubtedly varies with the type of material originally registered, the method by which retention is probed, and the interval between learning and later recall. With complex or extensive material the effect of interference is negligible, since original registration is too slight to allow for its operation. The magnitude of the registration defect in general, i.e., the patient's poor performance on instant test of recall, diminishes the significance of any evidence for retroactive interference effects in amnesic patients" (1964, p. 461).

(ii) Learning narrative material. The narrative learning used by Talland and Ekdahl (1959) illustrates (see Figure 4.3 above) the comparative forgetting curves over an extended period of time for the Korsakoff and the control group. The former group again shows much more drastic initial decrement than the latter. In addition the control group actually shows an increase in performance after the first 24 hours. This resembles the "reminiscence effect" first described by Ballard (1913) in which an increment is found in learning after a period without overt practice. Such an effect does not appear in the performance of the Korsakoff patients who forget faster initially and continue to show a decrement thereafter.

This brief account of Talland's work with Korsakoff patients neglects many of the complexities and subtleties of his studies. However, even this oversimplification may serve to outline some of the contributions that can be made by a behavioral attack on the problems of so-called memory disorder.

When this kind of impairment is dissected in terms of some of the possible components of the learning sequence, it is apparent that no simple, single aspect of function is alone defective. Most, if not all, of the input and holding stages that seem to underlie learning appear to be affected. We as yet lack the means of estimating how these effects may interact and cumulate, but it can now at least be seen how carefully we must try to separate out a whole range of contributing factors. What is principally required is a thorough examination of each of the components whose malfunction may issue in the appearance of a derangement of memory.

Senile Dementia

This section will deal with the kind of memory disorder that afflicts some elderly psychiatric patients to whom the label "senile dement" is then often attached. Payne and Inglis (1960) have pointed out that dementia is an equivocal word carrying different implications that are not perfectly correlated with one another. One of its implications is etiological and refers to physical damage in the central nervous system; the other is descriptive and refers to a falling away from a previously higher level of behavioral competence. These two kinds of phenomena need not be related on a one-to-one basis.

Allison (1962) and Corsellis (1962) have given accounts of some of the etiological considerations. Their studies confirm that extremes of senile behavior deficit tend to be associated with rather gross and general cerebral pathology. Less is known about the relation between the particular locus of senile brain changes and specific impairments. It is of interest to note, however, that a number of EEG studies (Busse, Barnes, Friedman, & Kelty, 1956; Barnes, Busse, & Friedman, 1956) which reflect the integrity of the physical substrate, have reported a relatively high incidence of electrical disturbance in the area of the temporal lobes in elderly persons, especially in the ones with defects in learning ability (Busse, 1962). These data again show that the integrity of tissue in and around this brain region is of importance for the maintenance of human learning skill. Kral (1956, 1966) has similarly indicted the mammillary bodies as an important site of lesions in elderly patients with memory disorder.

This section of the chapter will deal with the descriptive rather than with the etiological aspects of senile disorders of learning. A review of most of the relevant studies carried out up to a decade ago has already been made (Inglis, 1958), so that little of that earlier work need be considered here. A selective overview of more recent studies may be subdivided under three main headings—clinical, psychometric, and descriptive-analytic (these labels reflect the principal but not the sole content of these subdivisions).

Clinical Implications

Description and Treatment

One of the longest series of therapeutic investigations of senile dementia was directed by D. E. Cameron. These studies have periodically been described in summarized form by Cameron (1963, 1966) and by Cameron, Kral, Solyom, Sved, Wainrib, Beaulieu, and Enesco, (1966).

Most recently these workers have used supplements of nucleic acids. Part of the rationale for this treatment is as follows. It is known that certain programs of inheritable form and function are coded at the macro-molecular level of cell activity. There is also some suggestive evidence that learned activity involves changes of nucleoprotein in the nervous system (John, 1967). Cameron reasoned that a defect at this level might underlie senile memory disorder and that replacement of this substrate might produce behavioral improvement. Cameron (1963) quotes one study (by S. Sved) that found evidence of elevated levels of ribonuclease (the enzyme that breaks down ribonucleic acid) in elderly patients with memory disorder. This, Cameron says, suggests that one factor in memory disturbance may be the overactivity of ribonuclease.

Cameron (1958) initially reported on the effects of the intravenous administration of both deoxyribonucleic acid (DNA) and ribonucleic acid (RNA) and the oral administration of RNA. At that time it seemed that the best effects were produced by RNA taken by mouth.

More detailed accounts of a larger study have been provided by Cameron, Solyom, and Beach (1961) and Cameron and Solyom (1961). The indices of learning behavior were provided by a Counting Test, intended to estimate the subject's "retention span" (Beaulieu & Solyom, 1963), the Wechsler Memory Scale (Wechsler, 1945), and some aspects of performance in a classical conditioning situation. There were two main groups of patients. Group I comprised elderly patients with memory disturbance; Group II had more severe disorder. The second group was divided into two subgroups; one of them got RNA and the other a placebo. In both groups, patients diagnosed as arteriosclerotic did better than the ones suffering from senile dementia. Since none of the relevant control comparisons between groups were made, however, firm conclusions seem unwarranted.

A further comparison of the oral and the intravenous administration of RNA has also been reported [Cameron, Solyom, Sved, & Wainrib (1963); Cameron, Sved, Solyom, Wainrib, & Barik (1963); Cameron, Sved, Solyom, & Wainrib (1964)]. These results suggested that the intravenous route had better effects than the oral, with the less impaired patients benefiting most. The lack of a comparable control group again vitiates any inference that could be drawn. Enesco (1967), furthermore, cites evidence that yeast RNA of the kind used in the above studies is neither incorporated in brain tissue nor increases brain synthetic activity.

A study of Talland, Mendelson, Koz, and Aaron (1965), using the drug tricyanoaminopropene, reputed to raise the level of nervous system RNA, failed to show changes in elderly subjects with memory disorder. Cameron (1966) also studied the effects of magnesium pemoline ("Cylert") on memory disorder. Glasky and Simon (1966) had found that this substance enhanced brain RNA, and Plotnikoff (1966) initially reported that it improved a conditioned-avoidance response in rats. Cameron (1966) gave an enthusiastic description of the performance of a drug-treated group who were tested at the same time as a placebo-treated group on the Wechsler Memory Scale. Most of the improvement in the treated group was found in the patients who were less than 70 years of age and who had a pretreatment MQ of over 60. Again, no direct comparisons of the two groups over treatments has been provided. Differences at the end of one week seem very small indeed. Talland (1966) and Talland and McGuire (1967) studied this drug and a placebo in normal volunteers and found the drug to act as a general stimulant rather than as one affecting the learning process directly. We are forced to conclude of these studies thus far, that the more they exercise appropriate controls the less encouraging are their results.

Prognosis

The predictive implication of memory dysfunction in the aged has been intensively studied by V. A. Kral (1959; 1965; 1966), who found that he was able to distinguish clinically between two different kinds of memory dysfunction in elderly patients. In one study (1958a; 1958b), 60 percent of the residents in an old people's home showed some degree of memory loss, and this deficit increased beyond the sixtieth year. About one third of the residents with this disorder showed mild (or "benign") impairment characterized by inconsistent failures of recall of the less recent past. This did not progress very rapidly and was found as often in men as in women. The other two thirds showed a more severe (or "malignant") kind of memory disorder characterized by the subject's inability to recall events of the recent past. This loss was usually progressive and accompanied by disorientation. The ratio of women to men in this group was about two to one.

Kral (1958b) found no significant association between either of these memory dysfunctions and signs of physical pathology. Although the memory disordered tended to be older than the others, age did not differentiate the mild cases from the severe.

Kral (1966) has suggested that the severe or malignant kind of disorder is due to a failure in the registration or acquisition phase of learning. This fits in with other findings already reviewed that concern the peculiar vulnerability of this part of the learning sequence, and is consistent with more analytic studies of learning in these patients to be reviewed below. The mild or benign form, Kral believes, may be based on a difficulty of retrieval, because these patients, who fail to reproduce data on one occasion, are often able to recall it at another time.

In addition to the descriptive distinction, these categories of memory dysfunction in the elderly also prove to have predictive value. It had already been shown by Inglis (1959a) that the learning ability of elderly patients was significantly related to their mortality over a period of two years. This observation was further confirmed by Sanderson and Inglis (1961).

In the meantime, similar investigations were being carried out by Wigdor and Kral (1961) and Kral (1962) who reported on the four-year follow-up study of elderly subjects from an old people's home; about 20 percent of them showed mild and 35 percent severe memory impairment. None of the others had difficulties in remembering. These groups were not significantly different in age.

These subjects were tested on an adaptation of the Wechsler Memory Scale as described by Kral and Durost (1953). This test differentiated the severe cases from all the other groups, who were themselves not significantly different from one another.

Over the four-year period more of the group with severe memory disorder died (see Table 4.2).

Table 4.2 Incidence of Deaths within a Four-Year Observation Period

Memory function	Subjects	Deaths	percent of Deaths
Normal	40	11	27.5
Benign dysfunction	20	8	38.2
Malignant dysfunction	34	21	61.7
Total	94	40	42.6

Source. Kral, 1962.

Furthermore, the survival time after testing was shorter for the severe group than for the others (see Table 4.3). There were also significant correlations *within* the groups between test score and survival: individuals with poor scores died sooner than the ones with good scores.

To see how these results from a special group might be generalized, other studies were carried out on larger groups of mental hospital patients. Kral, Cahn, and Mueller (1964) have reported on a three-year follow-up of 695 geriatric patients on whom 1290 assessments were made. They found that the patients with amnestic syndrome on the basis of senile psychosis or cerebral arteriosclerosis had a significantly shorter survival time and a higher mortality rate than comparable patients with other diagnoses. They concluded that the presence of an amnestic syndrome in an old person, whether in a mental hospital or not, is an important sign of *senium ex morbo*, whereas the presence of the benign type of senescent forgetfulness could be taken as an expression of *senium naturale*. Kral and Mueller (1966) have since published a further two-year follow-up on the same population, using the same criteria, with the same results.

Kral has also studied a number of methods of treating memory dysfunction in elderly patients. Because there was a consistent preponderance of women in the groups suffering from the malignant form of the disorder, Kral and Wigdor (1959) argued that some factors, perhaps hormonal, in the male might provide protection against this kind of

Table 4.3 Association between Average Memory Scale Score and Survival Time of Those Who Died during the Four-Year Follow-Up Period

Memory Function	Subjects	Deaths	Memory Scale Score	Length of Survival in Months
Normal	40	11	80.03	24.40
Benign dysfunction	20	8	67.25	23.50
Malignant dysfunction	34	21	26.71	15.20
Total	94	40	57.99	21.03

Source. Wigdor and Kral, 1961.

disorder. They gave an oral androgen to 13 residents of an old people's home, 6 of whom showed the malignant form of memory disorder. Their performance on the Kral and Durost (1953) Memory Scale was compared over an average period of 4 months with 13 similar control patients of whom 7 were severe cases. The only significant improvement that did take place was on one subtest in the case of the experimental patients with mild disorder.

Kral and Wigdor (1961) then went on to find out if a longer period of treatment or higher dosage of these androgens would further influence the effects. Neither of these factors produced remarkably different results.

Among other treatment studies, Kral, Cahn, Deutsch, Mueller, and Solyom (1962) have assessed Aslan's (1962) claims for the beneficial effects of procaine on aging processes. No significant effect was found. A further study of brief oral RNA treatment (Kral, Solyom, & Enesco, 1967) in senile and senescent subjects failed to show statistically significant improvement in memory test scores.

These studies clearly show that, even in memory disorder in the elderly, there is need to distinguish at least two kinds of disturbance; a mild or benign form that probably depends on some defect in retrieval; and a severe or malignant form that probably reflects a defect in registration. The latter carries a poor prognosis for shorter survival and greater mortality.

It will be seen that some psychometric studies have mainly been concerned with the registration or acquisition phase of learning and may have their main use in the detection of malignant memory dysfunctions.

Psychometric Considerations

Consideration may be given to one test that has been well standardized in the geriatric field.

This test has been developed by a number of investigators, and these variations are considered in order.

New Word Learning and Retention Test (NWLRT)

This test was originally devised by Shapiro and Nelson (1955) to find out if some groups of psychiatric patients differ from others in their capacity for new learning. Shapiro and Nelson outlined their method as follows:

> "Present ability to learn and retain the meanings of words was measured by teaching the subject the meaning of new words he did not know. The words chosen were the first five consecutive words which were previously missed by the subject on the vocabulary test (Terman and Merrill, 1937). The examiner repeats the definitions of each of the five words until the subject can give the meaning correctly three times without help. Precautions are taken to prevent automatic learning, each time the examiner gives a word definition, he changes the wording slightly. After an interval of twenty-four hours, the subject is re-tested to establish how many of the five newly learned words are retained" (1955, p. 251).

One advantage claimed for this test is that it tries to equate "difficulty level" over subjects by using, as the material to be learned, words adjusted according to the subject's actual vocabulary score.

Shapiro and Nelson (1955) after testing various groups of patients were not overenthusiastic about their findings only stating that

"The ability to retain the definitions of words significantly differentiated all psychiatric groups (except neurotics and acute schizophrenics) from normals. This retention test also differentiated between a number of psychiatric groups" (1955, p. 251).

Modified Word Learning Test (MWLT)

Walton and Black (1957) altered the original test so that the subject was now required to learn a minimum of six out of ten new words. The administration and scoring of this early version of the test were rather complicated and are best described in the authors' own words.

"The Terman Merrill (Form L) Vocabulary Test was used. This test was administered until the subject was unable to give the meanings of ten consecutive words. The examiner then told the subject the meanings of these ten words. Immediately he had done this he read to the subject each of the ten words in turn, the subject replying with the meanings as far as he had remembered them. The criterion of a successful performance was that the subject was able to give the meanings of any six of ten definitions. If the subject failed to do this the meanings of all ten words were repeated, though the wording was changed to avoid rote learning . . . The most rapid learning possible to the required criterion was obviously for the subject to give the correct meanings after the first presentation. This achieved a score of one. If the subject was able to give six correct meanings, but only achieved his sixth success on the seventh word his score was two. If he was only able to give six definitions by the tenth and final word his score was five . . . As a further example of scoring, let us suppose a patient was unable to learn the meanings of six of the words before the third full presentation of the ten words. It was also not until the ninth word in the third presentation that he was able to complete the sixth definition correctly. His score would therefore be fourteen" (1957, pp. 271–272).

In the first standardization, Walton and Black (1957) reported the results of 279 cases. Here the organic criterion group was probably mainly characterized by the presence of some degree of the amnestic syndrome. In this case although the patients were chosen on what seem "etiological" grounds, they were also probably quite homogeneous in behavior abnormality as well. The distribution of scores obtained is shown in Table 4.4. The overlap between the organics—presumably memory-disordered—and others is remarkably small. If a cut-off point is made at a score of 22, only one organic is misclassified, that is, more than 97 percent are correctly placed as are 97 percent in all the other groups together. Age and intelligence did not, in this case, seem markedly to affect the scores.

Walton, White, Black, and Young (1959) reported on a cross-validation study with slight scoring modifications. There were 304 subjects among whom the organic criterion group was again mainly made up of patients who were likely to have been amnestic. A cutoff score of 26 now created the smallest

Table 4.4 Distributions of MWLT Scores for the Various Criterion Groups

MWLT Scores	Normals	Neurotics	Psychotics	Mental Defectives	Organics
1–5	42	69	16	5	—
6–10	9	34	6	6	1
11–15	6	12	4	2	—
16–20	—	6	3	6	—
21–25	—	4	1	1	2
26–30	—	—	—	—	1
31–35	—	—	—	1	5
36–40	—	—	—	—	11
Over 40	—	—	—	—	26
Totals	57	125	30	21	46

Source. Walton and Black, 1957.

amount of misclassification (see Table 4.5).

It is not surprising that 19 of the 45 defectives were misclassified by the recommended cutting-score, since many of them presumably suffered from some learning disability.

Walton (1958) also showed that in elderly psychiatric patients, initial test scores were already closely associated with independent changes made in diagnosis after two years. Inglis (1959a) showed that there was also a close relation between poor learning scores and mortality. Walton and Black (1959) also showed a high association between test scores and independent objective signs of generalized brain damage. White and Knox (1965) also found poor test scores to be related to abnormal EEG's in elderly psychiatric patients.

Synonym Learning Test (SLT). Yet another version of the test has been developed by Kendrick, Parboosingh, and Post (1965). Instead of varying word definitions the subjects are presented with synonyms for the first ten consecutive words failed on the Mill Hill Vocabulary Scale (Raven, 1958). Results on 97 patients and 11 normal elderly subjects showed that the correlation between test score and independent psychiatric diagnosis was +.97, poor learning being associated with "brain damage." Factor analysis showed the test to be highly loaded on short-term memory.

Kendrick (1965) favors a Bayesian statistical approach (Meyer, 1966) that requires the consecutive testing and the establishment of different cutoff points for a brief battery of items (Kendrick, 1967; Kendrick & Post, 1967) to distinguish "diffuse brain damage" from other psychiatric conditions in the elderly.

The author's reservation about these tests attaches to the founding of psychological measures on etiological propositions of the kind implied by such a diagnosis as "brain damage." There is little reason to believe that criterion groups composed on the basis of this diagnosis are homogeneous in any useful sense. It may be more profitable to pursue the study of abnormality through the analytic description of the behavior itself, which thus may lead to the discovery of relevant independent variables that can give us the power to secure prophylaxis and change.

Descriptive Analytic Studies

Standardized tests for the detection of memory disorder suffer from many defects. Even the carefully studied word-learning tests involve only auditory-verbal learning. They also fail to detect the components of learning that may be most responsible for output in terms of the scores obtained. With some of these lacks in mind, the next series of studies was begun.

In the first of these studies (Inglis, 1957), tests were used that could yield objective measures of the main phases of learning. The

Table 4.5 Distributions of MWLT Scores for the Various Criterion Groups of a Cross-Validation Study

MWLT Scores	Normals	Neurotics	Psychotics	Mental Defectives	Organics
1–5	49	28	10	9	4
6–10	22	24	6	6	1
11–15	8	9	8	3	3
16–20	2	4	4	4	1
21–25	2	1	4	4	3
26–30	—	—	—	1	5
31–35	—	—	—	2	13
36–40	—	—	—	8	11
Over 40	—	—	—	8	37
Totals	83	66	32	45	78

Source. Walton et al., 1959.

technique chosen involved easy paired-associates. It also seemed desirable to account for various difficulties that might arise, as in the learning of material through different modalities (for example, auditory or visual) or in the different modes of reproduction (for example, recognition or recall). The following four subtests were devised.

Auditory recall. This test (Inglis, 1959b) involved verbal presentation and the recall of three pairs of words. The instructions were like the ones for the Paired Associate subtest of the Wechsler Memory Scale (Wechsler, 1945).

The acquisition score was the number of stimulus presentations before the first of the three consecutive correct criterion trials (up to a maximum of 30 presentations); the performance represented in Figure 4.4 would score 11; each circled trial counting one point.

With this method of scoring, the minimum (that is, the "best") is three, and the maximum (that is, the "worst") score is 93.

Visual recall. The three stimulus-response pairs were simple line drawings. Except for visual presentation, administration and scoring were the same as in the auditory recall subtest.

Auditory recognition. The subjects had to associate three pairs of words auditorily presented. In his reproduction, the patient had to choose (that is, recognize) correctly from the list of three responses read aloud. The criterion of learning and the method of scoring were the same as before.

Visual recognition. The items were again simple drawings. After the initial presentation, the correct response had to be chosen from the set of three shown by the examiner. The learning criterion and the scoring of this subtest remained the same.

In one pilot study (Inglis, 1957) these tests were given to two groups of elderly patients, one group with and the other without clinical evidence of memory disorder. They were matched in terms of age, Verbal Scale Intelligence (Wechsler, 1944), social class, and sex. Some results of this investigation are shown in Table 4.6.

It is possible to obtain scores for both acquisition and retention from paired-associate learning tests. In this study only measures of acquisition were taken. The significant differences on all the learning tests indicated that the memory disordered took more trials to learn to the criterion. Just as Kral has proposed, it seems that a defect in the first phase of the learning sequence (that is, acquisition or registration) is an important factor in the "memory disorder" shown by some elderly psychiatric patients. This disability was found in both of the modalities tested and for both recall and recognition.

The main finding was congruent with our review thus far, namely, that elderly psychiatric patients with memory disorder have a marked disability in acquisition. It also agrees with the clinical impression that they have a "poor memory for recent events," even if they remember more remote events. The results suggest a faulty recording of recent events of which there can therefore be no adequate playback. More remote events

PALT: auditory-recall

Stimulus	Response	Initial presentation	Test trials 1	2	3	4	5	6 ··· 30
a. Flower	Spark	⊖	⊖	⊕	⊖	+	+	+
b. Table	River	⊖	⊕	⊖	+	+	+	
c. Bottle	Comb	⊖	⊖	⊕	⊖	+	+	+

Figure 4.4 Scoring for the Inglis Paired Associate Learning Test (Auditory Recall) (From Inglis, 1966.)

Table 4.6 Means, Standard Deviations, and the Significance of the Differences between the Means of the Memory Disordered and Nonmemory Disordered Groups in Age, Verbal Intelligence, and Paired Associate Learning Test Scores

Variables	Memory Disordered		Nonmemory Disordered			
	M	S.D.	M	S.D.	< A >	< P >
Age	67.75	8.19	67.25	7.17	0.306	NS
Wechsler Verbal Scale W.S.	33.88	8.90	30.50	8.42	0.284	NS
Paired associate learning tests						
Auditory recall	59.25	23.60	14.13	4.55	0.150	<.001
Visual recall	50.25	29.20	6.63	3.70	0.169	<.01
Auditory recognition	51.88	29.61	7.50	3.42	0.174	<.01
Visual recognition	35.38	22.59	6.00	2.51	0.185	<.01

Source. Inglis, 1957.

were stored before the recording breakdown and may still be available for reproduction, even when current events can no longer be held in mind.

Inglis (1959c) then set out to see if these results could be confirmed in an experiment that used different groups of similar patients. It was further intended to learn if there were an impairment of retention over and above the acquisition defect.

The Auditory Recall test alone was given, since the four learning subtests showed good equivalence. This test was given twice in order also to get two scores of retention. These comprised a relearning score and a retained members score.

The significance of the difference between the two criterion groups is shown in Table 4.7.

We can observe that the experimental group was again significantly inferior to the control group in acquisition and on both the relearning and retained members scores. It seems that memory-disordered patients suffer not only from a defect in registration but also from a defect of retention.

The usefulness of the paired-associate learning test has been further explored by other workers. Caird, Sanderson, and Inglis (1962) carried out a cross-validation study that confirmed the original findings.

Riddell (1962a) studied the equivalence of two forms of the auditory verbal recall test. The correlation between the two was 0.507.

Studies of the "diagnostic" use of this test have also been carried out. Riddell (1962b) found tetrachoric correlations of 0.60 and 0.64 between two forms of the test and "organic" and "functional" diagnosis. Isaacs (1962) found that normal old people performed better than hospital patients. Patients with diffuse brain damage did worse than the ones with focal brain damage, and incontinent patients were worse than continent patients. Test scores were also related to response to rehabilitation. Isaacs and Walkley (1964), by using slightly simpler tests, concluded that the worst performances were found in female patients aged 75 and over, hospitalized for more than six months, and diagnosed as demented. Newcombe and Steinberg (1964) found that the test differentiated two groups of elderly patients, one with organic cerebral disease and the other with functional psychiatric illness. The rank order correlation between two forms, given at an interval of three months, was 0.615. The discriminative power of the test has been further confirmed by Kendrick, Parboosingh, and Post (1965), who also found that it had a high loading on the same short-term memory factor as their Synonym Learning Test. The kinds of errors that may result from the "diagnostic" use of these tests have been pointed out elsewhere (Inglis, 1966); even relatively high

Table 4.7 Means, Standard Deviations and the Significance of the Differences between the Means of the Memory-Disordered and Nonmemory Disordered Groups, in Age, Verbal Intelligence and Paired Associate Learning Test Scores

Variables	Memory Disordered		Nonmemory Disordered			
	M	S.D.	M	S.D.	A	P
Age	70.80	5.67	71.50	5.36	2.837	NS
Wechsler Verbal Scale I.Q.	89.80	8.79	92.50	6.38	1.009	NS
Paired associate learning test						
Acquisition	54.80	28.07	10.70	5.16	0.135	<.001
Relearning	56.80	34.93	3.90	3.48	0.136	<.001
Retained members	0.20	0.63	1.30	1.16	0.174	.01-.001

Source. Inglis, 1959 c.

correlations between test scores and diagnostic criteria can result in very great errors of misclassification.

The same test was also used in a prognostic study by Sanderson and Inglis (1961). There was shown to be a closer association between the test scores and mortality than between mortality and initial diagnosis.

This kind of measure produces results of practical value. However, it seemed necessary to describe more precisely those aspects of the learning process most vulnerable to senility.

As a means of analysis of the short-term storage phase of the learning sequence, the method of dichotic listening performance (Broadbent, 1958) was chosen.

Broadbent (1957) had shown that when digit-span stimuli were relayed at a speed of 2 per second through headphones, one half of the span to one ear and, simultaneously, the other half of the span to the other ear, subjects could reproduce the digits sequentially. In such reproduction, elements from the one half of the span were rarely alternated with elements from the other half. The first half-set recalled commonly contained fewer errors than the second half. Broadbent suggested that two kinds of mechanism may underlie this kind of performance. First, there is a "p-system" which can only pass information successively. Second, there is an "s-system" or short-term store which can hold excess information arriving when the p-mechanism is already fully occupied in transmitting information from another channel. Thus, the half-set of digits recalled first passes directly through the p-system while the half-set recalled second spends time in storage.

In practice, spoken digits are recorded on two channels of a stereophonic tape so that different numbers may be played back simultaneously to both ears. The technique of dichotic stimulation can be represented diagrammatically as in Figure 4.5.

C_1 and C_2 are two separate tape channels. The digits in the arrowheads are the different, simultaneous stimuli. The letters t_1, t_2, t_3, and t_4 show the time sequence. Thus, this subject first hears "five" read in his right ear and "two" in his left, both at time t_1, and so on for subsequent simultaneous pairs.

Inglis (1960) has suggested that some forms of memory disorder might be based on a breakdown of the kind of short-term storage mechanism involved in performance on this task. This should show as an impairment of recall in those half-sets of digits reproduced second. This expectation was tested by Inglis and Sanderson (1961).

The significance of the difference between the means of their memory-disordered and non-memory-disordered groups is shown in Table 4.8.

These results confirmed that memory disorder in elderly psychiatric patients may be based, at least in part, on a breakdown of

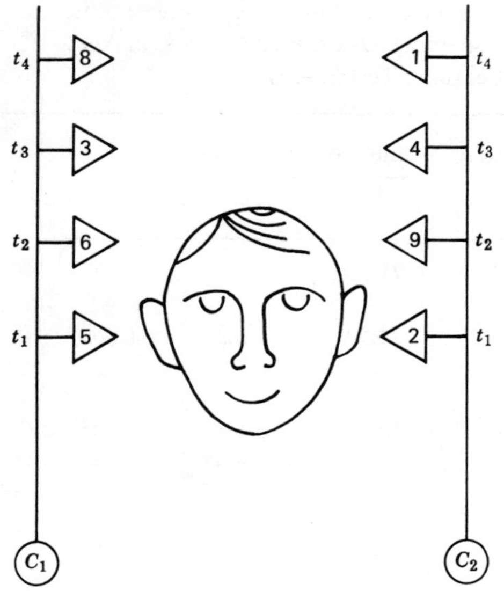

Figure 4.5 Diagrammatic representation of the technique of dichotic stimulation. (From Mackay and Inglis, 1963.)

the kind of storage mechanism (s-system) proposed by Broadbent to account for the capacity of young normal adults to respond successively to information delivered to them simultaneously.

We can also observe that there were significant differences of lesser magnitude between the groups in their responses to information in the immediate channel for the two longest half-sets.

The results of this experiment can be shown even more clearly in the form of the graph in Figure 4.6.

A second study (Caird and Inglis, 1961), using different groups of similar elderly psychiatric patients, produced results in close accord with the initial study, as may be seen from Figure 4.7.

In both of these studies, then, the memory-disordered patients showed an impaired ability in the second half-spans recalled, which were, by hypothesis, the ones that spent some time in a short-term store. These

Table 4.8 Means, Standard Deviations, and the Significance of the Differences between the Means of the Memory Disordered and Nonmemory Disordered Groups in Age, Verbal Intelligence, and Dichotic Listening Performance

Variables	Memory Disordered			Nonmemory Disordered			Between Group Differences	
	Mean	S.D.		Mean	S.D.		t	p
Age	75.73	4.42		75.00	4.46		0.57	n.s.
WAIS IQ's Verbal Scale	89.00	9.27		95.40	10.38		1.78	n.s.
Dichotic stimulation	Within Group Difference			Within Group Difference				
1 Digit								
1st channel	0.98	0.14	<.01	1.00	0.00	n.s.	0.55	n.s.
2nd channel	0.47	0.41		0.95	0.44		3.10	<.01
2 Digits								
1st channel	1.83	0.20	<.001	1.95	0.20	n.s.	1.64	n.s.
2nd channel	0.09	0.63		1.80	0.45		8.30	<.001
3 Digits								
1st channel	2.42	0.48	<.001	2.90	0.17	<.01	3.64	<.01
2nd channel	0.05	0.14		2.15	0.67		11.86	<.001
4 Digits								
1st channel	2.82	1.06	<.001	3.63	0.45	<.001	2.72	<.02
2nd channel	0.09	0.63		0.95	0.66		3.55	<.01

Source. Inglis and Sanderson, 1961.

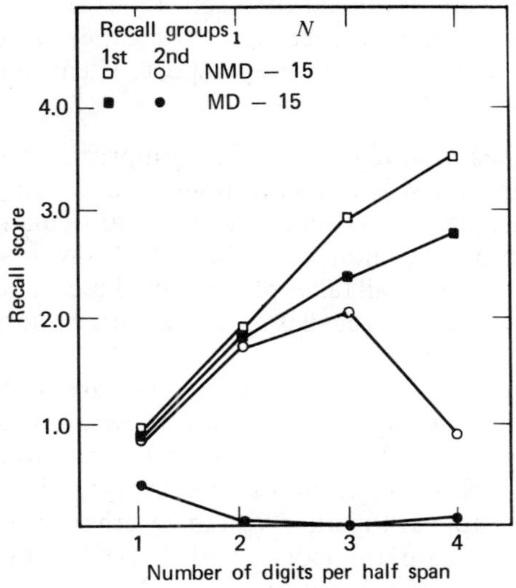

Figure 4.6 Graph of the scores made by elderly psychiatric patients on the first dichotic listening experiment. (From Inglis, 1965.)

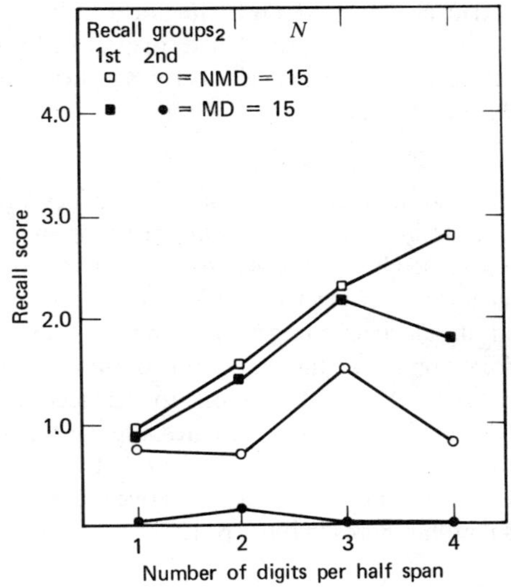

Figure 4.7 Graph of the scores made by elderly psychiatric patients on the second dichotic listening experiment. (From Inglis, 1965.)

findings, of course, do not preclude the possibility that other concurrent but independent functions may also become progressively less efficient, or break down altogether in senile disorders. However, the implication of these findings seems to be that the short-term storage process described by Broadbent is an important link in the learning chain. If the chain is broken at this point, then the whole sequence of learning may be disrupted with the consequent appearance of the kind of severe memory disorder and disorientation found in senile dementia.

The differences found between such groups of elderly psychiatric patients on dichotic listening performance has been confirmed once again by Caird and Hannah (1964).

Another intriguing means of analysis of these defect states in the elderly has been developed by Gedye (1967) who has adapted the method of the teaching machine to this purpose. Mackay and Inglis (1965) have also explored the application of operant learning principles to these problems.

In the case of senile dementia, as in the case of Korsakoff's psychosis, then, there is good evidence that the analysis of disorder by the experimental study of learning can bring us to a closer understanding of the nature of these dysfunctions.

Another source of this understanding is also to be found in studies that actually alter human learning ability, and it is to them that our attention is now turned.

EFFECTS OF INTERVENTION

Major advances in experimental psychopathology are likely to come from attempts to control behavior. Efforts are usually directly devoted to the amelioration of disorder, but insight may even spring from the specification of conditions that have other, indirect effects. Some knowledge may thus be gained from a brief consideration of two kinds of deliberate intervention which, whatever beneficial influence they otherwise have, may also incidentally disrupt human learning.

Electroconvulsive Treatment (ECT)

There are already available three excellent summaries of this topic. Campbell (1961) has made a general review of the psychological effects of ECT, and Brengelmann (1959) and Williams (1966) have dealt with its effects on memory. A brief account of a few of the more systematic studies should suffice to show what this kind of intervention can teach us about human learning dysfunction.

The treatment called ECT was launched in psychiatry by Cerletti and Bini (1938). There are now many methods used to produce general convulsions by passing a brief electric current through the human brain, usually as a treatment for depression. One method has been described by Kalinowsky (1967) as follows:

> "In the standard technique, electrodes are applied to both temples . . . Skin resistance must be decreased by a salt water solution or with the safer method of electro-jelly, similar to the one used in electrocardiography. The amount of current applied by the originators of the method was 70 to 130 volts for 0.1 to 0.5 seconds. Attempts have been made to measure the actual amount of current that passes through the brain, but the amounts found varied between 200 and 1600 milliamperes" (1967, p. 1279).

The passage of electricity induces a generalized convulsion—nowadays commonly controlled or modified by the administration of an anaesthetic and a muscle relaxant—the patient being rendered unconscious. The immediate behavioral effects of unmodified ECT were in some ways not unlike the ones of concussion. The patient usually awoke in a transiently confused, disoriented state (Lunn & Trolle, 1949) and might complain of memory disturbance (Holland, 1950). Glueck, Reiss, and Bernard (1957) have stated that if these treatments are given with sufficient frequency over a sufficiently long period of time (for example, 3 times a day for about 10 days) patients can be "regressed" into a state much resembling senile dementia. Cameron, Lohrenz, and Handcock (1962), however, have disputed the use of the term "regression" and insist that a disturbance of memory is here the central phenomenon.

Whatever may be the mode of therapeutic action of ECT on the depressive conditions for which it is usually administered, these latter observations certainly suggest a direct effect of shock on human learning processes. Taken together with information on the effects of unilateral ECT (v.i.), they cast much doubt on the views of workers like Bogoch (1954) who have contended that shock may merely serve to reduce the availability in recall of events associated with negative affect.

Foremost among studies of the effects of ECT are the ones that have been reported from Sweden by B. Cronholm and his associates.

Cronholm and Ottosson (1963a) have described the three main tests they have used to examine different aspects of learning after ECT, as follows.

The 30 word pair test. This comprises three lists of ten stimulus-response word pairs. Each list is read once and then recall demanded on presentation of the stimulus words. The first recall takes place immediately and then delayed recall is requested three hours afterwards.

The 20 figures test. This is a picture containing twenty line drawings; these are first exposed to the subject who is then required to pick them out from a larger array in which they appear together with thirty other drawings. Again, immediate and delayed recognition are both required.

Short story test. This involves the reading of a brief story, on the content of which twenty-five questions are asked, again, both immediately and three hours later.

From these items were taken inferential measures of learning, retention, and forgetting. "Learning" scores come from the degree of accuracy of immediate reproduction. "Retention" involves the quotient of delayed report over immediate recall. "Forgetting" is obtained by subtracting delayed report from immediate recall.

The first investigations of this group dealt with learning impairment *after* ECT. Cronholm and Molander (1957) described the results from 24 patients who were given one form of their test battery some days before the first ECT and an alternative form six hours after a second electroshock. A non-shock control group of 12 patients was also tested. The experimental group was significantly worse postshock on the learning variable for both the word pair and the figures test. It was also worse in terms of retention and forgetting for all three tests. Similar effects six hours after the first treatment were reported by Ottosson (1960a).

Cronholm and Blomquist (1959) then tested 30 patients with one form of the test battery a few days before the initial ECT, and with the second form one week after the last electroshock treatment of a series. There was a decrease in retention and an increase in forgetting in the word pair test one week after electroshock.

Cronholm and Molander (1964) then examined the performance of 28 patients one day before and then a month after the last treatment of a series. In none of the measures studied was there any decline found one month after the termination of treatment.

These results suggest that, for the post-shock period, any effect on "learning" (that is, immediate reproduction) occurs close to the time of shock. At greater distances in time between shock and learning the effect remains on "retention" and "forgetting," but even this diminishes with longer intervals between treatment and testing. Cronholm and Ottosson (1961), in fact, conclude that, as defined by their measures, the depressive state itself mainly impairs learning, while ECT mainly impairs retention. Thus, when a depressive state has been alleviated by ECT, learning is improved, whereas—initially at least—retention is impaired. They further note (Cronholm & Ottosson, 1963b) that the recovered depressed patient is more likely to attend to the immediate aspect of performance and report improvement in memory, even while his retention is objectively poorer.

Given the present state of our knowledge concerning the measurement of human learning functions, no final decision can be made about the appropriateness of particular tests, nor can agreement necessarily be reached about particular functions that may underlie specific performance. The way in which these Scandinavian authors stipulatively define "learning" and "retention," however, might not appeal to all investigators. For example, it would be possible to contend that the time they allow between "immediate reproduction" and "delayed reproduction" is simply one that permits of a period of consolidation, which therefore could be held to be impaired shortly after the administration of ECT.

This latter view fits in with other observations made by Cronholm and his co-workers. As has been noted in our consideration of concussion, it is not only the recording of events *after* trauma that is impaired. Prior events are also affected, and the nearer they are to the moment of trauma the more they are affected.

Cronholm and Molander (1961) studied three groups (one ECT, one drug control, and one untreated control group of 16 subjects each.) All groups were tested on the first day before any treatment was given on the standard three tests described above. In this case, there was a six-hour delay between immediate and delayed reproduction. The same procedure was followed on the next day, but within the first hour after initial testing the members of one group got ECT and those in the second group got the drug treatment. These authors describe their results as follows:

> "In all three tests performances were much worse six hours after learning at the second day of examination in Group 1, where an ECS was interpolated one hour after learning. The same holds true of the scores for forgetting. In the other groups there were only small differences between these performances at the first and second day of examination" (1961, p. 88).

A more extensive study of the consolidation hypothesis has been reported by Cronholm and Lagergren (1959) who studied the recall of a single number that had been presented 5 or 15 or 60 seconds before administration of electroshock. After he recovered consciousness the patient was asked at intervals (initially about every 10 minutes) to say what number he had been asked to remember. Rapidity of recall was measured by the increase of the proportion of patients reproducing the number correctly. There were, unfortunately, no precautions taken in this study against mere guesswork in the reproduction of the correct number. Various nosological groups were tested, and Figure 4.8 shows the results for a mixed group of psychoneurotics and endogenously depressed patients.

These authors concluded that,

> ". . . our findings indicate that a memory trace is weakened more when the learning-shock interval is short, that recovery takes place at the same rate independent of this interval, that recovery ceases about 160 min. after ECS, and that the memory trace reaches a lower final level when the learning-shock (interval) is short. Our findings and conclusions are in line with the hypothesis that for some time after learning a process is going on, usually called consolidation, that makes memory traces less sensitive to disturbance" (1959, p. 306).

These findings supplement, in a more controlled and systematic way, the clinical observations of the learning defects found in concussion. Furthermore, results suggest

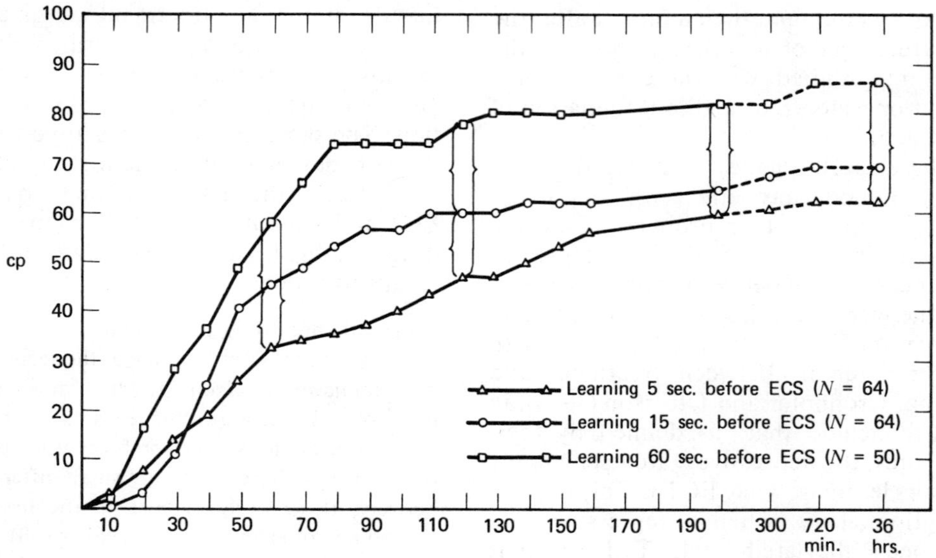

Figure 4.8 Cumulative percentages of patients having recalled the number learned before ECS relative to the time after ECS in the combined group of psychoneurosis and endogenous depression. (From Cronholm and Lagergren, 1959.)

that these defects and the therapeutic action of ECT on depressive symptoms may be relatively independent. Ottosson (1960b) summarized the findings of a very careful set of experiments as follows,

"By an experimental approach which allows variation of the stimulus intensity while the seizure discharge is under experimental control and, further, of a well defined alteration of the seizure discharge without interference with other effects of the electrical stimulation, it has thus been shown that the ECT effects studied arise through different mechanisms. The therapeutic, depression relieving effect and the EEG changes following treatment are mainly dependent on the seizure activity, whereas the memory disturbance is to a great extent dependent on other effects of the electrical stimulation" (1960b, p. 141).

One particular adaptation of ECT, namely unilateral treatment, gives further evidence of this independence and also provides more information about the possible mechanisms underlying the effects of shock on learning.

The technique of placing both electrodes on the same side of the head instead of bilaterally seems to have been first described by Friedman and Wilcox (1942), however, they were mainly concerned to show that their method could also produce major convulsions, and they did not comment on comparative effects. Blaurock, Lorimer, Segal, and Gibbs (1950) compared bilateral and unilateral ECT (left side versus right) in groups of paranoid schizophrenics and found most improvement in the right-side group. Perhaps, in light of the later evidence to be reviewed, this apparent improvement, in fact, may have been the result of a lesser degree of confusion produced by the shock in the case of the latter group. Impastato and Pacella (1952) further described the technique and also found (Pacella & Impastato, 1954) less memory disturbance and disorientation with unilateral shock. Lancaster, Steinert, and Frost (1958) specifically examined this effect of bilateral versus unilateral shock on depressive symptoms and on memory test scores. They found no difference in the therapeutic action but found a much less disrupting effect of the unilateral shock on memory function. They chose the nondominant side of the head only because they believed that any damage here would not be so important as damage to the dominant side. A larger series was similarly tested by Cannicott (1962), who has described his technique in some detail (Cannicott, 1963). He confirmed that unilateral ECT alleviated depression but caused less memory impairment. Confirmation of this finding has also come from a study by Martin, Ford, McDanald, and Towler (1965). Cannicott and Waggoner (1967) have also carried out systematic investigations of the difference between the two shock techniques, by using tests of immediate and recent memory and by stimulating only the nondominant side. Again, the bilateral group was found to be worse on the memory tests than the unilateral group. They also reported confusion and disorientation in a patient shocked on the dominant side in error.

The crucial contribution of the actual *side* of unilateral stimulation to learning deficit has been neatly demonstrated by Zamora and Kaelbling (1965). They observed that none of the previous studies could reveal whether the lesser dysmnesic effect of unilateral shock was because of the fact that only one side of the brain bore the brunt of the electrical stimulation, or whether dominance was the decisive factor. In view of Ottosson's (1960b) conclusions, it may even have been the lesser amount of electrical stimulation itself that produced the difference. Accordingly, they examined 28 patients on a 12-item battery of tests for cerebral dominance and on the Wechsler Memory Scale (Wechsler, 1945), excluding the visual items. This scale was again given after the fifth shock treatment. All the patients proved to be right-handed, and half were shocked on the dominant (that is, left) and half on the nondominant (that is, right) side. It was found that, although the groups were not significantly different *before* treatment, the dominant shock group was significantly impaired on the memory scale as compared with the nondominant group after treatment. There was no difference in the clinical improvement rate for the two groups. Confirmation of these findings has come from the clinical assessment of changes after bilateral and nondominant unilateral ECT by Impastato and Karliner (1966) who found just as much improvement in depression by using unilateral ECT but less memory disturbance and confusion. A study by Gottlieb and Wilson (1965) has shown reduced speed of recall of verbal material after dominant, unilateral ECT.[2]

Despite the fact that these studies have often lacked desirable controls (for example, double-blind design, objective assessments of recovery, and the like) these data carry some very interesting implications for further study. First, they suggest that the so-called memory impairment produced by ECT can be separated from its therapeutic action. Second, they cast grave doubt on the notion that shock-produced avoidance is in itself the reason for the failure of human performance that comes to be labeled as memory disorder after ECT. Third, they reinforce the notion that structures on the dominant side of the brain in man, perhaps mainly in the region of the temporal lobe, have a crucial part to play in at least some aspects of human learning. Fourth, they again support the view that the phase of transition of information from short-term to long-term storage, via some process of consolidation, is one particularly vulnerable to disruption. Finally, they confirm that there is a critical need for the objective analytic study of human learning functions whose disturbance may issue in the kind of product clinically labeled as memory disorder.

The studies we consider next give ample support to at least some of these conclusions.

Temporal Lobectomy

The role played by the temporal lobes and their underlying structures in human learning has now been frequently emphasized. They have been accorded importance by Brierley (1961; 1966a; 1966b) and by Ojemann (1966) in their general reviews of brain lesions associated with disorders of human learning. The effect of temporal lobe lesions has been summarized by Milner (1966). Particular attention has been paid to the role of the hippocampus in learning by Barbizet (1963) and by Meissner (1966). This section will only deal briefly with two complementary sets of studies of temporal lobe lesions that carry important implications for the further exploration of human learning disorder.

Temporal lobectomy in man has most often been carried out for the relief of attacks of psychomotor epilepsy (Gibbs, Gibbs, & Fuster, 1948) when these attacks have been triggered by an abnormal functioning of one or other temporal lobe, and

---

[2]A more comprehensive and up-to-date review of the effects of different sites of electrode placement in ECT has been published by the author (Inglis 1969).

when these fits have proved insusceptible to control by drugs (Hill, 1953). The surgical procedures used have been described by Penfield and Baldwin (1952) and by Falconer (1953).

It had long been known (Bekhterev, 1900; Kolodny, 1928; Keschner, Bender, & Strauss, 1936) that memory disorder might accompany tissue damage in the temporal lobes. It remained, however, for the systematic clinical observation of two cases described by Milner and Penfield (1955) and Penfield and Milner (1958) to show that unilateral temporal lobectomy, carried out on the side of the brain dominant for speech, could result in a drastic defect of recent memory. These authors inferred that such general defects must have been because of additional accompanying pathology of the opposite lobe; this has been confirmed in one of these cases at postmortem (Milner, 1966).

Meanwhile, more specific learning defects were being found by other investigators. Thus, Meyer and Yates (1955) described the effects of temporal lobectomy on 18 cases, account being taken both of the side of the lesion and also brain dominance for speech, right-handed patients being regarded as left-brain dominant. Of these 18 cases, 11 had surgery in the dominant hemisphere, 6 in the nondominant hemisphere, the remaining case was said to be of "doubtful" dominance. In this study, two kinds of learning tests were given; the New Word Learning and Retention Test (Shapiro & Nelson, 1955) and the Paired Associate Learning Test from the Wechsler Memory Scale (Wechsler, 1945). The patients were first tested about a week before, and retested about one month after the operation.

The results on tests of learning and retention were quite striking and systematic, as can be seen from Table 4.9. This is a consolidated version of a number of Meyer and Yates' (1955) separate tables. The dominant cases alone showed a marked impairment of learning one month after operation. They took more trials to learn up to a set criterion, and they retained less of this learning after an interval. Four dominant cases were again retested one year after the operation and still showed the learning defect. The nondominant cases showed no such defects.

A more extensive investigation was then carried out by Meyer (1959), with the following aims.

First, it was necessary to determine if the learning defect was specific to the single modality through which the material to be learned had been presented. Both tests had involved only the auditory modality. It was therefore necessary to determine if other kinds of learning tests (for example, visual, tactual) would also show defects.

Second, it remained to be seen if the learning difficulty was specific to the single kind of material used. Both tests used had been verbal in content. It was not known how the same patients would perform with, for example, pictorial material.

The recall mode of reproduction might be more difficult for a patient with expressive dysphasia than the recognition of

Table 4.9 Results on the Learning and Retention Tests before and after Temporal Lobectomy

	Dominant Group Means					Nondominant Group Means				
	N	*Pre*	*Post*	*t*	*p*	*N*	*Pre*	*Post*	*t*	*p*
New Word Test										
Learning scores	6	10.67	41.33	3.155	.01	2	6.5	5.5	—	NS
Retention scores (after 24 hours)		4.00	1.83	4.255	.001		5.0	5.0	—	NS
Wechsler Paired Associates										
Easy pairs	6	5.67	4.17	2.680	$< .05$	2	6.00	6.00	—	NS
Hard pairs		3.00	0.17	5.896	.001		4.00	4.00	—	NS

Source. Meyer and Yates, 1955.

correct responses and this factor had to be taken into account.

Meyer (1959) designed a number of different kinds of learning tests to examine these problems. They are as follows.

Auditory Verbal Recall, (*A.V.R.*). This paired associate learning test requires the subject to learn 8 pairs of words to a criterion of 3 consecutive correct responses and involves auditory presentation and the recall mode of response reproduction.

Auditory Verbal Recognition (*A.V.Rg.*). This subtest uses material similar to the A.V.R. test, but involves the recognition mode of response reproduction. This subtest investigated the notion that expressive dysphasia might produce poor results on the A.V.R. test, since this disorder mainly impairs the capacity for the spontaneous recall of words.

Visual Verbal Recognition, (*V.V.Rg.*). These items resemble the A.V.Rg. test, but both stimulus and response words are each printed on separate cards that are shown to the subject. It was used to enable the effect of verbal material to be distinguished from the effect of auditory presentation.

Visual Design Recognition, (*V.D.Rg.*). This test involves the association of 5 pairs of designs by the same means as the V.V.Rg. subtest. It involves the visual modality without involving words.

Visual Design Recall, (*V.D.R.*). These items, 6 pairs in all, require the subject to reproduce simple abstract designs as responses to stimuli provided by line drawings of common objects.

Tactile Design Recognition, (*T.D.Rg.*). This test requires the subject, while blindfolded, to associate pairs of simple wire patterns and to recognize the correct response from the series of responses while holding the stimulus object in his preferred hand.

The New Word Learning and Retention Test (Shapiro and Nelson, 1955), on which the original deficit had been shown, was also given.

In this study, 25 temporal lobectomy patients were tested; 14 were dominant cases, and 11 were nondominant. The preoperative testing took place from 1 to 28 days before the operation. Retesting was carried out from 20 to 35 days after the operation. Seventeen of the subjects (10 dominant and 7 nondominant) were tested yet again 11 to 15 months after the operation.

One month after the operation, no significant difference in learning scores was found in the nondominant group. In the dominant group, however, the results on the learning tests were indeed striking. The New Word Learning Test, as before, showed gross postoperative impairment. The same type of impairment was reflected in both the Auditory Verbal Recall and the Auditory Verbal Recognition subtests. These results suggested that expressive dysphasia alone could not account for the apparent learning deficit, since recognition as well as recall was affected. The Visual Verbal Recognition test, moreover, was apparently unaffected by the operation in this group. In other words, it did *not* appear that the verbal nature of the material alone could account for deficit after operation. The lack of impairment in any of the other subtests also suggested that the impairment was, in fact, restricted to verbal learning in the auditory modality.

For the one-year postoperative retest, no retest differences were found in the nondominant group. The performance of the dominant group was *still* significantly impaired on the learning tests that involved the auditory modality. This result was again contrary to the notion that dysphasia could explain these results, since all dysphasic symptoms had remitted after a year.

Meyer's (1959) study showed that the main effect of dominant temporal lobectomy in human patients is a verbal learning defect specific to the auditory modality. This disability, unlike transient dysphasia and visual field defects, was shown to be present one year (and, on one case, also four years) after the operation. Since the dominant cases could learn to associate verbal material when this was presented visually, this suggested that the content of learning was not crucial.

In a parallel but independent investigation, Milner (1958) obtained data from testing 30 temporal lobe cases, all left-brain speech dominant. Half of this group were operated on in the left (dominant) temporal lobe, half in the right (nondominant) temporal lobe; all were tested before and about three weeks after the operation.

After dominant temporal lobectomy Milner (1958) also reported defects of learning. She, however, held them to be defects specific to verbal material and found them to exist before the operation and to be exacerbated afterward. They were shown by results obtained on the Wechsler Memory Scale (1945). This is a poor test for any analytic purposes since it contains such a mixture of heterogeneous items; it tests old and new learning, verbal and nonverbal learning and also confounds verbal material and the auditory mode of presentation. Milner chose to show the learning defect, however, by comparing the mean scores of her various groups on the Wechsler Intelligence Scale (Wechsler, 1944) with their mean scores on the Wechsler Memory Scale (Wechsler, 1945).

Analysis of variance confirmed that the dominant temporal lobe group was significantly worse in IQ minus MQ scores than either of the other two groups. Milner (1958) realized that the overall Wechsler Memory Scale score could not be held convincingly to demonstrate a specific verbal defect. She noted, therefore, that the dominant group did not show impairment on such nonverbal items as the "Memory-for-designs" subtest. Furthermore, she found the greatest differences between the groups on the "Logical memory" subtest, in which subjects are required to recall as many elements as possible of a brief narrative after it has been read aloud to them. In addition to the usual immediate recall, she required delayed recall from her subjects about one and one-half hours after they had heard the story. Milner reported a preoperative difference between the groups significant at well beyond the .001 level. She also later (Milner, 1962) reported similar data both before *and* after the operation for 15 dominant cases and, for these few patients, found that learning ability was still impaired years after the operation.

These results supply a substantial confirmation of Meyer's findings that dominant temporal lobectomy in man produces a defect of learning. Milner's conclusion that this is an impairment of *verbal* learning is not, however, as convincingly supported by the data, as was Meyer's conclusion that the defect is one of verbal learning in the auditory modality, since the tests Milner used confound material and modality. It is, however, of great interest that even so heterogeneous a test as the Wechsler Memory Scale showed a defect to exist even before operation, a fact not ascertained by Meyer's more analytic paired associate items.

It has been found by Kimura (1963) that right temporal lobe cases show greater difficulty than left temporal lobe patients both in the immediate tachistoscopic perception, and in the recognition of previously presented, unfamiliar visual designs. Additional defects in memory for tonal patterns (Milner, 1962), for visually- (Milner, 1965) and proprioceptively-guided (Corkin, 1965) stylus-maze learning have also been reported following surgery of the nondominant temporal lobe.

General, gross memory impairment is usually clinically evident after bilateral temporal resection in human patients. Such cases have been described by Scoville and Milner (1957) and by Milner (1959). The particularly deleterious effect of bilateral removal might, perhaps, be due to two factors. In the first place, if the dominant lobe is removed, then the minor lobe may still to some extent be able to compensate directly for the consequent defects by some process of transfer of auditory learning ability between the two lobes. It may be that the dominant-side patients who only suffer from an auditory learning defect also partly compensate for this by coming to rely more heavily on, for example, visual cues and other aids to new learning. Removal of both the nondominant *and* the dominant lobe would rob the patient both of the possibility of transfer and of the possibility of substituting one kind of cue for another, thus resulting in the crippling, generalized memory disorder which has been reported in cases of bilateral temporal lobe removal.

These studies, then, provide us with direct evidence of the crucial contribution made by the temporal lobes and their underlying structures to learning in man. They also illustrate the need for an analytic approach to so-called memory disorder and accordingly make an indispensable contribution to the conclusions suggested by this review. Tasks must deal with modes of perception, type of perceptual input, and means of reproduction that may all have a crucial part to play in the detection and description of disorders.

CONCLUSIONS

It is evident from the data reviewed that "memory disorder" is a descriptive term of the coarsest kind. It may even be misleading insofar as it directs attention toward simple forgetting and treats of learning in terms derived from faculty psychology. In the analysis of defective behavioral processes, of which deranged memory may appear as the disordered product, we must bear in mind the complexity of those functions that underlie the chain of events involved in the read-in, storage, and output of information by any organism, not least by man.

The defects in the learning chain that produce this kind of behavior disorder do not always necessarily affect the same link in this chain, nor indeed is there any good reason for supposing that only one link at a time need be solely affected. Many of the findings, however, secured from very diverse measures of different conditions, suggest that the stage between prehension or primary memory and entry into longer-term storage is one that is peculiarly vulnerable to trauma and disease and even to the effects of some drugs (Overton, 1967) in man. Any test that we wish to construct or use for the more exact description of such disorders should certainly attend to this fact.

Much of what is clinically labeled as memory disorder would be more appropriately described as learning disorder. New events may impinge on the patient and even be clearly perceived by him, but they fail to make a lasting impression. When stored knowledge is called for, patients with such a disorder must make do with knowledge stored *before* the recording process broke down. The normal individual adjusts his behavior from moment to moment in terms of past information, anticipating what is to come from what has already taken place. The patient suffering from learning disorder, on the other hand, may not be able to call on the crucial behavioral supports derived from the internal maintenance of cues from the recent past and, hence, may even come to be disoriented in both time and space.

It need not be supposed that the integrity of any part of the sequence of learning is necessarily affected by disease or injury in an all-or-none manner. We must allow for the possibility of partial damage as well as for total destruction. Tasks designed to study any defective components of the human learning sequence must allow for normal variance as well as for the abnormal range of dysfunction.

Allowance must also be made for the possibility of discrete dysfunction in the different learning systems in man. This contention is well illustrated by the findings from studies of the effects of temporal lobectomy. Defects may exist in the sphere of auditory-verbal learning that do not exist for other materials or other modalities. Milner (1966) has even found that one of her temporal lobectomy cases with clinically apparent gross disorder was nevertheless able to learn a mirror-drawing task, although he would fail to recognize the apparatus from occasion to occasion. This same patient has been studied in an operant situation by Sidman, Stoddard, and Mohr (1966), who found him able to learn a visual discrimination task that he was quite unable to describe verbally after subsequent interruption. Clinical anecdotes about drastically memory disordered patients who were chary of the repetition of traumatic events like ECT (Barbizet, 1963) or even remembered the vicariously experienced misery of others (Talland, 1965) must also be borne in mind.

Emphasis deserves to be laid on the need for an analytic approach to the description of learning disorders in man. Here, as in other areas of dysfunction, it may be argued (Inglis, 1966) that major advances are likely to come mainly from a *direct* attack on the measurement and manipulation of disordered behaviors. There is little to be gained, and much to be lost, by the creation of further psychological tests founded on diagnostic guesswork. Data from the temporal lobe studies alone are sufficient to show the futility of talking about "brain damage" as if this were a unitary entity.

In spite of the danger of false inference that may arise when the psychologist tries to relate behavioral measures to etiological factors, interesting clues about important brain-behavior relationships have begun to emerge from studies of memory disorder. In all the conditions in which learning dysfunction in man appears as a significant element, there also often appears evidence to indict malfunctioning of the temporal lobes and their underlying structures. This is not to claim that these regions are in any sense the site of storage. Their integrity, however, seems vital for the maintenance of the cycle of recording; perhaps more especially for the transfer of learning from a temporary to a more permanent store.

If broad guidelines for future developments are to be specified, what we require are sensitive measures of all of the various phases or stages of the learning processes, transmissable through the whole range of sensory modalities and susceptible to various methods of reproduction. They should sample, too, a wide band of the spectrum of material that may be handled by any single sense. These measures should be capable of detecting, not simply breakdown, but the whole range of variation in function. They should not be dependent on the prior determination of what commonly prove to be quite nonspecific nosological classifications of disordered persons.

None of the tests or batteries of tests discussed in this review fulfil all, or even many of these criteria. If a guess had to be made, it would seem that the developments and adaptations of operant principles being pioneered by such workers as Gedye (1967) and Sidman, Stoddard and Mohr (1966) hold most promise for our purpose. We still seem to stand, however, only at the very threshold of our work.

REFERENCES

Adams, R. D. Nutritional diseases of the nervous system. *Trans. Amer. Clin. Climatol. Assoc.*, 1959, **71**, 59–93.

Adams, R. D., Collins, G. H., & Victor, M. Troubles de la memoire et de l'apprentissage chez l'homme: leurs relations avec des lésions des lobes temporaux et du diencéphale. In, *Physiologie de l'hippocampe*. Paris; Centre Nationale de la Recherche Scientifique, 1962.

Allison, R. S. *The senile brain: a clinical study*. Baltimore; Williams and Wilkins, 1962.

Aslan, Anna. The therapeutics of old age: the action of procaine. In, H. T. Blumenthal (ed.), *Aging around the world: medical and clinical aspects of aging*. New York: Columbia Univ. Press, 1962.

Ballard, P. B. Obliviscence and reminiscence. *Brit. J. Psychol. Monogr. Supp.* 1913, No 2.

Barbizet, J. Defect of memorizing of hippocampal-mammillary origin: a review. *J. neurol. neurosurg. Psychiat.*, 1963, **26**, 127–135.

Barnes, R. H., Busse, E. W., & Friedman, E. L. Psychological functioning of aged individuals with normal and abnormal electroencephalograms II. A study of hospitalized individuals. *J. nerv. ment. Dis.*, 1956, **124**, 585–593.

Beaulieu, C., & Solyom, L. The Counting Test: a test for measuring short term retention. Unpublished manuscript: McGill University, 1963.

Bekhterev, V. M. Demonstration eines Gehirns mit Zerstörung der vorderen und inneren Theile der Hirnrinde beider Schläfenlappen. *Neurol. Zentbl.*, 1900, **19**, 990–991.

Betlheim, S., & Hartmann, H. On parapraxes in the Korsakow psychosis. In, D. Rapaport (ed.) *Organization and pathology of thought*. New York, Columbia Univ. Press, 1951.

Blaurock, M. F., Lorimer, F. M., Segal, M. M., & Gibbs, F. A. Focal electroencephalographic changes in unilateral electric convulsion therapy. *Arch. Neurol. Psychiat.*, 1950, **64**, 220–226.

Bogoch, S. A preliminary study of post-shock amnesia by Amytal interview., *Amer. J. Psychiat.*, 1954, **111**, 108–111.

Bonhöffer, K. *Die akuten Geisteskrankheiten der Gewohnheitstrinker*. Jena: Fischer, 1901.

Brazier, Mary A. B. (ed.) *Brain function, Vol II: RNA and brain function memory and learning*. Los Angeles: Univ. California Press, 1964.

Brengelmann, J. C. *The effect of repeated electroshock on learning in depressives*. New York: Springer, 1959.

Brierley, J. B. Clinico-pathological correlations in amnesia. *Geront. clin.*, 1961, **3**, 97–109.

Brierley, J. B. The neuropathology of amnesic states. In, C. W. M. Whitty and O. L. Zangwill (eds.) *Amnesia*. London, Butterworths, 1966a.

Brierley, J. B. Some aspects of the disorders of memory due to brain damage. In, D. Richter (ed.) *Aspects of learning and memory*. New York: Basic Books, 1966b.

Broadbent, D. E. Immediate memory and simultaneous stimuli. *Quart. J. exp. Psychol.*, 1957, **9**, 1–11.

Broadbent, D. E. *Perception and communication*. London: Pergamon Press, 1958.

Busse, E. W. Findings from the Duke geriatrics research project on the effects of aging upon the nervous system. In, H. T. Blumenthal (ed.) *Aging around the world: medical and clinical aspects of aging*. New York: Columbia Univ. Press, 1962.

Busse, E. W., Barnes, R. H., Friedman, E. L., & Kelty, E. J. Psychological functioning of aged individuals with normal and abnormal electroencephalograms. I. A study of non-hospitalized community volunteers. *J. nerv. ment. Dis.*, 1956, **124**, 135–141.

Caird, W. K., & Hannah, F. Short-term memory disorder in elderly psychiatric patients. *Dis. nerv. System*, 1964, **25**, 564–568.

Caird, W. K., & Inglis, J. The short-term storage of auditory and visual two-channel digits by elderly patients with memory disorder. *J. ment. Sci.* 1961, **107**, 1062–1069.

Caird, W. K., Sanderson, R. E., & Inglis, J. Cross-validation of a learning test for use with elderly psychiatric patients *J. ment. Sci.* 1962, **108**, 368–370.

Cameron, D. E. The use of nucleic acid in aged patients with memory impairment. *Amer. J. Psychiat.* 1958, **114**, 943.

Cameron, D. E. The processes of remembering. *Brit. J. Psychiat.*, 1963, **109**, 325–340.

Cameron, D. E. Evolving concepts of memory. Presidential Address to the Society of Biological Psychiatry, Washington, D.C., June 1966.

Cameron, D. E., Kral, V. A., Solyom, L., Sved, S., Wainrib, B., Beaulieu, C., & Enesco, H. RNA and memory. In, J. Gaito (ed.) *Macromolecules and behavior*. New York: Appleton-Century-Crofts, 1966.

Cameron, D. E., Lohrenz, J. G., & Handcock, K. A. The depatterning treatment of schizophrenia. *Comprehensive Psychiat.*, 1962, **3**, 65–76.

Cameron, D. E., & Solyom, L. Effects of ribonucleic acid on memory. *Geriatrics*, 1961, **16**, 74–81.

Cameron, D. E., Solyom, L., & Beach, L. Further studies upon the effects of the administration of ribonucleic acid in aged patients suffering from memory (retention) failure. In, E. Rothlin (ed.) *Neuro-psychopharmacology*. Amsterdam: Elsevier, 1961.

Cameron, D. E., Solyom, L., Sved, S., & Wainrib, B. Effects of intravenous administration of ribonucleic acid upon failure of memory for recent events in pre-senile and aged individuals. In, J. Wortis (ed.) *Recent advances in biological psychiatry*. New York, Plenum Press, 1963.

Cameron, D. E., Sved, S., Solyom, L., & Wainrib, B. Ribonucleic acid in psychiatric therapy. In, J. H. Masserman (ed.) *Current psychiatric therapies*. New York: Grune & Stratton, 1964.

Cameron, D. E., Sved, S., Solyom, L., Wainrib, B., & Barik, H. Effects of ribonucleic acid on memory defect in the aged. *Amer. J. Psychiat.*, 1963, **120**, 320–325.

Campbell, D. The psychological effects of cerebral electroshock. In, H. J. Eysenck (ed.) *Handbook of abnormal psychology: an experimental approach*. New York: Basic Books, 1961.

Cannicott, S. M. Unilateral electroconvulsive therapy. *Postgrad. med. J.*, 1962, **38**, 451–459.

Cannicott, S. M. The technique of unilateral electroconvulsive therapy. *Amer. J. Psychiat.*, 1963, **120**, 477–480.

Cannicott, S. M., & Waggoner, R. W. Unilateral and bilateral electroconvulsive therapy; a comparative study. *Arch. gen. Psychiat.*, 1967, **16**, 229–232.

Cerletti, U., & Bini, L. L'elettroshock. *Arch. gen. Neurol. Psichiat. Psicoanal.*, 1938, **19**, 266–268.

Chorover, S. L. Comments on McGaugh's "Facilitation and impairment of memory storage processes." In, D. P. Kimble (ed.) *The anatomy of memory*. Palo Alto, Calif; Science and Behavior Books, Inc., 1965.

Conkey, Ruth C. Psychological changes associated with head injuries. *Arch. Psychol.*, 1938, No. 232.
Corkin, Suzanne. Tactually-guided maze learning in man: effects of unilateral cortical excisions and bilateral hippocampal lesions. *Neuropsychologia*, 1965, **3**, 339–352.
Corsellis, J. A. N. *Mental illness and the aging brain: the distribution of pathological change in a mental hospital population.* London: Oxford Univ. Press, 1962.
Courville, C. B. *Commotio cerebri*, Los Angeles: San Lucas Press, 1953.
Cronholm, B., & Blomquist, C. Memory disturbances after electroconvulsive therapy. 2. Conditions one week after a series of treatments. *Acta psychiat. neurol. Scand.*, 1959, **34**, 18–25.
Cronholm, B., & Lagergren, A. Memory disturbances after electroconvulsive therapy. 3. An experimental study of retrograde amnesia after electroconvulsive shock., *Acta psychiat. neurol. Scand.*, 1959, **34**, 283–310.
Cronholm, B., & Molander, L. Memory disturbances after electroconvulsive therapy. 1. Conditions 6 hours after electroshock treatment. *Acta psychiat. neurol. Scand.*, 1957, **32**, 280–306.
Cronholm, B., & Molander, L. Memory disturbances after electroconvulsive therapy. 4. Influence of an interpolated electroconvulsive shock on retention of memory material. *Acta psychiat. neurol. Scand.*, 1961, **36**, 83–90.
Cronholm, B., & Molander, L. Memory disturbances after electroconvulsive therapy. 5. Conditions one month after a series of treatments. *Acta psychiat. Scand.*, 1964, **40**, 212–216.
Cronholm, B., & Ottosson, J-O. Memory functions in endogenous depression before and after electroconvulsive therapy. *Arch. gen. Psychiat.*, 1961, **5**, 193–199.
Cronholm, B., & Ottosson, J-O. Reliability and validity of a memory test battery. *Acta psychiat. Scand.*, 1963a, **39**, 218–234.
Cronholm, B., & Ottosson, J-O. The experience of memory function after electroconvulsive therapy. *Brit. J. Psychiat.*, 1963b, **109**, 251–258.
Delay, J., & Brion, S. Syndrome de Korsakoff et corps mamillaires. *Encéphale*, 1954, **43**, 193–200.
Denny-Brown, D., & Russell, W. R. Experimental cerebral concussion. *Brain*, 1941, **64**, 93–164.
Deutsch, J. A. Higher nervous function: the physiological basis of memory. *Annu. Rev. Physiol.*, 1962, **24**, 259–286.
Ellis, N. R. (ed.) *Handbook of mental deficiency: psychological theory and research.* New York; McGraw Hill, 1963.
Enesco, Hildegard E. RNA and memory: a re-evaluation of present data. *Canad. Psychiat. Assoc. J.* 1967, **12**, 29–34.
Falconer, M. A. Discussion on the surgery of temporal lobe epilepsy: surgical and pathological aspects. *Proc. Roy. Soc. Med.*, 1953, **46**, 971–974.
Friedman, E., & Wilcox, P. H. Electrostimulated convulsive doses in intact humans by means of unidirectional currents. *J. nerv. ment. Dis.*, 1942, **96**, 56–63.
Gedye, J. L. A teaching machine programme for use as a test of learning ability. *Proceedings of a Programmed Learning Conference, Loughborough, England, April 1966.* London: Methuen, 1967.
Gibbs, E. L., Gibbs, F. A., & Fuster, B. Psychomotor epilepsy. *Arch. Neurol. Psychiat.*, 1948, **60**, 331–339.
Gillespie, R. D. Amnesia: component functions in remembering. *Brit. med. J.*, 1936, **2**, 1179–1183.
Glasky, A. J., & Simon, L. N. Magnesium pemoline: enhancement of brain RNA polymerases. *Science*, 1966, **151**, 702–703.
Glickman, S. E. Perseverative neural processes and consolidation of the memory trace. *Psychol. Bull.*, 1961, **58**, 218–233.
Glueck, B. C., Reiss, H., & Bernard, L. E. Regressive electric shock therapy: preliminary report on 100 cases. *Psychiat. Quart.*, 1957, **31**, 117–136.
Gottlieb, G., & Wilson, I. Cerebral dominance: temporary disruption of verbal memory

by unilateral electroconvulsive shock treatment. *J. comp. physiol. Psychol.*, 1965, **60**, 368–372.

Gruner, J. E. Sur la pathologie des encephalopathies alcooliques. *Revue Neurol.*, 1956, **94**, 682–689.

Hebb, D. O. *The organization of behavior: a neuropsychological theory*. New York: Wiley, 1949.

Hill, D. Discussion on the surgery of temporal lobe epilepsy: the clinical study and selection of patients. *Proc. Roy. Soc. Med.*, 1953, **46**, 965–971.

Holbourn, A. H. S. Mechanics of head injury. *Lancet*, 1943, **2**, 438–441.

Holland, C. G. The complaint of "forgetting" following electroshock. *Virginia med. Monthly*, 1950, **77**, 221–226.

Hull, C. L. The formation and retention of associations among the insane. *Amer. J. Psychol.* 1917, **28**, 419–435.

Impastato, D. J., & Karliner, W. Control of memory impairment in EST by unilateral stimulation of the non-dominant hemisphere. *Dis. nerv. System*, 1966, **27**, 182–188.

Impastato, D. J., & Pacella, B. L. Electrically produced unilateral convulsions (a new method of electrocerebrotherapy). *Dis. nerv. System*, 1952, **13**, 368–369.

Inglis, J. An experimental study of learning and "memory function" in elderly psychiatric patients. *J. ment. Sci.*, 1957, **103**, 796–803.

Inglis, J. Psychological investigations of cognitive deficit in elderly psychiatric patients. *Psychol. Bull.*, 1958, **55**, 197–214.

Inglis, J. On the prognostic value of the Modified Word Learning Test in psychiatric patients over 65. *J. ment. Sci.*, 1959a, **105**, 1100–1101.

Inglis, J. A paired-associate learning test for use with elderly psychiatric patients. *J. ment. Sci.*, 1959b, **105**, 440–448.

Inglis, J. Learning, retention and conceptual usage in elderly patients with memory disorder. *J. abnorm. soc. Psychol.*, 1959c, **59**, 210–215.

Inglis, J. Dichotic stimulation and memory disorder. *Nature*, 1960, **186**, 181–182.

Inglis, J. Abnormalities of motivation and "ego functions." In, H. J. Eysenck (ed.) *Handbook of abnormal psychology: an experimental approach*. New York: Basic Books, 1961.

Inglis, J. Immediate memory, age and brain function. In, A. T. Welford & J. E. Birren (eds.) *Behavior, aging and the nervous system*, Springfield, Ill., C. C. Thomas, 1965.

Inglis, J. *The scientific study of abnormal behavior; experimental and clinical research*. Chicago: Aldine, 1966.

Inglis, J. Electrode placement and the effect of ECT on mood and memory in depression: a brief review and some guesswork. *Canad. Psychiat. Assoc. J.*, 1969, In press.

Inglis, J., & Sanderson, R. E. Successive responses to simultaneous stimulation in elderly patients with memory disorder. *J. abnorm. soc. Psychol.*, 1961, **62**, 709–712.

Isaacs, B. A preliminary evaluation of a paired-associate verbal learning test in geriatric practice. *Geront. clin.*, 1962, **4**, 43–55.

Isaacs, B., & Walkley, F. A. A simplified paired-associate test for elderly hospital patients. *Brit. J. Psychiat.*, 1964, **110**, 80–83.

Jacobs, J. Experiments on prehension. *Mind*, 1887, **12**, 75–79.

John, E. R. *Mechanisms of memory*. New York: Academic Press, 1967.

Kalinowsky, L. B. The convulsive therapies, In, A. M. Freedman & H. I. Kaplan (eds.) *Comprehensive textbook of psychiatry*. Baltimore: Williams and Wilkins, 1967.

Kendrick, D. C. Speed and learning in the diagnosis of diffuse brain damage in elderly subjects: a Bayesian statistical approach. *Brit. J. soc. clin. Psychol.*, 1965, **4**, 141–148.

Kendrick, D. C. A cross-validation study of the use of the SLT and DCT in screening for diffuse brain pathology in elderly subjects. *Brit. J. med. Psychol.* 1967, **40**, 173–177.

Kendrick, D. C., Parboosingh, Rose-Cecile & Post, F. A. synonym learning test for use with elderly psychiatric patients: a validation study. *Brit. J. soc. clin. Psychol.*, 1965, **4**, 63–71.

Kendrick, D. C., & Post, F. Differences in cognitive status between healthy, psychiatrically ill, and diffusely brain-damaged elderly subjects. *Brit. J. Psychiat.*, 1967. **113**, 75–81.

Keschner, M., Bender, M. B., & Strauss, I. Mental symptoms in cases of tumors of the temporal lobe. *Arch. neurol. Psychiat.*, 1936, **35**, 572–596.

Kessler, J. W. *Psychopathology of childhood.*, Englewood Cliffs, N.J.: Prentice Hall, 1966.

Kimble, D.P. (ed.) *The anatomy of memory.* Palo Alto, Calif.: Science and Behavior Books, Inc., 1965.

Kimura, Doreen. Right temporal-lobe damage: perception of unfamiliar stimuli after damage. *Arch. Neurol.*, 1963, **8**, 264–271.

Kolodny, A. The symptomatology of tumours of the temporal lobe. *Brain*, 1928, **51**, 385–417.

Korsakoff, S. S. Étude médico-psychologique sur une forme des maladies de la mémoire. *Rev. Phil.*, 1889, **28**, 501–530.

Kral, V. A. The amnestic syndrome. *Mschr. Psychiat. Neurol.*, 1956, **132**, 65–80.

Kral, V. A. Senescent memory decline and senescent amnestic syndrome. *Amer. J. Psychiat.*, 1958a, **115**, 361–362.

Kral, V. A. Neuropsychiatric observations in an old people's home. Studies of memory function in senescence. *J. Gerontol.*, 1958b, **13**, 169–176.

Kral, V. A. Amnesia and the amnestic syndrome. *Canad. Psychiat. Assoc. J.*, 1959, **4**, 61–68.

Kral, V. A. Senescent forgetfulness: benign and malignant. *Canad. Med. Assoc. J.*, 1962, **86**, 257–260.

Kral, V. A. Recent research in geriatric psychiatry. *Med. Serv. J. Canad.*, 1965, **21**, 553–562.

Kral, V. A. Memory loss in the aged. *Dis. nerv. System*, 1966, **27**, 51–54.

Kral, V. A., Cahn, C., Deutsch, M., Mueller, H., & Solyom, L. Procaine (Novocain) treatment of patients with senile and arteriosclerotic brain disease. *Canad. med. Assoc. J.*, 1962, **87**, 1109–1113.

Kral, V, A., Cahn, C., & Mueller, H. Senescent memory impairment and its relation to the general health of the aging individual. *J. Amer. Geriatric Soc.*, 1964, **12**, 101–113.

Kral, V. A., & Durost, H. B. A comparative study of the amnestic syndrome in various organic conditions. *Amer. J. Psychiat.*, 1953, **110**, 41–47.

Kral, V. A., & Mueller, H. Memory dysfunction: a prognostic indicator in geriatric patients. *Canad. Psychiat. Assoc. J.*, 1966, **11**, 343–349.

Kral, V. A., Solyom, L., & Enesco, H. E. Effect of short-term oral RNA therapy on the serum uric acid level and memory function in senile versus senescent subjects. *J. Amer. Geriatric Soc.*, 1967, **15**, 364–372.

Kral, V. A., & Wigdor, Blossom T. Androgen effect on senescent memory function. *Geriatrics*, 1959, **14**, 450–456.

Kral, V. A., & Wigdor, Blossom T. Further studies on the androgen effect on senescent memory function. *Canad. Psychiat. Assoc. J.*, 1961, **6**, 345–352.

Lancaster, N. P., Steinert, R. R., & Frost, I. Unilateral electroconvulsive therapy. *J. ment. Sci.*, 1958, **104**, 221–227.

Lunn, V., & Trolle, E. On the initial impairment of consciousness following electric convulsive therapy: preliminary communication. *Acta psychiat. neurol. Scand.*, 1949, **24**, 33–58.

Lynn, J., Levine, Kate N., & Hewson, Louise, R. Psychologic tests for the clinical evaluation of late "diffuse organic," "neurotic" and "normal" reactions after closed head injury. *Proc. Assoc. Res. nerv. ment. Dis.*, 1945, **24**, 296–378.

McGaugh, J. L. Facilitation and impairment of memory storage processes. In, D. P. Kimble (ed.) *The anatomy of memory.* Palo Alto, Calif., Science and Behavior Books, Inc., 1965.

Mackay, H. A., & Inglis, J. The effect of age on a short-term auditory storage process. *Gerontologia*, 1963, **8**, 193–200.

Mackay, H. A., & Inglis, J. The reinforcement of simple responses in elderly psychiatric patients with and without memory disorder. Paper read at EPA meeting, Atlantic City, N.J., April 1965.

Martin, W. L., Ford, H. F., McDanald, E. C., & Towler, M. L. Clinical evaluation of unilateral EST. *Amer. J. Psychiat.*, 1965, **121**, 1087–1090.

Meissner, W. Hippocampal functions in learning. *J. Psychiat. Res.*, 1966, **4**, 235–304.

Meyer, D. L. Bayesian statistics. *Rev. Educ. Res.*, 1966, **36**, 503–516.

Meyer, V. Cognitive changes following temporal lobectomy for relief of temporal lobe epilepsy. *Arch. Neurol. Psychiat.*, 1959, **81**, 299–309.

Meyer, V. Psychological effects of brain damage. In, H. J. Eysenck (ed.) *Handbook of abnormal psychology: an experimental approach.* New York: Basic Books. 1961.

Meyer, V., & Yates, A. J. Intellectual changes following temporal lobectomy for psychomotor epilepsy. Preliminary communication. *J. neurol. neurosurg. Psychiat.*, 1955, **18**, 44–52.

Milner, Brenda. Psychological defects produced by temporal lobe excision. *Proc. Assoc. Res. nerv. ment. Dis.*, 1958, **36**, 244–257.

Milner, Brenda. The memory defect in bilateral hippocampal lesions. *Psychiat. Res. Reports*, 1959, **11**, 43–58.

Milner, Brenda, Laterality effects in audition. In, V. B. Mountcastle (ed.) *Interhemispheric relations and cerebral dominance.* Baltimore: John Hopkins Press, 1962.

Milner, Brenda. Visually-guided maze learning in man: effects of bilateral hippocampal, bilateral frontal, and unilateral cerebral lesions. *Neuropsychologia*, 1965, **3**, 317–338.

Milner, Brenda. Amnesia following operation on the temporal lobes. In, C. W. M. Whitty and O. L. Zangwill (eds.) *Amnesia.* London: Butterworths, 1966.

Milner, Brenda, & Penfield, W. The effect of hippocampal lesions on recent memory. *Trans. Amer. Neurol. Assoc.*, 1955, **80**, 42–48.

Moore, B. E., & Ruesch, J. Prolonged disturbances of consciousness following head injuries. *New England J. Med.*, 1944, **230**, 445–452.

Newcombe, Freda, & Steinberg, B. Some aspects of learning and memory function in older psychiatric patients. *J. Gerontol.*, 1964, **19**, 490–493.

Ojemann, R. G. Correlations between specific human brain lesions and memory changes. *Neurosciences Res. Prog. Bull.*, 1966, **4**, 1–70.

Ottosson, J-O. Experimental studies of memory impairment after electroconvulsive therapy. The role of the electrical stimulation and of the seizure studied by variation of stimulus intensity and modification by lidocaine of seizure discharge. *Acta Psychiat. Neurol. Scand.*, 1960a., Suppl., 145, **35**, 103–131.

Ottosson, J-O. (ed.) Experimental studies of the mode of action of electroconvulsive therapy. *Acta psychiat. neurol. Scand.* 1960b, Suppl. 145, **35**, 1–141.

Overton, D. A. Acquired control of learned responses by drug states (state-dependent learning.) Paper read at American College of Neuropharmacology, San Juan, Puerto Rico, December 1967.

Pacella, B. L., & Impastato, D. J. Focal stimulation therapy. *Amer. J. Psychiat.*, 1954, **110**, 576–578.

Payne, R. W., & Inglis, J. Testing for intellectual impairment—some comments reconsidered. *J. ment. Sci.*, 1960, **106**, 1134–1138.

Penfield, W., & Baldwin, M. Temporal lobe seizures and the technique of sub-total temporal lobectomy. *Ann. Surg.*, 1952, **136**, 625–634.

Penfield, W., & Milner, Brenda. Memory deficit produced by bilateral lesions in the hippocampal zone. *Arch. neurol. Psychiat.*, 1958, **79**, 475–497.

Piercy M. The effects of cerebral lesions on intellectual function: a review of current research trends. *Brit. J. Psychiat.*, 1964, **110**, 310–352.

Pilcher, C., & Angelucci, R. Analysis of three hundred and seventy-three cases of acute craniocerebral injury. *War. Med.*, 1942, **2**, 114–131.

Plotnikoff, N. Magnesium pemoline: enhancement of learning and memory of a conditioned avoidance response. *Science*, 1966, **151**, 703–704.

Raven, J. C. *Guide to using the Mill Hill Vocabulary Scale with the Progressive Matrices.* London: H. K. Lewis, 1958.

Rémy, M. Contribution a l'étude de la maladie de Korsakow. Étude anatomo-clinique. *Mschr. Psychiat. Neurol.*, 1942, **106**, 128–144.

Richter, D. (ed.). *Aspects of learning and memory*. New York: Basic Books, 1966.

Riddell, Sylvia A. The performance of elderly psychiatric patients on equivalent forms of tests of memory and learning. *Brit. J. soc. clin. Psychol.*, 1962a, **1**, 70–71.

Riddell, Sylvia, A. The relationships between tests of organic involvement, memory impairment and diagnosis in elderly psychiatric patients. *Brit. J. soc. clin. Psychol.*, 1962b, **1**, 228–231.

Ruesch, J. Intellectual impairment in head injuries. *Amer. J. Psychiat.*, 1944, **100**, 480–496.

Ruesch, J., & Bowman, K. M. Prolonged post-traumatic syndromes following head injury. *Amer. J. Psychiat.*, 1945, **102**, 145–163.

Ruesch, J., Harris, R. E., & Bowman, K. M. Pre and post-traumatic personality in head injuries. *Proc. Assoc. Res. nerv. ment. Dis.*, 1945, **24**, 507–544.

Ruesch, J., & Moore, B. E. Measurement of intellectual functions in the acute stage of head injury. *Arch. Neurol. Psychiat.*, 1943, **50**, 165–170.

Russell, W. R. *Brain, memory, learning: a neurologist's view*. London: Oxford University Press, 1959.

Russell, W. R., & Nathan, P. W. Traumatic amnesia, *Brain*, 1946, **69**, 280–300.

Russell, W. R., & Schiller, F., Crushing injuries to the skull: clinical and experimental observations. *J. Neurol. Neurosurg. Psychiat.*, 1949, **12**, 52–60.

Sanderson, R. E., & Inglis, J., Learning and mortality in elderly psychiatric patients. *J. Gerontol.*, 1961, **16**, 375–376.

Scoville, W. B., & Milner, Brenda. Loss of recent memory after bilateral hippocampal lesions. *J. neurol. neurosurg. Psychiat.*, 1957, **20**, 11–21.

Shapiro, M. B., & Nelson, Elizabeth H. An investigation of the nature of cognitive impairment in cooperative psychiatric patients. *Brit. J. med. Psychol.*, 1955, **28**, 239–256.

Sidman, M., Stoddard, L. T., & Mohr, J. P. Some additional quantitative observations of immediate memory in a patient with bilateral hippocampal lesions. Unpublished report: Behavior Laboratories of the Neurology Service, Massachusetts General Hospital, Boston, 1966.

Strich, Sabina J., Shearing of nerve fibres as a cause of brain damage due to head injury: a pathological study of twenty cases. *Lancet*, 1961, **2**, 443–448.

Syz, H. Recovery from loss of mnemic retention after head trauma. *J. gen. Psychol.*, 1937, **17**, 355–387.

Talland, G. A. Psychological studies of Korsakoff's psychosis: II Perceptual functions. *J. nerv. ment. Dis.*, 1958a, **127**, 197–219.

Talland, G. A. Perception of apparent movement in Korsakoff's psychosis. *J. Pers.*, 1958b, **26**, 337–348.

Talland, G. A. Psychological studies of Korsakoff's psychosis: III Concept formation. *J. nerv. ment. Dis.*, 1959a, **128**, 214–226.

Talland, G. A. The interference theory of forgetting and the amnesic syndrome. *J. abnorm. soc. Psychol.*, 1959b, **59**, 10–16.

Talland, G. A. A microgenetic approach to the amnesic syndrome. *J. abnorm. soc. Psychol.*, 1960a, **61**, 255–262.

Talland, G. A. Psychological studies of Korsakoff's psychosis: VI. Memory and learning. *J. nerv. ment. Dis.*, 1960b, **130**, 366–385.

Talland, G. A. The psychopathology of the amnesic syndrome. *Mod. Prob. Psychiat. Neurol.*, 1964, **1**, 443–469.

Talland, G. A. *Deranged memory: A psychonomic study of the amnesic syndrome*. New York: Academic Press, 1965.

Talland, G. A. Improvement of sustained attention with Cylert. *Psychon. Sci.*, 1966, **6**, 494.

Talland, G. A. Amnesia: a world without continuity. *Psychol. Today*, 1967, **1**, 43–50.

Talland, G. A., & Ekdahl, Marilyn. Psychological studies of Korsakoff's psychosis. IV The rate and mode of forgetting narrative material. *J. nerv. ment. Dis.*, 1959, **129**, 391–404.

Talland, G. A., & McGuire, M. T. Tests of learning and memory with Cylert. *Psychopharmacologia*, 1967, **10**, 445–451.

Talland, G. A., Mendelson, J. H., Koz, G., & Aaron, R. Experimental studies of the effects of tricyanoaminopropene on the memory and learning capacities of geriatric patients. *J. Psychiat. Res.*, 1965, **3**, 171–179.

Talland, G. A., & Miller, Alicemarie. Perceptual sets in Korsakoff's psychosis. *J. abnorm. soc. Psychol.*, 1959, **58**, 234–240.

Terman, L. M., & Merrill, Maud. *Measuring intelligence: a guide to the administration of the new revised Stanford-Binet tests of intelligence.* London: Harrap, 1937.

Trotter, W., Certain minor injuries of the brain. *Lancet*, 1924, **1**, 935–939.

Victor, M., & Adams, R. D., The effect of alcohol on the nervous system. *Proc. Assoc. Res. nerv. ment. Dis.* 1953, **32**, 526–573.

Victor, M., Talland, G. A., & Adams, R. D., Psychological studies of Korsakoff's psychosis. I. General intellectual functions. *J. nerv. ment. Dis.*, 1959, **128**, 528–537.

Victor, M., & Yakovlev, P. I. S. S. Korsakoff's psychic disorder in conjunction with peripheral neuritis. A translation of Korsakoff's original article with brief comments on the author and his contribution to clinical medicine. *Neurology*, 1955, **5**, 394–407.

Walker, A. E., Kollros, J. J., & Case, T. J. The physiological basis of cerebral concussion. *Proc. Assoc. Res. nerv. ment. Dis.*, 1945, **24**, 437–466.

Walton, D. The diagnostic and predictive accuracy of the modified word learning test in psychiatric patients over 65. *J. ment. Sci.*, 1958, **104**, 1119–1122.

Walton, D., & Black, D. A. The validity of a psychological test of brain damage. *Brit. J. med. Psychol.*, 1957, **30**, 270–279.

Walton, D., & Black, D. A. The predictive validity of a psychological test of brain damage. *J. ment. Sci.*, 1959, **105**, 807–810.

Walton, D., White, J. G., Black, D. A., & Young, A. J. The modified word learning test: a cross-validation study. *Brit. J. med. Psychol.*, 1959, **32**, 213–220.

Wechsler, D. A study of retention in Korsakoff psychosis. *Psychiat. Bull. N.Y. State Hosp.*, 1917, **2**, 403–451.

Wechsler, D. *The measurement of adult intelligence* (*3rd ed.*) Baltimore: Williams and Wilkins, 1944.

Wechsler, D. A standardized memory scale for clinical use. *J. Psychol.*, 1945, **19**, 87–95.

Welford, A. T. *Ageing and human skill.* London: Oxford Univ. Press, 1958.

Wernicke, C. *Lehrbuch der Gehirnkrankheiten für Artze und Studierende.* Berlin: Fischer, 1881.

White, J. G., & Knox, S. J. Some psychological correlates of age and dementia. *Brit. J. soc. clin. Psychol.*, 1965, **4**, 259–265.

Whitty, C. W. M., & Zangwill, O. L. (eds.) *Amnesia*. London: Butterworths, 1966.

Wigdor, Blossom T., & Kral, V. A. Senescent memory function as an indicator of the general preservation of the aging human organism. In, *Proceedings of the Third World Congress of Psychiatry*. Toronto; Univ. Toronto Press, 1961.

Williams, D., & Denny-Brown, D. Cerebral electrical changes in experimental concussion. *Brain*, 1941, **64**, 223–238.

Williams, Moyra. Investigation of amnesic defects by progressive prompting. *J. neurol. neurosurg. Psychiat.*, 1953, **16**, 14–18.

Williams, Moyra, Memory disorders associated with electroconvulsive therapy. In, C. W. M. Whitty & O. L. Zangwill (eds.) *Amnesia*, London, Butterworths, 1966.

Williams, Moyra & Zangwill, O. L. Memory defects after head injury. *J. Neurol. Neurosurg. Psychiat.*, 1952, **15**, 54–58.

Zamora, E. N., & Kaelbling, R. Memory and electroconvulsive therapy. *Amer. J. Psychiat.*, 1965, **122**, 546–554.

Zangwill, O. L. Clinical tests of memory impairment. *Proc. Roy. Soc. Med.*, 1943, **36**, 576–580.

Zangwill, O. L. Some clinical applications of the Rey-Davis performance test. *J. ment. Sci.*, 1946, **92**, 19–34.

Zangwill, O. L. The Grünthal-Störring case of amnesic syndrome. *Brit. J. Psychiat.*, 1967, **113**, 113–128.

Chapter 5

Disorders of Attention and Concentration

J. A. EASTERBROOK and C. G. COSTELLO

INTRODUCTION

A frequent complaint of the psychiatric patient is that he is unable to attend to and concentrate on things. Sometimes, even when the patient does not make this complaint, it is found that a disorder of attention and/or concentration underlies his more obvious symptoms of illness. This may occur, for instance, when a patient is brain damaged.

White (1964) has written that when we are attending

> ". . . something has been made the center or object or topic in regard to which we are actively busy or occupied whether perceptually or intellectually or even practically."

It is this behavioristic approach to the concept "attention" that will be adopted in this chapter; it will be seen to encompass concentration, at least in the short term.

Western investigators have demonstrated that more than one environmental event at a time can influence animals or men (Tolman, 1948; Hebb & Thompson, 1954; Nissen, 1951; Mackintosh, 1965) and that an organism may select between stimuli that seem to be equally stimulating (Berlyne, 1951). But these demonstrations and the lively research and controversies that they have provoked have not been used to any great extent in the understanding of disorders of attention. Soviet investigators have used their own theoretical notions and experimental data in an attempt to understand attention disorders, and it is their ideas that will be discussed first in this chapter.

THE ORIENTATION REACTION AND ITS DISORDERS

Overtly the orientation reaction or reflex (OR) is marked by the cessation of ongoing activity, turning of the head toward the stimulus and, in dogs, by pricking of the ears and sniffing. Covertly, general muscle tonus rises and there are energy mobilizing changes in the activity of the autonomic nervous system. There are also changes in cortical EEG patterns of the "alerting" kind and increases in the sensitivity of the sense organs and/or analyzers. The OR resembles the startle reflex in many ways. Situational novelty and complexity as well as conflicting reaction tendencies (for example, difficulties of discrimination) are known to produce the orientation reaction (Berlyne, 1960; Sokolov, 1963a, 1963b; Lynn, 1966). It is readily habituated in healthy animals and humans when stimuli of normal intensities are repeated.

The physiological elements in the OR vary greatly from person to person. Changes may occur in the galvanic skin response (GSR) with an increase in conductance, there may be an increase in receptor sensitivity (for example, dilation of pupils), a rise in general muscle tonus, and increase in frequency and decrease in amplitude of EEGs, a delay in respiration followed by an increase in amplitude and decrease in frequency of respiration, a slowing of heart rate—this latter being characteristic of humans as distinct from animals (Obrist, 1963; Lynn, 1966).

Although, as we have noted, individuals

differ in the physiological pattern of the OR, the most nearly universal response is the GSR, according to Lynn (1966). The relations between attention and emotional states or reactions remain to be worked out in detail. Some distinctions made by Soviet investigators between ORs and OR-like responses are relevant to this question.

Orientation reactions vary in strength and there is some basis for distinguishing between generalized (G) and localized (L) ORs. According to Lynn's (1966) account, metabolic reactions are less intense in the LOR than in the GOR. According to Sokolov (1963b), less intense or less novel stimuli produce localized ORs. Repetition of low intensity stimulation elicits changes from GOR to LOR. There is also some evidence reviewed by Lynn (1966) that tranquilizers will reduce GORs to LORs. One of the means suggested for distinguishing LORs from GORs is that in the LORs cortical rhythms show local desynchronization and in the GOR they show a general desynchronization.

As we have noted before, orientation reactions resemble startle-defensive reactions (SDR). But some writers maintain they are not the same. The reported critical differences between ORs and SDRs are as follows: (1) They differ in the vaso reactions (Sokolov, 1963b); constriction is general in the SDR and occurs both in the forehead and the forelimbs, but in the case of the OR, while constriction still occurs in the forelimbs, vaso dilation occurs in the forehead. (2) They differ in the evoked potentials from the hypocampus which are synchronized in the OR and desynchronized in the SDR (Grastyan, 1959). On the other hand, Lynn (1966) has noted suggestions that the SDR is simply more intense than the OR. The SDR is provoked by very high intensity stimuli almost always and by repeated moderately high intensity stimuli sometimes, while ORs are produced by low intensity stimuli. It may be that a similar kind of positioning of the SDR and OR can be made on a continuum related to the novelty attributes of stimuli. Grastyan (1961) has maintained that completely novel stimuli always elicit SDRs and that the ORs occur only when an organism has some familiarity with the stimulus. According to Lynn (1966) conditioning gives "signal value" to an intense stimulus and converts the reaction to it from an SDR to an OR.

The Soviet investigations have revealed a further distinction among LORs, GORs and SDRs. The cessation of ongoing activity which characterizes ORs is less complete in the case of LORs than that of GORs. By contrast, it is quite complete in the case of SDRs in which "freezing" or flight may be substituted for the prior activity. The ORs, of course, are regarded as investigative while the behavior accompanying SDRs includes at best a quick phasic movement of the head toward the stimulus (Grastyan, 1961). In terms of the response capacity they leave to the organism during their occurrence, therefore, the arousal reactions of the Soviet system seem to fall on a continuum from the greatest to the least as follows: LOR, GOR, SDR.

The importance of the orientation response for psychopathology lies in the fact that it appears to occur only in a weak form in many patients. The review of Lynn (1963) indicates that when stimulated either by tone, bell, ring, whistle, light, touch, or electric shock, schizophrenics, for instance, give no autonomic, pupillary, EEG or motor reaction, or if an OR does occur the autonomic components are much weaker than the motor components.

Luria (1963) and Vinogradova (cited by Lynn, 1966) have reported that weak ORs also occur in some mental defectives. When stronger ORs occur in mental defectives, they are unusually susceptible to habituation. Whether or not the weak ORs that occur in schizophrenics are abnormally easy or abnormally difficult to habituate appears to be undecided (Bernstein, 1964; Israel, 1966; Maltzman & Raskin, 1966).

Not all schizophrenics appear to show weak ORs and, indeed, there are some (paranoids and young, acute, agitated, or tense and anxious schizophrenics) who show strong ORs and SDRs. These strong responses appear to be unusually resistant to extinction. There is also evidence that strong ORs and SDRs occur when cerebral impairment has been caused by infection, head injury, senility, alcoholic brain disease, and some of the more severe of mental deficiencies. Shmavonian, Yarmat, and Cohen (1965) have also noted that similar behavior occurs in old people and suggest that the aged organism reacts to novel stimuli with total mobilization.

According to the Soviet investigators, *weak* ORs are a consequence of the occurrence of widespread protective inhibition which affects subcortical as well as cortical processes. Compatible with this interpretation are reports that failures of OR are more frequent late in the day than in the morning, and also that prolonged sleep reduces the frequency of such failures. The theory that these investigators favor to account for *strong* ORs is that a state of protective inhibition has developed but that it affects only cortical and not subcortical processes.

Although the measurement of these orienting responses in full detail necessitates the use of elaborate recording equipment, it seems clear that they are worthy of further investigation by those who are interested in disorders of attention. At the present time, the defective ORs, whether too weak or too strong, appear to occur in too many kinds of disorders for the responses to be used as diagnostic aids. But, as argued in a number of places in this book, the use of most measurements in psychology for diagnostic purposes is premature because these measurements need so much more work on them.

Because both weak and strong ORs are considered by the Soviet investigators to be the result of the development of protective inhibition, sleep therapy is considered by them to be of value in both instances. Weak ORs may be modified also, they have suggested, by the administration of CNS stimulants to enhance the excitatory and counteract the inhibitory effect of stimulation. The pharmacological stimulants that have been used include caffeine (in small doses) cocaine, insulin, atropine, and meretran. Bernstein (1964) found that the phenothiazines were ineffective.

In the case of strong ORs, meretran and prolonged chloropromazine treatment have been reported to be beneficial, at least, for the less deteriorated paranoids (Lynn, 1963, 1966). It is also suggested by Soviet conceptions that OR strength may be reduced by training patients to do something about the relevant stimuli, in other words, by giving the test stimuli "signal value." The problem here, however, is that, although conditioning may be relatively easy with some neurotics, it is apparently difficult with some psychotics and with the aged and brain damaged.

VIGILANCE AND ITS DISORDERS

If a person is instructed to watch for a signal and do something about it, he has a signal detection task. If the signals are sufficiently infrequent and low in magnitude, he has a vigilance task.

A number of sophisticated methods of analyzing vigilance data have recently been developed (Swets, Tanner, & Birdsall, 1964; Broadbent & Gregory, 1963; Price, 1966; & Broadbent, 1965). The more recent of these differentiates signal sensitivity from response sensitivity. But since they have not been used in investigation of disorders of vigilance, they will not be discussed here. They, of course, could not be neglected by any researcher wishing to do work in this area.

One means of assessing a person's vigilance is to measure his reaction time to signals. The work on reaction time done by Venables and his colleagues and reviewed by him, in Venables (1965), provides an interesting link between the vigilance work and the theoretical system of the Russian investigators. One of the conditions under which protective inhibition develops is that in which a stimulus becomes too intense. Venables' review indicates that the reaction times of schizophrenics become slower with an increase in stimulus intensity. This paradoxical effect appears to occur, however, only on the first occasion of testing; that is, with novel stimuli only. Another noteworthy point is that the paradoxical effect, although it occurs with reaction time to visual stimuli, has not been found in reaction times to auditory stimuli.

The work of Venables on the relationship between stimulus intensity and reaction time has not received as much attention by Western investigators as have the studies on the relationship between preparatory intervals, warning signals, and reaction time. Talland (1965) has reported that with aged, chronic schizophrenic, and brain damaged patients, a warning light does not improve response speed as it does with normals, but impairs performance.

Another paradoxical effect is that, whereas normals benefit from the use of a constant preparatory interval (PI) in the reaction-time situation by apparently developing expectancies, many patients do not show any benefit. It is true that with normals the benefit of this "set" is slightly reduced by increases in the duration of the PI up to about 25 seconds, but with schizophrenic patients the optimum preparatory interval is about 4 seconds and performance at intervals beyond $7\frac{1}{2}$ seconds is worse that under irregular PI conditions. A vigilance proficiency index based on a ratio of speeds at long PIs to speeds at short PIs reliably discriminates normals from schizophrenics (Rodnick & Shakow, 1940; Zahn & Rosenthal, 1965; Shakow & McCormick, 1965). The more rapid the loss of set—in other words, the higher the index—the lower are the patients liable to be rated in mental health. For instance, Rosenthal, Lawlor, Zahn and Shakow (1960) report a rank order correlation between these two variables of −0.89.

This inability to maintain a set in the reaction-time situation does not appear to be restricted to schizophrenic patients. Terrell and Ellis (1964) and Hawkins and Baumeister (1965) have reported an abnormally great loss of vigilance with increasing PI among mental defectives.

The data with regard to the influence of PI among brain-damaged patients are conflicting. Contrary to Costa (1962), McDonald (1964) found that his apparently comparable brain-damaged patients were disproportionately slower than normals with 15 second than with 3 second PIs.

Although, given long PIs, schizophrenics may do worse with constant than with irregular PI conditions, irregularity in PI may also show up a defect in "set" development among schizophrenics. Zahn, Rosenthal, and Shakow (1963) have shown that the reaction times of both normals and schizophrenics may be adversely influenced if a long PI is followed by a short PI for any particular trial. The schizophrenic reactions were abnormally prolonged as if, in neglect of the structure of the experiment as a whole, they expected the current trial to be like the last. Comparable results for schizophrenics have been reported by Shakow and McCormick (1965) and for brain-damaged patients by McDonald (1964).

The vigilance of a person may also be assessed by investigating the effects of a distracting stimulus on his reaction time. McGhie, Chapman, and Lawson (1965b) found that, when either visual or auditory distractors were presented, the visual reaction time of schizophrenics was more impaired than that of normals. In the case of auditory reaction time, only visual distraction produced this greater impairment in schizophrenics. Similar effects of distracting extraneous stimulation were found with depressives and paranoid psychotics.

Payne and Caird (1967) have suggested that overinclusive thinking could be associated with a slow and variable reaction time because irrelevant stimulation would be attended to and processed along with relevant stimuli. Forty-five patients (15 deluded and 15 nondeluded schizophrenics plus 15 nonschizophrenic psychiatric patients) were tested for simple and choice reaction times to tones, with and without distracting sounds. Measures of overinclusiveness and retardation were also taken for the patients. In the absence of distracting noise, reaction time was related to the retardation scores. In the presence of distracting noise, however, reaction time was closely related to overinclusiveness scores and not to retardation scores.

Payne (1966) suggested that the distractability of schizophrenics, particularly overinclusive schizophrenics, is because of a weakness of "filter," a term which was used by Broadbent in relation to selective listening. This hypothesis is also favored by McGhie, Chapman, and Lawson (1965a, 1965b). Shakow (1966), on the other hand, has suggested that the impaired vigilance of schizophrenics is the result of a tendency to establish minor "segmental sets." These segmental sets are made up of irrelevant response tendencies related to distractors in the environment and from past experience.

Luria (1963) has attributed the impaired attention of mentally defective children as demonstrated in reaction-time experiments to a weakness in the conditioned orienting response. This weakness, he suggests, is a result partly of poor conditionability and partly of the weak ORs found in mentally defective people.

A further hypothesis has been suggested by Broen (1966) and Broen and Storms (1961, 1966). They have argued that some schizophrenic attention disorders are produced by distracting stimuli because some normally weak reaction potentials have become more competitive as a consequence of increased drive.

Belmont, Birch and Karp (1966) reported findings with hemiplegic patients that can also be explained within an activation framework. They found that if control subjects were given five minutes of auditory stimulation part way through a visual reaction-time task, their vigilance was impaired. This did not tend to occur with the hemiplegic patients and, indeed, some of the patients gave faster reactions. This suggests the possibility that the patients were initially in an inhibitory state and that the intervening stimulation was disinhibitory or activating. Another finding that may be fitted into this activation framework is that of McDonald and Burns (1964). They found that the reduced vigilance of a brain-damaged patient occurred primarily at a low signal rate and that this impairment was attenuated at a high signal rate, which one may consider as being more activating or arousing.

The more fully developed forms of general vigilance theory imply therapeutic hypotheses. Expectancy ("set") theory due to Baker (1958, 1959a, 1959b) has been particularly fruitful in general psychology. It implies that failures of signal detection will be reduced by increasing the rate and predictability of signals, as Shakow and his associates have demonstrated from schizophrenics. Broadbent's current (1963, 1964, 1965) response competition theory has elements of his earlier stimulus competition theory and of activation theory. It implies that vigilance can be improved by making alterations to a patient's motivational matrix, by raising or lowering drive level, and by training to alter response biases. McCormack (1962) uses both an activation and an extinction-inhibition construct to imply that vigilance can be improved by raising activation level and by dissipating or counteracting an inhibitory state. Mackworth's (1964) review on inhibition in watchkeeping tasks documents the counteracting effect of chemical analeptics or stimulants. Finally, Holland (1957, 1958), Jerison and Pickett (1963), and Solley and Murphy (1960) have presented an interpretation of vigilance behavior in terms of operantly conditioned observing responses. Gardner (1964) refers to this interpretation as "scanning control," so as to imply that operant techniques will reduce those perceptual anomalies attributable to defective scanning, which are found in schizophrenics according to Silverman (1964a, 1964b). The same therapeutic hypothesis may be applied to attentional disorders of ego-defensive isolation, for this mechanism has been linked to extensive scanning by Gardner and Long (1962) and by Benfari (1966).

The work on vigilance and its relation to psychopathology has been done primarily by researchers. Vigilance situations are rarely, if ever, used by the clinician to assess disorders of attention in their patients. The research findings that have been reviewed suggest that they would repay consideration by clinicians.

DISORDERED PERCEPTUAL ARTICULATION

The areas of research that we consider very briefly in this section are perhaps only indirectly related to attention and concentration, although some writers on attention have insisted that the concept must encompass differential response to particular attributes of a stimulus (for example, Deutsch & Deutsch, 1963; Mackintosh, 1965) and others have assumed it (for example, Weckowicz & Blewett, 1959; Zeaman & House, 1963; Santostefano & Stayton, 1967). They are, in any case, important areas of research, and this brief reference to them is more appropriate in this chapter than in the others of the book. The first area of research has concerned perceptual proficiency, for example, through camouflage, and the number of dimensions of stimulation that a person can simultaneously appreciate (Thurstone, 1944; Roff, 1952). Deficiency in this ability appears to be related to the inadequate analysis of stimuli, or to the inadequate discrimination between adjacent form outlines.

A test that appears to measure analytical ability is the Embedded Figures Test (EFT), which is a modification by Witkin of the Gottschaldt figures. In this test the subject is shown one card bearing a simple geometric form. He is then given a colored card on which that form appears, sharing some of its boundaries with alternative figures. The task is to find the embedded figure, and the score is the time it takes to do so. Slowness on the EFT has been shown to be related to low scores on those Wechsler intelligence tests that define a factor labeled with terms like "perceptual organization" or "analytic intelligence": Block Design, Object Assembly, and Picture Completion (Goodenough & Karp, 1961; Karp, 1963; Witkin, Faterson, Goodenough &, Birnbaum, 1966).

Slow scores on the EFT have also been found to be related to scores on a body adjustment test and also on a rod and frame test, both of which indicate susceptibility to influence by distorted sensory input (Witkin, Dyk, Faterson, Goodenough, & Karp, 1962). Because of these findings, Witkin (1965) describes individuals with slow scores on the EFT as being "field dependent" and postulates that they are unable to keep item apart from context in a wide variety of perceptual situations.

Both Perez (1961) and Weckowicz (1960) have found that schizophrenics are more field dependent than normals in terms of embedded figures and similar tests. Weckowicz on the basis of his review of the literature, suggests that brain-damaged patients are even more field dependent than schizophrenics. Related findings for psychotic and brain-damaged patients have been reported by Teuber (1950) and Canter (1963, 1966). Field dependence has been found among mental retardates by Witkin, Faterson, Goodenough, and Birnbaum (1966) and may also be recognized in the attentional deficiency of retardates postulated by Zeaman and House (1963).

Witkin (1965) has suggested that field dependence represents a failure of, or retardation in, cognitive and perceptual differentiation that is presumably due to the inadequate formation of the nervous system and is genetically determined. Field dependence, in other words, is assumed by Witkin to be an enduring aspect of personality. In support of his view are high test-retest correlations for some measures of it and evidence that alcohol, electroconvulsive shock, anxiety because of the anticipation of heart surgery, special training, hypnosis, and change in life circumstances did not change the presumed cognitive style.

Elliott (1961), on the other hand, has suggested that so-called "field dependent" people are merely individuals who are liable to become ineffective in the face of strange and unstructured stimulus configurations. Elliott watched his subjects learning a finger maze and made records of the time spent on the first trial. These time scores were taken as an index of uncertainty. He found that field dependence, as measured by the Embedded Figures and the Rod and Frame tests was related to uncertainty as measured on the finger maze.

Weckowicz (1960) has suggested that field dependence represents a loss of an abstract or categorical attitude in Goldstein's sense. He found (Weckowicz & Blewett, 1959) that abstraction level, as measured by the Goldstein-Sheerer Color Form Test, was significantly related to proficiency in locating figures in the Embedded Figures Test.

Negative induction constructs may also be applicable for interpretation of findings related to field dependence. Kinsbourne and Warrington (1962a, 1962b) have demonstrated that a random pattern presented shortly after a target pattern would prevent recognition of the target. Moreover, this effect occurs even if the target pattern is presented to one eye and a masking pattern to the other, indicating that the masking is a central phenomenon. The masking effect has also been shown to depend on the duration of the two stimuli and their similarity of pattern (Fehrer, 1966).

In view of the variety of theoretical explanations proposed for field dependence and independence, it is not surprising that there has been very little in the way of procedures developed to modify or ameliorate this deficiency. A training program in the discrimination of stimulus dimensions that builds on the work of Zeaman and House (1963) however, has been designed by Santostefano and Stayton (1967) for mental retardates. This is a training program that is to be executed by parents and which can be tested for transfer on attention-related tasks. The program was conceived as an aid in the development of "focal attention", that is

> ". . . the act of engaging an object fully with one's attention over a sufficient period of time so that one can observe, register, and comprehend the unique properties and functions of that object and its possible relationship with other objects."

Santostefano and Stayton report that the children in their experimental training program had a mean IQ of 50 and a mean age of

5 to 6 years. They were given 22 object classification problems. Both the experimental (32 children) and the matched control group (32 children) were tested before and after the four-month training period. The tests used were: tracing a double S maze, finding an object pictured among others on a card (adapted from the Stanford-Binet Picture-Matching Test), sorting white, black, and grey buttons, sorting objects differing at two levels on two dimensions (shape and color), and imitating arm movements. In addition, records were made of the coaching given during these tests and the benefit in terms of improvement in test scores that was obtained from this coaching. The results indicated that there was a significant transfer of the discrimination training to all but the imitations test, but that there was no general "factor" of improvement as indicated by intercorrelation coefficients. The children who had been given the training benefited more from coaching during the post-tests, and required less of it. Preprogram intelligence test scores were moderately related to pretest scores but unrelated to difference scores, that is, the gain in scores produced by the training program. Some qualitative observations were presented by the investigators suggesting that the ones who had gone through the discrimination training course showed improved social interaction with their mothers.

Another area of research which can be included under this heading has been concerned with the ability of a person to search among alternatives for a target item, for example, a letter, card, or object. The person is scored for the speed with which he can find the target item. Although the targets are not usually embedded or camouflaged, their context may be inhibiting and, indeed, it has been demonstrated that the speed of detection is decreased by increased contextual complexity (for example, Shantz, Rubin, & Smock, 1962; Tecce & Testa, 1965). These search discrimination tasks verge on others, including vigilance tasks.

Search tests in which target figures are to be recognized among others are particularly difficult for patients with parietal and occipital lobe brain damage, according to Teuber (1950) and Teuber, Battersby, and Bender (1960). We note here that slow performance in multistimulus discrimination RT tasks is also characteristic of brain-damaged people (Costa, Horowitz, & Vaughan, 1965). Welford (1964), Birren (1964) and Nobel, Baker and Jones (1964) have also presented evidence indicating that this task becomes more difficult with increasing age.

In an attempt to understand the nature of a deficit in search discrimination, Venables (1963) asked his schizophrenics to sort decks of cards for the presence of an A or Z among a set of irrelevant letters. Then a predicted time to sort a fifth deck was obtained. The fifth set of cards had a different set of irrelevant letters. Sorting times that were longer than predicted were regarded as evidence of attention to the novel irrelevant stimuli. In addition, two-flash fusion thresholds were measured as the longest interval between two flashes which the patient reported as one and not two flashes. The greatest delays in sorting because of the novel irrelevant stimuli were made by the patients with the poorest flash resolution ($r = 0.64$). This deficit may be considered as a result of a general attention defect in which an hypothetical "filter" is ineffective in screening out irrelevant data. We have already referred to this hypothesis and detailed discussion of it will be found in Chapter 3.

Venables has presented a second hypothesis about the schizophrenic's slowness in search discrimination. He regarded the two-flash fusion thresholds as being an index of cortical activation, with poor flash resolution an index of low activation. In view of the relationship that he found between slowness in sorting and poor flash resolution, he has suggested that delays in sorting by schizophrenics may result from a low level of cortical activation.

There is a little experimental evidence that can guide us in the modification of this deficit in search time. Solley and Murphy (1960) have reported on a study in which the investigators vocally rewarded children for looking at one of a number of figurines and then measure the search discrimination time for these and other figures in a field of 40. The rewarded figures were more rapidly detected. Fisch and McNamara (1963) conditioned attention to one visual half field and found shorter search discrimination times for objects in that half field. A related finding was earlier reported by Walters (1958).

DISORDERS OF THE BREADTH OF ATTENTION

Kinsbourne and Warrington (1962c) report that Balint in 1909 was the first to use the term "attention" in connection with the disordered perception of simultaneous visual stimuli—a disorder produced by neurological damage. When a patient with brain damage in either hemisphere was presented with a stimulus in the affected visual half field, he could usually report it. However, when two stimuli were presented simultaneously the one in the affected half field became unavailable. This phenomenon has been well confirmed (for example, Teuber, Battersby, & Bender, 1960). It has been called "extinction," "precipitation," and "simultagnosia."

By using a tachistoscopic duration threshold procedure, Kinsbourne and Warrington (1962c) studied simultagnosia with four patients damaged in the anterior left occipital area. They found an inordinate increase in recognition thresholds as a result of adding a second stimulus. All of these patients also had severe reading difficulties and problems in spelling (dyslexia). Welford (1964) has concluded that aging people also show delays in recognition of tachistoscopically exposed stimuli, particularly (although not solely) when competitive or embedding stimulation is present.

Simultagnostic phenomena as a consequence of brain lesions in the somatosensory area have also been observed (Bender, 1945; Bender, Fink, & Green, 1951; Birch, Belmont, & Karp, 1964). This may be because of parietal lobe damage particularly (Teuber, 1950), and is evident in paraplegics (Birch, Belmont, & Karp, 1964).

Auditory versions of simultagnosia tests have recently come into research use (for example, Reitan, 1966). The dichotic listening technique is one of them. Lesions in the left anterior temporal lobe appear to be particularly implicated in these disorders according to Zangwill (1964). Inglis (1962) and Inglis and Caird (1963) report impairment as a result of aging. That these results are found when a conventional digits forward measure of memory span is unaffected by age, Welford (1964) attributes to the "shift of attention" required for reporting of the simultaneous stimuli.

In the dichotic listening technique, two series of cues are presented simultaneously, and the person is asked to follow one series to the exclusion of another. Generally, adults can do this, thereby demonstrating the existence of an attention mechanism which Broadbent (1958) has designated a "filter". McGhie, Chapman, and Lawson (1965a) have reported that chronic schizophrenics are particularly ineffective at a modified form of dichotic listening task by comparison to normals, chronic paranoid, or depressed patients. This deficit was evident when sequences of six digits or letters were presented in a female voice and irrelevant numbers or letters in a male voice were interspersed. It was also evident when the primary series to be remembered was presented visually with simultaneous auditory stimulation, and when the primary series was auditory and the distraction series visual.

A visual analogue of the dichotic task is the Stroop test of color word interference. In this test, three sets of stimuli are to be read as rapidly as possible, a list of color words, one of color patches, and a third of colors printed in the form of conflicting color words. The difference in time taken to read the two latter sets of cards is the interference score and has been found to be quite reliable (Santos & Montgomery, 1962). Schizophrenics (Wapner & Krus, 1960), young children with two or three years' reading experience, and aged people (Comalli, Wapner, & Werner, 1962) appear to be particularly liable to such interference.

Treisman (1964, 1966) has reviewed evidence on the parameters of effective and ineffective filtering. Good performance is facilitated not only by sensitivity to purely physical cues to channel differentiation but also by knowledge of the contingent probabilities of the language used. Performance may be impaired by the presence, in the irrelevant channel, of words that presumably elicit strong habitual response tendencies or have high probability in the relevant context. Availability of habits for response to printed color names seems also to be a condition of interference in Stroop test performance, according to evidence presented by Schiller (1966), by Rand, Wapner, Werner, and McFarland (1963) and by Comalli, Wapner and Werner (1962).

In general, perhaps, serially organized performances can be impaired by strong response links to irrelevant stimuli.

The work of Chapman, Chapman and Miller (1964) implies that an unusually strong association to one member of a series of words impairs use of context cues by chronic schizophrenics. Also, acute schizophrenics gave figurative (contextual) interpretations of some proverbs according to Lewinsohn and Riggs (1962), but not of proverbs with affective themes. Brodsky (1963) reports a comparable finding with pictorial material.

We have dealt with disorders in the range of attention when the individual had to attend to stimuli presented simultaneously. In the two latter cases, serially organized response to distributed cues is required, in addition to perceptual selection. We come now to the (presumably simpler) cases of serial response to successive stimuli in which interference is not deliberately supplied. A test of this sort is the digit span test of "immediate memory." The mean Wechsler subtest scores for various functional groups, reported by Payne (1961), indicate below average proficiency at the digit span subtest for all psychotic groups but not for epileptics nor for neurotics. Similar results for neurotics have been reported by Frank (1964) who found that only mental defectives and character disordered patients showed any serious impairment.

Poor digit span performance has been reported for children with functional defects in speech articulation (Ferrier, 1966) and retarded readers (Katz & Deutsch, 1964).

The visual retention test designed by Benton (1963) measures immediate memory for up to three geometric forms. Impairments in immediate memory assessed in this manner have been found to increase with age (Kendall, 1962; Thompson, Opton, & Cohen, 1963) and are particularly prevalent as a result of brain damage, especially right hemispheric brain damage (Teuber, 1950). Although apparently the impairment may occur as a result of functional disorders, L'Abate, Boelling, Hutton and Mathews (1962) found that brain damage produced more impairment than schizophrenia. The impairment is found also with mental deficiency (Benton & McGavren, 1962; Kendall, 1962, 1966; Ritchie & Butler, 1964).

The digit symbol or coding test may be included under this heading, and it has generally been found that severely ill patients such as psychotics and brain damaged do poorly on it. A recent review has been written by Beck, Feshbach, and Legg (1962). Reitan (1966) reports this test to be perhaps the most sensitive to brain damage of all the Wechsler scales.

Receptor effector (RE) spans can be measured with various maze tests, in terms of either tracing speed or the complexity of maze that can be traced without error. WISC mazes scores load on the same factor as the coding, digit span, digit symbol, and arithmetic sub-tests, sometimes called the attention-concentration factor. Besides Porteus' series of mazes and the ones from the WISC, other pencil and paper mazes in fairly common use are Reitans Trailmaking Test (TMT), the Tsai-Parkington Numbers Test, and Elithorn's dots maze (Elithorn, Kerr, & Mott, 1960; Davies, 1965). Various apparatus mazes (for example, finger and stylus) and maze analogues (for example, temporal patterns) are also available.

It was not clear to Payne (1961) that neurotics as a class show restricted RE-spans on maze tests. Nonetheless, anxiety evidently produces these effects according to McNamara and Fisch (1964), Agnew and Agnew (1963), Eysenck and Willett (1962, 1966), Parsons, Maslow, Morris, and Denny (1964), Murphy (1964), and Freedman (1966).

The Elithorn perceptual maze is notably sensitive to brain damage, according to Elithorn (1955) and to Benton, Elithorn, Fogel, and Kerr (1963). Davies (1965) reports that old age also impairs proficiency on this test. Proficiency on the TMT is impaired by brain damage, especially when the damage is recent (Fitzhugh, Fitzhugh, & Reitan, 1962, 1963). The same result occurs with mental retardation, according to Smith (1963).

Schizophrenics perform badly on the TMT, according to Smith and Boyce (1962), L'Abate, Boelling, Hutton, and Mathews (1962) and Goldstein and Neuringer (1966). The latter investigators found that schizophrenic patients, more than brain-damaged subjects, tended to lose the alternation patterns in the number-letter part of the test. Depressives may also perform slowly on maze tests, according to Payne (1961), but

Alvarez (1962) has reported reactive depressives superior to brain-damaged patients on the TMT.

No research seems to have been done concerning the amelioration of the reduced range of attention shown in span tasks. The theoretical possibilities are presumably numerous, and may include all of the ones raised above because successful performance of these tasks seems likely to depend on all of the aspects of attentive behavior thus far considered.

THE POSSIBILITY OF A GENERAL THEORY

Research into the causes and correction of disorders of attention has been pursued piecemeal, with little guidance by an explicit conception of how the various pieces treated above may be interrelated. This conception may not be feasible; however, some integrative possibilities can be outlined for future exploration.

All attentive behavior displays differential sensitivity to item and context. When behavior is determined primarily by an item, it may be said to be focused. When it shows that contextual cues have been employed, a certain breadth of attention must be inferred. Focus and range are complementary aspects of attentive behavior, like figure and ground; hence, focusing cannot be defined without reference to context. Complete knowledge of attentive behavior demands a theory that deals with both the intensity and the extent of involvement and that accounts for changes between extremes on the two dimensions. Accordingly, great importance must be attached to Kulpe's (1902) proposal of a reciprocity of focus ("clearness") and to range in attention as investigated by Chapman and Brown (1935) and by Morton (1941). Rendered into objective terminology, this proposition would imply a reciprocity between intensity and range in the distribution of behavioral resources.

The orienting response of Soviet theory is supposed to achieve the concentration and sensory clarification of narrow attention. By all accounts, too, it does so at the cost of current alternatives and previously ongoing behavior, although this aspect of the process seems not to have been explicitly studied in the USSR. The participation of the OR in the postulated reciprocity of focus and range in behavior can be inferred from other evidence.

Orienting responses are produced by stimuli that are unfamiliar. When these stimuli occur among a series of familiar stimuli in a serial task, they serve to "disintegrate" performance. For instance, in oral reading or in maze tracing, the occurrence of these stimuli reduces receptor-effector spans, the number of overlapping processes (Woodworth, 1938). Immediate memory spans are likewise reduced when unusual forms of common cyphers are employed, according to Mackworth (1966). Conversely, receptor-effector spans are reported to be increased when the probability of transition between items is raised, according to Treisman (1965) and Morton (1964) for reading, and to Warrington, Kinsbourne and James (1966) for the span of apprehension. Expectancies (relevant) and knowledge of transitional probabilities increase "filtered" memory spans in dichotic listening studies according to Treisman (1964, 1966). In the absence of this information, both the filtering and the breadth aspects of attentive performance are imparied. Stimuli that elicit ORs evidently reduce the breadth of attentive behavior.

According to Soviet writers, ORs can be too weak or too strong. Chronic schizophrenics are reported to show weak ORs, and hence the foregoing analysis implies that they should display weakened concentration. Their behavior should be influenced by divergent determinants—by "segmental sets" in Shakow's terms. Young, acute schizophrenics and other patients, such as brain-damaged people, are reported to produce strong ORs, so that their attentive abnormalities should reveal loss of context. Some supportive studies have been cited. This formulation of loss of context may extend to those disorders of perceptual relativity which have been discussed in terms of attention by Callaway and Thompson (1953), by Piaget, Vinh-Bang and Matalon (1958), by Weckowicz and Blewett (1959), and by Gardner (1964). It may also extend to dissociation phenomena, which Pillsbury (1908) treated as disorders of attention, and to hypnotic phenomena and suggestibility, which have been analyzed in terms of a reduction in the number of determining tendencies (Allport, 1954). The experimental data required to check these speculations are not yet available.

There are other important points in relation to which more evidence is needed for the development of an integrative conception of attentive disorders. In particular, the interaction of emotion and ORs has not been thoroughly worked out. At the metabolic or neurohumoral level, it is possible that emotional reactions differ from ORs principally in duration and intensity. Perhaps ORs occur with reduced intensity in emotion, in accordance with the "law of initial value," to which Venables (1964) has alluded. Another possible interaction has to do with the effect of emotion on serial integration in behavior. To the extent that emotion impedes anticipatory adjustment, it may increase the probability and intensity of ORs. Whether the two sorts of abnormality in OR can be construed in terms of emotion remains to be seen.

The OR is a dominant response, possibly acquired, and its effect in focusing behavior expresses this dominance. That other kinds of response can achieve considerable dominance is widely known, particularly through Hull's use of the concepts of habit strength and reaction potential. In that theory, it is implied that when a set of stimuli are presented, every increase in the probability of response potentiated by (a dominant) one of them implies a complementary decrease in the probability that the others will influence behavior. If the words in a sentence are such a set, then the utility of the contextual cues of the sentence should be reduced by increasing the strength of habitual response to any one word. This result was obtained by Chapman, Chapman, and Miller (1964) and led to production of literal rather than abstract verbal responses. The effect was particularly strong among chronic schizophrenics, who accordingly seem excessively prone to behavioral focusing from this cause. Their supposed liability to weak ORs evidently does not mean that chronic schizophrenics lack an effective mechanism to bring about the focusing on a single stimulus that is normally associated with a strong OR. The dominance concept, it seems, describes focusing in a more inclusive sense than the concept of OR.

The response strength concept of focusing has important utility in the general literature on incidental and intentional learning (McLaughlin, 1965). It also finds support in the fact that unstructured, "meaningless," irrelevant stimuli are ineffective or only very briefly effective as distractors among normals. A good deal of the evidence on insensitivity to contextual cues can still be understood in terms of response strength, and an integrative theory of attentive disorders must reflect this fact.

Finally, an integrative theory of attentive disorders must deal with the paradox reflected above. In one group of experiments, familiarity constructs have been employed to explain broad attention: ORs are supposed to occur in the absence of familiarity and to reduce the range of attention. In another group of experiments, by contrast, other familiarity constructs—strong response tendencies—seem to mimic ORs in reducing the effectiveness of contextual cues. It is an attraction of Broadbent's new (1965) theory of attentive behavior that it seems to encompass this paradox of familiarity by postulating two such constructs, stimulus expectancy and response bias. In any case, it is clear that attentive phenomena cannot be explained solely in terms of a monotonic relation with stimulus familiarity.

REFERENCES

Agnew N. M., & Agnew, Mary. Drive level effects on tasks of narrow and broad attention. *Quart. J. exp. Psychol.*, 1963, **15**, 58–62.

Allport, G. W. The historical background of modern social psychology. In G. Lindzey (Ed.), *Handbook of Social Psychology*. Cambridge, Mass.: Addison-Wesley, 1954, pp. 3–56.

Alvarez, R. R. Comparison of depressive and brain injured subjects on the trail making test. *Percept. mot. skills*, 1962, **14**, 91–96.

Baker, C. H. Attention to visual displays during a vigilance task. I Biasing attention. *Brit. J. Psychol.*, 1958, **49**, 279–288.

Baker, C. H. Towards a theory of vigilance. *Canad. J. Psychol.*, 1959a, **13**, 35–42.

Baker, C. H. Attention to visual displays during a vigilance task. II Maintaining the level of vigilance. *Brit. J. Psychol.*, 1959b, **50**, 30–36.
Beck, A. T., Feshbach, S., & Legg, D. The clinical utility of the digit-symbol test. *J. consult. Psychol.*, 1962, **26**, 263–268.
Belmont, I., Birch, H. G., & Karp, E. The disordering of intersensory and intrasensory integration by brain damage. *J. nerv. ment. Dis.*, 1966, **141**, 410–418.
Bender, M. B. Extinction and precipitation of cutaneous sensations. *Arch. Neurol. Psychiat.*, 1945, **54**, 1–9.
Bender, M. B., Fink, M., & Green, M. Patterns in perception on simultaneous tests of face and hand. *Arch. Neurol. Psychiat.*, 1951, **66**, 355–362.
Benfari, R. Defense and control: further indications. *Percept. mot. Skills*, 1966, **22**, 736–738.
Benton, A. L. *The revised visual retention test*. Iowa City: The State University of Iowa, 1963.
Benton, A. L., & McGavren, Musetta. Qualitative aspects of visual memory test performance in mental defectives. *Amer. J. ment. Def.*, 1962, **66**, 878–883.
Benton, A. L., Elithorn, A., Fogel, M. L., & Kerr, M. A perceptual maze test sensitive to brain damage. *J. neurol. neurosurg. Psychiat.*, 1963, **26**, 540–544.
Berlyne, D. E. Attention, perception and behavior theory. *Psychol. Rev.*, 1951, **58**, 137–146.
Berlyne, D. E. *Conflict, arousal and curiosity*. New York: McGraw-Hill, 1960.
Bernstein, A. S. The galvanic skin response orienting reflex among chronic schizophrenics. *Psychonom. Sci.*, 1964, **1**, 391–392.
Birch, H. G., Belmont, I., & Karp, E. Excitation-inhibition balance in brain-damaged patients. *J. nerv. ment. Dis.*, 1964, **139**, 537–544.
Birren, J. E. *The psychology of aging*. Englewood Cliffs, N.J.: Prentice-Hall, 1964.
Broadbent, D. E. *Perception and communication*. London: Pergamon, 1958.
Broadbent, D. E. Differences and interactions between stresses. *Quart. J. exp. Psychol.*, 1963, **15**, 205–211.
Broadbent, D. E. Vigilance. *Brit. med. Bull.*, 1964, **20**, 17–20.
Broadbent, D. E. A reformulation of the Yerkes-Dodson law. *Brit. J. Math. Stat. Psychol.*, 1965, **18**, 145–157.
Broadbent, D. E., & Gregory, Margaret. Vigilance considered as a statistical decision. *Brit. J. Psychol.*, 1963, **54**, 309–323.
Brodsky, M. Interpersonal stimuli as interference in a sorting task. *J. Pers.*, 1963, **31**, 517–533.
Broen, W. E., Jr. Response disorganization and breadth of observation in schizophrenia. *Psychol. Rev.*, 1966, **73**, 579–585.
Broen, W. E., Jr., & Storms, L. H. A reaction potential ceiling and response decrements in complex situations. *Psychol. Rev.*, 1961, **68**, 405–415.
Broen, W. E., Jr., & Storms, L. H. Lawful disorganization: the process underlying a schizophrenic syndrome. *Psychol. Rev.*, 1966, **73**, 265–279.
Callaway, E. J., III, & Thompson, S. V. Sympathetic activity and perception. *Psychosom. Med.*, 1953, **15**, 443–455.
Canter, A. A background interference procedure for graphomotor tests in the study of deficit. *Percept. mot. Skills*, 1963, **16**, 914.
Canter, A. A background interference procedure to increase sensitivity of the Bender-Gestalt test to organic brain disorder. *J. consult. Psychol.*, 1966, **30**, 91–97.
Chapman, D. W., & Brown, H. E. The reciprocity of clearness and range of attention. *J. gen. Psychol.*, 1935, **13**, 357–266.
Chapman, L. J., Chapman, Jean P., & Miller, G. A. A theory of verbal behavior in schizophrenia. In B. Maher (ed.) *Progress in Experimental Personality Research*, Vol. I. New York: Academic Press, 1964, pp. 49–77.
Comalli, P. E., Wapner, S., & Werner, H. Interference effects of Stroop Color-Word Test in childhood, adulthood and aging. *J. genet. Psychol.*, 1962, **100**, 47–53.
Costa, L. D. Visual reaction time of patients with cerebral disease as a function of length and constancy of preparatory interval. *Percept. mot. Skills*, 1962, **14**, 391–397.

Costa, L. D., Horowitz, M., & Vaughan, H. G., Jr. Choice reaction time as a function of stimulus uncertainty in patients with brain lesions. *Percept. mot. Skills*, 1965, **21**, 885–886.

Davies, Ann D. M. The perceptual maze test in a normal population. *Percept. mot. Skills*, 1965, **20**, 287–293.

Deutsch, J. A., & Deutsch, D. Attention: some theoretical considerations. *Psychol. Rev.*, 1963, **70**, 80–90.

Elithorn, A. A perceptual maze sensitive to brain damage: a preliminary report. *J. neurol. neurosurg. Psychiat.*, 1955, **18**, 287.

Elithorn, A., Kerr, M., & Mott, J. A group version of a perceptual maze test. *Brit. J. Psychol.*, 1960, **51**, 19–26.

Elliott, R. Interrelationships among measures of field dependence, ability and personality traits. *J. abnorm. soc. Psychol.*, 1961, **63**, 27–36.

Eysenck, H. J., & Willett, R. A. Cue utilization as a function of drive, an experimental study. *Percept. mot. Skills*, 1962, **15**, 229–230.

Eysenck, H. J., & Willett, R. A. The effect of drive on performance and reminiscence in a complex tracing task. *Brit. J. Psychol.*, 1966, **57**, 107–112.

Fehrer, Elizabeth. Effect of stimulus similarity on retroactive masking. *J. exp. Psychol.*, 1966, **71**, 612–615.

Ferrier, E. E. An investigation of the ITPA performance of children with functional defects of articulation. *Exceptional Children*, 1966, **32**, 625–629.

Fisch, R. I., & McNamara, H. J. Conditioning of attention as factor in perceptual learning. *Percept. mot. Skills*, 1963, **17**, 891–907.

Fitzhugh, Kathleen, Fitzhugh, Loren C., & Reitan, R. M. Relation of acuteness of organic brain dysfunction to trail making test performances. *Percept. mot. Skills*, 1962, **15**, 399–403.

Fitzhugh, Kathleen, Fitzhugh, Loren C., & Reitan, R. M. Effects of "chronic" and "current" lateralized and non-lateralized cerebral lesions upon trail making test performance. *J. nerv. ment. Dis.*, 1963, **137**, 82–87.

Frank, G. H. The validity of retention of digits as a measure of attention. *J. gen. Psychol.*, 1964, **71**, 329–336.

Freedman, P. E. Human maze learning as a function of stress and partial reinforcement. *Psychol. Rep.*, 1966, **18**, 975–981.

Gardner, R. W. The development of cognitive structures. In Constance Scheerer, (ed.) *Cognition: Theory, Research, Promise*. New York: Harper, 1964, pp. 147–171.

Gardner, R. W., & Long, R. I. Control, defence and concentration effect: a study of scanning behavior. *Brit. J. Psychol.*, 1962, **53**, 129–140.

Goldstein, G., & Neuringer, C. Schizophrenic and organic signs on the trail making test. *Percept. mot. Skills*, 1966, **22**, 347–350.

Goodenough, D. R., & Karp, S. A. Field dependence and intellectual functioning. *J. abnorm. soc. Psychol.*, 1961, **63**, 241–246.

Grastyan, E. The hippocampus and higher nervous activity. In Marion A. Brazier, (ed.) *The Central Nervous System and Behavior*. New York: Macy, 1959.

Grastyan, E. The significance of the earliest manifestations of conditioning in the mechanism of learning. In A. Fessard and others (eds.) *Brain Mechanisms and Learning*. Oxford: Blackwall, 1961.

Hawkins, W. F., & Baumeister, A. A. Effect of duration of warning signal on reaction times of mental defectives. *Percept. mot. Skills*, 1965, **21**, 179–182.

Hebb, D. O., & Thompson, W. R. The social significance of animal studies. In G. Lindzey, (Ed.) *Handbook of Social Psychology*, Cambridge, Mass.: Addison-Wesley, 1954, pp. 532–562.

Holland, J. G. Technique for behavioral analysis of human observing. *Science*, 1957, **125**, 348–350.

Holland, J. G. Human vigilance. *Science*, 1958, **128**, 61–67.

Inglis J. Effect of age on responses to dichotic stimulation. *Nature*, 1962, **194**, 1101.

Inglis, J., & Caird, W. K. Age differences in successive responses to simultaneous stimulation. *Canad. J. Psychol.*, 1963, **17**, 98–105.

Israel, Nancy R. Individual differences in GSR orienting response and cognitive control. *J. exp. res. Pers.*, 1966. **1**, 244—248.

Jerison, H. J., & Pickett, R. M. Vigilance: a review and re-evaluation. *Human Factors*, 1963, **5**, 211–238.

Karp, S. A. Field dependence and overcoming embeddedness. *J. consult. Psychol.*, 1963, **27**, 294–302.

Katz, Phyllis A., & Deutsch, M. Modality of stimulus presentation in serial learning for retarded and normal readers. *Percept. mot. Skills*, 1964, **19**, 627–633.

Kendall, Barbara S. Memory-for-design performance in the seventh and eighth decades of life. *Percept. mot. Skills*, 1962, **14**, 399–405.

Kendall, Barbara S. Orientation errors in the memory-for-designs test: tentative findings and recommendations. *Percept. mot. Skills*, 1966, **22**, 335–345.

Kinsbourne, M., & Warrington, Elizabeth K. The effect of an after-coming random pattern on the perception of brief visual stimuli. *Quart. J. exp. Psychol.*, 1962a, **14**, 223–234.

Kinsbourne, M., & Warrington, Elizabeth K. Further studies in the masking of brief visual stimuli by a random pattern. *Quart. J. exp. Psychol.*, 1962b, **14**, 235–245.

Kinsbourne, M., & Warrington, Elizabeth K. A disorder of simultaneous form perception. *Brain*, 1962c, **85**, 461–486.

Kulpe, O. The problem of attention. *Monist*, 1902, **13**, 36–68.

L'Abate, L., Boelling, G. M., Hutton, R. D., & Mathews, D. L., Jr. The diagnostic usefulness of four potential tests of brain damage. *J. consult Psychol.*, 1962, **26**, 479.

Lewinsohn, P. M., & Riggs, Ann. The effect of content upon the thinking of acute and chronic schizophrenics. *J. abnorm. soc. Psychol.*, 1962, **65**, 206–207.

Luria, A. R. Peculiarities of the orientation reflexes of child oligophrenics. *The Mentally Retarded Child.* New York: Pergamon, 1963.

Lynn, R. Russian theory and research on schizophrenia. *Psychol. Bull.*, 1963, **60**, 486–498.

Lynn, R. *Attention, arousal and the orientation reflex.* London: Pergamon, 1966.

Mackintosh, N. J. Selective attention in animal discrimination learning. *Psychol. Bull.*, 1965, **64**, 124–150.

Mackworth, Jane F. Performance decrement in vigilance, threshold and high-speed perceptual motor tasks. *Canad. J. Psychol.*, 1964, **18**, 209–223.

Mackworth, Jane F. Perceptual coding as a factor in short term memory. *Canad. J. Psychol.*, 1966, **20**, 18–33.

Maltzman, I., & Raskin, D. S. Effects of individual differences in the orienting reflex in conditioning and complex processes. *J. exp. res. Pers.*, 1966, **1**, 1–16.

McCormack, P. D. A two factor theory of vigilance. *Brit. J. Psychol.*, 1962, **53**, 357–363.

McDonald, R. D. Effect of brain damage on adaptability. *J. nerv. ment. Dis.*, 1964, **138**, 241–247.

McDonald, R. D., & Burns, S. B. Visual vigilance and brain damage: an empirical study. *J. neurol neurosurg. Psychiat.*, 1964, **27**, 206–209.
241–247.

McGhie, A., Chapman, J., & Lawson, J. S. The effect of distraction on schizophrenic performance, (1) Perception and immediate memory. *Brit. J. Psychiat.*, 1965a, **111**, 383–390.

MaGhie, A., Chapman, J., & Lawson, J. S. The effect of distraction on schizophrenic performance, (2) Psychomotor ability. *Brit. J. Psychiat.*, 1965b, **111**, 391–398.

McLaughlin, B. "Intentional" and "incidental" learning in human subjects: the role of instructions to learn and motivation. *Psychol. Bull.*, 1965, **63**, 359–376.

McNamara, H. J., & Fisch, R. I. Effect of high and low motivation on two aspects of attention. *Percept. mot. Skills*, 1964, **19**, 571–578.

Morton, J. The effect of context upon speed of reading, eye movements and eye-voice span. *Quart. J. exp. Psychol.*, 1964, **16**, 340–354.

Morton, N. W. The reciprocity of visual clearness and the span of apprehension. *Amer. J. Psychol.*, 1941, **54**, 553–558.
Murphy, I. C. Serial learning, conditionability and the choice of an independent measure of anxiety. *J. abnorm. soc. Psychol.*, 1964, **69**, 614–619.
Nissen, H. W. Phylogenetic comparison. In S. S. Stevens (ed.) *Handbook of Experimental Psychology*. New York: Wiley, 1951, pp. 347–386.
Noble, C. E., Baker, B. L., & Jones, T. A. Age and sex parameters in psychomotor learning. *Percept. mot. Skills*, 1964, **19**, 935–945.
Obrist, P. A. Cardiovascular differentiation of sensory stimuli. *Psychosom. Med.*, 1963, **25**, 450–459.
Parsons, O. A., Maslow, Harriet I., Morris, Freda, & Denny, J. P. Trail making test performance in relation to certain experimenter, test and subject variables. *Percept. mot. Skills*, 1964, **19**, 199–206.
Payne, R. W. Cognitive abnormalities. In H. J. Eysenck (ed.) *Handbook of Abnormal Psychology*. New York: Basic Books, 1961, pp. 193–261.
Payne, R. W. The measurement and significance of overinclusive thinking and retardation in schizophrenic patients. In P. H. Hoch and J. Zubin (eds.) *Psychopathology and Schizophrenia: XX*. New York: Grune and Stratton, 1966, pp. 77–97.
Payne, R. W., & Caird, W. K. Reaction time, distractability and overinclusive thinking in psychotics. *J. abnorm. Psychol.*, 1967, **72**, 112–121.
Perez, P. Size constancy in normals and schizophrenics. In W. H. Ittelson and S. B. Kutash (eds.) *Perceptual Changes in Psychopathology*. New Brunswick, N.J.: Rutgers Univ. Press, 1961, pp. 39–55.
Piaget, J., Vinh-Bang, & Matalon, B. Note on the law of the temporal maximum of some optic-geometric illusions. *Amer. J. Psychol.*, 1958, **71**, 277–282.
Pillsbury, W. B. *Attention*. New York: MacMillan, 1908.
Price, R. H. Signal detection methods in personality and perception. *Psychol. Bull.*, 1966, **66**, 55–62.
Rand, G., Wapner, S., Werner, H., & McFarland, J. H. Age differences in performance on the Stroop Color-Word Test. *J. Pers.*, 1963, **31**, 534–538.
Reitan, R. M. A research program on the psychological effects of brain lesions in human beings. In N. R. Ellis (ed.) *International Review of Research in Mental Retardation*. New York: Academic Press, 1966.
Ritchie, Jean, & Butler, A. J. Performance of retardates in the memory-for-design tests. *J. clin. Psychol.*, 1964, **20**, 108–110.
Rodnick, E. H., & Shakow, D. Set in the schizophrenic as measured by a composite reaction time index. *Amer. J. Psychiat.*, 1940, **97**, 214–225.
Roff, M. A factorial study of tests in the perceptual area. *Psychometric Monogr.*, 1952, **8**.
Rosenthal, D., Lawlor, W. G., Zahn, T. P., & Shakow, D. The relationship of some aspects of mental set to degree of schizophrenic disorganization. *J. Pers.*, 1960, **28**, 26–33.
Santostefano, S., & Stayton, S. Training the preschool retarded child in focusing attention: a program for parents. *Amer. J. Orthopsychiat.*, 1967, **37**, 732–743.
Santos, D. F., & Montgomery J. R. Stability of performance on the color-word test. *Percept. mot. Skills*, 1962, **15**, 397–398.
Schiller, P. H. Developmental study of color-word interference. *J. exp. Psychol.*, 1966, **72**, 105–108.
Shakow, D. Segmental set. *Arch. gen. Psychiat.*, 1966, **6**, 1–17.
Shakow, D., & McCormick, M. Y. Mental set in schizophrenia studied in a discrimination reaction setting. *J. pers. soc. Psychol.*, 1965, **1**, 88–95.
Shantz, D. W., Rubin, B. M., & Smock, C. D. Utilization of visual information as a function of incentive motivation. *Percept. mot. Skills*, 1962, **15**, 357–358.
Shmavonian, B. M., Yarmat, A., & Cohen, S. I. Relationship between the autonomic nervous system and the central nervous system in age differences in behavior. In A. T. Welford and J. E. Birren (eds.) *Behavior, Aging and the Nervous System*. Springfield, Ill.: Thomas, 1965, pp. 235–258.

Silverman, J. The problem of attention in research and theory in schizophrenia. *Psychol. Rev.*, 1964a, **71**, 352–379.

Silverman, J. Scanning-control mechanism and "cognitive filtering" in paranoid and nonparanoid schizophrenia. *J. consult. Psychol.*, 1964b, **28**, 385–393.

Smith, T., & Boyce, E. The relationship of the trail making test to psychiatric symptomatology. *J. clin. Psychol.*, 1962, **18**, 450–453.

Smith, T. E. Relationship of the trail making test to mental retardation. *Percept. mot. Skills*, 1963, **17**, 719–722.

Sokolov, Y. N. Higher nervous functions: the orienting reflex. *Ann. Rev. Physiol.*, 1963a, **25**, 545–580.

Sokolov. Y. N. (S. W. Waydenfeld, Tr.) *Perception and the Conditioned Reflex*. London: Pergamon, 1963b.

Solley, C. M., & Murphy, G. *Development of the Perceptual World.* New York: Basic Books, 1960.

Swets, J. A., Tanner, W. P., & Birdsall, T. G. Decision procedures in perception. In J. A. Swets (ed.), *Signal Detection and Recognition by human observers.* New York: Wiley, 1964, pp. 3–57.

Talland, G. A. Initiation of response and reaction time in aging and with brain damage. In A. T. Welford and J. E. Birren (eds.), *Behavior, Aging and the Nervous System.* Springfield, Ill.: Thomas, 1965, pp. 526–561.

Tecce, J. J., & Testa, Donna H. Effects of heightened drive (shock) on 2-, 4-, and 8-choice card sorting. *Percept. mot. Skills*, 1965, **16**, 93–94.

Terrell, Catherine G., & Ellis, N. R. Reaction time in normal and defective subjects following varied warning conditions. *J. abnorm. soc. Psychol.*, 1964, **69**, 449–452.

Teuber, H. L. Neuropsychology. In Molly R. Harrower (ed.) *Recent Advances in Diagnostic Psychological Testing*. Toronto: Ryerson, 1950, pp. 30–52.

Teuber, H. L., Battersby, W. S., & Bender, M. B. *Visual field defects after missile wounds of the brain*. Cambridge, Mass.: Harvard Univ. Press, 1960.

Thompson, L. W., Opton, E., Jr., & Cohen, L. D. Effects of age, presentation speed and sensory modality on performance on a "vigilance" task. *J. Gerontol.*, 1963, **18**, 366–369.

Thurstone, L. L. A factorial study of perception. *Psychometric Monogr.*, 1944, **4**.

Tolman, E. C. Cognitive maps in rats and men. *Psychol. Rev.*, 1948, **55**, 189–208.

Treisman, Anne M. Selective attention in man. *Brit. med. Bull.*, 1964, **20**, 12–16.

Treisman, Anne M. Reading rate, word information and auditory monitoring of speech. *Nature*, 1965, **205**, 1297–3000.

Treisman, Anne M. Our limited attention. *Adv. Sci.*, 1966, **22**, 600–611.

Venables, P. H. Selectivity of attention, withdrawal, and cortical activation: studies in chronic schizophrenia. *Arch. gen. Psychiat.*, 1963, **9**, 74–78.

Venables, P. H. Input dysfunction in schizophrenia. In B. Maher (ed.) *Progress in Experimental Personality Research*. Vol. 1, New York: Academic Press, 1964, pp. 1–47.

Venables, P. H. Slowness in schizophrenia. In. A. T. Welford and J. E. Birren (eds.) *Behavior, Aging and the Nervous System*. Springfield, Ill.: Thomas, 1965.

Walters, R. H. Conditioning of attention as a source of autistic effects in perception. *J. abnorm. soc. Psychol.*, 1958, **57**, 197–201.

Wapner, S., & Krus, D. M. Effects of lysergic acid diethylamide and differences between normals and schizophrenics on the Stroop Color-Word Test. *J. Neuropsychiat.*, 1960, **2**, 76–81.

Warrington, Elizabeth K., Kinsbourne, M., & James, M. Uncertainty and transitional probability in the span of apprehension. *Brit. J. Psychol.*, 1966, **57**, 7–16.

Weckowicz, T. E. Perception of hidden pictures by schizophrenic patients. *Arch. gen. Psychiat.*, 1960, **2**, 521–527.

Weckowicz, T. E., & Blewett, D. B. Size constancy and abstract thinking in schizophrenic patients. *J. ment. Sci.*, 1959, **105**, 709–734.

Welford, A. T. The study of aging. *Brit. med. Bull.*, 1964, **20**, 65–69.

White, A. R. *Attention*. Oxford: Basil Blackwell, 1964.

Witkin, H. A. Psychological differentiation and forms of pathology. *J. abnorm. Psychol.*, 1965, **70**, 317–336.

Witkin, H. A., Dyk, Ruth B., Faterson, Hanna F., Goodenough, D. R., & Karp, S. A. *Psychological Differentiation*. New York: Wiley, 1962.

Witkin, H. A., Faterson, Hanna F., Goodenough, D. R., & Birnbaum, Judith. Cognitive patterning in mildly retarded boys. *Child Developm.*, 1966, **37**, 301–316.

Woodworth, R. S. *Experimental Psychology*. New York: Holt, 1938.

Zahn, T. P., & Rosenthal, D. Preparatory set in acute schizophrenia. *J. nerv. ment. Dis.*, 1965, **141**, 352–358.

Zahn, T. P., Rosenthal, D., & Shakow, D. Reaction time in schizophrenic and normal subjects in relation to the sequence of series of regular preparatory intervals. *J. abnorm. soc. Psychol.*, 1963, **63**, 161–168.

Zangwill, O. L. Neurological studies and human behaviour. *Brit. Med. Bull.*, 1964, **20**, 43–48.

Zeaman, D., & House, Betty J. The role of attention in retardate discrimination learning. In N. R. Ellis (ed.) *Handbook of Mental Deficiency*. New York: McGraw-Hill, 1963.

Chapter 6

Depersonalization

T. WECKOWICZ[1]

INTRODUCTION

Depersonalization is a concept difficult to delineate. It can be regarded as a symptom or as a loosely associated group of symptoms that occurs in psychiatric patients. It can be induced experimentally and also occurs spontaneously in normal subjects. A major obstacle to clearer definition of this concept lies in the fact that it refers to exceedingly private events in the individual's experience. These prove very difficult to describe by a language geared to the description of public (consensually validated) events or private events, such as pain, that occur usually in clearly defined social settings. When it comes to describing and conveying something as ineffable as depersonalization or derealization, the subject resorts to metaphors, "as if" expressions, and figures of speech. The result is semantic confusion. Different authors mean different things when they use the term depersonalization.

The concept of depersonalization merges by imperceptible degrees with the concept derealization, the concept of altered body image and self, *déjà vu, jamais vu*, altered time and space perception and so on—the whole gamut of phenomenological descriptions of the experiences of mental patients. Therefore, it is rather difficult to evaluate and to review objectively the psychiatric literature on the phenomena of depersonalization.

DEFINITION

There are several definitions of Depersonalization, which are really descriptions of the symptom. The one offered by Schilder (1914) is perhaps most clear and precise. It is given here in a free English translation:

> "The individual feels totally different from his previous being; he does not recognise himself as a person. His actions seem automatic he behaves as if he were an observer of his own actions. The outside world appears to him strange and new and it has lost the character of reality. The 'self' does not behave any longer in its former way" (p. 54).

From this definition it can be seen that the core of the symptom is a change in appearance, a "strangeness" of the object of experience: either the self or the external world or both. There is also a disturbance in the subject-object relationship producing perplexity and interfering with the smooth flow of conscious experience. These aspects of depersonalization are stressed in one form or another by all the investigators of this phenomenon.

HISTORY

Krishaber (1872) gave the first description of depersonalization under the name of

[1] The author wishes to acknowledge the help in translating papers from German and the constructive criticism of his wife Dr. Helen Liebel-Weckowicz.

"cerebro-cardiac neuropathy." The term "depersonalization" was used first by Dugas (1898) who subsequently published a monograph and a paper on the subject (Dugas, 1933; Dugas & Moutier, 1911). Schilder (1914, 1928, 1935, 1939) in several publications gave perhaps the most thorough description of the depersonalization symptom. Mapother (Mayer-Gross, 1935) differentiated between depersonalization as concerned with the self and derealization as concerned with the external world. A similar differentiation into the auto- and allopsychic depersonalizations was made by Wernicke (1900). He also distinguished somatopsychic depersonalization which was an expression of a disturbed relationship to one's body. Kurt Schneider (1921) treated the discussion of depersonalization from a phenomenological point of view. Janet (1903) considered depersonalization from the point of view of his theory of levels of psychic tension. Freud (1936) devoted a paper to his personal experience of derealization on seeing the Acropolis for the first time in his life. Several other psychoanalytic writers have contributed to the subject (Nunberg, 1955a; Federn, 1928; Hartmann, 1922; Sadger, 1928; Oberndorf, 1934; Bergler & Eidelberg, 1935; Bychowski, 1943). More recently psychoanalytic writers, interested in "ego psychology," have discussed depersonalization phenomena from the point of view of the self-object split in the ego (Jacobson, 1959; Sarlin, 1962; Stamm, 1962). Meyer (1957, 1959), von Gebsattel (1937), and Kimura (1963) have discussed depersonalization in terms of the phenomenological and existential schools of psychiatry. Important contributions to the topic have also been made by descriptive, nosological psychiatrists in the Kraepelinian tradition, like Mayer-Gross (1935), Shorvon (1946), Ackner (1954a, 1954b), and Roth (1959). Three monographs on the subject were published by Goppert (1960), Vella (1960), and Megrabyan (1962) in German, Italian, and Russian, respectively. Cattell (1966) has given the most recent review of literature on the depersonalization phenomenon.

DESCRIPTION AND PHENOMENOLOGY

In this section the phenomena of depersonalization will be described. Phenomenology of depersonalization is a description of the contents of consciousness of depersonalized subjects. It must be distinguished from any theoretical interpretation of depersonalization undertaken by writers of the phenomenological school of philosophy and psychiatry. The various kinds of phenomenological interpretations will be presented in a subsequent section. According to Ackner (1954a) who investigated 50 patients suffering from depersonalization, their experience can be characterized by six salient features: (1) feeling of change, (2) feeling of unreality, (3) unpleasant quality of the experience, (4) the non-delusional quality of the experience, and (5) a loss of affective response.

Feeling of Change

The subject feels himself changed completely in comparison with his former state. This change extends to both himself and the external world. He feels strange, cannot recognize himself. Both his inner and outer worlds have undergone a profound change. This feeling of change comes on very often quite suddenly, often after awakening with a fright from a light sleep or after an attack of syncope (Mayer-Gross, 1935; Shorvon, 1946; Meyer, 1959). The subject is bewildered, perplexed, and cannot understand the meaning of this change.

Feeling of Unreality

The self and the body appear unreal, as if the subject were dreaming. When the phenomenon of depersonalization is accompanied by derealization, as it very often is, the feeling of unreality extends to the external world. The individual says that his body feels as if it were not made of flesh and bone but of the same "stuff that dreams are made of." The subject feels as if he were dead. The external world lacks vividness, the colors are dull. The houses and trees look as if they were not real, but were mere props made of cardboard. There is a lack of depth and a flatness in the perceived external world. People do not look real, they appear to be robots moving mechanically. The subject's movements have also a robotlike, mechanical quality; they do not seem to be under control of the self. Loewy (Mayer-Gross, 1935) refers to this aspect of depersonalization as a loss of the specific feelings that accompany action (*Aktionsgefühle*) and considers it as the basic symptom in depersonalization. The feeling of unreality does not necessarily mean that the experienced sensations and feelings are fainter than ordinarily. Sometimes there is a hyperawareness and a nightmarish quality about them (Cattell, 1966). The subjects use metaphors and figures of speech to convey the strange feeling of unreality experienced with regard to themselves and the outer world.

The Unpleasant Quality of Experience

Characteristically the subject finds the experience of depersonalization unpleasant. This quality of unpleasantness distinguishes true depersonalization from a feeling of change and detachment that occurs occasionally in alcoholics, and in LSD_{25} and mescaline intoxication, although these two drugs produce quite often a state of true depersonalization. Sometimes the feelings of change and detachment, for example, produced by alcohol or in some mystical experiences, are highly pleasant and are connected with a state of euphoria. It is a debatable question whether these phenomena are the same as clinical depersonalization. Some psychoanalysts, for example, Stamm (1962) claim that some of their patients find depersonalization pleasant, but it is doubtful if they are describing the same phenomenon. True depersonalization is very unpleasant. In a patient of Cattell (1966), a young woman, this unpleasant feeling of depersonalization was so intense that she had a strong urge to inflict pain on herself in order to produce a real feeling. The unpleasant feeling in the case of depersonalization is very often associated with a fear of going insane, dying, or fainting.

The Nondelusional Quality

The true depersonalization symptom has an interesting "as if" quality. The subjects are aware that their bodies are real, they only feel "as if" they were not real. The external world is real; it only appears to be unreal. The individual finds the experience quite perplexing and in conflict with his system of beliefs. The state of depersonalization can pass by imperceptible degrees into a delusional state with the individual having delusions about his body, his identity, and the external world. Delusions of this type, for example, of being dead, of the body being made of some inorganic material, of having no blood, and nihilistic delusions out the external world are particularly common in involutional melancholia, although they occur also in schizophrenia. Once the patient has developed delusions to account for his experiences, he becomes less perplexed, more reconciled to his fate, and more accepting of his experience. His system of beliefs and his experiences become congruent with one another. Some state of equilibrium is achieved. Many patients in incipient stages of schizophrenia, involutional melancholia, or depression, experience depersonalization and derealization. Subsequently these phenomena are replaced by frank delusions. Roth (1959) has described a syndrome in which a short psychotic episode with frank delusions is followed by a prolonged state of depersonalization and derealization. Ackner (1954a) describes a group of patients in whom there is a fluctuation between a complaint having an "as if" formulation and a frankly delusional conviction. These may be borderline cases of schizophrenia.

Loss of Affective Response

The subjects complain of a loss of capacity to experience feelings. They complain of having lost affection for the members of their families, of losing all their interest, of not being capable of loving and empathizing with others (Lewis, 1934; Mayer-Gross, 1935). At the same time there is no objective evidence of flatness of affect (Schilder, 1914). On the contrary, the subjects are very distressed and worried because they are not capable of experiencing emotions. Thus, there is a paradox of the subject being emotionally disturbed and emotional about not being able to experience emotions. Kurt Schneider (1921) stressed this inability to experience genuine emotions as being the core symptom in depersonalization and the basic mechanism underlying it.

Depersonalization usually occurs in conjunction with some other symptoms. Some of them are very closely related to depersonalization and cannot be easily separated. Thus derealization: feeling of strangeness and unreality of the external world accompanies depersonalization in a majority of cases. Other symptoms that occur quite often together with depersonalization are distortion of body image, alteration in self-concept, changed time and space perception, distortion of perception of forms, *déjà vu* and *jamais vu* feelings, states of altered consciousness, complaints about inability to visualize, hypermnesia, and tendency to ruminate about the past. More loosely associated with depersonalization are depression, frankly schizophrenic symptoms (such as hallucinations, delusions, and disorder of thought), phobic states, mildly obsessional states, and temporal lobe epilepsy. Of these symptoms, distortion of space and time perceptions, inability to visualize, and hypermnesia drew particular attention of various phenomenologically inclined writers on depersonalization. In describing depersonalization and derealization they pointed out that perception of space was distorted, that very often there was no depth perception, that objects appeared flat and two dimensional, that there was a distortion of perceived distances, and that the shapes of perceived objects were also distorted. The perception of time in many patients is altered. Time appears to move very slowly or to be at a standstill. The patients sometimes experience being outside time. Time and self become separated. Also experience becomes fragmented, there is no continuity in time any longer. Inability to visualize all possible aspects of perceived objects which could be potentially experienced detracts from meaningfulness of percepts. Janet (1903) attached a great significance to hypermnesia and the tendency to ruminate about the premorbid state and to compare it with the present state of illness.

As we can observe from the above, depersonalization is far from being a clearly delineated, operationally definable symptom. It is more like a loosely knit complex of symptoms, a poorly delineated sphere of experiences.

INCIDENCE

Symptoms very like those of depersonalization occur quite often in psychiatric patients as well as in normals. The difficulty in arriving at precise figures of their incidence is caused by the lack of agreement among the authors on what constitutes a full-fledged depersonalization syndrome. This is inevitable in view of the vagueness of the concept. Depersonalization and derealization have been described as occurring in many cases of psychotic depression (Lewis, 1934). They occur quite often in early stages of schizophrenia, particularly of the hebephrenic type (Mayer-Gross et al., 1954). According to Shorvon (1946):

> "depersonalization can occur in any morbid psychological condition and is common in manic-depressive states, schizophrenia, obsessional neurosis and involutional melancholia. It also occurs in anxiety states and hysteria. It is seen in states of altered consciousness and occurs in encephalitis lethargica, in epilepsy, intoxications, delirium, hypoglycemia and exhaustion. It has been described in organic conditions such as brain tumour and trauma, athetosis, hypoparathyroidism, carbon monoxide poisoning and mescalin intoxication" (p. 780).

To this can be added depersonalization that occurs in subjects undergoing sensory deprivation experiments, in prisoners, in weightlessness produced by space travel, and its relatively frequent occurrence reported in samples of normal population, particularly in adolescence. The prevalence of the depersonalization symptoms among psychoneurotics is indicated by the fact that Shorvon (1946), during a relatively short period of time, collected 66 cases, and that Roth (1959) had no difficulty in finding 135 cases. Roberts (1960) investigated occurrence of depersonalization in a sample of the British student population. By using an open-ended questionnaire he found that out of the sample of 57, twenty-three subjects reported having experienced depersonalization symptoms. Dixon (1963), by using more objective questionnaires on a sample of 112 American students, found that between one third and one half had genuine depersonalisation experiences. All the above authors with the exception of Dixon have found a higher incidence of depersonalization in women than in men, a fact also stressed by Mayer-Gross (1935).

The most frequently reported age of the onset of depersonalization is in the twenties (Mayer-Gross, 1935; Shorvon, 1946). However, Roberts (1960) and several psychoanalytical authors (Jacobson, 1959; Blank, 1954; Stamm, 1962) reported first occurrence of depersonalization in childhood. Roth (1959) had in his series a relatively high proportion of patients in whom the first onset of depersonalization was at the age of over 45.

PREVIOUS PERSONALITY AND PRECIPITATING CAUSES

It has been consistently reported that there is a relation between depersonalization and obsessional symptoms. Thus, Shorvon (1946) reported obsessional traits in 88 percent of his series of cases, Roth (1959) 74 percent, and Meyer (1959) regards obsessional neurosis and depersonalization as two alternative mechanisms of dealing with the external world and as occurring in the same personality type. The obsessional characteristics that occur in depersonalized individuals are personality traits rather than symptoms of a fully developed compulsive-obsessional neurosis. Roth (1959) describes the predepersonalization personality as being dependent, immature, obsessional, rigid, anxiety prone and afflicted with mild chronic phobias. These patients are conscientious, scrupulous individuals. They like order, are cautious and routine bound. Sedman and Reed (1963) pointed out that the type of personality described by Roth is very similar to the anankastic-sensitive personality type described by Kurt Schneider (1958). These authors reported that depersonalization occurred very often in depressive patients whose premorbid personality can be categorized as anankastic-sensitive. It is possible that, in the case of individuals described as having anankastic personalities, some developmental factors lead to a poorly integrated "body schema" or a poorly developed self-concept that predisposes them to depersonalization. Other premorbid personality types have been reported in patients suffering from depersonalization. Thus, Mayer-Gross (1935) found relatively frequent extroverted personality, and Janet (1903) mentions psychosthenic personality. Hysterical personality has also been implicated. Thus, one third of Shorvon's depersonalized patients had hysterical symptoms. Ackner (1954b) and Meyer (1959) also described a hysterical type of depersonalization. If the anankastic-insecure personality is accepted as a predisposing factor, it would indicate that, using Eysenck's terminology, depersonalization occurs more frequently in dysthymics and, therefore, is typical rather of introversion than extroversion (Eysenck, 1947). On the other hand, if the hysterical personality is implicated, the connection will be between depersonalization and extroversion. Regarding the previous history of the patients, Shorvon (1946) and several psychoanalytic writers (Wittles, 1940; Oberndorf 1934), reported disturbed child-parent, particularly child-father relations in persons suffering from depersonalization. However, Roth (1959) could not confirm this finding in his sample. When discussing onset and precipitating causes, most of the authors stress the suddenness of onset in many cases of depersonalization (Mayer-Gross, 1935; Shorvon, 1946; Roth, 1959). In many cases there is a history of trauma preceding the onset of depersonalization. Thus, Roth (1959) has found a psychic shock, a bereavement or some threat to the individual, significantly more often preceding the onset of depersonalization than preceding the onset of other neurotic conditions. He mentions as precipitating causes: personal calamity, physical illness, exhaustion, and anaesthesia—all conditions that produce an acute threat to the patient and that overwhelm him by a sudden fear. Shorvon (1946) made an interesting observation that the onset of depersonalization is very often preceded by a relaxation that follows prolonged fatigue or psychological stress or both.

The duration and pattern of the depersonalization episodes can vary a great deal. Some depersonalization attacks, particularly the ones which occur in normal people, are momentary, others may last for years. Some subjects can have repeated depersonalization episodes (Roberts, 1960). As mentioned previously, sometimes depersonalization precedes a frankly delusional-psychotic state, at other times it may follow a brief psychotic episode (Roth, 1959).

THE NOSOLOGICAL STATUS OF DEPERSONALIZATION

As could be expected, the vagueness of the concept of depersonalization caused a controversy among Kraepelinian psychiatrists as to whether to regard it as a symptom, a syndrome, or a full-fledged disease entity. Mayer-Gross (1935) came to the conclusion that depersonalization was a biopsychological reaction, probably an unspecific "preformed" functional response of the brain which could be produced in the predisposed individuals by many causes. He regarded it as a physiologically determined reaction which could be triggered off by a variety of factors. It is even possible that depersonalization may be related to temporal lobe epilepsy. The fact that Shorvon (1946) reported a high incidence of nonspecific EEG abnormalities in patients suffering from depersonalization adds some additional plausibility to this hypothesis. However, Roth (1959) found that EEG abnormalities in depersonalized patients, although common are not more common than in other neurotics. Ackner (1954b) believes that the depersonalization syndrome can occur in the framework of several different mental diseases. He describes six depersonalization syndrome settings: (1) Depersonalization in an organic brain disease. (2) Schizoid disturbance of identity, described by Glauber (1949) as "primary anhedonia," by Eisenstein (1951) as "narcissistic neurosis," and by Deutch (1942) as "as if" personalities. (3) Hysterical disturbance of identity. (4) Other hysterical depersonalization syndromes mainly produced by repression or denial. (5) Depressive depersonalization syndrome. (6) "Tension" depersonalization syndrome. The last is produced by repression of hostile feelings and aggressive urges. In addition to these six types, he mentions two more: multiple depersonalization syndrome and mixed depersonalization syndrome. The multiple depersonalization syndrome in which subjects can have a succession of different kinds of depersonalization as of the "depressive" type and of the "tension" type is of some theoretical importance. It indicates, according to Ackner, that depersonalization is not a "disease entity" and that it could be produced in the same individual by different "disease processes."

Meyer (1959) classified nonpsychotic cases of depersonalization on the basis of the factors that triggered the symptom into the following groups: (1) Depersonalization and derealization as a disturbance of the relationship between the ego and the environment (the anankastic depersonalization). (2) Depersonalization as an acute reaction to a traumatic experience. (3) Depersonalization as a symptom of chronic neurosis. (4) Hysterical depersonalization. (5) Depersonalization accompanying mystical experience. This phenomenon although it bears a great similarity to depersonalization proper, is different from the latter because it leads to a richer spiritual life. (6) Depersonalization occurring in puberty, particularly when associated with an identity crisis. Other writers of Kraepelinian tradition stand on the side of a disease entity "depersonalization" which has to be differentiated from the depersonalization as a symptom of other "mental diseases." Shorvon (1946) talks about "primary idiopathic depersonalization" occurring in adolescence. Roth (1959) described a new "form of neurotic illness" with a typical onset and history that is characterized by a combination of depersonalization and a characteristic form of phobic anxiety. In 40 percent of cases of this "new illness" there are "features reminiscent of disturbance in temporal lobe function such as *déjà vu* phenomena, metamorphopsia, and panoramic memory and, in a higher proportion, more variable obsessional, hysterical, depressive features and vasomotor disturbances" (p. 594). Individuals with an anankastic personality seem to be predisposed to this condition. It appears to the author of this chapter that, until causal mechanisms are known, it is rather futile to talk about "disease entities."

Some attempts have also been made to delineate the depersonalization syndrome more precisely. Roberts (1960) differentiated depersonalization syndrome (DP) from depersonalization symptom (dp). Depersonalization syndrome is a wider category and includes apart from depersonalization symptoms proper symptoms of derealization (dr), desomatization (ds), loss of feeling (dE), loss of visualization (dv), and slowing up of subjective time (dT). The descriptions of depersonalization experiences by normal subjects were scored by two independent investigators for the above categories, and a high degree of agreement was obtained. The most objective study was that of Dixon (1963). A Lickert-type of self-administered rating scale of various aspects of depersonalization together with the Guilford R scale for introversion-extroversion (of the Guilford STDCR battery) and the Taylor Manifest Anxiety Scale (TMAS) were administered to 117 students. The scores of 112 subjects were intercorrelated and analyzed by cluster analysis. One large cluster of "self-alienation" and two smaller ones: "mystical experience" and "hallucinatory experiences" were found. When a centroid axis of the "self-alienation" cluster was found, ten items of the depersonalization self-rating scale loaded highly on it. As far as the other personality variables were concerned, there was no relation between the Guilford R introversion-extroversion scale and depersonalization score for men. For women a small negative correlation ($r = -.22$) was found. Furthermore, there was a positive correlation between the depersonalization and anxiety measures ($r = .54$ for women and $r = .32$ for men). The study of King and Little (1959) throws some additional light on the relation of depersonalization to introversion-extroversion and anxiety. These authors found that thiapentone (a barbiturate) produced improvement in cases of depersonalization. It reduced phobic anxiety by lowering arousal and also, if the theory of Eysenck (1963) is true, it shifted the subjects in the direction of extroversion. This would indicate that depersonalization is more likely to be a dysthymic than a hysterical symptom. There is a great need for more correlational studies on the line of Dixon's study, using both normals and psychiatric patients, suffering from depersonalization, as subjects.

THEORIES OF DEPERSONALIZATION

Many theories of depersonalization have been offered. Some of them are only restatements of the description of the phenomenon, others are purely speculative. There is a dearth of experimental studies. All the theories of depersonalization can be divided into the following groups: (1) One aspect of depersonalization is selected and put forward as an explanation of the phenomenon, (2) organic theories of depersonalization, (3) psychoanalytic and psychodynamic theories, (4) theories in the framework of the phenomenological and existential schools of psychiatry. It will not be possible to discuss all the theories in detail, and only the most important ones will be reviewed.

One-Aspect Theories

Most of the early theorists of depersonalization singled out one feature of the symptom and built their explanation of depersonalization around it. These early theories were summarized by Ackner (1954b) and the present summary follows his summary closely. Thus, Krishaber (1872) and Ribot (1882) considered depersonalization as being the result of a disturbance of sense perception. Pick (1904), Oesterreich (1910), and Loewy (1908) stressed the emotional disturbance as primary. Loewy postulated a loss of specific feelings accompanying action and movements. Janet (1903) believed that a hyperactivity of memory, which prompted the patient to contrast his illness with the recollection of the healthy state, was the cause of depersonalization. Heymans (1911) incriminated the loss of feeling of familiarity as the basis of the syndrome. Schilder (1914) in his early paper stated the "increased self observation" produced depersonalization. Ackner (1954b) points out that, apart from the ad hoc nature of this theorizing, it was based on the now unacceptable assumption that the mind is composed of a collection of different functions any one of which may be singly disturbed. More recent theorists think in terms of the totality of the personality functions. Thus, Störring (1933) postulated a disturbance of a number of different psychological functions as the cause of depersonalization. Ackner (1954b) himself suggested

> "that it is the relative failure of integration of an experience and not the experience itself which gives rise to the feeling of unreality or strangeness. As such failure of integration may originate from more than one source and as many different experiences may be affected, depersonalization complaints may have many different origins" (p. 864).

Particularly, integration of experience with the system of beliefs appears to be important.

Organic Theories of Depersonalization

Attempts have been made to explain depersonalization on the basis of organic disturbance of the brain functions. As we mentioned in the section on the incidence of depersonalization, the phenomenon occurs in many organic diseases of the brain, particularly the ones that involve the parietal, the temporal lobes, and the lymbic system. Schilder (1935) in his later discussion of depersonalization and L'Hermitte (1939) related depersonalization to a disturbance of "body schema" (body image). Tumours or lesions localized in the region of the inferior parietal, angular and marginal gyri of the brain produce body-schema disturbance and often depersonalization-like symptoms. However, cases with an organic brain damage in these regions constitute only a small minority of all the cases with depersonalization symptoms. In an earlier paper Schilder (1928) suggested that abnormal afferent stimuli which result from certain vestibular disorders can cause sudden changes in the individual's experience of his body or of the world. More recently, Weckowicz and Sommer (1960) related the impoverishment of self-concept in chronic schizophrenics to a disturbance of the body image and space perception. Penfield and Rasmussen (1950) produced feelings of unreality, derealization, and phenomena resembling depersonalization by electrical stimulation of various areas of the temporal lobes in conscious patients. However, these symptoms were associated with states of altered consciousness such as clouding and mild confusion, and thus were different from typical depersonalization symptoms. Some similarity between depersonalization and temporal lobe epilepsy has already been pointed out. Mayer-Gross (1935) and Shorvon (1946) postulated a "preformed functional response of the brain" as the basis of depersonalization. The fact that depersonalization occurs at puberty and also at the involutional period of life, points to the possibility that harmonal changes occurring in these two periods of life may cause depersonalization.

Hallucinogenic drugs produce very often symptoms similar to depersonalization that are sometimes indistinguishable from the depersonalization symptoms occurring in psychiatric patients and occasionally lasting several days. Guttmann and Maclay (1936) described depersonalization symptoms produced by mescalin intoxication. Mering, Morimoto, Hyde, and Rinkel (1957) described depersonalization induced by LSD_{25}. Luby, Cohen, Rosenbaum, Gottlieb, and Kelley (1959) produced schizophrenia-like depersonalization by another hallucinogenic drug, Sernyl. These psychopharmacological studies indicate that depersonalization may be produced not only by an anatomical lesion of the brain, but also by a biochemical lesion. Unfortunately, too little is known about the specific effects of these drugs on the brain to postulate a hypothesis about the mechanisms by which they produce depersonalization.

In between the organic theories and psychodynamic theories of depersonalization, there are some explanations based on occasional depersonalization-like phenomena produced by experimental means in psychological laboratories. Thus, sensory deprivation experiments occasionally produce depersonalization-like experiences in subjects (Wexler, Mendelson, Liederman, and Solomon, 1958). Similar effects are sometimes produced by a delayed auditory feedback and "white noise" (Cattell, 1966). Thus it seems that a disruption of the normal input of information into the brain and, also, lasting changes in arousal could produce depersonalization. Experiments in which subjects received conflicting information occasionally produced symptoms somewhat resembling depersonalization. Witkin and Asch (1948a, b) reported that conflicting vestibular and visual cues for the orientation of the body in space, as in the tilted room or tilted chair situation, occasionally produce symptoms somewhat resembling depersonalization. Weightlessness, as in space travel, was also reported to produce some perceptual disturbance and ego disorientation which were similar to the ones occurring in depersonalization (Mercury Project Summary, 1963). These experiments throw some light on the frame of reference of the theory of ego functioning, which will be discussed together with other psychoanalytic and psychodynamic theories. The fact that it is almost impossible to define depersonalization operationally renders an experimental approach to this problem extremely difficult.

Psychoanalytic and Psychodynamic Theories

Following the example of Cattell (1966) psychoanalytic theories of depersonalization can be divided into three groups: (1) Those that explain depersonalization as a result of the function of defence mechanisms, (2) those that stress intrapsychic splitting and (3) those that are based on recent developments in ego psychology and stress perception, apperception, the concept of self, and ego development.

The early psychoanalytical theories of depersonalization stressed conventional ego-defence mechanisms, particularly the one of denial. The paradigm for this type of defence is the description by Freud (1900) of dream within dream. The dreamer defends himself against forbidden impulses becoming conscious in the dream by saying to himself "this is only a dream, therefore it is not real." In this way a feeling of unreality, derealization, and depersonalization may serve as a denial of forbidden impulses. Freud (1936) in a later paper described a personal experience of derealization when seeing the Akropolis for the first time in his life and explained this experience as a defence against a feeling of triumph and guilt. Bergler and Eidelberg (1935) put forward the hypothesis that depersonalization is a defence against unacceptable anal-exhibitionistic wishes. Sadger (1928) and Searl (1932) regarded depersonalization as a defence against fear of castration. More recently Sarlin (1962) advanced the idea that depersonalization is a defence against sadistic-aggressive impulses directed against an internalized object. Arlow (1959) has described the *déjà vu* experience, a phenomenon closely related to depersonalization, as being defensive in the sense that it assures the subject there is no danger; he has passed through this threatening situation safely once before. Blank (1954), Rosen (1955), Bird (1957), and Stamm (1962) also stressed the defensive function of depersonalization. With the greater stress on the personality structure as against instinctive impulses in more recent psychoanalytical theorizing, there has been an increasing tendency among psychoanalytical writers to explain the depersonalization phenomena in terms of intrapsychic conflict and splitting. The split is between the ego and the superego, or within the ego itself. Nunberg (1955) postulated that in depersonalization destructive impulses stored in the ego are turned back against the ego and threaten the ego with destruction, treating it as if it were a genital. Thus one part of the ego becomes dissociated from another part and ignores it. Oberndorf (1934, 1950) postulated that depersonalization is caused by a conflict between the ego and the superego, produced by an identification with the parent of the wrong sex. Thus a disharmony results between the ego which is of one sex and the superego which is of the other sex. The resulting anxiety is denied by erotization of thinking. Wittles (1940) believed that depersonalization was produced by a poor integration and a split within the ego because of multiple incompatible identifications with several objects (phantom images). Sarlin (1962) also considered conflicting identifications as being important in the causation of depersonalization. The last four authors consider unsatisfactory child-parent relations an important factor in the genesis of depersonalization in later life.

Jacobson (1959) who described depersonalization symptoms occurring in political prisoners, also emphasized a split within the ego. In these prisoners one part of the ego tended to identify with the jailers and the other with the self of the prisoner, with a resulting regression to a pregenital level and a narcissistic conflict of a sado-masochistic pattern. The depersonalization was due to a denial of the existence of one part of the ego by the other. Fenichel (1945) believed that depersonalization resulted from a withdrawal of the libidinal cathexes from the external world and the investment of them in the ego. At the time countercathexes tended to deny this libidinization of the ego. Federn (1928) put forward a similar explanation of depersonalization but also stated that different parts of the ego, for example, the boundary as against the core, may be invested with different amounts of libido. The last group of psychoanalytical theories is a logical extension of the previous group. Their ideas are based on the more recent work of psychoanalytical ego theorists such as Hartmann (1950) and Jacobson (1954). The latter stress the integrative, conflict-free aspects of the ego which are responsible for an intrinsic personality growth quite apart from neurotic conflicts. They also stress the self of the individual as being not the same as his ego. While the ego is a mental apparatus, the self is an internalized image of the individual. Both the self and various external objects become parts of the ego. In narcissism, libido is invested not in the whole of the ego, but only in the self-image. The distinction between the ego and the self is similar to that made in social psychology (Mead, 1934) between "I" and "me." "I" is the subject and "me" the percept of oneself as seen by others and the subject. It will be seen that this distinction is extremely important for the theorizing of phenomenological and existentialist writers. Another important point of the new ego psychology is an attempt to investigate ego functions by the methods and within the framework of experimental psychology. Thus, perception and cognitive processes are considered as important ego functions. Kubie (1953) stresses the importance of the body schema as the foundation of the knowledge of the external world. Roberts (1960) in the theoretical part of his paper uses a similar idea to explain depersonalization and derealization. According to this author the self-image is at the core of all experience. In perception of the external world, this self-image is exteriorized in imagination and gives meaning to the perceived objects. If this process is not functioning properly, derealization and depersonalization occur. Stewart (1964) comments that a satisfactory child-mother relationship is necessary for subsequent fusion of percepts with memory traces, thus, rendering them meaningful. A lack of such a fusion may cause the perceived world to be meaningless, thus, producing feelings of derealization. McReynolds (1960) postulated that in schizophrenic patients, who often suffer from depersonalization and derealization, percepts are not assimilated to the "conceptual schema." As a result, objects look strange and unfamiliar and cause anxiety in the patients. Weckowicz (1964) reported experimental findings that support McReynolds' theory. Arlow (1959) believes that in depersonalization phenomena there is a split in the self-representation into a participating self and an observing self, the participitating self being "me" and the observing self being "I." The participating self is dissociated from the rest of the ego, producing the feeling of estrangement. The theory of Schilder (1914) discussed earlier that depersonalization is the result of a morbidly exaggerated self-observation, is relevant in this connection. The most important contribution in this group of theories is the article: "The self, the sense of self and perception" by Spiegel (1959). This author offers a closely reasoned theory of "self-feeling" and self-perception. He bases his theorizing on perceptual and conceptual phenomena such as figure-ground relations, adaptation level (Helson, 1948), and frame of reference (Sherif & Cantril, 1947). The unusual "self-feelings" and self-perceptions are produced where there is a marked discrepancy between an inner sensation or a self-perception and the frame of reference. This discrepancy may be produced by an unusual inner sensation, deviating markedly from the frame of reference (for example, sensations produced by hallucinogenic drugs) or the frame of reference itself is unstable because of the lack of stability of the experienced environment. Thus a disturbance of constancy of internal perception and the constancy of "self-feeling" produce disturbances in the feelings of identity and in the feelings of reality, leading to depersonalization phenomena. Depersonalization occurring during puberty and adolescence, very often connected with the identity crisis, can be explained on the basis of Spiegel's theory as a dissonance between novel "self-feelings" and previously formed self-concept.

An apparent convergence between psychoanalytical theory and contemporary experimental psychology, as indicated by Spiegel's paper, is of some importance for the general development of psychology. We shall observe in the next section on the views regarding depersonalization of the phenomenological and existential schools of psychiatry that there is also some convergence between the views of these two schools on the one hand and that of psychoanalysis and experimental psychology on the other. We turn now to the discussion of the views of phenomenologists and existentialists.

Theories in the Framework of the Phenomenological and Existential Schools of Psychiatry

Since depersonalization is a phenomenon concerned with the innermost core of the individual's experience, with his existence, it is not surprising that it stimulated particular interest in philosophically minded phenomenological and existentialist European psychiatrists. The depersonalization theories put forward by these psychiatrists are based on the philosophies of Husserl and Heidegger. They are difficult to present in a concise manner.

An early theory of depersonalization was put forward by Kurt Schneider (1921) on the basis of a phenomenological analysis of the emotions of feelings. This author was particularly concerned with subjective genuineness and authenticity of feelings. Depersonalization was described by him as caused by a loss of authenticity of self-feelings. They appeared only as contents of consciousness without being properly assimilated into the ego. Von Gebsattel (1937) offered an explanation of depersonalization from the existential point of view. He sees depersonalization as a disturbance of Being-in-the-World (*Daseinswelt*). The basis of normal experiencing, of normal perception and cognition, is sympathy between man and the world or "togetherness-of-man-with-the-world" (*Miteinander von Mensch und Welt*). This then becomes the basis of the feeling of reality of one's experience and of the harmony of the subject-object relation. The perception of the external objects and of oneself is an intentional act of the *Dasein*. It endows percepts with meaning. If there is a disturbance of the *Dasein*, the perceived world and the self become meaningless. (For the purpose of exposition *Dasein* in this connection may be equated with the ego of the individual.) Normal *Dasein* depends on the feeling of possibility (*Seinsmöglichkeit*) and being able to (*können*) accept some aspects of the world and reject other aspects, to reshape the world and oneself, in one word, to exercise freedom of choice. On this possibility of freedom depends the smooth flow of conscious experience, normal development of personality, and self-actualization. If this function is disturbed, as it very often is disturbed in melancholia, life becomes meaningless, and there is existential void, emptiness. According to von Gebsattel, this emptiness is projected on the perceived world and produces phenomena of depersonalization and derealization? There is a gulf, a split (*Spaltungserlebnis*) between the self and the world. The world is sensed passively, is meaningless and unreal. It is just a play of shadows. It cannot be reached for, its wholeness is lost and it becomes fragmented. Being-in-the-world (*Daseinswelt*) vanishes, feeling of self is altered. Kimura (1963) carried this analysis one step further. He disagrees with von Gelbsattel that the feeling of derealization is secondary to the projected inner emptiness on the external world. He believes that the disturbance is even more basic. To understand his theory, it is necessary to sketch briefly some of the ideas of Husserl (1962) on perception and experience. In perception, when all the presuppositions are bracketed, it is possible to distinguish *noema* which are contents of consciousness (*Bewusstseinsinhalt*) from *noesis* which is "being-in-consciousness" (*Bewusstsein*). The first have a character of sensations.[2] The second are real objects of the world, are created by intentional acts of the ego, and are called actual facts (*Tatsachen*). The pure transcendental ego, by the process called reflection, objectifies itself in an image which is, however, not a perfect representation of the pure ego. Thus we have "I" as the observer or actor and "me" as the observed object. Kimura states that Western philosophy tended to put a greater emphasis on the analysis or "me" aspect of the self, regarding the "I" aspect as unknowable. The Zen-Buddhist Japanese tradition with its tendency not to separate the subject from the object, seeks the transcendental pure ego ("I") in the experienced external world, in the world's immediately given "myness" character. By using Husserl's terminology, one can say that facts (*Tatsachen*), created by intentional acts of the ego, reflect this ego by the

[2] Perhaps it would be more correct to say that they have the character of "pure phenomena," pure appearance as against real objects.

inescapable impression of reality and the "myness" they produce in the perceiver. In the case of depersonalization, perceived facts (*Tatsachen*) do not exist. The perceived world is robbed of reality and meaning and becomes a meaningless combination of sense stimuli passively received. The world is "de-aesthetisized," "de-physiognomized," and "de-sympathetized," and remains a mere bunch of sense stimuli. Space, the perception of which depends on carrying out various transactions with external objects, loses its meaning. Experiencing becomes fragmented into episodes without continuity in time because the sense of continuity of time is closely related to the stream of consciousness of "being-in-the-world" (*Daseinswelt*). Time is an a priori given internal intuition of the becoming of self, its development, and actualization. Time integrates individual experiences in a continuous flow. Hence, in depersonalization, experiences are fragmented; they do not occur in time. If *Dasein* is crippled by restriction of the possibility of existing (*Seinsmöglichkeit*) or self-actualization, the perceived world loses its reality and becomes dead. The activity of the ego is no longer reflected in it. Self becomes separated from the world, and thus depersonalization and derealization ensue. They are primary and not secondary to the perceived inner emptiness which is projected to the external world, as stated by von Gebsattel. Meyer (1957, 1959) also discusses depersonalization from the existential point of view. He stresses the fact that the depersonalization and derealization phenomena are a manifestation of the ego-outer world relations. He believes that obsessional-compulsive neurosis and depersonalization are two opposite poles of the same type of disturbance. The obsessional-compulsive neurotic is completely controlled by the external world. He comes into a close contact with the world, cannot detach himself from it. The external world obtrudes itself on the obsessional neurotic and "possesses" him. He cannot put a distance between himself and the world. The external world is *too real* for him. The depersonalized patient on the contrary loses contact with the world. There is an unbridgable gap between him and the external world, and since the reality of the external world depends on the resisttence it offers to the subject, the world becomes unreal to him. The obsessional-compulsive and depersonalized patients occupy the opposite poles of an axis which can be described in terms of being close to or far away from the external world. These patients can move along this axis either away, from or toward the world. As we have stated previously, Meyer believes that the subjects with anankastic personalities are prone to these two opposite types of mental disorder with occasional shifting from one to the other.

This concludes the discussion of various theories of depersonalization. However, before this section is ended, it is worthwhile to indicate some convergences between the theorizing within the framework of psychoanalysis, existential psychiatry, and experimental psychology with regard to the psychic functions involved in the phenomena of depersonalization and derealization. Contemporary psychoanalysts stress in connection with depersonalization the impairment of the integrative functions of the ego, the separation of the representation of the self from the representation of the object and a disturbance of relationship between individual experiences and their frame of reference. Similarly, the existential psychiatrists stress a lack of the activity of the ego, a lack of the active integration of experience, a split between the self and the external world, and the fragmenting of experience with a disruption of its continuity, as the factors that produce depersonalization. Although there is no well developed theory of depersonalization and derealization, there is some recent theorizing in experimental psychology of perception that points to a possibility of convergence between the psychoanalytical, existential, and experimental points of view. Gibson (1966) stated that perception of real objects in the world depends on active "obtaining," active extracting of information that is contained in the energy impinging on the organism by its perceptual systems. Stimulation input which is "imposed" and passively received, does not lead to the perception of real objects but only to sensory experiences. Thus he stressed active exploration of the environment and active extraction of information as determining the degree of reality of the perceived meaningful objects. Passive reception of "imposed" as contrasted to "obtained" stimulation could lead to meaningless sensation.[3] This offers a possibility of an experimental investigation of perceptual processes in patients suffering from depersonalization and derealization. A hypothesis can be formulated that depersonalized subjects do not use actively their perceptual systems to extract information from the environment or that they use them to a lesser extent than normal controls. Investigation of possible disturbance of the frames of reference of perceptual processes is another possible line of experimental approach to the problem of depersonalization.

PROGNOSIS AND TREATMENT

There is not much to be said as far as the prognosis in depersonalization cases is concerned. It depends entirely on the circumstances in which depersonalization occurs. In many cases depersonalization lasts a short period of time and clears up spontaneously. Other cases are resistant to treatment and last for years. Mayer-Gross et al. (1954) state that depersonalization is a bad prognostic sign in depression and does not respond well to treatment. Roth (1959) reported that depersonalization does not respond to ECT and that some depressive patients develop depersonalization following this treatment. Ackner and Grant (1960) could not confirm this report and found that depressive patients with depersonalization symptoms responded equally well to ECT as did patients without these symptoms, although neurotic depersonalized patients could be made worse by ECT.

Several kinds of treatment have been tried in depersonalization with various results. Shorvon (1946) used in his series of cases: ECT, continuous narcosis, Benzidrine and Epanutin, vasodilators, ether abreaction, cardiazol induced shocks, modified insulin, and even prefrontal lobotomy in one case. Ether abreaction produced the best results. King and Little (1959) obtained good results in cases suffering from depersonalization by repeated light sleep treatments induced by Thiopentan. Cattell (1966) reported good results with the administration of dextro-amphetamin together with amytal. Chlorpromazine was found to be useful in cases complicated by severe anxiety. Psychoanalysts treat depersonalization by psychotherapy on analytical lines with varying results.

CONCLUSION AND SUMMARY

Depersonalization and derealization phenomena are of great theoretical interest since they are concerned with the core of personal experience. They are linked up with the sense of ultimate reality of the external world and the self and, therefore, they are of great importance for epistemology, ontology, and other problems of philosophy of mind. Because of the metaphorical language in which they are described and because they belong to a "field in which physical world and the world of symbols overlap, and where 'mythical' thinking interpenetrates reality thinking" (Mayer-Gross, 1935, p. 112), depersonalization phenomena offer great difficulty to an experimental attack. For this reason they have been largely ignored by experimentally oriented psychologists. However, with a new experimental approach to higher cognitive and symbolic processes, it may become possible to investigate depersonalization more objectively than has been done thus far.

[3] In an earlier publication Gibson (1950) differentiated two types of visual experiences: "visual world" and "visual field." The "visual world" is three-dimensional, has depth, and obeys the constancy of perception laws. The "visual field" is flat, two-dimensional and obeys the laws of perspective. Meaningful objects are contained in the "visual world," while meaningless sensations, unless they play a representational role, belong to the "visual field." Since depersonalized subjects complain of a lack of depth, of flatness of the perceived world, it is likely that they tend to see more in terms of the "visual field" than the "visual world." The fact that in schizophrenic patients, frequently subject to depersonalization, constancy of perception is impaired, points in the same direction (Weckowicz, 1964).

REFERENCES

Ackner, B. Depersonalization, I Aetiology and phenomenology. *J. ment. Sci.*, 1954a, **100**, 838–853.

Ackner, B. Depersonalization, II Clinical syndromes. *J. ment. Sci.*, 1954b, **100**, 854–872.

Ackner, B. and Grant, Q. A. F. R. The prognostic significance of depersonalization in depressive illness treated with electric convulsive therapy. *J. neurol. neurosurg. Psychiat.*, 1960, **23**, 243–246.

Arlow, J. A. The structure of *Déjà vu* experience. *J. Amer. Psychoanal. Assoc.*, 1959, **7**, 611–631.

Bergler, E. and Eidelberg, L. Der Mechanismus der Depersonalisation. *Internationale Zeitschrift für Psychoanalyse*, 1935, **21**, 258–285.

Bird, B. Feelings of unreality. *Int. J. Psychoanal.*, 1957, **38**, 256–265.

Blank, H. R. Depression, hypomania and depersonalization. *Psychoanal. Quart.*, 1954, **23**, 20–37.

Bychowski, G. Disorders in the body image in the clinical pictures of psychoses. *J. nerv. ment. Dis.*, 1943, **97**, 310.

Cattell, J. P. Depersonalization phenomena. In *American Handbook of Psychiatry*, Vol. III, ed. S. Arieti. New York: Basic Books, 1966.

Deutch, Helene. Some forms of emotional disturbance and their relationship to schizophrenia. *Psychoanal. Quart.*, 1942, **11**, 301–321.

Dixon, J. C. Depersonalization phenomena in a sample of population of college students. *Brit. J. Psychiat.*, 1963, **109**, 371–375.

Dugas, L. Un cas de dépersonalisation. *Revue de philosophie de la France et de l'étranger*, 1898, **23**, 500–507.

Dugas, L. Sur la dépersonalisation. *Journal de la psychologie normale et pathologique*, 1933, **33**, 276.

Dugas, L. and Moutier, F. *La dépersonnalisation*. Paris: Alcan, 1911.

Eisenstein, V. W. Differential psychotherapy of borderline states. *Psychiat. Quart.*, 1951, **25**, 379–433.

Eysenck, H. J. *Dimensions of Personality*. London: Rutledge and Kegan Paul, 1947.

Eysenck, H. J. Personality and drug effects. In *Experiments with Drugs*. H. J. Eysenck (ed.) New York: MacMillan, 1963.

Federn, P. Some variation in ego-feelings. *Int. J. Psychoanal*, 1928, **9**, 401.

Fenichel, O. *The Psychoanalytic Theory of Neurosis*. New York: Norton, 1945.

Freud, S. A distance of memory on the Akropolis (1936), *Int. J. Psychoanal*, 1941, **22**, 93–101.

Freud, S. *The Interpretation of Dreams* (1900). New York: Basic Books, 1955.

Gibson, J. J. *The Perception of the Visual World*. Boston: Houghton Mifflin, 1950.

Gibson, J. J. *The Senses Considered as Perceptual Systems*. Boston: Houghton Mifflin, 1966.

Glauber, L. P. Observations on a primary form of anhedonia. *Psychoanal. Quart.*, 1949, **18**, 67–78.

Goppert, H. Zwangskrankheit und Depersonalisation. *Bibliotheca Psychiatrica et Neurologica Fasc.*, 1960, **108**, 1–84.

Guttmann, E. and Maclay, W. S. Mescalin and depersonalization, Therapeutic experiments. *J. neurol. neurosurg. Psychopath.*, 1936, **16**, 193.

Hartmann, H. Ein Fall von Depersonalisation. *Zeitschrift der Gesellschaft für Neurologie und Psychiatrie*, 1922, **74**, 592–601.

Hartmann, H. Comments on the psychoanalytic theory of the ego. *The Psychoanalytic Study of the Child*, Vol. 5, pp. 74–96. New York: International Universities Press, 1950.

Helson, H. Adaptation-level as a basis for a quantitative theory of frame of reference. *Psychol. Rev.*, 1948, **55**, 297–313.

Heymans, G. Weitere Daten ¨ber Depersonalisation und "Fausse Reconnaissance." *Zeitschrift für Psychologie, Physiologie und Sinnesorgane*, 1911, **48**, 112.

Husserl, E. *Phänomenologische Psychologie*. Hague: Martinus Nijhoff, 1962.
Jacobson, Edith. The self and the object world. *The Psychoanalytic Study of the Child*, Vol. 9, pp. 75–127. New York: International Universities Press, 1954.
Jacobson, Edith. Depersonalization. *J. Amer. Psychoanal. Assoc.*, 1959, **7**, 581–610.
Janet, P. *Les obsessions et la psychasthénie*. Paris, 1903.
Kimura, B. Zur Phänomenologie der Depersonalization. *Der Nervenarzt*, 1963, **34**, 391–397.
King, A. and Little, J. C. Thiopentone treatment of the phobic anxiety-depersonalization syndrome. *Proc. Roy. soc. Med.*, 1959, **52**, 595–596.
Krishaber, M. De la névropathie cerebrocardiaque. *Gazette Science Médicine*, Bordeaux, 1872.
Kubie, L. Central representation of the symbolic process in psychosomatic disorders. *Psychosom. Med.*, 1953, **15**, 1–7.
Lewis, A. Melancholia: a clinical survey of depressive states. *J. ment. Sci.*, 1934, **80**, 277.
L'Hermitte, J. *L'Image de notre corps*. Paris: Editions de la Nouvelle Revue Critique, 1939.
Loewy, H. Die Aktionsgefühle. *Prager medizinische Wochenschrift*, 1908, **33**, 443.
Luby, E. D., Cohen, B. D., Rosenbaum, G., Gottlieb, J. S. Kelley, R. Study of a new schizophrenomimetic drug Sernyl. *Arch. neurol. Psychiat.*, 1959, **81**, 363–369.
Mayer-Gross, W. On depersonalization. *Brit. J. med. Psychol.*, 1935, **15**, 103–121.
Mayer-Gross, W., Slater, E., Roth, M. *Clinical Psychiatry*. London: Cassell, 1954.
McReynolds, P. Anxiety, perception and schizophrenia. In D. D. Jackson (ed.), *The Etiology of Schizophrenia*. New York: Basic Books, 1960.
Mead, G. H. *Mind, Self and Society*. Chicago: University of Chicago Press, 1934.
Megrabyan, G. A. *Depersonalizatsiya* (Depersonalization). Erevan: Armyanskoe, 1962.
Mercury Project Summary. (Including results of the fourth manned orbital flight). Washington, D.C.: NASA, 1963.
Mering, Von D., Morimoto, K., Hyde, R. W. and Rinkel, M. Experimentally induced depersonalization. In P. H. Hoch and J. Zubin (eds.) *Experimental Psychopathology*. New York: Grune and Stratton, 1957.
Meyer, J. E. Studien zur Depersonalisation, II. Depersonalisation und Zwang als polare Störungen der Ich-Aussenwelt-Beziehung. *Psychiatrie und Neurologie*, 1957, **133**, 63–79.
Meyer, J. E. Die Entfremdungserlebnisse. Über Herkunft und Entstehungsweise der Depersonalisation. *Sammlung psychiatrischer und neurologischer Einzeldarstellungen*. Hrgg. K. Conrad, W. Scheid, H. J. Weibrecht (eds.), Stuttgart: Georg Thieme Verlag, 1959.
Nunberg, H. States of depersonalization in the light of the libido theory (1924), *in Practice and Theory of Psychoanalysis*. New York: International Universities Press, 1955a.
Nunberg, H. *Principles of Psychoanalysis*. New York: International Universities Press, 1955b.
Oberndorf, C. P. Depersonalization in relation to erotization of thought. *Int. J. Psychoanal.*, 1934, **15**, 271.
Oberndorf, C. P. The role of anxiety in depersonalization. *Int. J. Psychoanal.*, 1950, **31**, 1–5.
Oesterreich, K. *Phänomenologie des Ich*. Leipzig, 1910.
Penfield, W. and Rasmussen, T. *The Cerebral Cortex of Man*. New York: Macmillan, 1950.
Pick, A. Zur Pathologie des Ichbewusstseins. *Archiv für Psychiatrie und Nervenkrankheiten*, 1904, **38**, 22.
Ribot, Th. *Diseases of Memory*. London, 1882.
Roberts, W. W. Normal and abnormal depersonalization. *J. ment. Sci.*, 1960, **106**, 478–493.
Rosen, V. H. The reconstruction of a traumatic childhood event in a case of depersonalization. *J. Amer. Psychoanal. Soc.*, 1955, **3**, 211–220.
Roth, M. The phobic anxiety-depersonalization syndrome. *Proc. Roy. Soc. Med.*, 1959, **52**, 587–595.

Sadger, J. J. Über Depersonalization. *Internationale Zeitschrift für Psychoanalyse*, 1928, **14**, 315.

Sarlin, C. N. Depersonalization and derealization. *J. Amer. Psychoanal. Assoc.*, 1962, **10**, 784–804.

Schilder, P. *Selbstbewusstsein und Persönlichkeitsbewusstsein*. Berlin: Julius Springer, 1914.

Schilder, P. Depersonalization, in *Introduction to Psychoanalytic Psychiatry*. New York: Nervous and Mental Disease Monograph Series, 50, 1928.

Schilder, P. *The Image and Appearance of the Human Body*. London: Kegan Paul, Trench, Trubner, 1935.

Schilder, P. The treatment of depersonalization. *Bull. N.Y. Acad. Med.*, 1939, **15**, 258.

Schneider, Kurt. Pathopsychologische Beiträge zur psychologischen Phänomenologie von Liebe und Mitfühlen. *Zeitschrift für gesamte Neurologie und Psychiatrie*, 1921, **65**, 109–140.

Schneider, Kurt. *Psychopathic Personalities*. London: Cassel, 1958.

Searl, M. N. Note on depersonalization. *Int. J. Psychoanal.* 1932, **13**, 329.

Sedman, G. and Reed, G. F. Depersonalization phenomena in obsessional personalities and in depression. *Brit. J. Psychiat.*, 1963, **109**, 376–379.

Sherif, M. and Cantril, H. *The Psychology of Ego-Involvement*. New York: John Wiley, 1947.

Shorvon, H. J. The depersonalization syndrome. *Proc. Roy. Soc. Med.*, 1946, **39**, 779–792.

Spiegel, L. A. The self, the sense of self and perception. *The Psychoanalytic Study of the Child*, Vol. **14**, 1959, pp. 81–109.

Stamm, J. L. Altered ego states allied to depersonalization. *J. Amer. Psychoanal. Assoc.*, 1962, **10**, 762–783.

Stewart, W. A. "Panel on depersonalization, 1963." *J. Amer. Psychoanal. Assoc.*, 1964, **12**, 171–186.

Störring, E. Die Depersonalisation. *Zeitschrift für gesamte Neurologie und Psychiatrie*, 1933, **98**, 462.

Vella, G. *Il Concetto dipersonalizzazione*. Rome: Editrice Studium, 1960.

Von Gebsattel, V. E. Freiherr. Zur Frage der Depersonalisation. (Ein Beitrag zur Theorie der Melancholie.) *Der Nervenarzt*, 1937, **10**, 169–178, 248–257.

Weckowicz, T. E. Shape constancy in schizophrenic patients. *J. abnorm. Soc. Psychol.*, 1964, **68**, 177–183.

Weckowicz, T. E. and Sommer, R. Body image and self-concept in schizophrenia. *J. ment. Sci.*, 1960, **106**, 17–39.

Wernicke, C. *Grundriss der Psychiatrie*. Leipzig: Georg Thieme Verlag, 1900.

Wexler, D., Mendelson, J., Leiderman, P. H. and Solomon, P. Sensory deprivation: a technique for studying psychiatric aspects of stress. *Arch. neurol. Psychiat.*, 1958, **79**, 225.

Witkin, H. A. and Asch, S. E. Studies in space orientation. III. Perception of the upright in the absence of visual field. *J. exp. Psychol.*, 1948a, **38**, 603–614.

Witkin, H. A. and Asch, S. E. Studies in space orientation. IV. Further experiments on perception of the upright with displaced visual fields. *J. exp. Psychol.*, 1948b, **38**, 762–782.

Wittles, F. Psychology and treatment of depersonalization. *Psychoanal. Rev.*, 1940, **27**, 57.

Part II

Disorders of Affect

Chapter 7

Depression: Assessment and Aetiology[1]

JOHN A. STERN, JAMES. N. McCLURE., JR.,
and C. G. COSTELLO.

INTRODUCTION

To laymen depression generally suggests a normal human response (for example, grief) to certain upsetting events, especially losses, disappointments, and bereavements. Such "normal" depressions are usually brief, benign, time-locked to some particular event, time-limited, and are rarely seen by physicians and even more rarely by psychiatrists. Fortunately, only a small part of any population has depression of the kind that impels them to seek professional help, but clinicians often see a psychological syndrome, with depressed mood as a central theme, that is quite distinctive in its manifestations from ordinary grief.

In this chapter we discuss primarily the symptom of severe depression. As opposed to normal depressions, it is severe, distressing, often disabling, may lead to fatal consequences, and constitutes perhaps the bulk of admissions to private acute psychiatric hospitals in the United States (Kraines, 1957; Zigler & Phillips, 1961).

Mayer-Gross, Slater, and Roth (1960) have suggested that approximately three or four out of 1000 people suffer from affective disorders that require treatment. Roth (1959) has suggested elsewhere that the incidence of the disorder may be as high as 4 percent in men and 8 percent in women. A study by Kay, Beamish, and Roth (1964) indicated that 26 percent of patients over 65 years of age suffer from depression. Ratcliffe (1964) reported that depressive illness was present in 40 percent of males and 60 percent of females admitted to a typical Scottish Hospital between 1955 and 1959.

Perhaps the most significant single contributor to the delineation of depression as a clinical entity was Kraepelin (1896) and, although we are concerned in this chapter with the symptom rather than with the syndrome of depression, some historical background is necessary. He identified specific psychiatric syndromes in order to elucidate the natural history of the disorder. This would then permit an evaluation of treatment efforts and a search for specific aetiological factors. He found that patients who suffered from manic depressive disorders quite often remitted spontaneously and that patients who suffered from schizophrenia generally did not. Kraepelin also made the very fundamental connection between manic and depressive symptoms, which had apparently eluded most students of the disorder until that time. He stated:

"We include here certain slight and slightest colorings of mood, some of them periodic, some of them continuously morbid which on the one hand are to be regarded as a rudiment of more severe disorders, on the other hand pass over without sharp boundary into the domain of personal predisposition. In the course of years, we have become more and more convinced that all of the above-mentioned states (periodic and circular insanity, mania and melancholia) only

[1]This investigation was supported in part by USPHS Grant No. MH 13002.

represent manifestations of a single morbid process."

Kraeplin believed that the depressive disorders were a definite disease process with a hereditary and constitutional basis. The opposite point of view was taken by Sigmund Freud who perhaps has been the most influential in the theoretical and clinical approach to depressive disorders in the United States. In "Mourning and Melancholia" (1955) he developed the concept that depression was completely analogous to the experience of an ordinary loss, and in so doing postulated the unitary concept of depression. Freud believed that for the depressed patient in whom one could not perceive a loss appropriate to the severity of the symptoms there was an unconscious loss not known to the patient. The patient feels hostility toward someone close to him who has disappointed him. He identifies with the person and turns his unconscious rage and hostility inward against the incorporated person, thus, producing the severe depression with self-depreciation and suicidal ideas. Thus, many psychotherapists consider their goal with a depressed patient to be to help him release his hostility. Melanie Klein (1957) postulated that depressions later in life were replications of depressive experiences during infancy. Fenichel (1945) believed that less severe neurotic and reactive depressions stem from situations in which the person felt disappointed and developed some hostility and feelings of guilt but could clearly maintain ego boundaries. In more severe depressed states the patient became more regressed and his concept of reality became disorganized. These writers and the ones following them have more or less set the tenor of what American psychiatrists have thought about depression. It is generally assumed that all depressions are reactions to loss that may be predisposed to by childhood losses, separations, and disappointments; it is further assumed that psychotherapy is the treatment of choice in most cases, and there is a tendency to disregard theories implying some role for biological causes.

Among the followers we may mention, Bibring (1953) who wrote that depression occurred when "the organism can perceive its goal and at the same time be aware of a helplessness to obtain it." Gittleson developing this idea (1966) suggested that the anally oriented (obsessive compulsive) patient may become depressed when he is aware of his murderous preoccupations along with his "clean" and noble expectations of himself. The orally oriented (fixated or reressed) patient may become depressed when he is unable to be taken care of and realizes that he will have to stand on his own feet. The genitally-oriented patient may become depressed when he finds himself sexually inadequate, weak, or not admired. Spitz (1946) following more Freudian ideas seemed to assume that it was the curtailment of aggressive outlets produced by being confined in bed that resulted in anaclitic depression. Bowlby (1960) suggested that anaclitic depression is the result of the rupture of a key relationship with the consequent pain of yearning that occurs in a young child. He felt that suppressed rage was not an important precusor of depression.

Engel (1962) emphasized the survival value of depression which leads to conservation of energy. Kaufman and Rosenbloom (1957) reported that monkeys raised in a monkey community and then separated from their mothers first went through a stage of distress, accompanied by increased activity. This was followed by a depression withdrawal phase which he also assumed led to conservation of energy. It also served the purpose of eliciting adoptive behavior on the part of some adult animal such as the father monkey.

We shall return briefly to these ideas toward the end of the chapter when we discuss the aetiology of depression. Let us first look at the important problem of the assessment of depression.

ASSESSMENT OF DEPRESSION

Self-report and Rating Scales

Most rating scales and self-report measures for measuring depression have been designed to measure depression as a syndrome rather than a specific symptom of disordered affect. Because of this fact they are not discussed in detail here, but some references to these scales may be of value to the reader, particularly the reader who does not fully accept the premise of this book. One such scale has been named the Inventory for Measuring Depression and was first described by Beck and his colleagues (1961). This scale has been factor analyzed [Weckowitz, Muir, & Cropley, (1967), Cropley & Weckowitz (1966)] and some evidence concerning its validity has been published by Metcalfe and Goldman (1965). Similar scales have been developed by Zung (1965), Wechsler, Grosser, and Busfield (1963), and Hamilton (1960). Hamilton's scale has been used for measuring psychiatric patients' responses to antidepressant medications (LeGassicke, Boyd, & McPherson, 1964; Rose, Leahy, Martin, & Westhead, 1965; Waldron, & Bates, 1965). It has also been used for evaluating depression in medical inpatients (Schwab, Bialow, Clemmons, & Holzer, 1967). Humphrey (1967) has combined some of the items of the Zung Scale with items of his own that are designed to measure functional disturbances occurring as the result of the illness such as performance at work, sexual relationships, and so on. The combined scale he calls a Function Mood Scale.

Instruments designed to measure overall pathology usually incorporate items that concern depression and here too the approach of the scale developers has been to regard depression as a syndrome. Examples of these scales are the MMPI (Hathaway & McKinley, 1951), the Malamud Sands Psychiatric Rating Scale (Malamud & Sands, 1947), the Lorr Multi-Dimensional Scale (Lorr et. al., 1953), and the Wittenborn Scales (Wittenborn, 1955).

A scale designed to measure depression as a particular disordered affect distinguishing it in particular from anxiety has been presented by Costello and Comrey (1967) with some evidence for its construct validity.

Depression has generally been one of the mood factors obtained in studies concerned with factor analyses of mood states measured by means of adjective check list and scales. A recent review of this literature can be found in Lorr, Daston, and Smith (1967). Because of this, adjective check lists designed to measure depression alone or along with other mood states have been developed. Examples are (1) the Lubin Scale (Lubin, 1965), which has the particular advantage of incorporating a number of parallel versions, the comparability of which has been presented by Lubin, Dubres and Lubin (1967), and (2) the Clyde Mood Scale (Clyde, 1963).

It seems very likely that, even when an attempt is made to measure depression simply as a particular type of disordered affect, rather than as a complex syndrome, scales such as the one designed by Costello and Comrey (1967) will have a limited, if initially important, role for this particular problem of the science of psychopathology. It is quite likely that they can serve as nothing more than fairly coarse nomothetic nets used to identify groups of people that appear to differ considerably in their depressive tendencies, and with the help of which more precise and sensitive tests can be developed. It is noteworthy here that Becker (1964) in a study of the communality of manic depressive and "mild" cyclothymic characteristics found that the intercorrelation between their various mood measures were insignificant, defeating their efforts to measure a common cyclothymic factor.

It may very well be that these more adequate measuring instruments will be further refined adjective check lists or something similar. At the moment, however, they seem more likely to be physiological or biochemical in nature. At least more active research seems to be proceeding with measures of this kind, and we now review some of them.

Endocrine Aspects of Depression

The relationship between hormones, emotional states, and psychiatric disorders has interested investigators from the first knowledge of the endocrine system and its disorders. There are several recent excellent reviews of this topic (Gibson, 1962; Michael & Gibbons, 1963; Rubin & Mandell, 1966). Addison (1855) in describing hypofunction of the adrenal cortex mentioned, as accompanying symptoms, anxiety, insomnia, and confusion, and later authors included symptoms of apathy, irritability, mild depression, and a lack of initiative often with some degree of organic brain impairment. Hormone therapy usually produces improvement in these symptoms (Michael & Gibbons, 1963). The opposite disorder, hyperfunction of the adrenal cortex was first described by Cushing in 1932. It is associated with some degree of psychiatric disturbance in about 50 percent of the reported cases. Most authors report severe mental disturbances in 15 percent to 20 percent. A wide range of psychiatric symptoms has been described that includes acute excitement, anxiety, paranoid delusions, and auditory hallucinations, but the most frequent kind of symptom appears to be depression of mood (Michael & Gibbons, 1963). Adding to the evidence of a connection between hormonal factors and psychological symptoms are the findings that administration of ACTH and cortisone may produce acute psychoses including schizophrenic symptoms, deleria marked by unusually bizarre hallucinations, excitement or stupor, with euphoria the most commonly occurring symptom. How these substances produce the psychotic reactions is not known, and Quarton et al. (1955) review 35 separate hypotheses advanced to account for them. Michael and Gibbons (1963) point out that, although both the Cushing syndrome and the administration of adrenocortical hormones or ACTH produce elevations of circulating adrenal corticosteroids, yet Cushing's syndrome is associated with a high incidence of depression and the introduction of exogenous hormones is associated with a high incidence of euphoria.

Disordered functioning of the thyroid gland has also long been known to produce profound psychological symptoms. Indeed, before the development of sensitive tests of thyroid function, the clinician found it difficult to distinguish between thyroid disease and severe states of depression. However, the administration of thyroid hormone does not seem to produce the high incidence of profound mental disturbance found with the use of cortisone. This is perhaps fortunate because of the proclivity of physicians to prescribe thyroid extract for menstrual disorders, general malaise, and tiredness, etc., in the absence of demonstrated hypofunction of the thyroid gland.

The assumption that thyroid disease was the result of psychic conflicts and stress led psychiatric theorists to believe that there was a connection between endocrine and psychiatric disorders. Selye's discovery (1950) that a wide variety of factors threatening the psychological and physical integrity of both animals and humans produce an increase in secretion of ACTH and adrenocortical hormones led him to elaborate a broad theory that involved a role for stress and abnormal steroid hormone release in many disease states. This gave considerable impetus to authors who felt that stress caused endocrine disorders and that endocrine disorders were related to psychiatric ones. Selye's work produced a great proliferation of research studying the various kinds of stressors that in experimental animals and humans have led to increased release of adrenocortical hormones. So common, in fact, is the release of these hormones that it has been proposed that this steroid release be used as an objective index of whether a stimulus was stressful or not (Ganong, 1963). A great deal of work in recent years has been devoted to elucidating the manner in which external noxious stimuli exert their influence on the anterior pituitary and the endocrine system. (Michael & Gibbons, 1963; Ganong, 1963). It is now fairly well accepted that neural events lead to the release of a humoral transmitter in the hypothalamus which travels down the portal veins surrounding the pituitary stalk, reaches the anterior pituitary, and triggers the release of pituitary hormones. They, in turn, cause the secretion of the appropriate hormones in the target endocrine glands (Harris, 1955). Destruction of the hypothalamus or the severing of the vascular connection between the hypothalamus and the pituitary blocks the stress-induced release of 17-hydroxycorticosteroids. Bunney, Mason, and Hamburg (1965), who found an increase in the urinary excretion of 17-hydroxycorticosteroid metabolites in depressed patients, assumed that increased stimulation of the hypothalamus from higher brain centers led to increased elaboration of the hypothalamic releasing factor.

The widespread interest in endocrine aspects of psychiatric disorder, of course, led to numerous studies of the endocrine status of psychiatric patients. At first the hope was that these studies would lead to causal relationships and such different psychiatrists as Freud (1955) and Kraepelin (1896) expressed the hope that psychiatric disorders might be found to be hormonally caused. However, this optimistic point of view faded with improvement in precision of endocrine measures. Early endocrine studies of psychiatric patients used, of necessity, indirect measures of endocrine function and produced results that were imprecise and ambiguous. The consensus of recent work that utilizes more precise measurements has been that no specific hormonal disturbance is associated with any psychiatric disorder, and it fails to support the notion that endocrine disorder is a specific, either direct or indirect, cause for any major psychiatric syndrome. Rubin and Mandell (1966) state that the research emphasis has shifted from "the concepts of disease specific alterations" to one looking for endocrine responses, "as a concomitant of such psychological variables as guilt, anxiety, absence of denial, insight into severity of the illness, and depressive affect." However, Mason (1963) suggests that it might still be fruitful to look for distinct patterns and profiles of various endocrine responses to psychiatric disorder. The isolation of these specific patterns might also aid in objective criteria for psychiatric diagnosis.

The disappointing fact that there seems to be no specific aetiological relationship between steroid disorder and psychiatric syndromes, however, should not obscure one of the most consistently found and reproducible objective laboratory findings concerning depression. It has been repeatedly demonstrated that there is a significant increase in the output of adrenal 17-hydroxycorticosteroids during acute severe depressions. Board et al. (1956), reporting one of the earlier investigations, studied blood levels of 17-OHCS. They used 30 acutely ill psychiatric patients on the morning after admission. All were found to have a significant elevation above the mean of a normal group. Those patients called "psychotic depressive" had a higher mean than the patient group in general. Another investigation of a group of 33 depressed patients (Board et al., 1957) showed again that, within a few days of admission, the mean 17-OHCS level of patients was 60 percent higher than that for normal controls. The patients with retarded depression (without motor hyperactivity, crying, and overt expressions of great anxiety) tended to show higher mean levels than the patients who were agitated and tearful. In both studies, clinical improvement was correlated with a fall in plasma corticosteroid levels. Several longitudinal studies of hospitalized depressed patients show a persistence of the elevated steroid level. Bunney, Hartmann, and Mason (1965) reported a female patient with a 48-hour cycle of alternating mania and depression. They found that, even months after admission to the hospital, she showed abrupt rises in the urinary 17-hydroxycorticosteroid output coincident with shifts of her behavior from mania to depression. Gibbons and McHugh (1962) found that the morning plasma cortisol level in 17 depressive patients was significantly elevated above the normal level. The patients were followed at weekly intervals until discharge and 70 percent of them showed a "fluctuating decline with clinical improvement."

Other studies confirm the finding of high urinary excretion of 17-hydroxycorticosteroid metabolites in depressed patients. Pryce (1964) found a 23 percent fall in urinary excretion of depressed female patients by recovery. Ferguson et al. (1964) found that the principal urinary metabolite of cortisol was significantly elevated before treatment of depressed patients and fell by 45 percent after improvement following electroconvulsive therapy. Similar findings have been reported by Hullin and his colleagues (1967), although they found that even after ECT their depressed patients showed higher than normal levels.

Not only do most authors report an elevated urinary 17-hydroxycorticosteroid output in acutely depressed patients but many of them report a positive correlation between blood steroid levels and severity of depression. Board et al. (1956) found that the patients rated as highly emotionally distressed had a higher blood cortisol level than the ones who were not. Gibbons and McHugh (1962) found that, in general, the more severe the depression the higher the blood cortisol level. Board et al. (1957) also found that the greater the "felt" anxiety and emotional distress the higher was the hormone level. McClure (1966) described a good correlation between ratings of severity of depression and plasma cortisol level.

As consistent as have been these steroid findings in depression, we must point out that there are a number of exceptions and that the elevation of steroid output is scarcely specific for depressive disorders. The stimuli that produce elevations in 17-hydroxycorticoid blood or urine levels include novel experiences (Fishman et al. 1962), stressful interviews (Hetzel et al. 1955), "arousing" motion pictures (Handlon et al. 1962), students during examination (Hodges et al. 1962), patients about to undergo surgery (Price et al. 1957). Persky et al. (1956) show that patients with anxiety alone have significant elevations of both plasma and urinary 17-hydroxycorticosteroid levels. Bliss et al. (1956), who studied 19 recently admitted disturbed psychiatric patients without any specific diagnosis, conclude that any psychiatric disorder marked by severe emotional turmoil was likely to produce elevated 17-hydroxycorticoid levels. Michael and Gibbons (1963), in their review, suggest that the intensity of the patient's emotional response is what is correlated with the rise in adrenocortical activity rather than the quality of the stimulus. Gibbons (1965) suggests that the elevation of corticoids found in depression and in other stresses is "a primitive response." He notes that the response is also found in infrahuman species and suggests that the 17-hydroxycorticosteroids being catabolic, would "help to make energy more readily available for a monkey in the wild state and equally for primitive man . . . If continued long enough (the response) might be harmful rather than helpful to the monkey in a laboratory and to modern man."

Another line of evidence that the adrenocorticoid elevation in depression is related to subjective discomfort rather than to the presence of the clinical disorder is that in manic patients (who share the basic disorder but not the discomfort), the most frequent cortico-steroid finding is depression below normal levels, despite the great activity and energy expenditure of these patients. Rizzo et al. (1954) followed the urinary 17-OHCS in a female patient and found extremely low levels during a phase of manic hyperactivity with return to normal with clinical recovery. Bunney and Hartmann (1965) found in their patient with rapidly alternating manic and depressive days that the urinary steroid level was above normal on depressed days and below normal on manic days. Michael and Gibbons (1963) report a "cyclothymic girl" with low plasma cortisol (7 micrograms per 100 cc) during an episode of mild elation and with marked rise (27 micrograms per 100 cc) during a depressed phase. Lingjaerde (1964) studied plasma hydrocortisone in a group of female patients and found that the level in patients who were "mostly hypomanic and manic" was considerably lower than that who were "mostly depressive" but that it was still slightly elevated above normal levels. The difference from normal was not statistically significant. However, there has been no systematic study of steroid levels in adequate samples of manic patients and there are some exceptions to the finding. Schwartz et al. (1966) followed one manic depressive patient through a cycle and found that the corticoids were elevated during depression but there were some periodic elevations during the manic stage as well (although there is some suggestion that these brief elevations reflected brief periods of depressive mood). Bliss et al. (1956) studied, on admission, an overactive manic patient who had 28 micrograms per 100 cc of 17-hydroxycorticosteroid that fell to 14 micrograms when calm. It has been suggested, however, that this might be an artifact of hospitalization. Gibbons and McHugh (1962) report one patient with mood swings in whom plasma cortisol was high during depressive periods and who returned to normal levels during periods of normal mood or mild elation. Bunney, Hartmann, and Mason (1965) in discussing their patient with regularly alternating moods associate the drop in steroids to "changes in defensive organization that occur during the manic stage." They felt that mania represented a denial of illness and "a defense against the pain of depression." We wonder, however, whether it is necessary to interpose a concept such as defense mechanism in considering steroid changes in mania. It seems more economical to assume that, as one of the symptoms of depression is discomfort, one of the symptoms of mania is overoptimistic lack of discomfort in most situations. The resultant discomfort level might be the determining factor in the corticoid output rather than something specific to manic-depressive disorder itself.

Granted the lack of specificity of the increased steroid output in depression, it still is an interesting finding and has a number of implications that have been explored in the literature. One of the suggestions made is that the steroid level and changes in it might be regarded as an objective correlate of clinical improvement. This would be true perhaps even if the pretreatment levels were not necessarily elevated since, as we have noted, Pryce (1964), Ferguson et al. (1964), and Hullin et al. (1967) found a decrease in urinary steroid excretion in patients recovering from depression.

In most of the studies reported in which

pretreatment 17-OHCS levels are above the normal mean, follow-up studies were available to show that they returned toward a normal level. It might be possible to regard the fluctuations in steroid levels as a reasonably sensitive indicator of the patient's internal psychic distress. Unfortunately, there are a number of exceptions both to the elevation initially and to decline after clinical improvement, and Gibbons and McHugh (1962) pointed out that 30 percent of their patients showed no particular decline with improvement.

Bunney and co-workers have suggested a number of imaginative ways in which the steroid levels might be used in a clinical setting. The first of them deals with its possible use as an indicator of unsuspected suicide potential. Bunney and Fawcett (1965) studied a group of patients with depression of whom three ultimately suicided. None was thought to be experiencing acute stress at the time of discharge or going home on pass, and all had been rated on the basis of ward behavior to have a low potential for committing suicide. Nonetheless, all three were significantly elevated in 17-hydroxycortiosteroids in urine, and their levels tended to be among the highest of the total group of depressed patients. Several other patients who had comparable high steroid levels did not actually suicide but exhibited seriously suicidal thoughts or attempts. A second suggestion generated from their study was that the steroid level was simply not equated with suicide risk but indicated a level of inner distress which might not be perceptible clinically and which should arouse the concern of those responsible for the patients. Gibbons et al. (1960) found a correlation between increase in adrenocortical products excreted in the urine of depressed patients and the occurrence of upsetting events. Bunney, Mason, Roatch, and Hamburg (1965) suggest that stressful events lead to exacerbation of symptoms and to increases in urinary steroid levels. Bunney, Mason, and Hamburg (1965) found two subgroups of depressed patients both of whom were given a high depression rating by ward nurses. One group had a high urinary steroid output, while the output of the other was close to the normal mean. They believed that the group with the higher steroid level complained more about their symptoms and had fewer defenses against them and were still fighting them, while the low group had equivalent depressive symptoms but tended to deny them and blame them on physical illness. The authors suggested that the urinary steroid differences were reflecting differences in the patient's ability to form defenses against the unpleasant psychological symptoms of depression.

Could steroid excretion studies be helpful in distinguishing schizophrenia from manic-depressive reaction? This is a differential diagnosis which, in the floridly disturbed patient, is often difficult to make. Ideally, if the majority of acutely depressed patients had elevated levels, one would hope that many schizophrenics would not. Unfortunately, the data on steroid output in schizophrenics is unclear. Patients labeled schizophrenic in general tend to show a great deal of variability in steroid response. However, Bliss et al. (1955) measuring plasma steroid levels in 26 chronic schizophrenics and 120 normals found no significant difference between the groups. Bliss et al. (1956) compared the plasma corticoid levels in 27 acutely psychiatric patients whose diagnoses were unfortunately not specified but of whom the "majority" were schizophrenic (but a number were diagnosed as depression and schizoaffective disorder) with 26 chronic schizophrenics who had been ill and hospitalized five years or more. The chronic schizophrenic population had a steroid level of 14 micrograms per 100 cc, which was not significantly elevated above normal. The 27 acutely ill patients were divided into 19 who were judged to be emotionally upset and 8 who were judged to be calm. The calm patients had a normal level while the emotionally upset, irrespective of diagnosis, had a significantly elevated level. However, they commented that one very disturbed patient had only 6 micrograms and several chronic schizophrenics and apparently undisturbed normals had 30 or more. They concluded that the steroid level, although influenced by emotional factors, must be controlled by other factors as well. Anderson and Dawson (1965) reported similar inconsistent results. They found that, although the steroid levels were higher than normal among depressive patients, many of their chronic schizophrenic patients also had high levels. Rey et al. (1961) followed three patients diagnosed as recurrent catatonic. Unlike many studies, they include a great deal of clinical material. Although all the patients showed episodes of bizarre, puzzling behavior, two of the three had, in the course of the illness, manic and depressive episodes which suggests that, rather than being schizophrenic, they might well have been suffering from an atypical affective disorder. All the patients had increases in urinary excretion of 17-OHCS at some point in their acute attack. Similarly, Sachar et al. (1963) report periods of heightened corticoid excretion in a group of four young male patients diagnosed schizophrenia. They also include a great deal of descriptive clinical material which makes it seem likely that, instead of being typical schizophrenics, the patients involved were atypical affective disorder patients. All of them are described as having extremely good recoveries and three of them returned to duty. Two of them responded well to EST. All four psychotic episodes were marked by fairly typical depressive features. The depressive episodes were referred to as "Anaclitic depression" with the increase in urinary 17-hydroxycorticoids occurring during this phase. One wonders indeed whether these patients were suffering from depressions rather than schizophrenia. It would be interesting to determine what the steroid levels are in acute young schizophrenics about whom there is less diagnostic ambiguity and in whom there is no prominent affective symptomatology. Coppen and his colleagues (1967) found the steroid levels to be "remarkably normal" in their male acute schizophrenics with a mean age of 34.2 years (S.E. = 1.8).

Although it is reasonably well documented that in the majority of cases acute depression is accompanied by an elevation of 17-hydroxycorticosteroids, there are many exceptions to this finding that are interesting themselves. In many cases the exceptions are apparently capricious, and Gibbons (1966) remarks of one depressed patient who showed no significant rise in either corticoid excretion rate or blood level that this is "another illustration that an increase in adrenocortical activity is not a necessary concomitant of depressive illness." Brambilla and Nuremberg (1963) measured 17-ketosteroids and 17-hydroxycorticosteroids in 24 patients with endogenous depression; all were found to be within normal limits and in most cases within the low normal range. Similarly, Stenback, Jakobsen, and Rimon (1966) studied 28 hospitalized depressions and found that the urinary 17-hydroxycorticosteroid levels at time of hospitalization were not as uniformly high as many others had found. In many cases the post-treatment rating of depression declined without a corresponding decline in 17-hydroxycorticoid levels. These authors suggested, however, that perhaps many of their patients had milder depressions than the patients hospitalized in other countries and pointed out that in their hospital even very mildly depressed patients are hospitalized.

Another possibility for variance among reported steroid responses in depressed patients is that more than one type of depression was involved. Board et al. (1956), for example, found that patients diagnosed neurotic depressions had a lower level of blood steroid than the ones diagnosed psychotic depression. Stenback et al. (1966), divided their patients into 7 considered to be manic depressive and 20 neurotic depressive and concluded that they were dealing with two types of depression, one with no significant elevation and one more likely to have an elevation, since 4 of the 7 called manic depressives had an elevated steroid level.

Other factors which affect steroid secretion may well play a part in inconsistent reports across studies. One factor certainly is the stress of being newly admitted to a psychiatric ward. Anderson and Dawson (1965) found that depressed patients with very similar clinical pictures had much lower 17-hydroxycorticosteroids on the experimental metabolic ward than depressed patients did on the admitting ward. Board et al. (1956) demonstrated significant elevations in steroid levels in patients whose blood was drawn the morning after admission. Even patients with an already elevated steroid level responded with an even greater elevation when confronted with upsetting environmental events, Anderson and Dawson (1965); Bunney, Mason, and Hamburg (1965). Whether the patient had received shock treatment may affect results, since Bliss et al. (1954) show that electroconvulsive therapy gave an acute elevation on the day of the treatment but that steroids returned to normal within four hours. Schwartz et al. (1965) found both nonspecific discomfort levels and motility of the patient affected the steroid output and recommended that studies control for both. Curtis et al. (1966) found a striking difference in the diurnal variation of the urinary excretion curves for 17-hydroxycorticoids in males and females. They suggested that the male patients metabolized or excreted cortisol products at a higher rate and that this would affect the blood levels as well. Other factors such as length of illness and hospitalization could possibly make a difference in adrenal-steroid response.

Nonetheless, with all the exceptions there still seems to be a significant association between depression and elevated 17-hydroxycorticosteroid output in humans. The significance of the relationship is, of course, poorly understood. Rubin and Mandell (1966) suggest that perhaps both the depressive state and the hyperstimulation of the pituitary are "concomitants of a suprahypophyseal brain dysfunction." They cite the case reported by Wolff et al. (1964) of an adolescent male patient who along with other evidence of hypothalamic dysfunction had a marked increase in output of adrenal steroids concurrent with symptoms of severe depression. All symptoms occurred so predictably each month that the patient's family avoided any activity that would conflict with them. It is still possible, as suggested by some authors, that the adrenocortical outpouring is responsible for some psychiatric symptoms. However, it is the opinion of others (Bunney, Hartmann, & Mason, 1965) that the associated changes in adrenal output follow rather than precede clinical changes in mood. The most generally accepted opinion at this time seems to be that the steroid changes are an indicator of nonspecific emotional distress (Rubin & Mandell, 1966).

Thyroid Disturbances and Depressive Disorder

The relationship between depression and thyroid output has been much less consistent and less studied. Although neuroendocrine releasing systems similar to that of the adrenal cortex exists for the thyroid gland, the thyroid output does not have the great variability or quick responsiveness to changes in the environment so prominent with the adrenal cortex. There is evidence that the thyroid gland is responsive to severe stress, but in the direction of marked inhibition of function (Brown-Grant, Harris, & Reichlin, 1954). Acute cold exposure seems to be one of the few environmental stimuli that can precipitate an increase in thyroid function (Andersson et al., 1962). Neither inhibition nor excitation of thyroid functions in humans has been demonstrated to be related to stress in any systematic way, despite the frequent clinical papers implicating stress as an aetiological factor in hyperthyroidism. Therefore, it is not surprising to find that there have been relatively few studies that show significant changes of thyroid metabolism in psychiatric patients as compared to normal subjects. Even in some papers where differences have been found (Kelsey et al., 1957), the differences have later been found to be the result of, for example, iodine deficiencies in hospital diet. Studies of radioactive iodine uptake are particularly susceptible to changes in dietary iodine, and this may account for diametrically opposing reports in studies of schizophrenic patients (Michael & Gibbons, 1963). Several studies have shown normal values of protein-bound iodine (PBI) in the blood of psychiatric patients (Starr et al., 1950; Brody & Man, 1950; and Gibbons et al., 1960). Bowman et al. (1950) reported a lower mean PBI in depressed patients than in normal controls (5.5 versus 6.2 micrograms per 100 cc). Michael and Gibbons (1963) report that as patients recovered from a depressive episode there was a decline of 0.5 micrograms in the mean level "which was just statistically significant but hardly so clinically." There is, therefore, some suggestion that prolonged emotional disturbance in depression might be associated with slight increases in the serum protein-bound iodine level.

Gonadal Function and Depressive Disorder

Very little work has been reported concerning the levels of gonadal or gonadotrophic hormones in psychiatric patients. This is perhaps unfortunate, since one wonders whether ovarian or pituitary hormone levels have any role to play in the so-called postpartum depressions, or more especially in the acute self-limited brief syndrome popularly known as "baby blues." A number of investigators believe that exacerbations in depressive illness, hospital admissions, and suicides are all more likely to occur in the premenstrual phase of the menstrual cycle (Dalton, 1964). It is interesting to speculate whether the hormonal flux that occurs at this time has any role in the production of the psychological symptoms. It is also striking how similar the symptoms of the so-called premenstrual tension syndrome are to that of an acute brief depressive episode. There seems to be some clinical evidence (Dalton, 1964) that progesterone administration during the latter part of the menstrual cycle serves to alleviate these psychic symptoms. The mechanism, of course, is not known.

Salivary Output

Studies dealing with salivary output in depression date back to Strongin and Hinsie (1938, 1939). Prior to this time, of course, authors had noticed that depressed patients complained, among a host of other symptoms, of feelings of dryness of the mouth. Techniques for measuring salivary output have ranged from the placing of cups over salivary ducts to the simple expedient of placing dental cotton rolls in the subject's mouth for specific time periods. Most of the data reported on below utilized this latter technique. More specifically, the method usually involves placing three dental rolls in the mouth of the subject, two buccally and one sublingually. They are left in place for 2 minutes, after which they are removed and placed in a screw-top jar. The jar plus the rolls having been weighed on an analytic balance is now reweighed in order to get a measure of salivation rate in grams per minute.

All of the studies in this area demonstrate that depressed patients have a significantly lower salivary output when compared to normal subjects. Unfortunately, this response does not appear to be unique to depression. Davies and Gurland (1961), Giddon and Lisanti (1962), and Palmai and Blackwell (1965) have all demonstrated that schizophrenic patients under conditions of rest demonstrate a salivary output as low as the one of depressed patients. On the other hand, Peck (1959) and Busfield et al. (1961) have reported significantly lower salivary output for depressed patients as compared with schizophrenic patients. That the matter is even more complicated is suggested by Strongin and Hinsie's results (1938) that chronic schizophrenics had a markedly elevated salivary output, while "early psychotics" (hebephrenics, one manic-depressive, and one obsessive-compulsive neurotic) had significantly low salivary outputs. Strongin and Hinsie describe these "early psychotics" as being tense and anxious about their problems, which suggests that this may be a contributing factor to the lower salivary output of this group. Loew (1965, 1966) has also suggested than an important contributing factor leading to a reduction in salivary output was anxious agitated behavior.

In addition to salivary inhibition, Palmai and Blackwell (1965) demonstrated that their depressed patients evinced an altered pattern of salivary output. They measured salivary output every two hours for a 24-hours period in a group of patients during the first 48 hours of hospitalisation, while they were receiving electroconvulsive therapy and again just before discharge. They found that, whereas normal control subjects have their maximal salivary output during the early morning hours (4 am) with the lowest output during the early evening hours (6 to 8 pm), depressed patients showed a reversal of this pattern with a slow but steady rise in salivary output during the day, with maximum output between 6 to 8 pm and the low level at 4 am. This pattern was observed at first measurement and on the measurements obtained during the series of ECT. Salivary output just prior to hospital discharge demonstrated the same pattern shown by the normal subjects as well as levels of salivary output identical to the ones of the normal subjects. The 20 female depressed patients in this study suffered from early morning awakening and a diurnal variation in mood. In a more recent study (Palmai et al., 1967), 20 female depressed patients were studied in whom the symptoms of early morning awakening or marked diurnal fluctuation were absent. Once again readings were taken at 2-hour intervals for a 24-hour cycle on three occasions—within one week of admission, after two weeks treatment, and again just before discharge. A further reading at 8 am only was obtained at weekly intervals. Four of the patients received treatment with ECT and 16 with imipramine 50 mg four times a day. Measurement were also made on 10 control subjects selected from the nursing staff. Eight of them received imipramine in the same dosage as the patients for a period of ten weeks commencing after the first salivary measurement.

In line with previous findings the patients before treatment showed a significantly lower salivary output than the one shown by the control subjects. Even more interesting was the finding that the diurnal patterns of flow was the same in the patients in this study as the controls and was a mirror image of the one obtained for the patients in the previous study (Palmai & Blackwell, 1965).

The measurements taken before discharge indicate that both the patients treated with ECT and the ones treated with imipramine were now showing salivary output closer to the outputs of the normal controls. The patients who had received ECT returned to a normal level while the ones treated with imipramine still showed significantly less salivation than the normal controls ($p < 0.001$). The authors suggest that, since both ECT and imipramine-treated patients were clinically improved on discharge, imipramine may have been specifically depressing salivation. Some support is given for this suggestion in that the control subjects who received imiparmine also showed reduced salivary output.

The recovery of the salivary output in the patients who received ECT in the last study is, of course, of particular importance. Davies and Palmai (1964) and Davies and Gurland (1961) also report that effective treatment produces a return of salivary output to normal ranges. Clearly related to the treatment effect are the findings of Strongin and Hinsie (1938) that, in the two cyclic manic-depressive patients they studied, during the manic phase the secretory rate fell within the normal range, whereas during the depressed phase the secretory rate was below the normal range. Davies and Palmai (1964) also reported that severity of depression was related to salivary output with the more severely depressed patients having a lower output than the less severely depressed ones. These findings have been corroborated to some extent by the findings of Busfield and Wechsler (1962). If we can assume that severity of depression is related to recovery, with the more severe depression having a poorer prognosis, these authors' results, which demonstrate that patients who improve on antidepressant medication have a significantly higher resting level of salivary output than patients who do not or who, on the contrary, respond poorly to treatment, fit in with the above results. There is, however, one conflicting report by Gottlieb and Paulson (1961) who found that their depressed patients did not demonstrate an increase in salivary output on recovery. It may well be, however, that the drugs that they used, which included imipramine, may have specifically depressed salivation.

Davies and Palmai (1964) also studied the effects of methacholine, a drug that increases salivary output and produces blood pressure drops, and found that depressed patients like normal subjects demonstrated marked increases in salivary output, suggesting that the mechanism for production of salivary output is not impaired but that the inhibition is rostral to the hypothalamus.

Although in keeping with the theme of this book, we shall not become involved with the complications of the classification of depressive illnesses, it is noteworthy that Loew (1965, 1966), Gottlieb and Paulson (1961), and Busfield and Wechsler (1962) found that endogenous depressions have lower salivary output than do exogenous depressions. Some indications of the complexity into which one can enter from a classification point of view is indicated by the fact that Loew found patients with involutional depressions to have salivary outputs nearer to the control level than any of the other depressed patients he studied, whereas Busfield and Wechsler found this group of depressed patients to have low salivary output.

As we noted previously, Loew has suggested that anxiety-agitation may be an important factor in depression of salivary output. More specifically, he divided his psychogenic depression group into three subgroups—a reactive depression, exhaustion state depression, and a neurotic depression group. He found that the latter group has an average salivary output that was lower than the one for any other group, including the manic-depressive group. On the basis of this finding, he suggested that two factors, which may be independent, are producing a reduction in salivary output. The first factor being an endogenous factor principally found in the M-D group, and the second factor being an anxiety-agitation one associated with Selye's general adaptation syndrome.

It seems clear from this review of the literature on salivary output that this is a promising and simple procedure that deserves further study not only to clear up the points of obvious difference between studies reviewed but also in an attempt to develop this procedure as a diagnostic one. Further studies are needed that deal with the diurnal patterns of salivary output, the effects of "activating" procedures on salivary output, the differences in chemical composition of saliva across groups, and the manner in which patients may fall into subgroups in relation to the level and pattern of salivary output. In this way, we may be able to identify the mechanisms through which these changes are mediated as potential clues to aetiology and to more rational treatment procedures.

Electrolytes and Depressive Disorder

Fluids that are good conductors because of ionization are called electrolytes. The studies we review here have been concerned with the relative masses and concentration of electrolytes in the cells and in the extracellular fluid. The importance of these studies lies in the fact that the resting potential of neurons depends on the ratio of the concentration of potassium inside and outside the cell. The action potential of neurons is dependent on the ratio of the concentrations of intracellular to extracellular sodium.

One of the earlier studies is the one by Klein and Nunn (1945), who studied one male manic-depressive patient and found that, when he was depressed, he retained water and sodium which was lost during his days of mania.

Russell (1960) studied the water, sodium, and potassium balance in 15 depressed patients. The patients were on a constant intake of sodium and potassium, and the urinary losses of these electrolytes were estimated daily for a period of up to 5 weeks while they were treated by ECT. Russell found no significant alteration in the balance of water, potassium, and sodium as the depressed patient recovered from his illness.

A more recently developed technique is isotope dilution. By using this technique, it is possible to measure exchangeable sodium. In other words, one can determine the mass of body sodium with which the isotope mixes in a given time—usually 24 hours. By using this method, Gibbons (1960) found that, in the 16 depressed patients who recovered from their illness, the 24-hour exchangeable sodium decreased by about 10 percent. Eight patients who did not improve during the period of testing showed no significant alteration in exchangeable sodium. These findings, of course, contradict the findings of Russell, who reported no change in sodium balance during recovery from depression. Coppen, Shaw, and Mangoni (1962) also reported that there was no change in exchangeable sodium during the recovery from depression of their 12 patients. But Coppen and Shaw (1963) found that "residual sodium"—the sodium outside the extracellular space—was increased by nearly 50 percent during a depressive illness and returned to normal after recovery. Coppen (1967) has suggested that this increase in residual sodium, which probably represents an increase in intracellular sodium, would reduce the action potential of cell membranes by some 7 millivolts. Coppen (1960) also found that the rate of transfer of sodium from blood to cerebrospinal fluid was half the normal rate when the 20 depressed patients of this study were depressed, and that the rate was normal when they recovered. These findings were confirmed by Fotherby et al. (1963).

Coppen and his colleagues (1966) investigated electrolytes in a series of 22 patients suffering from mania. They found that the "residual sodium" showed an average 200 percent increase over normal when the patients were manic. Some of the manic patients became depressed, and these patients showed a 50 percent increase in residual sodium. After recovery from their illness the patients' residual sodium returned to normal. It seems, therefore, that manic patients show a similar but greater deviation from normals than do depressive patients.

Coppen (1967) has pointed out that because it has not been possible to manipulate body water and electrolytes back to normal by dietary or pharmacological methods, such as the administration of a low salt diet, we have been unable to answer the question whether the changes in electrolytes are causal or secondary to the changes in mood. Some work suggests that changes in water and electrolyte distribution may alter mental state. Busfield (1950) gave water and vasopressin to patients suffering from mania or depression and found that the patients became very much worse. Karstens (1951) found that the same procedure repeated on 6 normal subjects produced the symptoms of a depressive illness.

Brown, Hullin, and Roberts (1963) demonstrated an increase in the extracellular fluid volume in 22 of 28 patients when they recovered from their primary depressive disorders as a result of treatment with ECT or imipramine.

Hullin et al. (1967) investigated 14 depressed patients who received a course of ECT. During the first two weeks of ECT, they found a significant increase in extracellular fluid and a significant increase in the total body water, suggesting that the increase in the extracellular fluid was the result of water retention. But, after the completion of the course of ECT, these measurements began to approach once more the pretreatment measurements. During treatment the "solid weight" of patients decreased, but it showed a significant increase following treatment. The authors suggest that the observed changes in bodily composition are more closely associated with recovery from depression than they are a direct result of ECT. No clear tests of these alternatives have been made, however, and the authors can point only to the fact that one patient who did not receive ECT, but recovered spontaneously, showed similar body-water changes and that two patients, who received ECT but whose depressive symptoms were not relieved, did not show these changes.

Hullin and his colleagues (1967b) also found that two patients who exhibited the classical features of manic-depressive psychosis, showed increases in total body water and a decrease in "solid weight" during the transition from depression to normality and that during the manic phases, which followed the normal phases, these variables continued to alter in the same direction, so that in the later stages of mania the total body water and weight attained maximum values and the "solid weight" a minimum value. The return of normal mood that was associated with the disappearance of manic symptoms were characterized by an increase once more in "solid weight" and a decrease in total body water. These changes continued until the depression returned.

The Electroencephalogram in Depression

The literature dealing with EEG changes in manic or depressive states is, to say the least, contradictory. One common finding is that the incidence of gross abnormalities is no higher in this patient group than in a normal population. Ellingson (1954), reviewing the literature on EEG abnormalities in depression, arrives at a conclusion still valid today. To quote: "It is clear that there is not sufficient evidence to draw any final conclusions concerning the incidence or nature of EEG abnormality in the manic-depressive psychoses" (p. 266). Itil (1964) arrives at a similar conclusion. Let us, however, briefly review the pertinent published findings.

Under conditions of rest Davis (1941, 1942) found that patients in the depressive phase evinced alpha frequencies at 10 cps or slower, while the manic group tended to have alpha frequencies of 10 cps or faster and that one characteristic of EEG's of manic-depressives was a "choppy" EEG. Bonnet and Bennet (1960) similarly observed that choppy EEG's (classified by them as dysrhythmic and borderline abnormal) were found more frequently in manic-depressives than in normals. Lemere (1941) on the other hand did not obtain such a differentiation but did find that high-voltage alpha activity was more characteristic of M-D patients, regardless of status at time of evaluation, than was true of either normals or schizophrenics. Finley (1944) found high-frequency activity to be greatest in the psychotic depressions, with remission of symptoms associated with a reduction of this activity.

Hurst et al. (1954) corroborate aspects of both Davis' and Finley's studies in finding mean alpha activity to be higher in manic than in depressed patients, as well as a higher incidence of low-voltage fast activity (LVF) in their manic-depressive group. Not only was there a higher incidence of LVF activity but the dominant frequency of this activity was also higher than in the control group.

These authors also evaluated the effect of photic stimulation on M-D and a control group. In the lower frequency band (4–20 cps) their M-D group demonstrated better photic driving than the control group, while at higher frequencies (21–26 cps) the relationship reversed.

Shagass (1955a, b) evaluated photic

driving at 10 and 15 cps in patients suffering from anxiety states ($N = 31$) neurotic depression (30), psychotic depression (38), paranoid schizophrenia (29), simple schizophrenia (6), and control (29). Although he presents his conclusions in terms of the ratio of driving at these two frequencies (15:10), he also presents the average driving response in each group of subjects at each of the two frequencies. He concludes that the response ratios were significantly higher in anxiety states as compared to depressions (whether neurotic or psychotic), with control subjects and with paranoid schizophrenics falling between these two extremes. The anxiety group had significantly higher ratios than the two depression groups. These differences appear to be a function of more driving at the higher frequency for the anxiety group, and better driving at the lower frequency for the neurotic depression group, with less driving at the higher frequency for both the neurotic and psychotic depressions. These results have not been replicated in other laboratories and constitute an interesting hypothesis deserving further investigation. Thus, at least two laboratories report changes in the photic driving response in depressive states. Both agree that there is inhibition of driving at higher frequencies, with the evidence for low-frequency driving changes somewhat more equivocal. The recent Russian literature has related photic driving to adequacy of cortical functioning or to "functional mobility of the brain" (Pevzner, 1961). Impaired driving at higher frequencies is taken as evidence for impaired functioning.

Wilson and Wilson (1961) and Zung, Wilson, and Dodson (1964) studied EEG alpha desynchronization in depressed patients—the first study using patients awake, the second study using patients during various stages of sleep. Wilson and Wilson report that habituation of alpha desynchronization was more rapid in the control group, that habituation was less regular in the depressed group, and that the latter group demonstrated longer periods of alpha desynchronization than characterized the control group. The major fault with this study is the marked age discrepancy between their patients ($\bar{x}$ 49 yrs) and control ($\bar{x}$ 27 yrs) group, although we hasten to add that we know of no study that has demonstrated age to be an important variable in affecting the aspects of alpha desynchronization described above as discriminating between normal and depressed patients. Not only are depressed patients more responsive to stimuli while awake but they demonstrate the same difference during all stages of sleep as evaluated electroencephalographically. Zung et al. (1964) further found that after treatment the difference between the patient and control group was no longer statistically reliable.

Thus we observe that although the EEG, when taken under conditions of rest, appears to be a poor tool for aiding in the diagnosis of depression, when it is studied with respect to changes produced by stimulation, there is hope that it may yet become a respectable diagnostic instrument for psychiatry.

Under this heading may be mentioned the provocative work of Shagass and his colleagues on evoked cerebral potentials. Shagass and Schwartz (1962, 1963a, 1963b) found that when they compared patients suffering from psychotic depressions, on the one hand, and healthy or psychoneurotic patients, on the other hand, the amplitude of the initial negative-positive component of somatosensory cerebral evoked responses was larger in the psychotic depressives. They also found that its recovery as determined by administering paired "conditioning" and "test" stimuli was retarded in the depressed patients. In a later study (Shagass & Schwartz, 1966) they confirmed previous findings that recovery of the initial component was less in psychotic depressions than in controls, particularly during the first 20 msec. They did not confirm that responses to unpaired stimuli are larger in depression, and they suggested that previous differences might be attributed to a lack of control for age.

Although Shagass, Schwartz, and Amadeo (1962) found that imipramine had no effect on the recovery measure, they did find that after successful therapy the recovery measure changed in the direction of "normal." Clearly related to these findings of Shagass and Schwartz is the finding that recoveries from depression may be facilitated by scalp positive transcranial direct current polarization (Costain et al., 1964; Lipold & Redfearn, 1964; Redfearn et al., 1964). It has been suggested that this effect may be produced by increasing the excitability of mesencephalic reticular formation neurons. We should note, however, that Sheffield and Mowbray (1968) did not find polarizing current to have any marked effect on their six normal subjects.

The Sedation Threshold

Shagass and Jones (1958) review the work of Shagass and collaborators who for a number of years had been engaged in assessing the utility of the sedation threshold as a psychiatric diagnostic device. The sedation threshold measurement involves the intravenous injection of 0.5 mg/kg doses of sodium amytal every 40 seconds until "sedation" is achieved. The point of sedation is identified by slurring of speech and an inflection of the increase in 15–30 cps EEG activity as recorded from anterior cortical derivations. By using these measures and by reviewing results based on some 750 patients, these authors came to the conclusion that

> "It is clear that the neurotic and psychotic depression groups constituted two separate populations with respect to the sedation threshold. This difference is perhaps the most clinically useful one provided by the sedation threshold" (p. 1007).

All but 5.2 percent of their psychotic depression group were sedated before 4 mgm/kg of amytal had been injected while 90 percent of the neurotic depressions needed more than 4 mgm for sedation. Although it discriminates well between these groups, they found, for example, that in addition to the psychotic depressions, hysterics, organic patients, the ones suffering from acute and simple schizophrenia, schizoaffective disturbance, and paranoid state had low sedation thresholds, while the neurotic depression group had for its bedfellow patients diagnosed as anxiety state, chronic schizophrenia, borderline schizophrenia (pseudoneurotic) and, to a lesser extent, anxiety neurotics, and obsessive-compulsive neurotics.

A flurry of research studies were sparked by this and earlier reports by Shagass and his co-workers. A number of them experienced difficulties in repeating the Shagass procedure. Most studies found considerable difficulty in determining the point at which speech became slurred, or the point at which the increase in 15–30 cps EEG activity leveled off. According to Shagass these two points should coincide. Most authors had considerable difficulty in defining this point with either of these techniques, since patients, for example, would demonstrate slurring of speech, show a recovery of normal speech, and require a number of further injections before slurring was again manifested. In addition, slurred speech could not be used in some studies because of speech retardation. Authors who reported this difficulty include Boudreau (1958); Ackner and Pampiglione (1959); Nymgaard (1959); Martin and Davies (1962, 1965). A number of solutions have been offered, the first of which was to eliminate the slurring of speech criterion and to stick to the EEG measure. Thus, Nymgaard defined the inflection point as the first time the downward slope of the curve relating amount of 15–30 cps activity to total quantity of drug injection had an angle of 140° or less. By using this criterion he replicated Shagass' results, psychotic depressions having an average sedation threshold of 2.23 mg/kg versus 3.27 mg/kg for a neurotic-depressive group. No one else has used Nymgaard's simple rule for defining the EEG inflection point. Boudreau (1958), although he had trouble defining the inflection point, as well as losing 28/60 tests because of too much muscle artifact in his recordings, generally corroborated Shagass' results. Perez-Reyes et al. (1962) utilized inhibition of the electrodermal response associated with the repetition of 3 digit numbers and found that the electrodermal responses disappeared before the verbal response (sleep threshold) disappeared. By using EDR inhibition threshold, they found their psychotic depressions to have a significantly lower threshold ($\bar{x}$ 1.81 mg/kg) than was true for either a neurotic depressive ($\bar{x}$ 3.44) or a normal control group ($\bar{x}$ 3.32). Similar results were found in a later study (Perez-Reyes & Cochrane, 1967). Perris and Brattemo (1963) also replicated Shagass' results and, in addition, demonstrated that with treatment there was a rise in the sedation threshold for the endogenous depression group (which was greater than that shown by his exogenous depression group).

With respect to negative results, we have the studies by Martin and Davies (1962, 1965) both of which are based on the same data. Sleep threshold was defined as the point where the patient no longer responded to verbal stimuli. Claridge and Herrington (1960) had demonstrated that this measure was equally efficient as the sedation threshold in discriminating between psychotic and neurotic depressions. Martin and Davies report that they were unable to obtain consistent relations between any of the measures obtained (ratings of agitation, anxiety, retardation, and severity of depression) and the sleep threshold.

Muscle Tension

A number of studies have been conducted in recent years which suggest that depression is accompanied by a heightened state of muscle tension (hyperponesis). Thus, Whatmore and Ellis (1959, 1962) demonstrated that electromyographic (EMG) activity is elevated in patients suffering from both endogenous as well as reactive depressions. In their endogenous depression study they followed five patients through periods of remission and found that these patients maintained their high level of activity even though they were clinically recovered. Whatmore (1966) has suggested that depressives differ from schizophrenics in that the former show constant and the latter labile hyperponesis. Their results of maintenance of EMG activity during periods of remission are somewhat at variance with other studies. Martin and Davies (1965) report the highest level of muscle tension in their endogenous depression group, followed by the reactive depression group, with both significantly different from a normal control group. There was some suggestive evidence from their study that the higher level of muscle tension may be situationally induced. In any case, the depressive patients demonstrated more of a drop in EMG activity during the recording period than was true of control subjects.

Goldstein (1965) studied EMG activity in nonpsychotic depressives and found them to have a higher level of muscle activity under conditions of stimulation (white noise) than either another neurotic or a control group. Under conditions of rest, unlike the previous authors, she obtained no significant differences between groups. Wilson and Wilson (1961) similarly report a high level of muscle tension in severely depressed patients, with an intensification of EMG activity in response to photic stimulation.

Rimon, Stenback, and Huhmar (1966) evaluated EMG activity from various muscle groups in a series of 45 depressed patients. Eight of these were diagnosed as manic-depressives, with 37 diagnosed as reactive or neurotic depression. These authors obtained no differences in EMG output between these two groups. They related EMG activity to severity of depression as measured by the Beck inventory (1961), as well as to clinical improvement. Severity of depression was found to be significantly correlated with EMG activity of the masseter muscle group. The *milder* the depression the *greater* the amount of tension manifested in this muscle group. Clinical improvement was measured by change in symptomatology of depression as evaluated by the Beck inventory. Patients were categorized as showing good versus poor remission. Recovery was associated with a *rise* in EMG activity in all muscle groups measured with exception of the hand. However, a significant increase was only found for the masseter muscle group. To complete our review of this area of contradictory results, we can quote the studies of Shipman et al. (1964) who found muscle tension not to be, or to be only poorly related to either the state of depression or anxiety.

Wulfeck (1941a and b) measured muscle tension indirectly by having subjects hold a ball in their hand with instructions to depress it to a level most comfortable for him. They recorded pressure exerted on the ball pneumographically. Manic-depressives demonstrated higher levels of baseline (rest) tension than normals, but less than was true of schizophrenics. Patients in both the manic and depressive phase had similar tension levels. In response to difficult motor coordination tasks (involving the other hand) manic depressives as well as schizophrenics demonstrate greater increases in tension than is true of normal or neurotic subjects.

Although the published results are often at variance with each other, like Malmo and Shagass (1949), we still believe that

> "... the study of muscular tension in the psychiatric disorders should provide important data concerning the physiology of the pathological emotional states associated with these disorders."

However, we could continue to quote them a

bit further and indicate that the state of affairs with respect to research has not improved much since 1949. To quote:

> "However, very little experimental work has been carried out in this field. The available information is meager and may be summarized by the statement that most investigators find evidence of greater than normal muscle tension in psychiatric patients."

Motor Reaction Time

Since one of the common observations made about depressed patients is that they demonstrate psychomotor retardation, it is surprising that not more studies have been conducted to evaluate this variable. Shakow and Huston (1936) in their studies of motor function in schizophrenia report on a small group of manic-depressive patients, finding them to be much like schizophrenics in that they had significantly slower tapping rates than was true of normal subjects.

Wulfeck (1941a, b) found depressed patients to demonstrate psychomotor retardation, while manics performed at higher speed levels than all other groups and also made more errors. Brower and Oppenheim (1951) related changes in psychomotor performance in depressed patients to clinical improvement. They observed an increase in adequacy of performance of psychomotor tasks that was associated with amelioration of symptoms of depression. Martin and Rees (1966), similarly, found depressed subjects to have longer reaction times with severity of depression correlated with reaction time. The only negative data was presented by Hall and Stride (1954) who reported that the depressives did not differ significantly from normals in reaction time, while neurotics were found to be significantly faster than depressed patients. These authors stress the need to match subjects for age in order to draw valid conclusions in reaction-time studies.

The motor reaction-time studies have not attempted to discriminate between the various depressive types. Reaction times as measured by physiological response measures such as latency of EEG alpha desynchronization, and latency of orienting responses as measured in other physiological systems does not appear to discriminate between depressed and normal subjects. One might thus agree with Shakow and Huston (1936) that the slower response times on voluntary tasks are probably a function of motivational deficits.

Conditional Response Studies

Astrup (1962) reviews a relatively large Russian literature in this area (25 studies) and points out that disturbances, both unconditional as well as conditional, are often observed in M-D patients. Inhibition of unconditional responses was observed by Astrup in looking at vascular responses (forearm plethysmography) to cold stimulation, as well as electrodermal responses to electric shock stimulation.

Protopopov, quoted by Astrup, however, found that manic patients demonstrated a hypersensitivity to both cold as well as to low levels of electric shock stimulation. He did not observe this hypersensitivity in depressed patients. Voluntary motor inhibition of responses to shock stimulation could not be obtained in either manic or depressed patients by this author. We suspect that these results are really not at variance with Astrup's results, but that the latter author limited his investigations to patients in the depressive phase of the M-D illness.

Protopopov's studies dealing with conditional responses indicate that manic patients develop simple conditional (motor) responses more rapidly than normals and that depression slows down the development of these responses. In manics, conditional responses developed rapidly and inhibitory responses slowly while, in depressed patients, conditional responses were established more slowly, latency of the response was prolonged, and the response was weaker than the one found in manic patients. Inhibitory responses were, as in the manic, difficult to elaborate.

Ivanov-Smolensky (1925) studied the development of conditional responses in a group ($N = 7$) of manic-depressed patients in the depressed phase. The unconditional stimulus was the verbal instruction to press a rubber ball (attached to a manometer so that latency and strength of the response could be measured), the conditional stimulus was a tone or more complex auditory stimulus presented immediately prior to the instruction to press. Conditioning was carried out over a 4-day period with 2 to 25 trials administered per day.

Conditioning consisted of the presentation of an auditory stimulus followed by verbal instruction. Normal subjects, after 5 to 8 combinations, demonstrated good evidence of conditioning (bulb pressing during tone and prior to instruction to press), while in depressed patients these responses were first elaborated after 40 trials. The conditional response, in normals, was established rapidly (5 to 8 trials), its latency was short, the amplitude constant, and the response was described as energetic and rapid. For the depressed group, it was established slowly (20 to 70 combinations), its latency was long, the amplitude inconsistent and variable, and the response was characterized as slow and gradual in nature.

Extinction of the response by instruction "don't press" was extremely rapid in the depressed [(1 to 2 trials) and slower in the control group (3 to 5 trials)]. Reinstatement of the UCR (press to instruction to press) was slower in the depressed than in the normal group. Thus, both unconditional responses as well as conditional motor responses are seen to be impaired in depressed patients.

In a subsample (3 normals and 4 depressives) the author assessed the generalization of CR's. The CR was established to tones of 3 different frequencies (123, 132, 1161 cps), the response was then extinguished to 123 cps. In depressed patients there was greater generalization of extinction than was found for the normal subjects. The extinction procedure was repeated a number of times (after reestablishment of the CR) with the finding that sleep-inhibition developed in the depressed but not in normal subjects. These results are interpreted within the Pavlovian framework of greater irradiation of inhibitory responses in the cortex of depressed as compared to normal subjects.

Although Ivanov-Smolensky published some of his results in German (1925) as well as in English (1928), they seem to have made little impact on Western psychiatry with the possible exception of Gantt and, more recently, Astrup. It is not until the 1960's that we observe a renewal or development of interest in conditioning studies as applied to depression. Ban et al. (1966) studied 28 subjects, 7 each diagnosed as neurotic depression, endogenous depression, schizophrenia with depression, and 7 normal volunteers. The experimental procedure involved the study of orienting responses (OR), unconditional responses (UCR), simple conditioning, and differential conditioning. The response measure utilized was the electrodermal response, the CS a white or yellow light, and the UCS an intense auditory stimulus.

Control subjects gave significantly greater amplitude OR's than any of the three patient groups. The neurotic group was also significantly differentiated from both the psychotic groups. Qualitatively, both the control and the neurotic group demonstrated clear and smooth habituation curves over trials, while the two psychotic groups demonstrated inconsistent habituation over trials. With respect to the UCR, the control group was again differentiated from all of the patient groups, with the schizophrenic group differentiable from the two depression groups (lowest amplitude UCR for the schizophrenic group).

Disinhibition of the OR to the CS by the pairing of the CS with a UCS, as measured by an increase in amplitude of the OR, occurred maximally in the control and the neurotic depression groups, with the two psychotic groups demonstrating little disinhibition. With respect to the CR, it was found that the control group gave significantly more CR's than any of the patient groups, with the latter groups not differentiable from each other on this measure.

The authors conclude that one can, on the basis of conditioning studies, discriminate between patients and nonpatients as well as between diagnostic groups.

> "The qualitatively different OR behavior and the potential for disinhibition clearly differentiate the neurotic depression from the other two pathological groups. Significantly stronger amplitudes of the UCR, with a prolonged latency time, and impaired CS discrimination, characterize schizophrenic depression and discriminate it from endogenous depression. The latter group is further characterized by slowly-formed but stable conditional reflexes" (p. 102).

Unfortunately no attempt is made to use a discriminant function or other analytic procedure to determine how well patients in the various groups can be appropriately identified by the conditioning procedures. The results presented in these two studies (reviewed in some detail here) appear to be reasonably concordant, although one used a simple motor and the other used an autonomic response measure. Both studies report poorer and less consistent conditioning in depressed patients.

That other unconditional responses are also disturbed in depression is documented in a study by Kielholz and Beck (1962). These authors studied autonomic function in depression, and they present results of a study that is concerned with the return of acral warmth after the immersion of the forearm in cool water. Patients who suffered from "exhaustion depression" were found to have significantly lower initial skin temperatures than was true of normal subjects, and in response to forearm cooling and rewarming there was a distinct delay of acral warmth return in the depressed as compared to the control group. These authors state that sympathetic hyperfunction with signs of decompensation characterized 18 of the 20 patients studied, while two demonstrated pure sympathetic overexcitation. These abnormal vegetative responses are reported by these authors to also characterize patients suffering from neurotic depressions.

Unfortunately, the delay of return of forearm warmth after application of the cold pressor test is not diagnostic for depression since similar results have been demonstrated in schizophrenia (Shattock, 1950).

Stewart et al. (1959) evaluated extinction of electrodermal OR's and the development and extinction of CR's in 4 groups of patients (M-D 27; schizophrenic 18; personality disorders 15; anxiety neurosis 10). Habituation of OR's was slowest in the anxiety neurosis group with no differences between the other three groups. With respect to conditional anticipatory responses, the only group from which the M-D's could be differentiated was the personality disorder group—the latter subjects giving significantly more conditional responses. The conditional defensive response (response to the "UCS" when the latter was no longer presented during extinction trials) discriminated the M-D's from both the anxiety neurotics and the personality disorder group. These results thus suggest that differentiation between schizophrenia and manic-depressive psychosis was not possible, although, on one or more of the measures used, both of these disturbances could be discriminated from the other two groups.

AETIOLOGY OF DEPRESSION

In our introduction, we have already referred to the main theories that have been proposed to account for the development of depression. Most of them have not been adequately tested, primarily, because their formulations do not readily lead to testable hypotheses. Bowlby's notion concerning the aetiological role of parental separation in childhood, however, has resulted in a considerable amount of research.

Parental Deprivation and Depressive Disorder

Beck, Sethi, and Tuthill (1963) reported in their study that patients who were severely depressed had suffered more parental bereavement before their sixteenth birthday than the patients who were mildly depressed. Relationships between early separation and depression have also been reported by Earle and Earle (1961), Sethi (1964), Munro (1966), Brown (1966), and Denneby (1966). Hill and Price (1967) compared the incidence of child bereavement in 1483 depressed patients and 1059 nondepressed adult psychiatric inpatients. They found that their depressed patients lost more fathers because of death before their sixteenth birthday and that this finding was most marked for female depressives. Wilson, Alltop, and Buffaloe (1967) also report findings similar to those of Beck and those of Munro concerning the relationship between parental deprivation and the severity of depression. They studied 92 depressed patients and found that the parentally bereaved group ($N = 64$) showed higher scores on the psychotic triad of the MMPI than the patients not so bereaved. They also found that, in the bereaved group, the mean scores of the basic scales of the MMPI of the patients who had lost their mothers ($N = 10$) were significantly higher than the mean scores of the patients who had lost their fathers. Hopkinson and Reed (1966), on the other hand, found no significant relationship between bereavement in childhood and adult depressive psychosis.

Some investigators have studied the effects of parental separation on animals. We referred in the introduction to Kaufman and Rosenbloom's (1957) finding that infant monkeys separated from their mothers went into a depression-withdrawal phase.

Senay (1966) has studied the effects of separation on dogs. He first formed a relationship with each litter of six three-week old German shepherd pups and for the next nine months was their sole consistent human figure. Then for a two-month separation period the animals had no contact with the author. During this period a caretaker fed the animals and recorded data from photoelectric counters, but he did not speak to the animals, touch them, or observe them in any way. This was followed by a one-month reunion period. Before separation the animals were ranked in an approach-avoidance test and their temperament characterized in approach-avoidance terms. It was found that separation was associated with increases in object seeking for animals with approach temperament and with increases in object avoidance and aggressive behavior for animals of the avoidance temperament. The author admits that there are too few subjects for any reliable conclusions to be drawn but suggests that his work can be considered a model for animal studies of the effects of separation in producing depression.

Seay, Hansen, and Harlow (1962) studied the effects on four monkeys of three weeks separation from the mother. The initial response of the monkeys was one of "violent and prolonged protest." This was followed by what the authors felt was clearly despair marked mainly by a depression of play activities. They suggest that the findings are generally in accord with Bowlby's theory of primary separation anxiety as an explanatory principle for the basic primary separation mechanisms, but they suggest further that the human being, even the human child, is capable of more subtle and profound behavioral disturbances than any nonhuman animal.

For the rest we have a number of scattered studies attacking the problem in a variety of ways. We review them briefly.

A series of studies by Winokur and his colleagues (Winokur & Pitts, 1965; Pitts & Winokur, 1966; Winokur & Clayton, 1967) suggest that affective disorder is more frequent in females than in males. It was also found that in the parents of probands a statistically significant excess of mothers as compared with fathers were found to have suffered from the same illness. Brothers and sisters of male probands and sisters of female probands showed essentially the same morbidity risk for affective disorder, the difference being observed in brothers of female probands. It was also found that alcoholism was significantly more prevalent in fathers and siblings of the affective disorder group than in a matched control series.

Another series of studies has been concerned with the ideas presented by Cohen et al. (1954). They suggested that manic-depressive patients shared common characteristics of excessive conformity, dependency, and a need for social approval, and that they were frequently used by their families as "esteem getting" instruments. In line with this hypothesis, Becker (1964) found that manic-depressives valued achievement more for the approval it obtained from others than for its own sake. He also found that manic-depressives showed strong conformity tendencies and subscribed to authoritarian values. Further supporting evidence has been obtained in studies by Spielberger, Parker, and Becker (1963) with a manic-depressed group, and also by Becker and Nichols (1964) for a sample of nonpsychiatric cyclothymic college students. Katkin, Sasmor, and Tan (1966) studied conformity and achievement related characteristics in an experimental group made up of patients suffering from involutional depression or psychotic depressive reaction and in a control group of psychiatric patients diagnosed as schizophrenic with no history of depressive disorder. Apart from this clinical criteria the patients had to satisfy a psychometric criterion based on the Depression scale of the MMPI before they were included in either the experimental or the control group. They found that depressed patients showed more conformity than a schizophrenic control when conformity was measured by the degree to which the patients shifted their responses to a 15-item inventory after hearing tape recordings of extreme opinions on these items. No significant differences between the groups were found on a questionnaire measure of authoritarian ideology, on a fascism scale, or on a value achievement scale. Contrary to prediction the schizophrenics showed higher scores on a social desirability scale than did the depressives. The authors suggest that the higher score on the social desirability scale may be because of the greater defensiveness of the schizophrenic patients. In support of this suggestion they refer to Edwards (1965) findings of a negative correlation (–0.65) between the MMPI depression scale and the social desirability scale.

It is generally assumed that depressed patients have a low evaluation of themselves. A series of studies suggests that the situation is not that simple. In his first study, Laxer (1964a) found, by using the Semantic Differential, that depressed patients showed lower real self-ratings at admission than other psychiatric patients and showed a greater move toward higher real self-rating from admission to discharge. In a second study, Laxer (1964b) found evidence that depressed patients blamed themselves more and rated their moods lower than other psychiatric patients. But he also found that patients in very low mood showed low self-rating only if they blamed themselves for their failures, whereas the ones who tended to blame others when they were in an unhappy mood did not show such a devaluative concept. He suggests that a combination of very low mood and high self-blame characteristic of neurotic depressives is a necessary if not sufficient condition for the syndrome of neurotic depression. His suggestion is an important one in that it results in the conclusion that

> "low mood is not synonymous with the syndrome of depression and is not by itself to be taken as a prototype in normals for depression in psychiatric patients. A necessary additional factor it seems is aggression against the self as psychoanalytic theory suggests" (Laxer, 1964, p. 545).

Before Laxer's conclusions are accepted it would be necessary to show that depressed patients did not also have a low evaluation of things other than themselves. Costello and Comrey (1967) also used the Semantic Differential and found that normal subjects with depressive tendencies gave low evaluations to both self and nonself-concepts. A similar finding by Mayo (1967) is that a measure of *general* punitiveness based on the scale developed by Foulds (1965) was positively related to the severity of depression.

This is as good a place as any, perhaps, to mention that Friedman (1964) basing his conclusions on performance on 33 psychometric tests concluded that the actual ability in performance during severe psychotic depression is not consistent with the patient's unrealistically low image of himself. He suggested that the experience of ego helplessness is more subjective than objective, more imaginary than real. He suggested further that his results were not in line with the traditional psychoanalytic energy and libido exhaustion concept of depression.

Beck has done two studies concerned with the dreams and fantasies of depressed patients. In one study, Beck (1961), by classifying his psychiatric patients depressed or not depressed in terms of scores on his inventory for measuring depression (Beck et al., 1961), found that the depressed group had significantly more masochistic dreams and early memories than a nondepressed group, and that the masochism scores on a fantasy test and on a masochism inventory were also significantly higher in the depressed group. It is not clear whether these patients were in treatment at the time. Certainly in an earlier study by Beck and Hurvich (1959), which was also concerned with masochistic dream content, the patients were in psychoanalytic therapy. If this is true in the later study, then we cannot rule out the possible influence on the dreams and fantasy of the patient of the analyst's ideas concerning depression and masochism.

Also with regard to the study by Beck and Hurvich (1959) we must note that the authors state:

> "Further although the dream sample was not explicitly used as the basis for construction of the rating scale, it is probable that some aspects of the rating scale are at least partly based on the dreams of the patients in the present sample since these dreams were known to the senior author when the scoring manual was developed. It is clear that both cross-validation and multiple validation studies are necessary to confirm these findings and allow a specification of their general ability."

It is perhaps noteworthy that the data in this study were obtained from only six matched pairs of subjects. In a better controlled study with a much larger sample of patients, Beck and Ward (1961) obtained supportive evidence for the relationship between depression and masochistic dream content.

There is one other matter to which we refer because of its general interest. As is well known, mood changes produced by progestational agents have been reported (for example, Kane et al., 1967), but it appears that adequate control studies have not been done, and it would seem particularly important here to separate out the direct pharmacological effects and the indirect psychological effects.

CONCLUSION

Despite the fact that depression is one of the most, if not the most, common complaint of psychiatric patients, very little is known about it. We shall never know anything more about it if we do not keep two things in mind:

1. Difficult as it may be, strict scientific principles must be adhered to at all times. Research in this, as in most areas, of clinical psychological research is expensive, time consuming, and questions of ethics must play a role. Instant, not too costly research is not likely to get us far.
2. Unlike the physical scientists, we are not dealing with passive objects. This introduces another very difficult problem into our science (see Rosenthal (1966) for a discussion of this issue).

It may well be that depressive illnesses will be best understood eventually as a number of syndromes with depressed mood as one of the symptoms. It is argued in Chapter 1 that until depressed mood and the many other symptoms discussed in this book are better measured and understood, it is probably advisable not to try to cluster them in any manner.

However, clinical practice will not stand still until the above is done. We must remember that clinical disorders (both medical as well as psychiatric) have been described for centuries, and that their descriptions appear to be remarkably constant over the years (Lindsay, 1963). Although the focus of this volume is on individual symptoms, many clinicians are persuaded that syndromes of depression, in which clusters of symptoms are intercorrelated, are concepts that are useful in the treatment of patients.

What constitutes the syndromes and, indeed, whether they are valid at all, has been heatedly debated in the literature for the past 50 years. Nonetheless, a number of recent studies present evidence in favor of the attempt to delineate syndromes (Cassidy et al., 1957; Kiloh and Garside, 1963; Zung, 1965; Pollitt, 1965; Sandifer et al., 1966; Rosenthal and Klerman, 1966; Winokur and Pitts, 1964; Hunt et al., 1967; Mendels and Cochrane 1968). The evidence has been critically reviewed in Chapter I. Others fail to find evidence of a depressive syndrome (McConaghy et al., 1967). The issue has by no means been resolved but the possibility that depressive syndromes can be defined for both research and clinical purposes cannot be discarded. One of the major problems concerning research on any of the psychiatric conditions is the definition of what should be included under the diagnostic entity being studied. The problem, of course, is a two-pronged one: (1) definition of the attributes that one wants to accept for arriving at a definitive diagnosis, and (2) reliable identification of these attributes in a given patient population. As is apparent from our review of the literature, the definition of depression is quite vague, running from "depressive symptoms in hospitalized patients" to rigorously defined criteria for arriving at a diagnosis of manic-depressive disease.

There are a number of studies using historical data and the structured psychiatric interview alone that have succeeded in extracting data from groups of psychiatric patients—a subgroup of patients that displays the cluster of endogenous depression symptoms and that fits objective predefined criteria of the disorder (Pitts et al., 1966; Winokur & Pitts, 1964; Woodruff, Pitts, & Winokur, 1964; Pitts & Winokur, 1966). We believe that this technique can be used to collect a group of patients who can be defined with some rigor and who can be assumed to be homogenous with respect to the presence of endogenous depression. The immediate usefulness of defining such a group is that it permits prognostic statements with a considerable degree of reliability. Patients who fit certain well-defined, objective, historical criteria for depression will, in the great majority of instances, have a self-limiting course of illness and will exhibit a virtually complete recovery. This is quite a different outcome from the majority of schizophrenic patients if they are selected with similar care and objectivity. Furthermore, the definition of a group of patients in this fashion permits the more rational application of the therapies that are currently available.

Investigators who use the structured psychiatric interview in defining groups of patients believe that it is useful in delineating groups that are discrete and separate from each other, and they have shown that patients so diagnosed retain their diagnosis when followed up after a period of time (Perley & Guze, 1962). They believe that the structured interview has advantages over questionnaires in that, if the clinician administers the interview, he can be sure that the subject understands the question, he can evaluate the clinical significance of symptoms that the patient reports, he can take care to determine whether the symptoms reported fall into episodes, and he can get dates of onset of symptoms, etc. In whatever way patients are diagnosed, however, we believe that it is important for investigators to make as explicit as possible the criteria for including patients into diagnostic groups in order that their results may be replicated and tested in other centers. Our experience in this review of the literature convinces us that it is far better for the investigators to establish their own criteria for diagnostic inclusion in advance of the study and to make their own diagnosis on the patient material used, rather than to rely on the diagnosis made by the clinicians actually caring for patients, which is notoriously impressionistic and unreliable. If possible, case history material or, at least, specimen case history should be included to indicate the application of the diagnostic criteria used by researchers.

The diagnosis, whether rigorously defined or "all-inclusive," currently is based exclusively on historical material, that is, self-report or case history material. Self-report data is principally based on interview material which is usually obtained in a psychiatric interview, with interviews ranging from open-ended impressionistic ones to highly structured interview schedules. Akin to this latter procedure are questionnaire schedules filled out by the patient and/or relatives. To what extent "structured interviews" elaborate information different from and more reliable than questionnaire data has to the best of our knowledge (and surprise) not been systematically investigated. Although proponents of face-to-face interviewing techniques hold that information so obtained is more reliable than the information procured by a paper-and-pencil questionnaire that covers the same material, the limited evidence available does not corroborate this position. There appear to be as many difficulties in reliably eliciting information in face-to-face contact as through the paper-and-pencil medium.

Case history material, has often been used in retrospective studies and, of course, suffers from the inadequacy of both of the above techniques as well as from the fact that the information recorded has gone through considerable "selective filtering" and may not cover all the points one can readily cover in a prospective study.

These, then, are the self-report measures available to the researcher in this difficult field. What are the other avenues available for obtaining information on which to base one's diagnostic label? One can observe patient behavior rather than obtaining self-report data from him. It is of considerable theoretical as well as practical importance that information obtained by these two routes is often not highly related. Thus, for example, the study by Grinker et al. (1961) which used both types of data, fortunately conducted a separate factor analyses of the interview and the observation derived data. Factors identified by these two techniques bore surprisingly little relationship to each other. Analysis of the interview material elaborated factors associated with a number of clusters of symptoms associated with depression (which is based on the same type of material), while the factor structure of the observation derived data came up with a more complicated and less "explanatory" factor structure. The studies by Lorr et al., (1953) based purely on observational data bear out the above results. Any relationship between the factors arrived at by these authors and the clinical diagnostic labels in current usage in psychiatric practice were more obvious by their absence than by their presence. It is of interest that the factors described in the Lorr book have been replicated a number of times and might lead to a radical revision of psychiatric labeling if they can be demonstrated to be better prognostic tools and tools for the assignment of therapies on a rational basis than the ones currently in vogue in clinical psychiatric practice (see the further discussion of Lorr's work in Chapter 1).

The last measure, which to date has been principally used as a dependent variable in research on depression, is a direct measure on the patient that uses physiological recording techniques such as the EEG for measuring adequacy of sleep or more objective measures of "observable" behavior such as monitoring the movements of a patient in bed.

It should really come as no "shock" that there is little agreement across studies that attempt to use physiological measures to arrive at more definitive psychiatric diagnoses. Although the physiological measures hopefully can be replicated across different laboratories, the criteria used to define the independent variable often bear little relationship to each other. One man's "periodic catatonia" becomes another man's "atypical depression."

REFERENCES

Ackner, B., & Pampiglione, G. An evaluation of the sedation threshold test. *J. Psychosom. Res.*, 1959, **3**, 271–281.

Addison, J. *On the constitutional and local effects of disease of the suprarenal capsules.* London: 1855.

Anderson, W. M., & Dawson, J. The variability of plasma 17-hydroxycorticosteroid levels in affective illness and schizophrenia. *J. Psychosom. Res.*, 1965, **9**, 237–248.

Andersson, B., Ekman, L., Gale, C., & Sundsten, J. W. Activation of the thyroid gland by cooling of the pre-optic area in the goat. *Acta Physiol. Scand.*, 1962, **54**, 191–192.

Astrup, C. Schizophrenia: Conditional reflex studies. Springfield, Ill.: Charles C. Thomas, 1962.

Ban, T. A., Choi, S. M., Lehmann, H. E., & Adamo, E. Conditional reflex studies in depression. *Canad. Psychiat. Assoc. J.*, 1966, **11**, Spec. Suppl., 98–104.

Beck, A. T. A systematic investigation of depression. *Comprehensive Psychiat.*, 1961, **2**, 163–170.

Beck, A. T., & Hurvich, M. S. Psychological correlates of depression. I. Frequency of "masochistic" dream content in a private practice sample. *Psychosom. Med.*, 1959, **21**, 50–55.

Beck, A. T., Sethi, B. B., & Tuthill, R. W. Childhood bereavement and adult depression. *Arch. gen. Psychiat.*, 1963, **9**, 295–302.

Beck, A. T., & Ward, C. H. Dreams of depressed patients. *Arch. gen. Psychiat.*, 1961, **5**, 462–467.

Beck, A. T., Ward, C. H., Mendelson, M., Mock, J., & Erbaugh, J. An inventory for measuring depression. *Arch. gen. Psychiat.*, 1961, **4**, 561–571.

Becker, J. Achievement related characteristics of manic depressives. *J. abnorm. soc. Psychol.*, 1964, **69**, 531–538.

Becker, J., & Nichols, C. H. Communality of manic depressive and "mild" cyclothymic characteristics. *J. abnorm. soc. Psychol.*, 1964, **69**, 531–538.

Bibring, E. The mechanism of depression. In P. Greenacre (ed.), *Affective disorders*. New York: International University Press, 1953.

Bliss, E. L., Migeon, C. J. Branch, C. H., & Samuels. L. T. Adrenocortical function in schizophrenia. *Amer. J. Psychiat.*, 1955, **112**, 358–365.

Bliss, E. L., Migeon, C. J., Branch, C. H., & Samuels, L. T. Reaction of adrenal cortex to emotional stress. *Psychosom. Med.*, 1956, **18**, 56–76.

Bliss, E. L., Migeon, C. J., Nelson, D. H., Samuels, L. T., & Branch C. H. Influence of E.C.T. and insulin coma on level of adrenocortical steroids in peripheral circulation. *Arch. Neurol. Psychiat.*, 1954, **72**, 352–361.

Board, F., Persky, H., & Hamburg, D. A. Psychological stress and endocrine functions: Blood levels of adrenocortical and thyroid hormones in acutely disturbed patients. *Psychosom. Med.*, 1956, **18**, 324–333.

Board, F., Wadeson, R., & Persky, H. Depressive affect and endocrine functions: Blood levels of adrenal cortex and thyroid hormones in patients suffering from depressive reactions. *Arch. Neurol. Psychiat.*, 1957, **78**, 612–620.

Bonnet, H. & Bennet, H. Das EEG bei Depressionszustanden. La revue Lyonnaise Med. 1960.

Boudreau, D. Evaluation of the sedation threshold. *Arch. Neurol. Psychiat.*, 1958, **80**, 771–775.

Bowlby, J. Grief and mourning in infancy and early childhood. *Psychoanalytic study of the child.* 1960, **15**, 9–52.

Bowman, K. M., Miller, E. R., Dailey, M. E., Simon, A., & Mayer, B. F. Thyroid function in mental disease: a multiple test survey. *J. nerv. ment. Dis.*, 1950, **112**, 404–424.

Brambilla, F., & Nuremberg, T. Adrenal cortex function of cyclothymic patients in depressive phase. *Dis. Nerv. Syst.*, 1963, **24**, 727–731.

Brody, E. B., & Man, E. B. Thyroid function measured by serum precipitable iodine determinations in schizophrenic patients. *Amer. J. Psychiat.*, 1950, **107**, 357–359.

Brower, D. & Oppenheim, S. The effects of electroshock therapy on mental functioning as revealed by psychological tests. *J. gen. Psychol.*, 1951, **45**, 171–188.

Brown, D. G., Hullin, R. P., Roberts, J. M. Fluid distribution and the response of depression to ECT and imipramine. *Brit. J. Psychiat.*, 1963, **109**, 395–398.

Brown, F. Childhood bereavement and subsequent psychiatric disorder. *Brit. J. Psychiat.*, 1966, **112**, 1035–1041.

Brown-Grant, K., Harris, G. W., & Reichlin, S. The effect of emotional and physical stress on thyroid activity. *J. Physiol.*, 1954, **126**, 29–40.

Bunney, W. E., Jr., & Fawcett, J. A. Possibility of a biochemical test for suicide potential. *Arch. gen. Psychiat.*, 1965, **13**, 232–239.

Bunney, W. E., Jr., & Hartmann, E. L. Study of a patient with 48-hour manic depressive cycles. I. An analysis of behavioral factors. *Arch. gen. Psychiat.*, 1965, **13**, 611–618.

Bunney, W. E., Jr., Hartmann, E. L., & Mason, J. W. Study of a patient with 48-hour manic depressive cycles. II. Strong positive correlation between endocrine factors in manic defense patterns. *Arch. gen. Psychiat.*, 1965, **12**, 619–625.

Bunney, W. E., Jr., Mason, J. W., & Hamburg, D. A. Correlations between behavior variables and urinary 17-hydroxycorticosteroid in depressed patients. *Psychosom. Med.*, 1965, **27**, 299–308.

Bunney, W. E., Jr., Mason, J. W., Roatch, J. F., & Hamburg, D. A. A psychoendocrine study of severe psychotic depressive crises. *Amer. J. Psychiat.*, 1965, **122**, 72–80.

Busfield, B. L., Jr., & Wechsler, H. Salivation rate: A physiologic correlate of improvement in hospitalized depressed patients treated with three anti-depressant medications. *Psychosom. Med.*, 1962, **24**, 337–342.

Busfield, B. L., Jr., Wechsler, H., & Barnum, W. J. Studies of salivation in depression. II: Physiological differentiation of reactive and endogenous depression. *Arch. gen. Psychiat.*, 1961, **5**, 472–477.

Cassidy, W. L., Flanagan, N. B., Spellman, M. and Cohen, M. E. Clinical observations in manic-depressive disease. A quantitative study of one hundred manic-depressive patients and fifty medically sick controls, *J. Amer. Med. Assn.*, 1957, **164**, 1535–1546.

Claridge, G. S., & Herrington, R. N. Sedation threshold, personality and the theory of neurosis, *J. Ment. Sci.*, 1960, **106**, 1568–1583.

Clyde, D. J. *Clyde Mood Scale Manual.* Coral Gables, Florida: University of Miami, Biometrics Laboratory, 1963.

Cohen, Mabel B., Baker, Grace, Cohen, R. A., Fromm-Reichmann, Frieda, & Weigart, Edith A. An intensive study of twelve cases of manic depressive psychosis. *Psychiatry*, 1954, **17**, 103–137.

Coppen, A. Abnormality of the blood cerebrospinal-fluid barrier of patients suffering from a depressive illness. *J. neurol. neurosurg. Psychiat.*, 1960, **23**, 156–161.

Coppen, A. The biochemistry of affective disorders. *Brit. J. Psychiat.*, 1967, **113**, 1237–1264.

Coppen, A., Julian, Thelma, Fry, D. E., & Marks, V. Body build and urinary steroid excretion in mental illness. *Brit. J. Psychiat.*, 1967, **113**, 269–275.

Coppen, A., & Shaw, D. M. Mineral metabolism in melancholia. *Brit. Med. J.* 1963, **2**, 1439–1444.

Coppen, A., Shaw, D. M., Malleson, A., & Costain, R. Mineral metabolism in mania. *Brit. Med. J.*, 1966, **1**, 71–75.

Coppen, A., Shaw, D. M., & Mangoni, A. Total exchangeable sodium in depressive illness. *Brit. Med. J.*, 1962, **2**, 295–298.

Costain, R., Redfearn, J. W. T., & Lippold, O. C. J. A controlled trail of the therapeutic effects of polarization of the brain in depressive illness. *Brit. J. Psychiat.*, 1964, **110**, 786–799.

Costello, C. G., & Comrey, A. L. Scales for measuring depression and anxiety. *J. Psychol.*, 1967, **66**, 303–313.

Cropley, A. J., & Weckowitz, T. The dimensionality of clinical depression. *Austr. J. Psychol.*, 1966, **18**, 18–25.

Curtis, G. C., Fogel, M. C., McEvoy, D., & Zarate, C. The effect of sustained affect on diurnal rhythm of adrenal cortical activity. *Psychosom. Med.*, 1966, **28**, 696–713.

Cushing, H. Basophil adenomas of pituitary body and their clinical manifestations (pituitary basophilism). *Bull. Johns Hopkins Hosp.*, 1932, **50**, 137–195.

Dalton, Katherina. *The Premenstrual Syndrome*. Springfield, Ill.: Charles C. Thomas, 1964.

Davies, B. M., & Gurland, J. B. Salivary secretions in depressive illness. *J. Psychosom. Res.*, 1961, **5**, 269–271.

Davies, B. M., & Palmai, G. Salivary and blood pressure responses to methacholine in depressive illness. *Brit. J. Psychiat.*, 1964, **110**, 594–598.

Davis, P. A. Electroencephalograms of manic-depressive patients. *Amer. J. Psychiat.*. 1941, **98**, 430–433.

Davis, P. A. Comparative study of the EEG's of schizophrenic and manic depressive patients. *Amer. J. Psychiat.*, 1942, **99**, 210–217.

Denneby, C. M. Childhood bereavement and psychiatric illness. *Brit. J. Psychiat.*, 1966, **112**, 1049–1069.

Earle, A. M., & Earle, B. V. Early maternal deprivation and later psychiatric illness. *Amer. J. Orthopsychiat.*, 1961, **31**, 181–186.

Edwards, A. L. Correlation of a "unidimensional depression scale for the MMPI" with the SD scale. *J. Consult. Psychol.*, 1965, **29**, 271–273.

Ellingson, R. J. The incidence of EEG abnormality among patients with mental disorders of apparently non-organic origin. A critical review. *Amer. J. Psychiat.*, 1954, **111**, 263–275.

Engel, G. Anxiety and depression-withdrawal: the primary affects of displeasure. *Int. J. Psychoanal.*, 1962, **43**, 89–97.

Fenichel, O. *The psychoanalytic theory of neurosis*. (2nd ed.) New York: W. W. Norton, 1945.

Ferguson, H. C., Bartram, A. C., & Fowlie, H. C. A preliminary investigation of steroid excretion in depressed patients before and after electroconvulsive therapy. *Acta. Endocr.* (Kobenhaun), 1964, **47**, 58–68.

Finley, K. H. On the occurrence of rapid frequency potential changes in the human EEG. *Amer. J. Psychiat*, 1944, **101**, 194–200.

Fishman, J. R., Hamburg, D. A., Handlon, J. H., Mason, J. W., & Sachar, E. Emotional and adrenocortical responses to a new experience. *Arch. gen. Psychiat.*, 1962, **6**, 271–278.

Fotherby, K., Ashcroft, G. W., Affleck, J. W., & Forrest, A. D. Studies on sodium transfer and 5-hydroxyindoles in depressive illness. *J. Neurol. Neurosurg. Psychiat.*, 1963, **26**, 71–73.

Foulds, G. A. *Personality and Personal Illness*. London: Tavistock Publications, 1965.

Freud, S. *Mourning and melancholia*. London: Hogarth Press, 1955.

Friedman, A S. Minimal effects of severe depression on cognitive functioning. *J. abnorm. soc. Psychol.*, 1964, **69**, 237–243.

Ganong, W. F. The central nervous system and release of adrenocorticotropic hormone. In A. V. Nalbandov (ed.), *Advances in neuroendocrinology*. Urbana, Ill.: University of Illinois, 1963.

Gibbons, J. L. Total body sodium and potassium in depressive illness. *Clin. Sci.*, 1960, **19**, 133–138.

Gibbons, J. L. Endocrine changes in depressive illness. *Proc. Roy. Soc. Med.*, 1965, **58**, 519–521.

Gibbons, J. L. The secretion rate of corticosterone in depressive illness. *J. Psychosom. Res.*, 1966, **10**, 263–266.

Gibbons, J. L., Gibson, J. G., Maxwell, A. E., & Willcox, D. R. C. An endocrine study of depressive illness. *J. Psychosom. Res.*, 1960, **5**, 32–41.

Gibbons, J. L., & McHugh, P. R. Plasma cortisol in depressive illness. *J. Psychiat. Res.*, 1962, **1**, 162–171.

Gibson, J. B. Emotions and the thyroid gland. A critical appraisal. *J. Psychosom. Res.*, 1962, **6**, 93–116.

Giddon, D. B., & Lisanti, V. F. Cholinesterase—like substance in the parotid saliva of normal and psychiatric patients. *Lancet*, 1962, **1**, 725–726.

Gittleson, N. L. The phenomenology of obsessions in depressive psychosis. *Brit. J. Psychiat.*, 1966, **112**, 261–264.

Goldstein, I. B. The relationship of muscle tension and autonomic activity to psychiatric disorders. *Psychosom. Med.*, 1965, **27**, 39–52.

Gottlieb, G., & Paulson, G. Salivation in depressed patients. *Arch. gen. Psychiat.*, 1961, **5**, 468–471.

Grinker, R. R., Miller, J., Sabshin, M., Nunn, R., & Nunnally, J. C. *The phenomena of depression*. New York: Hoeber, 1961.

Hall, K. R. L., & Stride, E. Some factors affecting reaction time to auditory stimuli in mental patients. *J. ment. Sci.*, 1954, **100**, 462–477.

Hamilton, M. A rating scale for depression. *J. Neurol. Neurosurg. Psychiat.*, 1960, **23**, 56–62.

Handlon, J. H., Wadeson, R. W., Fishman, J. R., Sachar, E. J., Hamburg, D. A., & Mason, J. W. Psychological factors lowering plasma 17-hydroxycorticosteroid concentration. *Psychosom. Res.*, 1962, **24**, 535–541.

Harris, G. W. *Neural control of the pituitary gland*. London: E. Arnold, 1955.

Hathaway, S., & McKinley, C. *Minnesota Multiphasic Personality Inventory*. New York: Psychol. Corp., 1951.

Hetzel, B. S., Schottstaedt, W. W., Grace, W. J. & Wolff, H. G. Changes in urinary 17-hydroxycorticosteriod. *J. clin. endocrinol. Metab.*, 1955, **15**, 1057–1068.

Hill, O. W., & Price, J. S. Childhood bereavement and adult depression. *Brit. J. Psychiat.* 1967, **113**, 743–751.

Hodges, J. R., Jones, M. T., & Stockham, M. A. Effect of emotion on blood corticotrophin and cortisol concentrations in man. *Nature*, 1962, **193**, 1187–1188.

Hopkinson, G., & Reed, G. F. Bereavement in childhood and depressive psychosis. *Brit. J. Psychiat.* 1966, **112**, 459–463.

Hullin, R. P., Bailey, A. D., McDonald, R., Dransfield, G. A., & Milne, H. B. Variations in body water during recovery from depression. *Brit. J. Psychiat.*, 1967a, **113**, 573–583.

Hullin, R. P., Bailey, A. D., McDonald, R., Dransfield, G. A., & Milne, H. B. Body water variations in manic-depressive psychosis. *Brit. J. Psychiat.*, 1967b, **113**, 584–592.

Hullin, R. P., Bailey, A. D., McDonald, R., Dransfield, G. A., & Milne, H. B. Variations in 11-hydroxycorticosteroids in depression and manic-depressive psychosis. *Brit. J. Psychiat.*, 1967c, **113**, 593–600.

Humphrey, M. Functional impairment in psychiatric patients. *Brit. J. Psychiat.*, 1967, **113**, 1141–1151.

Hunt, S. M., Jr., Singer, K., & Cobb, S. Components of depression, *Arch. gen. Psychiat.*, 1967, **16**, 441–447.

Hurst, L. A., Mundy-Castle, A. C., & Beerstecher, D. M. The EEG in manic-depressive psychosis. *J. ment. Sci.*, 1954, **100**, 220–240.

Itil, M. T. *Elektroencephalographische studien by Endogenen Psychosen und deren Behandlung mit Psychotropen Medikamenten unter besonderer berucksichtigung des Pentothal—Elektroencephalogramms. Istanbul*: Ahmet Sait Matbassi, 1964.

Ivanov-Smolensky, A. G. Uber die bedingten reflex in der depressiven phase der manic-depressiven irreseins. *Mschr. Psychiat. Neurol.*, 1925, **58**, 376–388.

Ivanov-Smolensky, A. G. The pathology of conditioned reflexes and the so-called psychogenic depression. *J. nerv. ment. Dis.*, 1928, **67**, 346–350.

Kane, F. J., Jr., Daly, R. J., Ewing, J. A., & Keller, M. H. Mood and behavioral changes with progestational agents. *Brit. J. Psychiat.*, 1967, **113**, 265–268.

Karstens, P. Über die beeinflussung des psychischen zustandes normaler durch aufnahme und retention unphysiologisch grosser wassermengen. *Arch. Psychiat. Nerventr.* 1951, **186**, 231.

Katkin, E. A., Sasmor, D. B., & Tan, R. Conformity and achievement related characteristics of depressed patients. *J. abnorm. soc. Psychol.*, 1966, **71**, 407–412.

Kaufman, I. C. Rosenbloom, L. A. Depression in infant monkeys separated from their mothers. *Science*, 1957, **55**, 1030–1031.

Kay, D. W., Beamish, P., & Roth, M. Old age mental disorders in Newcastle-upon-Tyne. I. Study of prevalence. *Brit. J. Psychiat.*, 1964, **110**, 146–158.

Kelsey, F. O., Gullock, A. H., & Kelsey, F. E. Thyroid activity in hospitalized psychiatric patients—relation of dietary iodine to I^{131} uptake. *Arch. Neurol. Psychiat.*, 1957, **77**, 543–548.

Kielholz, P., & Beck, D. Diagnosis, autonomic tests, treatment and prognosis of exhaustion depression. *Comp. Psychiat.*, 1962, **3**, 8–14.

Kiloh, L. G. and Garside, R. F. The independence of neurotic depression and endogenous depression, *Brit. J. Psychiat.*, 1963, **109**, 451–463.

Klein, Melanie. *New directions in psychoanalysis*. New York: Basic Books, 1957.

Klein, R., & Nunn, R. F. Clinical and biochemical analysis of a case of manic-depressive psychosis showing regular weekly cycles. *J. ment. Sci.*, 1945, **26**, 323–336.

Kraepelin, E. *Psychiatrie* (5th ed.) Leipzig: Barth, 1896.

Kraines, S. H. *Mental depressions and their treatment*. New York: McMillan Press, 1957.

Laxer, R. M. Self concept changes of depressive patients in general hospital treatment. *J. consult. Psychol.*, 1964a, **28**, 214–219.

Laxer, R. M. Relation of real self-rating to mood and blame and their interaction in depression. *J. consult. Psychol.*, 1964b, **28**, 538–546.

Le Gassicke, J., Boyd, W., & McPherson, F. A controlled out-patient evaluation with fencamfamin. *Brit. J. Psychiat.*, 1964, **110**, 267–269.

Lemere, F. Cortical energy production in the psychoses. *Psychosom. Med.*, 1941, **3**, 152–156.

Lindsay, J. H. Fashions in psychiatry, melancholia 1621 and depression 1961 *Canad. Psychiat. Assoc. J.*, 1963, **8**, 155–161.

Lingjaerde, P. S. Plasma hydrocortisone in mental disease. *Brit. J. Psychiat.*, 1964, **110**, 423–432

Lipold, O. C. J., & Redfearn, J. W. T. Mental changes resulting from the passage of small direct currents through the human brain. *Brit. J. Psychiat.*, 1964, **110**, 768–772.

Loew, D. Syndrome, Diagnose, Und Speichelsekretion Dei depressiven patienten. *Psychopharmacologia*, 1965, **7**, 339–348.

Loew, D. Die Einordnung des Symptoms "Mundtrockenheit" in die psychiatrische Diagnostike von Depressionen. *Psychiat. Neurol. (Basel)*, 1966, **151**, 366–378.

Lorr, M., Daston, P., & Smith, Iola R. An analysis of mood states. *Educ. psychol. Measmt.*, 1967, **27**, 89–96.

Lorr, M., Jenkins, R. L., & Hopsopple, J. O. Multidimensional Scale for Rating Psychiatric Patients, Hospital Form. *U.S. Vet. Admin. tech. Bull. TB 10-507*, Veterans

Administration, Washington, D. C., 1953.

Lubin, B. Adjective checklists for measurement of depression. *Arch. gen. Psychiat.*, 1965, **12**, 57–62.

Lubin, B., Dupres, V. A., & Lubin, Alice, W. Comparability and sensitivity of set 2 (Lists E, F, and G) of the Depression Adjective Check Lists. *Psychol. Rep.*, 1967, **20**, 756–758.

McClure, D. J. The diurnal variation of plasma cortisol levels in depression. *J. psychosom. Res.*, 1966, **10**, 189–195.

McConaghy, N., Joffe, A. D., and Murphy, B. The independence of neurotic and endogenous depression. *Brit. J. Psychiat.*, 1967, **113**, 479–484.

Malamud, W., & Sands, S. L. A revision of the psychiatric rating scale. *Amer. J. Psychiat.*, 1947, **104**, 231–237.

Malmo, R. B., & Shagass, C. Physiologic studies of reaction to stress in anxiety and early schizophrenia. *Psychosom. Med.*, 1949, **11**, 9–17.

Martin, I., & Davies, B. M. Sleep threshold in depression. *J. ment. Sci.*, 1962, **108**, 466–473.

Martin, I., & Davies, B. M. The effect of sodium amytal on autonomic and muscle activity in patients with depressive illness. *Brit. J. Psychiat.*, 1965, **111**, 168–175.

Martin, I., & Rees, L. Reaction times and somatic reactivity in depressed patients. *J. psychosom. Res.*, 1966, **9**, 375–382.

Mason, J. W. Book review. The physiology of emotions. Simon, A., Herbert, C. C., & Straus, R. (eds.), Springfield, Ill.: Charles C. Thomas, 1961. *Psychosom. Med.*, 1963, **25**, 499–500.

Mayer-Gross, W., Slater, E., & Roth, M. *Clinical Psychiatry* (2nd ed.), London: Cassell, 1960.

Mayo, P. R. Some psychological changes associated with improvement in depression. *Brit. J. soc. clin. Psychol.*, 1967, **6**, 63–68.

Mendels, J., and Cochrane, C. The nosology of depression: The endogenous-reactive concept. *Amer. J. Psychiat.*, 1968, **124**, supplement, 1–11.

Metcalfe, M., & Goldman, E. Validation of an inventory for measuring depression. *Brit. J. Psychiat.*, 1965, **111**, 240–242.

Michael, R. P., & Gibbons, J. L. Interrelationships between the endocrine system and neuropsychiatry. *Int. Rev. Neurobiology*, 1963, **5**, 243–302.

Munro, A. Parental deprivation in depressive patients. *Brit. J. Psychiat.*, 1966, **112**, 443–457.

Nymgaard, K. Studies on the sedation threshold. *Arch. gen. Psychiat.*, 1959, **1**, 530–536.

Palmai, G., & Blackwell, B. The diurnal pattern of salivary flow in normal and depressed patients. *Brit. J. Psychiat.*, 1965, **111**, 334–338.

Palmai, G., Blackwell, B., Maxwell, A. E., & Morgenstern, F. Patterns of salivary flow in depressive illness and during treatment. *Brit. J. Psychiat.*, 1967, **113**, 1297–1308.

Peck, R. E. The S. H. P. test—an aid in the detection and measurement of depression. *Arch. gen. Psychiat.*, 1959, **1**, 35–40.

Perez-Reyes, M., & Cochrane, C. Differences in sodium thiopental susceptibility of depressed patients as evidenced by the galvanic skin reflex inhibition threshold. *J. Psychiat. Res.*, 1967, **5**, 335–347

Perez-Reyes, M., Shands, H. C., & Johnson, G. Galvanic skin reflex inhibition threshold: A new psychophysiologic technique. *Psychosom. Med.*, 1962, **24**, 274–277.

Perley, M., & Guze, S. Hysteria—the stability and usefulness of clinical criteria. *New Eng. J. Med.*, 1962, **266**, 421–426.

Perris, C., & Brattemo, C. E. The sedation threshold as a method of evaluating antidepressive treatments. *Acta. Psychiat. Scand.*, 1963, **39**, Suppl. 169, 111–119.

Persky, H., Grinker, B. R., Hamburg, D. A., Sabshin, M. A., Korchin, S. J., Basowitz, H., & Chevalier, J. A. Adrenal cortical function in anxious human subjects. *Arch. neurol., Psychiat.*, 1956, **76**, 549–558.

Pevzner, M. S. *Oligophrenia—Mental deficiency in children*. Consultants Bureau, N.Y. 1961.

Pitts, F. N., Jr., & Winokur, G. Affective disorder. VII. Alcoholism and affective disorder. *J. Psychiat. Res.*, 1966, **4**, 37–50.
Pollitt, J. D. Suggestions for a physiological classification of depression. *Brit. J. Psychiat.*, 1965, **111**, 489–495.
Price, D. B., Thaler, M., & Mason, J. W. Preoperative emotional stability and adrenal cortical activity. *Arch. neurol. Psychiat.*, 1957, **77**, 646–656.
Pryce, I. G. The relationship between 17-hydroxycorticosteroid excretion and glucose utilization in depression. *Brit. J. Psychiat.*, 1964, **110**, 90–94.
Quarton, G. C., Clark, L. D., Cobb, S., & Bauer, W. Mental disturbances associated with ACTH and cortisone: A review of explanatory hypotheses. *Med.*, 1955, **34**, 131–150.
Ratcliffe, R. A. W. The change in character of admission to Scottish mental hospitals. 1945–1959. *Brit. J. Psychiat.*, 1964, **110**, 22–27.
Redfearn, J. W. T., Lippold, O. C. J., & Costain, R. A preliminary account of the clinical effects of polarizing the brain in certain psychiatric disorders. *Brit. J. Psychiat.*, 1964, **110**, 773–785.
Rey, J. H., Willcox, D. R., Gibbons, J. L., Tait, H., & Lewis, D. J. Serial biochemical and endocrine investigations in recurrent mental illness. *J. Psychosom. Res.*, 1961, **5**, 155–169.
Rimon, R., Stenback, A., & Huhmar, E. EMG findings in depressive patients. *J. Psychosom. Res.*, 1966, **10**, 159–170.
Rizzo, N. D., Fox, H. N., Laidlaw, J. C., & Thorn, G. W. Concurrent observations of behavior change and adrenocortical variations in a cyclothymic patient during a period of twelve months. *Ann. Intern. Med.*, 1954, **41**, 798–815.
Rose, J. T., Leahy, M. R., Martin, I. C. A., & Westhead, T. T. A comparison of nortriptyline and amitriptyline in depression. *Brit. J. Psychiat.*, 1965, **111**, 1101–1103.
Rosenthal, R. *Experimenter effects in behavioral research*. New York: Appleton, 1966.
Rosenthal, S. H., & Klerman, G. L. Content and consistency in the endogenous depressive pattern, *Brit. J. Psychiat.* 1966, **112**, 471–484.
Roth, M. The phenomenology of depressive states. *Canad. Psychiat. Assoc. J.*, 1959, **4** (Suppl.), 32–54.
Rubin, R. T., & Mandell, A. J. Adrenal cortical activity in pathological emotional states: A review. *Amer. J. Psychiat.*, 1966, **123**, 387–400.
Russell, G. F. M. Body weight and balance of water, sodium and potassium in depressed patients given electroconvulsive therapy. *Clin. Sci.*, 1960, **19**, 327–336.
Sachar, E. J., Mason, J. W., Kolmer, H. S., Jr., & Artiss, K. L. Psychoendocrine aspects of acute schizophrenic reactions. *Psychosom. Med.*, 1963, **25**, 510–537.
Sandifer, M. G., Wilson, I. C., & Green, L. The two type thesis of depressive disorders. *Amer. J. Psychiat.* 1966, **123**, 93–97.
Schwab, J. J. Bialow, M. R., Clemmons, R. B., & Holzer, C. E. Hamilton rating scale for depression with medical inpatients. *Brit. J. Psychiat.*, 1967, **113**, 83–88.
Schwartz, M., Mandell, A. J., Green, R., & Ferman, R. Mood, motility, and 17-hydroxycorticoid excretion; a polyvariable case study. *Brit. J. Psychiat.*, 1966, **112**, 149–156.
Seay, B., Hansen, E., & Harlow, H. F. Mother-infant separation in monkeys. *J. child psychol. Psychiat.*, 1962, **3**, 123–132.
Selye, H. *The physiology and pathology of exposure to stress.* Montreal: Acta Inc., 1950.
Senay, E. C. Toward an animal model of depression: A study of separation behavior in dogs. *J. Psychiat. Res.*, 1966, **4**, 65–71.
Sethi, B. B. Relationship of separation to depression. *Arch. gen. Psychiat.*, 1964, **10**, 486–496.
Shagass, C. Differentiation between anxiety and depression by the photically activated EEG. *Amer. J. Psychiat.*, 1955a, **112**, 41–46.
Shagass, C. Anxiety, depression and the photically driven EEG. *Arch. neurol. Psychiat.*, 1955b, **74**, 3–10.
Shagass, C., & Jones, A. L. A neurophysiological test for psychiatric diagnosis results in 750 patients. *Amer. J. Psychiat.*, 1958, **114**, 1002–1010.

Shagass, C., & Schwartz, M. Cerebral cortical reactivity in psychotic depressions. *Arch. gen. Psychiat.*, 1962, **6**, 235–242.

Shagass, C., & Schwartz, M. Psychiatric disorder and deviant cerebral responsiveness to sensory stimulation. In. J. Wortis (ed.), *Recent advances in biological psychiatry*, Vol. V., New York: 1963. (a)

Shagass, C., & Schwartz, M. Psychiatric correlates of evoked cerebral cortical potentials. *Amer. J. Psychiat.*, 1963b, **119**, 1055–1061.

Shagass, C., & Schwartz, M. Somatosensory cerebral evoked responses in psychotic depression. *Brit. J. Psychiat.*, 1966, **112**, 799–807.

Shagass, C., Schwartz, M., & Anadeo, M. Some drug effects on evoked cerebral potentials in man. *J. Neuropsychiat.*, 1962, **3**, 5549–5558.

Shakow, D., & Huston, P. E. Studies of motor function in schizophrenia. I. Speed of tapping. *J. gen. Psychol.*, 1936, **15**, 63–108.

Shattock, F. M. The somatic manifestations of schizophrenia: A clinical study of their significance. *J. ment. Sci.*, 1950, **96**, 32–142.

Sheffield, L. J., & Mowbray, R. M. The effects of polarization on normal subjects. *Brit. J. Psychiat.*, 1968, **114**, 225–232.

Shipman, W. G., Oken, D., Goldstein, I. B., Grinker, R. R., & Heath, H. A. Study in psychophysiology of muscle tension. *Arch. gen. Psychiat.*, 1964, **11**, 330–345.

Spielberger, C. D., Parker, J. B., & Becker, J. Conformity and achievement in remitted manic depressive patients. *J. nerv. ment. Dis.*, 1963, **137**, 162–172.

Spitz, R. Anaclitic Depression. *Psychoanalytic study of the child*, 1946, **2**, 313–342.

Starr, P., Petit, D. W., Chaney, A. L., Rollman, H., Aiken, J. B., Jamieson, B., & Kling, I. Clinical experience with the blood protein-bound iodine determination as a routine procedure. *J. clin. Endocrinol.*, 1950, **10**, 1237–1250.

Stenback, A., Jakobson, T., & Rimon, R. Depression and anxiety ratings in relation to the excretion of urinary total 17-hydroxycorticosteroid in depressive subjects. *J. Psychosom. Res.*, 1966, **9**, 355–362.

Stewart, M. A., Winokur, G., Stern, J. A., Guze, S. B., Pfeiffer, E., & Hornung, F. Adaptation and conditioning of the galvanic skin response in psychiatric patients. *J. ment. Sci.*, 1959, **105**, 1102–1111.

Strongin, E. I., & Hinsie, L. E. Parotid gland secretions in schizophrenic patients. *J. nerv. ment. Dis.*, 1938, **87**, 715–718.

Strongin, E. I., & Hinsie, L. E. Parotid gland secretions in manic-depressive patients. *Amer. J. Psychiat.*, 1939, **94**, 1459–1462.

Waldron, J., & Bates, T. J. N. The management of depression in hospital. *Brit. J. Psychiat.*, 1965, **111**, 511–516.

Wechsler, H., Grosser, G. H. & Busfield, B. L., Jr. The depression rating scale. *Arch. gen. Psychiat.*, 1963, **9**, 334–343.

Weckowicz, T. E., Muir, W., & Cropley, A. J. A factor analysis of the Beck Inventory of Depression. *J. consult. Psychol.*, 1967, **31**, 23–28.

Whatmore, G. B. Some neurophysiologic differences between schizophrenia and depression. *Amer. J. Psychiat.*, 1966, **123**, 712–716.

Whatmore, G. B., & Ellis, R. M., Jr. Some neurophysiologic aspects of depressed states: an electromyographic study. *Arch. gen. Psychiat.*, 1959, **1**, 70–80.

Whatmore, G. B., & Ellis, R. M., Jr. Further neurophysiologic aspects of depressed states: an electromyographic study. *Arch. gen. Psychiat.*, 1962, **6**, 243–253.

Wilson, I. C., Alltop, L. B., & Buffaloe, W. J. Parental bereavement in childhood: MMPI profiles in a depressed population. *Brit. J. Psychiat.*, 1967, **113**, 761–764.

Wilson, W. P., & Wilson, N. Observation on the duration of photically elicited arousal responses in depressive psychoses. *J. nerv. ment. Dis.*, 1961, **133**, 438–440.

Winokur, G., Clayton, Paula. Family history studies II: Sex differences and alcoholism in primary affective illness. *Brit. J. Psychiat.*, 1967, **113**, 973–979.

Winokur, G. and Pitts, F. N., Jr. Affective disorder: I. Is reactive depression an entity? *J. nerv. ment. Dis.*, 1964, **138**, 541–547.

Winokur, G., & Pitts, F. N., Jr. Affective disorder: VI. A family history of prevalences, sex differences and possible genetic factors. *J. Psychiat. Res.*, 1965, **3**, 113–123.

Wittenborn, J. R. *Wittenborn psychiatric rating scales*. New York: Psychol. Corp., 1955.

Wolff, S. M., Adler, R. C., Buskirk, R. R., & Thompson, T. H. A syndrome of periodic hypothalamic discharge. *Amer. J. Med.*, 1964, **36**, 956–967.

Woodruff, R., Jr., Pitts, F. N. Jr., & Winokur, G. Affective disorder II: a comparison of patients with endogenous depressions with and without family history of affective disorder. *J. nerv. ment. Dis.*, 1964, **139**, 49–52.

Wulfeck, W. H. Motor functions in the mentally disordered—Part I. *Psychol. Rec.*, 1941a, **4**, 271–322.

Wulfeck, W. H. Motor functions in the mentally disordered—Part II. *Psychol. Rec.*, 1941b **4**, 326–348.

Zigler, E., & Phillips, L. Psychiatric diagnosis and symptomatology. *J. abnorm. soc. Psychol.*, 1961, **58**, 69–75.

Zung, W. W. K. A self-rating depression scale. *Arch. gen. Psychiat.*, 1965, **12**, 63–70.

Zung, W. W. K., Wilson, W. P., & Dodson, W.E. Effect of depressive disorders on sleep EEG responses. *Arch. gen. Psychiat.*, 1964, **10**, 439–445.

Chapter 8

Depression: Treatment

C. G. COSTELLO and G. P. BELTON

Both psychotherapy and somatic therapies have been used in an attempt to alleviate depression. Many suggestions have been made in the literature as to the best way to give psychotherapy to the depressed patient, but they are based on clinical lore and are not substantiated by any empirical data.

The new developments in behavior modification techniques, which are described in a number of places in this book, have not been applied to depressive illnesses. Even the newer theoretical developments along these lines tend to ignore depression. For instance, "depression" does not occur in the index of the excellent book, *Psychotherapy and the Psychology of Behaviour Change*, by Goldstein, Heller, & Sechrest (1966). A start has been made in that Ferster (1966) has discussed depressive illnesses in terms of operant conditioning principles but without any empirical data to support his notions or any clear guidelines concerning modification techniques.

Somatic therapies have played a much greater role up to this time, and we shall now look at the two main current therapies—electroconvulsive shock and antidepressant drugs.

ELECTROCONVULSIVE SHOCK TREATMENT

Because electric shock treatment is so widely and generally accepted as an effective form of treatment for depressive illnesses it is particularly important that the experimental evidence for its efficacy be carefully evaluated. The studies have tended to regard depression as a syndrome rather than as a symptom. But they have usually considered depressed mood to be an important feature of the patient's illness. In any case, the whole question of ECT treatment is of such importance that it would seem quite wrong not to include discussion of it somewhere in a book of this sort. This chapter is the most appropriate place.

RETROSPECTIVE STUDIES

One group of studies has been retrospective in nature. These studies will not be reviewed in detail because methodological deficiencies make it impossible to place any reliance on the data presented by them. The kind of difficulty to which we refer may best be specified by discussing in detail one particular study. This, of course, should not be taken to mean that this is the most deficient of all the studies of this nature.

Huston and Locher (1948) compared the course of manic-depressive psychosis in two groups of patients. One group of 75 patients was treated with ECT and the other control group of 80 patients did not receive ECT. The groups were ". . . fairly comparable with respect to age of onset, percentage with typical depressions and duration of illness before admission." They did differ, however, in one important respect in that the control group consisted of patients admitted to a hospital during the period of 1930 to 1938 while the treated group consisted of patients admitted to the same hospital from 1941 to 1943. Huston and

Locher found the recovery rates to be 79 percent for the control group and 88 percent for the treated group. The difference between these percentages was not statistically significant. It was found, however, that the median duration of hospitalization after treatment was longer in the nonshock group (15 months) than in the treated group (9 months). They also found that the incidence of suicide was lower in the shock group—1 percent, than in the nontreated group—7 percent.

Huston and Locher concluded that ECT was indicated for the treatment of manic-depressive disorders on the basis that "... shock therapy produces a rate of recovery as high as that of spontaneous recovery, reduces the incidence of suicide, probably prevents death and shortens the duration of hospitalization."

Let us first look at the results of this study. The differences between the two groups in terms of the incidence of suicide was not tested for statistical significance by Huston and Locher but, when such a test was done by the present authors, it was clearly found to be not significant. Again, the difference between the two groups in terms of the number of deaths from causes other than suicide (5 percent of the control group and 1 percent of the shock group) was found not to be significant. Huston and Locher did not test the significance of the difference between the two groups with respect to the duration of the depression being treated. Unfortunately, although they give means, medians, and ranges for those groups, they do not give the all important standard deviations of the scores; and without the standard deviations it is not possible to test for the significance of the difference.

Huston and Locher also provided data concerning the recurrence of depression after the depression that was being treated had remitted. At the end of their comparison they made this somewhat cryptic statement: "shock therapy therefore did not appear to predispose to subsequent depressions." Actually, 11 of the 52 control patients who recovered from their initial depressions relapsed as did 11 of the 54 experimental or shock patients who had initially recovered. Perhaps a more appropriate concluding statement could have been that shock therapy does not appear to reduce the probability of recurrence of depression.

This study is quite often referred to as evidence in support of the therapeutic efficacy of ECT (for example, Campbell, 1961). Even if we consider the data presented to be reliable, we still do not have any evidence to support such a conclusion. One may question the justifiability of going on to look at the reliability of data that results in no significant findings but, as we have already noted, Huston and Locher's study provides us with a good example of the methodological deficiencies of the retrospective studies of ECT.

The deficiencies of the study are as follows.

1. The reliability of the information seems doubtful in view of the fact that it was obtained from "... letters from relatives, social agents, referring physicians, local hospitals, county homes, private sanitariums, and the patients themselves." To what extent data from such a variety of sources would be comparable is quite unknown.

2. The authors note that "in evaluation of the post-admission course, the clinical status at discharge was graded as complete recovery, pronounced improvement, improvement, and no improvement." The operations by which one determines for any given patient his position on such a crude scale is not given.

3. It was noted that the control patients received psychotherapy or occupational therapy, hydrotherapy, and "participation in group activities." No statement is made concerning the treatment other than electric shock that the experimental group may have received. It is almost certain that they received other kinds of treatment, and once again this vitiates any conclusions that can be made from this study.

4. Although the authors reassure us that the two groups were comparable in terms of their diagnoses, one cannot indeed be very reassured. No evidence is given that concerns the manner in which the patients were diagnosed or the reliability of the diagnostic categories used.

5. The control group was followed up for a period of up to 14 years. The maximum follow-up for the treated group was only 4 years. This in itself, of course, would be enough to cast doubt on the whole study. It is true that the authors note that "whenever the differences in the length of the

follow-up period might make a comparison questionable equal follow-up periods were used." But exactly how this was done and how many patients had to be excluded as a result is not stated.

Similar comments can be made about the study by Norman and Shea (1946) which compares discharge rates for a shock-treated group and a control group, and we, of course, can question "discharge from hospital" as an index of a recovery from depression. It is well known that discharge from hospital often depends on factors other than the patients' condition. Statements like the following one also make one reluctant to place too much reliance on the results of this study:

> "In a small number of cases an attempt was made during treatment to give more intensive psychotherapy in the hope that this would decrease the number of shock treatments required and at the same time give the patient a deeper insight into his problems" (p. 857). "... there are also certain patients who after treatment had a full remission that lasted sufficiently long to accomplish their discharge from the hospital but promptly developed another episode, were readmitted as new cases, were treated again and were once more released. Others were subsequently admitted to other hospitals for treatment" (p. 858).

Salzman (1947) matched two groups of patients for age, duration of illness, and previous admissions, the only difference being that one group had received previous ECT while the other had not. He then reviewed the past admission history of each patient. For some patients this information was obtained from abstracts and summaries of treatments in hospitals other than the one in which the patient was staying at the time of the study. It is clear, of course, that this immediately introduces the problem of the differences between the hospitals in the criteria used for admission, discharge, diagnosis, and so on. Salzman did not even mention the reasons why the patients in the control group were excluded from treatment by ECT.

For convenience, other studies in this area will be noted. They are Hinko and Lipschutz (1943); Hamilton and Ward (1948); Friedman (1949); Karagulla (1950). We can state with considerable assurance that the reader who reviews these studies will soon realize that they all suffer from serious methodological faults. It is also true, of course, that the very nature of retrospective studies makes them unsatisfactory. To compare experimental and control groups separated by long periods of time makes it extremely difficult to be sure that any difference found between the groups is not the result of this time factor.

Before leaving the retrospective studies, Karagulla's study (1950) should be given a little more attention. She concluded that

> "the percentage rate of recovery does not vary greatly whether the patients are treated conservatively or with electric convulsion therapy. Such slight differences as may exist are statistically insignificant."

Slater (1951) attempted to use Karagulla's own figures to show that her conclusions were unwarranted and that ECT did indeed lead to greater improvement. Slater's main point appears to be that death from causes other than suicide occurred to a much greater extent in the control group than in the shock group. He suggests that Karagulla was wrong to discount this data, as she did, on the basis that death, unless in the form of suicide, cannot be attributed to a depressive process. Slater argued that on the contrary death may be "... due to exhaustion or intercurrent infection or to other causes which would never have arisen if the patient had not been mentally ill." He suggests that the deaths occurred because the patients had been left untreated by ECT. But Karagulla notes that the main control groups consisted of "... those patients who, for various reasons, e.g., age, poor physique, concomitant physical illness, were judged unsuitable for convulsive therapy—they were in fact the 'poor risk' patients." Clearly as the experimental and control groups were not matched initially on variables related to the occurrence of death such as age and physical illness, one can say nothing at all about the different mortality rates in relation to treatment versus no treatment. We can also add, of course, that in view of the numerous methodological faults in Karagulla's study, controversy concerning the conclusions of her study is unwarranted.

STUDIES INCLUDING A PLACEBO DRUG GROUP

The next group of studies that we consider, although they do not include the most important no-treatment control or placebo ECT, do include a placebo drug group which may be regarded as an approximation to a no-treatment group. Kiloh, Child, and Latner (1960a) allocated their 81 patients labeled endogenous depression in "strict rotation" to one of three groups: (1) iproniazid 50 mg. t.d.s. for a minimum of three weeks; (2) Iproniazid placebo given under the same conditions, and (3) ECT. The patients were assessed after the treatment period on a 5-point scale which was subsequently divided into "good result" and "poor result." The results indicated that iproniazid had a beneficial effect on 54 percent of the cases treated, whereas placebo had a similar effect on 11 percent of the cases, and ECT on 89 percent of the cases. The differences between the groups were statistically significant. But we cannot place much reliance on these results for the following reasons.

1. It is quite clear from the term "strict rotation" that random assignment of the patients was not involved.
2. No evidence is presented concerning the reliability and validity of the rating system employed.
3. No attempt was made to standardize ECT treatment—patients being given the "optimum number of convulsions for their condition."
4. Although the authors refer to their study as a double-blind one, this is much in doubt since they themselves state that ". . . to all those concerned with the trial though the truth was long suspected."
5. Evaluations for the ECT group were done 7 to 10 days after the last treatment, but we do not know how many treatments the patients had or for how long. It would certainly seem that the treatment lasted to 5 or 6 weeks in some cases.

The patients on medication, on the other hand, were on it for a period of only 3 weeks. A follow-up study done by the same authors (Kiloh et al., 1960b) is even more difficult to evaluate. For example, patients who showed an initial poor result had been given another form of treatment prior to the assessment. Another troublesome feature of this follow-up study is that the clinical assessments were carried out by the authors, and clearly, by this time they were aware of the treatment groups to which the patients belonged.

In a similar study, Wittenborn, Plante, Burgess, and Livermore (1961) examined the relative efficacy of ECT, iproniazid, and placebo in the treatment of 87 hospitalized premenopausal women with a primary diagnosis of depression. The patients were randomly assigned to the 3 treatments and were tested on a large number of tests during 5-day pretreatment and postreatment periods. Comparison of the ECT and placebo groups revealed significant differences in a direction that favored ECT on the MMPI Psychasthenia and Depression scores, on the "Friendly," "Clear thinking," and "Depressed" scales of the Clyde-Mood Scale, on the latency of reversals on the necker cube, and in caloric intake. There were differences between the two groups on the Depression and Anxiety scales of the Wittenborn Psychiatric Rating Scales, on the Rozenweig Picture Frustration Test, on the Similarities and Digit Symbol subscales of the WAIS, on the Numerical Ability subtest of the Differential Aptitude Test, in choice reaction time, the latency of response to a series of questions, and the number of somatic complaints as indicated by a physicians' checklist. None of these differences was significant. Of course, when we make a number of multiple comparisons of this sort, all of which presumably are relevant comparisons, it is difficult to know what conclusions to draw from such a mixture of significant and nonsignificant findings. Certainly the authors' suggestion that the results support the conclusion that ECT is superior to placebo is a doubtful one. Of course, we can go further and question the relevance of many of the measures used. For instance, the work of Messick and Jackson (1961) and Comrey (1957) casts doubt on the status of the Depression and Psychasthenia scales of the MMPI as scales that are suitable for the measurement of any specific type of disordered affect or behavior. The Rosenzweig test was included on the assumption that it provides evidence on the ". . . outward direction of assertive needs which seem to be so deficient in depressed states." We believe that a considerably greater amount of data would be needed on this particular hypothesis before the test could be used in assessing the effects of treatment for depression. Similar comments can be made with regard to the various cognitive and motor tests used in the study.

Apart from the problem of the multiple comparisons made with measuring instruments of doubtful relevance, we have the problem related to the fact that only the comparison of iproniazid and placebo was run on a double-blind basis. Of course, it is almost impossible to keep patients blind regarding their treatment by ECT. All the more reason then, why those making assessments of the patients' condition should not know the treatments received by them. This single blind condition was not satisfied in the study.

Similar criticisms can be made of a second study (Wittenborn et al., 1963) in which the effects of imipramine rather than of iproniazid were compared with the effects of ECT and drug-placebo conditions. An additional problem, which cannot be discussed in detail here, arises from the fact that the imipramine group in the second study was compared with the ECT and placebo group of the first study, to which some new patients were added for the purpose of this second study. The assumption by the authors that the patients can be regarded as having been randomly assigned to treatments is a questionable one.

In 1965 there was a report to the Medical Research Council by its Clinical Psychiatry Committee on the treatment of depressive illness. This report was based on a study in which 250 depressed patients were randomly assigned to a four-week period of treatment with either imipramine, phenelzine, ECT, or placebo. The assessments of the patients, which were made at weekly intervals during the four weeks of treatment and up to twenty-four weeks after termination of therapy, indicated that ECT was therapeutically superior to the placebo-drug treatment. But, once again, unfortunately, the study is too vulnerable to criticism for any sound conclusion to be made.

Among the criticisms that can be made are the following.

1. Although the double-blind condition applied to the drug administrations, it did not apply to the ECT administration. As we have previously stated, it is difficult to apply this condition to ECT treatment but, at least, the person making the assessment of patients need not have known the treatment group.

2. Assessment of the patients' condition were based on an overall rating of the illness and on ratings of 15 separate symptoms such as suicidal ideas, fatigue, ideas of reference, and so on. No other information about the rating procedure is provided other than the statement that "for each of the symptoms and for the overall rating a scale of severity was laid down." In view of the fact that the data were obtained from assessments from three different regions of the country with 55 physicians in 30 different hospitals participating, it would seem necessary for more information to have been given on the scales including, of course, their reliability.

3. At the end of the four-week treatment period, the physician in charge of each case was given the choice of prescribing an alternative treatment. Only 39 percent of the total group remained on the originally prescribed treatment over the whole six-month period. This, as the authors of the report note, ". . . clearly makes impossible any direct comparison of the progress made by the four original treatment groups."

4. As a result of this feature of the study, it was decided at the 24-week assessments to compare the groups in terms of time of discharge from hospital. We have already suggested, in connection with another study, that to equate recovery from illness with discharge from hospital introduces a somewhat less than precise equation. Although the authors' own comments indicate they realized that this is true, their realization does not do anything to alter the validity of the data.

Once again we must conclude, as we did with the review of retrospective studies, that in the case of this group of studies, which compares ECT treatment with a placebo-drug treatment, the studies have been too poorly designed to enable us to reach any firm conclusion concerning the efficacy of ECT.

STUDIES INCLUDING A PLACEBO-ECT GROUP

The next group of studies compared the patients receiving ECT with patients receiving simulated or placebo ECT. The first study of this nature was conducted by Ulett, Smith, and Gleser (1956). In this study, 84 patients with diagnoses of schizophrenic, involutional psychotic, psychotic-depressive, neurotic-depressive, and manic-depressive (depressed) reaction were divided into four groups of patients matched on diagnosis, sex, age, education, and incidence of previous attacks. The four groups were assigned, respectively, to convulsive photoshock, subconvulsive photoshock, electroshock, and control treatments. The control was actually a placebo-ECT group, since all the patients were sedated by means of intravenous secobarbital sodium to a light stage of sleep prior to treatment, and the handling of patients in all the groups was kept as uniform as possible. All of the patients were treated three times a week up to 12 to 15 treatments. Response to treatment was evaluated by means of a psychiatric rating on a 5-point rating scale and on the Malamud Psychiatric Rating Scale. These ratings were made three days after the last treatment by one of the psychiatrists who was not informed of the treatments the patient received. Follow-up studies after three and six months of those patients who received no further treatments were also made. Our concern here is with the comparison between the ECT and the placebo group. The assessments after three days suggested that the therapeutic response of the ECT group was superior to the one of the placebo shock group, and the same general trend was evident three months and six months after the cessation of therapy, although comparisons at this point are somewhat difficult, since at three months there were only 16 patients remaining in the ECT group and 6 in the placebo group, all the others having required further treatment. And at six months the comparison was made between 11 ECT patients and 5 placebo patients. More important, perhaps χ^2 tests carried out by the present authors on the data obtained at the three post-treatment points failed to reveal any significant differences.

Sainz (1959) divided his 20 patients diagnosed as manic-depressives (depressed) or involutional depressives into two groups of 10 each "... by selecting each alternate admission." One group received ECT and the other group was given "mock" electroshock with intravenous sodium pentothal only. The patients of the "mock" group were unaware of the fact that they had not received ECT. Nine of the ten patients on ECT recovered, and one was moderately improved. Nine out of the ten "mock" ECT patients did not recover and, when they were then given the full course of ECT, seven of these patients subsequently showed full remission. It would seem from the report that assessments were made by Sainz himself in full knowledge of the group to which the patient belonged. We cannot be sure about this because insufficient details are given and because most other things in the study make it quite impossible to evaluate the data adequately.

Brills and his colleagues (1959) investigated the role played by the various components of treatment with electric shock in producing recovery. They assigned 97 male patients to one of five treatment groups: (1) ECT with succinyl choline chloride; (2) orthodox ECT; (3) ECT under thiopental sodium eliminating the motor convulsion; (4) thiopental sodium alone; and (5) nitrous oxide alone. The last two treatments induced unconsciousness without shock, although electrodes were applied in each treatment. Roughly two thirds of the patients were diagnosed as schizophrenic reaction, while the remainder were diagnosed as schizoaffective reaction, psychotic depression, involutional depression, reactive depression, and manic-depressive psychosis. Assessments were made one month before and one month after treatment by ratings of psychiatric status on a 9-point scale, by the Lorr Psychiatric Rating Scale applied by both psychiatrists and nurses, and by ratings of psychological status derived from a psychological test battery. A global rating was also made that combined scores derived from these three methods. The ratings were made without knowledge of group membership.

No statistically significant differences were found in the therapeutic effectiveness of the variations of ECT and simulated ECT. There are also no reliable differences between the combined shock group and the combined nonshock group. The fact that the groups were not precisely equal in the actual proportions of schizophrenics and depressives necessitated further analyses. No significant differences in improvement were found for the treatment groups when the depressives were considered separately. But any conclusion based on the findings with the depressives is somewhat precarious because of the fact that only 30 of the patients diagnosed were depressed and even some of them were diagnosed as having schizoaffective disorders. Quite clearly the study does not provide evidence for the particular therapeutic value of administering electric shock to patients but, again, the study is by no means tight enough to enable one to arrive at any firm conclusions one way or the other.

Wilson and his colleagues (1963) reported the results of an investigation carried out in two phases. In the first phase of the study, 24 patients were randomly assigned to four groups:

1. The electroshock imipramine group—all the patients in this group received both electric shock and imipramine. The electric shock was administered following intravenous thiopental sodium and succinyl choline chloride, and there were two treatments per week for a total of six treatments. Two of the patients in this group were lost to the study so that the final data were obtained on only 22 patients.
2. The electric shock placebo-drug group.
3. The anesthesia-imipramine group.
4. The anesthesia placebo-drug group.

The patients in the third and fourth group received intravenous thiopental twice weekly for a total of six treatments but were not given succinyl choline chloride, nor was an electric shock given. Response to treatment was assessed by the change from pretreatment to protreatment in psychiatric ratings based on the Hamilton Scale (Hamilton, 1960) and by the change in MMPI Depression scores. The assessment interviews on which the Hamilton Scale scores were based were done by three raters at the same interview, one of whom was aware of the treatment received by each patient. The agreement between the raters was extremely good. The comparison of particular interest is that between the ECT placebo-drug group and the anesthesia placebo-drug group. Unfortunately, these results are based on only six patients in each group, making one unsure as to how much weight one can put on the finding that the improvement in the ECT drug-placebo group was significantly greater than the improvement in the anesthesia drug-placebo group. Of course, there is also the problem of the fact that one of the interviewers did know to which group the patient belonged.

STUDIES INCLUDING A NO-TREATMENT GROUP

In the final group of studies to be reviewed a no-treatment control group was included in the design. The first of these studies was conducted by Bagachi, Howell, and Schmale (1945). They studied the therapeutic response and electroencephalic patterns of a group of 54 neurotic and psychotic patients treated with electroshock, and they compared these patients with a control group of 64 patients who did not receive shock. One half of the patients in the treatment group were diagnosed as schizophrenic (with or without depression) and the remainder were classified as belonging to one of the following three categories: (1) psychoneurosis with depression, (2) psychoneurosis—obsessive, compulsive, and depressive, and (3) endogenous depression—manic depressive and involutional. The patient's status at discharge was classified as made worse (scored as − 1), no change (scored as 0), improved (scored as + 1), and recoverd (scored as + 2). The index of *efficiency of shock treatment* was calculated by finding the ratio between total weight (sum of number of cases under each discharge status times discharge score or weight) and total number of cases. The percentage of efficiency of treatment was determined by obtaining the ratio between perfect efficiency, which is "recovery" and which was assumed to have the weight of 2, and the obtained index of efficiency. It was found that the percentage of efficiency of treatment for the shock group was 49 percent as compared with the percentage of efficiency of treatment for a control group of 30.5 percent the difference between these two percentages being significant.

A number of criticisms apply to this study.

1. Both groups also received other treatments—"psychotherapy in all its forms."
2. Composition of the two groups in

terms of diagnoses and other relevant variables is not given.

3. The way in which the control group was selected and the reason for exclusion of control patients from treatment with ECT is not specified.

4. No details are given about the method of assessment that resulted in the classification in terms of improvement.

5. Neither double-blind nor single-blind conditions seemed to have been included.

The study by Tillotson and Sulzbach (1945) cannot be evaluated, since the authors simply present their results all of which favor ECT over no-treatment, and no other details of the study are given.

Janis (1950a and b) developed a number of self-rating scales of affective attitudes for the purpose of evaluating the hypothesis that the occurrence of post-treatment amnesias are closely related to the decline in affective disturbances. The questionnaires were administered to patients receiving ECT shortly before they began the treatment and four weeks after completion of the electroshock series. Identical procedures were applied to a nonshock control group. None of the control patients were specifically excluded from ECT on the basis of any psychiatric considerations, and the treated and untreated groups were matched in age, education, diagnosis, and duration of hospitalization. The number of patients that was studied is not given. It was found that the ECT group in contrast to the control group showed a marked decline in affective disturbance scores. Although two thirds of the patients were diagnosed as schizophrenic and the remainder were classified as psychoneurotic or borderline psychotics, and although it is difficult to know to what extent Janis' results may be applied to patients suffering primarily from depression, the study does provide some evidence to support the conclusion that, at least four weeks after the completion of treatment, the patients that receive ECT show better affective attitudes than do patients in a no-treatment control group.

Scherer (1951) reported the results of a study concerned with both ECT and lobotomy. We are concerned here with this study's investigation of the effects of ECT. A battery of tests was administered to 41 patients before and after a course of ECT, and to 26 control patients. Improvement evaluation was made two to four weeks after the last treatment in the shock group, and a comparable time was used for the control patient. When the ECT patients and the control patients were compared, the rate of improvement was not found to differ significantly. However, this study does not enable us to have much confidence in any conclusion. The types of patients who made up the groups are not indicated, and the assessments leave much to be desired—in the authors' own words:

> "the evaluation of improvement or unimprovement was based on a combined judgment of psychiatrists, nurses, aides, and therapists, i.e., occupational therapists, recreational therapy instructors and the manual arts department personnel. This estimate was obtained at a meeting of the staff where a majority decision by a show of hands was the deciding factor."

Democracy has no place in science.

The purpose of the study reported by Shapiro and his colleagues (1958) was to investigate the effects of ECT on psychomotor slowness and on the "distraction effect" in depressed patients. The study, however, did include an estimate of the therapeutic efficacy of ECT. Thirty depressed patients were studied. Unfortunately, although it was intended that the patients be assigned at random to the treatment and no-treatment groups, the first 5 of the 15 treatment patients were assigned specifically to the treatment group. No significant differences between the two groups were found in clinical assessments after cessation of therapy. There is one barely significant difference on one aspect of the Hildreth Feeling Scale in favor of the ECT group. But we wonder whether much reliance can be put on this result. As we have already indicated, random assignment was not complete. The authors also suspected that "... there might have been a tendency to avoid referring the very ill patient to the psychologist when it was realized that it might result in their being held off treatment for a period of time." Neither double-blind nor single-blind conditions seem to have been included in this study. It is perhaps noteworthy also that ECT had a tendency to increase psychomotor slowness.

In view of the fact that there is no good experimental evidence that ECT is of particular therapeutic value, we do not intend to review here the differential effects of unilateral versus bilateral ECT, particularly, since none of these studies has included a placebo or no-treatment group. Clearly, the therapeutic efficacy of ECT must be demonstrated before one investigates the relative effectiveness of varying modifications of the treatment. The data concerning the differential amnesic effects of unilateral versus bilateral ECT have been reviewed in Chapter 4.

Of course, even if it had been demonstrated that the administration of electroconvulsive shock was of particular therapeutic efficacy, it would be essential to determine what aspects of a somewhat complex treatment process were producing the effects—for instance, what would be the effects of simply the threat of electroconvulsive shock, or the effects of electric shock administered to other parts of the body. It is a pity that, despite the clinical conviction of the therapeutic efficacy of ECT, there are no sound data to substantiate this conviction. Mental health professionals would appear to have a serious responsibility to properly evaluate this method of treatment if its continued use is intended.

ANTIDEPRESSANT DRUGS

Studies that are concerned with evaluating the efficacy of various treatments of depression have not always been concerned primarily with the effects of the treatment on depressive affect. Their approach frequently has been to treat depression as a syndrome or a disease entity and to evaluate the treatment's effectiveness with regard to the changes on all of the symptoms associated with the syndrome or the disease. On the other hand, as with studies of ECT, depressive affect has usually been one of the most important symptoms of the illness treated and, indeed, in many of the studies, the presence of a primary affective disturbance has been the criterion used in selecting patients for the study. It was appropriate, therefore, for us to review these studies here but, of course, the nature of these studies with regard to the symptom-syndrome distinction should be kept in mind.

We shall not review the studies in which neither a placebo nor a no-treatment group was included. The results from such studies, although, as is well known (for example, Foulds, 1958), more optimistic generally than control studies, provide little in the way of meaningful data for a scientist or scientifically oriented clinician. This results, of course, in the exclusion of many studies that compare different kinds of drugs. It would seem essential to unequivocally demonstrate some therapeutic effectiveness for one drug before comparing other drugs with it. A word more can be said about placebo controls. They are, of course, important in all drug research but, as Werner (1962) has pointed out, they may be even more important in the case of antidepressants than in the case of other drugs. He suggests that if, as Trouton (1957) contends, placebo reaction is a learned or conditioned response, placebo responses may be more prominent in patients suffering from depression, since introverts, according to Eysenck's theory, condition more readily than extraverts. In Eysenck's theory, patients suffering from depressive illnesses are considered to be usually of introverted personality. Therefore, they would be expected to acquire placebo responses more quickly and to retain them longer than does the extravert.

Let us look first at the studies that report significantly greater effects for the active drugs than for the placebo condition. There are 14 of these studies, and one's initial reaction might be that this is proof enough. Perhaps, then, we should note here that 14 studies present negative results! But we return for the moment to the ones that report positive results. Most of them have such serious methodological deficiencies that we cannot place a great deal of reliance on their findings.

Needless to say it is important in evaluating the effects of a drug that the double-blind condition be met. Some of the studies have failed wittingly or otherwise in this regard. Friedman, DeMowbray, and Hamilton (1961) make this unusual comment:

> "We feel that the traditional double-blind method is not applicable to an investigation of the pharmacotherapy of depression. When treatment is discontinued depressive conditions do not necessarily recur when switching to a placebo . . . In addition in a trial such as ours conducted with in-patients remission of symptoms leads to the patient's discharge and

hence a new variable is introduced into the situation."

It is difficult to follow this argument, but in any case it is unlikely that many would agree with this conclusion of a lack of applicability of the double-blind condition. It may be as well to note here another of their statements:

> "In the final analysis of results only those 36 cases are considered where the raters agreed on the direction of post treatment changes."

This statement also undermines one's confidence in the data presented.

In a number of the papers (Leyberg & Denmark, 1959; Ball & Kiloh, 1959; Abraham et al., 1963) the authors note that there were considerable side effects in the patients that received the drug, and one wonders to what extent this may have spoiled the double-blind condition. One study (Ball & Kiloh, 1959) notes that 27 of the 49 patients given imipramine showed side effects, whereas they were shown in only 13 of the 48 patients given a placebo. A chi square test by the present authors of this difference clearly indicates statistical significance ($\chi^2 = 9.054$ $df = 1$ $p < .01$).

It, of course, can be quite difficult to obviate this problem of side effects. But, even when we recognise this, we cannot be any more accepting of the results of the studies. It perhaps should be noted also that we cannot help but wonder how many of the other studies were beset by this problem despite the absence of comment on it in the papers.

Two of the studies (Kenning, Richardson, & Tucker, 1960; Browne, Kreeger, & Kazamias, 1963) failed to ensure that the patients were randomly assigned to the treatment groups. Kenning, Richardson, and Tucker (1960) note that

> ". . . where a doctor indicated that his patient was very sick, the author may have been biased to give the drug to more patients who were very ill and the placebo to others when this was not indicated. This, however, would load the experiment against the drug, making the results more significant than they actually appear."

Unfortunately, this is not a safe assumption to make and, on the contrary, it may well be that patients who were intially considered to be very ill were more readily seen as being improved, although in actuality, the real improvement was slight. It may also very well be that Wilder's Law of Initial Value holds true here, and that the patients who are more sick initially tend to improve to a greater extent after a constant period of time.

A number of studies (Leyberg & Denmark, 1959; Abraham et al., 1963; Garry & Leonard, 1963; Skarbek, 1963; Rickels, Ward, & Schut, 1964; Master, 1963) have used a crossover design without adequately facing the problems posed by this design. These problems include the following:

1. The possibility of carry-over effect. If a drug is given first, its pharmacological effects may still be present when the placebo is given. On the other hand, if the placebo is given first and there is little effect, the psychological effect of the disappointment may carry over to the drug administration.

2. The crossover design with the usual application of t tests or χ^2 to the data does not adequately test for the effects of order of administration and for the interaction between the drug and order effects. In order to do this adequately, the design, instead of being the simple *AB*, *BA* type, would have to be a more complicated one, such as *AB*, *BA*, *AA*, *BB*, *-A*, *-B*. Now anyone that knows the difficulties involved in getting sufficient data, even for a simple crossover study, may regard this suggestion as quite unrealistic, and yet the progress of science always involves the surmounting of seemingly impossible obstacles.

A closer look at one of these studies may make the nature of the problem involved a little clearer. In the study by Rickels, Ward and Schut (1964) the analysis was done on difference scores. Either an active drug or a placebo was given for two weeks, and this was followed for two weeks by the alternative treatment. The difference scores used were based on the pre- and post-drug and the pre- and post-placebo measures. To do this, the post first two-week scores were used as the baseline measures for the post four-week scores. Now apart from the fact that differences may have been present between the two groups that had the two different orders of treatments, despite random assignment on the measures before any treatment was given (testing for this possibility is generally omitted in all of the studies), differences between the groups almost certainly existed after the first two-week treatment. This makes the difference scores pre- and post-first two weeks and pre- and post-second two weeks not comparable, and would probably require transformations of the data, covariance analyses, or both. Further discussion of the problems in cross-over designs can be found in Chassan (1967) and Costello (1966).

Another problem with some of the studies (Abraham, et, al., 1963; Daneman, 1961; Overall et al., 1962) is that little attempt was made to control other treatment variables. For instance, in a study otherwise well designed (Daneman, 1961), psychoanalytically oriented psychotherapy was continued with all of the patients.

Even if, for the moment, we were to shut our eyes to these problems, the differences in favor of the drugs administered are not always that marked or very long lasting. Often we find that a number of assessment procedures have been used and that the significant difference has occurred only in one or two of them (for example, Kenning et al., 1960; Overall et al., 1962), immediately presenting the problem of the occurrence by chance of significant findings in multiple comparisons.

Some of the investigators found that whatever difference existed initially (after two or three weeks) between the drug and placebo groups, no difference was found after a longer period, that is after 4 to 12 weeks (Overall et al., 1962; Robin & Langley, 1964; Master, 1963; Abraham et al., 1963).

The many variables that are involved in drug evaluation studies and the need for much tighter control of these variables is suggested in studies like the one by Weintraub and Aronson (1963) in which the patients, who were assigned randomly either to the imipramine group or to a placebo group, were assessed by the psychiatric resident assigned to the patient and also by the chief resident. The double-blind condition was satisfied in the study. The judgment of response to treatment by the psychiatric resident indicated that imipramine was having a greater effect than the placebo. The judgments by the chief resident showed no significant differences between the active drug and the placebo. The degree of agreement between the therapist and the chief resident, both with regard to the pretreatment condition of the patient and with regard to the degree of improvement, was very small indeed.

We may mention also here the findings of Honigfeld (1963) that depressed patients showed greater improvement after administration of placebo tablets, the more favorable was their own attitude to medication and the more favorable was the therapeutic milieu defined in terms of the attitudes of physicians and nurses in the ward.

The following studies reported no significant difference in effect between the drug and the placebo group: Hohn et al., 1961; Ashby & Collins, 1961; Roulet et al., 1962; Rothman, Grayson, & Ferguson, 1962; Greenblatt, Grosser, & Wechsler, 1964; Wilson et al., 1963; Hollister et al., 1963; Ulenhuth & Park, 1964; Hollister et al., 1964; Fink, Klein, & Kramer, 1965; Friedman et al., 1966; Prange, McCurdy, & Cochrane, 1967.

Because some may believe that Fink, Klein, and Kramer (1965) should not be included in the above list, a little more detail will be given. They compared imipramine and placebo with a chlorpromazine-procyclidine combination. Random assignment of patients and the double-blind condition was met. The ten depressed patients who received placebo showed less improvement on clinical outcome ratings than either the imipramine group or the chlorpromazine-procyclidine group. But, on a Melancholy Agitation factor derived from the Lorr MSRPP scales (Multidimensional Scale for Rating Psychiatric Patients), only the chlorpromazine-procyclidine group made significant improvement. On the Sleepy score of the Clyde Mood Scale both the chlorpromazine-procyclidine group and the placebo group showed improvement with the improvement of the placebo group being significantly greater than the improvement of the imipramine group. These results do not seem particularly encouraging as far as the therapeutic effects of psychoactive drugs are concerned.

This brings the number of studies that report negative results to 12. There are two other studies in which the authors conclude that their data provide evidence in favor of the drug but which can nevertheless be added to the list of negative studies. The reasons for this will now be given.

Miller, Baker, Lewis, and Jones (1960)

compared the effectiveness of imipramine, iproniazid, dexedrine, and placebo. Twenty-four patients were selected on the basis of having depression as the central or prominent clinical feature. A double-blind procedure was used, and it seems that all of the patients took all of the drugs presumably in the order imipramine, iproniazid, dexedrine, and placebo, although this aspect of the procedure is not too clear. A simple scale was used to indicate four categories of response: recovered, markedly improved, slightly improved, unimproved. The authors suggest that the most spectacular response in terms of improvement occurred with imipramine and note that 30 percent of these patients who responded have either recovered or markedly improved. Unfortunately, they made no statistical test of the significance of the results. The present authors found that Chi tests, by either collapsing some of the categories to get rid of zero entries or without this collapsing and by applying Yate's correction, resulted in insignificant values.

The patients in the study by Rees, Brown, and Benaim (1961) were assigned at random to the two different orders of imipramine and placebo in a crossover design. An analysis was done only after the first three weeks before the patients were switched. Of the 11 patients on imipramine, there were 10 percent totally recovered, 25 percent markedly improved, 15 percent moderately improved, 50 percent with slight or no improvement, and 0 percent slightly worse. The corresponding figures for the 9 patients in the placebo group were: 10 percent, 0 percent, 20 percent, 65 percent and 5 percent. It may be difficult to envisage 5 percent of 9 patients but these are the figures presented. Although the authors, concentrating on the totally recovered and markedly improved categories, suggest that this is evidence in favor of imipramine, a χ^2 test of the whole table results in an insignificant finding.

Generally, of course, these studies contain methodological deficiencies similar to the ones in the positive studies. However, it would not seem particularly necessary to detail them in the case of negative studies.

We mention here two studies (Wittenborn, Maurer, & Plante, 1963; Honigfeld & Lasky, 1962) that attempted to assess the effects of an antidepressant drug one year following treatment. Unfortunately, many of the patients had received other treatments during the course of the year, making the data somewhat meaningless.

Reviews of the same literature come to different conclusions. The review by Klerman and Cole (1965) is not as pessimistic as the one presented here; nevertheless, they are not particularly enthusiastic about the drugs. Hordern (1966), on the other hand, although aware of many of the methodological problems involved in the evaluation of the drugs, appeared to be much more optimistic about them, and Werner's (1962) review is more optimistic. But Liberman's (1961) review is as pessimistic as the present one.

It should be emphasized that the present authors believe that it is not unlikely that imipramine or some similar compound will be shown to have a significant therapeutic effect on depressive illnesses. Indeed, DiMascio, Meyer, and Stifler (1963) found that a week's administration of imipramine significantly reduced the level of depression of a group of *normal* subjects selected because their scores fell two standard deviations above the mean on the depression scale of the MMPI. The effects of the drug on a low depressed group was not significantly greater than the effects of a placebo. But again we have a problem. The changes in depression were also measured on the MMPI scale, and Comrey (1957), in a factor analytic study, has found that only six of the items of the depression scale were loaded on a factor that could justifiably be labeled depression.

More thorough work must be done before antidepressant drugs can be given a satisfactory status. Studies in humans of the pharmacological action of imipramine, like the study of Haskovec and Rysanek (1967), might throw some light on the most effective use of imipramine as may work such as that of Stein (Stein & Seifter, 1961; Stein 1962) on the effects of imipramine on self-stimulation in animals. Stein found that amphetemine lowered the threshold for reinforcement, thus, increasing the rate of self-stimulation, whereas imipramine had weak inhibitory effects on self-stimulation. On the other hand, imipramine had a "profound potentiating effect on the response to amphetemine." Irwin (1968) suggests, however, that this effect of imipramine to increase the response to amphetemine is a nonselective action shared by other drugs which are not antidepressant.

REFERENCES

Abraham, H. C., Kanter, V. B., Rosen, I., & Standen, J. L. A controlled clinical trial of imipramine (Tofranil) with out-patients. *Brit. J. Psychiat.*, 1963, **109**, 286–293.

Ashby, W. R., & Collins, G. H. A clinical trial of imipramine ("Tofranil") on depressed patients. *J. ment. Sci.*, 1961, **107**, 547–551.

Bagachi, B. K., Howell, R. W., Schmale, H. T. The electroencephalographic and clinical effects of electrically induced convulsions in the treatment of mental disorders. *Amer. J. Psychiat.*, 1945, **102**, 49–60.

Ball, F. R. B., & Kiloh, L. G. A controlled trial of imipramine in treatment of depressive states. *Brit. Med. J.*, 1959, **2**, 1052–1055.

Brills, N. Q., Crumpton, E., Eiduson, S., Crayson, H. M., Hillman, L. J. & Richards, R.A. Relative effectiveness of various components of electroconvulsive therapy. *Arch. Neurol. Psychiat.*, 1959, **81**, 627–635.

Browne, M. W., Kreeger, L. C., & Kazamias, N. G. A clinical trial of amitriptyline in depressive patients. *Brit. J. Psychiat.*, 1963, **109**, 692–694.

Campbell, D. The psychological effects of cerebral electroshock. In H. J. Eysenck (ed.), *Handbook of abnormal psychology*. New York: Basic Books, 1961.

Chassan, J. B. *Research design in clinical psychology and psychiatry*. New York: Appleton-Century-Crofts, 1967.

Clinical Psychiatry Committee, Medical Research Council, Great Britain. Clinical trial of the treatment of depressive illness. *Brit. Med. J.*, 1965, **2**, 881–886.

Comrey, A. L. A factor analysis of items on the MMPI depression scale. *Educ. psychol. Measmt.*, 1957, **18**, 578–585.

Costello, C. G. *Psychology for psychiatrists*. New York: Pergamon Press, 1966.

Daneman, E. A. Imipramine in office management of depressive reactions (a double blind clinical study). *Dis. nerv. Syst.*, 1961, **22**, 213–217.

Di Mascio, A., Meyer, R. E., & Stifler, L. Effects of imipramine on individuals varying in level of depression. *Amer. J. Psychiat.*, 1968, **124** (suppl.), 55–58.

Ferster, C. B. Animal behavior and mental illness. *Psychol. Rec.*, 1966, **16**, 345–356.

Fink, M., Klein, D. F., & Kramer, J. C. Clinical efficacy of chlorpromazine-procyclidine combinations, imipramine and placebo in depressive disorders. *Psychopharmacologia*, 1965, **7**, 27–36.

Foulds, G. A. Clinical research in psychiatry. *J. ment. Sci.*, 1958, **104**, 259–265.

Friedman, A. S., Granik, S., Cohen, H. W., & Cowitz, B. Imipramine (Tofranil) vs. placebo in hospitalized psychotic depressives. *J. Psychiat. Res.*, 1966, **4**, 13–36.

Friedman, C., De Mowbray, M. S., & Hamilton, V. Imipramine (Tofranil) in depressive states: controlled trial with in-patients. *J. ment. Sci.*, 1961, **107**, 948–953.

Friedman, E. Unidirectional electro-stimulated convulsive therapy. II. Therapeutic results in 536 patients. *J. nerv. ment. Dis.*, 1949, **109**, 540–549.

Garry, J. W., & Leonard, T. J. Trial of amitriptyline in chronic depression. *Brit. J. Psychiat.*, 1963, **109**, 54–55.

Goldstein, A. P., Heller, K., & Sechrest, L. B. *Psychotherapy and the psychology of behavior change*. New York: John Wiley, 1966.

Greenblatt, M., Grosser, G. H., & Wechsler, H. Differential response of hospitalized depressed patients to somatic therapy. *Amer. J. Psychiat.*, 1964, **120**, 935–943.

Hamilton, D. M., & Ward, G. M. The hospital treatment of involutional psychoses. *Amer. J. Psychiat.*, 1948, **104**, 801–804.

Hamilton, M. A rating scale for depression. *J. Neurol. Neurosurg. Psychiat.*, 1960, **23**, 56–62.

Haskovec, L., & Rysanek, K. Excretion of 3-Methoxy-4-hydroxymandelic acid and 5-hydroxyindoleacetic acid in depressed patients treated with imipramine. *J. Psychiat. Res.*, 1967, **5**, 213–220.

Hinko, E. N., & Lipschutz, L. S. Five years after shock therapy. A preliminary report. *Amer. J. Psychiat.*, 1948, **104**, 387–390.

Höhn, R. Gross, Gertrude M., Gross, M. & Lasagna, L. A double-blind comparison of placebo and imipramine in the treatment of depressed patients in a state hospital. *J. Psychiat. Res.*, 1961, **1**, 76–91.

Hollister, L. E., Overall, J. E., Johnson, M., Katz, G., Kimbel, I., Jr., & Honigfeld, G. Evaluation of desipramine in depressive states. *J. new Drugs*, 1963, **3**, 161–166.

Hollister, L. E., Overall, J. E., Johnson, M., Pennington, V., Katz, G., & Shelton, J. Controlled comparison of amitriptyline, imipramine and placebo in hospitalized depressed patients. *J. nerv. ment. Dis.*, 1964, **139**, 370–375.

Honigfeld, G. Physician and patient attitudes as factors influencing placebo responses in depression. *Dis. nerv. Systm.*, 1963, **24**, 343–347.

Honigfeld, G. & Lasky, J. J. A one year follow-up of depressed patients treated in a multi-hospital drug study. I. Social workers' evaluations. VA Cooperative Studies in Psychiatry, Report No. 30, 1962.

Horden, A. The anti-depressant drugs. *Int. J. Psychiat.*, 1966, **2**, 48–67.

Huston, P. E. & Locher, L. M. Manic-depressive psychosis. Course when treated and untreated with electric shock. *Arch. Neurol. Psychiat.*, 1948, **60**, 37–48.

Irwin, S. A rational framework for the development, evaluation and use of psychoactive drugs. *Amer. J. Psychiat.*, 1968, **124** (suppl.), 1–19.

Janis, I. L. Psychologic effects of electric convulsive treatments. I. Post-treatment amnesia. *J. nerv. ment. Dis.*, 1950a, **111**, 359–382.

Janis, I. L. Psychologic effects of electric convulsive treatments. III. Changes in affective disturbances. *J. nerv. ment. Dis.*, 1950b, **111**, 469–489.

Karagulla, S. Evaluation of electric convulsive therapy as compared with conservative methods of treatment in depressive states. *J. ment. Sci.*, 1950, **96**, 1060–1091.

Kenning, I. S., Richardson, N. L., & Tucker, F. G. Treatment of depressive states with imipramine hydrochloride, *Canad. Psychiat. Ass. J.*, 1960, **5**, 60–64.

Kiloh, L. G., Child, J. P., & Latner, G. A controlled trial of iproniazid in the treatment of endogenous depression. *J. ment. Sci.*, 1960a, **106**, 1139–1144.

Kiloh, L. G., Child, J. P., & Latner, G. Endogenous depression treated with iproniazid: a follow-up study. *J. ment. Sci.*, 1960b, **106**, 1425–1428.

Klerman, G. H., & Cole, J. O. Clinical pharmacology of imipramine and related anti-depressant compounds. *Pharm. Review*, 1965, **17**, 101–141.

Leyberg, J. T., & Denmark, J. C. Treatment of depressive states with imipramine hydrochloride (Tofranil). *J. ment. Sci.*, 1959, **105**, 1123–1126.

Liberman, R. A criticism of drug therapy in psychiatry. *Arch. gen. Psychiat.*, 1961, **4**, 131–136.

Master, R. S. Amitriptyline in depressive states: a controlled trial in India. *Brit. J. Psychiat.*, 1963, **109**, 826–829.

Messick, S., & Jackson, D. N. Acquiescence and the factorial interpretation of the MMPI. *Psychol. Bull.*, 1961, **58**, 299—304.

Miller, A., Baker, E. F. W., Lewis, D., & Jones, A. Imipramine, a clinical evaluation in a variety of settings. *Canad. Psychiat. Ass. J.*, 1960, **5**, 150–160.

Norman, J., & Shea, J. T. Three years' experience with electric convulsion therapy. *New England J. Med.*, 1946, **234**, 857–860.

Overall, J. E., Hollister, L. E., Pokorny, A. D., Casey, J. F., & Katz, G. Drug therapy in depressions. Controlled evaluation of imipramine, isocarboxazide, dextroamphetamine-amobarbital, and placebo. *Clin. Pharmacol. Ther.*, 1962, **3**, 16–22.

Prange, A. J., McCurdy, R. L., & Cochrane, C. M. The systolic blood pressure response of depressed patients to infused norepinephrine. *J. Psychiat. Res.*, 1967, **5**, 1–13.

Rees, L., Brown, A. C., & Benaim, S. Controlled trial of imipramine (Tofranil) in treatment of severe depressive states. *J. ment. Sci.*, 1961, **107**, 552–559.

Rickels, K., Ward, C. H., & Schut, L. Different populations, different drug responses: comparative study of two anti-depressants, each used in two different patient groups. *Amer. J. Med. Sci.*, 1964, **247**, 328–335.

Robin, A. A., & Langley, G. E. Controlled trial of imipramine. *Brit. J. Psychiat.*, 1964, **110**, 419–442.

Rothman, T., Grayson, H., & Ferguson, J. A comparative investigation of isocarboxazid and imipramine in depressive syndromes. *J. Neuropsychiat.*, 1962. **3**, 234–240.
Roulet, N., Alvarez, R. R., Duffy, J. P., Lenkoski, L. D., & Bidder, T. G. Imipramine in depression: a controlled study. *Amer. J. Psychiat.*, 1962, **119**, 427–431.
Sainz, A. Clarification of the action of successful treatment in the depressions, *Dis. Nerv. Syst.*, (Suppl.), 1959, **20**, 53–57.
Salzman, L. An evaluation of shock therapy. *Amer. J. Psychiat.*, 1947, **103**, 669–679.
Scherer, I. W. Prognosis and psychological scores in electroconvulsive therapy, psychosurgery, and spontaneous remission. *Amer. J. Psychiat.*, 1951, **107**, 926–931.
Shapiro, M. B., Campbell, D., Harris, A., & Dewsberry, J. The effects of ECT upon psychomotor speed and the "distraction effect" in depressed psychotic patients. *J. ment. Sci.*, 1958, **104**, 681–695.
Skarbek, A. Trial of amitriptyline in chronic depression. *Dis. nerv. System.*, 1963, **24**, 115–119.
Slater, E. T. O. Evaluation of electroconvulsive therapy as compared with conservative methods of treatment in depressive states. *J. ment. Sci.*, 1951, **97**, 567–569.
Stein, L. Effects and interactions of imipramine, chloropromazine, reserpine and amphetamine on self-stimulation: Possible neurophysiological basis of depression. In J. Wortis (ed.), *Recent advances in biological psychiatry, Vol. IV.* New York: Plenum Press, 1962.
Stein, L., & Steifter, J. Possible mode of anti-depressive action of imipramine. *Sci.*, 1961. **134**, 286–287.
Tillotson, K. J., & Sulzbach, W. A comparative study and evaluation of electric shock therapy in depressive states. *Amer. J. Psychiat.*, 1945, **101**, 455–459.
Trouton, D. S. Placebos and their psychological effects. *J. ment. Sci.*, 1957, **103**, 344–354.
Uhlenhuth, E. H., & Park, L. C. The influence of medication (imipramine) and doctor in relieving depressed psychoneurotic outpatients. *J. Psychiat. Res.*, 1964, **2**, 101–122.
Ulett, G. A., Smith, K., & Gleser, G. C. Evaluation of convulsive and subconvulsive shock therapies utilizing a control group. *Amer. J. Psychiat.*, 1956, **112**, 795–802.
Weintraub, W., & Aronson, H. Clinical judgment in psychopharmacological research, *J. Neuropsychiat.*, 1963, **5**, 65–70.
Werner, G. Clinical pharmacology of central stimulant and anti-depressant drugs. *Clin. Pharmacol. Ther.*, 1962, **3**, 59–96.
Wilson, I. C., Vernon, J. T., Guin, T., & Sandfifer, M. G., Jr. A Controlled study of treatments of depression. *J. Neuropsychiat.*, 1963, **4**, 331–337.
Wittenborn, J. R., Maurer, H., & Plante, M. Methods for treating depression evaluated after the lapse of one year. *J. nerv. ment. Dis.*, 1963, **136**, 492–499.
Wittenborn, J. R. Plante, M., Burgess, F., & Livermore, N. The efficacy of electroconvulsive therapy, iproniazid, and placebo in the treatment of young depressed women. *J. nerv. ment. Dis.*, 1961, **133**, 316–332.

Chapter 9

Anxiety

BARCLAY MARTIN AND L. ALAN SROUFE

SOME PROBLEMS OF DEFINITION

In the clinical literature there is considerable agreement as to what constitutes the more extreme manifestations of anxiety. A typical description is provided by Portnoy (1959) in the *American Handbook of Psychiatry* as follows:

> "... subjectively experienced uneasiness, apprehension, anticipation of danger, doom, disintegration, and going to pieces, the source of which is unknown by the individual and toward which he feels helpless, with a characteristic somatic pattern. This somatic pattern shows evidence of increased tension in the skeletal muscles (stiffness, tremors, weakness, unsteadiness of voice, etc.); the cardiovascular system (palpitation, blushing or pallor, faintness, rapid pulse, increased blood pressure, etc.); and the gastrointestinal system (nausea, vomiting, diarrhea, etc.). There may also be other manifestations such as cold wet extremities, rapid or irregular breathing, frequency of urination, and sleep disturbances ..."

The quantification or scaling of degrees of anxiety for purposes of assessment or experimental studies of change, poses a number of troublesome problems. These problems of definition and measurement are not nearly so great with respect to symptoms such as tics, thumbsucking, enuresis, alcoholism, hypertension, etc., where usually a single overt response *is* the symptom, there is no debate about definition, and measurement is a technical problem with little theoretical implication. Anxiety on the other hand, as the above clinical description indicates, is usually approached from a multiple-response point of view. Few people are willing to limit their conceptions of anxiety to one response and, for example, say that anxiety *is* rapid heart rate, or that anxiety *is* the self-report of a feeling of anxiousness. Common sense tells us that a person's heart may beat more rapidly for a variety of reasons that have no relationship to anxiety, and that what one person reports as a subjective feeling of anxiousness may be quite different from what another person would report. One solution to this problem is to toss out the whole concept of anxiety and just work with specific responses such as heart rate, muscular tremors, and various self-reports about subjective experiences. This is a tempting solution and one for which the present authors have some sympathy. However, such a solution ignores the possibility that there may be underlying neurophysiological and/or hormonal processes that should properly be conceptualized as the central, although as yet not directly measurable, anxiety response(s).

For present purposes, then, we shall conceive of anxiety as a neurophysiological response that has especially strong manifestations in the hypothalamic-sympathetic-adrenal medullary system, and in the hypothalamic-pituitary-adrenal cortical system, and in the reticular systems. Pathological intensity and persistence of anxiety reflects chronic over-reaction in some aspect of these neurophysiological systems. This reaction will have measurable effects in physiological, behavioral, and self-report systems. It is further assumed that the anxiety response, although innately available in human organisms, is highly learnable, that is, it can become readily attached to previously noneliciting stimuli, probably on the basis of simple contiguity.

Eysenck has proposed that there are two primary underlying dimensions of neurotic disorder, neuroticism and extroversion-introversion, and that both have strong hereditary determinants.

> "Neuroticism is conceived of as an inherited autonomic over-reactivity, while introversion is characterized by strong conditionability; hence, anxiety as a conditioned fear reaction appears most frequently in dysthymics, i.e. neurotic introverts" (Eysenck, 1961, p. 21).

The evidence for inheritance of individual differences in autonomic reactivity is based on rather modest differences in correlation between small samples of identical and fraternal twins (Jost and Sontag, 1944), and more definitive work is needed on this question. The present writers would also question the independence of autonomic over-reactivity and conditionability implied in the statement quoted above from Eysenck. For the purposes of this chapter, we shall not conceptualize anxiety within the framework of the neuroticism and extroversion-introversion dimensions of Eysenck, although a virtue of this theory is that it suggests some testable hypotheses.

It is important to distinguish between stimulus-oriented definitions and response-oriented definitions. The distinction that is usually made, for example, between castration anxiety and separation anxiety would seem to be in terms of what the person is afraid of, that is, the stimulus, rather than in terms of a difference in the anxiety response itself. The usual distinction between fear and anxiety in terms of the former being reality based and the latter being irrational also refers primarily to a difference in stimuli rather than to a difference in response. We shall emphasize a response-oriented definition, and take the position that until shown otherwise the anxiety response is the same even though elicited by different stimuli. The terms fear and anxiety will be considered synonomous unless explicitly stated otherwise.

This emphasis on a response-oriented definition is contrary to much of the clinical literature where, for example, psychoanalytic writers distinguish between anxiety precipitated by fantasied threats of castration and overwhelming stimulation of any kind; and May (1959), writing about the existential approach, states that anxiety results from "a threat to the foundation, the center of existence. It is the experiencing of the threat of non-being . . ." (p. 1354). Goldstein (1939) maintained that anxiety is part of a catastrophic response that occurs when the individual does not have the capacity to live up to the demands made on him. These tend to be stimulus-oriented definitions. For some individuals cues associated with the "threat of non-being" may well elicit anxiety, for other individuals cues associated with the fantasies of castration do indeed elicit anxiety. The logical distinction that we make here is that the anxiety response itself is not defined in terms of these eliciting stimuli but rather as a response system that can, by learning, become associated with almost any kind of stimulus.

It is, of course, important for most clinical and research purposes to be able to identify the cues that elicit the anxiety response. These cues can be internal as well as external, and include "response-produced cues" associated with thoughts, images, fantasies, somatic drive states, etc.

Another kind of response that should be logically distinguished from anxiety is a response that has been learned in order to reduce anxiety, variously referred to as defensive, coping, or avoidance responses. It is common for clinicians to infer the existence of anxiety from the presence of avoidance responses. For example, a person who avoids close interpersonal ties would be said to be anxious about close interpersonal relationships. It should be kept in mind that such avoidance responses are not anxiety and, indeed, if the avoidance responses are serving their assumed purpose, they may indicate low anxiety.

In the following studies, anxiety is introduced as a variable in two ways: (1) by groups selected to represent different degrees of anxiety present in the individuals, for example, psychiatric patients classified as anxiety reaction, or subjects selected by an assessment procedure such as the Taylor Manifest Anxiety Scale (MAS), and (2) by experimental manipulations or selection of real-life situations thought to be anxiety arousing. In evaluating the relevance of various measures to the construct of anxiety, we shall usually look for evidence that the measure relates to both subject-defined and situation-induced anxiety.

ASSESSMENT: PHYSIOLOGICAL MEASURES

There seems to be little question that physiological changes can be effected through stressful experimental manipulations, or that psychiatric groups can be discriminated from normal controls via physiological response differences.

Weinar (1962) has pointed out that physiological changes similar to the ones in experiments thought to arouse fear "... can be wrought by simple and novel stimuli, such as sound and light ..." (p. 117). Subjects respond with an increase in skin conductance with the presentation of virtually any stimulus (I. Martin, 1961; Venables, 1960), and Davis et al. (1955) have reported that the log of this change is a linear function of the stimulus intensity. Davis et al. (1955) also present similar data for other autonomic responses and for muscle tension.

We assume that there are various arousal states associated with processes such as "orienting" to new stimuli, physical effort, deprivation (for example, water or sleep), intense physical stimulation (for example, electric shock), mental effort (for example, mental arithmetic), *and* emotions such as fear. If there are characteristic responses associated with fear then they will be seen more clearly when not measured under conditions known to introduce confounding arousal states. To take an extreme example, it would be inadvisable to frighten a person while he is performing a task that requires strenuous physical exertion with the aim of measuring physiological responses associated with fear. The kind of experimental procedure that would seem to be least confounded with other arousal states is the kind in which the measures are taken in an anticipatory period where either no external stimuli are given (other than some kind of initial instruction in which the subject is forewarned of some impending event) or physically mild stimuli are provided which are associated with some impending event (for example, a conditioned stimulus that serves as a signal). Likewise measures obtained in a post-stimulation recovery period might be less confounded with other arousal states due to the stimulation per se. Few of the studies to be reported, however, were designed to elicit a relatively "pure" fear response. We shall emphasize studies that, at least, minimize some of the more obvious alternative interpretations.

Other complexities involved in the physiological assessment of fear, or any other emotion, should be mentioned at the outset. Studies by Haggard (1943), Lazarus and Opton (1966), and Schachter (1966) make it clear that cognitive factors influence physiological responses or the subject's interpretation of his physiological responses Lazarus and Opton, for example, report studies in which an "intellectualized" cognitive set reduces the autonomic response to an otherwise arousing film. There is also evidence for individual differences in "preferred" mode and patterning of response (for example, Lacey et al., 1953), making multiple physiological measures advisable.

Another source of complexity is that many autonomic responses involve an interaction between sympathetic and parasympathetic activity (Gellhorn & Loofbourrow, 1963). Some responses, heart rate, for example, are biphasic or "homeostatic" (Sternbach, 1966). Should one measure the immediate acceleration, the subsequent deceleration, the "peak-valley" distance, time to return to baseline, or some combination of these and other measures? More generally, in physiological assessment, should one measure average level, change in average level, discrete changes, spontaneous activity, habituation, recovery, or conditionability? Each of these approaches has been used, and examples will be found on subsequent pages.

Partly because single measure studies still predominate, and partly for expositional clarity, experimental and correlational data relevant to individual physiological response systems will be presented initially. Discussion of studies using multiple responses and attempts to distinguish anxiety from other emotional states by differences in physiological patterns of response will follow.

Cardiovascular Responses

Heart Rate

Heart rate has been widely used as a dependent variable in experimental stress studies. A large number of studies have shown heart-rate acceleration to be the immediate response to strong aversive stimuli. These studies have been reviewed by Graham and Clifton (1966) and include responses to intense cold (for example, Engel, 1960; Obrist, 1963), loud sounds (for example, Uno & Grings, 1965), and shock (for example, Zeaman, et al., 1954). Graham and Clifton conclude that for simple, nonsignal stimuli, heart-rate acceleration is characteristic for sudden, intense stimuli, and that such acceleration responses are slow to habituate. On this basis, perhaps, "startle" responses can be distinguished from "orienting" responses.

In addition to aversive stimuli, Lacey (1959) has reported that a variety of situations (for example, mental arithmetic), which he interprets as demanding "rejection" of the external environment, cause heart-rate acceleration. Darrow (1929a, 1929b) and Campos and Johnson (1966) have also demonstrated cardiac acceleration in response to ideation and verbalization. Clearly it would be inappropriate to interpret these accelerative responses as indicative of anxiety.

Heart-rate responses in anticipation of aversive stimuli might be more relevant to many clinicians' concept of anxiety. Most recent studies have used anticipation of electric shock, and Hodges and Spielberger (1966), for example, found a significant increase in heart rate to the threat of shock. However, subjects who scored high and low on the Taylor MAS did not show differential increases, but a self-report measure of high fear of shock obtained one month previously did predict greater rate increment. Deane (1961, 1964) performed an experiment in which prior experience with shock and knowledge of time of onset of shock were manipulated. All subjects tended to show acceleration during the 30-second period preceding shock. The group that had *not* experienced the shock prior to the test trial showed greater acceleration than the group that had experienced the shock. However, the group told merely that the shock would occur at some time as a memory drum displayed the numbers 1 to 12 could not be differentiated from the group specifically informed that the shock would occur on number 10. The shock intensities used were mild, and stronger intensities might have altered the results.

Elliot (1966) provides further information on these issues in a similar study. Whether the shock was strong (4.0 ma.) or mild (.2 ma.), subjects without prior experience with the shocks showed greater acceleration. Of course, it is possible that "no experience" subjects expected an even stronger shock, but it is noteworthy that, among the subjects who experienced the shock, the strong shocks did not produce greater acceleration. Although knowledge of time of onset was again nonsignificant, differences in the response curves were noted. The subjects who knew when the shock was coming *decelerated* just before the shock. Such a deceleration, however, usually occurs just prior to any expected stimulus, even if this stimulus is nonaversive (for example, Steward, 1962; Coquery & Lacey, 1966).

Heart-rate acceleration also occurs in response to more complex stress situations; for example, stressful films (Lazarus & Opton, 1966), anticipation of oral exams (Hickham et al., 1948), and criticism (Malmo et al., 1957). The several studies on fear versus other emotions (Ax, 1953; Funkenstein et al., 1957; Lewinsohn, 1956; Schachter, 1957) also indicate cardiac rate increase under complex experimental fear conditions.

Heart-rate responses have also been used to distinguish psychiatric groups with anxiety symptoms from normal controls. Malmo and Shagass (1952), for example, report higher heart rates for a group of neurotics, in whom anxiety was a prominent symptom, than for normals during mirror tracing and a rapid discrimination task. Wishner (1953) found resting heart rates to be higher in 11 anxiety neurotics than in 10 normals. Glickstein et al. (1957), in a factor-analytic study, were able to distinguish two groups of patients. One group, rated higher in anxiety, showed generally faster heart rates, which reliably reflected a series of stresses in time.

Vascular Responses

Malmo and Shagass (1952), in the study just mentioned above, also compared the systolic blood pressure of the anxious neurotic patients to that of a group of schizophrenics and a group of normals. The anxious neurotic group had a higher average systolic blood pressure before the task was introduced and showed a steady increase throughout the task. Both the schizophrenic and normal groups showed an initial increase, followed by a leveling off. Thus, the anxious neurotics showed no sign of habituating to the stress, unlike the other two groups. Systolic blood pressure has also been found to be associated with clinically assessed or experimentally aroused anxiety by other investigators (Ax, 1953; Funkenstein et al., 1957; Malmo et al., 1951; Milliken, 1964; Wolf et al., 1948).

Increased cardiac output and blood flow (Adsett et al., 1962; Clancy & Vanderhoof, 1963; Funkenstein et al., 1957) and peripheral vasoconstriction (Ackner, 1956a, 1956b; Obrist, 1963) have also been implicated as responses to stress. For a discussion of skin temperature, which is largely a function of blood flow and blood volume, see Plutchik (1956). Generally, the cardiovascular changes discussed can be called "sympathetic" (Obrist, 1963).

Skin Responses

Detailed methodological considerations with respect to skin responses in emotion are beyond the scope of this chapter, and recent papers are readily available (Darrow, 1964; Martin & Venables, 1966; Montagu & Coles, 1966). It seems that when one records skin potential or skin resistance (the resistance of the skin to an applied current) some combination of sweat gland and epidermous activity is being measured. Even when considered individually, the responses of these components may be quite complex. For example, at higher levels of arousal it is possible, as Harrison (1964) notes, that there is some inhibition of sweat gland activity interacting with the sympathetic excitation, because the sweat gland (a cholinergic mechanism) may be inhibited by noradrenaline. He has recently reported data that indicate increased sweat gland activity (number of glands) occurs only at the onset of stress. This is followed by decreased activity "associated with increased pituitary-adrenal activity." Not having parasympathetic innervation, the sweat gland is at least free from the problems of negative feedback discussed earlier (Sternbach, 1966). It is also clear that the sweat gland has important ties to "arousal" centers (Wang, 1964).

Average Level and the Galvanic Skin Response (GSR)

Studies attempting to discriminate patient from normal groups by using *resting* skin conductance level have been largely negative or equivocal (Malmo, 1957). There have been numerous successful attempts to discriminate groups during stress.

Lader and Wing (1964) conducted a study noteworthy for the care with which measures were obtained, for the selection of a group of patients in which anxiety was prominent and other symptoms secondary, and for a well-matched normal control group. The "stress" consisted of a series of 100 db tones. Habituation rate (the decreasing magnitude of GSR to successive tones) was significantly lower, and the number of spontaneous GSR fluctuations was significantly higher in the anxious patients. Lader (1967) repeated this procedure on the following groups of subjects: (a) anxiety with depression, (b) anxiety state, (c) agoraphobia, (d) social phobia, (e) specific phobia, and (f) normal. Again, both habituation rate and number of spontaneous GSR's were significantly related to these groupings in the order of the above listing—that is, the habituation rate was lowest for the anxiety with depression group and highest with the normal group, and the number of spontaneous GSR's was highest for the anxiety with depression group and lowest for the normal group. In another report, Lader, Gelder, and Marks (1967) indicate that for a subsample of these same patients, low habituation rate and high frequency of spontaneous GSR's are related to poor treatment prognosis.

Experimental stress studies with normal subjects have also used the GSR as a dependent variable. In a recent study (Geer,

1966b), subjects with high fear of spiders, as measured by the Fear Survey Schedule (Geer, 1965), showed GSR's of greater magnitude and duration to the first presentation of a spider photograph than did three other groups, including a group of subjects with high fear of snakes but low fear of spiders. An important methodological aspect of this study was the habituation of the GSR to neutral pictures before presentation of the test stimuli, although it is still possible that the results reflect only differences in "interest" in snakes and spiders. Epstein (1962) conducted a classic study on life stress. He found that novice parachutists showed higher skin conductance levels before than after a jump, and also greater GSR's to words and pictures related to jumping on the day of a jump than at a time two weeks away from a jump.

Katkin (1965; 1966) and Miller and Shmavonian (1965) have found that both skin conductance and GSR nonspecifics (fluctuations in skin resistance in the absence of known stimulation) significantly increased during experimental stress (threat of shock).

Palmar Sweat

Ferreira and Winter (1963) provide important data on the most widely used measure of palmar sweat, the Palmar Sweat Index (PSI), which results in a stain which can be quantified by using a densitometer. In addition to describing the process in detail (see also Lore, 1966), they also present data on interfinger correlations (average $r = .48$) and on the importance of duration but not pressure. Brutten (1959) and Lore (1966) present across-time reliabilities that suggest this measure compares well to other physiological indexes in terms of reliability. Palmar sweat has been reported to significantly correlate with skin conductance (Wenger & Gilchrist, 1948). It is a simple, inexpensive measure, but it cannot be used in studies where continuous measurement is required.

At least one study rather clearly points to a link between palmar sweat and anxiety. In this study Beam (1955) found increased sweating prior to doctoral examinations and opening night appearance in plays. Lore (1966) found increased palmar sweating when kindergarteners listened to frightening stories, but he failed to control for story content. Nonfrightening stories may have produced similar changes. Finally, studies that find increased sweat during therapy interviews (Mowrer, 1953), during nonsolveable problems (Solley & Stagner, 1956), and while listening to incomprehensible verbal messages (Haywood, 1962) probably confound mental effort with anxiety.

GSR Nonspecifics

GSR nonspecifics or spontaneous GSR's have been shown to be reliable (for example, Lacey & Lacey, 1958; Dykman et al., 1963). Studies previously mentioned, for example, Lader & Wing (1964), and Katkin (1965, 1966), have found this measure to relate to both subject and situation defined anxiety. Eysenck (1956) has suggested that this lability is a characteristic of neurotics, but Burdick (1966) failed to find a significant relationship between this measure and the Maudsley Personality Inventory (MPI) neuroticism scale, using 27 subjects. Katkin (1966), however, found a significant positive relationship between GSR nonspecifics and Zuckerman's Affect Adjective Check List (AACL), a self-report measure of anxiety, after a stress experience (threat of shock).

GSR Conditioning

Several studies have found that anxious subjects, as assessed by diagnostic classification or verbal report, show greater ease of GSR conditioning than normals (Bitterman & Holtzman, 1952; Welch & Kubis, 1947). Howe (1958) found anxious patients to extinguish more slowly than normals after GSR conditioning and to have higher initial conductance levels. Obrist (1958) found that adequately conditioned subjects exhibited higher conductance levels ("anxiety") and less decrement in conductance levels over the course of conditioning. Finally, Beam (1955) reported greater GSR conditioning before doctoral examinations and opening nights of plays.

Skeletal Muscle Activity

Many investigators have argued that GSR is not *the* measure of anxiety or arousal (Duffy, 1962; I. Martin, 1961; Malmo, 1966). Muscle tension, and measures related to it, is often the heir apparent. In his theory, Jacobson (1942) argues that muscle tension is a necessary part of the anxiety response.

Malmo (1966) reports that GSR oscillation increases during a period preceding pain, but that finger movements increase even more, and although GSR conditioning can distinguish patient from normal groups, ease of eyeblink conditioning is an even more powerful discriminator.

Finger movement and eyeblink conditioning suggest the wide range of responses that have been used in assessing skeletal muscle involvement in anxiety. Others include gross movements, restlessness (fidgeting), hand-grip pressure, body posture, gestures, tremor, magnitude of knee jerk, eyeblink rate, and electromyographic (EMG) measurement of muscle activity. Malmo (1957) has also suggested that respiratory irregularities are characteristic of tense persons. Jurko et al. (1952), and Malmo and Shagass (1949) present data that support this notion. Goldstein (1964b) reports that these measures do not seem to be strongly intercorrelated.

Sainsbury (1964) has recently reported on a series of studies with anxious patients. He and his colleagues have demonstrated that anxiety-state patients, although under relaxation conditions, give a greater number of spontaneous EMG's than normal controls (soldiers). He also reports significant correlations between a combination of arm and frontalis responsivity and an inventory of somatic anxiety symptoms ($r = .49$) and between the number of movements (while sitting alone) and the Taylor MAS (mixed patients, $r = .47$). Malmo and Smith (1955) present data on the superiority of the frontalis (versus the forearm) in distinguishing anxiety neurotics.

Other studies have shown that high anxious normal subjects (for example, as assessed by the Taylor MAS) show greater muscle activity (Balshan, 1962) and eyeblink rate (Doehring, 1957) in response to white noise, and that the EMG can reflect experimental stress in undifferentiated normal subjects (Davis & Malmo, 1951; Newman, 1962).

Both Goldstein (1964a), who has reviewed the literature on muscle tension, and Malmo (1966) have suggested that the anxious patient is more distinguished by his prolonged response to stress than by resting levels, and that these patients may be suffering from a failure of some homeostatic mechanism, probably located in the reticular systems. For example, in the Malmo et al. (1950) study, using strong auditory stimuli, pathologically anxious patients did not show greater forearm action potentials at rest, or in immediate response to the stimulus (startle). However, the responses of the normal controls quickly returned to baseline, whereas the response of the anxious subjects continued and increased during the entire stimulus period, reaching its peak much later. Likewise, Davis, Malmo, and Shagass (1954) found a somewhat larger initial response by anxious patients to bursts of white noise, but an even greater difference was found .3 to .4 seconds after stimulation. These findings are similar to the ones for blood pressure, skin conductance, and GSR conditioning reported previously.

Stomach Activity

Wolf and Wolff (1947) found anxiety ("a wish to flee") associated with a *decrease* in acid output and gastric motility in psychiatric patients. This sympathetic response seems consonant with the heart rate acceleration and other responses discussed above. However, other data indicate an increase in gastrointestinal activity in various stress situations. Mahl and Karpe (1953), in a case study, found that increased secretion of hydrochloric acid (HCl) was associated with increased self-reported anxiety. Mahl (1949, 1950) also reports that, with nonavoidant shock conditioning with dogs, acid concentration in the stomach increased with anxiety reactions (trembling, awkward postures, etc.), and that there is more free HCl in the stomachs of students about to take an examination. A well-known study of gastric activity in stress is that of Brady's (1958) "executive monkeys" in which monkeys "responsible" for preventing regularly scheduled shocks developed peptic ulcers and yoked control monkeys that received the same number of unavoidable shocks did not. One of the most interesting findings here was that HCl secretion was greater following than during shock-avoidance. Davis and Berry (1963) have conducted a similar study with humans. By using muscle-action potentials associated with movements of the stomach, "executive students" (responsible for preventing intense noise in an avoidance condition) showed a greater stomach-muscle response during, but not after, the task than students in a nonavoidance condition. Stomach-muscle contractions may not, of course, be directly related to HCl secretion. Mahl (1950) has argued that such parasympathetic dominance is characteristic of *chronic* anxiety only. For example, in his study with dogs, the increase in acid secretion did not occur until the fifth day of training.

Pupillary Reactivity

Dilation of the pupil in dark and constriction in light can be used as indixes of adrenergic and cholinergic mechanisms. Rubin (1962) has argued that for a maximal generalized adrenergic ("sympathetic") response to stress (an adaptive emergency reaction) there must also be a concurrent decrease in cholinergic activity. He predicted, therefore, that, under stress, normal subjects would show increased pupillary dilation to dark and decreased constriction to light. With intense cold as the stressor, these results were obtained. He has also reported discrepancies from this pattern for psychotic and neurotic subjects. McCawley, Stroebel, and Glueck (1966) replicated Rubin's procedures with samples of psychotics and normals more closely matched for age, and were unable to discriminate between the groups on the basis of aberrant pupillary reactivity. Psychoneurotics (Rubin, 1964) were characterized by a prolonged response to the cold stimulus, the adrenergic-cholinergic imbalance persisting far beyond the normal response. Again, delayed recovery is indicated as characteristic of anxious states.

Studies Using Multiple Measures

Association with Anxiety

The studies discussed in this section employ multiple physiological measures, but do not attempt to discern a pattern of response unique to anxiety. Studies of this type will be discussed subsequently. The studies reviewed here permit the reader to note the differential effectiveness of various measures in a given stress situation.

Multiple measure studies generally confirm that physiological measures are responsive to stress and can be used to distinguish patient groups from normal controls. Malmo and Shagass (1949), for example, by using pain, found more finger and head movements, greater neck-muscle potential and heart-rate variability, and more respiration irregularities in anxious patients and early schizophrenics than in normal subjects. Percent change of GSR was not significant.

There have been few attempts to combine physiological measures into a weighted index. Wenger (1942, 1948) provides a notable exception. Based on repeated factor analytic studies of children and adults, he found certain variables that grouped themselves into a clear autonomic factor. For adults, in order of their beta weights, these are: heart period, sublingual temperature, diastolic blood pressure, log conductance change, salivary output, volar forearm conductance, and palmar conductance. Such weighted scores are called autonomic balance ($\bar{A}$) scores, and a lower score indicates sympathetic dominance. $\bar{A}$ scores are found to be normally distributed in resting subjects and increase under parasympathomimetic drugs. For a more complete discussion of autonomic balance and the early Wenger studies, see Sternbach (1966, Chapter 3).

Early studies by Wenger (1948) and Gunderson (1953) showed lower $\bar{A}$ scores for battle fatigue groups and early schizophrenics. A study assessing changes in autonomic balance during oral examinations has been conducted by Smith and Wenger (1965). Eleven graduate students were measured at rest just prior to, and one month before and after their exams. $\bar{A}$ scores significantly decreased at the time of the examinations, all 11 subjects showing the effect. Six of the eight variables in the score were individually significant (decreased salivary output, higher sublingual temperature, shorter heart period, greater systolic and diastolic blood pressure, and less change in log palmar conductance). Although the authors do not report how an index based on equal (or some other) beta weights would have compared to their index, the fact that the two nonsignificant variables have the lowest weights in the $\bar{A}$ score argues for the validity of their weightings.

Goldstein (1964b) subjected 21 female psychiatric patients, defined as anxious by very high scores on the Taylor and Freeman anxiety scales, as well as symptomatology, and 21 nonpatient control subjects to one minute of intense white noise. Skin resistance, respiration, heart rate, blood pressure, and EMG from 7 muscles (frontalis, masseter, right trapezius, biceps, and forearm, and left sternomastoid and gastroenemius) were recorded. All muscle groups except trapezius showed greater increases from rest to noise in the anxious patients than in the nonanxious controls. Systolic blood pressure and respiration rate were higher during rest for the anxious patients than for the nonanxious controls, but showed no differential reaction to noise. Other measures were not significantly related to anxiety level.

Wing (1964) compared 20 anxiety state patients and 20 nonpatient controls, matched for age and sex, during a high-speed color-naming task. The patients tended to be higher on skin conductance and spontaneous activity, pulse rate, and forearm extensor tension during both rest and stress. Change scores, however, were not significant, except in the case of muscle tension, which showed a greater increase for the nonpatient controls. This finding, however, may well be related to the fact that the patient group had higher levels of muscle tension in the prestress period. Initial levels were not partialed out because they failed to correlate with change. An important finding was that the skin conductance level of the control subjects returned to normal following the stress, while that of the anxious group continued to rise. Once again, a recovery period measure shows promise in discriminating groups. In both the Goldstein and Wing studies the presence and absence of anxiety is confounded with the patient-nonpatient status of the subjects. This is unfortunate in that, for example, the psychological meaning of the "experiment" might be quite different for patients and nonpatients.

One of the most systematic series of stress studies is that of the Lazarus group using films (for example, Lazarus et al., 1963; Lazarus & Alfert 1964; Mordkoff, 1964; Speisman et al., 1961; Speisman et al., 1964). Their use of self-report as well as physiological measures, within-subject correlations, and cognitive variables make these studies particularly worthy of our attention (for a recent review see Lazarus & Opton, 1966). They have repeatedly shown that heart rate, skin conductance and other measures reliably follow stress episodes. For example, in the study by Mordkoff (1964), continuous measures of heart rate, skin resistance, respiration, and hand-squeeze pressure were obtained during subincision and circumcision films. The Nowlis Adjective Check List was given before and after, and self-ratings were obtained repeatedly during the film. The results showed that skin resistance level dropped at the stress points of the film (as judged a priori and from subject ratings). Heart rate, a slow response, could not follow the ups and downs of the film as closely, but did reflect the stress. Respiration results were largely nonsignificant, and squeeze-pressure results were called "moderate to good."

Between Subject Intercorrelations

From a survey of the generally consistent literature discussed above, one would expect substantial intercorrelations among the various stress indixes. However, B. Martin (1961), after reviewing the work of Ax (1953), Lewinsohn (1956), Terry (1953), Wenger (1948), and others, was forced to conclude that ". . . intercorrelations among physiological measures obtained under either resting states or under stress tend to be low and frequently insignificant" (p. 245). He points out, however, that few studies had intercorrelated measures under clearly fear-arousing conditions or used change score measures with initial level partialed out (see Lacey, 1956). This conclusion is not substantially modified by subsequent research.

Within-Subject Intercorrelations

That there are individual patterns of autonomic response, which are reproducible over time and across stressors, has been clearly demonstrated by Lacey (for example, Lacey, 1959; Lacey et al., 1953; Lacey et al., 1963), Engel (1960), and others. Related to this is Malmo's (1950) notion of symptom specificity. Subjects seem to differ in their "preferred" mode of response. Mandler, Mandler, Kremen, and Sholiton (1961), for example, found nonsignificant correlations between individual autonomic responses and the Taylor MAS, but, when MAS scores were correlated with each subject's highest autonomic score, the correlation was .60 ($p < .01$). Thus a given subject may show only a small increase in heart rate while giving a strong GSR to stress, and his relative position in a group would be quite different for these two measures. These individual differences could completely wash out *inter*subject correlations, but to the extent that each autonomic response rises and falls with changes in stress, *within*-individual correlations may still be substantial. The Lazarus group (for example, Lazarus et al., 1963; Mordkoff, 1964) have reported substantial intraindividual relationships. Lazarus et al. (1963), for example, report a median intrasubject correlation of +.545 between heart rate and skin conductance within a group of 50 subjects. Schnore (1959) has also strongly advocated the use of within-subject analysis. Although he does not actually report correlations, he does present substantial concordances (Kendall's *W*) among nine physiological variables across four arousal conditions within the same subjects. For level measures the *W*s ranged from .995 to .336, with a median of .801, and were significant for 42 of 43 subjects. The median for change measures was .513. These concordances at least imply substantial within-subject correlations.

Summary of Autonomic and Skeletal Muscle Measures

Many individual autonomic measures seem related to anxiety in that they (1) discriminate between high and low anxious groups under stress, although perhaps not so well at resting levels, and (2) are affected in normal subjects by "anxiety arousing" experimental or real-life situations. Increases in heart rate, systolic blood pressure, skin conductance, GSR, and muscle tension have been associated with subject and experimental anxiety in many studies. Increases in GSR nonspecifics, respiration rate, heart-rate variability, and HCl in stomach have also been associated with anxiety, but with perhaps less certainty.

Differences between high and low anxious groups appear during anticipation, the stress itself, and in a poststress recovery period. The trend of response in stress and subsequent poststress periods may be especially sensitive in distinguishing groups, with the stress response of the normal subjects peaking sooner and recovering more rapidly. There is some indication that anticipating a possibly harmful event without knowing by direct experience what it is like accentuates the degree of autonomic arousal. The generally inconsistent results for measures obtained under "resting" conditions may reflect the fact that "rest" is not a highly controlled situation, and there may be a great deal of variability in subjects' expectations while they are told to wait, or not, before an experiment. Back et al. (1967) report an interesting analysis and research on the "in-between times" part of an experiment when "nothing" is happening. The biochemical results of this study are mentioned in the next section.

The implications of the multiple response studies for anxiety assessment are (1) that the individual's characteristic pattern of autonomic response must be taken into account before degree of anxiety relative to other individuals can be inferred, and (2) that relative changes in different autonomic responses within the same individual tend to be correlated, and each response may have some validity for reflecting anxiety level.

Biochemical Measures

Adrenocortical

For a biochemical introduction to the adrenocortical steroids, see Sourkes (1962). Cortisol (hydrocortisone; 17-OH-CS), the most common in man, has been most widely investigated. A number of studies, particularly by the Grinker-Persky group (for example, Persky, 1962) find adrenocortical hormone levels to be higher in psychiatric patients. Persky (1962) reports that they have repeatedly replicated the findings by Bliss et al. (1956) that patients rated high on anxiety (acutes) show 70 percent greater ($p < .001$) adrenocortical hormone levels than normals, although patients judged calm could not be discriminated from normals. In one study (Persky et al., 1956) both plasma cortisol and urinary 17-hydroxycorticosterone (17-OH-CS) discriminated anxious patients from nonanxious patients, and these differences were maintained over a four-day period. The plasma cortisol measure also reflected rated interview stress. It has been found that anxious subjects lose intravenously administered cortisol from the plasma at a much faster rate (Persky, 1957a), are more responsive to ACTH (Persky, 1957b), and produce more ACTH (Persky, 1962). These facts taken together strongly suggest that production of adrenocortical hormones must be greatly increased in anxiety. Other studies by this group have shown increased plasma hydrocortisone under hypnotically induced anxiety and correlations with Rorschach anxiety indexes (Pure C, F + %) and numerous paper-and-pencil scales, including those of Taylor, Zuckerman, and Baron (Persky, 1962). Fiorica and Muehl (1962) have also found subjects high and low on the Taylor MAS to be discriminated by Plasma 17-OH-CS.

A number of studies have shown that normal subjects show heightened adrenocortical activity under stress. In a study of flying stress Marchbanks (1960) found urinary 17-OH-CS levels (after 10 and 20 hours) to be greater than on a control day. Schwartz and Shields (1956) found excretions of formaldehydrogenic steroids to be greater on the day of an important examination (versus before or after), and subjects that rated themselves low in tension during this stress had significantly lower values. Hormonal changes have also been reported to reflect everyday stresses (Handlon, 1962). Zuckerman et al. (1966) found higher plasma thyrotropin, increased 17-ketosteroids, and a borderline increase in 17-ketogenicsteroids ($p < .10$) in eight hours of social-perceptual deprivation, compared to a social-isolation control group. These differences were accompanied by differences in self-rated anxiety on the Affect Adjective Check List (AACL).

Table 9.1 Effects of Epinephrine and Norepinephrine on the Cardiovascular System

Measure	Epinephrine	Norepinephrine
Cardiac output	+	0 or −
Blood pressure		
Systolic	+	+
Diastolic	0	++
Mean	+	++
Peripheral resistance	−	+
Pulse rate	+	−

[a]Based on presentation by Sourkes, T. L. *Biochemistry of Mental Disease*. New York: Harper and Row, 1962.

Adrenomedullary

The adrenal gland extracts (the catecholamines) have been found to simulate effects caused by stimulation of sympathetic postganglionic nerves. Two of the catecholamines, epinephrine (adrenaline) and norepinephrine (noradrenaline), have been most widely investigated.

Perhaps the obvious first step in seeking an association between the catecholamines and stress is to inject subjects with epinephrine and/or norepinephrine and to note autonomic and experiential effects. Breggin (1964) has reviewed this literature. The effects of epinephrine and norepinephrine on the cardiovascular system seem to be as shown in Table 9–1 (Sourkes, 1962). B. Martin (1961), in a review of six studies, concluded that epinephrine

> "... leads to increased skin conductance, systolic blood pressure, heart rate, cardiac output, forehead temperature, central nervous system stimulation, blood sugar level, and decreased diastolic blood pressure, peripheral vascular resistance, hand temperature, and salivary output" (pp. 237–238).

Other papers also suggest the sympathomimetic capability of epinephrine (Hawkins et al., 1960; Frankenhaeuser et al., 1961; Frankenhaeuser & Järpe, 1962). In the Frankenhaeuser et al. (1961) study norepinephrine was also found to produce subjective and somatic symptoms of "anxiety."

Breggin (1964) has pointed to the importance of the experimental setting in such infusion studies. He believes that the marked anxiety and performance changes found by Basowitz et al. (1955) in response to minimal doses of epinephrine were at least in part because of the presence of a psychiatrist, which reinforced these changes. Schachter (e.g., 1966) presents data demonstrating that self-report and behavioral responses of subjects to these infusions can be effected by the "mood" portrayed by a confederate purportedly given the drug also. Breggin has also suggested, citing Rothballer's (1959) data, that large amounts of epinephrine may produce parasympathetic (feedback) and sedative effects. Frankenhaeuser and Järpe (1963), however, found a progressive increase in response with increased dosages within the range employed (.05, .10, .15, and .20 ug/kg body wt/min.).

In another infusion study, Frankenhaeuser and Järpe (1962) assessed psychophysiological reactions to continuous intravenous infusions of a mixture (1:1) of norepinephrine and epinephrine. Eleven subjects, mostly medical students, were observed under both drug and placebo conditions. It is not specified whether the subjects knew a placebo would be given on one occasion. By using this combined treatment, they found especially marked subjective (self-ratings), overt (particularly tremor and discomfort), and autonomic changes. Four of the subjects reported feeling "as if" they were anxious under the drug; none made this report under the placebo. The dominance of epinephrine was indicated by a decrease in diastolic blood pressure, along with increased systolic blood pressure and heart rate. Catecholamines in the urine were increased under both drug and placebo conditions.

There have also been a number of studies in which catecholamine levels have been used as dependent variables. Several studies, relevant to the hypothesis of Funkenstein et al. (1957), to be discussed later, have found associations between anxiety (passive anticipation) and urinary epinephrine and between anger (aggressive or active states or, more generally, muscular tension) and norepinephrine (for example, Elmadjian, 1959 & Elmadjian et al., 1957, 1958; Silverman et al., 1957). Interesting studies of a quite different nature have found excessive adrenaline in fearful, retreating animals (for example, rabbits) as opposed to aggressive animals (Goodall, 1951). Bloom et al. (1963) found a significant increase in epinephrine in paratroop trainees during jump periods as opposed to night rest and, importantly, also to ground activites. They also found differences between some later jump periods and ground activities for norepinephrine. Zubek and Schutte (1966) found that subjects who "quit" after the second day of a week of perceptual isolation showed a significant increase in urinary epinephrine. Effects for norepinephrine were not significant, nor were overall experimental-control group differences on either measure. Finally, studies that used insolveable tasks (Frankenhaeuser & Patkai, 1964) and that simulated weightlessness (Goodall et al., 1964) as stressors obtained significant increases of urinary epinephrine but not of norepinephrine.

Related Measures

Numerous indirect biochemical measures, usually thought to be related to adrenocortical or adrenomedullary functioning, have been used in stress studies. In an early paper Hoagland (1949) found that a number of stress situations (cold, heat, examinations, a frustrating game, etc.) led to an increased loss of certain blood cells (eosinophils and lymphocytes), much as is the case following injections of adrenocorticotropic hormone (ACTH). Likewise, Schottstaedt et al. (1956) have reported increased renal excretion of fluids and electrolytes in stress. In a recent study Gottschalk et al. (1965) reported that ratings of anxiety, during free association, correlated positively with plasma free fatty acids, but not with a direct measure of adrenocortical function (17-OH-CS). Back, Wilson, Bogdonoff and, Troyer (1967) found the level of plasma free fatty acids (FFA) in the circulating plasma to be affected by conditions associated with a conformity experiment. Subjects with high Social Desirability scores (Crowne & Marlowe, 1964) showed higher levels of FFA than did those with low scores. Increased plasma fibrinolytic activity (Ogston, 1964) and decreased blood eosinophils (Bloom et al., 1963; Dreyfuss, 1956; Persky, 1953) have also been demonstrated as stress concomitants.

In a carefully conducted study, Pitts and McClure (1967) report the experimental induction of anxiety reactions in patients with anxiety neurosis and in normals by the infusion of sodium lactate. A control infusion of glucose in saline solution produced no change in anxiety level. When sodium lactate was accompanied by calcium chloride infusion there was a marked reduction in magnitude of anxiety reaction. The authors suggest that increased lactate production in response to increased epinephrine release is central to the anxiety reaction. The calcium ion in some way inhibits the effect of the lactate ion. A contributing factor, not considered by the authors, is the possibility of enteroceptive conditioning, that is, excessive lactate ions may produce certain primary reactions such as dizziness, tremors, paresthesias, etc., which in turn may serve as conditioned stimuli for additional anxiety responses. It should be noted that the patients gave much stronger reactions than the normals.

A great deal of work has been done with hippuric acid, an index of the liver's detoxifying action. Grinker (1966) has recently reviewed this work. Basowitz et al. (1955) found increased hippuric acid in the urine of paratroop trainees assessed to be anxious by ratings. Grinker (1966) has also reported that level of anxiety and treatment progress are reflected by the speed of excretion of injected hippuric acid by patients. They have even used hippuric acid as a validating criterion in the establishment of a rating system, and these anxiety ratings have been successfully used to predict adrenocortical and cardiovascular responses to stress. There have also been less satisfactory results. For example, Persky (1953) found no difference in parachutists prior to jumps versus neutral periods. Johannsen et al. (1962) report small, although occasionally significant, correlations between hippuric acid excretion, interview ratings, and numerous MMPI-like scales.

It is important to point out the need for stringent dietary and pharmacological controls in biochemical studies, particularly where they involve the comparison of groups. For example, in the well-known study by LaBrosse and Mann (see Pollin, 1962) hippuric acid was found to be related to schizophrenicity. However, an even stronger relationship was found between hippuric acid and coffee intake. When the latter variable was partialed out, the initial relationship vanished.

Biochemical Measures: Summary

Subjects assessed as anxious or subjects made anxious by experimental stress show increased output of adrenocortical hormones, increased urinary epinephrine, and urinary hippuric acid. Experimental injection of both epinephrine and norepinephrine, either separately or simultaneously, can lead to anxiety-like responses of a physiological, behavioral and self-report nature. Infusion of the lactate ion may be an especially powerful way to induce an anxiety reaction. The importance of the situation and the subject's cognitive interpretations in affecting these anxiety-like responses should be recognized.

The Physiological Differentiation of Fear from Other Arousal States

B. Martin (1961) reviewed in detail four experimental studies (Ax, 1953; Funkenstein et al., 1957; Lewinsohn, 1956; Schachter, 1957) which attempted to distinguish fear from anger and pain. In the three studies where fear and anger states were thought to be aroused, diastolic blood pressure increased more in anger than in fear, whereas heart rate increased more in fear. Cardiac output increased, and peripheral resistance decreased, significantly more in fear in the two studies where they were reported. Likewise, both studies that included measures of palmar conductance and respiration rate found a greater increase in these responses for fear than for anger. Martin concluded at that time:

> "In spite of some inconsistencies . . . there does appear to be evidence for distinguishable response patterns that can be tentatively associated with the constructs of fear (anxiety) and anger" (p. 236).

There are important methodological problems in research of this kind, however, that are not easily solved. The general intensity of arousal should be approximately the same for the different conditions, order of presentation should be counterbalanced (it was not in Schachter's study), and independent behavioral and self-report evidence should be obtained to verify the arousal of distinctive emotional states.

Sternbach (1962) recorded the skin resistance, heart and respiration rates, gastric motility, eyeblink rate, and finger-pulse volume of ten children while they watched the film, "Bambi." By analyzing film segments rated by each child as "scary" (agreement among children was low), Sternbach was unable to discern any consistent pattern for fear, nor was he able to differentiate these "scary" parts from the ones rated by the group as happy or sad. The number of subjects in this study was small, and more distinctive manipulations of fearful, happy, and sad conditions are desirable.

Wolf and Wolff (1947) report differential gastric responses associated with anger and anxiety. Acid output, vascularity, and gastric motility decreased in anxiety, but increased in anger.

Funkenstein et al. (1957) suggested on the basis of their own findings, plus the findings of Ax and Schachter, that the physiological reaction accompanying anxiety is epinephrinelike, whereas that for anger is norepinephrinelike. The catecholamine infusion studies presented earlier lend credence to this hypothesis. By dividing their subjects into epinephrinelike and norepinephrinelike responders, Funkenstein et al. found the expected relationship with a rated tendency to respond to stress with anxiety or anger.

Some physiological investigations have attempted even finer distinctions; for example, between anxiety and tension. Diethelm et al. (1949) have defined three types of emotional reaction from psychiatric interviews: (1) tension, characterized by feelings of muscle tautness and a definite effort at control, (2) anxiety, with subjective feelings of uneasiness and apprehension, and (3) "guilt or acute anger." Blood was drawn from these subjects and was used to activate rabbit and frog muscle tissue previously calibrated for electromyographic reaction to acetylcholine, eserine, epinephrine, and norepinephrine. These investigators believed that they could predict the muscle tissue reaction from the interview data, although rater reliabilities were not clearly specified, blindness was not insured, and the data were not treated statistically. An epinephrinelike response was found in anxiety, acetylcholinelike in tension, and norepinephrinelike in guilt and anger. Schottstaedt (1960) also reports that he can distinguish anxiety from tension within subjects. Urine specimens were taken four times a day from five medical residents over a period of years. The subjects kept detailed records of their feelings and diets (an important control), and were asked to characterize their general mood (apprehensive, anxious, tense, etc.) at each collection period. Schottstaedt was able to discriminate anxious periods from tense periods by urinary volume, sodium excretion, and endogenous creatine excretion, all of which increased in anxiety and decreased in tension. Neutral periods and periods in which subjects felt *both* tense and anxious fell in between. There were few significant differences for potassium excretion. Examples of situations that were labeled by the subjects as arousing anxiety were the meeting of a husband's relatives, the first drive in a new car, and a deadline near with no decision. Situations arousing tension were driving in heavy traffic, extra duties, and too many things to do. It is not altogether clear to what extent the distinction between anxiety and tension was defined by the investigators or by the five subjects.

Mason et al. (1961) report, largely on the basis of the study of one monkey, that in predictable situations that involve a noxious stimulus, such as avoidance learning, there is an increase in 17-OH-CS and norepinephrine levels but not an increase in epinephrine level. When noxious stimuli occur in complicated and unpredictable fashion, then levels of epinephrine as well as 17-OH-CS and norepinephrine increase.

An important attempt to differentiate an anxiety-response pattern from other arousal patterns is the factor analytic work of Cattell (for example, Cattell & Scheier, 1961). On the basis of several studies in which change scores on the same subjects were factor analysed, Cattell concluded that anxiety could be differentiated from effort stress. Both factors, however, involved increases in corticosteroid excretion, heart rate, and trapezius muscle tension. Opposite loadings occurred on glutamic acid in urine (high in anxiety, low in effort stress), cholinesterase (low in anxiety, high in effort stress), and hippuric acid (high in anxiety, little change in effort stress). The tables of factor loadings presented by Cattell and Scheier, however, are not very convincing with respect to demonstrating an anxiety factor that is distinctive from other physiological response patterns.

Physiological Differentiation of Fear from Other Arousal States: Summary

Investigators differ as to whether they consider the question of differential patterns of physiological responses associated with different arousal states to be a fruitful one to ask. If one can avoid the dangers inherent in reification of states such as fear (anxiety), anger, etc., then the search for subsystems of functionally related physiological responses that covary with behavioral and self-report measures of fear is worthwhile. Empirically, however, the evidence remains unclear.

Although it seems likely that an epinephrine-like response is associated with fear, it is probably also associated with other arousal conditions and does not provide a distinctive basis for assessing the magnitude of fear.

ASSESSMENT: BEHAVIORAL MEASURES

Disturbances in skeletal-motor activity, speech, perception, memory, learning, and problem solving have been attributed to anxiety. Like physiological responses, behavioral disturbances can be produced in many ways, and every instance of motor tremor, impairment of memory, or learning cannot be interpreted as a manifestation of anxiety. Many of these disturbances are treated in more detail in other chapters, including the consideration of contributing factors other than anxiety. In this section, our discussion will focus on research that implies an association between anxiety and the behavioral disturbance.

We suggest several empirical generalizations at the outset to provide a frame of reference in considering these findings.

1. For strongly dominant response, increasing anxiety results in even greater probability of occurrence of the response. If the initially dominant response is the "correct" response by some task definition, then increasing anxiety results in improvement in the quality of performance. There is some indication, less strongly supported than the above, that responses which are strongly dominant initially suffer some impairment relative to other responses at extreme levels of anxiety.
2. When a "correct" response is only moderately dominant initially, increasing anxiety results in the inverted U function in which quality of performance initially increases with anxiety and then shows marked impairment with further increase in anxiety.
3. When an initially nondominant response is defined as "correct," then increasing anxiety results in even less likelihood of occurrence of this response and, accordingly, a monotonic decrease in quality of performance.

Again, we must emphasize that the behavioral measures described below can be affected by many factors other than anxiety. For example, an increase in incentive value or in the arousal of achievement motivation (based on either hope for success or avoidance of failure) would tend to improve performance in many instances and to affect the empirical generalizations just described. Likewise, subject variables such as intelligence may interact with stress manipulations to effect the extent to which anxiety is aroused.

Motor Disturbance

Buss, Wiener, Durkee, and Baer (1955) found rated restlessness (involving agitation, tremors, and tics) of psychiatric patients in an interview to correlate .66 with an overall anxiety rating and .37 with the Taylor MAS. Sainsbury (1955) likewise found a greater number of gestures during discussion of stressful than of nonstressful topics during a psychiatric interview and cross-validated the finding in a second session. Luria (1932) and Ebaugh (1936) report greater disturbance in hand and finger movements when subjects are presented with emotionally significant words in a word-association test than for words without emotional significance. Malmo and Shagass (1949) and Malmo, Shagass, Belanger, and Smith (1951), by using more sophisticated measurement techniques, found left-hand finger irregularity (movements not synchronous with the task-required movement of the right finger) strongly associated with clinically diagnosed anxiety. See the section on physiological responses in this chapter for a discussion of electromyographic measures of muscle potentials.

Speech

Korobow (1955) measured speech disturbances as a function of three degrees of delayed auditory feedback, and correlated the different types of disturbances with self-report measures obtained immediately after the experiment. Some low but significant correlations suggested that subjects who felt ill at ease, stupid, and jumpy were more inclined to speak softly, briefly, and to omit words and word endings.

Mahl (1956, 1959) and Kasl and Mahl (1965) have systematically studied the relationship between speech disturbance and anxiety. "Ah" as a speech disturbance does not correlate positively with other speech disturbances, nor does it seem to be directly related to anxiety. Other speech disturbances, usually referred to as "non-ah" disturbances, include the following: sentence change, repetition, stutter, omission, sentence incompletion, tongue slips, and intruding incoherent sound. The ratio of all "non-ah" disturbances to total words used has been shown to increase when a patient talks about anxiety-arousing topics in psychotherapy (Mahl, 1959). Assessment of the anxiety relatedness of the topic was done without knowledge of the degree of speech disturbance. In another study (Kasl & Mahl, 1965) the anxiety-arousing content was experimentally manipulated in interviews with normal subjects, and the "non-ah" ratio was found to be significantly higher under anxiety-arousing conditions. Panek and Martin (1959) found increases in both "ahs" and repetitions to be associated with individual GSR's in psychotherapy interviews. Geer (1966a) found a higher "non-ah" ratio, more silences, and a slower rate in the speech of subjects who were expecting to make a public speech in the next few minutes than in a control group.

Speech disturbances are rather complicated in nature, and the findings with respect to them do not provide especially strong evidence for the empirical generalizations previously described. Post hoc, correct speech responses can be viewed as only moderately dominant responses, which is probably true in the case of extemporaneous speech as compared, for example, with a highly memorized and overlearned speech. Increases in anxiety, then, would be expected to lead eventually to a greater frequency of incorrect responses such as sentence change, repetition, sentence incompletion, and tongue slips, as suggested by the second generalization. However, it is also likely that some speech disturbances, especially stuttering and long silences, may reflect responses learned originally as ways of reducing anxiety. Many theories of stuttering, for example, propose that various features of stuttering are learned on the basis of anxiety reduction. See Barbara (1959) and Chapter 13 of this boook for a discussion of the role of anxiety in stuttering.

Perceptual-motor

Davis (1949), by using perceptual-motor tracking tasks similar to the tasks required of airplane pilots, found that neurotics generally performed more poorly than normals. Individuals suffering from anxiety reactions made more overactive and extensive responses than normals, but hysterics showed the opposite, making more underactive responses with long reaction times than did normals. Beier (1951) found subjects to take longer and make more errors in mirror drawing under experimental threat than under nonthreatening conditions. Threat was introduced by implying that the subject was neurotic on the basis of Rorschach responses. Wechsler and Hartogs (1945) found anxious patients to perform more poorly than normals on mirror tracing.

Stennett (1957) independently assessed activation or drive level by skin conductance and muscle potentials, and found quality of performance on a tracking task to increase at first as experimental stress increased, and then to decrease under more extreme stress (large bonus for accurate performance, threat of shock if not performed adequately).

Mandler and Sarason (1952) found high anxiety subjects (Test Anxiety Scale) performed better than low anxiety subjects on the Kohs Block Design Test under neutral conditions. Under both failure and stress conditions the reverse was true. Ryan and Lakie (1965) report a similar result for a ring-peg task done via mirror images.

When incorrect responses are initially dominant, as in mirror tracing, an increase in subject or situational anxiety produces impairment in performance. Some of the increase in adequacy of performance in the unselected normal sample of Stennett or in low anxiety groups (subject defined) in the Mandler and Sarason studies is probably because of increase in incentive or achievement motivation arousal.

Perception

Postman and Bruner (1948) reported impairment in the tachistoscopic perception of three-word sentences under failure stress. Moffitt and Stagner (1956) found increased perceptual closure (identifying incomplete figure as complete under tachistoscopically shortened presentations) under the same kind of experimental threat that Beier used, implying that subjects were neurotic. Korchin and Basowitz (1954) also found greater perceptual closure tendencies for paratroop trainees in the morning before a scheduled jump than in the evening following the jump. Trainees with high levels of hippuric acid in their urine showed greater impairment than the trainees with low levels.

Since all measures of perception depend on some kind of response, it is impossible to know with certainty whether the subject actually fails to "see" the stimulus accurately, or whether the failure occurs in the response system. However, this distinction in interpretation can be converged on, and Eriksen and Wechsler (1955) made an ingenious attempt to separate the effects of anxiety on response processes as opposed to sensory discrimination. In their study, shock-induced anxiety resulted in restricted and stereotyped response preferences, but did not impair sensory discrimination.

In studies that used group comparisons, Angyal (1948) found more impairment in the recognition of patterns of letters under brief exposure conditions in high anxiety patients than in other types of patients. Krugman (1947) and Goldstone (1955) found the threshold for flicker-fusion to occur at a lower frequency for anxious than for nonanxious subjects. See Granger (1961), however, for a discussion of the many variables that affect flicker-fusion thresholds.

To summarize, when conditions are such that accurate perceptual discrimination is difficult, that is, when incorrect competing perceptions are relatively strong, anxiety tends to produce impairment.

Stimulus Generalization

The above studies suggest that difficult perceptual discriminations are impaired for anxious subjects, and it would seem reasonable to conclude from this finding that anxious subjects should show flatter stimulus generalization gradients than should nonanxious subjects. Rosenbaum (1956) did find greater generalization (by using rectangles of varying height as stimuli) for clinically anxious patients when they were under the threat of shock than when they were not so threatened. Wenar (1954), by using a switch-pressing response, reported high anxiety subjects (Taylor MAS) to show flatter temporal generalization gradients than low anxiety subjects. Arnhoff (1959), Buss (1955), Fager, and Knopf (1958), and S. A. Mednick (1957) failed, however, to find a relationship between stimulus generalization and subject anxiety as measured by the Taylor MAS. Martha T. Mednick (1957) did find a high anxiety group to show more verbally mediated GSR generalization than a low anxiety group (Forced-Choice Taylor MAS) but, unfortunately, her anxiety groups were badly confounded with different sex proportions. Buss and Buss (1966) used words with anxiety meanings (worried, startled, fearful, etc.) as stimuli and did not find increased stimulus generalization under shock-induced threat. Broen, Storms, and Goldberg (1963) and Broen and Storms (1964), however, in several carefully performed studies, did find flattened stimulus generalization curves under hand dynamometer induced increases in drive levels. If anxiety is associated with generally higher levels of drive, then these studies of Broen and his colleagues indirectly support the hypothesis of flatter stimulus generalization gradients under high anxiety.

The relationship between anxiety and stimulus generalization is not clear. It would probably be premature to accept the null hypothesis that there is no relatioship at this time. The Taylor MAS does not have high validity as a measure of anxiety (see the section on self-report measures), and stimulus generalization studies with humans require careful attention to procedural details.

Memory

Impairment in immediate memory, as measured by digit span, has been shown to be associated with failure-criticism stress (Moldawsky and Moldawsky, 1952), with paratroop trainees compared to a control group (Basowitz, Persky, Korchin & Grinker, 1955), and in patients confronted with the threat of surgery (Wright, 1954). The Moldawsky and Moldawsky study is especially informative because subjects were also given a vocabulary test that was found not to be affected by the failure-criticism stress. Lucas (1952) found an interaction between subject anxiety (Taylor MAS) and experimental stress (failure-criticism). High anxious subjects showed more impairment under stress on memory for a list of consonants than low anxious subjects, but under a nonstress condition there was a slight superiority for the high anxiety group. Kaye, Kirschner, and Mandler (1953) also found high anxious subjects (Test Anxiety Scale) to have shorter memory span than low anxious subjects.

Immediate memory for new material such as a particular sequence of digits or consonants can be readily viewed as a task in which the correct response is weak, relative to numerous, almost equally strong, competing responses. It is not possible in any of these "memory" experiments to rule out the possibility that the impairment resulted from lack of attention or poor "learning" of the response, rather than from more rapid forgetting. Easterbrook (1959), in fact, proposed that most impairing effects of stress or emotion might be thought of in terms of the restricted range of relevant cues to which the subject attends.

Learning

Simple Conditioning

This heading refers only to studies in which a single response is being learned to a single stimulus. Spence (1964) surveyed the literature and reported that, in some 25 independent comparisons, it was found in all but four instances that high anxiety subjects, selected by the Taylor MAS, showed greater ease of eyelid conditioning than did low anxiety subjects. When anxiety has been experimentally aroused in the form of instructions to expect increasing strengths of the UCS (air puff) or by the use of shock or the threat of shock, the experimental groups showed higher levels of eyelid conditioning (Spence, 1958; Spence, Farber, & Taylor, 1954; Spence & Goldstein, 1961).

Facilitation of simple GSR conditioning has also been found to be associated with situational anxiety (Beam, 1955) and with clinically assessed anxiety (Bitterman & Holtzman, 1952; Welsh & Kubis, 1947).

These results are consistent with the generalization that, when the correct response is strongly dominant, increases in anxiety will further enchance the relative strength of the correct response. Taylor and Spence (1966) also report two studies of eyelid conditioning in which performance of high and low anxiety subjects diverge as conditioning proceeds, with high anxious subjects getting progressively better. This is to be expected from the point of view of Spence-Taylor theory in which response strength is a multiplicative function of habit and strength and drive (anxiety in this case). Any increases in habit strength as a result of conditioning trials are multiplied by a higher drive factor in the high anxiety group.

Complex Learning

Studies that use serial verbal or spatial mazes with two response alternatives (right or left) being presented at each choice point have generally shown that high anxiety subjects (Taylor MAS) make more errors than do low anxiety subjects (Axelrod, Cowen, & Heilizer, 1956; Farber & Spence, 1953; Matarazzo, Ulett, & Saslow, 1955; Taylor & Spence, 1952). In most of these studies a tendency was observed for high anxiety subjects to make proportionately more errors at "difficult" choice points (empirically determined) than at "easy" choice points. Hughes, Sprague, and Bendig (1954), and Katahn (1966) did not find poorer performance by high anxiety subjects on verbal mazes. Katahn, in fact, found that, among the subjects who were above the median on a Mathematical Aptitude Test, the high anxiety subjects performed better than the low anxiety subjects.

Other studies have used the more traditional serial-learning procedure in which the subject is presented with successive items and is required to anticipate the next item on the list. On a serial-learning task, Beam (1955) found more errors under real-life stress, and Malmo and Amsel (1948) found anxious patients to make more errors than normals. Montague (1953) found high anxious subjects (Taylor MAS) to perform better than low anxious subjects when intra-list similarity of nonsense syllables was low, but found low anxious subjects to be superior to high anxious subjects when intra-list similarity was high. He assumed that competition by incorrect responses was lower with low intra-list similarity. Saltz and Hoehn (1957) attempted to manipulate task difficulty independently of the number of incorrect competing responses, and they found an interaction between anxiety level (Taylor MAS) and task difficulty, but did not find a relationship between anxiety level and the degree of incorrect competing responses. See Taylor (1958), however, for a critical evaluation of the Saltz and Hoehn study.

In four separate studies that used serial

lists of nonsense syllables Nicholson (1958), Sarason (1956, 1957a, and 1957b) an interaction was found between subject anxiety (Taylor MAS) and experimental stress (neutral versus "ego oriented" instructions or failure-criticism). High anxiety subjects show relatively greater impairment in performance as stress increases than do low anxiety subjects, who sometimes show improvement under increasing stress. Sarason and Harmatz (1965) found similar results by using a Test Anxiety Scale and high school students as subjects. When stress is introduced by electric shock or threat of shock, this interaction has not been generally found (Silverman & Blitz, 1956; Deese, Lazarus, & Keenan, 1953; Lazarus, Deese, & Hamilton, 1954). These latter studies also differ from the previous studies in that avoidance and nonavoidance conditions were employed.

Studies that use paired associate learning provide the strongest, least equivocal evidence for the contribution of incorrect competing responses to the impairment of performance in anxious subjects. Lists have been prepared to minimize incorrect competing responses by selecting words for which there is a strong initial association between each stimulus and response pair (for example, barren-fruitless) and for which there are relatively weak associations among the different stimulus words or among the different response words. High anxiety subjects (Taylor MAS) have shown superior performance on these lists to low anxiety subjects (Spence, Farber, & McFann, 1956; Spence, Taylor, & Ketchel, 1956). There was a tendency, however, in both of these studies for the high anxiety group to show a decrement in performance near the end of the learning trials. Broen and Storms (1961) use the concept of response-strength ceiling to account for this decrement. Their argument is to the effect that response strength can reach a ceiling level by either increasing drive or, in this case, by increasing associative strength and that, when it does reach the ceiling, the correct response begins to lose its competitive advantage over incorrect responses, which may continue to increase in associative strength.

Paired-associate lists have also been devised that increase the strength of incorrect competing responses relative to the correct response. This has been done by creating some S-R pairs that have high initial associative connections (for example, tranquil-placid) and by creating others that have low associative connections. In the latter pairs, stimulus words are used that are similar in meaning to a stimulus word used in high-association pairs (for example, serene-headstrong). It is assumed that an incorrect response would be initially dominant over the correct response in such a pair. Studies have shown (Ramond, 1953; Spence, Farber, & McFann, 1956; Spence, Taylor, & Ketchel, 1956) that high anxiety subjects (Taylor MAS) are inferior in performance to low anxiety subjects on these "competitive" pairs *on the initial learning trials*. Standish and Champion (1960), by using somewhat different procedures, found similar results.

Katahn (1964) and Katahn and Lyda (1966), by using a different format than the usual paired-associate procedure, had subjects first learn a highly dominant response word to a stimulus word, and then the *same* subjects learned a nondominant response to the same stimulus word. High anxious subjects (Taylor MAS) learned the dominant response more readily than low anxious subjects; the reverse was true for the subsequent nondominant response. Castaneda and Palermo (1955) experimentally manipulated associative strengths by varying periods of prior practice with paired associates that involved five colored lights as stimuli and five buttons for responses. Stress was also introduced experimentally in the form of speed instructions for half the subjects. They found stress tended to impair performance when the dominant response was incorrect and to facilitate performance when the dominant response was correct.

Another kind of finding that emphasizes the role of the incorrect competing responses involves paired-associate lists in which each S-R pair is isolated as much as possible from all others by minimizing associative connections between S-R pairs as well as within the list of stimulus and response words. All associations, correct and incorrect, should initially be weak but, as learning progresses, the correct response should gradually become dominant, and the influence of incorrect competing responses should become less. Three separate studies (Spence, 1958; Taylor, 1958; Taylor & Chapman, 1955) have found high anxiety subjects (Taylor MAS) to perform about the same as low anxiety subjects in the early stages of learning, but have found high anxiety subjects to gradually become superior as learning progresses. Kamin and Fedorchak (1957) used a similar list and did not confirm this finding.

When stress is introduced in paired-associate learning by failure (Gordon and Berlyne, 1954) or by immediate versus delayed intertrial spacing (Korchin and Levine, 1957), the interaction of subject anxiety by experimental stress is found, with the high anxious subjects showing the greater decrement in performance with increasing stress. In the Korchin and Levine study this interaction existed for the comparison between psychiatric patients with anxiety symptoms versus normals, but not for the comparison between normal groups divided on the basis of the Taylor MAS. Again, when shock is used as the stressor in paired-associate learning, this interaction did not occur (Besch, 1959).

The Digit-Symbol-Substitution type task is a variant of the paired-associate learning task in which new and rather unfamiliar symbols (stimuli such as the following: Λ, L, Γ, ⊥) must be learned as responses to specific digits. It is not a "pure" paired-associate task, since performance depends to some extent on the perceptual-motor acts involved in looking back at the code key and in writing the correct response. This task is usually performed under time pressure, and it is clear that the incorrect responses are initially more numerous and, at least, equally strong as correct responses. It has been found to be quite sensitive to the effects of anxiety (Geer, 1966, S. B. Sarason, Mandler, & Craighill, 1952; I. G. Sarason, & Palola, 1960; Westrope, 1953).

Other tasks that have also been found to be affected by anxiety are the following: motor learning in children (Castaneda, 1961; Castaneda, Palermo, & McCandless, 1956), complex verbal coding task (Katchmar, Ross, & Andrews, 1958) difficult anagrams task (I. G. Sarason, 1961) and incidental learning (Aborn, 1953).

We have not dealt extensively with theory in this section. The Spence-Taylor "drive" theory, with its fundamental assumption that response strength is a multiplicative function of habit strength and drive, accounts moderately well for certain features of these results. The concept of response-strength ceiling elaborated by Broen and Storms (1961) is a plausible addition to the assumptions of Spence and Taylor which helps to account for the fact that increases in drive sometimes result in a relative decrease in occurrence of a response that was only moderately dominant at the low-drive levels. The drive theories of Spence and Taylor, and Broen and Storms, of course, apply to any kind of drive and are not limited to drive associated with anxiety. An increase in general activation level is a likely accompaniment of the anxiety response as we conceptualize it and, accordingly, these drive theories are quite relevant.

Other factors have also been emphasized as contributing to the empirically observed effects of anxiety. Anxious subjects have undoubtedly learned to make responses under high stress or threat conditions that differ from the responses made by low anxiety subjects under similar conditions. These responses may be elicited by cues associated with the internal anxiety state itself or by cues in the external situation. The high anxious subject, for example, may have intruding thoughts about fear of failure, wishes to flee, etc., that would seriously interfere with "correct" performance. Child (1954) and Sarason, Mandler and Craighill (1952) have stressed these interfering responses in their interpretations of the effects of anxiety.

Behavioral Measures: Summary and Conclusions

Subject-defined and situationally induced anxiety have been shown to affect performance in many areas: motor activity, speech, perceptual-motor, perception, memory, and simple and complex learning. Results for stimulus generalization are less clear. The findings concerning the paired-associate procedure are most convincing with respect to the empirical generalizations proposed at the beginning of this section. The paired-associate procedure lends itself well to the experimental manipulation or control of associative strength between individual stimulus-response pairs, and relative dominance of "correct" and "incorrect" responses, thus, can be varied or controlled. Also, these generalizations are supported most strongly when anxiety is introduced experimentally by failure-criticism. Results for shock-induced anxiety are inconsistent.

To summarize, studies indicate the following.

1. For strongly dominant responses, increasing anxiety results in even greater probability of occurrence of the response.

2. When a correct response is only moderately dominant, increasing anxiety results in the inverted U function in which quality of performance initially increases with anxiety and then shows impairment with further increase in anxiety.

3. When a "correct" response is non-dominant, that is, "incorrect" responses are dominant, then increasing anxiety results in even less likelihood of occurrence of the "correct" response and, accordingly, it yields a monotonic decrease in quality of performance.

ASSESSMENT: SELF-REPORT MEASURES

Self-Report Measures: Commonly Used Scales

Self-report measures include reports by the subject about his physiological or behavioral responses that might be measured independently by another observer as well as reports about subjective states that cannot be independently measured by another observer. An example of the former would be, "My heart beats rapidly," and an example of the latter would be, "I feel like I am going to pieces."

The most widely used paper-and-pencil self-report scales that have been considered to be measures of anxiety in adults are the Taylor Manifest Anxiety Scale (1953), the Pt Scale, the Welsh Anxiety Index, and the Winne Neuroticism Scale from the MMPI (Welsh, 1952; Winne, 1951), the IPAT Adult Anxiety Scale (Cattell, 1957), the Eight-Parallel-Form Anxiety Battery (Scheier and Cattell, 1960), and the Neuroticism Scale of the Maudsley Personality Inventory (Eysenck, 1959). These scales correlate highly with one another. For example, the IPAT Adult Anxiety Scale has been found to correlate about .80 with the Taylor Anxiety Scale (Bendig, 1959; Cattell & Scheier, 1961), .77 with the Neuroticism Scale of the Maudsley Personality Inventory (Bendig, 1959), and about .80 with the Pt Scale of the MMPI (Karson & Pool, 1957). Likewise, in three separate studies, the Taylor MAS has been found to correlate .92, .81, and .72 with the Pt Scale of the MMPI (Eriksen & Davids, 1955; Deese, Lazarus, & Keenan, 1953; Eriksen, 1954), and in two separate studies to correlate .77 and .80 with the Neuroticism Scale of the Maudsley Personality Inventory (Bendig, 1959; Spence & Spence, 1964). Not all studies yield correlations of these magnitudes, but the evidence strongly suggests that these various self-report measures intercorrelate with each other about as highly as their reliabilities permit, and that they are interchangeable for most purposes.

Inspection of the items in these scales suggests that they are primarily measuring reports of worry, difficulty in concentrating, apprehension, taking things hard, restlessness, and feelings of personal inadequacy. Some of the scales, especially the Taylor MAS, also have items that refer to somatic disturbance such as blushing, sweating, rapid heart rates, gastrointestinal upsets etc. These items do not seem to contribute consistently to the main variance (Siegman, 1956), and usually they come out as separate factors in factor analytic studies (O'Connor, Lorr, & Stafford, 1956). Hamilton (1959) and Buss (1962) also confirm this separation of specific autonomic components from the more general cognitive and affective components of anxiety when self-report data obtained by interview is factor analysed. However, self-reports of high muscular tension, tended to be associated with the cognitive-affective factor rather than with the autonomic factor in both of these studies. Hamilton's study (1959) was limited to anxiety neurotics, and the following symptom clusters describe the two ends of the obtained bipolar factor: muscular tension, fears, insomnia, apprehension, and difficulty in concentrating versus gastro-intestinal, genito-urinary, respiratory, and cardiovascular complaints.

Costello and Comrey (1967) have developed separate self-report scales for anxiety and depression that would seem to represent an improvement on the above mentioned scales. The scales intercorrelate about .50, which perhaps reflects the real level of correlation between these variables. The anxiety scale is found to be more highly related to diagnosed anxiety than to diagnosed depression, and the depression scale more highly related to diagnosed depression than anxiety.

Anxiety in children has also been assessed by paper-and-pencil self-report tests; for example, the Childrens Manifest Anxiety Scale, CMAS (Castaneda, Palermo, & McCandless, 1956), and the General Anxiety Scale for Children, GASC (Sarason, Davidson, Lighthall, Waite, & Ruebush, 1960). These scales are similar in construction to the adult anxiety scales. The CMAS, in fact, is almost identical to the adult Taylor MAS except for the exclusion of a few items and some item rewording.

Validity Considerations

The validity of self-report measures must be determined by their relation to behavioral and physiological measures. This relationship will be attenuated by the fact that there is no simple, unitary behavioral-physiological response associated with anxiety, as well as by any inherent lack of validity in the self-report measure itself.

These self-report measures discriminate quite well between patient groups diagnosed as neurotic and matched normal control groups (Eysenck, 1961; Matarazzo, Guze, & Matarazzo, 1955). The association of these measures with different degrees of rated behavioral manifestations of anxiety *within* groups of neurotic patients is frequently better than chance, but on an absolute basis very low. Buss, Weiner, Durkee, and Baer (1955) report Taylor MAS correlations of .16 with rated distractability, and .37 with rated restlessness within a sample of psychiatric patients, and Sainsbury (1964) reports a correlation of .47 between number of movements while sitting alone and the Taylor MAS. Kendall (1954) had nurses rate tuberculosis patients on various behavioral indixes of anxiety (probably confounded to some extent with self-report information), and he found a nonsignificant difference on mean anxiety ratings between groups representing the upper and lower 27 percent of the Taylor MAS distribution. When groups based on the upper and lower 13 percent of the distribution were compared, the difference was significant, $p < .01$. Gleser and Ulett (1952) and Lauterbach (1958) likewise report low but significant relationships between Taylor MAS and rated anxiety.

The obtained relationships of the Taylor MAS to classical aversive conditioning (primarily eyeblink conditioning) and to complex learning phenomena, described previously, provide some support for the validity of this scale. It should be borne in mind, however, that most of these studies emphasized the construct of drive or activation in predicting and in accounting for the results. Also, the relationships obtained were very weak, usually based on comparisons between extreme groups selected by the Taylor MAS. Correlations of 25 or less between the Taylor MAS and the corresponding behavioral measure would probably account for most of the results.

The relationship of these self-report measures to physiological measures is also weak at best. There are occasional instances of significant relationships; for example, Becker and Matteson (1961) found high anxious subjects (IPAT Anxiety Scale) to have higher initial skin conductance and to show more rapid GSR conditioning, with initial level partialed out, than low anxious subjects. Rossi (1959) found a significant correlation between muscle action potentials and the Taylor MAS, and Fiorica and Muehl (1962) found a relation between plasma 17-OH-CS and the Taylor MAS. Most published researches, however, report nonsignificant relationships between this type of self-report scale and autonomic measures. This has been especially true for various skin conductance and palmar sweat measures (Beam, 1955; Burdick, 1966; Calvin, McGuigan, Tyrrell, & Soyars, 1956; Endler, Hunt, & Rosenstein, 1962; Katkin, 1965; Lotsof & Downing, 1956; Martin, 1959; and Silverman, 1957). Heart-rate measures are not usually associated with the Taylor MAS (for example, Hodges & Spielberger, 1966).

There are two important exceptions to these generally negative studies. Mandler, Mandler, Kremen and Sholitan (1961) found nonsignificant correlations between the Taylor MAS and 11 *individual* autonomic measures, but determined a correlation of .60 ($p < .01$) when each subject's highest autonomic response was used. Opton and Lazarus (1967) found no differences on self-report items in high- and low-autonomic responders (heart-rate and skin conductance) to a film showing bloody shop accidents or to shock threat. When subjects were divided into those showing higher autonomic response to the film than to shock threat (an ipsative comparison based on each subject's responses), then the high responders to the film were found by empirical item analysis of self-report items to be lacking in impulse expression, socially inhibited, introverted, submissive, insecure, passive, and anxious. These findings parallel the ones reported on page 224 where within subject comparisons of autonomic response were reported to yield higher intercorrelations among autonomic measures than between subject comparisons.

Summary Evaluation of these Commonly Used Scales

It is probably a misnomer to label these scales as measures of anxiety as we are using this term. The "face validity" of the items employed in these scales certainly suggests something broader than a persistent, intense fear response as indicated, for example, by the following items taken from the IPAT Adult Anxiety Scale (Cattell & Scheier, 1961):

> "If I had my life to live over again I would (a) *plan very differently*, (b) in-between, (c) want it the same; In discussion with some people, I get so annoyed that I can hardly trust myself to speak (a) *sometimes*, (b) rarely, (c) never; Most people are a little queer mentally though they do not like to admit it (a) *true*, (b) uncertain, (c) false."

In general items on these scales reflect not only fearfulness but other affect states such as depression and anger, somatic symptoms, ways of coping with unpleasant affect states, and attitudes and beliefs. A broader term such as neuroticism might well be a more appropriate label for what these scales measure.

The generally low relationships found between these scales and behavioral measures and the generally nonsignificant relationships found with physiological measures also argue against the validity of these scales as measures of anxiety. In view of the poor showing of the above scales, the authors urge serious attention to the following considerations for improving the validity of self-report anxiety scales.

Self-Report Measures: Factors that Improve Validity

Time Interval

First, the time interval over which anxiety level is reported should be specified; for example, during the last six months, during the last three years, or today. It would be necessary to reword items as well as to include the time interval in the introductory instructions. Not much systematic research has been done on the effects of time-interval manipulation, but a few studies suggest that it may be an important variable. (Bergs & Martin, 1961; Martin, 1959; Zuckerman, 1960).

We propose that the distinction between trait and state anxiety proposed by Cattell and Scheier (1961) is basically a time-interval distinction. State or momentary anxiety level refers to anxiety assessed during a brief time interval and trait anxiety refers to a kind of average that is estimated over a long-time interval. Measures that may be relatively valid for long time-interval assessment (trait) may not be especially valid for short time-interval (state) assessment and, likewise, may not be especially valid as measures of change in anxiety level. Any measure of change must involve some kind of time-interval specification, preferably an explicit specification, although this is not always the case.

Some of the most interesting research coming from Cattell's laboratory is the research that involves "state" anxiety in which either many repeated self-report, behavioral, and physiological measures are obtained on the same individual (P technique), or the same measures are obtained at two different times for a fairly large sample of individuals (incremental-R technique). Both procedures yield factors representing co-varying clusters of change scores. For example, Cattell and Scheier (1958), by using the incremental-R technique, found the following measures to load on a factor interpreted as "state" anxiety: anxiety-tension checklist (self-report), .41; questionnaire measure of "ergic tension" (self-report), .40; less confidence in assuming skill in untried performance (self-report), .35; predominance of short-term goals (self-report), .32; less persistence in unrewarding situations (self-report), .31; higher systolic pulse pressure (physiological), .30; and lower mean handwriting pressure (behavioral), .30. If a strong case can be made for identifying factors of this kind with anxiety, then the measures involved should have good validity for measuring change.

Situation

Specification of the situation is a second important consideration. It is only common sense to expect that a person may be consistently anxious in some situations but not in others. The Test Anxiety Scale developed by Sarason and Mandler, and Craighill (1952) and the Test Anxiety Scale for Children (Sarason, S. B. et al., 1960) represent attempts to specify the situation (in this case academic examinations) with respect to which the individual is asked to report his anxiety. The series of studies that involve these two scales suggest that both are moderately valid as measures of anxiety tendencies in this class of situations.

The most systematic and sophisticated attempt to take situation variables into account in constructing an anxiety scale has been made by Endler, Hunt, and Rosenstein (1962). The scale is referred to as an "S-R Inventory of Anxiousness" and systematically asks for self-reports about 14 different kinds of responses in each of 11 different situations. Examples of situations included are: going to meet a new date, getting up to give a speech before a large group, entering a final examination in an important course, and crawling along a ledge high on a mountain side. The importance of the situation in measuring anxiety is shown by the finding of these authors that variance attributable to situations was 11 times that attributable to individual differences among subjects. The relative contribution of situations to variance, of course, can be readily manipulated by the range of situations included in the test. Nevertheless, these results show that a reasonable sampling of situations contributes enormously to the variance. Endler et al. factor analysed their situations correlation matrix and found that these situations clustered into two main factors—one representing interpersonal situations and one representing inanimate or bodily harm situations.

Another example of a self-report measure that systematically includes the situation is the Fear Survey Schedule (Geer, 1965). The subject rates himself on how fearful he is with respect to each of a long list of objects or situations. It has been used successfully as a selection instrument in studies of snake phobia (Lang & Lazovik, 1963), and to differentially predict magnitude of GSR to photographs of spiders and snakes (Geer, 1966).

Studies that have used a simple rating scale of fear applied to a specific situation *and* a specific time are able to obtain moderately valid measures, as indicated by correlation with other concurrent measures or by sensitivity to experimental manipulation. Lang and Lazovik (1963), for example, used such a rating scale to measure fear of a snake, and Basowitz, Persky, Korchin, and Grinker (1955), and Walk (1956) used a similar scale to measure fear in paratroop trainees. The Anxiety Scale of the Zuckerman (1960) Affect Adjective Check List, when applied to a specific time and situation, has been shown to be related to the number of GSR non-specifics in a recovery period that followed the threat of shock (Katkin, 1966), and to imminence of academic examinations (Winter, Ferreira, & Ransom, 1963; Zuckerman, 1960; Zuckerman & Biase, 1962). It should be mentioned, however, that in the Winter et al. study the AACL did not correlate with the Palmar Sweat Index. More recently, Zuckerman, Lubin, Vogel, and Valerius (1964) reported the AACL to reflect film-induced anxiety and the threat of an examination. The same manipulations also affected a newly added scale of depression and, in the case of the threat of examination, a newly added scale of hostility.

Response Sampling

A third consideration in self-report anxiety measurement is the sampling of responses. These responses can range from adjectives, phrases, or sentences, describing subjective emotional or cognitive states, to specific autonomic responses or somatic symptoms. As we mentioned previously, Endler et al. (1962) included 14 kinds of responses in their S-R Inventory. They factor analysed their interresponse correlation matrix and obtained one large general factor that included both subjective feeling and somatic symptoms that they labeled "distress." There were also two smaller factors labeled, respectively, "exhilaration" and "autonomic." The latter was determined almost entirely by need to urinate frequently, loose bowels, and experiencing nausea so that "autonomic" may be too broad a term. These results are somewhat different from the results of O'Connor, Lorr, and Stafford (1956), Buss (1962), and Hamilton (1959), which were described previously in this chapter.

Systematic inclusion of a variety of responses in the development of self-report measures will permit investigators to take individual response tendencies into account in the self-report system, as did Mandler et al. (1961) in the autonomic system. This would be especially useful in measures of change where, for example, responses that showed the strongest tendency to reflect an initial stress reaction for a given individual, for instance, to a public speaking experience, would be used to measure change in degree of reaction after a "treatment" experience. Matched subject controls, of course, would be necessary.

Response Bias

A fourth consideration in self-report anxiety measurement is that of response bias. Acquiescence, the simple tendency to answer "yes" to an item without regard to the meaning of the item, is probably not a major source of error (Rorer, 1965). Defensiveness or the tendency to answer in a socially desirable manner probably *is* an important source of bias. Epstein (1962), for example, found verbal indications of fear in stories told to pictures highly relevant to parachute jumping to decrease on the day of a jump while GSR and other indications of fear increased. Likewise, Lazarus and Alfert (1964) found that subjects who were high on the personality trait of denial (repressive personality), as measured by various MMPI scales, did indeed verbally deny affect arousal under film-induced threat, but that they showed greater heart-rate and skin-conductance arousal than subjects who were low on the trait of denial.

There have been several attempts to reduce social desirability variance in anxiety measures by using a forced-choice format (Bergs & Martin, 1961; Heineman, 1953; Martin, 1959). The evidence is not clear regarding the extent to which the forced-choice format actually improves validity. One reason that the forced-choice measures have not been used more frequently is that they take much longer to administer. Many investigators have tried to reduce the effects of defensiveness on the Taylor MAS by eliminating subjects that score high on the MMPI Lie Scale. The validity of the Lie Scale for this purpose has not been established to the present writers' knowledge. The Defensiveness Scale for Children was developed by Sarason et al. (1960) to be used in conjunction with the Test Anxiety Scale for Children, and it would seem to improve the validity of the latter (Zimbardo, Barnard, & Berkowitz, 1963). The opposite of defensiveness, saying that one is more anxious than one really is, can be a source of error also. Lang (for example, Lang & Lazovik, 1963) after initially selecting phobic subjects by the Fear Survey Schedule routinely interviews them to eliminate subjects who have inappropriately responded highly.

Self-Report Measures: Summary and Conclusions

Most commonly used "anxiety" scales such as the Taylor MAS, the IPAT Anxiety Scale, and the MMPI Pt Scale intercorrelate highly and, to a large extent, are measuring the same thing. These scales do not correlate highly with behavioral manifestations of anxiety, and frequently do not correlate at all with physiological measures. These scales should probably be considered as tapping a more general neuroticism or maladjustment dimension, with anxiety contributing a relatively small proportion of the variance. The validity of self-report anxiety measurement has been improved to some extent and can be further improved by taking into account the following factors.

1. The time interval being assessed
2. The specification of the situation
3. The responses sampled
4. Response biases

MODIFICATION OF ANXIETY

Psychological Procedures

Ideally, we would like to present results from studies in which (a) anxiety was objectively assessed pre- and post-treatment; (b) the treatment procedures were objectively specified; and (c) there was random assignment of subjects to various experimental and control conditions. Unfortunately, these restrictions narrow the available studies to a small number, indeed; hence, we must depart somewhat from this ideal in our selection of studies.

Traditional Interview Psychotherapy

A few studies in which traditional psychotherapeutic methods, largely lacking in operational specification, have been used found changes in self-report anxiety scales of the type previously discussed. Schofield (1953) found several MMPI scales, including *Pt*, to be significantly reduced by outpatient psychotherapy, and Gallagher (1953) found a significant decrease in Taylor MAS scores with client-centered therapy, but there was no control group. The research reported by Rogers and Dymond (1954) and Shlien (1964) might be relevant in that the significant decrease in self-ideal discrepancy on the *Q*-sort procedure for their client-centered and Adlerian treatment, as compared with a "waiting list" control group, is probably tapping the same neuroticism dimension as the Taylor MAS type measure. Since we consider anxiety to be only a small part of the variance measured by scales such as the Taylor MAS, these researches, who use traditional interview-type procedures, do not shed much light on the question of anxiety modification.

Martin, Lundy, and Lewin (1960) in a five-session experimental psychotherapy study manipulated three degrees of "communicative feedback" in groups that experienced (1) traditional interview psychotherapy of a client-centered orientation, (2) talked to a therapist who attended and listened but did not respond verbally, and (3) talked to a tape recorder with no therapist present. Pre- and post-measures were also obtained on a fourth (no-treatment) group. This study was primarily concerned with within-therapy processes, but a forced-choice adjective checklist measure of anxiety, which included time-interval specification, was given before and after treatment. The traditional and nonverbal therapist groups both showed significantly greater decreases in self-reported anxiety than did the no-treatment control group. The tape-recorder group fell in between and was not significantly different from any other group. The subjects in this study, however, were not clinic patients, but college students who were selected on the basis of (1) high Forced-Choice Taylor MAS scores, (2) presence of at least moderate psychological disturbance assessed by an interview, and (3) motivation for a brief treatment experience.

Systematic Desensitization

The studies that best meet the criteria stated at the beginning of this section are those of Lang and Lazovik (1963), Lang, Lazovik, and Reynolds (1965), and Paul (1965). These studies used the systematic desensitization (or counterconditioning) procedures developed by Wolpe (1958). The theory and detailed description of these procedures are provided in Chapter 10, Phobias, and will not be repeated here. Lang and his colleagues have shown that relaxation training, hierarchy formation, suggestion of cure, and an interview-type relationship with a therapist could not account for all the behavioral and self-report changes in fear of nonpoisonous snakes in college students resulting from the desensitization procedure. An interview-type relationship group fell midway between the relaxation-training-only group and the systematic desensitization group in effectiveness, and it was not significantly different from either. Follow-up data indicated that the decreased fear in the desensitization group persisted without "symptom substitution." Land (1969) also reports work done in collaboration with Melamed which shows that the desensitization procedure can be effective when programmed by a tape recording with *no therapist present*.

Paul (1965) found greater reduction in fear associated with public speaking after five sessions of systematic desensitization than after five sessions of traditional insight therapy, a placebo experience, or no treatment. Traditional insight therapy and placebo experience were about equally effective, and both were better than no treatment. Fear was assessed by self-report (S-R Inventory of Anxiousness), behavior ratings, pulse rate, and palmar sweat. Paul and Shannon (1966) applied desensitization procedures within five-person groups for nine sessions. All subjects were chronically anxious in a number of situations as measured on two occasions that were spaced several months apart on self-report anxiety scales, including the IPAT Anxiety Scale and the S-R Inventory of Anxiousness (the situations involved a speech before a large group, a competitive contest, a job interview, and a final course examination). The group-treatment approach resulted in a significant decrease on all these self-report measures *and* a significant increase in gradepoint average relative to a nontreated control group, matched on degree of initial anxiety.

In a well executed study, Cassell (1965) found that children who had received one session of "puppet therapy" prior to cardiac catheterization were less disturbed during the procedure and subsequently expressed to their parents more willingness to return to the hospital than did children in a control group. The "puppet therapy" consisted of acting out the catheterization procedure with "doctor" and "child" puppets.

Cautela (1966), Lazarus (1966), and Wolpe and Lazarus (1966) provide clinical descriptions of the application of desensitization-type procedures with patients in whom anxiety is a prominent symptom. Costello (1964) reports effective use of desensitization procedures in one lengthy session when LSD was used to enhance vividness in imagining the anxiety-producing scenes, and also to increase the degree of relaxation and feeling of wellbeing, as the response presumed to be incompatible with anxiety.

Stampfl and Levis (1967) have developed a treatment procedure referred to as implosive therapy in which they dispense with both the relaxation induction and the graded hierarchy and have the patient visualize the central, frightening experience. They assume that anxiety will extinguish under these circumstances, and report clinical cases to support this assumption.

The relative contribution of relaxation induction, hypnosis, graded hierarchies, the interpersonal relationship, cognitive factors, "in vivo" versus imagined scenes, etc., have just begun to be studied. See, for example, Cooke (1966), Davison (1968), Folkins et al. (1968), Kirchner & Hogan (1966), Lang (1969), and Lomont & Edwards (1967).

Modification of a Physiological Response by Operant Procedures

It has often been suggested that anxiety symptoms have a circular effect, reinforcing and intensifying each other, and that breaking into this circle at any point can be beneficial (for example, Jacobson, 1942; Malmo, 1962). Despite suggestions of authorities (for example, Morgan, 1965; Kimble, 1961) that autonomic responses are not amenable to instrumental conditioning or voluntary control, there is now considerable evidence that the GSR (Kimmel, 1967), heart-rate acceleration (for example, Shearn, 1962; Frazier, 1966; Brenner, 1966; DiCara & Miller, 1966), and heart-rate deceleration (Engel & Hanson, 1966; DiCara & Miller, 1966) may be amenable to operant techniques. Hnatiow and Lang (1965) and Lang, Sroufe, and Hastings (1967) have demonstrated "voluntary" control of both acceleration and deceleration in an overall reduction of cardiac variability that was accomplished by presenting subjects with a visual display of their own cardiac activity and by instructing them to keep their rate stable. They conclude that findings such as these ". . . prompt new clinical strategies for the modification of emotional responses, implying that autonomic components of fear and anxiety may be shaped directly." Engel and Hanson (1966) have reported successful treatment of atrial fibulation through these operant techniques. For a more extensive discussion of the implications and directions of this research see Lang (1969).

Drugs

Pharmacological modification of anxiety has been the subject of massive research. Thousands of studies have been reported on the effectiveness of drugs for treatment of anxiety, and a paper by Davis (1965) has 410 references to controlled studies on tranquilizers. We must necessarily limit our review to a representative sampling of mostly recent, well-controlled studies, and must deal extensively only with the studies most relevant to anxiety. Although our primary purpose is to present results, any discussion of drug studies must begin with some methodological comments.

The nonspecific nature of drug action has been discussed by Dews (1962) and Kety (1960). As Dews has stated: "Probably all drugs have more than one type of action. This is especially true of drugs affecting the central nervous system" (p. 428). Also, in making inferences from observed behavior changes, it is difficult to distinguish between primary and secondary responses.

Related to this is Maher's (1966) discussion of the general effects of certain anxiety reducing drugs, particularly the ataractics ("major tranquilizers," such as the phenothiazines). Studies with animals often find that attempts to affect conditioned emotional responses and avoidance responses are successful only when dosages are large enough to produce a general depression of behavior. Strong dosages of chlorpromazine, for example, seem to affect the oxygen uptake by the brain (Eiduson et al., 1964), which would have global effects on behavior. With respect to the most widely studied major tranquilizer, Heilezer (1960) has concluded that, "The clearest conclusion is that chlorpromazine has a salutary general effect upon psychotic subjects; there is no convincing evidence that it has one or more specific effects." His criticism is particularly directed at studies that employ global improvement ratings. Unfortunately, it is mainly for such general drugs (and large dosages) that reviewers have found the work "definitive" (for example, Davis, 1965; Rickels, 1966; and Wortis, 1965).

In addition to global action, stronger drugs often produce readily observable side effects. For example, chlorpromazine (thorazine) can cause photosensitivity, rashes, heart-rate changes, nasal congestion, and extrapyramidal symptoms, including Parkinsonism (Blair, 1963). These effects can be reduced by additional medication (Fann, 1966), but this, of course, leads to other control problems. These side effects have consequences for experimental design. The typical study purports to be "double-blind" (neither subject nor experimenter knows which subjects have been given the drug). In many studies, however, procedures are not specified and guarantees of "blindness" are not enunciated. For example, Gundlach et al. (1966) cite two studies (Hare, 1963; Cromwell, 1963) in which treatments were not individually coded. Subjects are merely given drugs labeled, "1" and "2." If one or two subjects in group "2" develop a rash, the subjects and experimenters are no longer "blind."

Finally, crossover designs, where each subject takes drug and placebo in a counterbalance order, are also the rule. Raab et al. (1966) have recently shown how this can lead to difficulties. In general, whenever an interaction between drug and order exists, treatment effects are confounded (Grant, 1948).

Major Tranquilizers

Despite the difficulties in assessing the effects of major tranquilizers, some recent, controlled studies will be summarized. A study by DiMascio et al. (1963) with normal subjects, will serve as an introduction to studies with physiological dependent variables. They investigated the effects of chlorpromazine and three other phenothiazines on physiological, self-report, and rating measures. They found that at the highest dosage employed (200 mg/d) chlorpromazine produced a significant drop in blood pressure and a significant constriction of the pupil ("parasympathetic" effects). Smaller dosages (for example, 25 mg/d) also produced the pupil constriction. None of the drugs affected the Taylor MAS or Cattell IPAT scores, but these subjects had low initial anxiety. There was some evidence from the Clyde Mood Scale that chlorpromazine subjects were less friendly, sleepier, and less clear in their thinking, particularly with increased dosage. They were also rated as more sluggish by a physician. In conclusion: chlorpromazine produced predominantly hypnotic effects that were dose related.

Mitchell and Zax (1959) report a reduction in ease of GSR conditioning to a loud tone following chlorpromazine for a sample of schizophrenic patients. Goldstein et al. (1966), to show that the preceding results were not merely local (that is, a drying of the skin which can be produced by chlorpromazine) measured heart rate, finger-pulse volume and skin conductance while 40 chronic schizophrenics watched two frightening movies with a one-week interval. Half of the subjects were treated with thiordizane (a phenothiazine which does not produce "Parkinsonism") during the interval; half received placebo. All subjects had been on placebo for at least two weeks prior to the first film, and the assignment to groups was randomized within wards. Two of three GSR measures (total range of skin conductance and average of the three largest GSR's) significantly discriminated the two groups, as did heart-rate change scores adjusted for initial level. Neither order of film nor drug by order was significant. The groups did not differ in plot comprehension but, on an additional clinical measure, the drug group showed a decrease in remote associations. These results would have been more convincing with respect to anxiety reduction had a neutral, pleasant, or sad film also been used. Perhaps a general reduction in emotional response has been effected.

Whatmore and Ellis (1964), in a longitudinal study of schizophrenics, found that chlorpromazine sharply reduced muscle action potential, and that this seemed to be associated with a subsequent reduction in symptomatology.

Finally, Sourkes (1962) has reported that reserpine (from the plant Rauwolfia Serpentina) reduces urinary and plasma catecholamines.

Minor Tranquilizers

The "minor tranquilizers" are not antipsychotic and, generally, are not prone to producing side effects and global suppression. They have been used more often in studies with neurotics and normal subjects under laboratory stress.

Gundlach et al. (1966), by using a Target Symptom Rating Scale (TSRS), an adjective checklist, and the Taylor MAS, as well as global ratings, found evidence for improvement of outpatients treated with diazepam on the specific measures, but this was not significantly beyond that of placebo subjects. An important point to be made here is that the finding of a significant improvement in a treated group, while not finding significance for a control group, does *not* allow the conclusion that the drug was effective. To reach this conclusion, one must demonstrate a statistically significant difference between the change scores of the two groups. Smith and Chassan (1964), however, found diazepam significantly superior to two phenothiazines in overall improvement ratings of anxiety patients. Both diazepam and chlorpromazine were superior to trifluperazine as assessed by specific ratings of anxiety. However, there was no placebo group in this study, and procedures (who did the ratings under what conditions) were not clearly specified.

Rickels et al. (1966) report that meprobamate (Milltown), a muscle-relaxing drug which is subject to the problem of global effects, coupled with psychotherapy is superior to psychotherapy and placebo in private psychiatric practice. This was only true for global measures and ratings by physicians, and there is the possibility of a "halo" effect, because the physicians were able to tell which patients were on the drug (see also Paredes et al 1966). Self-report measures, the Clyde Mood Scale, and the IPAT, did not indicate superiority for the drug plus psychotherapy group. Rickels and Snow (1964) earlier found meprobamate superior to placebo in a crossover design, by using these same measures with a group of anxiety state patients. Side effects were equally common during drug and placebo conditions. The results of McNair et al. (1965), however, are not favorable to meprobamate. They used their Psychiatric Outpatient Mood Scale, global and specific ratings by the patients, and a somatic distress scale, in a noncrossover design. Although the results were almost totally negative for meprobamate, chlordiazepoxide was significantly more effective than placebo on most measures, including somatic distress. Results favorable to chlordiazepoxide had also been reported earlier by this same group (Lorr et al., 1964). Those results suggested not only less reported "tension" and "anxiety," but also more vigor, counterindicating global suppression.

Studies that use normal subjects more often employ fixed dosages and other controls that are not always possible in a hospital setting. Two of these studies found meprobamate ineffective (Barrett & DiMascio, 1966, by using specific anxiety scales) and detrimental (Reitan, 1957) by using test performance. The Barrett and DiMascio study, exemplary for its control, did find *smaller* dosages of chlordiazepoxide and diazepam effective with high anxious subjects (those with high scores on the Taylor MAS).

Several studies have investigated autonomic changes under minor tranquilizers. In perhaps the most extensive study that uses meprobamate, Pronko and Kenyon (1959) assessed heart rate, blood pressure, EMG, GSR, and eosinophil count under conditions of delayed auditory feedback with college students. Meprobamate (small dosage), placebo, and no capsule were used in the following repeated measures format:

Order 1: *M*eprobamate *P*lacebo *N*o capsule
Order 2: Placebo No capsule Meprobamate
Order 3: No capsule Meprobamate Placebo

Although order is counterbalanced, it will be noticed that N never immediately follows M, and M never immediately follows N. Possible sequence effects may account for some of the confusing results. Partial ordering was often observed; for example, meprobamate decreased GSR with respect to placebo, but not with respect to no capsule. Meprobamate *increased* EMG with respect to placebo, but not to no capsule. There were no significant results for heart rate, blood pressure, or eosinophil count. A limiting effect (low initial anxiety) may, at least, partially account for these results. Pronko and Kenyon cite other data indicating that large dosages of meprobamate reduce muscle tonus and that GSR results have been conflicting (Berger, 1954; Laties, 1957; Marquis et al., 1957). The conclusion to be reached in 1959 was that "... the definitive value of meprobamate has yet to be firmly established" (p. 236).

Recent data have been more favorable concerning meprobamate. In a study with anxiety patients, as well as normals, Williams and Williams (1966) assessed the effects of meprobamate on muscle activity and digital volume pulse by using delayed auditory feedback as a stressor, in a crossover design. Alcohol and coffee intake were controlled. For the patients the drug significantly lessened the percent decrease in digital volume pulse and lowered EMG level. It was also found that, under placebo, patients showed significantly higher EMG level than normals, whereas the two groups did not differ under the drug. As was true for Pronko and Kenyon, there were no significant effects for normal subjects. Importantly, the investigators tested for blindess in the subjects. Exactly half of the subjects (chance) were able to guess which treatment they had received first. Other studies on the effects of meprobamate on muscle tension are provided by Berger (1954) and Gillette (1956). An excellent study by Frankenhaeuser and Kareby (1962) found meprobamate effective in counteracting catecholamine excretion during stress (for example, Stroop test, mirror tracings) with normal subjects. Finally, the data of Pfeiffer et al. (1964) suggest meprobamate produces low frequency EEG without behavioral sleepiness.

One study that uses chlordiazepoxide is at least partially favorable. Homberg et al. (1964) found that, relative to a placebo group, blood pressure was significantly lower, and other measures in the predicted direction, for a group of drug-treated patients.

Summary: Modification of Anxiety

There have been few well-controlled experimental studies that use psychological procedures to modify anxiety. Most convincing among them have been the studies that employ systematic desensitization, which suggest that fear of public speaking, snakes, and other situational anxieties, can be reduced by behavioral techniques.

The effectiveness of drugs in the specific treatment of anxiety is as yet not completely resolved. Although major tranquilizers reduce symptoms of anxiety, it has been difficult to demonstrate these changes in the absence of a general suppression of behavior. Several recent studies that use minor tranquilizers, in which physiological dependent variables have been used, provide some evidence that these drugs are specifically effective in reducing anxiety. The controlled studies that use various rating measures have been less successful. A discouraging number of studies continue to have experimental and statistical inadequacies.

Drug studies would benefit from an incorporation of some of the findings that are described in the section on physiological assessment and that point to conditions where anxiety effects are highlighted. For example, curves of autonomic responses and EMG recordings frequently show greater divergence between high and low anxious subjects in the later stages of stress or in a poststress recovery period than at the beginning of stress. Habituation rate of GSR and number of spontaneous GSR's seemed to be especially sensitive to different levels of anxiety in patient groups. Drug studies in which physiological or behavioral measures were obtained during these more precisely defined conditions might be a better test of the effectiveness of the drug than are averages over an entire stress period or global ratings of general ward behavior.

Finally, there has recently been experimental work that demonstrates autonomic responses such as heart rate and GSR may be amenable to direct manipulation by using operant techniques. These studies suggest the possibility of directly modifying the autonomic symptoms of anxiety.

REFERENCES

Aborn, M. The influence of experimentally-induced failure on the retention of material acquired through set and incidental learning. *J. exp. Psychol.*, 1953, **45**, 225–231.

Ackner, B. Emotions and the peripheral vasomotor system: a review of previous work. *J. psychosom. Res.*, 1956, **1**, 3–20. (a)

Ackner, B. The relationship between anxiety and the level of peripheral vasomotor activity. *J. psychosom. Res.*, 1956, **1**, 21–48. (b)

Adsett, C. A., Schottstaedt, W. W., & Wolf, S. G. Change in coronary blood flow and other hemodynamic indicators induced by stressful interviews. *Psychosom. Med.*, 1962, **24**, 331–336.

Angyal, Alice F. The diagnosis of neurotic traits by means of a new perceptual test. *J. Psychol.*, 1948, **25**, 105–135.

Arnhoff, F. N. Stimulus generalization and anxiety. *J. gen. Psychol.*, 1959, **60**, 131–136.

Ax, A. F. The physiological differentiation between fear and anger in humans. *Psychosom. Med.*, 1953, **15**, 433–442.

Axelrod, H. D., Cowen, E. L., & Heilizer, F. The correlates of manifest anxiety in stylus maze learning. *J. exp. Psychol.*, 1956, **51**, 131–138.

Back, K. W., Wilson, S. R., Bogdonoff, M. D., & Troyer, W. G. In-between times and experimental stress. *J. pers.*, 1967, **35**, 456–473.

Balshan, Iris D. Muscle tension and personality in women. *Arch. gen. Psychiat.*, 1962, **7**, 436–448.

Barbara, D. A. Stuttering. In S. Arieti (ed.), *American Handbook of Psychiatry,* Vol. I. New York: Basic Books, 1959.

Barrett, J. E., & DiMascio, A. Comparative effects on anxiety of the "minor tranquilizers" in "high" and "low" anxious student volunteers. *Dis. nerv. Syst.*, 1966, **27**, 483–486.

Basowitz, H., Persky, H., Korchin, S. J., & Grinker, R. R. *Anxiety and Stress.* New York: McGraw-Hill, 1955.

Beam, J. C. Serial learning and conditioning under real life stress. *J. abnorm. soc. Psychol.*, 1955, **51**, 543–551.

Becker, W. C., & Matteson, H. H. GSR conditioning, anxiety, and extraversion. *J. abnorm. soc. Psychol.*, 1961, **62**, 427–430.

Beier, E. G. The effect of induced anxiety on flexibility of intellectual functioning. *Psychol. Monogr.*, 1951, **65**, No. 9 (Whole No. 326).

Bendig, A. W. College norms for and concurrent validity of Cattell's I. P. A. T. Anxiety Scale. *Psychol. Newsltr.*, 1959, **10**, 263–267.

Berger, F. M. The pharmacological properties of 2-methyl-2-n-proplyl-1, 3-propanediol dicarbamate (Milltown), a new interneural blocking agent. *J. Pharmacol. exp. Ther.*, 1954, **112**, 413–423.

Bergs, L. P., & Martin, B. The effect of instructional time interval and social desirability on the validity of a forced-choice anxiety scale. *J. consult. Psychol.*, 1961, **25**, 528–532.

Besch, Norma, F. Paired-associates learning as a function of anxiety level and shock. *J. Pers.*, 1959, **27**, 116–124.

Bitterman, M., & Holtzman, W. Conditioning and extinction of the galvanic skin response as a function of anxiety. *J. abnorm. soc. Psychol.*, 1952, **47**, 615–623.

Blair, D. *Modern drugs for the treatment of mental illness.* London: Staples Press, 1963.

Bliss, E. L., Migeon, C. J., Branch, C. H. H., & Samuels, L. T. Reaction of the adrenal cortex to emotional stress. *Psychosom. Med.*, 1956, **18**, 56–76.

Bloom, G., Von Euler, U. S., & Frankenhaeuser, M. Catecholamine excretion and personality traits in paratroop trainees. *Acta. physiol. Scand.*, 1963, **58**, 77–89.

Brady, J. V. Ulcers in executive monkies. *Sci. Amer.*, 1958, **199**, 95–100.

Breggin, P. R. The psychophysiology of anxiety. *J. nerv. ment. dis.*, 1964, **139**, 558–568.

Brenner, J. Heart rate as an avoidance response. *Psychol. Record*, 1966, **16**, 329–336.

Broen, W. E., & Storms, L. H. A reaction potential ceiling and response decrements in complex situations. *Psychol. Rev.*, 1961, **68**, 405–415.

Broen, W. E., & Storms, L. H. The differential effect of induced muscular tension (drive) on discrimination in schizophrenics and normals. *J. abnorm. soc. Psychol.*, 1964, **68**, 349–353.

Broen, W. E., Storms, L. H., & Goldberg, D. H. Decreased discrimination as a function of increased drive. *J. abnorm. soc. Psychol.*, 1963, **67**, 266–273.

Brutten, E. J. Colormetric measurement of anxiety: a clinical and experimental procedure. *Speech Monogr.*, 1959, **26**, 282–287.

Burdick, J. A. Autonomic lability and neuroticism. *J. psychosom. Res.*, 1966, **9**, 339–342.

Buss, A. H. Stimulus generalization as a function of clinical anxiety and stimulus generalization. *J. abnorm. soc. Psychol.*, 1955, **50**, 271–273.

Buss, A. H. Two anxiety factors in psychiatric patients. *J. abnorm. soc. Psychol.*, 1962, **65**, 426–427.

Buss, A. H., & Buss, Edith H. Stimulus generalization with words connoting anxiety. *J. pers. soc. Psychol.*, 1966, **4**, 707–710.

Buss, A. H., Wiener, M., Durkee, Ann, & Baer, M. The measurement of anxiety in clinical situations. *J. consult. Psychol.*, 1955, **19**, 125–129.

Calvin, A. D., McGuigan, F. J., Tyrrell, Sybil, & Soyars, M. Manifest anxiety and the palmar perspiration index. *J. consult. Psychol.*, 1956, **20**, 356.

Campos, J. J., & Johnson, H. J. The effects of verbalization instructions and visual attention on heart rate and skin conductance. *Psychophysiol.*, 1966, **2**, 305–310.

Cassell, Sylvia. Effect of brief puppet therapy upon the emotional responses of children undergoing cardiac catheterization. *J. consult. Psychol.*, 1965, **29**, 1–8.

Castaneda, A. Supplementary report: Differential position habits and anxiety in children as determinants of performance in learning. *J. exp. Psychol.*, 1961, **61**, 257–258.

Castaneda, A., & Palermo, D. S. Psychomotor performance as a function of amount of training and stress. *J. exp. Psychol.*, 1955, **50**, 175–179.

Castaneda, A., Palermo, D. S., & McCandless, B. R. Complex learning and performance as a function of anxiety in children and task difficulty. *Child Develpm.*, 1956, **27**, 327–332.

Cattell, R. B. *Handbook for the I. P. A. T. Anxiety Scale.* Champaign, Ill.: Inst. for Pers. and Abil. Testing, 1957.

Cattell, R. B., & Scheier, I. H. *Factors in personality change: a discussion of the condition-response incremental design and application to 69 personality response measures and three stimulus conditions.* Urbana, Ill.: Lab. of Pers. Assess. and Group Behavior, Advance Publ. No. 9, 1958.

Cattell, R. B., & Scheier, I. H. *The Meaning and Measurement of Neuroticism and Anxiety.* New York: Ronald, 1961.

Cautela, J. R. A behavior therapy approach to pervasive anxiety. *Behav. Res. Therapy*, 1966, **4**, 99–109.

Child, I. L. Personality. *Annu. Rev. Psychol.*, 1954, **5**, 149–170.

Clancy, J., & Vanderhoof, E. Physiological responses in therapeutic relationships. *Dis. nerv. Syst.*, 1963, **24**, 491–498.

Cooke, G. Identification of the efficacious components of reciprocal inhibition therapy. Unpublished Ph.D. thesis, Univ. of Iowa, 1966.

Coquery, J., & Lacey, J. I. The effect of foreperiod duration on the components of the cardiac response during the foreperiod of a reaction time experiment. Paper read at the Fifth Annual Meeting of the Society for Psychophysiological Research, October, 1966.

Costello, C. G. Lysergic acid diethylamide (LSD 25) and behavior therapy. *Behav. Res. Therapy*, 1964, **2**, 117–130.

Costello, C. G., & Comrey, A. L. Scales for measuring anxiety and depression. *Brit. J. Psychol.*, 1967, **66**, 303–313.

Cromwell, H. A. Controlled evaluation of psychotherapeutic drug in internal medicine. *Clin. Med.*, 1963, **70**, 2239–2244.

Crowne, D. P., & Marlowe, D. *The approval motive.* New York: Wiley, 1964.

Darrow, C. W. Differences in the physiological reactions to sensory and ideational stimuli. *Psychol. Bull.*, 1929, **26**, 85–201. (a)

Darrow, C. W. Electrical and circulatory responses to brief sensory and ideational stimuli. *J. exp. Psychol.*, 1929, **12**, 267–300. (b)

Darrow, C. W. The rationale for treating the change in galvanic skin response as a change in conductance. *Psychophysiol.*, 1964, **1**, 31–38.

Davis, D. R. Increase in strength of a secondary drive as a cause for disorganization. *Quart. J. exp. Psychol.*, 1949, **1**, 22–28.

Davis, F. H., & Malmo, R. B. Electromyographic recording during interview. *Amer. J. Psychiat.*, 1951, **107**, 908–916.

Davis, F. H., Malmo, R. B., & Shagass, C. Electromyographic reaction to strong auditory stimulation in psychiatric patients. *Canad. J. Psychol.*, 1954, **8**, 177–186.

Davis, J. M. Efficacy of tranquilizing and anti-depressant drugs. *Arch. gen. Psychiat.*, 1965, **13**, 552–572.

Davis, R. C., & Berry, F. Gastrointestinal reactions during a noise avoidance task. *Psychol. Rep.*, 1963, **12**, 135–137.

Davis, R. C., Buchwald, A. M., & Frankmann, R. W. Autonomic and muscular responses and their relation to simple stimuli. *Psychol. Monogr.*, 1955, **69**, No. 20, 1–71 (Whole No. 405).

Davison, G. C. Systematic desensitization as a counterconditioning process. *J. abnorm. Psychol.*, 1968, **73**, 91–99.

Deane, G. E. Human heart rate responses during experimentally induced anxiety. *J. exp. Psychol.*, 1961, **61**, 489–493.

Deane, G. E. Human heart-rate responses during experimentally induced anxiety: a follow-up with controlled respiration. *J. exp. Psychol.*, 1964, **67**, 193–195.

Deese, J., Lazarus, R. S., & Keenan, J. Anxiety, anxiety reduction, and stress in learning. *J. exp. Psychol.*, 1953, **46**, 55–60.

Dews, P. B. Psychopharmacology. In A. J. Bachrach (ed.), *Experimental Foundations of Clinical Psychology*. New York: Basic Books, Inc., 1962.

DiCara, L., & Miller, N. E. Shaping of heart rate changes by reward in curarized rats. Paper presented at the 37th annual meeting of the Eastern Psychological Association, New York City, April, 1966.

Diethelm, O., Fleetwood, M. R., & Milhorat, A. T. The predictable association of certain emotions and biochemical changes in the blood. *Proceedings A. R. N. M. D.*, 1949, **29**, 262–278.

DiMascio, A., Havens, L. L., & Klerman, G. L. The psychopharmacology of phenothiazine compounds: a comparative study of the effects of chlorpromazine, promethazine, trifluoperazine, and perphenazine in normal males. II. Results and discussion. *J. nerv. ment. Dis.*, 1963, **136**, 168–186.

Doehring, D. G. The relation between manifest anxiety and rate of eyeblink in a stress situation. *USN Sch. Aviat. Med. Res. Rep.*, 1957, No. 6.

Dreyfuss, F. Coagulation time of the blood, level of blood eosinophils and thrombocytes under emotional stress. *J. psychosom. Res.*, 1956, **1**, 252–257.

Duffy, E. *Activation and Behavior*. New York: Wiley, 1962.

Dykman, R. A., Ackerman, P. T., Galbrecht, C. R., & Reese, W. G. Physiological reactivity to different stressors and methods of evaluation. *Psychosom. Med.*, 1963, **25**, 37–48.

Easterbrook, J. A. The effect of emotion on cue utilization and the organization of behavior. *Psychol. Rev.*, 1959, **66**, 183–201.

Ebaugh, F. G. Association-motor investigation in clinical psychiatry. *J. ment. Sci.*, 1936, **82**, 731–743.

Eiduson, S., Geller, E., Yuwiler, A., & Eiduson, B. T. *Biochemistry and Behavior*. New York: Van Nostrand, 1964.

Elliot, R. Effects of uncertainty about the nature and advent of a noxious stimulus (shock) upon heart rate. *J. pers. soc. Psychol.*, 1966, **3**, 353–356.

Elmadjian, F. Excretion and metabolism of epinephrine. *Pharmacol. Rev.*, 1959, **11**, 409–415.

Elmadjian, F., Hope, J. M., & Lamson, E. T. Excretion of epinephrine and norepinephrine in various emotional states. *J. clin. Endocrin. & Metab.*, 1957, **17**, 608–620.

Elmadjian, F., Hope, J. M., & Lamson, E. T. Excretion of epinephrine and norepinephrine under stress. *Recent Progr. Hormone Research*, 1958, **14**, 513–521.

Endler, N. S., Hunt, J. McV., & Rosenstein, A. J. An S-R inventory of anxiousness. *Psychol. monogr.*, 1962, **76** (17, Whole No. 536).

Engel, B. T. Stimulus-response and individual-response specificity. *AMA Arch. gen. Psychiat.*, 1960, **2**, 305–313.

Engel, B. T., & Hanson, S. P. Operant conditioning of heart rate slowing. *Psychophysiology*, 1966, **3**, 176–187.

Epstein, S. The measurement of drive and conflict in humans: theory and experiment. In M. R. Jones (ed.), Nebraska symposium on motivation. Lincoln: Univer. of Nebraska Press, 1962.

Eriksen, C. W. Some personality correlates of stimulus generalization under stress. *J. abnorm. soc. Psychol.*, 1954, **49**, 561–565.

Eriksen, C. W., & Davids, A. The meaning and clinical validity of the Taylor anxiety scale and the hysteria-psychasthenia scales from the MMPI. *J. abnorm. soc. Psychol.*, 1955, **50**, 135–137.

Eriksen, C. W., & Wechsler, H. Some effects of experimentally induced anxiety upon discrimination behavior. *J. abnorm. soc. Psychol.*, 1955, **51**, 458–463.

Eysenck, H. J. *The Maudsley Personality Inventory*. London: Univer. of London Press, 1959.

Eysenck, H. J. Classification and the problem of diagnosis. In H. J. Eysenck (ed.), *Handbook of Abnormal Psychology*. New York: Basic Books, 1961.

Eysenck, S. B. G. An experimental study of psycho-galvanic reflex responses of normal, neurotic, and psychotic subjects. *J. psychosom. Res.*, 1956, **1**, 258–272.

Fager, R. E., & Knopf, I. J. Relationship of manifest anxiety to stimulus generalization. *J. abnorm. soc. Psychol.*, 1958, **57**, 125–126.

Fann, W. E. Use of methylphenedate to counteract acute dystonic effects of phenothiazines. *Amer. J. Psychiat.*, 1966, **122**, 1293–1294.

Farber, I. E., & Spence, K. W. Effects of anxiety, stress, and task variables on reaction time. *J. exp. Psychol.*, 1953, **45**, 120–125.

Ferreira, A. J., & Winter, W. D. The palmar sweat print: a methodological study. *Psychosom. Med.*, 1963, **25**, 377–384.

Fiorica, V., & Muehl, S. Relationship between plasma levels of 17-hydroxy-corticsteroids (17-OH-CS) and a psychological measure of manifest anxiety. *Psychosom. Med.*, 1962, **24**, 596–599.

Folkins, C. H., Lawson, Karen D., Opton, E. M. Jr., & Lazarus, R. S. Desensitization and the experimental reduction of threat. *J. abnorm. Psychol.*, 1968, **2**, 100–113.

Frankenhaeuser, M., & Jarpe, G. Psychophysiological reactions to infusions of a mixture of adrenaline and noradrenaline. *Scand. J. Psychol.*, 1962, **3**, 21–29.

Frankenhaeuser, M., & Jarpe, G. Psychophysiological changes during infusions of adrenaline in various doses. *Psychopharmacol.*, 1963, **4**, 424–432.

Frankenhaeuser, M., Jarpe, G., & Matell, G. Effects of intravenous infusions of adrenaline and noradrenaline on certain psychological and physiological functions. *Acta physiol. Scand.*, 1961, **51**, 175–186.

Frankenhaeuser, M., & Kareby, S. Effect of meprobamate on catecholamine excretion during mental stress. *Percept. Mot. Skills*, 1962, **15**, 571–577.

Frankenhaeuser, M., & Patkai, P. Inter-individual differences in catecholamine excretion during stress. Report of the Psychological Laboratory, Univer. of Stockholm, 1964, No. 178.

Frazier, T. W. Avoidance conditioning of heart rate in humans. *Psychophysiology*, 1966, **3**, 188–202.

Funkenstein, D. H., King, S. H., & Drolette, M. E. *Mastery of stress*. Cambridge: Harvard Univer. Press, 1957.

Gallagher, J. J. Manifest anxiety changes concomitant with client-centered therapy. *J. consult. Psychol.*, 1953, **17**, 443–446.

Geer, J. H. The development of a scale to measure fear. *Behav. Res. Therapy*, 1965, **3**, 45–53.
Geer, J. H. Effect of fear arousal upon task performance and verbal behavior. *J. abnorm. Psychol.*, 1966a, **71**, 119–123.
Geer, J. H. Fear and autonomic arousal. *J. abnorm. soc. Psychol.*, 1966b, **71**, 253–255.
Gellhorn, E., & Loofbourrow, G. N. *Emotions and emotional disorders*. New York: Harper & Row, Hoeber division, 1963.
Gillette, H. E. Resultant effects of meprobamate in disabilities resulting from musculoskeletal and central nervous system disorders. *Int. Rec. Med. & gen. pract. Clinics*, 1956, **169**, 453–468.
Gleser, Goldine, & Ulett, G. The Saslow Screening Test as a measure of anxiety-proneness, *J. clin. Psychol.*, 1952, **8**, 279–283.
Glickstein, M., Chevalier, J. A., Korchin, S. J., Basowitz, H., Sabshin, M., Hamburg, D. A., & Grinker, R. R. Temporal heart rate patterns in anxious patients. *Arch. Neurol Psychiat.*, 1957, **78**, 101–106.
Goldstein, I. B. Role of muscle tension in personality theory. *Psychol. Bull.*, 1964, **61**, 413–425. (a)
Goldstein, I. B. Physiological responses in anxious women patients. *Arch. gen. Psychiat.*, 1964, **10**, 382–388. (b)
Goldstein, K. *The Organism*. New York: American Book, 1939.
Goldstein, M. J., Acker, C. W., Crockett, J. T., & Riddle, J. J. Psychophysiological reactions to films by chronic schizophrenics. *J. abnorm. Psychol.*, 1966, **71**, 335–344.
Goldstone, S. Flicker fusion measurements and anxiety level. *J. exp. Psychol.*, 1955, **49**, 200–202.
Goodall, M. Studies of adrenaline and noradrenaline in mammalian heart and suprarenals. *Acta. Physiol. Scandinav.*, 1951, **24**, Suppl. 85.
Goodall, M., McCally, M., & Graveline, D. E. Urinary adrenaline and noradrenaline response to simulated weightless state. *Amer. J. Physiol.*, 1964, **206**, 431–436.
Gordon, W. M., & Berlyne, D. E. Drive-level and flexibility in paired-associate nonsense syllable learning. *Quart. J. exp. Psychol.*, 1954, **6**, 181–185.
Gottschalk, L. A., Cleghorn, J. M., Gleser, G. C., & Iacona, J. M. Studies of relationships of emotions to plasma lipids. *Psychosom. Med.*, 1965, **27**, 102–111.
Graham, F. K. & Clifton, R. K. Heart-rate change as a component of the orienting response. *Psychol. Bull.*, 1966, **65**, 305–320.
Granger, G. W. Abnormalities of sensory perception. In H. J. Eysenck (ed.), *Handbook of Abnormal Psychology*. New York: Basic Books, 1961.
Grant, D. A. The Latin square principle in the design and analysis of psychological experiments. *Psychol. Bull.*, 1948, **45**, 427–442.
Grinker, R. R. The psychosomatic aspects of anxiety. In C. D. Spielberger (ed.), *Anxiety and Behavior*. New York: The Academic Press, 1966.
Gunderson, E. K. Autonomic balance in schizophrenia. Unpublished doctoral dissertation, University of California, Los Angeles, 1953.
Gundlach, R., Engelhardt, D. M., Hankoff, L., Paley, H., Rudorfer, L., & Bird, E. A double-blind outpatient study of Diazepam (Valium) and placebo. *Psychopharmacol.*, 1966, **9**, 81–92.
Haggard, E. Some conditions determining adjustment during and readjustment following experimentally induced stress. In S. Tomkins (ed.), *Contemporary psychopathology*. Cambridge, Mass.: Harvard Univ. Press, 1943.
Hamilton, M. The assessment of anxiety states by rating. *Brit. J. Med. Psychol.*, 1959, **32**, 50–59.
Handlon, J. H. Hormonal activity and individual responses to stresses and easements in everyday living. In R. Roessler and N. S. Greenfield (eds.), *Physiological Correlates of Psychological disorders*. Madison: Univ. of Wisconsin Press, 1962.
Hare, H. P., Jr. Comparison of diazepam, chlorpromazine, and a placebo in psychiatric practice. *J. new Drugs*, 1963, **3**, 233–240.
Harrison, J. The behavior of the palmar sweat glands in stress. *J. psychosom. Res.*, 1964, **8**, 187–191.

Hawkins, E. R., Monroe, J. D., Sandifer, M. G., and Vernon, C. R. Psychological and physiological responses to continuous epinephrine infusion. *Psychiat. Res. Rep. Amer. Psychiat. Ass.*, 1960, **12**, 40–52.

Haywood, H. C. Novelty seeking behavior as a function of manifest anxiety and physiological arousal. *J. pers.*, 1962, **30**, 63–74.

Heilezer, F. A critical review of some published experiments with chlorpromazine in schizophrenic, neurotic, and normal humans. *J. chronic Dis.*, 1960, **11**, 102–148.

Heineman, C. E. A forced-choice form of the Taylor Anxiety Scale. *J. consult. Psychol.*, 1953, **17**, 447–454.

Hickham, J. B., Cargill, W. H., & Golden, G. Cardiovascular reactions to emotional stimuli: Effect on cardiac output, A-V oxygen difference, arterial pressure and peripheral resistance. *J. clin. Invest.*, 1948, **27**, 290–298.

Hnatiow, M., & Lang, P. J. Learned stabilization of cardiac rate. *Psychophysiology*, 1965, **1**, 330–336.

Hoagland, H. Stress and the adrenal cortex with special reference to potassium metabolism. *Proceedings, ARNMD*, 1949.

Hodges, W. F., & Spielberger, C. D. The effects of threat of shock on heart rate for subjects who differ in manifest anxiety and fear of shock. *Psychophysiol.*, 1966, **2**, 287–294.

Homberg, G., & William-Olsson, U. Effects of benzquinamide, in comparison with chlordiazepoxide and placebo, on subjective experiences and autonomic phenomena in stress experiences. *Psychopharmacol.*, 1964, **5**, 147–157.

Howe, E. S. GSR conditioning in anxiety states, normals, and chronic functional schizophrenic subjects. *J. abnorm. soc. Psychol.*, 1958, **56**, 183–189.

Hughes, J. B., II, Sprague, J. L., & Bendig, A. W. Anxiety level, response alternation, and performance in serial learning. *J. Psychol.*, 1954, **38**, 421–426.

Jacobson, E. The physiological conception and treatment of certain anxiety states. *Psychol. Bull.*, 1942, **39**, 599–613.

Johannsen, W. J., Friedman, S. H., Feldman, E. I., & Negrete, A. A re-examination of the hippuric acid-anxiety relationship. *Psychosom. Med.*, 1962, **24**, 569–578.

Jost, H. & Sontag, L. W. The genetic factor in autonomic nervous system function. *Psychosom. Med.*, 1944, **6**, 308–310.

Jurko, M., Jost, H., & Hill, T. S. Pathology of the energy system: An experimental-clinical study of physiological adaptive capacities in a nonpatient, a psychoneurotic, and an early paranoid schizophrenic group. *J. Psychol.*, 1952, **33**, 183–198.

Kamin, L. J., & Fedorchak, Olga. The Taylor scale, hunger, and verbal learning. *Canad. J. Psychol.*, 1957, **11**, 212–218.

Karson, S., & Pool, K. B. The construct validity of the Sixteen Personality Factors Test. *J. clin. Psychol.*, 1957, **13**, 245–252.

Kasl, S. V., & Mahl, G. F. The relationship of disturbances and hesitations in spontaneous speech to anxiety. *J. pers. soc. Psychol.*, 1965, **I**, 425–433.

Katahn, M. Effects of anxiety (drive) on the acquisition and avoidance of a dominant intratask response. *J. Pers.*, 1964, **32**, 642–650.

Katahn, M. Interaction of anxiety and ability in complex learning situations. *J. pers. soc. Psychol.*, 1966, **3**, 475–479.

Katahn, M., & Lyda, L. L. Anxiety and the learning of responses varying in initial rank in the response hierarchy. *J. Pers.*, 1966, **34**, 287–299.

Katchmar, L. T., Ross, S., & Andrews, T. G. Effects of stress and anxiety on performance of a complex verbal-coding task. *J. exp. Psychol.*, 1958, **55**, 559–564.

Katkin, E. S. Relationship between manifest anxiety and two indices of autonomic stress. *J. pers. soc. Psychol.*, 1965, **2**, 324–333.

Katkin, E. S. The relationship between a measure of transitory anxiety and spontaneous autonomic activity. *J. abnorm. Psychol.*, 1966, **71**, 142–146.

Kaye, D., Kirschner, P., & Mandler, G. The effect of test anxiety on memory span in a group test situation. *J. consult. Psychol.*, 1953, **17**, 265–266.

Kendall, E. The validity of Taylor's Manifest Anxiety Scale. *J. consult. Psychol.*, 1954, **18**, 429–432.

Kety, S. S. Recent biochemical theories of schizophrenia. In D. D. Jackson (ed.) The Etiology of Schizophrenia. New York: Basic Books, Inc., 1960, 120–145.

Kimble, G. A. *Hilgard and Marquis' Conditioning and Learning*. New York: Appleton-Century-Crofts, 1961.

Kimmel, H. D. Instrumental conditioning of autonomically mediated behavior. *Psych. Bull.*, 1967, **67**, 337–345.

Kirchner, J. H., & Hogan, R. A. The therapist variable in the implosion of phobias. *Psychotherapy: Theory, research and practice*, 1966, **3**, 102–104.

Korchin, S. J., & Basowitz, H. Perceptual adequacy in a life stress. *J. Psychol.*, 1954, **38**, 495–502.

Korchin, S. J., & Levine, S. Anxiety and verbal learning. *J. abnorm. soc. Psychol.*, 1957, **54**, 234–240.

Korobow, N. Reactions to stress: a reflection of personality trait organization. *J. abnorm. soc. Psychol.*, 1955, **51**, 464–468.

Krugman, M. Flicker fusion frequency as a function of anxiety reaction: an exploratory study. *Psychosom. Med.*, 1947, **9**, 269–272.

Lacey, J. I. The evaluation of autonomic responses: toward a general solution. *Ann. N.Y. Acad. Sci.*, 1956, **67**, 123–164.

Lacey, J. I. Psychophysiological approaches to the evaluation of psychotherapeutic process and outcome. In E. A. Rubinstein and M. B. Parloff (eds.) *Research in Psychotherapy*. Washington, D.C.: National Publishing Co., 1959.

Lacey, J. I., Bateman, D. E., & Van Lehn, R. Autonomic response specificity: an experimental study. *Psychosom. Med.*, 1953, **15**, 8–21.

Lacey, J. I., Kagan, J., Lacey, B. C., & Moss, H. The visceral level: situational determinants and behavioral correlates of autonomic response patterns. In P. H. Knapp (ed.) *Expression of the Emotions in Man*. New York: International Univer. Press, 1963.

Lacey, J. I., & Lacey, B. C. The relationship of resting autonomic activity to motor impulsivity. In *The Brain and Human Behavior* (Proceedings of the Assn. Res. Nerv. Ment. Dis.). Baltimore: Williams & Wilkins, 1958.

Lader, M. H. Palmar skin conductance measures in anxiety and phobic states. *J. psychosom. Res.*, 1967, **11**, 271–281.

Lader, M. H., & Wing, Lorna. Habituation of the psycho-galvanic reflex in patients with anxiety states and in normal subjects. *J. Neurol., Neurosurg., Psychiat.*, 1964, **27**, 210–218.

Lader, M. H., Gelder, M. G., & Marks, I. M. Palmar skin conductance measures as predictors of response to desensitization. *J. psychosom. Res.*, 1967, **11**, 283–290.

Lang, P. J. The mechanics of desensitization and the laboratory study of human fear. In Franks, C. M. (ed.), *Assessment and Status of the Behavior Therapies*. New York: McGraw-Hill, 1969.

Lang, P. J., & Lazovik, A. D. Experimental desensitization of a phobia. *J. abnorm. soc. Psychol.*, 1963, **66**, 519–525.

Lang, P. J., Lazovik, A. D., & Reynolds, D. J. Desensitization, suggestibility, and pseudotherapy. *J. abnorm. Psychol.*, 1965, **70**, 395–402.

Lang, P. J., Sroufe, L. A., & Hastings, J. E. Effects of feedback and instructional set on the control of cardiac rate variability. *J. exp. Psychol.*, 1967, **75**, 425–431.

Laties, V. G. Effects of meprobamate on fear and palmar sweating. *Fed. Proc.*, 1957, **16**, 315 (abstract).

Lauterbach, C. G. The Taylor A scale and clinical measures of anxiety. *J. consult. Psychol.*, 1958, **22**, 314.

Lazarus, A. A. Broad-spectrum behavior therapy and the treatment of agoraphobia. *Behav. Res. Therapy*, 1966, **4**, 95–97.

Lazarus, R. S., & Alfert, Elizabeth. Short-circuiting of threat by experimentally altering cognitive appraisal. *J. abnorm. soc. Psychol.*, 1964, **69**, 195–205.

Lazarus, R. S., Deese, J., & Hamilton, R. Anxiety and stress in learning: the role of intraserial duplication. *J. exp. Psychol.*, 1954, **47**, 111–114.

Lazarus, R. S., & Opton, E. M., Jr. The study of psychological stress: a summary of theoretical formulations and experimental findings. In C. D. Spielberger (ed.) *Anxiety and Behavior*. New York: The Academic Press, 1966.

Lazarus, R. S., Speisman, J. C., & Mordkoff, A. M. The relationship between autonomica indicators and psychological stress: heart rate and skin conductance. *Psychosom. Med.*, 1963, **25**, 19–30.

Lewinsohn, P. M. Some individual differences in physiological reactivity to stress. *J. comp. physiol. Psychol.*, 1956, **49**, 271–277.

Lomont, J. F., & Edwards, J. E. The role of relaxation in systematic desensitization. *Behavior Research and Therapy*, 1967, **5**, 11–25.

Lore, R. K. Palmar sweating and transitory anxiety in children. *Child Develpm.*, 1966, **37**, 115–124.

Lorr, M., McNair, D. M., & Weinstein, G. J. Early effects of chlordiazepoxide used with psychotherapy. *J. Psychiat. Res.*, 1964, **1**, 257–270.

Lotsof, E. J., & Downing, W. L. Two measures of anxiety. *J. consult. Psychol.*, 1956, **20**, 170.

Lucas, J. D. The interactive effects of anxiety, failure, and intraserial duplication. *Amer. J. Psychol.*, 1952, **65**, 59–66.

Luria, A. R. *The Nature of Human Conflicts*. New York: Liveright, 1932.

Maher, B. *Principles of Psychopathology*. New York: McGraw-Hill, 1966.

Mahl, G. F. Chronic fear and gastric secretion of HCl in dogs. *Psychosom. Med.*, 1949, **11**, 30–44.

Mahl, G. F. Anxiety, HCl secretion, and peptic ulcer etiology. *Psychosom. Med.*, 1950, **12**, 158–169.

Mahl, G. F. Disturbances and silences in the patient's speech in psychotherapy. *J. abnorm. soc. Psychol.*, 1956, **53**, 1–15.

Mahl, G. F. Measuring the patient's anxiety during interviews from "expressive" aspects of his speech. *Transact. New York Acad. Sci.*, 1959, **21**, 249–257.

Mahl, G. F., & Karpe, R. Emotions and hydrochloric acid secretion during psychoanalytic hours. *Psychosom. Med.*, 1953, **15**, 312–327.

Malmo, R. B. Experimental studies of mental patients under stress. In M. Reymert (ed.) *Feelings and Emotions*. New York: McGraw-Hill, 1950.

Malmo, R. B. Anxiety and behavioral arousal. *Psychol. Rev.*, 1957, **64**, 276–287.

Malmo, R. B. Activation. In A. J. Bachrach (ed.) *Experimental Foundations of Clinical Psychology*. New York: Basic Books, Inc., 1962.

Malmo, R. B. Studies of anxiety: some clinical origins of the activation concept. In C. D. Spielberger (ed.) *Anxiety and Behavior*. New York: Academic Press, 1966.

Malmo, R. B., & Amsel, A. Anxiety-produced interference in serial rote learning with observations on rote learning after partial frontal lobectomy. *J. exp. Psychol.*, 1948, **38**, 440–454.

Malmo, R. B., Boag, T. J., & Smith, A. A. Physiological study of personal interaction. *Psychosom. Med.*, 1957, **19**, 105–119.

Malmo, R. B., & Shagass, C. Physiological studies of reaction to stress in anxiety and early schizophrenia. *Psychosom. Med.*, 1949, **11**, 9–24.

Malmo, R. B., & Shagass, C. Studies of blood pressure in psychiatric patients under stress. *Psychosom. Med.*, 1952, **14**, 82–93.

Malmo, R. B., Shagass, C., Belanger, D. J., & Smith, A. A. Motor control in psychiatric patients under experimental stress. *J. abnorm. soc. Psychol.*, 1951, **46**, 539–547.

Malmo, R. B., Shagass, C., & Davis, F. H. A method for the investigation of somatic response mechanisms in psychoneurosis. *Science*, 1950, **112**, 325–328

Malmo, R. B., Shagass, C., & Smith, A. A. Responsiveness of chronic schizophrenia. *J. Pers.*, 1951, **19**, 359–375.

Malmo, R. B., & Smith, A. A. Forehead tension and motor irregularities in psychoneurotic patients under stress. *J. Pers.*, 1955, **23**, 391–406.

Mandler, G., Mandler, Jean M., Kremen, I., & Sholitan, R. D. The response to threat: relations among verbal and physiological indices. *Psychol. Monogr.*, 1961, **75** (Whole No. 513).

Mandler, G., & Sarason, S. B. A study of anxiety and learning. *J. abnorm. soc. Psychol.*, 1952, **47**, 166–173.

Marchbanks, V. H. Flying stress and urinary 17-hydroxycorticosteroid levels during 20 hour missions. *Aerospace Med.*, 1960, **31**, 639–643.

Marquis, D. G., Kelley, E. L., Miller, J. G., Gerard, R. W., & Rapoport, A. Experimental studies of behavioral effects of meprobamate on normal subjects. *Ann. N.Y. Acad. Sci.*, 1957, **67**, 701–710.

Martin, B. The validity of a self-report measure of anxiety as a function of the time interval covered by the instructions. *J. consult. Psychol.*, 1959, **23**, 468.

Martin, B. The assessment of anxiety by physiological-behavioral measures. *Psychol. Bull.*, 1961, **58**, 234–255.

Martin, B., Lundy, R. M., & Lewin, M. H. Verbal and GSR responses in experimental interviews as a function of three degrees of "therapist" communication. *J. abnorm. soc. Psychol.*, 1960, **60**, 234–240.

Martin, I. Somatic reactivity. In H. J. Eysenck (ed.) *Handbook of Abnormal Psychology.* New York: Basic Books, Inc., 1961.

Martin, I., & Venables, P. H. Mechanisms of palmar skin resistance and skin potential. *Psychol. Bull.*, 1966, **65**, 347–357.

Mason, J. W., Mangan, G., Brady, J. V., Conrad, D., & Rioch, D. McK. Concurrent plasma epinephrine, norepinephrine and 17-hydroxycorticosteroid levels during conditioned emotional disturbances in monkeys. *Psychosom. Med.*, 1961, **23**, 344–353.

Matarazzo, J. D., Guze, S. B., & Matarazzo, Ruth G. An approach to the validity of the Taylor anxiety scale: scores of medical and psychiatric patients. *J. abnorm. soc. Psychol.*, 1955, **51**, 276–280.

Matarazzo, J. D., Ulett, G. A., & Saslow, G. Human maze performance as a function of increasing levels of anxiety. *J. gen. Psychol.*, 1955, **43**, 79–95.

May, R. The existential approach. In S. Arieti (ed.), *American Handbook of Psychiatry.* Vol. II. New York: Basic Books, 1959.

McCawley, A., Stroebel, C. F., & Glueck, B. C. Pupillary reactivity, psychologic disorder, and age. *Arch. gen. Psychiat.*, 1966, **14**, 415–418.

McNair, D. M., Goldstein, A. P., Lorr, M., Cibelli, L. A., & Roth, I. Some effects of chlordiazepoxide and meprobamate with psychiatric outpatients. *Psychopharmacol.*, 1965, **7**, 256–265.

Mednick, Martha T. Mediated generalization and the incubation effect as a function of manifest anxiety. *J. abnorm. soc. Psychol.*, 1957, **55**, 315–321.

Mednick, S. A. Generalization as a function of manifest anxiety and adaptation to psychological experiments. *J. consult. Psychol.*, 1957, **21**, 491–494.

Miller, L. H., & Shmavonian, B. M. Replicability of two GSR indices as a function of stress and cognitive activity. *J. pers. soc. Psychol.*, 1965, **2**, 753–756.

Milliken, R. L. Mathematical-verbal ability differentials of situational anxiety as measured by blood pressure change. *J. exp. Educ.*, 1964, **32**, 309–311.

Mitchell, L. E., & Zax, M. The effects of chlorpromazine on GSR conditioning. *J. abnorm. soc. Psychol.*, 1959, **59**, 246–249.

Moffitt, J. W., & Stagner, R. Perceptual rigidity and closure as functions of anxiety. *J. abnorm. soc. Psychol.*, 1956, **52**, 354–357.

Moldawsky, S., & Moldawsky, Patricia C. Digit span as an anxiety indicator. *J. consult. Psychol.*, 1952, **16**, 115–118.

Montagu, J. D., & Coles, E. M. Mechanism and measurement of the galvanic skin response. *Psychol. Bull.*, 1966, **65**, 261–279.

Montague, E. K. The role of anxiety in serial rote learning. *J. exp. Psychol.*, 1953, **45**, 91–96.

Mordkoff, A. M. The relationship between psychological and physiological response to stress. *Psychosom. Med.*, 1964, **26**, 135–150.

Morgan, C. T. Physiological psychology. New York: McGraw-Hill, 1965.
Mowrer, O. H. Psychotherapy, theory and research. New York: Ronald Press Co., 1953.
Newman, P. P. EMG studies of emotional states in normal subjects. *J. Neurol. Neurosurg. Psychiat.*, 1962, **3**, 29–36.
Nicholson, W. M. The influence of anxiety upon learning: Interference or drive increment? *J. Pers.*, 1958, **26**, 303–319.
Obrist, P. A. GSR conditioning and anxiety as measured by basal conductance. Paper presented at E.P.A. Meetings, Philadelphia, April 11, 1958.
Obrist, P. A. Cardiovascular differentiation of sensory stimuli. *Psychosomatic Med.*, 1963, **25**, 450–459.
O'Connor, J. P., Lorr, M., & Stafford, J. W. Some patterns of manifest anxiety. *J. clin. Psychol.*, 1956, **12**, 160–163.
Ogston, D. Fibrinolytic activity and anxiety and its relation to coronary artery disease. *J. psychosom. Res.*, 1964, **8**, 219–222.
Opton, E. M., & Lazarus, R. S. Personality determinants of psychophysiological response to stress: a theoretical analysis and experiment. *J. pers. soc. Psychol.*, 1967, **6**, 291–303.
Panek, D. M., & Martin, B. The relationship between GSR and speech disturbance in psychotherapy. *J. abnorm. soc. Psychol.*, 1959, **58**, 402–405.
Paredes, A., Baumgold, J., Pugh, L. A., & Ragland, R. Clinical judgment in the assessment of psychopharmacological effects. *J. nerv. ment. Dis.*, 1966, **142**, 153–160.
Paul, G. L. *Insight versus desensitization in psychotherapy: An experiment in anxiety reduction*. Stanford: Stanford University Press, 1965.
Paul, G. L., & Shannon, D. T. Treatment of anxiety through systematic desensitization in therapy groups. *J. abnorm. Psychol.*, 1966, **71**, 124–135.
Persky, H. Response to a life stress: An evaluation of some biochemical indexes. *J. applied Physiol.*, 1953, **6**, 369–372.
Persky, H. Adrenocortical function in anxious human subjects: the disappearance of hydrocortisone from plasma and its metabolic fate. *J. clin. Endocrin. & Metabl.*, 1957, **17**, 760–765. (a)
Persky, H. Adrenalcortical function in anxious human subjects. *Arch. Neurol. Psychiat.*, 1957, **78**, 95–100. (b)
Persky, H. Adrenocortical function in anxiety. In R. Roessler & N. S. Greenfield (eds.) *Physiological correlates of psychological disorders*. Madison: Univ. of Wisconsin Press, 1962.
Persky, H., Grinker, R. R., Hamburg, D. A., Sabshin, M. A., Korchin, S. J., Basowitz, H., & Chevalier, J. A. Adrenal cortical function in anxious human subjects. *Arch. Neurol. Psychiat.*, 1956, **76**, 549–558.
Pfeiffer, C. C., Goldstein, L., Murphree, H. B., & Jenney, E. H. Electroencephalographic assay of anti-anxiety drugs. *Arch. gen. Psychiat.*, 1964, **10**, 446–453.
Pitts, F. N., & McClure, J. N. Lactate Metabolism in anxiety neurosis. *New England J. Med.*, 1967, **277**, 1329–1336.
Plutchik, R. The psychophysiology of skin temperature: a critical review. *J. gen. Psychol.*, 1956, **55**, 249–268.
Pollin, W. Control and artifact in psychophysiological research. In R. Roessler & N. S. Greenfield (eds.), *Physiological correlates of psychological disorders*. Madison: Univ. of Wisconsin Press, 1962, 171–191.
Portnoy, I. The anxiety states. In S. Ariete (ed.), *American Handbook of Psychiatry*, Vol. 1, New York: Basic Books, 1959.
Postman, L., & Bruner, J. S. Perception under stress. *Psychol. Rev.*, 1948, **55**, 314–324.
Pronko, N. H., & Kenyon, G. Y. Meprobamate and laboratory-induced anxiety. *Psychol. Rep.*, 1959, **5**, 217–238.
Raab, E., Carranza, J., Heaney, J., & Rickels, K. Deanol (paxanol) in anxiety. *Dis. nerv. Syst.*, 1966, **27**, 544–546.
Ramond, C. K. Anxiety and task as determiners of verbal performance. *J. exp. Psychol.*, 1953, **46**, 120–124.

Reitan, R. M. The comparative effects of placebo, Ultran, and meprobamate on psychological test performance. *Antibiotic Med. Clin. Therapy*, 1957, **4**, 158–165.

Rickels, K. Developments in psychopharmacology. *Psychosomatics*, 1966, **7**, 274–277.

Rickels, K., Cattell, R. B., Weise, C., Gray, B., Yee, R., Mallin, A., & Aaronson, H. G. Controlled psychopharmacological research in private psychiatric practice. *Psychopharmacologia*, 1966, **9**, 288–306.

Rickels, K., & Snow, L. Meprobamate and phenobarbital sodium in anxiety neurotic psychiatric and medical clinical outpatients. *Psychopharmacol.*, 1964, **5**, 339–348.

Rogers, C. R., & Dymond, Rosalind F. (eds.) *Psychotherapy and Personality Change*. Chicago: Univ. of Chicago Press, 1954.

Rorer, L. G. The great response-style myth. *Psychol Bull.*, 1965, **63**, 129–156.

Rosenbaum, G. Stimulus generalization as a function of clinical anxiety. *J. abnorm. soc. Psychol.*, 1956, **53**, 281–285.

Rossi, A. M. An evaluation of the Manifest Anxiety Scale by the use of electromyography. *J. exp. Psychol.*, 1959, **58**, 64–69.

Rothballer, A. B. The effect of catecholamines on the central nervous system. *Pharmacol. Rev.*, 1959, **11**, 494–544.

Rubin, L. S. Patterns of adrenergic-cholinergic imbalance in the functional psychoses. *Psychol. Rev.*, 1962, **69**, 501–519.

Rubin, L. S. Autonomic Dysfunction as a concomitant of neurotic behavior. *J. nerv. ment. Dis.*, 1964, **138**, 558–573.

Ryan, E. D., & Lakie, W. L. Competitive and noncompetitive performance in relation to achievement motive and manifest anxiety. *J. pers. soc. Psychol.*, 1965, **1**, 342–345.

Sainsbury, P. Gestural movement during psychiatric interview. *Psychosom. Med.*, 1955, **17**, 458–469.

Sainsbury, P. Muscle responses: Muscle tension and expressive movements. *J. psychosom. Res.*, 1964, **8**, 179–186.

Saltz, E., & Hoehn, A. J. A test of the Taylor-Spence theory of anxiety. *J. abnorm. soc. Psychol.*, 1957, **54**, 114–117.

Sarason, I. G. Effect of anxiety, motivational instructions, and failure on serial learning. *J. exp. Psychol.*, 1956, **51**, 253–260.

Sarason, I. G. Effect of anxiety and two kinds of motivating instructions on verbal learning. *J. abnorm. soc. Psychol.*, 1957a, **54**, 166–171.

Sarason, I. G. The effect of anxiety and two kinds of failure on serial learning. *J. Pers.*, 1957b, **25**, 283–291.

Sarason, I. G. A note on anxiety, instructions, and word association performance. *J. abnorm. soc. Psychol.*, 1961, **62**, 153–154.

Sarason, I. G., & Harmatz, M. G. Sex differences and experimental conditions in serial learning. *J. pers. soc. Psychol.*, 1965, **1**, 499–505.

Sarason, I. G., & Palola, E. G. The relationship of test and general anxiety, difficulty of task, and experimental instructions to performance. *J. exp. Psychol.*, 1960, **59**, 185–191.

Sarason, S. B., Davidson, K. S., Lighthall, F. F., Waite, R. R., & Ruebush, B. K. *Anxiety in Elementary School Children*. New York: Wiley, 1960.

Sarason, S. B., Mandler, G., & Craighill, P. G. The effect of differential instructions on anxiety and learning. *J. abnorm. soc. Psychol.*, 1952, **47**, 561–565.

Schachter, J. Pain, fear and anger in hypertensives and normotensives. *Psychosom. Med.*, 1957, **19**, 17–29.

Schachter, S. The interaction of cognitive and physiological determinants of emotional state. In C. D. Spielberger (ed.), *Anxiety and Behavior*. New York: The Academic Press, 1966.

Scheier, I. H., & Cattell, R. B. *Temporary Handbook for the I.P.A.T. 8-Parallel-Form Anxiety Battery*. Champaign, Ill.: Inst. for Pers. and Abil. Testing, 1960.

Schnore, M. M. Individual patterns of physiological activity as a function of task differences and degree of arousal. *J. exp. Psychol.*, 1959, **58**, 117–128.

Schofield, W. A further study of the effects of therapies on MMPI responses. *J. abnorm. soc. Psychol.*, 1953, **48**, 67–77.

Schottstaedt, W. W. Some differential physiological correlates of anxiety and tension. In L. J. West and M. Greenblatt (eds.), *Explorations in the physiology of emotions*. Psychiatric Res. Rep. APA, No. 12, 1960.

Schottstaedt, W. W., Grace, W. J., & Wolff, H. G. Life situations, behavior, attitudes, emotions, and renal excretion of fluids and electrolytes. *J. psychosom. Res.*, 1956–58, **1–2**, 75–83, 147–159, 203–211.

Schwartz, T. B., & Shields, D. R. Urinary excretion of formaldehydrogenic steroids and creatinine. *Psychosom. Med.*, 1956, **18**, 159–172.

Shearn, D. W. Operant conditioning of heart rate. *Science*, 1962, **137**, 530–531.

Shlien, J. M. Comparison of results with different forms of psychotherapy. *Amer. J. Psychotherapy*, 1964, **18**, 15–22.

Siegman, A. W. Cognitive, affective, and psychopathological correlates of the Taylor MAS. *J. consult. Psychol.*, 1956, **20**, 137–141.

Silverman, A. J., Cohen, S. I., & Zuidema, C. Psychophysiological investigations in cardiovascular stress. *Amer. J. Psychiat.*, 1957, **113**, 691–693.

Silverman, R. E. The manifest anxiety scale as a measure of drive. *J. abnorm. soc. Psychol.*, 1957, **55**, 94–97.

Silverman, R. E., & Blitz, B. Learning and two kinds of anxiety. *J. abnorm. soc. Psychol.*, 1956, **52**, 301–303.

Smith, D. B. D., & Wenger, M. A. Changes in autonomic balance during phasic anxiety. *Psychophysiol.*, 1965, **1**, 267–271.

Smith, M. E., & Chassan, J. B. Comparisons of diazepam, chlorpromazine, and trifluo-perazine in a double-blind clinical investigation. *J. Neuropsychiat.*, 1964, **5**, 593–600.

Solley, S. M., & Stagner, R. Effects of magnitude of temporal barriers, type of goal, and perception of self. *J. exp. Psychol.*, 1956, **51**, 62–70.

Sourkes, T. L. *Biochemistry of Mental Disease*. New York: Harper and Row, 1962.

Speisman, J. C., Lazarus, R. S., Mordkoff, A. M., & Davison, L. A. Experimental reduction of stress based on ego-defense theory. *J. abnorm. soc. Psychol.*, 1964, **68**, 367–380.

Speisman, J. C., Osborn, J., & Lazarus, R. S. Cluster analysis of skin resistance and heart rate at rest and under stress. *Psychosom. Med.*, 1961, **23**, 323–343.

Spence, K. W. A theory of emotionally based drive (D) and its relation to performance in simple learning situations. *Amer. Psychologist*, 1958, **13**, 131–141.

Spence, K. W. Anxiety (drive) level and performance in eyelid conditioning. *Psychol. Bull.*, 1964, **61**, 129–139.

Spence, K. W., Farber, I. E., & McFann, H. H. The relation of anxiety (drive) level to performance in competitional and non-competitional paired-associates learning. *J. exp. Psychol.*, 1956, **52**, 296–305.

Spence, K. W., Farber, I. E., & Taylor, Elaine. The relation of electric shock and anxiety to level of performance in eyelid conditioning. *J. exp. Psychol.*, 1954, **48**, 404–408.

Spence, K. W., & Goldstein, H. Eyelid conditioning as a function of emotion-producing instructions. *J. exp. Psychol.*, 1961, **62**, 291–294.

Spence, K. W., & Spence, Janet T. Relation of eyelid conditioning to manifest anxiety, extraversion, and rigidity. *J. abnorm. soc. Psychol.*, 1964, **68**, 144–149.

Spence, K. W., Taylor, Janet, A., & Ketchel, Rhoda. Anxiety (drive) level and degree of competition in paired-associates learning. *J. exp. Psychol.*, 1956, **52**, 306–310.

Stampfl, T. G., & Levis, D. J. Essentials of implosive therapy: a learning-theory-based psychodynamic behavioral therapy. *J. abnorm. Psychol.*, 1967, **72**, 496–503.

Standish, R. R., & Champion, R. A. Task difficulty and drive in verbal learning. *J. exp. Psychol.*, 1960, **59**, 361–365.

Stennett, R. G. The relationship of performance level to level of arousal. *J. exp. Psychol.*, 1957, **54**, 54–61.

Sternbach, R. A. Assessing differential autonomic patterns in emotion. *J. Psychosom. Res.*, 1962, **6**, 87–91.

Sternbach, R. A. *Principles of psychophysiology*. New York: Academic Press, 1966.

Steward, J. R. The effect on heart rate of warnings and receipt of pleasant and aversive auditory stimuli. *Diss. Abstr.*, 1962, **23**, 1803.

Taylor, Janet A. A personality scale of manifest anxiety. *J. abnorm. soc. Psychol.*, 1953, **48**, 285–290.

Taylor, Janet A. The effects of anxiety level and psychological stress on verbal learning. *J. abnorm. soc. Psychol.*, 1958, **57**, 55–60.

Taylor, Janet A., & Chapman, Jean P. Anxiety and the learning of paired-associates. *Amer. J. Psychol.*, 1955, **68**, 671.

Taylor, Janet A., & Spence, K. W. The motivational components of manifest anxiety: drive and drive stimuli. In C. D. Spielberger (ed.), *Anxiety and Behavior*. New York: Academic Press, 1966.

Taylor, Janet A., & Spence, K. W. The relationship of anxiety level to performance in serial learning. *J. exp. Psychol.*, 1952, **44**, 61–64.

Terry, R. A. Autonomic balance and temperament. *J. comp. physiol. Psychol.*, 1953, **46**, 454–460.

Uno, T., & Grings, W. W. Autonomic components of orienting behavior. *Psychophysiology*, 1965, **1**, 311–321.

Venables, P. H. The effect of auditory and visual stimuli on the skin potential response of schizophrenics. *Brain*, 1960, **83**, 77–86.

Walk, R. D. Self-ratings of fear in a fear-invoking situation. *J. abnorm. soc. Psychol.*, 1956, **52**, 171–178.

Wang, G. H. *The neural control of sweating*. Madison: The Univ. of Wisconsin Press, 1964.

Wechsler, D., & Hartogs, R. The clinical measurement of anxiety. *Psychiat. Quart.*, 1945, **19**, 618–635.

Weinar, H. Some psychological factors related to cardiovascular responses: a logical and empirical analysis. In R. Roessler & N. S. Greenfield (eds.), *Physiological correlates of psychological disorders*. Madison: Univ. of Wisconsin Press, 1962.

Welsh, G. S. An anxiety index and an internalization ratio for the MMPI. *J. consult. Psychol.*, 1952, **16**, 65–72.

Welch, L., & Kubis, J. F. Conditioned PGR (psychogalvanic response) in states of pathological anxiety. *J. nerv. ment. Dis.*, 1947, **105**, 372–381.

Wenar, C. Reaction time as a function of manifest anxiety and stimulus intensity. *J. abnorm. soc. Psychol.*, 1954, **49**, 335–340.

Wenger, M. A. The stability of measurement of autonomic balance. *Psychosom. Med.*, 1942, **4**, 94–95.

Wenger, M. A. Studies of autonomic balance in Army Air Force personnel. *Comp. psychol. Monogr.*, 1948, No. **101**.

Wenger, M. A. Pattern analyses of autonomic variables during rest. *Psychosom. Med.*, 1957, **19**, 240–244.

Wenger, M. A., & Gilchrist, J. C. A comparison of two indices of palmar sweating. *J. exp. Psychol.*, 1948, **38**, 757–761.

Westrope, Martha R. Relations among Rorschach indices, manifest anxiety and performance under stress. *J. abnorm. soc. Psychol.*, 1953, **48**, 515–524.

Whatmore, G. B., & Ellis, R. M. Some neurophysiologic aspects of schizophrenia: An electromyographic study. *Amer. J. Psychiat.*, 1964, **120**, 1161–1169.

Williams, J. G. L., & Williams, Barbara. The effect of meprobamate on the somatic responses of anxious patients and normal controls. Paper presented at the Sixth Annual Meeting of the Society for Psychophysiological Research, October, 1966.

Wing, Lorna. Physiological effects of performing a difficult task in patients with anxiety states. *J. Psychosom. Res.*, 1964, **7**, 283–294.

Winne, J. F. A scale of neuroticism: An adaptation of the Minnesota Multiphasic Personality Inventory. *J. clin. Psychol.*, 1951, **7**, 117–122.

Winter, W. D., Ferreira, A. J., & Ransom, R. Two measures of anxiety: A validation. *J. Consult. Psychol.*, 1963, **27**, 520–524.

Wishner, J. Neurosis and tension: An exploratory study of the relation of physiological and Rorschach measures. *J. abnorm soc. Psychol.*, 1953, **2**, 253–260.

Wolf, S., Pfeiffer, J. B. Ripley, H. S., Winter, O. S., & Wolff, H. G. Hypertension as a reaction pattern to stress. *Ann. int. Med.*, 1948, **29**, 1056–1076.

Wolf, S., & Wolff, H. G. *Human gastric function* (2nd ed.). New York: Oxford Univ. Press, 1947.

Wolpe, J. *Psychotherapy by reciprocal inhibition.* Stanford, Calif.: Stanford Univer. Press, 1958.

Wolpe, J., & Lazarus, A. A. Behavior Therapy Techniques. New York: Pergamon, 1966.

Wortis, J. Psychopharmacological and physiological treatment. *Amer. J. Psychiat.*, 1965, **121**, 648–652.

Wright, M. W. A study of anxiety in a general hospital setting. *Canad. J. Psychol.*, 1954, **8**, 195–203.

Zeaman, D., Deane, G., & Wenger, N. Amplitude and latency characteristics of the conditioned heart response. *J. exp. Psychol.*, 1954, **38**, 235–250.

Zimbardo, P. G., Barnard, J. W., & Berkowitz, L. The role of anxiety and defensiveness in children's verbal behavior. *J. Pers.*, 1963, **31**, 79–98.

Zubek, J. P., & Schutte, W. Urinary excretion of adrenaline and noradrenaline during prolonged perceptual deprivation. *J. abnorm. Psychol.*, 1966, **71**, 328–334.

Zuckerman, M. The development of an Affect Adjective Check List for the measurement of anxiety. *J. consult. Psychol.*, 1960, **24**, 457–462.

Zuckerman, M., & Biase, D. V. Replication and further data on the validity of the Affect Adjective Check List measure of anxiety. *J. consult. Psychol.*, 1962, **26**, 291.

Zuckerman, M., Lubin, B., Vogel, L., & Valerius, Elizabeth. Measurement of experimentally induced affects. *J. consult. Psychol.*, 1964, **28**, 418–425.

Zuckerman, M., Persky, H., Hopkins, T. R., Murtaugh, T., Basu, G. K., & Schilling, M. Comparison of stress effects of perceptual and social isolation. *Arch. gen. Psychiat.*, 1966, **14**, 356–365.

Part III

Disorders of Behavior

Chapter 10

Phobias[1]

V. MEYER AND A. H. CRISP

At first acquaintance the phobia may seem to be one of the more tangible as well as circumscribed of abnormal behaviors presenting in the psychiatric clinic. Its definition, which rests at a descriptive level, is of a recurrent, intrusive, excessive, specific fear which is recognized as unreasonable or even absurd by the person who experiences it. This unreasonable but compelling fear can be of things such as an object (for example, a knife), a natural force, (for example, thunder; the dark), a disease (for example, cancer; venereal disease), another living thing (for example, wasps; policemen), a social situation (for example, crowded shops; restaurants) or a place (for example, anywhere other than the home; public lavatories). It may occasionally be associated with an idea or impulse, personally resisted, and also regarded as unreasonable and out of character, but more or less identifiable by the patient, who may be able to express it to the doctor along with the phobia. For example, a young mother may be able to express her unreasonable fear that her baby may be injured by scissors or knives and at the same time disclose her hidden impulse to harm the baby. A fear of heights may be spoken of in the same breath as a recurring but resisted impulse to suicide. A fear of going to the theater may be linked, in the patient's mind, with his impulse to stand up and shout out during the performance. A fear of traveling on buses or trains may be described in association with a compulsion to snatch at a fellow passenger's genitals. Alternatively, the patient or relative may present with a complaint that the former behaves in a handicapping, ritualistic manner, for instance, frequently washing and cleaning, and the patient may or may not readily describe an accompanying fear or other feeling, for instance, a fear of or disgust with dirt. Some of these patients may associate intensification of such rituals with the experience of frightening, aggressive or sexual impulses. The majority will not do this, although some psychiatrists will infer such associations and origins.

Some phobic objects and situations more than others lend themselves to being avoided. Although the fear of dirt and the need to keep it at bay may involve the obsessional patient in a persistent and unavoidable struggle, the patient who fears heights, wasps, or open spaces may, for the most part, successfully avoid these things. These patients are often then characterized clinically by their freedom from anxiety. Indeed, they may sometimes appear bland and uncomplaining. However, they continue to feel fear for the experience of fear in the given

[1]This chapter covers the literature up to the first half of 1968.

situation, also fear of being seen to be so disturbed; their phobia is now of fear itself (Lewis 1956). Freud has delineated a category of anxiety hysteria for these patients. He (see Diethelm, 1950) regarded them clinically as falling midway between the hysterical and the obsessional states.

There are no useful studies of the natural history of this latter category of neurotic illnesses, often called anxiety phobic states. However, there are a number of studies of the course of the related obsessional illnesses. Work by Lewis (1936), Rudin (1953), Muller (1957), Ingram (1961), and Kringlen (1965) all show the tendency for such illnesses to persist for a very long time even when treatment, whether it be psychotherapy, drugs, leucotomy, or E.C.T., is interposed. These workers have found poor prognosis to be usually related to factors such as the severity of the obsessional symptom, the presence of ritualistic behavior, the existence of a premorbid obsessional personality, and the absence of concurrent depressive affect. Although Pollitt (1957) found a somewhat better prognosis among a group of less severely disturbed outpatients with obsessional neurosis, it is evident that the high spontaneous recovery rates claimed for other psychoneurotic illnesses [Denker (1946), Saslow and Peters (1956), Hastings (1958), Wallace and White (1959), and Stevenson (1961)] are not a feature of obsessional neurosis.

Although the natural history of anxiety phobic states per se has not been reported on, Roberts (1964) has reported a $1\frac{1}{2}$- to 6-year follow-up after treatment of 38 women with agoraphobia which had rendered them effectively housebound. Nine were recovered, nine were still completely housebound, and twenty were no longer housebound but still experienced the same or similar phobic anxiety symptoms. He found a good prognosis was associated with a gradual and late age of onset, less severe disability, and marked depression. His patients were described as being normally tense but effective people with superficially adequate social and marital adjustments. However, he noted a high incidence of frigidity.

Some clinicians (Walker, 1959) believe that a depressive mood underlies some anxiety phobic states and will dictate the intensity, prognosis, and treatment method of the latter. However, Gittleson (1966) has recently shown that obsessional symptoms and behavior can just as well disappear as intensify with the emergence of severe depression. Other investigators regard depression as another symptom operating at the same level as other neurotic symptoms, subject to the same conditions of change, and sensitive to the same nonspecific variables. Gehl (1965) has recently proposed on clinical grounds that some anxiety phobic symptoms arise in a cyclical relationship to states of depression, each state successively emerging from the other during the passage of time. Certainly, it is common in the clinic to find patients with obsessional personalities who are depressed in the involutional phase of their lives.

Many adult patients with phobias describe having had fears, now regarded by them as having been unreasonable, during childhood. These have usually been of the dark, of animals, of thunder, or of meeting people. Kringlen (1965) found that about one fourth of these patients reported phobic symptoms in childhood as against one fifth of a control group of psychosomatic patients who did not have a current diagnosis of phobic or obsessional state. This latter finding emphasize the point that many adult patients and healthy subjects without surrent complaints of phobias also describe such childhood experiences. Furthermore, Brandon's (1960) epidemiological study has shown that, in a Northern English urban community, an estimated 38 percent of the girls and 20 percent of the boys have phobias of some degree. Brandon found only a slightly higher percentage of phobias among a group of maladjusted children. However, Lewis (1954) and Craig (1956), by using stricter criteria, found the percentage to be only 12 percent and 16 percent, respectively, among groups of children.

The percentage of obsessive and phobic disorders among inpatient psychiatric populations is reported as varying between 0.2 and 3.1 percent (Ingram, 1961). Most studies report a high proportion of females among these populations. This is probably particularly true of the anxiety phobic patient group. A significantly greater percentage, found by most investigators, of obsessional behavior and symptoms among the families of obsessional and phobic patients does nothing to resolve the nature versus nurture problem. However, most authorities (Kringlen, 1965) are agreed that these patients come from backgrounds in which the parental attitude has been strict and puritanical.

In the past, phobias have been treated by many means; with psychotherapy, psychotropic drugs (Sargent, 1966), including intravenous pentobarbitone (Roth, 1959), electroconvulsive therapy, and leucotomy (Sargent, 1962). Claims for the value of any specific therapeutic measure have rarely taken into account the natural history of the disorder or the importance of nonspecific therapeutic factors. Furthermore, once sedative or tranquilizing drugs have been prescribed, phobic patients often come to depend on high doses of these drugs without any major benefit.

The theories concerning the origins of phobias have been mainly posed by psychoanalytically orientated workers. Phobia formation has been regarded as one of the neurotic defence mechanisms available to some persons who thereby become more able to cope with their lives. Mechanisms of displacement, projection, and denial are conceptualized by such clinicians to explain the development of the symptoms. The individual displaces or projects anxiety from other sources on to an object or environment, often having a symbolic link, which can then be avoided and the source of their anxiety thereby denied. The anxiety is thought to have originally arisen out of a conflict situation in which the individual has been unable to adequately express his or her sexual and/or aggressive impulses. These are often thought of as having arisen or having been evoked within dependency relationships essential for the individual's wellbeing. Thus the housebound agoraphobic housewife binds herself to the expected and safe marital role and thereby avoids exposure to the temptations of freedom contained within her otherwise actively ambivalent attitude to her role. Anxiety that arises out of unsatisfied dependency needs and fears of separation would also be expected sometimes to motivate and reinforce such phobias.

In the present chapter we hope to describe the beginnings of an understanding of phobias based on learning principles and on experimental evidence concerning the acquisition and removal of fear responses both in animals and man. This background provides some of the basis for current behavior therapy as applied to the treatment of phobias.

AETIOLOGY OF PHOBIAS—A BEHAVIORIST VIEW

Watson and Rayner's famous experiment (1920) has been frequently cited as a paradigm of phobic symptom formation on the basis of a simple process of classical Pavlovian conditioning (Pavlov, 1927). Watson created a "phobia" of white rats in a 11-months boy, who had been fond of white rats, by striking a steel bar whenever the boy reached out for the rat. The loud noise (unconditioned stimulus—US, using Pavlovian terminology) produced a fear response (unconditioned response—UR) in the boy and the fear of the sound, as expected, transferred or became conditioned (conditioned response—CR) to the rat (conditioned stimulus—CS). Watson also demonstrated that, following this procedure, the boy displayed fear reactions to other furry animals (dogs and rabbits) and to furry objects (fur coats), although these stimuli were not used in the original conditioning. This well-known phenomenon of the conditioning process is called stimulus generalization: an organism conditioned to one stimulus also responds to other stimuli which resemble the original CS along some continuum. The strongest reaction occurs in response to the CS and the strength of it gradually diminishes as other stimuli become less and less similar to the original CS (generalization gradient).

The fear of rats, thus conditioned, is unadaptive and considered abnormal because in this situation rats are not dangerous in any way. Had the fear been conditioned by the same procedure to a dangerous animal, the response would have been regarded as adaptive and normal. Freud and Breuer (1892) drew attention many years ago to the importance of such "associations" for the development of a specific phobia or an hysterical symptom in humans. However, as previously mentioned, Freud considered that such patterns of behavior persisted or reemerged only because they provided a vehicle for the expression of the patients' repressed needs and fears arising both before and after the acquisition of the associations and, thus, reinforcing or "over determining" it.

From all standpoints it appears then, that

the process of classical conditioning is highly relevant for the acquisition of irrational fears. Thus, phobic reactions may develop by means of such conditioning where, as a a result of pairing a traumatic event evoking fear with a neutral environmental stimulus, the latter acquires the ability to elicit conditioned fear. Let us now consider the question whether this simple model can adequately account for the development and persistence of all phobic manifestations.

The first problem to be considered is this: How are we to account for the persistence of phobic symptoms? According to general learning principles, the elicitation of a habit without reinforcement (omission of reward or punishment) leads to the extinction of the habit. Thus, each time the phobic encounters the phobic CS without a recurrence of the noxious UCS which evoked the original fear, no reinforcement of the conditioned fear occurs and extinction of it should follow in time. That this course of events leads to extinction has been demonstrated in laboratory studies of classical conditioning where the animal is relatively immobilized and irrespective of its behavior is forced to experience the association of the CS—no reinforcement. Most of the phobic patients, however, persist in displaying fear reactions when confronted with the CS. It is the conditioning of instrumental responses produced to reduce or to eliminate the conditioned fear reactions which provides a reasonable answer to this problem. The paradigm of anticipatory traumatic avoidance learning serves best to illustrate this (Solomon & Brush, 1956). Typically, the animal is placed on an electrified grid and presented with a neutral signal (for example, buzzer) followed by an electric shock. The shock activates a pain-fear response, involving central, neuroendocrine and autonomic reactions, and the animal engages in various aversive skeletal responses. Following the performance of one of these skeletal responses, the experimenter terminates the shock and after a few such trials the animal makes this response (escape response) promptly to the onset of the shock. At the same time indications of fear become more and more evident in response to the buzzer, and with further trials the escape response occurs to the onset of the buzzer and becomes an avoidance response. By responding promptly to the signal, the animal learns to avoid the shock. Avoidance responses, thus developed, unlike other instrumental responses, have been shown to persist through hundreds of extinction trials without the readministration of shock. (More recently, Turner & Solomon 1962, have extended this technique to human subjects and have demonstrated that it is possible to set up stable avoidance responses to a neutral CS which are resistant to extinction.)

The avoidance response occurs not to the painful stimulation provided by the shock but to the non-noxious buzzer. The explanation for this is that on early trials of conditioning the sound of the buzzer acquires the ability to evoke a fear response and that this acquired fear then provides the motivation for performing the avoidance response originally elicited by the shock. Since the usual arrangement is that the avoidance response turns off the buzzer and the animal's fear, on the assumption that such fear reduction is rewarding, the fear-reducing response is learned. Thus, the acquired fear, just like the primary fear, possesses drive properties and in its role as a drive energizes, and, by its reduction, reinforces various instrumental avoidance responses. These avoidance responses make the process of extinction impossible because they prevent the organism experiencing the relationship of the CS—no reinforcement. The term anxiety has been commonly applied to the concept of conditioned fear, some learning theorists, however, prefer a more neutral term such as "conditioned avoidance drive," (CAD) which includes such experientially different feelings as anxiety, guilt, and disgust.

There still remains the problem of explaining the persistence of CAD. In order to account for the failure of CAD extinction, Solomon and Wynne (1954) put forward two principles, anxiety conservation and a partial irreversibility of the CAD. According to the first principle, an avoidance response attains a very short latency and removes the conditioned stimulus before the long-latency CAD has a chance to develop fully. However, since in this case no CAD reduction is possible, a decrement in habit strength of the avoidance response occurs. This decrement is revealed in an increased latency of the avoidance response which leads to the full development of the CAD and to the strengthening of the habit (decreased latency) once more through reinforcement (CAD reduction). Thus, massed evocations of the CAD are not possible and, for this reason, the CAD is protected from rapid extinction. However, since the CS is not followed by the UCS, gradual weakening of the CAD would be expected and extinction of the avoidance response should ensue, although extremely slowly. To account for the apparent failure of extinction procedures, the authors postulated the second principle. According to it, severe trauma causes irreversible physiological changes, and possibly endocrinological changes, which result in a partial irreversibility of the CAD. Complete evocation of the CAD may also include such reactions and, consistently with the principle of irreversibility, the original traumatic conditions would be reinstated, leading to a vicious circle. The evidence in support of these principles is far from being clear-cut and, at the present stage of our knowledge, all that can be said is that ordinary extinction procedures are not very effective for instrumental avoidance responses established on the basis of traumatic learning.

In traumatic avoidance experiments the animals do not usually develop disturbed behavior which could merit the term "neurotic." This is understandable because the escape and avoidance responses are successful and the CAD plays an adjustive role. When animals are submitted to traumatic shocks from which they are unable to escape, they usually display behavior that could be more reasonably described as "neurotic." In such experiments various autonomic and skeletal responses, originally elicited by the shock, persistently appear not only in the apparatus but also outside it in response to stimuli associated with the traumatic situation. Mowrer and Viek's experiment (1948) indicates that such marked behavioral disturbances are because no effective escape or avoidance responses may be established. The persistence of "experimental neurosis," however, requires an explanation since the animal is frequently exposed to the CS-s without the UCS, and extinction would be expected. In attempting to account for the persistence, Wolpe (1958) argues that each time the animal is passively removed from the experimental cage, the ongoing CAD at the time is reduced and this reinforces "neurotic reactions." (Wolpe rejects the principle of partial irreversibility of the CAD and similar theories, all of which imply some organic damage, on the grounds that in such a case the elimination of neurotic responses by learning processes would not be possible.) If this formulation is correct then one would expect a prolonged confinement of the organism in a feared situation to lead to the extinction of fear and avoidance responses. Evidence for this will be considered later.

It appears then that traumatic avoidance learning serves as an analogue of the development and persistence of phobias. Such a formulation presupposes two stages: (a) classical conditioning of an autonomic disturbance (CAD), resulting from a traumatic experience, to incidental environmental stimuli; and (b) instrumental conditioning of responses which lead to the avoidance of the conditioned stimuli. It is this second stage of development which prevents the process of extinction from taking place. By acquiring the habit of avoidance, the phobic eventually manages to exclude the possibility of encountering the phobic stimulus at all (for example, housebound housewife). In psychiatric parlance "spontaneous remission" does not occur because avoidance behavior makes it impossible for the patient to "test reality" (Eysenck, 1963).

The next problem to be considered is the nature of aversive stimuli on the basis of which phobias may develop. Thus far, we have concerned ourselves with physical pain of traumatic dimensions as an extreme and prototypal instance of environmental stress and have seen that conditioning is possible with a few trials involving such stimuli. The first pertinent question here is whether a single, severe, traumatic trial and whether a series of subtraumatic events may produce similar effects as will a few traumatic events. The available evidence about the dynamics of this process in individual cases is too scanty to permit a satisfactory answer. However, experimental confirmation of one-trial traumatic conditioning in the rat has been provided by Hudson (1950). Recently, Campbell et al. (1964) demonstrated that a single experience of respiratory paralysis in human subjects, produced by Scoline, established a conditioned response to a neutral stimulus that persisted and became stronger in time over 100 extinction trials. (In this case, however, the effect of the UCS—horrifying experience—cannot be equated with physical pain.) From laboratory studies many instances have been reported of conditioning being established in animals and human subjects after as few as two reinforcement trials with relatively mild noxious stimuli (Franks, 1960), and a series of these reinforcements may have effects equivalent to a few reinforcements with powerful noxious stimuli (Wolpe, 1958). To explain how a severe CAD could develop with repeated conditioning of a mild CAD, Wolpe postulates that anxiety has additive properties. The slight amount of fear evoked by the UCS and the even smaller CAD, conditioned to the CS on the previous trial, add together, allowing a greater amount of the combination of fear and anxiety to be conditioned. This leads to a greater amount of the CAD to be added to the fear on the next trial. As the trials proceed, the amount of the CAD increases at an accelerated rate. Wolpe admits that his hypothesis merely suggests a possible mechanism by which intensities of the CAD may be conditioned by the use of mild noxious stimuli and that other variables may complicate it.

A considerable amount of evidence indicates that the development of a CAD may derive from stimuli other than the ones that produce direct physical pain. Jones (1960) drew attention to reports on individuals with congenital insensitivity to pain which suggest that pain is not the sole precursor of a CAD. "Experimental neurosis" can be induced in animals in situations that require the learning of progressively more difficult discriminations without the use of a noxious UCS. Disturbed behavior ensues when the animal is unable to make the required discriminations. Whatever the merits of various formulations put forward to account for this induced "neurotic behaviour" (see Broadhurst, 1960), the important implication is that ambivalent stimulation, eliciting opposing response tendencies simultaneously, may give rise to anxiety. That the nature of a CAD produced by this stimulation is similar to the one precipitated by noxious stimuli appears to find support in an experiment by Fonberg (1956). By using noxious stimuli, she trained dogs to perform instrumental avoidance responses to various conditioned stimuli. Subsequently, the dogs were made "neurotic" by increasing the difficulty of a discriminatory salivary response to different stimuli. Simultaneously with the emergence of disturbed behavior, the previously established avoidance responses reappeared. Ambiguous stimulation may be considered as an experimental equivalent of a psychological conflict situation. For humans, many of these situations involve forceful but incompatible response tendencies derived from the process of socialization where strongly motivated but socially undesirable patterns of behavior are punished by various means. Frustration, in the sense of failing to attain a desired or important goal, may constitute another possible source for the generation of aversive reactions. (Readers interested in experimental studies of conflict and frustration are referred to Yates 1962.) It is important to bear in mind in this context that any CS that has acquired the power to elicit a CAD may serve as a basis for further (higher-order) conditioning to take place. This has been well demonstrated by Wolpe (1958) in a cat. By pairing an auditory stimulus, to which strong anxiety reactions had been previously conditioned, with various environmental stimuli, the latter acquired the ability to evoke anxiety and withdrawal responses in the animal.

The above analysis has been based almost entirely on findings and principles derived from laboratory animal experiments. Few would doubt the value and relevance of these experiments in relation to aetiological considerations of phobic disorders. However, attempts to extrapolate animal psychology to human behavior may be seriously questioned. In addition to the usual distance separating controlled laboratory experiments from learning in a free environment, there is the gap resulting from the fact that much human learning involves complex conceptual processes, aided by linguistic symbolization. Furthermore, a great deal of human learning takes place in a social context. Indeed, there is some evidence to indicate that in humans the features of avoidance learning and extinction may be drastically more complex.

Examination of the literature reveals that phobic disorders may be acquired with no personal experience of traumatic stimuli. Probably the first and the most direct demonstration of this can be found in a study by Jones (1924b). A child with no fear of rabbits and another who was afraid of them were put together into a pen with a rabbit; the first child immediately developed anxiety reactions to the animal which persisted for over two days. Jones suggested that social imitation was perhaps the most common source of irrational fear in children. Murphy et al. (1955) and Miller et al. (1962, 1963) have shown that monkeys can acquire a CAD merely by seeing another monkey receive shocks. The real gap in the behavioristic account of social conduct has been only recently filled by Bandura and Walters (1963) who emphasize the role of social variables in the development and modification of human behavior. In particular, they make an impressive case for social imitation as one of the most important primary modes of learning. Recent investigations on children and adults demonstrate that CAD can be acquired by observers who merely witness aversive stimuli being administered to performing individuals (Breger 1962, Bandura 1965, Bandura & Rosenthal 1966).

An experiment carried out by Bridger and Mandel (1964) demonstrates that verbal cues can give rise to a CAD. A group of subjects was told that they would receive one strong electric shock following a CS. Then the CS was repeatedly presented, and all subjects showed galvanic skin responses (GSR), although they did not receive the shock. The magnitude of GSR was just as large as that found in another group of subjects that actually received the shock on every trial. However, when the shock electrodes were removed and the subjects informed that they would not be shocked, in contrast to the reinforcement group, there was an immediate extinction in the threatened group. This finding may have important implications for treatment and will be discussed later.

Whatever the original conditioned stimulus, by the process of stimulus generalization and higher-order conditioning, a CAD may spread to a range of stimuli which may appear to share no common features with each other. Studies on semantic generalization (Razran, 1964) indicate that verbal links may also facilitate generalization. Furthermore, it is reasonable to suppose that a spread of a CAD to new stimuli may take place on the basis of symbolic associations. It has been shown that many learning processes may occur without the individual being aware of them: a response may be conditioned to a stimulus or a class of stimuli while the subject is unaware of any connection or of any reinforcement (for example, Lacey & Smith, 1954; Greenspoon, 1962). Finally, secondary gains derived from phobic conditions may facilitate the development and maintenance of phobias. Once the symptom has been acquired, it may become rewarding in some circumstances and the newly acquired rewards may reinforce and maintain it. Lazarus (1966) drew attention to social reinforcement for the persistence of avoidance behavior in cases of agoraphobia. Typically, in order to offset social isolation, the agoraphobic forms strong and dependent interpersonal relationships.

The central conceptual theme originally advanced seemed pretty simple, that is, the acquisition of anxiety on the basis of traumatic stimuli in relation to concurrent external stimuli and the development of instrumental avoidance behavior mediated by the acquired drive. However, additional considerations have revealed a number of complicating factors, and it is not surprising that at present there is no reliable and valid way of tracing the historical development of phobias in an individual case. At this point, even a sympathetic reader may, quite justifiably, raise two objections against the basic formulations. First, he may point out that it does not account for the low incidence of phobias in the population. Second, he may argue that since the common problem that characterizes neurotic patients in general is anxiety and various behavioral "defences" built against it, the formulation advanced here does not explain why only a proportion of patients present classical phobic conditions. Ample evidence for a wide range of relevant individual differences, both physiological and psychological in nature, appears to go some way in meeting these objections. Particularly pertinent in this context is Eysenck's dimensional system of "neuroticism" and "introversion—extraversion" (Eysenck, 1957). According to this theory, neuroticism implies a labile or overreactive autonomic nervous system in response to any stressful stimuli. The more autonomically reactive, the more prone is the individual to develop neurotic disorders. The introversion—extraversion dimension, on the other hand, determines the speed and firmness with which conditioned responses are built up; introverts and extraverts are characterized by the ease and difficulty, respectively, with which they form conditioned responses.

An explanatory neurological concept of "inhibition—excitation" has been put forward by Eysenck to account for the behavior of introverts and extraverts. It is postulated that individuals scoring high on neuroticism and introversion (dysthymics) are predisposed to develop symptoms of an excitatory nature, such as anxieties, phobias, compulsions and ruminations, reactive depressions; those high on neuroticism and extraversion (hysterics), on the other hand, are predestined to display inhibitory symptoms, such as paralyses, amnesias, anaesthesias, and psychopathic patterns of behavior. The evidence and arguments advanced by Eysenck in support of the theory appear to be impressive in general, but a number of studies have been reported that do not support, or even contradict, certain aspects of the theory (for example, Davidson et al., 1964, 1966; Becker & Matteson, 1961); also no general factor of conditioning has been established (for example, Bunt & Barendregt, 1961). Eysenck (1965), however, has argued that these studies failed to take a number of relevant considerations into account. Nonetheless the theory does not specifically account for a wide range of symptoms stemming from similar dynamics, that is, avoidance behavior by which conditioned stimuli are removed and, hence, the CAD reduced. Such a dynamic system is hard put to explain, for example, why some patients develop avoidance responses of somatic nature (for example, hysterical conversion symptoms) or why dysthymics as a group display a variety of symptoms. The already available evidence that different autonomic and motor mechanisms are specifically susceptible in different individuals to activation by stress and are related to symptoms (for example, Lacey et al., 1953; Malmo & Shagass, 1949) indicates the need for further research in this area, which will no doubt pay a dividend in the attempts to develop a comprehensive aetiological theory.

One factor which has not been considered thus far, and which no doubt plays an important role in contributing to differences on the behavioral level among dysthymic patients, is the nature of conditioned stimuli. Thus, if a nonpersonal, external anxiety-producing stimulus is under the individual's control, in that it can be sucessfully avoided, a classical phobia as clinically defined may be expected. In the case when a conditioned stimulus occurs frequently and cannot be completely eliminated from the environment, repeated rituals may take place to reduce the evoked anxiety. Ubiquitous and poorly defined stimulus configurations of which the individual is not aware may give rise to so-called "free floating anxiety." Stimuli involved in the individual's own behavior during stress may also become conditioned stimuli. For instance, if an individual experiences positive sexual or aggressive impulses during stress, these covert responses give rise to associated internal stimulation which in turn may acquire the ability to evoke anxiety. Similar effects may develop on the basis of the mediation hypothesis, when actual overt sexual or aggressive acts are punished. Thus, conditioned avoidance responses may develop not only to external stimuli that arouse such positive responses, but also to internal stimulation associated with such responses. Since these internal stimuli are, in a sense, self-generated, they would be least likely to be avoided successfully (Jones, 1960). If these sources of anxiety are frequently recurring impulses or ideas which are not under the patient's voluntary control, repeated and apparently "senseless" ritualistic actions may ensue. One may ask in this context whether there are any known dimensions that could determine which particular stimulus, among a number of stimuli present during stress, would most likely become a conditioned stimulus for an individual subject. Little is known about it, but on theoretical grounds one would expect that a stimulus which particularly engages the individual's attention at the time of stress would be the most likely. In addition, a stimulus that in the past acquired the ability to elicit mild anxiety would have a greater chance.

In conclusion, it should be emphasized that the aetiological theory of phobias based on learning principles derived from animal experiments is, at least, a simplified version of the true state of affairs; much modification and elaboration will be required. Criticism on this score is justified, but an outright rejection of such a formulation is not warranted in view of the impressive experimental evidence. Several critics voiced an opinion, directly or indirectly, that learning theory accounts for the course of some "simple" phobias but not for "complex" phobias (for example, Shafer & Jaffe, 1965; Marks & Gelder, 1966); Fish (1964) divides phobias into the ones which are conditioned or learned and the hysterical, and obsessional categories, the implication is that the latter complex phobias, for which an "underlying conflict" can be found, are not subject to learning processes. It is not stated what kind of different machanisms are involved. The argument advanced here is that "underlying disturbances"—themselves learned—may lead on the basis of higher-order conditioning to the development of phobias. In other words, learning processes may still be operating in the development of complex phobias and may offer a rational link between "conflicts" and phobias. Granting the complexity of human learning, much of it can be explained by a simultaneous application of a series of simple events and basic principles derived from animal experiments. Even internal processes may turn out to be subject to the same principles as external behavior patterns. A number of learning theorists have provided arguments in favor of the mediational behavioristic position according to which covert responses, such as "thoughts" and "feelings" are regarded in the same manner as overt responses (for example, Osgood, 1953; Mowrer, 1960); also the central role played by "covert thinking responses" in operant conditioning has been recognized (for example, Hefferline, 1962; Staats & Staats, 1963; Homme, 1965).

A simple formulation in the initial stages of development has a distinct advantage in that it yields clear-cut testable hypotheses. Apart from that, it should be remembered that all theory is of necessity a simplified, and therefore incomplete, account of the actual facts.

ASSESSMENT TECHNIQUES

In clinical practice the diagnosis of phobic symptoms is often straightforward. Patients with phobic symptoms are aware of their irrational fears, and a careful questioning can elicit sufficient information about the specific stimulus antecedents of anxiety, subjective experiences of anxiety (for example, sweating, palpitation, trembling, tight sensation in the stomach, etc.) and the nature of avoidance behavior. Confronting the patient with the phobic object or situation, when possible, can provide more objective evidence for the patient's complaints. It is not surprising, therefore, that no specific attempts have been made to develop a diagnostic test for this condition. Nonetheless, systematic and objective measures of the relevant variables would be highly desirable and valuable to clinicians and researchers for designing treatment and for evaluating changes. Let us examine briefly some of these attempts and the possible developments in this area.

Recently several attempts have been made to construct and to evaluate rating scales (Fear Survey Schedules) designed to provide brief measures of commonly occurring fears. Each inventory consists of a list of stimulus situations which cover a wide range of most common sources of anxiety. The content of these scales are situations to which it is unadaptive for a person to experience anything more than mild anxiety. Each item is rated by the subject on a point scale that yields a measure of intensity of specific "phobias" and a total score. Wolpe and Lang (1964) developed such an inventory on the basis of clinical observations and offer it for clinical use. Grossberg and Wilson (1965) applied this schedule to undergraduate students and demonstrated a positive correlation between the total score and Taylor's Manifest Anxiety Scale. However, the amount of common variance indicates that the scales cannot be used interchangeably. Geer (1965) constructed a similar inventory from the responses of a college population and carried out several studies employed in evaluating the scale. He found the internal consistency reliability of the scale to be high and demonstrated its correlations with several personality scales, confirming Grossberg and Wilson's finding. He also conducted validation studies in which subjects were divided into high, medium and low, or high and low fear groups selected on the basis of their response to specific items of the scale, and in which they were asked to approach the actual feared stimuli as closely as they could. The dependent variables used were measures of the following: the distance that the subject stopped from the stimulus, "latency" scores, that is, the time from the end of instructions to the final approach point, the subject's rating of the intensity of fear experienced when nearest to the stimulus, Affective Adjective Check List, and the experimenter's rating of the subject's fear. The fear groups were differentiated in the expected direction on almost all the variables, and all the correlations between them were significant. Lanyon and Manosevits (1966) investigated the relationship between scores on a self-report fear survey schedule and independent measures of behavior in a fear-arousing situation. Subjects who reported mild, moderate and intense fear of spiders were found to differ on most of the situational measures from subjects who did not report spider fear. However, subjects who initially reported different degrees of fear did not differ among themselves on the situational measures. Lang and Lazovik (1963) and Cooke (1966) used Fear Survey Schedules to assess changes in "phobic" behavior of college students in an experimental study of desensitization therapy. They have shown a positive relationship between changes in overt avoidance behavior in response to the "phobic" stimulus (snake) and the subjects' ratings of their fear. It appears then that self-report measures of fear tend to be valid indicators of fear behavior in an actual fear-evoking situation.

Since the norms and findings reported on Fear Survey Schedules have been entirely derived from university nonpsychiatric samples, the application of these measures to psychiatric patients has limited usefulness. The mere fact that irrational fears have been found to be quite common among the student populations, yet none of them sought psychiatric help, indicates the necessity of extending research to psychiatric populations. It may well turn out that the main differentiating characteristics between "phobic" individuals who are not attending a psychiatric clinic and phobic patients are not so much the intensity of fear but the extent to which the disturbance interferes with their social mobility, interpersonal relationships and work, and also the presence of other symptoms. Clinical evidence indicates that patients with clear-cut, circumscribed phobias are not common. In the present stage of development the greatest value of the available Fear Survey Schedules is their use as research tools, particularly for the selection of subjects and evaluation of changes. To a lesser extent they can also be useful in clinical practice. For instance, they can quickly provide the information whether one or several stimuli are the sources of disturbance in individual patients; for patients who endorse several stimuli, the relative intensities of disturbance can be obtained. However, Rubin et al.'s (1968) factor analytic study of Geer's schedule indicates that the 51 items that comprise the inventory were drawn from four major areas and are not entirely independent fears. According to the authors, the implication of this is that the total score is a misleading criteria in terms of which to select subjects for comparative studies. It seems then that fear survey schedules must take into account the areas from which individual items are drawn. The authors advocate the use of factor scores rather than general or single-item scores.

Useful as they are, inventories and rating scales have certain limitations because they can be faked and, in addition, some patients may not be fully aware of all the sources of anxiety. At least two methods that could overcome these limitations and that yield more precise information are worth considering. One of them is based on the concept of "perceptual defence" (see review by Inglis, 1960). In essence, this phenomenon shows that the time for recognition of emotionally-toned stimuli presented for very brief exposures increases as compared with recognition thresholds for neutral stimuli. It has been postulated that recognition is avoided as an anxiety-reducing device. One of the serious complications in this method is that subjects with very a high-anxiety reaction to stress may recognise emotionally toned stimuli very quickly. It has been argued that this "sensitization" or "vigilance" may be because of the disruptive effects of strong anxiety on the process of successful perceptual avoidance. Apart from that, no norms are available for this method. The second method of assessing anxiety involves the recording of various somatic reactions that seem to be related to the experience of anxiety (see the review by Martin, 1960, and Chapter 9 of this book by Martin and Sroufe). Kelly (1966) has recently shown that "basal" forearm blood flow may be used as an index of anxiety which can be of diagnostic value. Limited attempts to use recordings of various indexes of anxiety to trace changes during treatment have been reported (for example, Agras, 1965, 1967; Hoenig & Reed, 1966). Thus, Hoenig and Reed, in their study, suggest that recordings of anxiety by means of psychogalvanic skin response (PGR) to key anxiety words, and to imaginary and to real stimuli do not always conform to the results assessed by the usual clinical methods, which largely rely on the patients' verbal reports of progress in treatment. The superiority claimed for these techniques is that they provide involuntary and, therefore, more direct measures of anxiety or arousal. On the other hand, this method requires an expensive and elaborate recording apparatus and the evaluation of tracings presents considerable difficulties. Moreover, so far as social and clinical recovery is concerned, the patient's report of his feelings of anxiety and his behavior may prove to be more relevant than any record of autonomic changes. Thus, although both methods have obvious advantages and are useful for research purposes, their usefulness for clinical work will remain restricted until the limitations and complications involved are resolved.

A great majority of phobics are patients who either display multiple phobias or, in addition to the main phobic complaint, present other symptoms. To adopt appropriate and comprehensive treatment programs for patients with these more complex symptom patterns, the behavior therapist is obliged from the outset to ferret out and to identify the relevant dimensions along which therapy should proceed. In cases of multiple phobias, it is important to determine whether they are independent or whether they can be subsumed under some generalisation continuum. When additional symptoms are present, it is essential to determine whether they are reactions to the phobic condition or whether they are primary symptoms on the basis of which the main complaint has developed. Finally, the relevance of any ongoing stress in the patient's environment as well as the possibility of secondary gains in relation to the development and the maintenance of the phobia must be considered. At the moment, there are no objective assessment methods which provide a valid answer to these problems.

One method which may eventually prove useful is Kelly's Repertory Grid Technique for measuring relationships between concepts (Kelly, 1955). The main advantages of the technique are the following: it can be used for a systematic study of the individual case; it does not involve a direct report; the subject is allowed to deal with vital and meaningful material in terms of his personal life; precise quantification of the responses is possible. Recently, the use of the technique, with various modifications, and the theory underlying it has been steadily extended to the fields of clinical psychology and psychiatry (Bannister, 1965, 1966; Bannister & Mair, 1968; Crisp, 1966). It appears that this method can be adapted for establishing hierarchies of stimulus situations evoking anxiety and for providing some insight into the underlying meaning of a symptom for a patient. This approach might also be useful as a means of checking whether or not some consistent thread of meaning runs through a variety of apparently unconnected symptoms in one patient.

The foregoing considerations indicate that at present Fear Survey Schedules, rating scales, and direct estimates of avoidance behavior are practicable and informative objective aids at the disposal of the behavior therapist for planning treatment and evaluating progress. Extension of the preliminary work on these methods to psychiatric patients will no doubt increase their usefulness. However, there still remain a number of important aspects of the condition for which no adequate and readily applicable methods of assessment are available. In this connection there appears to be no substitute for a carefully conducted interview of the patient and for clinical experience.

MODIFICATION TECHNIQUES — treatment

Description

Mary Cover Jones' study (1924a and b) of methods for removing irrational fears in children, crude and naive as it may appear, was the first demonstration of the therapeutic properties of direct deconditioning of phobias and provided the springboard for new advances in treatment of symptoms mediated by anxiety. Among several methods investigated, which unfortunately were not used in pure form, she claimed to have found success with two—direct deconditioning and social imitation. The case of Peter illustrates the procedures. The child was seated in a high chair and given food he liked. The experimenter introduced a rabbit (the feared stimulus) in a cage at a distance at which eating response was not interfered with. While Peter was eating, the animal was gradually brought nearer to him and eventually released from the cage. Occasionally, other children not afraid of the rabbit were brought in "to help with the unconditioning." Eventually the fear response was diminished in favor of the positive response which "transferred" without training to other anxiety-provoking stimuli resembling the animal.

The method of direct deconditioning essentially involved the process of counterconditioning whereby the fear-object was associated with a stimulus (food) capable of arousing a positive reaction. Since direct confrontation with the phobic stimulus aroused anxiety so intense that it was not possible to initiate and sustain alternative behavior, the generalization principle was made use of and exploited therapeutically. In this instance, the boy was presented with a stimulus situation that resembled the original one but that evoked a reduced amount of anxiety. This enabled the substitution of an adaptive, normal reaction for the original, unadaptive anxiety response. The normal reaction became dominant and, because of its own generalization gradient, the process was repeated along a graded continuum of similar situations, moving toward the original one. Eventually the normal response became prepotent in all circumstances. This is essentially one of the methods advocated by Jersild and Holmes (1935) for treating children's fears and continues to be used occasionally for phobic patients in general (for example, Meyer & Gelder, 1963; Marks & Gelder, 1965; Gelder & Marks, 1966). The method, sometimes referred to as gradual habituation or toleration technique, utilises mainly a graduated presentation of the actual fear stimulus, and no special effort is made to instigate in the situations a specific response incompatible with anxiety. For example, agoraphobics are required to walk with the therapist and then, on their own, gradually increasing distances; acrophobics are requested to climb increasing heights; claustrophobics are placed in rooms of gradually decreasing dimensions. The application of this technique is well illustrated by Freeman and Kendrick (1960) in the treatment of a case of cat phobia. The patient had to handle the following series of stimuli: materials graded in texture and appearance from very unlike to very like cat fur, a toy kitten, pictures of cats, a live kitten which eventually the patient was required to take home and keep. It was expected that as the kitten grew the positive response would be maintained and would generalize to all strange cats. Before treatment is undertaken the therapist must first of all identify the relevant sources of anxiety pertaining to the phobic stimulus or situation and then compile them in a hierarchical order. The usual procedure is to ask the patient to rank the items in terms of the amount of anxiety experienced with each.

On the basis of his theory of neurosis, Wolpe (1958) has elaborated a therapeutic system based on the principle of counterconditioning, called by him reciprocal inhibition, which states:

> "If a response inhibitory to anxiety can be made to occur in the presence of anxiety—evoking stimuli so that it is accompanied by a complete or partial suppression of the anxiety response, the bond between these stimuli and the anxiety responses will be weakened."

He proposed and applied a number of responses which are "physiologically antagonistic to or incompatible with anxiety," but the behavioral response that has had the widest application in reciprocal inhibition therapy is deep muscular relaxation. It has been the basis of what is known now as systematic desensitization technique which has been most widely adopted by behavior therapists for treatment of phobias.

Only a brief description of the operations involved in systematic desensitization will be given here since a detailed account of the technique has been published (Wolpe, 1961; Wolpe & Lazarus, 1966). A detailed history of the symptom is taken and a particular effort is made to elicit those characteristics of the phobic stimulus which produces greatest anxiety. For example, for a patient with a pathological fear of wasps, they may turn out to be size (the larger the wasp the greater the fear), buzzing (the louder the buzzing the more the anxiety), proximity (the nearer the wasp the more fear evoked), and movement (the more active the insect the greater the fear). These dimensions provide the basis for constructing a list of graded items or an anxiety hierarchy. Gradually, working up through the list, each element is changed until a large, noisily buzzing wasp, flying close to the patient's face would be the strongest item.

At about the same time the patient undergoes relaxation training which essentially consists of making him tense up and relax various muscles and of drawing his attention to the differences between bodily sensations thus produced. When training has produced a "sufficient" degree of relaxation, desensitization proper begins. The patient is asked to relax in the way he has learned and to signal whenever feeling disturbed. He is then required to imagine a scene representing the weakest stimulus item on the anxiety hierarchy. If relaxation remains unimpaired, this is followed by having the patient imagine the next item and so on, until the strongest anxiety-provoking item can be imagined without the evocation of anxiety.

The usual practice, advocated by Wolpe, is to conduct desensitization under hypnosis with the patient sitting on a comfortable chair. However, hypnosis is not an essential requirement and, with patients who cannot be hypnotized or object to it, the procedure is omitted and nonhypnotic relaxation is employed. Lazarus (1964) drew attention to "crucial procedural factors" involved in desensitization proper and provided "a logical and consistent modus operandi." The most important thing is to maintain deep relaxation throughout to prevent the desensitization process per se from assuming anxiety-mediating properties. If the patient signals anxiety, he is told to stop imagining an on-going scene and is instructed to relax. The item is presented again when the patient attains a deep relaxation level. Repeated signalling at the commencement of the hierarchy indicates that the gradient requires extension to weaker items. Occurrence of repeated signalling after a few items have been successfully desensitized is handled by withdrawing the stimulus, reinstating deep relaxation, and by presenting the items which have been successfully dealt with. No session should be terminated when a disturbance is reported, since the last item of any learning series is well retained. The duration of scene presentations is a matter of a few seconds for the first few items, and the time is gradually increased as the treatment progresses. The patient's ability to arrive at a clear image and the nature of the on-going activity in the scene determine the timing of it. The interval between the presentation of individual scenes is again a matter of a few seconds when no disturbance is indicated; otherwise, the duration is determined by the time taken to reinduce deep relaxation. As regards the number of items per session, the general rule advocated is to start 2 to 4 and then to augment the number as the therapy proceeds. The main considerations regarding the duration of sessions are the availability of time and the endurance of the patient; the usual time is approximately 30 minutes. No specific rules are given as to the spacing of sessions. Wolpe (1961) states:

> "Whether sessions are massed or widely dispersed, there is almost always a close relation between the extent to which desensitization has been accomplished and the degree of diminution of anxiety responses to real stimuli."

Lazarus (1961) described an adaptation of systematic desensitization to the group treatment of phobic disorders. Patients displaying the same kind of phobia (for example, claustrophobia) were all given the same hierarchy for desensitization. A group of patients with mixed phobias were handed the items of their relevant hierarchies on slips of paper.

Perusal of the literature reveals that sometimes systematic desensitization is used with real stimuli; sometimes systematic desensitization in imagination is combined with graded retraining with real stimuli. (Marks & Gelder, 1965; Meyer & Crisp, 1966.) Other responses than relaxation, capable of inhibiting anxiety, have been occasionally utilized. For instance, in treating children's phobias, Lazarus (1959) made use of feeding responses and drugs (amobarbital and phenalglycodol) while presenting imaginary and real stimuli. Friedman (1966) used methohexitine sodium in systematic desensitization of phobias in adults. Lazarus and Abramovitz (1962) reported the use of "emotive imagery" capable of arousing positive feelings. The phobic child was required "to imagine a sequence of events which is close enough to his everyday life to be creditable, but within which is woven a story concerning his favorite hero or alter-ego." Recently Lazarus (1965) has shown the possibility of exploiting vigorous and well timed muscular activity (for example, blows at a punching bag) as a suitable anxiety-inhibiting response. Wolpe (1958) drew attention to the usefulness of avoidance responses (anxiety-relief responses) in the framework of reciprocal inhibition. The rationale underlying this technique is as follows: if the termination of a traumatic stimulation is repeatedly associated with a stimulus, that stimulus acquires the ability to evoke relief responses which follow the cessation of the noxious stimulation and which provide means of inhibiting anxiety. Isolated examples of the application of this technique have been documented (Meyer, 1957; Lazarus, 1959, 1963; Thorpe et al., 1964; Solyom & Miller, 1967). The usual procedure is to administer an electric shock that is terminated as soon as the patient utters either the word "calm" or the word representing the phobic stimulus.

These specific techniques have been rarely used since they were mainly intended for those individuals who were incapable of deriving benefit from systematic desensitization based on relaxation. Furthermore, they have usually been applied in conjunction with other methods.

Results: Psychiatric Patients

Since most systematic attempts to apply learning principles to the problem of treatment have adopted more or less orthodox Hullian stimulus-response theory, the S-R model has determined to a great extent the selection of cases and symptoms for treatment. Consequently, one finds that a majority of reports on behavior therapy are concerned with patients with relatively well-defined behavioral abnormalities elicitable by clear-cut stimuli. From a practicable point of view this trend is understandable because it is easier to apply learning principles to disorders in which the concepts of stimulus and response can be relatively clearly defined. For this reason, the number of phobic patients treated by behavior therapy is greater than other types of patients. However, despite an extensive literature, when we inquire about the efficacy of reciprocal inhibition as applied to phobias, we are struck by the dearth of critical evidence. Most of the published reports deal with isolated cases and offer illustrations of the method rather than proofs of the efficacy of treatment. Several reports, describing results of more extensive series of phobics, are subject to damaging criticism on a number of counts (Breger & McGaugh, 1965). Most have not dealt adequately with important design problems: sampling biases are common in that patients who had not completed a certain number of sessions were excluded; the degree of improvement is frequently assessed by the therapist who conducted treatment or by people who are sufficiently acquainted with the design and treatment to be subject to observer's bias; where ratings are used, intra- and inter-rater reliabilities are not reported; more than one specific learning technique of treatment is often employed and other therapeutic procedures included but experimental control is seldom exerted which would enable one to assign results unequivocally to a specific technique; few studies include a satisfactory follow-up and control groups to allow for "spontaneous recovery." Furthermore, results of various reports are not comparable because samples of patients differ in terms of diagnostic classification, severity of phobias, the number and nature of other symptoms, and differences also exist concerning criteria of improvement. While examining the reported results one should consider these issues, bearing in mind immense difficulties inherent in any experimental investigation of therapy (Gottschalk & Auerbach, 1966).

Wolpe (1961) reports results of systematic desensitization based on relaxation as applied to "68 phobias and allied neurotic anxiety habits" in 39 patients who composed one third of the total population so treated by him and are considered to be a representative sample of his total treated population. From the description of the patients it appears that only a few could be classified as classical phobias. Wolpe seems to extend the term phobia to anxiety reactions to a variety of social, interpersonal, and sexual situations. Apart from that, many patients had "other neurotic response habits as well, that were treated by methods appropriate to them." Bearing this in mind, his results are as follows: in a mean of 11.2 sessions, 35 of 39 patients (90 percent) "responded to treatment" and 62 of 68 neurotic habits (91 percent) were "overcome or markedly improved"; of 8 classical phobias (5 agoraphobics and 3 claustrophobics), two agoraphobics failed to respond. A follow-up study, involving a period from six months to four years, of 20 successfully treated cases revealed no relapse or the emergence of new symptoms. It should be noted that Wolpe's sample consists of outpatients with relatively mild degrees of disturbances and that the study is subject to most of the criticisms listed earlier.

Lazarus (1963) presents the outcome of treatment for a sample of 126 outpatients of "severe and widespread neurosis" selected from a total of 408 patients treated by the author. Included in the sample are 28 phobics "where unitary and specific stimulus situations evoke anxiety in the patient." The main method of treatment was systematic desensitization based on relaxation but other subsidiary conditioning techniques were also used. In addition, we are told that during ordinary interviews some patients tended to abreact and at "judicious intervals patients' relevations were interpreted in a manner which endeavoured to clarify irrationalities in their behavior patterns and to correct misconceptions in general." The data concerning mean number of sessions (14.07), reasons for failure and follow-up are not given for the separate diagnostic categories. Fifty-nine percent of phobias were rated as "markedly improved or completely recovered" at the termination of treatment. This work suffers from as many flaws as Wolpe's report.

Four other reports are available which fail to incorporate most of the necessary controls and which provide only scanty information about patients and techniques used. Schmidt et al. (1965) give results of behavior therapy achieved with 10 phobics who formed a subgroup of the total sample of 42 cases (mainly inpatients). A variety of techniques, some of which are not well-known, were used, and it is not stated which were applied to phobics. At the end of treatment, 6 phobics were rated as showing "marked or moderate improvement." The follow-up data do not refer to phobics specifically. Friedman (1966), by using systematic desensitization based on relaxation induced by intravenous injection of methohexitone sodium of subanaesthetic doses, claims 100 precent success in an average of 12 sessions with 25 outpatients suffering with "phobic symptoms." No follow-up is reported. Lazarus and Abramovitz (1962), employing "emotive imagery" as an anxiety inhibiting response, achieved "recovery in seven out of nine phobic children" in a mean of 3.3 sessions. Follow-up inquiries up to 12 months later indicated no relapses or "symptom substitution." The same author (1959) treated 18 phobic children with systematic desensitization based on relaxation, feeding responses, and drugs, and he also made use of conditioned avoidance responses. All cases are reported as either recovered or much improved at the end of treatment (mean number of sessions, 9.4) and at follow-up conducted over a period of 6 months to $2\frac{1}{2}$ years.

Controlled retrospective studies of a group of 77 patients treated with behavior therapy and a matched group of 55 controls who had treatment other than behavior therapy have been carried out at the Maudsley Hospital, and detailed information is available in three published reports (Cooper, 1963; Marks & Gelder, 1965; Cooper et al., 1965). In the total sample were included 29 agoraphobics (mostly inpatients) and 12 "other phobics" (mainly outpatients) all of whom received graded practical retraining; 8 agoraphobics and 4 "other phobics" also had desensitization in imagination. In addition, some patients were also given sedative drugs, antidepressants, E.C.T., supportive interviews, and even psychotherapy. The control cases with the same diagnoses (29 agoraphobics and 11 "other phobics") were matched with behavior therapy cases for sex and type of symptom, and then as closely as possible for age, and for duration and severity of symptoms. Most of the controls received supportive interviews, sometimes alone and sometimes in combination with sedatives and tranquilizers; 10 were submitted to intensive psychotherapy; and some "were encouraged to go for walks, but not in a systematic or graded fashion as employed in behavior therapy." The authors point out that the two groups were roughly matched in terms of other treatments and a comparison should reveal the contribution of behavior therapy over and above that of other treatments. On the basis of information extracted from the case notes, the patients were assessed clinically by two independent judges on a specific symptom improvement scale and also on a general improvement scale. Assessments were made at several points of time, extending to one year follow-up. At the end of treatment, 69 percent of agoraphobics treated with behavior therapy showed improvement on the symptom scale and 72 percent at one year follow-up. The respective figures for controls are 55 percent and 60 percent. In other phobias immediate results of behavior therapy achieved 100 percent of improvement which dropped to 67 percent at one year follow-up. For controls the respective figures are 27 percent and 45 percent. Thus patients with other phobias did significantly better than controls at the end of treatment, but some relapsed and at one year follow-up their superiority was diminished to an insignificant level. The mean number of sessions was identical (27) for both groups, but the mean duration of treatment was 9 months for controls and only 4 months for the behavior therapy group. Agoraphobics who had behavior therapy did only slightly better than controls, but their mean number of sessions was 59 and the duration of treatment 6 months, whereas for the controls these figures were 30 and 5, respectively. Marks and Gelder (1965) carried out a more detailed analysis of 32 phobics and their controls, and they report that the general scale of improvement tentatively suggests the same overall pattern of change in controls and patients treated with behavior therapy. The greater improvement of agoraphobics as compared with controls on the symptom scale is shown to be partly a function of increased frequency and duration of treatment received by the former group. A few patients developed fresh symptoms but these occurred as frequently in controls (3) as in patients receiving behavior therapy (4). The improvement rate in both groups of agoraphobics masked considerable residual disability on the follow-up. Agoraphobics were severely handicapped and displayed a fluctuating course of disturbance associated with depression, generalized anxiety, and depersonalization, whereas other phobias were less disturbed and more often showed a fairly circumscribed and continuous disturbance.

Apart from the usual drawbacks of retrospective studies in general, the wide variety of therapeutic ministrations applied in this investigation precludes an unequivocal assignment of results to any specific method. Furthermore, some of the authors' far-reaching assertions and conclusions do not seem to be warranted. For example, they are not justified to compare their results with those published by other workers and to conclude that *behavior therapy* is not useful for complex agoraphobics since the main treatment technique used was practical graded retraining. This is only one method of behavior therapy and, as we shall see later, not the best method; the authors themselves (Marks & Gelder, 1965) remark that there was slight evidence that patients who received systematic desensitization in imagination did rather better. Moreover, the treatment program of behavior therapy for complex cases was too narrow and incomplete in that it was directed solely at the main complaint, while other symptoms were disregarded. Their statements about inapplicability of learning principle to many features displayed by some agoraphobics and to some aspects of traditional therapy are premature.

Recently Gelder and Marks (1966) carried out a prospective follow-up trial of behavior therapy in patients with severe agoraphobia. Ten patients were submitted to practical graded retraining together with systematic desensitization in imagination, while ten controls were given a brief re-educative psychotherapy. An equal number of patients in each group received the same drugs and both groups were well matched on a number of clinical variables. Frequent and detailed assessments were carried out with symptoms and social adjustment rating scales and other tools. The results obtained appear to correspond to the ones reported in the previous study. Seven patients in each group showed evidence of improvement in the main phobic symptom at the end of treatment. Mean ratings of the treated phobia revealed slightly greater improvement in the behavior therapy group, but the authors attribute this to slightly longer treatment received by this group. During follow-up, the intensity of the main phobia increased in both groups but did not attain the pretreatment level. Other symptoms ran a parallel course in both groups, showing little change during treatment and follow-up. As regards social adjustment, a significant improvement occurred at the end of treatment in work adjustment of the behavior therapy group, whereas the control group showed a significant improvement in interpersonal relationships outside their families. These gains were more or less lost at follow-up. A progressive worsening of the rating of family relationships was shown to take place in the control group. The groups as a whole were not drastically changed, and most patients were left with considerable residual social disability. The development of fresh symptoms was noted in three patients, but these symptoms were not taken as evidence of "symptom substitution" since they emerged before the main symptom subsided. The authors adduced some evidence from this and another study (Gelder et al., 1964) that patients who had few symptoms other than phobias did best. They also concluded that their findings lend some support for greater effectiveness of systematic desensitization over control treatments in producing symptomatic improvement, when this method was applied to mildly disturbed agoraphobics but not to severe agoraphobics with other complicated problems.

Compared with other studies discussed above, this is the best designed and controlled investigation. However, as in the other studies, a limited number of behavior therapy techniques was tried, and the treatment program was too narrow and incomplete. In view of this, the authors are not justified to conclude that behavior therapy as such is not particularly useful in severe agoraphobics.

Recently Gelder et al. (1967) compared the efficacy of desensitization with two forms of psychotherapy in phobic outpatients. Sixteen patients received desensitization in imagination for 9 months, 10 individual psychotherapy for a year, and 16 group psychotherapy for 18 months. Treatment sessions were carried out once a week, and the patients' symptoms and social adjustment were assessed by rating scales at various intervals over a period of two years throughout treatment and follow-up. The findings indicate that desensitization produced more patients whose symptoms improved at the end of treatment and follow-up than either form of psychotherapy. Also, improvement was faster with desensitization than with psychotherapy. Furthermore, greater and more rapid improvement took place in occupational and leisure adjustment with desensitization. Group therapy and desensitization effected equal changes in interpersonal relationships. With desensitization these changes occurred only after symptoms had changed, whereas with group psychotherapy the changes occurred irrespective of symptom improvement. There was no evidence of symptom substitution.

Apart from that, the authors attempted to determine which of the 26 variables recorded were related to improvement and which particular items could predict the outcome.

The findings indicate that poor response to either treatment tended to be positively associated with the diagnosis of agoraphobia, the presence of many neurotic symptoms, severe obsessional features accompanying the phobias, and age at treatment. On the whole, similar variables were associated with poor response to desensitization, but the diagnosis of agoraphobia and a high level of anxiety at the start of treatment were relatively more important, and age at treatment was unimportant.

To summarize, the published reports, limited as they are, demonstrate no evidence that behavior therapy methods have produced results inferior to other methods of treatment. In fact, there is considerable evidence in favor of behavior therapy, particularly systematic desensitization, being an effective treatment for patients with circumscribed phobias. In cases with severe agoraphobia, behavior therapy, although relatively not as efficacious, nonetheless has been shown to have an edge on other methods of treatment. The number of treatment sessions and incidence of relapses are not unfavorable as compared with other forms of treatment. The "emergence" of new symptoms during and following treatment has sometimes been reported (Crisp, 1966), but Crisp has described the difficulty in defining a symptom and assessing its significance in relation to the symptom under treatment. Many other workers have remarked on the absence of such phenomena despite predictions, on the basis of psychoanalytic theory, to the contrary. Finally, it seems possible in many cases to remove a phobia without knowledge of its origin and without needing to attempt to modify the patient's "basic personality characteristics."

"Phobic" subjects not attending a Psychiatric Clinic

In addition to specific therapeutic measures, all therapy involves a number of nonspecific agents, for example, hospital care, suggestion, complex interpersonal relationship ("transference") (see Frank, 1961). Any attempt to isolate factors or mechanisms that determine the success or failure of a treatment method requires the introduction of rigorous experimental control. This is extremely difficult, if not impossible, to attain with clinical material where the therapist's moral obligation is to provide the patient with the best legitimate treatment. For this reason a number of workers used volunteers who had no psychiatric history but who displayed fear reactions to stimuli such as heights, snakes, spiders, or rats. The advantage of working with those samples are obvious, but the findings cannot be uncritically taken as applicable to psychiatric patients (Mair & Crisp, 1968).

In the attempt to explore the possibility of adapting systematic desensitization to the group treatment, Lazarus (1961) compared the effects of group desensitization with "more conventional forms of interpretive psychotherapy" on matched volunteers with "phobias." The total group included 11 acrophobics, 15 claustrophobics, four mixed phobics, and five impotent men ("sexual phobia"). Group desensitization was applied to 18 subjects of whom 13 "recovered" after an average of 20 sessions and three relapsed after an average of nine-months follow-up. Group interpretive psychotherapy was given to nine individuals, and there were no recoveries in this sample. Group psychotherapy and relaxation was administered to eight subjects of whom two recovered and one relapsed. The mean number of therapeutic sessions for the latter two groups was 22. The 15 cases who had not benefited from the interpretive treatment were treated by group desensitization and ten recovered after an average of ten sessions. The investigation is extremely useful in demonstrating that desensitization can be adapted to group treatment, but the demonstrated superiority of desensitization over group psychotherapy may be questioned mainly because the matching of subjects was incomplete and the author himself carried out both treatments and the assessment of progress.

Lang and Lazovik (1963) conducted a well-controlled experiment set out to determine which variable involved in systematic desensitization in imagination produces fear reduction. They used 24 college students with an excessive fear of snakes. Four subgroups matched for severity of fear were created so that the effects of repeating an overt avoidance test to a real snake, pretherapy training (muscular relaxation and hypnosis), and desensitization itself could be separately evaluated. Subjective and independent objective ratings of anxiety indicated that subjects who underwent desensitization (11 sessions) showed a greater reduction of phobic reactions than did nonparticipating controls. The measures of anxiety reduction were positively related to the number of hierarchy items successfully desensitized. Improvement in the specifically treated fear appeared to generalize to other fears. On the follow-up after six months, the experimental group exhibited further improvement and no signs of "symptom substitution." On the basis of their findings the authors cautiously conclude that improvement was due to desensitization and could not be attributed to relaxation, hypnosis, therapist-patient relationship, or to suggestibility.

This experiment was recently extended (Lang et al., 1965) to 23 desensitization subjects, 11 untreated controls, and 10 subjects who were submitted to the identical procedures as the desensitization group, except that instead of desensitization they received "psychotherapy." In this procedure the anxiety-hierarchy items provided "a starting point for a discussion of non-anxiety evoking aspects of the subject's life. The procedure is described as "therapeutically neutral except for the therapist-client relationship." No follow-up study was carried out. All the indixes of snake phobic behavior showed a significant reduction only in the desensitization group. The two control groups were indistinguishable in regard to the change of fear reactions. The other findings reported in the previous study were confirmed.

Paul (1965) also investigated the efficacy of systematic desensitization relative to other procedures. Ninety-six college students debilitated by interpersonal performance anxiety were assigned to four procedure groups: systematic desensitization in imagination, insight oriented psychotherapy aimed "to gain insight and self-understanding of the historical and current basis and interrelationships of the subject's problem," attention-placebo condition designed to determine nonspecific treatment effects such as suggestion, faith, attention, and interest of the therapist, and an untreated control group. The desensitization group served as its own control by the introduction of a "wait-period" before the actual treatment was undertaken. Assessments of progress included cognitive, physiological, and observable measures under stress conditions. All these measures revealed a significantly greater reduction of anxiety from pre- to post-treatment for the desensitization group than for the other groups. The improvement was sustained at a six-week follow-up with no evidence of "symptom substitution." As regards the demonstrated superiority of desensitization over other forms of treatment, one may raise an objection. It is generally agreed that such therapies, particularly insight therapy, require a much longer time than that allotted by Paul and, therefore, the investigation cannot be regarded as a fair test of the relative efficacy of the "insight therapy." At the same time, however, one cannot argue that the better results obtained with desensitization were attributable to nonspecific agents that are assumed to operate in "insight therapy."

By using a similar design and the same type of subjects, Paul and Shannon (1966), allocated 50 subjects to five conditions which included all four from the previous study plus a group-desensitization sample which this time served as its own control. No follow-up was carried out, but the immediate results of the previous investigation were confirmed. Group desensitization treatment also produced a significant reduction of social anxiety and brought about diminution of general anxiety as revealed by increased extraversion and decreased emotionality scores. In addition, compared with untreated controls, academic performance of the group-treatment sample improved significantly. All changes demonstrated for the group desensitization sample "equalled or excelled" the ones obtained by the individual desensitization group on all measures. Since the former sample received, in addition to systematic desensitization, intensive group discussion "with re-educative goals aimed at increasing confidence, skills and awareness of effects of personal relationships," the results for this group cannot be attributed to desensitization only.

By employing the experimental design modeled on the one constructed by Lang and Lazovik, Rachman (1965) made an attempt to investigate the separate effects of systematic desensitization and relaxation. Twelve subjects with fear of spiders were assigned to four treatment groups: desensitization with relaxation, desensitization without relaxation, relaxation only, and no treatment controls. A significant reduction in fear was obtained only in the desensitization with relaxation group, and the improvement was maintained at the three-months follow-up. In view of the small number of subjects, the author tentatively concludes that "the combined effects of relaxation and desensitization are greater than their separate effects."

Davison (1968) assigned 28 female volunteers fearful of snakes to one of four conditions: eight subjects received systematic desensitization in the usual manner. Eight girls had pseudodesensitization; this procedure was identical to the first except that imaginal stimuli paired with relaxation were essentially neutral and irrelevant to snakes (common childhood events). Eight subjects (exposure group) were presented with the same items of the snake hierarchy as the systematic desensitization group, but without relaxation. Four girls received no treatment. All groups were matched in terms of intensity of their snake-avoidance behavior. Subjects in the second and third group were "yoked" to their matched partners in the systematic desensitization group to ensure that all girls received the same number of sessions, the duration of each session, the number of stimulus exposures per session, and the duration of each exposure. All subjects were assessed before and after the experiment on the avoidance test (similar to the one used by Lang and Lazovik, 1963) and on a ten-point self-rating scale. A maximum of nine sessions was given. Assessments were conducted by an experimenter who did not participate in the treatment.

The results showed that a significant reduction in avoidance behavior and in anxiety rating occurred only in the systematic desensitization group. The two other treatment groups did not differ significantly in approach behavior from no treatment controls, nor did they differ from each other. The obtained correlation of .81

between anxiety reduction and approach behavior, indicated that subjects who experienced the greatest amount of anxiety reduction also displayed the greatest increment in approach behavior.

This well controlled study confirmed Rachman's findings and indirectly indicated that nonspecific variables such as relationship, expectations of beneficial outcomes could not per se account for improvement obtained with systematic desensitization.

In a rather poorly controlled study, Kondas (1967) obtained positive results with group desensitization of pupils and students with examination anxiety ("stage fright"). Groups of subjects treated with autogenic relaxation, presentation of hierarchy items without relaxation, or left untreated did not show improvement.

Relevant in this context are two investigations of desensitization, although both studies used nonphobic patients. In a crossover design, by using 12 asthmatic patients who served as their own controls, Moore (1965) obtained a greater degree of improvement with systematic desensitization than with either relaxation or relaxation and suggestion. An interesting aspect of the treatment outcome was that subjective reports and respiratory function tests improved together with desensitization, whereas with the other two procedures subjective improvement was greater than the objective one. Zeisset (1968) selected interview anxiety for treatment. Forty-eight patients (3 psychoneurotics and 45 functionally psychotics) were assigned to one of four conditions: systematic desensitization; relaxation-plus-application (subjects were trained in differential relaxation with strong suggestion that they could learn to control anxiety with relaxation in real-life situations), attention-placebo (a procedure similar to the one introduced by Paul, 1965), and no treatment control. This well-controlled study showed a significantly great reduction of anxiety on observed behavioral and self-report measures in the desensitization and relaxation-plus-application groups than in the other two groups. No differences were found between desensitization and relaxation-plus-application and between attention-placebo and no-treatment controls.

Since Zeisset did not attempt counterconditioning with his relaxation-plus-application method, and in view of the previously reported findings showing relative ineffectiveness of relaxation alone, the apparent difficulty is to account for the effects of this treatment procedure. It is highly unlikely that suggestion played a significant part, since the attention-placebo group did not improve. It seems highly likely, however, that desensitization did occur in the relaxation-plus-application group. After all, the subjects did practice relaxation in the context of an interview situation which constituted post-treatment assessment. Furthermore, on practicing relaxation between treatment sessions, they could have been desensitizing some related anxieties on their own. A significant improvement obtained by Kondas (1967) with a group of children given relaxation only may reflect a similar contamination of procedures. Kondas requested the children to practice relaxation in the classroom situation.

Cooke (1966) attempted to compare the effects of systematic desensitization by using real or imaginary phobic stimuli. He also investigated the differential effects of reciprocal inhibition treatment on subjects with different general anxiety levels. Twelve subjects afraid of rats were assigned to three treatment conditions: desensitization to the actual fear stimulus (direct treatment), desensitization to the imagined fear stimulus (indirect treatment), and no-treatment control. The subjects in each group were subdivided into high and low general anxiety on the basis of their scores on an emotionality scale. Ratings of fear in an avoidance test, carried out by independent judges, revealed a significant reduction of fear in the desensitization groups only. There was a slight, although insignificant, difference in favor of the direct treatment, despite the fact that subjects in this group attained less complete relaxation because of the nature of the procedure and were anxious on significantly more items of the hierarchy than subjects given the indirect treatment.

Under the direct treatment, equal numbers of items were completed by high and low anxiety subjects and general anxiety level was not related to the outcome of treatment. Under the indirect treatment, however, low-anxiety subjects completed significantly more items than high-anxiety subjects and, despite this, high-anxious subjects showed a greater reduction of the treated fear. This finding, albeit based on a small number of cases, does not support occasional suggestions in the literature that a high level of general anxiety is detrimental to the progress of desensitization. In view of the small number of cases involved, this study needs to be replicated.

Garfield et al. (1967) reported a pilot study purporting to investigate whether actual exposure to a "phobic" object would accelerate the effects of desensitization. Seven volunteers with extreme fear of snakes were selected and randomly assigned to two groups. One group had eight sessions of systematic desensitization; the other groups also received eight sessions of desensitization but had four additional "in vivo" training sessions. All subjects showed a reduction in "phobic" behavior, but a significantly greater improvement was obtained with the "in vivo" training procedure. The findings suggest that a combination of desensitization and practical retraining may be more efficacious than desensitization alone.

Recently Bandura et al. (1967), carried out an investigation designed to explore the "vicarious extinction" of children's avoidant responses toward dogs. Forty-eight children were assigned to the following treatment conditions: one group participated in "modelling sessions" in which they observed a "fearless peer model" engage in progressively longer and closer interactions with a dog within a pleasurable context (party); a second group of children were submitted to the same modelling situations, but in a neutral context; in order to control for the effects of exposure to the dog per se, a third group observed the dog in the pleasurable context but without the peer model; a fourth group engaged in the pleasurable activities but was not exposed to either the dog or the peer model. At the completion of the treatment sessions and one month later, the children were readministered the situational tests (graded interaction tasks) with the test dog and with an unfamiliar dog. All groups showed reduction in avoidant behavior but the two modelling groups exhibited significantly greater, more stable, and generalised improvements. The positive context, however, added little to the outcome.

Ritter (1968) compared the effectiveness of "vicarious" and "contact desensitization" in the group treatment of children afraid of snakes. Forty-four preadolescent boys and girls served as subjects. Vicarious desensitization consisted of the same basic procedure as that employed by Bandura for his second group of subjects. Contact desensitization involved, in addition to observation, a physical contact with models and a snake. Treatment consisted of two 35-minute sessions. Contact desensitization produced a significantly greater reduction in avoidance behavior than vicarious desensitization. Both experimental groups showed a significantly greater reduction than a no-treatment control group. The most stringent terminal task was achieved by 80 percent of the children in the contact desensitization group, 53 percent of the children in the vicarious desensitization group, and none in the control group. This study provides additional evidence that the combination of desensitization and practical retraining may be more effective than desensitization on its own.

Attempts have also been made to investigate several other aspects of systematic desensitization. It is generally assumed that anxiety should be reduced to zero to each step of the anxiety hierarchy. According to Wolpe's proposition, however, anxiety-provoking stimuli should be accompanied by a complete or *partial* suppression of the anxiety response. Rachman and Hodgson (1967) made an attempt to investigate the degree of anxiety reduction that must be achieved before proceeding to the next item in the hierarchy. Ten spider "phobic" volunteers were divided into two groups, matched for the initial degree of fear. A subjective rating for fear for each scene was obtained initially for each subject and then again after every third presentation of the scene. In one group, anxiety was reduced to zero for each item. In the other group, anxiety was only reduced by 50 percent before proceeding to the next item. By using objective measures (avoidance test) and subjective ratings of anxiety, the first group showed insignificantly greater improvement than the second group. Thus, without a significant loss of effectiveness, the length of treatment for the second group was reduced by over 25 percent. Needless to say that this study should be repeated, particularly with psychiatric patients. However, considering Wolpe's hypothesis about additive properties of anxiety, it is difficult to see why a partial suppression of anxiety should lead to its reduction. Also, it could be argued that, if anxiety is only partially suppressed, the learning of new connections may be impaired (Beech, 1966).

Lang and Lazovik (1963) found that, following desensitization, subjective reports of anxiety reduction lag in time behind overt behavior. Although avoidance test scores differentiated their experimental subjects from controls immediately following experiment, it was not until the follow-up assessment that the subjective ratings produced the same findings. More recently questions have been raised about generalization of the effects of systematic desensitization to real-life situations in psychiatric patients (for example, Meyer & Crisp, 1966; Hain, *et al.* 1966). Davison (1968) pointed out that on theoretical grounds a complete transfer from imaginal scenes to real life would not be expected, since hierarchies for desensitization are unlikely to cover all elements contained in the patient's phobia. Transfer of learning appears, then, to pose a theoretical and practical problem for behavior therapists using desensitization. Two attempts have been made to throw some light on these problems.

Rachman (1966b) conducted an exploratory investigation into the speed of generalization from desensitization to real-life stimuli. The main aims of the study were "to search for time lags and to pin down the time at which the generalization occurs." Apart from that he attempted to investigate further the occurrence of relapses after desensitization.

Three spider-phobic subjects were exposed to an anxiety-provoking stimulus involving spiders and were required to estimate the degree of fear. This procedure was immediately followed by systematic desensitization of the identical stimulus that was used in the pretreatment avoidance test. Immediately after the completion of desensitization, the subjects were exposed again to the original life-stimulus and requested to rate their fear. This procedure was repeated 24 hours, three days, or one week later. Generalization from desensitization to real stimuli occurred almost immediately in 82 percent of the observations. This transfer was partial in all instances. Immediate reductions of anxiety were not always stable and recovery of some degree of fear occurred in approximately 40 percent of the observations. In some cases further improvement took place during the follow-up period. In a small proportion of instances an increase in anxiety was observed.

On a practical level, Rachman's findings support those of Agras (1965). Some phobic patients in Agras' study exhibited a partial recurrence of anxiety reactions to items that were successfully desensitized in earlier treatment sessions. It is by no means clear why these relapses take place but, according to Agras, these findings may offer one possible explanation for clinical relapses following desensitization. If some items in a hierarchy are not completely desensitized, then a potential source of relapse is present, since reinforcement of these items would lead to the strengthening of avoidance behavior and, by generalization, to a total relapse.

Relevant in this connection are Wolpe's findings (1963) which indicate that the number of scene presentations to eliminate anxiety is not uniform. As desensitization progresses, the type of phobia determines the pattern. Thus, in claustrophobia and phobias in which anxiety rises with increasing proximity to a feared object, the number of desensitization trials increases as the distance decreases. In phobias in which anxiety increases with distance from a safe place (for example, agoraphobia) or with increasing number of phobic objects (for example, fear of public speaking), the number of presentations is initially high and progressively diminishes. This proximity model finds support in Rachman's study (1966b).

Agras (1967) attempted to investigate the problem of transfer by using five agoraphobic patients. The transfer of anxiety reduction from systematic desensitization to two different situations was explored. The first involved the patients' imagining five items selected from the hierarchy, and the measure of progress was the galvanic skin response. The second was the patients' actual performance in the feared situation, obtained from a detailed self-report. Four patients were improved or much improved at the end of desensitization treatment, which required 15 to 70 sessions to reach the final criterion. In three patients, including the one who failed to improve, reduction in GSR closely followed the course of desensitization, suggesting a good transfer of improvement in treatment to imagining a scene in the test situation. One patient exhibited a delay of this transfer and another showed almost a total lack of generalization for the most part of treatment. Improvement in objective performance lagged behind the progress on desensitization in three out of four patients. The patient who did not display such a lag showed no transfer to test items in imagination.

The findings of this study on objective performance appear to be discrepant with the ones reported by Rachman (1966b). Agras drew attention to several factors that may account for the discrepancy. Rachman used nonpsychiatric subjects and tested generalization to each specific stimulus immediately after desensitization. Moreover, an immediate exposure to the feared object in the presence of the therapist may have constituted a form of transfer retraining. These procedures may have given rise to spuriously high results with regard to generalization obtained by Rachman. Agras also suggested that a transfer lag may be due to the therapist reinforcing the patient's approach responses to the feared situations by paying a selective attention to reports of progress only during the final phases of desensitization. Finally, he concluded that GSR evoked by the imagination of feared situations was not a useful measure of actual therapeutic improvement.

The exploratory nature of these studies preclude any firm conclusions as to the reasons why some individuals do not generalize from desensitization to real-life situations and why some display a partial recurrence of anxiety to items previously desensitized. Whatever the reasons, the introduction of real stimuli immediately after desensitization would be expected to enhance generalization. Since phobic patients do not expose themselves in a systematic manner to the feared situations immediately after each desensitization session, they would not profit from the effects of immediate transfer. Consistent with this are findings reported by Garfield et al. (1967) and Ritter (1968) showing that a therapeutic strategy combining desensitization with practical retraining is more effective than desensitization alone.

Finally, Ramsey et al. (1966) investigated the relative effectiveness of massed and spaced systematic desensitization sessions. Twenty volunteer psychology students with fears of insects, reptiles, and animals were given systematic desensitization under conditions of massed and distributed practice. In the spaced condition, the subject received four 20-minute sessions (one per day) whereas in the massed procedure the subjects were given two 40-minute sessions (one per day). All subjects were submitted to both procedures, with half receiving one the first week and the other the second week. Effects of the treatment conditions were assessed by the usual fear estimates during an avoidance test before and after the experiment. Both procedures produced a significant reduction of fear, but the spaced practice was significantly superior to massed practice.

In conclusion, the above investigations have accumulated considerable evidence that systematic desensitization is effective in diminishing fears in nonpsychiatric subjects. The evidence is more convincing than that advanced for psychiatric patients. Attempts to isolate and to determine the separate effects of various operations in systematic desensitization indicate that improvement is related to the combination of progressive presentations of the feared stimuli and relaxation. Some evidence has been adduced that the incorporation of practical retraining in desensitization may be therapeutically more efficacious. A number of studies purporting to explore certain additional aspects of desensitization and subject variables have produced interesting findings that require further investigation. In addition, it appears that nonspecific therapeutic agents are not in themselves conducive to improvement.

It should be borne in mind, however, that the relevance of these studies to psychiatric patients has not been established.

Theoretical Considerations

Empirical demonstration that any treatment works still leaves the problem of explaining how it works. It is pertinent then to examine the validity of Wolpe's explanation of systematic desensitization in terms of reciprocal inhibition. The evidence thus far presented appears to be consistent with Wolpe's formulation (Rachman, 1965, Moore, 1965, Kondas, 1967, Davison, 1968). On the basis of relevant animal studies, however, Lomont (1965) advanced an argument that an alternative explanation in terms of classical extinction cannot be dismissed. That the classical anxiety extinction procedure is common to the reciprocal inhibition method is apparent in that the patient is required to experience conditioned stimuli for a period of time without any reinforcement of subsequent punishment. In other words, these stimuli cease to be signals for danger. Since the patient is prevented from freely escaping from the conditioned stimuli, conditioned avoidance responses do not persist as in an ordinary free avoidance procedure. Thus, the problem to be answered is whether the effects of systematic desensitization result from the conditioning of new responses to anxiety-evoking conditioned stimuli that are inhibitory of anxiety, or from the classical extinction procedure.

Before examining the relevant evidence, it is important to point out that workers in this field frequently confuse experimental procedures with theoretical explanations put forward to account for their effects. (Evans & Wilson, 1968). The term extinction refers only to a specific procedure operationally defined. The term "counter-conditioning" is sometimes used operationally, that is, as specific procedure that intentionally and explicitly involves the conditioning of new responses to the CS; sometimes it is used as a theoretical explanation to account for the phenomenon of extinction. In view of psychological and neurophysiological processes assumed by Wolpe to operate in "reciprocal inhibition," the term should be reserved for a theoretical explanation of reciprocal inhibition therapy. However, Wolpe uses the terms reciprocal inhibition and counterconditioning interchangeably, showing preference for the former in view of his inferences about neurological processes, and it is not often clear in what sense these terms are used. The lack of precision in defining how these terms are used causes confusion, and one wonders, for example, about the meaning of a statement such as: "It means that the learning process involved is probably conditioned inhibition rather than extinction" (Rachman, 1965).

Lomont (1965) cited a number of animal studies which strongly furnish support for his formulation in that preventing or delaying escape from a feared situation markedly reduces the number of trials to extinguish that response and anxiety reaction to the CS. There have been a few attempts to make controlled comparisons between counterconditioning and extinction procedures as methods of eliminating fear in rats. Gale et al. (1966) demonstrated that a group of rats which had a gradual presentation of a CS with the addition of food attained a significantly faster reduction of conditioned fear than a group for which food was omitted. However, the latter group also showed a significant decrease of fear which did not occur in a control group (passage of time only). Thus, the findings indicate that the effectiveness of counterconditioning cannot be accounted for on the basis of extinction alone. Gambrill (1967) attempted to evaluate and to compare the effectiveness of a counterconditioning procedure in eliminating instrumental avoidance behavior with an extinction procedure and to assess the relative contribution of components of a competing instrumental response in eliminating the avoidance response. Only a counterconditioning procedure that elicited and reinforced the instrumental response was significantly more effective than a classical extinction procedure in producing a decrease in avoidance responding. This effect was only evident on the first session and, when the opportunity of performing the competing response was eliminated, the animals in this group showed a significant increase in avoidance responding. Other procedures, each differing in the degree to which a competing response was introduced, were equally effective over ten extinction trials, and a delay in effectiveness was related to the degree to which a procedure involved a competing response. This study supports Gale *et al.* findings in that a counterconditioning procedure effects a significantly faster reduction rate of avoidance responding than an extinction procedure alone. Both studies indicate that extinction alone does reduce avoidance behavior. Gambrill's study, however, adduces some evidence that counterconditioning, like punishment combined with extinction, produces an immediate suppression in the rate of responding but that, when special procedures allowing for other responses are removed, an increase in avoidance responding occurs.

Gambrill's procedure did not involve a gradual presentation of stimuli associated with the avoidance response, and this feature of reciprocal inhibition method may be an important aspect that cannot be attributed to the extinction operation the method entails. Lomont (1965) considered some relevant literature on the significance of the "progressive principle." He concluded that this variable has not been adequately investigated, and the results bearing on this problem are conflicting. Lomont did not refer to one study (Kimble & Kendall, 1953) which showed that a procedure which involved a gradual increment of the intensity of CS was more effective in producing extinction than a normal extinction procedure.

In support of his thesis, Lomont cites Agras' study (1965) that demonstrated a considerable degree of spontaneous recurrence of anxiety to items already successfully desensitized. Spontaneous recovery is a familiar phenomenon in extinction, but it is not easy to attribute it to a counter-conditioning procedure in which disappearance of an old response is the result of replacement by a new response.

Recently Lomont and Edwards (1967) tested some of Lomont's theoretical deductions with human subjects fearful of snakes. The study used a complex design and was very tightly controlled. One group received systematic desensitization. The procedure differed from the usual one. During each stimulus visualisation, the subjects were required to sustain a mild degree of muscular tension. The end of the visualisation period or the signaling of anxiety, whichever came first, was followed by 20 seconds of relaxation. The other group was submitted to a similar procedure, except that relaxation was omitted (extinction procedure). Systematic desensitization produced significantly greater or nearly significantly greater fear reduction than the extinction procedure on three out of five measures of snake fear change. Extinction appeared to be ineffective. However, since no no-treatment control group was included, it cannot be concluded that extinction was totally ineffective.

Thus, the bulk of the experimental studies with animals and human subjects, bearing in mind the limitations and differences in experimental procedures and designs, appears to provide impressive evidence that the effects of systematic desensitization cannot be accounted for on the basis of classical extinction alone. Counterconditioning seems to explain better the effectiveness of Wolpe's desensitization method.

Additional evidence appears to have a bearing on this problem. Polin (1959) demonstrated in rats a greater effectiveness of an extinction procedure which employed massed exposures of disturbing stimuli ("flooding") than that obtained with normal (spaced) extinction trials. Other workers found flooding therapeutically beneficial for phobic patients. Malleson (1959) required a student with "examination panic" to imagine intensely disturbing examination situations without being relaxed. Although strong emotional reactions were provoked, the procedure proved to be successful. (The author also briefly states that a similar technique proved successful in treatment of agoraphobics.) Wolpin and Raines (1966) submitted six cases (five psychiatric patients) with a fear of snakes to three different procedures. These procedures were (1) a presentation of a graded hierarchy for visualisation with no training or instructions in relaxation, (2) a presentation of the same hierarchy with instructions to tense up, and (3) an administration of the most stressful item from the hierarchy with no relaxation. All six subjects were able to handle the original feared snake after five sessions and the marked improvement was maintained in five cases at three-to-five-weeks follow up. Rachman (1966a) on the other hand, failed to achieve improvement with three subjects, who were afraid of spiders, by subjecting them to ten sessions of "flooding." They were requested to imagine the most frightening situations involving spiders. In an attempt to account for these disparate results, he drew on two animal experiments which suggest that the duration, intensity, and mode of presentation of anxiety-provoking stimuli may be critical factors in producing extinction. Malleson massed the exposure trials, and Wolpin and Raines used prolonged exposure, whereas Rachman employed brief presentations. Apart from that, Wolpin and Raines report that the first part of each session was spent "simply getting to know the person and giving her a chance to discuss anything that might have been of concern." Furthermore, Wilson (1967) suggested that the nature of the imagined scenes may account for the discrepant results. Whereas Wolpin and Raines instructed their patients to imagine the accomplishment of the final act (holding a snake), Rachman required his subjects to rehearse in imagination fear responses to the most horrifying situations.

Relevant in this connection is Stampfl's "implosive therapy," which is essentially flooding. (Stampfl & Levis, 1967; 1968). His procedure consists of having the subject imagine, right from the start, rather horrifying scenes. This is repeated several times, and it is argued that these circumstances lead to the extinction of anxiety. Reports on clinical trials and controlled studies have recently appeared. (Hogan, 1966; Hogan & Kirchner, 1967; Kirchner & Hogan, 1966; Levis & Carrera, 1967). Hogan and Kirchner (1967) required their subjects to imagine intensely disturbing scenes involving rats without rehearsing the accomplishment of the final criterion response (picking up a rat). This procedure was limited to one session (average duration 39 minutes), and the subjects were exposed continuously to a series of interconnected images until, apparently, they displayed no further anxiety reaction to the imagined scenes. A control group was exposed to neutral scenes. A significantly greater proportion of subjects in the experimental group performed the final criterion behavior. According to Staub (1968), these findings suggest that the critical factor determining success in flooding procedures may be the duration of exposure to fear-evoking situations.

Research to sort out these issues is greatly needed since, if it develops that reciprocal inhibition therapy produces beneficial effects by extinction, then treatment procedures would become simpler and more economical. The therapist would not have to be concerned about constructing graded hierarchies and inducing responses inhibitory of anxiety. Furthermore, Lomont points out that these variables that effect extinction and conditioning differently (for example, massed versus distributed trials, and some drugs) would have to be manipulated accordingly. Meanwhile, however, particularly in view of the accumulated practical knowledge in the clinical field, behavior therapists are justified in designing treatment programs on the basis of the principle of counter-conditioning.

Apart from these experimental investigations of various aspects of systematic desensitization, a few authors critically examined the rationale of systematic desensitization. Two workers in this field questioned the assumption that *muscular relaxation* is the essential ingredient of systematic desensitization. Davison (1966) drew attention to various studies with paralytic drugs which show that, under a complete muscular paralysis where little, if any, feedback from relaxed muscles is possible, animals are able to acquire fear responses. This evidence is at odds with the view that the absence of proprioceptive stimulation from relaxed muscles is incompatible with the experience of anxiety. Davison put forward tentatively two hypotheses to account for anxiety suppression with relaxation. One is derived from the fact that, in a variety of responses incompatible with anxiety, which have been used in reciprocal inhibition method, muscular relaxation is not common to all of them. They all seem to generate positive affective states. Thus it may be that muscular relaxation produces such a state which inhibits anxiety. The second hypothesis emphasizes a possible difference between active self-induced relaxation and passive relaxation induced by drugs.

Rachman (1968) puts forward a thesis that is similar to Davison's first hypothesis. He argues that, although relaxation appears to be a necessary component of desensitization, there is no evidence that *muscular relaxation* is necessary. In support of his argument he makes the following points: therapeutic effects have been obtained with very brief training in relaxation; successful outcomes have also been reported with practical retraining where subjects are physically active during treatment sessions; some evidence indicates that, during relaxation induced by Wolpe's technique, the subject's reports of calmness and relaxation are often unaccompanied by a decrease or lack of muscular activity traced by means of electromyography; a number of other responses, including purely imaginal devices (for example, imagining a calm summer day), have been used in reciprocal inhibition therapy.

On the basis of this evidence he suggests that what may be necessary is not muscular relaxation but the experience of calmness or "mental relaxation." He then draws on various sources of information which suggest that such a state could be induced by verbal instructions and suggestions, preferably given in a monotonous fashion, combined with a deliberate stimulation of imaginary scenes of a peaceful quality. However, at the present state of knowledge, it would be unwise to abandon muscular relaxation. Highly anxious psychiatric patients may require muscular relaxation as a means of inducing calmness. Furthermore, for those patients who have difficulty in obtaining vivid images of scenes verbal suggestions of calmness may be ineffective.

Lader and Wing (1966) offered another possible interpretation of desensitization on the basis of findings obtained from a series of experiments purporting to determine reliable physiological indixes of anxiety which would discriminate anxious from normal subjects and which would be sensitive to sedative drugs used in treatment of morbid anxiety. They found that spontaneous fluctuations of GSR responses at rest and a gradual decrement of GSR responses to repetitive auditory stimuli (habituation) met this criteria. The rate of habituation in patients suffering from morbid anxiety was inversely related to the level of activity (arousal). They postulated that the rate of habituation of any person, at any particular time, depends on two variables, an innate habituation property and the level of activity at that time. On the basis of their findings and theoretical considerations, Lader and Wing suggested that desensitization can be interpreted in terms of habituation. By means of relaxation, the patient's level of anxiety is reduced, and then he is exposed to repeated minimal stimulation when the habituation rate is optimal. The basic difference between Wolpe's and Lader and Wing's views is that, whereas Wolpe's emphasizes a close temporal connection between anxiety reactions and responses inhibiting anxiety, Lader and Wing's model stresses ensuring a decrease in arousal level so that habituation can occur rapidly. A resolution of these alternative hypotheses is important for obvious practical implications.

A number of findings appear to be consistent with Lader and Wing's view, and the model could be maintained if the experimental data indicated that desensitization followed the extinction paradigm. However, we have seen that desensitization fits better a counterconditioning model. Other objections to Lader and Wing's position are indicated. The term habituation has been reserved for the phenomenon of a gradual decrease of unlearned, natural reactions (for example, orienting or startle responses) associated with a repetitive or continuous presentation of stimuli eliciting these responses; the term extinction refers to a decrease of acquired responses to conditioned stimuli. A distinction between these two procedures is justified not only because they involve responses of a different nature, but also because the effects of habituation are generally transient, whereas the effects of extinction usually produce an enduring reduction in response strength. Moreover, the relative ineffectiveness of procedures involving only a gradual presentation of aversive stimuli to nonpsychiatric subjects, as well as some evidence demonstrating successful therapeutic effects of flooding with psychiatric patients, seem to run counter to Lader and Wing's hypothesis. Without further research, it would be premature to make a final decision about the validity of either position.

Treatment of phobias by orthodox psychotherapy is well known to constitute a therapeutic problem. Curran and Partridge (1955), for instance, state: "phobic symptoms are notoriously resistent to treatment, and their complete removal is rarely achieved." Nevertheless, a certain proportion of patients benefit from these treatment procedures, and learning theorists are hard put to account for this. They postulate that the occurrence of phobic verbal behavior could lead to a positive change because of reciprocal inhibition: these responses are elicited while the patient's anxiety is inhibited by comfort and a relaxed atmosphere provided by the therapist. The fact that reciprocal inhibition is not applied specifically and systematically is put forward to account for poor results. The need for phobic patients to undergo some form of graded retraining in practical situations was recognised long ago (for example, Freud, 1919, Janet, 1925). Bridger and Mandel's findings described previously are relevant in this context. Their results suggest that verbal manipulations may not be effective for patients whose phobias developed on the basis of direct experience of trauma and, in order to change their expectancies and maladaptive patterns of behavior, the undergoing of a new direct experience may be necessary. Using Pavlovian terms, modification of behavior acquired through "the first signaling system" (direct experience) requires submitting this system to new experiences; whereas in cases where "the second signaling system" (speech) is only involved, it is sufficient to remove subjective expectancy through the second signaling instructions.

In addition to the problems inherent in the techniques of treatment, there have been frequent comments in the literature concerning the apparent importance of the patient's motivation, level of anxiety, personality type, and other clinical variables (Lazarus, 1963; Schmidt et al., 1965; Meyer & Crisp, 1966; Gelder et al., 1967). Some findings indicate that high neuroticism and introversion may be relatively poor prognostic signs. The comparatively poorer response to treatment of complex phobics may be accounted for in terms of a theory which holds that anxiety as a drive is indiscriminate in the habits it energizes (generality of motivation, see Kimble, 1961). Thus the presence of anxiety due to any external or internal stress or conflict experienced by the phobic patient may hamper any attempt at treating the main symptom only.

With regard to the role of nonspecific agents such as insight, suggestion, patient-therapist relationship, there is no evidence from the controlled studies that they per se are responsible for successes obtained with behavior therapy (see also Grossberg, 1964; Bandura, 1967). Statements to the contrary are unfounded and meaningless unless critical factors and mechanisms underlying these nonspecific variables are specified. However, the experimental evidence cited here cannot be unquestioningly accepted because of the limited nature of samples used and because various nonspecific agents have not been entirely isolated. Although the importance of these agents has been widely recognized clinically long ago and sometimes received experimental support (see Frank, 1961), there has been a lack of agreement and paucity of adequate evidence on their nature and critical factors involved. Mainly for this reason, behavior therapists have tended to disregard such "intangibles." Recently this area has received more attention. Crisp, for example, has attempted to develop a measure of "transference" (1964a and b) and has applied this to behavior therapy situations (1964b, 1966). The view under investigation has been that neurotic symptoms may arise out of unsatisfactory neurotic dependency relationships with other people and that they may therefore become modified if the patient's dependency needs are "transferred" into a mutually gratifying therapeutic relationship. His tentative findings are that, among female patients, at least, the patient's initial attitude toward the therapist, both as a protective, parental figure and as a phantasised sexual partner, is related to therapeutic outcome. Such findings, if confirmed, may be regarded as a potentially universal therapeutic variable.

Eysenck (1963) believes that the patient can become deeply involved with, dependent on and grateful to the therapist, independently of his previous interpersonal and especially childhood experiences, and that the patient's attitude is specifically related to the beneficial effects of treatment provided by the therapist, but having implications for the symptom only.

Skinnerians have adduced a considerable amount of evidence that the therapist becomes a powerful source of discriminative and reinforcing stimuli. As a social reinforcer, using verbal and nonverbal cues, he can influence and control behavior (see Bandura, 1961). Perhaps the most impressive work in this field is that of Truax who has attempted to investigate the role of certain aspects of the therapist's behavior. His findings indicate that the therapist's "empathy, warmth, and unconditional acceptance" are significantly related to therapeutic change (Truax & Carkhuff, 1964; Truax, 1966a). He also showed (1966b) that when Carl Rogers responded differentially to certain aspects of a patient's verbal behavior during treatment sessions, unwittingly on Rogers' part, significant reinforcement effect occurred as evidenced by changes in the patient's behavior.

Thus, research in this area is beginning to uncover some interesting findings, and it becomes apparent that various "intangibles" can be restated in terms of learning principles and can be profitably investigated within this theoretical framework. Uncovering critical factors and the mechanisms involved, and their systematic implementation in therapy, will no doubt make these agents more powerful therapeutic tools for behavior modification and control.

In conclusion, the most impressive fact

about desensitization as applied to irrational fears, considering its relatively short existance, is the amount of experimental work carried out and the willingness of behavior therapists to examine critically their basic assumptions. The relative simplicity and clarity of theoretical formulations make this possible. Considerable amounts of evidence indicate that specific operations in systematic desensitization are responsible for elimination of "phobic" behavior. This empirical evidence provides some support for principles and theoretical formulations from which these procedures are derived, but thus far there is a lack of conclusive knowledge as to how they work.

Practical Problems

In this section reference will be made to the most common practical problems encountered in treating patients with the above methods. Whenever possible, suggestions for overcoming these difficulties, partly derived from theoretical considerations and partly from clinical practice will be outlined.

The initial difficulty for the behavior therapist is sometimes the one of paving the way for therapy. First, it is important for the outcome of treatment to put the symptom under control not only during specific treatment situations but also between them. Recurrence of the symptom between the treatment sessions is thought to be detrimental to the progress. Thus, it is advisable to admit for inpatient treatment those individuals whose chances of coming into contact with phobic stimuli or situations cannot be completely controlled.

The next step, that is, the construction of an anxiety hierarchy for desensitization, constitutes the most difficult and taxing procedure. In the section on the assessment techniques, some of the problems were briefly mentioned and possible ways of exploring them were suggested. In practice, however, at the present stage of development, the therapist is obliged to rely mainly on skillfully conducted interviews with the patient. The object of these interviews is to pinpoint all anxiety-producing dimensions of the phobic situation and to provide a fine grading of relevant stimuli. Needless to say, the hierarchy must contain the items that constitute all the relevant stimulus elements of anxiety. In many instances the construction of a hierarchy is relatively a simple matter. Thus, in cases of acrophobia, it is usually found that the only relevant dimension is height (the greater the height the greater the fear); similarly, the size of enclosed spaces may be the only pertinent aspect of claustrophobia. Even in these conditions, however, additional dimensions may be involved; thus, presence or absence of people may play a part, spatial proximity to an opening (for example, a window) may be important in some acrophobics, or the height of the ceiling in some claustrophobics. The above-mentioned case of wasp phobia illustrates the possible complexity of elements involved. In many agoraphobics merely being out alone at a distance from the place of safety may not be the relevant aspect of the phobic situation; fears of traffic, accidents, strange people, or contamination due to petrol fumes may be at the basis of the condition. For patients who report more than one source of anxiety it is important to establish whether these sources are unrelated or whether there is a common thread running through them. In the former case, separate anxiety hierarchies are constructed for each source of disturbance; in the latter, whether one or several hierarchies are necessary, the nature of items is determined by the main theme. For instance, a patient complained of phobias of cinemas, theaters, train journeys, boardroom meetings, and airplane trips. At first it was tempting to have one hierarchy based on these situations which according to the patient evoked increasing degrees of anxiety in the enumerated order. It turned out, however, that the main theme associated with these situations was fear of confinement—the more difficult for the patient to leave a situation at will the greater the anxiety. Merely asking the patient what he avoids is often inadequate, and only a careful probing can determine the real sources of anxiety. Frequently, probing involves situations that the patient has not experienced and, in this case, he is required to imagine whether he would expect to feel anxious in such situations.

The grading of items for each thematic group is achieved by presenting the items on separate cards and by having the patient rank them according to the degree of anxiety they evoke. It is not possible to be certain beforehand whether a fine grading has been achieved, and the lack of smooth transition from step to step becomes apparent during desensitization. If an item in a hierarchy produces more anxiety than can be counteracted, then additional weaker items must be sought and inserted between the steps.

The principle of reciprocal inhibition demands that the patient must learn to associate the phobic stimulus complex with feelings other than the ones of anxiety, and these alternative responses must be sufficiently strong to counteract whatever anxiety is present at each stage of desensitization. Consistent with this principle, the second step in reciprocal inhibition therapy entails introduction of responses that inhibit anxiety. The most commonly used response has been deep muscular relaxation. However, some patients, particularly children, fail to respond to training in relaxation for no apparent reason. Furthermore, claims that such relaxation is always accompanied by mental relaxation have been questioned. A number of alternative responses advocated for those individuals who are unable to profit from relaxation training have already been mentioned. However, they have not been adequately tried out, their effectiveness in inhibiting anxiety has not been established, and some have a limited range of applicability (for example, feeding responses, emotive imagery, relaxation under hypnosis). Preliminary reports (Friedman, 1966; Brady, 1966, 1967; Kraft, 1967; Worsley & Freeman, 1967) suggest that the answer to these problems may lie in the use of adequate drugs. It appears that a predictable degree of emotional calmness and reduced autonomic activity can be induced rapidly with intravenous methohexitone sodium, the effects of which wear off within a few minutes. In order to maintain relaxation the administration of the drug is continued throughout the treatment. Reed (1966), however, finds the use of methohexitone sodium, as a means of inducing relaxation, to be of limited value. The main disadvantages are that the drug does not always produce relaxation in all spheres; some patients dislike the prospect of injections; some find the effects of the drug unpleasant.

The treatment itself, whether carried out in the form of systematic desensitization in imagination or practical retraining, has certain limitations and a number of problems. With regard to systematic desensitization the following are encountered.

(a) There is no standard administration procedure the value of which has been demonstrated experimentally. Lazarus' (1964) general instructions concerning "crucial procedural factors" are mainly derived from uncontrolled clinical observations and, as such, require to be submitted to experimentation. We have already observed that occasional violations of some "prescribed procedures" did not prove to be detrimental to the outcome of treatment. A successful desensitization of a snake phobia in one session (Wolpin & Pearsall, 1965) brings into question the suggestion that presenting more than a few items from a hierarchy in a given session can be damaging. Duration of imagined scenes should be timed from the onset of a clear image. It is essential, therefore, to establish the time required by the patient to conjure up clear images.

(b) Some patients are unable to imagine vividly and maintain that the procedure is artificial and could not evoke anxiety in them. There is evidence to suggest that in some individuals different sense modalities, used for imagination, have varying effects on the degree of anxiety produced (Clark, 1963; Meyer & Crisp, 1966). Therefore, it is advisable to encourage patients to use all sense modalities when required to imagine scenes. Also, asking patients to talk about items may in some cases increase their reality and aid imagination (Badri 1967).

(c) Reliance on the patient's signaling the experience of anxiety may be questioned. Some patients appear to become anxious but do not report the experience of anxiety and vice versa. Any observable change in posture or facial expression suggesting increased tension should be acted on. There is a great need for the development of some reliable measure of anxiety during desensitization.

(d) It will be recalled that some patients exhibit a partial recurrence of anxiety reactions to items which were desensitized in earlier treatment sessions (Agras, 1965; Rachman, 1966b). To prevent this potential source of clinical relapse, the therapist should check at the commencement of each treatment session the permanency of the items dealt with in the previous session.

(e) Some patients fail to generalise from

the therapeutic situation to real life. This is particularly common in cases where phobic objects or situations normally produce mild anxiety (for example, wasps, thunder, flying).

Graded practical retraining would seem to obviate the difficulties related to imagination and generalization since the stimuli and the patient's reactions to them may be brought under direct control. A number of practical difficulties, however, have rendered this technique less practicable than systematic desensitization.

(a) The first problem is the one of translating an anxiety hierarchy into practical situations. In some cases this is possible but the task often becomes cumbersome and requires a great deal of ingenuity on the part of the therapist. In some instances it is, if not impossible, extremely difficult to effect a fine grading (for example, phobics with steep stimulus generalization). In other cases symptom-provoking stimuli are not really available (for example, shortlived insects, thunder). For some phobias it is possible to overcome these difficulties to some extent by making use of visual and auditory aids (for example, filming or tape recording of relevant stimuli).

(b) Treatment itself is often tedious and time consuming since the therapist is required to participate actively by presenting, or taking the patient to, progressively increasing symptom-provoking situations. This is relatively easy in phobic disorders involving objects that can be introduced into the consulting room. In cases involving complex situations, for example, fear of traveling, going out, social gathering, treatment has to be carried out in these situations.

(c) In applying this technique as in desensitization in imagination, it is essential to keep anxiety under control. If the nature of phobic stimuli permits their presentation in the consulting room, while the patient sits in a chair, muscular relaxation is the obvious means of control. Such control may become extremely difficult to exert while the patient is active in situations outside the consulting room. In this case, a smooth transition from step to step and the patient's feeling of security in the presence of the therapist are mainly capitalized. If an adequate control cannot be exerted by these means, then tranquilizers are used.

The above considerations provide the basis for a treatment approach that, in the authors' opinion, should prove to be most effective. The essence of this approach is the simultaneous application of desensitization and, at least, a modicum of practical retraining.

For patients whose whole treatment can be conducted in the consulting room each session consists of the following procedures.

(a) The systematic desensitization in imagination combined with verbalization of scenes, using any available means for inducing deep relaxation.

(b) The gradual presentation of at least some real stimuli, corresponding to items dealt with in (a), while the patient is still held in a state of relaxation.

(c) As in (b), while the patient is in his normal state; meanwhile the therapist gradually withdraws himself from the treatment room during the presentation of each item.

For patients whose practical retraining cannot be carried out in the consulting room simply because of the nature of stimulus configurations, each session involves the following operations.

(a) As in (a) above.

(b) If possible, immediately after (a) the patient is required to participate in situations corresponding as closely as possible to the items dealt with in fantasy; the therapist again gradually withdraws himself from these situations.

(c) The patient is urged to participate in similar situations between treatment sessions.

The latter may be more fully illustrated by applying this approach to agoraphobics. The patient is familiarized in the presence of the therapist with a specific trip. This distance is divided into a number of stages of gradually increasing distance from the hospital. The patient is required to visualize the shortest trip while completely relaxed, and then is instructed to carry out the trip on his own. If he does not report experiencing anxiety, he is instructed to practice the task in his own time between sessions. If anxiety is reported then, of course, the first procedure is repeated.

This approach combines the advantages of both techniques. Furthermore the initial desensitization eases the transition to practical retraining so that a fine grading of real stimuli or situations does not have to be strictly observed. Finally, it enables an immediate check on the progress and helps to prevent any doubts that the patient may entertain about generalization to real life.

Relapses after successful treatment can be reasonably well explained in terms of learning principles. Incomplete desensitization has been already referred to as one, probably the most common, cause for relapses. A new, repeated traumatic event or experience of anxiety because of any stress in the presence of old stimuli may give rise to the recurrence of the same phobia. Apart from that, a new phobia may be acquired if different stimuli are involved. There have been no studies of treatment of relapsed cases, but there are no apparent reasons why the same treatment method should not be administered.

Apart from the practical problems inherent in the methods used, a number of complications may arise during treatment. Occasionally, unexpected fluctuations in response to treatment occur. This is perhaps the best evidence at the behavioral level that the original analysis of the patient's phobia was inadequate and that reappraisal of the case and treatment approach is called for (Meyer & Crisp, 1966). Occasionally, new symptoms emerge during treatment that may hamper the progress in the treated phobia (Meyer & Crisp, 1966, Marks et al., 1966). Sometimes these changes can be related to obvious causes.

Thus far, our discussion has not considered complex phobic patients who present other symptoms. Experience has shown that some respond well not only in regard to treated phobias but also in regard to untreated symptoms. More often than not, however, improvement in phobias occurs without any change in untreated symptoms, and some patients fail altogether to respond. As stated earlier, there is no acceptable way to determine beforehand the significance of other symptoms in relation to phobic disorders in individual patients, and it is not possible to predict with any degree of certainty the effects of treatment of the main complaint on other symptoms. The fact remains that the presence of other symptoms may impede progress in treatment of phobias and enhance the chances of relapse (Meyer & Crisp, 1966; Marks et al., 1966).

As experience with behavior therapy grows, it is becoming increasingly evident that current difficulties in the patient's life situation play a part in triggering or maintaining the symptom. Secondary gains in the patient's domestic or work situation and relationships that arise as a result of the symptom may also serve to entrench the latter.

A number of criticisms can be directed at practicing behavior therapists. They frequently design treatment procedures without a careful consideration of relevant experimental data and fail to observe the basic requirements of the learning principles adopted. Furthermore, in the effort to adhere to some recommended procedure, they often do not pay sufficient attention to individual differences in patients' responses to specific therapeutic strategies. The most pertinent criticism is that behavior therapists tend to adopt a narrow view of symptomatology which leads to inappropriate and incomplete treatment. The basic problem of what constitutes a symptom for treatment is often not considered carefully. Thus, treatment of phobias is often undertaken without an attempt to consider the possibility that other symptoms, secondary gains, and stresses in the patient's life are related or even basic to the production of the phobias. Disregard of the above can be held responsible for therapeutic failures.

The practicing behavior therapists who accept the previously stated wider aetiological considerations begin to abandon the original tendency to confine their therapeutic efforts to circumscribed areas of maladaptive behavior and have adopted a more comprehensive "broad spectrum" approach (for example, Lazarus, 1966; Davison, 1969).

This approach adopts a combination of treatment methods directed at all possible sources of deviant behavior. Consistent with this behavior, therapists are beginning to be more concerned with the meaning of symptoms, the patient's cognitive processes, that is, attitudes and beliefs, and do not restrict themselves exclusively to autonomic and motor responses. They also consider, and when relevant, attempt to deal with current stresses in the patient's life, his interpersonal relationships with significant persons and the therapist. Many of these problems can and have been dealt with by behavior therapy methods. Whatever therapeutic strategies the behavior therapist adopts, he attempts to apply explicitly and systematically his data and principles.

A number of attempts have been made to find a common ground between learning theorists and workers with a psychodynamic orientation and to integrate the two theoretical approaches (Alexander, 1963; Bandura, 1961; Crisp, 1966; Dollard & Miller, 1950; Kanfer, 1961; Marks & Gelder, 1966; Mowrer, 1950). It may be that, in time, these two approaches will be found to have more in common than divides them. However, the role of behavior therapy aimed, in the most effective manner, according to our current understanding of learning processes, at enabling the patient to shed unwanted behavior patterns and to acquire fresh forms of behavior, is likely to remain a distinct contribution. The reported results of behavior therapy aimed at phobic symptoms are already encouraging despite considerable disagreements concerning theoretical interpretations of experimental findings in the field of learning. (Breger & McGaugh, 1965; Hilgard, 1965; Kimble, 1961.) It should be borne in mind, however, that there is sufficient agreement regarding some of the facts and generalizations concerning learning to make possible their practical application.

Behavior therapy, as applied to phobic disorders, has already been established as a useful adjunct to the clinic, but it is bound to fall into disrepute if it is uncritically accepted as a ready-made, routine form of treatment. If theoretical and practical advances are to be made, a rigorous and planned experimental approach to the problems outlined here is greatly needed. Meanwhile, the clinical practitioner may contribute to such advances by testing specific hypotheses in individual patients undergoing treatment.

In our view, to isolate factors and mechanisms that determine success or failure of any treatment method would be most fruitful in advancing our theoretical and practical knowledge.

REFERENCES

Agras, W. S. An investigation of the decrement of anxiety responses during systematic desensitization therapy. *Behav. Res. Ther.*, 1965, **2**, 267–270.

Agras, W. S. Transfer during systematic desensitization therapy. *Behav. Res. Ther.*, 1967, **5**, 193–199.

Alexander, F. The dynamics of psychotherapy in the light of learning theory. *Amer. J. Psychiat.*, 1963, **120**, 440–448.

Badri, M. B. A new technique for the systematic desensitization of pervasive anxiety and phobic reactions. *J. Psychol.*, 1967, **65**, 201–208.

Bandura, A. Psychotherapy as a learning process. *Psychol. Bull.*, 1961, **58**, 143–159.

Bandura, A. Vicarious processes: a case of no trial learning. In L. Berkowitz (Ed.), *Advances in experimental social psychology* Vol. II. New York: Academic Press, 1965.

Bandura, A., Grusec, J. E., & Menlove, F. L. Vicarious extinction of avoidance behavior. *J. Personal & Soc. Psychol.*, 1967, **5**, 16–23.

Bandura, A., & Rosenthal, T. L. Vicarious classical conditioning as a function of arousal level. *J. Personal & Soc. Psychol.*, 1966, **3**, 54–62.

Bandura, A., & Walters, R. H. *Social learning and personality*. New York: Holt, Rinehart & Winston, 1963.

Bannister, D. The rationale and clinical relevance of repertory grid technique. *Brit. J. Psychiat.*, 1965, **111**, 972–982.

Bannister, D. A new theory of personality. In B. M. Foss (Ed.), *New Horizons in Psychology*. London. Penguin Books Ltd, 1966.

Bannister, D., & Mair, J. M. M. *The evaluation of personal constructs*. London: Academic Press, 1968.

Becker, W. C., & Matteson, H. H. GSR conditioning, anxiety and extraversion. *J. abnorm. & soc. Psychol.*, 1961, **62**, 427-430.

Beech, H. R. Personality theories and behaviour therapy. In B. M. Foss (Ed.), *New Horizons in Psychology*. London: Penguin Books Ltd, 1966.

Brady, J. P. Brevital-relaxation treatment in frigidity. *Behav. Res. Ther.*, 1966, **4**, 71–77.

Brady, J. P. Comments on methohexitone-aided systematic desensitization. *Behav. Res. Ther.*, 1967, **5**, 259–260.

Brandon, S. An epidemiological study of maladjustment in childhood. Unpublished M.D. Thesis. University of Durham, England. 1960.

Breger, S. M. Conditioning through vicarious instigation. *Psychol. Rev.*, 1962, **69**, 450–460.

Breger, L., & McGaugh, J. L. Critique and reformation of "learning theory" approach to psychotherapy and neurosis. *Psychol. Bull.*, 1965, **63**, 338–358.

Bridger, W. H., & Mandel, I. J. A comparison of G.S.R. fear responses produced by threat and electric shock. *J. Psychol. Res.*, 1964, **2,** 31–40.

Broadhurst, P. L. Abnormal animal behavior. In H. J. Eysenck (Ed.) *Handbook of Abnormal Behaviour*, London: Pitman, 1960.

Bunt, A., Van De, & Barendregt, J. T. Intercorrelations in three measures of conditioning. In J. T. Barendregt (Ed.) *Research in psycho-diagnostics*. The Hague: Mouton, 1961.

Campbell, D., Sanderson, R. E., & Laverty, S. G. Characteristics of a conditional response in human subjects during extinction trials following a single traumatic conditioning trial. *J. abnorm. & soc. Psychol.*, 1964, **68**, 627–659.

Clark, D. F. The treatment of hysterical spasm and agoraphobia by behaviour therapy. *Behav. Res. Ther.*, 1963, **1**, 245–250.

Cooke, G. The efficacy of two desensitization procedures: An analogue study. *Behav. Res. Ther.*, 1966, **4**, 17–24.

Cooper, J. E. A study of behaviour therapy in thirty psychiatric patients. *Lancet*, 1963, **i**, 411–415.

Cooper, J. E., Gelder, M. G., & Marks, I. M. Results of behaviour therapy in 77 psychiatric patients. *Brit. med. J.*, 1965, **i**, 1222–1225.

Craig, W. S. The child in the maladjusted household. *Practitioner*, 1956, **177**, 21–32.

Crisp, A. H. An attempt to measure an aspect of "transference." *Brit. J. med. Psychol.*, 1964a, **37**, 17–30.

Crisp, A. H. Development and application of a measure of "transference." *J. Psychosom. Res.*, 1964b, **8**, 327–335.

Crisp, A. H. "Transference," "symptom emergence" and "social repercussion" in behaviour therapy. A study of 54 treated patients. *Brit. J. med. Psychol.*, 1966, **39**, 179–196.

Curran, D., & Partridge, M. *Psychological medicine*. Edinburgh: Livingstone, 1955.

Davidson, P. O., Payne, R. W., & Sloane, R. B. Introversion, neuroticism and conditioning. *J. abnormal. soc. Psychol.*, 1964, **68**, 136–143.

Davidson, P. O., Payne, R. W., & Sloane, R. B. Cortical inhibition, drive level, and conditioning. *J. abnorm. Psychol.*, 1966, **71**, 310–314.

Davison, G. C. Anxiety under total curarisation: Implications for the role of muscular relaxation in the desensitization of neurotic fears. *J. nerv. ment. Dis.*, 1966, **143**, 443–448.

Davison, G. C. Systematic desensitization as a counter-conditioning process *J. abnorm. Psychol.*, 1968, **73**, 91–99.

Davison, G. C. Appraisal of behaviour modification techniques with adults in institutional settings. In C. M. Franks (Ed.), *Assessment and status of the behavioural therapies and associated developments*. New York: McGraw-Hill, 1968b.

Denker, P. G. Results of treatment of psychoneurosis by the general practitioner. A follow-up study of 500 cases. *New York State Journal of Medicine*, 1946, **46**, 2164–2166.

Diethelm, O. *Treatment in psychiatry*. Springfield, Ill: C. C. Thomas, 1950.

Dollard, J., & Miller, N. E. *Personality and psychotherapy*. New York: McGraw-Hill, 1950.

Evans, I., & Wilson, T. Note on the terminological confusion surrounding systematic desensitization. *Psychol. Rep.*, 1968, **22**, 187–191.

Eysenck, H. J. *The dynamics of anxiety and hysteria*. London: Routledge and Kegan Paul, 1957.

Eysenck, H. J. Behaviour therapy, symptom remission and transference in neurotics. *Amer. J. Psychiat.*, 1963, **119**, 867–871.

Eysenck, H. J. Extraversion and the acquisition of eyeblink and GSR conditioned responses. *Psychol. Bull.*, 1965, **63**, 258–270.

Fish, H. J. *An outline of psychiatry*. Bristol: John Wright & Sons, 1964.

Fonberg, E. On the manifestation of conditioned defensive reactions in stress, 1956. Cited in Wolpe, J. *Psychotherapy by reciprocal inhibition*. Stanford: Stanford Univ. Press, 1958, p. 65 and 92.

Frank, J. D. *Persuasion and Healing*. Baltimore: Johns Hopkins Press, 1961.

Franks, C. M. Conditioning and abnormal behaviour. In H. J. Eysenck (Ed.), *Handbook of abnormal psychology*. London: Pitman, 1960.

Friedman, D. A new technique for the systematic desensitization of phobic symptoms. *Behav. Res. Ther.*, 1966, **4**, 139–140.

Freeman, H. S., & Kendrick, D. C. A case of cat phobia. *Brit. med. J.*, 1960, **2**, 497–502.

Freud, S. *Collected papers*, **2**, 392. London: Hogarth Press, 1919.

Freud, S., & Breuer, J. Hysterical attacks. *Collected Papers*, Sigmund Freud, Vol. V. London: Hogarth press, 1892.

Gale, D. S., Sturmfels, G., & Gale, E. N. A comparison of reciprocal inhibition and experimental extinction in the psychotherapeutic process. *Behav. Res. Ther.*, 1966, **4**, 149–155.

Gambrill, E. Effectiveness of the counterconditioning procedure in eliminating avoidance behaviour. *Behav. Res. Ther.*, 1967, **5**, 263–273.

Garfield, Z. A., Darwin, P. L., Singer, B. A., & McBrearty J. F. Effect of "in vivo" training on experimental desensitization of a phobia. *Psychol. Rep.*, 1967, **20**, 515–519.

Geer, J. H. The development of a scale to measure fear. *Behav. Res. Ther.*, 1965, **3**, 45–53.

Gehl, R. H. Depression and claustrophobia. *Rev. Franc. Psychoanal*, 1965, **29**, 233–255.

Gelder, M G., & Marks, I. M. Severe agoraphobia: a controlled prospective trial of behaviour therapy. *Brit. J. Psychiat.*, 1966, **112**, 309–319.

Gelder, M. G., Marks, I. M., Sakinofsky, I., & Wolff, H. H. Behaviour therapy and psychotherapy in phobic disorders: alternative or complementary procedures? Paper given at Learning Theory Symposium of the 6th Int. Congr. Psychoth. London, 1964.

Gelder, M. G., Marks, I. M., & Wolff, H. H. Desensitization and psychotherapy in the treatment of phobic states: A controlled inquiry *Brit. J. Psychiat.*, 1967, **113**, 53–73.

Gittleson, N. L. The fate of obsessions in depressive psychosis. *Brit. J. Psychiat.*, 1966 **112**, 705–708.

Gottschalk, L. A., & Auerbach, A. H. *Methods of research in psychotherapy*. New York: Appleton-Century-Crofts, 1966.

Greenspoon, J. Verbal conditioning and clinical psychology. In A. S. Bachrach (Ed.), *Experimental foundations of clinical psychology*. New York: Basic Books, 1962.

Grossberg, J. M. Behaviour therapy: a review. *Psychol. Bull.*, 1964, **62**, 73–88.

Grossberg, J. M., & Wilson, H. K. A correlational comparison of the Wolpe-Lang fear survey schedule and Taylor Manifest Anxiety Scale. *Behav. Res. Ther.*, 1965, **3**, 125–128.

Hain, J. D., Butcher, R. H. G., & Stevenson, I. Systematic desensitization therapy: An analysis of results in 27 patients. *Brit. J. Psychiat.*, 1966, **112**, 295–307.

Hastings, D. W. Follow-up results in psychiatric illness. *Amer. J. Psychiat.*, 1958, **114**, 1057–1066.

Hefferline, R. F. Learning theory and clinical psychology—an eventual symbiosis? In A. J. Bachrach (Ed.), *Experimental foundations of clinical psychology*. New York: Basic Books, 1962.

Hilgard, E. R. *Theories of learning*. New York: Appleton-Century-Crofts, 1965.

Hoenig, J., & Reed, G. F. The objective assessment of desensitization. *Brit. J. Psychiat.*, 1966, **112**, 1279–1283.

Hogan, R. A. Implosive therapy in the short-term treatment of psychotics. *Psychother.: Theory, Research and Practice*. 1966, **3**, 25–32.

Hogan, R. A., & Kirchner, J. H. Preliminary report of the extinction of learned fears via short-term implosive therapy. *J. abnorm. Psychol.*, 1967, **72**, 106–109.

Homme, L. Perspective in psychology—XXIV. Control of coverants, the operants of the mind. *Psychol. Rec.*, 1965, **15**, 501–511.

Hudson, B. B. One-trial learning in the domestic rat. *Genet. Psychol. Monogr.*, 1950, **57**, 173–180.

Inglis, J. Abnormalities of motivation and "ego-functions." In H. J. Eysenck (Ed.), *Handbook of abnormal psychology* London: Pitman, 1960.

Ingram, I. M. Obsessional illness in mental hospital patients. *J. ment. Sci.*, 1961, **107**, 382–402.

Janet, P. *Psychological healing 2*. London: George Allen and Unwin, 1925.

Jersild, A. T., & Holmes, F. B. Children's fears. *J. Psychol.*, 1935, **1**, 75–104.

Jones, H. G. Learning and abnormal behaviour. In H. J. Eysenck (Ed.), *Handbook of Abnormal Psychology*. London: Pitman, 1960.

Jones, M. C. A laboratory study of fear: The case of Peter. *Pedagogical Sem.*, 1924a, **31**, 308–315.

Jones, M. C. The elimination of children's fears. *J. exp. Psychol.*, 1924b, **7**, 383–390.

Kondas, O. Reduction of examination anxiety and "stage fright" by group desensitization and relaxation. *Behav. Res. Ther.*, 1967, **5**, 275–281.

Kanfer, F. H. Comments on learning in psychotherapy. *Psychol. Rep.*, 1961, **9**, 681–699.

Kelly, D. H. Measurement of anxiety by forearm blood flow. *Brit. J. Psychiat*, 1966, **112**, 789–798.

Kelly, G. *The psychology of personal constructs*, Vols. I and II. New York: Norton, 1955.

Kimble, G. A. *Revised version of conditioning and learning*. London: Methuen, 1961.

Kimble, G. A., & Kendall, J. A comparison of two methods of producing experimental extinction. *J. exper. Psychol.*, 1953, **45**, 87–89.

Kirchner, J. H., & Hogan, R. A. The therapist variable in the implosion of phobias. *Psychother.: Theory, Research and Practice.*, 1966, **3**, 102–104.

Kraft, T. The use of methohexitone sodium in behaviour therapy. *Behav. Res. Ther.*, 1967, **5**, 257.

Kringlen, E. Obsessional neurotics: A long term follow-up. *Brit. J. Psychiat.*, 1965, **111**, 709–722.

Lacey, J. I., Bateman, D. E., & VanLehn, R. Autonomic response specificity. *Psychosom. Med.*, 1953, **15**, 8–21.

Lacey, J. I., & Smith, R. L. Conditioning and generalization of unconscious anxiety. *Science*, 1954, **120**, 1045–1052.

Lader, M. H., & Wing, L. *Physiological measures, sedative drugs and morbid anxiety.* London: Oxford University Press, 1966.

Lang, P. J., & Lazovik, A. D. The experimental desensitization of a phobia. *J. abnorm. soc. Psychol.*, 1963, **66**, 519–525.

Lang, P. J., Lazovik, A. D., & Reynolds, D. J. Desensitization, suggestibility and pseudotherapy. *J. abnorm. Psychol.*, 1965, **70**, 395–402.

Lanyon, R. I., & Manosevits, M. Validity of self-reported fear. *Behav. Res. Ther.*, 1966, **4**, 259–263.

Lazarus, A. A. The diminution of children's phobias by deconditioning. *Med. Proc. (South Africa)*, 1959, **5**, 261–265.

Lazarus, A. A. Group therapy of phobic disorders by systematic desensitization. *J. abnorm. soc. Psychol.*, 1961, **63**, 504–510.

Lazarus, A. A. The results of behaviour therapy in 126 cases of severe neurosis. *Behav. Res. Ther.*, 1963, **1**, 69–79.

Lazarus, A. A. Crucial procedural factors in desensitization therapy. *Behav. Res. Ther.*, 1964, **2**, 65–70.

Lazarus, A. A. A preliminary report on the use of directed muscular activity in counter-conditioning. *Behav. Res. Ther.*, 1965, **2**, 301–303.

Lazarus, A. A. Broad spectrum behaviour therapy and the treatment of agoraphobia. *Behav. Res. Ther.*, 1966, **4**, 95–97.

Lazarus, A. A., & Abramovitz, A. The use of "emotive imagery" in the treatment of children's phobias. *J. ment. Sci.*, 1962, **108**, 131–135.

Levis, D. J., & Carrera, R. N. Effects of 10 hours of implosive therapy in the treatment of outpatients. A preliminary report. *J. abnorm. Psychol.*, 1967, **72**, 504–508.

Lewis, A. J. Problems of obsessional illness. *Proc. Roy. Soc. Med.*, 1936, **29**, 325–336.

Lewis, A. J. Obsessional disorder. *Price's textbook of the practice of medicine*. London: Oxford University Press, 1956.

Lewis, H. Deprived children. *The Mersham experiment, a social and clinical study*. Nuffield Foundation. London: Oxford University Press, 1954.

Lomont, J. F. Reciprocal inhibition or extinction? *Behav. Res. Ther.*, 1965, **3**, 209–219.

Lomont, J. F., & Edwards, J. E. The role of relaxation in systematic desensitization. *Behav. Res. Ther.*, 1967, **5**, 11–25.

Mair, J. M. M., & Crisp, A. H. Estimating psychological organization, meaning and change in relation to clinical practice. *Brit. J. Med. Psychol.*, 1968, **41**, 15–29.

Malleson, N. Panic and phobia. *Lancet.*, 1959, **i**, 225–227.

Malmo, R. B., & Shagass, C. Physiologic study of symptom mechanisms in psychiatric patients under stress. *Psychosom. Med.*, 1949, **11**, 25–29.

Marks, I. M., Birley, J. L. T., & Gelder, M. G. Modified leucotomy in severe agoraphobia: A controlled serial inquiry. *Brit. J. Psychiat.*, 1966, **112**, 757–769.

Marks, I. M., & Gelder, M. G. A controlled retrospective study of behaviour therapy in phobic patients. *Brit. J. Psychiat.*, 1965, **111**, 561–573.

Marks, I. M., & Gelder, M. G. Common ground between behaviour therapy and psychodynamic methods. *Brit. J. med. Psychol.*, 1966, **33**, 11–23.

Martin, I. Somatic reactivity. In H. J. Eysenck (Ed.), *Handbook of abnormal psychology*. London: Pitman, 1960.

Meyer, V. The treatment of two phobic patients on the basis of learning principles. *J. abnorm. soc. Psychol.*, 1957, **55**, 261–266.

Meyer, V., & Crisp. A. H. Some problems in behaviour therapy. *Brit. J. Psychiat.*, 1966, **112**, 367–381.

Meyer, V., & Gelder, M. G. Behaviour therapy and phobic disorders. *Brit. J. Psychiat.*, 1963, **109**, 19–28.

Miller, R. E., Banks, J. H., & Ogawa, N. Communication of affect in "cooperative conditioning" of rhesus monkeys. *J. abnorm. Soc. Psychol.*, 1962, **64**, 343–348.

Miller, R. E., Banks, J. H., & Ogawa, N. Role of facial expression in "cooperative avoidance conditioning" in monkeys. *J. abnorm. soc. Psychol.*, 1963, **67**, 24–30.

Moore, N. Behaviour therapy in bronchial asthma: A controlled study. *J. psychosom. Res.*, 1965, **9**, 257–276.

Mowrer, O. H. *Learning theory and personality dynamics*. New York: Roland Press, 1950.

Mowrer, O. H. *Learning theory and behaviour*. New York: Wiley, 1960.

Mowrer, O. H., & Viek, P. An experimental analogue of fear from a sense of helplessness. *J. abnorm. soc. Psychol.*, 1948, **67**, 24–30.

Muller, C. Weitere Beobachtungen zum Verlauf der Zwangskrankheit. *Mschr. Psychiat. Neurol.*, 1957, **133**, 80–94.

Murphy, J. V., Miller, R. E., & Mirsky, I. A. Interanimal conditioning in the monkey. *J. comp. physiol. Psychol.*, 1955, **48**, 211–214.

Osgood, C. E. *Method and theory in experimental psychology*. New York: Oxford University Press, 1953.

Paul, G. L. *Insight versus desensitization in psychotherapy: An experiment in anxiety reduction*. Stanford: Stanford University Press, 1965.

Paul, G. L., & Shannon, D. T. Treatment of anxiety through systematic desensitization in therapy groups. *J. abnorm. Psychol.*, 1966, **2**, 124–135.

Pavlov, I. P. *Conditioned reflexes*. Oxford: Oxford University Press, 1927.

Pollitt, J. Natural history of obsessional states. A study of 150 cases. *Brit. med. J.*, 1957, **i**, 194–198.

Polin, A. T. The effect of flooding and physical suppression as extinction techniques on an anxiety-motivated avoidance locomotor response. *J. Psychol.*, 1959, **47**, 253–255.

Rachman, S. Studies in desensitization—1: The separate effects of relaxation and desensitization. *Behav. Res. Ther.*, 1965, **3**, 245–251.

Rachman, S. Studies in desensitization—11: Flooding. *Behav. Res. Ther.*, 1966a, **4**, 1–6.

Rachman, S. Studies in desensitization—111: Speed of generalisation. *Behav. Res. Ther.*, 1966b, **4**, 7–15.

Rachman, S. The role of muscular relaxation in desensitization therapy. *Behav. Res. Ther.*, 1968, **6**, 159–166.

Rachman, S., & Hodgson, R. J. Studies in desensitization—IV: optimum degree of anxiety reduction. *Behav. Res. Ther.*, 1967, **5**, 249–250.

Ramsay, R. W., Barends, J., Brucher, J., & Kruseman, A. Massed versus spaced desensitization of fear. *Behav. Res. Ther.*, 1966, **4**, 205–207.

Razran, G. R. The place of the conditioned reflex in psychology and psychiatry in Pavlovian conditioning and American psychiatry. In G. R. Razran & W. H. Bridger (Eds.), *G.A.P. symposium No. 9, group for advancement of psychiatry*. New York, 1964.

Reed, J. L. Comments on the use of methohexitone sodium as a means of inducing relaxation. *Behav. Res. Ther.*, 1966, **4**, 323.

Ritter, B. The group desensitization of children's snake phobios using vicarious and contact desensitization procedures. *Behav. Res. Therap.*, 1968, **6**, 1–6.

Roberts, A. H. Housebound housewives—A follow-up study of phobic anxiety states. *Brit. J. Psychiat.*, 1964, **110**, 191–197.

Roth, M. The Phobic anxiety—depersonalization syndrome. *Proc. Roy. Soc. Med.*, 1959, **52**, 587–596.

Rubin, B. M., Katkin, E. S., Weiss, B. W., & Efran, J. S. Factor analysis of a fear survey schedule. *Behav. Res. Ther.*, 1968, **6**, 65–75.

Rudin, E. Ein Beitrag zur Frage der Zwangskrankheit, insbesondere ihrer hereditaren Beziehugen. *Arch. Psychiat. Z. ges. Neurol. Psychiat.*, 1953, **191**, 14–54.

Sargent, W. The present indications for leucotomy. *Lancet*, 1962, **ii**, 1197–2000.

Sargent, W. Psychiatry in general teaching hospitals. *Brit. Med. J.*, 1966, **ii**, 257–262.

Saslow, G., & Peters, A. D. A follow-up study of untreated patients with various behaviour disorders. *Psychiat. Quart.*, 1956, **30**, 283–302.

Schmidt, E., Castell, D., & Brown, P. A retrospective study of 42 cases of behaviour therapy. *Behav. Res. Ther.*, 1965, **3**, 9–19.

Shafer, S., & Jaffe, J. R. Behaviour therapy in the treatment of psychoneurosis. *Brit. J. Psychiat.*, 1965, **111**, 1199–1203.

Solomon, R. L., & Brush, E. S. Experimentally derived conceptions of anxiety and aversion. In M. R. Jones (ed.) *Nebraska symposium on motivation*, Lincoln, Nebraska: University of Nebraska Press, 1956.

Solomon, R. L., & Wynne, L. C. Traumatic avoidance learning: The principle of anxiety conservation and partial irreversibility. *Psychol. Rev.*, 1954, **81**, 353–385.

Solyom, L., & Miller, S. B. Reciprocal inhibition by aversion relief in the treatment of phobias. *Behav. Res. Ther.*, 1967, **5**, 313–324.

Staats, A. W., Staats, C. K. *Complex human behaviour: A systematic extension of learning principles*. New York: Holt, Rinehart & Winston, 1963.

Stampfl, T. G., & Levis, D. J. The essentials of implosive therapy: a learning theory based psychodynamic behavioural therapy. *J. abnorm. Psychol.*, 1967, **72**, 496–503.

Stampfl, T. G., & Levis, D. J. Implosive therapy—a behavioural therapy? *Behav. Res. Ther.*, 1968, **6**, 31–36.

Staub, E. Duration of stimulus-exposure as determinant of the efficacy of flooding procedures in the elimination of fear. *Behav. Res. Ther.*, 1968, **6**, 131–132.

Stevenson, I. Processes of "spontaneous" recovery from psychoneurosis. *Amer. J. Psychiat.*, 1961, **117**, 1057–1064.

Thorpe, J. G., Schmidt, E., Brown, P. T., & Castell, D. Aversion-relief therapy: A new method for general application. *Behav. Res. Ther.*, 1964, **2**, 71–82.

Truax, C. B. Therapist empathy, warmth and genuineness & patient personality change in group psychotherapy: a comparison between interaction unit measures, time sample measures, patient perception measures. *J. Clin. Psychol.*, 1966a, **22**, 225–229.

Truax, C. B. Reinforcement and non-reinforcement in Rogersian psychotherapy *J. abnorm. Psychol.*, 1966b, **71**, 1–9.

Truax, C. B., & Carkhuff R. R. Significant developments in psychotherapy research. In L. E. Abt & B. F. Reiss (Eds.), *Progress in clinical psychology*. New York: Grune and Stratton, 1964.

Turner, L. H., & Solomon, R. L. Human traumatic avoidance learning: theory and experiments on the operant-respondent distinction and failure to learn. *Psychol. Monogr.*, 1962, **76** (Whole No. 559).

Wallace, H. E. & White, M. B. Natural history of the psychoneuroses. *Brit. Med. J.*, 1959, **i**, 144–148.

Walker, L. Prognosis for affective illness. *J. Neurol. Neurosurg. Psychiat.*, 1959, **22**, 338–341.

Watson, J. B. & Rayner, R. Conditioned emotional reactions. *J. exp. Psychol.*, 1920, **3**, 1–14.

Watson, J. B., & Rayner, R. Studies in infant psychology. *Sci. Monogr.*, New York, 1921.

Wilson, G. D. Efficacy of "flooding" procedures in desensitization of fear: a theoretical note. *Behav. Res. Ther.*, 1967, **5**, 138.

Wolpe, J. *Psychotherapy by reciprocal inhibition*. Stanford: Stanford University Press, 1958.

Wolpe, J. The systematic desensitization treatment of neurosis. *J nerv. ment. Dis.*, 1961, **132**, 189–203.

Wolpe, J. Quantitative relationships in the systematic desensitization of phobias. *Amer. J. Psychiat.*, 1963, **119**, 1062–1068.

Wolpe, J., & Lang, P. J. A fear schedule for use in behaviour therapy. *Behav. Res. Ther.*, 1964, **2**, 27–30.

Wolpe, J., & Lazarus, A. A. *Behaviour therapy techniques*. Oxford: Pergamon Press, 1966.

Wolpin, M., & Pearsall, L. Rapid deconditioning of a fear of snakes. *Behav. Res. Ther.* 1965, **3**, 107–111.

Wolpin, M., & Raines, J. Visual imagery, expected roles and extinction as possible factors in reducing fear and avoidance behaviour. *Behav. Res. Ther.*, 1966, **4**, 25–37.

Worsley, J. L., & Freeman, H. Further comments on the use of methohexitone sodium as a means of inducing relaxation. *Behav. Res. Ther.*, 1967, **5**, 258.

Yates, A. J. *Frustration and conflict*. New York: Methuen, 1962.

Zeisset, R. M. Desensitization and relaxation in the modification of psychiatric patients' interview behaviour. *J. abnorm. Psychol.*, 1968, **73**, 18–24.

Chapter 11

Obsessions and Compulsions

M. D. MATHER

INTRODUCTION

Obsessions or compulsions may take the form of an act, a thought, a fear, or an urge that is *repetitive*, irrational, and out of the voluntary control of the individual. It is usually unchanging in the form it takes and is unmodified throughout the process of repetition. In this sense it is said to be *stereotyped*. The motor sequences in an act, for example, are exact in detail, and the verbalizations of a thought sequence are unchanging. Another feature of the obsession is the *internal resistance* (Mayer-Gross, Slater, & Roth, 1955). The individual is subject to the compulsion against his own will, and it often has a quality of disgust, repulsion, or aversion to him. This the authors call "contrast ideas." The impulse to kill one's child or to carry out something undesirable is an example of this. There is not only insight into the irrational quality of the symptom, as in other neuroses, but distaste relating to it.

Examples of obsessions are repetitive counting, ritualistic hand washing, pseudo-philosophical questions, impulses to do harm. The motor acts may often have some symbolic significance and are attempts to allay fears or doubts of an irrational kind. Superstitious behavior has been classified as obsessional. Such symptoms occur in anxiety states. They may also be seen in schizophrenia or manic-depressive psychoses and involutional melancholia. In the psychoses, there may be no insight into the irrational nature of the obsession, and it is held with delusional intensity. There is an increased incidence in states of fatigue, and in some instances of organic deterioration.

Metzner (1963) has stressed the "Janus-like" quality of the obsession. It appears to serve two purposes at the same time. The individual may wish to guard himself against the gratification of an urge, either sexual or aggressive, by carrying out some act that may gratify the need against which it was a defence. This dual characteristic of the obsession may contribute to the inner resistance already mentioned.

EXPERIMENTAL EVIDENCE FOR COMPULSIVE BEHAVIOR AND ITS ASSESSMENT

Experimental Evidence

Behavior that appears to be compulsive has been produced experimentally in both animals and humans. Different terms have been used to describe this behavior, including fixation, perseveration, absence of variability, resistance to extinction, and behavior constancy. In most of the experiments, the behavior has been demonstrated as repetitive, stereotyped, and irrational, in so far as it often does not appear to meet environmental demands of the experimental setup. It is questionable, however, whether the behavior variously described in the experimental literature is always strictly comparable because of the different methods of determining and assessing it.

Some of the most important experimental work on fixations or compulsions in the rat, has been carried out by N. R. F. Maier and his colleagues (Maier, 1949; and Maier, Glaser, & Klee, 1940). They assessed the behavior of rats under two different experimental conditions—one, the condition of normal motivation in the learning of a discrimination problem and the other, the condition of "frustration" or the presentation of a discrimination problem that was insoluble. It is the latter that may be regarded as an analogue.

In the normally motivating conditions of learning, the rat was required to discriminate between two doors, either by its position or by the symbol displayed. The choice of the correct door was consistently rewarded by food, and the "incorrect" choice consistently punished (the door being locked caused the rat to receive a bump on the nose and fall into the net below).

In the insoluble situation, the doors were locked in random sequence, thus, preventing the reward of food from being associated with either door. If the rat refused to jump it was forced to do so by an air blast or tap on the tail. Under these conditions, rats tended to adopt a position response which became "fixated" or resistant to change. Maier, Glaser, and Klee (1940) demonstrated that rats who had not been subjected to the insoluble situation, but only to the soluble one, could learn an alternative response if it were appropriately and consistently reinforced. Rats who had experienced insolubility, on the other hand, could not abandon the responses produced by this condition when an alternative was reinforced. There was, nonetheless, a differential delay in responding to the "correct" and "incorrect" doors, as confirmed by Feldman (1953), suggesting that the rat had learned to discriminate between the doors although it did not change its response accordingly.

This is considered by Maier to be sufficient evidence for the compelling nature of the response acquired under insoluble conditions. It would be in line with the clinical observations of compulsive behavior in humans. Although the patient knows his response to be unadaptive, he is unable to change it and often experiences some aversion to carrying it out.

Similar experimental conditions have been employed to produce fixated behavior in humans (Marquart & Arnold, 1952, and Jones, 1954). Marquart and Arnold presented to normal human subjects an insoluble problem consisting of two doors each bearing a symbol (a triangle, a circle, or a square) in different combinations. The subjects were required to open the correct door. An incorrect choice was punished by the appearance of a red light. Without prior warning the problem became soluble. Fixated behavior was observed in some subjects during the soluble problem; subjects who did not learn the problem tended to adhere consistently to an erroneous principle and to make stereotyped remarks. These subjects were not clinically obsessionals, and their behavior appeared to arise from the experimental conditions.

Marquart and Arnold observed that the subjects who showed stereotyped behavior took over 129 trials to learn the soluble problem, whereas those subjects who did not, learned the soluble problem within 100 trials. In agreement with Maier and his colleagues in their observations of rats, Marquart and Arnold claim to have demonstrated the different nature of the fixated response from the normally reinforced responses which will change and be adapted to altered environmental conditions. Whether or not it is qualitatively different, at least, it appears resistant to change.

Jones (1954) obtained fixated responses in humans by an insoluble T-maze problem in which left or right responses were randomly rewarded or punished. The subject's choice was made by pressing a morse key that would produce a reward in the form of a white light or a punishment in the form of a buzzer. A subsequent soluble problem revelaed the presence of unchanged repetitive responses in some of the subjects.

Fixated behavior has also been observed in learning experiments in both animals and humans. Responses that have been reinforced consistently may, under certain conditions, become fixated and resistant to change. The investigators have commonly employed a T-maze or multiple-choice apparatus in which a particular choice is reinforced by reward (Hamilton & Krechevsky, 1933; Elliott, 1934; Patrick, 1934a and 1934b; Everall, 1935; O'Kelly, 1940a and 1940b; Kleemeier, 1942; Farber, 1948). The responses that are normally subject to extinction when the reward is shifted to an alternative path of the apparatus, may become persistent and resistant to extinction under certain conditions. They will be discussed in more detail in the later section on the development of compulsive behavior. It suffices in this section to mention that experimentally induced conditions of shock, emotional upset, or altered levels of motivation have appeared to produce the fixation of a previously learned response.

Kleemeier (1942) has rightly differentiated between the learned response that is unchanging and repetitive but which may be adapted to meet the demands of the situation (as a repetitive response adopted under shock), and a response that continues in unvarying manner when the demands of the situation have changed. The former behavior he describes as lack of variability, and the latter he defines as true fixation. It is this latter behavior with which one is chiefly concerned in the clinical setting.

Methods of Assessment

In the determination and assessment of a fixated response, authors have usually employed a new learning situation in which the continuance of this particular response would be described as inappropriate. It prevents the organism from acquiring an alternative response to meet the demands of the situation.

Maier and his colleagues assessed the strength of the responses in their experiments by the number of trials in which a rat persisted in his position response during the new symbol discrimination problem. It was found that failure to abandon the response in 200 trials indicated that the rat would also be incapable of doing so in any subsequent trials.

Knöpfelmacher (1952) suggested that the concentration of fixated responses was as important as the number of trials to extinction.

Marquart and Arnold (1952) obtained fixated responses in human subjects by the same method as Maier and his colleagues. They employed a similar measure of *stereotypy* which was defined as "consistency of choice," that is, the number of times a subject made an identical response on two successive presentations. This criterion differentiated between "normal" learners and "slow" learners; the latter group taking over 129 trials and appearing to base their responses continuously on an erroneous principle.

Jones (1954) considered several measures of fixated responses which occurred in his previously "frustrated" human subjects during the administration of the soluble problem. A succession of six responses to one of the possible two choices of keys was used as the criterion of fixation, since he found that the subjects who were not subjected to frustration could learn the problem after responding this number of times on one key. He employed two measures of fixation, namely, the duration of the fixated response and the proportion of repetitive responses to the total number of responses given. He measured also the degree of vacillation or variation in pressure on the key by means of a rubber bulb under the key that was connected to a pen-recording on a drum-kymograph. Vacillation decreased during periods in which the repetitive responses occurred, suggesting that these responses were enabling the subject to make some form of adjustment to the problem-solving situation.

Learning in the multiple-choice situation, employed by some authors, allowed a wider range of choice of response for the subject and facilitated different ways of assessing a fixated response.

Kleemeier (1942) measured two kinds of behavior in rats in a 4-alley-multiple-choice apparatus. Having trained the rats to follow one alley to obtain food and then an alternative alley, he subjected the rats to changed conditions in which they were shocked. *Lack of variability* was noted by the number of times a particular alley was chosen in these shocked conditions. Removal of shock and shift of reward to an alternative alley allowed a measure of *fixation*. Distribution of choices to the various alleys on shock-free trials indicated the persistence of a choice when demands had changed.

Kleemeier used a further test by blocking the alley continually chosen by the rat. This he called forcing variability on the rat. In this case, no alternative response was adopted by the rat, suggesting that it could not find an adequate substitute even when it was prevented from carrying out the response, and that it was dominated by the fixated behavior.

A similar method of assessing fixated behavior in humans has been used by Patrick (1934). He presented human subjects with a choice of four possible responses in a multiple-choice apparatus that consisted of a roomlike enclosure, an entrance hall, and four exit doors. The doors were locked or unlocked according to an ever-varying principle. The solution, that is the correct choice of door on each trial could never be attained by the subject. Under conditions of insolubility, Patrick classified his subjects' reactions to ascertain stereotypy of response.

Patrick assessed the number of classified reactions under normal conditions of problem-solving and under emotionally disturbing stimuli. The relative preponderance of one type of reaction over another in a series of trials was the method of assessment he employed. Kleemeier's methods of assessing fixated responses in changed conditions of learning could be applied to the human field and would give a better indication of the strength of the particular mode of response adopted. Patrick did not alter the learning situation to test the *persistence* of what he described as *stereotypy.*

There are other aspects of human fixation that could be assessed—the tendency to repeat a particular motor sequence, such as trying the same door repetitively, and the tendency to adhere rigidly to a particular hypothesis or idea. Everall (1935) has observed that a motor response or a hypothesis may be subject to perseveration in rats.

Application of Methods of Assessment to The Compulsive Symptom

Thus far these methods of assessment have not been fully applied in the clinical situation. Measures of the frequency and duration of the compulsive response to specific stimuli would be important in assessing its strength. A measure of the concentration of the response, or the consistency with which it is evoked by these stimuli, would also be relevant in determining the extent to which the response has a compulsive hold on the subject. It is probably necessary to know if other incompatible responses are sometimes evoked by the same stimuli in order to have some assessment of the proportion of these responses (Knöpfelmacher, 1952; Marquart & Arnold, 1952).

Assessing frequency and duration of a response would seem to be appropriate to both the ideational compulsion or the recurring thought and the motor compulsion. With particular regard to the motor compulsion, which often appears clinically to be more situation-bound, it would be possible to have some assessment of the varying strengths of response evoked by a range of stimuli. This would also give some measure of the extent of generalization of a response pattern. It is noticeable, for instance, that some obsessional patients are almost completely handicapped, being unable to undertake any activities without becoming involved in some compulsive ritual. The symptoms in this sense may be pervasive. Yet the number of repetitions of the compulsive act once it is evoked and its *duration* may not be relatively excessive. The range of generalization may be an independent facet of compulsive behavior which may be important in assessment.

EXPERIMENTAL EVIDENCE RELATING TO IMPORTANT FACTORS IN THE DEVELOPMENT OF THE COMPULSIVE SYMPTOM

Frustration or Insolubility

A frustrating situation has already been demonstrated as productive of fixation (Maier, Glaser, & Klee, 1940; Maier, 1949). The definition of frustration within the context of Maier's work is an insoluble problem in which either of two stimuli are *randomly* rewarded and punished, so that either give 50 percent rewarded trials and 50 percent punished trials. The fact that neither stimulus can become consistently associated with reward or punishment has been considered one cause of the fixation. Other important components of the insoluble problem are the pressure to respond (produced by the air blast) and the absence of any escape.

The random pattern of reinforcement in the frustration situation is an essential feature in producing fixation since 50 percent orderly punishment and reward in the motivating condition of the soluble discrimination problem did not cause rats to fixate (Maier & Klee, 1943).

In another study, in which the same experimental conditions were employed, Maier and Feldman (1948) established that the longer the durations of the insoluble problem, the greater the strength of the fixation. Comparable durations of practice under motivating soluble conditions, however, produced no significant increases in the strength of the learned response.

Punishment and Frustration

The proportion of punishment to reward may also be an important determinant of fixations. It has been established that fixated responses may be produced in human subjects when presented with a similar kind of insoluble discrimination problem (Marquart, 1948; Marquart & Arnold, 1952). A response would be rewarded by a light flashing and would be punished by a shock. These authors found that by varying the absolute amount of punishment and the concentration of punishment within the insoluble problem, they obtained different degrees of fixation. Not only was the amount and concentration of punishment relevant but also the extent to which the subject wished to succeed in finding a solution. They presented their groups of subjects with an insoluble problem of different durations and of different proportions of punished trials within each. A longer period of frustration with a lower concentration of punished trials was found to have a more fixating effect on a response when the junior author was experimenter (Marquart & Arnold, 1952) whereas a shorter period of insolubility with a higher concentration of punished trials was more fixating when the senior author was experimenter (Marquart & Arnold, 1952; Marquart, 1948). From this they conclude that in the former conditions, where there may have been lower motivation to succeed, the duration of the insoluble problem determined the fixating of the response. In the latter conditions, the motivation to succeed being higher, the concentration of punishment became a more important determinant.

As in Maier's experiments with rats, qualitative differences were observed in the responses of the human subjects. Subjects could either abandon their responses within 80 to 91 trials of a subsequent soluble problem, *or* they required over 94 trials. This bimodal distribution appeared to confirm the qualitative difference between "learners" and "slow-learners." Complete fixation, however, was never observed in the human subject in these experiments.

The important components of the frustrating situation that cause a response to become fixated may be summarized as follows. The essentially random pattern of the insoluble problem does not allow the learning of an association between any stimulus and reward, and a fixated response occurs as a result of this. The orderly reinforcement of a soluble problem allows the learning of an appropriate response that can be abandoned when demands subsequently change. However, the orderly reinforcement may constitute the same frequency of rewarded and punished trials. From this, the authors conclude that it is the pattern of reinforcement that is a major determinant of whether a response becomes fixated.

Secondly, it must be imperative to the animal or human to respond, and there must be no escape from the field or substitute goal. The pressure to respond may constitute in humans a high motivation to succeed in the problem.

The duration of frustration may be an important factor, although in humans it appears to depend on how involved they may be in the situation, and on the percentage of punished trials received. The more involved the individual is, and the greater the concentration of punishment, the more likely it is that a short period of frustration will fixate the response.

The duration of frustration may generally be considered to have a greater reinforcing effect on the strength of a fixation than has the frequency of repetition on the strength of a response acquired in normal conditions of learning.

One study (Krechevsky & Honzik, 1932) has not been confirmed, and it would seem fixate a reinforced response. However, this has not been confirmed, and it would seem that repetition in itself is not sufficient to produce fixations.

Frustration and Partial Reinforcement

An important aspect of the insoluble problem has been considered the partial reinforcement of a response (Wilcoxon, 1952). Evidence suggests that, if a response is partially reinforced in a learning situation, it is more persistent than if it is reinforced 100 percent of the time (Jenkins & Stanley, 1950). Wilcoxon considers that the "insoluble" problem, in fact, constitutes just such ideal conditions for learning. Any response the rat adopts during the insoluble problem receives 50 percent reward and 50 percent punishment. Although it is randomized the reinforcement is essentially partial reinforcement. Wilcoxon argues that any learning situation in which these conditions hold true should fixate a response. To demonstrate that it was the nature of the reinforcement rather than the insolubility itself that produced fixations in Maier's rats, Wilcoxon subjected three groups of rats to different conditions of reinforcement using Maier's discrimination apparatus. One group received continuous reinforcement; the other two received partial reinforcement in a soluble and insoluble situation, respectively. As Wilcoxon predicted according to learning principles, conditions of partial reinforcement in a soluble problem produced the greatest fixation.

Although it is fairly well substantiated that partial reinforcement contributes to the persistence of a response, its relative importance in the production of fixations has not been established. As Maier (1956) states, Wilcoxon did not take account of the different proportions of punishment in his three experimental conditions. (They were in fact not equivalent to the proportions of reward.) He rightly points out that this variable alone could have explained the results. It is already known that punishment increases the strength of a fixation.

Emotion and Shock

There is considerable experimental evidence to suggest that any emotionally disturbing stimulus introduced in a problem-solving situation may fixate a response. In these experiments, rats have been required to learn a T-maze or multiple-choice maze in which a particular choice of alley has been reinforced by reward. Some emotionally disturbing stimulus introduced at the choice point has been found to cause the fixation of the learned response.

Hamilton & Krechevsky (1933) and Everall (1935) found that shock at the choice-point of a T-maze tended to fixate a previously learned response in rats. Increase in the length of practice in the original training of this response did not result in its becoming fixated, a finding consistent with Maier's. The frequency of repetition of a habit does not appear to be a determinant of fixation.

Fixation of a reinforced right-turning response in a T-maze could also be produced by withholding the rats in a cage at the choice-point for two minutes (Everall, 1935). The author suggests that emotional upset, whether produced by shock or the blocking of two pathways to a goal, causes the fixation of a response.

The same fixating effects of shock have been found in both humans and rats when they have been trained in multiple-choice apparatus (Everall, 1935; Kleemeier, 1942; Patrick, 1934). Everall found that rats shocked in an insoluble multiple-choice situation not only repeatedly chose the same alleys but also adhered to hypotheses regarding visual and spatial sequences of the alleys. As Everall points out, "Perseveration, both of a motor and ideational sort . . . is the result of emotional excitement."

Similar results have been obtained in human subjects (Patrick, 1934). Patrick prepared an insoluble problem in a multiple-choice apparatus in which any one of four doors would be open to permit an exit from an enclosure. The other three would be locked. The open door was ever-varying, thus, making the problem insoluble. Emotionally disturbing stimuli at the choice-point consisted either of an electric shock, a loud noise from a horn, or a cold shower. Patrick showed that any one of these stimuli tended to make the subjects repeat the same choice of door on a series of trials. The presentation of the problem without shock did not result in this perseverative behavior, but rather a tendency to deduce some rational principle on which to base a choice. In the presence of emotional excitement this rational behavior appears to be replaced by repetitive stereotyped behavior in humans and in rats.

Kleemeier (1942) showed that rats which are presented with a *soluble* multiple-choice situation may also become fixated if shocked at the choice-point. He emphasizes the motivational aspect of shock and suggests that fixations occurring in Maier's experiments are because of the emotional consequences of the frustration and the compelling motivation of the air-blast.

The evidence seems fairly conclusive in showing the fixating effect of emotion. Any response may become fixated under emotion-arousing conditions. Frustration or insolubility in itself may not be a determining factor but rather the emotional excitement evoked by it. A disturbing stimulus in the context of a soluble problem may be sufficient to fixate a response. The nature of the fixation may be a previously learned habit (Kleemeier, 1942; Hamilton & Krechevsky, 1933; Everall, 1935) or a response which is most available. Kleemeier found that alleys in his multiple-choice apparatus that were more accessible to the rat tended to be fixated on more frequently during shocked trials.

The Reduction of Anxiety and Fixation

Some learning theorists have argued that responses may become fixated when they are instrumental in reducing anxiety that has been evoked by intense stimuli, such as electric shock (Farber, 1948; Wolpe, 1953). In conditions of shock, the anxiety aroused becomes conditioned to stimuli in the environment or situation, and any response adopted that facilitates escape from these stimuli is strongly reinforced. Thus the response may become resistant to extinction.

Farber (1948) attempted to show that responses which had become fixated under shock were sustained by anxiety, and that by inhibition of the anxiety the responses could be eliminated. He trained rats by food reward to take a left turn in a T-maze. Half of them were then subjected to conditions in which they were shocked at the choice-point. When the food reward was subsequently shifted to the alternative side, there was greater fixation to the original left turn among shocked rats as predicted. However, Farber demonstrated that feeding some of the shocked rats after their runs caused them to abandon their fixated left-turning responses. Feeding only facilitated the faster extinction of the responses of the shocked rats and not the ones of the non-shocked rats. Thus it appears that feeding had the specific effect of removing the anxiety that sustained the fixated response, rather than influencing the particular response itself.

Wolpe (1953) has similarly argued that the jumping fixation in Maier's "frustrated" rats is reinforced by escape from the noxious stimulus—the air blast. In the insoluble problem, in which the rat is forced to respond by an air blast, the motive of the rat may change from one of seeking food to one of reducing anxiety occasioned by the air blast. The jump following the air blast, thus, is satisfactorily anxiety-reducing and is strongly reinforced.

Although there is evidence to support the importance of anxiety-reduction in the learning of responses (Solomon & Wynne, 1954), this cannot be considered the sole factor responsible for the fixated behavior of Maier's rats (Maier & Ellen, 1951; Ellen, 1956). As Yates (1962) has pointed out, Farber's rats were not frustrated in Maier's sense and, furthermore, did not show such a degree of fixation; all of them ultimately extinguished their responses.

The degree of anxiety is clearly a relevant variable in the fixation of responses, and Maier himself has emphasized the importance of "frustration threshold" of the rats. Some of the rats in the soluble learning problem became fixated presumably as a result of their "frustration level" having been exceeded (Maier, 1956). This may be synonymous with their "anxiety level."

Primary-Drive Reduction, Motivation, and Fixation

It has already been suggested that an animal's involvement in the situation or its motivation to find a solution may be one determinant in the development of a fixation. In the case of rats in a problem-solving situation in which they must learn the response that will be rewarded by food, the intensity of the hunger drive may be important both in the learning and in the fixating of the response adopted. The evidence produced thus far, however, suggests that the relationship between fixation and primary drive reduction is not a simple linear one (Elliott, 1934; O'Kelly, 1940b; Jones, 1954).

Elliott (1934) found that increase in hunger in rats produced repetitive responses which appeared fixated. He used a multiple-choice apparatus in which all the alleys were rewarded by food. In this sense, the situation was not problem-solving, and no response was punished. He ran three groups of rats on different degrees of food deprivation, two groups being commenced with minimal hunger and subjected to increases in degrees of hunger and one group being commenced on maximal hunger and subjected to decreases in hunger level. Although four alternative equally rewarded responses were available to the rats, increased hunger produced repeated choices of the same response. It tended to persist even in the rats whose drive level was subsequently decreased. High motivation or hunger drive appears to decrease variability in behavior.

Klee (1944) suggests that the development of fixations in Maier's insoluble problem may be determined by the degree of involvement in the situation. He investigated the responses of rats in Maier's insoluble problem, under two kinds of motivation: air-motivation and food-motivation. One group was forced to respond by the air blast, whereas a second group only underwent food deprivation. Klee found a greater incidence of fixations in the former group which, he argued, was more involved in the situation. The latter group usually did not respond. Increasing the motivation and involvement by prolonged food-deprivation, however, was sufficient to produce fixations in this group also.

Very similar results have been obtained in the human field (Jones, 1954). Jones studied the effects of increasing motivation of human subjects in an insoluble problem similar to the one used by Maier. He employed a temporal maze in which responses could be recorded by pressing one of two keys. Six groups of subjects received different lengths of "frustration" (5, 50, and 100 trials) and either "incentive" or "non-incentive" conditions. The incentive conditions consisted of telling the subjects that it was an intelligence test and that they should be able to solve it in two minutes. In non-incentive conditions the subjects were told that the experimenter wished to discover the difficulty of the task. As in Maier's experiment, the insoluble problem was followed by a soluble one with no warning given. Jones found that the incentive groups showed more stereotyped, fixated behavior. Increased duration of frustration had similar effects on the behavior. Fixated responses, therefore, appeared to be a function of both duration of frustration and degree of involvement in the experiment. These results appear to be consistent with the findings of Marquart and Arnold (1952). It is worth noting, however, that there appeared to be a "ceiling" of 50 trials beyond which a further increase in duration of frustration did not produce stronger fixations. This is in agreement with the results of Maier and Feldman (1948).

Jones was not investigating the influence of a primary drive such as hunger in his human subjects, as was Klee. The important conclusion, however, from both animal and human studies, is that increase in motivation to find a solution and to obtain a reward in the experimental set-up, no matter whether a primary or secondary learned drive is employed, may contribute to the fixation of the response.

There is limited evidence to suggest that lowered motivation or satiation may also increase the possibility of fixation in rats. This might suggest that there is a bimodal relationship between motivational level and the occurrence of fixated behavior. This is only tentative. O'Kelly (1940a and b) produced fixated responses in rats by either of two kinds of conditions that he considered were emotionally disturbing to the rats, namely, electric shock and satiation by water intake. He trained rats in a T-maze to take one of two paths to water reward, and subsequently he subjected them to an electric shock at the entrance of the maze. His results confirmed the ones of Hamilton and Krechevsky (1933); when water reward was shifted to the alternative path following shocked trials, fixation of the initial habit occurred.

O'Kelly then trained rats equally on both the right and the left path of the T-maze, following 24 hours of water deprivation. Running the same rats, subsequently, under conditions of satiation had the effect of fixating the rats on the first path they had learned. O'Kelly concluded that both satiation and shock produce an emotional disturbance in the organism, which is responsible for the development of the fixation. The response fixated may be perseverative (persistence of the on-going behavior) if only one response has been learned, or it may be regressive (return to the first habit) if two responses have been learned.

The weight of evidence seems to support more the importance of high levels of motivation rather than satiation in the fixation of a response.

Generalized Cortical Damage and Fixation

There is some tentative evidence that generalized brain damage in rats may contribute to the persistence of behavior. Hamilton and Ellis (1933a and b) found that rats who had been subjected to an operation causing generalized brain damage tended to persist in habits in which they had previously been trained, more than did non-operated rats. Even under conditions of satiation and, thus, absence of motivation, brain-damaged rats persisted in a response they had previously learned to obtain food. Normal rats which were similarly satiated abandoned any response previously reinforced by food.

The authors differentiate the fixated behavior of operated rats from persistent behavior that is goal-seeking and perpetuated by motivation.

Gottsdanker (1939) has shown that poor differentiation among choice possibilities may produce fixation in human subjects. This seems pertinent to the occurrence of fixated behavior in brain-damaged subjects where there may be poor ability to make finer discriminations. He used a multiple-choice keyboard involving 300 possible choices. To some groups of subjects he confined the field of choice, and to others he did not. He introduced another condition of blindfoldness, so that some subjects could not see their choices. The group which was blindfolded and had no boundaries within which to make their choices of response, became more fixated. In this group, there was poorer discrimination between keys. The inability to differentiate between stimuli in this situation leads one to speculate that it may be subjectively insoluble and, thus, present conditions similar to Maier's "frustration" situation.

Conflict and Fixation

Masserman (1943) has made the distinction between frustration and conflict. "The consequences of frustration must be distinguished from those of conflict since frustration as such does not appear to result in experimental neurosis." Compulsive behavior was produced in cats (Masserman, 1943) by engendering a motivational conflict. Cats were trained to receive food from a box at a sound or light signal. Placing a barrier to the goal by locking the lid caused the animals to ignore the food signals. They did not, however, display any anxiety or phobic reactions. When the animals were presented with an air blast across the box at the moment of taking food, they showed signs of anxiety at the food signals, and adopted some behavior pattern in which they persisted no matter how painful. Some would circumvent the food box in a ritualistic manner or would hide their heads in the box without taking food.

Mowrer (1940) demonstrated an apparently compulsive phenomenon in rats in a conflict situation. Rats were trained to press a pedal to terminate a shock through the grill of their cage floor. The pedal itself was then electrically charged. Shock from the grill floor then caused the rats to retreat from the pedal, which they had previously used to terminate it. Anxiety was aroused by the learned response of touching the pedal. However, when the floor shock increased, the rat returned to press the pedal. Mowrer observed that the rat was compelled to press it in the face of the increasing grill shock. The nature of the pedal-pressing response changed in that it was now accompanied by agitation and in that the response was repetitive. There was a state of conflict or competing impulses in which there was both the tendency to approach the pedal and not to approach it. Mowrer has supported this causative factor in compulsions (Mowrer, 1960) by reference to other experiments. Deese (1952) noted alternating movements toward and away from a stick that had previously been associated with both anxiety and food. The rat experienced, fear on approach toward the stick, and relief when it reversed. Approach toward the stick on the other hand was reinforced by the food reward. The rat reduced, fear but did not reduce hunger, and so progressed forward again.

It seems to the present author that similar experimental conditions of motivational conflict (in the sense in which Masserman uses the term) have been created in many of the afore-mentioned experiments, although the authors may have emphasized the importance of other variables.

Maier's work has not always gained full recognition because he holds the view that fixations are not the result of a learning process but are abnormal responses arising from frustration. Maier's definition of frustration is insolubility and the absence of motivational conditions for learning. His insoluble problem, however, might be considered as a conflict situation as described by Masserman. Either choice of response which the rat may adopt is both rewarded and punished and, therefore, receives reinforcement that is conflicting. Partial reinforcement may increase the strength of a response, but it does not seem to be an adequate explanation for the fixations obtained by Maier. Partial reinforcement consists of 50 percent reward and 50 percent *non-reward*. The results of these conditions have not been compared with the results of 50 percent reward and 50 percent *punishment*, constituting the insoluble problem. The different degrees of fixation in Wilcoxon's experiment (1952) were essentially obtained by varying the proportions of reward and punishment.

Furthermore, conflicting reinforcement appears to be an important variable in the investigations on the effects of shock (Farber, 1948; Hamilton & Krechevsky, 1933; O'Kelly, 1940; Everall, 1935; Kleemeier, 1942). In learning situations in which a response is reinforced by food reward, a subsequent aversive stimulus, such as shock, introduces a motivational conflict, and the on-going behavior becomes both rewarded and punished. In Farber's experiment (1948), the most fixated rats were the ones who had received shock following reinforcement by food. Subsequent feeding may have reduced anxiety in the rats and may have caused extinction of the fixation. It may equally well have reduced the conflict, because of a preponderance of reward.

Metzner (1963) has suggested that a response may become fixated when it has been a successful avoidance response and, subsequently, becomes unsuccessful as a result of its having been punished. This seems to be essentially the same condition of conflict of reinforcement that has already been described above. Learning of approach-avoidance associations to the same stimulus may be one of the conditions for the development of a fixation. A plausible reason for this has been offered by Mowrer (1940) in terms of conflict.

Implications of the Animal Studies to Human Obsessional Behavior

Although there has been far more extensive experimental work with animals than with humans, the animal work seems to have important relevance to the understanding of human compulsions. The insoluble problem in Maier's experiments with rats can be seen to have some similarity with the conditions to which humans may be subjected in real life, and which seem to evoke obsessional behavior. One example of this is the frequent obsessional preoccupation with disease, germs, death, etc. The occurrence of disease, etc., is under no adequate control by the individual, that is to say, there is no behavior which can be adopted which will satisfactorily avert it, and in this sense the situation is insoluble. The compulsive rituals (for example, hand-washing, counting, etc.) may be the only way available to the individual to produce some degree of certainty in an essentially uncertain and insoluble problem. The inability of the individual to escape and the extent of his involvement in this kind of situation need not be emphasized.

The importance of partial reinforcement in these conditions is also apparent. It seems to be an essential facet of the insoluble situation where prediction is impossible, that undesirable events may be consequent on behavior in a random or chance fashion. Disease or illness, for example, may be expected to occur in a random and unpredictable way; on the other hand, it may often not occur and, therefore, may appear to be averted following behavioral sequences that have been adopted.

The degree of punishment experienced seems to be a causative variable in animal experiments. Painful life experiences relevant to the content of the obsessional preoccupation and compulsion may be found in human subjects. The obsessional fear of cancer can be seen in patients who have experienced traumatic incidents of death from cancer in relatives.

Guilt often appears to be a concomitant of the obsessional idea or habit. This is most apparent in the obsessional fears of doing harm and of killing. The guilt may be a secondary reaction to the symptom, but this does not seem to be a totally adequate explanation. The purpose of the obsessional symptom to guard against the gratification of a need has already been mentioned in the introduction. It is in these cases that one may see the importance of motivational conflict in the development of the symptom. In the earlier experiences of the individual, a behavior pattern that gratified a need may have been punished and, thus, may have generated anxiety and guilt.

The degree of anxiety or emotion aroused by experimental conditions has also contributed to compulsive behavior in the animal experiments. Obsessional behavior in humans may be a function both of certain external conditions and of the degree of emotional arousal in the individual. In both animal and human studies, the innate emotional lability and responsiveness has been somewhat neglected. Extreme emotionality was found to be one trait which significantly differentiated those who were fixated and those who were not (Marquart & Arnold, 1952).

These would appear to be the only analogies that we may justifiably draw between animal and human compulsive behavior. Far more research is needed in the human field in order to understand the greater complexities seen in human obsessions, particularly the ruminative obsessions, and some of the compulsions that appear to have symbolic significance.

EXPERIMENTAL EVIDENCE AND TECHNIQUES FOR MODIFYING THE COMPULSIVE SYMPTOM

Modification by Guidance

As previously shown in the sections on assessment and development, rats who have adopted responses under insoluble conditions cannot abandon them when subsequently faced with a soluble problem. Subjecting these rats to motivating conditions of trail and error learning fails to change their behavior. However, Maier and Klee (1945) discovered a technique that altered the fixated behavior. In the motivated discrimination problem following frustration, they manually guided the rats to jump to the correct window. Whenever a rat was about to carry out its stereotyped response, the experimenter would place a hand against the rat, thus, preventing it from performing the response. It, therefore, had either to avoid jumping or to jump to the correct window.

Maier and Klee (1945) compared the effectiveness of two slightly different methods of guidance with trial and error learning in altering both habits and fixations. Two groups of rats, one having first learned position responses in motivating conditions, and one having adopted position stereotypes under frustration, were both subdivided and received either the method of trial and error to alter their response, or the method of trial and error in conjunction with guidance. This latter method consisted of concentrated guidance trials followed by trial and error.

The whole procedure was repeated in a second part of the experiment with the guidance trials now alternated with the trial and error trials, instead of their being concentrated at the beginning. The results showed that both the massed and the spaced guidance techniques were more effective for abolishing both habits and fixations than the ordinary learning trials. Fixated rats were unable to benefit from trial and error learning alone, as has been confirmed in previous studies, but guidance enabled them to abandon their fixations. This technique did not, however, facilitate new learning and, once the fixation was abolished, there was a stage of variability before the new discriminating response was adopted. The rats who were not fixated adopted the new response by trial and error soon after abandoning the position response. Maier and Klee conclude that guidance may break an old response (whether it be a habit or fixation) but that it is not effective in teaching a new one.

There are two phases in the modification of a fixation, its abandonment, and then a period of relearning. Maier claims that this vitiates against learning theory which states that change in behavior can be brought about by modifying the relative strength of behavior tendencies (Spence, 1936). In Maier's work the freeing of the rat from the old response is not sufficient to evoke an alternative response, hence, the intervening period of variability before alternative behavior is learned.

Furthermore, guidance not only had "therapeutic" value in animal fixations, but was shown to have preventative effects (Maier & Ellen, 1952). Two groups of rats were trained in Maier's symbol discrimination problem. One group was required to learn by trial and error. The other group learned with 10 guided trials for every 40 unguided trials. All the animals were then subjected to the insoluble problem and finally to a further discrimination problem. All rats who did not fixate under these conditions received further trials, 25 percent of which were randomly punished.

The group that received guidance initially showed less tendency to fixate during the subsequent frustrating conditions, and also showed more rapid learning of the second discrimination problem. Guidance, thus, seemed to reduce the tendency to fixation and also allowed the animal to benefit from subsequent reward and punishment.

However, the therapeutic component in guidance has not been established. It has been found that there is no difference between three techniques of breaking fixations; manual guidance, mechanical guidance by a mechanical transparent barrier, and handling with emotional soothing (Haslerud, Bradbard, & Johnstone, 1954). There is apparently some factor, which is neither pure guidance nor simple handling, that has the effect of breaking a fixation and of enabling the rat to learn an alternative response. The authors used these techniques in the same experimental conditions as Maier, alternating the guidance or soothing trials with trial and error in a discrimination problem subsequent to frustration.

Masserman (1943) showed that emotional soothing of compulsive cats, consisting of the experimenter handling the cat and stroking it manually, within the conflict situation failed to have any generalizing effect.

The Modification of Compulsive Behavior by Electroshock

Some evidence has shown that electroshock may have an influence on a perseverative response. Murphee and Peters (1956) assessed the relative effects of electroshock, insulin comas and of Chlorpromazine on fixated responses in rats. The fixations were produced by an insoluble problem employing a T-maze. These fixations were significantly reduced by electroshock. There was no significant change following the other treatments. Some other studies have supported this evidence (Masserman & Jaques, 1947; Hunt & Brady, 1951).

It is, however, by no means conclusive that electroshock has a therapeutic effect on fixations, even of recent origin. Neet and Feldman (1954) assessed the effect of 25 days and 10 days of electroshock on fixations that were produced under insoluble conditions. These two differing lengths of electroshock treatment failed to have any significant influence on the strength of the fixation and were no better than equivalent lengths of rest periods. The authors concluded that neither electroshock nor rest periods have any beneficial effect on fixated behavior.

In a subsequent study (Feldman & Neet, 1954), the same authors subjected rats to electroshock supplemented by guidance. The rats were presented with a discrimination problem and guided on every alternate trial. Half of the rats received electroshock once a day for ten days. There was no suggestion that electroshock supplemented by guidance enabled the rats to abandon their fixations more readily than by guidance alone. Feldman and Neet (1957) also established that electroshock fails to modify fixations of differing strengths.

Maier and Klee (1941) assessed the effect of metrazol-induced convulsions in altering fixated behavior but found that it had no effect.

From the contradictory evidence regarding the effects of electroshock, it is doubtful that this would be a choice of treatment for fixated behavior.

Modification of Compulsive Behavior by Reward and Punishment

The results of the experimental work on the effects of reward and punishment on the fixation is also somewhat contradictory. Maier and Ellen (1955) studied the effects of different proportions of punishment and reward on the fixations of rats, and concluded that all the conditions were, on the whole, ineffective in modifying fixated behavior. The results of Knöpfelmacher (1952) suggested that punishment may weaken a fixated response in rats. However, the fact that Knöpfelmacher used no such additional stimulus as an air blast in the frustrating situation that originally produced the fixations would lead us to suppose that his rats were less "frustrated." Maier and Klee (1943), on the other hand, showed that punishment may increase the strength of a fixation.

The results of these animal experiments suggest that punishment has little beneficial effect on a severe compulsion and that its therapeutic value may depend on the strength of the response, or the extent to which the animal has previously experienced punishing stimuli in the insoluble situation.

The results of these experiments are not

sufficient either to support or to contra-indicate therapy based on learning principles of reward and punishment.

Modification of Compulsive Behavior by the Application of Learning Principles (Human Studies)

Reciprocal inhibition and desensitization

Wolpe who has been one of the chief supporters of learning theory and anxiety-reduction (Wolpe, 1958) has reported the relief of compulsive habits (both of ideational and motor kind) following therapy based on this theory. He argues that anxiety is prominent in learned neurotic reactions. They become persistent because of their anxiety-reducing properties. Wolpe's techniques in treating obsessional or compulsive habits have involved essentially the reduction of the anxiety by the evocation of a response inhibitory to it (reciprocal inhibition).

In one case of a youth, who suffered from a compulsion of hand-washing (Wolpe, 1964), Wolpe reduced the anxiety that appeared to be reinforcing the symptom. The young man feared his urine would contaminate objects and people and took to extensive washing rituals to allay the anxiety. By inhibiting the man's anxiety about urine by desensitization, the motor compulsion was abolished.

In cases of an ideational compulsion or rumination (recurring thought), Taylor (1963) and Wolpe (1958) have demonstrated the effectiveness of inhibition of the habit by introducing a disruptive stimulus. The patient is required to repeat voluntarily the thought sequence, and either a sharp buzzer or the command "stop" is introduced. This stimulus inhibits the thoughts after a number of repetitions.

According to the learning principles of anxiety-reduction, there are two facets of the compulsive neurosis, the conditional anxiety or drive, and the response that is instrumental in reducing the anxiety and that may take the form of a motor act or thought. This is described as the compulsion. In the cases quoted, the first instance (Wolpe, 1964) is that of removal of the anxiety maintaining the compulsion. In the last two cases (Taylor, 1963; Wolpe, 1958), the compulsion itself has been treated without regard to the anxiety.

The relative effectiveness of treating either aspect of the behavior depends on the duration of the symptoms (Walton & Mather, 1964; Walton, 1960). Walton (1960) first showed that the attempts to remove a stone-kicking compulsion in a protracted case were unsuccessful until the therapy was accompanied by the inhibition of the anxiety over certain social issues that originally seemed to have caused the development of the compulsion.

By removing anxiety that related to aggressive impulses and to social stimuli by assertive training, Walton and Mather (1964) successfully alleviated two cases displaying compulsive habits. They were in the acute phase of illness, having only suffered for a few weeks or months. In chronic cases, this was found to be insufficient treatment. Treatment of both the motor habit and the anxiety sustaining it was found necessary to produce a remission in more long-standing cases. The motor compulsion may become partly autonomous of the historically earlier anxiety. Both aspects seem to need separate treatment. The methods used were desensitization and reciprocal inhibition, using graded hierarchies of the anxiety-provoking stimuli.

The cases reported thus far have been treated on the premise that the compulsion is essentially anxiety-reducing, although there is some doubt still concerning the results of dealing separately with either the anxiety or the compulsive habit.

Punishment

Wolpe (1958) has also suggested that obsessional symptoms may be at times anxiety-elevating. Eysenck and Rachman (1965) have suggested that remorse, guilt, or anxiety may be a *consequence* of carrying out the compulsive act rather than an antecedent of it. Taylor (1963) has argued that social disapproval of the act tends to perpetuate it because it increases the person's concern over his behavior, and this anxiety may have initially been responsible for the emergence of the habit. Punishment may aggravate a compulsion as has been shown earlier (Maier & Klee, 1943). However, Taylor argues that, if there is less delay between any social criticism and the act, then the criticism may be more successful in inhibiting the act. He demonstrates with one case of a lady who plucked her eyebrows compulsively. She was instructed to stop herself voluntarily every time she felt the urge to raise her hand to her eyebrow. This method is similar to that of vocal inhibition described earlier (see page 314). Treatment of fixations by punishment probably has limited use as suggested by the experimental evidence related thus far. It is also not at all convincing that the secondary anxiety aroused by punitive social attitudes toward the symptom is the most important factor to control.

Negative Practice

Humphrey and Rachman (1963) employed negative practice or satiation to treat the motor compulsion of chewing, biting, and tearing materials in a young boy. The voluntary performance of the compulsion for 20-minute sessions ultimately abolished the habit.

Other Methods

Meyer (1966) has suggested an alternative method of reducing anxiety that mediates the compulsive symptom. He has argued that the stimuli which evoke anxiety in the obsessional may be particularly difficult to avoid and that the patient is unable to withdraw from them (unlike the phobic who can successfully avoid the phobic objects). The performance of obsessional rituals may allay the fear of some untoward eventuality. On the basis of this argument, Meyer suggested a therapy that is based on "modification of expectations"; if the patient is allowed to see that not performing his rituals does not lead to the feared situation, his expectancies are changed, and this should mediate new behavior. Meyer successfully treated two patients by this method. The patients were merely prevented from carrying out their rituals.

There have been no systematic studies of the relative effectiveness of these different methods of behavior therapy in the alleviation of compulsive symptoms. Desensitization or reciprocal inhibition of anxiety through assertive training seem to have been most often employed. The compulsion or obsessional thought may be separately treated by avoidance conditioning, by negative practice, and by vocal or motor inhibition. Occasionally removal of the secondary anxiety that relates to the compulsive act may have an ameliorative effect.

Further Development of Modification Techniques

Advance in the therapy of compulsions may depend on understanding more of the complex variables that contribute to their development. It has already been suggested that anxiety-reduction may not account solely for the persistent nature of the behavior. Therapy based on this theory may be only partially successful. As Meyer (1966) has stated, the anxiety-provoking stimuli can be particularly difficult to avoid for a variety of different reasons. One such reason could be that the stimuli are conditioned to reward as well as to punishment. Many compulsions seem to arise from anxiety conditioned to aggressive or sexual impulses, the expression of which are highly rewarding and also almost impossible to avoid.

Masserman (1943) treated the compulsive reactions of cats who had been faced with a conflict situation by reducing one of the conflictful drives. Before placing the cats in the food box, he fed them. This proved ineffective, since the compulsions returned later when the cats were again hungry and placed in the same situation. No other treatment appears to have been developed and applied to compulsive behavior that has been produced under conditions of motivational conflict. If one is to understand fixated responses in Maier's frustration situation to be the product of a conflict situation, as has been defined earlier, guidance may be a technique of choice. The work of Maier has certainly not been fully applied to the human field.

Furthermore, confusion and poor discrimination between stimuli, suggested to be one of the causative factors in compulsive behavior, (Gottsdanker, 1939) do not appear to have been fully appreciated in the therapeutic situation. It is, for instance, typical of the obsessional patient with a fear of dirt and a compulsive hand-washing ritual that he is unable to make any clear differentiation between what is *actually* dirty and what is not. He is beset with doubts, and with an inability to pass a definite judgment on the stimuli that are anxiety-provoking. In this sense, also, the obsessional fear is unlike the phobia. The obsessional patient characteristically spends much time pondering and trying to make a decision. It is possible that this indecision and compulsiveness is the outcome either of a conflict situation or a learning situation in which discriminations are made difficult or impossible (Fonberg, 1956; Gottsdanker, 1939).

We suggested, therefore, that a possible beneficial approach in therapy might be "guidance" followed by a discrimination learning situation in which the patient is taught to make appropriate judgments on the presence or absence of the feared stimulus. In the case of the ritualistic handwasher, with his obsession for contamination, it might be possible to gear reward and punishment (perhaps, in the form of social approval or disapproval) to realistic decision making regarding dirty and clean objects. Discrimination learning of this kind might aid clearer differentiation and, thus, reduce obsessional doubts and fears.

Summary and Conclusions

Compulsive behavior may be defined as any act or thought that becomes repetitive, stereotyped in the form it takes, and unmodified by external conditions. This kind of behavior has been produced in both animals and humans in learning experiments. The compulsive character of the response was determined by its having remained unaltered in changed experimental conditions in which an alternative response was demanded. It is apparent from the experimental literature that authors may not be agreed on the nature of the compulsive response. A response that may become repetitive when it has once been evoked by certain external stimuli, may be abandoned when the stimuli are removed. This may be lack of variability in response, but not fixation or compulsion. The strength of the compulsive response has been variously assessed by its frequency of occurrence, its duration, and the consistency with which it occurs in proportion to alternative responses.

Methods of assessing the strength of a compulsive response have not generally been applied to the clinical field, although there seems to be sufficient evidence to suggest that the fixated responses adopted under experimental conditions are analogous to the compulsive symptom.

The most extensive experimental work on the development of the compulsion has been carried out by N. R. F. Maier, who has demonstrated the important causative factor of frustration, or the insolubility of a discrimination problem. This involves the inconsistent and random association of reward and punishment with either of two possible alternative responses. The strength of the compulsive response adopted may be increased by the duration of the "frustration" and by the higher proportion of punished trials in the insoluble problem. The important facets of frustration relevant to the development of the fixations have been discussed. They include the degree of the organism's involvement or pressure to respond, the absence of "escape," or alternative goal-seeking, and the partial reinforcement of a response.

The arousal of emotion by the introduction of a disturbing stimulus in motivating conditions of learning may contribute to the development of a fixation. The emotional upset appears to be responsible for the fixation of the reinforced response, which otherwise would have been subject to the normal extinction process. If alternative responses are made available to the organism, one of them may be adopted in the emotionally disturbing condition in preference to the response. The emotional arousal nonetheless seems to fixate whichever response is chosen.

The importance of anxiety in the reinforcement and perseveration of a response is discussed in relation to Maier's conditions of frustration and conditions of motivation. A response may become strongly reinforced and, thus, resistant to extinction because it successfully reduces the anxiety evoked by noxious stimuli, as the air blast used by Maier in the insoluble frustrating condition or the shock introduced in a soluble motivating condition.

Some evidence supports the view that a high level of drive, whether primary (hunger or thirst), or secondary learned drives in human subjects to find a solution, to obtain a reward, or to become involved, may be an important condition for the development of a fixation.

Generalized cortical damage may be a causative factor, and the possibility of poor discrimination between stimuli, contributing to fixations in such conditions, is suggested.

Motivational conflict defined as the development of approach-avoidance associations to the same stimulus is posited as a causation of fixation. It is suggested that the presence of this conflict has been overlooked in the foregoing experiments that involve so-called insoluble problems (the rewarding and the punishing of a response) and in the soluble learning problems in which shock is introduced (the punishing of a previously rewarded response). Discriminations cannot be made in these conditions.

There is less adequate experimental literature on the modification of fixations. Guidance and electroshock appear to have been most extensively investigated. Guidance appears to have great therapeutic value for animal fixations. The importance of reward and punishment in modification has not been established.

Most of the human studies on the modification of compulsive symptoms have been single-case studies. There is no convincing experimental evidence from which the value of any technique may be reliably judged. The methods used have been based for the most part on the theory of anxiety-reduction. The evidence suggests that the evocation of a response incompatible with anxiety inhibits it (reciprocal inhibition) (Wolpe, 1958) and, therefore, the compulsive response that is instrumental in reducing the anxiety may also extinguish (Wolpe, 1964). If the compulsive behavior is of recent origin, this principle may operate. In the chronic case the compulsion may be partly autonomous of this anxiety and, therefore, may require separate attention. Reciprocal inhibition has been used to modify both the learned anxieties and the compulsive habits of both a motor and an ideational kind.

Punishment by social disapproval has also been employed to disrupt compulsive behavior. Negative practice or the development of satiation in performing a compulsive habit may also have some value.

An important theoretical point relevant to the modification of compulsions has been raised by Meyer (1966). Stimuli evoking anxiety in the obsessional may be difficult or impossible to avoid. Unlike the phobic, he cannot withdraw from these stimuli. The obsessional may fear some eventuality that he cannot predict or control and, therefore, cannot successfully avoid. The prevention of the performance of a compulsive ritual in these obsessionals may succeed in demonstrating that non-performace does not lead to the feared eventuality (modification of expectations).

This inability to predict the results (reward or punishment) of external stimuli or events seems to be an essential aspect of obsessionals which has not been fully considered in their treatment. Random reward and punishment, insolubility, or motivational conflict, can be observed to result in impossible prediction. This can be interpreted as poor discrimination, that is the difficulty in differentiating between the rewarding stimuli and the punishing stimuli. The abolishing of compulsive symptoms may lie in enabling the obsessional to learn appropriate differentiation of the stimuli that are punishing and rationally to be avoided, and the ones that are not.

REFERENCES

Deese, J. *The Psychology of learning*. New York: McGraw-Hill, 1952.

Duncan, C. P. Habit reversal induced by electroshock in the rat. *J. comp. physiol. Psychol.*, 1948, **41**, 11.

Ellen, P. The compulsive nature of abnormal fixations. *J. comp. physiol. Psychol.*, 1956, **49**, 309–317.

Elliott, M. H. The effect of hunger on variability of performance. *Amer. J. Psychol.*, 1934, **46**, 107–112.

Everall, Eleanor E. Perseveration in the rat. *J. comp. physiol. Psychol.*, 1935, **19**, 343–369.

Eysenck, H. J., & Rachman, S. *The causes and cures of Neurosis*. London: Routledge and Kegan Paul, 1965.

Farber, I. E. Response fixation under anxiety and non-anxiety conditions. *J. exp. Psychol.*, 1948, **38**, 111–131.

Feldman, R. S. The specificity of the fixated response in the rat. *J. comp. physiol. Psychol.*, 1953, **46**, 487–492.

Feldman, R. S., & Neet, C. C. The effect of electroconvulsive shock on fixated behavior in the rat. II. The effect of ECS supplemented by guidance. *J. comp. physiol. Psychol.*, 1954, **47**, 210–212.

Feldman, R. S., & Neet, C. C. The effect of electroconvulsive shock on fixated behavior of the rat. III. The effect of ECS as a function of the duration of conflict. *J. comp. physiol. Psychol.*, 1957, **50**, 97–99.

Fonberg, E. On the manifestation of conditioned defensive reactions in stress, 1956. Cited by J. Wolpe, *Psychotherapy by reciprocal inhibition*. Stanford: Stanford Univer. Press, 1958, p. 92.

Gottsdanker, R. M. An experimental study of fixation of response by college students in a multiple-choice situation. *J. exp. Psychol.*, 1939, **25**, 431–443.

Hamilton, J. A., & Ellis, W. D. Behavior constancy in rats. *J. genet. Psychol.*, 1933a, **42**, 120–139.

Hamilton, J. A., & Ellis, W. D. Persistence and behavior constancy. *J. genet. Psychol.*, 1933b, **42**, 140–153.

Hamilton, J. A., & Krechevsky, I. Studies in the effect of shock upon behavior plasticity in the rat. *J. comp. physiol. Psychol.*, 1933, **16**, 237–253.

Haslerud, G. M., Bradbard, L., & Johnstone, R. P. Pure guidance and handling as components of the Maier technique for breaking abnormal fixations. *J. Psychol.*, 1954, **37**, 27–30.

Humphrey, J., & Rachman, S. Case data 1963. Cited by H. J. Eysenck & S. Rachman in *The causes and cures of Neurosis.* London: Routledge and Kegan Paul, 1965, p. 137.

Hunt, H. F., & Brady, J. V. Some effects of electroconvulsive shock on conditioned emotional response ("Anxiety"). *J. comp. physiol. Psychol.*, 1951, **44**, 88–98.

Jenkins, W. O., & Stanley, J. C. Partial reinforcement: a review and critique. *Psychol. Bull.*, 1950, **47**, 193–234.

Jones, L. C. T. Frustration and stereotyped behaviour in human subjects. *Quart. J. exp. Psychol.*, 1954, **6**, 12–20.

Klee, J. B. The relation of frustration and motivation to the production of abnormal fixations in the rat. *Psychol. Monogr.*, 1944, **56**, No. 4 (whole 257), p. 45.

Kleemeier, R. W. Fixation and regression in the rat. *Psychol. Monogr.*, 1942, **54**, No. 4 (whole 246), p. 34.

Knöpfelmacher, F. Some effects of reward on the strength of position stereotypes in the white rat. *Quart. J. exp. Psychol.*, 1952, **4**, 78–86.

Krechevsky, I., & Honzik, C. H. Fixation in the rat. *Univer. Calif. Publ. Psychol.*, 1932, **6**, 13–26.

Maier, N. R. F. *Frustration: The study of behavior without a goal.* New York: McGraw-Hill, 1949.

Maier, N. R. F. Frustration theory: restatement and extension. *Psychol. Rev.*, 1956, **63**, 370–388.

Maier, N. R. F., & Ellen, P. Can the anxiety reduction theory explain abnormal fixations? *Psychol. Rev.*, 1951, **58**, 435–455.

Maier, N. R. F., & Ellen, P. Studies of abnormal behavior in the rat. XXIII. The prophylactic effects of "guidance" in reducing rigid behavior. *J. abnorm. soc. Psychol.*, 1952, **47**, 109–116.

Maier, N. R. F., & Ellen, P. The effect of three reinforcement patterns on positional stereotypes. *Amer. J. Psychol.*, 1955, **68**, 83–95.

Maier, N. R. F., & Feldman, R. S. Studies of abnormal behavior in the rat. XXII. Strength of fixation and duration of frustration. *J. comp. physiol. Psychol.*, 1948, **41**, 348–363.

Maier, N. R. F., Glaser, N. M., & Klee, J. B. Studies of abnormal behavior in the rat. III. The development of behavior fixations through frustration. *J. exp. Psychol.*, 1940, **26**, 521–546.

Maier, N. R. F., & Klee, J. B. Studies of abnormal behavior in the rat. VII. The permanent nature of abnormal fixations and their relation to convulsive tendencies. *J. exp. Psychol.*, 1941, **29**, 380–389.

Maier, N. R. F., & Klee, J. B. Studies of abnormal behavior in the rat. XII. The pattern of punishment and its relation to abnormal fixations. *J. exp. Psychol.*, 1943, **32**, 377–398.

Maier, N. R. F., & Klee, J. B. Studies of abnormal behavior in the rat. XVII. Guidance versus trial and error in the alteration of habits and fixations. *J. Psychol.*, 1945, **19**, 133–163.

Marquart, D. I. The pattern of punishment and its relation to abnormal fixation in adult human subjects. *J. gen. Psychol.*, 1948, **39**, 107–144.

Marquart, D. I., & Arnold, L. P. A study in the frustration of human adults. *J. gen. Psychol.*, 1952, **47**, 43–63.

Masserman, J. H. *Behavior and neurosis.* Chicago: Univer. of Chicago Press, 1943.

Masserman, J. H., & Jacques, M. G .Effects of cerebral electroshock on experimental neurosis in cats. *Amer. J. Psychiat.*, 1947, **104**, 92–99.

Mayer-Gross, W., Slater, E., & Roth, M. *Clinical Psychiatry.* London: Cassel, 1955.

Metzner, R. Some experimental analogues of obsession. *Behav. Res. & Ther.*, 1963, **1**, No. 3, 231–236.

Meyer, V. Modification of expectations in cases with obsessional rituals. *Behav. Res. & Ther.*, 1966, **4**, No. 4, 273–280.

Mowrer, O. H. An experimental analogue of regression with incidental observations on reaction formation. *J. abnorm. soc. Psychol.*, 1940, **35**, 56–87.

Mowrer, O. H. *Learning theory and behavior.* New York: Wiley, 1960.

Murphee, O. D., & Peters, J. E. The effect of electroconvulsions, insulin comas, and certain chemical agents on fixations in the rat. *J. nerv. ment. Dis.*, 1956, **124**, 78–83.

Neet, C. C., & Feldman, R. S. The effect of electroconvulsive shock on fixated behavior in the rat. I. The effect of a ten- and of a twenty-five-day series of ECS on the stability of the fixated response. *J. comp. physiol. Psychol.*, 1954, **47**, 124–129.

O'Kelly, L. I. An experimental study of regression. I. Behaviour characteristics of the regressive response. *J. comp. physiol. Psychol.*, 1940a, **31**, 41–53.

O'Kelly, L. I. An experimental study of regression. II. Some motivational determinants of regression and perseveration. *J. comp. physiol. Psychol.*, 1940b, **30**, 55–95.

Patrick, J. B. Studies in rational behavior and emotional excitement. I. Rational behavior in human subjects. II. The effect of emotional excitement on rational behavior in human subjects. *J. comp. physiol. Psychol.*, 1934, **18**, 1–22 and 153–195.

Solomon, R. L., & Wynne, L. C. Traumatic avoidance learning: The principles of anxiety conservation and partial irreversibility. *Psychol. Rev.*, 1954, **61**, 353–385.

Spence, K. W. The nature of discrimination learning. *Psychol. Rev.*, 1936, **43**, 427–449.

Taylor, J. G. A behavioural interpretation of obsessive-compulsive neurosis. *Behav. Res. & Ther.*, 1963, **1**, No. 3, 237.

Walton, D. The relevance of learning theory to the treatment of an obsessive-compulsive state. In H. J. Eysenck (Ed.), *Behaviour therapy and the neuroses.* Oxford: Pergamon Press, 1960.

Walton, D., & Mather, Marcia D. The application of learning principles to the treatment of obsessive-compulsive states in the acute and chronic phases of illness. In H. J. Eysenck (Ed.), *Experiments in behaviour therapy.* Oxford: Pergamon Press, 1964.

Wilcoxon, H. C. "Abnormal fixation" and learning. *J. exp. Psychol.*, 1952, **44**, 324–333.

Wolpe, J. Learning theory and "abnormal fixations." *Psychol. Rev.*, 1953, **60**, 111–116.

Wolpe, J. *Psychotherapy by reciprocal inhibition.* Stanford: Stanford Univer. Press, 1958.

Wolpe, J. Behaviour therapy in complex neurotic states. *Brit. J. Psychiat.*, 1964, **110**, 28–34.

Yates, A. J. *Frustration and conflict.* London: Methuen, 1962.

Chapter 12

Tics

AUBREY J. YATES

Interest in the explanation and treatment of tics has shown very marked fluctuation in the history of psychiatry. In the late nineteenth century rapidly increasing attention to the problem culminated in the classical treatise of Meige and Feindel (1907). The rapid rise in influence of Freudian psychoanalytic psychology about this time, however, quickly replaced the reeducative methods advocated by Brissaud, and by Meige and Feindel, with the psychodynamic approach to treatment. Since, however, tics, like obsessions, are extremely refractory to any form of treatment, the disorder became neglected for several decades, apart from the efforts of a few psychoanalysts. Tiqueurs tended to be regarded by psychiatrists as intractable patients, with whom little success could be expected from the expenditure of a great deal of effort. In recent years, however, there has been some revival of interest in the problem, both from a theoretical and a behavior modification point of view. From the theoretical viewpoint, tics are of especial interest, since their frequency, and intensity, etc., can readily be measured and, hence, formulated theories about their genesis and treatment can be easily tested. From the behavior modification viewpoint, it is more readily possible than in the case of many other disorders to determine changes in the state of the disorder following the application of various methods of treatment.

The definition of a tic given by Meige and Feindel has not been improved on and, therefore, is repeated here.

> A tic is a coordinated purposive act, provoked in the first instance by some external cause or by an idea; repetition leads to its becoming habitual, and finally to its involuntary reproduction without cause and for no purpose, at the same time as its form, intensity and frequency are exaggerated; it thus assumes the character of a convulsive movement, inopportune and excessive; its execution is often preceded by an irresistible impulse, its suppression associated with malaise. The effect of distraction or of volitional effort is to diminish its activity; in sleep it disappears. It occurs in predisposed individuals who usually show other indications of mental instability (Meige & Feindel, 1907, pp. 260–261).

The clarity and comprehensiveness of this definition, however, do not suffice, as Meige and Feindel were well aware, to make the operational or clinical definition of the presence or absence of a tic a matter of simplicity. Insofar as any tic involves motor movement it must be differentiated out from other movements which may have many of the characteristics of a tic, but which do not merit remedial action. Second, there are several classes of abnormal behaviors which must be differentiated from tics. Third, it should be differentiated from classes of movements which are often very difficult behaviorally to distinguish from tics, but which have a clearly organic origin and should be considered separately from tics, even though this separation is not meant to imply that "organically-based tics" cannot be behaviorally treated by the same methods as are used with tics.

ASSESSMENT TECHNIQUES

The problems to be considered here fall into three categories: differential diagnosis, the types of tics, and the measurement of "movement" in children and adults.

Differential Diagnosis

Differential diagnosis of tics from other conditions is important because of the implications for treatment. Ticlike movements may occur in many organic conditions, involving brain injury or physiological malfunction. In these cases, successful medical direct treatment of the disease-process will usually, although not always, result in the disappearance of the ticlike behavior. (The analogy would be with the delusions and hallucinations found to accompany abnormal blood-sugar level; direct treatment of the latter will ameliorate the former.)

The principal *organic* conditions with which tics may be confused are spasms, choreas, and cerebellar and cerebello-rubrospinal tremor. Although the differential diagnosis, in individual cases, may be extremely difficult, the general differences are relatively easily specified. Table 12.1 incorporates the principal distinguishing signs, as elaborated by Meige and Feindel (1907), Wilson (1927), Williams (1932), and Hassin, Stenn, & Burstein (1930).

The principal *functional* conditions from which tics must be differentiated have included stereotyped acts (for example, continuous rhythmic rocking, repetition of phrases, etc.) and psychiatric conditions such as compulsions and phobias, which often involve repetitive sequences of acts (Bender & Schilder, 1940, 1941; Hall, 1935; Mahler, 1944). The main distinction here lies in the nature of the compulsive acts or phobic inhibition of behavior, in that the phobias and compulsions usually involve

Table 12.1 Differential Diagnosis of Tics from Organic Conditions Producing Ticlike Movements

Spasm	Tic	Chorea	Tremor
Not subject to voluntary control	Subject to voluntary control	Not subject to voluntary control	Not subject to voluntary control
No correlation with personality	Personality defect always present	No correlation with personality	No correlation with personality
Cannot be modified by external control (attention, distraction)	May be modified by external control (attention, distraction)	Cannot be modified by external control (attention, distraction)	Cannot be modified by external control (attention, distraction)
Abrupt, instantaneous	Brusque but slower	Still slower	Regular, increased by movement
Specific reflexes modified	Reflexes unimpaired	Reflexes often modified	Reflexes increased
Strength proporional to strength of stimulus	Not proporional to strength of stimulus	Not proporional to strength of stimulus	Not proporional to strength of stimulus

Table 12.1 (continued)

Spasm	Tic	Chorea	Tremor
Continues during sleep	Disappears during sleep	Continues during sleep	Disappears during sleep
Muscle may atrophy	No muscular atrophy	Myasthenia, hypotonia	Myasthenia, hypotonia, or reverse
Painful/distressing	Painless	Sometimes painful	Painless
Purposeless	Purposeful	Purposeless	Purposeless
Cannot be reproduced voluntarily	Can be reproduced voluntarily	Cannot be reproduced voluntarily	Cannot be reproduced voluntarily
Cannot be inhibited	Inhibition increases tension level	Cannot be inhibited	Cannot be inhibited
Execution brings no tension reduction	Execution brings tension reduction	Execution brings no tension reduction	Execution brings no tension reduction
Aetiology organic: peripheral irritation (lesion)	Aetiology nonorganic	Hereditarily determined	Aetiology organic: brain lesion or tumor

much more extensive and complex sequences of behavior.

Types of Tics

Several attempts have been made to classify tics into various categories, but most of them are of little value. Thus, Meige and Feindel (1907, pp. 142–205) spent a good deal of time describing the various kinds of tics in terms of the musculature involved (face, eyes, neck, arms, etc.), but such a classification is probably irrelevant as far as treatment is concerned. A more important distinction may be that between clonic and tonic tics. Clonic tics are those where the movement or contraction is abrupt and short-lived; whereas in tonic tics the contractions are long-lasting and more or less continuous. In the latter case, discrimination from athetoid or choreic movements becomes more difficult. From the theoretical and treatment viewpoint, as we shall observe later, the most important fact about a tic may be its degree of complexity, which will determine in part the degree to which the subject can accurately reproduce the movement on a voluntary basis. Finally, we note that only one clear-cut "tic-syndrome" has ever been described, and it is still uncertain whether it is organically based or not. This is the famous Gilles de la Tourette syndrome,[1] which is characterized by compulsive jerkings of the voluntary

[1] Also called *maladie des tics, maladie des tics convulsifs, maladie des tics impulsifs, maladie des tics des degeneres, Koordinierte Erinnerungskraempfe, mimischer Krampf*, and *Myospasia impulsiva*. In Mahler's (1949) distinction between tic syndrome and neurotic tic, the former term is equivalent to the Gilles de la Tourette syndrome.

musculature of a widespread nature, but particularly affecting the face, neck, and extremities. The syndrome is differentiated from other complex tics, however, by the accompaniment of coprolalia (compulsive obscene utterances) and by echolalia (repetition of other persons' words and phrases) and, more rarely, echokinesis (repetition of other persons' actions). The condition is very rare, but its existence as an entity seems well established (Ascher, 1948; Kelman, 1965; Fernando, 1967).

The Methodological Problem

Careful observation of any individual will reveal the existence of stereotyped movements of which the individual is often completely unaware. The basic methodological problem, therefore, is one of deriving standard procedures for defining the presence of a tic, for which treatment would be desirable, as opposed to the presence of a movement that, although habitual, does not justify or require treatment. Mention should be made here of the *time-sampling* technique in which the individual is observed over standard time periods, and in which every movement of a specified type is recorded if it occurs during that time period. The methodological problems involved in the use of time-sampling techniques have been very thoroughly documented (Arrington, 1939, 1943), and the methods have been applied to the study of movements in children from preschool (Blatz & Ringland, 1935; Koch, 1935) through school (Seham and Boardman, 1934) to high school (Young, 1947), as well as with abnormal groups, such as psychotics (Jones, 1941). The observations have been made in a wide variety of situations which include free play, indoors and outdoors, controlled play with or without verbal restraint, and regular teaching sessions. They have been made under conditions that involved rest or the performance of distracting tasks, the taking of examinations, and the subjection to severe stress (inhibition of micturition) (Blatz & Ringland, 1935; Koch, 1935; Seham & Boardman, 1934; Jones, 1941, 1943a, 1943b; Young, 1947). The movements observed have covered a very wide range indeed, mostly derived from the original classification of Olson (1929) into oral, nasal, hirsutal, irritational, manual, ocular, aural, genital, and facial. The measurement techniques have varied from the crude to the sophisticated, with more recent studies taking account of the necessity for training the observers carefully, for establishing within- and between-rater reliability, for establishing base lines of movement frequency from which to estimate the influence of introducing new independent variables, and so forth. Of particular interest in this connection is the work of Sainsbury (1954a, 1954b) who correlated natural observational data with data obtained at leisure from film records and EMG records. Sainsbury (1954b) found that very short film records would produce highly reliable data; and that EMG records correlated quite highly (.83) with time-sampling techniques.

With respect to the definition of a tic, however, the methodological problems are of less significance than the clear-cut results that have been established on the basis of these studies. It has been clearly shown (for example, Blatz & Ringland, 1935; Seham & Boardman, 1934) that practically all children demonstrate one or more persisting movements of a repetitive kind; and that a high proportion (72 percent in the Blatz and Ringland study) show two or more of these movements. The existence of these movements may be reasonably attributed to *the instability of the developing nervous system* which leads to a failure of inhibition of excitatory nervous activity (Epstein, 1927). The gradual decline (but by no means the entire disappearance) of these movements with increasing age may likewise be attributed to increased maturation of the nervous system.

The two basic questions then become: first, are some tics simply the persistence of these involuntary movements in some children, because of defective development of inhibitory control; second, are some tics developed quite independently of increasing maturation of the nervous system and hence, in a sense, *qualitatively* different from repetitive movements of a "normal" kind?

There would appear to be two ways of approaching the problem of defining a tic in the light of the foregoing discussion. First, the presence of a tic as opposed to a persisting involuntary movement may be *empirically* determined by the systematic developmental study of tiqueurs with respect to questions such as whether the tic movements were present in embryonic form in childhood and, as such, indistinguishable from similar movements in children in whom these movements later disappeared. If this were the case, then the tics would simply be exaggerated forms of movements present in childhood and which had become very strong habits because of frequent repetition resulting from the failure of inhibitory processes. Second, it is possible that the definition of a tic must be made, not on an empirical basis (since the *form* of the tic may be indistinguishable from movements that are not regarded as tics), but on a *theoretical* basis. That is, either a movement which is present in the individual's repertoire may become fixated because of the intervention of a new independent variable, not commonly experienced by most children (such as a highly traumatic event that may lead to the movement by chance being capitalized on as an aggressive or defensive reaction in the threatening situation); or the insertion of a traumatic event into the life history may produce a completely *new* movement that serves the same purpose. The importance of the distinction is indicated by the problem of *preventive* treatment, that is, the possibility that, if a tic could be differentiated from a nontic movement in its embryonic stages, appropriate action might be taken to prevent its development. Clearly, if a tic, whatever its origin, ultimately becomes a strong habit, it will, like all strong habits, become extremely resistant to any form of modification.

In another sense, of course, the identification of a tic is made by the patient when he decides that the particular movement he manifests is socially embarrassing and that he would like to be rid of it, but finds that he cannot abolish it himself, and hence presents himself for treatment. At present, this is, of course, the usual way in which a tiqueur is identified.

Methodologically, therefore, future research with respect to the definition of a tic should concentrate on the problems of *predicting* the transformation of an early movement into an adolescent or adult tic by attempting to define characteristics of those movements present in all children which indicate that the movement is likely to increase in severity and frequency with increase in age, rather than the reverse; and of identifying those traumatic experiences (if the theory of the traumatic origin of *some* tics is correct—see below) that are likely to produce severe and apparently irreversible and involuntary movements, which produce social incompetence because they lead to an avoidance of social situations.

MODIFICATION TECHNIQUES

In this section, we discuss behavioristic theories of the genesis and maintenance of tics; theories on which treatment techniques have been based; the techniques themselves and the principal results obtained with their use; and the methodological problems involved in relation to future directions of research and practice.

The Genesis and Maintenance of Tics

Approaches to developing theories of the genesis and maintenance of tics have been based largely on two models derived from general experimental psychology. On the one hand, theories have been derived from the work of Hull and his colleagues and, on the other, from the work of Skinner and his colleagues (operant conditioning). In both approaches, however, the tic is regarded as a learned response.

A Model Derived from the Theory of Hull

Early attempts were made to consider the tic as a conditioned response. Thus, Brain (1928) provides the paradigm of conjunctivitis as an unconditioned stimulus (US) that produces the unconditioned response (UR) of blinking. Parental reactions and/or subjective thoughts will act as conditioned stimuli (CS) that become capable of evoking the UR as a conditioned response (CR) via classical conditioning. This model, however, has difficulty in accounting for the long-term persistence of the tic as a CR in the absence of the original US (conjunctivitis).

More recently, Yates (1958) conceptualized the tic as a drive-reducing conditioned avoidance response (CAR), originally evoked in a highly traumatic situation. In such a situation, intense fear may be aroused, but *direct* escape from the situation may be impossible. Hence, a truncated movement of withdrawal or aggression may be the only possible response. If, however, the movement produces, or coincides with the cessation of the fear-inducing stimulus, it will be strengthened by reinforcement. On subsequent occasions, through stimulus-generalization (including internal symbolization), conditioned fear (specific anxiety) may be aroused, which is then reduced by performance of the movement. In this way, the tic may ultimately come to be elicited by a wide variety of stimuli and may achieve the status of a powerful habit.

It should be noted that no direct evidence has ever been provided for this theoretical formulation, but indirect evidence suggests it is not unreasonable. Solomon and Wynne (1954) have demonstrated that animals placed in a highly traumatic situation develop CARs which appear to reduce the anxiety associated with the original situation and which are highly resistant to extinction. It is also interesting to note that some psychoanalytic investigators have arrived at essentially the same theory of the genesis of tics (for example, Gerard, 1946) from the detailed study of the developmental history of tiqueurs. The model also follows closely the original two-factor theory of Mowrer (1950) in which classically conditioned fear presents the individual with a problem that is resolved by the deliberate or random discovery of an instrumental response which reduces the fear. In terms of Hullian learning theory, the reaction potential (${}_SE_R$) of the tic at a given moment may be conceptualized as a multiplicative function of the habit strength (${}_SH_R$) of the tic (determined mainly by the number of times it has previously been evoked) and the momentary drive strength of anxiety (D), which fluctuates from time to time. Since habit strength increases as a simple negatively accelerated positive growth function and, eventually, reaches asymptotic level, further performance of the tic cannot increase its habit strength beyond a given point.

The author has more recently produced a considerably modified and extended version of the theory outlined above. This extension cannot be discussed in detail here.[2] Briefly, however, the theory argues that a fundamental distinction must be made between the concepts of neuroticism and neurosis in relation to abnormalities of behavior. Neuroticism is conceived of as a constitutional predisposition involving a high degree of autonomic lability, so that in early childhood almost any stimulus that exceeds an abnormally low threshold will trigger off excessive autonomic responses. Thus, a person high in neuroticism will react to objectively low stress situations by the formation of a wide range of CARs, the particular form of which will be determined by the nature of the situation in which the stress is experienced. In the case of tics, these individuals will tend to develop polysymptomatic tics. On the other hand, individuals low in neuroticism will not develop CARs unless they are subjected to an abnormally high degree of stress, and then they will tend to develop specific or monosymptomatic tics. Hence, an important distinction must be made between the individual with multiple tics and the individual with a single circumscribed tic in relation to the inferred neuroticism dimension and the degree of original stress involved. The revised model also has important implications for the expectation of treatment success. If a monosymptomatic tic is successfully treated, the reoccurrence of the tic or the development of new tics would not be expected unless the individual again is subjected to very high stress; whereas, in the case of the multiple tiqueur, it would be predicted that successful treatment would have little effect on the development of new tics or the reoccurrence of the old ones.[3] Finally, the revised theory argues that monosymptomatic tics are most likely to occur in nonneurotic individuals; whereas polysymptomatic tics are most likely to occur in highly neurotic individuals.

A Model Derived from the Theory of Skinner[4]

Basically, the operant conditioning model turns out to be very similar to the theory put forward by Yates (1958). It would be argued by the operant workers that tics are generated and maintained by their consequences

[2]The theory is described in detail in Yates (1969).

[3]In neither case, of course, are we referring to the phenomenon of symptom substitution as formulated by psychodynamic psychologists.

[4]Although Skinner has tended to argue for an atheoretical or strictly empirical approach, the term theory is deliberately used here, in one of its senses, namely, the use of a coordinated body of knowledge from which to formulate ideas about the genesis and maintenance of tics.

in just the same way that any other movements are. The contingencies that tics produce, either in the external environment, or within the organism via internal feedback systems, are reinforcing and, hence, maintain the behavior. The implications for treatment may then be derived directly and empirically from knowledge of the effects of reinforcing and aversive contingencies.

The Experimental Modification of Tics

We consider first the derivation of a method of treatment based on Hullian learning theory and, second, one based on the operant conditioning paradigm.

Treatment Based on Hullian Learning Theory

According to the model proposed above, the tic may be conceptualized as a learned habit that has (in adults, at least) probably attained maximum habit strength ($_SH_R$). In terms of the theory it should be possible to extinguish this habit by building up a negative or incompatible habit of "not performing the tic." If the subject is given massed practice in the tic, then reactive inhibition (I_R) should build up rapidly. When I_R reaches a critical point, the subject will be forced to "rest" or not perform the tic. Of course, this fact, by itself, is trivial; however, the importance of the method lies in the further prediction that the dissipation of I_R during rest will be a reinforcing state of affairs for any responses performed by the subject during that period. The basic prediction is that what will be reinforced during the rest period will be the response of not responding (that is, of not being able to perform the tic). Note carefully that this habit ($_SI_R$) of "not-responding" is not the *absence* of response, but rather an incompatible *positive* response.[5] The habit ($_SI_R$) of not performing the tic will be associated with drive-reduction as a result of the dissipation of I_R and, hence, will be reinforced. With repeated massed practice, therefore, a "negative" habit will be strengthened, incompatible with the positive habit of performing the tic. Furthermore, repeated voluntary evocation of the tic should *not* increase the strength of the positive habit since t is already asymptotic and, consequently, not subject to strengthening by massed practice.

At any given moment, therefore, the effective reaction potential of the tic ($_S\bar{E}_R$) (that is, the ability of the subject to perform the tic) will be a resultant of the forces in the equation

$$_S\bar{E}_R = (_SH_R \times D) - (I_R + {_SI_R})$$

As $_SI_R$ increases, $_S\bar{E}_R$ should diminish to a point at which the excitatory and inhibitory parts of the equation are equal. The positive response tendency of the tic will then be counterbalanced by the response tendency not to perform the tic, and behaviorally extinction should be complete. During the learning process, of course, $_S\bar{E}_R$ would be expected to fluctuate, since its momentary strength is affected by several unstable factors (for example, variations in drive level); and any increase in drive may temporarily mask the effects of increasing ($_SI_R$).

The theoretical constructs of reactive and conditioned inhibition were derived largely from animal studies and some human studies that involved massed and spaced practice in relation to the phenomenon of reminiscence. The optimum conditions of massed practice under which conditioned inhibition ($_SI_R$) might be expected to grow most rapidly and effectively were, of course, unknown with respect to the extinction of tics. Yates' prolonged study of the effects of varying conditions of massed practice and rest with a single patient was, therefore, avowedly an *experimental* rather than a treatment study, and this was made plain to the patient, who willingly accepted the experimenter's statement that no therapeutic benefits might be obtained. The subject was a female psychiatric patient, 25 years old, of high average intelligence, who was markedly neurotic and somewhat extraverted. She manifested four clear-cut tics, varying in complexity: a complex stomach-contraction/breathing tic; a nasal "explosion" (expiration) tic; a "throat-clearing" tic; and a bilateral eyeblink tic. These tics formed a related complex in so far as they appeared to have started following two very traumatic experiences about 10 years earlier when

[5] The analogy would be with the halting of a train when the engine is shut off. The train halts, not because the engine is shut off, but because of "inhibition" of ongoing motion by friction—which is a positive force producing, as it were, a negative result. Similarly, inhibition in Hull's system is unfortunately named, since it is a positive process, not the absence of process.

the patient felt she was being suffocated while undergoing anaesthesia. She reported being terrified that she was going to die and could not tolerate any object being placed over her face. The tics (which could occur independently) thus appeared to be CARs and appeared to reduce anxiety since the patient reported a need to perform the tics and relief following their performance.

The series of experiments carried out are reported in detail in Yates (1958). They involved varying combinations of massed practice and rest. Initially, the massed practice periods were of one minute's duration, followed by one minute's rest (the "standard procedure"). In any one session, each tic was practiced for five trials, and there were two sessions per day, one carried out under direct supervision of the experimenter, the other carried out by the patient alone at home. In later experiments the massed practice periods were extended to fifteen minutes and then to one hour, followed by a prolonged rest period of several days to several weeks.[6] In all, some 315 experimental periods were utilized over a period of nine months.

The results of the experiments are shown in Figure 12.1, from which it can be seen that highly significant decrements in capacity to produce the tics voluntarily resulted. The patient also reported a significant decline in the involuntary occurrence of the tics in social situations, although no objective measures of this were available. The effect of the massed practice was most striking in relation to the relatively simple nasal tic; and least striking in relation to the complex stomach tic.

That the results obtained were in accordance with expectations from the theory is indicated by several factors: the shape of the curves suggests the obverse of a learning curve; a "negative" reminiscence effect was obtained following rest periods (that is, a *decline* over rest of the capacity to produce the tics) and the failure to obtain a rise in frequency in the initial practice sessions (suggesting that, for this patient, $_{S}H_{R}$ was asymptotic).

Yates' study with this patient was continued by Jones (1960) who found no recovery of function on transfer of the patient from one experimenter to another; and who was able to reduce very markedly the capacity of the patient to reproduce the complex stomach contraction tic. Generalization to "real-life" remained incomplete.

Several subsequent studies on other tiqueurs have offered fairly strong support for the validity of the theory and technique put forward by Yates. Thus, Rafi (1962) found a very significant decline in frequency of a head jerk and facial grimace in a patient subjected to 25 two-hour sessions of massed practice. The "standard procedure" of Yates (one-minute massed practice periods) and slightly longer periods (five minutes) were unsuccessful, however, in reducing the rate of voluntary evocation of a foot-tapping tic in a second subject. (Both of these subjects were much older than Yates' patient.) The patient in whom no reduction of frequency with massed practice was obtained was slightly introverted; whereas Yates' patient was slightly extraverted, and Rafi's other patient markedly so. In both of Rafi's patients, there was a significant decline in frequency of the involuntary movements, but they did not remit completely.

Two studies by Walton also obtained theory-congruent results. In the first study (Walton, 1961) a twelve-year-old boy with multiple tics was given prolonged periods of massed practice in the major tic and shorter periods of massed practice in the others. An interesting innovation of Walton's was the use of largactil to reduce drive-level and, hence, to initiate involuntary rest pauses earlier; he also assumed that the drug would reduce tolerance for the buildup of reactive inhibition. A significant reduction in both voluntary and involuntary evocation of the tics was produced; and this improvement was maintained over a one-year follow-up period. In the second study (Walton, 1964) he subjected a second child (with three tics—nasal explosion, hiccoughing, and head-shaking of 11 years' duration) to very prolonged periods of massed practice ($\frac{1}{2}$ to 1-and-$\frac{1}{2}$ hours) over no less than 109 sessions, this time by using amylobarbitone as the drive-reducing drug. Again, there was a significant reduction in frequency of the tics over a five-month follow-up.

Lazarus (1960) also successfully used massed practice with a youth with severe

[6] These prolonged periods of massed practice were not distressing to the patient since, after the first few minutes, most of the time was spent in involuntary rest pauses.

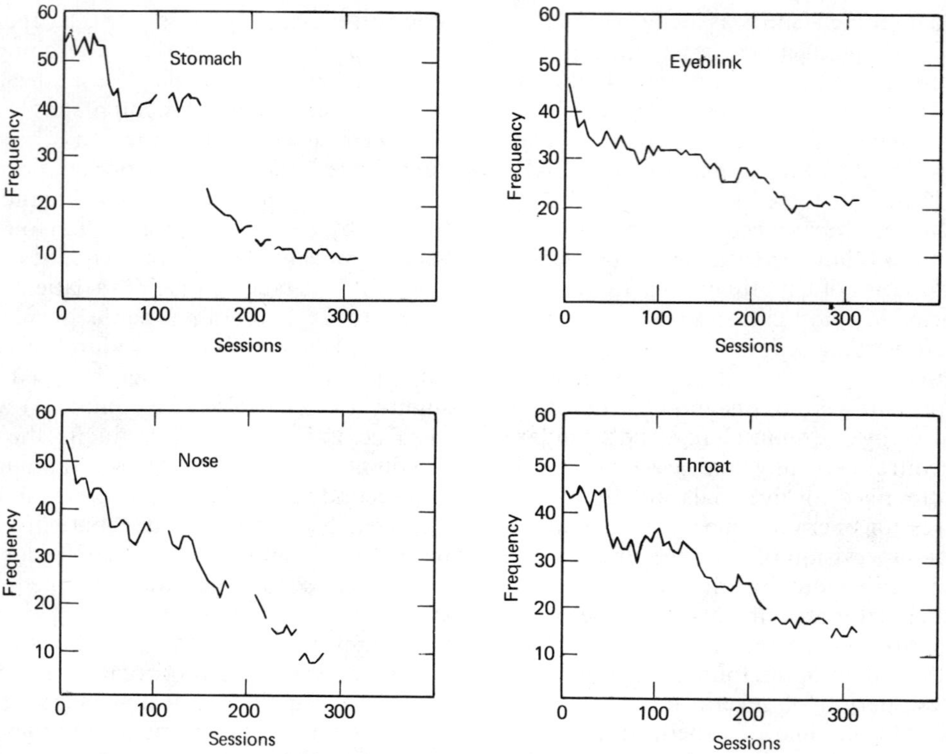

Figure 12.1 Changes in the frequency of four tics voluntarily evoked under various conditions of massed practice. (*Source*. Yates, 1958.)

mouth and head movements that accompanied stuttering.

Finally, Clark (1966) has recently reported the successful application of massed practice to the compulsive obscene utterances found in Gilles de la Tourette's syndrome. One of his three cases withdrew from treatment (nevertheless, showing decrements in the predicted direction), but the other two cases have remained symptom-free over a follow-up period of four years, have shown no signs of symptom substitution, and have improved generally in their social adjustment (not surprising, in view of the socially crippling nature of compulsive obscene utterances).[7]

Thus, no less than seven studies provide partial or strong support for both the theory and the technique. In light of this, it is disappointing and disconcerting to find completely contradictory findings in a recent important study by Feldman and Werry (1966). They studied a 13-year-old boy with multiple tics of face, neck, and head of six years' duration. Of these tics, the head jerk was subjected to massed practice of periods of five minutes' duration (with a later attempt at periods of fifteen minutes' duration). Not only did they not find any evidence of a decline in frequency of voluntary evocation following massed practice, but both voluntary and involuntary evocation increased very significantly, and an old tic reappeared. The treatment was eventually abandoned. The changing frequency of *involuntary* tics at various stages of the study is shown in Figure 12.2. The results obtained by Feldman and Werry are extremely puzzling in view of the uniformly positive results reported in the earlier studies. Feldman and Werry rightly reject any explanation in terms of the positive habit ($_SH_R$) being nonasym-

[7] Recent studies by Stevens and Blachly (1966) and by Shapiro and Shapiro (1968) have strongly confirmed earlier reports that the Gilles de la Tourette syndrome may be completely abolished by high dosages of the drug Haloperidol. Stevens and Blachly suggest that the syndrome may result from a metabolic disturbance which causes central nervous system enzyme or neurotransmitter dysfunction. These findings, of course, do not invalidate Clark's results, but suggest that the syndrome may be best treated by the drug rather than by the tedious procedures of massed practice, and tend to confirm the presumed organic basis of this syndrome.

ptotic at the commencement of massed practice (and, hence, being strengthened by practice), since evocation frequency returned to the original level when massed practice was discontinued. Their preferred explanation is in terms of an increase in drive-level produced by the stress of the experimental method in this particular patient. This explanation they regard as accounting for the raising above threshold of an old, apparently extinguished, tic. They also assume that, in the experimental situation, drive increased at a faster rate than reactive inhibition.

This explanation of the results does not seem to be adequate to the present author, although it is true that the patient was described as obsessive and somewhat depressed, that is, he was probably an introverted neurotic. The explanation may lie instead in the fact that the patient was introverted rather than extraverted and in methodological considerations relating to the ability of the patient to carry out the massed practice efficiently and to reproduce the tics accurately. These considerations will be discussed further below.

In view of the positive results obtained in earlier studies, it is unfortunate that Feldman and Werry were unable to carry out further controlled experimental studies in an effort to pinpoint the reasons for failure. Thus, in terms of their drive theory, they could have made use of Walton's technique of administering drive-reducing drugs; or they could have increased the extraversion

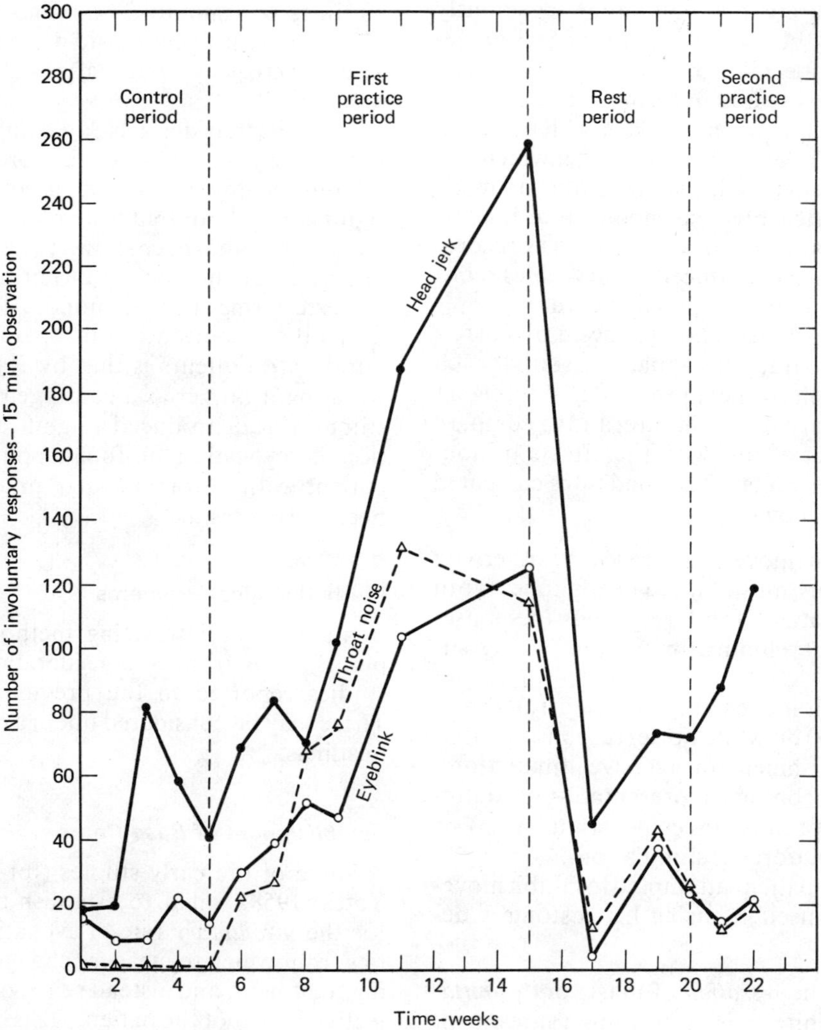

Figure 12.2 The frequency of involuntary tics during the four stages of the study. (*Source*. Feldman and Werry, 1966.)

of the patient by the administration of drugs (thus, altering the cortical excitation-inhibition balance). In the absence of these studies, it is unnecessary at present to conclude that massed practice is ineffective in reducing the evocation of tics, or that the theory is necessarily wrong. Certainly, however, the Feldman and Werry study vividly points up the need for more controlled work in this area.

Treatment Based on Operant Conditioning

The only major study of the application of operant techniques to the modification of tics is that of Barrett (1962). She studied a 38-year-old male with multiple tics of 14 years' duration. Barrett made no attempt to record the frequency and amptitude of each separate tic, but rather ingeniously recorded the overall occurrence of movement by special technical procedures. The patient was seated in a comfortable swivel-tilt armchair, to the back of which was attached a large U-shaped magnet which, via an induction coil, recorded the patient's most noticeable spasmodic movements, regardless of locus or amplitude. The recording was then transduced into a visible record on a cumulative response recorder.

The basic procedure followed by Barrett was to program her apparatus so that each recorded movement produced a contingent event of an aversive nature, and to compare the effects of this with the effects of noncontingent events. The conditions compared were as follows.

1. Each movement *turned off* otherwise continuous music in the headphones worn by the patient for 1.5 seconds (response-contingent elimination of reinforcing stimulus).
2. Each movement *initiated* a 1.5 second blast of 60 db white noise (response-contingent punishment or aversive stimulation).
3. Noncontingent presentation of continuous white noise (aversive stimulation) or music (reinforcing stimulation).
4. The patient attempted to inhibit movements himself by using his customary devices.

Thus, the *cessation* of music or the *initiation* of white noise following a movement may be regarded as the contingent instatement of aversive stimulation, and the effects of these procedures were compared with control conditions that involved attempted self-control or noncontingent aversive or nonaversive stimulation.

The operant or baselevel of the frequency of movement (that is, the rate produced in the absence of the above special procedures) varied from a minimal level of 64 movements per minute to a high of 116. Barrett found that continuous (noncontingent) noise did not change the baselevel; contingent noise reduced the rate to 40 movements per minute, as did noncontingent music. Contingent cessation of music was the most effective controller of movement rate, a reduction of 15 to 30 movements per minute resulting (a drop of 40 to 50 percent in frequency). Self-control procedures by the patient reduced the movement rate to 50 to 60 times per minute. The reliability of the effects of contingent music was established as satisfactory by a retest after a two-month break.

Thus, Barrett demonstrated quite clearly that operant schedules of reinforcement or nonreinforcement can be used to affect significantly the output of involuntary movements, just as has been shown equally clearly in studies of the control of normal speech and stuttering (Goldiamond, 1965). The only other reported use of operant procedures with tiqueurs is that by Rafi (1962). By using a buzzer as a contingent aversive stimulus, Rafi produced a significant reduction in evocation of foot-tapping in the patient with whom massed practice had been unsuccessful.

Methodological Problems

A number of interesting methodological points arise from a consideration of the studies reported in the previous section. These may be considered under a number of headings.

Establishment of Base Rates

Some of the early studies (for example, Yates, 1958) failed to establish base rates for the *involuntary* rate of evocation of the tics from which to measure changes following treatment, and instead relied on the subjective report of the patient. This deficiency was remedied in some subsequent studies (for example, Feldman & Werry, 1966).

Barrett (1962) also measured the base rate, but her study was essentially a laboratory experiment and, hence, no attempt was made to measure the involuntary rate "in real life." Clearly, it is desirable that base rates should be carefully established prior to the introduction of experimental conditions.

Intrasubject Control

In the study of Yates (1958) it would have been possible to apply one of the basic principles of behavior therapy, namely, the use of the subject as his own control (Shapiro, 1961a, 1961b) and, thus, to provide a more rigorous test of the theory on which the method of massed practice was based. In other words, if one of the tics had not been subjected to massed practice, then spot-checks on its frequency of voluntary evocation would have been expected to reveal little, if any, decline in rate because very little I_R would be generated by such spot-checks. Stimulus generalization might be expected to produce some decline in the unpracticed tic but, overall, the prediction would be expected to be fulfilled if the theory were correct. Unfortunately, for a number of reasons, Yates did not use this essential control. However, this kind of internal control was exercised in the study by Feldman and Werry (1966).

Voluntary Reproduction of the Tics

There is an interesting contrast between the massed-practice studies and the operant-conditioning study of Barrett. In terms of the theory of reactive and conditioned inhibition it seems essential that the tics be reproduced as accurately as possible. If this is not achieved by the subject, then slightly different groups of muscles will be involved in various reproductions of the tic, and this will retard the growth of I_R, and consequently of ${}_SI_R$. Some evidence of the validity of this requirement is to be found in Yates' (1958) study where the most significant changes were produced in the relatively less complex tics. This could well have been one critical variable in the study of Feldman and Werry (1966), who found that, at the end of the early stages of the study, the patient "had not been practising the tics as instructed, often shortening the session by one or two minutes and sometimes omitting it entirely" (p. 113—the reference is to the sessions practiced on his own by the patient). As we pointed out earlier, Barrett (1962) did not attempt to modify *individual* movements in her patient, but instead applied the contingencies to any movement or group of movements that activated the recorder sufficiently. More research is obviously required within the operant framework to determine the relative efficacy of this technique as against attaching various contingencies to specific movements.

Measures of Dependent Variable

Tics, of course, vary on a number of dimensions, including strength, frequency, and quality. Unfortunately, thus far, insufficient work has been carried out on techniques for objectively recording changes on these dimensions during treatment. Simple frequency counts are probably not adequate, since frequency could remain relatively stable while amplitude declines significantly, perhaps even to the point where the movements would no longer be perceived by an independent observer who was unaware of the nature of the subject's disorder.

Transfer from Laboratory to Real Life

It has become apparent in recent years that one of the major problems of the behavior therapist relates to the transfer of results obtained in a laboratory situation to real-life situations. There are a number of aspects to this problem. In so far as the maladaptive behavior is tied to *social* stimulus situations (probably the most common state of affairs), results produced in an impersonal laboratory situation are not very likely to transfer very strongly outside the laboratory. Hence, the strictly laboratory-based studies must be regarded as a preliminary to the attempt to abolish the behavior outside the laboratory. As Goldiamond (1965) has so clearly demonstrated in relation to stuttering, this is *not* just a case of obtaining instances of stimulus generalization, but may more often involve the instatement of entirely new forms of behavior, on the one hand, and the transfer (*not* through generalization) of laboratory-based stimulus control of this behavior to real-life-based stimulus control. As Goldiamond has also shown, this may involve training the subject to be his own experimenter.

In the case of tics treated by massed practice, Yates (1958) and Jones (1960) were well aware of the problem of extending conditioned inhibition to nonlaboratory real-life situations of a social nature in which the frequency of the involuntary tics tended to increase. One possible solution, which occurred to these authors, was to require the patient to indulge in massed practice in social situations as well as the laboratory and, thus, to attach conditioned inhibition to these situations. Such a procedure was obviously impractical in view of the possible undesirable side effects that might result from social embarrassment. An alternative solution, however, readily suggested itself. Since social situations by definition involved the presence of other people, then, instead of generalizing ${}_{S}H_{R}$ to *situations*, it could perhaps be generalized to *people*. Hence, a possible solution would be gradually to bring more and more people into the laboratory situation to observe the patient under conditions of massed practice, and to arrange for these observers gradually to behave in a more and more hostile fashion, thus, increasingly approximating the real-life conditions in which the tic is exacerbated. In this way, ${}_{S}I_{R}$ would become attached to people. Unfortunately, neither Yates nor Jones reached the stage of carring out these experiments.

Personality Factors and the Use of Drugs

Little attention has thus far been paid to the possible significance of individual differences in personality structure in relation to the use of massed practice. Since inhibitory processes are being generated in opposition to excitatory processes, then individual differences in neuroticism and extraversion-introversion may be of critical importance. A highly introverted neurotic (that is, a person with a combination of high autonomic drive and with a slow rate of buildup of reactive inhibition) may be a contraindication to probable successful treatment. In these circumstances, the use of appropriate drugs, which influence autonomic activity or alter the excitation-inhibition balance, may be in order on an experimental basis. The studies of Walton (1961, 1964), in particular, point the way for future research. Unfortunately, little work has thus far been carried out on the personality correlates of tiqueurs (Crown, 1953).

Follow-up Data

Virtually all of the studies reviewed are seriously defective in the adequacy of follow-up data. These data are of crucial importance in relation to the treatment of tics, since they are notoriously resistant to almost any form of treatment. Guttmann and Creak (1940) followed up eight cases (aged 5 to 15 years on admission) for ten years. At least 50 percent of the cases were still displaying the tic behaviors, and the authors doubted the validity of the reported remission in the other cases, this being based on letters from the subjects and not on direct observation (they were untreated cases). Mahler and Luke (1946) presented follow-up data on 10 cases aged 7 to 12 years on admission and treated by psychotherapy for periods that varied from seven weeks to three years. On discharge from treatment, no cases could be regarded as "cured"; seven were "slightly" to "much" improved; and four were unimproved. Unfortunately, the follow-up data are not very satisfactorily presented, but Mahler and Luke conclude that there was ". . . no direct correlation between recovery from the tic syndrome and length or method of psychotherapy . . ." nor were ". . . thoroughness of treatment and good therapeutic results . . . in direct proportion, even when the syndrome was of short duration and the child was relatively young" (Mahler & Luke, 1946, p. 435). Somewhat better results were reported, however, by Paterson (1945) for 21 cases of spasmodic torticollis of apparently nonorganic origin. Thus, the results reported by behavior therapists must be treated with extreme caution and should be regarded for the present as experimental studies of the control and the manipulation of these forms of maladaptive behavior, rather than as therapeutic in intent or result.

Methodology of Massed Practice

The necessity for accurate reproduction of the tic under massed practice conditions has already been pointed out. There is no doubt that a great deal more experimentation will be necessary before any standard techniques are available. Indeed, the present author is satisfied that one of the most dangerous trends evident at present in behavior therapy is the premature standardization of techniques which are then applied "routinely," with either "success" or "failure" being reported in relation to a given patient. It is essential that each new patient be regarded as a new *experimental* problem.[8] It may be expected, of course, that gradually some standard techniques will develop but, if behavior therapy should ever become a set of standard techniques, then, in this author's view, it will become subject to precisely the same problems and strictures that behavior therapists have heaped on psychoanalysis and psychotherapy. Thus, at the conclusion of his study, Yates (1958) tentatively concluded that the optimal conditions for the generation of conditioned inhibition were very prolonged periods of massed practice (possibly of the order of five to six hours, bearing in mind that the majority of this period would be spent "not performing the tic"), followed by very prolonged periods of rest (of the order of several weeks). Although it is possible, on this basis, to criticise subsequent studies on the grounds that the periods of massed practice have been too short, it does *not* follow that prolonged massed practice followed by prolonged rest should become a standard technique for the treatment of tiqueurs. As both Feldman and Werry (1966) and Rafi (1962) showed, some subjects are unable to tolerate much shorter periods of massed practice, although, of course, it may prove possible to increase tolerance for prolonged massed practice periods by the use of appropriate drugs. Essentially, however, each new subject must be regarded as presenting a new experimental challenge, although hopefully previous experimental results will provide, at least, a rational jumping-off point for the procedures to be used.

Methodology of Operant Conditioning

The study by Barrett (1962) was recognized by that author as being exploratory in nature, and one particular point (fully recognized by Barrett) may be of especial importance for future operant work. This relates to the importance of *partial reinforcement* techniques. Barrett used continuous rather than partial reinforcement methods, but it has been demonstrated repeatedly that the use of partial reinforcement techniques increases resistance to extinction—indeed, this factor may well account for the extreme tenacity of tics as motor habits.

In conclusion, clearly, the study of the application of theoretical and empirical knowledge, derived from studies of learning and extinction, has only begun to be applied to the control and modification of tics. The success, or otherwise, of the theories and the methods therapeutically, however, is of less importance than the fact that these studies are being carried out within a controlled experimental framework. Given greater methodological sophistication along the lines suggested above, there is every reason to anticipate a twofold reward: increase in basic knowledge of how fairly clear-cut and specific behavior may be modified and controlled with a feedback to general experimental psychology; and, ultimately at least, a very real advance in the capacity of the abnormal experimental psychologist to significantly modify in real-life a peculiarly disabling form of maladaptive behavior.

REFERENCES

Arrington, R. E. Time sampling studies of child behavior. *Psychol. Monogr.*, 1939, **51**, 1–193.

Arrington, R. E. Time sampling in studies of social behavior: a critical review of techniques and results. *Psychol. Bull.*, 1943, **40**, 81–124.

Ascher, E. Psychodynamic considerations in Gilles de la Tourette's disease (maladie des tics). *Amer. J. Psychiat.*, 1948, **105**, 267–276.

---

[8]As the author has attempted to show (Yates (1969)) behavior therapy developed, in England at least, out of Shapiro's (1961a, 1961b) work on the *experimental* investigation of the single case. In this sense, there are *no* standard techniques in behavior therapy.

Barrett, B. H. Reduction in rate of multiple tics by free operant conditioning methods. *J. nerv. ment. Dis.*, 1962, **135**, 187–195.

Bender, L., & Schilder, P. Impulsions: a specific disorder of the behavior of children. *Arch. Neurol. Psychiat.*, 1940, **44**, 900–1008.

Bender, L., & Schilder, P. Mannerisms as organic motility syndrome (paracortical disturbances) *Conf. Neurol.*, 1941, **3**, 321–330.

Blatz, W. E., & Ringland, M. C. *The study of tics in preschool children.* Univer. Toronto Studies (Child Development Series No. 3), 1935.

Brain, W. R. The treatment of tic (habit spasm). *Lancet*, 1928, **214**, 1295–1296.

Clark, D. F. Behavior therapy of Gilles de la Tourette's syndrome. *Brit. J. Psychiat.*, 1966, **112**, 771–778.

Crown, S. An experimental inquiry into some aspects of the motor behavior and personality of tiqueurs. *J. ment. Sci.*, 1953, **99**, 84–91.

Epstein, J. Functional spasms in children, their physiologic pathology, and their relation to the neuroses in later life. *Amer. J. med. Sci.*, 1927, **173**, 380–385.

Feldman, R. B., & Werry, J. S. An unsuccessful attempt to treat a tiqueur by massed practice. *Behav. Res. Ther.*, 1966, **4**, 111–117.

Fernando, S. J. Gilles de la Tourette's syndrome: a report on four cases and a review of published case reports. *Brit. J. Psychiat.*, 1967, **113**, 607–617.

Gerard, M. W. The psychogenic tic in ego development. In A. Freud and others (Eds.), *Psychoanalytic study of the child*, Vol. 2. New York: Internat. Univer. Press, 1946. Pp. 133–162

Goldiamond, I. Stuttering and fluency as manipulatable operant response classes. In L. Krasner & L. P. Ullman (Eds.) *Research in behavior modification.* New York: Holt, 1965. Pp. 106–156.

Guttmann, E., & Creak, M. A follow-up study of hyperkinetic children. *J. ment. Sci.*, 1940, **86**, 624–631.

Hall, M. B. Obsessive-compulsive states in childhood and their treatment. *Arch. Dis. Childhd.*, 1935, **10**, 49–59.

Hassin, G. B., Stenn, A., & Burstein, H. J. Stereotyped acts or attitude tics? A case with a peculiar anomaly of gait. *J. nerv. ment. Dis.*, 1930, **71**, 27–32.

Jones, H. J. Continuation of Yates' treatment of a tiqueur. In H. J. Eysenck (Ed.), *Behavior therapy and the neuroses*. Oxford: Pergamon, 1960. Pp. 250–258.

Jones, M. R. Measurement of spontaneous movements in adult psychotic patients by a time-sample technique: a methodological study. *J. Psychol.*, 1941, **11**, 285–295.

Jones, M. R. Studies in "nervous" movements: I. The effect of mental arithmetic on the frequency and patterning of movements. *J. gen. Psychol.*, 1943a, **29**, 47–62.

Jones, M. R. Studies in "nervous" movements: II. The effect of inhibition of micturition on the frequency and patterning of movements. *J. gen. Psychol.*, 1943b, **29**, 303–312.

Kelman, Diane H. Gilles de la Tourette's disease in children: a review of the literature. *J. Child Psychol. Psychiat.*, 1965, **6**, 219–226.

Koch, H. An analysis of certain forms of so-called "nervous habits" in young children. *J. genet. Psychol.*, 1935, **46**, 139–170.

Lazarus, A. A. Objective psychotherapy in the treatment of dysphemia. *J. South African Logopedic Soc.*, 1960, **66**, 8–10.

Mahler, M. S. Tics and impulsions in children: a study of motility. *Psychoanal. Quart.*, 1944, **17**, 430–444.

Mahler, M. S. A psychoanalytic evaluation of tic in psychopathology of children: Symptomatic and tic syndrome. In A. Freud and others (Eds.), *Psychoanalytic study of the child*, Vols. 3 and 4. New York: Internat. Univer. Press, 1949. Pp. 279–310.

Mahler, M. S., & Luke, J. A. Outcome of the tic syndrome. *J. nerv. ment. Dis.*, 1946, **103**, 433–445.

Meige, H., & Feindel, E. *Tics and their treatment*. London: Appleton, 1907.

Mowrer, O. H. *Learning theory and personality dynamics.* New York: Ronald, 1950.

Olson, W. C. *The measurement of nervous habits in normal children.* Minneapolis: Univer. Minnesota Press, 1929.

Paterson, M. T. Spasmodic torticollis: results of psychotherapy in 21 cases. *Lancet*, 1945, **2**, 556–559.

Rafi, A. A. Learning theory and the treatment of tics. *J. psychosom. Res.*, 1962, **6**, 71–76.

Sainsbury, P. The measurement and description of spontaneous movements before and after leucotomy. *J. ment. Sci.*, 1954a, **100**, 732–741.

Sainsbury, P. A method of measuring spontaneous movements by time-sampling motion pictures. *J. ment. Sci.*, 1954b, **100**, 742—748.

Seham. M., & Boardman, D. V. A study of motor automatisms. *Arch. Neurol. Psychiat.*, 1934, **32**, 154–173.

Shapiro, A. K., & Shapiro, E. Treatment of Gilles de la Tourette's syndrome with haloperidol. *Brit. J. Psychiat.*, 1968, **114**, 345–350.

Shapiro, M. B. A method of measuring psychological changes specific to the individual psychiatric patient. *Brit. J. med. Psychol.*, 1961a, **34**, 151–155.

Shapiro, M. B. The single case in fundamental clinical psychological research. Brit. J. med. Psychol., 1961b, **34**, 255–262.

Solomon, R. L., & Wynne, L. C. Traumatic avoidance learning: the principles of anxiety conservation and partial irreversibility. *Psychol. Rev.*, 1954, **61**, 353–385.

Stevens, J. R., & Blachly, P. H. Successful treatment of the maladie des tics. *Amer. J. Dis. Child.*, 1966, **112**, 541–545.

Walton, D. Experimental psychology and the treatment of a tiqueur. *J. Child Psychol. Psychiat.*, 1961, **2**, 148–155.

Walton, D. Massed practice and simultaneous reduction in drive-level—further evidence of the efficacy of this approach to the treatment of tics. In H. J. Eysenck (Ed.), Experiments in behavior therapy. Oxford: Pergamon, 1964. Pp. 398–400.

Williams, T. O. Abnormal movements (tic), their nature and treatment. *Internal. J. Med. Surg.*, 1932, **45**, 23– 26 and 101–103.

Wilson, S. A. K. The tics and allied conditions. J. Neurol. Psychopathol., 1927, **8**, 93–103.

Yates, A. J. The application of learning theory to the treatment of tics. *J. abnorm. soc. Psychol.*, 1958, **56**, 175–182.

Yates, A. J. *Behavior therapy*. New York: Wiley, 1969.

Young, F. M. The incidence of nervous habits in college students. *J. Personality*, 1947, **15**, 309–320.

Chapter 13

Stuttering

H. GWYNNE JONES

STUTTERING AND ASSOCIATED PHENOMENA

Stuttering or stammering, terms which are now considered to be synonymous, refer to a particular type of speech dysfluency, most typically characterized by blocks, repetitions, and prolongations of speech sounds, which occurs in the absence of anatomical abnormalities of the peripheral speech apparatus. They do not embrace "cluttering," another speech abnormality in which failure to control speed of utterance leads to truncated, incoherent, and dysrhythmic speech. More precise definition is difficult as stutterers exhibit a wide range of abnormalities, including many apparently remote from the mechanics of speech production. For example, although the condition is generally one easily recognisable by both laymen and speech experts, this recognition may require the stutterer to be seen as well as to be heard. Many authors refer to emotional reactions in their definition and description of the disorder. This chapter opens, therefore, with a brief survey of the main manifestations associated with stuttering.

Repetitions of Speech Sounds

Perhaps the most prominent feature of stuttering is the repetition of individual sounds, syllables, or even words of phrases, especially the ones that occur at the initial position in an utterance. Consonants may present particular difficulty. Syllable, word and phrase repetition is very common in the normal speech of young children, and hence diagnosis and assessment are frequently difficult at early ages.

Prolongations of Speech Sounds

Vowels particularly may be uttered in a drawn out fashion very seldom observed in fluent speakers at any age. This feature, therefore, may be of diagnostic importance in young children but is one which tends to occur later than repetition in the development of stuttering.

Blocks

Periods of silence may occur during which the sufferer, despite strenuous efforts, cannot utter the desired sound. Blocks are most frequently associated with initial words, phrases or sentences and evoke considerable distress. It is probably the visual observation of muscular tension during blocks and the empathic appreciation of the associated emotional distress that makes the diagnosis of seen stuttering more reliable than the diagnosis based on the hearing of tapes. Silent blocks may be associated with respiratory abnormalities, but they are more likely to be consequences of the block than to be causal in nature.

Accessory Motor Abnormalities

A variety of grimaces or other irrelevent motor behavior, mainly of the face but possibly involving the trunk and limbs, is frequently associated with occasions of speech difficulty. Many of these movements give the appearance of an ineffective struggle for release from the speech block, but often become stereotyped, automatic, and almost involuntary in nature. Other movements or even stereotyped utterances appear to function more as indirect aids to speech. Both forms, which may trouble the stutterer as much as his speaking difficulty, are probably secondary elaborations of stuttering. Bloodstein (1960a, 1960b, 1961) has shown that the incidence of these motor symptoms increases with age to a maximum of about 70 percent in older stutterers. It is suggested that they become fixed by a learning process brought about by their inevitable association with the ultimate release from a speech block.

Avoidance Behavior

Learning factors are also clearly important in the very common avoidance of stimuli that have become associated with speech difficulty. These stimuli may be particular letter sounds or words or more general environmental situations such as the use of a telephone. Avoidance of specific words may take the form of curcumlocution at which stutterers may become extremely adept.

Danger stimuli tend to multiply and generalize and, therefore, the stutterer tends to become more and more involved in avoidance, frequently to an extent that determines his whole way of life and is reflected in his attitudes, standards, and value systems. Kimmel (1938) has studied these effects in detail, and many therapists claim that they frequently produce a resistance to treatment which, if effective, must involve a radical modification of the patient's well practiced way of life. Bloodstein (1960b) claims that avoidance is the most common single feature in stuttering, and Johnson (1955, 1959), one of the major authorities in this field, actually defines the disorder as an "anticipatory, apprehensive, hypertonic avoidance reaction." Others, such as Douglass and Quarrington (1952, Quarrington & Douglass, 1960) and Freund (1966) have elaborated a concept of "interiorized stuttering," the end result of avoidance which becomes so expert as to mask the overt speech disorder.

Emotional Disorder

In view of the high prevalence of avoidance behavior, it is not surprising that there is evidence of a heightened general level of anxiety and, to some extent, hostility among stutterers (for example, Santostefano, 1960). There is, however, little objective support for the view that stuttering is a manifestation of a more basic neurotic disorder, or even that stutterers display any characteristic personality profile. However, the majority of personality studies can be severely criticized on methodological grounds (see Beech & Fransella, 1968), and there are indications of more specific personality characteristics. For example, Sheehan and Zelen (1955) showed experimentally that, as compared with controls, stutterers tend to underestimate their ability in a "level of aspiration" situation. Various abnormalities of the "self-concept" have also been suggested (for example, Sheehan, 1954). A recent study in this area was carried out by Fransella (1965), who compared concepts of "me" and "stutterer" by means of the semantic differential and Kelly's repertory grid technique. Stutterers agreed with normal controls in their unfavorable description of stutterers in general, but did not consider themselves as sharing these characteristics. This discrepancy tends to support Sheehan's view that stutterers tend to develop a dichotomous self-concept which includes contradictory elements of a "horrible stuttering self" and a "free speaking normal self." He claims that the speech disability has "secondary gain" features and that it serves to excuse shortcomings. Like Fransella, he believes that effective therapy must involve radical modification of this concept of the "self."

LAWFUL VARIABILITY IN STUTTERING

Any account of the phenomenology of stuttering must refer to three associated "effects" which have been much studied experimentally and which must be taken into account in designing assessment procedures, particularly when assessing the effectiveness of modification techniques. They are discussed in full detail by Beech and Fransella (1968).

The Consistency Effect

This refers to the tendency for stuttering to be evoked by the same cues on different occasions, even when those occasions are several weeks apart. The term was first used by Johnson and Kott (1937), and usually refers to stuttering on the same words in repeated readings of a passage. In a more general sense, it may also be applied to the tendency for stuttering to be associated with particular types of or specific environmental situations. Johnson and Knott found that some 60 percent to 70 percent of words stuttered during a reading were also stuttered in the previous reading of a passage, but Tate and Cullinan (1962) report high positive correlations between the degree of consistency and the severity of stuttering. These authors studied several measures of consistency and advocate a normal deviate score that makes allowance for chance expectation.

$$Z = \frac{O_0 - E_0 - \frac{1}{2}}{E_0(N - E_0)\ N}$$

where O_0 represents the observed number of nonstuttered words and E_0 the expected number.

The Expectancy Effect

As might be suggested from the consistency effect, most stutterers can predict with considerable accuracy those words with which they are likely to experience difficulty, even when several days intervene between prediction and test. Elimination of the anticipated difficult words from a passage reduces stuttering to an insignificant level, and even the degree of difficulty is predictable (Wischner, 1952). Bloodstein (1960b) considers the speech blocks to be largely determined by anticipatory responses to certain features of a speech sequence. Some children show consistency but are unable to predict stuttering. Conscious awareness, however, of a conditioned stimulus is not necessary for the establishment of a conditioned response. Cues vary from individual to individual, but (Johnson, 1955) the nature of the sound and the position, the function, and the length of the word appear to be important. In general, consonants tend to be more difficult than vowels, initial words than terminal words, adjectives, nouns, verbs, and adverbs than other parts of speech, and longer words than shorter words. Those words that carry a heavy share of the meaningful content of a communication also tend to evoke stuttering. Goldman-Eisler (1958) has shown that the pauses in normal speech tend to occur at the points where the transitional probabilities are low, that is, where what is to follow is least predictable and, therefore, highly meaningful in the sense that it has high information value. It is not surprising if those parts of a speech sequence that are difficult for normal speakers evoke stuttering in those vulnerable to this type of dysfluency.

The Adaptation Effect

This refers to the decrease in stuttering that occurs when a passage is read a number of times in succession (Johnson & Knott, 1937). The degree of adaptation tends to be negatively correlated with the initial frequency of words stuttered, and this must be taken into account in the measurement of adaptation, the scoring of which is anyway rather unreliable. The degree and speed of adaptation also varies with the difficulty of the material but, typically, a 50 percent reduction of stuttering is produced, with the largest decrease from the first to the second reading. The adaptation effect is reduced by increasing the interval between successive readings and is likely to disappear at a 24-hour-interval. If the reading situation is varied, for example by a change of audience, the effect is also reduced. A few experiments have been concerned with adaptation in spontaneous speech, for example when describing the same object on successive occasions. Adaptation occurs but at a slower rate than in the reading situation. Brutten (1963) took a palmer sweat print as a measure of anxiety at each successive reading in an adaptation experiment and found that reduction in sweat and therefore, by inference, in anxiety correlated with the degree of adaptation. In general, stuttering adaptation is a lawful phenomenon, but individual stutterers may produce flat, irregular, or even negative adaptation curves.

Johnson has described the adaptation effect as a "laboratory model of the improvement process," but there is little evidence of any correlation between adaptation and improvement scores during therapy. His explanation of the process is in terms of reduction in anxiety brought about by the stutterer's finding, when actually reading, that his difficulties are not as great as originally anticipated. Wischner (1950) has a similar view, but it is expressed more formally in terms of experimental extinction of anxiety. He describes experiments demonstrating "expectancy adaptation," a reduction in anticipated stuttering prior to successive readings. Gray and Brutten (1965) are typical of others who concentrate more on response adaptation and who account for the phenomenon in Hullian terms, making use of the concepts of reactive and conditioned inhibition. Certainly, spontaneous recovery occurs about four and one-half hours after adaptation, consistent with the dissipation of reactive inhibition. Peins (1961) extends this argument by invoking the satiation of meaning that occurs when verbal material is repeated aloud several times. As argued previously, the less propositional or meaningful a word, the less likely it is to be stuttered.

PREVALENCE AND ONSET OF STUTTERING

Reliable evidence concerning the prevalence of stuttering is only available for Britain and North America, but it has been suggested that there is considerable cross-cultural variability. Typical of the Anglo-American findings are the ones that derive from a study by Andrews and Harris (1964), who made a complete survey of the school population between the ages of nine and eleven in the City of Newcastle-upon-Tyne. Just over 1 percent of these children were persistent stutterers, but 4 percent to 5 percent had been transient stutterers at an earlier age. There is highly consistent evidence of a differential sex ratio with about 3:1 increased incidence in males. There is no convincing evidence that socioeconomic factors are important and, despite anecdotes linking stuttering with high intelligence, there is little difference on intelligence test scores between unselected groups of stutterers and appropriate control groups. Andrews and Harris found a slight but significantly lowered mean IQ for their stutterers, but the reverse has also been reported. This and other studies failed to show any "verbal/performance" discrepancy or other indications of specific verbal disability. However, among the educationally subnormal and other low-intelligence groups, the incidence of stuttering appears to rise (Loutit & Halls, 1936).

The onset of stuttering is usually early in life, almost always before the age of eight. Although later onset is rare, well-documented instances of stuttering that occurred for the first time in adulthood have been reported, but usually following severe physical or psychological trauma. Precise information about the typically early onset is difficult to obtain because of the difficulty of distinguishing between the early stages of stuttering and the normal dysfluencies characteristic of young children. Indeed, Johnson (1959) claims that "true" stuttering is brought about by parents' overanxious and critical reactions to their children's normal early speech.

Davis (1939, 1940a, 1940b) carried out a series of relevant studies of the early development of speech. Between the ages of two and five, repetitions are very common with phrase repetition most, word repetition rather less, and syllable repetition least frequently observed. Repetition of as many as one quarter of the words uttered is by no means abnormal. Phrase and word repetition tends to decrease as the child grows older, but syllable repetition tends to remain constant. In children who later become clearly deviant in speech behavior, however, syllable repetition tends to be relatively more common and to increase with age.

Even so, it is difficult with young children to distinguish normal speech from incipient stuttering, and Bloodstein et al. (1952) showed that the parents of stutterers are more likely than other parents to diagnosis stuttering when listening to tape recordings of children's speech. Other studies (for example, Glasner, 1949), however, indicate that there are objective, if mainly qualitative, differences between the early speech patterns and the speech development of stutterers and nonstutterers. As development proceeds, stuttering usually passes through a series of stages. Simple repetition is later accompanied by prolongations and blocking, accessory motor activity may then be added, avoidance may then be observed and, finally, various forms of emotional disturbance or social maladjustment may become evident. These stages may not necessarily occur in this order, and not all stutterers will pass through all stages.

Spontaneous recovery from the early stages of stuttering is common as is evident from the declining incidence (c. 4 percent to c. 1 percent) already described. A recent study by Sheehan and Martyn (1966) also indicates that later spontaneous recovery, without therapeutic intervention, is quite common among persistent well-established stutterers. Of an intake of 2406 students to the University of California, Berkeley, 58 were found to have been persistent stutterers at some stage of their lives, but only eleven of them were still active. Seventeen of the forty-seven recovered stutterers had received no formal therapy. There was, in fact, a significant negative relationship between recovery and speech therapy, but this is almost certainly mainly a consequence of the fact that the more severe the condition the less likely is recovery, and the more likely is attendance at a speech clinic.

ASSESSMENT TECHNIQUES

It will be clear from the preceding sections of this chapter that the assessment of stuttering is no simple matter and must include the taking of a detailed case history, interviews, and a prolonged observation in relation to all the manifestations described. A variety of investigatory clinical psychological techniques may also be usefully employed according to the requirements of the individual case, as in the investigation of psychiatric patients in general.

In addition to this general assessment, a detailed speech examination must be carried out along the lines described by Johnson et al. (1963), Van Riper (1963), and others. The techniques developed by these speech pathologists include rating scales, of which Johnson's Iowa Scale is the most elaborate, detailed self-rating questionnaires, and "attitude toward stuttering" scales. The core of the speech examination, however, is the counting and the analysis of dysfluencies during sample readings of standard paragraphs and spontaneous speech on set topics. The speed of reading and of speaking is highly correlated with the number of words stuttered and is a fairly reliable measure of change.

Although several objective measures of this nature are available, there are many difficulties involved in the comparison of findings from repeated assessments, for example, at different stages in the treatment of a patient. The adaptation effect is the most important of them. Apart from the experimental evidence already discussed, there is ample clinical evidence that stutterers adapt emotionally to the clinic situation in general and to the assessment situation in particular. If spurious gains are not to be recorded, it is essential that fresh assessors be introduced and that efforts be made to obtain records of spontaneous speech in everyday, novel, and threatening situations. Stutterers also tend to exhibit slow but extensive spontaneous fluctuations in the severity of their symptoms and, hence, repeated reassessment is necessary over a prolonged period.

AETIOLOGY OF STUTTERING[1]

A rational approach to the treatment of a disorder requires that the treatment be based on an adequate account of the underlying psychopathology and the processes involved in its development. In the writer's view an adequate account of the aetiology of stuttering must await an adequate analysis of the dynamic mechanisms underlying speech production, and not only in their final mature form but also in terms of their development during childhood. Speech is the outstanding characteristic of the human organism and involves the delicate and skilful coordination of the voluntary and involuntary musculature of a complex motor apparatus under the continuous control of neural processes at the highest levels of the cerebral cortex. As such, speech is naturally subject to a lengthy sequence of developmental changes. Typically, the onset of stuttering occurs at a crucial stage in this development, and it must, the writer believes, be regarded as a developmental disorder.

When we examine in any detail the development of even a relatively primitive and simple functional system that has many features common to human beings and lower species, it rapidly becomes evident that it involves a complex interaction of many factors and that distortions of the normal course of development may come about from a variety of causes. The development of voluntary and nocturnal control of bladder functions and the aetiology of enuresis provide an excellent example (Jones, 1960a; see also Chapter 15). The relevant course of development involves complex learning processes made possible by anatomical

[1]The remaining sections of this chapter, concerned with aetiology and modification, are an expanded version of a paper read at the V.R.A. International Seminar on Stuttering and Behavior Therapy, Carmel, California, November 1966.

maturation and by functional differentiation within the nervous system, and clearly the causation of enuresis is heterogeneous and usually multifactorial in that any one of various physiological, emotional, and environmental factors may disrupt the course of development. It is extremely likely that the same is true of stuttering and, indeed, the most superficial examination of its phenomenology suggests that this is true. For example, the dramatic inhibition of stuttering, produced by the prevention of self-monitoring activities through masking of auditory feedback (Cherry & Sayers, 1956), strongly suggests the importance of fairly specific neurological factors. Also, the commonplace observation that the speech of many chronic stutterers is undisturbed when they speak to animals is a clear demonstration that no complete explanation can be couched in neurological terms. There is also ample clinical evidence that anxiety may be extremely important, at least, in the maintenance of stuttering behavior. A number of influential and experimentally well-founded theories of stuttering are based on only one restricted field of evidence. To combine them, particularly when they readily integrate in terms of the developmental process, is not to indulge in an empty eclecticism or to neglect Occam's razor. An adequate theory, and one likely to lead to effective treatment, must account, or at least not be inconsistent with, the full range of relevant data.

Normal Speech Development

An accurate and detailed account of speech development is not possible at the present time. Here we shall attempt no more than an outline sketch of its main aspects, focusing on those which might go awry to bring about the manifestations of stuttering.

The work of Chomsky (1965) and others, which has produced strong evidence for highly organized, innate determinants of the deep syntactic structure of language, presents a major challenge to any purely empiricist account of the acquisition of language in humans. Nevertheless, such a latent structure can only become manifest in specific language behavior, the nature of which, despite unlearned restrictions on its grammatical form, is determined by experience. Learning theorists such as Skinner (1957), Osgood (1953), and Staats (Staats & Staats, 1962; Staats et al., 1962) provide a generally satisfying account of the way in which classical and operant conditioning interact and in which mediational processes operate, to allow parents and other social agents to steer the developing vocalizing ability of the child into standards speech units which come to signify objects or events in the external world, and which acquire complex cognitive and affective meanings that allow the interpersonal communication characteristic of humans.

It has been show (Rheingold et al., 1959) that even the early nonspeechlike sounds of a baby can function as operants whose frequency can be controlled by secondary reinforcers such as the smiles of parents. At a later stage, Osgood has shown that the infant's utterances include almost the entire repetoire of human speech sounds but that gradually there is a change toward the selection of sounds similar to the ones that occur in the speech of its parents. Ultimately the child's "babbling" will include sounds approximating words or phrases meaningful and pleasing to the parents, who produce immediate reinforcement. This serves to differentiate out and to shape into recognizable speech a rudimentary vocabulary much practiced by the child whose hearing of his own speech has probably acquired secondary reinforcing qualities. At this stage, the parent usually engages in frank educational activities that use the child's ability to echo or repeat on demand words said by the parent. Simultaneously, the child becomes trained to speak his words in the correct context of time and place. For example, reinforcement is only provided when the child says "daddy" in the presence of the father. In this way, discrimination learning occurs, and the word becomes firmly linked with the appropriate environmental object or event. Rapid growth of vocabulary can then take place by the parents' pointing out objects and naming them. Osgood, from his mediation hypothesis, has argued with force that when a word is presented in this way with a stimulus object, components of the response elicited by the concrete object become conditioned to the word. In this way the word alone comes to evoke some replica of the actual response to the object and, therefore, acquires representational properties or meaning. Furthermore, this "meaning" can become shared with other words with which the original word is associated, even if these other words are never paired with the concrete stimulus.

Luria (1961), by a fascinating experimental approach to the very simple motor activities of which a young child is capable, has linked them with successive stages in the acquisition of speech. In its early stages, speech cannot influence motor activity, which is regulated by direct feedback systems. Later, the child's speech initiates activities, but this excitatory function is independent of the meaning of the words used: "stop" has the same effect as "go." With further language development, speech takes over a regulative function dependent on meaning and, ultimately, becomes internalized as an essential component of thought. The meaning component of speech does not appear to be very important until the age of about five, which suggests that meaning may not be greatly involved in the onset of stammering, which generally occurs somewhat earlier.

Where knowledge is seriously lacking is concerning the neurophysiological mechanisms underlying the continuous control of speech, and still less is known of their development. One thing is certain, they must be complex and involve monitoring of feedback. At the present stage of knowledge any model of these mechanisms must be hypothetical. One such model, which owes much to Fairbanks (1954), is shown in Figure 13.1 which also includes components, external to the organism, which are important in the learning processes already mentioned.

The mature person placed in a social communication situation must plan what he intends to say in terms of meaningful content and, drawing on his knowledge of words, construct this content in the form of a verbal message. It is not known whether this is a continuous or intermittent process, but the fact that pauses in speech tend to occur at the points where the transitional probabilities are low perhaps suggests the latter. The message once formulated, the motor apparatus of speech is activated in accordance with an internal schema of speech sounds based on earlier learning. Information concerning the emitted speech must be fed back and matched with the original schema and the extent of error estimated. Information concerning this error modifies the fresh input so as to reduce subsequent errors. Anticipation is involved in this process so that, to some extent, the comparator mechanism must also be a predictor. There is also, almost certainly, some form of implicit speech or "rehearsal" mechanism which is certainly active in childhood and which may be important in stuttering. The diagram does not include the multiple channels of feedback—bone, tissue, and air which, because of their differential transmission rates, complicate the picture further. The speech apparatus itself is also complex and involves varying types of neural control.

The development of mastery of such an intricate servomechanism clearly demands efficient neural arrangements and very precise learning. It is not surprising that all children exhibit some degree of dysfluency during the period of rapid expansion of their speaking vocabulary which is also associated with a strong urge to communicate. Neither is it surprising that we all, however mature and however practiced, may lapse into dysfluency in situations of stress. When we speak normally, our well-practiced and efficient neural servomechanisms function in an automatic fashion without our conscious awareness of their operation.

Against the background of this type of model it becomes evident that each of many different factors may deflect the normal course of development and may lead to the appearance of a stutter. In Figure 13.2, the most obvious of these factors are arranged in groups representing a developmental sequence to which both maturational and learning processes contribute, although to a different degree at different stages.

First one needs to consider the contribution of heredity. The evidence concerning this is by no means clear, but the relatives of stutterers do appear to be at greater risk. Andrews and Harris (1964), for example, found a 3-to-4-times increased risk among the first degree relatives of their probands. Of course, a familial disorder is not necessarily genetically determined and, in the case of stuttering, apart from more general environmental influences, imitation of the speech model that is provided by a stuttering relative may be of particular importance. Andrews and Harris make a sophisticated genetic analysis of their data and conclude that nongenetic factors alone are unlikely

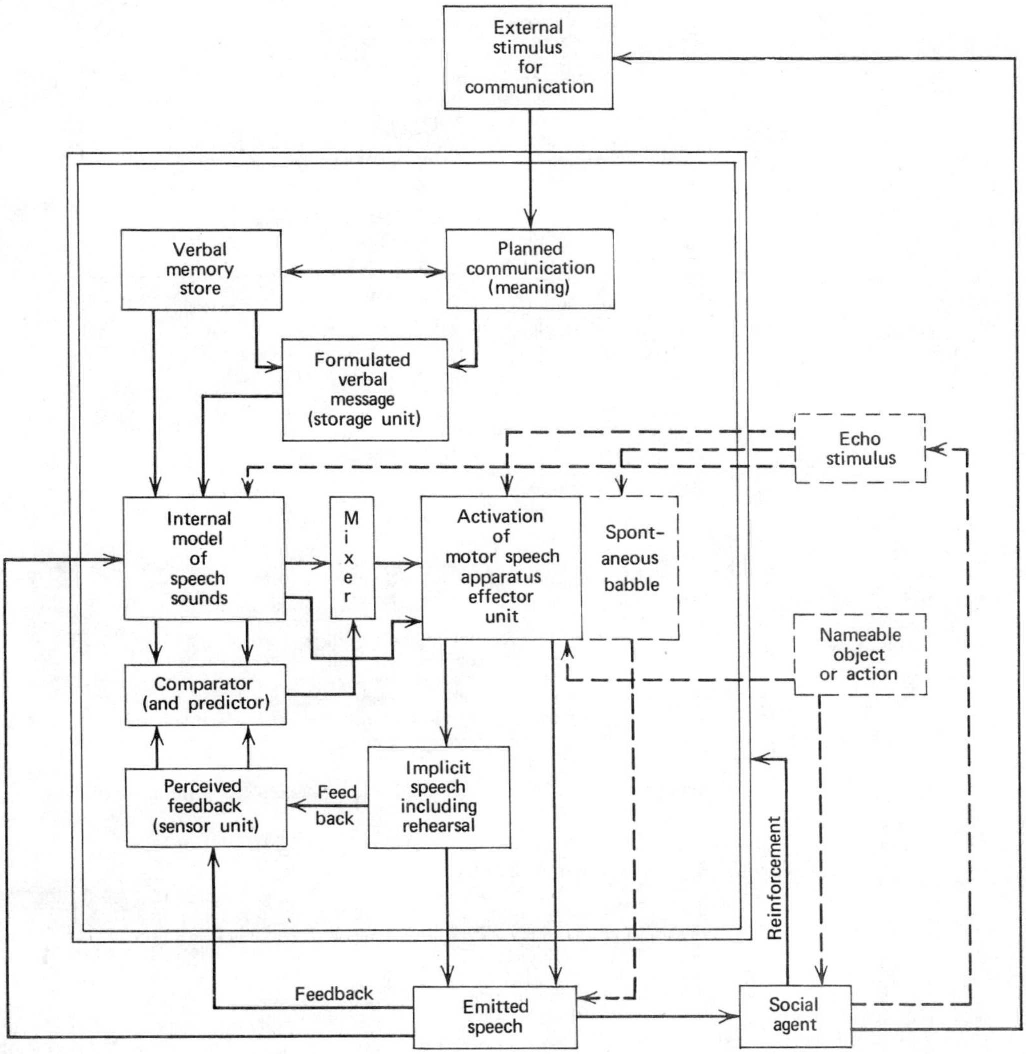

Figure 13.1 Model of self-regulating speech control mechanism. *Solid line*, mature state. *Dashed line*, developmental stages.

to account for the increase in risk. Thus, at least for their familial cases, they favour a genetic explanation and suggest two major alternatives. Transmission may be by a common dominant gene, but with a multifactorial background, or inheritance may be wholly polygenic. Presumably, many different genetic components are involved in the type of speech mechanism outlined.

Sex is, of course, genetically determined and, as already mentioned, a differential sex-incidence in stuttering is well established. Andrews and Harris claim that this probably implies sex-limitation by the action of female genes, which modify the effects of the genes specifically related to stuttering. Sex-linked genes do affect the physical and psychological development of children, and a tendency for girls to be superior to boys in language ability has been frequently noted. These authors also point out that it is consistent with polygenic inheritance that the sex of the proband affects the risk of stuttering among the relatives. The male relatives of female stutterers are at greatest risk, and the risk is least among the female relatives of male stutterers.

The laterality of cerebral language functions is one largely genetically determined factor of great interest in that laterality abnormalities, particularly uncertain dominance, have long been considered important in the genesis of stuttering. Earlier views such as

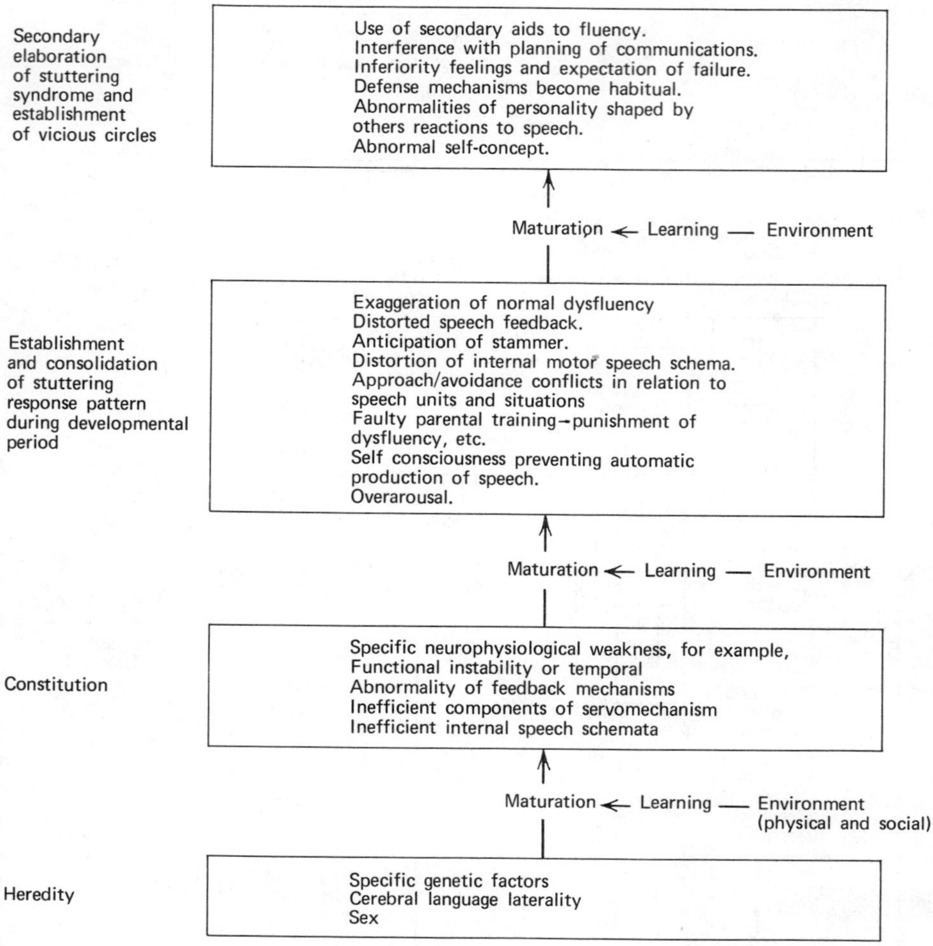

Figure 13.2 Hypothetical factors in the genesis and the maintenance of stuttering.

those of Travis that forced change of handedness leads to central confusion and, hence, to disturbance of speech output have had to be abandoned in the face of contrary evidence. The evidence concerning the effects of left-handedness itself is conflicting (see Beech & Fransella, 1968) but weak dominance, when assessed by methods that more or less directly reflect central processes (Jasper, 1932; Wada & Rasmussen, 1960) does appear to be associated with stuttering. This complicates twin studies concerned with the genetics of stuttering, as identical twins may show reversed laterality.

The most direct indication of cerebral speech laterality is obtained by the intracarotid amytal test which, unfortunately, carries certain risks and is only justified when the information is of great clinical importance as before some types of neurosurgery. During this test, sodium amytal is injected directly into the carotid artery on each side in turn while the subject counts aloud and makes rapid movements with the fingers of both hands. When the injection is on the nondominant side, the subject interrupts his counting only very briefly but his opposite side finger movements are disrupted for 5 minutes or more. Injection on the dominant side produces a considerably longer break in counting, and this is followed by confused counting and by difficulty in naming objects and in reading.

By employing this technique, Jones (1966) carried out an extremely interesting study but with only four lifelong stutterers, all with brain lesions that involved the speech areas. Each of the four patients became aphasic whichever side was injected, and this was taken as clear evidence for bilateral representation of speech. However, the most striking finding was that all four lost their stutter after neurosurgery, and subsequent amytal tests produced aphasia only when the injection took place on the undamaged side. This is interpreted as implying the secondary establishment of unilateral speech representation following the operation. Certainly, it would appear to be more efficient for the postulated type of complex speech servomechanism to be organized unilaterally within the cerebral cortex.

Genetic tendencies, subject to processes of learning and to other environmental factors, are reflected in the constitution of the individual. Any defect or functional weakness of any component of the speech servosystem would disturb the functioning of the whole. Functional instability or temporal abnormalities of the feedback circuits is a type of malfunctioning that appears to be particularly relevant to stuttering (Yates, 1963). Certainly, difficulties of initiation and termination of speech units appear to be the cardinal features of stuttering and are precisely the types of abnormality to be expected when feedback is interfered with during the performance of a complex tracking task as, in one sense, speech might be considered to be. Artificial interference, such as delaying the auditory feedback to a normal speaker, disrupts his speech in a manner that shares many of the features of stuttering. On the other hand, Cherry and Sayers (1956) found that prevention of the self-monitoring process, by a masking low frequency (120–180 c/s) continuous tone to eliminate bone-conducted feedback, produced a dramatic and total inhibition of stuttering in almost all stammerers.

Related constitutionally determined weaknesses would be likely to exaggerate and to increase the duration of dysfluency during the early developmental period, and would play an important part in the establishment and the consolidation of an early stuttering response pattern. The stuttering itself would cause further interference with auditory feedback and, presumably, with the formation of stable internal motor schemata for speech. Anticipation of a stutter would similarly lead to imprecise prediction within the servomechanism and, possibly, to poor coordination of speech response.

This too is the stage at which social learning becomes important and, in particular, emotional reactions complicate the picture. Sheehan (1953, 1958) accounts for the maintenance of stuttering in terms of blocking produced by double approach/avoidance conflicts in relation to specific words and to a variety of speech situations. Sheehan's overall theory is complex and closely argued in relation to a great deal of experimental and clinical evidence, but its essence can be stated fairly briefly. Most theories, he claims, are concerned with the onset of a speech block and do not account for the equally mysterious overcoming of the block and the continuation of speech. He analyses the situation in terms of Miller's double approach/avoidance conflict paradigm. The stutterers goal is communication, but in any particular speech situation he anticipates dysfluency. The anxiety associated with this anticipation creates an avoidance gradient that rises steeply as the feared word is approached. Ultimately, the approach and avoidance tendencies reach equilibrium and a block occurs. Sheehan's main hypothesis to account for the upsetting of this equilibrium is that, once the block occurs, the stuttering is manifest to the listener, and the stutterer must abandon his defences, thus, reducing his anxiety and lowering the avoidance gradient. In other words, the occurrence of stuttering reduces the fear that elicited it. As Yates (1963) points out, although this is the weakest part of Sheehan's explanation, which otherwise has much to support it, the general problem of the resolution of conflict when all forces are in equilibrium has never received a satisfactory theoretical solution.

In the writer's view, there is evidence that anticipation may be more painful than the reality of the anticipated event in a number of situations, for example expected "shock" and actual "shock" during aversive therapy. There is, however, one other factor in most conflict situations of this type that is seldom taken into account, namely the passage of time.

The usual type of diagram, suitably modified, is reproduced in Figure 13.3. The complete and broken lines in the diagram represent the balance of forces at the inception of the block. However, as is subjectively evident to all, the aversive qualities of silence in a social communication situation are a function of its duration and, therefore, the silence avoidance gradient gradually rises and is represented by the dotted line in the diagram at the point where speech is achieved.

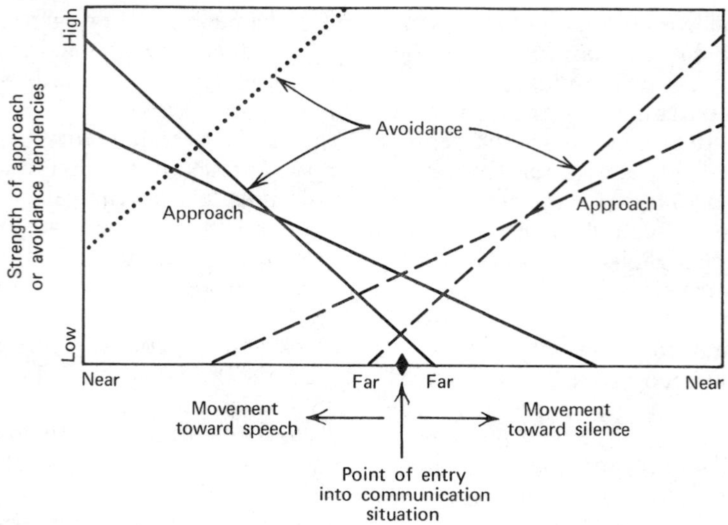

Figure 13.3 The stutterer's conflict in a communication situation. *Solid line*, tendencies to or from speech. *Dashed line*, tendencies to or from silence. *Dotted line*, silence avoidance tendency after the passage of time.

The implications of this become clearer from Figure 13.4 which shows the algebraic summation of approach and avoidance tendencies from Figure 13.3. The lower curve represents the initial state which would lead to vacillation at the midpoint. With the passage of time, this curve is gradually distorted toward the final (broken line) form, thus, producing a decelerating movement toward the act of speech which ultimately occurs but still with a high degree of conflict and, presumably, of anxiety. Essentially similar dynamics would apply to conflicts of this type in relation to particular words and to particular communication situations.

Sheehan's approach-avoidance model has recently been criticized from several points of view. In one important paper, Maher (1964) points out that Miller's model is frequently applied analogically in an uncritical way to human social behavior. In particular, he argues that, in conflict situations of the type referred to by Sheehan, both the presumed approach and avoidance tendencies arise from learned drives and, therefore, from a strict application of Miller's theory, there is no reason why the avoidance gradient should be steeper than the approach gradient and, therefore, the two need never cross to generate a conflict. Maher himself solves many of the difficulties that arise from this argument by adding a further postulate to the ones proposed by Miller. He suggests that the stronger of the two competing response tendencies mediates behavior only when its absolute momentary strength exceeds that of the weaker by an amount that is a constant fraction of the weaker.

Parental training is also an important factor at this stage of development, and Wendell Johnson (1955, 1959) has suggested faulty training as the actual cause of stuttering. Although it must be admitted that a form of secondary stuttering might arise in this way, the writer remains unconvinced that this is a sufficient explanation of the genesis of most stammers. Johnson's theory is essentially diagnosogenic. He argues that certain parents become alarmed at normal nonfluencies and express their disapproval or even punish their children to the extent that the child becomes anxious about his speech and develops avoidance responses that can lead to the development of Sheehan's type of approach/avoidance conflicts. A great deal of empirical research has been stimulated by Johnson's influential and important theory, and it is reviewed thoroughly by Beech and Fransella (1968), who conclude that much of the evidence is consistent with this model. Nevertheless, the type of parental reaction described by Johnson, although partly determined by the personality and attitudes of the parent, seems more likely to occur when the child's early dysfluency is prolonged or exaggerated, for the reasons already mentioned, and interferes with the longer practice and training required by these children before they acquire fluency.

Punishment may not be the only fault in parental training. Parents with too high a standard may not reward early inexact approximations to words and, thus, hamper the operant shaping process. Others, by being attentive in a warm way when dysfluencies occur, may actually positively reinforce their occurrence. Indeed, Wingate (1959), who stresses this point, experimentally demonstrated that critical evaluation of stutterers' dysfluencies can produce improvement.

Wischner (1950, 1952) is another authority who, on the basis of an experimental analysis of the consistency and adaptation effects, stresses the importance of learning processes in the consolidation and the maintenance of stuttering. He invokes both classical conditioning and instrumental learning, arguing that cues, which may be situational or word specific, become conditioned stimuli for the arousal of anxiety. This anxiety becomes the emotional substratum for the learning of a variety of avoidance responses and, when they are ineffective, reaches such a level as to be an important factor in the disruption of fluency. Once fluency is regained, however, there is a sharp reduction in drive and, therefore, the immediately preceding stuttering behavior is reinforced. This theory's main weakness is that, if stuttering is positively reinforced in this way, one would predict a continuous progressive deterioration of speech culminating in complete disruption. In fact, stuttering tends to stabilize at a severity level typical of the individual.

It is clear, however, that a number of factors can make the dysfluent child self-conscious concerning his speech, and this self-consciousness will interfere with the normal development of automatic speech and will foster too great an awareness of auditory feedback. When the self-consciousness is accompanied by anxiety for whatever reason, this will lead to overarousal and probably to inefficient regulation of the complex speech servomechanism in accordance with the Yerkes Dodson principle (Jones, 1960b).

Zhinkin's (1966) work at the Moscow institute of Psychology indicates a more direct way in which anxiety might affect speech production. He has carried out extensive radiographic research on the role of the pharynx as distinct from the buccal cavity, tongue and lips, in the production of vowel sounds and has demonstrated clearly that each sound is associated with a characteristic pharyngeal volume and shape, and also that distortions of this shape accompany stammering. He makes the theoretical point that the pharyngeal musculature is under the involuntary control of lower brain centers, whereas the mouth is controlled from cortical motor centers. Emotional arousal, therefore, is likely to disrupt pharyngeal control and to produce distortions of speech that voluntary effort cannot remedy.

Once the stuttering pattern becomes firmly established, it is likely to be secondarily elaborated into a complex and variable syndrome that involves several vicious circles which make spontaneous remission with further maturity unlikely. One of the most common elaborations, already mentioned, is the development of accessory movements or other activities which apparently aid in the struggle for fluent speech.

It is interesting that, in the work already referred to, Luria (1961) demonstrates the impellant, initiating, and controlling function that the speech of a child of 3 to 4 has in relation to its motor behavior. He claims that this is possible because, by this age, the neurodynamics of simple verbal reactions have become more perfect than the neurodynamics of the motor reactions. The

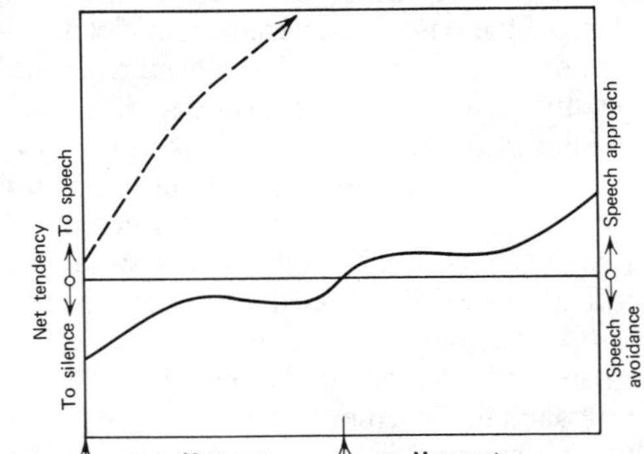

Figure 13.4 Summation of partial tendencies from Figure 13.3. *Solid line*, at time of entry into communication situation. *Dashed line*, after the passage of time.

accessory activities of stammerers suggest that the reverse may be true for them.

Another secondary effect of stuttering is that the attention which must be paid to speech production and to the avoidance of certain dangerous words or phrases is likely to interfere with the planning and the formulation of verbal communications, both in terms of their meaningful content and their linguistic form.

More important, perhaps, a whole set of neurotic reactions and defence mechanisms may be developed on the basis of inferiority feelings, expectations of failure, the approach/avoidance conflicts, and even reactions to failures of therapy. According to basic temperament, the stutterer's personality will be shaped in directions determined by his own and others reactions to his speech, and he will develop abnormalities of his self-concepts in terms of how he thinks and feels about himself, and of the way he believes others see him.

Thus, the terminal point in the development of stuttering is a complex syndrome which can vary widely from individual to individual. This, however, does not necessarily imply that stuttering is a disorder that cannot be considered as an entity. On present evidence there might well be a specific neurodynamic weakness of primary aetiological importance but which gives rise to a variety of secondary manifestations.

THE MODIFICATION OF STUTTERING

The main implication of the developmental and multifactorial account which has been given of the onset, maintenance, and elaboration of stuttering is that its treatment should also be multilateral and should include both specific modification techniques and more general forms of therapy. The latter would be aimed at reducing the anxiety and conflict associated with difficult speech situations and at modifying the stutterer's concepts of himself and of his speech. The need for an individually tailored, multidimensional approach to treatment is, in fact, recognized by most experienced workers. Thus, Sheehan (1958) states:

> "The fundamental goal of treatment . . . is . . . to eliminate all tendencies to avoidance whatever the source. Word fears and situation fears . . . are attacked most directly through speech therapy. Feelings, relationships and defences are reached through psychotherapy."

Most contemporary speech therapy clinics are much influenced by Van Riper's (1958, 1963) "expressive and dynamic symptomatic therapy." General counseling and psychotherapeutic procedures are aimed at enabling the stutterer to understand himself and the nature and fluctuations of his disorder, to increase his tolerance of his own stuttering and the reactions of listeners, and to become more independent and tough-minded. More specifically, along lines very similar to the "graduated desensitization" practices of behavior therapists, practice is given in entering progressively more stressful situations in an attempt to inhibit anxiety even though stuttering may continue to occur. Simultaneously, more direct forms of speech therapy are employed. They include differential relaxation of the speech musculature and rhythmic speaking games, but the main emphasis is on the teaching of "voluntary stuttering." In this the patient imitates his own pattern of stuttering, not only on feared words, but also on a proportion of words that would not be expected to cause difficulty. Another related method of learned voluntary control is called "cancellation." The patient stops after a stuttered word and repeats it without strain or with a voluntary stutter. When proficient at this he graduates to "pull-outs," the modification of speech before the stuttered word is completed. Van Riper also lays great stress on the modification of "preparatory sets" so as to enable the stutterer to approach a word on which he expects to stutter in the same way as any other word. At the end of therapy it is hoped that, even if stuttering is not eliminated, it will be "easy" rather than effortful, unrelated to anxiety, controlled, and brief. At follow-up, five years after therapy, Van Riper in fact reported that 50 percent of 137 severe stutterers no longer stuttered or that their dysfluency was so mild as not to constitute a handicap.

It is likely that the exceptional personal qualities of Van Riper contribute to some degree to these findings. In general, there is little objective evidence concerning the efficacy of the various forms of therapy, and most published reports have serious methodological faults, or do not allow sufficiently long follow-up periods to take account of the frequency of relapse, which is usually quite high. Thus, much of what is written in this section of the chapter is based on theoretical considerations and clinical experience.[2]

In terms of the latter it seems clear that, when attempting to modify a severe and long-standing stammer in an adult patient, the treatment must be intensive in order to have any marked effect. More may be gained from admitting the stammerer to the hospital for a few weeks, to follow a planned program of varied daily activities, than from two or more years of weekly outpatient visits. If the therapeutic task is regarded, as it is from the behaviorist standpoint, as a relearning one, this is by no means surprising when so many highly practiced and omnipresent reactions must be modified. Unless it is possible to retain a continuous fairly high measure of control of the patient's environment for a period, the gains made during the treatment sessions are likely to be rapidly offset by adverse relearning in everyday life.

From the type of model of the genesis of stuttering outlined in this chapter, one might hope to derive a specific technique that makes a direct attack on the postulated specific neurodynamic weakness. This would be most likely to be effective if it were possible to take the stutterer back, so to speak, to the critical stage of his speech development and to start retraining from there. Earlier, the analogy was drawn between stuttering and enuresis and, in the present connection, we note with interest that Mowrer (1938) followed precisely this approach in designing his "bell and pad" method for the conditioning treatment of enuresis.

Unfortunately, it is difficult to make a similar approach to the modification of stuttering because of the difficulties of circumventing the effects of the stutterer's speech experience and of his previous use of language. For example, the learning of a new foreign language does not appear to be helpful in that, in general, the stuttering pattern is transferred intact to the new language. The one exception to this rule that is known to the writer (Sheehan, 1966) in fact illustrates the complexity of relevant experiential factors in that the learning of the new language (Hebrew) followed radical changes in life-style, social roles, and cultural environment.

Cybernetic Approaches

Mysak (1966) examines the implications of regarding speech as a complex multiple-loop servomechanism, in great detail, and makes many specific therapeutic suggestions which could be incorporated within a more general plan of treatment. He stresses that there are, at least, two levels of activity: a higher cognitive level concerned with the monitoring of thought and the content of speech, and a lower, normally automatic level concerned with the monitoring of articulation variables. The prominence of the expectancy effect certainly suggests that the stutterer, at the lower-level, becomes too involved with monitoring ahead, and that this is likely to interfere with the higher level activities.

Of the modification techniques based on cybernetic models, the greatest interest has been shown in delayed auditory feedback (DAF), auditory masking, and in "shadowing." It has long been known (Harms & Malone, 1939) that stuttering is extremely rare in the deaf, and Lee's (1950) demonstration that delays of from 1/15th to 1/10th of a second in the hearing (via tape recorder and earphones) of their own voice tends to disrupt the speech of normal speakers attracted a great deal of attention. Delays of this duration very frequently produce speech blocks and prolongations of sounds similar in many ways to stuttering. It would be naive to suggest, as some have, that stutterers, because of abnormalities of cerebral functioning, are faced with a similar delay in feedback. In fact, repeated exposure to the experimental condition frequently results in adaptation, and Neeley (1961) has shown that it is relatively easy to distinguish between tape recordings of the speech of stutterers and that of normal speakers under the influence of DAF. However, time factors in feedback may have a more subtle role in stuttering. For example, proprioceptive, air-conducted, and bone-conducted feedback arrives at different rates. This presents a problem in integration which may be weak in some stutterers, and

[2]The clincial experience on which the author draws is largely that of his able colleague, Mrs. Berenice Krikler, a speech pathologist and clinical psychologist with a wide range of recorded relevant experience.

malintegration may bring about effects similar, in some respects, to the ones produced by simple DAF. DAF modifies the speech of stutterers and may, during its application, eliminate the usual stuttering manifestations. Its most thorough therapeutic application has been by Goldiamond (1964, 1966) but in the context of a program of operant behavior modification. This will be discussed with other operant procedures, in a later section.

Cherry and Sayers (1956) convincingly demonstrated the inhibitory effect on stuttering of the prevention of self-monitoring by masking bone-conducted auditory feedback. Their theorectical interpretation of this phenomenon is challenged by Sutton and Chase (1961) on the basis of an ingenious experiment in which three conditions of masking were compared with "no noise" conditions. Apart from the continuous masking used by Cherry and Sayers, noise was, in one condition, introduced only during subjects' phonation and, in another, only during the silent intervals between phonations. All noise conditions produced a significant reduction in stuttering dysfluency, but there was no differential effect between the three. Sutton and Chase, therefore, consider it unlikely that the increased fluency is a result of the stutterer being unable to hear his own voice. There is force to this argument, but all the noise conditions would be likely to interfere seriously with the auditory monitoring process. The extent and nature of this interference merit further experimental investigation.

Attempts have been made to exploit the masking effect in therapy, but there appears to be little or no "carry over" from the experimental condition, even after many trials, into the free speech of the stutterer. Therefore, with the aim of training stutterers into new perceptual habits that might generalize over all speech situations, Cherry and Sayers devised their "shadowing" technique. In order to transfer the stutterer's attention away from his own voice to that of another speaker, the experimenter reads from a book, and the stutterer has to "shadow" him, speaking a few words behind without seeing the text.[3] Skill at this imitative task is fairly readily acquired by most stutterers, and their practice can then be extended by shadowing radio talks or tape recordings between formal sessions at a clinic.

Marland, in an appendix to the Cherry and Sayers paper, reported promising initial therapeutic results with a variety of stutterers during preliminary clinical trials of these techniques. Similar findings are reported by Maclaren (1960, 1963) who, however, made simultaneous use of a wide range of speech therapy technique. Krikler (1966) carried out a more systematic study in which shadowing was practiced for eight weeks by 50 adult or adolescent severe stutterers, mainly between the ages of 20 and 30. They attended the clinic weekly, but undertook daily home shadowing practice from a graded series of recordings. The results have not been completely analyzed, but it is clear that, although a few patients improved dramatically, the overall success achieved is little, if any, greater than when more traditional methods are employed over a similar period.

More recently, Kondas (1967) makes a more favorable report, which covers an average 3.2 years follow-up period, on the treatment of nineteen children with severe stuttering. After therapy, fifteen were "cured" or "much improved," and only two of them showed any relapse during follow-up. For three very young children, Kondas successfully made use of a play form of shadowing that involved puppets. This author, like Maclaren, stresses an individual approach and makes use of a variety of subsidiary techniques in addition to shadowing. His findings, therefore, cannot be considered to relate specifically to shadowing, but it is likely that the main reason for the discrepency between them and those of Krikler is that shadowing is considerably more effective with young children than with older stutterers in whom the secondary manifestations have become prominent. A detailed examination of all reports indicates fairly strongly that this is true.

More research is required on feedback techniques in general (see Yates, 1963) and, in particular, the dramatic temporary effects need to be studied in detail to provide indications of ways in which generalized learning might be more effectively achieved. Indeed, no phenomenon that results in the

[3]As a note of warning to those whose speech, like that of the author's, is readily disrupted by DAF, it should be pointed out that the shadowing situation, from the listening point of the shadowee, is also a DAF situation.

experimental modification of stuttering should be neglected by the therapist, as each may offer a starting point for reeducation and may provide experience in fluent speaking.

Rhythm Effects

A good example of this experimental control is the rhythm effect. Imposed rhythms or syllabication of speech, which may be aided by external cues, although producing an artificial manner of speaking, frequently inhibit stuttering. Chorus reading or speaking have similar effects. Rhythmic control assisted by metronomelike instruments was at one time a popular form of therapy, and there has been a recent revival of interest in these techniques; but most experienced therapists claim that the therapeutic gains are seldom lasting.

Two main theoretical explanations have been suggested for the rhythm effect. Much evidence points to a pacemaker type of control of the motor skills involved in speech. Many writers, however, lay great stress on the distraction effects of rhythm, and it is certainly true that many forms of attention diversion, including possibly the accessory movements carried out by stutterers themselves, do increase the fluency of stutteres, at least temporarily. Johnson and Rosen (1937) make the distraction hypothesis more precise by relating it specifically to the expectation that stuttering will occur.

Beech and Fransella (1968) have experimentally tested several such hypotheses. For example, they found that an arhythmic metronome and instructions for the subjects to listen carefully for a pattern of beats failed to produce the usual effect, and they concluded that the underlying mechanism could not be distraction in any simple sense. These workers' own major hypothesis is that rhythm is effective by virtue of the fact that it makes predictable the point in time at which a vocalization should occur. They tested this version of the "pacemaker" hypothesis in an experiment on twenty stutterers who were required to read a series of words exposed on a screen for varying lengths of time. For one half of the words, the movement of a line on the screen clearly indicated and allowed prediction of the point in time at which the word should be uttered. The other words were required to be spoken at unspecified times during their exposure. Highly significant differences in the predicted direction indicated that predictability is an important factor, but possibly not sufficient of itself to account entirely for the effects of rhythm.

In most accounts of the therapeutic use of rhythmical speech, stress is laid on the early difficulty of maintaining this unnatural manner of speaking in everyday situations and on the later difficulty of weaning the patients from it. Meyer and Mair (1963) describe a portable metronome in the form of a deaf-aid worn by their stutterers outside the clinic and brought into use by means of an unobtrusive switch as and when required. A graded series of tasks aided the weaning process. Krikler (1966) finds a wave-sketching technique (by pencil on sheets of newspaper and later by finger in the air), which can be gradually internalized, to be as effective as other rhythmic procedures, and minimally productive of artificiality in speaking. She does not consider this an effective therapy used in isolation but a useful starting point for a wider program of treatment.

Much the same conclusion is reached by Andrews and Harris (1964), who trained 35 stutterers in "syllable-timed" speech. They were taught to speak syllable by syllable with equal stress and in time with a regular rhythm. Some 100 hours of practice produced considerable gains in fluency, but most patients relapsed a great deal in the following three months. Further follow-up during the next nine months indicated little further change. Children benefited more and relapsed less than adolescents and adults.

The Adaptation Effect

Brutten and Gray (1961) take seriously the description of the adaptation effect as a "laboratory model of the improvement process." They propose a technique in which those of a selection of words which are stuttered on a first reading are removed before the second reading, thus accelerating adaptation. This process is repeated over successive readings and, when fluency is achieved, the words are reinstated in the reverse order of their removal. In this way, cues related to success reinforcement should generalize to the reinserted words. This is a suggestion that is theoretically sound and has experimental support. With modifications, it might also be applied to continuous prose and, if a word continued to evoke stuttering after reinsertion, it could be included in a list for specific intensive remedial practice.

Stuttering Considered as Operant Behavior

Shames and Sherrick (1963) make an interesting case for regarding stuttering as the persistence and the elaboration of childhood dysfluency brought about by processes of operant conditioning that involve both positive and negative reinforcement. They point out, however, that the observed kinds and schedules of reinforcement are numerous and complex, there being no single contingency for stuttering.

Goldiamond and his co-workers, by using mainly escape and punishment procedures, have clearly demonstrated that stuttering behavior can be isolated from normal speech as a response unit, and that it can be controlled as an operant by manipulating response-contingent consequences. In laboratory situations, stuttering has been both suppressed and intensified in this way, and dysfluency encouraged in normal subjects. Perhaps, because of the very precision of the early experiments and the resultant prominence of the discriminatory cues associated with the laboratory, these effects were fairly rapidly reversed after each session. Thus, there was very little generalization into everyday life. In the field of behavior therapy generally, operant modification tends to have most therapeutic effect when carried out in a seminatural environment and when care is taken to carry over cues into real-life situations. This, of course, is quite possible in relation to stuttering and is attempted in the more recent studies. In this connection, the training of parents and other significant individuals as reinforcing agents in the stutterer's environment must not be neglected.

Flanagan, Goldiamond, and Azrin (1958), by using white noise as an aversive stimulus, provide an elegant demonstration of laboratory control of dysfluency by variation in reinforcement contingencies. In his later work, however, Goldiamond (1964, 1966) makes a full experimental analysis of stuttering, drawing, for his theoretical interpretation, on all aspects of the operant paradigm. In some of the earlier experiments DAF was employed as a reinforcer and was shown to be aversive. Certain discrepancies in the findings, however, led Goldiamond to make a more detailed study of the effects of DAF. The change from normal to delayed auditory feedback is a change in the constant stimulus context in which speech responses occur. This change tends initially to disrupt the usual behavior pattern and, in the longer term, leads to an adaptive change in the topography of the responses. Among such topographic modifications was noted a slowed rate of speech with prolongation of the speech elements. This was associated with a reduction in or elimination of stuttering. Goldiamond accounts for this change by postulating that auditory and proprioceptive feedback has a positive reinforcing function in the maintenance of the chained responses of speech. DAF has the effect of deferring this reinforcement, and one method of maintaining the speech behavior is to prolong each response until it again overlaps with the reinforcing stimulus.

On the basis of this and related arguments, Goldiamond elaborated a therapeutic program in four stages:

1. The first stage is concerned with the establishment of a new speech pattern—the prolongation and slowing down that has already been described. Four techniques are in various combinations employed for this purpose. In time DAF alone tends to produce this effect, but this time may be long. To speed the process the stutterer is instructed verbally on how he is to speak. Goldiamond acknowledges that instructions may be rapid and efficient controllers of behavior, and regards them as one type of discriminative stimuli, exercising control according to the differential consequences of obedience and disobedience. To further aid the acquisition of the new pattern, the visual presentation of material to be read can be mechanically paced, and differential reinforcement may be applied to different reading rates
2. Once the new pattern of speech has become established, attention is directed to altering its stimulus control. This is achieved by gradually fading the delay of feedback from 250 ms in gradual steps to no delay.
3. If the new response pattern is maintained without DAF, it is gradually shaped in the direction of normal speech by a programmed speeding up of the pace of presentation of reading material. If deterioration in fluency occurs, a retreat is made to an appropriate earlier stage in the program.

4. Finally, an attempt is made to transfer control from the experimenter and the laboratory devices to the patient himself and to allow him to operate this control in his normal environment. Goldiamond (1964) draws a sharp distinction between generalization procedures, which involve the experimental manipulation of discriminative stimuli, and self-control procedures, which involve the instruction of the subject in the operant analysis of the relations between his own behaviors and the environmental conditions under which they occur. By an interesting counseling/psychotherapeutic technique, this author guides his patients into changing their environment in ways likely to favor more adaptive behavior. This technique is used by Goldiamond in other contexts in relation to a variety of behavior problems and would certainly be suited to the modification of many of the secondary emotional manifestations of stuttering, although he seldom uses the term emotion.

From his accounts, Goldiamond's therapeutic program is certainly very promising, but final judgment must be reserved until longer follow-up data are available on a larger number of stutterers. It is perhaps noteworthy that his experimental work led him from the use of general universal reinforcers to a very special use of DAF, closely related to the servomechanistic aspects of speech.

Although Goldiamond's is the most comprehensive approach within a strictly operant framework, we must also mention the recent attempts at operant control of stuttering by using verbal reinforcers (for example, Shames, 1966) which demonstrate that similar control is possible by these means when contingency schedules are strictly observed. Punishment, in general, would be expected to arouse anxiety and, therefore, to exacerbate dysfluency and, in a series of experiments, Siegel and Martin (1965a, 1965b, 1966; Martin & Siegel, 1966a, 1966b) by employing both verbal and shock reinforcement on normal speakers and stutterers show that response contingent punishment does produce a significant decrease in dysfluencies, but that random punishment may result in increase. In one of these experiments, these workers demonstrated that a wrist strap could function as an effective discriminative stimulus for generalization purposes. After pairing with appropriate reinforcing verbal stimuli for a period, attachment of the strap alone decreased stuttering in a variety of experimental situations.

Negative Practice

One form of behavior-orientated therapy, negative practice, or the voluntary repetition of the maladaptive response, was early used in the treatment of stuttering by Dunlap (1944). Case (1960) also included this technique, among others, in a therapeutic study of 30 stutterers, but the reports are such that it is difficult to evaluate the outcome. In the writer's view, negative practice, which is a very peripheral approach to modification, is unlikely to be effective in conditions in which anxiety and other emotional reactions play a prominent part (Jones, 1960c).

Brutten (1966) and Shoemaker (1966), however, take account of this point both in their therapeutic approach and in the two-factor theory of stuttering from which it derives. These authors distinguish between the primary disorganization of speech, which they consider to result from classically conditioned anxiety or "negative emotionality," as they describe it, and secondary adjustive responses, such as eye-blinks and nose-wrinklings, which they suggest are acquired on the basis of instrumental learning. Their therapeutic attack is first directed against the former by the techniques referred to in the next section and, as reduction in anxiety becomes evident, negative practice is applied to the adjustive responses. Their actual technique depends more on Hullian concepts of reactive and conditioned inhibition than on Dunlap's original rationale and, thus, the voluntary evocation of responses is truly massed.

Graduated Desensitization by Reciprocal Inhibition

From the account given of the genesis and maintenance of stuttering, therapy, to be effective, should include techniques for the reduction of anxiety and, hence, the resolution of approach/avoidance conflicts. Provided that a careful study is made of the verbal, situational, and interpersonal stimuli that evoke anxiety in the individual case, techniques of desensitization by reciprocal inhibition (Wolpe, 1958) seem very appropriate for this purpose. Several reports suggest that this method has considerable value in the modification of stuttering, but objective and controlled evaluation data are not available.

The hierarchy of anxiety-provoking situations used for this technique may be presented to the subject via his own imagination or by means of a graded series of real-life situations. The former approach has many advantages but, in the writer's experience, some individual's appear to require an "in vivo" approach, at least, at some stages of the procedure. In particular, desensitization in reality situations is often necessary when the response to be eliminated, as with stuttering, involves a fair amount of well-practiced motor behavior. A useful compromise is to employ the imaginal technique for the more general social anxieties of the patient but to provide graduated training in actual more formal speech situations.

As an example of this approach, the patient might begin by reading to the therapist, initially employing, say, rhythmical aids until fluency is achieved. Then he might be given appropriate speaking assignments to prepare and to deliver, first to the therapist alone and, ultimately to groups of strangers. In the final stages, this audience might even heckle the speaker. Because of the secondary interference with the planning of communications that stuttering produces, the patient will need to be trained in the preliminary organization of what he has to say. Krikler (1966) claims that encouragement of and training in "picturization," the forming of visual images, is helpful in this training. Although inspired largely by contemporary concepts of behavior therapy, a program of this nature has much in common with Van Riper's (1958) approach.

Counseling and Psychotherapy

However effective the attempts at modifying the basic stuttering manifestations, when they have been long-standing there is likely to remain the more general neurotic tendencies, the diffuse, pervasive, but mainly social anxieties, and the distorted self-concepts of the typical severe established stutterer. Many of the techniques already described should do much to break the vicious circles that sustain these reactions and to foster self-confidence and reduce stress. Nevertheless, most therapeutic programs will need to include something very much akin to psychotherapy. This would be aimed partly at getting the stutterer to face the fact that he does stutter and, therefore, would reduce many of his unreal fears and expectancies concerning both himself and his listener. At a later stage in treatment he will also need to be helped to adapt to himself as a non-stutterer. Attempts to strengthen self-confidence and to increase sociability should also be made. It will be clear from this chapter that the author inclines to a behavioristic, experimental point of view, and approaches therapy as a problem of re-education. However, learning is not a concept that only embraces simple motor and autonomic aspects of behavior, but it is equally relevant to complex verbal, social and even "thinking" behavior. Behavior modification in these areas will inevitably involve a great deal of verbal interchange between the therapist and the patient and, at times, will look very much like orthodox psychotherapy, if not of the psychoanalytic variety. It is striking that such a rigorous behaviorist as Goldiamond, for example, makes considerable use of verbal methods.

Psychoanalytic views have not been reviewed in this chapter, although they are considered highly relevant to the understanding and the treatment of stuttering. However, the author has only very slight competence in this area, and most of the reports are based on single case studies which, taken together, do not suggest any specific psychopathology.

SUMMARY AND CONCLUSIONS

All the evidence reviewed indicates that stuttering is typically a complex disorder representing the culmination of a developmental process which possibly starts with the early childhood manifestation of a specific neurodynamic weakness affecting the control of speech. Learning processes are extremely important in the establishment and the maintenance of the primary disorder, and they may have a more fundamental aetiological role. Inevitably, secondary manifestations, which take different forms in different individuals, arise from and as reactions to the basic dysfunction. Anticipatory anxiety and a variety of avoidance responses are prominent among them.

There are equally strong indications that effective therapy must be comprehensive in nature and must be adapted to the individual case. It should incorporate specific modification techniques designed to eliminate the speech dysfluencies but should also include more general procedures for the reduction of anxiety and the modification of the patient's social responses and self-concepts.

Cherry and Sayer's "shadowing" technique and Goldiamond's use of delayed auditory feedback show particular promise as methods of modifying the basic dysfluency but, as yet, only the latter has been incorporated in a systematic reeducational program. This total program has many advantageous features but cannot be fully evaluated until more data are available.

Graduated desensitization techniques appear particularly valuable for the reduction of cue-evoked anxiety and for the modification of avoidance behavior. Again, however, hard data are lacking.

The major conclusion, as always, must be that more research is necessary and, particularly in relation to modification procedures. This must be of a more rigorous nature with adequate control data and follow-up for, at least, two years after the cessation of treatment. This is not meant to imply that modification research should take the form of a simple clinical trial of prescribed procedures. The most fruitful of the research reviewed in this chapter is characterized by a simultaneous experimental analysis of modification techniques and of the maladaptive processes that it is intended to modify.

REFERENCES

Andrews, G., & Harris, M. *The syndrome of stuttering*. London: Heinemann, 1964.

Beech, H. R., & Fransella, F. *Research and experiment in stuttering*. Oxford: Pergamon, 1968.

Bloodstein, O. The development of stuttering: I. Changes in nine basic features. *J. Sp. Hear. Dis.*, 1960a, **25**, 219–237.

Bloodstein, O. The development of stuttering: II. Developmental phases. *J. Sp. Hear. Dis.*, 1960b, **25**, 366–376.

Bloodstein, O. The development of stuttering: III. Theoretical and clinical implications. *J. Sp. Hear. Dis.*, 1961, **26**, 67–81.

Bloodstein, O., Jaeger, W., & Tureen, J. A study of the diagnosis of stuttering by parents of stutterers and nonstutterers. *J. Sp. Hear. Dis.*, 1952, **17**, 308–315.

Brutten, E. J. Palmar sweat investigation of disfluency and expectancy adaptation. *J. Sp. Hear. Res.*, 1963, **6**, 40–48.

Brutten, E. J. Stuttering: the disintegration of conditioned negative emotionality. Paper read at Int. Seminar on Stuttering and Behaviour Therapy, Carmel, California, November, 1966.

Brutten, E. J., & Gray, B. B. Effect of word cue removal on adaptation and adjacency: a clinical paradigm. *J. Sp. Hear. Dis.*, 1961, **26**, 385–389.

Case, H. Therapeutic methods in stuttering and speech-blocking. In H. J. Eysenck (Ed.), *Behaviour therapy and the neuroses*. Oxford: Pergamon, 1960.

Cherry, C., & Sayers, B. McA. Experiments upon the total inhibition of stammering by external control and some clinical results. *J. Psychosom. Res.*, 1956, **1**, 232–246.

Chomsky, N. *Aspects of the theory of syntax*. M.I.T. Press. 1965.

Davis, D. M. The relation of repetitions in the speech of young children to certain measures of language maturity and situational factors. Part I, *J. Sp. Dis.*, 1939, 4, 303–318; Part II, *J. Sp. Dis.*, 1940a, **5**, 235–241; Part III, *J. Sp. Dis.*, 1940b, **5**, 242–246.

Douglass, E., & Quarrington, B. The differentiation of interiorized and exteriorized secondary stuttering. *J. Sp. Hear. Dis.*, 1952, **17**, 377–385.

Dunlap, K. Stammering: its nature, aetiology and therapy. *J. Comp. Psychol.*, 1944, **37**, 187–202.

Fairbanks, G. Systematic research in experimental phonetics: I. A theory of the speech mechanism as a servomechanism. *J. Sp. Hear. Dis.*, 1954, **19**, 133–139.

Flanagan, B., Goldiamond, I., & Azrin, N. Operant stuttering: the control of stuttering behaviour through response-contingent consequences. *J. exp. Anal. Behav.*, 1958, **1**, 173–177.

Fransella, F. The effects of imposed rhythm and certain aspects of personality on the speech of stutterers. Ph.D. Thesis, University of London Library, 1965.

Freund, H. *Psychopathology and the problems of stuttering with special consideration of clinical and historical aspects*. Springfield, Ill: C. C. Thomas, 1966.

Glasner, P. Personality characteristics and emotional problems in stutterers under the age of five. *J. Sp. Hear. Dis.*, 1949, **14**, 135–138.

Goldiamond, I. Stuttering and fluency as manipulable operant response classes. In L. Krasner & L. P. Ullman (Eds.), *Research in behaviour modification*. New York: Holt, Rinehart & Winston, 1964.

Goldiamond, I. Experimental analysis of stuttering and carry over of fluency outside the laboratory. Paper read at Int. Seminar on Stuttering and Behavior Therapy, Carmel, California, November 1966.

Goldman-Eisler, F. Speech production and the predictability of words in context. *Quart. J. exp. Psychol.*, 1958, **10**, 96–106.

Gray, B. B., & Brutten, E. J. The relationship between anxiety, fatigue and spontaneous recovery in stuttering. *Behav. Res. and Ther.*, 1965, **2**, 251–259.

Harms, M. A., & Malone, J. Y. The relationship of hearing acuity to stammering. *J. Sp. Dis.*, 1939, **4**, 363–370.

Jasper, H. H. A laboratory study of diagnostic indices of bilateral neuromuscular organization in stutterers and normal speakers. *Psychol. Monogr.*, 1932, **43**, 72–174.

Johnson, W. (Ed.) *Stuttering in children and adults*. Univer. Minnesota Press, 1955.

Johnson, W. (Ed.) *The onset of stuttering*. Minneapolis: Univer. Minnesota Press, 1959.

Johnson, W., Darley, F. L., & Spriestersbach, D. C. *Diagnostic methods in speech pathology*. New York: Harper & Row, 1963.

Johnson, W., & Knott, J. Studies in the psychology of stuttering: I. The distribution of moments of stuttering in successive readings of the same material. *J. Sp. Dis.*, 1937, **2**, 17–19.

Johnson, W., & Rosen, L. Studies in the psychology of stuttering: VII. Effect of certain changes in speech pattern upon frequency of stuttering. *J. Sp. Dis.*, 1937, **2**, 105–109.

Jones, H. G. The behavioural treatment of enuresis nocturna. In H. J. Eysenck (Ed.), *Behaviour therapy and the neuroses*. Oxford: Pergamon, 1960. (a)

Jones, H. G. Learning and abnormal behaviour. In H. J. Eysenck (Ed.) *Handbook of abnormal psychology*. London: Pitman, 1960. (b)

Jones, H. G. Continuation of Yates' treatment of a ticqueur. In H. J. Eysenck (Ed.), *Behaviour therapy and the neuroses*. Oxford: Pergamon, 1960. (c)

Jones, H. G. Behavior therapy and stuttering: the need for a multifarious approach to a multiplex problem. Paper read at Int. Seminar on Stuttering and Behavior Therapy, Carmel, California, November 1966.

Jones, R. K. Observations on stammering after localised cerebral injury. *J. Neurol. Neurosurg. Psychiat.*, 1966, **29**, 192–195.

Kimmell, M. Studies in the psychology of stuttering: IX. The nature and effects of stutterers' avoidance reaction. *J. Sp. Dis.*, 1938, **3**, 95–100.

Kondas, O. The treatment of stammering in children by the shadowing method. *Behav. Res. & Therapy.*, 1967, **5**, 325–329.

Krikler, B. Personal communication 1966.

Lee, B. S., Effects of delayed speech feedback. *J. acoust. Soc. Am.*, 1950, **22**, 824–826.

Loutit, C. M., & Halls, E. C. Survey of speech defects. *J. Sp. Hear. Dis.*, 1936, **1**, 73.

Luria, A. R. *The role of speech in the regulation of normal and abnormal behaviour*. Oxford: Pergamon, 1961.

Maclaren, J. The treatment of stammering by the Cherry-Sayers method: clinical impression. In H. J. Eysenck (Ed.) *Behaviour therapy and the neuroses*. Oxford: Pergamon, 1960.

Maclaren, J. The treatment of stammering by shadowing. London: College of Speech Therapists, 1963.

Maher, B. A. The application of the approach-avoidance conflict model to social behavior. *Conflict resolution*, 1964, **8**, 287–291.
Martin, R. R., & Siegel, G. M. The effects of response contingent shock on stuttering. *J. Sp. Hear. Res.*, 1966a, **9**, 340–352.
Martin, R. R., & Siegel, G. M. The effects of simultaneously punishing stuttering and rewarding fluency. *J. Sp. Hear. Res.*, 1966b, **9**, 466–475.
Meyer, V., & Mair, J. M. M. A new technique to control stammering: a preliminary report. *Behav. Res. and Ther.*, 1963, **1**, 251–254.
Mowrer, O. H., & Mowrer, W. M. Enuresis: a method for its study and treatment. *Amer. J. Orthopsychiat.*, 1938, **8**, 436–459.
Mysak, E. D. *Speech pathology and feedback theory*. Springfield, Ill.: C. C. Thomas, 1966.
Neeley, J. N. A study of the speech behaviour of stutterers and nonstutterers under normal and delayed auditory feedback. *J. Sp. Hear. Dis*. Monogr. Suppl., No 7, June 1961, 63–82
Osgood, C. E. *Method and theory in experimental psychology*. New York: Oxford Univer. Press, 1953.
Peins, M. Adaptation effect and spontaneous recovery in stuttering expectancy. *J. Sp. Hear. Res.*, 1961, **4**, 91–99.
Quarrington, B., & Douglass, E. Audibility avoidance in nonvocalized stutterers. *J. Sp. Hear. Dis.*, 1960, **25**, 358–365.
Rheingold, H. L., Gewirtz, J. L., & Ross, H. W. Social conditioning of vocalizations in the infant. *J. comp. physiol. Psychol.*, 1959, **52**, 68–73.
Santostefano, S. Anxiety and hostility. *J. Sp. Hear. Res.*, 1960., **3**, 337–347.
Shames, G. H. Verbal reinforcement in therapy for stuttering. Paper read at Int. Seminar on Stuttering and Behavior Therapy, Carmel, California, November 1966.
Shames, G. H., & Sherrick, C. E., A discussion of nonfluency and stuttering as operant behaviour. *J. Sp. Hear. Dis.*, 1963, **28**, 3–18.
Sheehan, J. G. Theory and treatment of stuttering as an approach-avoidance conflict. *J. Psychol.*, 1953, **36**, 27–49.
Sheehan, J. G. An integration of psychotherapy and speech therapy through a conflict theory of stuttering. *J. Sp. Hear. Dis.*, 1954, **19**, 474–482.
Sheehan, J. G. Conflict theory of stuttering. In J. Eisenson (Ed.) Stuttering: a symposium. New York: Harper, 1958.
Sheehan, J. G. Personal communication. 1966.
Sheehan, J. G., & Martyn, M. M. Spontaneous recovery from stuttering. *J. Sp. Hear. Res.*, 1966, **9**, 121–135.
Sheehan, J. G., & Zelen, S. L. Level of aspiration in stutterers and nonstutterers. *J. abnorm. soc. Psychol.*, 1955, **51**, 83–86.
Shoemaker, D. A two-factor approach to the problem of stuttering. Paper read at Int. Seminar on Stuttering and Behavior Therapy, Carmel, California, November 1966.
Siegel, G. M., & Martin, R. R. Experimental modification of disfluency in normal speakers. *J. Sp. Hear. Res.*, 1965a, **8**, 236–244.
Siegel, G. M., & Martin, R. R. Verbal punishment of disfluencies in normal speakers. *J. Sp. Hear. Res.*, 1965b, **8**, 245–251.
Siegel, C. M., & Martin, R. R. Punishment of disfluencies in normal speakers. *J. Sp. Hear. Res.*, 1966, **9**, 208–217.
Skinner, B. F. *Verbal behavior*. New York: Appleton-Century-Crofts, 1957.
Staats, A. W., & Staats, C. K. A comparison of the development of speech and reading behaviour with implications for research. *Child Developm.*, 1962, **33**, 831–846.
Staats, A. W., Staats, C. K., & Crawford, H. L. First-order conditioning of meaning and the parallel conditioning of a G.S.R. *J. Gen. Psychol.*, 1962, **67**, 159–167.
Sutton, S., & Chase, R. A., White noise and stuttering. *J. Sp. Hear. Res.*, 1961, **4**, 72.
Tate, M. W., & Cullinan, W. L. Measurement of consistency of stuttering. *J. Sp. Hear. Res.*, 1962, **5**, 272–283.

Van Riper, C. Experiments in stuttering therapy. In J. Eisenson (Ed.), *Stuttering: a symposium*. New York: Harper, 1958.

Van Riper, C. *Speech correction: principles and methods*. 4th ed. Englewood Cliffs, N.J.: Prentice-Hall, 1963.

Wada, J., & Rasmussen, T. Intra-carotid injection of sodium amytal for the lateralization of cerebral speech dominance. Experimental and clinical observations. *J. Neurosurg.*, 1960, **17**, 266–282.

Wingate, M. E. Calling attention to stuttering *J. Sp. Hear. Res.*, 1959, **2**, 326–335.

Wischner, G. J. Stuttering behaviour and learning: a preliminary theoretical formulation. *J. Sp. Hear. Dis.*, 1950, **15**, 324–335.

Wischner, G. J. An experimental approach to expectancy and anxiety in stuttering behaviour. *J. Sp. Hear. Dis.*, 1952, **17**, 139–154.

Wolpe, J. *Psychotherapy by reciprocal inhibition.* Stanford Univer. Press, 1958.

Yates, A. J. Recent empirical and theoretical approaches to the experimental manipulation of speech in normal subjects and in stammerers. *Behav. Res. and Ther.*, 1963, **1**, 95–119.

Zhinkin, N. I. Personal communication. 1966.

Chapter 14

Thumbsucking

P. O. DAVIDSON

Sucking movements are one of the first forms of specific behavior to appear in the infant (Lubit & Lubit, 1948). Odor, taste, and temperature variations stimulate the sucking reflex in the newborn (Kelston, 1949), and this sucking reaction also occurs if muscle groups such as buccinator or tongue are stimulated (Barber, 1960). However, after the first week of life the sucking reaction is specific and occurs primarily to stimulation of lips or tongue.

During the first twenty-six weeks of life, sucking is a prime activity with the infant, averaging about two hours of sucking daily (Barber, 1960). Sucking activity appears to reach its maximum intensity at about the seventeenth week (Kelston, 1949).

From the second to the seventeenth week of age the most common position for the infant's arms is such that the hands rest between the waist and the top of the head (Herring, 1932); consequently, the fingers and thumbs often come into extensive contact with the mouth. It is not surprising, therefore, that the convenient shape of the thumb, on stimulating the lips, often results in thumbsucking.

Nonnutritive sucking of one form or another occurs in the infants of many orders of mammals (cf. Levy, 1934; Lawes, 1950; Ross, 1951; Smith, 1960). Digital sucking occurs in most primate infants (Benjamin, 1961), and the thumb is the preferred digit in rhesus monkey infants (Benjamin, 1962a) and in human infants (Sweet, 1948).[1]

INCIDENCE

There are relatively few studies reporting the frequency of nonnutritive sucking in children. An extensive amount of nonnutritive sucking was found by Brazelton (1956) to occur in 87 percent of 70 healthy babies. Klackenberg (1949) found that about 50 percent of 259 infants indulged in extensive nonnutritive sucking. Humphreys and Leighton (1950) reported that 58 percent of 1000 children showed extensive nonnutritive sucking activity of one kind or another.

Although most infants place their thumbs and fingers in their mouths and occasionally thumbsuck, this behavior often disappears by the time the child is twelve to eighteen months of age. Nevertheless, a considerable percentage of children beyond this age continue thumbsucking as a habit. Investigations of this habitual thumbsucking have reported incidences ranging from 17 percent to 46 percent, as shown in Table 14.1. Differences in the ages of the children examined (often not specifically noted) could account for this range in the incidences reported. In the Traisman and Traisman (1958) study, 75 percent of the infants who

---

[1] For this reason, only the term "thumbsucking" will be used in this chapter, although it will always mean "finger or thumbsucking."

Table 14.1 Reported Incidence of Habitual Thumbsucking

Author	Year	Country	No. of Children	Percent with Habit
Levy	1928	U.S.A.	112	25.0
Bliss	1945	New Zealand	500	17.0
Honzik	1948	U.S.A.	—	28.0
Humphreys[a] & Leighton	1950	England	1000	27.5
Sillman[b]	1951	U.S.A.	60	33.3
Bar-Yosef	1954	Israel	2500	44.2
Gardner	1956	England	1000	27.2
Traisman[c] & Traisman	1958	U.S.A.	2650	45.6
Schmidt	1960	U.S.A.	—	17.0

[a] 500 of sample had normal occlusion; 500 of sample had Class II malocclusion.
[b] Based on a private dental practice.
[c] Based on a pediatrics practice.

sucked their thumb began to do so within the first three months of age, while the remaining 25 percent did so within a year. The average age of quitting was 3.8 years although the distribution was highly skewed (some still thumbsucking at age 16). Oxar (1956) found that 5 percent of 1972 children examined at age four were actively sucking their thumbs, and Klackenberg (1949) reported that 14 percent of 259 four-year-olds seen in a Stockholm city health center were chronic thumbsuckers. Lapouse and Monk (1962) report that 2 percent of 482 school children aged 6 to 12 years were sucking their thumbs "almost all of the time." Out of a total of 173 children who were thumbsuckers, Johnson (1939) found that 24 percent quit by age one, and an additional 60 percent by age three, but 10 percent continued thumbsucking beyond age 10 years.

Reports of sex differences in the incidence of thumbsucking are conflicting. Traisman and Traisman (1958) found no differences in incidence between male and female children. Honzik (1948), Honzik and McKee (1962), and Heinstein (1963) report a higher incidence for females, although Gesell and Ilg (1937), and Kunst (1948) report a higher incidence for males. Smith (1960) and Benjamin (1961), observing infant rhesus monkeys, also report a higher incidence of thumbsucking for males.

ETIOLOGY

Speculation on the causes of nonnutritive sucking have been plentiful (cf. Freud, 1938; Ribble, 1944; Kaplan, 1950), but experimental studies have been few and contradictory.

Thumbsucking apparently increases under conditions of fatigue, sleep, boredom (Palermo, 1956), decreased motor activity (Benjamin & Mason, 1963), and time since last being fed (Levy, 1934; Kunst, 1948) Benjamin & Mason, 1963). It appears related to teething (Kunst, 1948) and to emotionally disturbing stimuli (Benjamin, 1962a), but not to cholic (Traisman & Traisman, 1958). Greater frequency of thumbsucking in children weaned late was found by Sears and Wise (1950) and Bernstein (1955), but not by Levy (1928), Roberts (1944), Yarrow (1954), or Mujamoto (1958). Breast feeding was found related to increased thumbsucking by Heinstein (1963), but not by Davis, by Sears, Miller, and Broadbeck (1948), by Traisman and Traisman (1958), or by Porter (1964).

Many of these contradictory experimental results relate to the theoretical controversy of whether the infantile oral-drive is inborn or acquired. According to the innate oral-drive theory, first investigated by Levy (1934), too little opportunity for nutritive sucking in early infancy results in a displacement of sucking energy in the form of nonnutritive sucking. This theory predicts increased thumbsucking would accompany decreased feeding time. The opposing view, put forward by Davis et al. (1948) and Palermo (1956), holds that the association of sucking with food reinforcement results in an oral drive that is, at least, in part acquired. This theory, viewing thumbsucking as a secondary goal response, predicts that increased thumbsucking would accompany increased early nutritive sucking (that is, increased feeding time). Experimental results that support the prediction from the innate oral-drive theory have been reported by Levy (1934), Roberts (1944), Lawes (1950), Ross (1951), Yarrow (1954), and Fleischl (1957). Experimental results that support the prediction from the acquired oral-drive theory have been found by Davis et al. (1948), Brodbeck (1950), Blau and Blau (1955), Traisman and Traisman (1958), Smith (1960), and Porter (1964). It has been suggested that the contradictory results of studies prior to 1957 may have been because of many methodological shortcomings (Ross, Fisher, & King, 1957). The more recent and carefully designed research by Benjamin (1961, 1962a, 1962b) clearly supported the acquired oral-drive theory (for rhesus monkeys, at least).

One of the few consistent etiological findings appears to be that the use of pacifiers reduces the incidence of chronic thumbsucking (cf. Bakwin, 1948; Klackenberg, 1949; Rittlemyer, 1955; Traisman & Traisman, 1958). Haryett (1967), in comparing 146 chronic thumbsucking children with carefully matched controls, found that the use of pacifiers was the only replicable difference on hundreds of variables between the two groups. Specifically, it was found that the nonthumbsucking children had used a pacifier consistently more than the thumbsuckers.

EFFECTS OF THUMBSUCKING

Psychological Effects

Palermo (1956), in reviewing social attitudes toward thumbsucking, noted several interesting changes which have occurred during the past century. Toward the end of the nineteenth century, the habitual thumbsucking baby was often looked on as being a happy baby. Three factors emerged at the turn of the century to produce an almost complete change in parental attitudes toward thumbsucking. First, there was the rise of modern medicine and the discovery of the germ. Protecting babies against germs became a major parental concern to the extent that many parents believed that nothing should enter the child's mouth that wasn't first boiled. Since it was obvious that the child's thumb couldn't be boiled, it seemed equally obvious that it should never be permitted to enter the mouth.

The second factor that resulted in a changed attitude toward thumbsucking was an increased concern by dentists about harmful effects to the jaws, palate, and the occlusion of the teeth (to be discussed separately later).

The third and final blow to the old viewpoint came with the rise in popularity of Freudian theory. Freud viewed thumbsucking as an infantile sexual response (cf. Freud, 1938) and, since open expression of sexual impulses was taboo in our culture, the child obviously should not be permitted to suck his thumb. Numerous theories derived from Freudian theory made the sins of thumbsucking quite explicit. It was suggested that the child who sucked his thumb was under emotional stress; he was bottle- not breast-fed; he was not getting enough sucking experience; he was weaned improperly, etc.; in any case, he was obviously not being raised by the parents in a proper psychological fashion.

In the 1940's and 1950's there was again a shift in attitudes concerning chronic thumbsucking. Thumbsucking had been discounted in the medical profession as a serious source of germ entry. The dental problems were generally ignored or thought to be exaggerated, and psychoanalytic ideas were being placed in a more realistic perspective. Furthermore, increasing numbers of pediatricians began to entertain the idea that the anxieties of the parents, induced by the child's thumbsucking habit, were far more deleterious to the child than the habit itself. Thumbsucking was viewed more and more as normal behavior in young children that should best be ignored, and there was a growing belief that trying to stop the habit was more dangerous to the child's well-being than permitting it to continue. If the thumbsucking did continue beyond infancy into the school age, then it was thought to be an anxiety-reducing response, symptomatic of some underlying disturbance—probably in child-parent relationships (cf. Barnett, 1956).

These divergent viewpoints on the psylogical effects of thumbsucking arose, were accepted, or rejected, with little reference to any empirical studies. The occasional case history was invoked to "clearly demonstrate" a particular viewpoint, but the rationale for most of these conclusions rested firmly on dogma rather than on data. This is not surprising since there are very few controlled experiments reported in this area. Such experiments have generally found no important psychological differences between thumbsucking children and normal controls. Gesell and Ilg (1937) report, for example, that the thumbsuckers are better sleepers, more active, and more content to play alone. Traisman and Traisman (1958) found no relation between thumbsucking and "psychological problems." Honzik (1948), in comparing two groups of children, followed from 21 months to 18 years, found that thumbsucking related to good marital harmony of the parents and a close bond between the mother and the child. Davidson and Haryett (1967) were unable to find any consistent psychological abnormalities in thumbsucking children aged 6 to 12 years by using a battery of tests of personality and adjustment. Haryett (1967) found no replicable differences in parental child-rearing practices, parent-child relationships, or emotional stability of the child, after comparing 146 thumbsucking children with matched controls. Differing results were reported by Mujamoto (1958) in a study of 39 thumbsucking children and 29 controls from grades one to six. He found the thumbsucking group to display more emotional instability, low frustration tolerance, and unsociability. It is not known to what extent these contrary findings of Mujamoto's could be a result of cultural differences between Japanese and North American children.

One of the most extensive studies on the psychological effects of thumbsucking was an 18-year longitudinal study of 47 boys and 47 girls conducted by Heinstein (1963). This study reported that thumbsucking was unrelated to disturbed emotional development and to troubled mother-child relationships. Furthermore, thumbsucking was negatively related to other behavior problems. Girls and boys who, as preschoolers, sucked their thumbs were less likely than others to have additional behavior problems.

It has often been observed, however, that children who suck their thumbs have concomitant behavior patterns which may or may not be considered problematic (these patterns include playing with a favorite blanket [cf. Schulz, 1960], hair, other parts of the body, or bedclothing). Haryett, Hansen, and Davidson (1967) found that 48 percent of their group of 65 thumbsucking children had such associated habits.

Dental Effects

The effects of thumbsucking on a child's teeth are more readily observable than the effects upon his "psyche" and, consequently, much better documented. However, the interpretation of this documentation has resulted in many controversies and disagreements.

The dental studies generally agree that thumbsucking and related habits *can* cause some dental problems. The disagreements relate to the incidence, seriousness, necessary antecedent conditions, and long range effects of thumbsucking as a cause of malocclusion. If one were to merely report a box score of the considerable number of dental studies of thumbsucking,[2] indicating which ones reported serious dental problems and which ones did not, the final tally would be close enough to make it easy for anybody to interpret the results as supporting their particular prejudices or theories. Most authors who wrote before 1950 availed themselves of this opportunity.

One of the problems in this controversy, as Benjamin (1962a) noted, was that the descriptions of thumbsucking have been far less adequate than the descriptions of malocclusion. Investigators usually cannot determine accurately how much any individual sucks his thumb in comparison with other individuals and, as Graber (1958) has shown, the extent of malocclusion depends to a large extent on the duration, frequency, and intensity of the thumbsucking habit.

Clinically, it has certainly been observed

[2]Borland, Sosnow, Kegeles, and Mims (1962) have abstracted over 600 references on studies related to psychology in dentistry, including 87 studies on oral habits (thumbsucking, fingersucking, etc.).

Table 14.2 Prevalence of Malocclusion in Children Who Suck Their Thumbs

Author	Description of Sample of Thumbsucking Children	Number	Percent with Malocclusion
Lewis (1930)	Ages 3 to 5 years	30	80
Kjellgren (1938)	School age	167	87
Johnson (1939)	Ages 2 to 14 years	153	48
Traisman & Traisman (1958)	Majority under age 4	1208	10
Gardner (1956)	Ages 5 to 15 years	275	51

that many children who are persistent thumbsuckers do have dental malocclusions. There are, however, enough cases of thumbsucking with no malocclusion and cases of malocclusion without thumbsucking to lead some writers to conclude that the two are relatively independent. Table 14.2 shows the results of some of the studies that report relationships between thumbsucking and malocclusion.

The large differences in results shown in Table 14.2 may again be the result of age differences in the samples. The Traisman and Traisman (1958) study reporting low percent malocclusion appears to have used younger subjects than did the other four studies. If we considered only this study, it would be easy to conclude that thumbsucking is not a cause of malocclusion. On the other hand, it would appear from studies such a Kjellgren's (1938) that, in school age children, thumbsucking is highly likely to result in malocclusion.

The definite relationship between chronic thumbsucking and malocclusion is much more evident when we look at large samples of children who have malocclusions and calculate the percentage of cases where the malocclusion was thought to result from a thumbsucking habit. Several of these studies are given in Table 14.3.

With the exception of Johnson's (1939) older study that used very young children, all the other results are in surprisingly close agreement. These studies clearly suggest that a large percentage of malocclusions in many children can be traced to a thumbsucking habit.

It appears, therefore, that thumbsucking may or may not produce malocclusions (depending, perhaps, on the number of years of thumbsucking), but that a significant percentage of malocclusions may be produced by thumbsucking. Most of the studies that minimize the seriousness of thumbsucking as a cause of malocclusion have examined

Table 14.3 Prevalence of Thumbsucking as an Etiological Factor in Children Having Malocclusions

Author	Description of Sample of Children Having Malocclusions	Number	Percent Thought to be because of Thumbsucking Habits
Johnson (1939)	Mostly under 3	989	17
Bar-Yosef (1954)	Ages 6 to 16 years	1840	60
Gorelick (1954)	Ages 2 to 5 years	47	60
Traisman & Traisman (1958)	Ages 1 to 16 years	211	55
Popovich (1956)	Ages 3 to 12 years	689	52
Nord (1962)	School age	15,000	60

children under the age of five years. Most of the studies that emphasize the serious dental effects of thumbsucking have examined children over the age of five years.

Findings by Sillman (1951a, 1951b) are an often quoted exception to this general rule. He suggested, on the basis of clinical observation, that thumbsucking affected the oral structure of children with poor bite, but had little effect on good bite. Benjamin (1962a, 1962b), in a series of carefully controlled experiments, disputes Sillman's conclusions. She found that, although genetic predisposition is indeed an important variable determining later malocclusion, the cumulative effects of thumbsucking on malocclusion produced marked increases with the passage of time—even after partialing out the effects of any genetic predisposition.

The specific effects that thumbsucking can have on dental structure have been described by Ruttle, Quigley, Crouch, and Ewan (1953) who studied the effects of prolonged finger and thumbsucking habits in 36 children, compared with a nonhabit control group of the same age. They reported that thumbsucking produces elongation of the anterior segment of the maxillary arch (seen in Figure 14.3), producing spacing, labial inclination, and protrusion of the maxillary incisor, with shallow and open-bite relationships of the anterior teeth. In addition, true and apparent overjet were increased strongly by the thumbsucking habit. Figure 14.1 shows an example of an open bite in a thumbsucking child. Haryett et al. (1967) describe the specific effects as follows.

> "The type of malocclusion associated with thumb and finger sucking is dependent upon the position of the thumb or fingers, the duration, intensity and frequency of the habit and the associated muscle contractions of the lips and cheeks. Pressure from the thumb causes protrusion of the maxillary anterior teeth. The crow bar effect of the thumb contributes to a flattening of the mandibular incisor segment which in turn causes mild crowding. As a result, shallow and open-bite relationships of the anterior teeth are developed. The maxillary lip is held out by the protruding incisors and becomes hypotonic. The mandibular lip may become positioned behind the maxillary incisors. In this manner, the malocclusion becomes stabilized. The strength of the cheek muscles during sucking produces contraction of the maxillary arch which becomes more tapered toward the front of the mouth. In some cases, the maxillary contraction may be so severe that tooth interferences occur in the molar regions. Compensatory lateral mandibular displacements often become necessary for chewing, and facial asymmetries may develop."

Other effects of thumbsucking, noted by Sweet (1948), include diminution of the important gag reflex; mouth breathing, which in turn leads to underdevelopment of nose and upper lip; facial asymmetry; incompetent lip posture; and frequently, callouses on the thumb. It is not surprising that Sweet decries parental indifference to continued thumbsucking in children of school age. Levitt (1948) points out that the aesthetic, oral, and facial disfigurement which he has found can be produced by thumbsucking may result in psychological disturbances that are overlooked by parents and psychologists who discount the seriousness of the thumbsucking habit in older children.

The anterior open-bite produced by chronic thumbsucking can itself have several undesirable effects. Klein (1952) found that this malocclusion of the incisor teeth encourages abnormal habits of the lips and tongue and of breathing and swallowing. Straub (1960, 1961) argues that the most serious of these habits is tongue thrusting into the gap created by the anterior open-bite (see Figure 14.2). Haryett et al. (1967) found that tongue thrusting through the open-bite during swallowing occurred in 88 percent of their thumbsucking sample. Since the tongue can be forcibly thrust into the open gap several hundred times a day in the act of swallowing, tongue thrusting can stabilize or even exaggerate the malocclusion originally initiated by thumbsucking. Some recent studies (cf. Marge, 1965; Harrington & Breinholt, 1963) have indicated that the tongue thrust associated with the open-bite of thumbsucking in children over the age of 5 or 6 can be a significant factor in articulatory problems in speech.

Most dentists would agree that there is likely to be little permanent damage to the dentition provided that thumbsucking (and associated habits such as tongue thrusting) cease prior to four years of age (cf. Mack, 1951; Schmidt, 1960; Capouya, 1959). Some authors prefer to set this limit at five or six

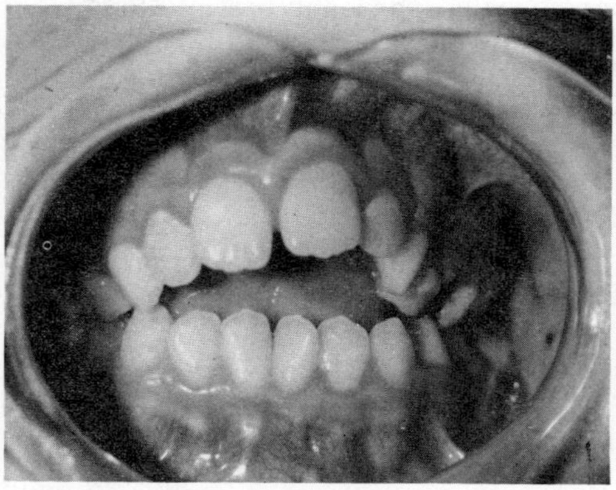

Figure 14.1 An anterior view of occlusion showing a typical open bite.

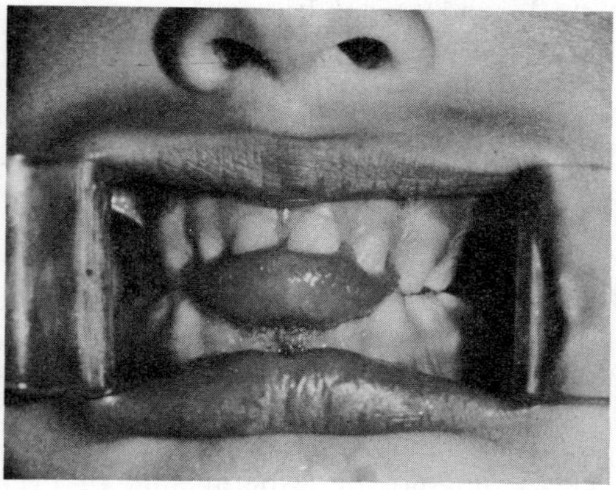

Figure 14.2 An anterior view of occlusion showing a tongue thrust during swallowing.

years of age (Hagen, 1956; Kugelmass, 1952) or at the time of eruption of the child's permanent anterior teeth (Haralambakis, 1957; Lencher, 1950). If the habit persists beyond this time, there is increasing likelihood of harmful effects. Most malocclusions caused by oral habits will generally be self-correcting, providing the faulty oral habit is discontinued at an early enough age. Hughes (1949), however, estimates that about 16 percent of thumbsucking cases develop a malocclusion so pronounced and so little inclined to self-correction that orthodontic treatment is necessary if the distortion is to be remedied.

TREATMENT

The major problem with modification of most symptoms of psychopathology is to find a method that is more effective than the base rate of spontaneous remission. The major problem with thumbsucking is not to *find* an effective treatment method, since one appears to exist, but *whether to use it*. This controversy has resulted largely from the changing social attitudes toward thumbsucking (discussed previously). Two of the currently popular attitudes toward thumbsucking both imply that trying to stop the habit could be damaging to the child.

If thumbsucking is seen as normal and harmless, then the parents may not only be frustrated in their attempts to stop the habit, but by focusing attention on it, they, perhaps, actually prolong it (cf. Ilg & Ames, 1955). Furthermore, the stresses produced by these attempts may strain relationships between parent and child and create new problems where previously none existed. By implication this view holds that the only problem with thumbsucking is needless parental overconcern. An objection that can be raised against this viewpoint is that it fails to take into account the age of the child. Although the preponderance of evidence and opinion agree that thumbsucking need not cause serious dental or psychological problems in infants and children to the age of three or four years, there is no such consensus concerning children five years and older. Dentists, for example, are by no means convinced that thumbsucking continued beyond age four or five years can be considered "harmless" without first checking for malocclusions of the child's teeth.

Even if the dentist finds serious malocclusions, however, he is constrained from interfering with the thumbsucking by another popular and prevalent belief. This viewpoint, based largely on psychoanalytic theory, sees thumbsucking as an anxiety reducing means of gratification for young children (cf. Pearson, 1948). If the child continues to suck his thumb beyond the usual age for quitting, then it could be viewed as a symptom of some sort of underlying emotional disturbance. (This opinion is at variance with what little experimental evidence is available—as discussed earlier.) To prevent the child from sucking his thumb would result, according to advocates of this viewpoint, in severe emotional repercussions (Every, 1948) such as night terrors and enuresis (Korner & Reider, 1955), emotional instability (Barnett, 1956), stuttering, masturbation, antisocial trends (cf. Schmidt,

1960), and sexual frigidity in later years (Pearson, 1948). These warnings are condensed into statements such as: "Is not malocclusion of the personality more serious than malocclusion of the teeth" (Weiss & English, 1957); or "Is it better to tolerate an unruly thumb than to develop a frustrated child. The cure may be worse than the habit" (Veeder & Pollock, 1952). Most of these dangers, unfortunately, appear in the dental journals as established psychological knowledge when, in fact, they are based upon unsubstantiated opinion or clinical inferences and not on experimental or even observable evidence (cf. Bakwin & Bakwin, 1938; Gandler, 1952; Barber, 1960).

Many will no doubt notice that this viewpoint represents one side of the current general controversy on "symptom substitution." The theoretical aspects of this controversy are beyond the scope of this chapter (see Chapter 10), but vis-à-vis thumbsucking this controversy reduces into a continuing argument of whether chronic thumbsucking in older children should be viewed as a symptom of an underlying emotional disturbance or merely as a learned habit—a conditioned reaction in Eysenck's (1960) terms (cf. Davidson & Haryett, 1967).

Although the available data do not support the view that thumbsucking children are more emotionally disturbed than controls, those who hold to this belief typically recommend that thumbsucking children be treated, if at all, by pediatricians (cf. Hagen, 1956) or by psychiatrists (cf. Levin, 1958) and not by dentists. The thumbsucking itself is usually ignored, and the attention focused on parent-child relations, parental attitudes, or unconscious anxieties in the child. In addition to recommending the use of psychotherapy (cf. Barnett, 1956), other methods, including hypnosis (Heron, 1954), suggestion (Stolzenberg, 1962), autosuggestion (Boyens, 1940), and psychoanalysis (Bonnard, 1960), have all been advocated. Starr (1956) has pointed out that these recommendations notwithstanding, psychiatric treatment of thumbsucking children is extremely difficult after five years of age.

There is no adequate experimental evidence available to assess the value of any of these treatment methods. This lack of evidence is not surprising since most proponents of these treatments also tend to see thumbsucking as, in itself, not a serious problem and one that is probably best left alone. Consequently, these treatments are not only seldom validated, but they are, in fact, seldom used.

The viewpoint that thumbsucking is a simple, learned habit (Palermo, 1956) has led to quite a different treatment approach. Direct intervention in the form of physical restraint or punishment exemplify the type of treatment recommended by proponents of this viewpoint. Many of these methods, which are essentially "home remedies," were designed to prevent thumbsucking in early infancy. Consequently, most of them are of dubious value in preventing thumbsucking in older children where the problem is in greater need of attention. For instance, when Chandler (1878) claimed, that "sleeveless night dresses are the *only* treatment that will work" he was probably not referring to school-age children. Other "home remedies" have included restraining the thumb in mittens, restraining the hand or arm in splints, bandaging the thumb, painting the thumb with bitter-tasting prescriptions, bribery, scolding, threats, physical punishment, etc. Like most home remedies, the effectiveness of any of these treatments has consensual validation, but not experimental validation. Flesher (1956), for example, in an uncontrolled study of 40 cases, found that the use of a bitter-tasting prescription resulted in cessation of thumbsucking within three days for 30 of the cases. He found most success in children aged seven to nine years.

The use of operant reinforcement instead of restraint or punishment has been reported in an interesting study by Baer (1962). He made the presentation of cartoons contingent on nonthumbsucking in a five-year-old boy who typically sucked his thumb while watching television. Although contingent withdrawal and re-presentation of the cartoon effectively controlled the thumbsucking during television viewing, there was little generalization to other situations.

Theoretically, one of the most effective ways to extinguish an undesired habit is to permit the response to occur but remove the reinforcements produced by that response (Eysenck, 1957). Although it is not known definitely what reinforcements are involved in thumbsucking, one method of treatment has evolved which seems to approximate closely this theoretical ideal.

A simple crib-shaped appliance is placed in the roof of the child's mouth (see Figures 14.3 and 14.4). The appliance is cemented onto the teeth and rests passively in the mouth. It is usually left in place for about 12 months (Haryett, 1962). If this palatal crib is properly constructed it serves three purposes. It breaks the suction between the thumb and the roof of the mouth, and it also prevents the thumb from stimulating the palate. The third purpose of the crib is to act as a restraining barrier on the tongue. This helps self-correction of the malocclusion to occur after the thumbsucking has stopped, by preventing the tongue from thrusting into the gap created by the anterior open-bite. The palatal crib imposes no physical restraint on the child, who is able to move his arms and place his thumb in his mouth. With the suction broken, however, the habit appears to be no longer enjoyable or satisfying (Haryett, 1962). A number of studies have found the palatal crib to be a highly effective and harmless method for arresting the thumbsucking habit (cf. Massler & Chopra, 1950; Brandhorst, 1957; Jarabak, 1959; Moyers, 1963). Graber (1963), for example, has successfully treated more than 600 cases by using this method, and has not observed a single case of symptom substitution over a 17-year-period.

Haryett et al. (1967), in a factorial experiment that used 66 subjects, comparing several treatment measures, found the palatal crib to be 100 percent effective, while all other treatment methods had no greater remission rate than the one found for untreated thumbsucking controls (about 10 percent). These groups were followed up for several years (cf. Davidson & Haryett, 1967), and it was found that two out of twenty-two who received cribs had started sucking again after one year. Twenty-three percent of the thumbsucking children who had had their habit arrested by a crib had developed other behaviors or mannerisms one year after treatment. The new behaviors included nailbiting, fondling clothing, etc. However, 36 percent of the thumbsucking children who were still actively sucking one year later had also developed other behaviors (the difference between these two results was not significant). Incidentally, of five cases of increased handling of genitals found on follow-up, none were in the group that received cribs. These results clearly failed to support psychoanalytic warnings about symptom substitution. Actually, it appeared as if forcefully stopping thumbsucking in children aged 4 to 16 years decreased the likelihood of more serious habits developing. Similar findings have been reported by other experimenters who have used cribs to break the thumbsucking habit. Sclare (1951), in a long-term study of 6 cases of thumbsucking corrected with a palatal crib, found that all showed personality improvement after the habit was arrested. Townsend (1951) found that not only were there no harmful effects from the use of a crib to arrest thumbsucking but, in a number of cases, the correction of the habit noticeably stepped up the process of maturation.

The crib itself does not appear to create any psychological problems in the child,

Figure 14.3 An occlusal view of the palatal crib.

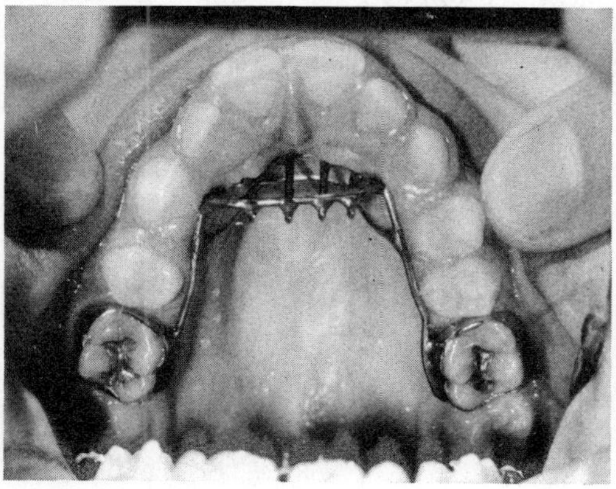

Figure 14.4 An anterior view of the crib after insertion.

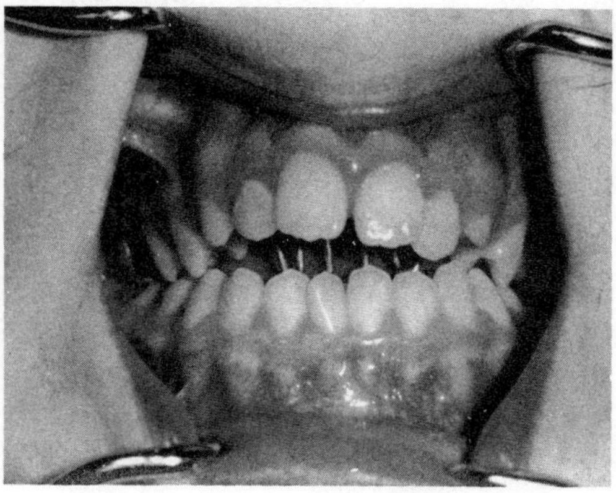

although Ilg and Ames (1955) describe it as a "really horrid looking device . . . with its vicious looking (and probably feeling) prongs . . . Merely looking at a picture of such a device would prevent most tender-minded parents from dreaming of using such a thing" (see Figure 14.3). Many of the early cribs did have sharpened spurs designed to inflict pain when the child sucked his thumb. Haryett, in his studies, has found that the spurs are probably more useful for stopping the tongue thrust rather than the thumbsucking. Cribs without spurs can be almost as effective in stopping thumbsucking (Haryett, 1967).

There appears to be two disadvantages to this kind of treatment for chronic thumbsucking. A temporary period of adjustment to the crib can take from a few days to one or two months. This primarily involves some temporary eating problems and some minor speech problems (lisping), which usually clear up within a week or two. On the other hand, children with speech problems sometimes show improvement after insertion of a crib, perhaps because of the cribbing effect on the tongue (Haryett et al., 1967).

In spite of the considerable number of studies reporting successful use of dental cribs in the treatment of large groups of thumbsucking subjects, it is surprising to find (cf. Gellin, 1964) that the two studies most frequently cited as evidence in the use of dental appliances both gave negative results. Korner and Reider (1955) reported on appliances placed briefly in three children's mouths, and all three continued thumbsucking. Traisman and Traisman (1958) reported successful treatment of only one out of four children. In the other three cases more physiological distress was found after than was seen during thumbsucking. The citation of these uncontrolled studies as evidence against the use of palatal cribs is doubly surprising since Korner and Reider suggest that the only conclusion one should reach from their study is that the cases they observed were too young, and Traisman and Traisman state that their sample is too small to reach any conclusion at all!

SUMMARY

Nonnutritive sucking, often in the form of thumbsucking, is a common occurrence in most infants. There are extreme differences in the frequency and duration of this habit, but most children have discontinued thumbsucking by age three or four years. Thumbsucking in infants and children to age three seems to have no serious psychopathological causes or effects—the best evidence appears to suggest that it is a simple learned habit. The old-fashioned idea that "a thumbsucking *baby* is a happy baby" is not without empirical support. The use of pacifiers in infancy seems to be a successful alternate in preventing chronic thumbsucking.

Thumbsucking in infancy can cause malocclusions of the teeth but, if the habit is discontinued, the malocclusions tend to be self-correcting. Beyond the age of four, and particularly beyond the age of six or eight, the amount of self-correction of malocclusion appears to progressively diminish.

Children beyond age four or five years who are actively or frequently sucking their thumb or fingers should be referred to a dentist (preferably an orthodontist) to assess the degree of malocclusion, if any, and the effects of the habit on that malocclusion, if any. If the thumbsucking is producing or maintaining serious malocclusions at this age, then arguments for arresting the habit merit serious consideration. The most effective method for stopping thumbsucking appears to be the insertion in the child's mouth of a properly constructed palatal crib. Since this is a somewhat expensive treatment, "home remedies" of one kind or another might be tried first (for example, suggestions, bitter-tasting prescriptions applied to the thumbs, etc.). In spite of frequent warnings in the literature, there is no conclusive evidence that abruptly stopping the thumbsucking habit in older children will result in any kind of psychological disturbance, and there is a growing amount of empirical data suggesting that arresting the habit may actually result in improved psychological adjustment.

REFERENCES

Baer, D. M. Laboratory control of thumbsucking by withdrawal and re-presentation of reinforcement. *J. exp. Anal. Behav.*, 1962, **5** (4), 525–528.
Bakwin, H. Thumb and fingersucking in children. *J. Pediat.*, 1948, **32**, 99–101.
Bakwin, R. M., & Bakwin, H. Psychologic care in infancy. *J. Pediat.*, 1938, **12**, 71–90.
Barber, T. K. Management of thumbsucking: A review. *North-West Dent.*, 1960, **39**, 177–181.
Barnett, I. H. Unhealthful oral habits. *Oral Hygiene*, 1956, **46**, 336–337.
Bar-Yosef, G. About the problem of sucking. *Habinuk*, 1954/55, **27**, 447–449.
Benjamin, Lorna S. The effect of bottle and cup feeding on the nonnutritive sucking of the infant rhesus monkey. *J. comp. physiol. Psychol.*, 1961, **54**, 230–237.
Benjamin, Lorna S. Non-nutritive sucking and dental malocclusion in the deciduous and permanent teeth of the rhesus monkey. *Child Developm.*, 1962, **33**, 29–35. (a)
Benjamin, Lorna S. Nonnutritive sucking and the development of malocclusion in the deciduous teeth of the infant rhesus monkey. *Child Developm.*, 1962, **33**, 57–64. (b)
Benjamin, Lorna S., & Mason, W. A. Effect of hunger on non-nutritive sucking in infant rhesus monkeys. *J. abnorm. soc. Psychol.*, 1963, **66**, 526–531.
Bernstein, A. Some relations between techniques of feeding and training during infancy and certain behavior in children. *Genet. psychol. Monogr.*, 1955, **51**, 3–44.
Blau, T. H., & Blau, Lili R. The sucking reflex. The effects of long feeding vs short feeding on the behavior of a human infant. *J. abnorm. soc. Psychol.*, 1955, **51**, 123–125.
Bliss, D. Thumb and fingersucking. *New Zeal. Dent. J.*, 1945, **41**, 103–104.
Bonnard, Augusta. The primal significance of the tongue. *Int. J. Psychoanal.*, 1960, **41**, 301–307.
Borland, L. R., Sosnow, I., Kegeles, S. S., & Mims, M. L. *Psychology in dentistry: Selected references and abstracts*, Public Health Services Publication No. 929. Washington: U.S. Dept. of Health, Education and Welfare, 1962.
Boyens, P. J. Value of autosuggestion in the therapy of bruxism and other biting habits. *J. Amer. Dent. Assoc.*, 1940, **27**, 1773–1777.
Brandhorst, W. S. Thumbsucking and its control. *Fortnightly Rev. Chicago Dent. Soc.*, 1957, **34**, 11–16.
Brazelton, T. B. Sucking in infancy. *Pediatrics*, 1956, **17**, 400–404.
Brodbeck, A. J. The effect of three feeding variables on the nonnutritive sucking of newborn infants. *Amer. Psychol.*, 1950, **5**, 292–293. (Abstract)
Capouya, M. N. A simple appliance for the elimination of thumbsucking. *J. Alabama Dent. Assoc.*, 1959, **43**, 9–11.
Chandler, T. H. Thumbsucking in children as a cause of subsequent irregularity of the teeth. *Dental Cosmos*, **1878**, 565–569.
Davidson, P. O., & Haryett, R. D. Thumbsucking: habit or symptom. *J. Dent. for Child.*, 1967, **33**, 252–259.
Davis, H. V., Sears, R. R., Miller, H. C., & Broadbeck, A. J. Effects of cup, bottle and breast feeding on oral activities of newborn infants. *Pediatrics*, 1948, **2**, 549.
Every, R. G. Problem of the thumbsucker. *Oral Health*, 1948, **38**, 103–106.
Eysenck, H. J. *The dynamics of anxiety and hysteria*. London: Routledge and Kegan Paul, 1957.
Eysenck, H. J. (Ed.) *Behavior therapy and the neuroses*. London: Pergamon Press, 1960.
Fleischl, M. F. The problem of sucking. *Amer. J. Psychother.*, 1957, **1**, 86–87.
Flesher, W. N. Thumbsucking can be corrected. *J. Oklahoma Dent. Assoc.*, 1956, **45**, 12–13.
Freud, S. Three contributions to a theory of sex. In Brill, A. A. (Ed.) *The basic writings of Sigmund Freud*. New York: Random, 1938.
Gandler, A. L. Nature and implications of thumbsucking; a review. *Arch. Pediat.*, 1952, **69**, 291–295.

Gardner, J. H. A survey of malocclusion and some aetiological factors in 1000 Sheffield school children. *Dent. Pract. Dent. Rec.*, 1956, **6**, 187–198.

Gellin, M. E. Management of patients with deleterious habits. *J. Dent. for Child.*, 1964, **31**, 274–283.

Gesell, A., & Ilg, F. L. *Feeding behavior of infants*, Philadelphia: Lippincott, 1937.

Gorelick, L. Thumbsucking in foster children, a comparative study. *N.Y. State Dent. J.*, 1954, **20**, 422.

Graber, T. M. Fingersucking habit and associated problems. *J. Dent. for Child.*, 1958, **25**, 145–151.

Graber, T. M. The "three M's": Muscles, malformation, and malocclusion. *Amer. J. Orthodont.*, 1963, **49**, 418–450.

Hagen, Kathryn. Thumbsucking. *Life and Health*, 1956, **71** (15), 27.

Haralambakis, H. Fingersucking as a cause of dentofacial anomalies. *Dent. Abstr.*, 1957, **2**, 157.

Harrington, R. & Breinholt, V. The relation of oral mechanism malfunction to dental and speech development. *Amer. J. Orthodont.*, 1963, **49**, 84–93.

Haryett, R. D. Malocclusion in public health. *Canad. Dent. Assoc. Journ.*, 1962, **28**, 372–386.

Haryett, R. D. A study of various treatments of thumb and fingersucking and their psychological and dental effects. National Health Grants Report 608–7–69. Ottawa: Department of Public Health, 1967.

Haryett, R. D., Hansen, F. C., & Davidson, P. O. Chronic thumbsucking: The psychological effects and the relative effectiveness of various methods of treatment. *Amer. J. Orthodont.*, 1967, **53** (8), 569–585.

Herring, G. A. A study of thumbsucking in infants from two to seventeen weeks of age. *Child Developm.*, 1932, **3**, 273.

Heinstein, M. I. *Behavioral correlates of breast-bottle regimes under varying parent-patient relationships*. Lafayette, Ind.: Child Development Publications, 1963.

Heron, W. T. Hypnosis and psychology. *North-West Dent.*, 1954, **33**, 215–220.

Honzik, Marjorie P. Biosocial aspects of thumbsucking. *Amer. Psychol.*, 1948, **3**, 351–352. (Abstract).

Honzik, Marjorie P., & McKee, J. P. The sex difference in thumbsucking. *J. Pediat.*, 1962, **61**, 726–732.

Hughes, B. O. The growth of children—psychological and hereditary factors. *Amer. J. Orthodont.*, 1949, **35**, 21–23.

Humphreys, H. F., & Leighton, B. C. Survey of antero-posterior abnormalities of the jaws of children between the ages of 2 and 5½ years of age. *Brit. Dent. J.*, 1950, **88**, 3–17.

Ilg, F., & Ames, L. B. *Child Behavior*. New York: Del Publishing Co., 1955.

Jarabak, J. R. Controlling malocclusion due to sucking habits. *Dental Clinics of North America*, 1959 (July), 364–383.

Johnson, L. R. The status of thumbsucking and fingersucking. *J. Amer. Dent. Assoc.*, 1939, **26**, 1245–1254.

Kaplan, M. A note on the psychological implications of thumbsucking. *J. Pediat.*, 1950, **37**, 555–560.

Kelston, L. Psychology of the sucking habit. *J. New Jersey Dent. Soc.*, 1949, **20**, 16–18.

Kjellgren, B. Fingersigningsvana has born from dental—orthopedisk synpunkt. *Nord. Med.*, 1938, 3.

Klackenberg, G. Thumbsucking: frequency and etiology. *Pediatrics*, 1949, **4**, 418–424.

Klein, E. T. Pressure habits factors in malocclusion. *Amer. J. Orthodont.*, 1952, **38**, 569–587.

Korner, Anneliese, & Reider, N. Psychologic aspects of disruption of thumbsucking by means of a dental appliance. *Angle Orthodontics*, 1955, **25**, 23–31.

Kugelmass, I. N. Pediatric approach to oral habits in children. *J. Dent. for Child.*, 1952, **19**, 166–168.

Kunst, Mary S. A study of thumb and fingersucking in infants. *Psychol. Monogr.*, 1948, **62**, 1–71.

Lapouse, R., & Monk, M. A. Fears and worries in a representative sample of children. *Amer. J. Orthopsychiat.*, 1962, **29**, 803–818.

Lawes, A. G. H. Psychosomatic study into the nature, prevention and treatment of thumbsucking and its relationship to dental deformity. Part I. *Dent. J. Austral.*, 1950, **22**, 167–194.

Lencher, N. H. Thumbsucking habit. *Dental Students' Magazine*, 1950, **28**, 9–12.

Levin, B. J. Chronic thumbsucking in older children. *J. Canad. Dent. Assoc.*, 1958, **24**, 148–150.

Levitt, L. M. Behavior problems of dental significance. *Georgetown Dent. J.*, 1948, **16**, 8–13.

Levy, D. M. Fingersucking and accessory movements in early infancy. An etiologic study. *Amer. J. Dent.*, 1928, **7**, 831–918.

Levy, D. M. Experiments on the sucking reflex and social behavior of dogs. *Amer. J. Orthopsychiat.*, 1934, **4**, 203–224.

Lewis, S. J. Thumbsucking: a cause of malocclusion in the deciduous teeth. *J. Amer. Dent. Assoc.*, 1930, **17**, 1060–1073.

Lubit, E., & Lubit, B. A. Psychological and dental aspects of thumbsucking. *Dent. Items of Interest*, 1948, **70**, 279–281.

Mack, E. S. Dilemma in the management of thumbsucking. *J. Amer. Dent. Assoc.*, 1951, **43**, 33–45.

Marge, M. Speech difficulties associated with dental anomalies in children. *J. Dent. for Child.*, 1965, **32**, 82–89.

Massler, M., & Chopra, B. The palatal crib for correction of oral habits. *J. Dent. for Child.*, 1950, **17**, 1–6.

Moyers, R. E. *Handbook of orthodontics.* (2nd ed.) Chicago: Yearbook Medical Publishers, 1963.

Mujamoto, M. A study of fingersucking in children. *Jap. J. educ. Psychol.*, 1958, **6**, 21–27.

Nord, C. F. L. The reader comments. *J. Amer. Dent. Assoc.*, 1962, **64**, 872–873.

Oxar, C. E. Public relations and the child patient. *J. Florida Dent. Soc.*, 1956, **26**, 10–11.

Palermo, D. S. Thumbsucking: a learned response. *Pediatrics*, 1956, **17**, 392–399.

Pearson, G. H. J. Psychology of fingersucking, tonguesucking and other oral habits. *Amer. J. Orthodont.*, 1948, **34**, 589–598.

Popovich, F. The incidence of sucking habits and its relationship to occlusion in 3-year-old children. Burlington Orthodontic Research Centre. Progress Report Series No. 1. Division of Dental Research, University of Toronto, 1956.

Porter, D. R. Implications and interrelations of oral habits. *J. Dent. for Child.*, 1964, **31**, 164–170.

Ribble, M. A. Infantile experience in relation to personality development. In J. McV. Hunt, (Ed.), *Personality and the behavior disorders*, Vol. II. New York: Ronald Press 1944.

Rittlemyer, L. F. Thumbsucking; a preventable problem. *Gen. Pract.*, 1955, **11**, 66.

Roberts, E. Thumb and fingersucking in relation to feeding in early infancy. *Amer. J. Dis. Child.*, 1944, **68**, 7–8.

Ross, S. Sucking behavior in neonate dogs. *J. abnorm. soc. Psychol.*, 1951, **46**, 142–149.

Ross, S., Fisher, A. E., & King, D. J. Sucking behavior: A review of the literature. *J. genet. Psychol.*, 1957, **91**, 63–81.

Ruttle, A. T., Quigley, W., Crouch, J. T., & Ewan, G. E. A serial study of the effects of fingersucking. *J. Dent. Res.*, 1953, **32**, 739.

Schmidt, D. A. An evaluation of a pernicious dental habit. *Dent. Dig.*, 1960, **66**, 323–326.

Schulz, C. M. *It's a dogs life, Charlie Brown.* New York: Holt Rinehart & Winston, 1960.

Sclare, R. Long arm of coincidence? *Brit. Dent. J.*, 1951, **91**, 60–63.

Sears, R. R., & Wise, G. W. Relation of cup feeding in infancy to thumbsucking and the oral drive. *Amer. J. Orthopsychiat.*, 1950, **20**, 123–138.

Sillman, J. H. Thumbsucking and the dentition: A serial study from birth to 13 years of age. *N.Y. Dent. J.*, 1951, **17**, 493–502. (a)
Sillman, J. H. Thumbsucking and the oral structures. *J. Pediat.*, 1951, **39**, 424–430. (b)
Smith, Lorna J. The nonnutritive sucking behavior of the infant rhesus monkey. Unpublished doctoral dissertation, University of Wisconsin, 1960.
Starr, P. H. Psychiatric aspects of thumbsucking as it related to dental malocclusion. *Washington Univer. Dent. J.*, 1956, **22**, 4–11.
Stolzenberg, J. Controlled suggestion in speech problems and tongue thrusting. *Amer. J. Orthodont.*, 1962, **48**, 604–608.
Straub, W. J. Malfunction of the tongue: Part 1. *Amer. J. Orthodont.*, 1960, **46**, 404–424.
Straub, W. J. Malfunction of the tongue: Part II. The abnormal swallowing habit: its cause, effects and results in relation to orthodontic treatment. *Amer. J. Orthodont.*, 1961, **47**, 596–617.
Sweet, C. A. Thumb and fingersucking in children. *Amer. J. Orthodont.*, 1948, **38**, 1017–1018.
Townsend, B. R. Critics corner. *Dent. Practitioner & Dent. Rec.*, 1951, **1**, 354–355.
Traisman, A. S., & Traisman, H. S. Thumb and fingersucking: A study of 2650 infants and children. *J. Pediat.*, 1958, **52**, 566–572.
Veeder C. L., & Pollock, N. Thumbsucking paradox. *Amer. J. Orthodont.*, 1952, **38**, 103.
Weiss, E. D., & English, O. S. *Psychosomatic medicine*. (3rd ed.) Philadelphia: W. B. Saunders Co., 1957.
Yarrow, L. J. The relationship between nutritive sucking experiences in infancy and non-nutritive sucking in childhood. *J. genet. Psychol.*, 1954, **84**, 149–162.

Chapter 15

Enuresis

S. H. LOVIBOND AND M. A. COOTE

INTRODUCTION

Nocturnal enuresis is conventionally defined as the involuntary discharge of urine during sleep after the age of 3 to 4 years in the absence of demonstrable organic pathology. It should be emphasized that any definition necessarily involves a number of arbitrary features. First, the incidence of bed-wetting in the general population declines almost exponentially from the first year to reach an apparent asymptote in adulthood. Second, the pattern of bed-wetting is highly variable, some children wetting the bed regularly several times a night, and others wetting only infrequently or in sporadic bursts. Third, the age at which children are expected to become dry at night shows considerable variation between communities and between social classes within communities.

Despite problems of definition, it is clear from recent surveys (for example, Bransby, Blomfield, & Douglas, 1955) that, at the age of 4 to 5 years, approximately 20 percent of all children in highly developed societies are still wetting the bed with sufficient frequency to constitute a management problem. By the age of 14 years the proportion of bed-wetters has fallen to about 2 to 3 percent. Thus it is clear that the great majority of enuretics will become continent before the age of 14 years in the absence of specific treatment. Nevertheless, the burden of dealing with soiled linen, and the psychological effects of enuresis on both the child and the parent, are such as to create a widespread interest in the etiology of the condition, as well as a considerable demand for an effective method of treatment.

In addition to drawing a distinction between regular and intermittent bed-wetters, it is usual to distinguish between primary enuresis (where the child has never become continent) and secondary enuresis (where the child resumes bed-wetting after a period of continence). There is as yet no compelling evidence that either of these distinctions is of prognostic significance. Evidence to be presented later suggests that the most important distinction which can be made is the one between nocturnal enuresis in the absence of other micturitional difficulties, and nocturnal enuresis accompanied by diurnal frequency and urgency.

THEORIES OF ENURESIS

The many differing conceptions of the nature and etiology of enuresis have been reviewed in an earlier publication (Lovibond, 1964) and only the main types of theory will be outlined briefly here. Theories of enuresis may be divided into two major categories: (a) psychodynamic theories, and (b) physiological/behavioristic theories.

Psychodynamic Theories

In psychodynamic theories, enuresis is regarded as a surface indicator or symptom of some underlying emotional disturbance of a general character. The etiology of enuresis, therefore, is to be sought in conditions that give rise to psychological conflict or stress. Psychodynamic theories have a number of clear implications. First, not only must psychotherapy be the treatment of choice, but any direct attack on the enuresis itself is likely to lead to consequences such as substitution of another symptom or exacerbation of anxiety. Second, a representative sample of enuretics should evidence a substantially greater degree of maladjustment than a matched group of nonenuretics.

Physiological/Behavioristic Theories

The essence of physiological/behavioristic theories of enuresis is that the disorder is conceived not as a symptom of emotional disturbance, but as a failure to develop adequate cortical control over subcortical reflex mechanisms. Cortical control is considered as involving both neural maturation and the development of complex sequences of conditioned reflexes. Individual theories differ chiefly in the degree to which maturation or conditioning is emphasized. In general, theorists with a medical background tend to stress neural maturation, whereas psychologists with an experimental bias tend to stress the role of conditioning. Enuresis is thus regarded as primarily a deficiency of neural maturation or a habit deficiency. Possible etiological factors include anomalies of neural development, the absence of environmental conditions necessary for the required learning of micturitional control, low levels of conditionability, and the presence of conditions ordinarily inimical to efficient learning of complex skills (for example, high levels of anxiety or nervous tension). An implication of physiological/behavioristic theories of enuresis is that the majority of enuretics should differ little from nonenuretics in general psychological adjustment. In some enuretics, secondary maladjustment may occur as a consequence of the negative social evaluation of bed-wetting, but this type of maladjustment would be expected to disappear following successful treatment. Another implication of physiological/behavioristic theories is that the only treatment of enuresis likely to be generally successful is some form of direct training, such as the conditioning therapy of Mowrer and Mowrer (1938) or the bladder-tolerance training of Muellner (1958, 1960) and Vincent (1964).

In general, recent evidence is overwhelmingly in favor of physiological/behavioristic theories, and against psychodynamic theories. Studies to be reviewed later indicate that there is little evidence of the efficacy of psychotherapy in the treatment of enuresis, whereas conditioning treatment has been shown to be highly effective. On the other hand, not only is there no evidence that symptom substitution follows the elimination of bed-wetting by conditioning methods, but the personality changes noted after successful conditioning treatment are almost invariably positive (Davidson & Douglass, 1950; Freyman, 1963; Geppert, 1953; Gillison & Skinner, 1958). Studies of personality change that involve before and after treatment measures have led to similar conclusions (Baller & Schalock, 1956; Behrle, Elkin, & Laybourne, 1956; Lovibond, 1964).

Comparative studies of the personalities of enuretics and of nonenuretics (for example, Lickorish, 1964; Lovibond, 1964) also support physiological/behavioristic theories rather than psychodynamic theories. These studies suggest that, although enuresis may sometimes occur as part of a complex of behavioral disturbances, the great majority of enuretic children differ little from nonenuretics in terms of general adjustment.

Cullen (1966) recently has provided further evidence for the view that childhood enuresis does not usually reflect an underlying behavior disturbance. In Cullen's study, experienced and qualified interviewers obtained information from 1000 mothers in an attempt to relate the prevalence of a wide variety of behavior disorders to events in the child's and the parent's medical history, and to aspects of the child's social and physical environment. Although nocturnal enuresis occurred frequently in the 3440 children of the sample, it was one of the few important behavior disorders that was found to be unrelated to other forms of behavioral disturbance or to a disturbed social environment. The only background factor to which enuresis was related was a history of childhood illnesses.

In contradiction to the child studies, several investigations (for example, Pierce,

Lipcon, McLary & Noble, 1956; Blackman & Goldstein, 1965) have demonstrated a higher incidence of behavioral disturbance in adult enuretics than in adult non-enuretics. This evidence is open to a number of interpretations but, in view of the evidence from studies of children, it seems likely that enuresis tends to persist into adulthood if it is accompanied by generalized behavioral disturbance.

THE PHYSIOLOGY OF MICTURITION

From the point of view of physiological/behavioristic theories, an understanding of the etiology, treatment, and prevention of enuresis must be based on an analysis of the mechanism of micturition and normal continence development. The physiological processes involved in the control of micturition are complex, and only the briefest outline can be given here.

As urine passes from the kidneys into the bladder via the ureters, the tone of the smooth detrusor muscle in the bladder wall is repeatedly adjusted to permit large increases in the volume of stored urine, with little increase in internal pressure. When the volume of the normal adult bladder reaches approximately 200 ml, the limits of tonal compensation are exceeded. With further distention of the bladder, rhythmical contractions of the detrusor begin, culminating in the micturitional reflex. This reflex consists of a strong contraction of the detrusor, and relaxation of the internal, followed by the external sphincter. (There is a reciprocally inhibitory relation between the detrusor and the internal sphincter.) The nervous impulses that provide the initial trigger for the micturitional reflex (or sequence of reflexes) result from stimulation of the sensory end organs in the bladder wall when the bladder is distended.

THE DEVELOPMENT OF CONTINENCE

Whereas, in the infant, micturition is an automatic reflex to bladder distention stimulation, the normal child or adult is able to inhibit micturition beyond the point of the first sensations of urgency, and to initiate micturition at low bladder volumes. The processes involved in the achievement of this degree of control are still a matter of controversy. It is probable that, as a consequence of neural maturation, the detrusor is brought under inhibitory influence from the cortex, but conditioning may also be involved. The evidence of Muellner (1958, 1960) and Vincent (1964) suggests that, in voluntary micturition, the detrusor is induced to contract by contracting the lower abdominal muscles, and by relaxing the pelvic floor muscles. This maneuver results in a rapid lowering of the bladder neck, and the descent of the bladder neck provides the stimulus for detrusor contraction. "Holding" of urine apparently is achieved by the opposite maneuver, although Basmajian (1962) believes that direct contraction of the external sphincter is also involved.[1] Toilet training is complete when the child is able to discriminate toilet from nontoilet situations and learns to initiate micturition only in the prescribed places.

It seems likely that practice in "holding" supplements the inhibitory control of detrusor activity by the higher centers, and results in gradually increasing tolerance for higher bladder volumes. Normally, the inhibitory control transfers to the sleeping state and, as a consequence of the increased functional capacity of the bladder, together with the reduced level of diuresis during sleep (Franczak, 1965), the child is able to sleep through the night without voiding. If, however, the limits of compensatory adjustment of the detrusor are exceeded during sleep, the degree of inhibitory control is sufficient to ensure that feedback stimuli from the filling bladder disperse sleep, so that the child awakens before the micturition reflex is triggered.

The problem of the etiology of enuresis thus becomes the problem of the conditions under which inhibitory control of micturition is inadequately developed, or incompletely transferred to the sleeping state.

[1]It is of interest to note that, in their efforts to prevent the urgent expulsion of urine, children with problems of diurnal urgency sometimes discover for themselves the efficacy of raising the bladder neck. Stephens (1965), for example, has described "the position of sitting on the floor, with knee flexed and heel tucked manually into the perineum to block the urethral passage." It is virtually certain that rather than blocking the urethral passage, this manoeuver raises the neck of the bladder in a manner similar to Vincent's (1964) perineal pressure appliance. (See section Diurnal Bladder Training.)

THE TREATMENT OF ENURESIS

General

There is evidence that enuresis has been a problem since ancient times (Glicklich, 1951) and, over the centuries, attempts at therapy have been made with an incredible variety of methods. Folk remedies have included such unlikely procedures as raising the foot of the bed, sleeping on the back, sleeping on cotton reels, and the consumption of numerous potions. Medical therapies have ranged from the administration of a wide range of drugs and hormones, to surgical procedures and the mechanical constriction of the urinary orifice. Present-day treatment methods include drug therapy, fluid restriction, hypnotherapy, psychotherapy, waking at intervals to urinate, diurnal bladder tolerance training, and direct conditioning.

Conditioning Treatment

Modern interest in the behavior therapy of enuresis by conditioning techniques dates from the paper by Mowrer and Mowrer (1938), although procedures essentially similar to the one described by the Mowrers had been used previously.

The Mowrer-type conditioning instrument makes use of a urine sensitive pad on which the child sleeps. When the child micturates, urine strikes the pad and triggers a relay in circuit with an electric bell. The bell causes micturition to cease, awakens the child and, in the case of young children, summons the attendant. The child is fully awakened and required to micturate. The apparatus is then reset and the child returns to bed. In the procedure followed by the Mowrers, treatment is continued until seven successive dry nights occur, followed by a further seven successive dry nights with an increased fluid intake before retiring.

The Mowrer's conception of the conditioning treatment process is illustrated by the following quotation.

"If some arrangement could be provided so that the sleeping child would be awakened *just after the onset of urination*, and only at this time, the resulting association of bladder distention and the response of awakening and inhibiting further urination should provide precisely the form of training which would seem to be most specifically appropriate" (Mowrer & Mowrer, 1938, p. 445).

Several writers, for example, Jones (1960), have elaborated this classical conditioning model of the treatment process. It should be noted that the model places very heavy emphasis on the "response of awakening." The first stage in treatment is viewed as training the child to awaken readily to the bell. Then the child must learn to awaken with the onset of micturition, and finally the response of awakening must be attached to the stimuli from bladder distention. The emphasis on awakening can also be seen in Mowrer and Mowrers' insistence that the child be fully awakened after triggering the bell during treatment.

A modification of the Mowrer technique, and a somewhat different version of the classical conditioning model, has been presented by Crosby (1950). Crosby's contribution has been discussed fully by Lovibond (1964) and will not be considered further here.

The model of conditioning treatment suggested by Mowrer and Mowrer (1938) and elaborated by other authors, has been criticized by Lovibond (1964) on two main grounds. First, unlike the CS in the classical Pavlovian model for salivary conditioning, the presumed CS in conditioning treatment (bladder distention) is not originally a neutral stimulus with respect to micturition, but is an unconditioned stimulus for the bladder emptying reflex. Second, if the classical paradigm holds true for conditioning treatment, the presumed CS-CR linkage should extinguish as soon as training is effective in preventing the occurrence of the reinforcement (the ringing of the bell). A more crucial criticism of the classical conditioning model is that it makes assumptions which are contradicted by available evidence.

It is commonly observed that during treatment the child at first urinates in his sleep; later he awakens to urinate, and still later he sleeps through the night without waking or micturating (not all children reach the stage of sleeping through the night dry). The second step, awakening to urinate, is seen as essential, since it is a manifestation of the conditioned linkage between bladder stimulation (CS) and the awakening response (CR). In fact, however, in any series of enuretics treated by conditioning methods, there will be found children who *never at any time awaken to urinate*, but who go straight from wetting during sleep to sleeping through the night dry. Furthermore, the senior author has eliminated wetting in a number of cases by the use of brief auditory stimuli without the child ever being awakened by the stimulus.

The classically conditioned-awakening response model of treatment meets further difficulty in accounting for the transition from self-awakening to sleeping through the night dry which occurs in a substantial proportion of treated cases. In order to encompass the development of the capacity to sleep through the night, following a phase of self-awakening to urinate, it is necessary to assume that the conditioned-wakening response is somehow inhibited during the last stage of treatment.

An alternative interpretation of the conditioning process may be made in terms of avoidance rather than classical conditioning (Lovibond, 1964). The paradigm experiment is described by Konorski (1948). Passive flexion of a dog's leg is followed by electric shock. After several pairings of flexion and shock, the dog strenuously resists leg flexion, and performs the antagonistic response of leg extension. It is assumed that feedback stimuli from leg flexion become a signal for shock, and produce the avoidance response of extension.

Applying this model to the conditioning treatment of enuresis, we have the following:

1. Contraction of the detrusor and relaxation of the sphincter are followed by a noxious stimulus (bell).
2. Feedback stimuli from detrusor contraction, sphincter relaxation, and the passage of urine through the urethra become the signal for the onset of the noxious stimulus, and induce the antagonistic response of sphincter contraction and detrusor relaxation.
3. Through the process of generalization, the initial onset of feedback stimuli from sphincter relaxation leads to sphincter contraction before wetting commences. The noxious stimulus is thus avoided, and bedwetting does not occur. (Generalization may extend to the point where bladder distention stimuli trigger the avoidance response, the result being increased inhibitory "tone" of the detrusor.)

The above formulation emphasizes direct sphincter control, and suggests that waking is not essential for successful treatment. The theory is thus able, without difficulty, to account for the observation that, during the latter stages of conditioning treatment, many enuretics acquire the capacity to sleep through the night without waking to urinate. Prior to treatment, detrusor contraction stimulation triggers micturition during sleep at relatively low bladder volumes. With the initial development of the conditioned avoidance response of sphincter contraction, wetting no longer occurs and, if functional low bladder capacity (Vincent, 1964) is not present, bladder distention stimulation may be insufficient to dispel sleep, and the child immediately passes from bed-wetting to sleeping through the night without wetting.

If, however, functional low bladder capacity is present prior to treatment, high bladder pressure produces stimulation of sufficient intensity to dispel sleep during the stage of initial response to treatment. The child thus awakens with an urge to urinate. On each occasion, however, maintenance of conditioned sphincter contraction for a period prior to awakening, permits training in increased bladder tolerance to take place. This training may be carried through to the point where abnormally high bladder pressure no longer accompanies the degree of bladder distention associated with usual levels of fluid intake prior to retiring. Bladder distention stimulation, and/or feedback stimulation from initial sphincter relaxation, continues to maintain conditioned avoidance sphincter contraction, however, so that wetting does not occur, and the child sleeps through the night dry.

When diurnal symptoms of frequency and urgency indicate severe functional low bladder capacity, the capacity to sleep through the night will not readily be acquired. If, however, children with severe functional low bladder capacity do reach the stage of sleeping through the night dry, diurnal symptoms of frequency and urgency will be relieved concomitantly.

On the basis of a reformulation of the process of conditioning treatment, Lovibond (1964) devised a modified brief auditory stimulus instrument (Twin Signal). This instrument was shown to produce more rapid elimination of wetting than the Mowrer-type instrument, but the rate of relapse was higher.

RESULTS OF DIFFERENT TREATMENT METHODS

Spontaneous Remission

A problem in the evaluation of any therapy is the definition of the base line against which to compare the proportion of recoveries in treated cases. This problem arises from the well-established tendency of behavior disturbances to recover "spontaneously," or as a result of unspecifiable influences. In the absence of suitable control groups, it has been suggested that a generally applicable spontaneous recovery base line for enuresis may be derived from the age-incidence curve of the disorder (Lovibond, 1964). Recent evidence from studies that employed untreated control groups (Werry & Cohrssen, 1965; De Leon & Mandell, 1966) permits a check on the validity of this conclusion.

In their comparison of psychotherapy and conditioning treatment of enuresis, Werry and Cohrssen (1965) included an untreated control group ($n = 27$). At the end of 4 months, one child in the untreated group was completely dry, and two others were greatly improved (that is, wetting was less than 35 percent as frequent as wetting prior to the 4-month-period). Thus, by using the very liberal criterion of a wetting frequency less than 35 percent of the former frequency, the spontaneous remission rate over 90 days was only 11 percent.

In the study of De Leon and Mandell (1966), 2 out of 18 untreated controls (11 percent) were found to have reached a criterion of 13 consecutive dry nights after 53 and 115 days, respectively. Notice that the spontaneous remission rates observed in these two studies occurred over a period considerably in excess of the period during which the great majority of enuretics respond to conditioning treatment. For example, De Leon and Mandell obtained a heavily skewed distribution of days to cure in their conditioning group, 83 percent of "cured" cases reaching the criterion of 13 days clear in 11 to 66 days. A strictly valid comparison between "spontaneous" and treated recovery rates would require the observation of matched pairs of treated and untreated subjects. This procedure has not yet been used, but it seems likely that its application would result in a spontaneous remission rate little different from that derived from the age-incidence curve.

Results of Psychotherapy

After reviewing the evidence available at the end of 1963, Lovibond (1964) concluded that the effectiveness of psychotherapy as a treatment for enuresis had still to be demonstrated conclusively. Since Lovibond's review, two controlled studies of psychotherapy have been published (Werry & Cohrssen, 1965; De Leon & Mandell, 1966). These studies, which will be reviewed in detail in a later section, failed to establish the value of the forms of psychotherapy used.

Results of Drug Treatment

A formidable list of drugs has been used in attempts to control enuresis but, by and large, the effects have been disappointing (Braithwaite, 1955). The most promising of the recently introduced drugs is the antidepressant imipramine (Tofranil). The earlier studies of the effects of imipramine were usually uncontrolled, or were conducted on disturbed children, unrepresentative of the general population of enuretics. Several investigators who have found imipramine to be effective in the control of enuresis have reported that relapse follows withdrawal of the drug (for example, Bostock, 1962; Munster, Stanley & Saunders, 1961). A return to earlier levels of wetting following the withdrawal of medication was also observed in two placebo-controlled studies of enuretic army and navy recruits (Dorison & Blackman, 1962; Hicks & Barnes, 1964). In each of these studies, however, the original response to imipramine was no greater than the significant placebo response.

Recently, Poussaint and Ditman (1965) conducted a placebo-controlled study of imipramine in the treatment of 47 subjects considered to be representative of enuretics typically seen by family physicians and pediatricians. The drug dosages in this study (up to 75 mg for children over 10 years) were higher than those usually employed, and the drug was gradually, rather than suddenly, withdrawn. At the end of 8 weeks, imipramine had produced a significantly greater reduction in wetting than the placebo. At this stage the dosage was increased, and the treatment response improved markedly. Eleven children (24 percent) became completely dry, and remained so when the drug was gradually withdrawn over a period of 4 to 6 weeks (follow-up 1 to 3 months). Only

7 children (15 percent) showed no improvement when the dose was raised to maximum levels. The authors concluded that gradual withdrawal of the drug was responsible for the "training" effects observed. Replication of these results would represent a significant advance in the drug therapy of enuresis.

Results of Conditioning Treatment

Jones (1960) and Lovibond (1964) and Young (1965a) have summarized the results of the studies of conditioning treatment that were available in the English language literature at the time of writing. Despite various inadequacies in many of the studies, and the use of different criteria of success by different investigators, the results as a whole permit the conclusion that, when properly applied, conditioning treatment is remarkably effective in arresting nocturnal enuresis. This conclusion is supported by the work of a number of other investigators (Franczak & Ignatowicz, 1964 (n = 32); Huijssoon, 1963 (n = 34); Pereira-D'Oliviera, 1961 (n = 75); Takeuchi, 1961 (n = 16), and Taylor, 1963 (n = 100).)

One of the present writers (M.A.C.) has treated over 1000 cases of enuresis by conditioning methods. Detailed analysis has been completed for only 216 of these cases, 123 males and 93 females aged 4 to 26 years. An initial success criterion of 2 weeks dry commencing within 12 weeks was achieved by 211 (98 percent) of the cases. For this number the mean time to last wetting was 26.3 days, with a median of 23 and a mode of 19 days. Seventy-three percent of the 211 cases reached the criterion of arrest within 30 days of commencement of treatment. Preliminary analysis indicates that the data from the full 1000 cases will not change this overall picture substantially.

The available evidence suggests that a reasonable estimate of the proportion of initial arrests of wetting that may be expected in an unselected group of enuretics is at least 90 percent. This rate of initial success is far in excess of the rate of spontaneous remission that would be expected during the usual period of treatment from the estimated age-incidence curve (Jones, 1960; Lovibond, 1964).

Since the efficacy of conditioning treatment in bringing about an initial arrest of wetting may be regarded as beyond question, further reference will be made only to studies that compare conditioning and other forms of therapy, or that investigate other variables in relation to conditioning therapy.

Comparisons of Conditioning and Psychotherapy

Two recent studies (Werry & Cohrssen, 1965; De Leon & Mandell, 1966) have made a comparison of conditioning and psychotherapy in the treatment of enuresis. The *S*s of Werry and Cohrssen were all referrals to an enuresis clinic who had never been dry for more than 3 months and who exhibited a wetting frequency of, at least, once per week. The mean age of the total group was 10 years. A no-treatment group (n = 27) was told that mothers would be contacted after a period of 4 months to check the child's progress. The psychotherapy group (n = 21) received 6 to 8 sessions of psychodynamically oriented supportive psychotherapy. Most of the therapy was carried out by a single therapist with 3 others assisting. The therapists generally felt that psychotherapy was a potentially useful form of treatment for enuresis. Subjects of the conditioning treatment group (n = 22) were treated by a Mowrer-type pad and buzzer apparatus in their own homes. The apparatus was set up only once per night, although a significant proportion of the children were found to be wetting more than once per night when the bed buzzer treatment was instituted. After the initial interview, no contact was made with the parents apart from an occasional telephone call. The instrument remained in place until the child had been dry for at least one month or until the 4-month-period had elapsed. At the end of 4 months, the parent was telephoned and asked how many times the child had wet the bed in the preceding month. The number of wet beds in the fourth month was expressed as a percentage of the pretrial monthly wetting frequency. Five categories of therapeutic response were defined: (1) 0 percent = cure (no wet beds during the preceding month), (2) 1 to 35 percent = greatly improved, (3) 36 to 69 percent = moderately improved, (4) 70 to 100 percent = unchanged, (5) 100 percent plus = worse.

The results of the Werry and Cohrssen study are shown in Table 15.1.

It is clear from the data in Table 15.1 that, whereas brief psychotherapy was ineffective, conditioning treatment resulted in a

Table 15.1 Comparison of Conditioning and Psychotherapy of Enuresis (after Werry & Cohrssen, 1965)

	Therapeutic Effect[a]				
Treatment Group (excluding dropouts)	Cure	Greatly Improved	Improved	Unchanged Worse	Dropout
A. No treatment ($N = 27$)	1 (5%)	2 (5%)	5 (20%)	19 (70%)	1
B. Brief psychotherapy ($N = 21$)	2 (10%)	2 (10%)	3 (15%)	14 (70%)	5
C. Bedbuzzer ($N = 22$)	7 (30%)	6 (30%)	4 (20%)	5 (20%)	4
Statistic	$X^2ABC = 17.09$		$X^2AB = .13$	$X^2BC = 9.13$	10
df	6		2	3	
p	0.01		N.S.	0.05 0.02	

[a]Percentages are rounded.

significantly higher rate of improvement than no treatment.

Despite the relative effectiveness of conditioning treatment in the Werry and Cohrssen study, however, the rate of initial arrest of enuresis was considerably lower than that usually reported. As the authors themselves note, the relative lack of supervision was probably responsible for the lowered success rate.

In the De Leon and Mandell study, the *S*s were 85 children of both sexes, aged 5 to 14 years, and referred with a diagnosis of functional enuresis to a mental health center. During an initial period of 2 weeks, mothers recorded whether or not the child's bed was wet (a) before the mother went to sleep, (b) at about 3.00 A.M., and (c) after the family awakened in the morning.

*S*s were assigned to one of three groups: conditioning ($n = 56$), psychotherapy-counseling ($n = 13$), and control ($n = 18$). The instrument used in conditioning treatment was of the Mowrer type. Following 3 nights when the child slept on the unconnected pad and wetting frequency was recorded, the instrument was switched on until the criteria of success or failure were reached. Success was defined as 7 successive dry nights on the operative pad, plus 3 successive dry nights on the unconnected pad, plus 3 successive dry nights with the instrument and pad out of the room. A failure was recorded if 90 days had elapsed without reaching the success criterion.

Subjects in the psychotherapy counseling group were seen for 12 sessions on a weekly basis. A session consisted of 40 minutes with the child and 20 minutes with the mother alone. The form of the therapy, which was unspecified, was carried out by a psychiatrist or a psychologist.

Subjects in the control group received no treatment, but nightly records of wetting frequency were kept. For the psychotherapy and control groups, success was defined as 13 successive dry nights. A failure was recorded for any *S* in the psychotherapy group who had not achieved 13 nights clear by the end of the 12 therapy sessions (about 90 days). The average follow-up period was 30 weeks and the range was 4 to 88 weeks. Seventy-five percent of the children were followed for at least 6 months. For those *S*s completing treatment, the percentage reaching the success criterion in the 3 groups was as follows: conditioning, 86.3, psychotherapy, 18.2, and control, 11.1. The difference between the success rates of the conditioning group and the other two groups combined was highly significant.

The results of the two studies reviewed, of course, do not permit the conclusion that psychotherapy per se is ineffective in the treatment of nocturnal enuresis. As De Leon and Mandell note:

> "Such conclusions must await the exploration of other related parameters such as the form of the therapy, the number of therapeutic sessions, intersession time, and individual differences among therapists as to skill and experience" (p. 330).

Nevertheless, in view of the demonstrated

effectiveness of conditioning methods, the results of the two studies must give pause to those who regard psychotherapy as the treatment of choice in dealing with the problem of enuresis.

Comparisons of Conditioning and Drug Therapy

Forrester, Stein, and Susser (1964) have reported a comparison of the effectiveness of conditioning and the drug Amphetamine. At the completion of the trial, there were 33 cases randomly assigned to treatment and followed for a six-month period. Failure to follow instructions and intolerance to the drug reduced the number of children who had received adequate treatment to 23. Enuresis was completely relieved in eight of the ten children receiving conditioning treatment (80 percent), and in three of the fifteen children receiving Amphetamine (23 percent). The difference between the two cure rates was statistically significant.

In another study, Young (1965a) compared the treatment responses of 273 enuretic children who received one of several drug treatments, and 105 enuretic children undergoing conditioning therapy. Bed-wetting was arrested in 65 percent of the conditioning group and in 36 percent of the combined drug group. Not only was the arrest rate significantly higher in the conditioning group, but arrest was more rapidly achieved and relapse less frequent.

The Combination of Drugs and Conditioning Treatment

Since there is evidence that CNS stimulant drugs facilitate laboratory conditioning (Pavlov, 1927), Young and Turner (1965) investigated the effect of administering the CNS stimulants Methedrine and Dexedrine during conditioning treatment. In accordance with prediction, initial arrest of wetting occurred significantly earlier in the drugs plus conditioning groups but, unexpectedly, retention of conditioning was significantly impaired. A long-term follow-up (Turner & Young, 1966) revealed that the frequency of relapse was particularly high in the group of subjects to whom Dexedrine had been administered. Turner and Young noted the parallel between their own results and those of Lovibond (1964), in which a modification of treatment technique also brought about a more rapid development of continence with an associated increase in the relapse rate. Further research into the use of drugs as an adjuvant to conditioning treatment is clearly indicated. (See section Implications For Future Research.)

Personality Factors in Response to Conditioning Treatment

Eysenck's theory of personality (Eysenck, 1957) assumes a general factor of conditionability, and predicts that introverts will condition more rapidly than extraverts. On this theory, introverted enuretics would be expected to show a better response to conditioning treatment than extraverted enuretics. By using behavioral ratings of enuretics' position on the introversion-extraversion dimension, Lovibond (1964) was unable to substantiate this prediction. More recently, Young (1965b) found evidence to support the related prediction that extraverted enuretics would show a higher relapse rate than introverted enuretics. Optimism concerning the outcome of future studies of the relationship between the introversion-extraversion personality dimension and the response to conditioning treatment must be tempered by doubts concerning the existence of an important general factor of conditionability (Lovibond, 1963a), and the relatively small amount of variance in conditioned-response acquisition accounted for by scores on available tests of extraversion (Willett, 1960).

Diurnal Bladder Training

Muellner (1960) has successfully treated enuresis by requiring bed-wetters to practise the "holding" of urine after the ingestion of increased quantities of fluid during the daytime. The purpose of this regime is to increase the functional capacity of the bladder, a deficiency in which is seen by Muellner as the essential cause of enuresis.

Vincent (1964) has also reported good results from the use of perineal pressure appliance. When the perineum is artificially elevated, children without structural abnormalities of the urinary system lose the desire to micturate, and training in increased bladder tolerance occurs. According to Vincent, the results are much better in cases with diurnal frequency and urgency as well as bed-wetting, than in cases of nocturnal enuresis without diurnal symptoms. Cases occur where there is no response to treatment in relation to either nocturnal or diurnal symptoms, despite the absence of structural abnormality. The present authors have been able to substantiate Vincent's results in a small number of cases.

The Combination of Bladder Training and Conditioning

Vincent (1966, 1967) has given preliminary reports of treatment procedures that combine conditioning with measures designed to increase functional bladder capacity. A Mowrer-type bed-pad has been arranged, in conjunction with electromechanical equipment, to operate a pneumatic perineal pressure appliance worn by the sleeping patient. The pressure appliance raises the bladder outlet and cuts off the stream of urine soon after it commences. Vincent has found that a similar, but more rapid, effect is achieved if, instead of mechanical perineal elevation, electrical stimulation is applied to the levator-ani muscle. Electrodes have been placed on the adjacent skin and into underlying tissue. More recently, electronic devices have been implanted in the muscle itself, and activated by an external stimulator, on the lines of the cardiac pacemaker.

There is little doubt that, instead of the bed-pad, impulses from EMG monitors could be used to trigger the pressure appliance or stimulator. Whether such a procedure would confer any therapeutic advantages cannot be predicted with any certainty.

The Problem of Relapse

In the preceding sections we have reviewed evidence that demonstrates the remarkable efficacy of conditioning treatment in bringing about an initial cessation of wetting. The term "initial" is used advisedly, since a substantial proportion of enuretics who become dry during the course of conditioning treatment subsequently relapse to something approaching the frequency of the original wetting.

Theoretically, the problem of defining relapse could present considerable difficulty, but in practice it tends to be relatively clear-cut. Evidence to be presented in a later section shows that the great majority of cases either wet the bed only occasionally after successful treatment, or return to a wetting frequency of more than once per week.

By using as a criterion of relapse a renewed frequency of wetting of more than once per week, Lovibond (1964) found that, over a period of 2 years, the relapse rate may reach 35 to 40 percent. As a consequence, he adopted the practice of advising parents that treatment should be regarded as involving the use of the conditioning instrument on two occasions. The relapse rate observed by Lovibond was very much higher than that usually reported, but it was noted that in the research literature there was a high positive correlation between the reported relapse rate and the length of the follow-up period. Several recent long-term follow-up studies have confirmed Lovibond's estimate of the relapse rate to be expected in an average group of enuretics whose wetting has been arrested by conditioning therapy. Freyman (1963) completed a 10-month follow-up study of 37 children who had initially become dry following conditioning treatment. Thirteen cases, or 35 percent, had relapsed to the point where reissue of the conditioning instrument was necessary. In a long-term follow-up study, conducted by Turner and Young (1966), the criterion of relapse was a wetting frequency of at least three nights in two successive weeks. It was found that, over a period of 40 to 63 months, 16 of 41 successfully treated enuretics (39 percent) had relapsed, although 3 relapsers had subsequently become dry.

Further work by the present authors, to be described in the next section, yielded comparable results.

The Prediction of Relapse

In an attempt to develop predictors of response to conditioning therapy, Lovibond (1964) examined a variety of background variables including age, sex, general adjustment, personality measures, and pattern of bed-wetting. None of these variables was significantly related to the outcome of treatment. It was found, however, that if the child wet the bed frequently, and particularly if he also suffered from urgency and frequency of micturition during the day, he was more likely to respond poorly to treatment and to relapse subsequently. The number of children in Lovibond's sample with these characteristics was very small, and, in an attempt to replicate his results, a retrospective outcome study was undertaken by

Table 15.2 Frequency of Renewed Wetting Following Successful Conditioning Treatment in the Diurnal and Control groups

Maximum Frequency of Renewed Wetting	Diurnal Group	Control Group
Practically every night	17	5
More than once per week on average	8	7
More than once per fortnight on average	0	1
Just occasional accidents	14	17
Nil	5	10

the present authors. From a sample of 408 children successfully treated by Coote with a Mowrer-type instrument during the preceding three years, 47 children were selected. These children had all presented with pronounced symptoms of diurnal frequency and/or urgency at the time of conditioning treatment.[2] The 47 children with diurnal difficulties (diurnal group) were matched with children presenting no signs of diurnal difficulty (control group). The matching criteria were age, sex, primary or secondary enuresis, and time since treatment.

A questionnaire was constructed to obtain information on the maximum frequency of renewed wetting following conditioning treatment, the extent of present diurnal urinary difficulties, and the extent to which the child was presently able to sleep through the night without rising to urinate. The questionnaire was sent by mail to the parents of the 94 children, and nonresponders were followed up to ensure a high rate of return. Completed questionnaires were returned by the parents of 44 diurnal *S*s and 40 control *S*s. Data on the initial response to treatment were available for all *S*s from the treatment records.

Table 15.2 summarizes responses of parents to the question concerning the maximum frequency of renewed wetting following attainment of the treatment criterion of 14 consecutive dry nights.

The first point of interest to emerge from the data in Table 15.2 is that, when relapse occurred, it tended to be quite clear-cut in both groups. Thus, in only one case was the maximum frequency of renewed wetting more than once per two weeks, but not more than once per week. In the remaining 83 cases, if wetting was resumed, it occurred only occasionally or with a frequency in excess of once per week. These results are consistent with the findings of Lovibond (1964), and indicate that the problem of defining relapse is not as serious as might be supposed.

The present data suggest that relapse should be defined as renewal of wetting with a frequency greater than once per week. On this definition the relapse rate in the control group (30 percent) is higher than that commonly reported, and closely parallels the rates observed in a series of studies by Lovibond (1964). It is apparent from Table 15.2, nevertheless, that the relapse rate in the diurnal group is even higher (57 percent), the difference being statistically significant ($\chi^2 = 6.11$, 1 *df*, $p < .02$, two tailed test). This finding supports the view of Vincent (1964) that enuretics with diurnal urgency and frequency should be treated as a separate group.

In one respect the present data failed to replicate an observation of Lovibond (1964). Contrary to Lovibond's findings, the difference between the diurnal and control groups in initial response to treatment did not approach significance.

Unexpectedly, no less than 35 of the 44 *S*s in the diurnal group were reported as no longer being troubled by diurnal frequency or urgency. The 35 *S*s included 20 who had relapsed. By contrast, nocturnal frequency seemed to have remained a problem for *S*s of the diurnal group. Relevant information could be obtained from only 28 *S*s, since the remainder either wet the bed most nights or were awakened during the night by a parent and required to urinate. Only 6 of

[2]In approximately 25 percent of the total Sample ($n = 408$), nocturnal enuresis was accompanied by discernible diurnal difficulties.

the 28 *S*s were reported as always being able to sleep through the night without getting out of bed to urinate. The proportion of control *S*s always able to sleep through the night was 22 out of 35. This difference between the diurnal and control groups is statistically significant ($\chi^2 = 10.81$, 1 *df*, $p < .01$, two tailed test).

It is unfortunate that the rate of spontaneous recovery from diurnal frequency and urgency is unknown, but it is highly improbable that the rate of recovery in the absence of treatment would approach the rate observed in the diurnal group. Hence, it seems reasonable to conclude that diurnal urgency and frequency are significantly ameliorated by conditioning therapy of nocturnal enuresis. Nevertheless, the failure of most of the present diurnal group *S*s to acquire the capacity to retain urine throughout the night, suggests that problems of inadequate bladder capacity remain, with consequent increased likelihood of relapse into nocturnal enuresis. In this connection it is interesting to note the observations made by Vincent (1964) on children treated for both diurnal urgency and frequency and nocturnal enuresis by means of a perineal pressure appliance. Vincent states that "the bedwetting sometimes stops in the first week of treatment. Unfortunately, whereas in some cases the cure is permanent, in others the bedwetting recurs *even though the diurnal symptoms are cured*" (p. 29, italics added).

IMPLICATIONS FOR FUTURE RESEARCH

The evidence reviewed indicates clearly that (a) when properly applied, conditioning treatment of enuresis is effective in a substantial majority of cases; (b) the efficacy of psychotherapeutic treatment has yet to be demonstrated convincingly; and (c) no drug yet investigated offers a degree of control of enuresis which approaches that of conditioning treatment. Nevertheless, despite the success of behavior therapy in this field, the need for further research is obvious. The areas that seem to the authors to offer the greatest promise of fruitful returns are the following.

1. *Electrophysiological studies*. In order to elucidate the mechanism of enuresis and conditioning treatment, there is a clear need to carry out electrophysiological studies of central neural activity and of the activity of the pelvic floor muscles in enuretics and nonenuretic controls.[3] It would be illuminating to carry out such studies under three conditions: (a) in the waking state prior to and during the acts of "holding" and voluntary micturition, (b) in the sleeping state prior to and during the act of bed-wetting, and (c) during the course of conditioning treatment.

Evidence of a relatively high incidence of EEG abnormality in enuretics is suggestive of a deficiency in cortical control (Gunnarson & Melin, 1951; Temmes & Toivakka, 1954; Turton & Spear, 1953), and Vincent (1964) has implicated inefficient activity of the pelvic floor musculature in enuresis.

It has long been suggested that deep sleep makes the enuretic less sensitive to the signals from the filling bladder, but the evidence is contradictory (Boyd, 1960). A related problem is the extent to which initiation of micturition during sleep involves the same mechanisms as voluntary micturition in the waking state. Vincent (1964) has observed that his appliance may inhibit voluntary micturition in a particular patient, but fail to prevent the same patient urinating in his sleep. Vincent suggests that in these cases the appliance becomes loose during sleep, or a powerful urge to micturate pushes the perineal floor down with great efficiency. There is suggestive evidence, however, that the process whereby micturition is initiated during sleep may differ in important ways from the process of voluntary waking micturition. Thus, Ditman and Blinn (1955) observed

[3]Since this chapter was written, a review of a series of electrophysiological studies of enuresis has become available (Broughton, 1968).

In these studies it was found that bedwetting usually takes place during arousal from slow-wave sleep, and is rarely related in any way to REM, or "dreaming sleep."

By comparison with normals, the enuretics studied showed an increase in the number and intensity of primary detrusor contractions during sleep, and a higher base-line bladder pressure. The enuretics were also found to have a longer period of non-REM sleep before the onset of rapid eye movements, higher heart rates during sleep, and less reduction in heart rate during sleep.

that in some enuretics there was no sign of activity in the rectus abdominus muscles prior to or during the act of bed-wetting, although these muscles are involved in voluntary micturition. In each of a small number of cases observed by the authors, micturition during sleep took the form of dribbling rather than the full urinary stream that is characteristic of waking micturition. No one has yet undertaken the task of closely observing the act of bed-wetting in a large and representative sample of enuretics. There is, nevertheless, a clear need for such observations to be made and, to be maximally fruitful, they should be combined with electrophysiological recordings under the conditions outlined above.

Among the questions that need to be raised in connection with electrophysiological recording during the course of conditioning treatment, the following immediately suggest themselves: What degree of cortical arousal by the bell or other stimulus is necessary for effective conditioning treatment? Can activity of the perineal musculature akin to that of voluntary "holding" of urine during the waking state be observed during sleep as conditioning treatment becomes effective?

2. *The combination of conditioning and drug therapy*. The results of Young and Turner (1965) make it clear that the investigation of the use of drugs as an adjuvant to conditioning therapy should be carried beyond the administration of cortical excitants throughout the course of conditioning therapy. Gerbrandt's (1965) analysis of the neural mechanisms of behavioral release and control suggests that the controlling mechanisms change significantly during the course of conditioning, and it is entirely possible that the type of drug that will facilitate the acquisition of control changes concomitantly. For example, it is possible that cortical excitants may have a facilitatory effect during the early stages of acquisition when excitatory mechanisms predominate, but that the use of *depressant* drugs may be indicated during the later phase of stabilization of the reflex when control passes to inhibitory mechanisms. Since these phases may well take a different course with different forms of conditioning (for example, classical versus passive avoidance), the need to elucidate the mechanism of conditioning treatment seems obvious. It seems likely that a program of studies of the effects of stimulant and depressant drugs administered at different stages of acquisition of conditioning would be illuminating. Until direct studies of conditioning treatment suggest a different mechanism, passive avoidance would seem to offer the best prospects for study.

3. *Direct bladder capacity training as an adjunct to conditioning treatment*. It has been demonstrated that relapse is the major problem of conditioning treatment, and that a history of diurnal micturitional difficulties is one of the few predictors of relapse. It seems probable that obvious signs of diurnal urgency and frequency are indicators of only the extremes of a continuum of functional low bladder capacity, and that lesser degrees of low bladder capacity exist in a substantial proportion of enuretics without obvious diurnal problems (Franczak, 1965).

In an earlier section it was suggested that conditioning treatment ordinarily results in substantially increased bladder capacity and that, when this fails to occur, relapse becomes likely. Since there is evidence that direct bladder capacity training in the waking state alone may eliminate enuresis in some cases (Vincent, 1964), the possibility of combining conditioning treatment and training with the Vincent appliance deserves thorough investigation.

Reduction of the Relapse Rate Following Conditioning Treatment

Clearly, from the evidence presented in earlier sections, the reduction of the relapse rate following conditioning treatment is a pressing research problem. Despite warnings given prior to treatment, the motivation of both parent and child is likely to drop when relapse occurs, and many parents do not actively seek retreatment. Furthermore, although most relapsers respond well to a second treatment and do not relapse again, a small minority responds poorly to retreatment and/or relapses repeatedly.

It is not infrequently suggested that the relapse rate might be reduced by overlearning during the initial treatment, that is, by extending the initial arrest criterion beyond the usual 14 days. In practice, the gains to be had by adopting this procedure are minimal. In the first place, the great majority of children who reach the criterion of 14 days dry will not wet again during the next two weeks, so that an extension of the criterion period to a month will result in no overlearning for these children. Secondly, if fluids are forced to increase the likelihood of further reinforcements, a child already sleeping through the night is likely to respond by waking to urinate. On the other hand, if the child is already waking to urinate, forcing fluids will simply increase the frequency of such waking.

Lovibond (1964) has studied the effects on the relapse rate of a number of variations of treatment procedure. The most promising was the use of intermittent reinforcement during training, although the results from a relatively small number of subjects were not decisive. Large-scale studies of intermittent reinforcement training schedules should provide a worthwhile investment of research resources. In addition, it is not unlikely that the use of the adjuvant procedures previously discussed will be found to improve both acquisition and retention of the conditioning that is presumed to underly the treatment response.

ADMINISTRATION OF CONDITIONING TREATMENT

As with any other conditioning therapy, the effectiveness of conditioning treatment of enuresis must depend both on the instrumentation and the expertise with which it is used. With its therapeutic value established beyond question, the general acceptance of conditioning treatment is hampered as much by mishandling in practice as by theoretical prejudice.

It is impossible to know how much success or disappointment has come of "do it yourself" treatments with equipment hired from departmental stores, or improvised from directions in hobby magazines. The only data available concerning the results of unsupervised treatment are those from a survey by Martin and Kubly (1955), and these data, tabulated by Jones (1960) alongside the results of many supervised series, are most unimpressive. It is not surprising that the majority of modern paediatric textbooks give the method only brief and cautious mention. As an example, *Textbook of Pediatrics* (Nelson, 1964) says

> "Some success is claimed for the conditioning type of treatment wherein a bell rings and wakens the child when the voided urine completes an electrical circuit in a pad placed beneath the child. This generally is ineffective, however, particularly if the enuresis is a symptom of neurosis."

One may dispute the etiological role of neurosis , but agree that the method may be ineffective if applied with primitive equipment and without expert supervision. Given satisfactory equipment and proper supervision, however, the dramatically successful results described elsewhere in this chapter may be expected.

A study of the treatment procedure to be described later will indicate that, although essentially simple, the method has many facets that are outside the competence of an intelligent parent armed with a set of instructions and a machine. Not only is sound equipment necessary, but also continuous and competent outside supervision.

Lovibond's (1964) emphasis on the need for the psychological preparation of the parent and the child, implies clearly that, when unsupervised, a vital aspect of the treatment is missing. The therapist-patient relationship is important even though the therapeutic effects are sought by the application of specific stimulus conditions. Furthermore, the usual rules apply, in that humane concern is shown for the patient's welfare as well as his whole system of attitudes relating to his disorder.

The child's attitudes may have to be modified to secure his rational cooperation. Social attitudes expressed to the child, and restrictions resulting from his disorder, may have led to anxiety, timidity, withdrawal, or feigned indifference.

Outright rejection of treatment by a patient is exceedingly rare, only three such instances being encountered in over 1000 cases treated by the authors. With adequate psychological preparation, emotional disturbance or fear reaction to the alarm is rare, and has never been known to persist for more than a few days. Serious general disturbance in a child requires detailed psychological assessment and a general therapeutic program, but there is some evidence to suggest that conditioning treatment of enuresis has no effect on the general disorder, although it may arrest the enuresis. Persistent fear reactions would, of course, be a contraindication to use of the method with such cases.

Far more frequently, pronounced general disturbance is encountered in a parent, and unless dealt with, can seriously hamper application of the method. The impossible or difficult home situation is not uncommon and must be discovered during the first interview. The medical practitioner's knowledge of these matters is often invaluable. In the homes of alcoholic, neurotic, intellectually dull, or self-obsessed parents there are obvious obstacles to treatment. There is also the "omniscient" parent who will vary the whole procedure laid down or will return an instrument after a 3-day proving period. Serious psychotherapeutic intervention is sometimes necessary, but problem parents commonly require only an unusual amount of supervision. Firm insistence on regular weekly reports may also become necessary.

The mother who has unsuccessfully applied a variety of treatments is apt to become pessimistic and discontinue therapeutic efforts prematurely. Some may regard the instrument as a magic box, a sort of Talisman, the mere presence of which will effect a cure without any effort by parents or child. The parent, and this usually means the mother, must be given an understanding of the treatment process as well as a clear appreciation of the demands it will make on those concerned and of its prospects for success. Every subtlety of the therapist-client relationship must be used to secure sustained cooperation.

Commercial firms in some cases perform a supervisory function but frequently this is with unqualified staff and without medical referral of the patient. Although Lovibond (1964) does not regard this state of affairs as desirable, he has pointed out that these firms provide a useful service which, under present circumstances, is not otherwise obtainable by many parents. Furthermore, even when incompetently handled, conditioning treatment is unlikely to harm the child significantly.

Several writers have envisaged not only incompetence but abuse of the method when used as a basis for punitive measures. Thus, Mowrer (1950) states that "In the hands of vindictive, sadistic persons this method can, to be sure, become just another means of assaulting the privacy and individuality of the enuretic child." As an example of such punitive procedures, the methods of a firm operating commercially in Australia may be cited. The firm offers a hiring and supervision service, and the details of its methods have been described to the authors quite gratuitously by at least 50 reliable exclients.

At first interview the child-patient is greeted with the remark that he is both stupid and dirty. If response to treatment is slow the parent is exhorted to "belt him all the way to the toilet and all the way back again each time the alarm rings." Next day he is to be dressed in a diaper, stood in a corner and the family is to gather round and jeer at him. Failure or relapse is ascribed to laziness or defiance, and a thrashing is prescribed.

It cannot be expected that this example is unique, and many will feel that it establishes the case against unqualified commercial operators quite convincingly. There will be little disagreement that a background of formal training in psychology, at least at undergraduate level, should be demanded of all who engage in this work. A special interest in the method and an acquaintance with its literature and research is also reasonably to be expected.

As an application of learning theory, conditioning treatment is the natural domain of the clinical psychologist with a thorough training in general psychological principles, but the general medical practitioner and paediatrician have been more ready to adopt the method, possibly because they are more frequently confronted with the problem of enuresis. Nevertheless, both medical practitioners and the older psychologists are deterred by unfamiliarity with the method and by reluctance to buy equipment that has acquired a reputation for exasperating unreliability.

Whether or not its members employ conditioning procedures, the involvement of the medical profession in the treatment of nocturnal enuresis is inevitable, and other workers will find medical liaison desirable. It is usually claimed that bed-wetting is of organic origin in somewhat less than 10 percent of cases, and certainly it is rarely an isolated symptom of an organic condition. If conditioning therapy precedes medical assessment, it is therefore seldom that diagnosis of an underlying physical factor will be confounded or delayed, provided that there is a search for other symptoms that will lead to an adequate investigation. However, although full urological examination is usually unrewarding in the absence of any other indication, and is not usually resorted to, the use of any type of therapy without preliminary medical assessment cannot be recommended.

There are other reasons for the involvement of the medical profession. The patient may need access to drug therapy as an adjuvant treatment, and medically trained judgment is often helpful in deciding when conditioning should be interrupted because of intervention of an illness. In countries where medical expenses are defrayed by government-assisted schemes and insurances, the medical profession may be at an advantage in being able to make the conditioning method available at little cost.

In many organic syndromes, bed-wetting is an accepted symptom, but is etiologically related in only a tenuous way. Bed-wetting may be arrested by conditioning in the presence of, for example, urinary tract infections, diabetes mellitus, cerebral palsy, mental retardation, and partial neurological defect. This suggests the need for exploration of the limits of applicability of conditioning methods.

Practical Treatment Procedure

The following procedure and observations are intended as a background for the development of the individual therapeutic program. They are presented particularly for those who are deterred by unfamiliarity from using the method, but the procedure is in no way mandatory; and the observations are, of necessity, fragmented. The equipment referred to is of the pad and bell type, such as Coote's (1965) in which the pad is wiped dry and immediately reused. Micturition triggers a light as well as the bell stimulus, and complete or nonintermittent reinforcement is used.

After routine medical assessment the enuresis alarm is demonstrated to child and parent(s). Saline from an eye dropper is used to trigger the alarm, and the child subsequently repeats this with one hand on the pad, thus being reassured that there is no shock and nothing to fear. The child is encouraged to make up his own saline and to demonstrate the alarm to the rest of the family.

The placing of the pad between drawsheet and waterproof and the alarm unit near the head of the bed are explained, and the child is asked to sleep without pyjama pants. After triggering the alarm during the night, the child is required to switch it off and attend the toilet. The pad is then wiped dry with a portion of the used drawsheet (which is replaced with a dry one) and the instrument is reset.

The amount of assistance required from the parent depends on the maturity of the child, teenagers usually being quite self-sufficient.

It is always emphasized, however, that for at least the first few nights, a parent should sleep within earshot to arouse a heavy sleeper. Ease of arousal, if not present at first, is in most cases rapidly acquired. The child is encouraged to "beat" his parent to the bell (this being recorded) and is told that, when he can win the competition for one week, he is really getting better. Then he tries to "beat the bell." Old procedures, such as lifting, fluid restrictions, and rewards are discontinued and, during the first week, fluid intake is increased to the point where, at least, one stimulus per night is recorded. In this respect the procedure differs in detail from that of other writers.

An attempt is made to explain the principles of the method at the child's own level of understanding by comparing the instrument to a teacher, although a somewhat more sophisticated explanation may be needed for the parent. Throughout the interview, the psychological preparation of the child and parent is undertaken as outlined in the previous section, and investigations are made of any domestic situations inimical to treatment, whether they be physical, or related to the behavior of others. Detailed study of the home situation is made without the child present.

A set of instructions and a record sheet are presented to the parent, and a weekly telephone report is arranged. The report is recorded on a duplicate sheet and an assessment of progress is given. In addition, any problems are dealt with, and frequently an opportunity is made to speak with and encourage the child. Mail contact is maintained with remote cases after personal interview.

Treatment is discontinued, and the instrument is returned after a dry proving period of two weeks. This criterion of success has been found very satisfactory, except in the case of those few enuretics who have a history of periodic bursts of wetting interspersed with long dry periods of two weeks or more duration.

It has become routine to warn the parent when the instrument is returned of the possible occurrence of lapses, and to explain how to deal with them in such a way as to avoid destruction of the patient's confidence. Frequently, isolated wetting episodes are associated with exhaustion following a series of late nights or with the presence of an ailment. In a very large number of cases, treatment is followed by sporadic lapses that may occur a few times in as many months but without any trend to consistent wetting being established. Retreatment is considered only with definite relapsers. As indicated in an earlier section, true relapsers comprise a class distinct from sporadic wetters. True relapse usually occurs within a few weeks, but seldom immediately after treatment. Retreatment is usually faster than initial treatment, but also fails completely with a few cases. In a very small minority, repeated relapse occurs.

It is not usually necessary to isolate the patient from siblings during treatment even if the alarm is nondirectional and of high intensity. Siblings may be disturbed during the first night or two but thereafter sleep soundly through each stimulus while the patient develops greater ease of arousal. It has thus been found possible successively and successfully to treat four children sleeping in the same room. There seems to be no record of attempts having been made to treat simultaneously a number of children in one room, and it would be expected that, unless the alarms were directional and quite distinct, difficulties would ensue. The burden of parental supervision would, in any case, be excessive. Where more than one child of the family is to be treated, there are psychological reasons for precedence of the elder.

Use of the bell alarm in a dormitory is impracticable because of the high probability of antagonistic attitudes arising. For institutional use, it is necessary to achieve at least semi-isolation of the patient, as was the case in the study of Davidson and Douglass (1950). The near presence and sympathetic assistance of an adult attendant is also required. These conditions are seldom realized in institutions, and efforts to treat institutionalized children have generally been disappointing.

Drug therapy of enuresis has been discussed, and has been shown to be a much less successful method than conditioning. The use of drugs as an adjuvant therapy with conditioning presents possibilities that are almost unexplored. A present problem with CNS stimulants is the increased tendency to relapse which follows their use. Pending further investigation, it is suggested that CNS stimulants should be avoided as adjuvants, except in the case of a few very deep sleepers who are not otherwise aroused by the alarm, and that, even with these cases, their use should be minimal.

When the enuretic under treatment immediately becomes dry or very intermittent, so that reinforcements are sparse, a diuretic is given nightly with a high fluid intake to encourage diuresis. In most cases, the rate of reinforcement is greatly increased. Other cases develop a pattern of consistently waking to void several times a night, and often continue their self-awakening after treatment is discontinued. The results of this regime pioneered by Coote are sufficiently encouraging to invite systematic investigation.

Use of the perineal pressure appliance of Vincent (1964) and of the bladder training method of Muellner (1958, 1960), or a combination of both, may well prove valuable as adjuvant therapy, but adjuvant therapy in general is still at the research stage. In view of the very high rate of arrest of enuresis, which is usually rapidly attainable with conditioning treatment alone, the need for adjuvant treatment is restricted largely to the management of special cases of enuresis.

INSTRUMENTATION IN CONDITIONING TREATMENT

Following publication by Pfaundler (1904) of his discovery of conditioning treatment of enuresis, a great profusion of equipment has become available, the common purpose being to provide an arousal stimulus rapidly after the onset of micturition.

Largely, this equipment has been built down to a price for direct sale to the public or for cheap hire. One English enuresis alarm is sold for 21 shillings, the price of half a dozen good cigars, but even far more expensive models will be found to be similar in all essential respects to Pfaundler's device used at the turn of the century. There are notable exceptions, but traditionally the crude design of the devices makes their use very complicated and their action erratic and even hazardous. Very little research has been devoted to improving the position, and treatment results commonly obtained fall so far short of those achievable that consideration must be given to the shortcomings of equipment as well as to the lack or complete absence of qualified supervision with which it is generally used.

In its most common form the enuresis alarm comprises a bed pad or mat which is covered by a drawsheet upon which the patient sleeps, preferably naked below the waist. The pad contains electrodes between which urine produces electrical conductivity, thus operating a nearby alarm unit, usually containing a bell.

The best-known published modification of this arrangement is that due to Crosby (1950), who replaced the auditory stimulus with an electric shock and the bed-pad with male and female structures in contact with the genitals and supporting electrodes as close as possible to the urethral meatus. The reader must be referred to the writings of Crosby (1950), Bostock and Shackleton (1957), and Lovibond (1964) for details and discussion of this apparatus.

Other writers, both before and after Crosby, used electrical stimuli and urine-detecting electrodes worn by the patient. In most cases, for instance, those of Takeuchi (1961) and the Laskow apparatus described by Franczak and Ignatowicz (1964), these electrodes are worn only loosely proximate to the genitals and are located by special pants or belts.

Compared with all such arrangements, the bed-pad urine detector provides a much longer CS-UCS interval but, according to Lovibond's (1963b, 1964) explanation of the mechanism of the treatment in terms of avoidance conditioning, the CS-UCS interval is not critical. Jones (1960), by using the classical, and Lovibond (1964), an aversive conditioning model, have both presented analyses disputing any theoretical advantages of electrical stimuli, and both reject their use on practical grounds. Published results do not indicate any advantages for instruments with shock stimuli and genital electrodes, but there are numerous accounts of difficulties in managing both patient and apparatus.

An interesting modification of the Crosby apparatus with a much more rational basis has recently been described by Millard (1966). The complete device, in portable form, was worn by a 19-year-old-female in the successful treatment of "giggle micturition," for which Millard has suggested the alternative name "ambivalent laughter micturition."

With the pad-and-bell-type instrument, the pad has always presented the central design difficulty. Frequent defects are insensitivity to small amounts of urine, false alarming because of perspiration conductivity or electrodes contacting, rapid electrode corrosion and, not least, the ability to inflict cutaneous ulcers as described by Gillison and Skinner (1958), Coote (1965), Borrie and Fenton (1965, 1966), and Forrester (1966). Ulcers may arise if, as a result of a disarranged drawsheet, there is contact between the skin and the two electrodes simultaneously, but they may also occur with an intact drawsheet interposed between the skin and the electrodes. The presence of an electrolyte facilitates passage of an electric current through the skin, giving rise to the lesions but, whereas the electrolyte has generally been assumed to be urine, Coote (1965) has established that perspiration alone is sufficient.

Borrie and Fenton (1966) have discussed in detail the electrochemical processes that lead to cell death and deep ulceration. These investigators have also pointed out that ulceration can occur in the presence of urine if (1) insufficient urine is present to trigger the alarm, (2) the alarm fails to operate because of a partially depleted battery, or (3) a patient is not roused by the alarm, which rings until battery depletion causes relay dropout, whereupon the electrodes again become alive.

Frequently appearing in crops, and often interspersed with a rash of red papules, the ulcers are typically circular, deeply punched out, and up to 2.5 cm in diameter with a central black haemorrhagic eschar. Relatively painless, they may arise overnight, be fully developed in 24 hours, and take several months to heal. The scars often show keloid formation and may be deeply and permanently colored by metallic ion transfer. The latter effect depends on the nature of the electrodes, but iontophoresis of copper involved in Coote's (1965) self-inflicted ulcers produced scar coloration which has not diminished in 3 years.

Figure 15.1, which is due to Borrie and Fenton, shows erythema and scars of healed ulcers on the same child. Forrester (1966) has described and illustrated ulcers sustained on the thigh, which were of sufficient severity to lead to plastic surgery. The site of the lesions may be the buttocks, arms, legs, or any area of the skin that a restless patient may appose to the electrodes or the drawsheet above them. The incidence of lesions is probably underestimated, as painless lesions may not be reported, but it is noteworthy that Gillison and Skinner found 11 out of 48 (23 percent) of their cases to be affected.

As the literature of physical medicine is replete with warnings of electrolytic "burns," and permanent "tattooing" because of ion transfer in direct current applications, one is left to wonder why these effects were not anticipated and prevented with enuresis alarms. There are several ways in which these effects may be overcome but, in considering them, we must break with tradition and accept the fact that refinements in equipment often make it more expensive. First, properly constructed Mowrer (1938) pads, presently to be described, are almost certainly ulcer free, but they have some practical disadvantages in use. Recessed electrode pads, also presently to be described, have a record of freedom from problems of all kinds. As a third approach, the use of alternating current across the pad electrodes almost completely prevents electrolytic corrosion as well as ulcers, but it usually presupposes the use of a mains operated unit. A high degree of intrinsic electrical safety can be achieved with such instruments, but trailing high tension leads are best avoided in bedrooms where there are small children, and portability must be sacrificed with reliance on mains operation.

A further approach to the design of ulcer-free equipment lies in the use of exceedingly small potential differences and currents across the electrodes. Ulcers produced experimentally by Coote (1965) arose out of the application for only 10 minutes of 6 volts and a current strength always less than 3 milliamperes. Borrie and Fenton (1966) did not report current strength, but succeeded with 3 volts applied for 25 minutes and failed with 1.5 volts used for 80 minutes. Potential differences much lower than the decomposition potential of urine could be used across the electrodes of bed-pads, because holding circuits have ample time to operate before polarization interrupts the current. Instead of applying a potential difference, it is possible on the other hand to use dissimilar electrodes that, when bridged by urine, form a primary cell of exceedingly low EMF. By using semi-conductor amplification, the operation of an instrument on this principle presents interesting possibilities. With very low voltages and currents, electrode corrosion must be greatly diminished but, unfortunately the problem of false alarming because of perspiration conduction remains. This may be controlled by purely electrical means with the sacrifice of sensitivity, but pad-structure is an important factor in its complete elimination.

There is a profusion of varieties of bed-pad in use but, insofar as they are known to the writers, they all appear to fall into a few distinct structural types.

The Pfaundler (1904) pad and its variants is still widely used. There are two wire screens, between which is sandwiched a layer of linen or other insulating fabric that, when wet with urine, provides an electrically conducting path between the screens, hence operating an alarm circuit. After wetting, a fresh dry sheet of linen is inserted between

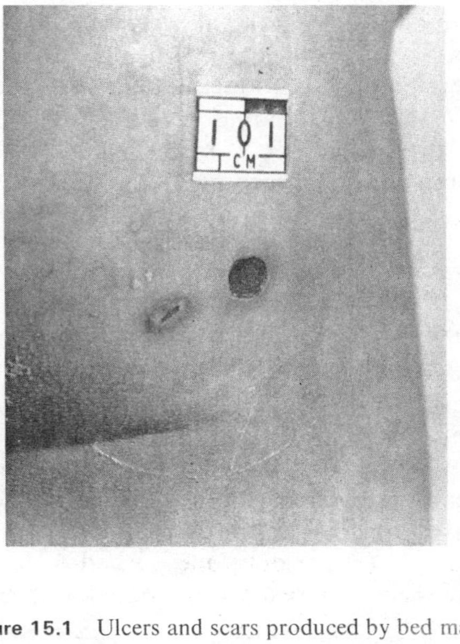

Figure 15.1 Ulcers and scars produced by bed mats. (*Source*. Lovibond & Coote.)

the screens before the alarm unit is reset. The screens may buckle and separate widely except where directly under the patient's weight, so that over a large area they cannot be bridged by urine and are rendered ineffective. False alarms may be caused by screens pressing through the fabric, by perspiration conduction or by misalignment of the 3 layers so that the screen perimeters touch. The most common variant is the use of aluminium foils, the upper one being perforated, as a highly expendable substitute for the screens. In a similar manner, sheets of electrically conductive rubber, plastic, and fabric have been used.

The Pfaundler (1904) pad structure can give rise to ulcers or electrolytic "burns" if the bed is disarranged by a restless patient, thus causing the electrodes to misalign, as can easily happen with smoothly sliding foils, so that both make contact with perspiration moistened skin. Otherwise misalignment can easily occur when the layers are assembled, and there is no reason to doubt that the lesions occur as a result of conduction through the urinous, or perspiration moistened, sheet.

Mowrer (1938) improved on the Pfaundler structure by quilting the screens and separator together. This ensured that the screens would be rapidly bridged by urine when wet, and would be quickly effective in producing a stimulus. The possibility of ulcers is eliminated if the screens are identical, correctly aligned, and particularly if the edges are bound with insulating material. Electrolysis can only occur in the fabric separator, and there can be no conductive path through the skin. Notwithstanding its advantages, the Mowrer structure has not replaced the Pfaundler one in general use. With both of them there is a need for as many as 6 complete pads or separators per patient and for a daily ritual of cleansing and drying.

A further improvement made by Mowrer (1938) was the inclusion of a relay in the pad circuit, thereby, greatly increasing its sensitivity to urine. This innovation, however, has not been included in some of the most widely distributed present-day equipment, which also employs foil pads essentially inferior to the 1904 wire screens.

Seiger (1952) developed a bed-pad that can easily be wiped dry for immediate reuse. The electrodes are thin parallel strips of sheet metal, preferably inconel, bonded and keyed into a rubber sheet. Alternate strips are linked to form two intermeshing sets. Other versions of the Seiger structure are widespread; wire sewn on rubber with a zigzag stitch, flat braided wire sewn on rubber, and strips of aluminium foil sewn to plastic being but a few. In common they have an evil reputation for producing cutaneous ulcers if used with direct current, and for rapid electrolytic corrosion of the electrode material. With a disarranged drawsheet the skin, moistened by perspiration or urine, provides a direct conductive path, and a parallel conductive path if separated from the electrodes by an intact but moistened drawsheet.

If the pad is flexible enough for crumpling, false alarms arise from electrode contact, but they are otherwise commonly caused by perspiration conduction unless the sensitivity of the alarm unit is carefully adjusted. Even when the drawsheet is not perceptibly moist, perspiration conduction is usually present, and measurements of current show fluctuations if there is a redistribution of the patient's weight on the drawsheet. That conduction by and electrolysis of perspiration are largely and probably mainly responsible for corrosion of the anode is shown by the fact that it proceeds apace when the pad is used on the bed of a nonenuretic.

Coote (1965) developed a pad in which the electrodes were recessed below the upper surface[4] to a depth empirically determined as, at least, one third of their least lateral dimension. Physical and electrical contact, between electrodes and the drawsheet or, if this is displaced, with the bare skin, is a near impossibility. These pads have been used with 6-volt battery-driven alarms in over 1000 treatments, and there have been no reports of cutaneous ulcers. Corrosion of the electrodes is extremely slow, and false-alarming because of perspiration conduction has been reported only once (with an instrument used in the tropics on a high circuit sensitivity setting).

The present form of the recessed-electrode pad is shown in Figures 15.2 and 15.3. A moulded sheet of neoprene is provided in its upper surface with parallel grooves which

---

[4]Australian Patent 236255 and New Zealand Patent 125511 apply to the recessed electrode principle.

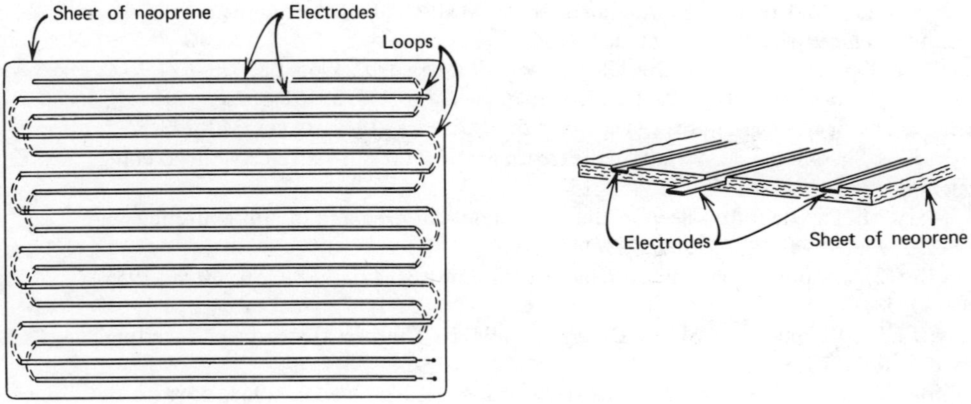

Figures 15.2 and **15.3** Recessed electrode pad construction. (*Source*. Lovibond & Coote.)

accommodate alternately arranged continuous nichrome wire braid electrodes looping underneath the ends of the pad through PVC insulation. The braid is held with terylene zigzag stitching which passes through fine stretch-nylon backing, moulded into the lower surface of the pad. The structure is easily wiped dry. Cleansing presents no problem; its flexibility enables it to be rolled for packaging, and the materials are chosen to withstand the effects of urine, oil based germicides, and autoclave temperatures. Materials costs and labor involved make these pads relatively expensive, but they are at the same time economical because of their high durability.

Recessed electrode pads require, in general, more sensitive alarm circuitry than others for their satisfactory operation, and these requirements, as well as detailed specifications of the pads, have been dealt with elsewhere by Coote (1965).[5] There have been subsequent modifications of details but not of principle. Because of their extreme simplicity, conventional circuits in common use will not be discussed here, but the reader is referred to the papers of Davidson and Douglass (1950), Borrie and Fenton (1966) and Seiger (1952).

A great deal of investigation remains to be carried out concerning auditory stimuli for enuresis alarms. The common electric doorbell, well adjusted, provides a cheap, satisfactory answer for most purposes, but is far from being the most physically efficient transducer, and for a given energy output it probably does not produce the most effective arousal stimulus. Although this is seldom a disadvantage, it is nondirectional. Present knowledge of auditory perception could provide some rational bases for selection and testing of stimuli from the existing unlimited range of electronically producible cacophony.

The Twin Signal and Brief Stimulus devices described by Lovibond (1964) need only be mentioned here; further investigations of these methods are at present being carried out, but as yet no results are available.

REFERENCES

Baller, W., & Schalock, H. Conditioned response treatment of enuresis. *Except. Child.* 1956, **22**, 233–236 and 247–248.

Basmajian, J. V. *Muscles alive*, Baltimore, Wilkins, 1962.

Behrle, F. C., Elkin, M. T., & Laybourne, P. C. Evaluation of a conditioning device in the treatment of nocturnal enuresis. *Pediatrics*, 1956, **17**, 849–854.

[5] The original publication contained an error in circuitry. Corrected reprints are available from the author.

Blackman, S., & Goldstein, K. M. A comparison of MMPI's of enuretic with non-enuretic adults. *J. clin. Psychol.*, 1965, **21,** 282–283.

Borrie, P., & Fenton, J. C. B. Buzzer Ulcers. *Proc. R. Soc. Med.*, 1965, **58**, 623–624.

Borrie, P., & Fenton, J. C. B. Buzzer Ulcers. *Brit. med. J.*, 1966, **2**, 151–152.

Bostock, J. The deep sleep-enuresis syndrome. *Med. J. Aust.*, 1962, **49** (1), 240–243.

Bostock, J., & Shackleton, M. Pitfalls in the treatment of enuresis by an electric awakening machine. *Med. J. Aust.*, 1957, **2**, 152–154.

Boyd, Mary M. The depth of sleep in enuretic school-children and in non-enuretic controls. *J. Psychosom. Res.*, 1960, **4**, 274–281.

Braithwaite, J. V. Some problems associated with enuresis. *Proc. Roy. Soc. Med.*, 1955, **49**, 33–38.

Bransby, E. R., Blomfield, J. M., & Douglas, J. W. B. The prevalence of bed-wetting. *Med. Offr.*, 1955, **94**, 5–7.

Broughton, R. J. Sleep Disorders: Disorders of arousal? *Science*, 1968, **159**, 1070–1078.

Coote, M. A. Apparatus for conditioning treatment of enuresis. *Behav. Res. Ther.*, 1965, **2**, 233–238.

Crosby, N. D. Essential enuresis: successful treatment based on physiological concepts. *Med. J. Aust.*, 1950, **2**, 533–543.

Cullen, K. J. Clinical observations concerning behaviour disorders in children. *Med. J. Aust.*, 1966, **1**, 712–715.

Davidson, J. R., & Douglass, E. Nocturnal enuresis: a special approach to treatment. *Brit. med. J.*, 1950, **1**, 1345–1350.

De Leon, G., & Mandell, W. A comparison of conditioning and psychotherapy in the treatment of functional enuresis. *J. clin. Psychol.*, 1966, **22**, 326–330.

Ditman, K. S., & Blinn, K. A. Sleep levels in enuresis. *Amer. J. Psychiat.*, 1955, **111**, 913–920.

Dorison, E. E., & Blackman, S. Imipramine in the treatment of adult enuretics. *Amer. J. Psychiat.*, 1962, **119**, 474.

Eysenck, H. J. *The dynamics of anxiety and hysteria.* London: Kegan Paul, 1957.

Forrester, R. M. Correspondence. *Brit. med. J.*, 1966, **2**, 302.

Forrester, R. M., Stein, Z., & Susser, M. W. A trial of conditioning therapy in nocturnal enuresis. *Develop. Med. & Child Neurol.*, 1964, **6**, 158–166.

Franczak, W. Daily rhythm of urinary excretion in children with urinary incontinence. *Pediatria Polska*, 1965, **40**, 405–408.

Franczak, W., & Ignatowicz, R. The treatment of nocturnal enuresis with the Laskow waking apparatus. *Z. Urol.*, 1964, **57**, 629–631.

Freyman, R. Follow-up study of enuresis treated with a bell apparatus. *J. Child Psychol. Psychiat.*, 1963, **4**, 199–206.

Geppert, T. V. Management of nocturnal enuresis by conditioned response. *J. Amer. med. Assoc.*, 1953, **152**, 318–383.

Gerbrandt, L. K. Neural systems of response release and control. *Psychol. Bull.*, 1965, **64**, 113–123.

Gillison, T. H., & Skinner, J. L. Treatment of nocturnal enuresis by the electric alarm. *Brit. med. J.*, 1958, **2**, 1268–1272.

Glicklich, L. B. An historical account of enuresis. *Pediatrics.* 1951, **8**, 859–876.

Gunnarson, S., & Melin, K. A. The electroencephalogram in enuresis. *Acta Paediat.*, 1951, **40**, 496–501.

Hicks, W. R., & Barnes, E. H. A double blind study of the effect of imipramine on enuresis in 100 Naval recruits. *Amer. J. Psychiat.*, 1964, **120**, 812.

Huijssoon, W. C. Treatment of nocturnal enuresis with an electric alarm. *Ned. Tijdschr. Geneesk.*, 1963, **107**, 159–162.

Jones, H. G. The behavioural treatment of enuresis nocturna. In H. J. Eysenck (Ed.), *Behavior therapy and the neuroses.* Oxford: Pergamon, 1960.

Konorski, J. *Conditioned reflexes and neuron organization.* Cambridge: Cambridge University Press, 1948.

Lickorish, J. R. One hundred enuretics. *J. Psychosom. Res.*, 1964, **7**, 263–267.

Lovibond, S. H. Positive and negative conditioning of the GSR. *Acta Psychologica*, 1963, **21**, 106–107. (a)

Lovibond, S. H. The mechanism of conditioning treatment of enuresis. *Behav. Res. Ther.*, 1963, **1**, 17–21. (b)

Lovibond, S. H. *Conditioning and enuresis*. Oxford: Pergamon, 1964.

Martin, B., & Kubly, D. Results of treatment of enuresis by a conditioned response method. *J. consult. Psychol.*, 1955, **19**, 71–73.

Millard, D. W. A conditioning treatment for "giggle micturition". *Behav. Res. Ther.*, 1966, **4**, 229–231

Mowrer, O. H. *Learning theory and personality dynamics*. New York: Ronald, 1950.

Mowrer, O. H. Apparatus for the study and treatment of enuresis. *Amer. J. Psychol.*, 1938, **51**, 163–166.

Mowrer, O. H., & Mowrer, W. A. Enuresis: a method for its study and treatment. *Amer. J. Orthopsychiat.*, 1938, **8**, 436–447.

Muellner, S. R. The voluntary control of micturition in man. *J. Urol.*, 1958, **80**, 473–478.

Muellner, S. R. Development of urinary control in children: a new concept in cause, prevention and treatment of primary enuresis. *J. Urol.*, 1960, **84**, 714–716.

Munster, A. J. Stanley, A. M., & Saunders, J. C. Imipramine (Tofranil) in the treatment of enuresis. *Amer. J. Psychiat.*, 1961, **118**, 76–77.

Nelson, W. E. *Textbook of pediatrics*. New York: Saunders, 1964.

Pavlov, I. P. *Conditioned reflexes*. (trans. by G. V. Anrep). London: Oxford University Press, 1927.

Pereira-D'Oliviera, E. Nocturnal enuresis treated by the alarm clock method. *Ned. Tijdschr. Geneesk.*, 1961, **105**, 867–870.

Pfaundler, M. Demonstration of an apparatus for automatic warning of the occurrence of bedwetting. *Verh. Ges. Kinderheilk*, 1904, **21**, 219–220.

Pierce, C. M., Lipcon, H. H., McLary, J. H., & Noble, H. F. Enuresis: psychiatric interview studies. *U.S. Armed Forces med. J.*, 1956, **7**, 1265–1280.

Poussaint, A. F., & Ditman, K. S. A controlled study of imipramine (tofranil) in the treatment of childhood enuresis. *J. Pediat.*, 1965, **67**, 283–290.

Seiger, H. W. Treatment of essential nocturnal enuresis. *J. Pediat.*, 1952, **40**, 738–749.

Stephens, F. D. Pediatric Society of Victoria: Symposium on urinary tract infection. *Med. J. Aust.*, 1965, **2**, 507.

Takeuchi, M. Trial of an apparatus for the treatment of nocturia and results of its use. *J. Ther. Tokyo*, 1961, **43**, 2183–2187.

Taylor, I. O. A scheme for the treatment of enuresis by electric buzzer apparatus. *Med. Offr.*, 1963, **110**, 139.

Temmes, Y., & Toivakka, E. Uber die EEG-Befunde bei Enuresis. *Acta paediatr., Stockh.*, 1954, **43**, 259–263.

Turner, R. K., & Young, G. C. CNS stimulant drugs and conditioning treatment of nocturnal enuresis. *Behav. Res. Ther.*, 1966, **4**, 225–228.

Turton, E. C., & Spear, A. B. EEG findings in 100 cases of severe enuresis. *Arch. Dis. Child.*, 1953, **28**, 316–320.

Vincent, S. A. Treatment of enuresis with a perineal pressure apparatus: the irritable bladder syndrome. *Develop. Med. Child Neurol.*, 1964, **6**, 23–31.

Vincent, S. A. Some aspects of bladder mechanics. *Bio-Medical Engineering*, 1966, **1**, 438–445.

Vincent, S. A. Paper given to the British Psychological Society Conference, Belfast, April, 1967.

Werry, J. S., & Cohrssen, J. Enuresis—an etiologic and therapeutic study. *J. Pediat.*, 1965, **67**, 423–431.

Willett, R. A. Measures of learning and conditioning. In H. J. Eysenck (Ed.) *Experiments in personality*. Vol. 2. London: Routledge and Kegan Paul, 1960.

Young, G. C. Conditioning treatment of enuresis. *Develop. Med. Child Neurol.*, 1965a, **7**, 557–562.

Young, G. C. Personality factors and the treatment of enuresis. *Behav. Res. Ther.*, 1965b, **3**, 103–105.

Young, G. C., & Turner, R. K. CNS stimulant drugs and conditioning treatment of nocturnal enuresis. *Behav. Res. Ther.*, 1965, **3**, 93–101.

Chapter 16

Hyperactivity[1]

JOHN S. WERRY AND ROBERT L. SPRAGUE

Hyperactivity is a conspicuous complaint made by adults about children's behavior. For example, Lapouse and Monk (1958) showed that approximately fifty percent of children aged 6 to 12 years were described by their mothers as being overactive, and about one third as restless. Thus, it is not surprising that hyperactivity should also be a common symptom of psychopathology in childhood. Chess (1960) found that about ten percent of children seen in her private practice were referred directly because of hyperactivity. Patterson (Patterson, Jones, Whittier, & Wright, 1965) found hyperactivity to be among the commonest problems for referral to four child guidance clinics.

Although it is possible to spend much time attempting to define what activity (and hence what hyperactivity) really is (Cromwell, Baumeister, & Hawkins, 1963), it seems clear that clinicians view it as *movement* not only locomotion, but increasingly also, any and all movements of the body, head, limb, and extremities including those occurring in the stationary position. The inclusion of motor responses other than movement, such as vocalization, seems less well established. For the purposes of this discussion, the authors will accept the above definition of activity as movement of all kinds and will exclude vocalization.

Hyperactivity tends to be viewed in the clinical literature most commonly as a stable behavioral or personality dimension; thus, the child is seen as having some kind of internal regulatory mechanism which tends to stabilize in a characteristic fashion, the total amount of movement made each day or the total energy output of the motor system (Schulman, Kaspar, & Throne, 1965). The hyperactive child then is one whose daily activity level lies at the upper end of the distribution of this behavioral trait in the population. The studies devoted to examining this hypothetical construct of activity level are sparse although, with the exception of that by Schulman et al. (1965), they give little support to the construct (Cromwell et al., 1963). However, they are too few in number to warrant the abandoning of such a popular clinical concept.

Activity level is essentially a quantitative dimension of behavior, but the clinician views hyperactivity also as having a qualitative element of situational inappropriateness, thus, bringing the child into conflict with his socio-familial environment (Schulman et al., 1965). As we shall learn below, assessment and modification techniques vary in the emphasis they give to these two dimensions but, in this chapter, the qualitative or *problem-behavior-in-the situation* dimension will receive greater

[1]The preparation of this review was supported by Public Health Service Research Grant NB 07346 from the National Institute of Mental Health.

emphasis. This is true because the authors believe that clinically it is more appropriate and useful not only for designing therapeutic programs but also for the much needed ongoing assessment of modification procedures, which ought to be part of every program of therapy.

ETIOLOGY

The earliest reports of hyperactivity in children viewed it as the direct result of damage to the developing brain, particularly from encephalitis, trauma, or anoxia (Ebaugh, 1923; Rosenfeld & Bradley, 1948; Strecker & Ebaugh, 1924). Strauss (Strauss & Lehtinen, 1947, p. 84), in his description of the "brain damaged" child, assigned to hyperactivity the status of a "hard" neurological sign apparently sufficient itself to make the firm diagnosis of brain damage even in the absence of other neurological evidence. In the past two decades other terms such as the hyperkinetic syndrome (Burks, 1960; Laufer & Denhoff, 1957; Ounsted, 1955; Sutherland, 1961) and minimal brain dysfunction (Clements, 1966, Clements & Peters, 1962) have tended to replace the more etiologically positive term of brain-damage syndrome. Nevertheless, the assumption that some kind of organic etiology, albeit obscure, is involved in this symptom-complex and that hyperactivity is its single most valuable diagnostic sign has remained (Clements, 1966). Studies that purport to examine this etiological hypothesis including the ones by Strauss himself (see Sarason, 1949) are generally of such poor quality that there is little substantial empirical evidence to support it.

In general, when the criteron for selection of subjects has been *brain damage* established by neurological (rather than behavioral) means (Ernhart, Graham, Eichman, Marshall, & Thurston, 1963; Prechtl & Dijkstra, 1960) or inferred from noxious events that carry a high probability of causing significant brain damage, for example, severe perinatal anoxia (Graham, Ernhart, Thurston, & Craft, 1962; Prechtl & Dijkstra, 1960; Schachter & Apgar, 1959), the studies, with the exception of those by Prechtl, fail to show that hyperactivity occurs more frequently in the brain-damaged group than in the controls. On the other hand, when the starting point of the study has been abnormal behavior, such as chronic hyperactivity or the hyperkinetic syndrome, a variety of mild neurological, electroencephalographic, perceptual and sensorimotor abnormalities are usually found also to be present in a frequency somewhat in excess of that observed in normal children (Burks, 1960; Laufer, Denhoff, & Solomons, 1957; Stewart, Pitts, Craig, & Dieruf, 1966; Werry, Weiss, & Douglas, 1964; Werry, Weiss, Douglas, & Martin, 1966). However, the neurological significance of these minor abnormalities is contentious, and although some investigators (Burks, 1960; Ingram, 1956; Ounsted, Lindsay, & Norman, 1966; Rosenfeld & Bradley, 1948; Werry et al., 1964) have found hyperactive children to exhibit an excess of events in their histories that might have caused brain damage, this excess is usually slight, and the frequency with which these events are actually attended by brain damage is likely to be relatively low. In other instances, the apparent excess may be explicable by the failure to control for IQ, since brain damage and IQ are negatively correlated. Other investigators (Stewart et al., 1966) or the same investigators, by using medical records instead of mothers' histories (Minde, Webb, & Sykes, 1968), have not been able to demonstrate any anamnestic differences.

Animal studies suggest that high activity level can be transmitted genetically (Cromwell et al., 1963; Fuller and Thompson, 1960) although such high activity in lower animals is often considered a sign of superior intelligence rather than an undesirable behavioral trait. Ablation studies in animals (Cromwell et al., 1963; Davis, 1957; French & Harlow, 1955) seem to have established fairly clearly that damage to several areas of the brain, notably, the frontal lobes, the basal ganglia, the hypothalamus, and the reticular activating system can produce significant changes in activity level. The clinical use of neuroleptic drugs such as the phenothiazines has demonstrated that they can produce akathisia or motor restlessness in adults. Thus, the evidence from animal studies and from clinical psychopharmacology tends to support the hypothesis that interference with cerebral function can result in hyperactivity.

On the other hand, as can readily be inferred from incidental remarks by apologists for the organic point of view (for example, Knobel, Wolman, & Mason, 1959; Clements & Peters, 1962), there has always been a strong body of opinion among clinicians working with children that psychological or experiential factors might be at least, if not more, important in the etiology of hyperactivity than organic disturbances. Evidence from animal studies (see Cromwell et al., 1963) suggests that gross early environmental restrictions can lead to hyperactivity, although in higher animals this tends to take the form of rather dramatic stereotypies. The effect of anxiety in producing acute bouts of restlessness is, of course, a universal human experience.

Multivariate studies of normal and behaviorally abnormal children (Digman, 1965; Rodin, Lucas & Simson, 1963; Schulman et al., 1965; Werry, 1968a) have thrown considerable doubt on the hypothesis that hyperactivity is part of a "minimal brain dysfunction syndrome." This seems to support the contention of others (Chess, 1960; Eisenberg, 1957; Werry et al., 1966) that hyperactivity can and does occur frequently without any other indications of brain dysfunction.

From the clinical point of view it seems legitimate to ask what difference a diagnosis of "organicity" makes in the practical handling of a child for whom hyperactivity is a problem? Does it necessitate a significantly different type of treatment or response by the child to a particular treatment? The studies by Eisenberg (Eisenberg, Gilbert, Cytryn, & Molling, 1961) suggest that the hyperactive child generally responds better to pharmacotherapy than to brief psychotherapy. But the diagnosis of hyperkinesis appears to have been strictly behavioral, and thus brain status has no *direct* relevance to treatment. Attempts to demonstrate a useful role for valid indixes of cerebral status, such as electroencephalographic or neurological abnormality in the treatment of the hyperactive child (nearly always in conjunction with pharmocological studies), have yielded conflicting results where IQ is held constant (Burks, 1964; Knobel, et al. 1959; Weiss, Werry, Minde, Douglas, & Sykes, in press; Werry et al., 1966), scarcely giving firm support to the idea that these indices have any substantial role to play in the management of hyperactivity. Although diagnosis of minimal brain dysfunction does seem to alert clinicians to the possibility of coexisting educational and perceptual motor deficits, as with Eisenberg's diagnostic category of hyperkinesis, assumptions about the state of the central nervous system do not contribute in any direct way to the assessment or remediation of these deficits. Hence, in the present state of knowledge, the validity of the organic etiological hypothesis appears to be for clinicians, an interesting although largely irrelevant question.

LEARNING IN HYPERACTIVITY

As noted, hyperactive children are often academically retarded, or display learning deficiencies, and perhaps one of the more interesting questions in the study of hyperactivity is why hyperactive children often show this poor learning performance. They are described as having short attention spans and as being distractable (see Ounsted et al., 1966). In most academic learning situations, it is necessary for the child actively to seek information for a considerable portion of his time relative to the task to be learned. Thus, motor behaviors that interfere with this active seeking of information may limit the amount of information he can obtain. This analysis can most readily be understood when we consider visual learning tasks. If the child is not properly oriented to the visual material when it is presented, he cannot make the proper associations expected of him by the teacher. Some evidence has accumulated, although by no means conclusive, that hyperactive children are deficient in visual learning tasks, perhaps because of irrelevant head turning movement. In a thorough study of the performance of bright, normal, and retarded children on a wide range of learning tasks, Carrier, Malpass, and Orton (1961) had raters judge the amount of movement of the child during learning tasks. As was expected, the bright and normal children showed significantly larger improvement scores over the range of learning tasks than did the retarded. However, while performing these tasks, the retarded children moved their heads significantly more than (1) the bright children, and (2) the normal children, although total movement was slightly greater for bright and normal children than for the retarded ones.

In a doctoral dissertation, Freibergs

(1965) had a group of normal and a group of hyperactive children, who were equated for IQ, perform a visual concept formation task. The hyperactive children took significantly more trials to learn the concepts. Under conditions of partial reinforcement (50 percent) the hyperactive children performed at significantly lower learning levels.

By using a delay of reinforcement task, which may maximize the interfering effects of hyperactivity by permitting more irrelevant intervening motor behaviors to occur. Sprague and Toppe (1966) found that a group of retarded children in the upper quartile on a direct activity measure made significantly fewer correct responses in a simple two-choice discrimination task than a group of children, matched on MA and chronological age, from the lower activity quartile.

These studies lend some support to the speculation that hyperactivity in the classroom may be more serious than its nuisance value to the social system. It appears that the hyperactivity may be actively interfering with the learning process. If this is the case, then it is relatively easy to understand how a hyperactive child could fall behind his peers in the class. Furthermore, it is quite possible that, when the child falls behind his peer group, he may develop an aversion or an avoidance response to academic material that is proving difficult for him, and thus becomes even more hyperactive.

If the behavior modification approach (vide infra) is used, one should perhaps attack directly the short attention span (for example, Quay, Werry, McQueen, & Sprague, 1966b; Quay, Sprague, Werry, & McQueen, 1967) as well as the excessive movement that may be interfering with learning particularly on visual tasks. By doing so, in the absence of cognitive handicaps, it might be possible to treat the hyperactive child early enough to prevent serious academic retardation, although Ounsted and his colleagues (Ounsted et al., 1966) view this problem with considerable pessimism, perhaps, an artifact of their studying retarded hyperkinetic children.

ASSESSMENT

We shall give attention now to the assessment of hyperactivity, but this does not in any way imply that the clinician ought not to be sensitive to other problem behaviors, particularly learning difficulties. As discussed above, we do believe, however, that medical-type assessments such as the electroencephalogram (see Freeman, 1967), neurological examination, and medical history are among the least helpful of all assessment procedures and should be kept to a minimum, except where there is suspicion of disease of the central nervous system *requiring medical treatment* excluding psychopharmacological drugs, the indications for which are not medical but rather behavioral.

Assessment techniques should meet three criteria—reliability, validity, and practicality, although it is doubtful if any of the well-established assessment techniques for hyperactivity meet all three criteria. Research workers, in general, have tended to concentrate on the problem of reliability, very often at the expense of validity and particularly by ignoring practicality. It seems trite to state that a good assessment technique should yield data useful to the clinician (1) in deciding whether there is a problem requiring treatment, (2) in planning how to modify particular problem behaviors, and (3) in assessing the results of therapeutic procedures. Yet, few psychometric or other psychodiagnostic techniques, reportedly developed to aid clinicians, have met these criteria hitherto. In this chapter, then, emphasis will be given to assessment techniques that appear to be useful and practical without, however, too much sacrifice of reliability.

Most assessment techniques to date have been principally quantitative. They have been concerned with assessing the amount of activity or, in short, the measurement of activity level. The assumption of a stable, internally determined activity level suggests that the assessment of activity in one situation, such as the laboratory or the clinic, might then be sufficient to be generalized to all other situations in the child's waking day. As we have pointed out above, the evidence for a stable activity level is by no means established, and there is evidence that children's activity can vary greatly not only from situation to situation (Patterson et al., 1965; Schulman et al., 1965) but also from day to day in the same situation (Patterson et al., 1965). Thus a prerequisite of any assessment purporting to be quantitative is that of adequate sampling across time and across situations.

Quantitative assessment can yield useful data both in evaluating the seriousness of a child's hyperactivity and as a dependent measure of therapeutic efforts, particularly pharmacotherapy. However, in the authors' opinion, quantitative type data needs, for purposes of meaningful therapeutic programs, even pharmacotherapy, to be complemented with some qualitative or functional-analytic type assessment that seeks to assess the motor behavior not only in terms of its amount but also in terms of its precipitants (stimuli) and its perpetuating consequences (reinforcements). Even those who had adhered most strongly to the organic point of view of hyperactivity, such as Strauss (Strauss & Lehtinen, 1947), have nevertheless laid great emphasis on structuring the environment or, in short, in altering stimuli (reduction of stimulus input, enhancement of stimulus value) and response-reinforcement contingencies (consistency). Neither is there any major contradiction to be found between this analytic approach and the pyschodynamic approach, which has always laid great emphasis on the precipitants and consequences of behavior. The latter has, perhaps, concentrated on remote rather than immediate causes of behavior, and has inferred, rather than demonstrated empirically, response-reinforcement contingencies. If we accept the basic premise that hyperactivity, indeed, is affected by environmental antecedents and by consequences, then some functional assessment would appear an essential part of assessment.

To conceptualize the assessment of hyperactive behaviors, so as to make the results as pertinent as possible to therapy, assessment may be considered as proceeding in three phases none of which is, of course, independent or completely distinct from others.

1. *Problem definition*. Assessment of hyperactivity must begin with some kind of overall inquiry that is aimed at eliciting from those complaining about the child's behavior the nature, the severity, and the situations in which hyperactivity appears to be a problem. In this way, a hierarchy of hyperactive behaviors according to nuisance value and/or the possibilities of modification attempts can be constructed.

2. *Problem analysis*. When the problem behaviors that are to serve as the focus of modification have been selected, except in those cases where pharmocotherapy is the only therapeutic approach, some assessment technique that attempts to detail the functional relationships (stimulus—response—reinforcement sequence) of these problem behaviors should be instituted since the information yielded will form the basis of planning the therapeutic program.

In attempting to make a meaningful assessment of stimuli, or precipitants, and of reinforcements, it is necessary to make two assumptions both of which have a fair degree of experimental support. They are the assumptions of immediacy and of the importance of social reinforcers. Immediacy suggests that stimuli and reinforcements, although particularly the latter, must stand in close temporal relationship to the problem behavior, thus, enabling the clinician to narrow the field for examination down to within a few seconds prior to and succeeding the problem behavior. The second assumption about the power of social reinforcers indicates that the factors perpetuating the problem behavior are most likely to be found in the responses of other persons in the child's immediate environment, particularly those who are held in high esteem by him or have power over him (Bandura & Walters, 1964). Similarly, the controlling stimuli are also likely to emanate from the same sources. Thus a functional analysis of the problem behavior should pay attention particularly to what significant persons in the child's environment are doing in the moments before and after the occurrance of the problem behavior. Although the definition of positive reinforcement as any environmental consequence that increases the frequency of a given behavior can be considered to represent the extreme in scientific empiricism, from the clinical point of view there is, nevertheless, merit in this definition, since it outlines a non-inferential purely descriptive approach to the analysis of the influence of the child's environment. In this way, it is sometimes possible to show that what observers judge to be punishment, for example, castigation, is in fact reinforcement, (Brown & Elliott, 1965). For some children, particularly the deprived and the unsuccessful, deviant behaviors are the most probable method available to them for obtaining social reinforcement. Cessation of presumed punishment may result in disappearance or reduction of the problem behavior. This illustrates that judgements about the impact of environmental events on the child, made on an emphatic rather than an empirical basis, at times, may be seriously in error.

3. *Problem measurement*. Some assessment techniques that give quantitative data, such as the frequency of a particular behavior in unit time, should be used then, or concurrent with (2), since this data will form the basis by which the efficacy of any therapeutic effects will be evaluated. They need not be limited to problem behaviors selected for treatment, since measurement of untreated behaviors may be used for control purposes. Hopefully, clinicians will not consider problem measurement as something that is of interest only to researchers, but as a means of the ongoing assessment of their own therapeutic efforts.

Assessment Techniques

Assessment techniques for hyperactivity are many and varied. The clinician should choose an assessment technique that is most suited to his own particular resources and that is likely to be most pertinent to his own clinical needs. A practical categorization of these techniques is (1) questionnaire-rating scale techniques, (2) the direct observations of behavior by using observers, and (3) the direct measurement of physical movement.

Questionnaire-Rating Scales

In this assessment technique, an adult [or occasionally a peer (Bower, 1960)], who is with the child for a significant period of time, usually on a fairly regular basis, such as a parent, a teacher, or a ward attendant, is asked to rate the child on items that pertain to motor behaviors. This method, of course, is fraught with all the well-known errors inherent in rating scale techniques. However, the disadvantages of using parents and teachers as raters have probably been overemphasized since certain investigators (Bower, 1960; Glidewell, Mensh, & Gildea, 1957; Novick, 1964; Quay, Sprague, Schulman & Miller, 1966a) have demonstrated that they can have a surprising degree of utility in the assessment of children's behavior problems. A lot depends on the nature of the questions. For example, in an epidemiological survey (Lapouse & Monk, 1958), 49 percent of children aged 6 to 12 years were described as "overactive" by their mothers and 30 percent as "restless." However, when hyperactivity is assessed by a series of operationalized questions such as "how many times does your child leave the table during a meal?" the answers to which are either self-quantifying or readily graded, satisfactory interrater reliability and the ability to discriminate between problem children and normals can be achieved (Werry et al., 1966). To abandon the questionnaire rating scale altogether would have the double disadvantage of losing an assessment technique that has the virtues of simplicity and inexpensiveness and of failing to use information coming from persons who are continuously sampling the child's behavior in many differing situations in a way which is difficult and expensive to reproduce by other means. Thus, for all their shortcomings, rating scales have a potential advantage over most other techniques, which ordinarily can be used to sample the child's behavior only for a sharply limited time or in an artificial situation.

There are several published rating scales (Burks, 1964; Graham, Ernhart, Craft, & Berman, 1963; McConnell, Cromwell, Bialer, & Son, 1964; Schrager, Lindy, Harrison, McDermott, & Killins, 1966; Sylvester, 1933).

A five-point Child Rating Scale with ten items was developed by McConnell et al. (1964) to measure the activity of institutionalized retardates. Although the reliability seems adequate (the average test-retest reliability over a one week interval was $r = .84$), the validity leaves something to be desired. The average correlation between the Child Rating Scale and ballistographic measures was $r = .20$, and another study (Sprague & Toppe, 1966) indicated that the correlation between the scale and a stabilimetric chair measurement was only $r = .30$. No reliability or validity information is given concerning the checklist published by Schrager et al. (1966). The Questionnaire in Regard to Hyperactive Traits published by Sylvester (1933) seems useful in that it attempts to measure some of the qualitative aspects of hyperactivity. The motor activity subsection of the questionnaire is divided into several areas: (1) content, (2) direction, (3) range, (4) tempo, and (5) variation. Unfortunately, however, no reliability or validity information was given in the published report of this particular checklist.

A rating scale designed by one of the authors (J.W.) in cooperation with Drs. John Peters and Gabrielle Weiss is set out in the Appendix A. It is essentially an amplification of a fairly reliable and valid scale used in earlier investigations of the effect of psychotropic drugs on hyperactivity (Werry et al., 1966). It should offer a means of problem definition, of quantification of activity level that is useful, particularly, in pharmacological work, and a crude quantification of problem behaviors as dependent variable measure. However, as presently constituted, it makes no effort to elicit either stimuli or response-reinforcement contingencies, although they could be added easily in two columns, the first one entitled "Immediate Precipitating Factors" and the second "Immediate Environmental Responses" (for example, praise, blame, physical punishment, etc.). Also, readers are warned that, with the exception of one study by Conners and Rothschild (1968), who found it drug sensitive, there is as yet no field work on the complete instrument and, hence, its practicability, reliability, and validity, are unknown. It is offered largely because there appears to be no satisfactory formally constituted alternative. Clinicians who wish to use it should be prepared to submit it to some scrutiny, albeit cursory.

Direct-Observations of Motor Activity Using Observers

In this assessment technique, the child is observed for a unit of time typically subdivided into cells of a few seconds' duration during which particular motor behaviors are noted as occurring on an all-or-none basis. The individual cells are then summed over the total period of time to give a quantitative score. The situation of observation is either some portion of the child's natural environment, such as the classroom (Patterson et al., 1965), or a laboratory situation (Hutt, Hutt, & Ounsted, 1965). The structure is ordinarily that of the free-field type where the child may behave as he normally does in similar situations. There are several reports of this technique of assessment (Becker, Madsen, Arnold, & Thomas, 1967; Berkson & Mason, 1963; Carrier et al., 1961; Cromwell et al., 1963; Doubros & Daniels, 1966; Hutt et al., 1965; Petterson et al., 1965; Werry et al., 1966; Werry & Quay, 1969), although all the investigators appear to have used somewhat different definitions of target motor behaviors, ranging from locomotion only (Cromwell et al., 1963) to inclusion of several kinds of motor behaviors (Becker et al., 1967; Doubros & Daniels, 1966; Patterson et al., 1965; Hutt et al., 1965; Werry et al., 1966; Werry & Quay, 1969). Reliability is of course likely to be highest where the definition is clear and the number of behaviors to be observed few. In the clinical situation, the target behaviors selected for observation would be the ones defined as problems and, hence, would vary somewhat from child to child and from observing situation to situation, although the variations are probably limited in number as far as hyperactive behaviors are concerned. Patterson et al. (1965) had seven categories of problem behaviors: movements directed toward the body, movements in chair, distraction (that is orientating of the head), gross movements of legs and feet, fiddling, communicative activity, and walking or standing. On the other hand, Cromwell et al. (1963) simply drew squares on a ward floor and counted the number of squares crossed in unit time. Thus, Patterson's technique is likely to be most useful for the classroom, whereas that Cromwell et al. (1963) is more appropriate to a free-field situation. None of the investigators above, however, have recorded any more than quantitative data by this technique, and an instrument that is to be most useful to the clinician, all probability, must be designed on an ad hoc basis, taking account of the needs of the particular child in the particular situation and designed so as to include functional analytic data.

The Berkson and Davenport scale (1962) is a checklist for stereotype movements. Often these stereotype movements are considered as part of the total hyperactivity syndrome. The reported interrater correlation varies between $r = .73$ to $r = .95$, which would appear to be satisfactory. The checklist has been used in a number of studies (Berkson, 1964; Berkson, 1965; Berkson & Mason, 1963; Berkson & Mason, 1964), and has been shown to relate to a number of environmental variables which indicate that the checklist has validity at least for an institutional setting. The Gross Body Movements Scale (Carrier et al., 1961) is a time-sampling checklist of body movements for the face, head, hand, arm and trunk, and feet and legs. This checklist was devised for a research project, and has been shown to be related to learning performance. The interjudge reliability is satisfactory; the mean correlation over several subjects and several of the subparts of the scale is $r = .86$.

The strength of this assessment technique lies in its objectivity and its capacity to yield what may be called "real-life" data. The weaknesses relate to the problems of adequate sampling of the child's behavior, the logistics of its implementation in real-life situations and the cost of the observers. However, there is reason to believe that the substitution of direct observation of this kind for, at least, a portion of the ordinary total time spent in clinical interviewing by professionals would be advantageous (see Cruickshank, Bentzen, Ratzeburg, & Tannhauser, 1961). Furthermore, it is possible to train relatively unskilled person to do this kind of observing who might then be used regularly by clinics to observe children in real-life situations, in place of the present concentration on the individual interview and the psychometric approach.

Direct Measurement of Movement

Here, activity is measured as it occurs by mechanical means. An excellent review of methodologies of direct measurement of activity level has been written by Cromwell et al. (1963). Since the time this article was written, some new techniques have been devised that show great promise in the area of measuring hyperactivity in children.

Open-Field Techniques

Self-winding calendar watches may be modified to measure movement as suggested by Schulman and Reisman (1959) and Bell (1968) so that, as the watch is moved through space, the hands advance. Thus, it is possible to attach the watch to a child at a given time and, at a later time, an adult—an attendant or a parent—can read the amount of movement in terms of hours and days that is recorded on the face of the watch. The advantages of this device are obvious. It does not require a human observer; it is relatively cheap and accurate; the child can be permitted to move about in his natural habitat; and it appears to have adequate reliability. The interday correlation varies between $r = .60$ to $r = .71$. However, it also has certain disadvantages. It does not produce a continuous record of the movement that would be valuable in subsequent analyses for response-reinforcement contingencies.

Ellis and Pryer (1959) have described an apparatus that used photoelectric cells to measure movement in a room. The apparatus they described embraced an eight feet by eight feet space, although obviously the room could be made larger. Lamps and photoelectric cells were placed in the room on opposite walls so that the light from the lamp would activate the photoelectric cell, unless the beam was interrupted by the movement of the subject. The lamps themselves were located 18 inches from the floor and two feet apart and, thus, the room was crisscrossed by a light grid. Each time a light beam was interrupted, the event was recorded on a counter that quantified the amount of movement in the room. The reliability of this technique proved quite satisfactory. By using an odd-even correlation for twenty-minute scores, the correlation was $r = .92$; by using ten-minute scores, $r = .87$. Some of the disadvantages of this technique are that it requires a specialized room, the equipment can be relatively costly, and it is possible for a subject to stand in one corner of the room and rock the upper part of his torso continuously without producing any activity count. Unless his legs were interrupting a light beam, this movement would not be detected by the apparatus. Such stereotype rocking motions are quite common in institutionalized children.

Lee and Hutt (1964) have described a playroom that has been designed to film the movements of children during play activities. A checkerboard pattern of black and gray squares was laid on the floor to assist in the identification of the movements of the children. In one corner of the room was located a camera with a wide angle lens which could cover the complete room. One of the advantages of this type of apparatus is that movement can be permanently recorded on film and judged at a later date by observers. The disadvantages are that the room can be relatively costly and, if much film is used in the process of recording activity, considerable time can be involved.

One of the problems of time-sampling techniques with animals has been the interpreting of records even when automatic equipment, using tilt cages or floors with moveable squares, has been utilized. Newbury (1956) has described a circuit that determines regularly recurring time intervals and that indicates on a permanent record the time intervals that contain activity, and which also records on a counter a cumulative total of the number of active periods. If one were using some time-sampling technique, this particular device would be of considerable value.

Ultrasonic generators have been used to measure the activity of animals. Peacock and Williams (1962) developed a circuit that included an ultrasonic generator and receiver. If the device is used in an enclosed cage or room, the ultrasonic generator radiates signals into the space and sets up standing waves. When these standing waves are disturbed by a subject moving, the receiver detects the signal. The output of the receiver then can be used to drive an oscillograph or a counter. The ultrasonic generator produces a 41-kilohertz signal which is well above the upper threshold of hearing in humans. Thus, the child in such a situation would not be aware that his movements were being monitored and would not be disturbed by the signal. Crawford and Nicora (1964) have used the ultrasonic generator and receiver to measure movement in a group of men, women, and children who participated in a fallout shelter demonstration. This device has the advantage of being able to monitor the movement of an unrestricted subject in a relatively large room without the subject's awareness. The disadvantages are the initial cost of the equipment and, also, it seems that the amplitude of the signal detected by the receiver is not independent of the distance of the moving object from the transmitter, that is, a small hand movement near the transmitter might produce as large an output as walking movement some distance from the transmitter (Werry, unpublished observations).

Sainsbury (1954) has described a technique for measuring movement from film. During the time the motion-picture camera is running, a light is flashed on for a few seconds and then off for a few seconds to signal the time intervals. After the film is developed, it is projected on a screen and an observer judges whether there is or is not movement during a given time interval. Sainsbury reports the interjudge reliability by using this technique to be $r = .86$, which is quite acceptable. Furthermore, he reports that the correlation between an electromyograph and the ratings of the observers viewing the film was $r = .83$. If one wishes to measure precisely the movement recorded on film, Kessen, Hendry, and Leutzendorff (1961) have described a technique whereby the movements of the limbs of an infant can be quantified very precisely. Certain frames from the film are taken, and the location of the limbs and other easily distinguishable features of the baby are noted on tracing paper, that is, the position of the left palm would be outlined on tracing paper. Then, at some specified number of frames later in the sequence, the position of the left palm and, hence, the amount of movement can again be ascertained. Although this technique quantifies limb movement very precisely, it is costly in terms of the equipment and the amount of man-hours needed to record and to measure the movement.

The authors are working on a telemetric device which seems to them to offer great promise for the recording of activity in an open-field situation. Although all of the above-mentioned devices can be used in a free-field situation, the free-field is nevertheless restricted to some specific place, either a checkerboard floor or a room especially equipped with ultrasonic generators and receivers. Stattelman and Cook (1966) have developed a small motion transducer transmitter which is about the size of a package of cigarettes. This small transmitter can be easily attached to a child. Without an antenna, the transmitter will readily broadcast up to distances of 100 feet. With an antenna this distance could be considerably increased. With this device, children could be permitted to move about freely at home or at school while their movements are continuously monitored by a central receiving station. This device, in fact, has been used in several studies (Davis, Sprague, & Werry, 1969; McArdle, 1968). The utility of similar telemetric devices has been reviewed by Herron and Ramsden (1967) and by Pronka (1968).

Restricted Field Techniques

A ballistocardiographic chair has been described by Foshee (1958) to measure movements of a child seated in the device. The chair was mounted on a platform and was supported at the corner by rubber stoppers. A lever was attached to the chair, and a magnet was attached to the end of the lever. Whenever the magnet moved in a coil of wire, a small voltage was produced in the coil. This signal was amplified and was fed into an integrator that counted the movement of the chair. The reliability of this ballistographic device was $r = .95$ when the measures were taken on two successive days. A series of studies (Cromwell & Foshee, 1960; Cromwell, Palk, & Foshee, 1961; Gardner, Cromwell, & Foshee, 1959) have been conducted by using this device indicating that it is a useful research tool.

A stabilimetric chair, similar to the ballistographic device mentioned above, has been developed by Sprague and Toppe (1966). The current version of this device is a small cushion which can be placed on any chair. The cushion is pivoted at the center and can tilt forward-backward or right-left. A movement of about 1/16 of an inch in any of these directions activates a silent switch in the cushion which in turn can be used to activate a counter and, thus, record the amount of wiggling in the chair. The device has satisfactory reliability; a correlation of $r = .97$ was obtained when alternating 12-second intervals were compared.

A similar stabilimeter for animal research, but which could be readily adapted for human research, has been described by Word and Stern (1958). It consists of a cage with a sheet-metal floor under which a permanent magnet speaker is located. The movements of the subject on the floor are detected by the vibrations in the speaker. The right kind of amplifier attached to the speaker will give an output that can be recorded and used to measure the movement of the subject in the cage. The cost of the floor and the speaker are quite minimal although the amplier is relatively more costly.

Although to date most of these devices appear to have been used in research only, some of them (for example, Bell's actometer, Sprague and Toppe's cushion, and Stattleman and Cook's motion transducer) may ultimately find a role in clinical assessment, and clinicians should be stimulated to explore their utility—hence, their presentation here.

MODIFICATION OR TREATMENT

Since there are few follow-up studies on hyperactive children, the natural history of hyperactivity is unknown, although common clinical belief (Bakwin & Bakwin, 1966; Chess, 1960; Laufer & Denhoff, 1957) holds that hyperactivity decreases with or without treatment as a function of age. Slight experimental support for this point of view is to be found in two studies by Cromwell et al. (1961) and Schulman et al. (1965). The activity of normal children or retardates of varying ages was measured directly and found to diminish in later childhood or early adult life. In one of the few follow-up studies of 14 hyperactive children, Menkes, Rowe, & Menkes (1967) found that hyperactivity in most had disappeared at adolescence. Menkes et al. also found that social adjustment in many was or had been poor, with a high frequency of psychosis and antisocial disorder. This study suffers from the weaknesses of a too broad definition of hyperactivity and retrospection, but the results are nevertheless of interest because of the great dearth of such studies. Follow-up studies on disturbed children which would be presumed to include hyperactive patients, namely, the ones on children diagnosed as conduct problem (Morris, Escoll, & Wexler, 1956; O'Neal & Robins, 1958) or "brain damaged" (Baumann, Ludwig, & Alexander, 1962; Laufer, 1962), suggest in confirmation of Menkes et al.'s findings that ultimate social adjustment in adulthood may often be poor. Thus, there is a need for studies that will permit a much better evaluation of the long-term prognosis of the hyperactive child. However, from a clinical point of view, there seems little doubt that the nuisance value of hyperactivity, particularly in the early grades of school, warrants some kind of therapeutic intervention even if the long-term prognosis for the symptom is promising.

That hyperactivity, at least in nondefective children, is modifiable for, at least, a few weeks seems well supported by a small number of controlled studies as well as by a much larger number of uncontrolled clinical reports. Treatment methods can be classified as (i) pharmacotherapy, (ii) psychotherapy, (iii) behavior modification, and (iv) other.

Pharmacotherapy

Although the quality of studies that evaluate drugs and the treatment of hyperactivity is generally poor (see Grant, 1962), two types of drugs seem to find favor with clinicians in the treatment of hyperactivity. The sympathomimetic amines or stimulants (such as the amphetamines and methylphenidate) have been used since 1937 (Bradley, 1937), and the few controlled studies extant confirm their value (Burks, 1964; Conners & Eisenberg, 1963; Conners, Eisenberg, & Barcai, 1967; Conners & Rothschild, 1968; Weiss et al., in press; Werry, 1968b; Zrull et al., 1964). These investigations have generally relied on *reports* of changes in activity level. Attempts to measure the effect of these drugs on activity level by direct means have been less successful. By using the ballistograph, McConnell and his colleagues (1964) were unable to show any change with administration of the drug. Millichap and Boldrey (1967) actually showed an increase in activity in four children, using Schulman's (Schulman & Reisman, 1959) actometer, with methylphenidate. Studies in monkeys made hyperactive by lesions in the caudate nucleus, however, did reveal objective evidence of reduction in activity (Davis, 1957). The study by Davis also confirmed the essential similarity of methylphenidate and the amphetamines, thus, substantiating studies in children (Eisenberg, Connors, & Lawrence, 1965). Recommended dosages for dextroamphetamine are from 2.5 to 20 mg. given once daily after breakfast and supplemented where necessary by a somewhat smaller noon dose (Laufer & Denhoff, 1957). Methylphenidate is probably somewhat weaker in action on a milligram-for-milligram basis since the upper limit (30 to 80 mg.) cited in the literature (Connors & Eisenberg, 1963; Knobel et al., 1959) is generally somewhat higher than that for dextroamphetamine. The method of administration for the two drugs is similar, beginning with small doses that are gradually increased until either a satisfactory reduction in hyperactive behaviors is achieved or until side effects such as anorexia, weight loss, or irritability appear.

The other group of clinically popular drugs is the phenothiazines such as chlorpromazine and thioridazine although, as with the stimulants, adequately controlled studies of their effects on hyperactivity are infrequent. The ones that do exist (Alderton & Hoddinott, 1964; Eisenberg et al., 1961; Fish, 1963; Freedman, Effron, & Bender, 1955; Garfield, Helper, Wilcott, & Muffly, 1962; Schulman & Clarinda, 1964; Werry et al., 1966) tend to be conflicting in their findings, so that the utility of the phenothiazines in the treatment of hyperactivity is by no means well established. Like dextroamphetamine, dosage is begun at a relatively low (for example, 10 to 25 mg.) once or twice daily, and either the dosage or the frequency of administration is gradually increased until a satisfactory reduction in hyperactivity is obtained or until side effects (principally somnolence, irritability, autonomic disturbances, parkinsonism) appear. As with dextroamphetamine, the limits of tolerance appear wide, but recent evidence suggests that high dosages, particularly over long periods of time, are to be avoided because of possible disturbances in pigment metabolism (Ayd, 1966; Greiner, & Nicolson, 1964).

A frequent question, which concerns parents, relates to any effect the administration of medication might have on the child's performance on academic task material in school. Surprisingly little attention has been devoted to this question by clinicians (Freeman, 1966), but studies which have (Barnes, 1968; Connors, 1966; Connors & Eisenberg, 1963; Connors et al., 1967; Connors & Rothschild, 1968; Helper, Wilcott, & Garfield, 1963; Weiss et al., in press; Werry et al., 1966) suggest that, when drugs are given in normal clinical dosage, any discernible effects on intellectual functioning are minimal, with the sympathomimetic amines tending slightly to facilitate performance and phenothiazines slightly to depress in some areas. Only one study (McArdle, 1968) has investigated retention in any systematic way, and her results seem to indicate reduced retention when learning occurs under thioridazine.

Few clinicians who favor the use of medication see pharmacotherapy as the only treatment of hyperactivity (Laufer & Denhoff, 1957). The structuring of the environment, remedial education, and psychotherapy are all emphasized in addition. We believe that medication can be an important aid in the treatment of hyperactivity, but that it should be considered in the context of a behavior modification paradigm where it serves as a means of facilitating the emission of prosocial behaviors (such as sitting still, attending, etc.) which then can be systematically consolidated by differential reinforcement procedures (vide infra). Furthermore, although drugs are likely to prove valuable in the treatment of hyperactivity, they are nevertheless weak in their effects as compared with psychological and educational variables. Thus, they should not be used as the *only* or even the primary treatment, except where circumstances preclude behavior modification procedures. Finally, the effect of drugs on the basic learning processes that are involved in behavior modification are as yet unknown. The studies in animals (Miller, 1966; Overton, 1966) and in children in the treatment of enuresis (Turner & Young, 1966) suggest that, although drugs may indeed promote the emission of the target behavior, these gains may be spurious in terms of a permanent alteration in the behavioral repertoire of the organism persisting after the withdrawal of medication.

Psychotherapy

Here this term is meant to imply therapeutic approaches that attempt to alter the child's behavior by some restructuring of his internal mental or mediating processes by using primarily verbal methods or behavior (such as play) reinterpreted in verbal terms. In this way it differs from behavior modification techniques where the primary emphasis is on some direct approach to the child's *behavior* itself rather than indirectly through his cognitive processes.

It is difficult to evaluate the usefulness of psychotherapy in the treatment of hyperactivity because it has been the subject of little systematic research. One of the few such studies, that by Eisenberg (Eisenberg et al., 1961) does suggest that short-term psychotherapy as ordinarily practiced is of little avail in influencing the behavior of hyperkinetic children. The extensive reviews by Levitt (1957, 1963) do not show psychotherapy as practiced in child guidance or psychiatric clinics to be effective in the treatment of *any kind* of psychopathology in children, although there are many objections to the validity of this conclusion. Furthermore, psychotherapy as currently practiced is not orientated toward the problem behavior or target symptom approach emphasized in this book, and the one with which we are in agreement. Also, we believe that, as presently constituted, the techniques of psychotherapy with children are so ill defined and the theories on which they are based so inadequately constructed that, from a research point of view, they are unlikely to yield the kind of data that will permit them to be assessed in any meaningful way in the foreseeable future.

Behavior Modification

Rationale

In this approach, in contrast to the one of psychotherapy, the emphasis is on discrete problem behaviors that are defined in terms not only of the behaviors themselves but also in terms of the situations in which these behaviors occur, such as "getting out of one's seat in the classroom." the emphasis in therapy is on direct approaches to these problem behaviors, very often in their naturalistic settings. Although verbal methods may be employed, they tend to be used as tools to achieve some direct changes in the target behaviors.

There is little firm support for the utility of psychoeducational maneuvers, in general, in the treatment of hyperactivity. Similarly, there is no evidence to support the contention that, in the treatment of hyperactivity, the behavior-modification approach is superior to pharmacotherapy, to psychotherapy, or other approaches, although it has been successful in, at least, four instances (Becker et al., 1967; Doubros & Daniels, 1966; Patterson et al., 1965; Ward, 1966). Nevertheless, the authors intend to emphasize behavior modification as the best available and primary technique for the treatment of hyperactivity. This position, therefore, requires some defending. The advantages of behavior modification would appear to be the following.

1. It is problem orientated and, thus, likely to be perceived as meaningful by

those complaining of the child's behavior. In this way, resistance to and lack of co-operation in treatment should be minimized. If successful, it is likely to result in definite, useful improvement in social functioning.

2. Because of its emphasis on behavior rather than on mental or mediating process, it would appear to be particularly suitable for use with younger children who are less verbally oriented, and in the treatment of conduct problems such as hyperactivity where verbal approaches are liable to be rejected by the child or to appear less effective than other types of problems (Johns & Quay, 1962).

3. Because its origins are in experimental psychology, the conceptualization and value system of behavior modification seems likely to lead more frequently to assessment of therapeutic procedures and to adequate research.

4. Because of its explicitness, it permits the formulation of prescriptions or plans of therapy that then can be implemented by relatively unskilled persons such as child-care workers, students, teachers, and parents (see Werry & Wollersheim, 1967).

The theory and techniques of behavior modification with children have been discussed in more detail elsewhere (Werry & Wollersheim, 1967). But the therapeutic goal in the case of hyperactivity can be summarized here as essentially a process of counterconditioning in which the aim is to replace the child's problem motor behaviors with incompatible but socially acceptable alternatives. This requires (1) the active promotion and establishment of incompatible alternative behaviors such as remaining in one's seat, and (2) the simultaneous implementation of ways to reduce problem behaviors such as getting out of one's seat. Fundamental to this process is an adequate assessment, as outlined above, which should have delineated (1) the precise kinds of motor behaviors that are bringing the child into conflict with his environment, (2) the situation in which these behaviors are occurring, (3) the environmental factors that are eliciting (stimuli) and are maintaining (reinforcements) these behaviors, (4) an order of priority among these behaviors, usually determined by their nuisance value or their potential amenability to treatment, and (5) the opportunities afforded by the child or his environment for the promotion and the consolidation of alternative incompatible prosocial behaviors.

Implementation

A therapeutic plan should then be drawn up according to the counterconditioning paradigm.

Conditioning Nonhyperactive Behaviors

The first detail is to design a variety of strategies that aim at maximizing the probability of the child's emitting prosocial behaviors (rather than hyperactive ones) and then that aim at strengthening these prosocial behaviors when they occur. No hyperactive child is perpetually in motion and, hence, can be expected to sit in his seat or be reasonably quiet for, at least, brief periods. The frequencies of these periods of quietude can be maximized through skillful use of both extrinsic and intrinsic motivation. The first attempts, by utilizing rewards or reinforcements that have a high reward value for this particular child, to make it "worth the child's while" to exhibit nonhyperactive behaviors. The types of reinforcement of this kind that are likely to prove most useful with children (see Bijou & Baer, 1966) are the following: praise from significant adults or peers (social reinforcement), preferred activities (Homme, DeBaca, Devine, Steinhorst, & Rickert, 1963), tokens that may be traded for objects, privileges, etc., or concrete rewards such as candies, toys, money, etc. The source of this reinforcement can come from adults or from peers, in the latter case, by making some kind of reward for the peer group contingent on the good behavior of the problem child (Patterson et al., 1965). It should be emphasized here that, in order to be successful, these reinforcements must be given in close temporal proximity (preferably within a few seconds) to the behavior to be strengthened.

Intrinsic motivation (Hunt, 1965) relies on reinforcement that accrues from problem solving, satisfaction of curiosity, or reduction of cognitive dissonance. This calls for a great deal of ingenuity and creativity in the design of academic and recreational activities for the hyperactive child. Typically, the major area of conflict for the hyperactive child will lie in the school situation and, because of a short attention span, behavioral difficulties, and specific cognitive deficits commonly associated with hyperactivity (Werry et al., 1966), the typical hyperactive child will often be academically retarded. It is likely then that, from a technical point of view, much of the hyperactive behavior present in the classroom situation, whatever its origins, at the time of consultation, will be representing an avoidance or an escape response to academic task material that, in the past, has produced for the child nothing but failure and frustration and, thus, has acquired the properties of an aversive stimulus. Hence, when the hyperactive child is also academically retarded, careful programming of academic material so as to ensure early and continued academic success is of paramount importance in facilating the emission of nonhyperactive behaviors. The use of extrinsic motivating factors will very frequently prove necessary to overcome the child's initial avoidance response to academic task material, even where the latter has been well programmed.

The use of the principle of successive approximation will maximize the likelihood of success. This means, simply, that we begin with rather limited goals as far as any change in behavior is concerned, and that we gradually increase these goals toward the social norm. Thus, initially, we might reward the child even though he were still wriggling and turning around, which behaviors, although still clearly deviant, are nevertheless, a great improvement on getting up out of one's seat. When the child is able to remain in his seat more or less as required, he would then be required to sit reasonably still for some period of time in order to gain rewards.

Extinguishing hyperactive Behaviors

The frequency of the motor behaviors selected for modification will, of course, inevitably decline in frequency with any increase in occurrence of incompatible prosocial alternatives such as remaining seated. However, the progress of therapy may be expedited by direct attempts to reduce the frequency or, in short, to extinguish the problem motor behaviors. This requires a removal of any reinforcers of the hyperactive behaviors as discovered in the assessment process (problem analysis), particularly attention from the parent, teacher, or peer group. Punishment such as isolation, the removal of privileges, or occasionally physical punishment (see Lovaas et al., 1965) may be employed as a further means of diminishing the frequency of problem behaviors. However, as we have pointed out above, with certain children, because of extreme rejection, social deprivation, or subcultural attitudes to authority, punishment may be considered by the child as rewarding.

This combined conditioning-extinction procedure just described is, of course, the one that is ordinarily used, if somewhat haphazardly, by parents and by educators. The hyperactive child, however, is very often the victim of environmental expectations in excess of his actual behavioral function, so that a vicious-cycle effect obtains. "Good" (for him) behavior is viewed as below the norm for his age and hence, at best, it goes unrewarded, whereas deviant behavior receives fairly regular punishment. Commonly used explanations of the organic (and, hence, involuntary) nature of hyperactivity are of help in interrupting this vicious cycle, although this is perhaps a case of being right for the wrong reason.

Generalization and Stabilization

Two further problems in therapy require emphasizing because of their neglect in most studies. The first of them is the problem of *generalization* of behavior outside the situation in which it was implemented. This is one which is particularly likely to obtain where behavior modification is carried out in an unnatural situation, such as a laboratory or a clinic. An essential part of the treatment program should then consist of an assessment of the extent to which the hyperactive behaviors have diminished in those real-life situations which brought the child to the attention of the clinician. When such an assessment, for example, by means of direct observations in those situations, reveals that no generalization has occurred, either the behavior-modification situation must be adapted to approximate more closely to the natural setting or, probably more frequently, the modification must then be executed in the naturalistic situation itself (for example, Patterson et al., 1965).

The second problem is that of *stabilization* of the nonhyperactive behaviors. This requires some reassessment of the child from time to time after cessation of treatment, since the hyperactive behaviors will have remained a part of the behavioral repertoire of the child, having been extinguished through discrimination learning only in certain situations such as school. Hopefully, the nonhyperactive behaviors will be self-perpetuating because of the resultant social approbation and relief of punishment. However, this cannot be assumed particularly where academic retardation is present since, unlike the hyperactive problem behaviors that can often be brought under control reasonably quickly, it will persist as a chronic problem always holding the threat of re-evocation of the deviant behavior.

Therapists and Situations for Therapy

Even in residential treatment settings, or special classes, it will prove impossible for therapists to supervise *the entire program of therapy*. Since the behavior modification paradigm assumes that most of the "therapy" will occur as a result of reordered environmental consequences of the problem behaviors, as they occur naturally; thus, one must use, as primary therapist, persons who have care of the child such as teachers, parents, child-care aides, etc., as indeed many behavior therapists have (see Werry & Wollersheim, 1967). Also, as we would expect from the nature of behavior modification, behavior therapists have shown an unusual willingness to leave their offices and clinics in order to assess and to initiate therapy in the child's natural environment. The real question facing the behavior therapists is what situation is likely to maximize the chances of substantial and lasting behavior change. With hyperactivity, each of the child's days can be thought of as consisting of an infinite number of successive learning trials in which hyperactivity is being strengthened or weakened. Thus, it is difficult to conceive of a successful behavior-modification program for hyperactivity that does not utilize at least a majority of these learning trials. This can be achieved in a significant way only by a substantial and significant alteration of the eliciting stimuli and response reinforcement contingencies or, in short, by a restructuring of the child's environment where these problem behaviors are manifest, using those who ordinarily dispense reward and punishment and who have control over eliciting stimuli. Although the emphasis in this chapter has been on the individual, the behavior-modification technique is eminently applicable to group situations, particularly to milieu therapy programs (Patterson et al., 1965), or even to group-therapy situations (Buehler et al., 1966). Techniques may vary, but the principles remain the same.

Other Procedures of Modification

Techniques such as individualized curriculum design, remedial education, reduction of stimulus input, and environmental structuring which have figured so prominantly in the treatment of the hyperactive or minimally brain-damaged child (Strauss & Lehtinen, 1947; Cruickshank et al., 1961; Haring & Phillips, 1962; Clements & Peters, 1962; Bakwin & Bakwin, 1966) can readily be encompassed in the behavior-modification framework that is discussed above as useful techniques for maximizing the emission of nonhyperactive behaviors, for minimizing the emission of hyperactive behaviors, and for promoting, as nearly as is possible in the complex human environment, the optimal conditions for the rapid learning of new patterns of behavior (elimination of stimulus and reinforcement ambiguity). When conceptualized in this way, their optimal utilization in the treatment of the hyperactive child appears more realizable than when they are viewed as independent therapeutic techniques.

SUMMARY AND CONCLUSION

Hyperactivity is a common and prominent symptom of psychopathology in childhood. In this chapter, it has been viewed as a disorder of movement which results in conflict with the social environment because of the amount of movement and/or its inappropriateness to the situation. Although hyperactivity is commonly considered in terms of a generalized disturbance of activity level, there is reason to believe that for clinical purposes the delineation of specific problem behaviors in their naturalistic situations is a more useful and heuristic approach. Thus, assessment techniques that meet the ordinary criteria of reliability which yield information about specific problem motor behaviors, the situations in which they occur, their precipitating events or controlling stimuli, and their environmental consequences or response-reinforcement contingencies are likely to be more useful than the ones that yield purely quantitative data about activity level. There is a need for the development of reliable, practical assessment techniques that will provide this kind of information. In contrast to purely quantitative techniques, which have attained some degree of sophistication, these functional or analytic assessment methods, to this point, have been largely of an ad hoc nature. It seems likely that the number of problem motor behaviors and their environmental consequences is limited and, thus, that some standardization of functional assessment techniques should ultimately be possible. Hyperactive behaviors have been viewed as operants, that is, as behaviors which act on the environment. This conceptualization is not incompatible with the widely held, although largely unsubstantiated, organic hypothesis of the origin of hyperactivity. Cerebral status could influence the probability of emission of hyperactive behaviors and perhaps also, the facility with which they respond to modification efforts (Quay et al., 1966b). To this date, however, the role of cerebral status in the etiology of hyperactive behaviors and, more importantly, in their response to therapy is quite unclear. The relevance of neurological and neurophysiological indixes must be established more firmly before these types of assessment can be considered essential or useful.

Pharmacotherapy appears able in certain instances to reduce the emission of hyperactive behaviors and, thus, should prove a valuable integral part of behavior modification procedures. Only where behavior modification procedures cannot be implemented because of practical difficulties should drugs be used as the sole means of treatment. Further work is rquired to establish the effect of medication on the learning processes involved in behavior modification, since experimental evidence in animals suggests that drugs may actually retard these processes (Miller, 1966; Overton, 1966). When given in normal clinical dosage, the effect of sympathomimetic amines and phenothiazines on cognitive function in children is unknown. What little work there is suggests that the former facilitate and that the latter depress, although in both cases effects are slight and difficult to detect.

The utility of psychotherapy whether individual, group, or family has not yet been established as a treatment of hyperactivity, and more rigorous attempts to evaluate these procedures seems necessary before their current popularity with clinicians can be vindicated. The behavior modification, learning theory, or problem-orientated approach has been described and has been presented as the preferred therapeutic method in hyperactivity. But, it is readily acknowledged that there is little evidence for the efficacy of behavior modification procedures. Thus, efforts to evaluate the usefulness of behavior modification as a treatment for hyperactivity must also be actively prosecuted.

As in the case with most symptoms of psychopathology, this review of hyperactivity has revealed clearly the lack of a firm knowledge base and the prevalent substitution of lore for law. Reliable and objective assessment techniques tied to some meaningful and testable theory about hyperactivity are fundamental to any substantial advance in our knowledge of the etiology and treatment of this common behavioral problem in children.

REFERENCES

Alderton, H. R., & Hoddinott, B. A. A controlled study of the use of thioridazine in the treatment of hyperactive and aggressive children in a children's psychiatric hospital. *Canad. Psychiat. Assoc. J.*, 1964, **9**, 239–247.

Ayd, F. J. Phenothiazines—Skin and eye complications. *Int. Drug. Ther. News.*, 1966, **1**, 1–3, 5.

Bakwin, H., & Bakwin, R. M. *Clinical management of behavior disorders in children.* Philadelphia: Saunders, 1966. P. 352.

Bandura, A., & Walters, R. H. *Social learning and personality.* New York: Holt, Rinehart & Winston Inc., 1964.

Barnes, K. Effects of methylphenidate and thioridazine on learning, reaction time and activity level in hyperactive emotionally disturbed children. Unpublished bachelor's thesis, University of Illinois, 1968.

Baumann, M. C., Ludwig, F. A., & Alexander, R. H. *A five year study of brain damaged children.* Springfield, Ill.: Mental Health Center, 1962.

Becker, W. C., Madsen, Jr., C. H., Arnold, C. R., & Thomas, D. R. The contingent use of teacher attention and praise in reducing classroom behavior problems. *J. Spec. Educ.*, 1967, **1**, 287–307.

Bell, R. Q. Adaptation of small wrist watches for mechanical recording of activity in infants and children. *J. Exp. Child. Psychol.*, 1968, **6**, 302–305.

Berkson, G. Stereotyped movements of mental defectives: V. Ward behavior and its relation to an experimental task. *Amer. J. ment. Defic.*, 1964, **69**, 253–264.

Berkson, G. Stereotyped movements of mental defectives: VI. No effect of amphetamine or a barbiturate. *Percep. motor Skills*, 1965, **21**, 698.

Berkson, G., & Davenport, R. K. Stereotyped movements of mental defectives. *Amer. J. ment. Defic.*, 1962, **66**, 849–852.

Berkson, G., & Mason, W. A. Stereotyped movements of mental defectives: III. Situation effects. *Amer. J. ment. Defic.*, 1963, **68**, 409–412.

Berkson, G., & Mason, W. A. Stereotyped movements of mental defectives: IV. The effects of toys and the character of the acts. *Amer. J. ment. Defic.*, 1964, **68**, 511–524.

Bijou, S. W., & Baer, D. M. Operant methods in child behavior and development. In W. K. Honig (Ed.), *Operant behavior areas of research and application.* New York: Appleton-Century-Crofts, 1966. Pp. 718–789.

Bower, E. M. *Early identification of emotionally handicapped children in school.* Springfield, Ill.: Charles C. Thomas, 1960. P. 73.

Bradley, C. The behavior of children receiving benzedrine. *Amer. J. Psychiat.*, 1937, **94**, 577–585.

Brown, P., & Elliott, R. Control of aggression in a nursery school class. *J. Exp. Child. Psychol.*, 1965, **2**, 103–107.

Buehler, R. E., Patterson, G. R., & Furniss, J. M. The reinforcement of behavior in institutional settings, *Behav. Res. Ther.*, 1966, **4**, 157–167.

Burks, H. F. The hyperkinetic child. *Except. Child,* 1960, **27**, 18–26.

Burks, H. F. Effects of amphetamine therapy on hyperkinetic children. *Arch. gen. Psychiat.*, 1964, **11**, 604–609.

Carrier, N. A., Malpass, L. F., & Orton, K. D. *Responses of bright, normal and retarded children to learning tasks.* Carbondale, Ill.: Southern Illinois University, Office of Educational Cooperative Research Project, 1961, No. 578.

Chess, S. Diagnosis and treatment of the hyperactive child. *N.Y. State. J. Med.*, 1960, **60**, 2379–2385.

Clements, S. D. Minimal brain dysfunction in children. Washington, D.C.: U.S.P.H.S. *NINDB Monog.* No. 3, 1966.

Clements, S. D., & Peters, J. E. Minimal brain dysfunctions in the school-age child. *Arch. gen. Psychiat.*, 1962, **6**, 185–197.

Conners, C. K. The effect of dexedrine on rapid discrimination and motor control of hyperkinetic children under mild stress. *J. nerv. ment. Dis.*, 1966, **142**, 429–433.

Conners, C. K., & Eisenberg, L. The effects of methylphenidate on symptomatology and learning in disturbed children. *Amer. J. Psychiat.*, 1963, **120**, 458–464.

Conners, C. K., Eisenberg, L., & Barcai, A. The effect of dextroamphetamine on children with learning disabilities and school behavior problems. *Arch. gen. Psychiat.*, 1967, **17**, 478–485.

Conners, C. K., & Rothschild, G. H. Drugs and learning in children. In *Learning Disorders.* Vol. III. Seattle, Washington: Special Child Publications, 1968. Pp. 191–218.

Crawford, M. L. J., & Nicora, B. D. Measurement of human group activity. *Psychol. Rep.*, 1964, **15**, 227–231.

Cromwell, R. L., Baumeister, A., & Hawkins, W. F. Research in activity level. In N. R. Ellis (Ed.), *Handbook of Mental Deficiency.*, New York: McGraw-Hill, 1963. Pp. 632–663.

Cromwell, R. L., & Foshee, J. G. Studies in activity level: IV. Effects of visual stimulation during task performance in mental defectives. *Amer. J. ment. Defic.*, 1960, **65**, 248–251.

Cromwell, R. L., Palk, B. E., & Foshee, J. G. Studies in activity level: V. The relationships among eyelid conditioning, intelligence, activity level and age. *Amer. J. ment. Defic.*, 1961, **65**, 744–748.

Cruickshank, W. M., Bentzen, F. A., Ratzeburg, F. H., & Tannhauser, M. T. *A teaching method for brain-injured and hyperactive children*. Syracuse, New York: Syracuse University Press, 1961. P. 429.

Davis, G. D. Effects of central excitant and depressant drugs on locomotor activity in the monkey. *Amer. J. Physiol.*, 1957, **188**, 619–623.

Davis, K. V., Sprague, R. L., & Werry, J. S. Stereotyped behavior and activity level in severe retardates: The effect of drugs. *Amer. J. ment. Defic.*, 1969, **75**, 725–727.

Digman, J. M. A test of a multiple-factor model of child personality. *Progress Report NIMH MH 08659–01*. Washington, D.C.: U.S.P.H.S. March, 1965.

Doubros, S. G., & Daniels, G. J. An experimental approach to the reduction of overactive behavior. *Behav. Res. Ther.*, 1966, **4**, 251–258.

Ebaugh, F. Neuropsychiatric sequelae of acute epidemic encephalitis in children. *Amer. J. Dis. Child.*, 1923, **25**, 89–97.

Eisenberg, L. Psychiatric implications of brain damage in children. *Psychiat. Quart.*, 1957, **31**, 72–92.

Eisenberg, L., Conners, C. K., & Lawrence, S. A controlled study of the differential application of outpatient psychiatric treatment for children *Jap. J. Child. Psychiat.*, 1965, **6**, 125–132.

Eisenberg, L., Gilbert, A., Cytryn, L., & Molling, P. A. The effectiveness of psychotherapy alone and in conjunction with perphenazine or placebo in treatment of neurotic and hyperkinetic children. *Amer. J. Psychiat.*, 1961, **117**, 1088–1093.

Ellis, N. R., & Pryer, R. S. Quantification of gross bodily activity in children with severe neuropathology. *Amer. J. ment. Defic.*, 1959, **63**, 1034–1037.

Ernhart, C. B., Graham, F. K., Eichman, P. L., Marshall, J. M., & Thurston, D. Brain injury in the preschool child: Some developmental considerations: II. Comparison of brain injured and normal children. *Psychol. Monogr.*, 1963, **77**, 17–33.

Fish, B. Pharmacotherapy in children's behavior disorders. In *Current Psychiatric Therapies*. New York: Grune & Stratton, 1963, **3**, 82–90.

Foshee, J. G. Studies in activity level: I. Simple and complex task performance in defectives. *Amer. J. ment. Defic.*, 1958, **62**, 882–886.

Freedman, A. M., Effron, A. S., & Bender, L. Pharmacotherapy in children with psychiatric illness. *J. nerv. ment. Dis.*, 1955, **122**, 479–486.

Freeman, R. D. Drug effects on learning in children: A selective review of the past thirty years. *J. Spec. Educ.*, 1966, **1**, 17–44.

Freeman, R. D. Special education and the electroencephalogram: Marriage of convenience. *J. Spec. Educ.*, 1967, **2**, 61–73.

Freibergs, V. Concept learning in hyperactive and normal children. Unpublished doctoral dissertation, McGill University, 1965.

French, G. M., & Harlow, H. F. Locomotor reaction decrement in normal and brain-damaged Rhesus monkeys. *J. comp. physiol. Psychol.*, 1955, **48**, 496–501.

Fuller, J. L., & Thompson, W. R. *Behavior genetics*. New York: John Wiley & Sons, Inc., 1960. Pp. 243–253.

Gardner, W., Cromwell, R. L., & Foshee, J. C. Studies in activity level: II. Effects of distal visual stimulation in organics, familials, hyperactives, and hypoactives. *Amer. J. ment. Defic.*, 1959, **63**, 1028–1033.

Garfield, S. L., Helper, M. M., Wilcott, R. C., & Muffly, R. Effects of chlorpromazine on behavior in emotionally disturbed children. *J. nerv. ment. Dis.*, 1962, **135**, 147–154.

Glidewell, J. C., Mensh, I. N., & Gildea, M. C. Behavior symptoms in children and degree of sickness. *Amer. J. Psychiat.*, 1957, **114**, 47–53.

Graham, F. K., Ernhart, C. B., Thurston, D., & Craft, M. Development three years after perinatal anoxia and other potentially damaging newborn experiences. *Psychol. Monogr.*, 1962, **76**, 1–53.

Graham, F. K. Ernhart, C. B., Craft, M., & Berman, P. W. Some developmental considerations: I. Performance of normal children. *Psychol. Monogr.*, 1963, **77** (10, Whole No. 573), 1–16.

Grant, Q. R. Psychopharmacology in childhood emotional and mental disorders. *Pediatrics*, 1962, **61**, 626–637.

Greiner, A. C., & Nicolson, G. A. Pigment deposition in viscera associated with prolonged chlorpromazine therapy. *Canad. med. assoc. J.*, 1964, **91**, 627–635.

Haring, N. G., & Phillips, E. L. *Educating emotionally disturbed children.* New York: McGraw-Hill, 1962.

Helper, M. M., Wilcott, R. C., & Garfield, S. L. Effects of chlorpromazine on learning and related processes in emotionally disturbed children. *J. consult. Psychol.*, 1963, **27**, 1–9.

Herron, R. E., & Ramsden, R. W. Continuous monitoring of overt human body movement by radio telemetry: A brief review. *Percept. motor Skills*, 1967, **24**, 1303–1308.

Homme, L. E., DeBaca, P. C., Devine, J. V., Steinhorst, R., & Rickert, E. J. Use of the Premack principle in controlling the behavior of nursery school children. *J. exp. anal. Behav.*, 1963, **6**, 544.

Hunt, J. McV. Intrinsic motivation and its role in psychological development. In D. Levine (Ed.), *Nebraska Symposium on Motivation.* Lincoln, Neb.: University of Nebraska Press, 1965. Pp. 189–282.

Hutt, C., Hutt, S. J., & Ounsted, C. The behavior of children with and without upper CNS lesions. *Behav.*, 1965, **24**, 246–268.

Ingram, T. T. S. A characteristic form of overactive behavior in brain damaged children. *J. ment. Sci.*, 1956, **102**, 550–558.

Johns, J. H., & Quay, H. C. The effect of social reward on verbal conditioning in psychopathic and neurotic military offenders. *J. consult. Psychol.*, 1962, **26**, 217–220.

Kessen, W., Hendry, L. S., & Leutzendorff, A. Measurement of movement in the human newborn: A new technique. *Child Develop.*, 1961, **32**, 95–105.

Knobel, M., Wolman, M. B., & Mason, E. Hyperkinesis and organicity in children. *Arch. gen. Psychiat.*, 1959, **1**, 310–321.

Lapouse, R., & Monk, M. A. An epidemiologic study of behavior characteristics in children. *Amer. J. publ. Helh.*, 1958, **48**, 1134–1144.

Laufer, M. W. Cerebral dysfunction and behavior disorders in adolescents. *Amer. J. Orthopsychiat.*, 1962, **32**, 501–506.

Laufer, M. W., & Denhoff, E. Hyperkinetic behavior syndrome in children. *Pediat.*, 1957, **50**, 463–474.

Laufer, M. W., Denhoff, E., & Solomons, G. Hyperkinetic impulse disorder in children's behavior problems. *Psychosom. Med.*, 1957, **19**, 38–49.

Lee, D., & Hutt, C. A play-room designed for filming children: A note. *J. child. psychol. Psychiat.*, 1964, **5**, 263–265.

Levitt, E. E. The results of psychotherapy with children: An evaluation. *J. consult. Psychol.*, 1957, **21**, 189–196.

Levitt, E. E. Psychotherapy with children: A further evaluation. *Behav. Res. Ther.*, 1963, **1**, 45–51.

Lovaas, O. I., Schaeffer, B., & Simmons, J. Q. Building social behavior in autistic children by use of electric shock. *J. exp. res. Pers.*, 1965, **1**, 99–109.

McArdle, J. Effects of thioridazine and methylphenidate on learning and retention in retardates. Unpublished master's thesis, University of Illinois, 1968.

McConnell, T. R., Cromwell, R. L., Bialer, I., & Son, C. D. Studies in activity level: VII. Effects of amphetamine drug administration on the activity level. *Amer. J. ment. Defic.*, 1964, **68**, 647–651.

Menkes, M. M., Rowe, J. S., & Menkes, J. H. A twenty-five year follow-up study on the hyperkinetic child with minimal brain dysfunction. *Pediat.*, 1967, **3**, 393–399.

Millichap, J. G., & Boldrey, E. E. Studies in hyperkinetic behavior II. Laboratory and clinical evaluations of drug treatments. *Neurol.*, 1967, **17**, 467–472.

Miller, N. E. Some animal experiments pertinent to the problem of combining psychotherapy with drug therapy. *Compr. Psychiat.*, 1966, **7**, 1–12.

Minde, K., Webb, G., & Sykes, D. Studies on the hyperactive child VI—Prenatal and paranatal factors associated with hyperactivity. *Develop. med. child. Neurol.*, 1968, **10**, 355–363.

Morris, H. H., Escoll, P. J., & Wexler, R. Aggressive behavior disorders of childhood: A follow-up study. *Amer. J. Psychiat.*, 1956, **112**, 991–997.

Newbry, E. Automatic measurement of general activity in time units. *Amer. J. Psychol.*, 1956, **69**, 655–659.

Novick, J. Ascertaining deviant behaviors in children. Paper presented at the meeting of the American Orthopsychiatric Association, Chicago, 1964.

O'Neal, P., & Robins, L. N. The relation of childhood behavior problems to adult psychiatric status: A thirty-year follow-up study of 150 subjects. *Amer. J. Psychiat.*, 1958, **114**, 961–969.

Ounsted, C. The hyperkinetic syndrome in epileptic children. *Lancet.*, 1955, **269**, 303–311.

Ounsted, C., Lindsay, J., & Norman, R. *Biological factors in temporal lobe epilepsy.* London: William Heinemann Medical Books, 1966. Pp . 72–81, 126.

Overton, D. A. State-dependent learning produced by depressant and atropine-line drugs. *Psychopharm.*, 1966, **10**, 6–31.

Patterson, G. R., Jones, R., Whittier, J., & Wright, M. A. A behavior modification technique for the hyperactive child. *Behav. Res. Ther.*, 1965, **2**, 217–226.

Peacock, L. J., & Williams, M. An ultrasonic device for recording activity. *Amer. J. Psychol.*, 1962, **75**, 648–652.

Prechtl, H. F. R., & Dijkstra, J. Neurological diagnosis of cerebral injury in the newborn. *Symposium on Prenatal Care*. The Netherlands: Noordhoff, 1960.

Pronko, N. H. Biotelemetry: Psychology's newest ally. *Psychol. Rec.*, 1968, **18**, 93–100.

Quay, H. C., Sprague, R. L., Shulman, H. S., & Miller, A. L. Some correlates of personality disorder and conduct disorder in a child guidance clinic sample. *Psychol. in Schools*, 1966a, **3**, 44–47.

Quay, H. C., Werry, J. S., McQueen, M. M., & Sprague, R. L. Remediation of the conduct problem child in the special class setting. *Except. Child.*, 1966b, **32**, 509–515.

Quay, H. C., Sprague, R. L., Werry, J. S., & McQueen, M. M. Conditioning visual orientation of conduct problem children in the classroom. *J. exp. child. Psy.*, 1967, **5**, 512–517.

Rodin, E., Lucas, A., & Simson, C. A study of behavior disorders in children by means of general purpose computers. *Proceedings of the Conference on Data Acquisition and Processing in Biological Medicine*. Oxford: Pergamon, 1963. Pp. 115–124.

Rosenfeld, G. B., & Bradley, C. Childhood behavior sequelae of asphyxia in infancy: With special reference to pertussis and asphyxia neonatorum. *Pediat.*, 1948, **2**, 74–84.

Sainsbury, P. A method of measuring spontaneous movements by time-sampling motion pictures. *J. ment. Sci.*, 1954, **100**, 742–748.

Sarason, S. B. *Psychological problems in mental deficiency*. New York: Harper, 1949, Pp. 52–58.

Schachter, F. F., & Apgar, V. Perinatal asphyxia and psychologic signs of brain damage in childhood. *Pediat.*, 1959, **24**, 1016–1025.

Schrager, J., Lindy, J., Harrison, S., McDermott, J., & Killins, E. The hyperkinetic child: Some consensually validated behavioral correlates. *Except. Child.*, 1966, **32**, 635–637.

Schulman, J. L., & Clarinda, S. M. The effect of promazine on the activity level of retarded children. *Pediat.*, 1964, **33**, 271–275.

Schulman, J. L., Kaspar, J. C., & Throne, F. M. *Brain damage and behavior: A clinical-experimental study*. Springfield, Ill: Charles C. Thomas, 1965.

Schulman, J. L., & Reisman, J. M. An objective measure of hyperactivity. *Amer. J. ment.*

Defic., 1959, **64**, 455–456.

Sprague, R. L., & Toppe, L. K. Relationship between activity level and delay of reinforcement in the retarded. *J. exp. Child Psychol.*, 1966, **3**, 390–397.

Stattelman, A., & Cook, H. A transducer for motion study by radio telemetry. *Proc. Soc. Exper. Biol. and Med.*, 1966, **121**, 505–508.

Stewart, M. A., Pitts, F. N., Craig, A. G., & Dieruf, W. The hyperactive child syndrome. *Amer. J. Orthopsychiat.*, 1966, **36**, 861–867.

Strauss, A. A., & Lehtinen, L. E. *Psychopathology and education of the brain-injured child.*, New York: Grune & Stratton, 1947.

Strecker, E. A., & Ebaugh, F. G. Neuropsychiatric sequelae of cerebral trauma in children. *Arch. neurol. Psychiat.*, 1924, **12**, 443–453.

Sutherland, I. F. Study of a hyperkinetic syndrome and resultant social disability in childhood. *Proc. of Third World Congress of Psychiat.*, Montreal, 1961, Pp. 724–725. (Abstract).

Sylvester, D. M. I. A descriptive definition of hyperactivity. *Smith Coll. Stud. Soc. Work*, 1933, **4**, 3–26.

Turner, R. K., & Young, G. C. CNS stimulant drugs and conditioning treatment of nocturnal enuresis: A long term follow-up study. *Behav. Res. Ther.*, 1966, **4**, 225–228.

Ward, M. H. Experimental modification of "hyperactive" behavior. Unpublished bachelor's thesis, University of Illinois, 1966.

Weiss, G., Werry, J. S., Minde, K., Douglas, V., & Sykes, D. Studies on the hyperactive child V: The effects of dextroamphetamine and chlorpromazine on behavior and intellectual functioning. *J. Child Psychol. Psychiat.*, in press.

Werry, J. S. Studies on the hyperactive child IV: An empirical analysis of the minimal brain dysfunction syndrome. *Arch. gen. Psychiat.*, 1968(a), **19**, 9–16.

Werry, J. S. The effects of methylphenidate and phenobarbital on the behavior of hyperactive and aggressive children. Paper presented at annual meeting of the American Psychiatric Association, Boston, 1968.(b)

Werry, J. S., & Quay, H. C. Observing the classroom behavior of elementary school children. *Except. Child.*, 1969, **35**, 461–470.

Werry, J. S., Weiss, G., & Douglas, V. Studies on the hyperactive child I—Some preliminary findings. *Can. Psychiat. Assoc. J.*, 1964, **9**, 120–130.

Werry, J. S., Weiss, G., Douglas, V., & Martin, J. Studies on the hyperactive child III—The effect of chlorpromazine upon behavior and learning. *J. Amer. Acad. Child Psychiat.*, 1966, **5**, 292–312.

Werry, J. S., & Wollersheim, J. P. Behavior therapy with children—A broad overview. *J. Amer. Acad. Child Psychiat.*, 1967, **6**, 346–370.

Word, T., & Stern, J. A. A simple stabilimeter. *J. exp. anal. Behav.*, 1958, **1**, 201–203.

Zrull, J. P., Westman, J. C., Arthur, B., & Rice, D. L. A comparison of diazepam, d-amphetamine and placebo in the treatment of hyperkinetic syndrome in children. *Amer. J. Psychiat.*, 1964, **121**; 388–389.

Appendix for chapter 16 see page 641
Werry-Weiss-Peters Activity Seale

Chapter 17

Psychopathology of Sleep[1]

ANTHONY KALES AND RALPH J. BERGER

INTRODUCTION

Disturbances of sleep and dreaming have often been implicated as causal or contributory factors to the development of psychological disorders. Until recently there have been few objective all-night studies of sleep disturbances or the effects of disease states or drugs on sleep patterns. The ones that have been carried out were often based on behavioral observations or on patient's reports. Although sleep could be classified in terms of electroencephalographic (EEG) patterns, it was considered as a unitary state that merely exhibited a continuum in depth. This view was disrupted by Aserinsky and Kleitman (1953, 1955), who observed that clusters of conjugate, rapid eye movements (REMs) occurred periodically throughout the night. Subsequent studies showed that these bursts were associated with a low voltage, high frequency EEG pattern (Dement, 1955; Dement & Kleitman, 1957a), and that dream recall was reported following 80 percent of awakenings from REM sleep and seldom reported (< 10 percent) following similar awakenings from nonrapid eye movement (NREM) sleep (Dement & Kleitman, 1957b).

Dement & Kleitman (1957a) modified the original EEG classification of 5 stages of sleep of Loomis, Harvey, and Hobart (1937) to four stages (Figure 17.1): stage 1, a low voltage, fast wave pattern without sleep spindles; stage 2, spindle activity of 14 to 16 cycles per second (cps) with a low voltage background; stages 3 and 4, high voltage, slow (delta) waves of one to two cps frequency. When half the record consists of this delta activity, it is classified as stage 4, while lesser amounts (20 percent) are classified as stage 3. REM sleep[2] usually occurs when a stage 1 EEG follows another sleep stage. REMs are associated with the low amplitude fast, stage 1 EEG activity, and a markedly decreased tonus of certain head and neck muscles (Berger, 1961; Jacobson et al., 1964). In contrast, when a stage 1 EEG is present as an individual falls asleep, REMs do not occur and the muscle tonus of the head and neck muscles is higher than during REM sleep. REM sleep has been referred to as REM period (REMP), stage 1-REM, rhombencephalic sleep, paradoxical sleep, dreaming sleep, activated sleep, deep sleep, and low voltage fast sleep.

[1] Supported in part by NIMH Training Grant 5 TI MH-6415 of the Brain Research Institute, University of California, Los Angeles, and the A.F. Office of Scientific Research of the Office of Aerospace Research under contract No. AF 49(638) -1387. This work was also assisted by the University of California, Los Angeles, Brain Information Service, a part of the National Information Network of the NINDB and was supported under contract PH-43-66-59.

[2] The terms REM sleep, REM periods, and stage REM are used interchangeably throughout this paper.

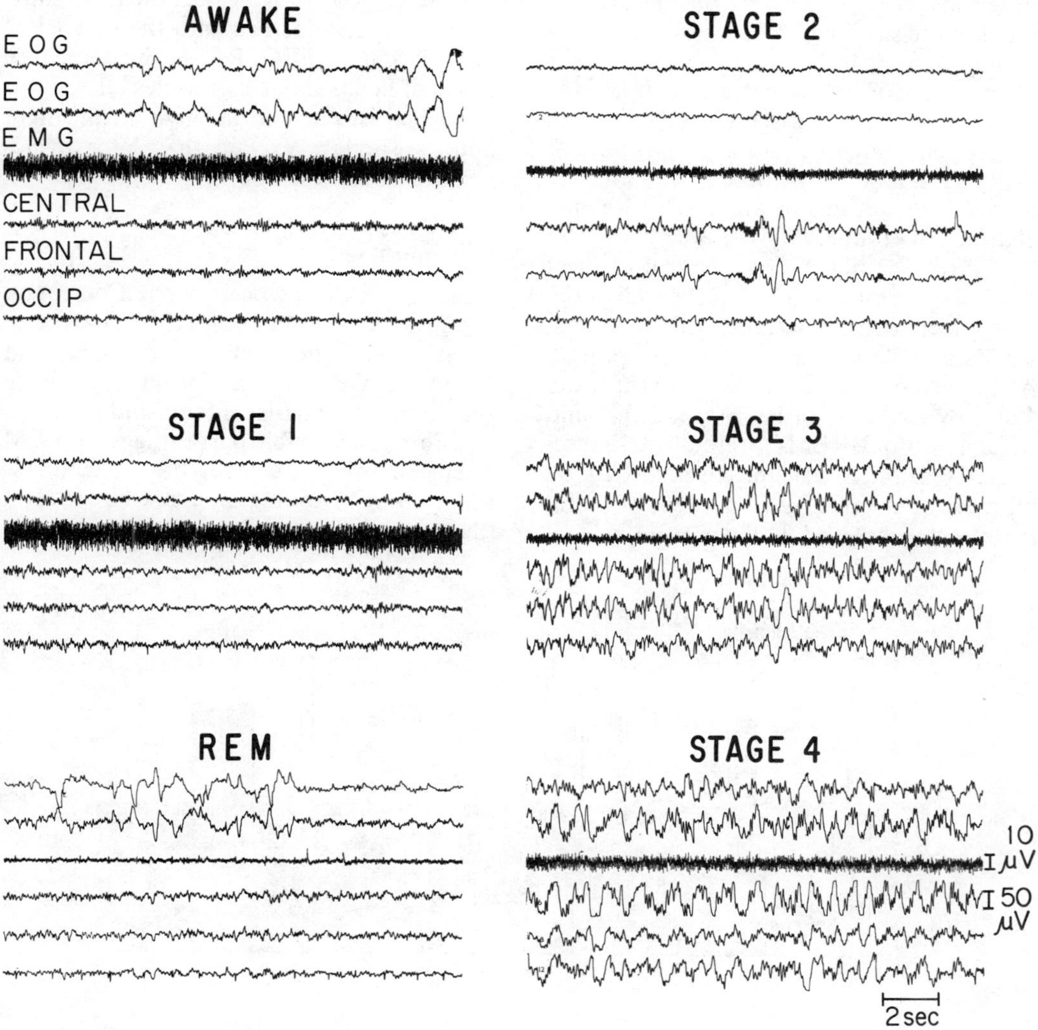

Figure 17.1 The stages of sleep. Amplitude changes in the electrooculogram (EOG) represent eye movements. The electromyogram (EMG) was recorded superficially from the submental muscles of the chin. Notice the high EMG and eye movements during wakefulness, the slow eye movements but absence of REMs during descending stage 1, and REMs with low EMG during stage REM. Stages 2, 3, and 4 are characterized by the slowing of frequency and an increase in amplitude of the EEG. The EEG channels were derived from the central, frontal, and occipital electrodes, compared with a reference electrode attached to the opposite ear.

Several years following the discovery of REM sleep, a sleep profile was described for young adult subjects (Dement & Kleitman, 1957a) which has been confirmed in many sleep laboratories (Feinberg, Koresko, & Heller, 1967; Kales et al., 1967b; Rechtschaffen & Verdone, 1964; Roffwarg, Dement, & Fisher, 1964; Williams, Agnew, & Webb, 1964, 1966). There are four to six REM periods in a nights' sleep, depending on the length. These periods occur cyclically at intervals of 70 to 100 minutes. The first several REM periods show a progressive increase in duration (Dement & Kleitman, 1957a; Feinberg, Koresko, & Heller, 1967; Kales et al., 1967b), so that the longer periods usually occur later in the morning. About 20 to 25 percent of the total sleep time of young adults is spent in stage REM, 5 to 10 percent in stage 1 (NREM), 50 percent in stage 2, and 20 percent in stages 3 and 4 combined. Many workers have noted an adaptation effect during the first night in the sleep laboratory consisting of a longer time required to fall asleep (sleep latency), more time spent awake following sleep onset, and less REM sleep than on subsequent nights (Agnew, Webb, & Williams, 1966; Antrobus, Dement, & Fisher, 1964; Kales et al., 1967b; Rechtschaffen & Verdone, 1964).

Figure 17.2 illustrates a typical night of sleep for a young adult. As the individual falls asleep, the initial stage 1 EEG appears; REMs do not accompany this sleep period. After the initial stage 1 EEG, stages 2, 3, and 4 usually appear in order. Stages 2, 3, 4, and stage 1 without REMs, are collectively referred to as NREM sleep. The first 70 to 100 minutes of sleep is NREM sleep, predominantly stages 3 and 4. Then, usually after a series of body movements, the EEG shifts to a stage 2, and then into the first REM period (Stage 1 EEG, REMs and decreased tonus of head and neck muscles). The cycle described is repeated throughout the night and is similar, except that later cycles usually do not include stage 4.

Age and Sleep

Sleep studies have been carried out in all age groups. Monod et al. (1964), Parmelee et al. (1967), Petre-Quadens (1966), and Roffwarg, Dement, and Fisher (1964) have shown that premature infants and full-term newborns have high percentages of REM sleep. In the premature, the percentages range from 60 to 80 percent, while at term the range is from 40 to 50 percent. The

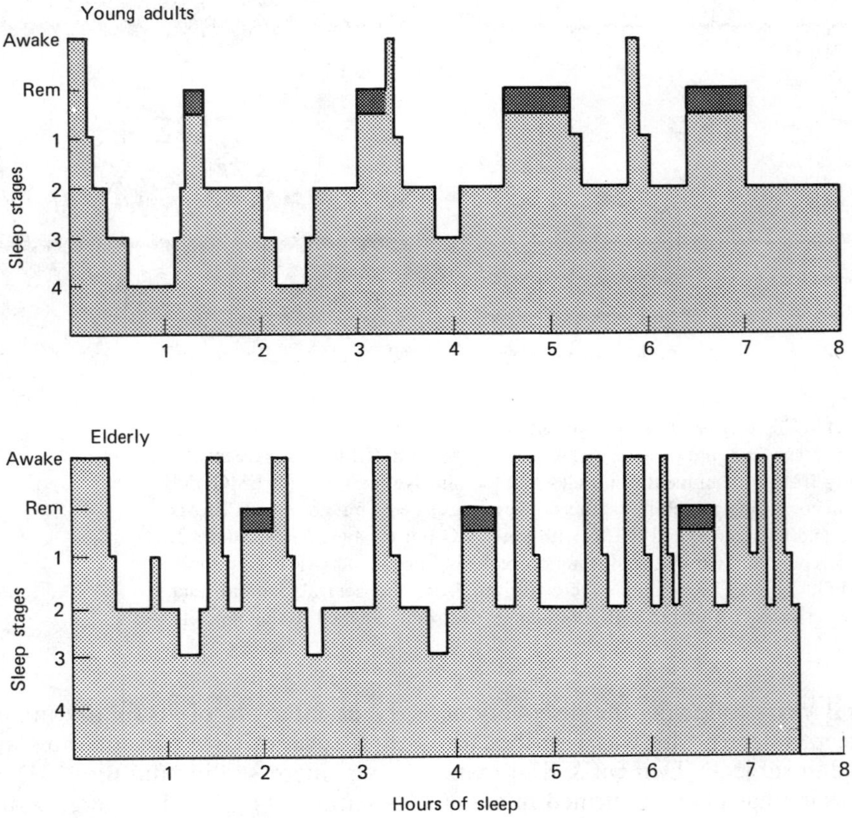

Figure 17.2 The comparison of sleep in normal young adults and elderly subjects. The sleep of young adults has considerable amounts of stage 4 sleep early in the night, progressive increases in the lengths of the first three REM periods, and infrequent brief awakenings. In the elderly, stage 4 is absent or small in amount, REM periods are relatively uniform in length, and awakenings are frequent especially in the latter part of the night.

percentage of REM sleep decreases progressively after birth, and at about 8 months is at a level of 20 to 25 percent which is maintained with slight variation throughout life. Since prematures, full-term newborns, and infants spend approximately $\frac{2}{3}$ to $\frac{3}{4}$ of the day asleep, the absolute REM time for this group is considerably higher than the absolute REM time for any other age group where the total sleep time is invariably less.

In the studies of Parmelee et al. (1967), 84 percent of sleep was stage REM at 30 weeks gestational age. This decreased to 68, 58, and 36 percent at 33 to 34 weeks, term (39 to 40 weeks) and 3 months past term, respectively. The percentages of REM sleep for premature infants at term and 3 months past term were similar to the ones for full-term infants at comparable ages. Parmelee, Wenner, and Schulz (1964) also studied the gross sleep patterns of 46 infants from birth to sixteen weeks of age. The mean amount of total sleep was 16.3 hours in the first week, and if decreased to 14.9 by the sixteenth week. The mean longest sleep period per day slightly more than doubled from 4.1 hours in the first week to 8.5 hours in the sixteenth week. The ratio of day sleep to night sleep was determined, and this changed from 0.9 in the first week to 0.5 in the sixteenth week. A definite diurnal cycle was present at 5 weeks in 66 percent of the infants and at 12 weeks in 98 percent of them.

Roffwarg, Dement, and Fisher (1964) reported on sleep patterns in age groups ranging from neonates to subjects who were 70 years of age. Neonates (1 to 15 days) were not studied with the EEG; however, REM periods were directly observed. The sleep cycles of REM (active) and NREM (quiet) sleep lasted 50 to 60 minutes. In the neonate, frequent sucking movements were observed during REM sleep as well as fine twitches, grimaces, tremors, and smiles. Roffwarg, Muzio and Dement (1966), speculating on the possible role of REM sleep in the newborn, hypothesized that REM sleep serves as an internal source of afferent stimulation to promote structural differention and maturation of the central nervous system (CNS). They argued that this is most necessary just prior to and following birth when sufficient external stimulation is lacking. Accordingly, the high ratio of REM sleep diminishes progressively with maturation following birth. One of us has recently emphasized the possible importance this intrinsic stimulation might have for the development of voluntary conjugate eye movements (Berger, 1969).

Neonates may pass directly from an awake state into REM sleep. In addition, the REM sleep periods in neonates and young infants tend to be of approximately uniform length throughout the night. After several years, there is considerable high voltage, slow wave sleep (stages 3 and 4) which occurs mostly early in the night. The first REM sleep does not occur until 2 to 3 hours after sleep onset, and the first several REM periods show a gradual increase in length as sleep progresses. In addition to the delay in the first REM period, the principal difference in the sleep patterns of children, adolescents, and young adults is a progressive decrease in slow wave sleep in the adolescent and young adult groups (Table 17.1).

In studies of normal, elderly subjects, compared to young adults, all investigators have reported less total sleep time, increased number of awakenings after sleep onset, and REM periods of fairly uniform duration. Initially it was reported that the normal elderly had REM sleep percentages of 13–18 percent which are considerably less than those reported for young adults (Lairy et al., 1962; Roffwarg, Dement, & Fisher, 1964). More recent studies have shown that after adaptation to the laboratory, normal elderly subjects have REM sleep percentages that approximate or are only slightly below the ones of young adults (Agnew, Webb, & Williams, 1967a; Feinberg, Koresko, & Heller, 1967; Kahn & Fisher, 1966; Kales et al., 1967c). However, since the total sleep time is less in the elderly, the absolute REM time is moderately reduced compared to young adults. The most striking difference in the elderly is a marked decrease to absence of stage 4 sleep. Agnew, Webb and Williams (1967a) reported a marked decrease in middle-aged subjects, while Feinberg, Koresko, and Heller (1967) and Kales et al. (1967c) found a further decrease in this sleep stage in elderly subjects. Thus, in the elderly, the percentage of REM sleep is slightly decreased, while the total sleep time is moderately reduced, and the percentage of stage 4

Table 17.1 Age and Changing Sleep Patterns

Age	Percentage REM Sleep of Total Sleep Time	Approximate Percentage Stage REM over 24 hours	Percentage Stage 4 of Total Sleep Time
Premature infant	60–84	40–56	—
Neonate	49–58	33–39	—
Infant	30–40	17–22	—
2–5 years	20–30	10–14	—
5–13 years	20–25	8–9	20–30
18–30 years	20–25	7–8	10–15
30–50 years	18–25	5–7	—
50–60 years	20–24	5–6	2–4
65–87 years	18–22	4–6	1–2

Compiled from data from several laboratories.

markedly decreased (See Table 17.1, Figure 17.2).

Dreaming and Sleep

It was concluded from early studies that dreaming was associated only with REM periods (Aserinsky & Kleitman, 1953; Dement & Kleitman, 1957b). It was believed that any NREM dream recall could be accounted for by attributing it to mental activity which had occurred while falling asleep, during an uninterrupted previous REM period, or while being awakened. However, subsequent studies by Foulkes (1962), Goodenough et al. (1959), Kamiya (1961), and Rechtschaffen, Verdone, and Wheaton (1963) reported much higher percentages of NREM dream recall. This was in part because of the use of more liberal criteria in defining a dream. Other factors strongly influencing the degree of NREM recall are the motivation of subjects and time of night (Kales & Jacobson, 1967). Goodenough et al. (1965), and Rechtschaffen, Hauri and Zeitlin (1966) have shown that auditory awakening thresholds for all stages of sleep decrease with accumulated sleep. Thus, late in the night, the thresholds are lowest, while dream recall from all stages is highest.

Presently, there is general agreement that dreaming can occur during NREM sleep, but that REM sleep dream recall most often closely resembles what individuals ordinarily regard as a dream. Monroe et al. (1965) were able to distinguish with 90 percent success between REM and NREM reports when they were unaware of which type of awakening elicited the report. More recently Foulkes and Vogel (1965) studied mental activity during sleep onset and found that dreamlike reports very similar to REM reports were quite common during descending EEG stages 1 and 2. Thus, dreaming is very frequently reported following stage REM and sleep onset awakenings. Following sleep onset, dreaming is occasionally reported following NREM period awakenings.

In other studies of dream recall, Dement and Wolpert (1958), Goodenough et al. (1965), and Whitman et al. (1962) found that the amount of dream recall depended more on the time of awakening than on the actual dream content, and that dream recall fell off proportionately as time elapsed from the end of a REM period to the awakening. In Dement and Wolpert's study, when more than eight minutes had elapsed from the end of the REM period to the awakening, dream recall practically disappeared. Goodenough et al. (1965) reported that abrupt awakenings resulted in considerably better dream recall than gradual awakenings, and that, in general, gradual arousal from any stage of sleep tended to produce more reports characterized as thoughtlike than dreamlike. These studies suggest that abrupt, brief, spontaneous awakenings during REM sleep probably facilitate dream recall on awakening in the morning.

Rechtschaffen, Vogel, and Shaikun (1963) studied dream content taken from REM periods at different times of the same night's sleep. Dreams from REM periods occurring later in the sleep period were more easily recalled and were more detailed, whereas dreams from early REM periods were poorly recalled and were fragmented in detail. Two factors appear to account for this: first, as already mentioned, the auditory awakening threshold is higher early in the sleep period; and second, the initial REM periods are brief in duration.

Goodenough et al. (1959) also studied two groups of subjects, one that recalled dreams frequently, and another that recalled them rarely, to see if there were any differences in their sleep-dream cycles. They found that REM periods occurred with equal frequency in both groups. Although the frequency of recall from awakenings made during REM periods was greater for the recallers, the nonrecallers still reported dreams from about half of the REM awakenings.

The role of the laboratory situation in the manifest dream content has been evaluated by Dement, Kahn, and Roffwarg (1965), Domhoff and Kamiya (1964a), and Whitman et al. (1962). Domhoff and Kamiya and Whitman et al. reported that many dreams dealt either directly or in a thinly disguised manner with the experimental situation. They also found that the frequency of dreams about the experiment was the same on a number of successive nights. Although Dement, Kahn, and Roffwarg also reported that the laboratory situation was present in a high number of the dreams of the first night, the influence of the laboratory was considerably reduced on subsequent nights. However, extensive studies by Domhoff and Kamiya (1964b) and Hall (1966) have demonstrated that laboratory dreams differ in many respects from the dreams recalled at home.

The effects of external stimuli on subjective experience during sleep have been studied by Berger (1963) and Dement and Wolpert (1958). Dement and Wolpert found that sounding a tone, flashing a light, or spraying water on the skin during NREM sleep did not initiate REM periods, indicating that REM periods occur autonomously rather than being elicited by external stimuli. The stimuli were incorporated into dream material that was reported on awakening one minute later on 10 to 60 percent of the occasions. Berger used spoken personal names as stimuli which were presented without the knowledge of his subjects. Incorporation of the stimuli into the dream narrative occurred about 50 percent of the time in a rather subtle manner, most frequently in the form of assonant connections between the stimuli and elicited dream content.

Physiology of the Sleep Cycle

There have been numerous studies of the neurophysiological changes associated with sleep, especially the REM phase. Most functions are quite variable or are activated during REM periods. The intrinsic neuronal activity of the brain as well as the general metabolic activity are similar in many respects to the levels observed in the waking state. In contrast, many neurophysiological parameters are at stable, decreased levels during NREM sleep.

The REMs usually occur intermittently in bursts during REM periods. Dement and Kleitman (1957b) proposed that the REMs may represent scanning movements as the dreamer follows the visual imagery of the dream, since they observed frequent correspondences between the direction of recorded eye movements and visual activity in the reported dream. In a later study Roffwarg et al. (1962), awakened subjects from REM periods soon after definitive eye movement patterns appeared, such as a run of horizontal or vertical movements. Another investigator without knowledge of the characteristics of the recording prior to awakening the subject, elicited dream recall and attempted to predict from the last portion of the dream narrative what type of eye movement pattern was present just prior to the awakening. In 80 percent of the instances where adequate dream recall was obtained, close correspondences resulted between predicted and recorded eye movement patterns. In other studies, Berger and Oswald (1962b) and Dement and Wolpert (1958) found positive correlations between the amount of recorded eye movement activity and the amount of visual dream activity recalled from subsequent awakenings. Berger, Olley, and Oswald (1962) found that adults who were congenitally blind, or who had become blind later in life but had lost the capacity to experience visual imagery, did not have electro-oculographically recordable REMs, although all other aspects of REM sleep were otherwise present. Subjects who still experienced visual imagery following the onset of their blindness, however, did exhibit normal REMs.

All of these above data are consistent with a scanning hypothesis concerning the REMs. However, other data might lead us to argue against such a hypothesis. Thus, the presence of REM sleep in neonatal kittens in whom the eyelids have not yet opened (Valatx, Jouvet, & Jouvet, 1964), and in both decorticate cats and humans, in whom we must presume all capacity for visual imagery to be lost (Jouvet, 1962; Jouvet, Pellin, & Mounier, 1961), is difficult to reconcile with this hypothesis without the introduction of a number of additional postulates (Roffwarg, Muzio, & Dement, 1966). These problems have been discussed at greater length elsewhere (Berger, 1967).

Numerous studies of pulse rate, respiration, and blood pressure have shown that REM sleep is characterized by wide variations and irregularity in these parameters in contrast to smaller variations during NREM sleep (Aserinsky & Kleitman, 1955; Jouvet, 1961; Kamiya, 1961; Snyder, Hobson, & Goldfrank, 1963; Snyder et al., 1964). A number of studies have been done of changes in muscle tonus and gross body movements during sleep. Jouvet, Michel, and Mounier (1960) reported that the posterior nuchal muscles of the cat showed a marked decrease of EMG activity with REM onset, and Berger (1961) observed a similar decreased tonus in the external laryngeal muscles of humans. Jacobson, et al. (1964) found that the tonus of most head and neck muscles studied decreased with the onset of REM sleep. The tonus of the trunk and limb muscles did not show any change with REM periods, however the tonus of these muscles decreased considerably with sleep onset and remained at low minimal levels throughout the night. Hodes and Dement (1964) showed that the H-reflex response elicited by electrical stimulation of the posterior tibial nerve in humans disappears during REM sleep.

Fisher, Gross, and Zuch (1965) and Karacan et al. (1966) studied the relationship between REM periods and penile erections. They found that a high percentage of the 86 REM periods they studied were accompanied by erections. The erections began and terminated in close temporal relationship to the onset and termination of REM sleep.

Weitzman et al. (1966) demonstrated a rise of plasma 17-hydroxycorticoids characterized by a series of peak elevations occurring during the latter part of the sleep period. Recently, Mandell et al. (1966a, b, and c) measured biochemical changes during REM periods, that consisted of a posterior pituitary hormone, ADH-like effect, and an increase in catecholamine metabolism as measured by an increase in 3-methoxy-4-hydroxymandelic acid (VMA) excretion and by an increase in urinary 17-hydroxycorticoids.

A number of neurophysiological studies revealed some of the mechanisms underlying sleep and wakefulness. The role of the ascending reticular activating system in maintaining an activated cortical EEG and alert behavior was well established (Moruzzi & Magoun, 1949). Moruzzi and his co-workers further showed the importance of the bulbar reticular substance for the normal occurrence of EEG slow wave sleep (Batini et al., 1959; Magnes et al., 1961). However, Clemente and Sterman (1967) and Hernández-Péon (1962) stressed the involvement of a basal forebrain cortical inhibitory system in the regulation of this sleep phase. Carli and Zanchetti (1965) and Jouvet (1962) demonstrated the necessary integrity of the rostral pons for the appearance of REM sleep. Destruction of this area led to disappearance of REM sleep, although NREM sleep and wakefulness persisted. On the other hand, decorticated cats showed no evidence of NREM sleep, although REM sleep and wakefulness were still seen (Jouvet, 1962). Accordingly, Jouvet has proposed that the pontine reticular formation is necessary and sufficient for REM sleep, but that NREM sleep is dependent on the presence of an intact cortex.

Other studies have furthered the concept of REM sleep as a unique state. Microelectrode implantations by Arduini, Berlucchi, and Strata (1963); Evarts (1962, 1964); and Huttenlocher (1961) in separate studies demonstrated that the firing rates of individual neurons in various parts of the brain are markedly increased during REM sleep. Kanzow, Krause, and Kühnel (1962) reported a sharp rise in cortical blood flow in cats during REM sleep of the same magnitude as that seen in waking states of fright or vigorous activity. Kawamura and

Sawyer (1965) and Rechtschaffen et al. (1965) reported significant rises in brain temperature associated with REM periods in the cat and the rabbit, respectively. Brebbia and Altshuler (1965) recently reported that there were significant differences in oxygen consumption between all stages of sleep with the highest level attained during REM sleep.

Although the degree of activation of most neurophysiological and biochemical parameters during REM sleep has been stressed, it may be incorrect to cassify any sleep stage as a "quiet" period (Johnson & Lubin, 1966). A number of studies have shown that galvanic skin responses and spontaneous electrodermal activity are significantly increased during stages 3 and 4 (Asahina, 1962; Broughton, Poire, & Tassinari, 1965; and Johnson & Lubin, 1966).

The sleep research described has provided investigators with an opportunity to study the sleep patterns in various sleep disturbances and disease states and the effects of drugs and total, partial, or selective sleep deprivation on sleep parameters. The purpose of this paper is to describe the findings of these studies from the viewpoint of the clinician.

SLEEP PATTERNS IN CLINICAL DISORDERS

In a number of clinical conditions such as schizophrenia, depression, hypothyroidism, mental retardation, and chronic brain syndrome, the sleep studies have focused on quantifying the stages of sleep present in each disorder. With other clinical entities such as enuresis, somnambulism, narcolepsy, epilepsy, coronary artery, duodenal ulcer disease, and bronchial asthma, the emphasis has been on relating the occurrence or exacerbation of the particular symptom to the sleep cycle.

Schizophrenia

It has frequently been proposed that the hallucinations of the schizophrenic actually represent the intrusion of dreaming into waking life. Many investigators thought that all-night sleep studies of schizophrenics, especially of those acutely ill, would reveal low percentages of REM sleep, since factors were being discharged during the waking state. By studying a group of chronic schizophrenic subjects, Dement (1955) found a normal percentage of REM sleep, and that dream recall from these patients tended to be fragmentary. Feinberg et al. (1964), Feinberg, Koresko, and Gottlieb (1965) and Koresko, Snyder, and Feinberg (1963) conducted two studies on the sleep of schizophrenic subjects, and found a similar percent of REM time in the schizophrenics and normal controls. Although those patients classified as hallucinating showed significantly higher frequency of eye-movement activity during REM periods than nonhallucinating schizophrenic patients, the values obtained in the hallucinating subjects did not exceed the ones of the normal controls. In a more recent study of chronic schizophrenics, Gulevich, Dement, and Zarcone (1967) reported a slight increase in the percentage of REM sleep together with a shorter latency from sleep onset to the first REM period.

Rechtschaffen, Schulsinger, and Mednick, (1964) attempted to demonstrate a correspondence between schizophrenic states and physiological indices of REM sleep, such as REMs, saw-toothed waves, stage 1 EEG, and loss of muscle tonus. The waking EEG, eye movement, and EMG tracings of five schizophrenics failed to show, even for short periods, any patterning that bore a convincing resemblance to the variables seen during REM periods. Studies of schizophrenic children by Onheiber et al. (1965) and Ornitz, Ritvo, and Walter (1965) also revealed no difference in amounts of sleep compared with normals. This sleep data does not support a clear-cut relationship between hallucinatory behavior in the waking state and dreaming in REM sleep. Most sleep studies of schizophrenics have focused on REM sleep, while measurements of other sleep stages have generally not been reported. In a recent study, Caldwell and Domino (1967) reported that stage 4 sleep was significantly decreased in a group of schizophrenic subjects. Moreover, when schizophrenics were sleep deprived (Luby & Caldwell, 1967), they failed to exhibit increases in stage 4 on recovery as are seen in normal subjects following sleep deprivation (Berger & Oswald, 1962a).

In a recent study, Zarcone, Gulevich,

Pivik, and Dement (1968) reported that actively ill schizophrenics failed to show a compensatory increase in REM sleep following REM deprivation, although schizophrenics in remission showed an exaggerated REM rebound increase following deprivation. However, Vogel and Traub (1968) reported that schizophrenics showed increases in REM sleep following REM deprivation similar in magnitude to those reported for non-schizophrenics. They suggested that schizophrenia is not related to increased REM pressure, increased REM discharge or an inability to compensate for REM deprivation. These authors suggested that in actively ill schizophrenics certain events of the REM sleep phase were being discharged in the waking state which resulted in a decreased need for the REM phase during sleep. Dement (1969) has suggested that the crucial factor in the REM-sleep deprivation and compensation phenomenon is the deprivation of the phasic pontine-geniculate-occipital (PGO) spikes which in normal conditions are predominantly discharged during REM sleep. In animal studies, depletion of cerebral seretonin was followed by an unrestricted discharge of PGO spikes (including the waking state) and a marked increase in drive-oriented behavior.

Depression

Sleep disturbance is among the most consistent symptoms of depressive illness. Prior to all-night EEG studies, less total sleep and early morning awakenings were described as characteristic of the disturbed sleep associated with depression. Diagnostic implications were frequently attributed to the type of sleep disturbance, and they were used by Kiloh and Garside (1963) as factors that differentiated between endogenous depressives, who had more frequent early awakenings, and reactive depressives, who experienced more frequent initial insomnia. However, a later study by Costello and Selby (1965) failed to confirm this difference. They found that the two types of depressives did not differ in their sleep patterns nor in their reports concerning the qualitative aspects of their sleep. Although both of the studies as well as a study by Hinton (1963) indicate that there is a reduction in total sleep time because of either increased early awakenings, initial insomnia, or both, in depressives, they all expose a need for physiological studies as an aid in finding diagnostic criteria for depression.

Before REMs were discovered Diaz-Guerrero et al. (1946) studied six patients with "manic-depressive psychosis, depressive type." The records were scored, using a slightly modified version of the criteria of Loomis, Harvey, and Hobart (1937). They characterized the sleep of the depressed patients as including difficulty in falling asleep, early or frequent awakenings, and a greater proportion of "light" sleep. Subsequent studies following the discovery of REMs have been carried out by Gresham, Agnew, and Williams (1965); Hawkins and Mendels (1966); Oswald et al. (1963); and Zung, Wilson, and Dodson (1964). All the studies reported less total sleep time and increased sleep latency for depressed patients as compared to normal controls. Stage 4 sleep was decreased in all the studies except the one of Oswald et al. (1963), which was complicated by the fact that heptabarbitone was administered to both patients and controls on half of the nights. Both Gresham, Agnew, and Williams (1965) and Hawkins and Mendels (1966) also reported a slightly decreased percentage of REM sleep, with a moderate increase following treatment. Snyder (1969) has recently conducted extensive longitudinal studies of psychotic depressed and non-psychotic depressed patients. In both groups of patients there were frequent and prolonged awakenings, total sleep was decreased, stages 3 and 4 were markedly decreased and REM sleep percentage was usually low. All changes were more pronounced in the psychotic depressed patients. In addition the psychotic depressed patients showed marked decreases in REM sleep latency. The most marked and consistent finding is the decrease to absence of stage 4 sleep. Following treatment, the recovery of stage 4 sleep is more delayed than that of the REM phase.

Zarcone, Gulevich, and Dement (1967) studied the effect of electroconvulsive (ECT) therapy on the sleep patterns of patients with varying degrees of depression and agitation. They found that ECT decreased the percentage of REM sleep, delayed the onset of the first REM period, and prolonged slow wave sleep time. These effects were still present two weeks after the course of ECT.

Hypothyroidism

The term myxedema was originally proposed by Ord (1878), and the first patient described in his paper was "always falling asleep." Sleepiness has continued to be noted as a characteristic of hypothyroidism. Heuser et al. (1966) and Kales et al. (1967a) reported on the all-night EEG sleep patterns of seven hypothyroid patients, four young adult, and three elderly patients. Four of these patients were again studied after several months of therapy with desiccated thyroid when they were euthyroid. The percentage of REM sleep both before and after treatment was similar to normal subjects of the same ages. In addition, total sleep time before and after treatment was similar. The most consistent and striking finding was that the percentage of stages 3 and 4 sleep was markedly reduced in all hypothyroid patients as compared to control subjects. The young adult hypothyroid patients showed a significant decrease in stage 4 sleep compared to normal young adult subjects, whereas the elderly hypothyroid patients had a significant decrease in stage 3 sleep compared to controls. After treatment, the percentage of time spent in stages 3 and 4 increased for each patient, so that the levels for these sleep stages were no longer significantly lower than those of controls. In addition, the waking alpha EEG frequency increased slightly for each subject together with an improvement in psychological test performance.

In addition to the changes in stage 4 sleep in hypothyroidism, marked decreases in stage 4 sleep have also been reported in normal elderly and middle-aged subjects by Agnew, Webb, and Williams (1967a); Feinberg, Koresko, and Heller (1967); and Kales et al. (1967c). Kales et al. (1968a) also noted that asthmatic patients have decreased levels of stage 4 sleep compared to controls. Other studies of stage 3 and 4 sleep may reflect on the clinical significance of these sleep stages. A high percentage of this sleep is present in childhood (Parmelee et al., 1967; Roffwarg, Dement, & Fisher, 1964); exercise increases the percentage of this sleep (Baekeland and Lasky, 1966); auditory awakening thresholds are much higher than in other sleep phases (Goodenough et al., 1965; Rechtschaffen, Hauri, & Zeitlin, 1966), and, as will be discussed later, following sleep deprivation, this sleep is recovered preferentially over REM sleep (Berger & Oswald, 1962a). It was our impression that decreases in the percentage of this sleep are more likely to be associated with the feeling that one has slept poorly than if REM sleep is altered. However, Monroe (1967) studied the psychological and physiological differences between good and poor sleepers. His results did not support our speculation regarding a correlation between the decreased stage 4 and the feeling that one has slept poorly. He reported that compared with good sleepers, the poor sleepers had a greater sleep latency, more awakenings, less total sleep, markedly less REM sleep, and an increase in stage 2. In addition, significant physiological differences between the groups were noted in skin resistance, phasic vasoconstriction, rectal temperature, and body movement measures.

Mental Retardation

Gibbs and Gibbs (1962) in an intensive review of young, mentally retarded patients found a striking exaggeration of normal sleep spindles, which they called "extreme spindles." These spindles have a frequency of 8 to 15 cycles per second, are a higher voltage, and are more continuous than normal sleep spindles. The finding was most often observed in children below 5 years of age, and it was not noted in any children over 12 years. Although no correlation was found between the extreme spindles and epilepsy, 70 to 80 percent of children with this pattern were mentally retarded. Only one of 3000 control subjects demonstrated this abnormal pattern. It was concluded from the various groups most affected that "extreme spindles are associated with damage to the extrapyramidal rather than pyramidal system."

Petre-Quadens, and Jouvet (1966) studied 45 mentally retarded patients ranging in age from 3 months to 62 years and compared the results with the ones from 25 normal controls. A number of differences were noted. Retarded subjects between 3 and 35 years showed a definite decrease in total sleep time as compared to the controls. The percentage of REM sleep in the mentally retarded decreased after 15 years while it remained constant in the controls. Whereas stage 4 sleep in the controls decreased uniformly with increasing age, it was irregular in the mentally retarded subjects. The percentages of the various sleep stages for the mentally retarded most closely approximated control values between the ages of 10 to 15 years. Petre-Quadens, and Jouvet also reported a paucity of sleep spindles in contrast to Gibbs' findings; however, they did not state if their report referred to children, older subjects, or both.

In a more recent study, Feinberg, Braun, and Schulman (1968) reported on sleep variables in 9 mongolian and 6 phenylpyruvic oligophrenia (PKU) subjects. The amount of stage REM in the retardates showed only an equivocal reduction compared with control subjects. However, the retardates showed markedly lower values for eye movement activity. Although the quantitative patterns were similar, the tracings of mongolian and PKU subjects differed in several respects, of which the most consistent was the presence of prolonged beta activity in the former group. Both groups showed reduction in sleep spindles, abnormally shaped K-complexes, and occasional or persistent abnormal discharges.

Chronic Brain Syndrome

Feinberg, Koresko, and Heller (1967) and Feinberg, Koresko, and Schaffner (1965) compared the sleep EEG and eye movement patterns in young and aged normal subjects, and in patients with chronic brain syndrome (CBS). The results showed that normal aging is associated with decreased total sleep, decreased stage 4, and a tendency toward decreased stage REM. Pathological aging, as manifested by the CBS group, resulted in an accentuation of the changes; compared to both normal groups, the CBS subjects had lower values for total sleep time, percentage stage REM, REM activity, and percentage stage 4. In the young normals, the first three REM periods increased successively in length, whereas in the aged normals and CBS subjects, all of the REM periods were of approximate equal duration. Within the CBS group, total sleep time was highly and significantly correlated with scores of intellectual function. In addition to these findings, several CBS subjects awakened regularly from REM sleep in states of agitation and delirium, and had to be physically restrained. These states lasted 5 to 10 minutes. Feinberg, Koresko, and Heller (1967) suggested that the regularly occurring delirious behavior of these CBS patients, arising from awakenings from REM sleep, may represent a relationship between REM sleep and the syndrome of nocturnal delirium and wandering and with the inability of an impaired cerebrum to distinguish between dream and reality. They suggest that drugs that decrease the intensity of REM processes could be helpful in the management and the treatment of these patients.

In their studies of normal elderly and CBS subjects, Feinberg and his associates have noted that many of the subjects with markedly abnormal sleep patterns had normal waking EEGs. They indicate that these findings, and the correlation of these changes with intellectual function, point to the value of sleep EEG as a diagnostic tool in geriatric psychiatry.

Somnambulism

All-night EEG sleep studies of sleepwalkers have been carried out by Gastaut and Broughton (1965), Jacobson et al. (1965), and Kales et al. (1966a). In the studies of Jacobson and Kales most of the somnambulists studied were children. Special cables and/or biotelemetry were used for recording purposes to allow motility about the laboratory. Contrary to the popular notion that sleepwalking is the acting out of a dream, the sleepwalking incidents occurred in nonrapid eye movement (NREM) sleep (typically stages 3 and 4) when mental recall is quite low, and not during rapid eye movement (REM) periods which are most frequently associated with dreaming. The somnambulistic incidents occurred predominantly during the first third of the night.

The sleepwalking episodes in the laboratory were less frequent than the ones reported at home and were brief, lasting from 30 seconds to several minutes. During the incidents, the subjects usually exhibited low levels of awareness, reactivity, and motor skill. Later, there was waking amnesia for all events. Investigators also were able to induce somnambulistic incidents by standing up the sleepwalkers during NREM sleep. All incidents, spontaneous or induced, characteristically began with a paroxysmal burst of high voltage, slow EEG activity, which also appeared at other times during stages 3 and 4 but was unassociated with somnambulistic incidents. Compared to normal children of the same age, the sleepwalkers showed a much greater frequency of duration of this EEG pattern. In this respect, they were similar to normal children of younger ages. This suggested a possible delay in the maturation of the CNS in sleepwalkers (Kales et al., 1966a). Usually, child somnambulists show a decrease in incidents as they grow older. It is possible that this is associated with a decrease in these bursts of high voltage, slow EEG pattern.

Comparison of the sleep patterns of the child somnambulists with control subjects did not reveal any differences in total sleep time, percentage of REM sleep, or other sleep stages (Kales et al., 1966a). Psychological testing and psychiatric interviews of 11 somnambulists showed a heterogeneity of personality patterns with a spectrum of psychopathology from mild to severe, considerable parental concern regarding the sleepwalking, but a less concerned attitude on the part of the somnambulists themselves (Kales et al., 1966b).

Enuresis

Bedwetting or enuresis is a common sleep disturbance with an incidence in children of 5 to 15 percent. Gastaut and Broughton (1965) and Pierce et al. (1961) showed that enuresis occurred predominantly out of NREM sleep. Although the bedwetting incidents occurred throughout the night, there was some preponderance in the first third of the night. Pierce et al. (1961) suggested that the enuretic episode might be a substitute for REM sleep, that is, it might replace the first REM period which as a result was "missed." This speculation was not borne out by the later studies of Gastaut and Broughton (1965), Hawkins, Scott, and Thrasher (1965), and Ritvo et al. (1967). These studies, however, did confirm that enuretic episodes generally occur during NREM sleep. Hawkins and his associates reported the occurrence of 47 wetting episodes as follows: stage 1, 1; stage 2, 19; stage 3, 16; stage 4, 7; stage REM, 4.

Gastaut and Broughton (1965) have described in detail the series of events that they call "the enuretic episode." Most of the incidents began in stage 4 sleep and were preceded by a K-complex or a burst of rhythmic delta waves associated with a general body movement. Broughton (1968) has recently proposed that enuresis, somnambulism and nightmares represent disorders of arousal. Sleep patterns then changed to a stage 2 or 1 (NREM), and the micturition occurred. If the subjects were awakened and changed, they did not report any dreams and on falling asleep, had normal sleep patterns. If left wet, however, stages 3 and 4 sleep did not appear for several hours and, if awakened in subsequent REM periods, the recall contained fragments of dreams of being wet.

Narcolepsy and Cataplexy

Prior to recent sleep research, wakeful and sleep EEG recordings on narcoleptics (Blake, Gerard, & Kleitman, 1939; Dynes & Finley, 1941) revealed no significant deviations from normal patterns. In more recent studies, Rechtschaffen et al. (1963) found that the nocturnal sleep of narcoleptics often began with REM sleep rather than with the initial NREM sleep of 60 to 100 minutes' duration observed in normal subjects. Further studies (Dement, Rechtschaffen, & Gulevich, 1966; Hishakawa & Kaneko, 1965) showed that the daytime sleep and sleep attacks of narcoleptic patients with cataplexy were characterized by sleep onset REM periods, accompanied by a marked decrease in muscle tone. Dement and his associates found that the sleep attacks in the majority of narcoleptics with a history of cataplexy were characterized by the immediate onset of REM sleep, whereas only 1 of 10 patients without cataplexy showed a sleep onset REM episode with their sleep attacks. In treating narcolepsy, drugs such as amphetamines, which markedly decrease REM time (Rechtschaffen & Maron, 1964), have long been used successfully.

Dement, Rechtschaffen, and Gulevich (1966) have proposed a redifinition of narcolepsy in which the necessary condition for the diagnosis is the establishment of the sleep onset REM period by laboratory test or, inferentially, by a history of cataplexy. They further suggest that those patients with a history of sleep attacks but who fail to show sleep onset REM periods in the laboratory should be placed in another diagnostic category.

Epilepsy

It is well established that seizures are not infrequent during sleep; some patients have seizures only during sleep. There have been several all-night EEG sleep studies of epileptic patients. Batini et al. (1962) and Cadilhac and Passouant (1965) reported that the 3 cps spike and wave complexes of petit mal are limited to NREM sleep, particularly at sleep onset and in stage 4. During REM sleep, the discharges completely disappeared, and they recurred only with passage to NREM sleep. The same investigators also found that generalized bilateral epilepsies, including grand mal and infantile myoclonus, had a decrease to absence of discharges during REM sleep and had a facilitation during NREM sleep, particularly stage 4. In focal cortical and temporal lobe epilepsies, Cadílhac and Passouant observed that the discharges were present in all phases of sleep, and in some patients were considerably enhanced during REM periods.

Ross, Johnson, and Walter (1966) obtained all-night recordings from 13 patients with petit mal attacks or grand mal seizures, or both. In all of the patients, waking interictal EEG showed bilateral synchronous paroxysmal spike and wave patterns. The majority of the records showed an increase in spike and wave discharge rate at sleep onset with a confirmed increase through slow wave sleep. In general, there was no augmentation of the clinical signs and symptoms with sleep onset; patients with subclinical discharges while awake continued to have subclinical discharges during sleep. There was a marked decrease in the discharge rate with the onset of REM periods. In addition, the presence of REMs further suppressed the discharge rate. No differences were noted in the overall sleep patterns of these patients as compared to nonepileptic subjects, indicating that the discharges had little effect on general sleep measurements.

Duodenal Ulcer

Dragstedt (1959) established that doudenal ulcer patients secrete 3 to 20 times more gastric acid at night than normal subjects. Armstrong et al. (1965) studied the relationship between sleep stages and gastric-secretion rates in duodenal ulcer patients and normal subjects. Marked increases in gastric-secretion rates frequently occurred during REM periods in the ulcer patients, whereas normals failed to demonstrate any consistent alteration in secretion rate during these periods. In the ulcer patients, of 24 secretion peaks noted, 22 occurred during REM sleep. The normal subjects, however, had low secretion levels for all periods of the night. The finding of a marked increase in gastric acid secretion during REM periods in duodenal ulcer patients may explain the nocturnal pain and discomfort frequently reported by this group.

Coronary Artery Disease

There has been much speculation as to which events of sleep could induce the anginal syndrome, which is a frequent nocturnal occurrence among patients with coronary artery disease. Nowlin et al. (1965) studied four patients with a history of exertional and nocturnal angina pectoris for several nights of sleep, with continuous recordings of EEG, EOG, and EKG. A total of 39 episodes of nocturnal angina with significant ST segment depression on the EKG were noted, and of them, 32 anginal attacks were associated with REM sleep.

It is not clear if the exacerbations in the ulcer and coronary subjects during REM sleep were correlated with a specific dream content that accompanies this sleep phase. No attempt was made in either study to elicit dream recall at the time of increased gastric secretion of EKG change. However, in the coronary study, the patients were questioned about any dream recall in the morning. Awareness of chest pain was common in all individuals who could recall dream content. The general characteristics of the dreams that preceded an awakening with chest pain tended to fall into two broad categories; the ones that involved strenuous physical activity and the ones that involed the emotions of fear, anger, or frustration.

Bronchial Asthma

Patients with asthma frequently have attacks of dyspnea at night and complain of their inability to sleep properly. Kales et al. (1968a) monitored 12 adult asthmatic patients for 35 subject nights. The asthmatic incidents occurred throughout the night and were not related to any specific stage of sleep. Of the 93 asthmatic episodes noted, 73 arose from NREM sleep and 18 from REM sleep, while 2 followed lengthy wakeful periods.

Compared to subjects of the same ages, the asthmatics had a significant increase in time awake and in decrease in stage 4 sleep. The increase in the total time spent awake was the result of frequent awakenings following sleep onset and early, final awakenings, rather than difficulty falling asleep. As for the decrease in stage 4 sleep, it is possible that the multiple awakenings with or without asthmatic attacks may not permit the subject to gradually descend to this stage. Or, it may be that as the subject goes into this sleep stage, there is increased respiratory difficulty, so that the sleep stage shifts to a stage 2 or 1, or the patient awakens.

In child asthmatics (Kales et al., 1968a) it was found that the asthmatic episodes occurred out of all sleep stages with a higher proportion occurring out of stage 2 sleep. The child asthmatic attacks were entirely confined to the last two thirds of the night as compared to the random distribution of the adult episodes; no incidents occurred in the first third when stage 4 sleep predominated.

It was concluded that adult asthmatic attacks occur in all stages of sleep with no clear-cut correlation with any part of the sleep cycle, although there may be considerable variability from subject to subject. Factors such as recumbency, 17-hydroxycorticosteroid levels, dreaming, and depth of sleep may play varying roles from subject to subject and night to night in precipitating asthmatic attacks. Nocturnal asthmatic attacks in adults may be multidetermined just as they are in the daytime. In children, nocturnal asthmatic attacks are essentially absent during stage 4 sleep.

The main changes in REM and NREM sleep in the various clinical disorders described above are summarized in Table 17.2.

EFFECTS OF SLEEP DEPRIVATION

Sleep deprivation has for long been of clinical interest, since it is well known that persons who go without sleep for extended periods frequently exhibit disorders of thought and perception that are sometimes indistinguishable from the ones observed in schizophrenia (Oswald, 1962).

The usual approach of experimental studies has been to deprive subjects either selectively of one phase of sleep, or of total sleep for varying periods of time, to determine what biochemical, physiological, or psychological changes might be produced by these procedures, and whether the pattern of sleep on recovery might be different from that which was observed prior to deprivation. Dement (1960) was the first to apply this procedure to the selective deprivation of REM sleep by arousing experimental subjects just after the onset of each REM period. He called it "dream deprivation," which was to some extent a misnomer, since it is now recognized that dreaming also occurs, although less frequently, during NREM sleep. Moreover, the use of such a term as "dream deprivation" lends undue emphasis to the psychological component of a total systemic process. Nevertheless, the results of Dement's experiment were extremely interesting and provocative. Dement observed that the frequency of occurrence of the REM periods increased at a rate greater than normal throughout each night, and that they became more marked during each successive night of REM sleep deprivation. The subjects exhibited significant elevations in percentage of time spent in REM sleep as compared with their previous base-line levels, when they were allowed to sleep undisturbed on subsequent recovery nights. No changes were observed in their sleep patterns following a later series of control nights during which the same subjects were awakened the same number of times that they had been awakened during REM sleep deprivation, but with the awakenings made during episodes of NREM sleep. Some psychological changes were reported in all subjects during the REM sleep deprivation period in the form of increased appetite, anxiety, irritability, and difficulties in concentrating. Similar psychological dis-

Table 17.2 Clinical Disorders and Sleep Patterns

Disorder	REM Sleep	NREM Sleep
Schizophrenia	No change, (?)↑REM	↓Stage 4
Depression	Sl.↓REM,↑with treatment	↓Stage 4,↑with treatment
Hypothyroidism	No change	↓Stage 4,↑with treatment
Mental retardation	↓REM (?),↓REMS	↓Spindles, abnormal K complexes
Chronic brain syndrome	↓REM, nocturnal wandering from REM	↓Spindles, abnormal K complexes
Enuresis	Few episodes	Most episodes
Somnambulism	Only one episode reported	Practically all episodes
Narcolepsy-cataplexy	Sleep onset REM periods Sleep attack = REM sleep	—
Epilepsy	↓Discharge rate	↑Discharge rate
Duodenal ulcer	Gastric acid secretion rate markedly increased	—
Coronary arteriosclerosis	Anginal attacks with EKG changes, awakenings	—
Bronchial asthma	Attacks in all stages of sleep	↓Stage 4

turbances were not seen on control nights. Dement (1960) concluded from these results that there was a specific need for REM sleep that had to be made up for at a later time when it was not allowed to occur naturally. Fisher and Dement (1963) have proposed that the hallucinations and the delusions commonly seen following total sleep deprivation might be because of the loss of REM sleep rather than of NREM sleep. They suggested that a pressure for REM sleep continuously builds up during sleep deprivation, until the dream hallucinations associated with this sleep state break through into waking thought. They suggested that the function of REM sleep with its associated dreaming process might be to preserve psychic stability and that it might be shown that REM sleep deprivation was involved in the etiology of schizophrenia. However, this has not been shown to date, and later studies on REM sleep deprivation, in many cases, failed to confirm the finding of significant psychological disturbances during deprivation (Kales et al., 1964; Sampson, 1966; Snyder, 1963; Vogel & Traub, 1968). Most of the later studies that have reported these disturbances have either not employed adequate control procedures or have used drugs containing amphetamine to suppress REM sleep, which contaminates the significance of their results (Agnew, Webb, & Williams, 1967b; Dement, 1964). However, a well-controlled recent study by Clemes and Dement (1967) did show significant psychological changes as revealed by projective tests during REM sleep deprivation.

If the psychotic-like disturbances produced by total sleep deprivation were caused by a direct breaking-through of the components of the REM sleep state into waking thought, then we should see short latencies of REM sleep onset, together with large increases in the percentage of REM sleep following total sleep deprivation. This is not the case; instead, there are significant increases in amounts of stage 4 sleep with reductions in percentage of REM sleep on the first recovery night following total sleep deprivation (Berger & Oswald, 1962a; Williams et al., 1964). On subsequent recovery nights there are compensatory increases in REM sleep. However, these may be secondary responses to the increases in stage 4 on the first recovery night at the expense of REM sleep and, thus, represent pseudo-REM deprivation effects. On the other hand, later studies that have involved more prolonged sleep deprivation (Johnson, Slye, & Dement,

1965; Kales et al., 1969) report an increase in both stage 1 REM and stage 4 on the first recovery night.

After 24 to 28 hours of total sleep deprivation, the EEG exhibits considerable slowing, often similar to a stage 1 sleep pattern, even though the subject may appear behaviorally awake and moving about with his eyes open (Armington & Mitnick, 1959; Johnson, Slye, & Dement, 1965). It seems likely that the hallucinations, the delusions, and the sometimes dreamlike speech of sleep-deprived persons are caused by downward drifts in cerebral vigilance, akin to the hypnagogic imagery that is frequently experienced in many people when normally falling asleep (Oswald, 1962), rather than being ascribed to an upsurge of REM sleep into wakefulness.

Dement, Greenberg, and Klein (1966) have recently demonstrated that the REM sleep-deprivation effect can be, so to speak, stored up. They allowed subjects to experience their normal amounts of REM sleep for several nights following near-total REM sleep deprivation, but awakened them from subsequent REM episodes when this normal percentage of REM sleep had been reached. On subsequent recovery nights, the subjects showed typical elevations in REM sleep, as if the recovery nights had immediately followed the REM sleep deprivation nights.

Agnew, Webb, and Williams (1964) demonstrated that selective recovery effects are not specific to REM sleep. They selectively deprived subjects of stage 4 sleep for two consecutive nights. Compensatory increases in stage 4 sleep were seen on recovery nights compared with base-line levels. In that study they did not report any psychological disturbances to have occurred during stage 4 deprivation. More recently they deprived one group of subjects of REM sleep for seven nights and another group of stage 4 sleep for seven nights (Agnew, Webb, & Williams, 1967b). They reported different changes in psychological measures following each type of deprivation. Stage 4 deprivation produced a depressive outlook, and REM deprivation resulted in a state of increased irritability and lability.

Selective deprivation of REM sleep in the cat leads to effects similar to the ones observed in the human (Jouvet et al., 1964). These effects are even observed in cats who have been subjected to almost complete extirpation of the forebrain, leaving only the pons intact—the brain-stem area which has been shown to be crucial for the normal occurrence of REM sleep (Jouvet, 1965). Cats, however, immediately make up for the loss of REM sleep, following total sleep deprivation, with increased percentages of REM sleep (Kiyono et al., 1965). This is in contrast to the effects of total sleep deprivation already described in the human, where stage 4 sleep takes priority on recovery. Other differences in cat and human are seen in response to partial sleep deprivation. The distribution of REM and NREM sleep within successive nights of restricted sleep remain unchanged in the human, although there is an increase in the amount of stage 4 within NREM sleep, mainly at the expense of stage 3 (Dement, Greenberg, & Klein, 1966; Webb & Agnew, 1965). However, in the cat, the percentage of REM sleep increases in proportion to the reduction in total sleep (Ferguson & Dement, 1967). It has been suggested (Berger, 1969) that the reason for these differences may lie in the different circadian patterns of sleep and wakefulness in man and cat. The human exhibits a diurnal sleep-wakefulness pattern, and a progressive decrease in the frequency of cycling of the two phases of sleep throughout his extended nocturnal sleep period (Feinberg, Koresko, & Heller, 1967; Kales, et al., 1967b.). The cat, on the other hand, has a polyphasic sleep-waking pattern, and a fairly constant frequency of cycling of the two phases throughout any sleep period (Sterman et al., 1965).

The newborn human infant may enter REM sleep directly from wakefulness without any intervening NREM sleep. The same is true for infant and juvenile monkeys (Meier & Berger, 1965), which renders it possible to carry out selective deprivation of either phase of sleep without unduly disturbing the normal amounts of the non-deprived phase. Berger & Meier (1966) found that, although it becomes progressively more difficult to selectively deprive newborn monkeys of either sleep state, they did not observe any compensatory increases in either of the deprived sleep states when the animals were allowed to sleep again undisturbed. They did report typical increases in REM sleep following REM sleep deprivation in juvenile animals, but the same was not true for NREM sleep following NREM sleep deprivation. It seems that there may be a basic metabolic process underlying the cyclic alternation of NREM and REM sleep that may limit the amount of time that can be spent in REM sleep. Following finite periods of REM sleep deprivation, continuation of deprivation beyond this period does not produce any further increase in REM sleep on recovery. One of us has recently proposed that a function of REM sleep may be to establish the neuromuscular pathways involved in voluntary coordinated eye movements during ontogenesis (Berger, 1969). Therefore, increases in the amount of REM sleep following its deprivation in the neonate would not be expected, since it is probably occurring to a maximal extent at that age compatible with the total economy of the organism.

The impairment in cognitive functioning following extended periods of sleep deprivation has already been noted, but we should also mention the effects of even moderate sleep loss on human performance. There have been many studies of performance under conditions of sleep deprivation that have failed to reveal any deteriorations compared with normal levels. It has become clear, especially from the work of Wilkinson (1961) and Williams and his associates (1959), that these negative results were obtained because the tasks administered were either too brief or were allowed unlimited time for completion. Sleep-deprived persons are capable of maintaining efficient performance for short periods, but when they must work continuously for long periods, especially under paced conditions, they begin to commit large numbers of errors of both commission and of omission. They cannot sustain sufficiently high levels of cerebral vigilance, and their lapses in performance are caused by periodic downward drifts to lower levels of arousal into the initial transitional phases of sleep.

Wilkinson, Edwards, and Haines (1966) have recently reported some interesting data on the effects of different amounts of partial sleep deprivation on two different performance tasks: one was an auditory detection task, the other required repeated arithmetic addition. The adding task was hardly affected by small amounts of sleep deprivation, but became more affected when subjects were obtaining less than 4 hours of sleep during one night—the first 4 hours of sleep being the period mostly spent in NREM sleep. On the other hand, the vigilance task was affected by reductions of 2 to 4 hours of a normal 8-hour sleep period, but no more deterioration occurred with further curtailment into the initial 4-hour sleep period. These effects on the vigilance task might possibly be ascribed to deprivation of REM sleep, which is normally concentrated in the latter half of an 8-hour sleep period. Wilkinson suggests that the two sleep phases may independently be related to different perceptual and cognitive functions in terms of their restorative function for normal levels of efficiency.

DRUGS, SLEEP, AND DREAMING

There have been a number of studies on the effects of various drugs on the sleep profile. Mainly short-term effects of drugs have been evaluated with the focus on alterations in REM sleep. In the majority of studies where sedatives, hypnotics, tranquilizers, antidepressants or stimulants have been administered, a slight to marked decrease in REM sleep has been noted.

CNS Depressants

Oswald et al. (1963) studied the effects of heptabarbitone on the sleep of six depressed patients and six sex- and age-matched controls. They found that heptabarbitone decreased the time awake, especially in patients in early morning hours, and decreased the frequency of shifts in sleep stages and the number of body movements. In both groups of subjects, heptabarbitone greatly decreased the duration of REM periods, and also the frequency of eye movements within those periods.

Oswald and Priest (1965) also studied the effects of a nonbarbiturate hypnotic, nitrazepam, and sodium amylobarbitone, when administered nightly, for up to 18 nights. They suggested that the difficulty many patients experience in renouncing the use of sleeping pills was related to the markedly altered sleep patterns both while the subjects were taking the drugs and following withdrawal. In the first experiment, after five base-line nights of sleep, two subjects received 15 mgm of nitrazepam for 14 consecutive nights. Initially, with the drug administration, there was a decrease in REM sleep, then a diminution of this effect over the 14 drug nights that was followed by a rebound in REM sleep after stopping the drug. On the second to the sixth recovery night the proportion of REM sleep was abnormally high, and time from sleep onset to the first REM period was considerably shortened (less than 45 minutes). As late as the twenty-fourth recovery night, REM sleep time was still elevated. In the second experiment, after five base-line nights, two subjects received 400 mgm of sodium amylobarbitone for nine nights. After the initial effect of the drug in decreasing REM sleep had appeared to lessen, the dosage was increased to 600 mgm for an additional nine consecutive nights, mimicking what is often done clinically. Again after an initial decrease, the proportion of REM sleep approximated base-line values. Drug withdrawal once more caused a rebound in REM sleep time, abnormally short delays from sleep onset to the first REM period, and an increased amount of REM sleep in the first two hours of the night. Some of these abnormalities were still present five weeks after the drug was withdrawn. Most important, in addition to the EEG changes, insomnia, nighmares, and a sense of having slept badly were noted following drug withdrawal.

Freeman et al. (1965) studied the effects of meprobamate given in dosages of 400 mgm at 9:00 P.M. and of 800 mgm at 12:00 A.M. The subjects spent significantly less time in stage REM and more time in stage 2 sleep. Stage REM time decreased from 101 minutes on base-line nights to 86 minutes on meprobamate nights. It was also noted that meprobamate markedly decreased the number of changes from one sleep stage to another.

Wender et al. (1964) reported that 200 mgm of chlorpromazine resulted in a 15 percent decrease in REM sleep. When chlorpromazine was administered in dosages of 600 mgm, there was a considerable increase in stage 1 sleep with sparse eye movements and many bursts of alpha activity. This stage 1 activity accounted for up to 80 percent of the time asleep. One subject also had a sleep onset REM period. Fisher and Dement (1963) also reported sleep onset REM periods in three subjects administered trifluoperazine 20 mgm daily in divided doses.

Hartmann (1966) studied the effects of single doses of 1.0 or 2.0 mgms of reserpine. Five of six subjects showed an increase in REM sleep when reserpine was administered. Several of the subjects also had a shortening of the time interval between sleep onset and the first REM period. Khazan and Sawyer (1964) noted that, although many drugs used in their studies in rabbits prevented the appearance of REM sleep, reserpine not only allowed the occurrence of REM sleep periods but actually appeared to lengthen them. Delorme, Jeannerod, and Jouvet (1965) reported that, although reserpine blocked the occurrence of REM sleep in the cat, it triggered monophasic spikes in the pons, lateral geniculate nuclei, and occipital cortex which were undistinguishable from the ones that are a normal characteristic feature of REM sleep in cats. Hoffman and Domino (1967) in a later study with humans found that higher doses of reserpine produced REM suppression with marked rebound on withdrawal. They stated that these results as well as the marked difference in the effects on REM sleep in man and cat require further study. Oswald et al. (1964, 1966) found that L-tryptophan resulted in delays of less than 45 minutes from sleep onset to the first REM period. They postulated that the effect on sleep is because of the metabolism of tryptophan to serotonin. The fact that the antiserotonin agent, methysergide, prevented the effect of tryptophan appeared to support this hypothesis. Recent studies suggest that certain CNS monoamines are related to specific sleep patterns and waking behavior. Jouvet (1969) has suggested that serotonin is related to NREM sleep while dopamine and norepinephrine, or both, are related to REM sleep and the awake state. Other investigators have reported conflicting findings concerning the relationship of monoamines and sleep patterns; the biochemistry of sleep is an area of intense investigation at this time.

Gresham, Webb, and Williams (1963) found that 1 g/kg of body weight of 95 percent ethyl alcohol (equivalent of 6 oz of 100 proof liquor for a 150 lb man) produced a moderate decrease in REM sleep time, whereas a moderate amount of caffeine

(2.5 to 3.0 cups of coffee for a 150 lb man) resulted in no significant change. This study was for only one night. A subsequent study of the effects of alcohol for several consecutive nights showed that the original findings may have been misleading. Yules, Freedman, and Chandler (1966) studied three subjects for 13 consecutive nights, 4 control, 5 alcohol, and 4 recovery nights. They administered 1 g of ethyl alcohol per kg of body weight on the alcohol nights. On the first alcohol night, the mean REM sleep time decreased from control values and, during the next four consecutive alcohol nights, REM sleep time increased to a peak value on the fifth alcohol night. During the four recovery nights, REM sleep time returned to control levels. The changes in REM sleep with alcohol administration occurred in the first half of the night when cerebro-spinal-fluid (CSF) alcohol levels were at maximum concentration. The decrease and subsequent increase in REM sleep with alcohol was accompanied by reciprocal changes in stage 2 sleep.

Gross et al. (1966) continuously monitored four patients who suffered from acute alcoholic psychosis, for periods ranging from 48 to 72 hours. Two of the four subjects who slept during this period showed varied increases in REM sleep. They concluded that the major consequence of extended drinking which leads to withdrawal psychoses is a profound disturbance of REM sleep. They assumed that during the drinking period there is severe REM deprivation which, on withdrawal, leads to extremely high compensatory percentages of REM sleep time accompanied by the hallucinations of the delirious state.

Kales et al. (1968b) studied the effects of several sedatives (chloral hydrate, glutethimide, methyprylon, pentobarbital, methaqualone, and a new drug under investigation, Dalmane, RO-56901). In addition, diphenhydramine HCL, an antihistamine, was evaluated because it is known to produce drowsiness. Each subject was studied for eight consecutive nights (3 base-line, 3 drug and 2 withdrawal nights) with each drug. 500 and 1000 mgms of glutethimide, 300 mgms of methyprylon, 100 mgms of pentobarbital, 300 mgms of methaqualone, 60 mgms of Dalmane, and 50 and 100 mgms of diphenhydramine HCL, all, produced varying decreases in REM sleep. glutelhimide and methyprylon resulted in marked REM suppression, although the other drugs had less pronounced effects. Wthdrawal of all the drugs except Dalmane produced rebound increases in the percentages of stage REM above base-line levels. Dalmane 30 mgms and chloral hydrate in doses of 500 and 1000 mgms did not alter sleep patterns either during drug administration or following withdrawal. Thus these drugs did not produce REM suppression when administered, and they did not result in REM increases above base line when withdrawn. On two occasions following the withdrawal of glutethimide and methyprylon, subjects reported repetitive terrifying nightmares on their recovery nights. One of the subjects, following the withdrawal of methyprylon, stated that they were the first nightmares she had experienced since childhood.

Hartmann (1968) reported on the effects of 100 mgms of phenobarbital, 100 mgms of chlordiazepoxide, and 30 mgms of Dalmane, given for one night. The percentage of REM sleep was somewhat reduced by phenobarbital but not significantly effected by chlorodiazepoxide and Dalmane.

CNS Stimulants

Rechtschaffen and Maron (1964) administered D-amphetamine sulphate to 8 subjects prior to sleep. It led to a significant decrease in the percentage of REM sleep time, compared with control nights when no drugs were given. Similarly, the administration of a combination of amphetamine and pentobarbital to 7 subjects resulted in a significant decrease in REM sleep time, compared with nights in which pentobarbital alone was administered. The administration of amphetamine and pentobarbital to 3 subjects for 3 to 4 consecutive nights produced REM sleep percentages below normal values. On withdrawal of the drugs, these subjects showed compensatory increases in the percentage of REM sleep time above normal values.

Oswald and Thacore (1963) studied 6 patients who were addicted to amphetamine or phenmetrazine. Although addicted to large or moderate quantities of these drugs, their sleep patterns differed little from normal in respect to three sleep measurements, which became highly abnormal following withdrawal of the drug. Total nocturnal REM time rose as high as 48 percent, REM time in the first two hours rose up to 70 minutes, and the delay between the first onset of spindles (sleep onset) and the first REM period was as low as 4 minutes. Moreover, these variables took from 3 to 8 weeks to return to normal.

Le Gassicke et al. (1965) studied a 24-year-old male who was addicted to tranylcypromine (Parnate). He consumed up to 700 mg daily and while taking the drug was restless, cheerful, and confident. Without it, he was apprehensive and housebound. Large tranylcypromine intake was associated with high muscle tension during sleep and sometimes with the abolition of the REM phase of sleep. REM sleep was wholly suppressed on five nights while the patient was taking the drug. Drug withdrawal was associated with complaints of dreaming by day and by night, and immediate onset and unprecedented duration of REM sleep with nightmares. On both withdrawal nights, a high proportion of the night's sleep was spent in REM sleep (76 percent and 50 percent). Once on each of those nights he awoke from REM sleep, emitting repeated bloodcurdling shrieks, and described a nightmare. These awakenings occurred from REM sleep. The direct transition to REM sleep following sleep onset occurred not only with the initial sleep onset of the night but also 12 times following 17 periods of wakefulness on the first drug withdrawal night, and twice following periods of wakefulness on the second withdrawal night.

Muzio, Roffwarg, and Kaufman (1966) found that small doses of LSD (7–22 μ total dose) produced a prolongation of the first or second REM period on most nights. In spite of this increase in REM sleep early in the night, total REM sleep for the whole night was not above base-line values. Because of the arousal effect of larger doses of LSD, it was not possible to study any dose-dependent relations in sleep patterns.

Several antidepressants, amitriptyline (Hartmann, 1968), imipramine (Ritvo et al., 1967; Ryba et al., 1965) and desmethylimipramine (Zung, 1968) have been studied. All produce moderate suppression of REM sleep. Hartmann (1968) noted that withdrawal of amitriptyline did not result in an increase in REM sleep, and he suggested that antidepressants may decrease the need for REM sleep. Zung (1968) also reported that desmethylimipramine, when given for several weeks to depressed patients was associated with increases in stage 4 sleep, which correlated with clinical improvement.

Whitman et al. (1961, 1964) conducted a number of studies evaluating the effects of various tranquilizers and antidepressants on dream content. One of the drugs studied was imipramine. They found that, following the administration of imipramine, the number of dreams per night were decreased significantly. In addition, the amount of hostility expressed in these dreams was increased to a significant degree. There was an increased amount of anxiety in dreams after imipramine, although there was also a tendency for anxiety to increase with each of the drugs.

The studies reviewed above, which are summarized in Table 17.3, indicate that most drugs, whether primarily depressant or excitatory, result in markedly altered sleep patterns, primarily in suppression of REM sleep. A number of investigations have been for only one night; the studies that have evaluated consecutive drug nights and subsequent withdrawal indicate that on stopping the drug, increases in REM sleep occur that are often associated with clinical disturbances such as nightmares and insomnia. The alterations in sleep patterns, primarily in REM sleep, caused by various drugs both during and following administration may provide a psychophysiological basis for addiction to or dependence on these drugs. Consequently, further research, especially with sleeping pills, should include the evaluation of drug and of withdrawal effects as well as of dose effects. This research should be directed toward finding compounds that not only induce sleep, but sleep which is comparable to a base-line ("normal") night's sleep.

SUMMARY

With the new techniques available in sleep research, answers have been provided to a number of questions which in the past were beyond the realm of investigative techniques. Recent sleep studies have attempted to relate nocturnal symptoms to specific sleep stages. Other studies have investigated

Table 17.3 Effects of Drugs on REM Sleep

Drug (Depressants)	Drug Effect	Withdrawal Effect
Barbiturate		
Amobarbital	Decrease	Increase
Heptabarbitone	Decrease	Increase
Pentobarbital	Decrease	Increase
Secobarbital	Decrease	Increase
Nonbarbiturate		
Chloral hydrate	None	None
Glutethimide	Decrease	Increase
Methyprylon	Decrease	Increase
Nitrazepam	Decrease	Increase
Dalmane	None	None
Methaqualone	Decrease	Increase
Ethyl alcohol	Decrease[a]	Increase
Chlordiazepoxide	None	—[d]
Chlorpromazine	—[b]	—[d]
Meprobamate	Decrease	—[d]
Reserpine	—[c]	Increase
Diphenhydramine	Decrease	Increase

Drug (Stimulants)	Drug Effect	Withdrawal Effect
Amphetamines		
Dextroamphetamine	Decrease	Increase
Antidepressants		
Amitriptyline	Decrease	None
Desmethylimipramine	Decrease	—[d]
Imipramine	Decrease	—[d]
Methylphenidate	Decrease	—[d]
Tranylcypromine	Decrease	Increase
LSD	Increase	—[d]
Tryptophane	Increase	—[d]

[a] After first night, REM time increased above base line.
[b] Decrease with small doses, increase with larger doses.
[c] Increase with small doses, decrease with larger doses.
[d] Not studied.
[e] First two REMs increased; total REM time not changed.

the effects of various disease states on basic sleep patterns.

Contrary to the widely held belief that sleepwalking is the acting out of a dream, recent studies show that sleepwalking incidents occur out of NREM sleep, predominantly stages 3 and 4. Enuresis also occurs predominantly out of stages 3 and 4 sleep, indicating that dreaming is not a major factor in precipitating these episodes. The very depth and soundness of stages 3 and 4 sleep also indicate that there is little if any volitional control over the somnambulistic and enuretic episodes.

Coronary artery and ulcer patients experience exacerbations of their symptoms during REM sleep. These exacerbations may be related to specific dream content or to the marked increase in neurophysiologic activity that accompanies this sleep phase. In narcolepsy with cataplexy, disturbances of the REM sleep mechanism are present; recent studies also suggest a redefinition of the criteria for narcolepsy. A number of conditions that include aging, depression, asthma, and hypothyroidism are associated with decreases in stage 4 sleep. Although insomniacs do not show marked differences from good sleepers in their sleep patterns, they tend to have a more "aroused" level of sleep, based on various physiologic measurements.

Sleep alterations are induced by most psychotropic drugs; REM sleep is generally suppressed during drug administration and is increased following drug withdrawal. Accompanying the increase in REM sleep after drug withdrawal may be an increase in dream recall, frequently of unpleasant dreams and occasionally of nightmares. These REM sleep changes together with the clinical observations of nightmares and insomnia following withdrawal may be of significance in the development of dependence and of addiction to these compounds.

Recent sleep research has contributed much to the understanding of various psychological disturbances. The most recent studies are emphasizing qualitative aspects of sleep, such as the measurement of physiological parameters and phasic events (eye movements, PGO spikes) rather than merely comparing percentages of sleep stages from one group to another. This research, along with other studies, poses a considerable promise for furthering our knowledge regarding the symptoms of psychopathology.

REFERENCES

Agnew, H. W., Webb, W. B., & Williams, R. L. The effects of stage four sleep deprivation. *Electroencephalog. Clin. Neurophysiol.*, 1964, **17**, 68–70.

Agnew, H. W., Webb, W. B., & Williams, R. L. The first night effect: an EEG study of sleep. *Psychophysiology*, 1966, **2**, 263–266.

Agnew, H. W., Webb, W. B., & Williams, R. L. Sleep patterns in late middle age males: an EEG study. *Electroencephalog. Clin. Neurophysiol.*, 1967, **23**, 168–171. (a)

Agnew, H. W., Webb, W. B., & Williams, R. L. Comparison of stage four and 1-REM sleep deprivation. *Percept. mot. Skills*, 1967, **24**, 851–858. (b)

Antrobus, J. S., Dement, W., & Fisher, C. Patterns of dreaming and dream recall: an EEG study. *J. abnorm. soc. Psychol.*, 1964, **69**, 341–344.

Arduini, A., Berlucchi, G., & Strata, P. Pyramidal activity during sleep and wakefulness. *Arch. Ital. Biol.*, 1963, **101**, 530–544.

Armington, J. D., & Mitnick, L. L. Electroencephalogram and sleep deprivation. *J. appl. Physiol.*, 1959, **14**, 247–250.

Armstrong, R. H., Burnap, D., Jacobson, A., Kales, A., Ward, S., & Golden, J. Dreams and gastric secretions in duodenal ulcer patients. *New Physician*, 1965, **14**, 241–243.

Asahina, K. Paradoxical phase and reverse paradoxical phase in human sleep. *J. Physiol. Soc. Japan*, 1962, **24**, 443–450.

Aserinsky, E., & Kleitman, N. Regularly occurring periods of eye motility, and concomitant phenomena during sleep. *Science*, 1953, **118**, 273–274.

Aserinsky, E., & Kleitman, N. Two types of ocular motility occurring in sleep. *J. appl. Physiol.*, 1955, **8**, 1–10.

Baekeland, F., & Lasky, R. Exercise and sleep patterns in college athletes. *Percept. mot. Skills*, 1966, **23**, 1203–1207.

Batini, C. F., Criticos, A., Fressey, J., & Gastaut, H. Nocturnal sleep in patients presenting epilepsy with bisynchronous EEG discharges. *Electroencephalog. Clin. Neurophysiol.*, 1962, **14**, 957.

Batini, C. F., Moruzzi, G., Palestini, M., Rossi, G. F., & Zanchetti, A. Effects of complete pontine transection on the sleep-wakefulness rhythm: The midpontine pretrigeminal preparation. *Arch. Ital. Biol.*, 1959, **97**, 1–12.

Berger, R. J. Tonus of extrinsic laryngeal muscles during sleep and dreaming. *Science*, 1961, **134**, 840.

Berger, R. J. Experimental modification of dream content by meaningful verbal stimuli. *Brit. J. Psychiat.*, 1963, **109**, 722–740.

Berger, R. J. When is a dream is a dream is a dream? In C.D. Clemente (Ed.) *Physiological Correlates of Dreaming, Exp. Neurol.*, 1967, Suppl. 4, 15–28.

Berger, R. J. Oculomotor control: a possible function of REM sleep. *Psychol. Rev.*, 1969, in press.

Berger, R. J., & Meier, G. W. The effects of selective deprivation of states of sleep in the developing monkey. *Psychophysiology*, 1966, **2**, 354–371.

Berger, R. J., Olley, P., & Oswald, I. The EEG, eye movements and dreams of the blind. *Quart. J. Exp. Psychol.*, 1962, **14**, 183–186.

Berger, R. J., & Oswald, I. Effects of sleep deprivation on behavior, subsequent sleep, and dreaming. *J. Ment. Sci.*, 1962, **108**, 457–465. (a)

Berger, R. J., & Oswald, I. Eye movements during active and passive dreams. *Science*, 1962, **137**, 601. (b)

Blake, H., Gerard, R. W., & Kleitman, N. Factors influencing brain potentials during sleep. *J. Neurophysiol.*, 1939, **2**, 48–60.

Brebbia, R. D., and Altshuler, K. Z. Oxygen consumption rate and electroencephalographic stage of sleep. *Science*, 1965, **150**, 1621–1623.

Broughton, R. J. Sleep disorders. Disorders of arousal? *Science*, 1968, **159**, 1070–1078.

Broughton, R. S., Poire, R., & Tassinari, C. A. The electrodermogram (Tarchanoff effect) during sleep. *Electroencephalog. Clin. Neurophysiol.*, 1965, **18**, 691–708.

Cadilhac, J., & Passouant, P. L'influence des différentes phases du sommeil nocturne sur les décharges épileptiques chez l'homme. In *Aspects Anatomofonctionnels de la Physiologie Du Sommeil*. V. 127, Lyon, 9–11 Sept. 1963. Centre National de la Recherche Scientifique, Paris, 1965. Pp. 555–570.

Caldwell, D. F., & Domino, E. F. Electroencephalographic and eye movement patterns during sleep in chronic schizophrenic patients. *Electroencephalog. Clin. Neurophysiol.*, 1967, **22**, 414–420.

Carli, G., & Zanchetti, A. A study of pontine lesions suppressing deep sleep in the cat. *Arch. Ital. Biol.*, 1965, **103**, 751–788.

Clemente, C. D., & Sterman, M. B. Limbic and other forebrain mechanisms in sleep induction and behavioral inhibition. *Progress in Brain Research*, 1967, **27**, 34–47.

Clemes, S. R., & Dement, W. C. Effect of REM sleep deprivation on psychological functioning. *J. Nerv. Ment. Dis.*, 1967, **144**, 485–491.

Costello, C. G., & Selby, M. M. The relationships between sleep patterns and reactive and endogenous depressions. *Brit. J. Psychiat.*, 1965, **111**, 497–501.

Delorme, F., Jeannerod, M., & Jouvet, M. Effets remarquables de la reserpine sur l'activite EEG phasique ponto-geniculo-occipitale. *C. R. Soc. Biol.*, 1965, **159**, 900–903.

Dement, W. C. Dream recall and eye movements during sleep in schizophrenics and normals. *J. Nerv. Ment. Dis.*, 1955, **122**, 263–269.

Dement, W. C. The effect of dream deprivation. *Science*, 1960, **131**, 1705–1707.

Dement, W. C. Experimental dream studies. In J. Masserman (Ed.) *Science and psychoanalysis: scientific proceedings of the Academy of Psychoanalysis*. Vol. 7. New York: Grune and Stratton, 1964. Pp. 129–184.

Dement, W. C. The biological role of REM sleep (circa 1968). In A. Kales (Ed) *Sleep: Physiology and Pathology*. Philadelphia: J. P. Lippincott Co. 1969.

Dement, W. C., Greenberg, S., & Klein, R. The effect of partial REM sleep deprivation and delayed recovery. *J. Psychiat. Res.*, 1966, **4**, 141–152.

Dement, W. C., Kahn, E., & Roffwarg, H. P. The influence of the laboratory situation on the dreams of the experimental subject. *J. Nerv. Ment. Dis.*, 1965, **140**, 119–131.

Dement, W. C., & Kleitman, N. Cyclic variations in EEG during sleep and their relation to eye movements, body motility and dreaming. *Electroencephalog. Clin. Neurophysiol.*, 1957, **9**, 673–690. (a)

Dement, W. C., & Kleitman, N. The relation of eye movements during sleep to dream activity: An objective method for the study of dreaming. *J. exp. Psychol.*, 1957, **53**, 339–346. (b)

Dement, W. C., Rechtschaffen, A., & Gulevich, G. The nature of narcoleptic sleep attack. *Neurology*, 1966, **16**, 18–33.

Dement, W. C., & Wolpert, E. A. The relationship of eye movement, body motility and external stimuli to dream content. *J. exp. Psychol.*, 1958, **55**, 543–553.

Diaz-Guerrero, R., Gottlieb, J. S., & Knott, J. R. The sleep of patients with manic-depressive psychosis, depressive type. An electroencephalographic study. *Psychosom. Med.*, 1946, **8**, 399–404.

Domhoff, B., & Kamiya, J. Problems in dream content study with objective indicators. I. A comparison of home and laboratory dreams. *Arch. gen. Psychiat.*, 1964, **11**, 519–524. (a)

Domhoff, B., & Kamiya, J. Problems in dream content study with objective indicators. II. Appearance of experimental situation in laboratory dream narratives. *Arch. gen. Psychiat.*, 1964, **11**, 525–528. (b)

Dragstedt, L. R. Causes of peptic ulcer. *J. A. M. A.*, 1959, **169**, 203–209.

Dynes, J. B., & Finley, K. H. The electroencephalograph as an aid in the study of narcolepsy. *Arch. Neurol. Psychiat.*, 1941, **46**, 598–612.

Evarts, E. V. Activity of neurons in visual cortex of the cat during sleep with low voltage fast EEG activity. *J. Neurophysiol.*, 1962, **25**, 812–816.

Evarts, E. V. Temporal patterns of discharge of pyramidal tract neurons during sleep and waking in the monkey. *J. Neurophysiol.*, 1964, **27**, 152–171.

Feinberg, I., Braun, M., & Schulman, E. Electrophysiological sleep patterns in mongolism and phenylpyruvic oligophrenia (PKU). (Abst.) *Psychophysiol.*, 1968, **4**, 395.

Feinberg, I., Koresko, R. L., & Gottlieb, F. Further observations on electrophysiological sleep patterns in schizophrenia. *Compr. Psychiat.*, 1965, **6**, 21–24.

Feinberg, I., Koresko, R. L., Gottlieb, F., & Wender, P. H. Sleep electroencephalographic and eye movement patterns in schizophrenic patients. *Compr. Psychiat.*, 1964, **5**, 44–53.

Feinberg, I., Koresko, R. L., & Heller, N. EEG sleep patterns as a function of normal and pathological aging in man. *J. Psychiat. Res.*, 1967, **5**, 107–144.

Feinberg, I., Koresko, R. L., & Schaffner, I. R. Sleep electroencephalographic and eye movement patterns in patients with chronic brain syndrome. *J. Psychiat. Res.*, 1965, **3**, 11–26.

Ferguson, J., & Dement, W. C. The effect of variations in total sleep time on the occurrence of rapid eye movement sleep in cats. *Electroencephalog. Clin. Neurophysiol.*, 1967, **22**, 2–10.

Fisher, C., & Dement, W. C. Studies on psychopathology of sleep and dreams. *Amer. J. Psychiat.*, 1963, **119**, 1160–1168.

Fisher, C., Gross, J., & Zuch, J. A cycle of penile erection synchronous with dreaming (REM) sleep. *Arch. gen. Psychiat.*, 1965, **12**, 29–45.

Foulkes, W. D. Dream reports from different stages of sleep. *J. abnorm. soc. Psychol.*, 1962, **65**, 14–25.

Foulkes, W. D., & Vogel, G. Mental activity at sleep onset. *J. abnorm. Psychol.*, 1965, **70**, 231–243.

Freeman, F. R., Agnew, H. W., & Williams, R. L. An electroencephalographic study of the effects of meprobamate on human sleep. *Clin. Pharm. Ther.*, 1965, **6**, 172.

Gastaut, H., & Broughton, R. A clinical and polygraphic study of episodic phenomena during sleep. In J. Wortis (Ed.) *Recent advances biological psychiatry*. Vol. 1: Plenum Press, 1965. Pp. 197–221.

Gibbs, E. L., & Gibbs, F. A. Extreme spindles: correlation of electroencephalographic sleep pattern with mental retardation. *Science*, 1962, **138**, 1106–1107.

Goodenough, D. R., Lewis, H. B., Shapiro, A., Jaret, L., & Sleser, I. Dream reporting following abrupt and gradual awakening from different types of sleep. *J. abnorm. soc. Psychol.*, 1965, **2**, 170–179.

Goodenough, D. R., Shapiro, A., Holden, M., & Steinschriber, L. A comparison of "dreamers" and "non-dreamers": eye movements, electroencephalograms, and recall of dreams. *J. abnorm. soc. Psychol.*, 1959, **59**, 295–302.

Gresham, S. C., Agnew, H. W., & Williams, R. L. The sleep of depressed patients. *Arch. gen. Psychiat.*, 1965, **13**, 503–507.

Gresham, S. C., Webb, W. B., & Williams, R. L. Alcohol and caffeine: effect on inferred visual dreaming. *Science*, 1963, **140**, 1226–1227.

Gross, M. M., Goodenough, D., Tobin, M., Halpert, E., Lepore, D., Perlstein, A., Sirota, M., Dibianco, J., Fuller, R., & Kishner, I. Sleep disturbances and hallucinations in the acute alcoholic psychosis. *J. Nerv. Ment. Dis.*, 1966, **142**, 493–514.

Gulevich, G. D., Dement, W. C., & Zarcone, V. P. All night sleep recordings of chronic schizophrenics in remission. *Compr. Psychiat.*, 1967, **8**, 141–149.

Hall, C. Studies of dreams reported in the laboratory and at home. Institute of Dream Research, Monogr. 1, Santa Cruz, California, 1966.

Hartmann, E. L. Reserpine: its effect on the sleep-dream cycle in man. *Psychopharmacologia*, 1966, **9**, 242–247.

Hartmann, E. L. Pharmacological sleep studies in man: pentobarbital (Nembutal) phenobarbital amitriptyline, (Elavil), chlorodiazepoxide (Librium) and RO 5–6901. (Dalmane) (Abst.) *Psychophysiol.*, 1968, **4**, 391.

Hawkins, D. R., & Mendels, J. Sleep disturbance in depressive syndromes. *Amer. J. Psychiat.*, 1966, **123**, 682–690.

Hawkins, D. R., Scott, J., & Thrasher, G. Sleep patterns in enuretic children. Presented to the Association for the Psychophysiological Study of Sleep, Washington, D. C., March 1965.

Hernández-Péon, R. Sleep induced by localized electrical or chemical stimulation of the forebrain. *Electroencephalog. Clin. Neurophysiol.*, 1962, **14**, 423–424.

Heuser, G., Kales, A., Jacobson, A., Paulson, M. J., Zweizig, J. R., Walter, R. D., & Kales, J. D. Sleep patterns in hypothyroid patients. *Physiologist*, 1966, **9**, 203.

Hinton, J. M. Patterns of insomnia in depressive states. *J. Neurol. Neurosurg. Psychiat.*, 1963, **26**, 184.

Hishikawa, Y., & Kaneko, Z. Electroencephalographic study on narcolepsy. *Electroencephalog. Clin. Neurophysiol.*, 1965, **18**, 249–259.

Hodes, R., & Dement, W. C. Depression of electrically induced reflexes ("H-reflexes") in man during low voltage EEG "sleep." *Electroencephalog. Clin. Neurophysiol.*, 1964, **17**, 617–629.

Hoffman, J. S., & Domino, E. F. Effects of reserpine on the sleep cycle in man and cat. Presented to Association for the Psychophysiological Study of Sleep, Santa Monica, California, April, 1967.

Huttenlocher, P. R. Evoked and spontaneous activity in single units of medial brain stem during natural sleep and waking. *J. Neurophysiol.*, 1961, **24**, 451–468.

Jacobson, A., Kales, A., Lehmann, D., & Hoedemaker, F. S. Muscle tonus in human subjects during sleep and dreaming. *Exp. Neurol.*, 1964, **10**, 418–424.

Jacobson, A., Kales, A., Lehmann, D., & Zweizig, J. R. Somnambulism: All night electroencephalographic studies. *Science*, 1965, **148**, 975–977.

Johnson, L. C., & Lubin, A. Spontaneous electrodermal activity during waking and sleeping. *Psychophysiology*, 1966, **3**, 8–17.

Johnson, L. C., Slye, E. S., & Dement, W. Electroencephalographic and autonomic activity during and after prolonged sleep deprivation. *Psychosomatic Med.*, 1965, **27**, 415–423.

Jouvet, D., Vimont, P., Delorme, F., & Jouvet, M. Étude de la privation sélectivé de la phase paradóxale de sommeil chez le chat. C. R. *Soc. Biol.*, 1964, **158**, 756–759.

Jouvet, M. Telencephalic and rhombencephalic sleep in cat. In G.E.W. Walstenholme and M. O'Connor (Eds.) *Nature of sleep*. Boston: Little, Brown and Company. 1961, 188–208.

Jouvet, M. Recherches sur les structures nerveuses et las mécanismes responsables des différentes phases du sommeil physiologique. *Arch. Ital. Biol.*, 1962, **100**, 125–206.

Jouvet, M. Behavioral and EEG effects of paradoxical sleep deprivation in the cat. Proc. XXIII Int. Cong. Physiol. Sci., Tokyo. *Excerpta Medica Internat.* Congr. Series, 1965, No. 87, 344–353.

Jouvet, M. Biogenic amines and the states of sleep. *Science*, 1969, **163**, 32–41.

Jouvet, M., Michel, F. and Mounier, D. Analysé electroencephalographique comparée du sommeil physiologique chez le chat et chez l'homme. *Rev. Neurol.*, 1960, **103**, 189–205.

Jouvet, M., Pellin, B. and Mounier, D. Étude polygraphique des différentes troubles de phases du sommeil au cours conscience chroniques (Comas prolongés). *Rev. Neurol.*, 1961, **105**, 181–186.

Kahn, E. and Fisher, C. Sleep characteristics and REM period erections of healthy elderly male subjects. Paper presented to the Association for the Psychophysiological Study of Sleep. Gainesville, Florida, March 1966.

Kales, A., Beall, G. N., Bajor, G., Jacobson, A., Kales, J. D., Slye, R. M. and Wilson, T. E. Sleep studies of adult and child asthmatics. (Abst.) *Psychophysiol.*, 1968, **4**, 397. (a)

Kales, A., Heuser, G., Jacobson, A., Kales, J. D., Hanley, J., Zweizig, J. R., & Paulson, M. J. All night sleep studies in hypothyroid patients, before and after treatment (sleep patterns and thyroid status). *J. Clin. End. Metabol.*, 1967, **27**, 1593–1599. (a)

Kales, A., Hoedemaker, F. S., Jacobson, A. and Lichtenstein, E. L. Dream deprivation: An experimental reappraisal. *Nature*, 1964, **204**, 1337–1338.

Kales, A., & Jacobson, A. Studies of mental activity: recall, somnambulism and effects of REM deprivation and drugs. In C. D. Clemente (Ed.) *Physiological Correlates of Dreaming*, 1967, *Exp. Neurol.*, Suppl. 4, 81–91.

Kales, A., Jacobson, A., Kales, J. D., Kun, T., & Weissbuch, R. All-night EEG sleep measurements in young adults. *Psychon. Sci.*, 1967, **7**, 67–68. (b)

Kales, A., Jacobson, A., Kales, J. D., Marusak, C., & Hanley, J. Effects of several drugs on sleep (Noludar, Doriden, Nembutal, Chloral Hydrate, Benadryl). (Abst.) *Psychophysiology*, 1968, **4**, 391–392.

Kales, A., Jacobson, A., Paulson, M. J., Kales, J. D., & Walter, R. D. Somnambulism: psychophysiological correlates. I. All-night EEG studies. *Arch. gen. Psychiat.*, 1966, **14**, 586–594. (a)

Kales, A., Kollar, E., Tan, L., & Kales, J. D. Sleep patterns following 205 hours of sleep deprivation. *Psychosom. Med.* 1969 (In press).

Kales, A., Paulson, M. J., Jacobson, A., & Kales, J. D. Somnambulism: psychophysiological correlates. II. Psychiatric interviews, psychological testing, and discussion. *Arch. gen. Psychiat.*, 1966, **14**, 595–604. (b)

Kales, A., Wilson, T., Kales, J. D., Jacobson, A., Paulson, M. J., Kollar, E., & Walter, R. D. Measurements of all-night sleep in normal elderly persons: effects of aging. *J. Amer. Gen. Soc.*, 1967, **15**, 405–414. (c)

Kamiya, J. Behavioral, subjective and physiological aspects of drowsiness and sleep. In D. W. Fiske and S. R. Maddi (Eds.) *Functions of varied experience*. Homewood, 1ll.: Dorsey Press, 1961, Pp. 145–174.

Kanzow, E., Krause, D., & Kühnel, H. Die Vasomotorik der Hirnrinde in den Phasen

Desynchronisierter. EEG–Aktivitat un naturlichen Schlaf der Katze. *Pflüg. Arch. ges. Physiol.*, 1962, **274**, 593–607.

Karacan, I., Goodenough, D. R., Shapiro, A., & Starker, S. Erection cycle during sleep in relation to dream anxiety. *Arch. gen. Psychiat.*, 1966, **15**, 183–189.

Kawamura, H., & Sawyer, C. H. Elevation in brain temperature during paradoxical sleep. *Science*, 1965, **150**, 912–913.

Khazan, N., & Sawyer, C. H. Mechanism of paradoxical sleep as revealed by neurophysiologic and pharmacologic approaches in the rabbit. *Psychopharmacologia*, 1964, **5**, 457–466.

Kiloh, L. G. and Garside, R. F. The independence of neurotic depression and endogenous depression. *Brit. J. Psychiat.*, 1963, **109**, 451–463.

Kiyono, S., Kawamoto, T., Sukakura, H., Iwama, K. Effects of sleep deprivation upon the paradoxical phase of sleep in cats. *Electroencephalog. Clin. Neurophysiol.*, 1965, **19**, 34–40.

Koresko, R. L., Snyder, F., & Feinberg, I. "Dream time" in hallucinating and non-hallucinating schizophrenic patients. *Nature*, 1963, **199**, 1118–1119.

Lairy, G. C.,Cormordret, M., Faure, R., & Ridjanovic, S. Etude E.E.G. du sommeil du viellard normal et pathologique. *Rev. Neurol.*, 1962, **107**, 188–202.

Le Gassicke, J., Ashcroft, G. W., Eccleston, D., Evans, J. I., Oswald, I., & Ritson, E. B. The clinical state, sleep and amine metabolism of a tranylcypromine (Parnate) addict. *Brit. J. Psychiat.*, 1965, **3**, 357–364.

Loomis, A. L., Harvey, E. N., & Hobart, G. A. Cerebral states during sleep as studied by human brain potentials. *J. Exp. Psychol.*, 1937, **21**, 127–144.

Luby, E. D., & Caldwell, D. F. Sleep deprivation and EEG slow wave activity in chronic schizophrenia. *Arch. gen. Psychiat.*, 1967, **17**, 361–364.

Magnes, J., Moruzzi, G., & Pompeiano, O. Electroencephalogram synchronizing structures in the lower brain stem. In G. E. W. Wolstenholme and M. O'Connor (Eds) *The nature of sleep*. Boston: Little, Brown and Company, 1961, 57–85.

Mandell, A. J., Brill, P. L., Mandell, M. P., Rodnick, J., Rubin, R. T., Sheff, R., & Chaffey, B. Urinary excretions of 3-methoxy-4-hydroxymandelic acid during dreaming sleep in man. *Life Sciences*, 1966, **5**, 169–173. (a)

Mandell, A. J., Chaffey, B., Brill, P., Mandell, M. P., Rodnick, J., Rubin, R. T., & Sheff, R. Dreaming sleep in man: changes in urine volume and osmolality. *Science*, 1966, **151**, 1558–1560. (b)

Mandell, M. P., Mandell, A. J., Rubin, R. T., Brill, P., Rodnick, J., Sheff, R., & Chaffey, B. Activation of the pituitary-adrenal axis during rapid eye movement sleep in man. *Life Sciences*, 1966, **5**, 583–587. (c)

Meier, G. W., & Berger, R. J. Development of sleep and wakefulness patterns in the infant rhesus monkey. *Exp. Neurol.*, 1965, **12**, 257–277.

Monod, N., Dreyfus-Brisac, C., Morel-Kahn, F., Pajot, N., & Plassard, E. Les premieres etapes de l'organisation du sommeil chez le premature et le nouveau-né. *Rev. Neurol.*, 1964, **110**, 304–305.

Monroe, L. J. Psychological and physiological differences between good and poor sleepers. *J. abnorm. Psychol.*, 1967, **72**, 255–264.

Monroe, L. J., Rechtschaffen, A., Foulkes, D., and Jensen, J. Discriminability of REM and NREM reports. *J. Pers. and Soc. Psychol.*, 1965, **2**, 456–460.

Moruzzi, G., & Magoun, H. W. Brainstem reticular formation and activation of the EEG. *Electroencephalog. Clin, Neurophysiol.*, 1949, **1**, 455–473.

Muzio, J. N., Roffwarg, H. P., & Kaufman, E. Alterations in the nocturnal sleep cycle resulting from LSD. *Electroencephalog. Clin. Neurophysiol.*, 1966, **21**, 313–324.

Nowlin, J. B., Troyer, W. G. Jr., Collins, W. S., Silverman, G., Nichols, C. R., McIntosh, H. D., Estes, E. H. Jr., & Bogdonoff, M. D. The association of nocturnal angina pectoris with dreaming. *Ann. Int. Med.*, 1965, **63**, 1040–1046.

Onheiber, P., White, P. T., Demyer, M. K., & Ottinger, D. R. Sleep and dream patterns of child schizophrenics. *Arch. gen. Psychiat.*, 1965, **12**, 568–571.

Ord, W. M. On myxoedema. *Roy. Med. Chir. Soc. Trans.*, 1878, **61**, 57–78.

Ornitz, E. M., Ritvo, E. R., & Walter, R. D. Dreaming sleep in autistic and schizophrenic children. *Amer. J. Psychiat.*, 1965, **122**, 419–424.

Oswald, I. *Sleeping and waking: physiology and psychology*. New York: Elsevier Pub. Co., 1962. 232 pages.

Oswald, I., Ashcroft, G. W., Berger, R. J., Eccleston, D., Evans, J. I., & Thacore, V. R. Some experiments in the chemistry of normal sleep. *Brit. J. Psychiat.*, 1966, **112**, 391–399.

Oswald, I., Berger, R. J. Evans, J. I. & Thacore, V. R. Effect of l-tryptophan upon human sleep. *Electroencephalog. Clin. Neurophysiol.*, 1964, **17**, 603.

Oswald, I., Berger, R. J., Jaramillo, R. A., Keddie, K. M. G., Olley, P. C., & Plunkett, G. B. Melancholia and barbiturates: A controlled EEG body and eye movement study of sleep. *Brit. J. Psychiat.*, 1963, **109**, 66–78.

Oswald, I., & Priest, R. G. Five weeks to escape the sleeping-pill habit. *Brit. Med. J.*, 1965, **2**, 1093–1099.

Oswald, I., & Thacore, V. R. Amphetamine and phenmetrazine addiction: physiological abnormalities in the abstinence syndrome. *Brit. Med. J.*, 1963, **2**, 427–431.

Parmelee, A. H. Jr., Wenner, W. H., Akiyama, Y., Schultz, M., & Stern, E. Sleep states in premature infants. *Develop. Med. Child Neurol.*, 1967, **9**, 70–77.

Parmelee, A. H. Jr., Wenner, W. H., & Schulz, H. R. Infant sleep patterns from birth to 16 weeks of age. *J. Pediat.*, 1964, **65**, 576–582.

Petre-Quadens, O. On the different phases of the sleep in the newborn with special reference to the activated phase, or phase D. *J. Neurol. Sci.*, 1966, **3**, 151–161.

Petre-Quadens, O., & Jouvet, M. Le sommeil paradoxal et le reve chez les debiles mentaux. *Acta Neur. Psychiat. Belg.*, 1966, **66**, 116–122.

Pierce, C. M., Whitman, R. M., Maas, J. W., & Gay, M. L. Enuresis and dreaming, experimental studies. *Arch. gen. Psychiat.*, 1961, **4**, 166–170.

Rechtschaffen, A., Cornwall, P., Zimmerman, W., & Bassam, M. Brain temperature variations with paradoxical sleep: implications for relationships among EEG, cerebral metabolism, sleep and consciousness. Proc. Symposium on Sleep and Consciousness, Lyon, France, 1965.

Rechtschaffen, A., Hauri, V., & Zeitlin, M. Auditory awakening thresholds in REM and NREM sleep stages. *Percept. mot. Skills*, 1966, **22**, 927–942.

Rechtschaffen, A., & Maron, L. The effect of amphetamine on the sleep cycle. *Electroencephalog. Clin. Neurophysiol.*, 1964, **16**, 438–445.

Rechtschaffen, A., Schulsinger, F., & Mednick, S. A. Schizophrenia and physiological indices of dreaming. *Arch. gen. Psychiat.*, 1964, **10**, 89–93.

Rechtschaffen, A., & Verdone, P. Amount of dreaming: effect of incentive, adaptation to laboratory, and individual differences. *Percept. mot. Skills*, 1964, **19**, 947–958.

Rechtschaffen, A., Verdone, P., & Wheaton, J. Reports of mental activity during sleep. *Can. Psychiat. Assn., J.*, 1963, **8**, 409–414.

Rechtschaffen, A., Vogel, G., & Shaikun, G. Interrelatedness of mental activity during sleep. *Arch. gen. Psychiat.*, 1963, **9**, 536–547.

Rechtschaffen, A., Wolpert, E. A., Dement, W. C., Mitchell, S. A., & Fisher, C. Nocturnal sleep of narcoleptics. *Electroencephalog. Clin. Neurophysiol.*, 1963, **15**, 599–609.

Ritvo, E. R., Ornitz, E. M., LaFranchi, S., & Walter, R. D. Effects of imipramine on the sleep-dream cycle: an EEG study in boys. Paper presented to the Association for the Psychophysiological Study of Sleep, Santa Monica, California, April, 1967.

Roffwarg, H. P., Dement, W. C., & Fisher, C. Preliminary observations of the sleep-dream patterns in neonates, infants, children and adults. In E. Harms (Ed.) *Problems of sleep and dream in children*: Monographs on Child Psychiatry. New York: Pergamon Press, 1964, pp. 60–72.

Roffwarg, H. P., Dement, W. C., Muzio, J. N., & Fisher, C. Dream imagery: relationship to rapid eye movements of sleep. *Arch. gen. Psychiat.*, 1962, **7**, 235–258.

Roffwarg, H. P., Muzio, J. N., & Dement, W. C. Ontogenetic development of the human sleep-dream cycle. *Science*, 1966, **152**, 604–619.

Ross, J. J., Johnson, L. C., & Walter, R. D. Spike and wave discharges during stages of sleep. *Arch. Neurol.*, 1966, **14**, 399–407.

Ryba, P., Shapiro, A., Friedman, N., Endicott, N., & Boyle, A. Physiological and psychological changes during several months of observation of a depressed patient: sleep, dream reporting and waking behavior. Presented to the Association for the Psychophysiological Study of Sleep, Washington, D. C., March, 1965.

Sampson, H. Psychological effects of deprivation of dreaming sleep. *J. Nerv. Ment. Disease*, 1966, **143**, 305–317.

Snyder, F. The new biology of dreaming. *Arch. gen. Psychiat.*, 1963, **8**, 381–391.

Snyder, F. Sleep disturbance in relation to acute psychosis. In A. Kales (Ed.) *Sleep: Physiology and Pathology*. Philadelphia: J. P. Lippincott Co., 1969.

Snyder, F., Hobson, J. A., & Goldfrank, F. Blood pressure changes during human sleep. *Science*, 1963, **142**, 1313–1314.

Snyder, F., Hobson, J. A., Morrison, D. F., & Goldfrank, F. Changes in respiration, heart rate, and systolic blood pressure in human sleep. *J. Appl. Physiol.*, 1964, **19**, 417–422.

Sterman, M. B., Knauss, T., Lehman, D., & Clemente, C. Circadian sleep and waking patterns in the laboratory cat. *Electronecephalog. Clin. Neurophysiol.*, 1965, **19**, 509–517.

Valatx, J. L., Jouvet, D., & Jouvet, M. Evolution électroencéphalographique des différents états de sommeil chez le chaton. *Electroencephalog. Clin. Neurophysiol.*, 1964, **17**, 218–233.

Vogel, G., & Traub, A. REM deprivation of schizophrenic patients. *Psychophysiol.*, 1968, **4**, 383.

Webb, W., & Agnew, H. The results of continued partial sleep deprivation. Paper presented to the Association for the Psychophysiological Study of Sleep, Washington, D. C., March, 1965.

Weitzman, E. A., Schaumburg, H., & Fishbein, W. Plasma 17-hydroxycorticosteroid levels during sleep in man. *J. Clin. Endocr.*, 1966, **26**, 121–127.

Wender, P., Koresko, R., Gottlieb, F. and Feinberg, I. Effects of drugs on sleep. Paper presented to the Association for the Psychophysiological Study of Sleep, Palo Alto, California, March, 1964.

Whitman, R. M., Ornstein, P. H., & Baldridge, B. An experimental approach to the psychoanalytic theory of dreams and conflicts. *Compreh. Psychiat.*, 1964, **5**, 349–363.

Whitman, R. M., Pierce, C. M., Maas, J. W., Baldridge, B. Drugs and dreams II: imipramine and prochlorperazine. *Compreh. Psychiat.*, 1961, **2**, 219–226.

Whitman, R. M., Pierce, C. M., Maas, J. W., & Baldridge, B. The dreams of the experimental subject. *J. Nerv. Ment. Dis.*, 1962, **134**, 431–439.

Wilkinson, R. T. Effects of sleep deprivation on performance and muscle tension. In G. E. W. Wolstenholm and M. O'Connor (Eds.) *The nature of sleep*. Boston: Little, Brown, and Company, 1961, pp. 329–336.

Wilkinson, R. T., Edwards, R. S., & Haines, E. Performance following a night of reduced sleep. *Psychon. Sci.*, 1966, **5**, 471–472.

Williams, H. L., Hammack, J. T., Daly, R. L., Dement, W. C., & Lubin, A. Responses to auditory stimulation, sleep loss and the EEG stages of sleep. *Electroencephalog. Clin. Neurophysiol.*, 1964, **16**, 269–279.

Williams, H. L., Lubin, A., & Goodnow, J. J. Impaired performance with acute sleep loss. *Psychol. Monog.*, 1959, **73**, 1–26.

Williams, R. L., Agnew, H. W., Jr., & Webb, W. B. Sleep patterns in young adults: an EEG study. *Electroencephalog. Clin. Neurophysiol.*, 1964, **17**, 376–381.

Williams, R. L., Agnew, H. W., Jr. & Webb, W. B. Sleep patterns in the young adult female: an EEG study. *Electroencephalog. Clin. Neurophysiol.* 1966, **20**, 264–266.

Yules, R. B., Freedman, D. X., & Chandler, K. A. The effect of ethyl alcohol on man's electroencephalographic sleep cycle. *Electroencephalog. Clin. Neurophysiol.*, 1966, **20**, 109–111.

Zarcone, V., Gulevich, G., & Dement, W. Sleep and electroconvulsive therapy. *Arch. gen. Psychiat.*, 1967, **16**, 567–573.

Zarcone, V., Gulevich, G., Pivik, T., & Dement, W. Partial REM phase deprivation and schizophrenia. *Arch. Gen. Psychiat.*, 1968, **18**, 194–202.

Zung, W. W. K. Antidepressant drugs and sleep in depressive disorders. (Abst.) *Psychophysiology*, 1968, **4**, 397.

Zung, W. W. K., Wilson, W. P., & Dodson, W. E. Effect of depressive disorders on sleep EEG responses. *Arch. gen. Psychiat.*, 1964, **10**, 439–445.

Chapter 18

Alcoholism

CYRIL M. FRANKS

INTRODUCTION, DEFINITION AND INCIDENCE

There is little doubt that alcoholism—however we define this term and however we assess its prevalence—presents a problem that has proved remarkably resistant to all attempts at understanding and at resolution. At the present author has documented more extensively elsewhere, concepts such as "cure" and "prevention" lie far ahead and even the more modest aspirations of large-scale containment and of controlling the urge to drink are little more than blueprints for the future (Franks, 1966). In 1942, Voegtlin and Lemere reviewed 20 different forms of treatment and found most of them wanting; in 1962, Gerard, Saenger, and Wile followed up 299 patients treated in a variety of clinics and found that less than 19 percent were able to maintain a period of abstinence for even one year following treatment. The situation then, in 1962, appeared to offer little more reason for optimism than in 1942. In an even more recent appraisal of psychotherapy with alcoholics, Hill and Blane (1967) concluded as follows: "We are unable to form any conclusive opinion as to the value of psychotherapeutic methods in the treatment of alcoholism." It may seem astounding that, despite many decades of research endeavor and much clinical ingenuity, matters of etiology and effective methods of coping with the problems presented remain largely in the realms of conjecture. The indications are that there is no single etiology and no single remedy and that etiology, treatment, and prevention alike will implicate a variety of disciples and a variety of approaches within any one discipline.

In this sense, the present chapter is limited, since it emphasizes the manifest concomitants of alcoholism and the approaches of the behavioral clinician. But there are several mitigating factors. First, the concern of this book is primarily with symptomatology. Second, as already stated, the record with respect to the value of existing methods of coping with the problem of alcoholism is far from impressive. Third, regardless of their value, existing treatment resources for the alcoholic patient are woefully inadequate (Barton, 1968) and, finally, the methods of the behavioral clinician, which are essentially what this chapter is about, represent an exciting new development in the field with much promise over a wide range of problem areas, of which alcoholism is but one (see Franks, 1969).

Disagreement, lack of knowledge, and confusion with respect to the etiologies and treatment of alcoholism are matched by an equal lack of unaminity concerning the concept of alcoholism and its definition (see Marconi, 1967). Quite apart from the emotional, religious, and moral overtones which frequently obscure basic issues, the controversy over whether alcoholism is a symptom or a disease is still diverting a lot of energy and effort that could be put to more productive use. In the present stage of knowledge, such disputes are futile, and the search for the disease process, if any, must continue while every effort is made to cope with the symptom or *behavior* of the alcoholic. This, then, is the point of view underlying the present chapter.

Within this context, the following definition appears to offer many advantages:

"Alcoholism is a chronic behavioral disorder manifested by repeated drinking of alcoholic beverages in excess of the dietary and social uses of the community and to an extent that interferes with the drinker's health or his social or economic functioning" (Keller, 1958).

No declaration is made in this definition with respect to unresolved problems pertaining to alcoholism as a disease or a symptom, to etiology, or to issues such as whether any addiction involved is physiological or psychological. This definition also begs the question as to whether the concept "alcoholism" is or is not a reification. In his last book, Jellinek (1960), although retaining the blanket term "alcoholism," stressed the need to differentiate among its various forms, and distinguished five new types: alpha, beta, gamma, delta, and epsilon. Only further research, possibly along factor-analytic lines, can determine the validity and the utility of this typology.

Zwerling and Rosenbaum (1959) seem to regard the omission of etiological considerations from such definitions as a strategic deficit. By contrast, the contention here is that improvements in definition should be along the lines of increased observational and behavioral precision rather than in terms of an at present futile insistence on matters that are beyond our present knowledge. For example, arguing that there *is* such a thing as an alcoholism syndrome, Korman and Stubblefield (1961) decided to test the underlying assumption that there must be a cluster of behaviors or traits that are common to the bulk of alcoholics. Their basic group consisted of 61 patients referred to an outpatient clinic with alcoholism as a primary presenting feature. Measures of 19 seemingly relevant variables were subjected to a factorial analysis in an attempt to isolate meaningful components. However, no such general factor or factors emerged, from which the authors concluded that "alcoholism is far from being a unitary tract, and that it is currently being defined in terms of characteristics that don't go well together." Of course, it is possible that these authors failed to isolate general factors because they failed to ask the right questions. But, certainly, this approach is of value, and it is possible that future dimensional analysis will yield a kind of behavioral botany that does adequately define an alcoholism syndrome or syndromes. Along related lines are the attempts of Mulford, Miller, and their associates (Mulford & Miller, 1960a, 1960b, 1963) to explore the definitions of alcohol held *by the drinker himself* in order to ascertain the individual's behavioral definitions of what alcohol does for and to him, and how he uses alcohol.

The "incidence" of alcoholism is clearly going to depend on the definition adopted, its interpretation, and the method used for applying this definition to the development of a working formula. As Clark (1966) points out, the most commonly used behavioral definitions of alcoholism show four elements: excessive intake, mental disturbance because of drinking, disturbance of social and economic functioning, and loss of control over drinking. As Clark demonstrated so well, different indicators yield different "incidence" data, and those indicators that do happen to yield similar rates often fail to identify the same category of individuals. This makes comparisons between studies unwarranted and, what is perhaps worse, misleading. A standardized approach to measuring prevalence is much needed, preferably one that is based on objective, quantifiable, and clearly delineated variables. (Parenthetically, we might note that a similar argument applies to alcoholism treatment and recovery concepts; see Pattison, 1966, 1967.)

Perhaps, the most widely used formula is the one derived by Jellinek (1952). Popham (1956) has devoted considerable attention to the Jellinek formula, its technical and logical deficiencies, and the development of sound alternatives.[1] Keller (1958) used this formula to estimate that there were approximately 5 million alcoholics in the United

[1] In the absence of a more direct means for determining the number of alcoholics, Jellinek's original formula was a method whereby the number of alcoholics with complications—those exhibiting a diagnosable physical or psychological change due to prolonged excessive drinking—could be estimated from the number of reported

States alone. Expressed in terms of rate, this yielded a figure of 7550 alcoholics per 100,000 adults of the population for men, and 1290 per 100,000 adults for females. It is sometimes argued that these rates are steadily increasing but, as with other data in social psychiatry and mental health surveys, the advancing rates over the years *may* well reflect not so much a true increase in the incidence of alcoholism as a steady improvement in reporting. The well publicized claims that alcoholism is steadily increasing, especially among women, may likewise be unwarranted (but see Keller, 1958, for an extended discussion of these issues).

DESCRIPTION AND ASSESSMENT OF THE ALCOHOLIC

The search for the so-called "alcoholic personality" may be or may not be an exploration in a blind alley. Although many reviewers rightly conclude that there is little or no evidence to suggest that persons of any one type are more likely to become alcoholics than those of any other type (for example, Sutherland, Schroeder, & Tordella, 1950; Syme, 1957), the problem is too complicated to be summarily dismissed in this fashion. A uniform definition of alcoholism and agreed behavioral criteria for pinpointing its incidence must precede effective research in this area. And, even if there were such common terms of reference, the failure to find a clinical diagnosis or behavioral description common to any given population of alcoholics would not necessarily preclude the presence of a specific "alcoholic personality." (It is quite conceivable for a small common variance contributed by the alcoholic personality *per se* to be thoroughly masked by many and diverse attributes of quite a different nature.) And, conversely, success in delineating a "personality" common to many alcoholics need not necessarily mean that these individuals possessed this particular communality *prior* to becoming alcoholic. Perhaps because of the immense difficulties inherent in the design and the execution of the necessary controlled longitudinal studies, the available literature sheds little light on these crucial issues. Attempts such as the one of Wittman (1939) to work back to the premorbid state by using retrograde information obtained from the patients themselves are commendable for their intent but of limited scientific value.

Incidentally, the biochemists and physiologists are confronted with similar dilemmas when they try to tease out information about some possible physical needs or deficiences in the premorbid alcoholic; for example, the fact that Diethelm and his associates (1955) found evidence of a chemical change in the "full blown" alcoholic adds little to our meagre knowledge of the biochemistry of the *potential* alcoholic. And even when the concern is with the alcoholic per se, the social and biological scientists are likely to encounter similar methodological problems; for example, Bates (1965) found all sorts of contaminating medical features in his study of what were supposed to be a "group" of alcoholics.

Theoretically, it would probably be of interest to study the development of alcoholism under controlled conditions but, even if practicable, such an artificial situation might well defeat its purpose. More feasible approaches must be evolved if the many strands involved in the study of the potential alcoholic are to be teased out. Of probably equal importance is the need to know more about the effects of alcohol in relation to individual behavioral and physiological differences. The complex notion, difficult both to delineate and to investigate, that people differ quantitatively, and perhaps qualitatively, in their responses to alcohol from the very onset of their lives remains largely unexplored in any systematic fashion.

---

deaths resulting from cirrhosis of the liver. The full formula, first presented in a WHO Report in 1951, is expressed as follows: $A = R\left(\frac{PD}{K}\right)$, where R = the ratio of all alcoholics to alcoholics with complications; D = the number of reported deaths from cirrhosis of the liver in a given year; P = the percentage of such deaths attributable to alcholoism; K = the percentage of all alcoholics with complications who die of cirrhosis of the liver; and A = the total number of alcoholics alive in a given year. The constants in the formula were later revised by Jellinek (1952) in the light of new actuarial data pertaining to causes of death. For further discussion of the Jellinek formula, its limitations, and its subsequent revisions, see Keller (1958), Manis and Hunt (1957), Popham (1956), and Popham and Schmidt (1962).

No wonder, then, that Armstrong (1958) wisely cautioned against the premature abandonment of the search for the alcoholic personality because of failure to date to develop adequate methods or even to isolate the appropriate investigative tools. As he goes on to observe:

"The ideal experiment is yet to be designed and carried out, one which will allow observation of an unsuspecting population, seemingly representative of a larger society, over a time span sufficiently long to watch the adolescent reach the age of social drinking and progress to the time when he or some of his fellows will show various unusual characteristics related to his drinking which will eventually be labeled alcoholic–all this to be accomplished without disturbing the study sample by the processes of observation" (p. 47).

One of the few longitudinal projects that is relevant to such a line of endeavor is the Oakland Growth Study, now in its fourth decade (see Jones, 1938; Jones, Macfarlane, & Eichorn, 1960). The members of this study, currently in their middle forties, were classified on the basis of their drinking patterns at 33, 38, and 43 years of age, respectively. These data were analyzed in relation to their personality characteristics as assessed by the California *Q* set (Block, 1961) when in junior and senior high schools and in adulthood. According to Jones (1968), the results clearly suggest that some of the attitudes, motives, and behaviors attributed to problem drinkers, moderate drinkers, or abstainers can be detected in the early years before drinking habits are established. The problem drinker tended to have a predrinking core of traits characterized by undercontrol, impulsivity, and rebelliousness. This work is of importance on three accounts: first, because it exemplifies the use of a normal longitudinal sample to consider questions that probably cannot be answered in any other way; second, because it does suggest that certain alcohol-related behavior is, at least in part, an expression of certain distinctive clusters of personality tendencies that are exhibited before drinking patterns have become established; third, because of its prophylactic implications, aimed at modifying the attitudes of such susceptible youngsters toward society in general, and toward alcohol as a symbol of virility and rebellion (see Lisansky, 1968).

Jones' findings are consistent with the previous work of some investigators (for example, McCord & McCord, 1960, 1962; Robins, Bates, & O'Neal, 1962; Sanford & Singer, 1967) but inconsistent with the work of others. As Sanford (1968) points out, these discrepancies will not be resolved until work as carefully conducted as that of Jones is carried out with larger samples and with more theoretically substantiated measures of personality. A schema for classifying alcohol-related behavior in terms that are both theoretically and practically significant has been recently outlined by Sanford (1967). Hopefully, some future investigator will combine systems like the one of Sanford with the methodology and painstaking thoroughness of Jones.

It may well be, as Lisansky (1960) suggests, that there is not a single common pattern but several. In one recent study, Walton (1968) compared addicts of the Jellinek "gamma" and "delta" types in terms of their profiles on Cattell's 16PF personality questionnaire. Clear-cut differences emerged, the "gamma" addicts (the loss-of-control or compulsive drinkers) were much more afraid of their own impulses and much more intrapunitively hostile than the "delta" (inability-to-abstain) drinkers. Although this tells us little about the premorbid personalities of the drinkers, it does suggest that personality differences might well partially determine the form the alcoholism will eventually take. It may be equally important to look not only at the presence or absence of certain traits but also at the *degree* to which these traits are present or absent, and at the peculiarities of the manner in which they coexist with certain other features.

Many individuals have systematically reviewed the extensive psychological test data that attempt to shed some light on the issues raised above (for example, Zwerling & Rosenbaum 1959; Hampton, 1951a, 1951b, 1951c, 1952). Since the majority of these tests are far removed from the terms of reference of the present chapter, they warrant only the most cursory treatment here. Their failure to contribute appreciably to the resolution of these issues provides additional justification for this policy of exclusion. Most projective techniques, and many psychometric tests, have yielded findings that are either inconsistent or not replicable. Perhaps the outstanding exceptions are those studies that employed the MMPI, although here again the reports are limited in their value on at least four major accounts:

1. In general, they pertain to established alcoholics and tell us nothing about an individual's premorbid potential for the development of alcoholism.
2. With certain noteable exceptions (for example, Rosen, 1960), they do not differentiate alcoholics from other deviant populations.
3. They are rarely cross-validated against other samples of alcoholics.
4. Many of these MMPI studies use scales other than the conventional ten on the profile sheet and, under the best of circumstances, the most that can be said of the majority of these new scales is that they are questionable.

Scale 4 (Psychopathic Deviation) is one of the few conventional scales that have been shown to differentiate alcoholics from both normals and various clinical groups with any degree of consistency. But even here—and not withstanding the distain of certain distinguished MMPI enthusiasts for the utilization of content (for example, Hathaway, 1960)—when MacAndrew and Geertsma (1963) conducted an impressive factor-analytic study of the MMPI with special relevance to this scale, they found that all significant differences could be attributed to three rather mundane items; that alcoholics report themselves as having used alcohol excessively, as having been in trouble with the law, and as feeling that they have not lived the right kinds of life.

If studies employing the conventional and well researched MMPI scales are vulnerable, the ones that use specifically derived MMPI alcoholism scales fare even worse. The reader interested in a devastating but valid critique of these secondary MMPI scales is referred to an appraisal by MacAndrew and Geertsma (1964), in which three different so-called "MMPI alcoholism scales" were shown to be primarily measures not of alcoholism but of general maladjustment. An independent study by Rotman and Vestre, also reported in 1966, arrived at a strikingly similar conclusion. These results are not surprising when we observe that all three scales were derived by contrasting diagnosed alcoholics with normals, thus begging the question of differentiation from matched nonalcoholic psychiatric patients—a question to which MacAndrew (1965) addressed himself in an apparently successful attempt to develop an MMPI scale that did validly and reliably satisfy such criteria. In this study, MacAndrew identified some 49 MMPI items which, even on cross-validation, were able to classify correctly 81.5 percent of a combined sample of 100 male alcoholic outpatients and 100 nonalcoholic male psychiatric outpatients (see MacAndrew, 1965 for the list of items concerned). In a later paper (MacAndrew, 1967), the 49 MMPI items were factor analyzed in an attempt to determine whether the responses of alcoholics to these items were unidimensional or multidimensional. A principle components analysis of the 49×49 item intercorrelational matrix yielded 13 factors which were then rotated to oblique simple structure. The factors thus obtained were so diverse in manifest content that MacAndrew was forced to conclude that, at least in self-representation, diagnosed male alcoholics differ significantly from nonalcoholic psychiatric male outpatients in a variety of ways that are not necessarily contingent on excessive alcohol intake—a conclusion which unfortunately does not take us much further in our understanding of alcoholism except in the recognition that alcoholics are rather more than "neurotics-who-also-happen-to-drink-too-much."

The two most well-known questionnaires constructed specifically for use with alcoholics are the Manson Evaluation Test (MET) (Manson, 1948a) and the Alcadd Test (Manson, 1948b). Gibbins, Smart, and Seeley (1959) have made a most penetrating analysis of the MET with respect to its origins, its validation, and its utility. Although Manson himself cautioned the user against so doing, the test is continually being used to differentiate alcoholic from nonalcoholic clinical deviates. As Gibbins et al. point out, even when properly used, the test has most serious limitations with respect to the selection of test items, the groups studied, and the derivation of the critical score employed to differentiate between alcoholics and nonalcoholics. In the concluding words of Gibbins et al., a test

> "designed to diagnose alcoholism is of little practical value in facilities where people go more or less voluntarily to seek treatment for their drinking problems. In fact, to use the test in such a situation seems more than pointless when one realizes that undertaking treatment for inebriety was basically the criterion employed for establishing its validity."

In a subsequent paper Smart (1961) turned his critical attentions to the Alcadd test. As with the MET, the vast majority of the subjects who were used in the validation study had already readily identified *themselves* as problem drinkers and, therefore, the test cannot be assumed to be effective in working with untreated or nonself-recognized problem drinkers. Furthermore, for statistical reasons, into which Smart goes in detail, the test cannot even be used to provide personality profiles of individual drinkers. Smart further elaborates on the non-applicability of the critical scores that are given in the manual, unless the user is working with a population already believed to contain about 43 percent alcoholics. His final conclusion about this test is that the "conditions upon which validity has been established appear to be so rare as to eliminate the Alcadd from any legitimate widespread use."

The assessment of the alcoholic and his differentiation from other groups may have to proceed along different lines. Attempts such as those of Mulford and Miller (1960a, 1960b, 1963) to develop scales of preoccupation with alcohol represent promising new applications of the questionnaire method, but perhaps one eventual solution lies in a total departure from traditional psychometrics. If the alcoholic is to be treated by techniques of behavioral modification, then likewise it would seem not unreasonable to try and ferret out matters pertaining to his identification in behavioral terms. At the present time, advances in both the theory and the practice of behavioral assessment lag dismally behind developments in the area of behavior modification. This is as true in the case of alcoholism as it is with respect to other disorders.

There is no doubt that the early conditioning attempts to modify deviant drinking behavior and nothing else met with limited success (see Franks, 1958, 1963, 1966, 1967b, 1967c). However, the indifferent success of these procedures cannot always be attributed exclusively to poor technique, and the many failures to remain abstinent suggest that perhaps abstinence alone is not the only behavior crucial to the alcoholic. As Narrol (1967) points out, it has often been noted that many chronic alcoholics who are willingly abstinent in the succorent atmosphere of the mental hospital (even if alcohol is made fairly readily available) often return to drinking soon after discharge.

It is therefore necessary to inquire what behavior or sets of behavior are crucial to the aberrant pattern, in this case drinking, that it is desired to change. To address himself to this question, Narrol developed a "token economy" environment in the hospital setting in which tokens were used to reinforce work on the hospital labor force. These tokens were exchangeable for virtually every kind of facility within the hospital, ranging from room and board, AA meetings, leaves of absence, through different kinds of drugs and therapy. A deprivation situation was established by starting patients in a closed ward of low status and limited material comfort, and the patient's task was described to him as working his way through a hierarchy of wards in order to improve his material status.

By a systematic study of the nature of the purchases made with the tokens as the patient progressed along the status-comfort hierarchy, Narrol was able both to measure and to change the behavior of the patients concerned. The hope is that, if behaviors crucial to the chronic hospitalized alcoholic can be identified and even manipulated, then an orderly systematic approach can be made to conditioning new, and perhaps alcohol-incompatible, behaviors in the place of the undesired alcohol response.

The next step in such a program, suggested by Narrol but not actually carried out, would be to have an "alcoholized" ward in which a token economy could include the use of alcohol as a reinforcer. To the best of the present writer's knowledge, the only studies reporting the operant use of alcohol with alcoholics in a self-determining situation are the ones of Mello and Mendelson, to be discussed in the next section.

LEARNING THEORY AND THE EFFECTS OF ALCOHOL: EARLY APPLICATIONS

To understand the alcoholic in learning theory terms, it is desirable to have an understanding of both the objective effects of alcohol and, perhaps equally important, the functions which alcohol serves for the individual who drinks it. Both aspects have been often but usually not well explored, and naiveté rather than scientific rigor and a knowledge of the hazards attending drug investigations characterizes many of these studies, especially the ones carried out prior to World War II (see the recent reviews by Carpenter, 1962, and Lester, 1966).

As sophistication in design and elegance in execution began to increase, so experimentally derived data began to yield results at variance not only with cherished popular beliefs but with previously "established" psychological findings (Keller, 1966). For example, recent studies by Carpenter and his associates (Carpenter, Moore, Snyder, & Lisansky, 1961; Carpenter & Ross, 1965) clearly challenge the hitherto accepted conclusion of Jellinek and McFarland (1940) that alcohol consistently deteriorates mental performance. It now seems likely that the action of alcohol is not a simple linear function of the amount ingested. In small amounts, alcohol may facilitate performance on certain task—even intellectual ones—and the traditionally accepted deterioration effect may not occur until the dosage is increased.

One of the more firmly established facts is that, if by tolerance is meant the ability of brain tissue to resist the effects of any given concentration of alcohol, then there is surprisingly little individual variation among different human beings. All persons show some impairment in driving ability, for example, at a blood alcohol concentration of 0.10 percent and, regardless of tolerance, the fatal concentration is 0.6 to 0.8 percent (AMA Committee on Medicolegal Problems, Sub-Committee on Alcohol, 1962). Yet, despite this fact, there are wide behavioral differences in reactions to alcohol that cannot be accounted for in any totally satisfactory manner. In an attempt to come to grips with the problem of those seemingly unaccountable individual differences, various limited theories have been proposed. McDougall's (1929) chemical theory of introversion-extraversion predicted that extraverts are more susceptable to the effects of alcohol; Sheldon and Stevens (1942) commented on the resistance of their "cerebrotonic" types of alcohol; and Pavlov (1958) reported differing sensitivities to alcohol among his dogs.

The only systematic attempt to set forth a general model for the investigation of predicted relationships between drug effects and personality variables is that of Eysenck. The pertinent ramifications of this unusually comprehensive theory are too involved to be described here, and the reader interested in a critical experimental appraisal of Eysenck's drug-personality postulate as it relates especially to the effects of alcohol is referred elsewhere (Franks, 1967d). Essentially, Eysenck's drug-personality postulate is part of a more general theory that relates physiological and psychological individuality in such a fashion that it purports to account for a whole range of phenomena, of which the effects of drugs is but one section. More specifically, it is suggested that central stimulants are introverting in nature, whereas central depressants—including alcohol—are extraverting.

Such an approach would be particularly valuable in an attempt to grapple with problems pertaining to alcohol and driving. From the several good reviews in this area (for example, Borkenstein, Crowther, Shumate, Ziel, & Zylman, 1964; Carpenter, 1962, 1968; Carpenter & Varley, 1962; Schmidt & Smart, 1959; Smart, 1967) it is evident that comparatively little progress has been made concerning our precise knowledge of how and why alcohol affects driving behavior. And yet, although the problems of experimental design, generalization from the laboratory to real life, subject variability, and so forth are formidable, they are by no means insolvable.

It is usual to investigate what alcohol does *to* the individual, and most investigations have been carried out along these lines. With few notable exceptions, scientific study of what alcohol does *for* the individual has been neglected. It is sometimes assumed that alcohol intoxication somehow favorably alters affect, but experimental verification of such assumptions, in the main, remains lacking. Those studies that are available *fail* to provide definitive answers to questions that pertain to the relative pharmacological and social aspects of drinking on affect, and to differences between alcoholics and nonalcoholics, or between normal and abnormal affective states with respect to the effects of alcohol on affect. In an attempt to shed light on these issues, Mayfield (1968a, 1968b) made use of the Clyde Mood Scale (Clyde, 1963). One of his conclusions, based on the laboratory study of hospitalized patients, was that alcohol is primarily a palliative for *disordered* affect. Although far from definitive, his studies certainly raise questions about those theories of alcohol effects which are based on the questionable assumption that affective improvement occurs with intoxication.

But, perhaps, the most important need is to develop good objective methods of assessing the effects of alcohol which can be readily applied outside the laboratory. Sometimes the available studies in this area have yielded data that are literally amazing. For example, Frankenhaeuser (1966) and Ekman, Frankenhaeuser, Goldberg, Hagdahl, and Myrsten (1964) report an astoundingly high concomitance between objective measurements of blood alcohol curves and subjective self-assessment of the perceived degree of intoxication. This is a surprising finding on many accounts, not least of which is the notoriously impaired judgment of subjects under the influence of alcohol, an impairment that *increases* as the alcohol intake is increased. This is not reflected in the Ekman et al. data.

The work of Hill and his associates appears to be promising (Haertzen & Fuller, 1967; Hill, Haertzen, Wolbach, & Miner, 1963; Haertzen, Hill, & Belleville, 1963). These authors developed the *Addiction Research Center Inventory (ARCI)*, a 550 item true-false questionnaire that was devised specifically for differentiation among the effects of different drugs, including alcohol. Their procedure appears to be superior to earlier attempts to assess subjective drug effects by the use of adjective checklists (for example, Petrie, 1958; Beecher, 1959; Nowlis & Nowlis, 1956; Clyde, 1960) in that the scales are aimed specifically at differentiating among various subjective drug effects. Considered *individually*, few subjective changes are unique to any one drug, (at least, as far as the drugs studied thus far with this technique are concerned: morphine, amphetamine, phenobarbital, alcohol, LSD-25, pyrahexyl, and chlorpromazine). And yet, collectively, there might be a kind of "pattern specificity" awaiting isolation and meaningful interpretation through the application of appropriate cluster and factor-analytic techniques.

A study by Docter and Bernal (1964) is of significance because it evaluates the effects of *sustained* alcohol intake in humans rather than that of a single drinking session. By employing the conventional methods and measures of the psychophysiological experiment, these investigators succeeded in investigating the effects of 14 days of sustained alcohol intake on two long-term male alcoholics. Such studies can shed considerable light on the enduring and transient changes that may follow prolonged drinking in both alcoholics and nonalcoholics. If Docter and Bernal's surmise is correct, then certain prolonged physiological effects which they observed could contribute to the maintenance of drinking behavior and, in part, account for the frequently expressed need of the alcoholic for a drink to "cure" his hangover. But these studies—significant and desirable as they are—contribute little to an analysis of the drinking *behavior* of the alcoholic and to the forces motivating him to drink in his daily milieu.

For obvious practical reasons, it is of extreme importance to know as much as we can about the effects of low doses of alcohol, and there is indeed a not inconsiderable amount of literature available on this subject, (for example, Carpenter, 1962; Drew, Colquhoun, & Long, 1958). But the exploration of this topic within a learning-theory context has been largely neglected. Conger (1951) has demonstrated that low doses of alcohol reduce the tendencies of rats to avoid punishment, while leaving unattended their approach for reward. But, with the exception of the work of Vogel-Sprott and her associates (Banks & Vogel-Sprott, 1965; Vogel-Sprott, 1966a, 1966b, 1967a, 1967b; Vogel-Sprott & Banks, 1965), such studies of "conflict" (that is, reward and punishment for the same response) have not been systematically pursued in human beings. There is a common belief that humans under low dosages of alcohol become less fearful or concerned about avoiding punishment, while they remain just as attracted by rewarding or pleasurable stimuli. Conger's work demonstrates that this is true in the case of rats, and Vogel-Sprott has recently succeeded in demonstrating that this applies also to man, at least in a laboratory situation. It remains now to explore this hypothesis in the clinical or more natural setting.

Sociological data on the drinking patterns of particular subcultures are available, and a number of investigators have made use of retrospective reports of drinking behavior that were obtained during sobriety, but the *behavioral* analysis of the alcoholic's drinking pattern, either in the laboratory or in the more naturalistic setting, has been largely neglected. In view of the readiness with which the operant analysis of behavior lends itself to the study of the ongoing drinking pattern of the alcoholic, this neglect seems particularly unfortunate. The work of Mello and Mendelson is a promising beginning in that their technique permits detailed examination of the periodicity and quantity of alcohol ingestion in relation to certain of its psychological determinants over long time-intervals. In conjunction with metabolic and psychophysiological assays, the method could be developed into an effective and powerful procedure both for the behavioral assessment of the effects of alcohol and the drinking pattern of the alcoholic.

Mello and Mendelson's initial subjects were two adult male volunteers, each with a 20-year history of drinking. They were placed on a standard metabolic ward regimen, complete with balanced diet and multiple vitamin supplementation. The first three days were devoted to obtaining a variety of base-line physical, psychological, and metabolic assessments. The two subjects were then given an opportunity to "work" for alcohol or money reinforcements in an operant conditioning paradigm in accordance with automatically programmed schedules of reinforcement (Mello & Mendelson, 1965). In a subsequent study, Mendelson and Mello (1966) added a simulated car-driving task in which both tracking accuracy and speed of reaction determined the frequency of reinforcement with alcohol. Each subject retained his own ignition key and was free to work at the machine whenever he chose, and for as long as he chose, provided that he confined himself to alternate hours (giving a maximum of 12 hours per day).

The particular advantage of this technique is that, in contrast with the more customary studies that involve the programmed administration of alcohol in a manner which is precisely controlled but extremely artificial, the amount and rate of drinking are controlled by the subject himself in a manner analagous to the real-life situation. Such procedures, especially if carried out as part of various group projects, may shed light on the vexing questions of why individuals start and stop drinking.

Any theory of alcoholism worth its salt has to cope with two possibly related but far from synonymous questions: Why do people drink? and Why do people become alcoholics? In attempting to provide answers to these questions a learning-theory model offers many advantages: it can be integrated into either a physiological drive or a need-deficit model (for example, that of Williams, 1954), a purely psychologically oriented model or, as Keller (1958) suggested, a school of thought that makes alcohol the culprit in that alcohol *per se* possesses some intrinsic property or properties whereby certain drinkers become "alcoholics." It can be applied regardless of the actual or hypothesized origins of the need to drink, for example, whether the need is regarded as socially acquired or physiologically determined. Once a response that satisfies a need or drive occurs—whether by accident or by design—it is more likely to occur the next time the individual is faced with a similar state of unsatisfied need, that is, learning occurs by a process of reinforcement, the reinforcement being a reduction in drive tension.

Until recently, learning theory offered many such speculations about alcoholism but, with the exception of Pavlovian aversive conditioning, little that could be readily applied to treatment. Much of this speculation stemmed from a few key animal studies, of which the ones carried out by Masserman and his associates are the most significant (Masserman, Jacques, & Nicholson, 1945; Masserman & Yum, 1966). Cats were trained to operate a switch in order to open a box and to obtain food. The cats were then subjected to shock or blasts of air whenever they opened the box, so that a "conflict" eventually developed between an avoidance-response tendency based on fear and an approach-response tendency based on hunger. Presumably as a consequence, the animals developed numerous "neurotic" behaviors such as feeding problems, refusal to operate the food-access switch, startle and phobic responses to sound and light stimuli, and aversive responses to various situations associated with the stimuli-food-experimenter complex.

However, when these same animals, which had previously refused even to approach the switch, were given alcohol, they once more operated the switch and fed themselves according to schedule. Masserman interpreted these results in terms of the alcohol disorganizing the more complex neurotic patterns, thus, permitting "simpler" feeding responses to reemerge. Several years later, Conger (1951) concluded from a fresh series of experiments that the effect of the alcohol was to produce a reduction in the fear drive which was keeping the animals from operating the switch. (We must note, parenthetically, that alcohol is not unique in this effect; for example, Bailey & Miller, 1952, later obtained similar results with sodium amytal). Further experiments led Conger to conclude that alcohol acts primarily by weakening the avoidance response based on fear rather than by strengthening the approach response based on hunger. This is a rather different explanation from that put forward by Masserman and Yum. But, on two occasions, Miller was unable to replicate Conger's work (Miller 1956; Miller & Barry, 1960). Weiss (1958) likewise failed to demonstrate the fear-reducing effects of alcohol in an unconditioned conflict situation; Kopmann and Hughes (1959) and McMurray and Jaques (1959) both found that alcohol did not reduce avoidance responses; Reynolds and Van Sommers (1960) found that dosage size itself was a crucial variable, low dosages increasing and high dosages decreasing avoidance responses; and Moskowitz and Asato (1966) found that the response decrement after alcohol was the same for positive and negative reinforcers. To add to the confusion, Barry and Miller (1962) reported a study which, they claimed, confirmed the original Masserman and Yum explanation. (If it is any consolation, let it be noted that Dews and Morse (1961) report a similarly conflicting state of affairs with respect to the documented effects of other drugs.)

Wolpe (1952) extended Masserman's studies by the addition of a nonconflict group. Following the training in opening a box to get food, the conflict animals were briefly shocked during feeding trials so that conflict was created between eating and shock-avoidance behavior. Each subject in the control group received shocks only while in the experimental cage and never at food approach. Redefining "neurotic" symptoms as "unadaptive responses characterized by anxiety and persistence," Wolpe found that *both* groups exhibited similar neurotic symptoms (such as escape and phobic behavior, resistance to being placed in the cage, feeding inhibitions, muscular tension, and mydriasis). From this, he concluded that conflict is *not* necessary for the development of neurotic behavior. More recently, Smart (1965a, 1965b) has criticized these experiments on methodological grounds. Nevertheless, following the experimental clarification of the Masserman-Wolpe studies, Smart likewise concluded that neurotic behavior depends, at least in part, on the conditioned aversive stimuli created, and that conflict is *not* necessary for the development of this behavior.

Apart from the confusion concerning the replication and interpretation of these studies, there is the problem of translating these findings into concepts that can be meaningfully applied to man. Fenichel (1954) and Dollard and Miller (1950) assume that the analogy between human and animal neurotic behaviors is close and that the induction of "experimental neuroses" in animals is comparable to the Freudian model for neuroses in man (hence, Masserman's use of his own experimental data within a psychoanalytic context). But, as both Eysenck (1959) and Wolpe (1952) point out, the behavior of Masserman's animals fails to meet criteria such as those of Hebb (1947) for states in animals to be regarded as analogous to human neuroses (an undesirable emotional condition which is generalized and persistent, occurring in a minority of the population, and having no origin in a gross neural lesion). Eysenck's contention that conflict is *not* an integral constituent for the generation of "neurotic" animal behavior would appear to gain support from both the Wolpe and Smart data.

Apparently, neurotic animal behavior depends not so much on the treatment of conflict situations as on the creation of conditioned avoidance and other responses.

Therefore, it would seem good strategy to avoid terms such as "conflict" in any learning-theory discussion of the application of animal-derived data to man. If alcohol reduces conditioned responses, and if certain tension and anxiety reactions are regarded as conditioned responses (anxiety may be regarded as having two components: an unconditioned or constitutional physiological component, perhaps a matter of autonomic nervous system hyperactivity; and a conditioned or acquired component), then drinking alcohol may well become a learned habit, the reinforcement being the reduction in tension which alcohol produces. And, if excessive drinking is a learned process, then the reduction of this response pattern likewise should be amenable to the laws of learning. Furthermore, as Conger (1956) pointed out, alcohol may be rewarding not only because it reduces conditioned anxiety but because this reduction in anxiety brings with it the additional reward of being successfully able to accomplish other tasks which, in their turn, lead to further security, prestige, and recognition (for example, make a sale, give a lecture, tell a joke). Supporting evidence comes from sources far removed from the laboratory. For example, the anthropologist Horton (1943) found that the strength of the drinking response in nonliterate societies tended to vary positively with the level of anxiety in the society. And the use of other central depressants which have been shown to reduce conditioned anxiety or fear responses, for example, barbiturates (Bailey & Miller, 1952) and oblivon (Bartholomew, Franks, & Marley, 1958), is also more prevalent in anxiety-ridden communities.

This, of course, is an oversimplification, and there are many complicating factors in a man's life. Rewards are competing and may carry different values for any one individual on any one occasion. It is conceivable that the fleeting relief afforded by alcohol on a day-to-day basis can be more rewarding than the promise of the eventual lasting achievement of future goals to be brought about only by continued abstinence. In similar fashion, the relief afforded by drinking can sometimes more than compensate for social disapproval. There is also ample evidence that alcohol depresses conditioned responses other than anxiety, some of which may be necessary ones. And there is little doubt that even anxiety responses are desireable to some extent; in accordance with the much neglected Yerkes-Dodson law, there may well be a curvilinear relationship between the alcohol and the desirability of its effects, a small amount being insufficient to reduce the conditioned anxiety, and a large amount extinguishing all anxiety, even those components necessary for prudent living. A further complication stems from the fact that alcohol can depress necessary partly *unconditioned* responses such as the ability to achieve errection prior to sexual intercourse. All these possibilities are, of course, subject to individual differences and, in particular, the presence of other neurotic drives. For example, if alcohol has in the past been primarily associated with painful experiences, then, conceivably, its consumption in the future could bring about a conditioned *increase* in anxiety (for a discussion of these issues and related ones see Conger, 1956; Franks, 1958, 1966).

Of particular relevance to a learning-theory approach to alcoholism is a recent paper by Ramsay and Van Dis (1967), in which it was established that rats could be trained to drink alcohol in order to escape from a punishing situation. The authors also reported that, once drinking had become a well-established habit, punishment lead to a decreased latency in taking the next drink. Although extrapolation from such data to alcoholism in man is highly hazardous, these findings are consistent with the ones that therapists know from experience.

The earliest efforts to apply some form of explicit learning or conditioning model to the treatment of alcoholism were predicated on the supposition that an aversion to alcohol can be induced in much the same way that one would develop a condition aversion to any other stimulus. These efforts (reviewed in detail elsewhere, for example, Franks, 1958, 1963, 1966, 1967b, 1967c), for the most part, were unrelated to any formal hypotheses about etiology. For centuries man had been attempting to induce a loathing for alcohol by primitive means such as the addition of putrid spiders to the drinker's glass. It was not until the advent of Pavlov and the formal conceptualization of the classical conditioned aversion model—primarily a matter of Aristotelian association by contiguity, it should be noted, rather than reinforcement theory—that more systematic and sophisticated methods were developed. The first attempts were to develop a conditioned aversion to the taste, sight, or smell of alcohol by the use of emetics such as apormorphine or emetine as the nausea-inducing agents. Perhaps the earliest recorded systematic attempt to treat alcoholism by an explicitly conditioning procedure was that of Kantorovich (1929). Unfortunately this study stimulated little interest, at least in the West, and it was not until the late 1930's and the early 1940's that application of the method of conditioned aversion to the treatment of excessive drinking became more extensively practiced.

These investigators of the thirties, forties, and early fifties were, for the most part, experimentally unsophisticated clinicians whose concern was with the empirical treatment of alcoholism rather than with the development of a theoretical model or with the rigorous application of conditioning principles. As a consequence, and with a very few exceptions, such as the work of Thimann (1949a, 1949b) and Voegtlin (1940, 1947), most of these investigations were characterized by a naive disregard for the known facts of conditioning, for the niceties of good experimental design, for consistent and rigorous application of procedures, and for systematic follow-up. For example, sedatives were given prior to treatment despite the fact that such procedures had long been shown by Pavlov and by others to affect the conditioning process adversely. And, seemingly regardless of the possibility that this, too, might well inhibit the conditioning process, patients were permitted to swallow the alcohol at each test trial. Similarly, the possible effects of the drugs commonly used to induce nausea on the conditioning process itself were rarely considered. And, despite some evidence that backward conditioning, if it occurs at all, is the most difficult way of attempting to bring about a conditioned response, the conditioned stimulus (the alcohol) was sometimes given *after* the onset of nausea. Finally, despite the obvious advantages of faradic aversion, reported by Kantorovich as early as 1929, virtually all the investigators of the 1930's and the 1940's employed nausea-inducing drugs.

It should be stressed that this disregard for the known principles of conditioning and learning stemmed from factors other than deliberate intent. Most of those individuals using the aversive conditioning were busy practitioners, trained in the empirical traditions of medicine rather than in the more rigorous thinking of the behavioral scientist (a term not even coined in those early days). Understandably enough, the concern of these physicians was with any technique that might help them in their immediate need to develop some effective way of treating too many alcoholics with too few staff in clinics not set-up for research or systematic investigation. Most investigators, therefore, gave little or no thought to problems of experimental design or to the theoretical implications of what they were doing. Those that did show some concern for these matters usually maintained that conditioned aversion was a method of treating the symptom of alcoholism, leaving them free to apply other methods—usually psychodynamic—to the so-called underlying causes. It is not surprising that, under these circumstances, *post hoc* attempts to evaluate the success of these procedures become meaningless. Insufficient reporting of procedure and lack of controls and follow-up were the order of the day, permitting a host of interpretations of the data and "success" rates, ranging from 100 percent effective to 100 percent futile. It was virtually inevitable that interest in conditioned aversion therapies began to wane, not to be revived until the renaissance of the 1960's and the integration of the behavioral scientist into the clinical milieu.

ALCOHOLISM AS A PROBLEM IN BEHAVIOR MODIFICATION

Until the present decade, learning *theory* (as contrasted with the more restricted use of the technique of aversive conditioning) as a practical aid in the treatment of the alcoholic was applied largely in the theoretical extrapolations from animal data of very forward looking psychologists such as Conger (1956) and Kingham (1958). With the present upsurge of interest in behavior modification and the advent of the behavioral clinician, the principles of learning and conditioning moved out of the laboratory into the world of the clinician. The present-day behavior therapist is an experimental clinician who is well versed both in the problems of the clinic and the methodology of the behavioral scientist. His concern is for the patient, but it is also with the rigorous application of experimental methods and of knowledge derived from the laboratory. He is not so much a specialist in alcoholism, or in any other disease, as a clinically sophisticated investigator who is interested in the general extension of a behavioral approach to every pertinent field of enquiry.

Under these circumstances, the total behavioral approach to alcoholism—as opposed to the haphazard utilization of a technique called conditioned aversion for the reduction of drinking—could not arise until these more general developments noted above had taken place. Since these developments have been effectively documented elsewhere (for example, Krasner & Ullmann, 1965; Ullmann & Krasner, 1965), the remaining portion of this chapter will focus on the application of these principles to the alcoholic.

The behavioral treatment of the alcoholic falls historically into three phases. First, there was the direct and narrow, if nonrigorous, application of Pavlovian conditioning procedures to the development of a conditioned avoidance response to alcohol. Second, there was the era of the more sophisticated application of classical and operant procedures to the development of a conditioned aversion to alcohol, and the provision of reinforcement for not selecting such drinks. Third, there *is* the inclusion of phase-two procedures as *part* of a total or "broad-spectrum" behavioral therapy program for the alcoholic, aimed at the modification of his whole life pattern if need be.

If conditioning techniques are to be applied either in a phase-two or phase-three type of operation, certain principles must be taken into consideration (see Feldman & MacCulloch, 1965; Franks, 1966). Their implementation, however, should be exercised with caution, since some of these principles are better established than others and some are derived partially from animal studies.

1. The CS and UCS must be amenable to exact control with respect to their intensity, duration, precision of onset, and cessation. Buildup must be rapid (Franks, 1958, 1960).
2. The CS-UCS interval must be precisely determinable and, once again, amenable to control. Ideally, contiguity should occur throughout, with the CS slightly preceding the UCS (Solomon & Brush, 1956).
3. Trials should be distributed over time rather than massed. Massed practice facilitates the generation of reactive inhibition and, hence, a possible decrement in the CR (Feldman, 1963).
4. Excessively high levels of UCS intensity are unnecessary since, as intensity increases, response time shortens, up to an asymptote beyond which the UCS has no additional effect. This has been demonstrated at least for electric shock (Kimble, 1955).
5. Gradually increasing the intensity of the UCS in successive trials is undesirable because this facilitates habituation (Miller, 1960).
6. UCS which have a sudden onset are more readily conditionable than drives with a gradual onset (Fromer, 1962).
7. Learning is most effective when the CS stands out from other stimuli in the background.
8. Partial and random reinforcement schedules are preferable to 100 percent reinforcement (for example, Humphreys, 1939, Lewis, 1960).
9. The overall training situation should be both as realistic and as varied as possible. The more the training situation and the real-life situation differ, the more rapidly will extinction occur (see Feldman & MacCulloch, 1965).
10. The USC should be one which, in its own right, has minimal effect on the conditioning process *per se*. In particular, the UCS should have no depressant or otherwise inhibiting effect on the central nervous system (Franks, 1960, 1963).
11. It is important to employ a number of different forms and attributes of alcohol as the CS (Quinn and Henbest, 1967).

In 1964, Raymond applied a number of these principles in a systematic procedure which employed apomorphine as his aversive producing agent. Following a discussion with the patient of the treatment and its underlying principles, Raymond made a careful determination of the minimum subcutaneous dosage of apomorphine needed to produce adequate nausea and of the interval between injection and onset of effect. In this way it was possible to time matters so that the patient received the CS (the alcohol) just before the onset of nausea. Only tiny amounts of alcohol were given, and the patient was not permitted to drink once nausea had ceased. The atmosphere was one of seriousness and of quiet encouragement, and the small variety of alcoholic beverages employed included both the patient's favorite beverage and, in the early stages, one to which he was ordinarily not predisposed. During the post-nausea stage, the patient was quietly but firmly involved in a discussion of the potentially harmful effects of drinking and was repeatedly told that it would henceforth be possible for him to manage his life effectively without the use of alcohol.

This procedure was maintained for about 10 days until the first clear sign of an aversion to alcohol became apparent. At this phase, and without any prior warning or explanation, the routine was abruptly changed. Saline solution was substituted for apomorphine and, on arrival in the treatment room, he found that his choice of beverages now included soft drinks as well as the usual alcoholic ones. When told to drink whatever he desired, the choice was invariably non-alcoholic. At this point the atmosphere was immediately relaxed, conversation was encouraged, and he was assured that all would be well. This was followed by two or three regular treatment sessions with apomorphine. Further "choice" situations were then introduced periodically, but always in such a way that the patient could not predict their likelihood of occurrence beforehand. This technique, a combination of operant and classical procedures, was calculated to reduce the anxiety created by the aversive situation by rewarding the patient for making the "correct" choice.

Following an average length of treatment of about three weeks and adequate explanations of the need to avoid "that first drink," the patient was placed on Antabuse therapy. Thus far, there is no report of any controlled study or systematic follow-up. Many questions present themselves. In particular there is the question of self-motivation to continue to take the Antabuse if the patient is not reinforced by the therapist or his agent. Procedures such as the ones advocated by Raymond, no matter how sophisticated, place most of the emphasis on preventing the alcoholic from drinking and little on the redirection or elimination of the drives that give rise to the alcoholism in the first place, that is, the emphasis is almost entirely upon phase 1.

A virtually insuperable difficulty with apomorphine is that it is extremely difficult to predict the exact time of onset of vomiting (and there are good reasons, both theoretical and empirical, for believing that the critical interval between the onset of the CS and the onset of the vomiting should be of the order of no more than a few seconds). Also, nauseants such as apomorphine are central depressants and, hence, are likely to impair the conditioning process *per se* (see Franks, 1966). Furthermore, the onset of nausea is usually gradual, and rapid conditioning requires the onset of the UCS and UCR to be sudden (for example, Fromer, 1962). Even more telling are the medical hazards involved in the use of relatively toxic emetics for repeatedly long treatment series.

For these reasons, Sanderson, Campbell, and Laverty (1963) developed a technique that employed a drug with a totally different action. Succinylcholine chloride dihydrate (Scoline) is a curarizing agent which brings about nerve-muscle depolarization by acting on the motor-endplates of the efferent neurons serving the skeletal musculature. Following an intravenous injection of 20 mg succinylcholine, the subject suddenly becomes totally paralyzed, unable to move, or even to breathe. This effect lasts for about 1 to $1\frac{1}{2}$ minutes, during which time the patient retains full consciousness and all his intellectual and emotional facilities. This terrifying experience is sudden in onset, precisely controllable, and truly traumatic, yet apparently safe medically.

Prior to treatment, the patient is fitted with electrodes permitting continuous polygraph recordings of his galvanic skin response (GSR), heart function (EKG and heart rate), respiration, and muscle tension. Changes in these four variables are used to indicate conditioned and unconditioned responses and to predict the onset of paralysis and the reestablishment of normal respiration. Once a constant base line of physiological function has been established, the patient is given a bottle containing his favorite beverage and told to grasp it, look at it, put it to his nose and sniff it, then put it to his lips and taste it, and then hand it back to the experimenter. After five such trials, the succinylcholine is injected intravenously via an already attached (saline) drip in such a way that the patient is unaware that it is being administered. As soon as the GSR measure indicates that the drug has entered the bloodstream, the patient is handed the bottle. This is so timed that the dramatic full effect of the drug takes place just as the bottle is about to touch the patient's lips. The bottle is then held to the patient's lips, and a few drops of alcohol are placed in his mouth, the bottle not being removed until signs of regular breathing reappear.

This harrowing experience, in which the subjects are told little of the nature of the treatment beforehand, except that it will be frightening but harmless, was carried out with 15 alcoholic patients. The treatment was ineffective in three patients who had experienced the same routine in a previous "run" without alcohol. Of the remaining 12 patients, a majority subsequently exhibited signs of aversion to all alcoholic beverages and even to suggestion of alcohol beverages. However, as the authors are careful to point out, the success—if any—of the method may well be attributable to mechanisms other than conditioning. Indeed, in a later study involving 45 patients, it was concluded that, although partially successful, the aversion produced is not sufficient to induce changes in drinking behavior that are marked enough or stable enough to recommend the technique as a complete treatment in itself (Madill, Campbell, Laverty, Sanderson, & Vandewater, 1966; Laverty, 1966).

Although several investigators (Clancy, Vanderhoff, & Campbell, 1967; Sanderson, Campbell, & Laverty, 1963) have reported favorable recovery rates with succinylcholine chloride, later studies by these same investigators and others have failed to substantiate their earlier findings (for example, Holzinger, Mortimer, & Van Dusen, 1967; Madill, Campbell, Laverty, Sanderson, & Vanderwater, 1966; Farrar, Powell, & Martin, 1968). Two other aspects of these studies merit comment. First, the authors also employed a pseudo-conditioning group in which no alcohol was presented in conjunction with the drug sessions. This group later manifested about the same degree of aversion to alcohol as the "conditioning" group. Second, the aversion condition procedure produced considerable anxiety, an anxiety that could conceivably incline the subjects concerned to imbibe alcohol to try and effect a reduction in their anxiety level. It is hardly necessary to dwell on the implications of this "doublebind" situation in which the behavioral scientist might well find himself immersed.

This rather unconventional procedure excepted, emetics are the usual pharmacological agents employed, and there is little doubt that the use of these drugs presents many hazards of a theoretical, medical, and practical nature (see Franks, 1966). Apart from the more obvious difficulties associated with the use of emetics (including the grossly unesthetic nature of the vomiting process for patient and for staff alike), there is the danger that, despite their primary unpleasant effects, drugs such as apomorphine could eventually develop reward values for alcoholics by virtue of their sedating actions, thereby weakening the effects of vomiting as negative reinforcement. Furthermore, as Quinn and Kerr (1963) point out, alcoholics frequently vomit as part of their normal drinking routine and, as Kimble (1955) has shown, adaptation of animals to a noxious stimulus prior to aversion learning weakens its effect as a negative reinforcer. Vomiting is not necessarily as strong an aversive response as its earlier protagonists believed.

Therefore, it is not surprising that recent investigators have been turning to faradic stimulation as a means of creating an aversive response. Electric shock possesses virtually all the desired advantages of an aversion inducing stimulus; it is precisely controllable, inexpensive, not unesthetic, and there are few medical contraindications other than cardiac malfunction (see Franks, 1966, Fried & Franks, 1964, Rachman, 1965). In abandoning pharmaceutical aversants, most contemporary investigators have likewise abandoned that limited, but historically inevitable, confinement to the traditional classical conditioning model that characterized the aversion therapies of the 1930's. The present trend is toward the sophisticated combination of classical and operant procedures which are aimed at the twins goals of an aversion for alcohol and a preference for non-alcoholic beverages. The more advanced investigators use this method as part of a total behavioral approach; others focus their attentions primarily on the alcoholism *per se*.

For example, at Pontiac State Hospital, Michigan, the patient is presented daily with a tray containing six separate beverages (beer, wine, whiskey, milk, water, and fruit juice) and told that he has to drink them all but in any order (Hsu, 1965). The six containers are so arranged that lifting a cup which contains an alcoholic beverage and sipping its contents results in a distressingly unpleasant (but not convulsive) electric shock being delivered to the patient's head. To develop an avoidance response the patient is told to select only five drinks out of the six on the fourth treatment day and, on the fifth treatment day, he is allowed to take only four. He is then released from the hospital and told to return in one month and in six months for a repetition of days four and five on each occasion.

The fact that the shock closely follows the alcohol intake is extremely important in view of the theoretical controversy centering around the distinctions between punishment and aversion and the possibility that, under certain circumstances, punishment can actually *increase* response strength (see Church, 1963; Eysenck & Rachman, 1965; Greenwald, 1965). This is direct punishment for the deviant behavior, thus meeting the criterion of punishment as usually defined, that is, when the occurrence of the noxious stimulus is contingent on the occurrence of a clearly specified, undesired response.

On the 40 male patients who volunteered for this procedure, only 20 completed the initial course and the first reinforcement session and, six months later, seven of these 20 patients had experienced at least one lapse. On the other hand, many patients reported loss of interest in drinking and extreme adverse bodily reactions at even the sight of alcohol. Hsu himself (personal communication, June 16, 1965) is not at all convinced that success, if any, is because of the direct creation of a conditioned aversion *per se*. Nevertheless, the method is one of promise which, if it does not prove to be totally unacceptable to patients because of its highly frightening nature, offers many advantages.

Before we conclude this survey of methods that are confined to the more or less direct treatment of the drinking problem itself, we must note two significant developments; they are the use of group aversive conditioning procedures and the method of covert stimuli. If the subject is sufficiently trained and motivated it might be possible to have the alcoholic patient give himself an electric shock at home whenever he feels the urge to drink. But if, despite all the telling arguments against their use, it is decided to employ drugs rather than electric shock, then direct supervision by the physician becomes mandatory. (Antabuse treatment, although a drug therapy, is not directly a classical conditioning procedure.) Such supervision, requiring much individualized and professional attention, is clearly not an economical proposition in terms of either facilities, cost, or demand. To offset these limitations, group aversion techniques have been suggested from time to time.

Typical of the very few good reports is that of Miller, Dvorak, and Turner (1960), who employed a more or less conventional aversive conditioning procedure, modeled on that of Voegtlin and his associated (for example, Voegtlin, 1940, 1947). In the first instance, the groups consisted of four patients and two physicians meeting for 10 daily sessions, a fresh group being started every two weeks. Both to help instruct the novices in matters of routine and to encourage nausea and wretching by virtue of his already conditioned predisposition to such behavior, one patient from the previous group was always included in each new group. To facilitate vomiting and avoid "dry heaves," all patients were encouraged to drink large amounts of tepid water during the 45-minute conditioning session. In an atmosphere of serious concentration, they were encouraged to sniff frequently at the alcoholic beverage of their choice but to sip only when gagging commenced. Each patient proceeded at his own rate, so that any patient could be at any phase of the procedure during any one treatment session. (To avoid a generalization of the aversive conditioning from alcohol to water, it is recommended by the present writer that, if this procedure is adopted, the patient be instructed to drink water frequently between sessions.)

All 20 patients treated in this fashion developed an aversion to alcohol and, of the 10 who were followed up for eight months, five were completely abstinent and three were abstinent apart from very brief lapses. Although no definitive conclusions can be drawn from these limited data and the few studies available, in principle the development of group aversion procedures would seem to merit further exploration, preferably by employing faradic aversion and as part of a more comprehensive behavioral approach to the alcoholic.

Aversive methods, no matter how designed and what stimuli are employed, are likely to offer many disadvantages, and any aversive stimulus that is strong enough to be truly traumatic is also likely to have at least some medical contraindications (see Bucher & Lovaas, 1968; Rachman & Teasdale, 1969). If, somehow, the subject could be persuaded to visualize an imaginary aversive stimulus with sufficient realism, then possibly all the desired attributes of aversion could be achieved without any of the medical hazards. It is perhaps with such a rationale in mind that Gold and Newfeld (1965) successfully developed a method of treating a male homosexual by training him to visualize himself in a potentially attractive homosexual situation that was invariably associated with a noxious one.

From such beginnings Cautela (1967) developed an ingenuous method whereby the alcoholic, having first been trained in relaxation and introduced to the principles and aims of *covert sensitization*, as the method is called, is shown how to visualize in detail both the pleasurable act of drinking alcohol and the unpleasant details of vomiting. Care is taken to ensure that the vomiting occurs *after* the patient visualizes seeing the alcohol and has the desire to drink but just *before* he visualizes reaching for the glass or bottle (see also Cautela, 1966a).

This method offers several advantages over the more conventional aversive procedures: medical hazards are avoided; no apparatus is involved; the techniques are inoffensive to the staff; and, perhaps most important, it is easy for the patient to carry out the treatment at home. But, on the negative side, not all patients are sufficiently good visualizers, even if facilitated by the induction of a light hypnotic trance, and the efficacy of the method awaits demonstration. And alternative explanations, such as suggestion and belief in the therapist, remain to be eliminated.

Anant treated 26 alcoholics by this method and reported total abstinence rates for periods ranging from 8 to 15 months. However, no control group was used, and it is therefore difficult to interpret his data (see Anant, 1966a, 1966b; 1967a, 1967b, 1967c; 1968a, 1968b). In an attempt to investigate this type of technique in a systematic and controlled manner, Ashem and Donner (1968) assigned patients at the residential male Alcoholic Unit of the Neuropsychiatric Institute in Princeton to one of three groups: a forward-conditioning group in which the method of covert sensitization was applied so that the imagined alcohol preceded the induced aversive images; a backward-conditioning group in which the method of covert sensitization was applied in such a sequence that the imagined alcohol following the induction of the aversive images; a no contact control group. Subjects were matched into triplets on the basis of IQ, age, and drinking experience, before being randomly assigned to one of the three groups. Throughout the study all subjects participated in the regular activities of the unit, including group psychotherapy. The treatment program consisted of nine sessions, each lasting 30 to 40 minutes.

It soon became evident that the backward-conditioning group was not, in effect, receiving no conditioning and, therefore, the data for both treatment groups, which did not differ significantly from each other, were combined. The results clearly showed a significant difference between the combined treatment and the control groups in drinking behavior at the 6-month follow-up. Whereas 40 percent of the treated subjects were not drinking, the corresponding figure for the control group was zero. In view of the fact that the subjects used in this study had been drinking for an average of 18.5 years, the authors were right to feel encouraged by their data. But the project really raises more questions than it answers, as the authors are well aware. It is still questionable whether the mechanism is indeed a conditioning one and, if effective, why this should be true. For long lasting effects to accrue, the association between alcohol and the aversive reaction must become an intrinsic part of the subject's behavioral repertoire and, as the authors point out, relatively little is known of the powers of internalized versus the external stimulus presentation on the control of behavior. According to Luria (1961), the regulation of nonverbal behavior by speech is effective only when the external verbal command becomes internalized.

Perhaps of even more interest is the adroit attempt of Cautela (1966b) to develop *group* covert sensitization procedures for the treatment of delinquent adolescent drinkers. First, he ascertained by questioning that his delinquent drinkers—all frequent car stealers—tended to do much of their drinking in the back seat of cars (the place where drinking occurs is very important to ascertain). The particularly favorite drink of each boy was also noted at this time. One boy preferred whiskey from a bottle, and the other three preferred drinking beer straight from a can.

The boys were instructed as follows (relaxation training was not given to them previously):

> "I want you to close your eyes and imagine this scene as clearly as you can: You are sitting in the back seat of a car and your buddy says to you: Want a drink? You say yes and as soon as you do, you get a funny feeling in the pit of your stomach. You start to feel sick and queasy and messy. As he is about to hand you the can or bottle you notice that there's a spider (or a little snake or a bee) on top of the can or bottle. As soon as you see this you immediately notice some bitter juice in your mouth. You really feel sick now. Pieces of food go into your throat. As you reach for the can or bottle, you puke all over the container, your hands, the car. There's beer or whiskey spilling all over the car. Snots are coming out of your mouth. Your eyes are watery. You feel sick as a dog. You can't help it—you vomit again and again. Oh, you can feel the vomit all over your hands and your clothes. Everything feels slimy. You can't stand it any longer. You jump out of the car away from the beer and whiskey. You feel much better outside the car. The air is fresh and clean. You're so happy to be away from the beer and whiskey."

The boys were carefully watched during this procedure for facial expressions of disgust or nausea. After the trial was over each boy was asked how he felt about the scenery and how clear the imagery was. On subsequent trials the word "drink" was used rather than either "beer" or "whiskey" and the subjects were told to imagine their own particularly favorite alcoholic beverage when the therapist said "drink." They were also told that, from this point on, whenever the therapist said "container" they were to imagine the usual kind of container from which they drank.

After three trials of this scene, the boys were given the following alternating instructions for the fourth trial:

> "I want you to close your eyes and imagine this scene as clearly as you can: You are sitting in the back seat of a car and your buddy says to you: Want a drink? You say no and as soon as you do you feel good. Your stomach feels good; you don't feel sick or queasy."

On subsequent trials during the session, and at later sessions, scenes were varied to include the subject's house, an alleyway, a bar, and so forth—in fact, any place where he may be likely to take a drink. The technique was also extended to alcoholic beverages other than the individual's favorite one.

BROAD-SPECTRUM BEHAVIORAL APPROACHES

The first phase in the behavioral approach to alcoholism began 40 years ago with the application of classical conditioning techniques to the development of aversive conditioning procedures. Alcoholism was probably the first major disorder to be treated in this fashion in any systematic manner. In the second phase, as outlined above, the limiting confines of the strictly Pavlovian model were expanded to encompass a variety of ingenious classical and operant techniques, all aimed directly at the drinking behavior *per se*. Phase two necessarily incorporated phase one, and the third or contemporary phase, in which attention is directed toward the total behavioral repertoire of the individual, including drinking-likes, incorporates as part of its procedures techniques developed in the preceding two phases.

Gradually, with the advent of the behavioral clinician as a therapist and as a scientist whose concern is with the application of modern learning theory to the modification of every variety of behavioral disorder (and what psychiatric disorder is not behavioral to some large extent!), the emphasis has become less on the treatment of the symptom alone and more on the behavioral modification of the total person, including the symptom. In 1964 Kepner suggested that the use of alcohol may represent a coping device whereby the person strives to deal with his anxieties and other unpleasant life situations. Presumably, if these tensions could be resolved, he would then have no need to resort to alcohol. With the advent of Wolpe's systematic desensitization (1958), a powerful tool became available for dealing constructively with the patient's anxieties. Kraft and Al-Issa (1967, 1968), for example, use systematic desensitization to restore their patients' emotional stability and social competence so that the need to resort to alcohol is no longer felt and they are able to engage in social intercourse, even with strangers, with equanimity. When neurotic behavior is motivated by fear or anxiety, it is possible that aversive conditioning might increase rather than eliminate such behavior (Eysenck & Rachman, 1965), and it is especially for patients of this type that Kraft and Al-Issa advocate systematic desensitization rather than aversive conditioning. In contrast, Vahl (1968) advocates the application of Stampfls' implosive therapy (see London, 1964, p. 95–109) to the extinction of anxieties in alcoholics, but it seems likely that the same limitations which apply to the use of aversive conditioning also apply to Stampfl's rather traumatic procedure, so that desensitization might well be a more appropriate technique for use with highly anxious alcoholics than is either aversive conditioning or implosive therapy.

But a human being is exquisitely complex, and social anxiety, no matter how evident, is usually but one component of his total maladaptive repertoire. It is therefore necessary to apply behavioral principles to a broad range of behavior and not just to one or two seemingly dominant aspects. This significant development is best summed up by Lazarus (1965) in his increasingly accepted concept of "broad-spectrum behavior therapy." This concept implies: first, that a variety of behavioral techniques be employed to eliminate the undesired drinking behavior; second, that, if necessary, a variety of behavioral techniques be employed to satisfy the patient's needs in other ways; third, that a variety of behavioral techniques be employed to modify other deviant aspects of the patients personality so that the individual is treated not as an otherwise normal person who happens to have learned to drink excessively but as a person with possibly numerous problems of which drinking is but one; fourth, that appropriate behavioral procedures be employed to ensure the continuance of the newly acquired patterns and the further development of the personality; fifth, that self-control behavioral procedures be emphasized; sixth, that these procedures be used in conjunction with any other principles of management that may be indicated.

This final aspect of broad-spectrum behavior therapy is most important, since it may implicate many individuals other than the therapist. Socioeconomic intervention may take the form of helping to bring about more appropriate employment or a change of residence; interpersonal incompatibilities may have to be resolved; new leisure pursuits inculcated; chemotherapy instigated; if necessary, the patient's current employer may need to be included in the overall treatment plan. In short, "the emphasis in the rehabilitation of the alcoholic must be on a *synthesis* that would include aversion therapy combined with psychotherapeutic and socioeconomic procedures, together with educative measures and environmental manipulation plus numerous adjunctive procedures as part of a wide and all-embracing reconditioning program" (Lazarus, 1965).

Very few behavior therapists other than Lazarus have developed such ambitious total behavior therapy programs; nevertheless, the contemporary trend is in this direction. For example, Mertens and Fuller (1964a, 1964b) have developed two manuals (one for the patient, one for the therapist) that spell out quite specifically the procedures and stages to be adopted in setting up a behavioral program for the alcoholic. For Mertens and Fuller, the principle goal is the development of self-control, defined as "the control of certain responses by stimuli produced by other responses of the individual" (Bijou & Baer, 1961). To achieve this self-control, it is first necessary to make a complex stimulus-response analysis of the total situation in the manner advocated by authorities such as Holland and Skinner (1961) and Ferster, Nurnberger, and Levitt 1962). The interested reader is advised to refer to the two manuals directly; they may readily be obtained from their author (care of the Research Department of Willmar State Hospital, Willmar, Minnesota).

Mertens describes his special training program as follows.

"1. Classroom sessions were held daily during which the alcholics were presented various aspects of a learning approach to behavior. This was accomplished by lectures, discussions, demonstrations, films and readings in *The Manual for the Alcoholic* and other selected readings. Tests were given on the materials presented.

"2. Participants also took part in a lab session. Here they had the opportunity to apply operant learning techniques to a rat in a Skinner Box. The same principles were then used to demonstrate how to teach a psychotic patient how to shave. The lab was planned as a shaping procedure whereby the individuals gradually increasing the complexity of the situation in which correct application of learning principles was called for. The end behavior being application of the behavioral principle of their own behavior. . . .

"3. Craft training, music training and relaxation training were also part of their program. The intent of these activities was to train the individual in responses that could be used when they returned to the community. If skills were learned in these areas while in the hospital, it was felt that the chances of the behavior being reinforced in the community were increased. The behaviors taught were those which could very possibly be reinforced in the individual's community. For example, the alcoholics' performance in the Craft Shop was part of an attempt to shape behavior that could be maintained quite readily through leathercraft chain-stores in the communities.

"4. Individual sessions were held with each participant to help with individual application for the program.

"5. Also in what we called "Behaviorodrama" an attempt was made to give the alcoholics practice in specific behaviors that could be useful to them in their daily lives in the community; for example, alternate ways of handling a problem situation. By practice in this controlled setting, an attempt was made to shape new behaviors useful in the community.

"6. Once the alcoholics were shown other possible avenues to control their drinking problem, an attempt was made to identify and make active the ultimate aversive consequences or unwanted effects of drinking. Acting out, repetition, and talking into a tape recorder for pay were means used to accomplish this phase."

It should be stressed that not all patients were accepted into this program, the criteria for selection being; verbalization of a desire to stop drinking; volunteering for the program once it was outlined; at least average intelligence level; age less than 55 years; and formal educational level at least 10 years.

Many of the attempts to develop broad-spectrum behavior therapy for the alcoholic become resolved into a combination of some form of aversive conditioning for the elimination of the drinking behavior and the application of techniques of relaxation and desensitization to both the drinking and to other undesirable behaviors, with perhaps the addition of some operant procedures. As Blake (1965) points out, this might appear to present certain theoretical contradictions, the argument being that relaxation is likely to inhibit drive and thus mitigate against the subsequent setting up of a conditioned aversion. But, as Blake succeeded in demonstrating, what actually happens is that, as the alcoholic patient becomes more competent at achieving relaxation, his self-confidence grows, he becomes less tense, and he requires little or no tranquilization or night sedation. This serves to strengthen his motivation for cure, and thus help the alcoholic individual (who is notoriously undermotivated with respect to staying with any form of treatment) focus on his need and desire to accept help. It is then possible to use a standard aversion procedure, either in isolation or, better, as part of a comprehensive behavioral program with the reasonable expectation that the patient will not be at too low a drive level for conditioning to occur.

In the method of "aversion relief," the unwanted behavior is first paired with an aversive stimulus, and is followed by the pairing of acceptable behavior with the termination of the aversive stimulus. Thus far, those methods have been applied primarily to the treatment of the sexual disorders (see Franks, 1967). In 1965 Blake reported a successful technique of aversion relief (or "relaxation-aversion therapy"), along with follow-up results at six and twelve months, respectively. In a later paper (Blake, 1967), two groups were compared: a relaxation-aversion and an aversion-only group. At a twelve-month follow-up of an unselected sample of inpatient hospital admissions, assigned on a matched basis to either of the two groups, the indications were that the relaxation-aversion method of treatment showed some evident but statistically insignificant advantages over treatment by electrical aversion alone. The question now remains as to what type of subject is best suited for each procedure.

However, so that optimism will not outweight prudence, a salutory note of caution must be sounded. For example, Feldman (1966) developed a learning technique that appeared to be rather effective in the treatment of homosexuality. But when MacCulloch, Feldman, Orford, and MacCulloch (1966) tried to apply a similar technique to the treatment of alcoholics, they ran into many difficulties. Their procedure consisted essentially of the setting up of a hierarchy that ranged from photographs of alcoholics beverages to actual alcohol in the glass via the sight of open and closed bottles. Slides of orange squash, and even actual orange squash, were used as aversion relief stimuli. But all four of their alcoholic subjects treated by this rather sophisticated form of anticipatory avoidance learning showed consistently poor responses to treatment. MacCulloch *et al.* rightly conclude that aversion therapy is far from being a complete panacea for alcoholism, and that both biochemical and psychophysiological factors need to be taken into account. But it would seem, at least to the present writer, that as far as the behavioral aspects of treatment are concerned, the weakness lies not in the employment of behavioral learning principles *per se*, but in their rather limited restriction to the treatment of the symptom alone.

One of the best examples of a systematic application of learning-theory principles to the treatment of the alcoholic as part of a "broad-spectrum" approach is the program developed by McBrearty and his associates (McBrearty, Dichter, Garfield, & Heath, 1968). The basic point of view is that the drinking response is but one facet in a complex series of closely linked or chained antedating responses that are essential to the culminating event, namely, drinking. The further assumption is that the efficiency of any total treatment strategy will depend not only on the manner in which the drinking response is directly interfered with but also on the degree to which the fractional antedating responses are manipulated. The problem, of course, is to determine the crucial elements in the behavioral chain and what are the most expedient ways of modifying these stages. The example cited by McBrearty is that of the anxiety response frequently elicited by male alcoholics when confronted with heterosexual stimulation; consumption of alcohol results in alleviation of the anxiety and the possibility of sexual response. Treatment maneuvers, therefore, would call for the interruption of the use of alcohol in this manner, an alleviation of anxiety in the company of the female, and the development of a repertoire of behavior that would lead to effective sexual performance without the presence of alcohol.

Arguing that drinking behavior is maintained in part by virtue of the *consequences* of that behavior, McBrearty further recommends that an attempt be made to employ an aversive relief technique in which the alcohol takes on some of the attributes of the aversive stimulus with which it has been paired. The use of alcohol, resulting in aversive consequences, would therefore be avoided; this avoidance behavior would become associated with relief, thus, strengthening the avoidance behavior.

McBrearty has ingeniously put these principles into practice in several state hospitals in Pennsylvania. His general policy is to organize a sophisticated treatment program which involves as many of the following phases as are deemed necessary and feasible:

A. *Didactic Training for Behavioral Change*
   1. Regular group meetings to discuss and practice the principles of behavior modification (each patient being given a copy of Mertens' and Fuller's "Manual for Alcoholics" for his personal use).

B. *Aversive Conditioning Procedures*
   1. *Visual-Verbal Sequence* involving an aversion relief technique whereby the appearance of "alcohol" words causes the patient to receive an electric shock, whereas "relief" words

(such as "relax") bring with them orange juice and *no* shock.

2. *Sip and Sniff Sequence*
Similar to the above except that actual beverages are used rather than "alcohol" words.

3. *Complex Sequence*
Following the operation of a lever when presented with an alcohol stimulus word, the patient is either shocked, told to drink (via the word "drink" placed on the stimulus screen) and then is shocked as he does so, or is presented with the word "relax" and fruit juices.

4. *Covert Sensitization*

C. *Relaxation Procedures*
1. Individual sessions (in which the patient is taught how to acquire control over relaxation).
2. Group sessions (in which three or four patients recline on couches and listen to a taped presentation of the various instructions for inducing a relaxation response).

D. *Desensitization Procedures*—employing the various hierarchical procedures of Wolpe.

E. *Training in Areas of Behavioral Deficit*
1. This can involve any aspect of the patient's total behavioral repertoire and require active collaboration with individuals such as his employer, other professionals, spouse or parent.

2. *Behaviordrama*
Although suggested by the work of Moreno in psychodrama, the rationale is based on the principles of learning (see Sturm, 1965, for a discussion of psychodrama in behavioral terms). In essence, it involves behavioral rehearsal of those situations for which there is behavioral deficit. If, for example, there is a lack of assertive behavior, the patient (after being first exposed to some of the methods outlined above) is exposed to stage-type situations and is required to practice adaptive behaviors. In learning-theory terms, this procedure increases the probability that this desirable adaptive behavior will appear under other circumstances.

3. *In Vivo Training*
This procedure involves the gradual real-life exposure of the patient to those situations that originally elicited the maladaptive behavior.

F. *Controlling Behavioral Excesses and Deficits by Systematic Application of Contingent Reinforcement Procedures*
Essentially, this represents an attempt to apply behavioral engineering or token economy principles (for example, see Atthowe & Krasner, 1968; Ayllon & Michael, 1959; Girardeau & Spradlin, 1964; Narrol, 1967) to the establishment of an operant word for alcoholics. Although McBrearty does not go this far, Narrol's (1967) outline for a comprehensive alcohol-ward program even includes the controlled use of alcohol as part of the reinforcement schedule, with a view not only to further understanding of the drinking process but to the possible alternative of moderate drinking.

The above strategy is by no means a cut-and-dried matter and is best viewed as a kind of blueprint or general guide for the conduct of behavioral modification programs with alcoholics in a hospital setting. When the formal part of the treatment program is completed, it might be advisable to effect and to consolidate the social rehabilitation by a device such as Kraft's (1967) "post behavior therapy club," in which patients learn how to make new and constructive social relationships as befitting their recently acquired status. As McBrearty is careful to point out, the effectiveness of these programs, no matter how promising, still awaits categorical demonstration. But, by the same token, the behavioral programmer might draw encouragement to proceed by the equally compelling fact that, thus far, the currently available literature reveals no alternative approach to the treatment of the alcoholic in which greater confidence can be placed.

CONCLUSIONS

The reader is reminded once again that the behavioral management of the alcoholic is but one crucial aspect of the total problem of alcoholism and its elimination. And perhaps the most interesting development of all is that modern behavior therapy, with its emphasis on the broad-spectrum approach, is increasingly recognizing this truth—hence, its emphasis on environmental, socioeconomic, biochemical, and directly physiological factors.[2] It is therefore abundantly obvious that basic research and the development of techniques of control in *all* these areas must become an integral part of any list of future needs with respect to the understanding and the treatment of alcoholism. It is with this caveat in mind that the following suggestions are offered. The emphasis is not on esoteric issues but on matters of practical significance of direct relevance to the working implementation of the sort of programs outlined in the previous section.

The development of behavioral assessment procedures has scarcely commenced. Although many possibilities have been raised, virtually nothing is known with confidence about the kind of alcoholic who is most likely to respond to any particular type of behavior modification. The rather naive and frequently conflicting lists of clinical contraindications of the 1930's (see Franks, 1966) are being replaced by more learning-theory oriented expectations, which nevertheless require verification. Vogel (1959, 1960), for example, was once accustomed to predicating all her expectations on the personality dimension of introversion-extraversion. Others have focused on anxiety and neuroticism as key dimensions to assessment. Thus, Menaker (1967) argues that, regardless of the source of the anxiety and unlike nonalcoholics, alcoholics will become increasingly anxious as they *anticipate* drinking. *If*, at the same time, it be accepted that alcohol indeed reduces anxiety, then drinking alcohol can be viewed as a device to reduce tension that is especially operative in the case of the alcoholic (even if it is not possible to do more than speculate as to why this might be true).

The situation is almost certainly much more complex than the above analysis suggests. In the first place, to say that alcohol has an anxiety-reducing effect, however true, is an oversimplification; many diverse behaviors can be observed during inebriation, depending on the subject, the situation, and the amount of alcohol ingested. In the second place, as Pollock (1966) points out, the initial relief of anxiety and tension because of taking alcohol may lead the drinker into previously avoided situations and, hence, to an ultimate *increase* in anxiety. Thus, the alcohol may provide potent reinforcement by releasing lower probability behaviors rather than by serving to reduce anxiety directly. In support of this contention, Pollock showed that alcohol significantly decreases the coping behavior of alcoholics (as measured by a Sentence Completion Test), whereas normal subjects showed an opposite pattern of change. The exploration of measures of anxiety as complex predictive devices, therefore, would seem to warrant further consideration.

The many serious weaknesses of pencil and paper ratings, especially of the self-reporting variety, have been documented elsewhere (Franks, Holden, & Phillips, 1961). The predilections of the present writer are toward prediction via *behavioral* means, such as laboratory measures of operant and classical conditioning, and general psychophysiological function. The probable absence of an appreciable general factor of conditioning need not preclude the possibility of specific laboratory procedures being used as valid predictions of successful attempts to modify drinking behavior by means of conditioning techniques.

As far as the development of actual behavior-modification techniques *per se* are concerned, a host of unresolved issues remain. As with many attempts to modify behavior (stuttering is a noteable example), the problem is to get the learned behavior to generalize to situations other than those of the treatment session and to periods after

[2] It is of interest to compare the behavior therapy of alcoholism with that of sexual disorders. Within less than a decade the behavioral therapist is beginning to develop sophisticated methods of treating the sexual disorders. The newest techniques are concerned with many aspects of the patient's life style and do not, as did most of the earlier studies, confine their role to one of the developments of a laboratory conditioned aversion to a fairly circumscribed deviational pattern. Historically, the events of the past ten years may be compared to a similar evolution in the development of behavioral methods in the treatment of the alcoholic. However, in the case of the alcoholic, these developments took place over some three or four decades and the impetus could not occur until behavior therapy became established as a branch of the behavioral sciences. It is probably for this reason that the advances made in the behavioral treatment of the sexual disorders have been telescoped into such a short period (Franks, 1967a).

direct treatment has ceased. Learning theorists are ever ready with stimulus-generalization explanations to account for the generation of widespread drinking behavior (e.g. Kepner, 1964), and experimentalists such as Vogel-Sprott (1964) are able to adduce convicing evidence in favor of response generation to other modalities *in the laboratory situation*. But the systematic study of these problems as they apply to the alcoholic and his life remains to be conducted.

Both control groups and follow-up studies are needed if the many parameters and alternative explanations of behavior change are to be understood. This is particularly true for those projects that include aversive procedures in their repertoire. An individual who voluntarily and knowingly enters into a program that involves nausea or electric shock must be highly motivated in the first instance and, as such, cannot be considered a random selection from the deviant population under study (in this case, alcoholics). If the various experimental and control groups are not somehow equated for levels of motivation (a most challenging problem for the experimenter), then interpretation of the results becomes hazardous, to say the least. Motivation may be different for different groups, and even for the same individual or group of individuals at different times. Just as sex differences in conditioning certain measures may be differentially operative in women for different measures and at various times (for example, see Graham, Cohen, & Shmavonian, 1966), so motivation may vary likewise in the alcoholic.

The volunteer for behavior modification may differ from those alcoholics who volunteer for other forms of treatment in respect to personality characteristic other than motivation, so that this factor also needs to be included in the control design. There is ample evidence that personality differences exist between volunteers and nonvolunteers for psychological experiments, but very little is known concerning the personality of those who volunteer for treatment in alcohol programs (see Corotto, 1963).

By definition, broad-spectrum behavior therapy must be concerned with life-long reinforcement schedules as well as with the acute phase of the alcoholic's rehabilitation. Although little is known about changes in motivation as the alcoholic progresses, there seems to be little doubt that patients who are willing to submit to an unpleasant conditioning process and to enforced abstinence immediately following an acute drinking problem will probably be less motivated to seek out treatment and to maintain abstinence as the months go by. As Clancy (1964) puts it, drinking and pain gradually begin to dissociate, and drinking and pleasure begin to reassociate. It is not until drinking begins to generate new painful associations—by which time it may be rather late—that the alcoholic is motivated to seek out further reinforcement or to apply the procedures he has already learned.

In practice, not only is the alcoholic often poorly motivated but also he is often blithely "unaware," despite repeated past experience, of the trouble he is likely to get into if he should embark on yet another drinking spree (see Merry, 1966). There is a great need for behavior therapy to develop some technique for overcoming this kind of denial behavior (or "rationalization," to use psychodynamic terminology).

These, then, are just a few of the myriad of problems that present themselves. As with endeavors in other areas, such as the possible biological factors predisposing to alcoholism, no breakthroughs appear imminent. Nevertheless, the methods of behavioral modification, as outlined here, seem to offer considerable promise for the future. Perhaps the most encouraging developments are as follows. First, there is the recognition of the need to focus on the total personality organization of the patient and not just on the drinking problem *per se*. In this respect, the gradual shift from the focus on the creation of a conditioned aversion in the 1930's and 1940's to the concept of the broad-spectrum behavior therapy of the 1960's represents a signal step forward. As Knight stated succinctly thirty years ago in a totally different context (see Voegtlin & Lemere, 1942, p. 797):

> "In all cases of chronic alcoholism there is a serious, underlying personality disorder. Cessation of the drinking, especially enforced cessation, does not solve the problem, but only throws the personality disorder into bolder relief."

But, in contrast with Knight, it is the contention of the present writer that the rehabilitation of the alcoholic involves not the invocation of speculative and subjective psychodynamic processes but the *synthesis* of behavioral, pharmacological, socioeconomic, and other environmental procedures that are embraced under the rubric of broad-spectrum behavior therapy.

The second encouraging development is that the behavioral clinician of the present decade is neither solely a laboratory scientist nor a clinical practitioner; he is both. Tempered by a realistic appraisal of the theoretical and practical limitations of most forms of behavior therapy, but recognizing the lack of any demonstrably superior alternative, hopefully he will be increasingly able to utilise the insights and the experience of the clinician in conjunction with the experimental methodology of the behavioral scientist (see Franks, Susskind & Franks, 1969).

The third development is the growing recognition that research into the variegated problems of alcoholism necessitates the establishment of special training programs. These programs should be aimed at the training of individuals of the highest scientific caliber to work in either clinical or research settings within an interdisciplinary framework that encompasses both the social and behavioral sciences as well as the biological (for example, see Blacker, 1968).

The point of view espoused in the present chapter—that of the learning theorist—is likely to achieve maximum effectiveness only to the extent that it is part of a broader program as outlined above. Hopefully, it is developments such as these which could bring about a climate of clinical research and practice that will one day provide society with an effective means of coping with the six million alcoholics in our midst.

REFERENCES

American Medical Association Committee on Medico Legal Problems, Sub-Committee on Alcohol. *J. Am. Med. Assoc.*, May 18, 1962, 638.

Anant, S. S. The treatment of alcoholics by a verbal aversion technique: a case report. *Manas*, 1966a, **13**, 79–86.

Anant, S. S. The use of verbal aversion technique with a group of alcoholics. *Saskatchewan Psychologist*, 1966b, **2**, 28–30.

Anant, S. S. A note on the treatment of alcoholics by a verbal aversion technique. *Canad. Psychol.*, 1967a, **8a**, 19–22.

Anant, S. S. Verbal aversion technique. *Interdiscipline*, 1967b, **4**, 1–14.

Anant, S. S. Treatment of alcoholics and drug addicts by verbal conditioning technique. Paper read at the Seventh International Congress of Psychotherapy, Wiesbaden, West Germany, August 21–26, 1967c.

Anant, S. S. The use of verbal aversion (negative conditioning) with an alcoholic: a case report. *Behav. Res. Ther.*, 1968a, **6**, 395–396.

Anant, S. S. Verbal aversion therapy with a promiscuous girl: case report. *Psychol. Reports*, 1968b, **22**, 795–796.

Armstrong, J. D. The search for the alcoholic personality in understanding alcoholism. *Annals of the American Academy of Political and Social Science*, 1958, **135**, 40–47.

Ashem, Beatrice, & Donner, L. Covert sensitization with alcoholics: a controlled replication. *Behav. Res. Ther.*, 1968, **6**, 7–12.

Atthowe, J. M. Jr., & Krasner, L. Preliminary report on the application of contingent reinforcement procedures (token economy) on a "chronic" psychiatric ward. *J. abnorm. Psychol.*, 1968, **73**, 37–43.

Ayllon, T., & Michael, J. The psychiatric nurse as a behavioral engineer. *J. exp. anal. Behav.*, 1959, **2**, 323–334.

Bailey, C. J., & Miller, N. E. Effect of sodium amytal on behavior of cats in an approach-avoidance conflict. *J. comp. physiol. Psychol.*, 1952, **45**, 205–208.

Banks, R. K., & Vogel-Sprott, M. D. Effect of delayed punishment on an immediately rewarded response in humans. *J. exp. Psychol.*, 1965, **70**, 357–359.

Barry, H., & Miller, N. E. Effects of drugs on approach-avoidance conflict tested repeatedly by means of a "telescope alley". *J. comp. physiol. Psychol.*, 1962, **55**, 201–210.

Bartholomew, A. A., Franks, C. M., & Marley, E. Susceptibility to methylpentynol—eyelid conditioning and P.G.R. response. *J. ment. Sci.*, 1958, **104**, 1167–1173.

Barton, W. E. Deficits in the treatment of alcoholism and recommendations for correction. *Amer. J. Psychiat.*, 1968, **124**, 1679–1686.

Bates, R. C. Pathology associates with alcoholism. *Quart. J. stud. Alcoh.*, 1965, **26**, 110.

Beecher, H. K. *Measurement of subjective responses.* New York: Oxford Univ. Press, 1959.

Bijou, S. W., & Baer, D. *Child development.* New York: Appleton-Century-Crofts, 1961.

Blacker, E. Training predoctoral social and behavioral science students in alcoholism research. *Amer. J. Psychiat.*, 1968, **124**, 1686–1691.

Blake, G. The application of behaviour therapy to the treatment of alcoholism. *Behav. Res. Ther.*, 1965 **3**, 75–85.

Blake, B. G. A follow-up of alcoholics treated by behaviour therapy. *Behav. Res. Ther.*, 1967, **5**, 89–94.

Block, J. *The Q-sort method of personality assessment and psychiatric research.* Springfield, Ill.: C. C. Thomas, 1961.

Borkenstein, R. F., Crowther, R. F., Shumate, R. P., Ziel, W. R., & Zylman, R. (ed. A. Dale). *The role of the drinking driver in traffic accidents.* Indiana Dept. of Police Admin., Ind. Univ., 1964. (Mimeo).

Bucher, B., & Lovaas, O. O. Use of aversive stimulation in behavior modification. In Jones, R. R. (ed.), *Miami Symposium on the prediction of behavior 1967: Aversive stimulation.* Coral Gables, Fla.: Univ. Miami Press, 1968 pp. 77–145.

Carpenter, J. A. Effects of alcohol on some psychological processes: A critical review with special reference to automobile driving skill. *Quart. J. Stud. Alcoh.*, 1962, **23**, 274–314.

Carpenter, J. A., & Ross, B. M. Effect of alcohol on short-term memory. *Quart. J. Stud. Alcoh.*, 1965, **26**, 561–579.

Carpenter, J. A. Contributions from psychology to the study of drinking and driving. *Quart. J. stud. Alcoh. Suppl.* No. 4. 1968, 234–251.

Carpenter, J. A., Moore, O. K., Snyder, C. R., & Lisansky, E. S. Alcohol and higher-order problem solving. *Quart. J. Stud. Alcoh.*, 1961, **22**, 183–222.

Carpenter, J. A., & Varley, Margaret. The joint action of tranquillizers and alcohol on driving. *Proceedings of the Third International Conference on Alcohol and Road Traffic*, London: British Med. Asso. 1962.

Cautela, J. R. Treatment of compulsive behavior by covert desensitization. *Psychol. Rec.*, 1966a, **16**, 33–41.

Cautela, J. R. Behavior Therapy and delinquency. Paper presented to the Division of Youth Service of Massachusetts, October 16, 1966b.

Cautela, J. R. Covert sensitization. *Psychol. Rep.*, 1967, **20**, 459–468.

Church, R. M. The varied effects of punishment on behavior. *Psychol. Rev.*, 1963, **70**, 369–402.

Clancy, J. Motivation conflicts of the alcohol addict. *Quart. J. Stud. Alcoh.*, 1964, **25**, 511–520.

Clancy, J., Vanderhoff, E. & Campbell, P. Evaluation of an aversive technique as a treatment for alcoholism; controlled with succinylcholine-induced apnea. *Quart. J. Stud. Alcoh.*, 1967, **28**, 476–485.

Clark, W. Operational definitions of drinking problems and associated prevalence rates. *Quart. J. Stud. Alcoh.*, 1966, **27**, 648–668.

Clyde, D. J. Self ratings, in L. Uhr & G. Miller (eds.). *Drugs and behavior.* New York: Wiley, 1960, Chapt. 47, pp. 583–586.

Clyde, D. J. *Manual for the Clyde Mood Scale.* Coral Gables, Fla.: Biometrics Lab., Univ. Miami, 1963.

Conger, J. J. The effects of alcohol on conflict behavior in the albino rat. *Quart. J. Stud. Alcoh.*, 1951, **12**, 1–29.

Conger, J. J. Alcoholism: Theory, problem and challenge. II. Reinforcement theory and the dynamics of alcoholism. *Quart. J. Stud. Alcoh.*, 1956, **17**, 291–324.

Corotto, L. V. An exploratory study of the personality characteristics of alcoholic patients who volunteer for continued treatment. *Quart. J. Stud. Alcoh.*, 1963, **24**, 432–442.

Dews, P. B., & Morse, W. A. Behavioral pharmacology. *Ann. Rev. Pharm.*, 1961, **1**, 145–174.

Diethelm, O. (ed.). *Etiology of chronic alcoholism.* Springfield, Ill.: C. C. Thomas, 1955, pp. 43–109.

Docter, R. F., & Bernal, Martha E. Immediate and prolonged psychophysiological effects of sustained alcohol intake in alcoholics. *Quart. J. Stud. Alcoh.*, 1964, **25**, 438–450.

Dollard, J., & Miller, N. *Personality and psychotherapy.* New York: McGraw-Hill, 1950.

Drew, G. C., Colquhoun, W. P., & Long, Hazel, A. Effects of small doses of alcohol on a skill resembling driving. *Brit. med. J.*, 1958, No. 5103, October 25, 993–999.

Ekman, G., Frankenhaeuser, M., Goldberg, L., Hagdahl, R., & Myrsten, A. L. Subjective and objective effects of alcohol as functions of dosage and time. *Psychopharmacologia*, 1964, **6**, 399–409.

Eysenck, H. J. Learning theory and behaviour therapy. *J. ment. Sci.*, 1959, **105**, 61–75.

Eysenck, H. J., & Rachman, S. *The causes and cures of neuroses: an introduction to modern behaviour therapy based on learning theory and the principles of conditioning.* London: Rouledge and Kegan Paul, 1965.

Farrar, C. H., Powell, Barbara J., & Martin, K. L. Punishment of alcohol consumption by apneic paralyses. *Behav. Res. Ther.*, 1968, **6**, 13–16.

Feldman, M. P. A reconsideration of the extinction of hypothesis of warm-up in motor behavior. *Psychol. Bull.*, 1963, **60**, 452–459.

Feldman, M. P. Aversion therapy for sexual deviations: a critical review. *Psychol. Bull.*, 1966, **65**, 65–79.

Feldman, M. P., & MacCulloch, M. J. The application of anticipatory avoidance learning to the treatment of homosexuality. 1. Theory, technique and preliminary results. *Behav. Res. Ther.*, 1965, **2**, 165–183.

Fenichel, O. *The psychoanalytic theory of neuroses.* New York: Norton, 1954.

Ferster, C. B., Nurnberger, J. I., & Levitt, E. B. The control of eating. *Journal of Mathetics*, 1962, **1**, 87–109.

Frankenhaeuser, Marianne. Relations between actual and estimated effects of central nervous system stimulants and depressants. *Reports from the Psychological Laboratories, Univ. Stockholm (Report No. 213)*, Stockholm, 1966.

Franks, C. M. Alcohol, alcoholism and conditioning: a review of the literature and some theoretical considerations. *J. ment. Sci.*, 1958, **104**, 14–33.

Franks, C. M. Conditioning and abnormal behaviour. In H. J. Eysenck (Ed.), *Handbook of abnormal Psychology.* London: Pitman Med. Pubs., 1960, pp. 457–487.

Franks, C. M. Behavior therapy, the principles of conditioning and the treatment of the alcoholic. *Quart. J. Stud. Alcoh.*, 1963, **24**, 511–529.

Franks, C. M. Conditioning and conditioned aversion therapies in the treatment of the alcoholic. *Int. J. Addict.*, 1966, **1**, 61–98.

Franks, C. M. Reflections upon the treatment of sexual disorders by the behavioral clinician: an historical comparison with the treatment of the alcoholic. *J. Sex. Res.*, 1967a, **3**, 212–222.

Franks, C. M. Behavior modification and the treatment of the alcoholic. In R. Fox (ed.), *Alcoholism-behavioral research, therapeutic approaches.* New York: Springer, 1967b, Chapt. 18, pp. 186–203.

Franks, C. M. Aversion and conditioning therapies. In B. Kissen (ed.)., *Evaluation of present drug modalities in the long term treatment of alcoholism.* Washington, D.C.: North Amer. Assoc. Alec. Prog., 1967c, pp. 21–31.

Franks, C. M. The use of alcohol in the investigation of drug-personality postulates. In R. Fox (ed.), *Alcoholism-Behavioral research, therapeutic approaches.* New York: Springer, 1967d, Chapt. 6, pp. 55–79.

Franks, C. M. (Ed.) *Behavior Therapy: Appraisal and Status*. N.Y.: McGraw-Hill, 1969.

Franks, C. M., Holden, E. A., & Phillips, M. Eysenck's "stratification" theory and the questionnaire method of measuring personality. *J. clin. Psychol.*, 1961, **17**, 248–253.

Franks, C. M., Susskind, D. J. & Franks, Violet. Behavior Modification and the School Psychologist. In G. B. Gottsegen & M. G. Gottsegen (Eds.). *Professional School Psychology*, Vol. III N.Y.: Grune & Stratton, 1969, pp. 359–396.

Fried, R., & Franks, C. M. Aversion therapy by electric shock: North American modification. In C. M. Franks (Ed.), *Conditioning techniques in clinical practice and research*. New York: Springer, 1964, pp. 184–185.

Fromer, R. The effect of several shock patterns on the acquisition of the secondary drive of fear. *J. Comp. physiol. Psychol.*, 1962, **52**, 142–144.

Gerard, D. L., Saenger, G., & Wile, R. The abstinent alcoholic. *Arch. gen. Psychiat.*, 1962, **6**, 83–95.

Gibbins, R. J., Smart, R. G., & Seeley, J. R. A critique of the Manson Evaluation Test. *Quart. J. Stud. Alcoh.*, 1959, **20**, 357–361.

Girandeau, F. L., & Spradlin, J. E. Token rewards on a cottage program. *Mental Retardation*, 1968, **2**, 345–351.

Gold, S., & Newfeld, I. L. A learning approach to the treatment of homosexuality. *Behav. Res. Ther.*, 1965, **2**, 201–204.

Graham, L. A., Cohen, S. I., & Shmavonian, B. M. Sex differences in autonomic responses during instrumental conditioning. *Psychosom. Med.*, 1966, **28**, 264–271.

Greenwald, A. G. Punishment as a means of increasing the "strength" of a response. Paper presented at the Annual Meeting of the Eastern Psychological Association, Atlantic City, April, 1965.

Haertzen, C. A., & Fuller, G. Subjective effects of acute withdrawal of alcohol as measured by the Addiction Research Center Inventory (ARCI). *Quart. J. Stud. Alcoh.*, 1967, **28**, 455–467.

Haertzen, C. A., Hill, H. E., & Belleville, R. E. Development of the Addiction Research Center Inventory (ARCI): Selection of items that are sensitive to the effects of various drugs. *Psychopharmacologia*, 1963, **4**, 155–166.

Hampton, P. J. Representative studies of alcoholism and personality: I. Naturalistic studies. *J. Soc. Psychol.*, 1951a, **34**, 203–210.

Hampton, P. J. Representative studies of alcoholism and personality: II. Clincial studies, *J. Soc. Psychol.*, 1951b, **34**, 211–222.

Hampton, P. J. Representative studies of alcoholism and personality: III. Psychometric studies. *J. Soc. Psychol.*, 1951c, **34**, 223–233.

Hampton, P. J. Representative studies of alcoholism and personality: IV. Psychoanalytic studies, *J. Soc. Psychol.*, 1952, **35**, 23–35.

Hathaway, S. R. Forward to Dahlstrom, W. G. & Welsh, G. S. *An MMPI handbook*: pp. vii–xi. Minneapolis, Minn.: Univ. Minn. Press, 1960.

Hebb, D. O. Spontaneous neurosis in chimpanzees: theoretical relations with clinical and experimental phenomena. *Psychosom. Med.*, 1947, **9**, 3–16.

Hill, H. E., Haertzen, C. A., Wolbach, A. B., & Miner, E. J. The Addiction Research Center Inventory: Standardization of scales which evaluate subjective effects of morphine, amphetamine, pentobarbital, alcohol, LSD-25, pyralexyl and chlorpromazine. *Psychopharmacologia*, 1963, **41**, 167–183.

Hill, M. J., & Blane, H. T. Evaluation of psychotherapy with alcoholics: a critical review. *Quart. J. Stud. Alcoh.*, 1967, **28**, 76–104.

Holland, J. G., & Skinner, B. F. *The analysis of behavior*. New York: McGraw-Hill, 1961.

Holzinger, R., Mortimer, R., & VanDusen, W. Aversion conditioning treatment of alcoholism. *Amer. J. Psychiat.*, 1967, **124**, 246–247.

Horton, D. The functions of alcohol in primitive societies: a cross-cultural study. *Quart. J. Stud. Alcoh.*, 1943, **4**, 199–320.

Hsu, J. J. Electroconditioning therapy of alcoholics. A preliminary report. *Quart. J. Stud. Alcoh.*, 1965, **26**, 449–459.

Humphreys, L. G. The effect of random alternation of reinforcement on the acquisition and extinction of conditioned eyelid reaction. *J. exp. Psychol.*, 1939, **25**, 141–158.

Jellinek, E. M., & MacFarland, R. A. Analysis of psychological experiments on the effects of alcohol. *Quart. J. Stud. Alchoh.*, 1940, **1**, 272–371.

Jellinek, E. M. The estimate of the number of alcoholics in the U.S.A. for 1949 in the light of the sixth revision of the international lists of cause of death. *Quart. J. Stud. Alcoh.*, 1952, **13**, 215–218.

Jellinek, E. M. *The disease concept of alcoholism*. Highland Park, N.J.: Hillhouse Press, 1960.

Jones, H. E. The California adolescent growth study. *J. educ. Res.*, 1938, **31**, 561–567.

Jones, H. E., MacFarlane, J. W., & Eichorn, D. H. A progress report on growth studies at the University of California. *Vita Humane*, 1960, **3**, 17–31.

Jones, Mary C. Personality correlates and antecedants of drinking patterns in adult males. *J. consult. clin. Psychol.*, 1968, **32**, 2–12.

Kantorovich, N. V. An attempt at associative-reflex therapy in alcoholism. (*Nov. Reflexol. Fixiol. Nerv.* Sist., 3: 436–447 1929) Abst. in *Psychol. Abstr.* 4: 493, 1930.

Keller, M. Alcoholism: nature and extent of the problem. *Annals of the American Academy of Political and Social Science*, 1958, **315**, 1–11.

Keller, M. Alcohol in health and disease: some historical perspectives. *Annals of the New York Academy of Sciences*, 1966, **133**, 820–827.

Kepner, Elaine. Application of learning theory to the etiology and treatment of alcoholism. *Quart. J. Stud. Alcoh.*, 1964, **25**, 279–291.

Kimble, G. Shock intensity and avoidance learning. *J. comp. physiol. Psychol.*, 1955, **48**, 281–284.

Kingham, R. J. Alcoholism and the reinforcement theory of learning. *Quart. J. Stud. Alcoh.*, 1958, **19**, 320–330.

Kopmann, E., & Hughes, F. W. The potentiating effect of alcohol on tranquilizers and other central depressants, *Arch. gen. Psychiat.*, 1959, **1**, 7–11.

Korman, M., Stubblefield, R. L. Definition of alcoholism. *J. amer. med. Assoc.*, 1961, **178**, 1184–1186.

Kraft, T. A post behavior therapy club. *Newsletter of the Association for Advancement of Behavior Therapy*, 1967, **2**, No. 2, 6–7.

Kraft, T., & Al-Issa, I. Alcoholism treated by desensitization: a case report. *Behav. Res. Ther.*, 1967, **5**, 69–70.

Kraft, T., & Al-Issa, I. Desensitization and the treatment of alcoholic addiction. *Brit. J. Addict.*, 1968, **63**, 19–23.

Krasner, L., & Ullmann, L. P. (Eds.) *Research in behavior modification*. New York: Rinehart & Winston, 1965.

Laverty, S. G. Aversion therapies in the treatment of alcoholism. *Psychosom. Med.*, 1966, **28**, 651–666.

Lazarus, A. A. Towards the understanding and effective treatment of alcoholism *S. A. Med. J.*, 1965, **39**, 736–741.

Lester, D. Self-selection of alcohol by animals, human variation, and the etiology of alcoholism: a critical review. *Quart. J. Stud. Alcoh.*, 1966, **27**, 395–438.

Lewis, D. J. Partial reinforcement: a selective review of the literature since 1950. *Psychol. Bull.*, 1960, **57**, 1–29.

Lisansky, Edith, S. The etiology of alcoholism: the role of psychological predisposition. *Quart. J. Stud. Alcoh.*, 1960, **21**, 314–343.

Lisansky-Gomberg, Edith S. Etiology of alcoholism. *J. consult. clin. Psychol.*, 1968, **32**, 18–20.

London, P. *The modes and morals of psychotherapy*. New York: Holt, Rinehart & Winston, 1964.

Luria, A. R. *The role of speech in the regulation of normal and abnormal behavior*. New York: Liveright, 1961.

MacAndrew, C. The differentiation of male alcoholic outpatients from nonalcoholic psychiatric outpatients by means of the MMPI. *Quart. J. Stud. Alcoh.*, 1965, **26**, 238–246

MacAndrw, C. Self-reports of male alcoholics: a dimensional analysis of certain differences from nonalcoholic male psychiatric outpatients. *Quart. J. Stud. Alcoh.*, 1967, **28**, 43–51.

MacAndrew, C., & Geertsma, R. H. An analysis of responses of alcoholics to scale 4 of the MMPI. *Quart. J. Stud. Alcoh.*, 1963, **24**, 23–28.

MacAndrew, C., & Geertsma, R. H. A critique of alcoholism scales derived from the MMPI. *Quart. J. Stud. Alcoh.*, 1964, **25**, 68–76.

MacCulloch, M. J., Feldman, M. P., Orford, J. F., & MacCulloch, M. L. Anticipatory avoidance learning in the treatment of alcoholism: a record of therapeutic failure. *Behav. Res. Ther.*, 1966, **4**, 187–196.

Madill, M. F., Campbell, S. G., Laverty, S. G., Sanderson, R. E., & Vanderwater, S. L. Aversion treatment of alcoholics by succinylcholine-induced apneic paralysis: an analysis of early changes in drinking behavior. *Quart. J. Stud. Alcoh.*, 1966, **27**, 483–509.

Manson, M. P. A psychometric differentiation of alcoholics from nonalcoholics. *Quart. J. Stud. Alcoh.*, 1948a, **9**, 175–205.

Manson, M. P. *The Alcadd Test.* Beverley Hills, Calif.: Western Psychological Service, 1948b.

Marconi, J. Scientific theory and operational definitions in psychopathology with special reference to alcoholism. *Quart. J. Stud. Alcoh.*, 1967, **28**, 631–640.

Masserman, J. H. Jacques, M. G., & Nicholson, M. R. Alcohol as preventive of experimental neuroses. *Quart. J. Stud. Alcoh.* 1945, **6**, 281–299.

Masserman, J. H., & Yum, K. S. An analysis of the influence of alcohol on experimental neuroses in cats. *Psychosom. Med.*, 1966, **8**, 36–52.

Mayfield, D. G. Psychopharmacology of alcohol. I. Affective change with intoxication, drinking behavior and affective state. *J. nerv. ment. Dis.*, 1968a, **146**, 314–321.

Mayfield, D. G. Psychopharmacology of alcohol. II. Affective tolerance in alcohol intoxication. *J. nerv. ment. Dis.*, 1968b, **146**, 322–327.

McBrearty, J. F., Dichter, M., Garfield, Z., & Heath, G. A behaviorally oriented treatment program for alcoholism. *Psychol. Rep.*, 1968, **22**, 287–298.

McCord, W., & McCord, J. *Origins of alcoholism.* Stanford, Calif.: Stanford Univ. Press, 1960.

McCord, W., & McCord, J. A longitudinal study of the personality of alcoholics. In D. P. Pitman & C. R. Snyder (eds.), *Society, culture, and drinking patterns.* New York: Wiley, 1962.

McDougall, W. The chemical theory of temperament applied to introversion and extraversion. *J. abnorm. Soc. Psychol.*, 1929, **24**, 293–369.

McMurray, G. A., & Jacques, L. B. The effects of drugs on a conditioned avoidance response. *Canad. J. Psychol.*, 1959, **13**, 186–192.

Mello, N. K., & Mendelson, J. H. Operant analysis of drinking patterns of chronic alcoholics. *Nature*, 1965, **206**, 43–46.

Menaker, T. Anxiety about drinking in alcoholics. *J. abnorm. Psychol.*, 1967, **72**, 43–49.

Mendelson, J. H., & Mello, Nancy, K. Experimental analysis of drinking behavior of chronic alcoholics. *Ann. N.Y. Acad. Sci.*, 1966, **133**, 828–845.

Merry, J. The "Loss of Control" myth. 1966 *Lancet*, **1**, 1257–1258.

Mertens, G. C. An operant approach to Self Control for alcoholics. Symposium on *Alcoholism and Conditioning Therapy*, American Psychological Association, 1964.

Mertens, G. C., & Fuller, G. B. *The therapist's manual.* Willmar, Minnesota: Willmar State Hospital, 1964a.

Mertens, G. C., & Fuller G. B. *The manual for the alcoholic.* Willmar, Minnesota: Willmar State Hospital, 1964b.

Miller, E. C., Dvorak, B. A., & Turner, D. W. A method of creating aversion to alcohol by reflex conditioning in a group setting. *Quart. J. Stud. Alcoh.*, 1960, **21**, 424–431.

Miller, N. E. Effects of drugs on motivation. *Ann. N.Y. Acad. Sci.*, 1956, **65**, 318–333.

Miller, N. E. Learning resistance to pain and fear: effects of overlearning exposure and rewarded exposure in context. *J. exp. Psychol.*, 1960, **60**, 137–146.

Miller, N. E., & Barry, H. Motivational effects of drugs: methods which illustrate some general problems in psychopharmacology. *Psychopharmacologia*, 1960, **1**, 169–199.

Moskowitz, H., & Asato, H. Effect of alcohol upon the latency of responses learned with positive and negative reinforcers. *Quart. J. Stud. Alcoh.*, 1966, **27**, 604–611.

Mulford, H. E., & Miller, D. E. Drinking in Iowa. III. A scale of definitions of alcohol related to drinking behavior. *Quart. J. Stud. Alcoh.*, 1960a, **21**, 267–278.

Mulford, H. E., & Miller, D. E. Drinking in Iowa. IV. Preoccupation with alcohol and definitions of alcohol, heavy drinking and trouble due to drinking. *Quart. J. Stud. Alcoh.*, 1960b, **21**, 279–291.

Mulford, H. E., & Miller, D. E. Preoccupation with alcohol and definitions of alcohol: a replication study of two cumulative scales. *Quart. J. Stud. Alcoh.*, 1963, **24**, 682–696.

Narrol, H. G. Experimental application of reinforcement principles to the analysis and treatment of hospitalized alcoholics. *Quart. J. Stud. Alcoh.*, 1967, **28**, 105–115.

Nowlis, V., & Nowlis, H. H. Description and analysis of mood. *Annals. N.Y. Acad. Sci.*, 1956, **65**, 345–355.

Pattison, E. M. A critique of alcoholism treatment concepts; with special reference to abstinence. *Quart. J. Stud. Alcoh.*, 1966, **27**, 49–71.

Pattison, E. M. Abstinence criteria in alcoholism treatment. *Addictions*, 1967, **14**, 1–19.

Pavlov, I. P. Experimental pathology of the higher nervous activity. In *Selected Works*. Moscow: Foreign Language Publishing House, 1958.

Petrie, A. Effects of chlorpromazine and brain lesions on personality. In H. H. Pennes (ed.), *Psychopharmacology*. New York: Hueber, 1958.

Pollack, D. Coping and avoidance in inebriated alcoholics and normals. *J. abnorm. Psychol.*, 1966, **71**, 417–419.

Popham, R. E. The Jellinek Alcoholism Estimation Formula and its application to Canadian data. *Quart. J. Stud. Alcoh.*, 1956, **17**, 559–593.

Popham, R. E., & Schmidt, W. *A decade of alcoholism research.* Toronto: Univ. Toronto Press, 1962.

Quinn, J. T., & Henbest, Rosalind. Partial failure of generalization in alcoholics following aversion therapy. *Quart. J. Stud. Alcoh.*, 1967, **28**, 70–75.

Quinn, J. T., & Kerr, W. S. The treatment of poor prognosis alcoholics by prolonged apomorphine aversion therapy. *J. Irish Med. Assoc.*, 1963, **53**, 50–54.

Rachman, S. Aversion therapy: chemical or electrical. *Behav. Res. Ther.*, 1965, **2**, 289–299.

Rachman, J., & Teasdale, J. Aversion therapy: An appraisal. In Franks, C. M. (ed.), *Behavior therapy: Appraisal and status*. New York: McGraw Hill, 1969.

Ramsay, R. W., & VanDis, H. The role of punishment in the aetiology and continuance of alcohol drinking in rats. *Behav. Res. Ther.*, 1967, **5**, 229–235.

Raymond, M. J. The treatment of addiction by aversion conditioning with apomorphine. *Behav. Res. Ther.*, 1964, **1**, 287–291.

Reynolds, G. S., & Van Sommers, P. Effects of ethyl alcohol on avoidance behavior. *Science*, 1960, **132**, 42–43.

Robins, N., Bates, W. M., & O'Neal, P. Adult drinking patterns of former problem children. In D. Pittman and C. Snyder (eds.), *Society, Culture and drinking patterns*. New York: Wiley, 1962.

Rosen, A. C. A comparative study of alcoholic and psychiatric patients with the MMPI. *Quart. J. Stud. Alcoh.*, 1960, **21**, 253–266.

Rotman, S. R., & Vestre, N. D. The use of the MMPI in identifying problem drinkers among psychiatric hospital admissions. *J. clin. Psychol.*, 1964, **20**, 526–530.

Sanderson, R. E., Campbell, D., & Laverty, S. G. An investigation of a new aversive conditioning treatment for alcoholism. *Quart. J. Stud. Alcoh.*, 1963, **24**, 261–275.

Sanford, N. *Where colleges fail.* San Francisco; Jossey-Bass, 1968.

Sanford, N., & Singer, S. Drinking and personality. In J. Katz (Ed.) *Psychological development and the impact of the college. Report of the student development study.* Stanford, Calif.: Inst. Study Hum. Prob., 1967 (Mimeo).

Sanford, N. Personality and patterns of alcohol consumption. *J. Consult. clin. Psychol.*, 1968, **32**, 13–17.

Schmidt, W. S., & Smart, R. G. Alcoholics, drinking and traffic accidents. *Quart. J. Stud. Alcoh.*, 1959, **20**, 631–644.

Sheldon, W. H., & Stevens, S. S. *The varieties of temperament: A psychology of constitutional differences*. New York: Harper, 1942.

Smart, R. G. A critical evaluation of the Alcadd test. *Ontario Psychological Association Quarterly*, December, 1961.

Smart, R. G. Effects of alcohol on conflict and avoidance behavior. *Quart. J. Stud. Alcoh.*, 1965a, **26**, 187–205.

Smart, R. G. Conflict and conditioned aversion stimuli in the development of experimental neuroses. *Canad. J. Psychol.*, 1965b, **19**, 208–223.

Smart, R. G. Alcohol and alcoholism in traffic accident research. *Addictions*, 1967, **14**, 21–33.

Solomon, R., & Brush, E. Experimentally derived concepts of anxiety and aversion. In M. R. Jones (Ed.), *Nebraska symposium on motivation*, **4**, Lincoln, Nebraska: Nebraska University Press, 1956.

Sturm, I. E. The behavioristic aspect of psychodrama. *Group Psychotherapy*, 1965, **18**, 50–64.

Sutherland, E. H., Schroeder, H. G., & Tordella, C. L. Personality traits and the alcoholic. *Quart. J. Stud. Alcoh.*, 1950, **11**, 547.

Syme, L. Personality characteristics of the alcoholic. *Quart. J. Stud. Alcoh.*, 1957, **18**, 288–30[illegible].

Thimann, J. Conditiond reflex treatment of alcoholism. I. Its rationale and technic. *New Eng. J. Med.*, 1949a, **241**, 368–370.

Thimann, J. Conditioned reflex treatment of alcoholism. II. The risks of its application, its indications, contraindications and psychotherapeutic aspects. *New Eng. J. Med.*, 1949b, **241**, 408–410.

Ullmann, L. P., & Krasner, L. (Eds.) *Case studies in behavior modification*. New York: Holt, Rinehart & Winston, 1965.

Vahl, R. Implosive therapy and the chronic alcoholic. Unpublished manuscript, RCA, Occoquan, Va., Aug, 1968.

Voegtlin, W. L. The treatment of alcoholism by establishing a conditioned reflex. *Amer. J. med. Sci.*, 1940, **199**, 802–809.

Voegtlin, W. L. Conditioned reflex therapy of chronic alcoholism. Ten years experience with the method. *Rocky Mountain Medical Journal*, 1947, **44**, 807–12.

Voegtlin, W. L., & Lemere, F. The treatment of alcohol addiction: A review of the literature. *Quart. J. Stud. Alcoh.*, 1942, **2**, 717–803.

Vogel, M. D. Alcohol, alcoholism and introversion-extraversion. *Canad. J. Psychol.*, 1959, **13**, 76–83.

Vogel, M. D. The relation of personality factors to GSR conditioning of alcoholics: an exploratory study. *Canad. J. Psychol.*, 1960, **14**, 275–280.

Vogel-Sprott, M. D. Response generalization under verbal conditioning in alcoholics, delinquents and students. *Behav. Res. Ther.*, 1964, **2**, 135–141.

Vogel-Sprott, M. D. A classical conditioning procedure to control suppression of a rewarded response punishment after a delay. *Psychol. Rep.*, 1966a, **19**, 91–98.

Vogel-Sprott, M. D. Suppression of a rewarded response by punishment as a function of reinforcement schedules. *Psychon. Sci.*, 1966b, **5**, 395–396.

Vogel-Sprott, M. D. Alcohol effects on human behaviour under reward and punishment. *Psychopharmacologia*, 1967a, **11**, 337–344.

Vogel-Sprott, M. D. Individual differences in the suppressing effect of punishment on a rewarded response in alcoholics and nonalcoholics. *Quart. J. Stud. Alcoh.*, 1967b **28**, 33–42.

Vogel-Sprott, M. D., & Banks, R. K. The effect of delayed punishment of a rewarded response in alcoholics and nonalcoholics. *Behav. Res. Ther.*, 1965, **3**, 69–73.

Walton, H. J. Personality as a determinant of the form of alcoholism. *Brit. J. Psychiat.*, 1968, **114**, 761–766.

Weiss, M. Alcohol as a depressant in psychological conflict in rats. *Quart. J. Stud. Alcoh.*, 1958, **19**, 226–237.

Whittman, M. P. Developmental characteristics and personalities of chronic alcoholics. *J. abnorm. Soc. Psychol.*, 1939, **34**, 361–377.

Williams, R. J. The genetotrophic concept—nutritional deficiences and alcoholism. *Ann. N.Y. Acad. Sci.*, 1954. **57**, 794–811.

Wolpe, J. Experimental neurosis as learned behaviour. *Brit. J. Psychol.*, 1952, **43**, 243–268.

Wolpe, J. *Psychotherapy by reciprocal inhibition.* Stanford: Stanford University Press, 1958.

World Health Organization, Expert Committee on Mental Health Report on the First Session of the Alcoholism Subcommittee, WHO Technical Report Series, No. 42, 1951 (Annex 2).

Zwerling, I., & Rosenbaum, M. Alcoholic addiction and personality (nonpsychotic conditions). In Arieti S. (ed.), *American Handbook of Psychiatry*. Vol. I. New York: Basic Books, 1959. Pp. 623–644.

Chapter 19

Aggression[1]

ERVIN STAUB AND LANE K. CONN

A central component of many forms of psychopathology, and an important problem in man's relationship to man, the phenomenon of aggression has long been the focus of theory, clinical observation, and research. Following the history of interest in aggression as a component of psychopathology (Freud, 1925; Horney, 1937; White, 1964), the last decade evidenced especially lively activity in the laboratory investigation of aggression (Bandura & Walters, 1963a, 1963b; Berkowitz, 1962, 1964; Buss, 1961). However, in spite of the attention aggression has received, there is still disagreement about its definition. The most common definition proposed that aggression[2] is a behavior that aims at inflicting injury or pain on others (Berkowitz, 1962; Buss, 1961; Dollard et al., 1939). The word "aims" refers to the motive underlying the act and implies intentionality. Often, however, there is no information other than the behavior itself to indicate intention of the actor; the description of the act may be the only clue to the motive. To increase objectivity, Buss (1961) defined aggression as a response that delivers noxious stimuli to another organism, whether pain was intended or not. Other writers argue, on the other hand, that motivational factors such as intention to reach a goal or expectation regarding the outcome of action are essential components of the definition of aggression (Feshbach, 1964; Kaufmann, 1965).

Accordingly, a number of writers have differentiated behavior that inflicts pain or injury in terms of the goal of the behavior. Behavior that aims to inflict pain or injury, referred to sometimes as "anger" aggression (Buss, 1961), and behavior that aims to accomplish other goals but inflicts injury and pain in the process, referred to as instrumental aggression, have been distinguished (Bandura & Walters, 1963a; Berkowitz, 1962; Buss, 1961; Feshbach, 1964). The example of a child who behaves aggressively in order to gain attention or to get another child's toy would appropriately represent this latter case.

The diagnostician or therapist has to attend both to manifestations of aggression—responses that inflict pain or injury on others—and to the question of what motive they may represent. Aggression may

---

[1]We wish to thank Robert Rosenthal for his helpful comments on the first draft of this chapter. We also extend our gratitude to Nancy Gregg and Lynn Feagans for their assistance in preparing the manuscript.

[2]The terms *aggression* and *hostility* will be used interchangeably in this chapter. This reflects the tendency of other writers in the field. Some writers use the term aggression exclusively (White, 1964); others differentiate between aggression and hostility (Buss, 1961). As Murstein has pointed out (1963), however, most of them use these two terms without clearcut differential meaning assigned to them. While in this chapter the two terms will be used interchangeably, some preference will be shown to *hostility* in reference to nonphysical forms of aggression.

be manifested at different levels of responding. At the behavioral level, aggression may be either physical or verbal. At the level of fantasy, aggression may be expressed through the imagined pain or suffering of others. At a cognitive or perceptual level, aggression may take the form of hostile attitudes, negative evaluation of others, or suspiciousness. Anger may intensify any or all forms of aggression, and may itself be manifested by physiological arousal. On the other hand, fear of punishment of, anxiety about, or guilt resulting from aggressive behavior, thoughts, or fantasy may suppress or modify manifestations of aggression. In addition to these manifestations and inhibitors of aggression, the conditions or influences that lead to aggressive behavior (frustration, norms of the subculture that encourage aggression, etc.) influence the type of treatment that may be effective and should, therefore, be considered in diagnosis and treatment.

Our plan in this chapter is first to describe and to evaluate the available instruments for the assessment of aggression, and to discuss problems of assessment. This will be followed by a discussion of two types of problems that arise in connection with the management of hostility: neurotic aggression and aggressive-antisocial tendencies. Research and theory related to the etiology of these two problems and approaches to their treatment will be discussed. Finally, a strategy for the diagnosis and the treatment of aggression will be suggested, emphasizing the form of expression and the determinants of aggression, and the use of specific techniques in its treatment.

We shall consider a variety of treatment approaches regardless of their theoretical orientation. However, a broad, but not eclectic, theoretical position is considered most profitable by the writers. The basic tenet of this theoretical stance is that behavior, affect, and cognition are all domains within which the principles of learning can be investigated and specified and that methods of treatment may be developed on the basis of these principles. Unconscious processes are best considered as unverbalized assumptions, beliefs, or motives that are manifested in some form of behavior. People are not always aware of the determinants of their actions. Through clarification, these determinants of behavior become available for modification according to principles of learning. The focus of treatment may be learning on the behavioral level, as well as on the cognitive or affective level, depending on the diagnosis. Experimental research from all areas of psychology may be employed to develop principles of learning at different levels, as well as techniques to apply these principles in clinical practice. The broadness of this approach suggests that both behavior modification (Ullmann & Krasner, 1965; Wolpe, 1958; Wolpe & Lazarus, 1966) and the recent example of the application of findings of laboratory investigations to psychotherapy (Goldstein, Heller, & Sechrest, 1966) be considered example of strategies for the development of theories and techniques of treatment. Goldstein et al. (1966), in a review of the literature, demonstrated a positive relationship between patient-therapist relationship and therapy outcome. Then, on the basis of a large body of research findings, they proposed methods to increase the interpersonal attraction between patient and therapist.

THE ASSESSMENT OF AGGRESSION

"Assessment for what purpose?" is a question to be clearly answered prior to formal testing and assessment. In a clinical setting the goal of assessment should be explicitly determined in relation to the goal of treatment and the techniques to be employed in therapy. For example, since the goal of treatment for the "dynamic" therapist centers around unconscious, dynamic disturbance, the purpose of assessment in this area of aggression and hostility may be to determine conflicts associated with aggression, such as severe anxiety and guilt about harboring hostile feelings and thoughts. The treatment goal and concern of the more behavioristic therapist, however, is focused primarily on the behavioral manifestations of aggression. This difference in treatment orientation should be reflected in the diagnostic goals and in the selection of assessment instruments to be employed.

To fulfill this ideal prescription for diagnosis, answers must be ascertained for basic questions such as the ability of various assessment instruments to measure aggression and hostility at various levels of responding and the relationship between test responses and various non-test-taking manifestations of aggression and hostility.

Relationship Between Test Responses and Behavioral Aggression

Assessment research, for a long time, has been preoccupied with the basic question of the relationship between aggressive and hostile test rsponses and behavioral expressions of aggression. Projective methods have been the most frequently employed assessment technique in this area and, accordingly, the vast majority of the research literature is concerned with the relationship between fantasy and overt aggression. Of all the projective tests, the TAT has been most frequently studied (estimated bibliographic references of over twelve hundred separate items) with the Rorschach running a distant second. The importance and necessity of demonstrating the relationship between test and behavioral aggressive responses seems obvious in terms of establishing predictive efficiency and validity. However, when the reasoning associated with the development of projective tests such as TAT and Rorschach is considered, attempts to relate fantasy expression of aggression to overt aggression are surprising.

The earlier writers on projective techniques derived their assumptions and postulates from psychoanalytic theory. Accordingly, they assumed that the motivating forces in personality are instinctive drives and impulses that are modified by ego-processes for overt behavior. Since the drives and impulses are part of the primary process, they are concealed from consciousness (ego); however, their expression is possible in fantasy because of the various ego defenses, for example, displacement, projection, etc. Thus it was assumed that TAT stories, like fantasy in general, revealed the respondent's underlying needs or drives. Henry Murray (1943) stated that he never expected the TAT to reflect overt behavior, nor to relate directly to self-report expressions of needs and impulses. Rather, Murray considered fantasy a safety valve for repressed impulses and, accordingly, expected to find negative relationships between fantasy responses, especially the ones related to motives negatively sanctioned by societal norms, and behavior. The earlier publications tended to agree with Murray's position and held that only needs that were socially approved might show a positive correlation between thematic and behavioral forms of expression. In contrast, needs expressed in fantasy that were socially disapproved would be expected to show no relationship, or a negative one, to overt behavior.

Findings obtained in both experimental and clinical settings have made it increasingly apparent that the relationship between projective test responses and overt behavior involves more variables than the neat psychoanalytic explanation incorporates. A few examples will suggest how complex is the relationship between fantasy and overt aggression. In studies of hunger, TAT stories did show more food imagery when people were hungry than when they were sated, but the relationship frequently became negative when hunger was severe (Lazarus et al., 1953; McClelland & Atkinson, 1948). Similarly, it was found that aggressive themes increased when subjects were exposed to irritating and frustrating situations before testing. However, only those subjects scoring high on the Manifest Hostility Scale tended to show this increase in aggressive themes, and lower scorers tended to have fewer aggressive responses on the TAT following instigation (Hokanson & Gordon, 1958). In studies on sleep deprivation (Murray, 1959), thematic expression of sleep was found to decrease with high levels of need for sleep.

In spite of the earlier conceptualization discussed above, some investigators assumed that a positive relationship existed between fantasy and behavioral aggression. A few authors report success in predicting overt aggression from straightforward frequency counts of fantasy aggression. It is more often the case, however, that no relationship is found, or at best a weak one, when fantasy aggression is evaluated by merely counting the number of times it occurs. A significant, straightforward relationship between fantasy and overt aggression tends to hold true only for deviant populations such as groups of assaultive and extremely hostile and aggressive, acting-out patients (Buss, 1961; Pittluck, 1950; Stone, 1956; Storment & Finney, 1953; Wolf, 1957). Although the relationship between fantasy and overt aggression in manifestly deviant populations is a consistently positive one, this finding is of little use to the practicing clinician. There is seldom a diagnostic or predictive problem with such extremely deviant populations concerning the probability of aggressive acting-out. Moreover, direct assessment techniques, such as observation and interview, are likely to yield as much pertinent information on these patients as projective testing, with considerably less time expenditure.

Turning to the vast body of studies on less deviant populations, we find great variation across reports on the relationship between fantasy and overt aggression. Although the reported degree of association ranges from inconclusive findings, to significant positive correlations, to significant negative correlations (Harrison, 1965; Lesser, 1957; Murstein, 1965), these complex findings taken together tend to support the proposition that a positive, moderately strong, significant relationship exists between fantasy and behavioral measures of aggression. It is necessary, however, to qualify this conclusion by adding that the relationship is modified by the presence of anxiety as an inhibitor of aggression.

Inhibitors and Defenses in Fantasy Responses

As early as 1950, Bellak was urging clinicians to consider the presence of anxiety in fantasy expression. He suggested that a shift was necessary from exclusive focus on drives to a consideration of ego processes and defenses against anxiety as manifested in thematic responses. It would appear that Bellak's urging has not gone unheeded. The research literature in the last fifteen years or so does reflect a greater concern with increasing sophistication in the understanding and measurement of inhibitory and defensive tendencies in fantasy expressions of aggression.

The general rationale for the measurement of inhibitors and defenses in thematic material can be summarized in the following way. Since aggressive behavior is generally punished and prohibited in our culture, individuals develop, in accordance with their history, varying degrees of anxiety and guilt over expressing aggression. Thus, in order to predict overt aggressive behavior, one must measure the amount and intensity of inhibition and defensiveness against the expression of aggression as well as the strength of the individual's aggressive drive. When a person consistently qualifies and defends against verbal expression of aggression in response to pictures, especially when the pictures regularly elicit aggressive content from most people, it suggests that anxiety or guilt concerning aggression is operating as an inhibitor. Furthermore, it is probable that an individual who is inhibited in an assessment situation about telling stories containing aggressive themes will also be inhibited in other situations from expressing overt aggression.

Furthermore, background factors that would presumably lead to inhibition of expressing aggression should be taken into consideration. For example, Lesser (1957) found a relationship between fantasy and overt aggression of adolescent boys, but only when maternal permissiveness toward expression of aggression was taken into account. A significant positive relationship existed between fantasy aggression and peer ratings on overt aggression for boys whose mothers encouraged overt aggression, whereas for boys whose mothers discouraged overt expressions of aggression, Lesser found a significant negative relationship between fantasy and peer ratings of aggressive behavior. If Lesser had merely correlated frequency of thematic aggression with peer ratings of aggressive behavior, the two significant but opposite relationships would have cancelled each other. In another study, Weatherley (1962) found a positive significant relationship between maternal permissiveness toward aggression in childhood and fantasy aggression on the TAT after instigation to aggression in adulthood.

The recent literature contains studies on the importance of measuring guilt in thematic aggression (Dill, 1961; Epstein, 1961; Feshbach, 1961; Saltz & Epstein, 1963; Shore et al., 1964). For example, reports from a series of related studies by Epstein (1962) and his students indicate that a positive relationship exists between aggressive drive[3] and thematic responses

[3]Epstein uses the concept *drive* to refer to a force with properties of activation and direction. It refers to a broad class of behavior which is a multiplicative function of activation and cue relevance, and is experienced by an individual as press to behave or think in a certain direction.

when guilt is low, and an inverse relationship exists when guilt is high. Unfortunately the results of studies on guilt have not been consistent; the results suggest that not only stimulus relevance but also the testing situation must be considered (Epstein, 1962; Kagan, 1967).

Another measure of inhibition of aggression which has been studied is the fear of punishment. One of the first investigations to incorporate a measure of fear of punishment along with frequency of fantasy aggression was conducted by Mussen and Naylor (1954). Their subjects were white and Negro boys confined to a juvenile detention center. It was found that boys with a relatively higher number of aggressive themes showed significantly more overt aggressive behavior than did boys with less fantasy aggression. However, prediction was enhanced when fear of punishment was considered. Boys who showed high fantasy aggression but low fear of punishment tended to be more overtly aggressive than were boys who showed high fantasy aggression with concomitant high fear of punishment. The most marked difference in overt aggression was found between boys with high TAT aggression and low TAT punishment scores and boys with low TAT aggression and high TAT punishment scores, the former being strikingly more overtly aggressive.

Whereas Mussen and Naylor (1954) focused primarily on expressions of external punishment, Purcell (1956), in a study of nonaggressive and antisocial-aggressive Army draftees who were psychiatric referrals, investigated the differential relationship between overt aggressiveness and themes of internal (self-deprecation, remorse, and feelings of guilt) and external sources of punishment. Consistent with findings of other studies, the antisocial group produced more fantasy aggression than the nonaggressive group. Anticipation of punishment as a consequence of aggression was no more prominent among overtly aggressive individuals than nonaggressive individuals. However, when the proportion of internal punishment to fantasy aggression was computed, the nonaggressive group had very significantly more internal punishment than the aggressive group. Thus, guilt as measured by anticipation of internal punishment was found to relate much more strongly than fear of retaliatory or external punishment to the absence of overt aggression. This finding has been supported in a more recent study by Schaefer and Norman (1967) that will be described below.

Clearly, the consideration of inhibitors of aggression like anxiety, guilt, and fear of punishment increases the ability to predict the relationship between fantasy and behavioral aggression. Moreover, it must be noted that information about these inhibitors themselves is important. For example, with patients whose strong anxiety over the expression of aggression inhibits even mild self-assertion, a reasonable treatment goal may be the weakening of some of the inhibitions that interfere with a moderate and adaptive degree of self-assertion. The identification of the forms and the degree of inhibition, therefore, would be an important part of diagnosis. Moreover, a tendency for overt aggressiveness may be the result of either a lack of inhibitions, or reinforcement for aggression from the environment, or a combination of these and other factors. It might be expected that prior evaluation of these factors would aid treatment.

Age as a Factor in Thematic Aggression

In a study (Schaefer & Norman, 1967) with antisocial and presumably normal preadolescent and adolescents boys, normal adolescents told more stories on the TAT with internal punishment themes than did antisocial adolescent boys. When the fantasy stories of preadolescents (ages 11 to 13) and adolescents (ages 14 to 18) were combined, antisocial boys showed more external punishment themes following an aggression theme than did normals. Schaefer and Norman's findings not only support previous findings that punishment variables are important to consider in understanding the relationship between overt antisocial behavior and fantasy aggression but, as we shall see, they also support previous findings that age or developmental differences are likewise important variables in this relationship. In addition to the above difference between antisocial and normal boys, Schaefer and Norman found that the stories of normal adolescents contained more internal punishment themes than did the stories of normal preadolescents. Furthermore, the fantasy of adolescent antisocial boys tended to contain less aggression than stories of the antisocial preadolescent boys, whereas the reverse tendency held for normal boys. These, and other research findings, suggest that there may be a rise in intellectual control and ego strength with a decrease in expression of primitive affect from preschool to the late teens (Balken & Vander Veer, 1944; Harrison, 1953; Suesholtz, 1948). Although younger adolescents are found to give freer expression to their impulses in fantasy than older adolescents, the latter are more likely to give stories that are higher in anxiety and aggression (Symonds, 1949; Symonds & Jensen, 1961). Also, the fantasy aggression of adolescents is often characterized as melodramatic violence (McDowell, 1952; Sanford, 1943). A descriptive analysis by Harrison (1953) of TAT stories of pre-pubescent and late adolescent girls indicates that by the time girls reach older adolescence there is a significant decrease in themes of violent melodrama.

Although the literature on differences in fantasy aggression for various age groups suggests strongly that clinicians should consider the age of their patients in interpreting the amount and type of fantasy aggression, much more evidence is needed to provide assistance in establishing reliable age norms and base rates. Without developmental norms for the interpretation of children's responses, there is a danger of misinterpreting as aberrant what is merely age appropriate.

Properties of the Test Stimulus

The new emphasis by both the clinical and the research-oriented psychologists on the cognitive, organizing, and synthetic functions underlying the production of fantasy responses has led to a revival of interest in the stimulus properties of the test stimuli (Brayer & Craig, 1960; Epstein, 1962; Kenny, 1961; Murstein, 1965). Generally, the earlier assumption that the degree of clinical richness in projective measures was a direct function of the degree of ambiguity has not been verified by empirical investigations. A general conclusion from the work on the stimulus properties of TAT pictures is that ambiguity and structure of pictures has an inverted U-shaped curvilinear relationship with productivity, with moderately ambiguous pictures yielding the best results. Murstein (1958a and b, 1965) concludes that the most highly ambiguous TAT pictures are the least useful for personality assessment, whereas pictures of medium ambiguity with regard to hostility content appear to be the most promising for clinical assessment. The standard Murray TAT cards have been rank-ordered in terms of scaled judgments for hostility "pull" (Murstein, 1963). Nine cards that were selected as being evenly spaced throughout the hostility continuum are, from most to least: 13MF, 18BM, 3GF, 9GF, 6GF, 7GF, 13B, 13G, and 10.

Epstein and his students (1962) reported work in progress in which series of pictures were constructed to represent a range along a dimension of increasing relevance for aggression. They found that pictures of low relevance produce the best measure of aggressive drive, and pictures of high relevance the best measure of guilt concerning the expression of aggression. With this approach, conflict in the area of aggression and hostility is indicated by over-responding with aggressive thematic content to the low end of the dimension and under-responding to the high end of the dimension. These findings fit nicely with the ones that were reviewed in the previous section relating to inhibition and defense in fantasy responses. The idea of employing TAT pictures with a built-in stimulus dimension for relevance may improve prediction of overt aggression from fantasy aggression. Unfortunately it tends to be the case that the specific conflict areas in the various diagnostic groups are not clear. Thus, on which of the many possible stimulus dimensions should the clinician assess the ulcer patient or the hypertensive patient? Or, as in the case of a new patient for whom there is no diagnostic evaluation, it would simply not be possible to administer to him 10 or more cards for each dimension of dependency, aggression, hostility, heterosexuality, etc. Once the salient areas of maladjustment are identified, however, the specific features of a patient's problems might be investigated profitably with this approach.

The absence of aggressive content in fantasy responses, when the stimulus is strongly prepotent in pull for such themes, can itself be successfully employed as a predictive indicator, or as Henry (1956) called it, "negative evidence," of conflict.

Kagan (1956) reported in one of the earliest studies to employ "negative evidence" that boys in grades one through three who failed to give aggressive themes to pictures that had strong pull for fighting content were significantly more often rated by their teachers as extremely nonaggressive. Dill (1961) found that persons who avoided relating thematic aggression to pictures with content obviously related to aggression were high in self-reported conflict over aggression. A number of other authors have also suggested that failure to produce fantasy aggression to test stimuli strongly suggestive of aggressive activity might provide the clinician with one index of anxiety associated with overt aggressiveness (Epstein, 1962; Murstein, 1965).

One implication of this work for the clinician lies in the need for awareness of the differential pull of the cards and of what constitutes a common response before attributing to it diagnostic significance of a pathological nature. An aggressive fantasy response might reflect good reality testing; it might also indicate gross reality distortion. The lack of an aggressive fantasy response might indicate blatant aversive denial of objective reality or an appropriate, nonpathological response.

Scoring Systems

Many scoring systems have been devised and used to measure thematic aggression. These scoring systems vary along a wide range of dimensions; some emphasize a subjective-wholistic rating and interpretive procedure, while others stress scoring of isolated parts of the stories with rigorous rules for quantification. Among the many different ways in which these themes can be categorized, analyzed, and rated there are the approaches of Murray's (1943) rating scale for needs and press, Tomkins' (1947) vector and level analysis, Kagan's (1961) method for scoring affect states, and Arnold's (1962) story sequence analysis.

One general conclusion that can be drawn from the great number of studies employing scoring systems for fantasy and hostility-aggression themes is that the inclusion of measures of anxiety, guilt, and fear of punishment leads to better prediction of behavioral aggression than measures of aggressive content alone. Other measures which have been demonstrated to predict overt aggressiveness are presence of tabooed aggressive activities (Jensen, 1957), realism of aggressive themes (Haskin, 1958), and intensity of verbalization (Pittluck, 1950).

TAT scoring systems on the degree of self-control in thematic responses of adolescents have successfully predicted those boys most likely to act-out aggressively and those most likely to improve in therapy (McNeil, 1962; Shore et al., 1964; Weissman, 1964). It has also been found that an increase in the future time perspective on the TAT of male adolescent delinquents followed psychotherapy directed toward vocational adjustment (Ricks et al., 1964).

An important question concerning the scoring systems is their usefulness to the clinician who works in an applied setting. First, appreciable amounts of time have to be expended in the use of most scoring systems. Second, the validity of most scoring methods is presented in nomothetical terms; although the magnitude of the significant findings suggests that these scoring systems may be adequate to differentiate between groups, they are not too helpful in making individual predictions and diagnoses. In individual diagnosis, a condition of the profitable use of a test, as well as a specific scoring system, may be the systematic combination of information from a number of sources, such as projective tests, behavioral observation, the patient's self-report, and nonprojective testing. Employment of all these sources of information may increase predictive validity as well as clarify the manifestations of the problem at various levels. Knowledge of the various forms of the expression of aggression may be helpful in setting goals for therapy and in planning therapy techniques.

The Draw-a-Person Test

Since the Draw-a-Person (DAP) test is frequently employed by clinicians to assess aggressive tendencies, especially among children, a brief review of the findings on the DAP will be presented.

The DAP test has received at best marginal, inconsistent support for its validity as a test of general personality adjustment, or as a predictive indicator of specific behaviors such as aggression (Goodman & Kotkov,

1953; Griffith & Peyman, 1959; Hammer & Piotrowski, 1953; Holzberg & Wexler, 1950; Spadaro, 1960; Stoltz & Coltharp, 1961; Watson, 1967; Whitmyre, 1953). Karen Machover's (1949) hypotheses that specify relationships between DAP responses and behavioral aggressiveness (for example, mouth detailing with teeth showing relates to verbal aggressiveness, overcritical, and sometimes sadistic subjects) have not been substantiated; for excellent reviews and discussions of the findings on the DAP we suggest the writings of Swensen (1965), Lewinsohn (1965), and Hiler and Nesvig (1965). In his review chapter, Swensen (1965) concludes that the majority of research findings actually contradict Machover's hypotheses. Reports continue to be published which state that most indixes of maladjustment based on figure drawing are highly correlated with estimates of the general artistic excellence of the drawing (Strumpfer & Nichols, 1962; Levy et al., 1963). Thus, it is possible that the supposed relationship between figure drawings and psychopathology is confounded by the drawer's ability to represent the human form accurately and artistically.

Despite the overwhelming evidence that the DAP has not been empirically validated, it is currently one of the most popular tests employed in clinical settings. Perhaps one reason for its popularity is that it is easy and quick to administer. In addition, some clinicians probably conclude that the findings from DAP studies are based on the judgments of inexperienced judges, whereas findings with experienced clinicians would reveal the DAP's true diagnostic and predictive value. A recent study of the diagnostic value of the DAP (Watson, 1967) showed that the judgments of 10 clinicians who regularly used the DAP were no better than the judgments of 10 practicing clinicians who seldom used the test; both sets of judges were slightly more accurate than chance. Furthermore, Hammer and Piotrowski (1953) found a significant relationship between hostility attributed to subjects' drawings by examiners and the judged hostility of the examiners themselves. If, however, the clinician chooses to use the DAP despite its serious limitations, it would appear that the most promising approach to the DAP would be an analysis of patterns of signs instead of scoring individual signs separately (Goldworth, 1950; Gutman, 1952; Machover, 1949; Swensen, 1965). Moreover, studies are needed that reliably predict overt behavior rather than psychiatric classifications (Griffith & Peyman, 1959). Swensen (1965) has suggested that studies be done in which DAP's are administered serially to patients undergoing therapy in an effort to determine which aspects of the drawings might vary concomitantly with changes in behavior. Lastly, the effects of age and IQ should be investigated and norms should be established in order to avoid confounding these factors in interpreting the drawings (Lewinsohn, 1965).

One goal of assessment is to predict to a criterion situation. Given the great variety of ways in which aggression and hostility can be expressed, from mild complaining to murderous physical assault, it is too much to expect that any assessment technique should provide a single predictive index of aggression. Moreover, situational determinants of aggression further reduce the likelihood that one test instrument can be a general predictor of aggression. These considerations apply unless one assumes that aggression is a trait or a general attribute that determines behavior without modification by the situation or by other factors. The present authors do not endorse this assumption. For a thought-provoking article on the need for more relativistic definitions in the social sciences, Kagan's (1967) article is excellent.

Nonprojective Assessment

Gordon Allport (1953) has remarked that "... normal subjects ... tell you by direct method precisely what they tell you by the projective method ... you may therefore take their motivational statements at their face value, for even if you probe you will not find anything substantially different." As a rejoinder to Allport's position, McGreevey (1962) has offered the following revision: "Nondefensive subjects tell you by direct methods precisely what they tell you by projective methods, but defensive subjects tell you something significantly different by direct methods from what they tell you by projective methods." Some investigators do report a greater defensiveness on the less "projective" tests like the Sentence Completion Test than on the more "projective" tests like the TAT, especially when socially unacceptable needs are being investigated (Thiner, 1962). However, others present findings that do not indicate this "defensiveness" difference between the Sentence Completion Test and the TAT (Filmore & Klopfer, 1962) and they report that they found no evidence to indicate that one taps behavior closer to awareness than does the other. Davids and Pildner (1959) conclude that there is less difference between projective and self-report tests in the level and in the validity of information they yield than is generally claimed. Detailed critical surveys of personality tests and questionnaires have been presented by Bass and Berg (1959), Buros (1959), Ellis and Conrad (1948), and Hathaway (1965).

The use of objective tests and personality inventories for the purpose of assessment of aggression and hostility has not been extensive. There have been five major attempts to build MMPI scales to assess aggression and hostility. Unfortunately, very little work has been done to establish the validity of these scales. The oldest hostility scale is Moldowsky's (1953) Iowa Hostility Inventory. It has been found to correlate significantly with psychotherapists' ratings of aggression and hostility of male therapy patients (Dinwiddie, 1954), global ratings of aggression and hostility based on interviews with male and female psychiatric patients, and verbal and physical forms of attacking behavior by female psychiatric patients (Buss, 1961).

Another MMPI hostility scale was constructed by Cook and Medley (1954), and has been coded by Dahlstrom and Welsh (1960) as the HO scale. Although the scale has been correlated with other personality tests (McGee, 1954), there is little direct evidence that it predicts overt aggression. The McGee (1954) findings suggest that the inventory is related to the perception of others as threatening (Buss, 1961).

A third MMPI-derived scale for assessing aggression and hostility is Schultz's (1954) Overt Hostility Scale (Hv). Schultz report a correlation of .38 between the Hv scale and ratings of frequency of overt hostility. Dahlstrom and Welsh (1960) conclude in a review of this scale that it has promising possibilities for predicting overt aggression, but that it needs additional validation work.

A fourth MMPI scale for measuring hostility was derived by Siegel (1956), the Manifest Hostility Scale (Jh). Additional normative data on Siegel's scale have been reported by Feldman and Siegel (1958). The only validity studies reported on this scale are correlational findings with other paper-and-pencil self-report measures.

Megargee, Cook and Mendelsohn (1967) have recently derived another MMPI scale (O-H) for assessing assaultiveness in overcontrolled people. They report moderately good success in detecting criminals of the overcontrolled assaultive type. This work is very promising, and hopefully more work will be undertaken to establish and to improve its validity. For additional material on this scale, see Megargee (1964), Megargee (1966), and Megargee and Mendelsohn (1962).

The Wechsler intelligence scales have been employed to assess conflicts over hostility. Wechsler (1958) originally suggested that a performance IQ greater than verbal IQ was diagnostically indicative of a psychopathic personality. In a review of the relevant literature, however, Guertin et al. (1962) reject Wechsler's suggestion as not being supported by empirical research. Blatt (1965) suggests that a pattern analysis of the Wechsler scale may be diagnostically employed to detect potential for acting out.

Concluding Remarks About Assessment

This short review of assessment instruments used for diagnosing aggression indicates that no available test is sufficient to the task of predicting individual behavior accurately. As this review has indicated, the use of projective instruments has been heavily emphasized, probably to the detriment of the careful exploration of alternative approaches. Nevertheless, a great deal has been learned. For example, knowledge has increased about the variables at work in the testing situation, such as temporary motivation, specific previous experiences that influence the content of projective responses, and the set created by testing itself (Epstein, 1962). Moreover, the presence of inhibitors of the expression of aggression such as anxiety, fear of punishment, and guilt has emerged as the most important modifier of the relationship between projective and behavioral expressions of aggression. Techniques for the measurement of these inhibitors have been and are being developed.

The usefulness of these techniques extends beyond the improvement of prediction of behavioral aggression, because either too strong or too weak inhibition of aggression constitutes a problem to be diagnosed and to be considered in treatment (see below).

One technique of "diagnosis," the sampling of the patient's behavior itself, has not been discussed. Little information is available about the use of behavior samples in aiding diagnosis, probably because they have not been systematically employed. In fact, behavior other than verbal, in spite of the concern over the relationship between projective responses and overt behavior, has neither been a focus of therapy nor has been considered an indicator of the nature of dynamic disturbance. In addition, of course, behavior sampling is often not practicable; it is difficult to observe and to record the behavior of patients in varied life situations. However, the use of behavior sampling in hospitals where patients could easily be observed has not been a frequent practice either. The recent efforts by behavior therapists to observe the behavior of hospitalized patients and to record the stimulus conditions that evoke undesirable behaviors, as well as the rewards that maintain them, represent a limited but very useful attempt (Ullmann & Krasner, 1965). Behavior sampling could also be employed, however, with nonhospitalized patients. Researchers, for example, often observe subjects in interactive situations. They may also vary properties of the environment, create expectancies and set goals, and then evaluate the resulting variation in behavior. Similar approaches may be used to evaluate patients' behavior.

A substitute for behavioral sampling, role playing, might also be employed. In changes of attitudes (King & Janis, 1956; Goldstein et al., 1966), in behavior therapy (Wolpe & Lazarus, 1966), or in psychodrama (Moreno, 1946) role playing has emerged as a successful technique of behavior change (see below). Behavior therapists in practice, evaluate in the course of role playing both the degree of inappropriateness of patients' responses and the degree of change following training. Psychodramatists also employ role playing as a diagnostic tool, both to learn how the patient behaves and to gain an understanding of his motives. Thus, when part of the treatment goal is to change behavior, both behavior sampling and role playing may be employed in diagnosis. It would be desirable, however, to systematically evaluate their properties as diagnostic techniques.

NEUROTIC AGGRESSION AND AGGRESSIVE-ANTISOCIAL TENDENCIES

Following this necessarily brief discussion of assessment, two types of problems, neurotic aggression and aggressive-antisocial tendencies, will be discussed. Neurotic aggression is characterized by hostile feelings and attitudes with strong inhibitions against their expression, so that hostility is expressed only indirectly or in fantasy. Occasionally, hostility may be expressed in some form of "acting out" (Abt & Weissman, 1965). Aggressive-antisocial tendencies are exemplified by overt aggressiveness and destructiveness, often accompanied by and sometimes manifested through certain forms of delinquency and criminality. These two types of problems represent syndromes, or groups of manifestations of problems with aggression that frequently co-occur. In the following pages they will be described in more detail, and some of their antecedents, together with treatment approaches, will be discussed. This discussion will include, then, problems related to both covert and overt aggression. However, because of the consideration of problems related to covert aggression in other sections of this book (for example, in the chapter on psychosomatic symptoms), somewhat more emphasis will be placed in this chapter on overt aggression.

Neurotic Aggression

According to the psychoanalytic view, repressed hostility is a central element in neurosis. White (1964) suggests that neurotic fears may involve fear of expression of impulses, especially aggressive impulses, ". . . because in childhood they imperiled a precarious parental relationship, and he (the neurotic) has never been able to learn that they no longer do so." Moreover, various "neurotic trends" involve difficulties with the management of hostility (White, 1964). For example, exaggerated needs for affection may be related to repressed hostility toward the parents; this hostility is stimulated by, and makes the development difficult for, every relationship the person enters in his search for affection. Moreover, exaggerated striving for power results from the belief that everyone is hostile, and possessing power decreases the likelihood of open hostility from others. In obsessional neurosis, problems with aggressive impulses take another form. Hostile, destructive, and even murderous fantasies and hostile and antisocial tendencies often characterize obsessional patients (White, 1964).

In addition to the repression of hostile impulses (Fenichel, 1945; White, 1964), the discharge of these impulses through various forms of acting out has also been discussed in a psychoanalytic framework (Bellak, 1965; Abt & Weissman, 1965). Acting out is interpreted as a transfer of repressed impulse to a new situation, and a "partial discharge of instinctual tension that is achieved by responding to the present situation as if it were the situation that originally gave rise to the instinctual demand" (Hinsie & Campbell, 1960).

Like psychoanalysts, behavior therapists often find that neurosis involves strong anxiety associated with the expression of anger and hostility (Wolpe, 1958; Wolpe & Lazarus, 1966). However, the concept of repression is not employed, and the origins of the problem are considered relatively unimportant. Rather, its present form, and the degree of interference with adaptive behavior, is considered of primary importance. Accordingly, the problem is seen as insufficient assertiveness; strong anxiety inhibits even appropriate expressions of self-assertion and justified resentment and anger (Salter, 1965; Wolpe, 1958). Somewhat similar views about the consequences of strong suppression of aggression have been expressed by others (Horney, 1937).

The involvement of hostility in neurosis seems to be corraborated by research findings. For example, on a test of constructing sentences out of scrambled words, (Wahler, 1959) sentence content of neurotic *S*s showed stronger hostility than that of normal controls, although this difference was restricted to hostility directed against people as opposed to objects. In another study (Haas, 1965) neurotic and psychotic trends, as measured by the MMPI, were correlated with covert and overt hostility, respectively, on the TAT and on other paper-and-pencil tests. It should be noted, however, that these research findings refer to hostile test responses, not to hostile interpersonal behavior. Because of their probable anxiety over hostility (see discussion in the assessment section), we might expect only a slight or no relationship between test hostility and the interpersonal hostility of neurotic persons.

In contrast to adults, in young children hostility is often expressed relatively directly, or it may be brought to expression through play activities or through interaction with a permissive adult. Normal children's expression of aggression in doll play is positively related to both frustrations at home and maternal punishment for aggressive behavior (Sears, 1951). In the course of several sessions in a permissive setting, doll-play aggression usually increases. This increase in aggression may be due, in part, to "disinhibition" (Bandura & Walters, 1963b). By studying the behavior of emotionally disturbed four-year-old children, Moustakas and Schlalock (1955) found that these children performed many more hostile responses in play and in their interaction with their nondirective therapist than normal four-year-olds. Emotionally disturbed children also engaged in some "severely" hostile acts, whereas the normal controls did not.

Individual differences in the inhibition of overt aggression appear early, and with increasing age these differences in the degree of inhibition become even greater. Inhibition may result from the development of anxiety or guilt specific to aggression. Or overt aggression may be one of the behaviors suppressed by general anxiety. In an extensive investigation of test anxiety, Sarason et al. (1960) have found that test-anxious children tend to blame themselves for failures or apparent failures and to inhibit overt expression of blame toward others, that is, they are nonaggressive in their overt behavior. However, judged by therapeutic experience, the fantasies of these children contain strong hostile impulses toward other people. It would appear that there is a similarity between neurotic individuals and persons high in test anxiety in their tendency to avoid overt expression of hostility. Whether associated with neurosis or test anxiety, feeling hostility without expressing it is likely to be the result of restrictive, suppressive parental behavior.

Aggressive-Antisocial Tendency

In contrast to problems centering around strong anxiety associated with hostility, overt aggressiveness and destructiveness result, in part, from lack of anxiety or other internal inhibitions of aggression. Aggressive, destructive behavioral tendencies may often be accompanied by other forms of antisocial behavior, such as delinquency and criminality (Bandura & Walters, 1959; McCord & McCord, 1964).

In investigating the antecedents of antisocial behavior McCord et al. (1959) found a lack of cohesiveness and inconsistency of discipline in the families of delinquent children. Similarly, Bandura and Walters (1959) found in their extensive study of aggressive adolescent boys that these children experienced conditions that were highly unfavorable for identification with their parents. Relationships between fathers and sons were especially poor, with either a severe break in the relationship or a generally poor relationship in which the fathers were typically hostile and rejecting. Bandura and Walters (1959) suggest that serious delinquency may be related not only to the lack of internalization of parental standards, but also to the development of hate and hostility toward the parents, and to the learning of active opposition to both parent and parental standards. The consequence may be a pattern of aggression combined with insistence on self-reliance and the rejection of interference; such boys fear, avoid, and repel close involvements except perhaps with members of their own group. A pattern of active rebellion and rejection of approach by others has also been reported by Redl and Wineman (1951) and McCord and McCord (1964). The tendency for suspicion and for the rejection of approach toward them may partially account for the difficulty of getting aggressive antisocial children and adults into treatment.

In the background of aggressive children, physical punishment predominates as a method of discipline, and love-oriented techniques are rarely used. Because of this, the probability of introjection of parental standards is decreased (Sears, et al., 1957). Moreover, by being physically punitive, the parents "teach" their children aggression through modeling (Bandura, Ross & Ross, 1963; Bandura & Walters, 1959, 1963a).

Direct evidence that aggressive-delinquent children are deficient in internal controls is also available. McCord and McCord (1956) found that children diagnosed as behavior disorders or psychopaths gave fewer guilt responses on a test with incomplete stories describing situations in which the central character has violated some standard of behavior than did children diagnosed in various other ways. Furthermore, Bandura and Walters (1959) found that aggressive boys were deterred from antisocial acts primarily by fear of external punishment, instead of by guilt or other forms of internal control. Other evidence pointing to the lack of internal controls in antisocial children was discussed in the assessment section. In addition to lacking internal controls, aggressive boys may lack empathy, the ability to experience vicariously others' emotions. The capacity to vicariously experience others' pain may be an important curb on aggression (Feshbach, 1964).

Determinants of aggressive-antisocial tendencies other than parent-child interactions have also been examined. The unconscious bases of aggressive behavior were stressed by contributors to a volume on "acting out" (Abt & Weissman, 1965). However, Bellak (1965) suggests that cultural milieu, social factors, and contemporary determinants have a great deal to do with the form "acting out" takes. For people in "culture conflict," living in ghettoes and large urban centers, murder, assault, rape and robbery may be a reflection of unfamiliarity, confusion, or rebellion against dominant values or norms (Chwert, 1965). Furthermore, children grow up often in cultural milieus that not only accept, but encourage certain forms of aggression, and they may later live in social groups that further encourage or even damand aggression. In an intensive and careful study of an average street corner group, Miller et al. (1961) found that the group had definite norms which determined the occasions that called for verbal or physical aggression as well as the forms and targets of aggressive behavior. It was also found that most of the verbal and physical aggression was performed without signs of anger, which suggests that often aggressive behavior may be the result of rules leading to habits, that is, it may be prescriptively rather than affectively determined.

In summary, aggressive delinquent adolescents lack internal controls, strive for self-reliance and react to interference with belligerance. They tend to learn aggression through modeling, and to interact with peers who may encourage, possibly even demand, hostile and aggressive behavior from them in a variety of situations. Aggressive antisocial adults seem to have many of the same characteristics (McCord & McCord, 1964).

In addition to neurotic aggression and the aggressive-antisocial behavior tendencies, aggression plays a role in a variety of other psychological problems. For example, hostility and belligerance are considered to be peripheral symptoms of schizophrenia (Solomon, 1966). In the manic phase of manic-depressive psychosis, the overactivity of the patient often leads to high-intensity behavior that may be judged aggressive and that contains the threat of injury. This, again, is thought of as a secondary, not a primary, feature of the psychosis (White, 1964). It is worth noting that, concerning the relationship between the more severe forms of psychopathology and the expression of aggression, in an extensive study of "mentally ill aggressiveness" (Brennan, 1964), hospitalized patients showed no physically aggressive behavior in approximately 75,000 hours of work, primarily in the community. Furthermore, Brennan quotes a New York State Department of Mental Health Study, according to which the arrest rate of former mental patients is about one fourth that of the general population. The composition of the patient population that Brennan examined was not specified, but it is likely that the patients who worked outside the hospital were carefully selected; moreover, some of them may have been under medication. Nevertheless, the findings suggest that no *a priori* assumption can be made about the relationship between hospitalization and aggressive behavior.

Treatment of Neurotic Aggression

Traditional Approaches

Psychoanalytic and nondirective therapies with adults do not usually employ special techniques of treatment with neurotic hostility. Whenever appropriate, the patient's hostility is either interpreted to him directly or reflected back to him by the therapist. In an analytic approach, negative transference would receive attention as a sign of displaced hostility; catharsis and abreaction would be considered special avenues for the discharge of hostility and anger; and various forms of aggressive acting out would be interpreted as discharge of repressed energies resulting from conflict over hostility. Hostile acting out may also be considered a form of communication, its content used by the therapist as a basis for interpretation (Ekstein, 1965). Abt (1965) suggests that acting out indicates an impaired ego, and one of the first steps in therapy would be to strengthen the ego. He states that this is achieved through interpretation that aims to bring the repressed fantasy into awareness, thereby connecting the fantasy to the behavior. In group therapy, the members of the group can be very useful in aiding the therapist in this process (Abt, 1965).

Traditionally, therapy with children has relied heavily on play activities, which have two important functions. Through play, children communicate their feelings, concerns, etc., to the therapist, and play also provides an opportunity for the expression and the release of various emotions, including hostility and anger. According to a cathartic hypothesis, the expression of hostility decreases further hostility. Nondirective therapists consider the expression of emotion, particularly when it takes place in a warm, accepting atmosphere, highly therapeutic (Axline, 1947; Haworth, 1964). Psychoanalysts consider catharsis helpful but insufficient, and emphasize the communicative aspect of play (Klein, 1932; Freud, 1946).

Several special techniques have been employed with children to aid them in expressing their feelings. One method that is regarded as especially useful when the expression of feelings is highly desirable is Levy's (1939) release therapy. Levy did not use interpretation, reflection, or clarification of emotions but relied on the therapeutic value of expression itself. Bender and Woltman (1936) employed another method to aid the expression of feelings. They used puppet shows in which children observed active, uninhibited behavior by various puppets. The children would get involved in the show by shouting advice to the puppets, thereby expressing their emotions relatively directly. The opportunity to observe other children and to note that they had similar feelings of hostility was also considered therapeutic.

Although clinical reports strongly suggest that the expression of hostility in a permissive atmosphere has beneficial effects, this claim still has to be carefully evaluated. Levitt (1957) reports, for example, no differential improvement of children in play therapy groups and no-treatment control groups. Seeman et al. (1964), in contrast, reported a significant reduction in teachers' ratings of aggressive behavior of children treated by play therapy in comparison to matched no-treatment controls. The decrease in ratings of aggressive behavior was presumably because of nondirective treatment in play therapy, but the specific effect of expression of hostility, independent of other factors, was not evaluated. Nevertheless, the authors make the point that permissiveness, instead of control, led to the reduction of aggression. In a more direct attempt to evaluate the effects of aggression on subsequent behavior (Kidd & Walton, 1966), 10- to 12-year-old participants in group therapy, who were originally diagnosed as aggressive, were encouraged to throw darts at photographs of individuals toward whom they expressed verbal hostility. Four half-hour dart-throwing sessions decreased overt aggression toward nonfamily members, but not toward family members, even though photographs of family members were most frequently used. No changes were reported in a control group, whose members participated in group therapy but did not throw darts.

A large body of experimental research has bearing on the issue of the therapeutic value of the expression of hostile feelings. The evidence that various opportunities for catharsis decrease subsequent aggressive behavior, or subsequent hostile fantasies, is equivocal. Buss (1961) and Bandura and Walters (1963b) made the generalization that expression of aggression reduces further aggressive behavior if subjects are angry and increases it if they are not angry. There is some research, however, that casts doubt on even this discriminative statement of the cathartic hypothesis. Some of this research showed that blood pressure of frustrated *S*s decreases subsequent to aggressive actions against the frustrator, but not if aggression is expressed against substitute targets (Hokanson et al., 1963). However, only physical and verbal expression of aggression reduced blood pressure, and fantasy aggression did not. In another study, moreover, *S*s who were not permitted to respond with aggression to a frustrator showed significantly more decrease in physiological arousal than *S*s who were permitted to respond with aggression (Holmes, 1966). The latter finding may support Berkowitz's conclusion that expectancy that an opportunity will arise to express aggression may influence aggressive behavior. Perhaps, when people do not expect that they will have an opportunity to express hostility or to respond with aggression to an insult, threat, or other form of instigation, then tension, anger, or the desire to be aggressive do not arise. Moreover, tension itself may be created by the opportunity to be aggressive, perhaps by activating conflicts relating to aggression. In a study by Taylor (1967) self-rated undercontrollers who reacted to provocation with counteraggression, showed more tension, as measured by basal conductance, than self-rated overcontrollers who were less aggressive behaviorally. "This finding is contrary to the hypothesis that people who characteristically inhibit their aggression experience greater tension than those who readily express their aggressive impulses" (Taylor, 1967).

A number of factors may act together to determine the effects of expression of aggression—whether its form is behavioral, verbal TAT responses, or questionnaire responses—on subsequent aggressive behavior, on aggressive fantasies, or on hostile feelings. Some of these factors may be the expectancy that aggression will be possible (Berkowitz, 1964), personality characteristics of the would-be aggressor (Fishman, 1965; Taylor, 1967), and the characteristics of the frustrator (Kaufmann & Marcus, 1965). Even though the above-mentioned research has generally been conducted under conditions far different from the usual interaction between patient and therapist, one must consider these findings to suggest that the beneficial effects of the expression of hostility in therapy cannot be taken for granted. Further clinical as well as experimental research is needed to determine the conditions under which the expression of hostility is beneficial, as well as the type of benefits that are likely to ensue.

One final note on the use of play therapy with children is in order. A novel view of the function of play in therapy, that shifts the emphasis from both the expressive and communicative value of play, has been proposed by White (1964). He suggests that play may provide children with an opportunity to develop mastery over their environment. In play, they may rehearse various situations, for example, the ones that instigate aggression, and may try out solutions for them. Whether this view is considered an extension of or an alternative to the traditional views of play discussed thus far, it is a view that suggests important applications. For example, in directed play, specific situations may be rehearsed and appropriate "solutions" or adaptive behaviors may be tried out.

Behavior Therapy

For behavior therapists the treatment of neurotic aggression means the decrease or elimination of anxiety that inhibits assertiveness—that is, inhibits the appropriate modes of the expression of anger and resentment—accompanied by training in adaptively assertive responses (Wolpe, 1958; Wolpe & Lazarus, 1966). Treatment techniques are selected to fit the patient, but desensitization and assertive training are the techniques most often used. In desensitization the stimuli that evoke anxiety for the patient are determined and then arranged in a hierarchy from least to most anxiety provoking. Patients are trained in relaxation and, while relaxed, scenes or images representing the anxiety-producing stimuli are presented to them verbally by the therapist. Relaxation and anxiety are viewed as incompatible responses, and relaxation is thus expected to reciprocally inhibit anxiety evoked by the stimuli presented to the patient (Wolpe, 1958; Wolpe & Lazarus, 1966).

Either following or accompanying desensitization, assertive training would be used to teach patients the expression of moderate forms of self-assertion, or to teach them to respond to hostility in an appropriate manner. Assertive training takes the form of role playing or rehearsal of specific interactions that patients are likely to encounter. The therapist may model assertive responses and may indicate to the patient how well he does in performing them, or the patient and the therapist may evolve together the behavior most appropriate to the patient and the situation. According to Wolpe, assertive training is important because assertive responses reciprocally inhibit anxiety (Wolpe, 1958). However, the primary importance of assertive training probably lies in teaching the patient the forms of behavior that successfully deal with the environment. In line with this goal, patients are often trained to act positively—to perform responses that express positive feelings toward others. Such responses may inhibit others' hostility and may result in various forms of reinforcement. Although behavior therapists use assertive training extensively, they have done little research on behavioral rehearsal and on role playing, which are the techniques used in assertive training. However, to some degree, the effectiveness of role playing in changing behavior or attitudes has been demonstrated (King & Janis, 1956; Goldstein, Heller, & Sechrest, 1966).

Another treatment technique employed by behavior therapists and relevant to the treatment of the problems that are involved in the management of hostility is "cognitive clarification" (Wolpe & Lazarus, 1966). The importance of cognitive clarification has usually been deemphasized in the literature on behavior therapy, perhaps because its aim can best be described as learning on a cognitive instead of on a behavioral level. Patients may be unaware of some of their assumptions about the appropriateness or inappropriateness of hostility, although these assumptions may manifest themselves in unadaptive behavior. Furthermore, patients may have norms, beliefs, and values that determine where, how, and when, if ever the expression of hostility is appropriate. Cognitive clarification aims at the verbalization of assumptions that the patient is unaware of; the therapist may actively call the patient's attention to previously unnoted consistencies in his behavior. Furthermore, the appropriateness of these newly verbalized assumptions, as well as of the patient's norms and beliefs that lead to unadaptive behavior, may be examined. In this process, information about societal norms, clarification of the consequences of action, and other means may be employed by the therapist. This description of cognitive clarification involves more than the one usually provided by behavior therapists; however, it seems to the present writers that the actual practice of cognitive clarification involves the processes described. The similarity to Ellis' (1962) rational therapy, and Kelly's (1955) emphasis on alternative constructs is obvious.

Through cognitive clarification the patient's norms about the appropriate nature of assertive behavior may be changed in conjunction with the elimination of anxiety and with training in assertive behavior; consequently, the possibility of conflicts between the newly learned behavior and the patient's feelings about behaving this way may be forestalled.

Assertive training employs modeling and reinforcement techniques to teach patients new forms of behavior. Principles of reinforcement (Bandura, 1961; Bandura & Walters, 1963a) have been frequently employed in behavior modification (Ullmann & Krasner, 1965). A few reports on their use with aggressive children are also available. O'Leary et al. (1967) reported the reduction of aggressive and destructive interactions between two siblings following the employment of a reinforcement schedule. Aggressive interactions were ignored, while cooperative interactions were reinforced by candy. Following the initial stages of treatment candy was replaced by token reinforcement which could be accumulated and exchanged for toys. Furthermore, O'Leary et al. added punishment to the techniques employed; assaultive or other undesirable behavior was followed by "time out," a period of brief isolation of the aggressor. The procedure sharply reduced the percentage of aggressive interactions, while it increased the percentage of cooperative interactions. In another study (Brown & Elliot, 1965), the aggressive behavior of nursery school children was reduced by a simple procedure; aggressive behavior was ignored, and alternative behavior was reinforced by attention.

The desired outcome of the behavior therapeutic treatment of neurotic aggression would be to enable the patient to engage in appropriately assertive behavior. If treatment is successful, hostility and anger which may have been previously elicited by stimuli, but inhibited by strong anxiety from coming to expression in overt behavior, will be replaced by appropriate assertive behavior that deals with the situation to the patient's satisfaction. The desired outcome of the treatment of overt aggressive behavior is the elimination of this behavior and its replacement with cooperative or other kinds of behavior that successfully deal with the environment and that result in desired reinforcements. In addition to the above examples (O'Leary et al., 1967, and Brown & Elliot, 1965) of the treatment of children's overt aggression, in the next section a variety of examples will be provided of the application of behavior modification principles to the decrease of aggressive-antisocial behavior.

Treatment of Aggressive-Antisocial Behavior

Treatment of overt aggressive behavior in young children may employ the techniques previously discussed: play therapy and its modifications, which emphasize expressions of emotions. Extreme forms of aggressive or destructive tendencies do not lend themselves, however, to conventional forms of treatment even at a relatively early age. With the development of aggressive-antisocial patterns of behavior, which may appear well before adolescence (Redl & Wineman, 1952), special difficulties for therapy arise. First, the rebellious, hostile, suspicious attitude of children, adolescents, and adults with an aggressive-antisocial behavior pattern makes it difficult to establish any relationship with them. Moreover, the norms of their culture are against participation in therapy. Nor do they perceive the need for help (Slack, 1960; Schwitzgebel, 1965). Secondly, the poor verbal ability, relatively poor fantasy, and predominantly motoric expressive style, which usually characterize individuals with this behavioral pattern, represent serious problems for therapy that focuses on verbal communication. Minuchin (1965) notes, in describing "multiproblem families" which produce delinquent children, that ". . . communication in such families involves an unusually large amount of disconnected monologue, meaning being most frequently expressed through paraverbal channels." Thirdly, aggressive-antisocial adolescents and adults often lack interest in socially acceptable vocational and, sometimes, recreational activities. Unless they develop socially acceptable goals, therapy is not likely to have lasting effects.

Several therapists have attempted to create some form of therapeutic milieu, group, or community. A small group of highly aggressive children, between the ages of 8 and 11 were treated in a residential treatment center, by Redl, Wineman, and their co-workers (1952). These children frequently reacted violently to small frustrations, destroyed property of their own and others, and abused and disobeyed the staff whenever possible. The authors suggest that the children were trying to defend themselves from interference by the staff and to eliminate interventions with their usual habits and with their styles of impulsiveness and of aggression. Treatment consisted of creating a total therapeutic environment. Children received good care, along with permissiveness and tolerance. However, certain essential rules and standards were firmly enforced. Furthermore, programs of activities were designed to develop interest in controlled behavior. Verbal therapy was deemphasized.

Treatment of adults, including psychopaths, in the framework of a therapeutic community was reported by Maxwell Jones (1953). The activities of patients in this community consisted of vocational training, social activities for which the patients themselves became increasingly responsible, and various forms of therapy, including group psychotherapy. Although the attitudes of the staff were intended to be positive, warm, and helpful, certain rules were enforced and the patients were carefully supervised.

Therapy through group participation was reported by Slavson (1943). His "activity groups" consisted of both dependent and aggressive children. Most of the children were probably much less maladjusted than the children treated by Redl and Wineman. These children, 8 to 13 years of age, participated in various activities like handicrafts, play, and trips. The leader of the group was friendly and completely permissive at the beginning, as well as impartial in his treatment of the children. However, he gave praise and recognition for all incidents of constructive behavior. The group moved from disorganization to organized orderly behavior that was initiated by the members. Members of the group imitated the leader in providing praise and recognition for others' behavior. In contrast to Redl et al., Slavson emphasized total permissiveness within these therapeutic groups.

Several elements may have contributed to patient improvement in these milieu or group treatments. The behavior of the staff members probably made it possible to perceive them as different from most people the patients had previously encountered; the negativism, the suspicion, and the hostility of the patients were probably reduced by the positive attitude of the staff. Under the guidance of the staff and through common participation in activities, group cohesiveness and positive group norms could develop. Positive behavior therefore, could be rewarded by the staff and, more importantly, by the members of the community or group. As group norms develop and members come to identity themselves with the group, adherence to group norms may itself become rewarding. In this process, new prosocial habits could be learned. Very importantly, occupational and social skills were learned that could provide alternatives to the previously dominant undesirable behaviors. Unfortunately, no information about the contributions of various components of treatment to the overall affect are available. Moreover, the costs of milieu therapy have been considered prohibitive. However, if careful evaluation of milieu treatments upholds the effectiveness suggested by the reports reviewed here, comparison of their costs with the costs of the detention of aggressive-antisocial individuals may make their use eminently reasonable on economic grounds alone.

Individual therapy has also been tried with delinquent boys. The Cambridge-Somerville Youth study aimed at the prevention of delinquency through treatment of potentially delinquent boys (Teuber & Powers, 1953). The boys were matched and divided into treatment and control groups. A large number of counselors were involved, and approaches to treatment varied. During a period of several years, boys in the treatment and control groups did not differ in the number of their arrests and court appearances. In contrast to this finding, and emphasizing the importance of control groups, was the counselors' belief that more than two thirds of the boys who were in treatment benefited from their association with the study, as well as the feeling by more than half of the boys themselves that they had benefited from participation. It is possible, of course, that the boys benefited in other ways than in the prevention of delinquent behavior, but no data are available to bear on this point.

Treatment with adult counterparts of these children is seldom successful. Looking at the severest cases, psychopaths, McCord and McCord (1964) begin their chapter on therapy with a quotation from the Doctor in *Macbeth*: "This disease is beyond my practice." Nevertheless, although most attempts with psychopaths have ended in failure, and although careful evaluation of treatment is almost uniformly lacking, some of the reports do sound optimistic. In most cases, it is not clear whether psychopaths were involved or not, but in all cases the patients were characterized by aggressive-antisocial behavioral tendencies. Group psychotherapy with emphasis on the development of identification was used by the Army, and the participants seemed to improve (Abrahams & McCorkle, 1947). Psychodrama was employed with a group of convicts, and was reported as a promising technique (Corsini, 1951). "Because the psychopath is seriously deficient in his ability to relate to other people, role playing might help in showing him the feelings of others" (McCord and McCord, 1964). Some success with hypnotherapy was also reported (Lindner, 1944). Rodgers (1947) suggests that hypnotherapy may break through the hostile suspicious barriers that ordinarily make relationships difficult. Schmideberg (1949) noted the difficulty in getting psychopaths to "endure kindness." Suspicious of all human beings and inexperienced at friendship, the psychopath rejects friendship. However, according to Schmideberg (1949), love, permissiveness, loyalty, and great patience seemed to ameliorate psychopathy. Drug therapy was also tried with psychopaths (McCord & McCord, 1964). Frequently temporary changes in mood or cooperativeness followed the administration of drugs, without lasting changes, however. It is not clear how therapy in some cases of reported success differed from the seemingly similar forms of therapy that were reported as unsuccessful. The answer may lie, at least partially, in the skill and the personality of the therapist as well as in the differences in evaluative criteria. Alternately, the secret of reported success may lie in the presence of factors that were not considered central components of the therapy. One of them may be the learning of vocational and social skills by patients that enable them to gain satisfaction in socially acceptable ways. If, however, this is an important factor, the origin of the motivation for this kind of learning, and the manner of the acquisition of interest in socially acceptable goals, or rewards, need to be explained. Perhaps pre-therapy interest in socially acceptable goals was a frequent precursor of improvement in successful cases; it seems to be generally true that our methods of therapy are more successful with patients who initially manifest less psychopathology.

Experimenter-Subject Psychotherapy

A novel approach to therapy with delinquents is represented by experimenter-subject psychotherapy (Slack, 1960), designed to establish a framework for therapy with "unreachable cases." Instead of being in therapy, the delinquent is paid as an employee for his help in research. Recent reports describe how contact with the potential employee is made at the usual hangouts of delinquent boys—the street corner, the poolhall (Schwitzgebel, 1965). Boys are offered a part-time job of talking into a tape recorder about anything they wish. By the use of various reinforcers (in addition to the salary) like bonus money for specific actions, the availability of food at the laboratory, etc., regular attendance was usually achieved. In one study (Schwitzgebel & Kolb, 1964) a "three-year follow up of the first 25 employees showed a significant reduction in the frequency and severity of crime when compared to a matched-pair control group." Members of the control group were never contacted, but were matched and followed up on the basis of correctional institutes' records.

This treatment approach relied on an employee-employer relationship (which is more acceptable to the delinquent), and on the discriminative use of reinforcement to overcome the difficulty of getting delinquents into therapy. The rewards, usually money or food, were appropriate for the occasion on which they were given. The treatment itself was not uniform, since the interviewer-counselors were volunteers who varied in background from social worker to priest. The content of the employee's talk was influenced at the beginning by small money bonuses or by praise. In general, however, the principle of self-determined growth was emphasized. Advice giving was avoided. Initial participation was motivated by money, but the comments by and the behavior of the boys indicated that, later, the experience itself became more important than the money. Clearly, this approach holds a great deal of promise, and is open for further innovations. One recent addition, for example, includes a communication system with portable units. Through this system, "employees" may be reached at any time, and they may contact the "laboratory" when they need support in overcoming the temptation of a delinquent act (Schwitzgebel, 1965).[4]

One application of operant conditioning to the treatment of institutionalized delinquent boys, which gained its inspiration from the experimenter-subject psychotherapy approach, was employed by one of the present authors (E. S.). Boys of 14 to 16 years of age, institutionalized at a children's center for moderately delinquent behavior, were seen in group therapy. These boys frequently displayed aggressive behavior and showed a tendency for explosions of anger. Activities related to the task of anger. Activities related to the task of the group—modification of behavior, feelings, and attitudes—were difficult to maintain. Behavior was often disorderly. However, on the introduction of a system of reinforcement, behavior in the group changed dramatically. Participants were told that they could "win" up to 75 cents in each session. Two preconditions for winning the money were stated: orderly behavior, and talking. Without them, the third requirement could not be fulfilled. The third determinant of winning money—the content of the talk that would be reinforced—group members had to figure out themselves. This arrangement made the differential reinforcement and the shaping of the content of discussions possible. The group leader had a pile of dimes in front of him, and rewarded task-related contributions to the discussion, such as participants' description of their own behavior and feelings, suggestions for change, comments about family, parents, and conditions of life at home and in the children's center. Behavior toward others in the group that was judged appropriate was also rewarded. Orderly participation was sometimes specifically rewarded by money bonuses at the end of a session. The most obvious change was increased orderliness, and continuous, intensive task-relevant participation in the discussion by most group members. Involvement, sometimes, reached the point where participants would continue to argue their point of view or to discuss a problem, even when their persistance resulted in periods of nonreinforcement.

On the one hand, the change in the group was probably simply the result of reinforcement for the new behavior. On the other hand, the money may also have provided participants with an excuse to talk about things that concerned them and to do what they would have liked to do anyway, but were inhibited from doing by the norms of their subculture. Talking about problems with an adult may mean you are a sissy! Getting money for just talking means you are getting the better of the situation.

Another application of a behavior-modification technique by the same author consisted of the use of assertive training (Wolpe & Lazarus, 1966) to decrease the tendency toward angry outbursts and verbal and physical aggressiveness by delinquent and neglected children. The rationale for treatment was that learning appropriately assertive behavior that deals with the challenge presented by the environment would decrease inappropriate aggressive behavior (for findings that support this rationale, see the final section of the chapter). Role playing and behavior rehearsal, the ingredients of assertive training, seemed especially suitable forms of therapy for these children, who could deal verbally with external events, but were not very good at the description of internal states. Assertive training seemed to

[4]Personal communication.

increase interest and involvement in therapy and to have beneficial effects on interaction with others. However, no systematic evaluation of behavior change is available.

The armamentarium of techniques for the treatment of hostility does not prove to be a collection of riches. Often treatment techniques are not specific to hostility, but are the same as the ones employed by the proponents of a therapeutic approach in the treatment of most, if not all, problems. Evaluation of the efficacy of most treatment procedures, especially of their usefulness in treating problems related to aggression, has been rare. Nevertheless, a few of the reports that were discussed were promising and provide building blocks for further progress.

As a conclusion to the review of various methods of therapy, a special problem that faces the therapist, that of the management of the patient's hostility within the therapeutic interaction, should be explored. According to Fromm-Reichman (1950), the therapist has to face not only the hostility the patient brings to therapy, but also the hostility that results from the patient's frustration as the therapist fights his resistances. Theoretically, especially in nondirective and psychoanalytically oriented therapy, free expression of hostility is important. There is evidence, however, that therapists with certain personlity characteristics—themselves having difficulty with expression of hostility—tend to inhibit patients' expression of hostility (Bandura et al., 1960). Furthermore, more experienced therapists encourage less patients' expressions of hostility toward themselves than less experienced therapists (Varble, 1964). Thereby, they decrease hostile verbalizations of patients. The experienced therapist's behavior may be defensive; alternatively it may be the result of his experience that negative cosequences ensue on free expression of hostility by the patient. Patients' expression of hostility toward the therapist may result in a decrease in the amount of status the patient attributes to the therapist, and thereby in a decrease in the therapist's influence over the patient. Moreover, expressing hostility may create too much anxiety or guilt in the patient. These speculations indicate that without relating "process" variables to "outcome" variables, the meaning of the former remains unclear.

SUGGESTIONS FOR A NEW APPROACH TO DIAGNOSIS AND TREATMENT

In the preceding discussion, two types of problems related to the management of hostility were described, and the treatments applicable to them were discussed. Although neurotic aggression and aggressive-antisocial tendencies were treated as unitary entities, they represent syndromes, or groups of symptoms, that frequently cooccur. In the following, it will be proposed that (a) diagnosis, following the identification of aggression as a problem area, should aim at the specification of all forms of manifestations of aggression (behavioral, emotional, and cognitive) as well as at the specification of inhibitors of aggression, such as anxiety, guilt, or fear of punishment. (b) As part of diagnosis all the currently operating influences in the patient's life that are likely to lead to manifestations of aggression should be specified, and (c) for treatment, specific techniques should be developed and employed to suit the specific manifestations and inhibitors of aggression as well as the determining conditions that operate in the patient's life. These goals may be considered ideals that can be fulfilled only in part at the present. The usefulness of the proposed approach is suggested by the apparent success of behavior modification (Paul, 1965; Ullmann & Krasner, 1965; Wolpe & Lazarus, 1966) since, like behavior modification, it aims at specificity in diagnosis and treatment, and at the application of learning principles to treatment. The present approach intends to suggest, in addition, that modification of cognitions and affects may be important, both as avenues of behavior change, and in providing for the consistency of change at different levels of responding.

First, diagnosis should aim at the specification of forms of expression of aggression. Some of them may be as follows: physical and verbal aggressiveness or assaultiveness, lack of appropriate assertive behavior, fantasy aggression, hostile attitudes, negative evaluation of others and a tendency to perceive others as hostile, and strong anxiety or guilt associated with aggression. Even when these forms of expression can be assessed, it is usually difficult to determine when any of these response tendencies at either the behavioral, imaginal, or affective level represent a problem. In diagnosing them as a problem, criteria such as frequency, intensity, appropriateness, and function, their deviation from the norms of the patient's own subculture, as well as their effects on other people may be useful to consider.

In addition to different forms of expression, currently operating determinants of aggression should be identified as part of diagnosis. Determinants of aggression are still conjectural, but a variety of determinants have been suggested, and some of them have been experimentally investigated. If aggression is considered instinctual (Freud, 1925; Lorenz, 1966), the only avenue for treatment left is the identification and the creation of conditions that are least likely to allow the expression of this instinct in an antisocial form. Other sources or determinants of aggression that have been proposed are frustration (Dollard et al., 1939), defined as interference with goal-directed activity, threats of attack or threats to the satisfaction of basic needs (Maslow, 1941), and threats to status or self-esteem (Worchel, 1961). Instrumental aggression may result from reinforcement of aggressive behavior (Buss, 1961; Bandura & Walters, 1963a and b). The norms of a subculture or of the group a person associates or identifies with (Miller et al., 1961) may determine whether different kinds of aggression are encouraged or discouraged; accordingly, these norms may be added to the list of potential determinants of aggression. Which manifestation of aggression, if any, these influences lead to, depends both on the presence or absence of inhibitors of aggression, such as anxiety or guilt, and on other personality characteristics (Fishman, 1965; Conn & Crowne, 1964; Taylor, 1967; Funkenstein, 1955). For example, the lack of impulse control or of the ability to delay one's response to environmental stimuli may increase the incidence of aggression. During delay, anger may dissipate. Moreover, Funkenstein (1955) found that some people tended to respond with anger, others with fear, to being verbally ridiculed. These differences may well be the result of past learning, specifically, of differences in childhood experience. Personality characteristics may be specifiable that predict such differential reactions to instigation; the need for approval (Conn & Crowne, 1964) may be one such predictor.

Following diagnosis, treatment should employ specific techniques appropriate to the problem. This is to add to general features of therapy, such as a positive relationship between the patient and the therapist, that were found to improve the outcome of treatment (Goldstein et al., 1966). An available example of a specific technique is desensitization (Wolpe, 1958; Wolpe & Lazarus, 1966), although further research is needed on the generality of its applicability. Other specific techniques for dealing with various manifestations of aggression may be developed on the basis of both past clinical experience and the findings of experimental research. For the latter, the impressive collection of research by Goldstein et al. (1966), which provided them with empirical foundations to propose methods that may increase therapists' influence over patients, may serve as an example.

The specific treatments used should aim at maximizing learning in the behavioral, cognitive, affective, and imaginal realms. This learning may be aimed at the elimination of the manifestations of problems with aggression, or at enabling patients to deal with the determinants of aggression, or at enabling patients to modify relevant environmental conditions, and so on. As a clarification of the suggested approach, and to provide some concrete illustrations, a few examples of treatment as a function of diagnosis will be discussed. Treatment may usually be expected to combine a number of specific techniques, as their appropriateness is indicated by the diagnosis.

1. *Hostile attitudes, negative evaluation of others, and a tendency to perceive others as hostile.* These manifestations of hostility may be grouped together because they all occur in the cognitive-perceptual domain, and are likely to appear together (Buss, 1961). Murstein found (1961a, b 1966) that people who were judged hostile by others, evaluated others' hostility less accurately than people who were judged friendly by others. The motives of people in general, and specifically of people close to the patient, may be discussed, and the patient's attention may be called to aspects of their behavior that he usually does not notice. Moreover, the patient may be encouraged to actively

test, in life situations, the motives of other people in following up and in extending the reevaluation attempted in therapy.

The therapist may concurrently attempt to evaluate the patients' habitual behavior; role playing may be one avenue. People who perceive others as hostile, or expect others to be hostile, may engage in self-fulfilling prophecy; their actions may invite hostility. The evidence that expectancies influence behavior is impressive (Rosenthal, 1966). If in the therapist's judgement the patient invites hostility by his actions, role playing may be used to point this out to the patient, and to teach him alternative modes of action. Finally, the perception of others as hostile may indicate a fear of hostility; learning appropriate responses to others' hostility may decrease perceived threat. Kaufman and Feshbach (1963), for example, found that a communication that suggested constructive, rational approaches for dealing with the instigation of aggression resulted in less aggression by the subject during a discussion which followed the instigation of aggression by the experimenter than any one of several other experimental treatments.

2. *Fantasy aggression*. Frequent and disturbing aggression in fantasy may be treated through the introduction of nonaggressive themes into the imagination. Images of events, of behavior sequences, and so on, that are neutral or incompatible with aggression may be introduced into the flow of images. For example, the image "two boys wrestle playfully, get angry, and start fighting" may be replaced by "two boys wrestle playfully, then exhausted, they go together to the drugstore and drink cokes." Initially, patients may be asked to imagine these scenes and others as the therapist describes them; later they may construct their own images. When fantasy aggression is instrumental, nonaggressive images that lead to the achievement of the same goal may be introduced. Procedures that McClelland (1965) employed to develop achievement imagery, and the direct reinforcement of verbalization of nonhostile imagery, may both be helpful in eliminating aggressive or violent images. The decrease in frequency and the reduction of intensity of fantasy aggression may reduce feelings of anxiety and guilt. Moreover, this decrease may reduce the probability of overt aggression. There is some indication that good imagination, the tendency to fantasize, is associated with more aggressive behavior following instigation for aggression than poor imagination. Good imagination may lead to the rehearsal of hostile images which may maintain anger or serve as cues for aggressive acts. Training in nonhostile imagery, therefore, may reduce the probability of aggression.

3. *Lack of association between aggression and anxiety*. The best opportunity for the belated socialization of individuals may be provided by a milieu or a group. However, specific techniques may also be employed for the conditioning of anxiety to aggression. One technique, aversive conditioning, employs the pairing of electric shocks or other unpleasant physical stimuli with the undesirable responses, which may be performed or simply imagined (Wolpe & Lazarus, 1966). A variant of this procedure employs images as aversive stimuli (Cautela, 1966). Through association with images that produce discomfort, the imagined or performed undesirable behavior comes to evoke discomfort also. With problems of obesity and alcoholism, Cautela used images that produced nausea. One of the authors (E.S.) used an extension of this procedure with a 14-year-old boy to decrease his inclination for stealing cars. He was to imagine himself stealing a car; the circumstances were realistically described. As he got into the car and was about to start it, the owner ran up to the car, pulled him out and beat him up, or a policeman grabbed him, and he was taken to the station; or, the car blew up and injured him and, as he got out of the car bleeding, the police got him for trying to steal a car. The realistic description of these events seemed to result in the experience of strong discomfort by the patient. The procedure was repeated with different makes of cars to ensure maximum generalization. During five months following the application of this procedure, the patient was not caught stealing a car, nor did he report the stealing of a car to the therapist, although he did report other illegal acts. Although clinical experience suggests the usefulness of aversive imagery in aversive conditioning (Cautela, 1966; Kolvin, 1967), no experimental demonstration of its efficacy is available.

Aversive conditioning and covert sensitization (Cautela, 1966), the procedure that uses images to create discomfort, may both be ineffective with patients who have extremely diminished capacity for anxiety. Psychopaths, for example, have been reported generally poor in affective capacity (Cleckley, 1950), even to the extent that they have difficulties in learning to avoid a painful stimulus (Lykken, 1957). Schachter and Latane (1964) found, nevertheless, that even chronically unemotional criminals showed signs of sympathetic hyperactivity. The two-factor theory of Schachter and Singer (1962) states that emotion is a function of both physiological arousal and the interpretation of arousal. By using this theory as a starting point, Valins (1967) suggests that "sociopaths may be unemotional because they ignore or do not utilize as cues whatever internal reactions they do experience," that is, because they do not interpret their arousal. If Valins' hypothesis is supported by further research, the problem (or, at least, one problem) becomes how to teach sociopaths to pay attention to and to interpret their arousal. Psychodrama may be employed, with emphasis on cues that indicate other people's emotions, and on the emotions that patients *should* experience under varied conditions. Training the patient to experience anxiety in association with aggressive behavior may be included.

4. *Low frustration tolerance, little impulse control.* Learning to delay responses to frustrating stimuli would be likely to decrease the probability of aggressive behavior. Holmes (1966) found, for example, that the elimination of aggressive cues from the environment resulted in a decrease of the physiological arousal of insulted subjects to the level of noninsulted ones, even though the former had no opportunity to express hostility. The findings suggest that delay of responding, the removal of instigating cues, and forgetting, may decrease anger and the probability of aggressive behavior. Delay may result from activities interpolated between stimulus and response. Some of these activities may be verbal self-instruction, fantasy activity, or motoric actions. Training to increase delay by fantasy activities that are interpolated between stimulus and action may follow the lines discussed above, under fantasy aggression. Training may also include self-instructions following stimuli—such as, "I'd better wait before I do anything; I should wait a moment until I am less angry before I act," etc. Finally, learning to respond to aggressive behavior with motoric action that is incompatible with aggressive behavior will result in delay of aggressive responses and, therefore, may decrease the probability of aggression.

5. *Frequent experience of frustrations, threats, and insults.* Frustrations may be the result of inappropriate goals; threats may be perceived that are not real. Here, however, the question of specific treatment techniques will be examined when the goals of the patient seem appropriate, and the threats and insults he suffers seem real. Aggression resulting from frustrations and threats may be decreased or may be eliminated by increasing the patient's skill or mastery in dealing with them. In a study by Rothaus and Worchel (1964) the most effective means of the reduction of hostility of subjects who were insulted and mistreated by the experimenter was an "instrumental communication," a complaint by a confederate-subject in the group, that changed the subsequent behavior of the experimenter. Control over the environment by nonaggressive means may be expected to reduce aggression. Depending on the area of activity where control is lacking, behavior that increases controlling capacity may be learned in assertive training, through training in occupational skills, or in other ways.

The procedures that were suggested as a function of either manifestations or determinants of aggression may be more or less appropriate, depending on the presence or absence of other manifestations or determinants of aggression. For example, strong submissiveness, dependency, or need for approval (Conn & Crowne, 1964), may decrease a patient's capacity to learn controlling behaviors. It is necessary to deal with a combination of factors the form of the problem, the characteristics of the individual and his life conditions. Nevertheless, specificity in diagnosis, in setting the goals for therapy, and in the application of treatment techniques are thought, by the present authors, to increase efficacy of treatment.

REFERENCES

Abt, L. E. Acting out in group psychotherapy. In L. E. Abt, & S. L. Weissman (Eds.), *Acting out: Theoretical and clinical aspects*. New York: Grune & Stratton, 1965.

Abt, L. E., & Weissman, S. L. (Eds.) *Acting out: Theoretical and clinical aspects*. New York: Grune & Stratton, 1965.

Abrahams, J., & McCorkle, L. Group psychotherapy at an army rehabilitation center. *Dis. nev. Syst*. 1947, **8**, 50–62.

Allport, G. W. The trends in motivational theory. *Amer. J. Ortho*. 1953, **23**, 108—119.

Arnold, M. B. *Story sequence analysis*. New York: Columbia University Press, 1962.

Axline, V. M. *Play therapy: The inner dynamics of childhood*. Cambridge, Mass.: Houghton Mifflin, 1947.

Balken, E. R., & Vander Veer, A. Clinical applications of the Thematic Apperception Test to neurotic children. *Amer. J. Ortho*., 1944, **14**, 421–440.

Bandura, A. Psychotherapy as a learning process. *Psychol. Bull*., 1961, **58**, 143–159.

Bandura, A., Lipsher, D. H., & Miller, P. E. Psychotherapists' approach-avoidance reactions to patients' expressions of hostility. *J. consult. Psychol*., 1960, **24**, 1–8.

Bandura, A., Ross, D., & Ross, S. A. Imitation of film-mediated aggressive models.*J. abnorm. soc. Psychol*., 1963, **66**, 3–11.

Bandura, A., & Walters, R. R. *Adolescent aggression: A study of the influence of child training practices and family interrelationships*. New York: Ronald Press, 1959.

Bandura, A., & Walters, R. H. *Social learning and personality development*, New York: Holt, Rinehart and Winston, 1963. (a)

Bandura, A., & Walters, R. H. Aggression. In Stevenson (Ed.), *Child psychology: The sixty-second yearbook of the National Society for the Study of Education. Part I*. Chicago: N.S.S.E., 1963. (b)

Bass, B. M., & Berg, I. A. (Eds.) *Objective approaches to personality assessment*. Princeton: Van Nostrand, 1959.

Bellak, L. The thematic apperception: Failures and the defenses. *Transactions of the New York Academy of Sciences*, 1950 (Series II), **12**, 122–126.

Bellak, L. The concept of acting out: Theoretical considerations. In L. E. Abt, & S. L. Weissman (Eds.), *Acting out: Theoretical and clinical aspects*. New York: Grune & Stratton, 1965.

Bender, L., & Woltman, A. G. The use of puppet shows as a psychotherapeutic method for behavior problems in children. *Amer. J. Ortho*., 1936, **6**, 341–354.

Berkowitz, L. *Aggression: A social psychological analysis*. New York: McGraw-Hill, 1962.

Berkowitz, L. Aggressive cues in aggressive behavior and hostility catharsis. *Psychol. Rev*., 1964, **71**, 104–122.

Blatt, S. The Wechsler scales and acting out. In L. E. Abt, & S. L. Weissman (Eds.), *Acting out: Theoretical and clinical aspects*. New York: Grune & Stratton, 1965.

Brayer, R., & Craig, G. The difficulty value of TAT cards. Paper presented at the Eastern Psychological Association meeting, 1960.

Brennan, J. J. Mentally ill aggressiveness: Popular delusion or reality. *Amer. J. Psychiat*., 1964, **120**, 1181–1184.

Brown, P., & Elliot, R. Control of aggression in a nursery school class. *J. exp. child Psychol*., 1965, **2**, 103–107.

Buros, O. K. *Fifth mental measurement yearbook*. Highland Park, N. J.: Gryphon Press, 1959.

Buss, A. H. *The psychology of aggression*. New York: Wiley, 1961.

Cautela, J. R. Treatment of compulsive behavior by covert sensitization. *Psychol. Rec*., 1966, **16**, 33–42.

Chwert, J. Delinquency and criminology: An acting out phenomenon. In L. E. Abt, & S. L. Weissman (Eds.), *Acting out: Theoretical and clinical aspects*. New York: Grune & Stratton, 1965.

Cleckley, H. *The mask of sanity*. (2nd ed.) St. Louis: C. V. Mosby, 1950.

Conn, L. K., & Crowne, D. P. Instigation to aggression, emotional arousal, and defensive emulation. *J. pers.*, 1964, **32**, 163–179.
Cook, W. W., & Medley, D. M. Proposed hostility and pharasaic-virtue scales for the MMPI. *J. appl. Psychol.*, 1954, **38**, 414–418.
Corsini, R. The method of psychodrama in prison. *Group Psychotherapy*, 1951, **3**, 321–326.
Dahlstrom, W. G., & Welsh, G. S. *An MMPI handbook: A guide to use in clinical practice and research*. Minneapolis: University of Minnesota Press, 1960.
Davids, A., & Pildner, H. Comparison of direct and projective methods of personality assessment under different conditions of motivation. *Psychol. Monogr.*, 1959, **72**, No. 464.
Dill, R. Effects of conflict over hostility and a preceding hostile picture on thematic responses to an ambiguous picture. Unpublished senior honors thesis, University of Massachusetts, 1961.
Dinwiddie, J. W. An application of the principle of response generalization to the prediction of aggressive responses. Unpublished doctoral dissertation, Catholic Univer. Of America, 1954.
Dollard, J., Doob, L. W., Miller, N. E., Mowrer, O. H., & Sears, R. R. *Frustration and aggression*. New Haven: Yale University Press, 1939.
Ekstein, R. General treatment philosophy of acting out. In L. E. Abt, & S. L. Weissman (Eds.), *Acting out: Theoretical and clinical aspects*. New York: Grune & Stratton, 1965.
Ellis, A., & Conrad, H. S. The vaidity of personality inventories in military practice. *Psychol. Bull.*, 1948, **45**, 385–426.
Ellis, A. *Reason and emotion in psychotherapy*. New York: Lyle Stuart, 1962.
Epstein, S. Food-related responses to ambiguous stimuli as a function of hunger and ego strength. *J. consult. Psychol.*, 1961, **25**, 463–469.
Epstein, S. The measurement of drive and conflict in humans: Theory and experiment. In *Nebraska Symposium on Motivation*. Lincoln, Nebraska: University of Nebraska Press, 1962, 127–206.
Feldman, M. J., & Siegel, S. M. The effect on self description of combining anxiety and hostility items on a single scale. *J. Clin. Psychol.*, 1958, **14**, 74–77.
Fenichel, O. *The psychoanalytic theory of neurosis*. New York: Norton, 1945.
Feshbach, S. The influence of drive arousal and conflict upon fantasy behavior. In J. Kagan, & G. S. Lesser (Eds.), *Contemporary issues in thematic apperception methods*. Springfield, Ill.: C. C. Thomas, 1961.
Feshbach, S. The function of aggression and the regulation of aggressive drive. *Psychol. Rev.*, 1964, **71**, 257–272.
Filmore, B. G., & Klopfer, W. G. Levels of awareness in projective tests. *J. proj. Tech.*, 1962, **26**, 34–35.
Fishman, C. Need for approval and the expression of aggression under varying conditions of frustration. *J. pers. soc. Psychol.*, 1965, **2**, 809–815.
Freud, A. *The psychoanalytical treatment of children*. London: Imago Publishing Co., 1946.
Freud, S. *Collected papers*. London: Hogarth Press, 1925.
Fromm-Reichman, F. *Principles of intensive psychotherapy*. Chicago: University of Chicago Press, 1950.
Funkenstein, D. H. The physiology of fear and anger. *Scientific American*, 1955, **192**, 74–80.
Goldstein, A. P., Heller, K., & Sechrest, L. B. *Psychotherapy and the psychology of behavior. change*. New York: Wiley, 1966.
Goldworth, S. A comparative study of the drawings of a man and a woman done by normal neurotic, schizophrenic, and brain-damaged individuals. Unpublished doctoral thesis, University of Pittsburgh, 1950.
Goodman, M., & Kotkov, B. Prediction of trait ranks from draw-a-person measures of obese and non-obese women. *J. clin. Psychol.*, 1953, **9**, 365–367.
Griffith, A. V., & Peyman, D. A. R. Eye-ear emphasis in DAP as indicating ideas of reference. *J. consult. Psychol.*, 1959, **23**, 560.

Guertin, W. H., Rabin, A. I., Frank, G. H., & Ladd, C. E. Research with the Wechsler intelligence scales for adults: 1955–1960. *Psychol. Bull.*, 1962, **59**, 1–26.

Gutman, B. An investigation of the applicability of the human figure drawing in predicting improvement in therapy. Unpublished doctoral thesis, New York University, 1952.

Haas, K. Direction of hostility and psychiatric symptoms. *Psychol. Rep.*, 1965, **16**, 555–556.

Hammer, E. F., & Piotrowski, Z. A. Hostility as a factor in the clinician's personality as it affects his interpretation of projective drawings. *J. proj. Tech.*, 1953, **17**, 210–216.

Harrison, R. Thematic Apperception Methods. In B. B. Wolman (Ed.), *Handbook of clinical psychology*. New York: McGraw-Hill, 1965, pp. 562–620.

Harrison, R. The Thematic Apperception Test. In L. K. Frank, et al., Personality development in adolescent girls. *Monographs of the Society for Research in Child Development*, 1953, **16**, 60–88, (Ser. No. 53).

Haskin, P. R. A study of the relationship between realistic and unrealistic aggression, reliance on categorical attitudes, and constructiveness of adjustment. Unpublished doctoral dissertation, Western Reserve University, 1958.

Hathaway, S. R. Personality inventories. In B. B. Wolman (Ed.), *Handbook of clinical psychology*. New York: McGraw-Hill, 1965.

Haworth, M. R. (Ed.) *Child psychotherapy: Practice and theory.* New York: Basic Books, 1964.

Henry, W. E. *The analysis of fantasy: The thematic apperception technique in the study of personality.* New York: Wiley, 1956.

Hiler, E. W., & Nesvig, D. An evaluation of criteria used by clinicians to infer pathology from figure drawings. *J. consult. Psychol.*, 1965, **29**, 520–529.

Hinsie, L. E., & Campbell, R. J. *Psychiatric dictionary.* (3rd ed.) New York: Oxford University Press, 1960.

Hokanson, J. E., Burgess, M., & Cohen, M. F. Effect of displaced aggression on systolic blood pressure. *J. abnorm. soc. Psychol.*, 1963, **67**, 214–218.

Hokanson, J. E., & Gordon, J. E. The expression and inhibition of hostility in imaginative and overt behavior. *J. abnorm. soc. Psychol.*, 1958, **57**, 327–333.

Holmes, D. S. Effects of overt aggression on level of physiological arousal. *J. pers. soc. Psychol.*, 1966, **4**, 189–194.

Holzberg, J. D., & Wexler, M. The validity of human form drawings as a measure of personality deviation. *J. proj. Tech.*, 1950, **14**, 343–361.

Horney, K. *The neurotic personality of our time.* New York: Norton, 1937.

Jensen, A. R. Aggression in fantasy and overt behavior. *Psychol. Monogr.*, 1957, **71**, No. 445.

Jones, M. *The therapeutic community: A new treatment method in psychiatry.* New York: Basic Books, 1953.

Kagan, J. The measurement of overt aggression from fantasy. *J. abnorm. soc. Psychol.*, 1956, **52**, 390–393.

Kagan, J. Stylistic variables in fantasy behavior: The ascription of affect states to social stimuli. In J. Kagan, & G. S. Lesser (Eds.), *Contemporary issues in thematic apperceptive methods*. Springfield, Ill.: C. C. Thomas, 1961.

Kagan, J. On the need for relativism. *Amer. Psychol.*, 1967, **22**, 131–142.

Kaufman, H. Definitions and methodology in the study of aggression. *Psychol. Bull.*, 1965, **64**, 351–364.

Kaufman, H., & Feshbach, S. Displaced aggression and its modification through exposure to antiaggressive communications. *J. abnorm. soc. Psychol.*, 1963, **67**, 79–83.

Kaufmann, H., & Marcus, A. M. Aggression as a function of similarity between aggressor and victim. *Percept. Mot. Skills*, 1965, **20**, 1013–1020.

Kelley, G. A. *The psychology of personal constructs*. New York: Norton, 1955.

Kenny, D. T. A theoretical and research appraisal of stimulus factors in the TAT. In J. Kagan, & G. S. Lesser (Eds.). *Contemporary issues in thematic apperceptive methods.* Springfield, Ill.: C. C. Thomas, 1961.

Kidd, A. H., & Walton, N. Dart throwing as a method of reducing extra-punitive aggression. *Psychol. Rep.* 1966, **19**, 88–90.

King, B. T., & Janis, I. L. Comparison of the effectiveness of improvised versus non-improvised role-playing in producing opinion changes. *Human Relations*, 1956, **9**, 177–186.

Klein, M. *The psychoanalysis of children.* London: Hogarth Press, 1932.

Kolvin, I. "Aversive imagery" treatment in adolescents. *Behav. Ther. Res.*, 1967, **5**, 245–249.

Lazarus, R. S., Yousem, J., & Arenberg, D. Hunger and perception. *J. Pers.*, 1953, **21**, 312–328.

Lesser, G. S. The relationship between overt and fantasy aggression as a function of material response to aggression. *J. abnorm. soc. Psychol.*, 1957, **55**, 218–221.

Levitt, E. E. The results of psychotherapy with children. *J. consult. Psychol.*, 1957, **21**, 189–196.

Levy, B. I., Lomax, J. V., Jr., & Minsky, R. An underlying variable in the clinical evaluation of drawings of human figures. *J. consult. Psychol.*, 1963, **27**, 508–512.

Levy, D. M. Release therapy. *Amer. J. Ortho.*, 1939, **9**, 713–736.

Lewinsohn, R. M. Psychological correlates of over-all quality of figure drawings. *J. consult. Psychol.*, 1965, **29**, 504–512.

Lindner, R. *Rebel without a cause—The hypnoanalysis of a criminal psychopath.* New York: Grune & Stratton, 1944.

Lorenz, K. *On aggression.* New York: Harcourt, Brace, & World, 1966, (Originally published in German edition, Vienna: G. Borotha-Schoeler Verlag, 1963).

Lykken, D. T. A study of anxiety in the sociopathic personality. *J. abnorm. soc. Psychol.*, 1957, **55**, 6–10.

Machover, K. *Personality projection in the drawing of the human figure.* Springfield, Ill.: C. C. Thomas, 1949.

Maslow, A. H. Deprivation, threat, and frustration. *Psychol. Rev.*, 1941, **48**, 364–366.

McClelland, D. C. Towards a theory of motive acquisition. *Amer. Psychol.*, 1965, **20**, 321–333.

McClelland, D. C., & Atkinson, J. W. The projective expression of needs. I. The effect of different intensities of hunger drive on perception. *J. Psychol.*, 1948, **25**, 205–222.

McCord, W., & McCord, J. *Psychotherapy and delinquency.* New York: Grune & Stratton, 1956.

McCord, W., & McCord, J. *The psychopath: An essay on the criminal mind.* Princeton: Van Nostrand, 1964.

McCord, W., & McCord, J., & Zola, I. *Origins of crime.* New York: Columbia University Press, 1959.

McDowell, J. V. Developmental aspects of fantasy production on the Thematic Apperception Test. Unpublished doctoral dissertation, Ohio State University, 1952.

McGee, S. Measurement of hostility: A pilot study. *J. clin. Psychol.*, 1954, **10**, 280–282.

McGreevey, J. C. Interlevel disparity and predictive efficiency. *J. proj. Tech.*, 1962, **26**, 80–87.

McNeil, E. B. Aggression in fantasy and behavior. *J. consult. Psychol.* 1962, **26**, 232–240.

Megargee, E. I. Undercontrol and overcontrol in assaultive and homicidal adolescents. Unpublished doctoral dissertation, University of California, 1964.

Megargee, E. I. Assault with intent to kill. *Transaction*, 1966, **2**, 27–31.

Megargee, E. I., Cook, P. E., & Mendelsohn, G. A. Development and validation of an MMPI scale of assaultiveness in overcontrolled individuals. *J. abnorm. Psychol.*, 1967, **72**, 519–528.

Megargee, E. I., & Mendelsohn, G. A. A cross-validation of twelve MMPI indices of hostility and control. *J. abnorm. soc. Psychol.*, 1962, **65**, 431–438.

Miller, W. B., Geretz, H., & Culter, H. S. Aggression in a boys' street corner group. *Psychiatry*, 1961, **24**, 283–298.

Minuchin, S. Conflict-resolution family therapy. Paper presented at the American Psychiatric Association Regional Research Conference, Galveston, Texas, 1965.

Moldowsky, P. A study of personality variables in patients with skin disorders. Unpublished doctoral dissertation, State University of Iowa, 1953.

Moreno, J. L. *Psychodrama, Part I.* New York: Beacon House, 1946.

Moustakas, C. E., & Schlalock, H. D. An analysis of therapist-child interaction in play therapy. *Child Development*, 1955, **26**, 143–157.

Murray, E. J. Conflict and repression during sleep deprivation. *J. abnorm. soc. Psychol.*, 1959, **59**, 95–101.

Murray, H. A. *Thematic Apperception Test manual.* Cambridge, Mass.: Harvard University Press, 1943.

Murstein, B. I. Nonprojective determinants of perception on the TAT. *J. consult. Psychol.*, 1958, **22**, 195–198. (a)

Murstein, B. I. The relationship of stimulus ambiguity on the TAT to the production of themes. *J. consult. Psychol.*, 1958, **22**, 348. (b)

Murstein, B. I. The effect of amount of possession of the trait of hostility on accuracy of perception of hostility in others. *J. abnorm. soc. Psychol.*, 1961, **62**, 216–220. (a)

Murstein, B. I. The role of the stimulus in the manifestation of fantasy. In J. Kagan, & G. S. Lesser (Eds.), *Contemporary issues in thematic apperceptive methods*. Springfield, Ill.: C. C. Thomas, 1961. (b)

Murstein, B. I. *Theory and research in projective techniques*. New York: Wiley, 1963.

Murstein, B. I. New thoughts about ambiguity and the TAT. *J. proj. Tech.*, 1965, **29**, 219–225.

Murstein, B. I. Possession of hostility and accuracy of perception of it in others: A cross-sex replication. *J. proj. Tech.*, 1966, **30**, 46–50.

Mussen, P. H., & Naylor, H. K. The relationship between overt and fantasy aggression. *J. abnorm. soc. Psychol.*, 1954, **49**, 235–240.

O'Leary, D. K., O'Leary, S., & Becker, W. L. Modification of deviant sibling interaction patterns in the home. *Behav. Res. Ther.*, 1967, **5**, 113–121.

Paul, G. *Insight versus desensitization in psychotherapy*. Stanford, Calif.: Stanford University Press, 1965.

Pittluck, P. The relation between aggressive fantasy and overt behavior. Unpublished doctoral dissertation, Yale University, 1950.

Purcell, K. The TAT and antisocial behavior. *J. consult. Psychol.,* 1956, **20**, 449–456.

Redl, F., & Wineman, D. *Children who hate*. Glencoe, Ill.: Free Press, 1951.

Redl, F., & Wineman, D. *Controls from within: Techniques for the treatment of the aggressive child.* Glencoe, Ill.: Free Press, 1952.

Ricks, D., Umbarger, C., & Mack, R. A measure of increased temporal perspective in successfully treated adolescent delinquent boys. *J. abnorm. soc. Psychol.*, 1964, **69**, 685–689.

Rodgers, T. Hypnotherapy and character neuroses. *J. clin. Psychopath.*, 1947, **8**, 519–524.

Rosenthal, R. *Experimenter effects in behavioral research*. New York: Appleton-Century-Crofts, 1966.

Rothaus, P., & Worchel, P. Ego-support, communication, catharsis, and hostility. *J. pers.*, 1964, **32**, 296–312.

Salter, A. The theory and practice of conditioned reflex therapy. In J. Wolpe, A. Salter, & L. J. Reyna (Eds.), *The conditioning therapies: The challenge in psychotherapies*. New York: Holt, Rinehart, & Winston, 1965.

Saltz, G., & Epstein, S. Thematic hostility and guilt responses as related to self-reported hostility, guilt, and conflict. *J. abnorm. soc. Psychol.*, 1963, **67**, 460–479.

Sanford, R. N. Thematic Apperception Test. In R. N. Sanford et al., Physique, personality and scholarship. *Monographs of the Society for Research in Child Development*, 1943, **8**, No. 1 (Ser. No. 34).

Sarason, S. B., Davidson, K. S., Lighthall, F. F., Waite, R. R., & Ruebush, B. K. *Anxiety in elementary school children*. New York: Wiley, 1960.

Schachter, S., & Latane, B. Crime, cognition, and the nervous system. In D. Levine (Ed.), *Nebraska Symposium on Motivation*. Lincoln, Nebraska: University of Nebraska Press, 1964.

Schachter, S. & Singer, J. E. Cognitive, social, and physiological determinants of emotional state. *Psychol. Rev.*, 1962, **69**, 379–399.

Schaefer, J., & Norman, M. Punishment and aggression in fantasy responses of boys with antisocial character traits. *J. pers. soc. Psychol.*, 1967, **6**, 237–240.

Schmideberg, M. The analytic treatment of major criminals: Therapeutic results and technical problems. Psychology and treatment of criminal psychopaths. *Int. J. Psychoan.*, 1949, **30**, 197. (Abstract)

Schultz, S. D. A differentiation of several forms of hostility by scales empirically constructed from significant items of the MMPI. Unpublished doctoral dissertation, Pennsylvania State College, 1954.

Schwitzgebel, R. *Streetcorner research: An experimental approach to the juvenile delinquent*. Cambridge, Mass.: Harvard University Press, 1965.

Schwitzgebel, R., & Kolb, D. Inducing behavior change in adolescent delinquents. *Behav. Res. Ther.*, 1964, **1**, 297–304.

Sears, R. R. Effects of frustration and anxiety on fantasy related aggression. *Amer. J. Ortho.*, 1951, **21**, 498–505.

Sears, R. R., Maccoby, E., & Levin, H. *Patterns of child rearing*. New York: Harper, 1957.

Seeman, J., Barry, E., & Ellinwood, C. Interpersonal assessment of play therapy outcome. *Psychotherapy: Theory, Research, and Practice*, 1964, **1**, 64–66.

Shore, M. F., Massimo, J. L., & Mack, H. The relationship between levels of guilt in thematic stories and unsocialized behavior. *J. proj. Tech.*, 1964, **28**, 346–349.

Siegel, S. M. The relationship of hostility to authoritarianism. *J. abnorm. soc. Psychol.*, 1956, **52**, 368–372.

Slack, C. W. Experimenter-subject psychotherapy: A new method of introducing intensive office treatment in unreachable cases. *Mental Hygiene*, 1960, **44**, 238–256.

Slavson, R. R. *An introduction to group therapy*. New York: Commonwealth Fund, 1943.

Solomon, P. (Ed.) *Psychiatric drugs: Proceedings of a research conference held in Boston*. New York: Grune & Stratton, 1966.

Spadaro, P. Contributo allo studio del test di Goodenough in varie categorie di criminal. *Quaderni di Criminologia Clinica*, 1960, **4**, 459–468.

Stoltz, R. E., & Coltharp, F. C. Clinical judgments and the Draw-a-Person test. *J. consult. Psychol.*, 1961, **16**, 79–83.

Stone, H. The TAT aggressive content scale. *J. proj. Tech.*, 1956, **20**, 445–452.

Storment, C., & Finney, B. B. Projection and behavior: A Rorschach study of assaultive mental hospital patients. *J. proj. Tech.*, 1953, **17**, 349–360.

Strumpfer, D. J. W., & Nichols, R. C. A study of some communicable measures for the evaluation of human figure drawings. *J. proj. Tech.*, 1962, **26**, 342–353.

Suesholtz, Z. Formal characteristics of children's fantasies as measured by the Thematic Apperception Test. Unpublished master's thesis, City College of New York, 1948.

Swensen, C. H. Empirical evaluation of human figure drawings. In B. I. Murstein (Ed.), *Handbook of projective techniques*. New York: Basic Books, 1965.

Symonds, P. M. *Adolescent fantasy: An investigation of the picture story method of personality study*. New York: Columbia University Press, 1949.

Symonds, P. M., & Jensen, A. R. *From adolescent to adult*. New York: Columbia University Press, 1961.

Taylor, S. P. Aggressive behavior and physiological arousal as a function of provocation and the tendency to inhibit aggression. *J. pers.*, 1967, **35**, 297–311.

Teuber, H., & Powers, E. Evaluating therapy in a delinquency prevention program. *Psychiatric Treatment*, 1953, **21**, 138–147.

Thiner, E. G. The magnitude of four experimental needs as expressed by two projective techniques. *J. proj. Tech.*, 1962, **26**, 354–365.

Tomkins, S. S. *The Thematic Apperception Test*. New York: Grune & Stratton, 1947.

Ullmann, L. P., & Krasner, L. (Eds.) *Case studies in behavior modification*. New York: Holt, Rinehart, & Winston, 1965.

Valins, S. Emotionality and information concerning internal reactions. *J. pers. soc. Psychol.*, 1967, **6**, 458–464.

Varble, D. L. An exploratory analysis of hostility in psychotherapy. Unpublished doctoral dissertation, Michigan State University, 1964.

Wahler, H. J. Hostility and aversion for expressing hostility in neurotics and controls. *J. abnorm. soc. Psychol.*, 1959, **59**, 193–198.

Watson, C. G. Relationship of distortion to DAP diagnostic accuracy among psychologists at three levels of sophistication. *J. consult. Psychol.*, 1967, **31**, 142–146.

Weatherley, D. Maternal permissiveness toward aggression and subsequent TAT aggression. *J. abnorm. soc. Psychol.*, 1962, **65**, 1–5.

Wechsler, D. *The measurement and appraisal of adult intelligence.* (14th ed.) Baltimore: Williams & Wilkins, 1958.

Weissman, S. L. Some indicators of acting out behavior from the Thematic Apperception Test. *J. proj. Tech.*, 1964, **28**, 366–367.

White, R. W. *The abnormal personality: A textbook.* New York: Ronald Press, 1964.

Whitmyre, J. W. The significance of artistic excellence in judgement of adjustment inferred from human figure drawings. *J. consult. Psychol.*, 1953, **17**, 421–424.

Wolf, I., Hostile acting out and Rorschach test content. *J. proj. Tech.*, 1957, **21**, 414–419.

Wolpe, J. *Psychotherapy by reciprocal inhibition.* Stanford, Calif.: Stanford University Press, 1958.

Wolpe, J., & Lazarus, A. A. *Behavior therapy techniques: A guide to the treatment of neuroses.* New York: Pergamon Press, 1966.

Worchel, P. Status restoration and the reduction of hostility. *J. abnorm. soc. Psychol.*, 1961, **63**, 443–445.

Chapter 20

Drug Addiction[1]

IVAN NORMAN MENSH

SYMPTOMATOLOGY

"Narcotic drug addiction is widely regarded as a grave national and international problem. No other issue affecting individual or public health arouses equal unanimity and equal zeal for reform and revenge; not radioactive fallout or pollution of rivers, not smog or smoking tobacco, not juvenile delinquency or alcoholism. Moreover, in the field of narcotic drug addiction and traffic, the United States is able to reach speedy and substantial international agreement with other governments; everyone seems to be strictly against narcotic drug addiction. There is no comparable consistency of outlook on any other subject relating to health, behavior or social responsibility" (Livingston, 1963).

This evaluation of drug addiction as an essentially unique phenomenon in national and international social structure suggests the social and psychological complexities of this area of psychopathology. Though data-gathering techniques are inadequate and therefore the data are not reliable (Chein, 1963, 1965; Chein et al., 1964; Eldridge, 1962), the best estimate is that the total number of drug addicts is far fewer than the number of persons addicted to alcohol and to other drugs than heroin and the opiates. Furthermore, there is dispute among the "experts" in the field over the enormity of the problem, many offering evidence that the "scare" headlines are justified neither by the incidence and frequency of drug addiction, nor by its association with delinquency, crime, and other major social problems.

Even the terminology of addiction is controversial. Chein et al. (1964) distinguish between habituates and "true addicts," and drug use and drug abuse (Wilner & Kassebaum, 1965). However, there is general agreement on the definition of drug addiction, although little agreement exists on the theories proposed to understand the phenomena of addiction (Hoch & Zubin, 1958). Following the repeated administration of a drug, there may develop a condition "such that continued use of the drug is necessary to maintain normal physiological function, and discontinuance of the drug results in definite physical and mental symptoms" (Isbell, 1951, 1955). Habit-forming but not addictive drugs are identified by a condition in which the habitué has a desire for the drug or drugs and uses them repeatedly but when for whatever reasons he discontinues their use he does not have any physical or psychological withdrawal symptoms (Tatum et al. 1929). It is the compulsive use of drugs, in spite of psychological changes, social disorganization, and phy-

---

[1]Grateful acknowledgement is made to Mrs. Marielle Fuller, Research associate, Department of Psychiatry, and Miss Phyllis Simon, Librarian, Biomedical Library, for their help in the bibliographic search and abstracting; and to Mrs. Faye E. Barnes, Division of Medical Psychology, for typing the manuscript.

sical changes secondary to the addiction, which identifies the addict (Ausubel, 1958). Some observers argue that these characteristics are found also with excessive use of stimulants, depressants, hypnotics, sedatives, alcohol, caffeine, tobacco, and laxatives. Following severe barbiturate addiction, withdrawal almost always produces symptoms, and they may be fatal if not immediately treated. Withdrawal following alcohol addiction sometimes results in a similar condition, and the withdrawal symptoms following opiate addiction are characterized by the well-known term of "kicking the habit," from the violent motor action among the symptoms of withdrawal.

The definition of drug addiction, in addition to the compulsive use and the severe symptoms following withdrawal because of physical dependence, also specifies a tolerance to the drug that requires with continued use an increased dosage to produce the desired effects. The challenges to the definitions of addiction to narcotic drugs also arise because of the patterns of drug availability over the decades. It is estimated that, prior to World War II, addicts bought heroin that was 87 percent pure; and, currently, the powders which are bought (one pound produces about 150,000 one-grain measures) are only 2 to 5 percent pure heroin (Wilner & Kassebaum, 1965). Even with the typical mixture of the 87 percent pure product with two parts of milk sugar, there is obviously great discrepancy between the potencies of the prewar drug and the currently sold heroin. Yet, the consumption per individual has not increased six- to eight-fold to match the reduced potency. This variation suggests "milder" habits presently, and there also are many more other drugs available now than previously, for example, barbiturates, tranquilizers, marijuana, and codeine derivatives, with which addicts experiment and rotate in use, to get greater "kicks" and at times because of their greater availability and lower cost than heroin. The wide variations in drug potency, with a factor as large as 2 to $2\frac{1}{2}$ in the 2 to 5 percent range of reported purity of heroin and in the daily dosage of addicts, also illustrate not only individual differences but also the interactions of their physical, social, and psychological characteristics.

In spite of these variants, the symptomatology of drug addiction to the opiates and heroin may be specified and identified by various techniques—pharmacological and biochemical, physical, social, and psychological—in decreasing order of reliability. An addict or "post addict" (a term introduced by the investigators at the USPHS Hospital at Lexington, Kentucky) when injected with N-allylnormorphine ("the Nalline" test; Wikler, 1963, 1965) is precipitated almost immediately into a withdrawal syndrome. Also, with modern chromatographic methods, traces of morphine in the urine can be detected up to ten days after the last injection of the drug. Both methods are in current use as checks on how "clean" postaddicts remain after their return to the community from hospitalization for their habit.

Withdrawal symptoms typically appear after about 12 hours, becoming progressively more severe and then fluctuating, lasting about ten days. The patients look like individuals with severe allergies or colds and have nausea, vomiting, running noses, dilated pupils, rapid pulse, elevated blood pressure, "goose flesh," itching, and other symptoms of severe physical upset. Needle marks and drug history differentiate the addict from patients with other severe illnesses. However, when the addict is regularly on drugs, it is difficult to identify him by physical examination or the usual laboratory tests, other than by needle marks on the arms and by urine chromatography. There do appear to be effects on smooth muscle tonus which result in severe constipation alternating with diarrhea, but other usually remarked changes in physical state are secondary to the habits of drug addicts, such as, loss of appetite and consequent weight loss, malnutrition and lower resistance to infection, decreased pain sensitivity and resultant inattention to sequelae of injections and accidents, and nonsterile injections followed by hepatitis or local, but severe, damage to the tissue (Ausubel, 1958). There also is the more lethal danger of an overdose because of variability in drug potency, and addicts not infrequently report their fear of this lethal possibility, accidentally occurring or by design, by a "pusher" or fellow addict.

The social symptoms of addiction are seen by some investigators as the hallmarks of drug abuse. The addict does not derive his personal satisfactions and rewards from social interactions in family, work, and leisure; nor from the stimuli of food, sex, and recreation. The reward characteristics of social relationships, security, prestige, and financial status do not appear to be significant for the addict (Ausubel, 1958). Wilner and Kassebaum (1965) suggest that, as a function of living in urban slums, within their ethnic minority group, drug users today may be more sociable and are spending more time with one another than appeared to be true in earlier decades. Chein and his co-workers (1964) also report, at least for the adolescent male addict, "mutual reinforcement of behavior patterns and greater autonomy of . . . (their) 'behavior world.'" With a few exceptions, this group of investigators believe that their data and conclusions generalize also to other subcultures of addicts.

The major social problems which the public press associates with drug addiction are those of crime and delinquency. Two decades ago, Lindesmith (1947) reported that about 25 percent of addicts had criminal records but emphasized that addicts lived primarily in slum areas where the crime rate was high for many other subgroups. Chapman (1962) points out that most addicts have exhibited delinquent behavior prior to their drug dependency. However, most serious investigators urge caution in interpreting data on crime and delinquency among addicts, because these data are necessarily based on *apprehended* addicts (Proceedings, White House Conference, 1962). Wilner and Kassebaum (1965) have shown the difficulty of explaining deviant behavior of the addict without studying non-institutionalized deviants living in the community, their social relationships and social groups. Chein (1963) states "This world that I have just depicted is not unique to drug users . . . other varieties of social deviants . . . come up with essentially the same picture. Narcotics do not offer the only maladaptive apparent escape hatch." Wilkins (1965) proposes a sociological model to explain, among other things, the oft-repeated difference between drug addict rates and the treatment of addicts in Great Britain and the United States. His model analyzes deviance in relation to the individual, social groups, and society at large. One of his conclusions is that "Perhaps a society can effectively control only those who perceive themselves to be members of that society. And perhaps the major point of distinction between a criminal and a sick person is that the . . . (latter) can still be identified and still identify himself as within the social system, whereas by definition a criminal cannot." This model introduces the question of the perception by the addict of his addiction, whether he is "sick." Few investigators report this perception just as few report crime and delinquency as specifically drug-associated behaviors, except that these deviant behaviors of the addicts, when they occur, may be for the purpose of obtaining drugs where, previously, the deviance had other targets. Furthermore, the widespread use of drugs by women, taken in patent medicines for many "aches and ailments" for several decades prior to World War I, no longer exists, that is, this socially acceptable relief now must be sought in such modern drugs as tranquilizers; hence, the use of opiates, except by addicts, has been replaced among women users by modern psychopharmacologia. Now there seems to be a majority of men, and younger users generally, among drug addicts.

At least part of the shift in the proportions of the sexes addicted may be associated with the advent of the Harrison Narcotics Act of 1914. The associated crime rate, if indeed there may be an association with drug addiction, likely may be an artifact of the shift of jurisdiction from personal and medical control, to the courts and correctional agencies. Unlike addicts of alcohol and tobacco, drug addicts when identified must submit to treatment. The alcohol or tobacco addict may continue addiction for years without involvement with legal authorities, but the history of drug addiction indicates that most confirmed users who are apprehended become known to the courts and the correctional agencies within two years after beginning their habit, through arrests for various crimes by male users, and for prostitution by female users. Chein's study of drug rates (1965) led him to report "a relative constancy" in the number of new users, for the 1953 to 1962 period, about 6800 annually (5700 to 6800 range over the ten years), and an equally "fairly stable" proportion becoming inactive each year. Yet, there has been reported an increase in crime rate during this period and up to the present. This discrepancy between the relatively stable rates, that is, the "chronic" state now existing in the drug addict subculture, if Chein is correct in his estimates and inferences, and the increased crime rates, suggests that addiction and crime are not associated. The unfortunate situation for the systematic investigator and student is that data for both addiction and crime are not reliable.

Cloward and Ohlin (1960) have elaborated a theory on delinquency, gang behavior, and addiction that postulates that "double failures," for example, individuals who have been failures in *both* the "legitimate" and criminal worlds, are those who are most likely to become addicts. Such a theory does not account for the addicts among physicians and nurses, or patients who became addicted by medication in illness or post-surgery, but these individuals are relatively few among the total number of addicts. Although physicians constitute 1 to 1.5 percent of admissions to the USPHS drug hospitals, in a proportion about ten times their number in the total population and a rate higher than for any other professional group, the absolute number is small and, more important, the "cure" rate is high.

The Chein study of delinquents and drug addicts (ibid) evaluated social and economic characteristics of 14 health areas with high drug rates in three boroughs of New York City. A few statistics illustrate that there does not appear to be any causal relation between juvenile delinquency and addiction, even though there is a statistically significant correlation of .63 between these two variables. Other correlations suggest the complex linking between delinquency and addiction—in 12 of the 14 health areas, Negroes and Puerto Ricans constitute over 70 percent of the population; the correlation between low income and drug rate is .76; between delinquency and poverty .68; and, in Manhattan "epidemic" and border areas, between the proportion of Negroes in the total population and drug rate, .77.

"... The highest drug-rate areas are all high-delinquency areas ... delinquency ... is not (a consequence of drug use), except in the sense that the varieties of delinquency tend to change to those most functional for drug use; the total amount of delinquency is independent of the drug use."

In their study of 18 gangs, Chein's group found that six could be classified with high-use of drugs (heroin and marijuana), eight with low-use, and four apparently were drug-free.

"There was a distinct subculture of drug users within the gangs of delinquents, they tended to have solitary or clique use of drugs, and... (this use) so affected the gang cohesiveness that negative feelings were generated toward the drug users, they were seen as unreliable, and were not in leadership roles."

As in the Chein study, the personal and individual variable in drug addiction also has been extensively studied, as have been the pharmacological and biochemical, medical and physical, and social and cultural variables. More than 250 years ago the significance of the individual in drug addiction already was remarked. In 1701, Jones drew analogies between the effects of opium and of alcoholic drinks and wrote "... the mischief is not really in the drug but in the people."

The craving for and compulsive use of drugs (Chein, 1964) has characterized the addict, and also his use of as high a dose as available, rather than smaller doses and the use of other, nonaddicting medicines, which one might infer would provide relief from pain and anxiety (Ausubel, 1958). Many observers feel that euphoria following drug intake is the primary motivating force and that the addict fears loss of this feeling if he abstains. Ausubel, for example, points out that morphine in 1/10 to 1/12 the usual dose of an addict can prevent the physical symptoms of withdrawal sickness, and that methadone, a drug widely used to "taper off" addicts, has minimal withdrawal symptoms, yet addiction to this drug appears to be as rapid as to other opiates. Furthermore, about three out of four addicts return to their addiction after intervals long enough that physical dependence probably is over. After a "fix," it is argued, euphoria appears and anxiety and pain are reduced, together with major reduction in the two basic drives of hunger and sex. The addict is quiet, unaggressive, withdrawn, with little interest in the outside environment or in his personal appearance. Psychomotor and verbal and learning tasks reflect the depressant effects of the drug, rather than the euphoria of the stimulating effect of the drug. There has not been recorded psychosis or psychological deficit of an irreversible nature as in the organic, intellectually deteriorated patient. Where psychosis has been observed, the investigators concluded that the condition existed independent of and prior to addiction (Gerard & Kornetsky, 1954; Ausubel, 1958).

The attraction of addiction for adolescents has been studied by many, with focus on individual symptomatology and generalization to addiction among adults. There is broad agreement (Gerard & Kornetsky, 1954; Toolan et al., 1952; Zimmering et al., 1952; Chein et al., 1964) that addiction does not arise *de nouveau*, except in the relatively small proportion of cases in which medication preceded addiction, but stems from personal and social maladjustment that exists prior to the addictive process. Typical of these generalizations and supported by the evidence of most investigators is Chapman's summary (1962):

> "... drug addiction is but a facet of the much larger problem of social and emotional maladjustment and the resultant disruptive and mentally disturbed behavior ... the addicts with which society is concerned ...have manifested delinquent behavior of some type prior to addiction, and increase their delinquency during addiction...."

As with all generalizations, caution is necessary, and Campbell (1962) has urged such caution:

> "I do not think it is helpful to define addiction as a personality disturbance and then conclude that anyone who can become addicted must have a disordered personality. While it can be conceded that most confirmed addicts do have difficulty in getting along with society in general, with their fellows and themselves, it is uncertain whether this is cause, or effect, or unrelated to the basic problems of addiction."

Campbell's experience led him to judge that half of the number of new addicts began by seeking relief from stress, pain, and anxiety; and that the remainder began out of "curiosity." This latter motivation has been offered by many addicts of both sexes, although whether this is a reliable evaluation of the etiology of addiction is questioned in a number of studies. Also, although Campbell states an opinion, not held by most observers, that "The classical picture of opium addiction is one of progressive mental deterioration...." his observation on intellectual inefficiency and loss of interest in the environment is generally accepted. Also, standard psychiatric nomenclature (APA, 1960) classifies drug addiction as "usually symptomatic of a personality disorder ... the proper personality classification is ... made as an additional diagnosis."

As with other habitual behaviors and disorders of personal and social adjustment, so studies of addiction by many investigators have not shed light on the constant question why "... the number of people with such (personality) traits who become addicted is relatively small as compared with the numbers of such persons with similar personality structures who do not become addicted" (Isbell, 1965). Lindesmith's theory (1947, 1965) of (1) the interaction of the awareness of the relationship between drug use and the relief of the distress of abstinence, and (2) a differential sensitivity to withdrawal symptoms (rather than predisposing personality factors or the euphoric properties of drugs) does not seem adequate to explain the addiction of many individuals. An extension of his theory, by specifying addiction as a primary adjustive mechanism, and three types of addiction—primary, symptomatic, and reactive—may offer the understanding of a larger number of addictions. His primary addict is seen as inadequate and poorly motivated for school or work, with a low threshold for frustration and little tolerance for anxiety, dependent, superficial and easily disrupted in interpersonal relations, frequently engaged in regressive fantasy, and quick to use addiction to reduce responses to conflicts and the anticipation of anxiety and pain. Wikler also has reported (1961) the anticipatory response as more significant in addiction than the reality of pain, and Lindesmith believes that the rarity of anxiety states or reactive depressions in primary addiction supports his theory. It is the reactive addict who uses drugs in response to the developmental stresses of adolescence and early adulthood—the individual who has neither trade nor vocation to support the drug habit, and who thus turns to crime and prostitution in an environment typically found in urban slums where drugs availability and peer-group tolerance and acceptance exist, and where a usual progression of drug experience begins with the smoking of marijuana and goes on to the sniffing of other drugs, then the subcutaneous and shortly thereafter the "main-line" injections of heroin. Finally, Lindesmith views only the symptomatic addict-type as the antisocial psychopath.

In summary of this position, then, there are the elements of Chein's emphasis on craving (Chein et al., 1964, & Chein, 1965) in addiction and of Wikler's conditioning theory (1962) in the earlier Lindesmith formulation (1947) of "A general theory of addiction. . .the characteristic craving of the opiate addict is generated in the repetition of the experience of using drugs to relieve withdrawal distress, provided that this distress is properly understood by the user." Furthermore, Lindesmith criticizes (1965) the concept of the "addiction-prone personality" because

> "The way in which personality types said to be predisposed to addiction are characterized appears to depend strongly on the nature of the investigator's specific experiences with addicts and upon his intellectual training and orientation."

Campbell (1962) writes of a "specific proneness to drugs . . . constitutionally determined" but does not specify the mechanisms of this influence. There also is the suggestion advanced by Williams (1952), in his study of alcoholism as a nutritional problem, in which he generalizes the concept of genetotropic disease in addictive behavior. Thus there is represented in the spectrum of theory and explanation of addiction the personal and psychological, social and cultural, physiological and medical, pharmacological and biochemical, and constitutional and genetic variables. This range leaves few disciplines or investigators unrepresented or ignored!

ASSESSMENT

The fact of drug addiction can be investigated not only by interviews, often unreliable, to obtain historical data on current or recent addiction but also, reliably, by Nalline injections and by urine chromatography (*vide supra*, p. 512, and by physical examination to locate needle marks and skin and tissue injuries from "main-line" injections. There are efforts to objectify interview methods, such as the ones by Ainslie et al. (1965) in which a "flexible" interview was devised to record signs and symptoms. This technique utilizes 34 symptoms and two global items on status and on change of behavior. However, systematic study of the personality patterns in addicted individuals, by means of psychological test instruments, will be primary focus of the assessment procedures and techniques to be reviewed.

Wikler (1962) and others (Hill et al., 1959, 1960, 1962) have reported their studies of hospitalized drug addicts by means of the MMPI. Typically, the profiles show an elevation of Pd, with Ma, Sc, and D, reflecting sociopathic and antisocial behaviors, by the self-report technique of the MMPI, together with, variously, a high energy level (surprising in view of the apathy, listlessness, and withdrawal of the addict, although it should be kept in mind that the subjects are hospitalized and no longer on drugs), disturbed and self-centered preoccupations, and depressive affect. Since this pattern of profile is found also among other samples of individuals with varying psychopathological conditions (Wilner & Kassebaum, 1965), there is no present evidence that elevations of scores on these subscales of the MMPI are unique to the drug addict. Rather, they reflect psychopathology without specifically revealing why the addicts seek this method of behavioral adjustment to their stresses instead of other pathological defenses such as psychosis or compulsive behaviors and rituals apart from the compulsive craving for and ingestion of drugs. There remains the question whether the MMPI reveals ". . . the importance of predisposing factors as essential conditions for the situational factors to produce the particular result of drug abuse."

We also consider the study of Hill, Haertzen, and Glaser (1960) on 270 hospitalized teen-aged and adult males, white and negro. They concluded that

> "Personality characteristics of narcotic

addicts are either associated with psychopathy or are predominantly psychopathic in nature, although they may include many of the classical psychoneurotic and psychotic features.... As indicated by the MMPI, personality characteristics of hospitalized adolescent addicts do not differ appreciably from those of adult addicts ... this similarity and the similarity between adolescent addicts and non-addict delinquents suggests that psychopathology has considerable significance in the etiology of addiction."

In another study by Hill and his coworkers (Hill, Haertzen, & Davis, 1962), MMPI profiles from the responses of hospitalized alcoholics, narcotic addicts, and "criminals," 200 subjects in each sample, were factor analyzed by the principal axis technique. Five factors were isolated, two of which were well defined. The first was labeled "undifferentiated psychopath," associated with social deviance and characterized by a "spike" on the Pd scale. The criminal sample had slightly greater loadings on this factor, with small, statistically significant but nondiagnostic differences from the other two samples. The second factor extracted was bipolar, with the positive pole associated with a composite profile of Pd and Ma, previously found (Hill et al., 1960) for drug addicts. This profile was labeled "primary psychopath." The negative pole was defined as "neurotic psychopath depressed," because of the significant elevation of the neurotic trial subscales, especially the D and Pd scales. The data showed the criminals more numerous on the positive pole, and the alcoholics more numerous on the negative pole, with the drug addicts intermediate.

The other three factors suggested psychopathologies, with social deviance, that is, elevated Pd, in all. The authors concluded:

"The present evidence suggests that, except for behavior which is peculiarly determined by the particular activity, no other personality characteristic is associated specifically with either alcoholism, narcotic addiction or criminality. Social deviance appears to be the common characteristic. If they cannot be differentiated from each other with regard to current personality class, except in minor quantitative terms, specific causal factors must be sought elsewhere" (Proceedings, White House Conference, 1962).

The ad hoc panel on drug abuse (ibid) also reported their observations in the area of assessment of crime—the crimes of the addict arise from his need for money for his habit, and not from any "basic" criminal tendencies; and these crimes are primarily committed against property rather than against persons. Because of the culture, prostitution among female addicts is common among the apprehended, with other illegal acts filling in during the period when the income from prostitution may not be sufficient for the purchase of drugs.

Lewis and Osberg (1958) summarized their assessment of institutionalized addicts by classing them as character disorders, "passive-aggressive or narcissistic; utilizing manipulation of others, corruption of others, provoking others to disagree among themselves and to overt anger ... a troublesome group to take care of."

The Addiction Research Center at Lexington has developed an ARC Inventory (Hill et al., 1963a, b; Haertzen et al., 1963 & Haertzen, 1965) specifically to assess the personality of addicts. The ARCI, a 550-item test, uses items similar to the ones of the MMPI, and adjective checklists. The items sample (1) attitudes toward individuals and institutions, (2) the respondent's philosophy of life, and (3) feelings of hostility. These areas of response are hypothesized by the authors as relatively little altered by drug use. Other items tap responses about drug effects on sensations, perceptions, bodily symptoms, moods, drives, motivations, and attitudes toward the test itself. The authors suggest that there must be techniques specifically designed for studying addiction, and that the effectiveness of the ARCI chiefly depends on its assessment of an "activity-sedation" continuum and on related shifts in the addict's pattern of motivation; alterations in mood along a "euphoria-dysphoric" continuum; and changes in sensation and perception and in the individual's physiological process. The responses to the items are analyzed in terms both of specific and of general and nonspecific actions and patterns of changes and shifts in the subjective effects of drug use.

Haertzen (1965) factor analyzed responses of 100 male post-addicts to the ARCI in a design that used seven drugs and a placebo. The drugs were alcohol, phenobarbital, amphetamine, chlorpromazine, scopolamine, LSD, and morphine. Two main factors emerged—reactivity and efficiency. All of the drugs produced changes on the reactivity factor and, in the efficiency dimension, there were differences between the subjective effects reported for placebo injections and for drug injections.

Other methods of measurement, not specifically designed for assessment of response characteristics of drug addicts, derive from studies of behavioral response other than addiction. There is, for example, Wikler's report (1962, 1963, 1965) of the utilization of the threshold for pain as a response indicator. He and his co-workers concluded from interview material that heroin and morphine have "a unique ability" to reduce

> "primary drives, notably those related to pain (in the sense of . . . physical discomfort) and sex—the latter being especially important in view of the emotional turmoil that this drive engenders during the adolescent period. . . . Because of the impractibility of conducting research on the sex drive in man, pain was selected as a model of a 'primary' drive. . . single doses of morphine selectively reduce anxiety associated with pain without impairing the ability to discriminate intensities of experimental pain. This property doesn't occur with phenobarbital."

A related area is that of placebo response, which has had wide study. There has been reported a broad range in which this phenomenon is found (Green, 1962; Honigfeld, 1964; Lasagna et al., 1955; Rickels & Downing, 1966; Sharp, 1965). There does not appear to be any consistency in the relationship between placebo response and personality characteristics. The reduction of potent drug in heroin mixtures from 85 to 90 percent to 2 to 5 percent during the post World War II years, the "rotation" among several drugs in the repertoire of addicts, the shift from a dominant proportion of women among addicts prior to the Harrison Act a half-century ago to a majority of male users currently, and the change in age at time of initial addiction to the teen years, all of these phenomena suggest that it may be appropriate also to systematically study placebo effects among drug addicts, except for the problem of the symptoms of withdrawal following physical dependency on heroin or morphine. It is important to observe that Lasagna, von Felsinger, and Beecher (1955), in studying drug-induced mood changes in normal male subjects in the 21 to 27 age range, reported that neither heroin nor morphine had an euphoric or pleasurable response when the subjects were comfortable and relaxed. Furthermore, the majority of subjects reported no euphoria or other mood effects—instead they voiced unpleasant feelings if any effects were noted—after the first injection, and they reported similar responses after a second injection. In contrast, among 50 chronically ill patients, men and women in middle and late adulthood, age range 45 to 87, one third reported being "happier" after an injection of the opiate, and the same proportion reported this response after injection of a placebo.

Complementing the assessment studies by the Lexington group are the evaluations of the teen-age delinquent, drug addict, and delinquent addict by Chein et al. (1964). This group used interviews, other observations, scales of social and psychological environment and behaviors, and psychological test instruments. Again, this study represents assessment of *known* users, as the authors are careful to point out. The subjects were drawn from the police files for 1952 to 1958 of the 16- to 20-year-old male users in three boroughs of New York City, and 96 percent of the total sample were studied. For the 15-year period, 1940 to 1954, the neighborhoods involved represented 15 percent of the census tracts, with 30 percent of all males in the 16 to 20 age range, and 80 percent of the total number of known users.

These addicts were characterized after study as pessimistic, unhappy, mistrusting, negative, defiant, manipulative, dysphoric in mood, and with a sense of futility. Teenagers who were neither drug users nor delinquent appeared to be actively resistant to the sociocultural pressures, had negative attitudes toward the addicts and delinquents, and dissociated themselves from them. The investigators emphasize the importance of a "delinquent orientation" that is characterized by attitudes unfavorable to parents, police, and middle-class behavior, "profound pessimism and alienation," and tolerant attitudes toward drug use. The study group had originally hoped to evaluate a sample of addicts from homes whose "psychological adequacy," as measured by scales designed for this purpose, was not deficient; and a sample of nondelinquent, nondrug users from psychologically deficient homes. However, data from the scaling measures showed "virtually no overlap between the two distributions."

Another part of the Chein study assessed 24 social and economic characteristics of areas epidemic in terms of drug use, and of nonepidemic areas. Fourteen variables consistently discriminated the two types of areas with the epidemic areas marked by concentrations of underprivileged minority groups, poverty and low economic status, low educational achievement, disrupted family life, disproportionately large numbers of adult females, very crowded housing, and a dense population of teen-agers. These qualities led the research group to observe that "drug use (is) essentially a metropolitan phenomenon." Also, it is important to observe that the two types of areas were not homogeneous with respect to these variables.

In summary of the Chein study, social and psychological observation and measurement methods were applied for the evaluation of teen-aged male addicts, delinquents, those with both sets of qualities, nondelinquents, and nondrug addicts; and also for a small sample of teen-aged female addicts and delinquents, as well as gang behaviors. Study areas were epidemic, for drug use and delinquency, and nonepidemic; and health-district areas. Although a study in depth and detail, we are again confronted with a dearth of information on other than known and apprehended addicts. Fortunately, the study paid attention to male teen-agers who actively resisted the pressures toward addiction and delinquency, unlike the major study sample.

Perhaps one of the most long-range studies of measurement of drug effects is the one by Wendt and his colleagues and students at the University of Rochester. Neither heroin nor morphine was used, and the subjects were normal college students, numbering 239. Cameron, Specht, and Wendt (1965) report, for example, the effects of amphetamines on moods, emotions, and motivations, as measured by adjective checklists of two types—long, free choice, and short, forced-choice lists. Nine studies during the decade of the program investigated methodological problems of drug research and drug-induced changes that are associated with the administration of amphetamine or of placebo. There were 239 drug and 438 placebo determinations on effects with the 239 male and female students, all 21 years of age or older. The long list had 132 self-descriptive adjectives, the short list 32 pairs in a forced-choice format. The design typically consisted of two days or more between sessions, responses to the lists prior to medication and again two hours later, in a modified double-blind method, with different subjects assigned to different drug sequences. The relevance of this research with normal subjects is apparent against the background of the problem of dependence on amphetamines and other stimulant drugs (AMA Committee on Alcoholism and Addiction, 1966).

Two other published measurement techniques are the Psychometric Index of Character Structure (PICS) developed by Levine and Monroe (1964) for use with drug addicts, and the California Psychological Inventory (Gough, 1957), which has been used to study delinquent boys (Stein et al., 1966) but not addicts. The PICS consists of 400 items among 20 scales and has been used to discriminate nonprisoner male addicts who leave the hospital against medical advice from those who remain until discharged. Among these nonprisoner addicts, 74 percent left AMA during the 1960 to 1961 study period. At one time, the Lexington hospital required a 9 to 12 month stay before the staff classified a patient as HTC (hospital treatment completed). This period later was reduced to 6 months and, since 1964, has been $4\frac{1}{2}$ months. In 1955, about two thirds of the patients left AMA, of whom about one third were considered as unimproved and the other third improved.

The other technique of assessment is considered primarily because of its 54-item socialization scale. Research to date suggests its utility in measuring the amount of socialization and the degree of asocial behavior (Stein et al., 1966). Gough reports (1965, 1966) that responses to the scale seem uninfluenced by intelligence, socioeconomic status, social desirability, or age; and are "relatively unrelated to race" (Stein et al., 1966). Cluster analysis of the responses of 318 boys of high school age (84 school disciplinary problems, 75 institutionalized delinquents, and 159 nondelinquents) yielded three dimensions:

"Stable home and school adjustment versus waywardness and dissatisfaction with family. . . . Optimism and trust in others versus dysphoria, distrust and alienation. . . . Observation of convention versus asocial role and attitude."

The variables of teen-age, male, sex, delinquency (Gough 1966), and attitudes are just the ones that, as noted in a number of studies reviewed in the preceding pages, characterize a majority of drug addicts in the United States today.

TREATMENT AND FOLLOW-UP

The modifications of behavior that are brought about by the addiction process is but one part of the total picture of behavioral modifications among individuals addicted to drugs. There are several phases in the addiction process—experimentation, early stages of addiction, chronic addiction and, in a proportion that is in controversy among both experts and nonexperts in the field, "cure" of the addiction, either temporary and transient or more permanently enduring. As in crime and delinquency, and perhaps an unfortunate choice of term especially when Livingston's comments are recalled (*vide supra* p. 511), the word recidivism is not infrequently applied to addicts who return to drug use and abuse after a period of withdrawal. Ausubel (1958) observes that a history of marijuana, alcohol, and various opiates is found among addicts in their periods of preaddiction and experimenting, but that, generally, the addict uses a specific drug after he becomes addicted and returns to this drug, even though he may "rotate" drugs because of financial pressures or the need to try other substances for a greater "kick."

Ausubel also is among those writers (Monroe & Hill, 1958) who believe that psychotherapy has only a limited function in the treatment of addiction. Group therapy may be more practical and feasible but

"Because of the addict's versatile capacity for rationalization, his resistance to gaining insight into the real causes of his addiction, and his peculiar group loyalty, group psychotherapy sessions may be easily transformed into group rationalization sessions. But if the group is skillfully chosen and supervised and directed fundamentally toward the individual motivations, defenses, and adaptations of the patient, beneficial results can be anticipated. At the present time, however, the long-term 'efficacy of group psychotherapy has yet to be evaluated'" (Wilker, 1965).

Rosenfeld (1962) also is pessimistic and writes that, in teenage addiction, "The motivation to cure oneself of the habit is vague, distant, in response to pressures of alarmed families, social workers, hospital staff." Similarly, Brill (1962) described the need for pretreatment preparation of addicts, for limited goals in treating them psychotherapeutically, for maintaining a less intensive relationship than is usual with other types of patients, for permissiveness, and for the arrangement of a flexible schedule which usually is met only when a crisis appears in the adjustment of the addict to nondrug existence. Furthermore, the "drop-outs" from treatment may later return for crisis or for other reasons, and often the families are seriously in need of psychological and other support. This latter easily is understood in the light of such observations as the ones of Wilner and Kassebaum (1965), who comment on the significance of Wikler's formulation of addiction (ibid):

"Relapse occurs so frequently that it is almost a part of the definition of the opiate addiction. If relapse can be induced at will in experimental animals . . . we have a powerful tool for studying how to prevent it. Secondly, if the conditioning hypothesis is correct, our current treatment systems are wrong, since simple withdrawal of the drug doesn't extinguish the conditioned response. Therefore we must try to devise ways to extinguish the conditioned response and apply these methods to extinction therapeutically."

The motivations of addicts for treatment also have been evaluated by Maddux (1965), who has described hospital management and aftercare procedures. It has been suggested at times that the lack of community agencies and, where they do exist, their geographical distance from the hospital and from the home environment of addicts create obstacles for follow-up treatment. Maddux attributes aftercare difficulties not to community agencies (he indicates their availability and cooperation) but to the lack of addicts' "motivations and the stability to use the service of a community agency.

Many need an active, reaching out service, and others need involuntary supervision."

Maddux instituted a milieu program in treatment efforts with hospitalized addicts. The goal was not to modify symptomatic behavior but to provide experience and training in the following:

"Basic educational and vocational skills for living in modern society . . . make the social milieu stable, firm, consistent, orderly, and giving . . . not . . . indulging . . . control and limit behavior of patients . . . prompt discipline, usually . . . deprivation of privileges and reduced autonomy . . . what Redl (1959) has called 'reality rub-in' . . . the hospital milieu permits the patient to learn that anxiety does not mean catastrophe . . . our . . . patients do not generally seem to have the relative freedom from anxiety which Cleckley (1955) observes in psychopathic states. Our patients have plenty of anxiety; the problem is that they are unable to endure it."

Although Maddux does not report any formal or systematic study of the effect of this milieu program, his clinical impressions were that the aggressive patient more likely was affected by the program than was the passive, conforming patient. In part, this may be related to an expedient of the staff and their own anxieties, to strike "a balance . . . between how much anxiety can be mobilized among the patient population and how much patient unrest the hospital can contain." The rationale for the hospital milieu program was based on the premise that "ego growth" was facilitated by imposing a social regression which, in turn, induced psychological regression, accompanied by anxiety and "some loosening of response patterns, and vulnerability to change, so that new identifications and new responses can be developed." Brill (1965) reports a similar experience at the New York Demonstration Center. Because of the addict's "marked unrelatedness to time . . . appointments must be (made) with great flexibility and patience" (on the part of the professional). Furthermore, there seemed to be an "unrelatedness" to the goals of the professional:

"In view of the tremendous individual gratification obtained from narcotics use . . . (the addict) is almost totally unrelated to psychological services involving the need for self-examination which the professional community believes he needs urgently. . . . It was frustrating . . . to . . . find ways of competing with drugs. . . ."

Brill concludes that only limited goals are appropriate or realistic because of the nature of the addiction proccess.

In evaluating various treatment programs the usual criterion is statistical. Hunt and Odoroff (1962) examined post-hospital records of nearly 1200 patients discharged from Lexington Hospital to return to New York City. Of these patients, 90 percent became readdicted within 1 to $4\frac{1}{2}$ years and, of them, 90 percent were readdicted within six months. Lower readdiction rates occurred with men over 30 years of age, for nonvoluntary, white patients and, for patients under 30, those who were in the hospital for more than a month.

Duvall et al. (1963) followed more than 450 patients who returned to New York City from Lexington. During a five-year follow-up, 87 percent were identified as returning to their addiction at some time in the study period. Yet, 25 percent were voluntarily abstinent by the fifth year after their discharge from the hospital. Significantly, more than a third of these abstinent patients were over 30 years of age, and Maddux has suggested that, eventually, as many as 90 percent may become abstinent, abstaining for periods of 20 years and more from their earlier addiction. This age relationship to abstinence, associated with the theory of "maturing out," will be discussed later in greater detail.

Lowry (1956) summarized the first 20 years of clinical experience in treating addicts at Lexington, with the goal of interrupting or removing "the habit of using . . . drugs as a pattern of living to relieve anxiety or for euphoria." This was to be accomplished by hospitalization which "provides the opportunity to initiate or complete treatment of the psychological addiction and to begin social and vocational rehabilitation." Of the nearly 24,000 patients admitted during the decades of 1935 to 1955, one third were discharged as unimproved, one third as improved, and a third as "hospital therapy completed." Nearly two thirds of the admissions were first admissions; 22 percent had a prior admission; and 14 percent had two or more prior admissions, accounting for 45 percent of all admissions. Lowry's characterization of hospital treatment of the addict concluded that a program of treatment "requires active participation of the patient. And therein lies the difficulty."

The criticism by O'Donnell (1965) of nearly a dozen follow-up studies indicates some of the confusion that is responsible for the many and differing opinions on relapse and recidivism rates. He examined the eleven follow-up studies of American drug addicts that have been reported in the literature (1936–1963), and he found that the range of relapse varied from as little as 8 percent (California physicians) to as much as 90 percent (adolescents and Lexington dischargees)! Furthermore, the sample sizes varied from as few as 30 to more than 4700, and included committed patients, physician addicts, parolees, voluntary patients, and patients in city, state, and federal hospitals. The length of follow-up also varied, from two months to six years.

In spite of these enormous variations in the sample characteristics, O'Donnell offered several generalizations. First, when relapse does occur, it tends to come shortly after abstinence, with 90 percent readdicting within six months and with most of the other relapses occurring within two years. Chein et al. (1964) report precisely the same proportions for initial addictions, 90 percent within a year of first use and the rest within a two-year period after their first use of drugs. Second, readdiction rates are sharply higher for addicts under the 25 to 30 age range. With respect to the variables of voluntary-involuntary treatment, race, length of hospitalization, and social class, there appear some trends among the differences but no clear patterns. In part, this is a function of the interaction among these several variables, for example, upper middle-class addicts, mostly physicians and other professionals, seem to have lowest relapse rates; and nonvoluntary patients have a lower relapse rate than do voluntary patients (*vide supra*, Hunt & Odoroff).

Six of the eleven studies reviewed by O'Donnell were of New York City addicts, and these six were among the highest seven high failure-rate studies: "... relapse ... (was) more probable in New York than elsewhere." Significantly, the critique notes the questions of (1) criteria of relapse or abstinence, (2) their reliability, (3) the frequency of measurement, history-taking, or data-gathering, and (4) validity criteria. The problems of physical measures (Nalline, urine chromatography), self-report reliability in interviews, and the length of the follow-up period, all loom large in evaluation of addiction relapse.

Kolb (1925, 1962) and Wikler (1961, 1965) have elaborated theories of treatment of addiction based on an anolog of conditioned response learning that is basic to the etiology of drug addiction and to possible treatment methods. However, only Wolpe (1965) has experimentally attempted to apply specific behavioral conditioning methodology to interrupt or to cure addiction and, unfortunately, with only one case. This was a physician addicted to meperidine, with a follow-up for three months at the time of the report. Thus, at best, the study serves at present only as a suggested model rather than a proved method. However, when one reviews other treatment modalities and successes there may not be so great a discrepancy in promise as there seems at first glance. Psychotherapy, for example, has not been demonstrated as an effective means for modifying behavior.

Wolpe's patient had a history of a three-year period of psychoanalysis and of addiction to meperidine for the relief of his emotionally disturbed response to the severe stresses of life. Craving for the drug developed after about two years. In the treatment regimen, the patient was trained to administer an electric shock to the forearm when a desire for the drug occurred. He administered nine shocks to himself during the first week of treatment, an additional one after a two-week interval, and reported decreased strength of his addiction and less frequent craving, with abstinence following and being maintained for three months after the last shock. Thus, the possibilities of the behavioral conditioning methods remain to be explored, in view of the paucity of report to date.

Another unconventional attempt is described by Yablonsky and Dederich (1965), the first a sociologist and the second the founder of the Synanon program. Although there may be a temptation for some to relate Synanon to the earlier movement by Addicts Anonymous, founded in 1947 in functioning on a basis similar to Alcoholics

Anonymous, or to group therapy processes, the Synanon group constantly emphasizes the uniqueness of their program. Begun in 1958, the program started with alcohol addicts, then shifted its focus to drug addicts. The program consists of "group discussions . . . extended-family living . . . educational seminars . . . cultural activities . . . (and) a work program." Yablonsky and Dederich report that "of those who stay at Synanon more than three months, over 70 percent . . . (are) abstinent." Typical of reports by this group, there are no data on the sample, population size, or other characteristics of those who are not "successes." For example, how many entered Synanon but did not remain three months? And how many others are not among the 400 who in 1964 were "leading constructive lives?" This emphasis on "success" is basic: "There is a tone of failure rather than success that pervades these institutions" (Lexington and other hospitals). Synanon is further described as

> "An open-end stratification system. A full measure of upward mobility is available . . .(a) prison or mental hospital has a caste system. . . . (First) The addict has to prove to the indoctrination committeee that he truly seeks help and wants to change his behavior."

Unfortunately, there are not recorded any systematic, objective criteria on which committee judgments are based. After being accepted, the member may

> "Achieve status and approval . . . only by good behavior—and not by the type of customary behavior in the sub-society of traditional settings . . . . The threat of ostracism, '30 days on the street,' is the ultimate punishment."

Two Synanon career goals are offered to their members, achievement as a Synanonist or therapist ("there are no professional therapists, only Synanonists") or in an "executive" role.

At the end of the first five years of their operations, Synanon reported 170 in the program (surprisingly, this number had jumped to 400 by the following year), with 50 percent "clean" for more than a year, 30 percent for two years, 22 percent for three years, and 15 percent for four years. Obviously, there are overlapping cases that produce the total of 117 percent. Synanon uses the "clean man-day unit" to measure success. Other characteristics of the 170 were reported—50 percent in the 20's, 35 percent in the 30's, 15 percent past 40 years of age; 15 percent Negro; 32 percent Catholic, 18 percent Jewish, and 12 percent Protestant; 70 percent of the total were males. What the ultimate measure of this movement will be must await some more systematic and detailed analysis of the sampling of addicts who arrive at the doors of Synanon, and the differences between those who are turned away and those who are admitted, and between the successes (70 percent in 1963) and the failures among those who enter the program. Yablonsky and Dederich assert that the usual measures are not applicable to the unique experiment of Synanon, but suggest no other methodology than the clean man-day unit.

There also is a gap in our knowledge of the history of addiction, treatment, and follow-up of nonapprehended addicts, as previously emphasized. The problems of sample selection and of criteria and reliability of measurement plague any report, especially when it deals with private patient care. Yet, because there is little in this area, we note with interest the experience of Pearson and Little (1965) with 84 addicts over a 30-year period. This number represented their total case load of addicts. After evaluating the 84 patients, the authors record 38 percent as "recovered," 8 percent "improved," 50 percent "failed," and 4 percent still in treatment.

Little has been written here about female addicts, because few studies of them exist. When women constituted the great majority of addicts, prior to 1914, there was not systematic study or even reporting of addiction. Even since that time there have been but few studies of female addicts—O'Donnell found only two reports among the eleven follow-up studies that he evaluated, and both had small numbers of cases; and Chein and his co-workers studied only 20 female adolescents in their intensive studies, which represented a 10 percent sample of the total admissions of teen-age, female addicts during the period of selection of subjects for the study. Similarities and differences between male and female adolescent addicts are interestingly presented by the group, but perhaps the only conclusion directly relevant to treatment is that "Whatever the basis of the differences, female addicts are unquestionably far more demanding of the time and energy of the staff than are male patients." In spite of, or because of, these differences, success rates do not distinguish the two sexes.

What associations geographical variables (and, therefore, social, cultural, political, and economic variables) may have with addiction and its treatment are in question also. Britain reports about 4000 addicts; Canada about 3200, of whom 74 percent have been law violators (AMA Council on Mental Health, 1957); 12 percent of all males and 60 percent of all male prisoners in Hong Kong are addicted to drugs (Way, 1965), but one third of the latter become abstinent and remain so for a year; and in the United States there may be 110,000 addicts, about one half of the number believed to be addicted around 1900. What these data mean for comparative or other purposes has not yet been demonstrated. Unfortunately, the public press and especially the Sunday supplements frequently use their unreliable figures, to the confusion and the fright of many.

Related to this confusion is a final note on maternal and neonatal addiction, a phenomenon occasionally also used by the press for "scare" purposes. Rarely occurring, this condition of neonatal narcotic addiction has been observed and reported by Steg (1957), Schneck (1958), Slobody and Cabrinik (1959), and Sussman (1963).

THEORIES OF ADDICTION

As may be expected from the complex variables of symptomatology, etiology, and treatment; and the interrelationships of physiological, biochemical, pharmacological, social, and psychological variables, there exists also a complex of theories and rationales of addiction ranging throughout the spectra of variables. Wikler (1961) long has argued for an understanding of addiction in terms of learning theory, specifically instrumental conditioning theory. In this context, he views each injection of drug as a reinforcer of drug-seeking behavior, reinforcing through reduction of the drive. The drive is postulated as deriving from early changes in feeling and sensation in the addict that were produced by the previous injection of drug. Furthermore, the preoccupation of addicts with "hustling" for drugs (that is drug-seeking behavior in an extra-legal sense") not only when they are in an active addiction phase but also during periods of nonaddiction, reported in terms of verbalized fantasy, especially in the presence of other addicts or "post addicts," suggests that drug-seeking behavior, "initially reinforced in the manner described, may become conditioned to 'secondary reinforcers' or stimuli (e.g., 'bad associates') regularly associated with acquisition of the drug during addiction." The theory also suggests that withdrawal phenomena may recur long after withdrawal of the drug, as in situations in which a "post-addict" finds himself again in an environment that includes ready availability of drugs. Further relapse shortly after withdrawal, with resumption of the drug addiction,

> "may be due simply to incomplete extinction of reinforced drug-seeking behavior. Later, relapse may be indicated by recurrence of at least some fragments of the abstinence syndrome as a conditioned response, coupled with traces of previously reinforced drug-seeking behavior that remained as a result of non-extinction during previous episodes of addiction and 'cure'."

Wikler (1962) further states (*vide supra*) that there is among addicts

> "initial preference for heroin or morphine because of the unique ability (of these drugs) to reduce all 'primary' drives, notably those related to pain (in the sense of any type of physical discomfort) and sex—the latter being especially important in view of the emotional turmoil that this drive engenders during the adolescent period."

One of the experimental tests of a part of this theory utilized pain as a stimulus.

> "Because of the impracticability of conducting research on the sex drive in man, pain was selected as a model of 'primary' drive . . . single doses of morphine selectively reduce anxiety associated with pain without impairing the ability to discriminate intensities of experimental pain. This property doesn't occur with phenobarbital . . . drug-seeking is 'instrumental' behavior."

Wikler (1965) also supports the concept of "decisive importance of euphoria as the main determinant of the addict's behavior, both in his initial addiction and in his subsequent relapses—for this is also the addict's explanation." Wikler then develops in detail his conditioning theory to explain the phenomena of addiction, relapse, and treatment. These concepts also have been advanced by Kolb (1939): "By building up a strong association between pleasure and pain and the taking of a narcotic he becomes conditioned to taking one in response to most any situation that may arise." As noted by others, Chein et al. (1964) state, however, "contrary to common belief, the drug does not contribute rich positive pleasure; it merely offers relief from misery."

Chein (1965) theorized that there are four "types" of addicts. His paradigm is essentially as follows.

Type	*Craving*	*"Personal Involvement"*	*Other Characteristics*
1	+	–	Psychopharmacologic effects primary
2	–	+	Little affected by drug tolerance
3	+	+	
4	–	–	Physical dependence

Types 1 and 3 are "true addicts," for craving is an essential characteristic of their condition, according to this schema.

Chein et al. (1964) also stress in dramatic style the other, societal complex of variables in a theory of addiction:

"how much drug-taking behavior would not take place were it not for the challenge of the risk; the attractiveness of the forbidden; the glamor of defying authority; the power of self-destructive needs given a socially validated channel of expression; the drawing power of an illicit subsociety to lonely individuals alieviated from the main stream and the lure of its ability to confer a sense of belonging, interdependence of fate, and common purpose to individuals who would otherwise feel themselves to be standing alone in a hostile world; and the inducements to drug use motivated by vast profits made possible by the very effectiveness of the law enforcement agencies and the operation of the economic law of supply and demand . . . the most dangerous consequences of addiction to the individual . . . (are) a direct outcome of the existence and enforcement of the law . . . the efforts of society to cope with the problem are models of irrationality."

Lindesmith (1965) asserts that craving for drugs is "the central and defining feature of addiction," with euphoria not a useful concept because of the reports by addicts. He states that

"the euphoric effect . . . tends to be greatly reduced or eliminated when physical dependence is established, and is, moreover, heavily counteracted by many dysphoric or unpleasant effects" (cf. also Maddux, 1965).

Lindesmith perceived addiction, as well as other deviant behaviors, arising from "anomie," the discrepancy between

"such culturally indoctrinated goals as that of achieving success and status and the perceived or available means of reaching such goals. . . . Addiction is conceived of as one such (adaptive) device (to relieve tension) by which the person escapes his problem by renouncing society's goals as well as established norms for attaining them" (cf. also Hill, et al., 1952a, b, 1955).

Cloward and Ohlin (1960) suggest in this same vein (*vide supra*, p. 514) that individuals who are "double failures, that is, in both the legitimate and the criminal worlds, are those who tend to become addicts."

Another theory is proposed by Lasagna and his associates (1955), based on the experiments and observations of both placebo and drug effects in normal and in addicted subjects.

". . . the usual effects of opiates (blunting of reactivity, reduction of urgency to action, interference with associational activity, and lassitude) may constitute a pleasant relief and temporary cessation of tension and struggle for the unbalanced personality. . . . Our (normal) group with atypical reactions resembled addicts in their preference for opiates; this group was made up of the more maladjusted subjects."

Ausubel (1958) has summarized the physiological, psychological, and sociological aspects of addiction in theorizing that there are four principal determinants—the availability of the drug, the immediate social milieu, the larger cultural environment, and the individual personality characteristics among which is a reward system of euphoric and pain-relieving responses to anxiety and to other stresses. After a "fix," the addict experiences a greatly reduced response, or even a disappearance of the response, to hunger, pain, and sexual stimuli. Ausubel, as does Wikler, then proposes that these changes in strengths of various drives and the now-habitual ways of responding to stress serve as reinforcers to the characteristic methods of response to personal and social stimuli. "Drug addiction is primarily a personality disorder. It represents one type of abortive adjustment to life that individuals with certain personality predispositions may choose under appropriate conditions of availability and sociocultural attitudinal tolerance." Lindesmith, as previously noted (1947), has introduced a controversial principle in his theory of addiction, postulating that addiction rests on the "awareness of the relation between drug use and the relief of distress associated with abstaining from the drug." His "general theory of addiction" postulated (1947) that "the characteristic craving of the opiate addict is generated in the repetition of the experiences of using drugs to relieve withdrawal distress, provided that this distress is properly understood by the user." Two decades earlier (1928), Terry and Pellens had suggested a similar theory. In 1965 (*vide supra*), Lindesmith reported that there had been a number of misinterpretations of his general theory. He used the concept of "a cognitive-conditioning process" to explain that the addict's attitudes and other behaviors in relation to a drug become established "as a conceptually controlled pattern. The withdrawal distress is indispensable only in the origin of this pattern, not in its continuance." This theory indicates an often overlooked point—that motivations for addiction, treatment, and relapse may vary as a function of the phase in which the addict finds himself, whether in the initial stage, continued use, abstinence, or relapse.

Furthermore,

> "The person does not become an addict because he defines himself as one, but defines himself as an addict because he realizes he is one. An addict does not relapse because of withdrawal distress but because of the previously established craving, which may be thought of as something like the results of conditioning in the lower animals except that it is conceptually elaborated . . . the craving is symbolically elaborated, and responses arising from it are directed and controlled by conceptual processes . . . the observed effects of addiction upon personality and character follow from the indirect conceptually mediated effects which addiction has upon the person's conceptions of himself and his status in society."

Lindesmith does not accept the "euphoria principle" of several addiction theories, nor the significance of predisposing personality characteristics, although he accepts the fact of differential sensitivity to withdrawal symptoms. As reported above (cf. page 515) his theory proposes three types of addicts to encompass the phenomena of addiction—primary, symptomatic, and reactive.

Chapman (1958, 1959, 1962) summarized (1962) his theoretical position in a similar vein:

> "drug addiction is but a facet of the much larger problems of social and emotional maladjustment and the resultant disruptive and mentally disturbed behavior . . . the addicts with which society is concerned . . . have manifested delinquent behavior of some type prior to addiction, and increase their delinquency during addiction. . . . They are passive-dependent, 'hangers-on' of peer groups. They suffer from weak ego development and have immature and inadequate life goals. Most have a strong fantasy life which drugs reinforce. . . . Not an inconsiderable number are psychotic or are on the borderline of psychosis. Paradoxically, drugs make possible some adjustment to reality."

Other observers, however, do not agree with Chapman's evaluation of the significant numbers of psychotic or borderline addicts.

Two theories have had little mention or discussion by other writers but do indicate the range of theoretical positions held in the field. Williams (1952) conceives of addiction to alcohol as a genetotropic disease, and there are lower animal studies that may lend support to this concept. However, addiction to drugs may be a very different phenomenon than addiction to alcohol, as suggested previously. The other theory, by Campbell (1962), suggests a constitutionally determined, specific proneness to drugs. Neither theory lends itself to experimental test in human addiction, but tests of the many other theories of addiction may be but little less difficult, although more widely adopted by investigators and clinicians in the theory, study, and treatment of drug addiction.

Wilkins (1965), as has Lindesmith (*vide supra*), developed a sociological theory of deviant behavior within social systems and has offered this theory in explanation of the differences between drug addiction in Great Britain and the United States. His model proposes that the definition of deviant behavior in a social system is a function of the relation of "certain types" of information to "certain" systems. This relationship means that more acts are "defined as deviant to the extent that the individuals so defined are 'cut off' from the values of the parent system." As more acts are "taken against those perceived as deviant" the individuals so defined begin to "perceive themselves as deviant." This cycle results in "isolation and alienation" of the deviants, and these latter then develop their own values which are counter to the system, so that they become "outlaws." The cycling effects produce "even more deviant behavior by the outlaws," and more forceful attempts to control by the system, and "around and around again."

Wilkins differentiates the drug addiction problems of Great Britain and the United States in terms of different images, in the two social systems, of (1) the use of drugs, (2) the addict, (3) the police, (4) the control system and the *perception* of this system, (5) definitions of "crimes," (6) the balance between legitimate and illegitimate means for obtaining drugs, and (7) the folklore. Wilkins concludes from his model that

> "Perhaps a society can effectively control only those who perceive themselves to be members of that society. And perhaps the major point of distinction between a criminal and a sick person is that the sick person can still be identified and still identify himself as within the social system, whereas by definition a criminal cannot."

Wilner and Kassebaum (1965) summarize "psychologic perspectives" of narcotics addiction in three formulations. The "symptomatologic, or psychobiologic, theory relates to the development of specific personality reaction patterns ... because of specific mental stresses arising from the individual's environment." In neurotics it is assumed that anxiety is a stress response and "negative pleasure" follows the use of drugs to reduce anxiety. Sociopaths, however, use drugs to obtain "positive pleasure" or euphoria (cf. also Kolb, 1925). Unlike the neurotics or sociopaths, "normals" are presumed to have "become addicted only as a result of the therapeutic use of drugs to relieve physical pain." The choice of drug depends on the availability of the particular drug, and the development of physical dependence and of tolerance are complications that tend to maintain the addiction process. Relapse is related to the personality pattern that is responsible for the initial addiction.

The psychoanalytic formulation (ibid) unfortunately does not distinguish addicts from other individuals with deviant behavior:

> "addicts (are) ... individuals whose psychosexual development has been arrested or has undergone regression to infantile or even more primitive levels. In infancy and early childhood a strong consistent father figure has generally been lacking, whereas the mother has been overindulgent and rejecting in an inconsistent way. The child, as a consequence, has been unable to learn that all his wants cannot be fulfilled in reality and has commonly regarded other persons, particularly the mother or mother substitutes, as objects to be used for self-gratification. Because of the arrested psychosexual development 'oral cravings' have become paramount, whereas genital pleasures are devoid of interest. Since such wants can never be fulfilled in reality, frustration results, and the narcissistic, oral-dependent individual reacts with hostility toward the mother and other women. Drugs are taken because of such conflict. Predisposition to use drugs is regarded as present before addiction begins. Addictive use of drugs is ascribed to the predisposition itself and to the contrast between the elated state induced by the drugs and the disillusionment which ensues when such effects wear off."

The third formulation, by Wikler and his associates, is classed as "pharmacodynamic." Wilner and Kassebaum (1965) see this latter theoretical model as especially useful because of the possibilities of experimental tests of the concepts and hypotheses. The theory emphasizes the specificity of drug actions and the psychologic importance of physical dependence on drugs. Different classes of drugs are regarded as having different effects on motivations of a "primary" and a "secondary" nature. Opiates depress the primary drives of pain, sex, hunger, and thirst. Thus an individual whose chief source of anxiety is related to pain, sexuality, or repression of aggressive drives will obtain specific relief from morphine. On the other hand, alcohol releases behavioral controls and, in this sense, enhances sexual and aggressive drives. Therefore, in individuals who characteristically "act out" in anxiety-provoking conflict situations, alcohol would be the preferred drug.

"In short, opiates take away the need for the solution of emotional problems, whereas alcohol prevents direct aggressive action against the source or symbols of the emotional conflict. Furthermore, the development of physical dependence on drugs creates a new biologic need comparable to hunger or thirst. Satisfaction of this need is directly and highly pleasurable, just as is satisfaction of hunger, thirst, or sexual gratification. Note that this concept is opposite to the concept of negative pleasure and that it presupposes that one of the chief gratifications of being an addict is to be dependent, or 'hooked,' so the new biologic need can be gratified.

"Wikler postulates that abstinence symptoms can be 'conditioned' and may appear in response to conditional stimuli of various sorts long after withdrawal has been accomplished and all classic manifestations of physical dependence have vanished. Thus the development of physical dependence creates a continuous cycle of alternating drug-induced biologic need and gratification of that need by obtaining the drug. Each dose of the drug reinforces behavior in which the addict must engage in order to obtain the drug by reduction of the drive produced by the previous one.

"The attraction of the pharmacodynamic formulation of Wilker is that it can be tested with currently available techniques.... Conditioning of abstinence phenomena can be developed in addicted rats, and such conditioned abstinence persists for months after discontinuance of opiates. Furthermore, addicted rats show a high tendency to 'relapse' to the drug (will drink more of the opiate than water) when placed in situations in which they have 'conditioned' symptoms of abstinence and a free choice of drinking either opiate or water.

"The importance of these observations is very great. Relapse occurs so frequently that it is almost a part of the definition of opiate addiction. If relapse can be induced at will in experimental animals, we have a powerful tool for studying how to prevent it. Secondly, if the conditioning hypothesis is correct, our current treatment systems are wrong, since simple withdrawal of the drug does not extinguish the conditioned response. Therefore we must try to devise ways to extinguish the conditioned response and apply these methods of extinction therapeutically."

Another theory of addiction has been offered by Chein and his associates (1964). This formulation is developed around the attitudes integral to "delinquent orientation" (cf. page 514 above) and a four-stage process of becoming involved with narcotics—experimentation, occasional use, regular or habitual use, and efforts to break the habit. The observations and data supporting this theory include the following: (1) 90 percent of those who become addicted are using drugs regularly within a year after the first trial, the remaining addicts are regular users within two years; (2) regular use precipitates changes in values, relationships, and other behaviors; (3) craving develops because the drug effects constitute a "coping mechanism" for frustration, anxiety, or other stress; and (4) those who attempt to break the habit generally are nondelinquent users whose attitudes toward significant adults, gang behaviors, and family differ from addicts with a delinquent orientation.

This group of investigators emphasize that

"there is no single type or syndrome of maladjustment specific to the adolescent opiate addict ... (no) single deep-lying need or conflict common to, or specific for, opiate addiction ... (no) unitary characteristic."

The generalizations proposed by Chein and his co-workers are set in the framework of concepts drawn from psychoanalytic psychology—ego pathology, narcissism, problems of sexual identification, and superego pathology.

"... addicts of all ages participate in an isolated in-group with its special mores, traditions, and argot which encourage suspicion, deceit, and manipulativeness toward both the in-group and the world of 'squares' . . . (there are) few barriers to membership in terms of race, religion, or maturity. Adolescent addicts are very democratic."

In commenting on the relative disproportion of female addicts in the male/female ratio (12 to 20 percent females/80 to 88 percent males), as in alcoholism, juvenile delinquency, and crime, Chein et al. observe that the ratio is not explained by greater psychological stability or more sheltering from stress among teenage girls and young women, since adolescent females and women predominate in psychiatric clinics and hospitals and, prior to the 1914 Harrison Act, there were many more female addicts. Women perhaps are "more apt to be protected from the social consequences of their actions," but this, too, does not appear to be an appropriate generalization. Perhaps females are "less likely than males to express tensions in ways that are detectably and flagrantly violative of prevailing social code . . . (there is) greater femine conventionality . . . (and) less experience and less contact with drug users." However, among the apprehended and hospitalized female adolescent addicts, unlike among the males, who generally try not to attract attention from the hospital staff, the female "*gets* herself noticed. . . . Whatever the basis of the difference, female adolescent addicts are unquestionably far more demanding of the time and energy of the staff than the male patients." Furthermore, there appeared in these studies different qualities of behavior between the male and female adolescent addicts. The former were aggressive and hostile and reported that these behaviors were rewarding to them or were "justified by their frustration and mistreatment by others." The girls, however, reported that feelings of anxiety and self-reproach followed the expression of anger and resentment. Since these data were based on studies of only 20 female and 32 male adolescents, there needs to be further sampling to determine the reliability of these generalizations. Yet, Chein concludes "though our study has focused on the adolescent addict, we believe that our findings are relevant for the majority of the addict population."

The learning theory context, as in Wikler's formulations, appears also in its application to addiction by Dollard and Miller (1950): "the use of drugs is effective in reducing drives, thus leaving the patient less motivated for therapy." Haertzen and Hill (1959) ". . . hypothesized that one important aspect in the development of addiction to opiates is initial reduction of discomfort, anxiety, and depression in those addicts who show neurotic tendencies." Also, Haertzen and Hill (1959) state ". . . one of the most important mechanisms through which drugs exert analgesic action is by reduction of anxiety associated with anticipation of pain. . . ." Kolb (1925) had anticipated these theoretical positions when he wrote:

> ". . . the relapse of drug addicts is due to the original cause of addiction to which has been added the increasing dependence upon drugs for the relief of any unpleasantness, the force of habit, and numerous impelling memory associations. The addict acquires a bundle of conditioned reflexes so that any stimulus formerly associated with the act of taking drugs will bring on the old desire."

There also is the historical and literary theory of Alfred Stille in 1894 (Felix, 1944):

> ". . . those who have propensity . . . to employ some artificial means of promoting the flow of agreeable thoughts, of emboldening the spirit to perform acts of daring, or of steeping in forgetfulness the sense of sorrow . . . are more likely to embrace narcotics and fall a victim of their enslaving characteristics than are those who do not possess these propensities."

Finally, there is an important theory relating to the "maturing out" of addicts which has been elaborated principally by Winick (Proceedings, White House Conference, 1962; *Bull. Narc.*, U.N., 1962, Wilner & Kassebaum, 1965). This phenomenon also has been reported for juvenile delinquency and psychopathic behavior by Glueck and Glueck (1959), the Bureau of Narcotics (1932), and O'Neal and Robins (1958). Observing the "drop-off" of rates of addiction in the 35- to 40-year-old age range, Winick states:

> "There is clearly a major concentration of addicts becoming inactive during their thirties. This may be a function not necessarily of the age of the addict, but of the life cycle of the disease of addiction itself . . . a large concentration of addicts becoming inactive in the first decade after their addiction began."

Winick reviewed the histories of nearly 17,000 addicts hospitalized in the 1953 to 1959 period, with over 7000 counted as active at the end of 1959, ranging in age from 18 to 76. By age 26, 25 percent no longer were reported as addicts; by age 30, 50 percent were inactive addicts; and by age 36, 75 percent no longer were reported as addicts. These data are "not an artifact of the proportions of addicts at these ages," and do suggest that addiction may be self-limiting for two thirds or more of drug addicts. There was a correlation between the age of initial use and the length of addiction, with longer periods of addiction among those who had begun their drug use early. The average period of drug use was 8·6 years, 7 percent had used drugs for periods of 15 or more years, and the maximum was 56 years.

Complicating this phenomenon, however, is the differential rates of relapse for the total proportion of addicts in at least four different metropolitan areas—67 percent in Chicago, 40 percent in New York, with much smaller rates for Philadelphia and Milwaukee. Winick concludes his study by asking whether "maturing out" may be a function of "less saliency and less urgency of problems facing addicts as they age;" or a "life-cycle phenomenon," that is, the length of the addiction process itself, or a combination of both factors.

SUMMARY

The use of drugs and addiction to them have been observed since the beginning of recorded history. Within the past half-century the phenomena of addiction have been viewed from many perspectives. Prior to the 20th century, the personal, social, and political dimensions of addiction had been remarked but, since the advent of increased national and international legislation for the attempted control of drug use, there has developed a particular aura around drug addiction. Livingston had summarized the uniqueness of drug addiction among the many behavioral patterns of man.

The complexities of the personal and social, pharmacological and biochemical, physical and psychological dimensions, and their interactions are many. Symptomatology, assessment techniques, therapeutic efforts, follow-up studies of addicts exposed to various treatment methods, and the theories proposed to understand addictive behaviors have been reviewed. The latter also involve the several stages of experiment, initial addiction, regular use, treatment and relapse, and post-addictive behaviors. Because of the studies of more than a generation of investigators, the phenomena of drug addiction essentially are known. Yet they remain enigmatic. This present state of knowledge is reflected especially in the many theories of addiction. Today there remain many unanswered questions within the context of interaction among the psychological, social, legal, political, medical, biochemical, and pharmacological variables of drug use and drug addiction.

REFERENCES

Ainslie, J. P., Jones, M. B., & Stiefel, J. R. Practical drug evaluation method. *Arch. gen. Psychiat.*, 1965, **12**, 368–373.

American Psychiatric Association. *Diagnostic and statistical manual: Mental disorders.* (13th ed.) Washington, D.C.: Amer. Psychiat. Assoc., 1960.

Ausubel, D. P. *Drug addiction: Physiological, psychological, and sociological aspects.* New York: Random House, 1958.

Brill, L. Agency treatment. In Bier, W. C. (Ed.), *Problems in addiction: Alcohol and drug addiction.* New York: Fordham Univ. Press, 1962.

Brill, L. Rehabilitation in drug addiction: A report of the New York Demonstration Center. In Wilner, D. M., & Kassebaum, G. G. (Eds.), *Narcotics.* New York: McGraw Hill, 1965.

Bureau of Narcotics, U.S. Treas. Dept., *Traffic in opium and other drugs for the year ended Dec. 31, 1931.* Washington, D.C.: Gov't Printing Office, 1932.

Cameron, Jean S., Specht, Priscilla G., & Wendt, G. R. Effects of amphetamines on moods, emotions, and motivations. *J. Psychol.*, 1965, **61**, 93–121.

Campbell, R. J. Etiology and personality factors. In Bier, W. C. (Ed.), *Problems in addiction: Alcohol and drug addiction*. New York: Fordham Univ. Press, 1962.
Chapman, K. W. Care and treatment of drug addicts. *Bull. Narcotics*, 1958, **10**, 25–58.
Chapman, K. W. Management and treatment of drug addiction. *J. chron. Dis.*, 1959, **9**, 315–326.
Chapman, K. W. The general problem. In Bier, W. C. (Ed.), *Problems in addiction: Alcohol and drug addiction*. New York: Fordham Univ. Press, 1962.
Chein, I. The status of sociological and social psychological knowledge concerning narcotics. In Livingston, R. B. (Ed.), *Narcotic drug addiction problems*. Publ. Hlth. Serv. Public., No. 1050, 1963.
Chein, I. The use of narcotics as a personal and social problem. In Wilner, D. M., & Kassebaum, G. G. (Eds.), *Narcotics*. New York: McGraw-Hill, 1965.
Chein, I., Gerard, D. L., Lee, R. S., Rosenfeld, Eva, & Wilner, D. M. *The road to H: Narcotics, delinquency, and social policy*. New York, Basic Books, 1964.
Cleckley, H. *The mask of sanity*. St. Louis: Mosby, 1955.
Cloward, R. A., & Ohlin, L. E. *Delinquency and opportunity: A theory of delinquent gangs*. New York: Free Press, 1960.
Committee on Alcoholism and Addiction, A.M.A. Council on Mental Health. Dependence on amphetamines and other stimulant drugs. *J. Amer. Med. Assoc.*, 1966, **197**, 1025–1027.
Committee on Narcotic Addiction, A.M.A. Council on Mental Health. Report on narcotic addiction. *J. Amer. Med. Assoc.*, 1957, **165**, 1834.
De Ropp, R. S. *Drugs and the mind*. New York: Martins Press, 1957.
Dollard, J., and Miller, N. *Personality and psychotherapy*. New York: McGraw-Hill, 1950.
Duvall, Henrietta J., Locke, B. Z., & Brill, L. Follow-up study of narcotic drug addicts five years after hospitalization. *Publ. Hlth. Rep.*, 1963, **78**, 185–193.
Eldridge, W. B. *Narcotics and the law. A critique of the American experiment in narcotic drug control*. New York: New York Univ. Press, 1962.
Felix, R. H. An appraisal of the personality types of the addict. *Amer. J. Psychiat.*, 1944, **100**, 462–467.
Gerard, D. L., & Kornetsky, C. Social and psychiatric studies of adolescent opiate addicts. *Psychiat. Quart.*, 1954, **28**, 113–125.
Glueck, S., & Eleanor. *Predicting delinquency and crime*. Cambridge, Mass.: Harvard Univ. Press, 1959.
Gough, H. G. *Manual for the California Psychological Inventory*. Consulting Psychology Press, Palo Alto, California, 1957.
Gough, H. G. Conceptual analysis of psychological test scores and other diagnostic variables. *J. abn. Psychol.*, 1965, **70**, 294–302.
Gough, H. G. Appraisal of social maturity by means of the CPI. *J. abn. Psychol.*, 1966, **71**, 189–195.
Green, D. M. Side effects. *Federation Proceedings*, 1962, **2**, 179.
Haertzen, C. A. Subjective drug effects: A factorial representation of subjective drug effects on the Addiction Research Center Inventory. *J. nerv. ment. Dis.*, 1965, **40**, 280–289.
Haertzen, C. A., & Hill, H. E. Effects of morphine and phenobarbital on differential MMPI profiles. *J. clin. Psychol.*, 1959, **15**, 434–437.
Haertzen, C. A., & Hill, H. E. Assessing subjective effects of drugs: An index of carelessness and confusion for use with the Addiction Research Center Inventory (ARCI). *J. clin. Psychol.*, 1963, **19**, 407–412.
Haertzen, C. A., Hill, H. E., & Belleville, R. E. Development of the Addiction Research Center Inventory (ARCI): Selection of items that are sensitive to the effects of various drugs. *Psychopharmacologia*, 1963, **4**, 155–166.
Hamburger, E. Barbiturate use in narcotic addicts. *J. Amer. Med. Assoc.*, 1964, **189**, 366–368.
Hill, H. E. The social deviant and initial addiction to narcotics and alcohol. *Quart. J. Stud. Alc.*, 1962, **23**, 562–582.

Hill, H. E. Belleville, R. E., & Wikler, A. Studies on anxiety associated with anticipation of pain. *A.M.A. Arch. Neurol. Psychiat.*, 1955, **73**, 602–608.

Hill, H. E., Haertzen, C. A., & Davis, H. An MMPI factor analytic study of alcoholics, narcotic addicts, and criminals. *Quart. J. Stud. Alc.*, 1962, **23**, 411–431.

Hill, H. E., Haertzen, C. A., & Glaser, R. Personality characteristics of narcotic addicts as indicated by the MMPI. *J. gen. Psychol.*, 1960, **62**, 127–139.

Hill, H. E., Haertzen, C. A., Wolbach, A. B. Jr., & Miner, E. J. The Addiction Research Center Inventory: Standardization of scales which evaluate subjective effects of morphine, amphetamine, phenobarbital, alcohol, LSD-25, pyrahexyl and chlorpromazine. *Psychopharmacologia*, 1963, **4**, 167–183.

Hill, H. E., Haertzen, C. A., Wolbach, A. B. Jr., & Miner, E. J. The Addiction Research Center Inventory: Appendix I. Items comprising empirical scales for seven drugs. II. Items which do not differentiate placebo from any drug condition. *Psychopharmacologia*, 1963, **4**, 184–205.

Hill, H. E., Kornetsky, C. H., Flanary, H. G., & Wikler, A. Studies on anxiety associated with anticipation of pain: I. Effects of morphine. *A.M.A. Arch. Neurol. Psychiat.*, 1952a, **67**, 612–619.

Hill, H. E., Kornetsky, C. H., Flanary, H. G., & Wikler, A. Effects of anxiety and morphine on the discrimination of intensities of painful stimulation, *J. clin. Investig.*, 1952b **31**, 473–480.

Hoch, P. H., & Zubin, J. (Eds.), Problems of addiction and habituation. New York: Grune and Stratton, 1958.

Honigfeld, G. Non-specific factors in treatment. I. Review of placebo reactions and placebo reactors. II. Review of social-psychological factors. *J. Dis. Nerv. System*, 1964, **25**, 145–156, 225–239.

Hunt, G. H., & Odoroff, M. E. Follow-up study of narcotic drug addicts after hospitalization. *Publ. Hlth. Rep.*, 1962, **77**, 41–54.

Isbell, H. Manifestations and treatment of addiction to narcotic drugs and barbiturates. *Med. Clin. No. Amer.*, 1950, **34**, 425–438.

Isbell, H. *What to do about drug addiction.* Publ. Hlth. Serv. Public., No. 94. Washington, D.C.: Gov't Printing Office, 1951.

Isbell, H. Medical aspects of opiate addiction. *Bull. N.Y. Acad. Med.*, 1955, **31**, 886–901.

Isbell, H. Perspectives in research on opiate addiction. In Wilner, D. M., & Kassebaum, G. G. (Eds.), *Narcotics*. New York: McGraw-Hill, 1965.

Jones, J. *The mysteries of opium reveal'd.* London: Richard Smith at the Angel and Bible, 1701.

Kolb, L. Pleasure and deterioration from narcotic addiction. *Ment. Hyg.*, 1925, **9**, 699–724.

Kolb, L. Clinical contributions to drug addiction. *Bull. N.Y. Acad. Med.*, 1955, **31**, 886–901.

Kolb, L. Drug addiction as a public health problem. *Sci. Monthly*, 1939, **48**, 391–400.

Kolb, L. *Drug addiction: A medical problem.* Springfield, Ill.: C. C. Thomas, 1962.

Lasagna, L., von Felsinger, J. M., & Beecher, H. K. Drug induced mood changes in man. *J. Amer. Med. Assoc.*, 1955, **157**, 1006–1020, 1113–1119.

Levine, J., & Monroe, J. J. Discharge of narcotic drug addicts against medical advice. *Publ. Hlth. Rep.*, 1964, **79**, 13–18.

Lewis, J. M., & Osberg, J. W. Observations on institutional treatment of character disorders. *Amer. J. Orthopsychiat.*, 1958, **28**, 730–744.

Lindesmith, A. R. *Opiate addiction.* Bloomington, Indiana: Principia Press, 1947.

Lindesmith, A. R. Problems in the social psychology of addiction. In Wilner, D. M., & Kassebaum, G. G. (Eds.), *Narcotics*. New York: McGraw-Hill, 1965.

Livingston, R. B. (ed.), *Narcotic drug addiction problems*. Bethesda, Md.: Publ. Hlth Serv. Public. No. 1050, 1963.

Lowry, J. V. Hospital treatment of the narcotic addict. *Fed. Proc. Quart.*, Dec, 1956.

Maddux, J. F. Hospital management of the narcotic addict. In Wilner D. M., & Kassebaum, G. G. (Eds.), *Narcotics*. New York: McGraw-Hill, 1965.

Monroe, J. J., & Hill, H. E. The Hill-Monroe Inventory for predicting acceptability for psychotherapy in the institutionalized narcotic addict. *J. clin. Psychol.*, 1958, **14**, 31–36.

O'Donnell, J. A. The relapse rate in narcotics addiction: A critique of follow-up studies. In Wilner, D. M., and Kassebaum, G. G. (eds.), *Narcotics*. New York: McGraw-Hill, 1965.

O'Neal, Patricia, & Robins, Lee N. Childhood patterns predictive of adult schizophrenia: A 30-year follow-up study. *Amer. J. Psychiat.*, 1958, **115**, 385–391.

Pearson, M. M., & Little, R. B. The treatment of drug addiction: Private practice experience with 84 addicts. *Amer. J. Psychiat.*, 1965, **122**, 164–169.

Proceedings (1962) White House Conference on Narcotics and Drug Abuse. Washington, D. C.: Gov't Printing Office, 1963.

Redl, F. Strategy and techniques of the Life Space Interview. *Amer. J. Orthopsychiat.*, 1959, **29**, 1–18.

Rickels, K., & Downing, R. Compliance and improvement in drug-treated and placebo-treated neurotic outpatients. *Arch. gen. Psychiat.*, 1966, **14**, 631–633.

Rosenfeld, Eva. Teen age addiction. In Bier, W. C. (Ed.), *Problems in addiction: Alcohol and drug addiction*. New York: Fordham Univ. Press, 1962.

Schneck, H. Narcotic withdrawal symptoms in newborn infant resulting from maternal addiction. *J. Pediat.*, 1958, **52**, 584–587.

Sharp, H. C. Identifying placebo reactors. *J. Psychol.*, 1965, **60**, 205–212.

Slobody, L. B., & Cabrinik, R. Neonatal narcotic addiction. *Quart. Rev. Pediat.*, 1959, **14**, 169–171.

Steg, Nina. Narcotic withdrawal reactions in newborn. *Amer. J. dis. Child.*, 1957, **94**, 286–288.

Stein, K. B., Gough, H. G., & Sarbin, T. R. The dimensionality of the CPI Socialization Scale and an empirically derived typology among delinquent and nondelinquent boys. *Multivar. Behav. Resch.*, 1966, **1**, 197–208.

Sussman, S. Narcotics and methamphetamine use during pregnancy; effect on newborn infants. *Amer. J. dis. Child.*, 1963, **106**, 325–330.

Tatum, A. L., Sievers, M. H., & Collins, K. H. Morphine addiction and its physiological interpretation based on experimental evidence. *J. pharmacol. & exper. Therap.*, 1929, **36**, 447–475.

Terry, C. E., & Pellens, Mildred. *The opium problem*. New York: Bur. Soc. Hygiene, 1928.

Toolan, J. M., Zimmering, P., & Wortis, S. B. Adolescent drug addiction. *N.Y. State J. Med.*, 1952, **52**, 72–74.

Way, E. L. Control and treatment of drug addiction in Hong Kong. In Wilner, D. M., & Kassebaum, G. G. (eds.) *Narcotics*. New York: McGraw-Hill, 1965. Wikler, A. Rationale of the diagnosis and treatment of addictions. *Conn. St. Med. J.*, 1955, **19**, 560–568.

Wikler, A. On the nature of addiction and habituation. *Brit. J. Addict.*, 1961, **57**, 73–79.

Wikler, A. Psychologic bases of drug abuse. (in *Proc., White House Conf.*, 1962.)

Wikler, A. *Opiate addiction: Psychological and neurophysiological aspects in relation to clinical problems*. Springfield, Ill.: C. C. Thomas, 1963.

Wikler, A. Conditioning factors in opiate addiction and relapse. In Wilner, D. M., & Kassebaum, G. G. (eds.) *Narcotics*. New York: McGraw-Hill, 1965.

Wilkins, L. T. Some sociologic factors in drug-addiction control. In Wilner, D. M., & Kassebaum, G. G. (eds.) *Narcotics*. New York: McGraw-Hill, 1965.

Williams, R. J. Alcoholism as a nutritional problem. *J. clin Nutrition*, 1952, **1**, 32–36.

Wilner, D. M., & Kassebaum, G. G. (eds.) Narcotics. New York: McGraw-Hill, 1965.

Winick, C. Maturing out of narcotic addiction. *Bull. Narc.*, U.N. Dept. Soc. Affairs, 1962, **14**, 1.

Winick, C. The 35 to 40 age drop-off. (in *Proc. White House Conference*, 1962.)

Winick, C. Epidemiology of narcotic use. In Wilner, D. M., & Kassebaum, G. G. (Eds.), *Narcotics*. New York: McGraw-Hill, 1965.

Wolpe, J. Conditional inhibition of Craving, *Behav. Res. Ther.*, 1965, **2**, 285–288.

Yablonsky, L., & Dederich, C. E. Synanon: An analysis of some dimensions of the social structure of an antiaddiction society. In D. M. Wilner & G. G. Kassebaum (eds.) *Narcotics*. N.Y.: McGraw-Hill, 1965.

Zimmering, P., Toolan, J. M., Safrin, R., & Wortis, S. B. Drug addiction in relation to problems of adolescence. *Amer. J. Psychiat.*, 1952, **109**, 272–278.

Chapter 21

Academic Underachievement[1]

WILLIAM R. MORROW

For present purposes, academic underachievement is defined as academic performance significantly below expected performance. Stated more fully, the underachiever is one whose performance as measured by school grades or by achievement test scores, relative to the performance of comparable peers in the same or comparable settings, is significantly below his expected performance as predicted from a measure of his scholastic aptitude or "intelligence."

By this definition, underachievers are distinguished from such categories as low achievers whose academic performance is in accord with what would be expected on the basis of their low scholastic aptitude; delinquents and emotionally disturbed youngsters whose academic performance is not significantly below their expected performance; and school dropouts (although some school dropouts may have been underachievers prior to their quitting school).

In this chapter we discuss first the problem of measuring underachievement and of identifying underachievers. Next we review research findings regarding the onset of underachievement, modifiable personal characteristics of underachievers, and peer-group and family influences on underachievers. With this background, we turn to remedial measures. We look briefly at psychodynamic counseling and other methods which are often recommended despite their apparent ineffectiveness. Then we review the key principles of reinforcement learning theory, and examine promising methods of behavior modification that are based on these principles. These methods include the behavioral guidance of parents, teachers, and other adults in modifying the reinforcement contingencies that control the individual underachiever's behavior, several forms of behavioral academic counseling (individual and group), and programs that saturate the school curriculum with high-interest "popular culture" materials and activities which are closely integrated with the pupils' nonschool world. We conclude by summarizing these remedial methods and by commenting briefly on needed further refinements and research.

MEASURING UNDERACHIEVEMENT AND IDENTIFYING UNDERACHIEVERS

Statistical Artifact Versus Actual Underachievement

Thorndike (1963), in a lucid discussion of methodological pitfalls in research on "underachievement," distinguishes four sources of discrepancy between predicted and observed achievement: (1) errors of measurement, both random and systematic,

[1] The writer wishes to thank Betty Northrup for her help in reviewing pertinent literature for this paper.

(2) heterogeneity in the measure of academic achievement, (3) relatively stable, "unmodifiable" characteristics of the individual or his background (or, viewed otherwise, difficult-to-modify, institutionalized patterns of social discrimination against broad classes in our society, of which the individual may be a member), and (4) personal and educational factors that are potentially subject to manipulation and modification. Educationally, real aspects of underachievement are related to the fourth category and, to some extent, the third category. To deal meaningfully with actual underachievement, we must first rule out statistical artifacts and methodological pitfalls which are associated particularly with the first two categories. Let us examine each category.

Errors of Measurement

Achievement fails to correspond perfectly with aptitude partly because of errors of measurement in assessing achievement and in assessing aptitude. For example, if we give one form of an aptitude test to a group of students this week and an equivalent form next week, the results will not be identical for each student. Among the reasons for discrepancies are that "by chance" some students will feel better, pay closer attention, or work harder at one testing than another; some students will be luckier in guessing at certain answers on one occasion than on the other; some students will be better able to do the specific tasks on one form than on the other, even though the tasks are equivalent "on the average," etc.

How likely is it that large discrepancies will occur between actual and predicted achievement scores because of errors of measurement? Thorndike (1963, pp. 8–10 and 69–71) suggests an answer by presenting the necessary formulas and by applying them to a hypothetical example, assuming typical values for the formula terms. Assume that the standard deviation of scores on an achievement test obtained by sixth graders in a given school is 1 grade-unit, and that the correlation between sixth grade achievement and a fifth grade IQ test (predictor) is .7. Discrepancies between actual and predicted achievement-test grade-scores will then have a frequency distribution with a standard deviation of about $\frac{7}{10}$ of a grade. How much of this spread is due to measurement error alone? Assume that the reliabilities are .9 for the predictor IQ test and .8 for the criterion achievement test. The standard deviation of discrepancies due solely to errors of measurement will then be $\frac{1}{2}$ grade-unit. Thus, if *nothing* but errors of measurement in predictor and criterion were operating, about 16 students out of 100 would obtain achievement scores half a grade-unit or more below their predicted scores (and about 16 would obtain achievement scores half a grade-unit or more above their predicted scores).

Thus the classification of an individual as an "underachiever" is rather "chancy," because of *random* errors of measurement. In addition, it is necessary to avoid introducing *systematic* error by identifying underachievers through procedures that unwittingly capitalize on the "regression effect." When the correlation between any two measures is less than perfect (that is, less than 1.00), individuals who fall well above average on one measure will, on the average, be less superior on the other (and those who fall well below average on one measure will be less inferior on the other). The extent of such "regression" toward the average score on the second measure depends on how imperfect (how much less than 1.00) the correlation is.

Thus, if we seek to identify "underachievers" by merely computing a simple difference between aptitude and achievement standard scores (or percentiles), or by a ratio of achievement to aptitude standard scores, then individuals high on aptitude will appear falsely to be "underachievers"—as a statistical artifact resulting from the "regression effect." Instead, we must define "underachievement" in terms of the discrepancy between actual and *predicted* achievement—predicted from the individual's aptitude score on the basis of a regression equation.

Heterogeneity in the Achievement (Criterion) Variable

The criterion measure of actual achievement, relative to predicted achievement, must be essentially the same measure for all cases in the group with reference to which the individual's achievement is being evaluated. Otherwise apparent discrepancies will occur because the achievement measure changes in a *systematic* way for different identifiable subgroups. To take an extreme example, suppose we combined data on the relationship between a scholastic aptitude test and the college grade-point average for 10 Ivy League university students and 100 "sticks" college students, and used the single common regression equation based on sticks students. Practically all Ivy League students would then be falsely classified as "underachievers" because of systematic heterogeneity in the achievement measure: A grade of "C" at Ivy League might indicate a higher level of absolute achievement than an "A" at sticks.

Such heterogeneity, although perhaps less extreme, may occur whenever the reference sample combines data from different schools, different curricula or programs, different teachers, or different identifiable subgroups, however defined, for which different standards of performance may apply. When these subgroups can be distinguished, the statistical technique of analysis of covariance (see a standard statistics text such as Lindquist, 1953; Walker & Lev, 1958) can be used to test whether all subgroups share a common line of regression in predicting achievement from aptitude. If not, predicted achievement should be determined separately for each subgroup, or for each set of subgroups sharing a common regression line.

Relatively Stable, Difficult-to-Modify Factors

An individual's score on a measure of achievement depends partly on relatively stable, difficult-to-modify characteristics of the individual or his background, or differences in environmental conditions associated with those characteristics. To some extent, an aptitude measure is one such characteristic. Others are sex and socioeconomic status.

For example, when achievement is measured by grades, most "underachievers" in a mixed group of elementary or high school pupils are boys; more "achievers" are girls. Therefore, it is advisable to use a regression equation for determining predicted achievement that is based on a reference group of the same sex.

Characteristics such as sex and socioeconomic status are not characteristics that the school, the clinician, or the researcher can modify directly. At the same time, certain achievement-related aspects of the student's educational and social environment which may be *associated* with his sex or his socioeconomic status can be changed. Thus, factors considered in this section shade off into the fourth category—modifiable factors.

When sources of discrepancy between predicted and observed achievement considered thus far are carefully controlled and statistically allowed for, a residue of underachievement remains that reflects factors in the fourth category.

Personal, Educational, and Environmental Factors Subject to Manipulation and Modification

How readily factors that influence underachievement can be manipulated and modified is a matter of degree. Some aspects of a pupil's educational and social environment can be changed fairly readily by school personnel, depending partly on available resources. He can be referred to a guidance counselor, or given remedial help, or given different assignments to appeal to his interests, and so on. Other aspects may be harder to change, for example, a parent's excessive criticism or lack of interest in the pupil's school work, or his close friends' ridiculing of regular study habits. These potentially modifiable factors are the main focus of concern for the educator, the researcher, and the clinician.

RECOMMENDED PROCEDURES FOR DETERMINING UNDERACHIEVEMENT

The identification of an individual as an underachiever requires: (1) a measure of his actual achievement, (2) the average achievement score predicted for an appropriate reference group (same scholastic aptitude score, same or comparable school, same sex and socioeconomic status), (3) the standard error of estimate of that predicted achievement score, and (4) a decision as to the degree of statistical confidence one wishes to have in the judgment that any discrepancy between actual and predicted achievement is more than a "chance" fluctuation.

What Measure of Achievement to Use

Two main types of achievement measures have been used: grade-point average (GPA), and standardized achievement test score.

GPA has the desirable characteristics of availability, quantifiability, some stability over time, some minimum trans-situational comparability, and social significance in terms of consequences for the individual. Undesirable characteristics are that grades may reflect somewhat variable criteria, are susceptible to rater bias, and are not standardized from one school, curriculum, or teacher to another.

When GPA is used as the criterion, it is recommended that only grades in academic courses be included (and not grades in activity courses such as physical education, typing, etc.). It is also recommended, in order to increase the reliability of the criterion, that cumulative GPA over several semesters be used.

Standardized achievement test scores share with grades the advantages of quantifiability and (probably greater) stability over time. They are superior to grades in objectivity and in comparability across schools, curricula, and teachers.

A major disadvantage of standardized achievement tests is that they correlate *too* highly with scholastic aptitude or intelligence tests. Test authors and publishers, in seeking to develop standardized achievement tests for use by school systems throughout the country, which vary in curricula and in other ways, have tended to avoid specificity of learning content measured. Instead, they have emphasized reading comprehension skills, reasoning ability, judgment, etc., as applied to various subject matters. As a result, there is much fairly direct overlap in what is measured by scholastic aptitude tests and by standardized school achievement tests (Coleman & Cureton, 1954; Kelley, 1927, pp. 193–209; Remmers & Gage, 1955, pp. 227). (This "duplication" may not necessarily apply to carefully developed, comprehensive achievement examinations that are used in a particular institution or school system.)

We are inclined to prefer the use of GPA, despite its serious limitations, as a criterion in assessing academic underachievement.

How to Estimate Predicted Achievement?

The aptitude measure used to predict the individual's expected achievement should be his score on a standardized scholastic aptitude or "intelligence" test. The reader is referred to a good text on psychological and educational tests (for example, see Cronbach, 1960) for a discussion of specific tests and of criteria for choosing a test to use in a particular situation.

The reliability of the aptitude measure will be improved by averaging measurements obtained on two or more occasions. Moreover, where there is some question as to the individual's "true" scholastic aptitude, an individual test should be used instead of relying solely on group tests.

Two alternative approaches are suggested for estimating expected achievement. One method is to apply the *regression line formula*. The data required (for a suitable reference group, for example, all pupils in the same grade, the same school, who study the same or equivalent curricula, the same sex, and, preferably, the same socioeconomic status) are the values to be entered in the following formulas.

$$C^1 = r_{pc}\left(\frac{SD_c}{SD_p}\right)\left(P - M_p\right) + M_c$$

$$SE_{c^1} = SD_c\sqrt{1 - r_{pc}^2}$$

$$t = \frac{C - C^1}{SE_{c^1}}$$

where C^1 Individual's expected score on criterion achievement measure

C Individual's obtained score on criterion achievement measure

P Individual's score on predictor aptitude measure

r_{pc} Correlation between predictor and criterion measures

SD_c Standard deviation of criterion measure

SD_p Standard deviation of predictor measure

SD_{c^1} Standard error of expected score on criterion measure

M_p Group mean on predictor measure

M_c Group mean on criterion measure

The probability that the discrepancy between actual and expected achievement is greater than "chance" is determined from a table of t, found in most statistics texts.

What if data are not available for calculating the regression line formula? An *alternative* is to calculate the mean and standard deviation of the achievement scores (for example, GPA) of a random sample of students of the same school, grade, sex, socioeconomic status, and approximate scholastic aptitude as the student in question. The sample mean yields an estimate of the individual's predicted achievement; the standard deviation represents the standard error of that estimate. The probability that the individual is an underachiever is determined by dividing his distance from the group mean on achievement by the standard error, and by looking up the obtained value of t. Even a small sample yields an estimate that is superior to guessing.

Evaluating the "Significance" of a Discrepancy

What probability value indicates that the individual is a "true" underachiever? No definite answer can be given to this question. One guideline is suggested by the research convention of treating the .05 significance level as a cutoff point; this is sometimes stretched to the .10 level.

In evaluating practical (not statistical) significance, other facts to consider are the absolute size of the discrepancy between the actual and the predicted achievement, the absolute achievement level, and the possible social consequences of continuing to perform at that level.

WHAT IF BOTH APTITUDE AND ACHIEVEMENT INDIXES ARE MARKEDLY DEPRESSED?

What if an individual's achievement is in line with his expected achievement as predicted from scholastic aptitude test score, but there is reason to suppose that the latter may be grossly depressed as a result of cultural deprivation or other environmental causes? "Intelligence" or scholastic "aptitude" tests measure learned performance, not any innate "given." Any inference from differences in "intelligence" test scores to differences in inborn ability or potential is based on the assumption of equal educational and of other environmental opportunities. Environmental opportunities are in fact grossly unequal. Empirical evidence indicates that unequal opportunities significantly influence "intelligence" test scores (Hunt, 1961), as well as achievement test scores and GPA. And once an individual (or a whole class of individuals) has been severely deprived of learning opportunities and incentives over an extended time period, and has fallen behind academically, the difficulties of "catching up" tend to be cumulative. The potentialities for "unfreezing" such patterns and for "catching up" in performance on "intelligence" tests as well as on achievement indixes, can be adequately assessed only by providing genuinely compensatory conditions for learning; these conditions may have to include convincingly equal occupational opportunities as incentives to work at school learning.

For these and related reasons, many clinicians, teachers, program developers, and researchers may wish to qualify some of the preceding sections in considering what criteria to apply in selecting "underachieving" individuals for certain types of remedial programs. Dramatic results have been obtained by Birnbrauer and his associates (1965) in teaching severely retarded children academic skills by systematic reinforcement procedures. Bijou (1965) has emphasized the broad implication of these results: When adequate data are not available to reach a conclusion as to what *any* category of individuals can or cannot do under more optimal conditions, an open-minded attitude should be maintained.

CHARACTERISTICS AND BACKGROUNDS OF UNDERACHIEVERS

Onset of Underachievement

How early is chronic underachievement likely to develop? Shaw and McCuren (1960) investigated this question for 11th and 12th graders who had remained in the same school district since the first grade, and stood in the upper 25 percent of the school population on scholastic aptitude (IQ above 110 on a group test given in grade 8). The subjects were classified as underachievers if their cumulative high school GPA was below their class mean; as normal achievers if their GPA was above the class mean (2.4, where A = 4, B = 3, C = 2, D = 1, F = 0). Underachieving boys were then compared with achieving boys, and underachieving girls with achieving girls, as to GPA for each grade from 1 through 11. Male underachievers as a group fell significantly ($p < .01$) below achievers at every grade beginning with the 3rd. Female underachievers did not differ significantly ($p > .05$) from achievers in any of the first 8 grades; they showed a clear difference ($p < .01$) in GPA only for the 9th, 10th, and 11th grades (on the basis of which they had been selected in the first place).

If Shaw and McCuren's findings hold true for other settings and samples, chronic underachievement by children of above-average scholastic aptitude may begin in the early elementary grades for boys, but not until high school for girls. Two other investigators (Appell, 1964; Barrett, 1957) have reported somewhat similar findings. Corresponding data do not seem to be available for students of average or lower scholastic aptitude.

MODIFIABLE PERSONAL CHARACTERISTICS OF UNDER-ACHIEVERS

We shall not attempt to review here in detail the extensive literature on academic underachievement. The interested reader is referred to Kornrich's (1965) anthology, recent reviews (Goldberg, 1965, pp. 24–34; Gowan, 1960; Miller, 1961, esp. Ch. 2; Taylor, 1964; Wellington & Wellington, 1965), and Gowan's (1961, esp. pp. 151–152; 1965, esp. p. 194) annotated bibliographies. This literature is quite uneven in methodological soundness, definitions of underachievers and comparison groups, grade levels studied, sex of samples, and measurement procedures used, etc. It is difficult to thread one's way through the resulting maze of reported findings. Moreover, since most of these studies are correlational or compare descriptive characteristics of criterion groups, it is difficult to derive from this literature firm support for causal interpretations and corresponding remedial procedures.

Below we summarize characteristics that have repeatedly been found to correlate significantly with underachievement in both sexes at various grade levels.

Broadly stated, the most clearcut and consistent research finding is that most underachievers, as compared with normal and overachievers, show less effective, persistent, and systematic work habits on academic tasks, instead show incompatible behavior to a greater extent, and more often fail to find academic work rewarding. Somewhat more specifically, the differences listed below have been reported at both the high school (junior and senior) level (Battle, 1957; Carter, 1956, 1960; Davids & Sidman, 1962; Frankel, 1960; Gawronski & Mathis, 1965; Gough, 1953; Lewis, 1941; Martin & Davidson, 1964; McBee & Duke, 1960; O'Leary, 1955; Payne & Farquhar, 1962; Pierce & Bowman, 1960; Silverman, Davids & Andrews, 1963; Sprinthall, 1964; Taylor, 1964; Taylor & Farquhar, 1965; Wilson & Morrow, 1962) and the college level (Aiken, 1964; Baker & Madell, 1965a, 1965b; Borow, 1945; Brown & Holtzman, 1955, 1964; Burgess, 1956; Diener, 1960; Dowd, 1952; Holtzman, Brown & Farquhar, 1954; Jones, 1955; McArthur, 1965; Morgan, 1952; Popham & Moore, 1960; Todd, Terrell & Frank, 1962; and Waters, 1964), although corresponding data at the elementary school level appear to be lacking.

1. The most marked differences appear to be in *study habits*. Most underachievers work less regularly and persistently at academic tasks, exert less effort and are more distractible when they do work, and leave uncompleted a greater (and substantial) amount of assigned work in one or more subjects.

2. In their *study methods*, underachievers tend to be more unsystematic, careless, and inefficient.

3. In their *attitudes, interests, and goals*, underachievers tend to have lower academic-achievement aspiration levels; to find school more unsatisfying and teachers more emotionally unsupportive, unreasonable, and erratic; to indicate somewhat less interest and satisfaction (as a group) in academic and intellectual activities, and (a minority) somewhat more interest in restless adventure and excitement; to be somewhat more uncertain regarding vocational goals, to have somewhat less professional-and-scientific goals, to be more impulsive and more concerned with immediate satisfactions, less future oriented and less planful regarding future goals; and, in general, to display a pattern of interests and values less similar to the ones of teachers.

4. The relationship between *anxiety* and academic performance appears to be complex. A certain degree of "test anxiety" may facilitate performance; in other instances, test anxiety may impair performance (Alpert & Haber, 1960; Dember, Nairne, & Miller, 1962). More generally, experimental studies have indicated an inverse-U relationship between the degree of anxiety or arousal and performance on complex tasks (Duffy, 1957; Malmo, 1957; Sarason, 1960; Jenness, 1962). With very low arousal, performance on complex tasks is impaired; with moderate arousal or anxiety, performance is optimum; more intense arousal interferes with refined cognitive processes and motor skills, impairing performance. Recent studies at the elementary school level (Feldhusen & Klausmeier, 1962) and the college level (Paul & Eriksen, 1964; Spielberger, 1962) point to a negative relationship between anxiety and achievement for students in the middle ranges of scholastic aptitude, and possibly for those of low aptitude, but not for those of very high aptitude—who tend to do well regardless.

The differentiating characteristics just cited refer essentially to *academic* behaviors and behavior-deficits, to certain interfering behaviors, and to the rewarding or punishing consequences of academic and interfering behaviors. In the writer's opinion, there is only weak and equivocal evidence for the hypothesis of an underachiever "personality" pattern or patterns, apart from situations that demand academic types of behavior. Although the evidence cited above is largely correlational, leaving interpretation uncertain, it seems likely that a major immediate "cause" of underachievement is insufficient study and ineffective study habits. Whatever the causal conditions controlling this behavior deficit, any remedial procedure that does not correct it seems unlikely to improve academic achievement.

GROUP INFLUENCES ON UNDERACHIEVERS

Some evidence suggests that behaviors associated with underachievement may be anchored in *peer-group norms*. Thus the friendship-clique norms of (a certain minority of) high school underachievers more often include negative reactions to school and to authority, violations of adult standards, and restless excitement-seeking, etc. (Conklin, 1940; Morrow & Wilson, 1961). At the college level, fraternity rushing and pledging are found to have adverse effects on academic achievement (Spielberger & Weitz, 1964).

As to the possible role of *family relations* in underachievement, two general findings have been reported with some consistency by a number of investigators: (a) Parents of underachievers, as contrasted with parents of normal and overachievers, tend to place *less emphasis on education* for their youngsters. This has been reported at the elementary school level (Kurtz & Swensen, 1961), the high school level (Pierce & Bowman, 1960; McGillivray, 1964; Morrow & Wilson, 1961), and the college level (Shore & Leiman, 1965). Parents of underachievers are less likely to express a value for education in specific ways such as making a study desk available, recognizing the amount of homework the student has done, having a reasonable idea of the grades expected of the student, participating actively in parent-teacher organizations, showing readiness to make financial sacrifices for the student's education, etc. (McGillivray, 1964). (b) Families of underachievers tend to be characterized by a *poorer family morale and integration*, which includes less mutual acceptance between parents and children, less satisfaction with family relations, less sharing and communication, and less consensus and awareness of each other. This type of finding has been reported at both the elementary level (Hattwick & Stowell, 1936; Peppin, 1963; Walsh, 1956), the high school level (Leibman, 1953; Morrow & Wilson, 1961; Shaw & Dutton, 1962; Shaw & White, 1965), and the college level (Field, 1953; Jones, 1955).

REMEDIAL PROCEDURES

Restatement of Problem

What are the crucial behaviors that must be modified in order to change underachievement into normal achievement? For some underachievers *attendance* at school or classes on a regular basis needs to be increased. Most underachievers probably need to *work* more regularly, with more concentration, and in many cases for longer periods on academic tasks, and to apply more effective *methods* when they do work. Approaches to remedying these deficiences may be divided into two categories which are based on contrasting assumptions: (a) the efforts to modify academic behaviors directly by applying learning principles; and (b) the efforts to modify emotional conflicts or attitudes that are assumed to be "underlying causes" expressed in "surface symptoms" that result in underachievement. The second category is often referred to as psychodynamic or insight-therapy methods.

In our view, certain direct behavioral methods are promising; we devote our main attention to them below. First, however, we comment briefly on psychodynamic methods and on certain direct methods that appear to be generally ineffective.

METHODS OF LIMITED EFFECTIVENESS

Psychodynamic Insight Counseling

The assumption has persisted, despite a lack of empirical support, that a "method of choice" for correcting underachievement is psychodynamically oriented counseling, individually or in small groups, aimed at increasing the underachiever's insight into emotional conflicts presumed to underlie his poor academic performance. Occasionally a similar type of counseling may be offered to parents, individually or in groups, on the assumption that disturbed family relations are a major source of the underachiever's emotional conflicts.

There have been relatively few experimental studies with before-after measurement and control groups which are designed to assess the effectiveness of this approach. Available experimental data suggest that such counseling, whether administered individually (Baymur & Patterson, 1960; Winkler, Teigland, Munger, & Kranzler, 1965) or in groups (Baymur & Patterson, 1960; Broedel, Ohlsen, Proff, & Southard, 1960; Chestnut, 1965; Cohn, 1966; Cubbedge & Hall, 1964; Hart, 1963; Keppers & Caplan, 1962; Mink, 1964; Sheldon & Landsman, 1950; Spielberger & Weitz, 1964; Winborn & Schmidt, 1962; Winkler, Teigland, Munger & Kranzler, 1965), has little or no effect on academic achievement.

This repeated finding is consistent with the conclusion of Eysenck (1961) and of Levitt (1957), based on extensive reviews of the literature, that there is little empirical support for the hypothesis that psychodynamic psychotherapy (whether psychoanalytic, nondirective, or some other variant) produces significant improvement in maladaptive behavior. Moreover, there is little empirical support for the key premises of psychodynamic psychotherapy, for example, the assumption that self-insight is either a necessary or a sufficient condition for the modification of behavior, maladaptive or otherwise (see for example Eysenck, 1960, esp. part I; Rachman, 1963).

"Enrichment," Work-Study, and Programmed Instruction

By themselves, "enrichment" work-study and programmed instruction have been found *insufficient* to modify underachievement, even though they embody pertinent principles. Specific examples that have included research evaluation are the following: (a) counseling elementary school teachers to provide challenging special enrichment projects for early identified bright underachievers (Jackson & Cleveland, 1966); (b) a work-study program for underachieving potential high school dropouts (Longstreth, Shanley, & Rice, 1964); (c) the use of programmed instructional materials with underachieving, emotionally disturbed students (Chittick, Eldred, & Brooks, 1966). Each of these programs started from the observation that underachievers often find traditional school programs uninteresting and unrewarding. Their solution was to provide learning content and form that, hopefully, would be closer to pupil interests and goals and/or would immediately reinforce desired behavior.

Two limitations may have accounted for the negative results. First, the principle of gearing the curriculum to student interest was not carried far enough to insure intrinsic reinforcement. More generally, these programs did not utilize sufficiently powerful reinforcers. Second, the programs did not make powerful reinforcers systematically contingent on the verified occurrence of desired academic behaviors.

BEHAVIOR MODIFICATION METHODS

Theoretical and Experimental Basis

If psychodynamic insight therapy has had little success in modifying underachievement, and if its basic assumptions lack empirical support, what alternatives are available? Before trying to answer this question, let us consider briefly what criteria should be met by an effective remedial approach. Ideally, corrective methods should be rationally derived from a body of basic theory that has firm empirical support, is relevant to planned modification of behavior, is operational, and that points clearly to identifiable conditions which are accessible, manipulable, and exert a powerful influence on behavior. In our opinion, the remedial approaches that best meet these criteria are (a) *behavior modification techniques* that are based on *reinforcement learning theory*, and (b) are *combined* as appropriate with techniques that harness the power (and economy) of *social system influences*, on the basis of pertinent group dynamics theory.

Key principles of reinforcement theory are summarized below. The reader is referred elsewhere for a comprehensive introduction to reinforcement theory (Holland & Skinner, 1961), applied behavior modification (Eysenck, 1960; Eysenck, 1964; Krasner & Ullman, 1965; Reese, 1966; Staats, 1964; Thomas & Goodman, 1965; Ullman & Krasner, 1965; Ulrich, Stachnik, & Mabry, 1966; Wolpe & Lazarus, 1966), and group dynamics (Cartwright & Zander, 1960; Hare, 1962).

The key principle of reinforcement theory is that *operant* ("voluntary," nonreflex) *behavior is governed by its consequences*. Some consequences strengthen or *increase* the subsequent rate of the behavior that produces them. If a hungry baby is repeatedly fed after he begins crying, he will soon cry regularly when hungry. If a child is given candy or attention while he is having a "temper tantrum," the probability is increased that he will use tantrums in the future to get what he wants. If a child is rewarded for completing certain chores by being given praise and approval, a special snack, access to a favorite TV program, freedom to go out and play, or etc.—provided that the particular form of "pay" is rewarding to the particular child—the future probability of doing chores willingly is apt to increase. The rewarding consequence in each of these examples is technically called a *positive reinforcer*.

Behavior is also accelerated if it results in the *removal* of aversive or painful stimulii; that is, if the behavior enables the individual to escape from, to delay, or to avoid altogether an aversive stimulus. Thus the parent's behavior of giving a child candy to stop his tantrum is reinforced by the ending of the unpleasant tantrum. The probability that the parent will repeat candy-giving behavior to escape (or avoid) future tantrums is thereby increased. This strengthening of the *parent's* behavior by its consequence of removing an aversive stimulus is termed *negative reinforcement*; the aversive stimulus in this context is called a negative reinforcer.

Behavior is weakened or *decreased* in rate when it is followed by (a) no consequences or only neutral consequences, or by (b) an aversive stimulus. The former process is termed extinction; the latter, punishment. In *extinction* a previously reinforced response, when repeatedly emitted but no longer followed by any reinforcing stimulus, declines in rate until it is extinguished. For example, if tantrums previously reinforced with attention now *consistently* produce neither attention nor any other reinforcer, tantrums will decline and disappear. If a child's questions about the world are consistently ignored, he will soon stop asking questions.

Punishment resulting from the impersonal operation of natural laws, when the consequence is clear and immediate, may expedite elimination of maladaptive behavior. The burnt child avoids touching the fire again. The toddler learns, partly by experiencing natural punishment, to detour around obstacles instead of bumping into them. *Social* punishment is more problematic in its effects. Unless the punishment is severe enough to completely suppress the unwanted behavior (which is being maintained by some positive reinforcement), that behavior may decline only temporarily and will increase again when punishment is discontinued (or sometimes even while punishment continues). Social punishment may also result in unwanted side consequences. The punishing agent may become a conditioned aversive stimulus and lose much of his reinforcing power for the punished individual; their social relationship may be disrupted, and the agent's further effectiveness as socializer and teacher may be impaired. However, if alternative behaviors to obtain reinforcement are readily available, a mild punishment such as a brief time-out (administered matter-of-factly) may expedite elimination of the unwanted behavior, with no untoward side effects.

A reinforcer will increase the rate of specified behavior (and punishment will decrease specified behavior) only if its presentation is systematically *contingent* on the occurrence of the specified behavior. If rewards and punishments are presented in a *noncontingent* manner, with no systematic relationship to the behavior that precedes them, little change of behavior is apt to result.

If the desired behavior is initially weak or nonexistent, *shaping* may be required. Shaping involves *differential reinforcement* of *successive approximations* to the final behavior. Differential reinforcement means that, on any given trial, only behavior that meets a specified criterion is reinforced. By gradually raising the criterion, behavior is altered through successive approximations to the final desired behavior. Thus, in training a high jumper, the coach may initially place the crossbar low, raise it a little after a few successful jumps, and so on. Similarly, children are more apt to develop the capacity for sustained concentration on school assignments if they are initially reinforced for concentrating on brief assignments, with a gradual increase in the duration required. This example points to another important concept, the *scheduling of reinforcement*.

In the *acquisition* of new behavior (or the strengthening of behavior that is very weak), it is often necessary to provide reinforcing consequences following every instance of the desired response, that is, to apply a *continuous* reinforcement schedule. As the response rate increases, the behavior can be *maintained* more efficiently by shifting gradually to a more *intermittent* schedule; for example, reinforcing every other response, then every third or fourth response, and so on. Here is an illustration from a classroom for boys with emotional problems (Whelan & Haring, 1966). A boy with a history of yelling, of running about the classroom, of destroying his work, and of failing to complete assigned tasks, was assigned 15 arithmetic problems to complete within 30 minutes. He spent the first 15 minutes looking about, tapping his feet, and playing with his pencil. The teacher had observed that he repeatedly tried to get her to stand beside his desk and to watch him work. Following this cue, she introduced a systematic reinforcement schedule in which the boy was required to do one problem without the teacher being present; then she watched him do one. Within the remaining 15 minutes he completed all the problems, and the teacher had successfully increased the criterion to a ratio of three problems done independently for each reinforcement (teacher presence and verbal praise) as he completed the next problem. Such a shift to larger and larger ratios of independent work per reinforcement is essential to maintain behavior efficiently. The shift is also necessary to develop skill in learning independently, and to develop self-control of the appropriate behavior by consequences that are intrinsic to completion of tasks, social approval, and self-approval.

The individual repeatedly has the experience that a certain behavior is reinforced when emitted in the presence of one stimulus, but not in the presence of another stimulus. When he emits the given behavior only on the first class of occasions and not on the second, he has formed a *discrimination*; the behavior has been brought under *stimulus control*. The positive stimulus in the presence of which the response is reinforced is a *discriminative stimulus* for that behavior. Before such a discrimination becomes established, the individual has shown "excessive" stimulus *generalization*. For example, the young child may initially say "Da-da" in the presence not only of his father but of any adult male. By experiencing differential reinforcement of his vocalization, he comes to discriminate; the response "Da-da" is then emitted only under the stimulus control of his father's presence as a discriminative stimulus for that response. In a similar way, the individual normally learns that "there is a time and a place for everything," that different kinds of behavior are appropriate in different situations, and that they are differentially reinforced.

Discrimination is often imperfect, however, and situations are often arranged in such a way as to be overlapping; hence, behavior appropriate to one situation may often interfere with behavior appropriate to another situation. In these circumstances *stimulus change*, that is rearrangement and rescheduling of stimulus situations so as to facilitate sharper discrimination, when *combined with new reinforcement contingencies*, may produce more rapid change than is possible in the old, unaltered situations. This is one reason for the frequent practice of holding "human relations" workshops in "cultural island" settings removed from "back-home" situations; likewise the practice of sending certain people away to "training schools" or "mental hospitals" to modify their deviant behavior. A major difficulty with this practice is that desired behavior-changes developed in the "cultural island" may fail to generalize to "back-home" situations. To be effective, stimulus change (combined with new reinforcement contingencies) must be introduced into those situations in which the altered behavior is to be maintained on a continuing basis; or else, the new behavior developed in cultural islands must generalize to back-home settings and then be maintained by the reinforcement contingencies operating in the "back-home" situations.

The ensuing sections describe several types of programs that apply these principles to the modification of behavior associated with underachievement.

New Reinforcement Contingencies Applied by Parents, Teachers, and Other Adults

The Arizona Behavioral Research Project has been developing new methods for dealing with potentially delinquent youngsters who both underachieve in school and show misbehaviors which range from truancy and classroom attention-getting behaviors to misdemeanors (Thorne, Tharp, & Wetzel, 1966, 1967). After parental permission to work with the referred child and his family is obtained, assessment procedures are directed toward specifying the following:

1. The problematic behaviors and their base-line (pretreatment) frequency, usually via a special record kept by a parent or a teacher.
2. The occasions and settings (discriminative stimuli) where the problematic behavior occurs.
3. The conditions that maintain the problematic behaviors and the behavior-deficits. The focus here is on ways in which the family (or teachers or others) may unwittingly reward unwanted behaviors (for instance, by giving the child special attention for substandard academic performances, for avoidance of study, or for distractible behavior); may completely fail to reward and punish the child *contingent* on his actions; may make excessive use of aversive stimuli (punishment and negative reinforcement), with insufficient use of positive rewards; or may show gross inconsistency in applying reinforcement.
4. The desired behavior-changes, that is, the academic and other prosocial behaviors to be increased, and the disapproved behaviors to be decreased.
5. The potential reinforcers and their relative strength for the particular child. Typical examples of reinforcers are receipt of social approval, attention, or affection from a specified adult; money, television watching, movie attendance, cosmetics, the use of the family car, permission to go on a date, participation in preferred activities, etc.

On the basis of this assessment, the behavior analyst (representing the Project) and the adult "mediator(s)" (parent, teacher, neighbor, relative, etc.) together formulate a *behavior modification plan* to be carried out by the mediator(s). (The project staff avoid direct contact with the child, except for the initial assessment.) In general, these plans call for the mediator(s) to administer positive reinforcers to the child in a systematic way, contingent on his emission of specific desired behaviors, and to consistently withhold reinforcers when unwanted behavior occurs.

The behavior analyst essentially teaches the mediator to apply more effective techniques of child management. However, he tries to avoid asking a mediator to behave toward the child in a way that is incompatible with the mediator's occupational or family roles, professional duties, or individual personality. Where possible, the first goal is to modify behaviors that are most annoying or serious to the parent or the teacher, and that are relatively frequent, in order to provide quick reinforcing feedback and encouragement to the mediator.

The behavior analysts are subprofessionals with bachelor's degrees in a variety of fields. The Project's senior staff give them four weeks of intensive training in reinforcement theory and practice, and remain available for consultation.

An interim report of the Project suggests a high degree of success in improving academic performance and in reducing misbehavior in most cases. The following case (Thorne, Tharp, & Wetzel, 1967) illustrates the approach.[2]

Claire is a bright, moderately attractive 16-year-old who was referred to the project for truancy, poor grades, and incorrigibility at home. The parents were divorced 6 years ago and the mother now supports the two of them as a maid. The father is out of state, as is Claire's older married sister.

When the referral came from a local high school, it stated that Claire was going to be expelled for truancy. The staff persuaded them to hold up expulsion for several days, which they were willing to do.

The mother was eager for help, although she lacked the physical or emotional resources to assist very much. Claire had been staying home from school for days and was now threatening to run away. Her mother had withdrawn all money, the use of the telephone, and dating privileges. These were all very powerful reinforcers to Claire but, unfortunately, her mother had not provided any clear way for Claire to earn them back.

Obviously, the most pressing problem was Claire's truancy and it was imperative that an intervention plan be prepared immediately to prevent suspension from school. Also, Claire's attending school would be very reinforcing to mother who was, at this time, somewhat dubious that a "noncounseling" approach would be successful. By winning her confidence, it would be possible to begin shaping her to regard Claire in a more positive perspective, which would be necessary before a more amicable relationship could be worked out between them.

An intervention plan was agreed upon by mother, Claire, and a staff member. Telephone privileges and weekend dates were contingent on attending school all day. The school attendance officer would dispense a note to Claire at the end of each day if she had attended all of her classes. On presenting the note to mother, Claire earned telephone usage (receiving and calling out) for that day. If she received four out of five notes during the week she earned one weekend date night, and five out of five notes earned two weekend date nights. Phone usage on the weekend was not included in this plan.

Much to mother's astonishment Claire accepted the plan. Mother herself felt the plan "childish" and was apprehensive about Claire complying with it. Staff emphasized the necessity and benefit of praising Claire whenever she brought a note home. This would be difficult for mother, who was inconsistent, ineffectual, and emotional in all her relations with Claire. However, she was given support through several brief phone calls every week.

Despite frequent family upsets, Claire attended school regularly from the first day of intervention. The plan was altered (in technical terms the schedule was "thinned") after a month so that Claire would receive only two notes a week. A note on Wednesdays would mean she attended all her classes on Monday, Tuesday, and Wednesday. This was backed up by the privilege of one weekend night out. A second note on Friday meant full attendance on Thursday and Friday, which was backed up by a second weekend night out. The telephone privileges were taken off contingency. About 7 weeks later the notes were stopped entirely.

The results were quite impressive. During the first 46 days of school (base-line period) Claire missed 30 days of school (65.2 percent). While working with the Project for less than 3 months she was illegally absent twice (6.6 percent). She was *never* illegally absent again following termination, which covers the entire second semester of school. Grades were beyond redemption during the first semester mainly because of absences, thus causing her to fail two subjects. This dropped to one failure during the second semester.

According to her counselor at school, Claire continued to experience a poor relationship with her mother but did begin expressing positive attitudes and interests in her classes. Thus, the project was successful in preventing this girl from being expelled

[2] Quoted with the kind permission of the authors and the publishers of *Federal Probation*.

from school and probably running away. This was accomplished with a very modest expenditure of staff time.

Behavioral Academic Counseling—Individual

Fox (1962) has described a pilot individual counseling application of reinforcement principles to effect the use of efficient study habits by five volunteer college students. The results were promising. They were GPA rise per student of from 1 to 3 full letter grades and the completion by four students of all study during the day, with evenings and weekends free, with the fifth student falling just short of this goal.

The principle of *shaping*, combined with *coaching* (Thomas & Goodman 1965), was applied throughout the program by building the study program for one course at a time, by establishing regularly scheduled study habits for a given course before working on efficient study techniques, and by bringing initiation of study under stimulus control first, and then gradually increasing the duration of study, etc.

Stimulus control of study initiation was developed by advising the student to undertake the study of a given course (working on one course at a time) at a specified time and place (unique to that course, and free of distractions) each weekday, taking only materials for that course with him. Sustained study of a given course was developed gradually by *making maximum use of available reinforcers* and by using the knowledge of *reinforcement schedules* and their effects. Aversive features such as the effort of sustained study of difficult material, having to forego completely competing social activities (friends, coffee, etc.), and the feelings of guilt and resentment on giving in to the temptation to quit studying, were minimized in the following way. The student was instructed (and thus formally authorized), if he experienced discomfort or began to daydream, to leave the study room immediately and to do whatever he pleased. However, to insure positive reinforcement before leaving, he was instructed to read one more page of the text or to solve one assigned problem and then to leave immediately. Each day for several days the amount of work to be performed, after a decision to leave, was increased (for example, to 5 pages of reading or 3 physics problems). Thereafter he was to do this amount of work at the outset and then make a decision whether to leave or to do exactly the same amount again—and so on, making an independent decision after each such work unit. The reinforcement of each work unit presumably included satisfaction over completing an assignment plus earning a right to leave. In technical terms the student was put on a fixed-ratio reinforcement schedule, which typically produces high rates of work and strong resistance to extinction (giving up), provided that the ratio of work per reinforcement is not too great ("strained"). In time, the student was studying each course (in a different room) for one full hour each day.

Once attendance in the study room for a given course was well established, the method of *successive approximations* was used to develop efficient study techniques. Robinson's (1946) SQ3R technique, with some modifications, was applied. SQ3R means "survey," "question," "read," "recite," "review." "Survey" means getting an overview of a chapter by skimming over the main headings (and reading the introductory or end-of-chapter summary, where provided). "Question" means reskimming and formulating questions suggested by the headings, in order to look for specific answers while reading. "Reading" means reading without underlining or notetaking. "Recitation" means outlining or otherwise reciting the material while the book is closed. "*It is during recitation that the student is emitting the essential behavior to be learned*; reading is like watching someone else perform." "Review" means checking the recitation outline against the book or rereading the chapter, for errors of omission and commission. For a given course, the student was trained in each of these 5 skills in succession. Training in each phase was broken down into steps or work units—with smaller units for the more difficult phases. Throughout the work on study techniques, the student was kept on a schedule according to which he made a separate decision, after each section of a chapter, whether to stay and study or to leave and play.

Fox suggests that the costliness of this approach in professional counseling time might be significantly reduced in three ways: (1) by developing an instruction book that might serve most students, (2) by developing machine programs (probably requiring complex branching), and (3) by training students as counselors.

Behavioral Academic Counseling—Group

Preventive Student-to-Student Academic Counseling of College Freshmen

Brown (1965) has conducted a carefully controlled experimental evaluation of a program that contains elements of Fox's (1962) approach, and that incorporates economizing measures (as Fox suggests) to reach more students. Although this method was developed as a failure-prevention program for all incoming freshmen, it is pertinent to correcting underachievement. Six hours of systematic academic counseling, as part of the orientation program for all freshmen, included three sequential activities: survival orientation meetings held in freshman dormitories, test-interpretation meetings held at the testing and guidance center, and study skills guidance sessions in the dormitories. All three activities used: (1) counseling by *peers*, that is, carefully selected, trained, and supervised upperclassmen; (2) small, same-sex discussion *groups* of four; (3) formal *assessment* and *feedback* regarding each freshman's academic behavior and attitudes. The student counselors were given 30 hours of intensive training the preceding spring, plus 10 hours of review in the fall just before the freshman orientation.

The aims of the survival orientation session were to survey common academic problems of freshmen, to advise on procedures for managing time effectively, to stimulate interest in developing study skills, and to inform students where and how they might get help with their problems. Special guidance materials used included a true-false *Effective Study Test* (Brown & Holtzman, 1961) and a 44-page *Effective Study Guide* booklet (Brown, 1961).

The second session fed back and interpreted individual results of previously administered tests of scholastic aptitude and achievement, and subscale scores on the revised Brown-Holtzman (1964) *Survey of Study Habits and Attitudes*. The focus was on identifying potential academic difficulties, deficient study habits, and motivational problems, and on providing some opportunity for corrective guidance.

The third session sought to identify inefficient study procedures and to demonstrate effective methods for studying textbooks, taking lecture notes, writing themes and reports, and taking examinations.

In a large-scale research evaluation of this program, experimental subjects earned first-semester grades averaging one half grade higher than controls carefully matched on sex, scholastic aptitude, study orientation, and high school GPA. Experimental subjects also showed large increases on the two inventories of study habits (while controls showed no change), and expressed extremely positive evaluations of the program on a 60-item questionnarie.

The most prominent feature of Fox's (1962) method that is missing from the program just outlined is Fox's meticulous shaping of successive approximations to efficient study habits over a number of weeks. Further development of techniques and materials, with careful research evaluation, is needed to explore ways in which the *successive approximation* feature, combined with checkup and corrective reprogramming, might be *incorporated* in Brown's mass-approach type of program with its economy features (student counselors, a group approach, the substitution of printed guides for some of the counselor's work, etc.)—especially for problem students (underachievers, probation students, etc.). Could this be accomplished, for example, by the further development of workable self-instruction booklets and self-record-keeping materials, combined with prearranged group checkup testing and counseling sessions? Would this extension significantly increase the payoff of such a program (already demonstrated to have considerable success)?

Combining Group Behavioral Academic Counseling with Systematic Desensitization for Test Anxiety

Katahn, Strenger, & Cherry (1966) have evaluated experimentally a short-term (eight 1-hour sessions) group counseling procedure for volunteer text-anxious college students. The procedure combined Wolpe's (1958, 1966) systematic desensitization treatment with behaviorally oriented counseling regarding time management, study habits, and techniques, etc. The two experimental groups showed a significant rise in GPA and a reduction in scores on Sarason's (1958) Test Anxiety Scale; equated controls failed to improve.

The desensitization technique involves three operations: (1) abbreviated training in deep muscle-relaxation; (2) the construction of anxiety hierarchies—in this instance relating to test-taking situations, studying, etc.; and (3) systematically counterposing relaxation to anxiety-evoking stimuli from the hierarchies. An anxiety hierarchy is a list of situations or stimuli with a common theme that elicits anxiety in the subject, and that is ordered as to degree of anxiety aroused. In the third step the subject, while deeply relaxed, imagines each scene several times for 5 to 10 seconds or longer, until the anxiety reaction for that scene is greatly reduced or eliminated. The sequence is from least to most anxiety-provoking scenes. The key principles are: (a) "*reciprocal inhibition*" ("If a response inhibitory of anxiety can be made to occur in the presence of anxiety-evoking stimuli, it will weaken the bond between these stimuli and the anxiety"—Wolpe, 1958, 1966), and (b) *stimulus-generalization* between scenes, and between imagined scenes and the corresponding real-life situations. In addition to clinical evidence (Wolpe, 1958, Wolpe & Lazarus, 1966), experimental evidence that this generalization occurs has been accummulating (Lang & Lazovik, 1963, 1965; Lazarus, 1961; Paul, 1966).

Katahn et al. (1966) report they are currently comparing the effects of systematic desensitization alone, behavioral counseling alone, and the combination.

Behavioral Group Counseling with Token-Economy Reinforcement of Delinquent Underachieving Children

Rose (1967) has evolved an imaginative combination of behavior modification procedures for small groups of delinquents, ages 8 to 15, who were referred following police contacts. The groups are homogeneous as to sex, age, and socioeconomic background, with from three to seven children in each group. Contacts by the group worker with the child's parents, teachers, etc., are largely limited to the initial behavioral assessment of the child's maladaptive behaviors and their base-line frequency, their settings and antecedent conditions, the consequences that appear to maintain them, and the subsequent monitoring of changes in the frequency of specified behaviors corresponding to treatment goals. Tentative but specific treatment goals are established in the first contact with the children.

The major means of influence are reinforcement procedures, combined with providing suitable activities, models, and other stimulus conditions likely to occasion those behaviors that the worker is trying to increase. To reinforce attendance and to establish the worker's reinforcing potency as a dispenser of both social and token reinforcement, in the first few sessions he dispenses huge amounts of appealing food (candy, soft drinks, potato chips, etc.) to the children on arrival—"just for coming." The main reinforcement leverage, however, is *tokens* which are given in the group sessions as immediate payment for documented reports of the completion of individual behavioral assignments, for conformity to a given rule for a given time period, or for performing spontaneously a specified desired behavior in a group session. Tokens can be exchanged at the end of each meeting in a "group store" that offers both display and catalog items. As desired behaviors increase and come to be reinforced by other people in extra-group settings, or as the behaviors become self-reinforcing, token reinforcement in the group is gradually removed, one activity at a time. Social reinforcement (praise, recognition, etc.) continues, but shifts from a continuous to a more intermittent schedule in order to increase the new behaviors' resistance to extinction.

Activities are varied and initially short, because of the children's limited attention span, and become longer as treatment progresses. Activities include simulated classroom-type activities (since all the children have school difficulties), role playing or behavioral rehearsal of difficult-to-learn behaviors, physical activities (since many of the children lack physical skills), miscellaneous attractive prosocial activities, behavioral assignments, given by the worker or the group to individual members with their agreement and participation, and that are directly related to the member's treatment and usually are to be performed before the next group meeting, planned visits and activities involving admired prosocial adult models, and certain other procedures.

The tokens provide powerful reinforcement for increasing desired behaviors. These include *academic behaviors* such as school attendance, study behaviors, writing, conforming to classroom requirements (for example, talking only when called on by the worker-teacher), etc. Simulated classroom-type activities and school-related behavioral assignments are major occasions for increasing academic behaviors. In making *behavioral assignments*, careful attention is paid to the specificity of the assignment, monitoring (including requiring notes from teachers that confirm the child's school attendance, the turning in of homework, etc.), the ability of the child to perform the required assignment, the existence of the necessary stimulus conditions for carrying out the assignment, and the progression by successive approximations to final desired behavior. Thus a child who had skipped school on the average of twice a week might be given the task of attending school for four complete days during the ensuing week.

When a child's termination is being considered, more thorough behavioral reassessment is carried out. In addition, the worker helps the child to find other sources of support (to replace the group) such as teachers, friends, a boys' club, parents, etc. Behavioral assignments, and if necessary special training by behavioral rehearsals, are usually given to facilitate this transfer. A six-month follow-up assessment is incorporated in the study.

Although the project is currently in process and no formal evaluation has been completed, preliminary observations are reported to be quite promising for the majority of boys who have been seen for from two to four months, somewhat less so for groups of delinquent adolescent girls.

Saturating the Curriculum with High-Interest "Popular Culture" Materials and Activities

Several programs have proceeded on twin assumptions: (a) that a major task in correcting problem pupils' deficient achievement and alienation from school is to motivate them; and (b) that this may be done by meaningfully integrating into the curriculum large quantities of high-interest materials and activities from the pupils' everyday popular culture. Emphasis is on reducing aversive features and on strengthening positively reinforcing features of school learning. Adequate research evaluation of this approach is not yet available. However, preliminary reports indicate considerable promise.

Special Self-Contained English-Social Studies Classes of Predelinquents

Hall (1966) has described a current experimental project (incorporating research evaluation) for delinquency-prone seventh-grade boys who were described by their regular teachers as unmanageable behaviorally and hopeless academically. Project boys participate in a specially designed version of the regular three-period, self-contained classes, conducted by a single teacher, in language arts, social studies, and geography. Teachers with demonstrated ability to work with these pupils are assigned to project classes (thus, perhaps, confounding teachers with methods, since control subjects are assigned to regular classes).

Project classes, although committed to covering the regular curriculum, include special units on work, school, family, law enforcement, and interpersonal relations, plus four weekly periods of remedial reading.[3] Great emphasis is placed on intrinsically interesting curriculum materials and activities that are relevant to the pupils' prior experience in working-class slums. A wide variety of presentation techniques are used. The remedial reading program provides a wide variety of high-interest materials of varied difficulty. These include newspapers and a large display of paperback books in each room; a series of reading workbooks judged to have both suitable content, interest appeal, and reading ease (Turner, 1962); one set of graded-difficulty, skill-building materials deemed suitable (*Readers Digest Skill Building Series*, 1958); and special exercises developed for the two paperback books that

[3] Copies of the project curriculum guide, with lesson plans and supplementary materials, are available from project director Dr. Nason E. Hall, Jr., Sociology Dept., Ohio State University, Columbus.

were read most frequently. This wide array of materials permits such "cafeteria" selection by the pupils, and enables them to work on their own much of the time at their own individual levels and speeds. Specially prepared reading test exercises and a teacher handbook enable the teachers to carry out remedial reading activities without highly specialized professional preparation.

The high-interest curriculum also facilitates elimination of punitive techniques of classroom discipline which alienate pupils and interfere with learning. A short period of "time out from reinforcement" is used to control deviant pupil behavior. When a pupil's behavior interferes with ongoing activities, the pupil is asked to isolate himself from the class for a short time. When he feels that he is ready to return and to respect others' rights, he does so.

The project is said to have demonstrated already that "problem boys can be interested and can enjoy learning," and "can be handled efficiently and effectively without resorting to punitive measures." Evaluative data which are being collected on each experimental and control subject include police contacts, school attendance, school achievement, and attitudes toward school and legal authorities. A preliminary report on the first project year (Hall & Waldo, 1965) indicated significantly greater gains in reading achievement for experimental pupils than for controls, particularly for pupils of measured IQ = 100 and above; although pupils in the lowest IQ category (79 and under) also showed substantial improvement.

Saturating an Entire School with High-Interest "Popular Culture"

Fader and his associates (Fader & Shaevitz, 1966; Fader & McNeil, 1968) have developed a total-school program aimed at promoting *functional* literacy among the "bottom-half" of the pupils in inner-city public schools in deprived neighborhoods. (Many of these pupils are probably underachievers by our formal definition; many more may be achieving below their potential by a broader definition which questions the validity of formal intelligence tests for many such pupils.) The essential features of the program are as follows: (a) "to so surround the student with newspapers, magazines, and paperbound books that he comes to perceive them as pleasurable means to necessary ends"; (b) to require a large quantity of writing for varied purposes, in forms acceptable to the pupils; and (c) to diffuse the program throughout every classroom. The program was shaped and pretested at a training school for delinquent boys, was extended to a number of public schools in Detroit and elsewhere, and is reportedly being experimentally evaluated in the District of Columbia public schools.

The emphasis is on surrounding pupils with a quantity of inviting materils that is closely related to the pupils' nonschool world, which they *will* read (not selected primarily as materials that pupils "should" read). Reading materials are displayed attractively on wall racks and on freestanding spinners, mobile book trailers are used, book trading is encouraged, and so on. Each child is allowed to choose two paperbound books for his own, is given a paperbound dictionary to keep, and receives from his English teacher a spiral notebook to use as a journal. He is told that the *quantity* of production in the journal is the *only* criterion on which his writing will be judged: not less than a certain number of pages each week. Copying is freely permitted; most pupils prefer to write original copy.

The program also requires that *all* teachers base a significant part of their course content and written exercises on newspapers, magazines, and paperbound books. Each English teacher acts as a resource person and guide for a team of teachers, helping to suggest materials and to set up a writing schedule that produces many short written exercises in all classes. Some papers are read for content by the class instructor, some are passed on to the English teacher who corrects grammar and rhetoric, some are filed *unread* in the students' folders. The assumption is made that a child can be taught to practice writing just as he can be taught to practice a musical instrument or an individual sport.

Anecdotal material, plus a partly controlled experimental evaluation, suggests that this program offers promise. Pupil performance gains in a training school that used the program exceeded gains in a control training school in measures of verbal proficiency, paragraph comprehension, and relevant attitudes. The superior gains were limited primarily to whites and to boys with initially higher scholastic aptitude and achievement test scores. Interpretation of the findings is uncertain because the experimental "variable" was confounded with possible differences in extraneous characteristics of setting, program, and personnel.

A limitation of this approach may be its too exclusive reliance on "instructional" materials' intrinsic interest appeal to reinforce learning behaviors that are defined only in rather general terms. Could its effectiveness be enhanced by the systematic use of other potential reinforcers and by specifying the desired academic performances on which those reinforcers could be made contingent, while still utilizing popular-culture materials extensively?

Programmed Educational Environments

Several investigators have combined programmed instruction, a contingent reward system, and precise behavioral measurement to design an educational environment that will accelerate academic performances and will modify interfering nonacademic behaviors. Target groups have been youthful correctional inmates, emotionally disturbed children, and other special-education groups likely to include a high percentage of underachievers.

In the CASE project (Cohen, 1968; Cohen, Filipczak, & Bis, 1966, 1967) at the National Training School for Boys, a special educational environment was designed. Subjects were all school dropouts with a record of academic failure and little or no interest in school work. The objectives were to develop effective study habits and attitudes, and to improve academic performance in basic subjects such as reading, language skills, and mathematics.

Pretests pinpointed each inmate's level of achievement and his specific deficiencies in each subject. Various instructional devices were used, with the emphasis on programmed instruction and teaching machines. Educational behaviors (for example, study responses, correct responses, program units completed with 90 percent or better correct responses, unit tests completed with 90 percent or better correct, final course examinations with 90 percent or better correct) and certain other behaviors were continuously recorded, measured, and the results were publicly displayed.

Powerful immediate extrinsic reinforcers were provided contingent on successful academic behaviors. Points (worth one cent each), obtainable only by specified academic behaviors, could be used by the student to buy soft drinks, milk, snacks, Polaroid snapshots, smoke breaks, entrance to and time in a "teen-town" lounge, entrance to and time in a library, the rental of private office space, the rental of books and magazines, additional classroom time, private tutoring, and anything listed in catalogs such as the Sears-Roebuck catalog. After several weeks, other events acquired increasing value as reinforcers for successful academic work—namely, being correct, the social approval of the staff and (increasingly) peers, and the prestige of taking an advanced course after completing a basic course.

To insure successful incorporation of the project within the constraints of a correctional institution, and its later continuation and extension under institution auspices, special training was provided for the administrative and professional staff, as well as line personnel. This training consisted of two courses—"environmental design" and "behavioral analysis and its extensions." Both courses, taught concurrently in 16 weekly three-hour sessions on work-time, used specially designed textbooks, lectures, demonstrations, and problem-solving laboratory exercises

The student-inmates were available 195 minutes daily (Monday through Friday) in the special educational environment which included the lounge, library, "free" bench, and restroom, as well as study areas. By the ninth week, they were spending an average of 109 minutes daily in recorded educational activity (not mere attendance). The reported results included impressive pre-post gains on standard reading, scholastic achievement, and general ability tests, as well as on tests covering programmed instructional materials.

McKee and his associates (McKee, 1967a, 1967b; McKee & Seay, 1966; Seay, 1967) at the Draper (Alabama) Correctional Center have developed a somewhat similar program for incarcerated young-offenders, most of whom were school dropouts with poor school records. Goals and instructional content were, however, primarily vocationally oriented. Remedial academic work was tailored to the individual's measured deficiencies in language and in computational skills that were clearly prerequisite to successful training for his specific vocational objective. Refined assessment permitted assigning selected parts of the instructional programs, instead of requiring the student to go through extensive material he had already mastered. By using Gilbert's (1962) system of mathetics, special instructional programs were developed, to accelerate the effective learning of technical skills in trades such as radio-TV repair, barbering, bricklaying, sign painting, welding, and as an automobile service station mechanic-attendant. The reinforcers used for maintaining a high rate of learning behaviors included: the opportunity to learn a salable vocational skill of the inmate's own choosing, the expectation of earlier parole via learning efforts, being correct most of the time with immediate feedback, money and points exchangeable for snacks, magazines, games, etc., in a special recreation room, and instructor approval. Reported results in this ongoing project have included impressive pre-post gains in tests covering programmed instructional content, as well as grade gains in remedial academic tool-subjects (average gain for 70 students, 1.3 grades over a six-month period with two hours of daily instruction totaling 206 hours per student).

Analogous procedures for use by teachers and parents of special-education pupils have been developed and have been applied by Lindsley and his associates (1968), with impressive results in accelerating academic performances and in decelerating undesired behaviors.

SUMMARY OF REMEDIAL PROCEDURES AND NEEDED FURTHER RESEARCH

We have reviewed behavioral methods for modifying academic underachievement that are based explicitly or implicitly on reinforcement learning principles. These methods appear promising, although experimental evidence regarding their effectiveness is as yet incomplete. Methods that have proved ineffectual were also reviewed briefly (psychodynamic "insight" counseling; "enrichment," work-study, or programmed instruction format alone).

At the college level, the behavioral methods described focus directly on guiding the student, individually or in small groups, to develop more efficient study habits. Such habits include bringing both the initiation and the maintenance of concentrated study under better stimulus control on a regular schedules, and using more efficient techniques in studying, writing papers, and taking tests. One program, specifically designed for "test-anxious" students, combines guidance in study habits with "systematic desensitization by relaxation" which is aimed at reducing the subjects' disorganizing levels of anxiety in test situations. Diagnostic assessment at the college level may include the use of study habit inventories (for example, Brown & Holtzman, 1964; Brown, 1961), the analysis of daily schedules and time-place logs, as a basis for developing more efficient schedules, Test Anxiety Questionnaire (Mandler & Cohen, 1958; Mandler & Sarason, 1952), interview probing to clarify specific problems and, in some instances, a standard reading test (Cronbach, 1960, pp. 388–392).

There is a need for experimentation with more economical ways of providing individualized guidance in efficient study habits. A promising direction may be to extend and to refine Brown's (1965) approach (intensive group workshop, student counselors, group testing and feedback, study-habits guidebook, etc.) so as to incorporate Fox's (1962) shaping of successive approximations to efficient study habits over a period of weeks. Further work is also needed on techniques for monitoring crucial study behaviors, and for recording and displaying student progress in these behaviors—both as verification and as reinforcing feedback to the student.

At the high school level and below, direct behavioral guidance in efficient study habits does not seem to have been experimentally evaluated as an approach to underachievement, except as a part of programs that use extrinsic incentives as leverage. With some (volunteer?) pupils, this guidance might prove effective. However, the methods reviewed have relied mainly on powerful reinforcers to accelerate desired study behavior, together with providing stimulus conditions (including appropriate assignments) calculated to occasion the desired behavior so that it might then be reinforced. Reinforcement procedures have included: new reinforcement contingencies (by using a variety of reinforcers) applied to individual children by parents, teachers, etc., in response to behavioral guidance (Thorne, Tharpe, & Wetzel, 1966, 1967); material reinforcers (food, token economy) gradually replaced by social reinforcers (approval, self-approval, etc.), presented contingent on performance of behavioral assignments given in a group counseling context (Rose, 1967), or contingent on specified academic or vocational-learning performances in a programmed educational environment (Cohen, 1968; Cohen et al., 1966, 1967; Lindsley et al., 1968; McKee, 1967a, 1967b); or saturation of an entire school, or of a substantial part or the curriculum, with high-interest "popular culture" materials and activities closely connected with the pupils' life outside the school (Hall, 1966; Fader & Shaevitz, 1966; Fader & McNeil, 1968).

Thorne and his associates (1965, 1967) promise in future reports to describe assessment procedures being developed to locate practical reinforcers, and to evaluate the flexibility of adult mediators in applying new reinforcement contingencies. Further experimentation to extend their approach might include *group* behavioral counseling of the parents of underachievers in the techniques of child management and (Della-Piana, Stahmann, & Allen, 1966) the stimulation of academic interests and activities, and analogous workshops for groups of teachers who would meet periodically instead of on a "one-shot" basis, etc. Further work appears to be needed also in refining practical techniques for monitoring student progress in crucial academic behaviors, and in the reduction of interfering behaviors. Additional information on this score may be expected in subsequent reports of the other current projects reviewed above.

REFERENCES

Aiken, L. R., Jr. The prediction of academic success and early attrition by means of a multiple-choice biographical inventory. *Amer. educ. Res. J.*, 1964, **1**, 127–135.

Alpert, R., & Haber, R. N. Anxiety in academic achievement situations. *J. abnorm. soc. Psychol.*, 1960, **61**, 207–215.

Appell, H. L. The relationship between certain aspects of the intellectually superior student's school record and his recollection of and expressed feelings about that record. *Dissert. Abstr.*, 1964, **24**, 3196–3197.

Baker, R. W., & Madell, T. O. Susceptibility to distraction in academically underachieving and achieving male college students. *J. consult. Psychol.*, 1965a, **29**, 173–177.

Baker, R. W., & Madell, T. O. A continued investigation of susceptibility to distraction in academically underachieving and achieving male college students. *J. educ. Psychol.*, 1965b, **56**, 254–258.

Barrett, H. O. An intensive study of 32 gifted children. *Personnel guid. J.*, 1957, **36**, 192–194.

Battle, H. J. Relation between personal values and scholastic achievement. *J. exp. Educ.*, 1957, **26**, 27–41.

Baymur, F. B., & Patterson, C. H. A comparison of three methods of assisting underachieving high school students. *J. counsel. Psychol.*, 1960, **7**, 83–90.

Bijou, S. W. Experimental studies of child behavior, normal and deviant. In L. Krasner & L. P. Ullmann (Eds.), *Research in behavior modification.* N.Y.: Holt, Rinehart, & Winston, 1965, Pp. 56–81.

Birnbrauer, J. S., Bijou, S. W., Wolf, M. M., & Kidder, J. D. Programmed instruction in the classroom. In L. P. Ullmann & L. Krasner (Eds.), *Case studies in behavior modification.* N.Y.: Holt, Rinehart, & Winston, 1965, Pp. 358–363.

Borow, H. A psychometric study of non-intellectual factors in college achievement. Unpublished doctoral dissertation, Pa. State College, 1945.

Broedel, J., Olsen, M., Proff, F., & Southard, C. The effects of group counseling on gifted underachieving adolescents. *J. counsel. Psychol.*, 1960, **7**, 163–170.

Brown, W. F. *Effective study test.* (Coll. level) San Marcos, Texas: Effective Study Materials, 1961.

Brown, W. F. Student-to-student counseling for academic adjustment. *Personnel guid. J.*, 1965, **43**, 811–817.

Brown, R. W., & Holtzman, W. H. A study-attitude questionnaire for predicting academic success. *J. educ. Psychol.*, 1955, **46**, 75–84.

Brown, W. F., & Holtzman, W. H. *Effective study guide.* (Coll. ed.) San Marcos, Texas: Effective Study Materials, 1961.

Brown, W. F., & Holtzman, W. H. *Survey of study habits and attitudes.* (Rev. ed., grades 12–14) N.Y.: Psychological Corp., 1964.

Burgess, Elva. Personality factors of over and underachievers in engineering. *J. educ. Psychol.*, 1956, **47**, 89–99.

Carter, H. D. Some validity coefficients for study test scores. *Calif. J. educ. Res.*, 1956, **7**, 112–114.

Carter, H. D. Over-achievers and under-achievers in the junior high school. *Calif. J. educ. Res.*, 1960, **12**, 51–56.

Cartwright, D., & Zander, A. (Eds.) *Group dynamics: research and theory.* (2nd ed.) Evanston, Ill.: Row, Peterson, 1960.

Chestnut, W. J. The effects of structured and unstructured group counseling on male college students' underachievement. *J. counsel. Psychol.*, 1965, **12**, 388–394.

Chittick, R. A., Eldred, M., & Brooks, G. W. *The use of programmed instruction with disturbed students.* Final progress report on National Institute of Mental Health, U.S.P.H.S. Grant No. MH-01076.

Cohen, H. L. Educational therapy: The design of learning environments. In J. M. Shielen, H. F. Hunt, J. D. Matarazzo, S. C. Savage (Eds.) *Research in Psychotherapy.* Washington, D.C.: American Psychological Association, 1968, 21–53.

Cohen, H. L. Filipczak, J. A., & Bis, J. S. CASE I: An initial study of contingencies applicable to special education. Silver Spring, Maryland: Educational Facility Press—Institute for Behavioral Research, 1967.

Cohen, H. L., Filipczak, J. A., & Bis, J. S. CASE Project: Contingencies applicable to special education. In R. E. Weber (Ed.), *A book on education and delinquency.* Washington, D.C.: D.H.E.W. Office of Juvenile Delinquency and Youth Development, 1966, Ch. 3.

Cohn, B. *The effects of group counseling on school adjustment of underachieving junior high school boys who demonstrate acting-out behavior* (Summary of Cooperative Research Project No. B-040). Moravia, N.Y.: Chronical Guidance Publications, 1966.

Coleman, W., & Cureton, E. E. Intelligence and achievement: the "jangle fallacy." *Educ. Psychol. Measmt.*, 1954, **14**, 347–351.

Conklin, Agnes M. Failures of highly intelligent pupils. *Teach. Coll. Contr. Educ.*, No. 792. 1940.

Cronbach, L. J. *Essentials of psychological testing.* (2nd ed.) N.Y.: Harper & Row, 1960.

Cubbedge, Georgia H., & Hall, M. M. A proposal for a workable approach in dealing with underachievers. *Psychol.*, 1964, **1**, 1–7.

Davids, A. & Sidman, J. A pilot study of impulsivity time-orientation and delayed gratification in future scientists and in underachieving high school students. *Except. Children*, 1962, **29**, 170–174.

Della-Piana, G., Stahmann, R. F., & Allen, J. E. *The influence of parental attitudes and child-parent interaction upon remedial reading progress.* Final report on Cooperative Research Project No. S-266, Univer. of Utah, mimeographed, 1966.

Dember, W. N., Nairne, F., & Miller, F. J. Further validation of the Alpert-Haber Achievement Anxiety Test. *J. abnorm. soc. Psychol.*, 1962, **65**, 427–428.

Diener, C. G. Similarities and differences between overachieving and underachieving students. *Personnel guid. J.*, 1960, **38**, 396–400.

Dowd, R. J. Underachieving students of high capacity. *J. higher Educ.*, 1952.
Duffy, E. The psychological significance of the concept of "arousal" or activation. *Psychol. Rev.*, 1957, **64**, 265–275.
Eysenck, H. J. (Ed.) *Behavior therapy and the neuroses*. N.Y.: Pergamon, 1960.
Eysenck, H. J. The effects of psychotherapy. In Eysenck, H. J. (Ed.), *Handbook of abnormal psychology: an experimental approach*. N.Y.: Basic Books, 1961, pp. 694–725.
Eysenck, H. J. (Ed.) *Experiments in behavior therapy*. N.Y.: Pergamon, 1964.
Fader, D. N., & NcNeil, E. B. *Hooked on books: program and proof.* N. Y.: Berkley, 1968.
Fader, D. N., & Shaevitz, M. H. *Hooked On books*. N.Y.: Berkley, 1966.
Feldhusen, J. F., & Klausmeier, H. J. Anxiety, intelligence, and achievement in children of low, average and high intelligence. *Child Developm.*, 1962, **33**, 403–409.
Field, L. W. Personality correlates of college achievements and major areas of study. Unpublished doctoral dissertation, Univer. of Houston, 1953.
Fox, L. Effecting the use of efficient study habits. *J. Mathetics*, 1962, **1**, 75–86.
Frankel, E. A comparative study of achieving and underachieving high school boys of high intellectual ability. *J. educ. Res.*, 1960, **53**, 172–180.
Gawronski, D. A., & Mathis, C. Differences between over-achieving, normal achieving, and under-achieving high school students. *Psychol. in the Schools*, 1965, **2**, 152–155.
Gilbert, T. F. Mathetics: The technology of education. *J. Mathetics*, 1962, **1**, 7–73.
Goldberg, Miriam L. *Research on the talented*. N.Y.: Columbia University Teachers College, 1965.
Gough, H. G. What determines the academic achievement of high school students? *J. educ. Res.*, 1953, **46**, 321–331.
Gowan, J. C. Factors of achievement in high school and college. *J. counsel. Psychol.*, 1960, **7**, 91–95.
Gowan, J. C. *An annotated bibliography on the academically talented*. Washington: National Educational Association, 1961.
Gowan, J. C. *Annotated bibliography on creativity and giftedness*. Northridge, Calif. San Fernando Valley State College Foundation, 1965.
Hall, N. E. The youth development project: A school-based delinquency prevention program. *J. school. Health*, 1966, **36**, 97–103.
Hall, N. E., & Waldo, G. P. Remedial reading for the disadvantaged, trouble prone pupil: An empirical Study. Ohio State University, mimeographed, 1965.
Hare, A. P. *Handbook of small group research*. N.Y.: Free Press—Macmillan, 1962.
Hart, D. H. A study of the effects of two types of group experiences on the academic achievement of college underachievers. Unpublished doctoral dissertation, Michigan State Univer., 1963.
Hattwick, Berta W., & Stowell, Margaret. Parental over-attentiveness and children's work habits and social adjustment in kindergarten and the first six grades. *J. educ. Res.*, 1936, Vol. 30, 169–176.
Holland, J. G. & Skinner, B. F. *The analysis of behavior*. N.Y.: McGraw-Hill, 1961.
Holtzman, W. H., Brown, W. F., & Farquhar, W. W. Survey of Study Habits and Attitudes: a new instrument. *Educ. psychol. Measmt.*, 1954.
Hunt, J. M. *Intelligence and experience*. N.Y.: Ronald, 1961.
Jackson, R. M., & Cleveland, J. C. *Results of early identification in guidance of underachievers*. Final report, Cooperative Research Project No. S-153. 1966.
Jenness, A. Personality dynamics. *Annu. Rev. Psychol.*, 1962, **13**, 479–514.
Jones, E. S. The probation student: what he is like and what can be done about it. *J. educ. Res.*, 1955, **49**, 93–102.
Katahn, M., Strenger, S., & Cherry, Nancy. Group counseling and behavior therapy with test-anxious college students. *J. consult. Psychol.*, 1966, **30**, 544–549.
Kelley, T. L. *Interpretation of educational measurements*. Yonkers, N.Y.: World, 1927.
Keppers, G. L., & Caplan, S. W. Group counseling with academically able underachieving students. *N. Mex. soc. Stud. educ. Res. Bull.*, 1962, **2**, 12–17.
Kornrich, M. (Ed.) *Underachievement*. Springfield, Ill.: Thomas, 1965.

Krasner, L., & Ullmann, L. P. (Eds.) *Research in behavior modification*. N.Y.: Holt, Rinehart, and Winston, 1965.

Kurtz, J. J., & Swenson, E. J. Factors related to over-achievement and under-achievement in school. *Sch. Rev.*, 1961, **59**, 472–480.

Lang, P. J., & Lazovik, A. D. The experimental desentization of a phobia. *J. abnorm. soc. Psychol.*, 1963, **66**, 519–525.

Lang, P. J., Lazovik, A. D. & Reynolds, P. Desensitization, suggestibility and pseudotherapy. *J. abnorm. Psychol.*, 1965, **70**, 395–402.

Lazarus, A. A. Group therapy of phobic disorders by systematic desensitization. *J. abnorm. soc. Psychol.*, 1961, **63**, 504–510.

Leibman, O. B. The relationship of personality and social adjustment to academic achievement in elementary school. Unpublished doctoral dissertation, Columbia Univer., 1953.

Levitt, E. E. The results of psychotherapy: an evaluation. *J. consult. Psychol.*, 1957, **21**, 189–196.

Lewis, W. D. A comparative study of personalities, interests, and home backgrounds of gifted children of superior and inferior educational achievement. *J. genet. Psychol.*, 1941, **59**, 207–218.

Lindquist, E. F. *Design and analysis of experiments in psychology and education*. Boston: Houghton-Mifflin, 1953.

Lindsley, O. R., and associates. Lectures presented in "Short course in precise behavioral management," Kansas City, Missouri, June 3–7, 1968.

Longstreth, L. E., Shanley, F. J., & Rice, R. E. Experimental evaluation of a high school program for potential dropouts. *J. educ. Psychol.*, 1964, **5**, 228–236.

McArthur, C. The validity of the Yale Strong Scales at Harvard. *J. counsel. Psychol.*, 1965, **12**, 35–38.

McBee, G., & Duke, R. L. Relationship between intelligence, scholastic motivation and academic achievement. *Psychol. Rep.*, 1960, **6**, 3–8.

McGillivray, R. H. Differences in home background between high-achieving and low-achieving gifted children: a study of 100 grade 8 pupils in the City of Toronto Public Schools. *Ont. J. educ. Res.*, 1964, **6**, 99–106.

McKee, J. M. Innovations in correctional programs—Draper's approach to correctional manpower training. Paper presented at Correctional Manpower Training Conference, University of Houston, College of Business Administration, Houston, July 26, 1967. (a)

McKee, J. M. Methods of motivating offenders for educational achievement. Paper presented at 97th Annual Congress of Corrections, Miami Beach, August 22, 1967. (b)

McKee, J. M., & Seay, D. M. Programmed instruction in vocational education—results of experiments with disadvantaged prison population. *Training and Development Journal*, 1966 (June), 37–40.

Malmo, R. B. Anxiety in behavioral arousal. *Psychol. Rev.*, 1957, **64**, 267–287.

Mandler, G., & Cohen, J. E. Test anxiety questionnaire. *J. consult. Psychol.*, 1958, **22**, 228–229.

Mandler, G., & Sarason, S. B. A study of anxiety and learning. *J. abnorm. soc. Psychol.*, 1952, **47**, 166–173.

Martin, J. G., & Davidson, Judy. Recall of completed and interrupted tasks by achievers and underachievers. *J. educ. Psychol.*, 1964, **55**, 314–316.

Miller, L. M. (Ed.) Guidance for the underachiever with superior ability. Washington, Office of Education Bull. 25, 1961.

Mink, O. G. Multiple counseling with underachieving junior high school pupils of bright, normal, and higher ability. *J. educ. Res.*, 1964, **58**, 31–34.

Morgan. H. H. A psychometric comparison of achieving and non-achieving college students of high ability. *J. consult. Psychol.*, 1952, **16**, 292–299.

Morrow, W. R., & Wilson, R. C. Family relations of bright high-achieving and underachieving high school boys. *Child Developm.*, 1961a, **32**, 501–510.

Morrow, W. R., & Wilson R. C. The self-reported personal and social adjustment of bright high-achieving and under-achieving high school boys. *J. Child Psychol. Psychiat.*, 1961b, **2**, 203–209.

O'Leary, M. J. Measurement and evaluation of work habits of over-achievers and under-achievers to determine the relationship of these to underachievement. *Dissert. Abstr.*, 1955, **15**, 2104–2105.

Paul, G. L. *Insight vs. desensitization in psycho-therapy: an experiment in anxiety reduction.* Stanford, Calif.: Stanford Univer. Press, 1966.

Paul, G. L., & Eriksen, C. W. Effects of test anxiety on "real-life" examinations. *J. Pers.*, 1964, **32**, 480–494.

Payne, D. A., & Farquhar, W. W. The dimensions of an objective measure of academic self-concept. *J. educ. Psychol.*, 1962, **53**, 187–192.

Pierce, J. D., & Bowman, P. H. Motivation patterns of superior high school students. *The gifted student*. Washington: Office of Education Coop. Res. Monogr. No. 2, 1960.

Peppin, B. H. Parental understanding, parental acceptance, and the self-concept of children as a function of academic over-and under-achievement. *Dissert. Abstr.*, 1963, **23**, 4422–4423.

Popham, W. J., & Moore, Mary R. A validity check on the Brown-Holtzman survey of Study Habits and Attitudes and Borow College Inventory of Academic Adjustment. *Personnel guid. J.*, 1960, **38**, 552–554.

Rachman, S. (Ed.) *Critical essays on psychoanalysis*. N.Y.: Pergamon, 1963.

Reader's Digest Skill Building Series. New York: Reader's Digest Services, 1958.

Reese, Ellen P. *The analysis of human operant behavior*. Dubuque, Iowa: Brown, 1966.

Remmers, H. H., & Gage, N. L. *Educational measurement and evaluation*. New York: Harper, 1955.

Robinson, F. P. *Effective study*. New York: Harper, 1946.

Rose, S. D. A behavioral approach to group treatment of children. In E. J. Thomas (Ed.), *The socio-behavioral approach and applications to social work*. New York: Council on Social Work Education, 1967, pp. 39–54.

Sarason, I. G. Interrelationships among individual difference variables, behavior in psychotherapy, and verbal conditioning. *J. abnorm. soc. Psychol.*, 1958, **56**, 339–351.

Sarason, I. G. Empirical findings and theoretical problems in the use of anxiety scales. *Psychol. Bull.*, 1960, **57**, 403–415.

Seay, D. M. Development, evaluation, and use of programmed materials as developed in the Draper experimental and demonstration project. Paper presented at Regional Manpower Development and Training Conference, Region IV, U.S.D.H.E.W. Bureau of Adult and Vocational Education, Atlanta, March 8, 1967.

Shaw, M. C., & Dutton, B. E. The use of the Parent Attitude Research Inventory with parents of bright academic underachievers. *J. educ. Psychol.*, 1962, **53**, 203–208.

Shaw, M., & McCuren, J. T. The onset of academic underachievement in bright children. *J. educ. Psychol.*, 1960, **51**, 103–109.

Shaw, M. C., & White, D. L. The relationship between child-parent identification and academic underachievement. *J. clin. Psychol.*, 1965, **21**, 10–14.

Sheldon, W. D., & Landsman, T. An investigation of non-directive group therapy with students in academic difficulty. *J. consult. Psychol.*, 1950, **14**, 210–15.

Shore, M. F., & Leiman, A. H. Parental perceptions of the student as related to academic achievement in junior college. *J. exp. Educ.*, 1965, **33**, 391–394.

Silverman, M., Davids, A., & Andrews, Jean M. Powers of attention and academic achievement. *Percept. motor Skills*, 1963, **17**, 243–449.

Spielberger, C. D. The effects of manifest anxiety on the academic achievement of college students. *Ment. Hyg.*, 1962, **46**, 420–426.

Spielberger, C. D., & Weitz, H. Improving the academic performance of anxious college freshmen: a group-counseling approach to the prevention of under-achievement. *Psychol. Monogr.*, 1964, No. 590.

Sprinthall, N. A. A comparison of values among teachers, academic underachievers, and achievers. *J. exp. Educ.*, 1964, **33**, 193–196.

Staats, A. W. (Ed.) *Human Learning*. N.Y.: Holt, Rinehart, & Winston, 1964.

Taylor, R. G. Personality traits and discrepant achievement: a review. *J. counsel. Psychol.*, 1964, **11**, 76–82.

Taylor, R. G., & Farquhar, W. Personality, motivation, and achievement: theoretical constructs and empirical factors. *J. counsel. Psychol.*, 1965, **12**, 186–191.

Thomas, E. J., & Goodman, Esther. (Eds.) *Socio-behavioral theory and inter-personal helping in social work*. Ann Arbor: Campus Publishers, 1965.

Thorndike, R. L. *The concepts of over- and underachievement*. N.Y.: Columbia University Teachers College, 1963.

Thorne, J. L., Tharp, R. G., & Wetzel, R. J. *Behavioral research project: an interim report on the first 14 months of operation*. Report, Office of Juvenile Delinquency and Youth Development Grants No. 65023 & 66020, 1966.

Thorne, J. L., Tharp, R. G., & Wetzel, R. J. Behavior modification techniques: new tools for probation officers. *Fed. Probation*, 1967, **31**, 21–27.

Todd, F. J., Terrell, G., & Frank, C. E. Difference between normal and underachievers of superior ability, *J. appl. Psychol.*, 1962, **46**, 183–190.

Turner, R. H. *Turner-Livingston Reading Series*. New York: Follett Publishing Co. & N.Y. Univer. Press, 1962.

Ullmann, L. P., & Krasner, L. (Eds.) *Case studies in behavior modification*. N.Y.: Holt, Rinehart, and Winston, 1965.

Ulrich, R. E., Stachnik, T., & Mabry, J. H. (Eds.) *Control of human behavior*. Glenview, Ill.: Scott, Foresman, 1966.

Walker, Helen M., & Lev, J. *Elementary statistical methods*: (2nd ed.) New York: Holt, 1958.

Walsh, Ann. M. *Self-concepts of bright boys with learning difficulties*. New York: Columbia University Teachers College, 1956.

Waters, Carrie W. Construction and validation of a forced-choice over- and under-achievement scale. *Educ. psychol. Measmt.*, 1964, **24**, 921–928.

Wellington, C. B., & Wellington, Jean. *The achiever: challenges and guidelines*. Chicago, Rand, McNally, 1965.

Whelan, R. J., & Haring, N. G. Modification and maintenance of behavior through systematic application of consequences. *Except. Child.*, 1966, **32**, 281–289.

Wilson, R. C., & Morrow, W. R. School and career adjustment of bright high-achieving and under-achieving high school boys. *J. genet. Psychol.*, 1962, **101**, 91–103.

Winborn, B., & Schmidt, L. G. The effectiveness of short-term group counseling upon the academic achievements of potentially superior but underachieving college freshmen. *J. educ. Res.*, 1962, **55**, 169–173.

Winkler, R. C., Teigland, J. J., Munger, E. F., & Kranzler, G. D. The effects of selected counselling and remedial techniques on underachieving elementary school students. *J. counsel. Psychol.*, 1965, **12**, 384–387.

Wolpe, J. *Psycho-therapy by reciprocal inhibition*. Stanford: Stanford Univer. Press, 1958.

Wolpe, J., & Lazarus, A. A. *Behavior therapy techniques*. N. Y.: Pergamon, 1966.

Chapter 22

Exhibitionism

DAVID R. EVANS

INTRODUCTION

Exhibitionism was first described and named by Charles Lasegue (1877), although McCawley (1965) makes reference to its occurence in the Greek Era. The definitions of Exhibitionism are many and varied, for instance, Arieff and Rotman (1942), Guttman (1953), and Rickles (1955). At the one extreme Henry (1955) defines it as "any self display made for the purpose of winning approval." At the other extreme, Rickles (1955) defines it as "the compulsive act by a male of exposing publicly his external genitalia to a female with conscious awareness on both parts." Both of these definitions are incorrect because the former would incorporate most of the population, and the second would exclude some cases of exhibitionism. Exhibitionism may be defined as the exposure of a part or the whole of the body for sexual or nonsexual rewards.

Before embarking on a discussion of exhibitionism, it should be pointed out that the literature in this field when compared to other fields, such as anxiety, is relatively scarce. One of the factors making the study of exhibitionism difficult is that the majority of exhibitionists demonstrate character disorders. An exhibitionist rarely, if ever, seeks medical help. He has to be coerced by the process of law. He can be equally difficult to retain in therapy.

Although basic research is sadly lacking in the realm of sexual deviations, some good statistical studies have been carried out on exhibitionism by authorities such as Ellis (1933), East (1946), Karpman (1948), Rickles (1955). Much of this material has been gathered together by Mohr et al. (1964) in their excellent book.

The Act

The act of exposure will vary according to the timidity or the boldness of the offender and the urgency of the compulsion. There are some relatively safe forms of exposure, for example, furtively from behind the drapes of a window, or while seated in a parked car. The culprit hopes that passing females will chance to see his organ and, if challenged, he is then able to plead that the incidence was an unfortunate accident. At the other extreme, the offender may totally disrobe behind a bush and spring out before his victim (Bond & Hutchison, 1960). While the majority of exhibitionists quite openly expose, some will hold their coats or other garments in such a way as to hide the view of their genitalia from all except their victim.

Some expose a flaccid penis, some an erect organ. In some cases masturbation will also accompany the act. In the majority of these cases the exposure preceeds masturbation, but the order may also be reversed. Often ejaculation ensues with or without masturbation. The act may be impulsive (Rickles 1955) or premeditated (Ellis 1933). For example, to some it is a full-scale commando-like exercise, while others report that they did not realize they had exhibited until the act had been completed. The majority of this latter group describe a "dazed," "trancelike" state or altered state of consciousness immediately prior to and during the act itself.

Allen (1949) suggests that this state is more common among psychopathic offenders. It may, however, be because of intense tension and sexual excitement accompanying the act, and is quickly followed by relief of tension and often feelings of guilt, shame, and remorse. Certainly, it has been noted in other than psychopathic exhibitionists.

In some cases the object of the act is to relieve nonsexual tension, but for the majority the act is carried out to gain sexual gratification. Although some cases show considerable variation in their act with regard to its nature and the place of occurrence, the majority report their symptomatology as very stereotyped. The usual course of events is for the exhibitionist to choose his victim, expose himself according to his peculiar foibles and, once the appropriate response has been registered, make off without undue delay.

The exhibitionist often has prior warning that he is going to act out. Although the apprehended offender may lie to avoid the consequences of his actions, the average exhibitionist will usually give an uncritical physician an exact description of his act. He is always able to describe the offense in detail despite the "trancelike" state often mentioned. He always emphasizes the irresistible nature of the urge and intimates that he is unable to control his actions. Yet, paradoxically, he will describe elaborate preparations made, journeyings to favourite spots, and the careful implementation of his special technique. Often an offender will "know" in the morning that he will likely expose in the afternoon, and he may decamp to a beach or a park where he knows he will find his victims. On other occasions, however, the exhibitionist will spontaneously and unexpectedly expose when stimulated without prior warning. The deliberate nature of the planning of the exposure so commonly met with does suggest that, although the act itself is, to some degree, instinctive, wilful behavior is involved and that the final offense is a complex mixture of habit, personality type, and deliberate acting out. The offender is fully aware of the absurdity of his action and usually rationalizes by viewing it as a substitute behavior because of sexual frustrations. He is quite unable to offer any reasonable explanation.

All authorities note and are baffled by exhibitionists who conduct themselves in such a way that arrest becomes inevitable. These individuals often remark that they feel considerable relief once they have been caught and the whole issue is in the open. This type of exhibitionist often exposes repeatedly in the same spot, making apprehension absurdly easy. Some will return to the scene of their crime or dawdle around and "wait" for the police to arrive. One individual is cited who exposed outside a police station and thus facilitated the work of the Force (Bond & Hutchison 1960). No satisfactory explanation of this phenomena has yet been given. It should be remembered that the act in many cases is a very strong habitual response. In such cases it may appear that the offender seeks arrest while in reality no such intention exists.

Opinions differ somewhat on the place of the offence. Radzinowicz (1957) in a study of exhibitionism in Cambridge, England, found that 47 percent of the offences occurred on the streets, 30 percent in parks and open spaces, mostly from the offender's car, 13 percent in public buildings, and 11 percent through a window. In a similar study by Mohr et al. (1964), in the Toronto area, it was reported that 74 percent exhibited in open places, of which 30 percent of the offences were from a parked car, 13 percent exhibited from public buildings, and 11 percent exposed through a window. Arieff and Rotman (1942) in a study of exhibitionism in the Chicago area indicated that 15 percent exhibited in their own home, 52 percent near their home, and 33 percent in public places, such as parks. Unfortunately, these statistics cannot be easily compared because of the lack of agreement among categories.

The incidence of exhibitionism as a sexual offence is reckoned to be high, accounting for about one third of all such offences. Arieff and Rotman (1942) state the percentage to be 35 percent. The figures presented by others (Apfelberg et al. 1944; Taylor 1947; Shaskan 1939; Ellis & Brancale 1956; Mohr et al. 1964) range from 24 to 36 percent. This does not represent, however, the true incidence of exhibitionism as probably only a minority of exhibitionists are apprehended.

Nevertheless, exhibitionism by its very nature, is most vulnerable to police action in comparison with other deviations.

The rate of recidivism is highest among exhibitionists as 20 to 25 percent of those appearing in Court have had previous convictions, and the follow-up rate of recidivism for a general group is 17 to 22 percent. About 20 percent of exhibitionists also have more sexual offences in their record. The habitual nature of the condition is largely held responsible for frequently repeated offences. Individual subjects vary considerably in their frequency of acting out, with some exhibiting several times daily, while others may exhibit only once in their lifetime. Some of the variance in frequency may be the result of environmental factors such as season and weather. Late spring and summer are peak seasons, due to scanty female wear and the greatly increased opportunity to accost females in parks, lanes, and beaches.

The Audience

The exhibitionist, except in a few rare instances, always exposes to strangers. Mohr et al. (1964) report that in only four of fifty-four cases were neighbors exposed to instead of strangers, and in three of these cases the neighbors were inadvertant victims. An exhibitionist never exposes to his wife, for obvious reasons, the conjugal contract would legitimize such behavior. The proportion of children as victims has been reported variously as anywhere from 20 to 50 percent (Arieff & Rotman 1942; Taylor 1947; Mohr et al. 1964). Although the preferred audience is usually female, both male adults and children have been exhibited to.

Taylor (1947) reported that of 67 exposures to adult women, 34 of the women were alone; in 14 cases there were two women, and in 19 cases more than two women were involved. Both Radzinowicz (1957) and Mohr et al. (1964) reported that exhibitionists exposing to adult women tended to expose to them individually, while those exposing to children were more likely to expose to them in groups. Where nubile female adults are involved, they are usually in the younger age groups, but middle aged and even elderly females have been the target on occasion.

Some exhibitionists are extremely specific in their choice of victims, that is to say, she must be dressed in a certain way, must appear educated and sophisticated or, on the other hand, vulgar and promiscuous, etc. Certain physical characteristics such as shapely legs, a pretty face, a large bust, etc., are important to some. Other deviants are omniverous in their tastes and are satisfied with any female who may be available.

It must be emphasized that an important factor in the act is the effect it has on the victim. This will apparently depend on the psychological needs of the exhibitionist. In a few cases, exposure constitutes a frank sexual invitation, and these men would respond if the female indicated reciprocal sexual interest. The majority of exhibitionists, however, do not anticipate sexual involvement with their victims and, indeed, would probably beat a hasty retreat if such were forthcoming. For the majority the intended reaction of the victim appears to be of three kinds: (a) fear and flight, (b) indignation and abuse of the exhibitionist, (c) pleasure and amusement. Ellis (1933) believed that (c) was the most desired reaction of the exhibitionist. Hirning (1947) and Hirschfeld (1948) believed that the victim must be impressed in order to give full satisfaction, although Apfelberg et al. (1944) and Allen (1949) suggest that the victim must appear shocked.

The Actor

Women do not appear to have an urge to expose their genitalia, which indeed, anatomically, is rather difficult. Only a handful of cases are reported in the literature, and the majority of these were obviously mentally ill. Wunnenberg (1963) describes a female exhibitionist, a transparently clad dancer, who experienced orgasm when before her audience, and two vaginal exhibitionists, one retarded, the other with a brain injury. The following descriptive data then refer to male exhibitionists.

The usual onset of exhibitionism is at puberty, and the peak period ranges between age fifteen and thirty. Its onset after age forty-five is extremely rare except when it is the result of organic factors. The intelligence of exhibitionists is normally distributed with a slight positive skew (Mohr et al. 1964). Educational achievements appear to be below capacity with a fairly high school drop-out, which is possibly because of the onset of symptoms and their repercussions.

Arieff and Rotman (1942) suggested that the occupations of their samples were diverse with the majority belonging to the laborer class. Other studies (Mohr et al. 1964; Hirning 1945; Radzinowicz 1957) support this observation. Although Mohr et al. (1964) found no executives in their sample, Hirning (1945) reported that 17 percent of his group were executives, and Radzinowicz (1955) reported that 3.2 percent of his group were professionals. No studies attempted to compare their figures with population statistics, hence, no conclusions can be drawn concerning this relationship. Mohr et al. (1964) report that, of 54 exhibitionists studied, the majority (61 percent) had good work records. Be‑ke (1952) reported a similar observation.

Several studies (Henninger 1941; Arieff & Rotman 1942; Mohr et al. 1964) report data that concern perental absenteeism in the homes of exhibitionists. No control, or population data are given in any of these studies, so that the meaningfulness of the data cannot be assessed. In these studies, statistics are also given regarding the relationship of exhibitionists to their parents and the type of child-rearing practices employed. Here, again, comparative data are lacking.

Hirning (1947) suggested that exhibitionists tend to marry at a later age than the average. This contention was not born out in the data collected by Mohr et al. (1964). They reported that the majority of their sample were married in their early twenties with a peak at ages 22 to 23. Most authors (Taylor 1947; Radzinowicz 1957; Mohr et al. 1964) found that between 58 and 63 percent of their sample were married. Mohr et al. (1964) suggest that the time of impending or recent marriage and childbirth are often times when exhibiting begins or increases.

The incidence of psychosis is no higher among exhibitionists than among other groups. The diagnosis of neurosis is so flexible as to be relatively useless from the statistical viewpoint. The neurotic basis of exhibitionism has been assessed from 26 percent (Arieff et al. 1942) to 3 percent (Apfelberg et al. 1944). Mohr et al. (1964) reported only one case in 15 (7 percent) to be neurotic. The compulsive nature of the condition in large numbers of exhibitionists, nevertheless, has been remarked upon (East 1946; Rickles 1955; Segal 1963). Mental deficiency has been suggested as causative in 22 percent of the cases by East (1924), and in 2 percent by Taylor (1947). Mohr et al. (1964) suggest that the former high incidence of feeblemindedness was the result of faulty assessment. Their investigations show a normal distribution of intelligence among exhibitionists. In a study of fifteen exhibitionists the author found only one subject with an IQ below 70.

A definite, but still unexplained, relationship exists between the deviation of voyerism and exhibitionism. Authors such as Henninger (1941), Caprio (1949), Bowman (1951), Guttman (1953), and Rickles (1955) have drawn attention to this association. No special affinity exists, however, between exhibitionism and other sexual deviations, although individual cases of its occurance with homosexuality, pedophilia, fetishism, etc., have been reported in the literature. The author knows of two cases of exhibitionism associated with prurient telephone-calling. Obscene remarks or lewd gestures during the act are rare and not typical of a true exhibitionist. As has been noted, children on occasion are the preferred audience. These cases are not usually classical, because the pedophile desires intimate contact with the victim, and the act of exposure is usually a device to persuade a child to fondle his genitals or masturbate him.

DIAGNOSTIC CONSIDERATIONS

Classification

There have been several attempts to classify exhibitionists, namely, Kraft Ebing (1912), Hirschfeld (1948), and Taylor (1947). The orientation of the majority of these efforts have been dictated by the assumptions concerning aetiological causes of exhibitionism. Early investigators such as Kraft-Ebing (1912), East (1924), and Ellis (1933) simply divided them into two groups, that is, organic and psychological. Later investigators have simply expanded these two groups into subgroups, for example, Hirschfeld (1948), Rickles (1950), and Taylor (1947). These subgroups include psychoneurotic, psychopathic, mental defective, epileptics, schizophrenics, alcoholics, and so on.

We suggest that the following broad two-way classification is the most useful at present.

1. Organic. Mentally retarded, epileptic, brain damaged, seniles, psychotic, diabetic.

2. Psychological. Psychoneurotic or psychopathic.

A great number of diseases will bring about a reactive exhibitionism. The act is a consequence of confusion, and the loss of self-esteem and moral values present in conditions that involve damage to the central nervous system. Typical examples are brain damage in degenerative conditions of the central nervous system, such as brain tumour, presenile psychosis, senile arteriosclerosis, and general paralysis of the insane, etc. Diabetics will expose when their blood sugar is poorly controlled, both in the hypoglycemic and hyperglycemic phases. Often a crude exposure that occurs in a person of previous blameless character is a warning that someting is greatly wrong and, indeed, some cases appear in court before the true nature of the illness is realized. The disease appears to lay bare or activate an archaic dormant mechanism. Such exhibitionism is not considered a true deviation, and the circumstances of the exposure are careless, befuddled, and not classical. It has been reported that exhibitionism may also result from chronic prostatitis.

Reactive exposure similar to that occuring in organic cases is sometimes seen in severe psychotics such as schizophrenics and manic depressives. The aetiology and mode of expression are identical. Mental defectives, who can experience sexual urges, are particularly apt to expose because of general silliness, lack of discretion, and sexual frustration with no possibility of attracting a suitable partner. The act is a crude sexual invitation that is performed by individuals who lack adequate judgment. This form of exposure cannot be considered as a classical deviation.

The first major decision to be made in diagnosis is whether the patient's acting out is precipitated by organic or psychological causes. Of primary importance in assessing the underlying cause or causes behind a patient's exhibiting, is a good medical and psychological history. On the basis of this, further tests can be planned in order to confirm the findings of the history. For example, one would be suspicious if the patient's history of exhibiting did not conform to the normative pattern of this disease. The author is acquainted with one such case in which the first occasion of acting out occurred in the subject's thirtieth year. This is the usual age at which exhibiting begins to diminish, rather than start. Also in the history was a case of diabetes in the patient's bloodline. On the basis of these findings the patient was referred for examination by an internal specialist. It was found that he suffered from hypoglycemia rather than from exhibitionism.

On the basis of a good case history and follow-up testing, it is usually possible to isolate the cases of exhibitionism that are of organic nature. Included in this category, as we have observed, are mental deficiency, psychosis, organic lesions, diabetes, epilepsy, and senility. If the history follows the normal pattern of development for exhibitionism, and organic factors as outlined above can be ruled out, then it may be assumed that the symptom is a psychogenic one. As in the situation where organic factors underly the deviant behavior, it is important where psychological factors underly the symptom that the nature of these factors be fully understood.

Blake (1965) suggested that alcoholism is "the result of a learned habit of uncontrollable drinking which is used by the individual in an effort to reduce a disturbance in psychological homeostasis." He further suggested that a variety of emotional conditions, namely, fear, anger, anxiety, etc., can be responsible for the disturbance in psychological homeostasis. Perhaps it will be useful to think of exhibitionism and, for that matter, all forms of deviant behavior in this manner.

Depending on the precipitating psychological problem, the form of treatment will vary. The act of exhibiting by the time of apprehension and treatment is, no doubt, habitual and, as such, can be treated by the aversive procedures to be discussed later, but the precipitating factor will vary and treatment must be planned accordingly.

Treatment with alcoholics (Evans & Day 1966) has indicated that treatment of the habitual act alone is insufficient. It is most important that the precipitating factor or factors be taken into consideration. Where anxiety appears to be the precipitating factor, a combination of reciprocal inhibition and aversion therapy might be the most effective treatment. Where lack of assertive behavior appears to be the precipitating factor, assertive psychotherapy might be the most effective treatment. For these reasons, adequate assessment is imperative in order to isolate the factor or factors, if any, that cause the patient to exhibit.

Psychological Testing

Psychological tests have rarely been used to diagnose exhibitionists. Perhaps this is because the symptom is usually quite obvious. On occasion there are cases, who deny the act, in which some assessment technique would be of value. Rubin (1960) administered Cattell's Personality Factor Questionnaire to 13 exhibitionists. Paitich (1957) administered projective tests to 10 exhibitionists, 10 homosexuals, and 10 control cases (nonsexual offenders). In a study of 20 exhibitionists, Spitz (1956) employed projective techniques. The obvious criticism of all of these studies is the small number of cases studied.

Of more value, perhaps, would be a study into the factors, which would permit prediction of therapy and prognosis. One obvious prognostic factor is the strength of the habit. Mild cases, who restrict themselves to safe exposing, may quietly exercise their habit throughout a lifetime without arrest or interference. The more compulsive exhibitionist, unless successfully treated, will exhibit repetitively on a daily or weekly basis until his drive diminishes as he approaches middle age. The habit may cease, or manifest itself but rarely after the fourth decade. To date, only a very small minority have had partial or total relief from successful therapy. The organic exhibitionist has a poor prognosis unless his physical problem is amenable to treatment.

MODIFICATION TECHNIQUES

Development of Symptoms

The dominance, until recently, of Freudian psychoanalytical theory in the field of sexual deviations, has been instrumental in obscuring the role of genetics in these conditions. Thus, most experts in sexology tend to ignore the role of constitutional factors in sexual disorders. The exceptions have been Schlegel (1963) and Roper (1966), who have drawn urgent attention to the need to investigate these hitherto neglected aspects of aetiology. Schlegel (1963) in a theoretical paper suggests that, when considered in terms of the andromorphic-gynacomorphic continuum, exhibitionists fall into either the gynacomorphic or the intermediate category. He notes, on the other hand, that there are many men falling into these categories who do not exhibit. The implications of these observations are worth further examination.

Roper (1966) notes the occurrence of exhibitionistic behavior in primates and subhuman species. He also describes its occurrence in primitive human cultures, for example the Zulus. Although both these areas (the body type and the anthropological) have received little attention to date, their investigation might reveal some basis for inferring genetic or constitutional factors in the development of exhibitionism. Although there is scant evidence concerning genetic factors in exhibitionism, the possibility of their existence cannot be ruled out.

Where the act of exhibiting leads to a reduction of anxiety, aggression, or fear, etc., in short arousal, the acquisition of the habit may be viewed in terms of the drive-reduction theorists. All cases of exhibitionism do not fit into this pattern, since there are many cases where the patient exhibits without apparently any drive reduction taking place.

Once the patient starts to exhibit, it is likely that the drive-reduction theory can be called on to explain its development into a habit. It should be noted that, after the first exposure, the patient does not necessarily have to exhibit for the act to be reinforced. McGuire, Carlisle, and Young (1964) have suggested that fantasy during masturbation can act to substantiate the learning process. They report two exhibitionists who demonstrate this phenomenon. Both had been surprised by an attractive female while surreptitiously urinating in a semipublic place. At first they were embarrassed and hurried away. Later the erotic circumstances occurred to them and became so sexually arousing that they were incorporated into their masturbatory fantasies. Eventually, they were unable to confine the activity and began to expose in public and were ultimately arrested.

In a recent study (Evans, 1968) it was demonstrated that, of two groups of exhibitionists treated by means of emotive imagery and aversive conditioning, the group with normal masturbatory fantasy was deconditioned significantly faster than the group with exhibitionistic masturbatory fantasy. This finding was interpreted to support the hypothesis of McGuire, Carlisle, and Young (1965) that masturbation to deviant fantasy tends to increase the habit strength of sexually deviant behavior.

One such case can be cited where the patient was urinating in an alley when a young female chanced to pass and noticed the act, which led to the patient's becoming an habitual exhibitor. It is likely that the act was also rewarded on that and future occasions by the thrill or pleasure ensuring. In other cases, vicarious learning may be responsible for the patient's initiation to the act. This can occur at any stage in the patient's development, whether it is during prepubescence, during sex play, or young adulthood, while observing another act out. Bandura and Walters (1965) cite a case of exhibitionism in which vicarious learning in the home was responsible for the deviant behavior.

It is also possible that exhibitionism in some cases is partly the result of the patient's failure to learn the values that normally inhibit the occurrence of the behavior. At present, there is no evidence to support or to negate this suggestion.

Displacement may be another concept that is useful in the understanding of incidents of exhibiting. Exhibitionism has been explained in these terms by Schlegel (1963). He suggested that, if considered in these terms, many of the peculiarities of exhibitionists can be explained. For example, the senselessness of the act is characteristic of all displacement phenomenon. Displacement is well defined and clearly recognized among lower animals. For instance, if males are fighting, they will often break off the encounter and go through the motions of seizing food or copulating with the nearest females or substitute. Energy displacement will thus spill over from one basic drive to another and particularly between the sex drive and aggression, which appear to be constitutionally linked in the male. Aggression will spill over into sexual behavior, for instance, and evidence of other drive displacements can be easily cited.

Another possible factor is the "releaser" mechanism so important among lower animals—for example, the duration of sunlight triggering off the mating instinct in birds. It cannot yet be ruled out that something similar does not happen with human exhibitionists. Perhaps the visual stimulus of the object in a particular locus or environment may act as an arousal signal through the hypothalamus and neuroendocrine metabolism to stimulate an old forgotten sexual mechanism.

From the above discussion the reader is probably aware by now of the status of aetiological theory in exhibitionism. Little evidence can be called forth in support of any of the factors outlined above. The factors outlined here are by no means exclusive, for example, the work of Berlyne (1960) in the area of curiosity could also be applied to exhibitionism and to other similar phenomena.

DESCRIPTION OF MODIFICATION TECHNIQUES

Current therapies for the treatment for exhibitionism and studies into their success are appallingly few.

Psychotherapy

Until recently, exhibitionism was treated almost exclusively with various forms of psychotherapy, that is, psychoanalysis, group psychotherapy, and individual psychotherapy. Opinions vary as to the efficiency of these conventional forms of treatment. More important, however, is the fact that there is no good evidence of their effectiveness. The use of supportive psychotherapy might benefit the morale of the patient as the average exhibitionist is usually a passive and dependent individual. Analytically oriented or "deep uncovering" psychotherapy would seem of dubious value, since it is unlikely that achieving intellectual insight can influence an habitual act to any great extent. The use of assertive psychotherapy, with strong emphasis on the manipulation of the environment, is probably worth further investigation, but only as an adjuvant to other active and more radical therapies. Salter's (1961) conditioned-reflex therapy is worth studying as a particular type of assertive psychotherapy. Group psychotherapy with the selection of suitable cases, such as the timid, self-conscious, and neurotic, may be of some value in the treatment program. Group psychotherapy could perhaps be extended to the wives of exhibitionists or to the patient and his wife counselled together in an abbreviated form of "family therapy." These maneuvers might well benefit generally the patient's psychological, domestic, and social health, but are not likely to modify greatly the deviation itself.

Hypnotherapy

Roper (1966) describes the successful use of hypnotherapy with three patients with a follow-up period of 5, $4\frac{1}{2}$, and 1 year, respectively. Roper noted the successful use of hypnosis in the treatment of other sexual perversions in the late nineteenth century by authorities such as Krafft-Ebing (1912) and von Schrank-Notzing (1895). No one, however, appears to have preceded Roper in its use with exhibitionism. Roper's technique is as follows: After preliminary work-up, the patient's response to hypnotic suggestion is assessed, and the proposed treatment carefully explained to the patient with the reassurance that it will be harmless. Hypnotic sessions are carried out on a couch in the therapist's office. A deep trance state is induced by a repetitive verbal technique of induction. At this time, attempts are made to get the patient to recall repressed memories concerning the events surrounding his initial act and subsequent reactions. The patient's exhibitionism is then reconstructed to him as an aberrant form of sexual activity performed while in a receptive state of mind because of various circumstances. The pleasure or satisfaction obtained had been sufficient for repetition to induce a habit pattern. This simple explanation is offered as a positive suggestion to the patient while he remains in a hypnotic trance, and it is further suggested to him that, as he now has insight into the habit, it no longer has the same control over him as previously and the need to repeat this behavior will not recur. These suggestions are repeated to the patient until he is able to affirm his agreement and acceptance of them. Subsequent posthypnotic suggestions are made along similar lines, with suggestions to increase his self-confidence. Sessions last about half an hour and are repeated at weekly intervals and more or less frequently as is thought necessary.

Roper noted in his cases that the symptoms ceased after the first deep trance was induced. Although admitting that it would be difficult to draw valid conclusions from only three cases, Roper believed that the key to success in his method of hypnotherapy lay in the degree of hypnosis, that is, the trance state must be deep. Without this criteria, success was unlikely. Whether any real significance could be attached to the explanations and the suggestions given to the patient, is not clear. Certainly, insight has shown no curative value on habits when it is used in psychotherapy. Perhaps the suggestions have only a general effect in the extinction of conditioned responses by nonreinforcement or reciprocal inhibition. It was noted that, in two cases, recrudescence of the symptom occurred but in a mild and attenuated form which yielded to further therapy. Presumably these relapses are a partial return of the previously extinguished conditioned response.

Reciprocal Inhibition Therapy

Reciprocal inhibition therapy, pioneered by Wolpe (1958), is based on the premise that neurotic behavior is an inappropriate learned response to environmental stress and that relearning is required to effect relief. The method, briefly, is to formulate a hierarchy of life situations in an ascending order of anxiety-provoking qualities. The patient is then taught muscular relaxation, with or without hypnotherapy, by Lazarus' method (Wolpe & Lazarus, 1966). When this skill is acquired, the patient is desensitized to the anxiety-provoking situation by repeatedly being asked to imagine the stimuli while in a relaxed state. The therapist begins with the least anxiety-provoking stimulus and moves up the hierarchy toward the most anxiety-provoking stimulus. The patient is instructed to signal with his hand if a situation disturbs him. When this occurs, the therapist starts two or three stimuli below this and works up the hierarchy once more.

The principle involved "is the piecemeal breaking down of neurotic anxiety-response habits, employing a physiological state incompatible with anxiety to inhibit the anxiety response to a stimulus that evokes it weakly, repeating the exposure until the stimulus looses completely its anxiety-evoking ability" (Wolpe & Lazarus 1966).

One suggested alteration of the technique

is the use of intravenous sodium brietal (Methohexital sodium, Lilly) to produce a swift and deeper degree of mental and physical relaxation. The procedure for the presentation of the hierarchy is the same as the one for reciprocal inhibition which is outlined above. Brady (1966) reports the use of this method with five cases of frigidity. To date this method has not been employed with exhibitionists, but it would seem worth investigation.

The rationale of reciprocal inhibition therapy is to reduce anxiety and, therefore, would be expected to be more successful with exhibitionists who demonstrate a high degree of tension and neuroticism. Although this assumption is a good one, its validity remains to be tested. The technique must be modified to be adjusted to the peculiar nature of the exhibitionist's behavior. The construction of a hierarchy is brought about by listing exposure-provoking stimuli. The patient is told to imagine, while relaxed, those series of scenes where a danger of acting out in real life would exist. Visual imagery can be assisted in some patients by their viewing written instructions on a small screen with regard to the required fantasy—for example, "Imagine yourself meeting an attractive young girl alone in a park," etc. Associations are built up in the patient's mind at these sessions to relax rather than to expose when the stimuli present themselves. The patient can often be trained to relax to the cue of the word "relax," which he may say or think to himself when he experiences a dangerous situation in real life.

Reciprocal inhibition therapy was first successfully applied to a case of exhibitionism by Bond and Hutchison (1960). We note with interest that, in this case, hypnotherapy was used as an aide to relaxation and, in view of Roper's later experiences, one may question whether the hypnosis was not partly or wholly responsible for a successful outcome rather than the reciprocal inhibition therapy. Wolpe (1958) also reports a case of chronic anxiety state with exhibitionism, in which he treated the man's anxiety to social situations by reciprocal inhibition therapy and by instigating assertive behavior. The patient's exhibitionism underwent an incidental and dramatic improvement with eventual recovery concurrently with a successful relief of the anxiety state.

Aversion Therapy

In aversion, or more correctly, avoidance conditioning, the aim of therapy is to train the subject to avoid the deviant response. The deviant response in exhibitionism is the exposure of the genitalia or, at the extreme, the whole body. Both of these responses are normal everyday activities, for instance, when the male goes to the bathroom, and so forth. In order to overcome this problem, some other response in the response chain of exhibiting must be associated with avoidance. The obvious choice is the thought component involved prior to and during the act. Wolpe (1958) reports one case in which he treated an exhibitionist by having him imagine the act and by shocking him when he signaled that a vivid image was present.

The author has had success with the Feldman and McCulloch (1964, 1965) paradigm in which deviant, normal, and neutral slides are employed in the treatment of various deviant behaviors. By building a hierarchy as it were of the exhibitionist's deviant behavior and of normal heterosexual behavior, and by devising a group of neutral statements, we were able to employ the Feldman and McCulloch (1965) paradigm. Examples of the stimuli are shown below.

The stimuli in the deviant and heterosexual selection are tailored to the individual. The statements are typed on paper and 35 mm negative slides are prepared of these statements.

The patient is seated before a rear projection screen, and he is able to control the onset of slides by means of a foot pedal; and shock is delivered through finger electrodes. Twenty of each type of slide are placed in a Kodak "Carousel" projector slide tray according to a predetermined program. The deviant slides are placed randomly among the sixty possible positions. Each deviant

Deviant	*Heterosexual*	*Neutral*
Thinking about exposing to a young girl in a park	Kissing your wife	Eating a sandwich
Exhibiting to a young woman on a street at noon	Petting with your wife	Washing a car

slide is followed by a normal heterosexual slide, and the neutral slides are placed in the remaining positions. The "Carousel" projector is modified so that the occurrence of a deviant slide starts a timer which, after a given time delay, starts the shock; shock is terminated when the patient goes on to the next slide. Before each session the shock level is set at the maximum the patient reports he can stand.

The statements on each slide are prepared so that they give the patient sufficient information to form an image, but also so that he can make the image as detailed as he wishes. The initial block of trials consists of an average of ten sessions once or twice a week. The initial block of trials is continued until the subject reports freedom from urges or thoughts about exhibiting for at least two weeks in succession. At this time he is seen every two weeks for three sessions, and then once a month for three sessions. The patients are then given a follow-up interview every three months for a period of two years (Bond & Evans, 1967). During trials, the delay between the onset of the deviant slide and the shock is varied randomly from three to six seconds in one-second intervals.

Evans (1967), has reported the results of the above method of treatment with seven exhibitionists. Six months following the initiation of treatment, five of the seven patients were no longer experiencing urges to act out nor were they acting out. The two other patients still reported urges to act out, and acted out at a decreased rate. It should be noted that, for six months prior to treatment, all seven exhibited once a month or more frequently. From observation it would appear that frequency of acting out (habit strength) is a sensitive predictor of the length of treatment and also of the likely success of treatment. We have stated previously, avoidance treatment such as this holds the greatest promise for symptom removal. However, it is suggested that a variety of other methods be employed for the treatment of the cause behind the symptom.

Operant Techniques

Some of the methods suggested by Mertens (1964) for the application of operant techniques to induce self-control for alcoholics may be applicable to exhibitionists. Three examples are as follows:

1. Social reward can be used by giving the patient a chart consisting of the days of the week and the hours of the day, and he has the task of not only avoiding exposure but of recording every hour of the day successfully passed without relapse; and this is inspected regularly by the therapist. This is also an effective measure of progress in treatment.
2. Chaining is another method. The patient is given a card that outlines a list of tasks he must perform if he should suddenly be attacked by the urge to expose. This list might include orders such as "look at watch and note exact time, walk swiftly around the block, etc." The patient is expected to consult this list the moment he becomes aware of the urge to exhibit. Again, motivation is needed in the patient and the maneuver is designed to distract attention from the stimulus and to displace sexual energy into motor and intellectual activity.
3. A very similar procedure is to furnish the patient with a typed list of "*pros and cons*" which he is to consult as soon as the desire to exhibit strikes. The "con" list brings to the awareness of the patient that the transient pleasure of gratification is heavily outweighed by disastrous possibilities for his job, family, and social reputation. The unpleasant sequelae of arrest, humiliation, jail, and ruin are emphasized. The fear of these possibilities may have an aversive effect.

Drug Therapy

Drug therapy is not likely, in the foreseeable future, to be of greater importance than as an adjuvant measure secondary to psychological therapies. In individual cases, however, the use of psychotropic drugs can be of great assistance. Exhibitionists, as can be expected, are prone to reactive anxiety states and depressions. Symptomatic relief may be urgently needed so that the sufferer can continue his normal life and be receptive to other therapies.

There is, however, one member of the phenothiazine group, Thioridazine (Sandoz), that deserves special mention because of its possible use with sexual deviants (Buki 1964). This drug, for reasons largely unknown, has a peculiarly depressing effect on the sexual drive (Kamm, 1965). When there is danger of acting out this drug may be of value. In some cases it may, in heavy doses, cause a temporary impotence or inability to ejaculate. Other side effects are minimal, such as drowsiness and drying of the mouth, so that it is a drug well fitted for use with ambulatory patients.

Hypothetically, this drug could well be used in cases where ejaculation and masturbation are the positive reinforcers of the exhibiting behavior. Thioridazine has been found to make this successful behavior impossible. Thus a deconditioning process could be set to work in the actual act of exhibiting. This result has been noted in one case by the author. It is believed that this hypothesis merits testing.

Surgery

Some European workers have used rather heroic measures to overcome the problem of the acting-out sexual psychopath. Some patients have been voluntarily castrated, usually with the satisfactory abatement of symptoms. The psychological effect of this dreaded and mutilating operation on the patient has not been adequately previewed. Castration has been applied to some severe cases of exhibitionism in Europe (Stürup 1961), and a successful outcome in seven cases has been reported. One would shrink from the idea of using such a radical procedure unless, of course, the patient was desperate, potentially very dangerous and liable to indefinite incarceration, and all other therapeutic help had been in vain.

As far as the author is aware, neurosurgical intervention to arrest exhibitionism has not been postulated or attempted. It is possible that either castration or neurological intervention might interrupt a malignantly compulsive type of exhibitionism; yet, this cannot now be considered the treatment of choice unless the situation were desperate and all other measures had failed. Electrical stimulation through implanted electrodes on vital areas of the brain, such as the thalamus, hypothalamus, and amygdala may also be worth investigation in the future, particularly, if nonsurgical procedures prove to be of limited value.

Sexual behavior is a very complex coordination of neuroendocrine factors and learning. Undoubtedly, sexual behavior as in other behavior is represented in the central nervous system by an extensive network of neural associations controlled or influenced by specific centers. The cerebral model of sexual excitation and inhibition has not yet been properly explored. Masserman (1966) points out that Sherrington in 1900 demonstrated that a spinal dog can copulate quite efficiently and a decerabrated bitch can conceive and deliver. Best and Taylor (1955) have noted several interesting physioanatomical correlations between olfactory-gustatory and sexual processes, namely, changes in the nasal mucosa are common in women during pregnancy and in monkeys during the estrus cycles, castration has produced degenerative changes in the nasal mucosa of rats, which are reversed by estrogen injections, the successful treatment of atrophic rhinitis by nasal application of follicular horone, etc. Masserman (1966) notes that lesions of the amygdalae render most monkeys overly tame, bulimic, and hypersexed. It has been reported that removal of the temporal lobe for epilepsy also resulted in the elimination of homosexuality in two cases (Walker 1966).

Lesions of the precuneus have resulted in hypersexuality in humans. In experimental rats, Heimer et al. (1964) found drastic changes in mating behavior following lesions at the junction of the diencephelon and mesencephelon. A "copulation reward" site has been discovered in the posterior hypothalamus of rats by Caggiula and Hoebel (1966). Most present-day psychosurgery is aimed at curbing aggression and is being performed on the amygdala and hypothalamus, whereas conventional surgery and stereotaxic procedures have been aimed at the frontal lobe and thalamus. The specific effect on sexual function of the drug thioridazine also hints at special centers that can be reached pharmacologically. A shadowy picture of cerebral sexuality is slowly emerging, but it requires a great deal of further research in neuroanatomy and neurophysiology before more advanced clinical use of neurosurgery can be foreseen. Masserman (1966) offers a caution to those who would omit neurophysiological theory from consideration. He states:

> "any 'metapsychologic' theory that neglects these factors and attributes all human behavior solely to an over-riding function called 'primal sexuality' may be attractive in a simple-minded

and pornographically titillating fashion, but at the price of physiologic and biodynamic naivete" (Masserman, 1966).

SUMMARY

Exhibitionism is defined as the exposure of a part or the whole of the body for sexual or nonsexual rewards. The lack of material other than statistical studies is pointed out. Certain aspects of the act of exhibiting are discussed such as its nature, place of occurrence, and frequency. The preferred audience is usually a strange female; however, children of both sexes and some adult males may be the audience in some cases. Salient characteristics of the exhibitionist are also discussed. For the most part, exhibitionism is confined to males between the ages of 12 and 40. In most other characteristics, there is little variance from the normal population.

Certain points concerning diagnosis are considered. After a review of the literature, it is suggested that a broad two-way classification of exhibitionists is most workable. The two categories are the organic and the psychological, depending on the genesis of the behavior. In diagnosis it is first necessary to determine which cause is appropriate. In most of the organic cases the exhibiting behavior can be modified by correct physical treatment. No adequate studies have been carried out that concern the use of psychological tests in diagnosis. Probably because in all cases, except the ones that involve denial, the symptomatology is quite obvious.

The second part of this chapter is devoted to various modification techniques applicable to exhibitionism. The development of symptoms is considered to be the result of a learning process. Often initial exposure occurs as a result of accidental learning, which with repeated activity becomes a habit. The usual reinforcement for continued behavior is the reduction of a sexual or a nonsexual arousal state.

The relative failure of most forms of psychotherapy is suggested; however, the use of assertive therapy as an adjunctive treatment is pointed out. Roper's (1966) method of treatment by hypnotherapy is outlined, and the need for further study and replication of this method is believed important. The use of reciprocal inhibition therapy by Wolpe (1958) and Bond and Hutchison (1960) is reviewed, and its usefulness is discussed. A modification of Feldman and McCulloch's (1965) paradigm, by using images instead of pictures, is outlined. This method is presently being studied by the author and, to date, the results look promising. Certain operant techniques are suggested that can be of use in the immediate treatment of exhibitionists.

The use of the drug Thioridazine (Sandoz) is discussed, and a hypothesis concerning its use in the treatment of exhibitionism is noted. Castration has been employed in some European countries, however, this is viewed as a most radical form of treatment. Some aspects of the physiology of sex are reviewed, and the importance of further investigation in this area is suggested.

REFERENCES

Allen, C. *The sexual perversions and abnormalities*. (2nd ed.) London: Oxford Med. Pub., 1949.

Apfelberg, B., Sugar, C., & Pfeffer, A. Z. A psychiatric study of 250 sex offenders. *Amer. J. Psychiat.*, 1944, **100**, 762–769.

Arieff, A. J., & Rotman, D. B. One hundred cases of indecent exposure. *J. Nerv. Ment. Dis*. 1942, **96**, 523–528.

Bandura, A., & Walters, R. H. *Social learning and personality development*, New York: Holt, Rinehart and Winston, 1965.

Bejke, R. A contribution to the theory of exhibitionism. *Acta. Psychiat. Scand.*, 1952, Supp. 80, 233–234.

Berlyne, D. E. *Conflict arousal and curiosity*. New York: McGraw-Hill, 1960.

Best, C. H., & Taylor, N. B. *The physiological basis of medical practice*. (6th. ed.). Baltimore: Williams and Wilkins, 1955.

Blake, B. G. The application of behaviour therapy to the treatment of alcoholism. *Behav. Res. Ther.*, 1965, **3**, 75–85.

Bond, I. K., & Evans, D. R. The application of avoidance therapy in two cases of underwear fetishists. *Can. Med. Ass.* J., 1967, **96**, 1160–1162.

Bond, I. K., & Hutchison, H. C. Application of reciprocal inhibition therapy to exhibitionism. *Can. Med. Ass. J.*, 1960, **83**, 23–25.

Bowman, K. M. The problem of the sex offender. *Amer. J. Psychiat.*, 1951, **108**, 250–257.

Brady, J. P. Brevital-relaxation treatment of frigidity. *Behav. Res. Ther.*, 1966, **4**, 71–77.

Buki, R. A. The use of psychotropic drugs in the rehabilitation of sex-deviated criminals. *Amer. J. Psychiat.*, 1964, **120**, 1170–1175.

Caggiula, A. R., & Hoebel, B. G. Copulation reward site in the posterior hypothalamus. *Sci.*, 1966, **153**, 1284–1285.

Caprio, F. S. Scoptophilia—exhibitionism: a case report. *J. Clin. Psychopath.*, 1949, **10**, 50–72.

East, W. N. Observations on exhibitionism. *Lancet*, 1924, **23**, 370–375.

East, W. N. Sexual offenders. *J. Nerv. Ment. Dis.*, 1946, **103**, 626–666.

Ellis, H. *Psychology of sex*. London: Heinemann, 1933.

Ellis, A., & Brancale, R. *The psychology of sex offenders*. Springfield, Ill.: Charles C. Thomas, 1956.

Evans, D. R. An exploratory study into the treatment of exhibitionism by means of emotive imagery and aversive conditioning. *Can. Psychol.*, 1967, **8**, 162.

Evans, D. R. Masturbatory fantasy and sexual deviation. *Behav. Res. Ther.*, 1968, **6**, 17–19.

Evans, D. R., & Day, H. I. A preliminary report on the conditioning of an avoidance response to alcohol drinking. *Can. Psychol.*, 1966, **7**, 156.

Feldman, M. P., & McCulloch, M. J. A systematic approach to the treatment of homosexuality by conditioned aversion: preliminary report. *Amer. J. Psychiat.*, 1964, **121**, 167–171.

Feldman, M. P., & McCulloch, M. J. The application of anticipatory avoidance learning to the treatment of homosexuality. *Behav. Res. Ther.*, 1965, **2**, 165–183.

Guttman, O. Exhibitionism. *J. Clin. Exp. Psychopath.*, 1953, **14**, 13–51.

Heimer, C. B., & Larsson, K. Drastic changes in the mating behaviour of male rats following lesions in the junction of diencephalon and mesencephalon. *Experientia*, 1964, **20**, 460–461.

Henninger, J. M. Exhibitionism. *J. Crim. Psychopath*, 1941, **2**, 357–366.

Henry, G. W. *All the sexes*. New York: Reinhart and Co., 1955.

Hirning, L. C. Genital exhibitionism, an interpretive study. *J. Clin. Psychopath.*, 1947, **8**, 557–564.

Hirschfeld, M. *Sexual anomalies and perversions*. London: Francis Alder, 1948.

Kamm, Ilse, Control of sexual hyperactivity with thioridazine. *Amer. J. Psychiat.*, 1965, **121**, 922–923.

Karpman, B. The psychopathology of exhibitionism. *J. Clin. Psychopath.*, 1948, **9**, 179–225.

Krafft-Ebing, R. von. *Psychopathia sexualis*. (12th ed.) New York: Rebman, 1912.

Lasegue, E. C. Les exhibitionistes. *L'union medicale*, troisieme serie, 1877.

McCawley, A. Exhibitionism and acting out. *Compreh. Psychiat.*, 1965, **6**, 396–409.

McGuire, R. L., & Carlisle, J. M., & Young, B. G., Sexual deviations as conditioned behaviour: a hypothesis. *Behav. Res. Ther.* 1965, **2**, 185–190.

Masserman, J. H. Sexuality re-evaluated. *Can. Psychiat. Ass. J.*, 1966, **11**, 379–388.

Mertens, G. C. An operant learning approach to self-control for alcoholics. Paper read at Amer. Psychol. Ass., Los Angeles, Sept. 1964.

Mohr, J. W., Turner, R. E., & Jerry, M. B. *Pedophilia and exhibitionism*. Toronto: University of Toronto Press, 1964.

Paitich, D. Exhibitionism: a comparative study. Paper read at Toronto Psychiat. Hosp. Journal Club, Toronto, March, 1957.

Radzinowicz, L. *Sexual offences*. London: Macmillan, 1957.

Rickles, N. K. *Exhibitionism*. Philadelphia: Lippencott, 1950.

Rickles, N. K. Exhibitionism. *J. Soc. Ther.*, 1955, **1**, 168–181.

Roper, P. The use of hypnosis in the treatment of exhibitionism. *Can. Med. Ass. J.*, 1966, **94**, 72–77.

Rubin, J. Some preliminary observations of types of exhibitionists. Paper read at Toronto Psychiat. Hosp. Journal Club, Toronto, April, 1960.

Salter, A. *Conditioned reflex therapy*. New York: Capricorn Books, 1961.

Schlegel, W. S. Der Exhibitionism des Mannes—eine Instinkt mechanische Übersprunghandlung? *Nervenarzt*, 1963, **34**, 365–368.

Segal, M. M. Impulsive sexuality: some clinical and theoretical observations. *Int. J. Psychoanal.*, 1963, **44**, 407–418.

Shaskan, D. One hundred sex offenders. *Amer. J. Orthopsychiat.*, 1939, **9**, 565–569.

Shrank-Notzing, A. von. *Therapeutic suggestion in psychopathia sexualis*. Philadelphia: F. A. Davis Co., 1895.

Spitz, H. H. A clinical investigation of certain personality characteristics of twenty male exhibitionists. *Diss. Abstr.*, 1956, **16**, 381–382.

Stürup, G. K. Correctional treatment and the criminal sexual offender. *Can. J. Correct.*, 1961, **3**, 250–265.

Taylor, F. H. Observations on some cases of exhibitionism. *J. Ment. Sci.*, 1947, **93**, 631–638.

Walker, E. H. Personal communication. 1966.

Wolpe, J. *Psychotherapy by reciprocal inhibition*. Stanford: Stanford University Press, 1958.

Wolpe, J., & Lazarus, A. A. *Behavior therapy techniques*. London: Pergamon Press, 1966.

Wunnenberg, W. Normality and abnormality in sexuality in homosexuality and exhibitionism. *Prax. Psychother.*, 1963, **8**, 243–257.

Chapter 23

Homosexuality

BASIL JAMES

The literature on homosexuality is bedeviled by the multiplicity of terms and the omission of operational definitions. Concepts of homosexuality range from actual genital contact between members of the same sex, through the conscious experience of homosexual fantasy, to so-called latent homosexuality. Although a dimensional approach underlines the fact that homosexuality may not be an all or nothing phenomenon, and that gradations can exist, the lack of precision in the use of terms, and their not infrequent interchangeability, adds to the confusion that tends to characterize thinking on the subject. Furthermore, correlations between certain items of nonsexual behavior and homosexuality, which have not been satisfactorily validated, are claimed or implied. Salzman (1965), for instance, in his critical review of the concept of latent homosexuality, shows how Freud's (1953d) ideas of male activity and female passivity have led to the doubtful conclusion that behavior characterized by timidity, sensitivity, or interest in the arts, when exhibited by a male, becomes "evidence" of homosexuality.

Kinsey's (1948) definition of homosexuality is, in the author's view, the clearest and most useful. Kinsey suggests that persons are not characterized as heterosexual or homosexual, but as individuals who have had certain amounts of heterosexual experience and certain amounts of homosexual experience. Instead of using these terms as substantives that stand for persons, or even as adjectives to describe persons, they may better be used to decribe the nature of the overt sexual relations, or of the stimuli to which an individual erotically responds. This definition includes not only the individual's observable behavior patterns, physiological as well as interpersonal, but also leaves open for inclusion the individual's fantasied stimuli and subjective responses. Furthermore, it in no way prejudges the questions of aetiology or of personality correlates.

Kinsey extended his view of sexual orientation as a continuum by devising his well-known heterosexual-homosexual rating scale (See Figure 23.1). An individual may be assigned a position on the scale according to his sexual experiences or responses, and in accordance with the following definitions of the various points on the scale.

0. Individuals are rated as 0's if they make no physical contacts that result in erotic arousal or orgasm, and make no psychic responses to individuals of their own sex. Their sociosexual contacts and responses are exclusively with individuals of the opposite sex.

1. Individuals are rated as 1's if they have only incidental homosexual contacts that have involved physical or psychic response, or incidental psychic responses without physical contact. The great preponderance of their sociosexual experience and reactions is directed toward individuals of the opposite sex. Such homosexual experiences

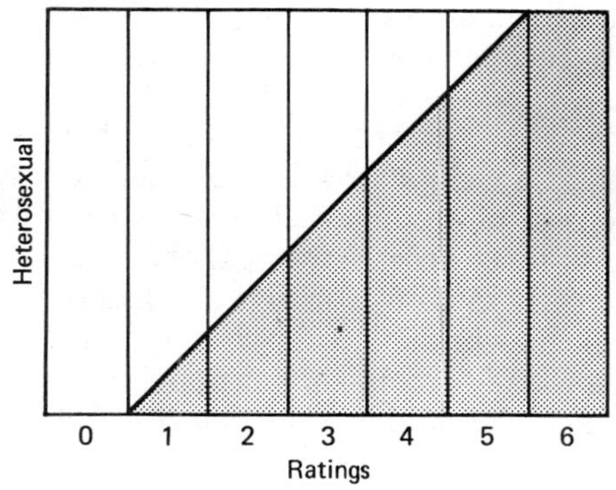

Figure 23.1 Heterosexual-homosexual rating scale. Based on both psychologic reactions and overt experience, individuals rate as follows: 0, exclusively heterosexual with no homosexual 1, predominantly heterosexual, only incidentally homosexual 2, predominantly heterosexual, but more than incidentally homosexual 3, equally hetrosexual and homosexual 4, predominantly homosexual, and more than incidentally heterosexual 5, predominantly homosexual, but incidentally heterosexual 6, exclusively homosexual.

as these individuals have may occur only a single time or two or, at least, infrequently in comparison to the amount of their heterosexual experience. Their homosexual experiences never involve as specific psychic reactions as they make to heterosexual stimuli. Sometimes the homosexual activities in which they engage may be inspired by curiosity, or may be more or less forced on them by other individuals, perhaps when they are asleep or when they are drunk, or under some other peculiar circumstance.

2. Individuals are rated as 2's if they have more than incidental homosexual experience, and/or if they respond rather definitely to homosexual stimuli. Their heterosexual experiences and/or reactions still surpass their homosexual experiences and/or reactions. These individuals may have only a small amount of homosexual experience or they may have a considerable amount of it, but in every case it is surpassed by the amount of heterosexual experience that they have within the same period of time. They usually recognize their quite specific arousal by homosexual stimuli, but their responses to the opposite sex are still stronger. A few of these individuals may even have all of their overt experience in the homosexual, but their psychic reactions to persons of the opposite sex indicate that they are still predominantly heterosexual. This latter situation is most often found among younger males who have not yet ventured to have actual intercourse with girls, although their orientation is definitely heterosexual. On the other hand, there are some males who should be rated as 2's because of their strong reactions to individuals of their own sex, even though they have never had overt relations with them.

3. Individuals who are rated 3's stand midway on the heterosexual-homosexual scale. They are about equally homosexual and heterosexual in their overt experience and/or their psychic reactions. In general, they accept and equally enjoy both types of contacts, and have no strong preferences for one or the other. Some persons are rated 3's, even though they may have a larger amount of experience of one sort, because they respond psychically to partners of both sexes, and it is only a matter of circumstance that brings them into more frequent contact with one of the sexes. This situation is not unusual among single males, for male contacts are often more available to them than female contacts. Married males, on the other hand, find it simpler to secure a sexual outlet through intercourse with their wives, even though some of them may be as interested in males as they are in females.

4. Individuals are rated as 4's if they have more overt activity and/or psychic reactions in the homosexual, while still maintaining a fair amount of heterosexual activity and/or responding rather definitely to heterosexual stimuli.

5. Individuals are rated 5's if they are almost entirely homosexual in their overt activities and/or reactions. They do have incidental experience with the opposite sex and sometimes react psychically to individuals of the opposite sex.

6. Individuals are rated as 6's if they are exclusively homosexual, both in regard to their overt experience and in regard to their psychic reactions.

INCIDENCE

Homosexuality does not seem to occur to a significant degree in all societies. In the most extensive analysis, Ford and Beach (1965) report that in 29 of the 76 societies for which information is available, homosexuality is "totally absent, rare, or carried out only in secrecy." However, Hooker (1965a) points out that careful and detailed data on homosexual behavior are lacking in many of the ethnographic descriptions in the Human Relations Area Files, on which Ford and Beach relied. Thus, although this work is the most reliable available, the findings should be accepted with caution.

As far as the incidence in our own culture is concerned, no investigation is comparable to that of Kinsey et al. They summarize their main findings as follows.

Thirty-seven percent of the total male population has at least some overt homosexual experience to the point of orgasm between adolescence and old age. This accounts for nearly 2 males out of every 5 that one may meet.

Fifty percent of the males who remain single until age 35 have had overt homosexual experience to the point of orgasm, since the onset of adolescence.

Fifty-eight percent of the males who belong to the group that goes into high school but not beyond, 50 percent of the grade school level, and 47 percent of the college level have had homosexual experience to the point of orgasm if they remain single to the age of 35.

Sixty-three percent of all males never have overt homosexual experience to the point of orgasm after the onset of adolescence.

Fifty percent of all males (approximately) have neither overt nor psychic experience in the homosexual after the onset of adolescence.

Thirteen percent of the males (approximately) react erotically to other males without having overt homosexual contacts after the onset of adolescence.

Thirty percent of all males have at least incidental homosexual experience or reactions (that is, rate 1 to 6) over at least a three-year period between the ages of 16 and 55. This accounts for one male out of every three in the population who is past the early years of adolescence.

Twenty-five percent of the male population has more than incidental homosexual experience or reactions (that is, rates 2 to 6) for at least three years between the ages of 16 and 55. In terms of averages, one male out of approximately every four has had or will have such distinct and continued homosexual experience.

Eighteen percent of the males have at least as much of the homosexual as the heterosexual in their histories (that is, rate 3 to 6) for at least three years between the ages of 16 and 55. This is more than one in six of the white male population.

Thirteen percent of the population has more of the homosexual than the heterosexual (that is, rates 4 to 6) for at least three years between the ages of 16 and 55. This is one in eight of the white male population.

Ten percent of the males are more or less exclusively homosexual (that is, rate 5 or 6) for at least three years between the ages of 16 and 55. This is one male in ten in the white male population.

Eight percent of the males are exclusively homosexual (that is, rate a 6) for at least three years between the ages of 16 and 55. This is one male in every 13.

Four percent of the white males are exclusively homosexual throughout their lives, after the onset of adolescence.

Heterosexual-Homosexual ratings for all white males in the study are shown in Figure 23.2 and in Table 23.1. In the latter, if the percentages are added from the right-hand side of each line, the cumulated percents will show the portion of the population that rates 1 or more, or 2 or more, etc., in each age period. A rating X indicates no sociosexual contacts or reactions.

AETIOLOGY

Although the incidence of the condition in the general population is high, and the literature voluminous, most of the clinical contributions are open to serious objections. Apart from the prejudicial effect of the theoretical framework from which most investigators work, the main criticisms can be expressed in terms of the limited numbers of the subjects involved, the superficiality of the investigations, or the biased selection. The question of biased selection is almost totally ignored, although it is an obvious hazard for the clinician. It is rarely homosexuality alone that brings the patient to the professional worker; it is accompanying anxiety, depression, dissatisfaction, and

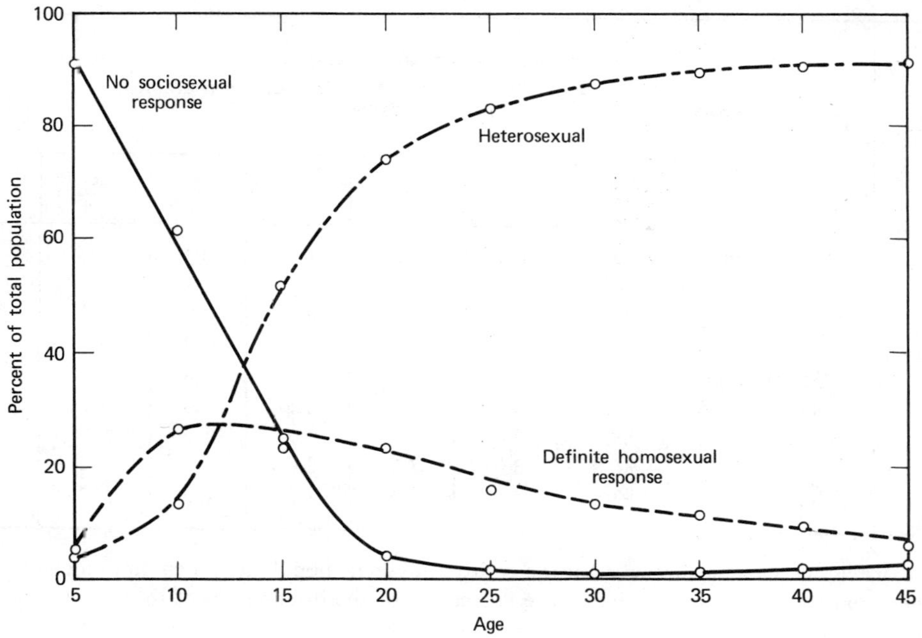

Figure 23.2 The development of heterosexuality and homosexuality by age periods. The active incidence curves are corrected for U. S. population. Males with no sociosexual response (rating X) rapidly disappear between the ages of 5 and 20. Males whose responses are chiefly heterosexual (rating 0 or 1) rapidly increase in number until they ultimately account for 90 percent of the whole population. Males who are more than incidentally homosexual in response or overt activity (rating 2–6) are most abundant in preadolescence and through the teens, gradually becoming less abundant with advancing age.

police prosecution, etc. Further reference will be made to the homosexuals who do not consult psychiatrists, but the point to be made here is that on the basis of clinical experience, it is impossible to draw the conclusion that otherwise well-adjusted people with homosexual tendancies do not exist in the community. Furthermore, it is obvious that those patients who undergo the most intense clinical investigations, that is, those who undertake psychoanalysis, are probably the most highly selected of all, having to meet those criteria, most often including intelligence, perseverence, and the ability to pay, that must be demanded by the analyst.

The question of numbers, of course, is linked with the intensity of investigation. It seems a valid general comment that investigations involving large numbers of patients can report only on very limited and perhaps superficial aspects of the subjects' personalities (Bourne, 1958). However, these aspects can be very important ones, and as against this, one has to set the fallibility of generalizing from a few cases, however well investigated clinically.

To judge most of the available clinical literature on homosexuality as confused or limited is not, however, to deny that it has any value. One can be tempted easily to throw out the baby with the bath water. What is important is to distinguish observation from inference; fact from fantasy. Such clinical observations and facts can then be examined along with data that are obtained from epidemiological, experimental, and other investigations in an attempt to understand the mechanisms of acquisition, maintenance, expression, and the change of homosexual propensity. The attempt to do so in this chapter will be confined mainly to male homosexuals, as the condition is much more common as a clinical problem in males, and the literature deals predominantly with the condition as presented by males. In addition, the processes involved are similar for both sexes, even though the

Table 23.1 Heterosexual-Homosexual Ratings for All White Males[a]

Age	Cases	Heterosexual-Homosexual Rating: Active Incidence Total Population—U.S. Corrections (Percent)							
		X	0	1	2	3	4	5	6
5	4297	90.6	4.2	0.2	0.3	1.2	0.3	0.2	3.0
10	4296	61.1	10.8	1.7	3.6	5.6	1.3	0.5	15.4
15	4284	23.6	48.4	3.6	6.0	4.7	3.7	2.6	7.4
20	3467	3.3	69.3	4.4	7.4	4.4	2.9	3.4	4.9
25	1835	1.0	79.2	3.9	5.1	3.2	2.4	2.3	2.9
30	1192	0.5	83.1	4.0	3.4	2.1	3.0	1.3	2.6
35	844	0.4	86.7	2.4	3.4	1.9	1.7	0.9	2.6
40	576	1.3	86.8	3.0	3.6	2.0	0.7	0.3	2.3
45	382	2.7	88.8	2.3	2.0	1.3	0.9	0.2	1.8

[a]These are active incidence figures for the entire white male population, including single, married, and post-marital histories, the final figure corrected for the distribution of the population in the U.S. Census of 1940.

roles, for example, of parents, may be reversed.

GENETICS

Despite the often quoted twin study of Kallman (1952), there is now little support for the notion that homosexuality has a predominantly inherited basis. The hypothesis that some male homosexuals are sex intergrades with male morphological sex characteristics, but a female chromosomal pattern (Lang, 1940) has been found untenable by Pritchard (1962). In reviewing the literature on the nuclear sex of homosexuals, he found investigations that involved 235 male homosexuals, all of whom had a typically male pattern. His own study of the somatic chromosomes in 6 male homosexuals also showed a male constitution. The evidence appearing to support Lang's theory, for example, the fact that homosexuality is associated with a low position in the family birth order, and with comparatively high maternal age (Slater, 1962), can equally support a psychogenesis. The importance of the interpersonal environment in the determination of gender role (see page 584) has been clearly shown by Hampson and Hampson (1961). In a study of the later gender role of intersex individuals, the sex of assignment by the parents appeared very much more important than the other possible determinants, that is, chromosomal sex, gonadal sex, hormonal sex, internal accessory reproductive structures, and external genital morphology. The only difficulties arose when the parents themselves had not resolved the problem of the sex to which the child should be assigned.

PSYCHOLOGICAL FACTOR

The general agreement concerning the importance of environmental rather than genetic influences in the genesis of homosexuality extends to a general emphasis on early life experiences. In addition, although the starting point of the varying theoretical schools is widely divergent, and although the psychological mechanisms involved in the acquisition of homosexual behavior are described in different terms, there is much in common between them. That this is so, can be illustrated by reference to studies that concern the personality characteristics and the interpersonal dynamics within the families of patients with homosexual problems.

Within the field of family study, certain consistent patterns of family relationships emerge. Brown (1963) describes the early relationship of the male patient with his mother as "close, strong, intimate"; the latter tended, in this study, to be dominating but with a propensity for fondling, petting, and caressing her son. It is perhaps equally significant that none of the 400 subjects studied had what was considered to be a satisfactory relationship with their father, many of them being described as either ineffective or hostile. The findings of O'Connor (1964) and Bieber et al. (1962) are very similar. The latter use the phrase "close-binding-intimate" to describe the attitude of mothers in their homosexual group, but also emphasize the pathogenic role of the fathers, who as a group were found to be detached, hostile, minimizing, and openly rejecting. In turn, the outstanding attitudes of homosexual patients to their fathers were characterized by hatred and fear, the father and son relationship being profoundly and unremittingly disturbed. They came to the conclusion that "a constructive supportive, warmly relating father *precludes* the possibility of a homosexual son." Bene (1965) in a less intensive study likewise stresses the incidence of a poor relationship with a paternal figure in her series of homosexuals, and she considers that this is the more important parental determinant.

This uniformity in the families of patients with homosexual problems is impressive, but it is open to the objection that the information was in each case a retrospective and subjective report. However, as a rule, by the time homosexuality is manifest, this may be the only method of obtaining information, and in the author's experience the frequency of idealization of early family relationships, and the denial of known family psychopathology, is greater than that of invention.

Reports of contemporaneous intrafamily transactions leading to sexual pathology are few, but that of Litin et al. (1956) nicely illustrates some of the interactional mechanisms involved. Thus, in a case of voyeurism described by the authors (case 7) the mother had permitted her six-year-old son to view her vagina on a number of occasions, and had condoned his peeping at a maid in the bath, and at a neighbor's daughter. Yet the boy's childish wish to "make a baby" evoked a severe scolding. Another boy of 12 (case 1) was described by the mother as "awfully sexy. When I lay in bed with him he gets an erection." When he showed interest in an eight-year-old girl, his mother told him "You're a sex maniac. If you want intercourse you need a girl of seventeen." Similar interactions involving overt or covert encouragement of deviant or precocious sexual behavior (homosexuality, transvestitism, etc.) are described. Although such cases are florid, the advent of family psychiatry, with the possibility of more objective study of interpersonal relationships, could well throw more light on the nature and the effect of the perhaps more subtle parent/child interactions, leading to homosexuality. Given the limitations of clinical investigations to date, however, there can be observed to be general agreement, not only that early experience is of paramount importance in the aetiology of homosexuality, but also regarding the general quality of that experience as provided by the family.

Data concerning the aetiology of human homosexuality resulting from experimental manipulation of the early environmental variables is, of course, lacking, but considerable evidence exists to illustrate the aberrance of mating and related behaviors in mature experimental animals consequent on interference with their early environment. Thus, Harlow (1963) reports that those of his rhesus monkeys deprived of normal mothering and sibling contact, later demonstrated marked anomalies of their courtship and mating behavior. Unusual behavior was shown by both males and females, but in addition when the unmothered females were eventually made pregnant and conceived, they showed very abnormal patterns of maternal behavior toward their young. Similarly, birds of many species, when isolated from their own kind early in life often show a later misdirection of sexual responses (for example, Fisher & Hale, 1957). Lorenz (1955) noted that some species when "imprinted" to man would later refuse to copulate with "conspecifics."

These findings raise the question of whether the effect of early environment in determining late sexual behavior constitutes a special and perhaps irreversible form of learning. Eysenck (1960) has stated that treatment is concerned with "habits existing at present; their historical development is largely irrelevant." Yet it may be that early learning of the kind described, if it occurs in the human, is somehow different from other forms of learning, and as this would have direct relevance to the question of its later modification, some consideration must be given to what is known of early-learning processes.

Most of what is known about early learning is derived from two fields of study, ethology and psychoanalysis, originally quite distinct but now converging. A great deal of discussion has been centered particularly on the two ethological concepts of "imprinting" and "critical periods." The concept of "critical periods" in early animal learning is now well established (Scott 1962), and there is a general consensus of opinion that in human development also, periods occur during which certain responses, for example, smiling, are evoked most readily, by certain stimulus configurations. The smiling response can be thought of as part of general attachment behavior, the development of which Bowlby (1957) considered to be basically an imprintinglike process. Money (1963) also refers to "imprinting" in human beings as being a possible determinant of homosexuality, but this view is somewhat speculative, being based on the finding that gender-specific psychological characters are acquired during the first 2 or 3 years of human life (Hampson 1955). Work by Money and the Hampsons also indicates that these gender-specific characteristics are extremely resistant to alteration by gender reallocation, and Money considers that the imprinting-like processes responsible are indelible and largely irreversible. However, there is no report of attempts to modify individual sex-linked behavior, and the question of the relationship between the development of human attachment behavior on the one hand, and later sexual anomalies on the other, must remain, for the moment, speculative.

Similarly, in animal work, imprinting experiments relevant to later sex-object choice are few, and attempts to apply the results to humans must be very cautious. In addition, many workers view imprinting as not fundamentally different from other forms of learning (Hinde 1955), and Klopfer (1961) expressed the opinion that only the existence of the "critical period" could be said to distinguish the two. Certainly many characteristics are shared by imprinting and other forms of learning, for example, stimulus generalization (Jaynes 1956, Moltz, 1960). In addition, imprinting has been found not to be an all-or-nothing phenomenon, discriminative ability (Sluckin & Salzen, 1961) and response frequency (Salzen & Sluckin, 1959) being determined by the time of exposure to the stimulus pattern. Moreover, Sluckin (1964) states that the durability and specificity of attachments depend, inter alia, on the total time of exposure, and the exclusiveness of exposure, to the figure.

Thus, although there is much to stimulate further research on all aspects of imprinting-like processes, particularly in the human, there is little experimental evidence at the present moment to encourage the view that adult human homosexuality derives from an irreversible imprinting-like process. In fact, rather the opposite is suggested by the fact that homosexual behavior is less common in women, who normally choose a sexual partner of the sex opposite to that of the person to whom their first attachment is made, and also by the therapeutic reversal of sexual orientation in some cases of homosexuality.

The psychoanalytical concepts of early learning as a determinant of later sexual orientation are less specific and less simple than the ones that may be derived from ethological studies to date, although many of the concepts bear some similarity to those of ethology. Thus, there are postulated several distinct stages in human psychosexual development during which highly specific and durable patterns of behavior are acquired. The psychoanalytic accounts of interaction between constitutional and early environmental factors as they relate to homosexuality are well known and will be but briefly reviewed here.

Freud's (1953a, b, and c) concept of bisexuality postulated a universal and permanent tendancy to homosexuality, a psychological homologue of the presence in the embryo (and vestigial remnants in the mature form) of both male and female morphology. He described various developmental mechanisms by which this tendancy may become the predominant one, leading to overt homosexual behavior. First, constitutionally intense libidinization of the anal zone would favor a homosexual propensity in the male, as would fixation at the anal stage of libidinal development because of anal experiences at this stage. In addition, there may be unsurmountable difficulties in coping with the oedipal situation, which again would result in fixation at, or regression to, the anal stage. Thus, Freud correlated the development of object relationships with the libidinal phases of sexual development. The failure to develop, normally, object cathexis results in the persistence of earlier tendancies to autoeroticism and narcissism, leading to the search for a love object representing himself, and therefore having to possess the male genital. He further postulated the existence of castration fears resulting from the discovery that certain individuals (girls) do not possess a penis, this fear leading to a reassuring avoidance and devaluation of females. Castration fear may arise or be intensified under the conditions which are said to prevail at the time of the oedipal complex, presumably especially if the situation includes a seductive mother and a harsh punitive father. The outcome according to Freud could be either identification with the opposite sexed parent, or a symbolic transformation of other men (representing the feared father) into women, thus devaluing them and at the same time covertly expressing hostility to them. The multiple roles frequently played in homosexual relationships are viewed according to this theory as representing the various determinants of the homosexual tendancy, this being overdetermined in each individual case.

Many other psychoanalytic theories also involve anxiety as a prime determinant of homosexuality. Thus, Klein et al. (1952) describe the vagina as representing, symbolically, the devouring mouth, the penis being equated with the comforting breast. Rado (1940, 1949), discarding the concept of bisexuality, writes nevertheless of homosexuality arising as an adaptation to hidden but incapacitating fears of the opposite sex, and Kardiner (1949), reviewing anthropological evidence, arrives at the conclusion that social efforts terrorize the child out of its normal sexual interests. Bieber et al. (1962), in their book, combine clinical study, in detail, with a large enough number of subjects to permit statistical handling. They state that the research was not designed as an experiment to test the association of controlled variables, as the problems they approached did not lend themselves to study at that level, but rather to delineate those variables that have the *most probable* relevance, or are most central to the problem of male homosexuality. Their conclusions are as follows.

> "[1] The capacity to adapt homosexually is, in a sense, a tribute to man's biosocial resources in the face of thwarted hetero-sexual goal achievement. Sexual gratification is not renounced; instead, fears and inhibitions associated with heterosexuality are circumvented and sexual responsivity with pleasure and excitement to a member of the same sex develops as a pathologic alternative. Any adaptation which is basically an accommodation to unrealistic fear is necessarily pathologic; in the adult homosexual, continued fear of heterosexuality is inappropriate to his current reality (pp. 303–304).
>
> [2] We consider homosexuality to be a pathologic biosocial adaptation consequent to pervasive fears surrounding the expression of heterosexual impulses." (P. 220.)

Many of these views invite the application of principles derived from the study of learning. The core of the analytic postulate is that stimuli characteristics of female sexuality (particularly female genitalia) produce anxiety leading to avoidance responses, and that sexual behavior with males is positively reinforced.

However, it would be oversimplifying the process of the acquisition of erotic attraction to various stimuli if one ignored the other variables subsumed under the term "gender role." These variables would include the following: general mannerisms, deportment and demeanor; play preferences and recreational interests; spontaneous topics of talk in unprompted conversation and casual comment; content of dreams, day dreams, and fantasies; replies to oblique inquiries and projective tests; evidence of erotic practice and finally the person's own replies to direct inquiry (Hampson & Hampson, 1961). It is difficult to believe that overt disclosures of behavior, socially judged as gender-linked, will be without effect in interpersonal relationships, and there can be little doubt that the availability and the choice of erotic objects will be at least partly determined by these interactions.

It is therefore surprising that virtually no consideration has been given, by exponents of therapy based on learning theory, to these important characterological gender-role behaviors. There is almost no mention of them in the nonanalytic literature, and although in an article reviewing the attempts of aversion therapy for sexual deviation, Feldman (1966) comments on the importance of the diagnosis of coexisting psychopathology and its treatment where necessary, he can only offer a classification based on Schneider (1959) as an attempt to set up predictive relationships between personality factors and the outcome of treatment. As far as the treatment of homosexuality itself is concerned, such an approach may be even less productive than Ferenczi's (1914) clinical distinction between the "invert, or passive male homoerotic" who "feels himself to be a woman, and this not only in genital intercourse, but in all relations of life," and the "active homosexual" who "feels himself a man in every respect. . . . The object of his inclination alone is exchanged . . ." (P. 300). Brown (1961) also distinguishes in a general way between the "invert" who has identified with, and adopted, the gender role of the other sex, and the "homosexual" who is an individual seeking sexual satisfaction with a member of the same sex. "Inversion is only *one* condition that may be related to *one* form of homosexuality." Hooker (1965b), however, reporting on 30 men, none of whom had sought psychiatric help, and who were carefully studied and followed up for 8 years, states that the relations between individual pairs—especially the ones who sustain a living relationship of some duration—appear to be additional determinants of the variation in sexual patterns and gender identity. Particularly significant is the description of one man whose gender-role behavior and fantasies underwent a very marked shift from female to male during the course of the study; this change was thought to be the result of the influence of the homosexual group of which he was a member, which disapproved of effeminate behavior and cross-dressing.

By using the MMPI, Aaronson and Grumpelt (1961) studied a group of homosexual men, with a control group, and found a subset in the former who seemed very masculine in orientation. The authors suggest a heterogenicity in dimensions of masculinity-femininity. Studies of this design and intent are uncommon, and a case exists for a very thorough typological study of homosexuals based not only on psychometric analysis but also on detailed clinical observation of behavior, especially interpersonal behavior. The analysis of verbal behavior (Gottschalk et. al. 1957) suggests a starting point. As has been pointed out, this analyses may reveal not only coexisting psychopathology, but behavior patterns of interaction relevant to the homosexual propensity itself and the possible manner of its modification. Such related behavior patterns are rarely volunteered as symptoms by a patient, and the behavior therapist, in particular, may do nothing more than note, in a general way, their presence, and select for treatment the symptom, that is, erotic behavior directed to the same sex, volunteered by the patient, as the dominant one, the removal of which is the sole direct aim of therapy. The question of whether other inappropriate gender-role behaviors disappear with the removal of the symptom of homosexuality remains unsettled, and may be very relevant to the question relapse. The number of published reports on the behavior therapy of homosexuality remains small, and apart from the understandable tendency to publish only successfully treated cases, no studies correlating the presence or absence of these related behavioral patterns, with treatment results, have been reported. In addition, there may be some selective bias, that is, obviously effeminate patients may be excluded from treatment because of the general belief that obvious effeminacy is unfavorable prognostically (Bieber et al., 1962).

An extension of the question of the effect of gender-role behavior on the outcome of treatment that is directed entirely at the object of genital eroticism, is the question of whether patterns of behavior, apparently originating as a result of identification mechanisms involving the opposite sex, can be treated by methods based on learning theory. How successful is such an approach likely to be? Although the answer to these queries awaits the appropriate experiments, there are no a priori grounds for believing that learning by identification differs fundamentally from other forms of learning. Kagan (1958) shows that the concept of identification can be satisfactorily accommodated within a learning theory framework. The motive for the acquisition of the identification response is, according to Kagan, a desire for the positive goal states (power, mastery over environment, and love and affection) commanded by the model, and the perceived similarity in attributes between the subject and the model is suggested as the reinforcing agent. The results of experiments by Bandura et al. (1963), which show that young children tend to identify most strongly with those adults who possess the greatest rewarding power, do not conflict with Kagan's views, and seem applicable to the problem of homosexuality, bearing in mind what is known about the distribution of power in the families of patients with this symptom. However, although this may account, at least in part, for the imitation learning of young children (aged 33 to 65 months, in the study of Bandura et al.), there seems little justification for the implication that inverted sex-role behavior is invariably, or even frequently, *maintained* by these mechanisms. As Kagan (1958) states, the strength of identification tendencies should decrease with age because, in general, the individual's ability to gratify his needs for mastery and love through his own behavior, rather than through a vicarious mechanism, should increase with development. In other words, it is at least very possible that sex-role behavior *develops* as a result of identification with adults possessing a high degree of rewarding power, but can be *maintained* by reinforcements of other kinds. One can only speculate on the nature of these other reinforcements, but the responses of other people, which may lead to, and include sexual relationships, are likely to be very important, (Hooker, 1965b). Hardy (1964) points out that instrumental behavior is a necessary part of (sexual) motivational expectations, these in turn being aroused by cues or stimuli which are associated with affective states due to some previous learning. Nonsexual responses by other people are also likely to be important, and Alexander (1963) analyses the psychotherapeutic process in learning-theory terms, although not specifically dealing with gender-role.

The potency of sexual activity, particularly in relation to orgasms, as a reinforcing agent, has been shown in dogs (Beach, 1950), in cats (Michael, 1961), and in rats (Kagan, 1958), but in the human it is more assumed than proved. Curran (1947) states "it is very easy for habit formation to occur in the sexual sphere, and the longer the habits persist, the more difficult are they to break." Kinsey et al. (1953) report that women who achieve orgasm by masturbation are more likely to continue the practice than are women who do not achieve orgasm in this way. McGuire et al. (1965) suggest that orgasm by masturbation to a deviant sexual fantasy or image has strong reinforcing properties for that (fantasied or real) stimulus, and Freud (1953b), expresses a similar belief. Whalen (1966) and Money (1961) both concede human arousability to have a physiological (hormonal) basis, but believe that experience exerts a strong influence, increasing the number of stimuli which can determine the actual state of arousal and the nature of the sexual acts by means of which reinforcement occurs. These views broadly form the theoretical basis on which behavior therapy stands. However, to view the symptoms of homosexuality as a response based solely on the reinforcing effect of sexual (orgasmic) gratification, without taking into consideration related behavioral manifestations, and other possible sources of reinforcement, is an oversimplification. To understand fully the nature of the processes that produce and maintain homosexual behavior, environmental influences—particularly interpersonal transactions within and without the family—as well as the individual's perception of himself as a sexual person, must be taken into account.

The role of parental and sibling influences in the genesis of homosexuality is not disputed. As stated earlier, most of the studies on families are concerned with (1) the patient's perception of his family, (2) the presence or absence of his parents in a physical sense, or (3) a statistical approach to sibship and maternal age. Few studies deal with here-and-now relationships, and no studies can be found of a psychiatric evaluation of the parents themselves, or of their own families. These last could make a valuable contribution as the influences brought to bear within a family have much of their origin in the previous life experience of the constituent members. The most simple situation is schematically represented in Figure 23.3.

SCHEMA REPRESENTING INFLUENCES EXERTED BY ONE GENERATION ON THE NEXT

This is a simple schema, and would have to be elaborated to include siblings, but the point to be underlined is that the roles played by the father or the mother, as well as their separate personal or interpersonal needs and contributions within the family relationships, can be observed to be determined to a considerable degree by their own early, developmental (notably family) experiences. It would seem that if the opportunity to grow up in the setting of a reasonably mature (parental) heterosexual relationship is denied, or if there is gross failure of the development of affectional systems between the child and the parent of each sex, then the child in turn, on reaching marriageable age, may also have a poorly developed ability to form stable, satisfying relationships, particularly with the opposite sex. Thus the failure to provide a healthy developmental environment within the family of one generation can "contaminate" the environment of the next generation. Furthermore, it is a frequent clinical finding that such an individual will marry a person with a similarly distorted capacity for sustained and satisfying heterosexual relationships. Even if such an arrangement appears, temporarily, to have mutual and reciprocal attractions, the advent of children disturbs the established relationship.

The possible outcomes of these altered relationships, as they apply to the sexual identity of the child, are many. One commonly observed in clinical practice is the investment, by the mother, of intense feelings of love and protection, in her relationship with her son—an investment not possible as far as husband is concerned.

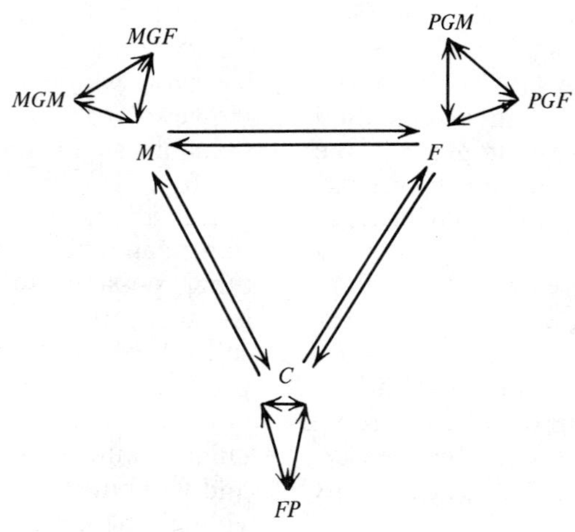

M, mother;
F, father;
C, child;
MGM, maternal grandmother;
MGF, maternal grandfather;
PGM, paternal grandmother;
PGF, paternal grandfather; and
FP, future parent.

Figure 23.3 M, mother; F, father; C, child; MGM, maternal grandmother; MGF maternal grandfather; PGM, paternal grandmother; PGF, paternal grandfather; and FP, future parent.

The husband's reaction to this situation is most frequently one of resentment and hostility, which serve to further exclude him from the developing close-binding, intimate mother-son relationship. The two latter are thrown ever closer together for mutual support and emotional gratifications, and a self-reinforcing and self-perpetuating series of interactions are set up. It would appear to the author that many significant so-called "oedipal situations" arise not as a normal emotional developmental milestone but rather as an expression of the child's responses to the behaviors of his parents, based in turn on their own pathological psychosexual immaturity.

Another common disturbed intrafamily situation is one in which a parent attempts to experience vicariously through her child, relationships wished for, but not experienced, in her own childhood. These experiences may be inappropriate for the individual child for many reasons, but notably because of its physical sex. Vicarious identification of a mother with her parent can also occur, and its emergence as a clinical problem is well described by Hilgard and Newman (1959) in their expansion of the concept of the anniversary phenomenon. As an illustration of how these processes can influence the sexual orientation of a child, the following case of the author's experience is quoted.

The mother of a girl with homosexual problems herself came from a sibship of unusual age distribution. The mother's children, of whom the patient was the fourth, were of almost identical age distribution, and during her fourth pregnancy, the mother became convinced that she was expecting a boy "like my mother." This assumption was reinforced by other members of the family, and so sure was she that she bought a complete set of boys (blue) baby clothes. She denied at the time of interview that when her daughter was born she experienced any disappointment. "In fact I burst into tears of joy!" That she was denying her true feelings was confirmed by the fact that the girl was treated in many ways much more like a boy than a girl.

Similar findings may not be unexpected when a baby is born of a sex contrary to the one wished for by a parent for any other reason. In these cases, the parents may quite unwittingly gratify their wishes for an opposite-sexed child by interactions with the child more appropriate to the other sex. This child may respond to the continuous multiplicity (Money, 1963) of parental signals in such a way that either his own concept of sexual *identity*, or his overt gender-role *behavior*, becomes partly reversed.

Such reactions between the child and the parent should be understood within the paradigm of simple operant conditioning, but crossed identification mechanism could also occur within a family in which either the physical membership, or the distribution of power, favored it. If the identification concept is kept too narrow, that is, concerned only with availability of suitable *parental* models, then cases may be encountered in which homosexuality may be expected but not found. Other available models, for example, older siblings, uncles, neighbors, etc., may be found to have substituted.

Such individuals, who show inappropropriate sex-role behavior, are likely to be exposed to a further multiplicity of interpersonal experiences that further alienate their position from the socially accepted sociosexual role—at school, at play, in relationships with the opposite sex, etc., and it can be postulated that social ease and sexual gratification can be attained only by joining a homosexually orientated subset. The seeking of such company would be reinforced by a diminution of unpleasant affect, and homosexual behavior reinforced by the experience of pleasant affect, notably orgasm. It is possible that as a result of homosexual relationships, stimulus generalization occurs that leads to the adoption of symbolic activities, and symbolic gratification. However, there is no general agreement regarding the nature of the symbolic (feminine) processes that may occur in homosexuality, and they are, in any case, largely superfluous concepts as far as the general theory being outlined is concerned.

But it has already been stated that not all homosexuals are "inverts"; indeed, it seems most probable that "inversion," meaning essentially an identifying with the opposite sex, is really a continuum (Kagan, 1958). In any case, misidentification does not appear to be the sole determinant of homosexuality. As has been stated above, fear may have been conditioned to heterosexual relationships, and to the internal mediating processes associated with it. The causes of such conditioned fear are limitless, and they may well include the presence of an intensely seductive mother, reinforced by childish fantasy, paternal attitudes, or more general negative family or social attitudes to heterosexuality. In these cases, although gender-role behavior may in other respects appear quite normal, genital sexual activity becomes possible only if it is other than heterosexual. The general personality dimension of activity—passivity may be an important determinant of the nature of the consequent sexual outlet—the more active, extroverted individual may be more inclined to indulge in direct genital relationships rather than indulge in sexual activity essentially more passive, such as voyeurism, fetishism, etc. It is also probable that chance also can play an important part in determining the nature of the deviation, for example, reinforcement by orgasm of an unplanned experience. The easier arousability of men than of women would thus account for the greater number of men than women with abnormal sexual objects, including homosexual objects.

Two further determinants of homosexual behavior seem important in the author's experience. Although, as stated, Kagan (1958) expresses the view that the individual's ability to gratify his needs for mastery and love through his own behavior, rather than through a vicarious mechanism, should increase with age, a childish wish for contact with a loving father, itself probably conditioned, can give rise to the seeking out of some same-sexed substitute. This mechanism, and the process of stimulus generalization, was well demonstrated by a patient, evacuated from London during the war, whose mother created for him an image of his father "doing all he could to help in the war." The fantasy created in the boy's mind was of a heroic soldier in uniform leading his men into battle and, although this was not the case, the fantasy was not corrected by the mother. When the family were reunited at the end of the war, the boy was shattered to find that his father had actually been managing a factory *manufacturing* uniforms. Although he recognized that this occupation was not dishonorable, his letdown was intense, and all admiration for his father vanished. He became instead, an ardent admirer of other men in army uniform, and began to seek dependant relationships with them. This situation soon led to a seduction, and by the time the patient presented for treatment, the stimuli he found most attractive were men in any uniform, even bus conductors and bandsmen, though army uniforms remained the most appealing. It is significant also that his favorite sexual fantasy was being manhandled by uniformed men, not roughly, but in a way which assured him of their strength and "manliness." In such a case, sexual liaisons reinforced the deviation; there was no doubt of his own ability to gratify his needs for mastery and love by more conventional methods.

Finally, it should be recognized that homosexual behavior may be reinforced by the individual's perception of himself, and perhaps by the perception of others and their response to him, as "different" and, therefore, interesting and admirable. Such an individual is not infrequently to be found among university undergraduates, a population that traditionally values nonconformity. These individuals are worthy of separate mention as the motivation for the change of their sexual habits is poor. The treatment, be it psychotherapy or aversion therapy, directed at their sexual behavior only may function as yet another reinforcer for their concept of themselves as a "special" and different—an effect militating against redirection of their sexual behavior.

ASSESSMENT OF HOMOSEXUALITY—SUMMARY

A definitive statement regarding the diagnosis of homosexuality is clearly indicated. An erotic response to a homosexual object as a symptom that is volunteered or is acknowledged by a patient is generally assumed to be unequivocal evidence on which to base the diagnosis. However, in practice, the situation sometimes occurs that homoerotism is suspected, or would from other evidence, be expected, but is denied by the patient. A clinician may sometimes be led to postulate "latent" homosexuality as a result of information about the following.

1. The developmental history, involving particularly the family dynamics

2. The nature of the current social relationships with one or both sexes.

3. The appearance and behavior of the patient during interview.

4. The result of psychological tests

Although certain family dynamics, operating during the earlier years, appear to make a contribution to the genesis of homosexuality, the currently available data are still comparatively crude and their significance for diagnostic purposes virtually unknown; there is certainly no known one-to-one causal relationship. Similarly, although current social relationships and personal mannerisms may alert a clinician to the possibility that the patient may have a homosexual problem, there is no justification for making a firm diagnosis of homosexuality, as defined, on these bases. Moreover, many clinical investigators are at pains to point out that the majority of presenting homosexual patients do not show even subtle signs of effeminacy in facial expression, voice, gestures, dress, or walk (for example, Braaten & Darling, 1965).

Nor are the usual psychological tests of value in themselves for making a diagnosis of homosexuality in the individual case. Reference has already been made (Aaronson & Grumfelt, 1961) to the fact that some patients acknowledging homosexuality appear very masculine on the MMPI, the test that seems to have been most extensively used in the assessment of homosexual patients. Aaronson and Grumfelt also point out that the optimal combination of three measures derived from the MMPI [the *T* score on the Mf scale, (Mfs), the rank of this scale in the profile (Mfr) consisting of the ten clinical sketches set forth in the MMPI test manual, and the score on the masculinity-femininity index (Mfi) (Aaronson, 1959)] resulted in a misclassification of 4 percent of the homosexual subjects and 16 percent of a heterosexual control group. They suggest furthermore that as the cutoff points of the various measures were chosen, in their investigation, to apply to the population under study, the diagnostic accuracy may be even less in a random clinical population. What these authors may have succeeded in doing, is to show that a combination of measures is diagnostically more accurate than the use of the Mf scale alone but, without further studies, the additional measures still appear to fall short of the "confirmatory evidence" necessary for the assumption of homosexual abnormality in a patient with a high Mf score (Hathaway & McKinley, 1951).

Thus the evaluation of developmental history, clinical examination, and psychometry all provide information that concerns only the basic general interest patterns—a variable known to be related to socioeconomic class. This information may be interpreted in terms of the appropriateness or the competence of the individual's general behavior, but it does not provide direct information about specific components of behavior, such as homosexuality. This must be obtained directly and, apart from acknowledgment by the patient, the only direct evidence of homosexuality is a measure of his physiological response to sexual stimuli in a test situation.

Two attempts at such direct evidence have been described—the use of plesythmography to measure changes in penile volume (Freund, 1963), and the change in pupillary size recorded by a movie camera (Hess et al., 1965), consequent on the exposure to male and female sexual stimuli. Both are still in the stage of experimental development, but they promise to offer the therapist not only direct objective evidence of denied or "latent" homosexuality, but also a measure of change during treatment. However, it should be anticipated that even if these techniques are successfully developed, there may still be a reluctance on the part of many clinicians to make use of them, because of the break of tradition that will be involved. However difficulties of this kind have been encountered in other branches of medicine, yet the use of elaborate and costly techniques such as cardiography and radiology is now standard.

It cannot be doubted that misdirection of sexual responsiveness, even though denied (consciously or otherwise) by the patient, can have a serious disruptive effect on many if not all social relationships and, although it is necessary for treatment to proceed in an orderly sequence, there seems no reason why again tradition must be maintained and psychological "resistances" or "denials" should be overcome before the treatment of homosexuality per se is undertaken. In other conditions, drugs and even electroplexy are very frequently used even in the absence of complete "insight" by the patient, and it may be sufficient justification for using a behavioral technique to treat objectively detected homosexuality, if the patient presents with a psychiatric problem that is thought by the therapist to be secondary to the patient's homosexuality.

Although of little help in arriving at a diagnosis of homosexuality per se, developmental history, behavioral and verbal analysis, etc., may yield information regarding more specific items of behavior that could be related at least to the persistence of homosexuality, or that could affect its potential for modification. As yet, except in terms of general clinical experience which suggests that the more typically effeminate male homosexual responds less well to treatment, little is known about the effect of treatment directed specifically at these apparently related behaviors.

THERAPY

So much has been written on the subject of psychodynamically orientated treatment that it is unnecessary to add more here. The most reliable and impressive results are the ones of Bieber et al. (1962), and they will be referred to when reference is made to the results of behavior therapy.

One of the earliest reports of aversion therapy for homosexuality was the often quoted case of Max (1935), who used electric shock as the aversive stimulus. A case of fetishism treated by aversion therapy, by using apomorphine (Raymond, 1956), and a report of a series of cases of homosexuality treated by a similar method (Freund, 1960), stimulated the more recent interest in the treatment of sexual deviation by aversive conditioning. Since that time, several reports have appeared in the literature that concern the aversive conditioning (both chemical and electrical) of homosexuality (Feldman, 1966). They have all had the aim of replacing the existing reinforcing pleasant sexual response to homosexual stimuli and behavior by an unpleasant response that leads to future avoidance. In addition, they have all, at least as far as the published reports reveal, concentrated only on the individual's erotic response, to the exclusion of related psychosocial, sex-linked behaviors. Although it may be true that the individual's customary erotic responses and behaviors form the cornerstone of his problems, and that once the former are suitably modified, the latter may vanish, this point has never been satisfactorily recorded or, apparently, tested.

The attempts at aversive conditioning, in many ways, have become progressively more sophisticated. The earlier reported cases involved mainly classical conditioning procedures, although James' (1962) technique also incorporated an attempt at positive instrumental conditioning, in that the patient was requested, if he felt any sexual excitement, to retire to his room which was appropriately adorned with photographs of "sexy" women, and was equipped with a record player and a record of a seductively-voiced female singer. Further direct attempts to treat the negative aspect of the patient's reaction to women were made by Thorpe et al. (1963), and have also been incorporated into treatment regimes that are described by Feldman and MacCulloch (1965), MacCulloch et al. (1965), and by Solyom and Miller (1965). These two last named reports illustrate the trend away from classical conditioning procedures toward the ones of operant conditioning. The technique of Feldman and MacCulloch is that of anticipatory avoidance learning. The patient is told that a male picture will be projected into a viewing box, and that several seconds later he might receive an unpleasant electric shock. He has the opportunity to terminate, or avoid, the shock by switching off the slide, hence learning an avoidance response to male sexual stimuli, which are presented in an ascending order of attractiveness previously ascertained. An attempt is also made to reduce any anxiety that may, prior to treatment, have occurred in association with female sexual stimuli, by introducing slides of female figures contiguous with the removal of the male slide. This female slide is always removed by the therapist, and not by the patient. Of twenty-six patients treated in this way, Feldman (1966) reports that eighteen, who were followed up for period of from 3 months to 2 years, show a complete absence of homosexual practice, together with a complete, or almost complete, absence of homosexual fantasy. In addition, it is claimed that these men are either actively practicing heterosexually, or have strong heterosexual fantasies. These results compare very favorably with those of Bieber et al. (1962), who reported 27 percent of patients becoming heterosexually adjusted as a result of psychoanalytic therapy (most of them having between 150 and 350 hours of treatment), and with those of apomorphine therapy as administered by Freund, who reported a little more than 25 percent heterosexual adaptation, which diminished to 12 percent after 2 years. Feldman (1966) lists those variables that have been shown to further increase resistance to extinction of the newly acquired heterosexual responses, and that it is desirable to incorporate into treatment:

1. Learning trials should be distributed rather than massed.
2. Contiguity of stimulus and response, particularly at onset, should be maintained throughout.
3. Shock should be introduced at whatever level has been found to be unpleasant for the patient, rather than gradually increased, thus, possible enabling the patient to habituate.
4. Partial reinforcement should be used in conjunction with instrumental techniques.
5. Reinforcement should be variable rather than fixed, both in ratio and in interval schedules.
6. There is a good deal of data which suggest that delaying a proportion of the patient's attempts to avoid should lead to greater resistance to extinction than immediate reinforcement.
7. In general, the greater the variation in the conditions of training, the more they will approximate the real-life situation, thus avoiding, as far as possible, generalization decrement, probably the most potent source of the rapidity of extinction.

Although the results of this treatment are impressive, the reader is given little idea of what biases of selection were involved, and although MacCulloch et al. (1965) indicate that the conditioning of pulse-rate changes to the conditioned stimulus may prove of some early predictive value, we must note that no clinical data are given that may be similarly of predictive value. Perhaps the eight who failed to respond are of more clinical and experimental interest than those who were improved. The predictive use of psychological tests, such as described by Morgenstern et al. (1965) in cases of transvestism, is clearly indicated.

There are two other aspects of aversion therapy to be considered. First, the continued use of visual, mainly pictorial, material Money (1963) has drawn attention not only to the difference in arousability between males and females but also to the possibility that eroticism occurs in response to pictorial stimuli more readily in males than in females. The possibility also exists that there also may exist a difference in this respect between heterosexual or homosexual males, and that perhaps the visual modality is not the best one via which to present stimuli. There seems no technical reason, for instance, why auditory stimuli should not be used, perhaps in isolated cases. That conditioning occurs readily to sounds is of course well known, and Platonov (1959) draws attention to the word as a signal—a physiological and therapeutic factor. In addition, Cameron et al. (1959, 1960) demonstrate how effective repetitive verbal stimuli can be, and the technique of James (1962) was to use a tape recorder, not only to produce homosexual stimuli, but also to intensify conditioned responses, both negative and positive. One obvious advantage is that a much wider variety of stimuli can be produced for the patient, fulfilling particularly Feldman's seventh criterion of treatment likely to resist extinction.

The second point that should be mentioned is the possibility that certain treatments, subsumed under the heading "Aversion Therapy," have effects greater than merely producing a simple conditioned aversive response. This does not seem to have been considered, although "brainwashing" is a term applied not only to aversion therapy but to a more thoroughgoing indoctrination (Sargant, 1957). Rachman (1965) discusses the advantages of electrical over chemical aversion therapy, but his arguments hold true only if the processes involved are the same. The case described by Raymond (1956) and those of Oswald (1962) and of Clark (1963) seem to have undergone a period of acute emotional crisis (resembling a psychotic break in Oswald's). It is notable also that satisfactory outcome was noted in those of Oswald's cases who experienced such a crisis. Many of the conditions required for the production of so-called "experimental neurosis" prevail in the usual regime which is involved in aversion therapy that uses apomorphine—an overwhelming, unpleasant, and frightening situation, with some degree of sensory deprivation, conflict (in the sense that at least, initially, the individual responds ambivalently to the sexual stimulus) and, perhaps most important, physical debility because of insomnia, inanition, vomiting, etc. Since the present author became interested in the possibility that the emotional crisis may represent Pavlovian ultra-paradoxical inhibition, the observations of patients undergoing aversion therapy have tended to support it. Although further confirmation is required, the responses of patients to elements in the situation strongly suggest that patients may undergo, successively, stages that represent the ones described in animal experiments as equivocal and paradoxical. It is of further interest that individuals by no means invariably produce a critical emotional state, and here again the question of personality variables requires further research. One quite striking fact, however, is that following the critical phase, when therapy is terminated, observations indicate that it is not only the sexual orientation of the patient that has changed. Often other quite notable aspects of interpersonal behavior also seem to be altered. Elevation of previously depressed mood and a general increase in assertiveness and effectiveness are often very obvious.

Surprisingly, in most forms of behavior therapy applied thus far to homosexuality, little attempt has been made to deal with the patient's anxiety, which so often seems to be associated with heterosexuality, by the process of desensitization by reciprocal inhibition. Ultimately, of course, it would be expected that satisfactory heterosexual intercourse will in itself act as an anxiety-inhibiting agent, but it would seem appropriate to consider the more usual forms of anxiety inhibition, relaxation. There also seems to be a place for directive counseling—many previously homosexual patients without prior heterosexual experience, once their homosexual inclinations have been treated by aversion therapy, experience adolescent-type awkwardness about dating, courtship, etc., quite apart from their problems concerning genital sexuality. Aversion therapy does not stand or fall on its ability to cure all symptoms related to homosexuality. It should rather be considered as part therapy.

CONCLUSION

Remarkably little is yet known about the aetiology and nature of homosexuality. It is certainly not a simple matter even to decide whether it should be considered a "disease" or an "illness." If these concepts imply any state less than optimum health, and if the health of an organism includes pursuing its biological destiny, including reproduction (Engel, 1962), then homosexuality can be so designated. To do so, of course, has the advantage of detracting from the idea that homosexuality per se is a crime, but the word "disease" or "illness" conjures up a fantasy of uniformity of psychological and behavioral characteristics, which would seem to be far from the truth. Epidemological, psychological, and clinical research is increasing in volume and sophistication, and the results to date permit certain broad and general conclusions. Homosexuality appears to be a maladaptive response that occurs in a variety of clinical conditions and psychological types. In a larger number of cases than was hitherto thought, it seems to be a reversible condition. However, what now appears to be indicated is a modification (not a complete rejection) of the ideas on the subject that are derived from psychoanalytic study, and a broadening of the learning theory approach, now currently in vogue. Each discipline has much to learn from the other on this subject.

REFERENCES

Aaronson, B. S. A comparison of 2 M.M.P.I. measures of masculinity-femininity. *J. Clin. Psychol.*, 1959, **15**, 48–50.

Aaronson, B. S., & Grumpelt, H. R. Homosexuality and some M.M.P.I. measures of masculinity-femininity. *J. Clin. Psychol.*, 1961, **17**, 245–247.

Alexander, F. Dynamics of psychotherapy in the Light of Learning Theory. *Am. J. Psychiatry*, 1963, **120**, 441–448.

Bandura, A., Ross, D., & Ross S. A comparative test of the status envy, social power, and the secondary reinforcement theories of identification learning. *J. Abnorm. Soc. Psychol*., 1963, **67**, 527–534.

Beach, F. A. Sexual behavior in animals and man. *The Harvey Lectures Ser*., 1950, **43**, 259–279.

Bene, Eva. On the genesis of male homosexuality: An attempt at clarifying the role of the parents. *Brit. J. Psychiat*., 1965, **111**, 803–813.

Bieber, I., Dain, H. J., Dince, P. R., Drellich, M. G., Grand, H. G., Gundlach, R. H., Kremer, M. W., Rifkin, A. H., Wilbur, C. B., & Bieber, T. B. *Homosexuality*. New York: Basic Books Inc., 1962.

Bourne, H. Tranquillizers and the general practitioner. *Med. J. Aus*., 1958, 189–191.

Bowlby, J. An ethological approach to research in child development. *Brit. J. Med. Psychol*., 1957, **30**, 230–240.

Braaten, L. J., & Darling, C. D. Overt and covert homosexual problems among male college students. *Genet. Psychol. Mon*., 1965, **71**, 269–310.

Brown, D. G. Transvestism and sex-role inversion. *The encyclopaedia of sexual behavior, Vol. II*. New York: Hawthorn Books, Inc., 1961.

Brown, D. G. Homosexuality and family dynamics. *Bull. Meninnger Clinic*, 1963, **27**, 227–232.

Cameron, D. E., Levy, L., & Rubenstein, L. The effects of repetition of verbal signals upon the behaviour of chronic psychoneurotic patients. *J. Ment. Sci*., 1960, **106**, 742–754.

Cameron, D. E., Levy, L., Rubenstein, L., & Malmo, R. B., Repetition of verbal signals: behavioral and physiological changes. *Am. J. Psychiat*., 1959, **115**, 985–991.

Clark, D. F. Fetishism treated by negative conditioning. *Brit. J. Psychiat*., 1963, 404–407.

Curran, D. Sexual perversions and their treatment. *Practitioner*, 1947, **158**, 343–348.

Engel, G. L. Psychological development in health and disease. Philadelphia: Saunders, 1962.

Eysenck, H. J. Learning theory and behaviour therapy. In H. H. Eysenck (ed.), *Behaviour therapy and the neurosis*. Oxford: Pergamon Press, 1960.

Feldman, M. P. Aversion therapy for sexual deviations: A critical review. *Psychol. Bull*., 1966, **65**, 65–79.

Feldman, M. P., & MacCulloch, M. J. The application of anticipatory avoidance learning to the treatment of homosexuality—1, theory, technique, and preliminary results. *Behav. Res. Ther*., 1965, **2**, 165–183.

Ferenczi, S. The nosology of male homosexuality (homo-erotism). (Translated by Ernest Jones). *Sex in psychoanalysis (1950)*. New York: Basic Books, Inc. 1914.

Fisher, E. A., & Hale, E. B. *Behaviour*, 1957, **10**, 309–323.

Ford, C. S., & Beach, F. A. *Patterns of sexual behaviour*. London: Methuen, 1965.

Freud, S. Three essays on the theory of sexuality. *The standard edition of the complete psychological works of Sigmund Freud*. Vol. 7. London: Hogarth, 1953a.

Freud, S. A special type of choice of object made by men. *The standard edition of the complete psychological works of Sigmund Freud*. Vol. 11. London: Hogarth, 1953b.

Freud, S. The infantile genital organization of the libido. *The standard edition of the complete psychological works of Sigmund Freud*. Vol. 19. London: Hogarth, 1953c.

Freud, S. The femininity of women. *The standard edition of the complete psychological works of Sigmund Freud*. Vol. 22. London: Hogarth, 1953d.

Freund, K. Some problems in the treatment of homosexuality. In H. J. Eysenck (ed.), *Behaviour therapy and the neurosis*. London: Pergamon, 1960.

Freund, K. A laboratory method for diagnosing predominance of homo- or hetero-erotic interest in the male. *Behav. Res. Ther*., 1963, **1**, 85–93.

Gottschalk, C. A., Goldine, C. G., & Hambidge, G. Verbal behaviour analysis. *Arch. Neuropsychiat*., 1957, **77**, 300–311.

Hampson, J. G. Hermaphroditic appearance, rearing and erotism in hyperadrenocorticism. *Bull. Johns Hopkins Hosp.*, 1955, **96**, 265–273.

Hampson, J. L., & Hampson, J. G. The ontogenesis of sexual behaviour in man. In W. C. Young (ed.), *Sex and internal secretions*. Baltimore: Williams and Wilkins, 1961.

Hardy, K. R. An appetitional theory of sexual motivation. *Psychol. Rev.*, 1964, **71**, 1–8.

Harlow, H. F. The maternal affectional system. In B. M. Foss (ed.), *Determinants of infant behaviour II*. London: Methuen, 1963.

Hathaway, S. R., & McKinley, J. C. Minnesota multiphasic personality inventory manual (rev. ed.). New York: Psychol. Corp., 1951.

Hess, E. H., Seltzer, A. L., & Shlien, J. M. Pupil responses of hetero and homosexual males to pictures of men and women. *J. Abnormal Psychol.*, 1965, **70**, 165–168.

Hilgard, Josephine R., & Newman, Martha F. Anniversaries in mental illness. *Psychiatry*, 1959, **22**, 113–121.

Hinde, R. A. The modifiability of instinctive behaviour. *Adv. Sci.*, 1955, **12**, 19–24.

Hooker, E. Male homosexuals and their "worlds." In J. Marmor (ed.), *Sexual inversion*. New York: Basic Books, 1965 a.

Hooker, E. An empirical study of some relations between sexual patterns and gender identity in male homosexuals. In John Money (ed.) *Sex research*. New York: Holt, Rinehart and Winston, 1965 b.

James, B. Case of homosexuality treated by aversion therapy. *Brit. Med. J.*, 1962, **1**, 768–770.

Jaynes, J. Imprinting: The interaction of learned and innate behaviour, 1., development and generalization. *J. Comp. Physiol. Psychol.*, 1956, **49**, 201–206.

Kagan, J. The Concept of identification. *Psychol. Rev.*, 1958, **65**, 296–305.

Kallman, F. Comparative twin studies on the genetic aspects of male homosexuality. *J. Nerv. and Ment. Dis.*, 1952, **115**, 283–298.

Kardiner, A. Discussion in P. Hock and J. Zubin (eds.) '*Psychosexual development in health and disease*.' New York: Grune and Stratton, 1949.

Kinsey, A. C., Pomeroy, W. B., & Martin, C. E. *Sexual behaviour in the human male*. Philadelphia: Saunders, 1948.

Kinsey, A. C., Pomeroy, W. B., Martin, C. E., & Gebhard, P. H. *Sexual behaviour in the human female*. Philadelphia: Saunders, 1953.

Klein, M., Heimann, P., Isaacs, S., & Riviere, J. *Developments in psychoanalysis*. London: Hogarth Press, 1952.

Klopfer, P. H. Imprinting. *Science*, 1961, **133**, 923–924.

Lang, T. Studies in the genetic determination of homosexuality. *J. Nerv. Ment. Dis.*, 1940, **92**, 55–64.

Litin, E. M., Giffen, M. E., & Johnson, A. M. Parental influence in unusual sexual behaviour in children. *Psychoanalytic Quarterly*, 1956, **25**, 37–55.

Lorenz. K. Morphology and behaviour patterns in closely allied species. In B. Schaffner (ed.), *Group processes*. New York: Macy Foundation, 1955.

MacCulloch, M. J., Feldman, M. P., & Pinshoff, J. M. The application of anticipatory avoidance learning to the treatment of homosexuality—II. Avoidance response latencies and pulse rate changes. *Behav. Res. Ther.*, 1965, **3**, 21–43.

Max, L. W. Breaking up a homosexual fixation by the conditional reaction technique: A case study. *Psych. Bull.*, 1935, **32**, 734.

McGuire, R. J., Carlisle, J. M., & Young, B. G. Sexual deviation as conditioned behaviour: A hypothesis. *Behav. Res. Ther.*, 1965, **2**, 185–190.

Michael, R. P. Hypersexuality in male cats without brain damage. *Science*, 1961, **134**, 553–554.

Moltz, H. Imprinting: empirical basis and theoretical significance. *Psychol. Bull.*, 1960, **57**, 291–314.

Money, J. Sex hormones and other variables in human eroticism. In W. C. Young (ed.) *Sex and internal secretions*. Baltimore: Williams and Wilkins, 1961.

Money, J. Developmental differentiation of femininity and masculinity compared. In S. M. Farber and R. H. L. Wilson. (eds.), *Man and civilization: The potential of women*. New York: McGraw-Hill, 1963.

Morgenstern, F. S., Pearce, J. F., & Rees, W. L. Predicting the outcome of behaviour therapy by psychological tests. *Behav. Res. Ther.*, 1965, **2**, 191–200.

O'Connor, P. J. Aetiological factors in homosexuality as seen in royal air force psychiatric practice. *Brit. J. Psychiat.*, 1964, **110**, 381–391.

Oswald, I. Induction of illusory and hallucinatory voices with considerations of behaviour therapy. *J. Ment. Sci.*, 1962, **108**, 196–212.

Platonov, K. *The Word as a physiological and therapeutic factor*. Moscow: Foreign Languages Publishing House, 1959.

Pritchard, M. Homosexuality and genetic sex. *Brit. J. Psychiat.*, 1962, **108**, 616–623.

Rachman, S. Aversion therapy: Chemical or electrical? *Behav. Res. Ther.*, 1965, **2**, 289–300.

Rado, S. A Critical examination of the theory of bisexuality. *Psychosomatic Med.*, 1940, **2**, 459–467.

Rado, S. An adaptational view of sexual behaviour. In P. Hock and J. Zubin (eds.) *Psychosexual development in health and disease*. New York: Grune & Stratton, 1949.

Raymond, M. J. Case of fetishism treated by aversion therapy. *Brit. Med. J.*, 1956, **2**, 854–857.

Report of the committee on homosexual offences and prostitution. *Wolfenden Report*. London. H.M.S.O., 1957.

Salzen, E. A., & Sluckin, W. The incidence of the following response and the duration of responsiveness in domestic fowl. *Animal behaviour*, 1959, **7**, 172–179.

Salzman, L. Latent homosexuality. In J. Marmor (ed.), *Sexual inversion*. New York: Basic Books, 1965.

Sargant, W. *Battle for the mind*. London: Heinemann, 1957.

Schneider, K. *Psychopathic personalities*. London: Cassell, 1959.

Scott, J. P. Critical periods in behavioural development. *Science*, 1962, **138**, 949–958.

Slater, E. Birth order and maternal age of homosexuals. *Lancet* 1962, *i* 69–71.

Sluckin, W. *Imprinting and early learning*. London: Methuen, 1964.

Sluckin, W., & Salzen, E. A. Imprinting and perceptual learning. *Quart. J. Exp. Psychol.*, 1961, **13**, 65–77.

Solyom, L., & Miller, S. A differential conditioning procedure as the initial phase of the behaviour therapy of homosexuality. *Behav. Res. Ther.*, 1965, **3**, 147–160.

Thorpe, J. G., Schmidt, E., & Castell, D. A. A comparison of positive and negative (aversive) conditioning in the treatment of homosexuality. *Behav. Res. Ther.*, 1963, **1** 357–362.

Whalen, R. E. Sexual motivation. *Psychol. Rev.*, 1966, **73**, 151–163.

Part IV

Psychosomatic Disorders

Chapter 24

Asthma[1]

KENNETH PURCELL AND JONATHAN H. WEISS

Historically, bronchial asthma has traversed the path from being first viewed as a symptom of central nervous system origin, then as a fundamentally immunological disorder, and now as a symptom whose interpretation depends on the particular professional spectacles through which one is peering. Most clinical allergists contend that asthma is caused primarily, if not exclusively, by sensitization to allergic elements in the patient's environment. Professionals in the mental health fields assert that psychological conflicts serve as the triggering agent and/or basic cause of asthma in many patients. Pediatricians and internists seem to fall somewhere in between, although usually they are closer to the allergist group. Often the medically oriented practitioner will note the aggravating effects of emotional stress on asthma while he exempts emotional processes from any significant etiologic role. The attitudes of each discipline are at least partially rooted in clinical reality in that a number of factors are relevant to the symptom of asthma, with the significance of each factor varying from one patient to the next, and even from one appearance of the symptom to the next in the same patient.

DESCRIPTION OF ASTHMA

Asthma is a symptom complex characterized by an increased responsiveness of the trachea, major bronchi, and peripheral bronchioles to various stimuli, and is manifested by extensive narrowing of the airways which causes impairment of air exchange, primarily in expiration, and wheezing. A narrowing of the airway may be because of edema of the walls, increased mucus secretion, spasm of the bronchial muscles, or the collapse of the posterior walls of the trachea and bronchi during certain types of forced expiration. The significance of these factors may vary from patient to patient and from attack to attack in the same patient. Similarly, the nature of the stimulation triggering these physiological processes may vary from patient to patient and from attack to attack. The audible wheezing sounds commonly associated with asthma are not invariably pathognomonic of the condition. Thus, in children, the presence of foreign bodies in the lung, or enlarged tracheobronchial lymph nodes, can give rise to wheezing and choking and, in adults, tumors, an enlarged thymus, or cardiac dyspnea can have similar results. Furthermore, some of the changes in breathing characteristics that may appear to be asthma are found in the "pain-fear" syndrome as well (Stein, 1962).

Psychologically, the patient during asthma appears to experience characteristic negative affect states that include anxiety, irritability, and depression. The frequency

[1] The writing of this chapter was supported by United States Public Health Research Grant HD 01060 to the Senior author.

and intensity with which these feelings occur depend on the history of the symptom, the degree to which the patient has successfully adapted to it, and the actual degree of disruption the symptom imposes. Thus, chronically asthmatic children who have had asthma since very early in life, and who were studied in an institutional setting that was designed to foster security, showed less in the way of negative moods during asthma (Weiss, 1966) than did adults who had a later age of onset and were studied under different circumstances (Knapp & Nemetz, 1960).

Mechanisms for the Operation of Psychological Variables

The intensive review of clinical experience and clinical research studies leads to the overriding impression that the kinds of behavioral antecedents most immediately relevant to asthma are emotional or affect states rather than personality types or patterns of interpersonal relationship. Certain interpersonal behaviors, for example, aggression, may or may not be accompanied by an affect, for example, anger. Similarly, an interpersonal action of another toward the patient, for example, rejection, may or may not elicit an emotional reaction such as anxiety, depression, or resentment. Yet, when the patient, or those observing the patient, describe the occasions in which psychological precipitants seem to trigger asthma, these precipitants are virtually always described in terms of one of four major affects: (a) anger; (b) excitement with pleasurable feeling; (c) anxiety or worry; and (d) depression. Often qualifying statements are made as to the importance of the intensity or duration of the emotional state. These observations are supported by the fact that substantial physiological and biochemical changes of the sort that might influence asthmatic symptoms are characteristic of emotional states, but not necessarily of interpersonal acts. Interpersonal transactions may be thought of as giving rise to emotional states. Therefore, they are more remote from and less directly related to the physiological symptom complex of asthma, even though an essential part of the sequence by which psychological events initiate or perpetuate asthmatic attacks.

There are at least three major mediating mechanisms through which emotional states may influence asthma. First, autonomic activity associated with emotional arousal can initiate the airway obstruction characteristic of an asthmatic attack by stimulating mucus secretion, vascular engorgement, or bronchial constriction. For example, it is known that vagal stimulation produces rapid bronchospasm and secretion. Second, emotional states are often associated with certain respiratory behaviors, for example, crying, laughing, coughing, and hyperventilation, which can lead to airway narrowing by a variety of mechanisms. The autonomic discharge and the respiratory mechanisms mediating the effects of emotions are by no means mutually exclusive. Hyperventilation, for example, may occur in association with certain emotional states and patterns of autonomic arousal. Or autonomic activity may initiate mucus secretion that provokes a cough followed by reflex bronchoconstriction.

Third, emotions have been shown to influence significantly endogenous adrenal steroid output (Hamburg, 1962; Handlon, Wadeson, Fishman, Sacher, Hamburg, & Mason, 1962) which may, in turn, alter the course of asthma. Reinberg et al. (1963), for example, have reported data that suggest some correspondence between the occurrence of nocturnal asthma attacks and the nightly periodic decrease in adrenocortical activity.

Finally, it is possible, but not yet demonstrated, that central nervous system processes may influence the immunologic phenomena (antigen-antibody reactions) that produce tissue change associated with narrowing of the airways.

Hereditary Factors

The incidence of asthma in the families of asthmatic patients appears to be relatively high when compared with a similar group of nonasthmatic patients (Criep, 1962; Ratner & Silberman, 1953; Schwartz, 1952). However, it is also possible to find substantial numbers of asthmatics with essentially negative family histories. After surveying their own experience, Ratner and Silberman comment:

> "It seems to us, from the data of Schwartz, that what may be inherited is not the capacity to become sensitized (immunologically), but a respiratory tract which may react with the production of asthma or rhinitis due to a multiplicity

of stimuli, one of which may be the antigen-antibody mechanism" (1953, p. 374).

This hypothesis of organ vulnerability is similar to what is postulated for patients who may develop cardiovascular or gastrointestinal symptoms.

Incidence

The incidence of asthma in the population has been observed to be between 2.5 and 5%, depending on the method of estimate. A survey by the Public Health Service in 1957 and 1958 suggested that nearly 4,500,000 persons in this country were suffering from asthma at that time. About 60% of the population of asthmatics was below the age of 17. Asthma occurs in boys twice as often as among girls, although the sex ratio evens out during the adult years. There are no well-documented explanations for this sex difference. Although asthma is relatively uncommon in infancy (Smyth, 1962), it has been diagnosed during the first few months of life, and has been reported to start as late as the seventh decade.

Symptom Course

On the one hand, there is reason to be moderately optimistic about the future of a large percentage of asthmatic patients who first exhibit the symptom in childhood. Rackeman and Edwards (1952) reviewed 449 patients who were first seen before 13 years of age and who were reevaluated 20 years later. Of the entire group, 71% had done extremely well, with improvement generally beginning sometime during or soon after adolescence. On the other hand, it is well to remember that asthma can be a life-threatening symptom. A report by Mustacchi, Lucia, and Jassy (1962) indicates that the fatality rate for this condition averages 1.5 deaths per 1000 asthmatic persons per year. Moreover, Gottlieb (1964) reports that each year since 1949, from 4000 to nearly 7000 deaths in the United States were certified as primarily due to asthma. He notes that,

> "Asthma was noted on death certificates in 1960 about one-half as often as pulmonary tuberculosis, about one-third as often as malignant neoplasms of the lung, eight times as often as meningococcal infections, and 13 times as often as accidents to occupants of commercial aircraft" (p. 276).

Some indication of the socially disabling nature of this symptom is contained in the data of the United States National Health Survey which indicates that in 1963 an average of about 64,000,000 days were lost to industry, schools, and other "necessary activities" because of asthma and hay fever. Asthma was estimated to be responsible for nearly one fourth of the days reported lost from school because of chronic illness conditions in children (Schiffer & Hunt, 1963).

In general, unfavorable prognosis is associated with the older patient, with disease of long duration, with the presence of organic disease in the respiratory or circulatory organs, with frequent and lengthy attacks, with incomplete recovery between attacks, with chronic cough, and with failure to detect a clear "triggering stimulus."

Assessing the Symptom

Asthma is a highly unstable symptom that requires careful evaluation to obtain a reasonably accurate assessment of frequency and severity. Some patients have long free periods between attacks. Others are chronically short of breath and begin wheezing very quickly in response to a whole array of stimuli, for example, exertion, dust, laughing hard, etc.

Very often, physicians who refer patients with asthma to psychologically oriented clinicians have only limited awareness of the extent of asthma. This is because patients go to physicians or, in the case of children, are brought to physicians, only at times of crisis. On many other occasions, flurries of asthma are managed by the patient himself with self-administered medication.

An accurate estimate of frequency and severity of the symptom is important for several reasons, one of which is to assist in gauging the impact of the symptom on the psychological well-being of the patient and his family. The inability to breathe is a frightening subjective experience. Patients who have experienced severe episodes of asthma may be prone to panic reactions even during mild to moderate attacks. These panic states sometimes accentuate the respiratory difficulty, as is suggested by the following excerpt from an interview with a 15-year-old girl.

> "I find that sometimes an attack will come on suddenly, my throat tightens up and I can't

get my breath. I try not to think about it, and the more I try not to think about it, the more difficulty I have in breathing, and I find as far as having a nebulizer along that if I don't, and I know I don't, I keep thinking, 'how am I breathing, can I take a deep breath?' And maybe within five minutes I have a real severe asthma attack and I can get so bad that I just go right out of the picture. I am unconscious, and this is when I get my most severe attacks when I know I'm not going to be able to get a neb for an hour or so and this is the most frightening, terrifying experience of my life. I have to have it with me at all times and if I don't, then that's it, I just get petrified, scared stiff, and I sit there thinking about it, and the more I think about it, the worse I get."

By way of contrast, teen-age boys or men, who need to present a strong masculine image, may underplay the severity of their symptoms. These individuals frequently delay taking medication, or take reduced amounts in the effort to convince themselves that they are "normal." As might be expected, this type of defensive denial sometimes leads to serious and incapacitating asthmatic episodes.

Still another form of distortion that is sometimes encountered in evaluating symptom severity arises from the belief that a somatic symptom induced by psychological provocation cannot really be serious—certainly not as serious as the same symptom induced by physical provocation. The belief that emotionally induced asthma is "fake asthma" has been found not only among relatives of the patient but also, on occasion, among physicians. The latter situation once led to a patient in the early stages of status asthmaticus (severe, continuous asthma resistant to treatment) being referred for psychotherapy with the physician believing that "It can't really be serious since everybody knows this patient's asthma is all psychic." A useful analogy in orienting both physicians and lay persons is that of the patient with a bleeding ulcer. It is commonly recognized that chronic tension may be one of the most significant antecedents of ulcer development. However, neither the gravity of the condition, nor the need for immediate symptomatic medically oriented treatment is questioned, despite acknowledgement of the fact that modification of relevant emotional processes may be the key tool for the prevention of future symptoms.

Some Measures of Asthma

Purcell, Brady, and Chai (1967), in a study assessing the effects of experimental separation from the family on asthma in children, report a series of intercorrelations between the following four measures of asthma: (a) the expiratory peak flow rate taken four times daily; (b) a physician's clinical examination scaling the severity of asthma at a given moment and done once daily; (c) a daily history of a child's asthma as reported by his mother; and (d) the amount of medication administered a child, as reported by his mother.

Intercorrelations among these measures were calculated for a group of 16 subjects with approximately 50 observations per subject. The highest average correlation was between the history of the severity of asthma and the amount of medication given (.60). This was not unexpected, since each of these two measures describes an entire 24-hour period as perceived by the same person—in this case, a child's mother. The other measures are momentary: the clinical examination describes the state of a child's symptom during a 1-minute period out of 24 hours, and the average peak flow represents lung function during four 1-minute periods of the day. All of the correlations were relatively low but in the expected direction, that is, better lung function (higher peak flow) is associated with reduced medication requirements (−.33) and with lower scores on clinical examination for wheezing (−.26). The correlation between peak flow rate and clinical examination is not higher because, for one thing, expiratory peak flow rate must drop between 25 percent and 40 percent before wheezing may be detected with a stethoscope. Therefore, there may be considerable variation in a peak flow measure with no noticeable variation in wheezing.

Of interest is the fact that the correlation between the history of asthma and the amount of medication for individual subjects ranged from a low of .25 to a high of .85. The amount of medication taken by a child was, in a number of instances, determined by many factors, for example, fluctuating anxiety, symptom denial, etc., other than simple symptom severity. Sometimes a parent adhered to a fixed quantity of medication regardless of symptom variability.

The intermittent character of the asthmatic symptom is dramatically shown in Figure 24.1, which compares a graph of expiratory peak flow rates that were obtained four times daily with once weekly measures from the same patient. The need for frequent assessment of the symptom, either historical or objective, is unmistakable if one is to obtain an accurate diagnostic portrait.

Patient and Family Attitudes Toward the Symptom

Between attacks, patients may regard their symptoms with anxiety and apprehension, or with disgust and embarrassment. They are frequently inhibited by the fear that their symptoms are conspicuous. They may feel different or weaker than others because they cannot keep up with them in physical activity. Persistent feelings of frustration about physical and social deficits are common. An episode of asthma that occurs among co-workers or other childen may be extremely discomfiting. For example, one adolescent girl told of the shattering experience of beginning to wheeze while kissing a boy. Relatively infrequently, the patient may regard asthma as an ally and a weapon to be used in a consciously manipulative way, either to obtain something he wants, or to avoid an undesirable situation. For example, some children can, by running around the block or hyperventilating, induce an attack of asthma in order to avoid going to school.

Resentment and bitterness may develop toward physicians for seeming to promise cures without results. Patients experience so many different schools of approach toward their asthma, for example, dietary, the creation of an allergenically controlled environment, psychological, etc., that they tend to become both confused and embittered if these approaches do not work. Asthmatic patients notoriously make the rounds of physicians in the community, and physicians often understandably react with frustration in seeking to cope with this difficult and refractory symptom.

The existence of a family member who is asthmatic, particularly if the condition is severe, is often felt as a potent emotional and financial burden by other family members. Parents frequently report a deep sense of guilt for having produced or fostered the development of asthma in a child. Sometimes they point to a genetic mode of transmission; sometimes they believe that bad behaviors on their part have created the symptom. When a patient's symptom is severe enough to warrant constant attention or significant financial drain, the parent or spouse may become irritable, resentful, and guilt-ridden. This guilt appears to be one of

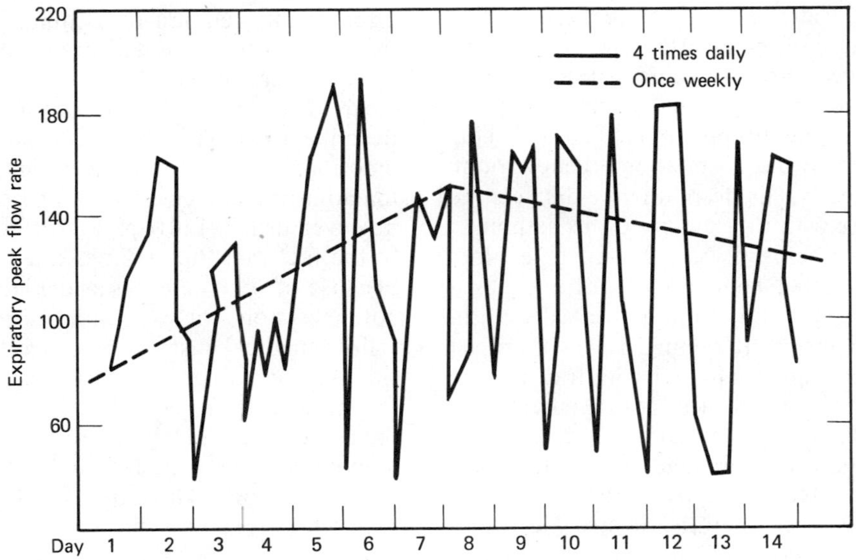

Figure 24.1 A comparison of expiratory peak flow rates four times daily and once weekly. *Solid line*, four times daily. *Dashed line*, once weekly.

the antecedents of the commonly observed over-protective maternal attitude toward the asthmatic child, with reciprocal over-dependence of the child on the mother.

Not infrequently, overprotective responses are elicited from physicians as well as from parents. The observation of a person in a severe asthmatic attack often arouses marked fear and, subsequent to this, sorts of restrictions may be urged on the patient by the physician to avoid the anxiety and the responsibility of peraps having to cope with an episode that can be life-threatening.

THE ROLE OF PSYCHOLOGICAL VARIABLES IN ASTHMA

The Case of L

The physicians treating him felt compelled to conclude that L's asthma must be psychological. Of late, his attacks had begun, without apparent reason, to become more frequent and more severe. Heavy doses of steroids failed to control the symptoms. Extensive physical examinations had repeatedly failed to turn up anything that would explain why this 12-year-old boy, who had initially done so well at the Children's Asthma Research Institute and Hospital (CARIH), had suddenly begun to slide downhill. Could it be that the anxiety and depression that had begun at just about the time his asthma had gotten worse were triggering the attacks? And could these, in turn, be because of the fact that L. was soon to be discharged to return home? These possibilities were given weight by nurses' reports that L. had lately appeared to "enjoy" being admitted to the hospital emergency room. And, clearly, his despondency did seem to correlate with the severity of his asthma.

Psychotherapy was initiated to explore the presumed contributions of emotional factors to L's condition, but revealed nothing conclusive. It seemed to his therapist that L's depression and withdrawal were more the product of discouragement over the failure of medication to control his symptoms, and his acute embarrassment over the effects corticosteroid drugs had on his appearance, than the reverse. Nevertheless, the hypothesis that L's asthma was emotionally induced, or perhaps even voluntarily brought on, was not easily rejected. For example, L. reported to his therapist, on the occasion of one severe attack, that he was relieved to be in the hospital and out of his cottage, because trouble had been brewing with the other boys.

The solution, when it finally came, was unexpectedly simple. L. had been, as mentioned, observed to be withdrawing more and more from social activities. He was spending a large part of his time in solitary pursuits. One of these pursuits, building models, he seemed particularly to enjoy. Since he had started spending time this way, L. had suspected that the smell of the glue he was using might be irritating his throat and lungs. However, he never mentioned this fact because he enjoyed building models and was afraid he might be stopped. Nor could he give up his hobby voluntarily. Thus, a vicious cycle had been in process. Model building aggravated L's asthma which, in turn, required him to spend more time alone, that is, building models.

With this discovery, a nonodorous glue was obtained for L. to use. His attacks subsided and his good spirits revived. At the latest follow-up since his discharge, L. is reported to be doing quite well at home.

This brief case excerpt illustrates a number of the important and often perplexing problems that face physicians and psychotherapists in their attempts to assess the role of emotions in asthma. First, there is the problem of distinguishing what in a patient's pattern of adjustment is cause and what is effect, in its relation to asthma. That behavioral problems and asthma may exist in a reciprocal cause-effect relationship is clear. Thus, reports from physicians that describe their patients' asthma as heavily emotional often refer to the patients' social maladjustments as evidence. These reports, however, usually fail to give adequate notice to the fact that the maladjustment may be because of such defenses as denial or overcompensation, for example, the refusal to follow medical instructions, overt aggression, or sexual promiscuity, instituted in response to symptoms. In these instances, then, the patient's response to his symptoms may be mistakenly interpreted as the cause of his symptoms. Of course, the distinction between cause and response is not hard and fast. Acting out behavior, such as refusal to take medication, may in fact foster more symptoms.

Second, there is the problem that derives from often accurate but incomplete observations about emotions in asthma. Thus, although L's withdrawal was indeed "antecedent" to his asthma, it was the unobserved event following withdrawal, that is, smelling the odor of glue, that actually provoked his asthma. Similarly, the observation that anger leads to asthma may be accurate, but overlooks the shouting, the storming about, and the crying that accompany the anger and that, in fact, may trigger the attack. To explore the psychodynamic significance of anger, as it relates causally to asthma in such an instance, could be fruitless and misleading.

The usefulness of conventional psychodiagnostic tests in evaluating the role of emotional factors in asthma is questionable because it is not now possible to specify with any precision the relevant test cues. Instead, as we shall try to show, the creation of specialized research instruments for evaluating the functional relationships between various classes of stimuli and the asthmatic response is a more promising approach. First, however, we shall discuss two important clinical and research issues which are more fully evaluated in recent review articles (Freeman, Feingold, Schlesinger, & Gorman, 1964; Lipton, Steinschneider, & Richmond, 1966; Purcell, 1965).

Is There a Personality Constellation Specific to Asthmatics?

Out of a large body of literature, mainly descriptive and nonexperimental case studies, has come suggestions regarding a common personality profile descriptive of asthmatic patients or of a specific type of nuclear conflict, for example, unresolved dependency on the mother, as especially applicable to asthmatics. Many authors have implied that these characteristics bear a causal relationship to the development of the asthmatic symptom; others have noted that they appeared secondary, resulting from the symptom and its effects on the patient and his family. Asthmatics, particularly children, have been described as anxious, dependent, conforming, insecure, lacking in self-confidence and hypersensitive. Our own view is that a careful examination of the literature does not suggest that any specific personality constellation, nuclear conflict, or form of interpersonal relationship is uniformly and etiologically associated with asthma. This assertion, which does not deny the observation that asthmatics and their families often manifest more behavioral disturbance than normal subjects, is based on several lines of evidence.

First, Neuhaus (1958) found that both asthmatic and cardiac patients (children) were significantly more maladjusted (anxious, insecure, and dependent) than a normal control group but did not differ from each other. He concluded that chronic illness may be the variable most relevant to the production of behavioral maladjustment in asthmatics rather than some process associated specifically with asthma.

A suggestion that unresolved dependency conflicts are central in the development of asthma is contained in the influential writings of French and Alexander (1941) who further hypothesize that asthma may often be viewed as a suppressed cry, with the stated implication that asthmatic children cry less than nonasthmatics, particularly around critical periods of separation conflict. To our knowledge, there is no systematic survey of crying behavior to support this assertion. Nevertheless, clinicians have sometimes noted a tendency for crying to be distorted in a silent, awkward way in certain of their patients. Purcell (1963) has suggested an alternative interpretation of this observation. He notes that a number of patients report that crying, like laughing and coughing, can trigger attacks of asthma and further, that these patients sometimes deliberately seek to avoid crying and laughing hard so as not to provoke asthma. Thus, the occasionally observed inability to cry or the silent, suppressed manner of crying may reflect a learned attempt to avoid initiating the uncomfortable experience of an asthmatic attack.

Second, evidence supporting the contention that asthma is a heterogeneous symptom has been mounting. Clinicians have long noted the wide variety of stimuli, for example, allergic, infective, emotional, and mechanical, capable of triggering asthma and have attempted to classify patients in terms of precipitant stimuli. The underlying assumption has been that success in categorizing the types of stimuli that initiate the physiological sequence leading to the clinical symptom of asthma should lead to more effective, individualized treatment. Many investigators have recognized that multiplicity of precipitating stimuli, for example, dust, infections, hyperventilation, is the rule and have been concerned with efforts to define the relative predominance of these factors and their reciprocal interactions for the individual case.

Differential Response to Institutionalization

Within this framework, Purcell and his collaborators (Purcell, 1963; Purcell, Bernstein, & Bukantz, 1961; Purcell & Metz, 1962; Purcell, Turnbull, & Bernstein, 1962) have separated subgroups on the basis of whether or not spontaneous remission of symptoms occurred within a short time after admission to CARIH. Certain psychological differences between groups, particularly between rapidly remitting (those who remain virtually symptom free and require no medication during the 18 to 24 month of residency) and steroid-dependent (those requiring continuous maintenance doses of corticosteroid drugs) groups have been found. For example, in response to a structured interview technique, rapidly remitting children report significantly more often than do steroid-dependent children that emotions such as anger, anxiety, and depression trigger asthma. Furthermore, the results of a questionnaire device to assess parental child-rearing attitudes have indicated that both mothers and fathers of rapidly remitting children show authoritarian and punitive attitudes to a greater degree than do the parents of steroid-dependent children.

The present hypothesis of these investigators suggests that among rapidly remitting children, in contrast to steroid-dependent children, the symptom of asthma may be more intimately associated with neurotic conflict and affective reactions. The asthmatic symptom of steroid-dependent children, on the other hand, is viewed as a response more regularly linked to the influences of allergic and infectious factors. The differences between these groups are regarded as relative rather than absolute.

The above remarks make it clear that a large segment of the population of severely asthmatic children become essentially asymptomatic without any medication when they leave their homes in all parts of the country and enter CARIH in Denver. The vast majority of the remainder of the population show substantial, although not as dramatic, improvement. Other residential centers for asthmatic children report similar experiences, as do pediatricians who hospitalize asthmatic children in hospitals for a brief time. Thus, there is clear evidence that removal from the family home and placement in an institutional setting often has a profoundly ameliorative effect on asthma in children.

However, removal from the family home represents a change in the total physical as well as the psychological environment of the child. The evidence implicating physical environmental factors in the perpetuation of asthma in certain patients is quite clear. Therefore, it becomes of central importance to find a way of drastically altering the significant psychological environment without modifying the physical environment.

Differential Response to Experimental Family Separation

One approach to this problem has been to measure the effects on asthma of separating a child from his family while maintaining an essentially constant physical environment. Purcell et al. (1967) studied chronically asthmatic children on a daily basis, both medically and psychologically, during periods in which they lived with their own families and during a period in which they had no contact with their families but were cared for in their own homes by a substitute mother. At the time of this writing a total of 22 children had been evaluated. On the basis of the selection instrument, a detailed, structured interview for assessing parental and child perceptions of the precipitants of asthma attacks, it was predicted that 13 of these children would respond positively to the experimental separation, while 9 would show no improvement in asthma. For the 13 predicted positives, all measures of asthma, including expiratory peak flow rates, amount of medication required, daily history of asthma, and daily clinical examination, indicated significant improvement occurring during the period of family separation for the group as a whole. For the group of 9 predicted nonresponders, only the daily history suggested improvement during separation.

None of the other measures showed any difference between the separation and nonseparation periods. Statistics for the individual showed that 70 percent (9) of the 13 predicted positives did indeed respond with improvement during separation, while only about 10 percent (1) of the 9 predicted nonresponders showed improvement.

Categorizing Allergic Potential

Finally, Block, Jennings, Harvey, and Simpson (1964) carried out a careful study that illustrated another method of subdividing asthmatic patients. These investigators developed an Allergic Potential Scale (APS) for evaluating a patient's predisposition to allergic reaction. The APS is based on items such as family history of allergy, skin test reactions, eosinophile count, ease with which a particular clinical symptom may be diagnosed as related to specific allergens, etc. By using a thematic analysis of projective tests, these investigators concluded that the low APS group (less disposed to allergy but not significantly different from the high APS group on severity of asthma) were more pessimistic, conforming, and had lower frustration tolerance. Mothers and fathers independently described these children more often as nervous, jealous, rebellious, and clinging than the high APS group. The results of the observations of mother-child interaction, quantified by an adjective *Q* sort technique, indicated that low APS mothers were more intrusive, angry, rejecting, depriving, etc. The scores on the Parental Attitude Research Instrument (PARI) substantiated this evidence of undesirable maternal attitudes. The personality assessment of the mothers, by using the MMPI, TAT, and Rorschach, suggested that low APS mothers were more fearful, anxious, and self-defeating with more evidence of psychopathology. The interviews and observations of mother-father interaction indicated that the low APS group of parents showed more ambivalent, destructive, and pathological relationships than the high APS group.

At the least, the results obtained from subgroup studies point to the heterogeneity of the asthmatic population. They also suggest the importance of discriminating among asthmatics so as not to obscure relationships that may exist only for a portion of the population. By inference, the data offer some assistance in making a more informed judgment about whether or not to include some form of psychotherapeutic intervention as a part of the treatment program for a particular asthmatic.

Can Asthma be Induced by Psychological Stimulation?

Asthma Induced by Emotional Provocation

Promising results have been obtained by investigators who employed emotional provocation techniques. Several studies have included direct clinical observation, often with some objective measurement, of an induced asthmatic attack. Stein (1962) noted that enclosing a patient in a whole body plethysmograph represented a severe emotional stress which in some patients precipitated an asthmatic attack. Dekker and Groen (1956) used the technique of selecting emotional stimuli from a patient's case history and then of applying psychological provocation tests. Of 12 patients, 3 showed minor respiratory symptoms and 3 exhibited frank asthmatic attacks. These investigators noted that high intensity of emotion in itself was not sufficient to produce an attack of asthma. Instead, they suggested that the emotional setting must not only have a certain intensity but must also be of a more or less specific quality. Owen (1964), by using another form of stimulus specificity, has shown that asthmatic children, contrasted to control subjects, showed (a) increased variability and amplitude of respiration, and (b) more abnormal patterns of respiration when listening to their own mother's voice as compared to the voice of an unknown female adult. Asthmatic wheezing, however, was not demonstrated.

Stevenson (1950) obtained respiratory tracings during an interview with a patient with bronchial asthma. He noted that the occurrence of wheezing coincided with the increased secretion of bronchial mucus associated with the feelings of resentment and anxiety that were provoked during the discussion of stressful situations. In another study of 22 patients (15 asthmatic and 7 with anxiety states) Stevenson and Ripley (1952) found that respiratory patterns varied closely with emotional state during an interview.

An increased rate or depth, or both, were found with anxiety and sometimes during anger; irregularity of respiration was frequently noted with anger and occurred during weeping. In 3 asthmatic patients, wheezing occurred that was related to both emotional changes and to changes in the pneumograph pattern.

Treuting and Ripley (1948) found that in 5 patients it was possible to induce asthma by a stress interview without exposure to pollen. In another investigation of hay fever sufferers (Holmes, Treuting & Wolff, 1950), the investigators demonstrated that a discussion of significant personal conflicts was capable of inducing nasal hyperemia, swelling, hypersecretion, and obstruction. It was noted that the nasal and bronchial mucosa are parts of a continuous membrane that is almost physiologically identical.

A rather different type of mechanism has been described by Faulkner (1941) who observed changes in the size of the bronchial lumen associated with emotional changes. While bronchoscoping one patient, he noticed that the recall of unpleasant incidents evoking resentment was accompanied by bronchial narrowing; in another, depressing thoughts caused the bronchial wall to lose tone, become flabby, and collapse.

Two studies have been aimed at evaluating a summation of stimuli hypothesis, that is, diverse stimuli such as emotional arousal and pollen may effectively combine to produce symptoms, although a given quantity of either type of stimulation is insufficient for symptom production. Holmes et al. (1950), in their study of nasal reactions, found that when ragweed sensitive subjects, who were exposed to a ragweed pollen room and reacted only mildly, were led to discuss conflictual, anxiety-arousing material, their hay fever symptoms became markedly exacerbated. As a result of observing nasal function following a brief unilateral stellate ganglion block, it was concluded that parasymptathetic neural impulses to the nose appeared to be the cause of the nasal hyperfunctioning accompanying the patient's reaction to a conflict situation. Treuting and Ripley (1948) were able to induce attacks of asthma in a pollen room during interviews that covered stressful topics, whereas pollen alone did not produce symptoms.

There are numerous anecdotal observations in the literature that report emotionally triggered asthma. One illustration from our experience in the experimental separation study will suffice. Two of the subjects were brothers and, on the basis of initial interviews, Mike was selected as a probable positive responder to separation (in terms of improvement in asthma), while Joey was identified as a probable nonresponder. The studies were carried out sequentially, and the data confirmed the predictions. The substitute mother, Miss K., who stayed with Mike (the responder) was a trained nurse and a careful observer. She had reported, and we confirmed this in our own interviews, that Mike's mother was a compulsively meticulous housekeeper who made a fetish of keeping everything around her spotless, including furniture, carpets, children, etc. Joe was described as a terror who was afraid of nothing. Mike, on the other hand, was said to be much more sensitive and attached to his mother. During the two weeks of separation, Mike was entirely free of asthma except for one 20-minute period of very mild wheezing. One evening Miss K. had some guests visiting her and noticed Mike standing hesitantly at the foot of the stairway. To quote Miss K.:

> "I went up to him and he was shivering and hyperventilating very hard and looked scared to death. There was just the start of a wheeze I could hear. He told me he had had an accident—wet his pants—and some had got on the carpet. I told him we could fix that easily and calmed him—and I was amazed. In less than 60 seconds his breathing was back to normal—no more wheezing and he didn't need a nebulizer."

Unfortunately, in many of the ingenious experimental studies that seek to tie together emotions and asthmatic responses, the sample of patients is often very limited (frequently one or two) and the frequency of observation is not reported. It is difficult to know, for example, in what proportion of patients or of occasions summative effects were or were not obtainable. This makes it difficult to estimate the generality of findings.

"Conditioned" asthma

In 1941, French and Alexander believed that the available evidence permitted them to conclude that there was ample support for the statement that asthma attacks may be precipitated by a conditioned reflex mechanism. The famous example given by MacKenzie in 1886 of a woman who was supposedly allergic to roses and who developed asthma when an artificial rose was held before her has been cited many times in the literature. The "hoarse, labored breathing" of Nick, the experimentally "neurotic" dog (Gantt, 1944), has also been frequently cited in support of the psychogenic production of asthma. In our judgment, however, "conditioned" asthma has yet to be demonstrated under controlled conditions in either humans or animals.

For example, references have often been made to the results of Liddell (1951), who produced experimental neuroses in sheep as well as to the results of Gantt (1944). In both, impressive evidence is presented of altered respiration accompanying the neurotic behavior in the dog and in the sheep. A number of writers have pointed to these data as evidence that asthma can be produced experimentally by psychological manipulation. However, examination of the monograph by Gantt discloses a clear statement that Nick was examined for asthma and that there was no evidence of the sounds of asthma despite the fact that respiration was clearly affected. Liddell, on the other hand, did not report any clinical examination for asthma. One of the early and widely cited reports is the one of Ottenberg, Stein, Lewis, and Hamilton (1958) who appeared to show successful classical conditioning of asthma in the guinea pig. The criterion for conditioned asthma was an observer's visual judgment about the animal's heavy, labored respiration and use of accessory muscles. Attempts to replicate these observations with the use of objective recordings of the respiratory pattern have not been successful. Stein (1962) has noted that all that was definitely established in the original study was that a marked respiratory disturbance occurred, perhaps associated with anxiety. Airway obstruction with the prolonged expiration characteristic of asthma was not demonstrated.

Herxheimer (1951) studied the response of human asthmatic subjects to inhalational challenge tests, that is, by having subjects breathe a substance to which they were sensitive. Part of Herxheimer's procedure was to have the subject blow hard into a spirometer (a device for measuring pulmonary function) prior to being exposed to the challenging substance. Herxheimer noted that in some subjects asthma appeared to develop after the subject had blown hard a few times, but *before* they were exposed to the antigen. A number of psychologically oriented investigators have referred to this as evidence of conditioning. It is, however, a known fact for all that is necessary to trigger asthma in some asthmatics is to have them blow hard several times. This respiratory stimulation is often accompanied by coughing and/or wheezing.

In the late 1950's, Dekker, Pelser, and Groen (1957) published an article that reported the successful classical conditioning of asthma in two subjects. Theese were two patients out of approximately 100 for whom conditioning was attempted. In a personal communication dated October, 1961, Dekker reported that he was unable to replicate even these results.

Knapp, who has been conducting a careful and elaborate series of experiments on conditioned asthma in human beings, summarizes his impressions as follows:

> "Our negative results would lead me at this moment to feel confident that conditioning, conceived in the most simple, mechanical model, cannot account for attacks of asthma in the human, but that 'learning,' particularly with the right kind of emotional concomitants, may well be important in certain individuals" (1963).

In summary, it appears accurate to state that, with either animals or human beings, the successful conditioning of asthma remains to be demonstrated, even in the opinion of those investigators whose original positive reports on conditioning are cited frequently.

TOOLS AND CUES FOR ASSESSING THE RELEVANT VARIABLES

Our review of some pertinent theoretical and empirical issues now leads us back to the problem of how the clinician may approach the evaluation of psychological factors in the particular asthmatic patient with whom he must deal. The tools and cues found useful clinically are the ones that have successfully, ableit imperfectly, discriminated among asthmatic subgroups.

There are four classes of information involved: (a) the patient's or, in the case of a child below the age of 8 or 9, his parents', perception of events related to the onset of asthma attacks; (b) the nature of the symptom response to separation from significant figures; (c) the biological characteristics of the patient; (d) patient and parental personality characteristics.

Perception of Events Related to the Onset of Asthma Attacks

This information is obtained from the structured interview that successfully distinguished rapid remitters from steroid-dependent children and that predicted responders and nonresponders rather successfully in the experimental separation study (Purcell et al., 1967). The patient is asked to list the things that he has noticed bring on asthma attacks. It is emphasized that the interviewer is interested in what the patient himself has noticed rather than what he has heard from his physician or, in the case of a child, from his parents. Detailed information is collected on items such as the time interval between the event, be it damp weather or an argument, and the development of asthma. After a patient spontaneously lists his observations, a list of additional asthma precipitants is read to him with the instruction that he indicate which, if any, apply. The total list of items is as follows: night asthma (unassociated in a patient's mind with any other precipitant), overexertion, weather (including change in season, dampness, heat, or cold), excitement (always with positive affect), emotional reactions (worry, upset, anger, sadness, or any other negative affect), laughing, crying, hard breathing, pollens (trees, grass, weeds), coughing, foods, colds, dust, other allergies, and "just get it."

After the patient's listing is obtained, he is asked to rank the precipitants in their order of importance (separately as to frequency and severity) in bringing on episodes of asthma. An estimate is obtained from him as to the absolute frequency with which a given precipitant is tied to the onset of asthma, for example, once a week, once a month or less. Asking the patient for illustrations of the operation of certain of the precipitants, for example, describe the last time that you were angry and felt that this caused you to have some asthma, or that you ate a certain food or were around some pollen, is especially useful in assisting the clinician to judge whether the patient is spontaneously reporting an occurrence from his own experience or is merely parroting something he has heard from those around him.

Sometimes it is possible, after an initial interview with the patient, to sensitize him (or the parents in the case of a young child) as an observer of the antecedents of asthma attacks. Reports on the importance or unimportance of emotional precipitants may become more convincing as the person involved becomes a better observer. The interviewer, of course, must be alerted to bias introduced by the patient's expectations as to what the psychologically oriented clinician wishes to hear. The bias may go in either direction. When it takes the form of compliance, the interviewer may test the substance of the observation by searching inquiries into the details of the onset of an attack that is supposedly precipitated by emotional stimuli. When the bias is expressed as an exaggerated and emotionally charged denial, one must withhold judgment as to the credibility of the denial.

Inquiry is also conducted about the usual techniques that the patient uses to try to stop an attack of asthma. In particular, the patient is asked whether he ever tries to stop asthma by "getting his mind off it" or by "trying to relax," and how effective these procedures are.

There is a number of precautions to be kept in mind during such an interview, some of which have already been alluded to. The first derives from the potential misinterpretation by the informant of a sequence of events that have led him to conclude that "emotions" cause asthma. The detailed inquiry into time relationships and the exact sequence of events between onset of the reported precipitating stimulus and the development of asthma is very helpful here. The question of how long a period of time before an asthmatic attack one ought to include in the search for emotional antecedents is important. From our standard interview studies with children and from parental reports and clinical observations, the strong impression is gained that emotional and respiratory events said to trigger asthma begin typically 1 to 30 minutes before the onset of wheezing and that they continue up to the time wheezing begins. That is, if a child became angry with another child, began to argue, then grew more upset and cried, and finally developed asthma, the whole process would generally take no more than 30 minutes. Only very infrequently does the beginning of a relevant emotional episode appear to precede asthma by as much as one hour. Even when there is evidence of a relevant episode beginning 2 or 3 or even 24 hours earlier, the effects persist and grow more pronounced the closer one gets to the report of onset of asthma. For example, let us assume that a child learns of a trip he is to take in 48 hours. The idea is quite exciting. Typically, as the time draws nearer and excitement mounts, the child may report excessive laughter, restlessness, jumping around, and then asthma. The point is that, even when the initiation of a seemingly relevant behavior sequence precedes asthma by more than 30 minutes, the characteristics of that behavior are present usually in a most intense form just prior to the development of asthma.

Second, definition of a stimulus does not automatically make the meaning of the stimulus clear. For example, a boy may report that anger leads to asthma whenever his mother tells him to wash the dishes. Without further exploration, which may require a psychotherapeutic relationship, one may not be able to tell whether the boy is rebelling against authority, or angry over the threat of being feminized, etc.

The third precaution derives from the repeated observation that there is often a gross discrepancy between subjective and objective reports of a patient's physical condition. Thus, information obtained regarding factors that precipitate and relieve asthma must be treated with appropriate skepticism. The report, for example, that "getting my mind off asthma" makes a patient better may simply reflect a change in perception of subjective distress in the absence of any physiological improvement. Similarly, the report that getting scared makes asthma worse may sometimes reflect only an increased awareness and responsiveness to a relatively unchanged amount of asthma.

A fourth precaution which is worth reemphasizing is the need to separate the informant's direct observation from what he may have been told by physicians, friends, parents, and other asthmatics, etc. This is especially necessary in the case of children, who will often dutifully report on the adverse effects of cold weather as a result of having been cautioned innumerable times to "dress warm" and "button up." Specific examples of each precipitant should be elicited to verify reports.

A fifth precaution will be readily apparent to clinicians since it is hardly exclusive to interviews regarding asthma. For a variety of defensive purposes, patients and/or parents or close relatives will either over- or underemphasize the role of emotions in asthma. On the one hand, the mother who feels intense guilt may flagellate herself by reciting the many ill effects her handling has had on her child's asthma. Or the parent who uses the child's asthma as a club with which to beat his or her partner may confide to the clinician the powerful ill effects on the child's asthma of the mishandling by that partner. Or again, the parent who fears that hereditary taint may be operating may prefer to see the child's problem as a psychological one, in much the same way as the brain-injured patient sometimes insists that "something psychological must be wrong with my mind." On the other hand, those parents or patients whose defenses tend to be in the direction of guarding against recognition of emotional problems may insist that "there is nothing wrong with me (my child), it's the weather, or the dust," or the myriad other things numerous consultations with physicians may have rightly or wrongly suggested. In these instances the clinician needs to be alert to these maneuvers and to deal with them before valid information can be obtained. Sometimes simple reassurance at the right time that, "We just don't know what causes asthma in your case," will suffice to cut through much guilt and anxiety. However, the occasions will undoubtedly arise where the work will need to be more involved and, at least, quasi-therapeutic to achieve the same result.

We have been arguing in favor of obtaining as much direct information as possible with regard to emotional events and asthma as opposed to the more general approach of assessing personality traits or psychopathology. A first step is to obtain detailed observations of the sequence of events culminating in asthma, including equally careful attention to physically defined precipitants. A second step may involve the determination of what the patient's perception of these events is in order to gain some idea of possible underlying mediators. These data all deal with "perceived" precipitants of asthmatic attacks, and the objection may be raised that these may be very different from the "real" precipitants. In general, it would appear that one is always dealing with "perceived" precipitants, but that on some occasions the perceptions are the ones of the patient or parent; on other occasions they are the ones of the pediatrician or allergist; and on still other occasions it is the psychologist or psychiatrist who is the perceiver. The task often lies in correlating and juxtaposing these perceptions.

Response to Separation

An effort is made to determine whether significant changes in the life situation have sometimes relieved asthma. Most often these changes have to do with separation from significant persons. For example, a very prompt response to hospitalization without the use of any potent medication is a frequent report. Parents have reported in the case of some children that there is a consistent improvement as the child reaches the vicinity of the hospital, even before getting to the emergency room.

It is important to inquire closely about the course of asthma during those periods when a husband has been separated from his wife or a child from his parents in the normal course of events. For example, husbands may go off on business trips or parents may take vacations for a few days or more at a time, leaving their child with a baby sitter. Or a child may visit with relatives or friends for a matter of days or of weeks. If the patient has noticed a change in the state of asthma during these times, it is useful to inquire as to the patient's perception of the reason for the change. The clinician must always keep in mind that frequently separation from significant persons is accompanied by a change in the physical environment that itself may be associated with alterations in asthmatic symptoms. Often it is not possible to do more than make an educated guess as to which factor is primarily responsible for a symptom change, and sometimes even an educated guess is all but impossible. When fairly unambiguous data are available on this point, for example, a patient who repeatedly improves during separation with any accompanying changes in the physical environment appearing insignificant, it deserves to be heavily weighted in evaluating the role of psychological variables.

Biological Characteristics

Much of the historical information in this category can be obtained directly by the psychologically oriented clinician. However, some of it must be sought from the physician involved in the case. The strength of constitutional disposition toward allergy varies directly with the degree of positive finding in the following items (Block et al., 1964).

Family History of Allergy

Evidence of major allergy (asthma, hay fever, eczema) in close relatives (parents and siblings) is positive.

Total Number of Allergies in Patient

The number of different allergic symptoms refers to the number of different shock organs involved. For example, a patient may suffer from bronchial asthma (lungs), eczema (skin), rhinitis (nose), etc.

Ease of Diagnosability of Specific Allergens

If a very clear correlation is discernible between allergic stress, for example, hyposensitization injections, exposure to an animal, and subsequent allergic symptoms, for example, asthma or a constitutional reaction, then a high rating is obtained on this variable. A reliable history that documents such a relationship is more important than any other single item as a clue to the existence of an immunologic problem.

Skin Test Reactivity

Responses to the scratch method of skin testing that are strong (better than 2+ in the conventional clinical measurement system of allergists) and multiple (to a variety of antigenic substances) make for a high rating.

Blood Eosinophile Percentage

Block et al. (1964) found that the highest percentage recorded during an allergic episode was a useful discriminator between high and low allergic groups. However, a practical difficulty is that such analyses are made extremely infrequently by the physician and, hence, are usually not available.

There are, in addition to the above five items which comprise the Allergic Potential Scale, two other pieces of relevant information. The first is evidence, preferably X-ray, of chest deformity. A high degree of hyperinflation, as shown by a markedly barrel-shaped chest, has been found to be associated more with the steroid-dependent than with the rapidly remitting subgrouping (Purcell & Bukantz, unpublished data). Second, a careful scrutiny of the correlation between infection and the occurrence of asthma is useful. Infection plays a major role in precipitating asthma frequently and severely in some patients and, where this is the case, psychological intervention is likely to be less effective.

A cautionary note in all of this is the fact that asthma is almost always a multiply triggered symptom. In the individual case, asthma precipitated by physically defined stimuli almost invariably coexists with asthma precipitated by psychologically defined stimuli. Therefore, a seemingly high score on biological characteristics does not preclude the significance of emotional stimuli, with the reverse being true as well.

Patient and/or Parental Personality Characteristics

The personality characteristics or attitudes said to be more typical of the low APS children and their parents (Block et al., 1964), the low skin reactivity in adult female patients (Feingold, Gorman, Singer, & Schlesinger, 1962), and the parents of rapidly remitting children (Purcell et al., 1961; Purcell & Metz, 1962) have already been noted. Although substantial evidence of a disturbed personality constellation is a cue to the operation of psychological influences on the production and maintenance of asthmatic symptoms, it is, in our opinion, a relatively weak one. For one thing, the evidence is more ambiguous on this point than on the others. Dekker, Barendregt, and de Vries (1961), for example, failed to find differences in neuroticism between a group of adult female asthmatics who showed "manifest allergy" and those who showed "no manifest allergy" based on skin reactivity and inhalation tests. Similarly, Purcell, Turnbull, and Bernstein (1962), by using a large battery of tests, found no difference in overall psychopathology between a group of rapidly remitting and steroid-dependent children.

Further Development of Assessment Techniques

Our own experience, as well as our evaluation of the literature, leads us away from increasingly refined studies on the general personality characteristics of the patient and/or his family to a focus on the antecedents and concomitants of the particular response in which we are interested—the asthmatic attack. The logic underlying this approach states that if "emotions" or "affects" are important in producing asthma, it should be possible to demonstrate a specific role for these variables in the precipitation of individual attacks.

Emotional Provocation Tests

As already described, interviews that focus on stressful life situations have been successfully used to induce asthma by several different investigators. Although the failure to provoke wheezing through discussion of stressful topics certainly does not eliminate the consideration of emotional elements, a positive finding clearly points toward some form of psychological treatment. Sometimes it may be possible to intensify emotions under hypnosis sufficiently to increase the probability of observing the development of asthmatic wheezing. Advances in assessment, we believe, will come about partly as a result of advances in our skills at reproducing, in the laboratory or office, the idiosyncratic emotional reactions relevant to asthma.

Effects of Separation

Another diagnostic tool that deserves exploration is the brief experimental separation. In our experience, symptomatic improvement, if it is going to occur at all following separation from significant figures, often happens within a few days or even sooner. Where feasible, one may suggest the possibility of a temporary separation (a few days to a week) of a husband and wife or parent and child as an evaluative technique. It may be possible to take advantage of naturally occurring events, for example, business trips, vacations, etc., with only a minor modification of living arrangements. Obviously, the presentation of such a concept to the patient and his family must be carefully thought out.

In the experimental separation study (Purcell et al., 1967) it was found helpful to emphasize (a) that this procedure was only one part of a thorough study of all of the factors affecting asthmatic symptoms, and (b) that if significant improvement were observed with change in the psychological environment, one must not assume that parents are "to blame" for their child's asthma. The situation is almost invariably more complicated, for example, fights with siblings may be a factor.

TREATMENT TECHNIQUES

From the foregoing review, it is evident that many questions that concern etiology, triggering mechanisms, and mediating pathways for the symptom of asthma remain as yet unanswered. This state of affairs imposes constraints on treatment efforts and is, at least, one factor responsible for their less than perfect record of success. Nevertheless, although a "cure" of asthma, by either psychological or medical means, remains a hope for the future, significant relief can often be afforded to the patient by the application of psychological techniques.

It is extremely important in setting the goals for therapy in asthma to recognize that the need to deal directly with the patient's reactions to his asthma is often matched by the need to deal with the feelings of "significant others" around his symptom. These feelings include fear, shame, anxiety, and resentment, and sometimes an investment in the patient's symptom as a means for solving family tensions. There can be no doubt that these feelings are readily communicated to the patient with potentially unfortunate results, both physically and emotionally. For example, one of the authors recently interviewed the parents of a 7-year-old girl who, in the year prior to coming to CARIH, had shown marked deterioration in her social relationships as well as in her asthma. With no apparent incident to which the onset of this deterioration could be traced, the patient had begun to show increasing irritability and demandingness, and had gradually become isolated from her peers. At home, she had become similarly more difficult, resenting and resisting efforts to treat her increasingly frequent attacks, and expressing a growing hopelessness that treatment would do her any good. Her parents were puzzled by this change in their daughter and could offer only the hypothesis that, with increasing maturity and self-awareness, she had begun to appraise her condition more realistically and was showing the frustration and rebellion that stemmed from this appraisal. Some probing into the parents' attitudes and behaviors revealed that the father had for some time been making a carefully detailed study of asthma. He had read much of the professional literature on the problem and had had consultations as well as correspondence with numerous physicians and investigators. He had concluded from these efforts that, for the most part, the treatment available to asthmatics was poor and that the potential effectiveness of this treatment was not to be regarded with much optimism. The father's fears and growing desperation were being communicated to and embroidered by his 7-year-old daughter. As a result, her pattern of behavior betrayed anxieties that were being only partially controlled by denial and displacement. When the parallel between the father's and the daughter's attitudes was suggested, the response was a genuinely surprised, "I never thought of it that way!"

Subjective and Objective Indices of Improvement

Before proceeding to a discussion of the various treatment techniques that have been brought to bear in cases of asthma, it will be useful to dwell, for a moment, on "subjective" and "objective" estimates of asthma, since they repeatedly arise as a consideration when assessment of the effectiveness of treatment techniques is attempted.

Generally, in assessing the effects of treatment, subjective and objective have referred to questionnaire or interview techniques, and to direct measures of pulmonary function, such as flow rates, respectively. From a research point of view, objective measures are greatly desired, and the conclusions of studies that lack them have been considered tentative at best. The reason for this is the repeated observation of gross discrepancies between subjective and objective measures, with subjective report generally overestimating the effectiveness of treatment (Beecher, 1959; Moore, 1965; White, 1961). Thus, patients whose flow rates show little or no change following treatment nevertheless report that they feel better, have fewer or less severe attacks, take less medication, engage in previously prohibited activities, are socially more outgoing, are hospitalized less frequently, and so on. Since we know that the degree of discomfort reported by the asthmatic patient is, at least, in part dependent on the degree to which his attention is directed to his breathing (Stevenson & Ripley, 1952) it may be that these subjective estimates reflect merely a withdrawal or redirection of attention with resultant faulty reporting. If this were entirely true, it would indicate that adequate assessment of treatment must rely on objective measurement. However, a second possibility is that, although the level of respiratory efficiency reflected in physiological measures, generally obtained *between* attacks, may remain unchanged, the range of triggering agents may in fact be narrower as a result of treatment. Thus, some asthmatics may function at a consistently impaired level, but vary in the degree to which they are subject to the eruption of clinical asthma. Third, it is conceivable that pulmonary function measures more sophisticated than flow rates might reveal variations in respiratory efficiency of which the patient is subjectively aware but which are not reflected in flow-rate variations.

In addition, it is unquestionably true that infrequently obtained pulmonary function tests are often less accurate as an index of asthma than a carefully maintained daily record of subjective evaluations of the symptom and reports of medication. Figure 24.1 shown earlier, shows the dramatic fluctuation in expiratory peak flow rates obtained four times daily. Nearly all studies that report marked discrepancies between subjective and objective evaluations used pulmonary function measures performed monthly or, at best, weekly. To compare a breathing record that samples a few minutes out of a month with the patient's self-observations, which cover a vastly greater proportion of the time, obviously contains a built-in error-producing system when dealing with a symptom as variable as asthma.

A final consideration, of special relevance to the setting of goals in psychotherapy, is that, when asthma has resulted in severe anxiety and social maladjustment, there is little reason to limit the assessment of therapeutic effectiveness to demonstrably improved physiologic function. If good results are even purely subjective but have important behavioral ramifications, the application of psychological techniques will be warranted. Of course, it will be necessary in all instances for the patient to be closely followed by a physician to maintain an adequate treatment regimen and to ward off the patient's undertaking activities that may remain beyond his physical capacity, despite his new found sense of well-being.

Selection of Treatment Technique and Mode of Operation

It is probably safe to state that, at one time or another, almost every variety of psychotherapeutic technique, including psychoanalysis, group psychotherapy, environmental manipulation, behavior therapy, hypnosis, and even ECT, has been applied in the treatment of bronchial asthma. With the single exception of ECT, claims of success have been filed in all instances. It is unfortunately true, however, that these claims have often been based on studies that have failed to meet one or another of the criteria of adequate treatment studies, namely: (a) unbiased subject selection procedures; (b) adequate therapist samples; (c) standardized treatment methods; (d) matched control groups not treated by the experimental method; (e) acceptable criteria for the evaluation of treatment effects; (f) a sufficiently long follow-up to rule out normal variability of the symptom; and (g) large enough samples for statistical evaluation. The absolute and relative values of each technique, therefore, remain difficult to evaluate, and apparent success is not a satisfactory criterion for the selection of a technique for the treatment of either asthmatics generally, or of particular patient subgroups.

There are several mechanisms whereby a technique may produce symptom change. They include: (a) the modification of some basic physiologic function, for example, an alteration in adrenocortical hormone output or autonomic reactivity which, according to Hahn (1966), differs in asthmatics and normals; (b) the reduction of the range of effective triggering stimuli, for example, removing the child from a tense family situation, treating the family to reduce tensions, or treating the child in order to alter his anxiety level; (c) the modification of the patient's attitude toward his symptom with the resulting reduction of what might be considered "secondary symptoms," for example, training the child to relax instead of panicing at the onset of an attack. The first two approaches might be considered "curative" or "preventive" in the sense that the goal is to eliminate or reduce attacks, and the third might be considered as having the reduction of the severity of symptoms as its primary goal. On the basis of current knowledge, it would appear that each technique, regardless of its primary aim, may result in any one or more of these changes.

An example of how symptom associated attitudes may exert feedback effects on symptom severity is contained in the following comments of Mrs. R., the mother of two boys who had been evaluated in the experimental separation study. Dr. G. refers to the physician who had been seeing the boys for medical examinations and whose simple relaxation suggestion, made in the context of daily contacts which may themselves have been reassuring, had far-reaching effects.

Mrs. R: Yes, I'd say since he's coming here his attitude towards asthma in particular . . . you know, he sometimes refused medicine and before he used to beg me for it, you know, and I think Dr. G. has a lot to do with it, you know . . . in, he, I don't know, he tells him to relax. He just tells him to relax when he blows into that peak flow. . . . And Michael takes it that he should relax all the time and he does. . . . And before, he used to cry, you know, and he doesn't cry as much as he used to when he would have an attack . . . you know, he'd get hysterical sometimes. . . . He doesn't get scared now. He's much better . . . and he's real happy. . . . Positive. Even outside—I was telling Dr. G.—he had an attack. He was playing in the yard with his little girl friend and he was so bad, Dr. P., he crawled in that front door, you know, he just crawled. He couldn't breathe, so I gave him the medicine and I told him to sit on the chair. He didn't cry or nothing. He just says, I think I need something, so I gave it to him and I went in the bedroom for something. He went out to play again, you know, and he was fine. Now if that was last year, he really would have been bad, you know, but he got over the attack with the inhaler and he went right out and played. . . . I think it's his emotions really, because when he used to cry and wouldn't relax . . . he used to get worse but he couldn't let the medicine work because he'd be crying and his mouth would stay open and the medicine . . . would just come out. . . . He wouldn't breathe the way he was supposed to.

Analytically Oriented Individual and Group Psychotherapy

The goal of analytically inspired individual and group psychotherapies is to provide the patient with insight into the dynamic meaning of his symptom and, by redirection of his impulses, to cause the symptom to become unnecessary. Thus, in Fenichel's terms, "The analyst's task is to complete analytic treatment of the pregenital structure that underlies the symptom" (1945, p. 322), and thereby provide a cure. It is assumed that asthma is a psychogenic condition and that alleviation of the psychological factors underlying the symptom will effectively erase the condition. There is much reason, however, to question the universality of this assumption. It appears to be more consistent with the evidence to view analytic treatment, or any psychotherapeutic treatment for that matter, as a means for reducing one portion of the sufficient stimuli responsible for the eruption of clinical asthma. Depending on the significance of emotional stimuli for the particular case, successful treatment may lead to minimal reduction or to virtual elimination of the clinical symptoms.

Miller and Baruch (1956) advocate the use of group psychotherapy as particularly appropriate for the treatment of asthmatics, based on their belief that the principal dynamic underlying asthma is the repression of hostility. Psychotherapy, according to these authors, must: (a) deal with the patient's affect hunger; (b) deal with his fear of rejection; (c) reduce the anxiety that motivates the repression of hostility; and (d) help him release his anger so that it hurts neither himself or others. Group psychotherapy, according to Miller and Baruch, is ideal for the accomplishment of these goals. The reason for this lies in the nature of the group process as they view it. Thus, a physically ill patient who enters the group is initially the object of the group's sympathy and concern. To the patient, this is equated with the affection he craves, so that his affect hunger is fed and his fear of rejection somewhat counteracted. With time, however, and a growing awareness on the part of the group of the emotional nature of the patient's symptoms, the initial, undue sympathy and concern are replaced by acceptance of the patient as another group member with emotional problems. From the patient's point of view, this results in his learning that he can get a reaction from others without resorting to physical symptoms. The group then assumes for him the value of the "good mother" and, as his sense of isolation decreases, his ego is strengthened. A crucial result of this increased security is a growth in the patient's ability to accept the criticism from the group and from the therapist that will, from time to time, be inevitable. He becomes aware that criticism is not always aimed at him alone, and also that in the past he has taken too much as total rejection. Simultaneously, as his fear of rejection is decreased, his anger is permitted greater awareness, and it thus becomes possible to help him admit, without undue anxiety and guilt, who the real object of this anger is. If this can be accomplished, the need for the symptom should theoretically diminish or disappear.

Although the theory underlying this approach may be questioned, the effectiveness of the approach may be evaluated in its own right. Groen and Pelser (1960) compared three groups: (a) patients treated with symptomatic medical treatment only; (b) patients treated with symptomatic therapy and ACTH; and (c) patients treated with group psychotherapy, if necessary combined with symptomatic therapy and/or ACTH. Their findings with 114, 35, and 33 subjects, respectively, showed a greater proportion of the patients in the group that received medical treatment plus group therapy to be judged "considerably improved" than in either of the other two groups, but no differences in the "clinically cured," "temporarily improved," or "worse" categories. Sclare and Crockett (1957), on the other hand, in a rather elaborate and complex study that used one experimental and six control groups, obtained negative results.

No systematic studies have yet been reported of the effects of individual psychotherapy with asthmatics, initiated either for treatment of asthma per se or for other emotional and behavioral problems. However, there are reports scattered through the clinical literature of cases in which symptomatic relief was said to be obtained by individual therapy (Abramson, 1956; Margolin, 1958; Miller & Baruch, 1953).

Hypnosis

There are basically three ways in which hypnosis may be used in the treatment of asthma. First, it can serve as an adjunct technique in psychotherapy to accelerate movement. Second, it can be used to teach the patient to relax rather than to panic when he detects the onset of symptoms. Third, it can be directed toward altering the patient's physiological reactions to precipitant stimuli directly.

The first application of hypnosis is not specific for the treatment of asthma, and will not be elaborated here for that reason. The second use of hypnosis, as a means of building confidence and reducing anxiety, has much to recommend it in cases of asthma or, more broadly, as has been pointed out by Kennedy (1957), in those instances where a condition may induce anxiety which, in turn, exacerbates the symptom. In these instances, hypnosis can be used to break the vicious cycle. It appears probable that the reports of success by using hypnosis are based for the most part on either this effect, or on what we have described earlier as a reduction in the range of effective precipitant stimuli. The evaluation of improvement has been based principally upon the subjective report of decreased symptom frequency and severity, on an increase in activity level, and on an improvement in mood (Edwards, 1960; Fry, 1957; Maher-Loughnan, MacDonald, Mason, & Fry, 1962; Smith & Burns, 1960; White, 1961).

There is some evidence in the literature that a variety of physiological changes may be induced by hypnosis (Barber, 1965), and two reports have appeared using asthmatic subjects in which some reduction in skin response to challenge tests was brought about by posthypnotic suggestion (Fry, Mason & Bruce Pearson, 1964; Mason & Black, 1958). In one instance, the suggestion regarding reduction of skin sensitivity was accompanied by a suggestion regarding similar reduction of asthma and hay fever and, by the patient's subjective report, the change in skin sensitivity paralleled overall symptom improvement.

The clinician who may be considering hypnosis for the treatment of asthma will want to know which patients are most likely to benefit from such treatment. Unfortunately, in only one study was an effort made to relate outcome of hypnotic treatment to patient variables (Maher-Loughnan et al., 1962). It appeared that patients who were younger, who had mild asthma of relatively short duration, who reported more emotional triggers and, finally, who were more easily hypnotizable, improved more. In addition, those patients who practiced autohypnosis reported greater improvement.

With regard to the selection of patients on the basis of "hypnotizability," some authors (Mason, 1960) report the usefulness of screening patients by this criterion, although others (Fry et al., 1964) suggest that a selection on this basis is unnecessary and that the willingness of the patient to cooperate is sufficient.

Institutionalization

It has long been observed that the removal of an asthmatic from his home situation often leads to symptom remission and that the return home is sometimes followed by relapse. Allergists have assumed that this is because of the presence in the home of a specific allergen. Psychiatrically oriented workers, however, have suspected the working of a psychological mechanism. Thus, Mullins (1960) in her description of the favorable effects on asthmatic children of a trip to "take the waters" at LaBourboule in France, noted that the psychological change during the trip was great, with the long lists of instructions given to the children by their parents being "cheerfully ignored." In an interesting experiment, Long, Lamont, Whipple, Bandler, Blom, Burgin, and Jessner (1958) found that dust-sensitive children who improved during hospitalization showed no clinical response when their hospital rooms were sprayed with dust taken from their own homes. Of course, the interpretation of this result is limited by the fact that only one allergen was tested and that the measures were clinical (stethoscopic). The role of allergens is thus not ruled out. More positive evidence for the beneficial effect of separation in selected cases emerges from the study by Purcell et al. (1967). On this basis, then, the clinician may wish to recommend institutionalization as the treatment of choice in chronic, severe cases where medical treatment at home has proved insufficient for adequate symptom control, and where psychological precipitants appear to be prominent. Institutionalization may result in an equally significant improvement in asthma where the patient is separated from an environment that contains allergens to which he is sensitive, or a high degree of air pollution, or any other physical agent that happens to be a potent asthmatic trigger for the particular patient. Impressions based on questionnaire and interview data suggest that, on the average, substantial improvement persists when the pediatric patient returns home (Bernstein & Purcell, 1963; Bukantz, 1962). However, a careful follow-up study of the long-term effects of institutionalization, including an appropriate control group, remains to be done in order to identify the variables associated with continued improvement or relapse.

There are certain problems associated with the recommendation for prolonged hospitalization. First, there is the simple, practical problem of limited availability of appropriate treatment facilities. In this connection, Bernstein, Allen, Kreindler, Ghory, and Wohl (1960) have described the use of part of a normal community hospital for the treatment of asthmatic children. This treatment unit was based upon the CARIH model, and the authors report encouraging results. Serious consideration should be given to the setting up of these units where the demand would justify doing so.

A second problem associated with the recommendation for separation of the patient from his family is that of convincing both the patient and his family of the wisdom of such a move. The negative feelings mobilized in parents by the threat of separation are numerous, and they include inadequacy and guilt over having exacerbated their child's asthma, shame over having an inferior child, concerns about the effects of separation on the child's adjustment as well as their own, fears that separation will change the child's feelings toward them, fear that, if no progress is made following separation, the child's future will be hopeless, since institutionalization is a last-ditch effort, and concerns about what effects the child's return home will have on the family function should the burdens of a sick child need to be resumed. A sense of desperation on the part of the family about the child's symptoms and their impact is most commonly the major motivating force. Rejection stemming from conscious or unconscious resentment may also be involved at times, with consequent guilt. As we noted earlier, it is useful to remind parents of the multiplicity of the factors that are relevant to asthma and to communicate a sense of sympathetic understanding rather than impatient condemnation.

Adequate preparation of the patient, especially in the case of a child, is equally important. Separation, as Gerard and Dukette (1954) have pointed out, should not be synonymous with total loss in the mind of the child. They have found that encouraging the child to talk about separation is a useful technique in promoting his acceptance of the move.

It is important that the separation be accomplished with the agreement of the parents and the understanding of the child that the length of separation will be determined by the institutional staff. Where this is not done, and some question is left in the mind of the child regarding the possibility of his parents removing him at an early date, he fails to adjust to his new environment, and the situation often leads to premature removal. This has been especially true in those instances where the question of premature removal exists in the mind of the parent as well. For example, we have found almost invariably, when parents relocate in Denver "for the duration of the child's residence at CARIH," that the child either fails to do well or is removed from the institute within a short time.

Precisely what the psychological factors are that bring about the favorable result of institutionalization cannot be stated with certainty. However, we are inclined to believe that, in addition to the removal of the patient from emotional tensions, the security fostered by the residential setting (Hallowitz, 1954) is an important factor. Anxiety around asthma, often induced by fearful parents, is considerably reduced in the residential setting.

Family treatment

There are two major reasons for seeing families of asthmatic patients in psychotherapy. First, it is now clear that the psychological environment of the asthmatic patient may be an important factor in determining the frequency and the severity of his asthma. It is likely to prove beneficial in the long run to treat the "environment," that is, the family, as well as the patient. Second, as we have repeatedly indicated, asthma often results in disruptive stresses for the entire family and these stresses deserve attention.

Some of the problems faced in engaging the families of asthmatics in treatment have already been alluded to, most specifically in our discussion of institutionalization. There, it will be recalled, a number of the reactions of the family to separation were described, including the guilt, shame, and anxiety that emerge when there is any hint that they are somehow responsible for the child's asthma. These feelings are not limited to families where separation is contemplated or has been accomplished, and can serve as motives for resistance to psychotherapy. Similarly, the frustrations accumulated over years of disappointed hopes for a "cure" of that child's asthma may be brought into therapy and manifested as a skeptical lack of motivation to become involved in yet another form of treatment. Where the patient's asthma has served as a factor in maintaining a neurotic adjustment in either or both of the parents, treatment will be resisted strenuously, and often ingeniously. This last point may be illustrated by our experience with the parents of a 12-year-old boy who was in residence at CARIH. Mrs. S., the boy's mother, was clearly playing the role of martyr in her family. For many years she had been torturing herself with the conviction that she was responsible both for her son's asthma, which she believed she had passed on to him hereditarily, as well as for his psychological problems, which she believed stemmed from her own panic when his asthma first appeared.

At the time of the boy's admission to CARIH, Mrs. S. had been encouraged to seek psychiatric treatment. She did, and contrary to what her therapist reported, wrote periodically to say that she was getting enormous help from treatment.

After approximately a year of the boy's residence at CARIH, both parents arrived for a summer visit and a joint interview was arranged for the purpose of discussing family treatment. As Mrs. S. had predicted, her husband was initially quite resistant. He was cynical with regard to psychotherapy in general, and could certainly see no reason for it in his case. After some discussion, during which Mrs. S. nodded to the interviewer meaningfully, satisfied that her prediction had been verified, Mr. S. was confronted directly with the fact that after his son was discharged from CARIH, he would no longer be our responsibility, but his parents! At that point Mr. S. relented. He agreed, although reluctantly, to a trial period of psychotherapy. No sooner had he done so than Mrs. S. turned to the interviewer, and, in a voice coated with innocence, asked, "Dr., I wanted to ask you, why is it that in the year I've been in treatment, I've made no progress at all?" Clearly, the threat of change in the family structure that might deprive her of her martyr's role motivated this remark which was intended as a warning and as a reinforcement for her husband's resistance.

With regard to the techniques of family treatment, Peshkin and Abramson (1957) have reported on the usefulness of a group with parents of asthmatic children. In their instance, the groups were composed of parents whose children were in residence at CARIH. The goal of the groups was to discuss the feelings of the parents around the separation as well as to explore the family conflicts that were responsible for precipitating their children's asthma. There is no reason, however, why the use of group therapy should be restricted to those families in which a separation from the child has been effected. Rather, the use of group therapy with the families of asthmatics would appear to have several basic advantages. First, the presence of the other group members can offer security to those families who fear that engaging in this therapy is tantamount to admitting responsibility for the asthma in their family. Second, there is a therapeutic gain to be obtained from the recognition that others share the fears, frustrations, and anxieties that attend having an asthmatic in the home. Third, the group sessions can be used didactically for the exchange of information regarding the care of an asthmatic, both psychologically and, where the therapist has had medical training, medically. In this connection, Peshkin and Abramson (1957) rightly point to the need for the therapist to have an adequate grasp of the fundamentals of asthma in order to deal with the realities of the family's expectations and responses to the effects of treatment. Fourth, where institutionalization is contemplated, it is often useful for parents to have the opportunity to discuss their reactions with other parents who have already had the opportunity to work through their own feelings around separation.

Behavior Therapy

Among the more recent additions to the repertoire of psychotherapeutic approaches is "behavior therapy," a group of techniques based in large part on principles of learning and conditioning (Wolpe, 1958). One of these techniques is termed "desensitization," and its goal is to train a patient to substitute an adaptive response, for example, relaxation, to a stimulus that has evoked an unadaptive one, for example, anxiety and phobic withdrawal. The relative simplicity of the technique employed, the brief time required to produce significant behavioral modifications and the impressive record of apparent success have led to experimentation with the technique with a broad variety of patients (Cf. Grossberg, 1964). Both the record of success and the theoretical explanations of the behavior therapists, however, have been subject to searching criticism (Cf. Breger & McGaugh, 1965).

In its application to the treatment of asthma, behavior therapy is closest in orientation to hypnosis, in that both seek to substitute new responses for old, for example, relaxation for anxiety, without exploring the history and the possible dynamic implications of the symptom. The major difference between what has been done with hypnosis outside of the behavior therapy framework and what has been attempted within it, is that the behavior therapists have not attempted to alter the asthmatic response per se. Rather, they have proceeded on the assumption that if the anxiety produced by a situation that eventuates in asthma can be alleviated, the asthma will similarly diminish. Thus, in the course of treatment, asthma may never be mentioned, but anxiety over sex, where asthma has become associated with sex, will be treated. For example, Cooper (1964) has reported the successful treatment of asthma in a 24-year-old woman whose attacks erupted in situations of severe stress which caused her to react with panic. In the usual fashion, a hierarchy of these situations, from the least to the most stressful, was obtained and the patient was taught to relax on command. She was then asked to imagine the least stressful situation in the hierarchy and, as soon as the first signs of anxiety appeared, she was instructed to relax. She was then taken through the entire hierarchy, learning at each stage to relax in the imagined presence of the stressful stimulus. A total of about 12 sessions were required for this phase of the treatment. The results, according to Cooper, were that during a period of 16 months post-treatment, the patient reported 4 attacks, 3 of which were stress-induced, as opposed to her reports of several attacks daily prior to treatment. A similar case was reported by Wolpe (1958), who indicated that he did not treat the asthma directly but, as in Cooper's case, dealt with the anxiety that the patient reported preceded the onset of her attacks.

Moore (1965) treated 12 asthmatic patients with either relaxation and reciprocal inhibition, relaxation with suggestions of improvement, or with relaxation alone. Reciprocal inhibition (teaching the patient to respond with relaxation specifically to stimuli associated with an asthmatic attack) was found to be the crucial factor, as it had a much greater positive effect on respiratory function than the other treatments, which did not differ from each other. All three treatments produced subjective improvement, but did not differ statistically in this respect. Subjective report and respiratory function improved together during reciprocal inhibition, while the other treatments were associated with greater subjective than objective improvement.

There is as yet relatively little literature on the use of behavior therapy in bronchial asthma, and the questions raised by Breger and McGaugh (1965) with regard to the technique more generally have yet to be answered. Nevertheless, behavior therapy appears to offer promise of a relatively simple and economic approach to the treatment of what is a distressful, complex, and puzzling symptom.

Tranquilizers

We have seen that anxiety may play at least three roles in the asthmatic syndrome. First, it may combine with other stimuli (for example, pollen) to provoke an attack, or it may provoke respiratory changes or asthma directly. Second, it may increase the distress or severity of an ongoing attack. And third, anxiety may be the result of the stress that the symptom imposes on the patient. Clearly, these three roles can interact to give rise to the "vicious cycle" described above. However, for purposes of describing the application of tranquilizers in the treatment of asthma, the separation is a useful one. Tranquilizers have been considered useful for the following reasons: (a) preventing the onset of attacks by reducing the emotional factors contributing to them (Friedman, 1963; McGovern, Oskaragoz, Barkin, Haywood, McEllheney, & Hensel, 1960; McGovern, Haywood, Thomas, & Fernandez, 1963; Thomas, 1962); (b) reducing the complicating panic that may accompany the onset of symptoms (Baum, Schotz, Gumpel, & Osgood, 1957); and (c) treating the emotional turmoil often observed in asthmatics, regardless of whether it affects the symptom status of the patient (Eisenberg, 1957). Thus, Eisenberg (1957) has reported both behavioral and asthmatic improvement with chlorpromazine and meprobamate, and Tuft (1959) indicates that prochlorperazine permitted reduction of steroid drugs in a majority of cases studied.

There are yet two other uses to which tranquilizers have been put, namely, to control the hyperstimulant effects of drugs such as ephedrine-theophylline (Fond, 1961) and to control the anxiety of children during the initial period of institutionalization (Tuft, 1959).

The tranquilizers, then, may be effective in treating some asthmatics. For example, Dietiker, Purcell, and Chai (1966) found, on the basis of preliminary data, that hydroxyzine pamoate (vistaril) had some beneficial effect in 16 of the 19 patients studied, but that the effect was more noticeable in those patients who reported emotional precipitants of asthma. However, tranquilizers should be used with great caution for several reasons. First, it is often difficult to achieve adequate tranquilization without at the same time depressing respiratory function (Baum et al., 1957). The occasionally fatal effects of morphine and barbiturates, which depress the respiratory center, decreasing alveolar ventilation and producing respiratory acidosis, are well known. Second, one must balance the gain to be made from using tranquilizers in a particular patient against the danger that "a happy, sedated, tranquil patient may not heed the warning signs of disease and thus delay important diagnosis and treatment" (Eisenberg, 1957, p. 934). Third, although the tranquilizers may be helpful in controlling the panic observed in status asthmaticus, they should be used guardedly "lest an already sedated, weakened patient be relaxed into a deepening sleep from which he never recovers" (Eisenberg, 1957, p. 936). At CARIH, the preference is to avoid the use of tranquilizers in status cases. The attitudes conveyed by the staff to the patients are relied on to do the work of calming and reassuring the patient.

SUMMARY

Asthma is conceptualized as a symptom that arises from an overreactivity of the respiratory apparatus (probably on a hereditary basis) to a multiplicity of stimuli, for example, infectious, allergic, and psychological. The prime psychological stimuli are affective states associated with major endocrine and autonomic system alterations as well as with certain respiratory behaviors (for example, crying, and hyperventilation) all of which may lead to the clinical symptom of asthma. However, it is clear that the simple presence of emotional disturbance is not sufficient evidence of its etiologic relevance, since disturbance often results from stresses imposed by the symptom.

In assessing the relative significance of emotional states to the initiation and perpetuation of asthma attacks, emphasis is placed on a specially designed, detailed interview rather than on standard psychologic tests. The focus is on the patient's (and/or parents') perceptions of the immediate antecedents of attacks and on the patient's symptom response to separation from significant figures in his life. A scale for evaluating the patient's allergic predisposition may also be helpful.

Once emotional factors have been judged relevant, psychological treatment may be oriented toward prevention of attacks or modification of the patient's attitude toward his symptoms. The latter sometimes leads to substantially greater social and occupational effectiveness without significant objective symptom change, or with a reduction in the severity but not the frequency of attacks. A variety of psychologically oriented interventions, for example, psychoanalysis, group therapy, behavior therapy, and tranquilizers, have been associated with partial success in the treatment of asthma. At this time there is little basis for selecting a particular treatment over any other, with the possible exception of institutionalization for patients whose symptoms are resistant to all conventional treatment in their home community. Systematic clinical research is much needed to evaluate the effectiveness of different psychological procedures in controlling asthma among different, but carefully defined, classes of asthmatic patients.

REFERENCES

Abramson, H. A. Psychic factors in allergy and their treatment. *Ann. Allergy*, 1956, **14**, 145–151.

Barber, T. X. Physiological effects of "hypnotic suggestion." *Psychol. Bull.*, 1965, **4**, 201–222.

Baum, G. L., Schotz, S. A., Gumpel, R. C., & Osgood, Catherine. The role of chlorpromazine in the treatment of bronchial asthma and chronic pulmonary emphysema. *Dis. Chest*, 1957, **32**, 574–575.

Beecher, H. K. *Measurement of subjective responses.* London: Oxford Univer. Press, 1959.

Bernstein, L. J., Allen, J. E., Kreindler, L., Ghory, J. E., & Wohl, T. H. A community approach to intractable asthma: A new concept in treatment. *Pediatrics*, 1960, **4**, 586–595.

Bernstein, L., & Purcell, K. Institutional treatment of asthmatic children. In H. I. Schneer (Ed.), *The asthmatic child.* New York: Harper & Row, 1963.

Block, Jeanne., Jennings, P. H., Harvey, Elinor., & Simpson, Elaine. Interaction between allergic potential and psychopathology in childhood asthma. *Psychosom. Med.*, 1964, **26**, 307–320.

Breger, L., & McGaugh, J. L. Critique and reformulation of "learning theory" approaches to psychotherapy and neurosis. *Psychol. Bull.*, 1965, **5**, 338–358.

Bukantz, S. C. Residential treatment and study of the intractable asthmatic child. *Allergol.*, 1962, 402–416.

Criep, L. H. *Clinical immunology and allergy*. New York: Grune & Stratton, 1962.

Cooper, A. J. A case of bronchial asthma treated by behavior therapy. *Behav. Res. Ther.*, 1964, **1**, 351–356.

Dekker, E., & Groen, J. Reproducible psychogenic attacks of asthma. *J. psychosom. Res.*, 1956, **1**, 58–67.

Dekker, E., Pelser, H. E., & Groen, J. Conditioning as a cause of asthmatic attacks. *J. psychosom. Res.*, 1957, **2**, 97–108.

Dietiker, K. E., Purcell, K., of Chai H. The effect of hydroxizine pamoate (vistaril) on asthma: distinctions among asthmatic children. *Unpublished data*, 1966.

Edwards, G. E. Hypnotic treatment of asthma: Real and illusory results. *Brit. med. J.*, 1960, **5197**, 492–497.

Eisenberg, B. C. Role of tranquilizing drugs in allergy. *J.A.M.A.*, 1957, **163**, 934–937.

Faulkner, W. B. Influence of suggestion on the size of the bronchial lumen. *Northwest Med.*, 1941, **40**, 367–368.

Feinchel, O. *The psychoanalytic theory of neurosis*. New York: Norton, 1945.

Fond, I. A. Hydroxyzine as a component of anti-asthmatic treatment. *Clin. Med.*, 1961, **8**, 1525–1528.

Freeman, Edith H., Feingold, B. F., Schlesinger, K., & Gorman, F. J. Psychological variables in allergic disorders: A review. *Psychosom. Med.*, 1964, **26**, 543–575.

Friedman, H. T. Librium-theophylline-ephedrine compound in bronchial asthma. *Ann. Allergy*, 1963, **21**, 163–167.

French, T. M., & Alexander, F. Psychogenic factors in bronchial asthma. *Psychosom. Med. Monogr.*, 1941, **4**, No. 1.

Fry, A. The scope for hypnosis in general practice. *Brit. med. J.*, 1957, **1**, 1323–1328.

Fry, L., Mason, A. A., & Bruce Pearson, R. S. Effect of hypnosis on allergic skin responses in asthma and hay fever. *Brit. med. J.*, 1964, **1**, 1145–1148.

Gantt, W. H. *Experimental basis of neurotic behavior*. New York: Harper & Brothers, 1944.

Gerard, Margaret W., & Dukette, Rita. Techniques for preventing separation trauma in child placement. *Amer. J. Orthopsychiat.*, 1954, **24**, 111–127.

Gottlieb, P. M. Changing mortality in bronchial asthma. *J.A.M.A.*, 1964, **187**, 276–280.

Groen, J. J., & Pelser, H. E. Experiences with, and results of, group psychotherapy in patients with bronchial asthma. *J. psychosom. Res.*, 1960, **4**, 191–205.

Grossberg, J. M. Behavior therapy: A review. *Psychol. Bull.*, 1964, **2**, 73–88.

Hahn, W. W. Autonomic responses of asthmatic children. *Psychosom. Med.*, 1966, **28**, 323–332.

Hallowitz, D. Residential treatment of chronic asthmatic children. *Amer. J. Orthopsychiat.*, 1954, **24**, 576–587.

Hamburg, D. A. Plasma and corticosteroid plasma levels in naturally occurring psychological stresses. In S. Korey (Ed.), *Ultrastructure and metabolism of the nervous system*. Baltimore: Williams & Wilkins, 1962.

Handlon, J. H., Wadeson, R. W., Fishman, J. R., Sacher, E. J., Hamburg, D. A., & Mason, J. W. Psychological factors lowering plasma 17-hydroxicortico-steroid concentration. *Psychosom. Med.*, 1962, **24**, 535–541.

Herxheimer, H. G. Induced asthma in man. *Lancet*, 1951, **1**, 1337–1341.

Holmes, T H., Treuting, T., & Wolff, H. Life situations, emotions and nasal disease. In H. G. Wolff (Ed.), *Life stress and bodily disease*. Proceedings of The Assoc. for Res. in Nerv. & Ment. Dis., Baltimore: Waverly Press, 1950.

Kennedy, A. The medical use of hypnotism. *Brit. med. J.*, 1957, **1**, 1317–1320.

Knapp, P. H. Emotional expression—past and present. In P. H. Knapp (Ed.), *Expression of the emotions in man*. New York Univer. Press, 1963.

Knapp, P. H., & Nemetz, S. J. Acute bronchial asthma: I. Concomitant depression and excitement, and varied antecedent patterns in 406 attacks. *Psychosom. Med.*, 1960, **22**, 42–56.

Liddell, H. The influence of experimental neuroses on respiratory function. In H. Abramson (Ed.), *Somatic and psychiatric treatment of asthma*. Baltimore: Williams & Wilkins, 1951.

Lipton, E., Steinschneider, A., & Richmond, J. B. Psychophysiologic disorders in children. In Lois W. Hoffman & M. L. Hoffman (Eds.), *Review of child development research*. Vol. 2. New York: Russell Sage Foundation, 1966.

Long, R. T., Lamont, J. H., Whipple, Babette, Bandler, Louise., Blom, G. E., Burgin, L., & Jessner, Lucie. A psychosomatic study of allergic and emotional factors in children with asthma. *Amer. J. Psychiat.*, 1958, **114**, 890–899.

McGovern, J. P., Haywood, T. J., Thomas, O. C., & Fernandez, A. A. Studies with a benzodiazepine derivative in various allergic diseases. *Psychosomatics*, 1963, **4**, 203–206.

McGovern, J. P., Oskaragoz, K., Barkin, G., Haywood, T., McEllheney, T., & Hensel, A. E. Studies of chlordiazepoxide in various allergic diseases. *Ann. Allergy*, 1960, **18**, 1193–1199.

Maher-Loughnan, G. P., MacDonald, N., Mason, A. A., & Fry, L. Controlled trial of hypnosis in the symptomatic treatment of asthma. *Brit. med. J.*, 1962, **11**, 371–376.

Margolin, S. G. On some principles of therapy. *Amer. J. Psychiat.*, 1958, **114**, 1087–1096.

Mason, A. A. Hypnosis and suggestion in the treatment of allergic phenomena. *Acta Allergy*, 1960, Suppl. VII, 332–338.

Mason, A. A., & Black, S. Allergic skin responses abolished under treatment of asthma and hay fever by hypnosis. *Lancet*, 1958, **1**, 877–880.

Miller, H., & Baruch, Dorothy W. Psychotherapy in acute attacks of bronchial asthma. *Ann. Allergy*, 1953, **11**, 438–444.

Miller, H., & Baruch, Dorothy, W. Allergies. In S. R. Slavson (Ed.), *The field of group psychotherapy*. New York: International Universities Press, 1956.

Moore, N. Behavior therapy in bronchial asthma: a controlled study. *J. Psychosom. Res.*, 1965, **9**, 257–276.

Mullins, Ann. Asthmatic children take the waters. *Lancet*, 1960, **21**, 440–441.

Mustacchi, P., Lucia, S. P., & Jassy, L. Bronchial asthma: Patterns of morbidity and mortality in United States. *Calif. Med.*, 1962, **96**, 196–200.

Neuhaus, E. C. Personality study of asthmatic and cardiac children. *Psychosom. Med.*, 1958, **3**, 181–186.

Ottenberg, P., Stein, M., Lewis, J., & Hamilton, C. Learned asthma in the guinea pig. *Psychosom. Med.*, 1958, **20**, 395–400.

Owen, Freya W. Patterns of respiratory disturbance in asthmatic children evoked by the stimulus of the mother's voice. *Acta Psychotherapeutica et Psychosomatica*, 1964, **2**, 228–241.

Peshkin, M. M., & Abramson, H. A. Psychosomatic group psychotherapy with parents of children having intractable asthma. *Ann. Allergy*, 1957, **17**, 344–349.

Purcell, K. Distinctions between subgroups of asthmatic children: Children's perceptions of events associated with asthma. *Pediatrics*, 1963, **31**, 486–494.

Purcell, K. Critical appraisal of psychosomatic studies of asthma. *N.Y.S. J. Med.*, 1965, **65**, 2107–2109.

Purcell, K., Bernstein, L., & Bukantz, S. C. A preliminary comparison of rapidly remitting and persistently "steroid dependent" asthmatic children. *Psychosom. Med.*, 1961, **23**, 305–310.

Purcell, K., Brady, K., & Chai, H. Effect of experimental separation from the family on asthma in children. Paper read at Sympos. on Res. in Asthma, Denver, April, 1967.

Purcell, K., & Bukantz, S. C. Distinctions between rapidly remitting and steroid dependent children: Incidence of chest abnormality as determined by X-ray. Unpublished data.

Purcell, K., & Metz, J. R. Distinctions between subgroups of asthmatic children: Some parent attitude variables related to age of onset of asthma. *J. psychosom. Res.*, 1962, **6**, 251–253.

Purcell, K., Turnbull, J. W., & Bernstein, L. Distinctions between subgroups of asthmatic children: Psychological test and behavior rating comparisons. J. psychosom. Res., 1962, **6**, 283–291.

Rackeman, F. H., & Edwards, M. D. Medical progress: Asthma in children: follow-up study of 688 patients after 20 years. *New England J. Med.*, 1952, **246**, 815–858.

Ratner, B., & Silberman, A. E. Critical analysis of the hereditary concept of allergy. *J. Allergy*, 1953, **24**, 371–378.

Reinberg, A., Chata, D., & Sidi, E. Nocturnal asthma attacks and their relationship to the circadian adrenal cycle. *J. Allergy*, 1963, **34**, 323–330.

Schiffer, Clara G., & Hunt, Eleanor P. Illness among children. *Children's Bureau, U.S. Dept. of Hlth. & Welf.*, 1963.

Schwartz, M. Heredity in bronchial asthma: A clinical and genetic study of 191 asthma probands. *Acta Allergol.*, 1952, **5** (Suppl. 2), 1–288.

Sclare, A. B., & Crockett, J. A. Group psychotherapy in bronchial asthma. *J. psychosom. Res.*, 1957, **2**, 157–171.

Smith, J. M., & Burns, C. L. C. The treatment of asthmatic children by hypnotic suggestion. *Brit. J. Dis. Chest*, 1960, **54**, 78–81.

Smyth, F. S. Allergy. In E. L. Holt, R. McIntosh, & H. L. Barnett (Eds.), *Pediatrics*. (13th ed.) New York: Appleton-Century, Crofts, 1962.

Stein, M. Etiology and mechanisms in the development of asthma. In J. H. Nodine & J. H. Moyer (Eds.), *Psychosomatic medicine*. Philadelphia: Lea & Febiger, 1962.

Stevenson, I. Variations in the secretion of bronchial mucus during periods of life stress. In H. G. Wolff (Ed.), *Life stress and bodily disease*. Proceedings of the Assoc. for Res. in Nerv. & Ment. Dis., Baltimore: Waverly Press, 1950.

Stevenson, I., & Ripley, H. S. Variations in respiration and in respiratory symptoms during changes in emotion. *Psychosom. Med.*, 1952, **14**, 476–490.

Thomas, J. W. Resprium in the treatment of bronchial asthma and respiratory allergy. *Ann. Allergy*, 1962, **20**, 789–793.

Treuting, T. F., & Ripley, H. S. Life situations, emotions and bronchial asthma. *J. nerv. & ment. Dis.*, 1948, **108**, 380–396.

Tuft, H. S. Prochlorperazine as an aid in the treatment of bronchial asthma. *Ann. Allergy*, 1959, **17**, 224–229.

Weiss, J. H. Mood states associated with asthma in children. *J. psychosom. Res.*, 1966, **10**, 267–273.

White, H. C. Hypnosis in bronchial asthma. *J. psychosom. Res.*, 1961, **5**, 272–279.

Wolpe, J. *Psychotherapy by reciprocal inhibition*. Stanford: Stanford Univer. Press, 1958.

Chapter 25

Headache

DONALD J. DALESSIO.

PAIN MECHANISMS

The nature of pain is a subject of continuous controversy in medicine. Pain is the primary symptom of most diseases and, as such, is of concern to all physicians. Problems related to pain and its relief cut across narrow boundaries of specialties or categories of disease. The presence or absence of pain has been the impetus for some systems of philosophy, aberrations of human behavior, and for not a little of the world's literature. Many penal codes are based in part on pain or the threat of pain as punishment for wrongdoing.

Furthermore, there are at least two attributes of pain that tend to differentiate it from other subjective experiences associated with ordinary sensation and perception, such as touch, vision, hearing, and the like. The first attribute is related to the significant emotional experience which usually occurs with pain or threats of pain. This is to a considerable extent related to personality variables which include fear, previous experience, and previous conditioning. The second attribute is closely related to the first, this being the proposition that pain is a subjective sensation peculiar to the individual which, at least in humans, requires an introspective report from the subject experiencing pain. This latter property of pain makes its precise measurement uncertain. Indeed, when dealing with clinical situations, it is often difficult to extract from the patient a reasonably close description of pain, which can be correlated with descriptions of pain from others. Pain may not always be noxious, and some types of pain, especially the ones associated with sexual perversion, may in perverted individuals be experienced as pleasure. Pavlov (1927) subjected dogs to shocks, burns, or cuts, associated with the presentation of food, and noted that the dogs could be trained to respond to these traumatic stimuli as signals for food without showing any signs of pain. Beecher (1946) questioned 215 American soldiers who were wounded at the Anzio landings concerning the intensity of their pain. Only 24 percent complained seriously of pain; the remainder were relatively comfortable. One may conclude from these observations that in some manner the brain is able to prevent noxious stimuli from producing pain, or is sometimes able to subvert these stimuli into a nonpainful experience, such as eating.

It is generally agreed that patterning of input is essential to the production of pain. The excessive peripheral stimulation which occurs when one hits one's thumb with a hammer quite obviously evokes pain of an acute nature. In addition, there are specific neural mechanisms which account for the summation of stimuli in clinical situations of chronic pain, where the provoking stimulus may not be so apparent. According to Livingston (1943) reverberating circuits in spinal internuncial pools can be set off by normally benign afferent input which could thereafter be interpreted centrally as painful. It is proposed that a specialized central system prevents this critical summation from occurring, in that it inhibits synaptic transmission of slowly conducting nerve fibers which ordinarily subserve pain. One must, therefore, evoke the dual concepts of central summation of pain and central inhibition of pain to explain pain as it occurs clinically. Melzack and Wall (1965) have modified this theory to propose that the substantia gelatinosa of the dorsal horn of the spinal cord functions as a gate control system that modulates the afferent stimuli before they are transmitted centrally. They suggest further that this gate control system may also serve to activate systems responsible for response to stimuli and perception.

Much information related to the study of pain has been obtained from the study of analgesic agents of varying types. It has been known for some time that receptors in the skin, termed nociceptors (responding to tissue damaging stimuli) have both myelinated and nonmyelinated afferent fibers. Not all nonmyelinated fibers (C-fibers) are specific for nociceptive stimuli, since it has been shown that C-fibers will respond to mechanical stimuli of only a few mg. of skin pressure, which does not cause pain (Iggo, 1960). It is important, therefore, to avoid the concept that C-fibers are specific in peripheral nerves for pain. Furthermore, it has been found that fluid obtained from areas where there has been tissue destruction, as in a blister which forms after burning, contains a pain-producing substance, which also has vasodilator and vasopermeability-increasing activity (Armstrong et al., 1957). It is suggested that this substance is a vasodilator polypeptide, related to the polypeptide bradykinin (Rocha e Silva et al., 1949). This polypeptide may be a terminal portion of the gamma globulin molecule from which it can be liberated or separated by proteolytic enzymes. It is suggested that injury to tissue will in some way activate an enzyme that leads to the formation of bradykinin (Lasagna, & Werner, 1966). Lim (1966) have injected bradykinin into the femoral artery of dogs, and evoked a consistent pain reaction. This same type of pain reaction can be elicited by the intraperitoneal injection of bradykinin in humans. Bradykinin does not cause pain when given subcutaneously, intramuscularly, or intravenously. By using this information, Lim has been able to show that the pain reaction is completely absent when aspirin was administered prior to the bradykinin injection. These data suggest that salicylates such as aspirin and related compounds exert a peripheral analgesic effect, at least during these experimental situations. When aspirin is given directly to the brain via the brachiocephalic artery, intraperitoneal pain produced by bradykinin is not blocked. On this basis, Lim suggests that a peripheral block of impulse transmission from chemoreceptors which mediate pain is produced by aspirin. Sodium salicylate, aminopyrine, and phenylbutazone are also found to act in this manner (Lim, 1966).

Chapman et al. (1959) have demonstrated that antidromic dorsal root activity plays some role in the liberation of vasodilator polypeptides of the bradykinin type. They suggest that neurogenically induced vasodilatation may represent a direct contribution of the nervous system to the inflammatory reaction. It is also evident that interactions within the spinal cord may play a great role in the central perception of pain. Hagbarth and Finer (1963) have studied the flexor response in man by recording electromyographically the response in the vastus medialis muscle when pain stimuli have been applied at different skin territories of the same limb. The flexor reflex consists of the contraction of the limb at the ankle, knee, and hip, when noxious stimulation is applied, in order to withdraw the limb from the site of noxious stimulation. This is an integrated and organized reflex, which serves as a withdrawal response. These investigators were able to show that under hypnotic analgesia, inhibition is evoked, and no excitatory activity follows. This illustrates that painful flexor reflexes in man are subject to modulation from higher centers.

Chapman et al. (1959) have demonstrated changes in tissue vulnerability induced during hypnotic suggestion. Following standard amounts of noxious stimulation of the forearm during hypnosis, decreased inflammatory reaction and tissue damage were observed when the suggestion was made that the arm was insensitive and numb, as compared to the reaction and tissue damage of the other arm which was suggested to be normally sensitive. When the suggestion was made that the forearm was tender, increased inflammatory reaction and tissue damage was observed, as compared with the normally sensitive arm. It was suggested, on the basis of these studies, that neural activity can alter inflammatory reactions in peripheral tissues.

Narcotics exert a suppressive action on spinal reflexes, probably by augmenting supraspinal cord reflexes. Reflex suppression by morphine is greater when the spinal cord is intact than when it is transected (Honde et al., 1951). Spinal cord reflexes can also be diminished by using medications that are not analgesics in the usual sense, especially anticonvulsants. Recent work on the use of the anticonvulsant carbamazepine in the well-determined pain syndrome tic douloureux suggests that inhibition of spinal cord reflexes may provide analgesia (Dalessio, 1966). In supprt of this hypothesis is the remarkable protective effect produced by carbamazepine in animals with convulsions evoked by strychnine. According to Eccles (1964) strychnine inhibits post-synaptic cortical inhibition and so promotes excitation. Strychnine will increase nervous excitation generally, with subsequent profound responses to minimal stimuli, as in human or animal strychnine poisoning. In animals, such as randomly bred mice, the intraperitoneal injection of 4 mg per kilogram of strychnine will evoke fatal convulsions uniformly within five minutes. If carbamazepine is given in a dose of 100 mg/kg intraperitoneally fifteen minutes before the injection of strychnine, these convulsions will be prevented, and all of the mice will survive the acute experiment. If the dose of carbamazepine is reduced to 50 mg/kg, 40 percent of the mice will exhibit tonic and extensor convulsions, although they will be short-lived, and again all of the mice will survive the acute experiment. It is suggested that carbamazepine blocks the effects of strychnine at the synaptic level in an unknown manner; it may be considered *as if* it were augmenting post-synaptic inhibition. Thus, tic douloureux, an extremely unpleasant pain syndrome, which will be described in detail later, may be manifested by a state of abnormal reactivity of the spinal trigeminal nuclei, related to a decreased or defective central integrative system that regulates sensory input. Tic douloureux has been proposed as a model for this type of syndrome, wherein the inability of the brain to suppress sensory input from normal or minimally damaged peripheral tissues evokes severe pain.

This latter proposition that pain is related to abnormal spinal reflex activity leads naturally to considerations of the central handling of pain in the brain. Here the dual functions in the somato-sensory system of man should be emphasized. One component of this system is represented by the lemniscal system, which is a precise, topographic system of somatic sensation which involves the peripheral nerves, the first order afferent fibers of the dorsal columns of the spinal cord, the neural elements of the medial lemniscus, and the cells of the ventrobasal nuclear complex of the thalamus and of the post central region of the cerebral cortex. A second, phylogenetically older system, designated as the antero-lateral system, originates in the dorsal horn of the spinal cord. Its spinothalamic component ascends to the thalamus partly to its midline nuclei, and from there to the posterior group nuclei which, in turn, project to the cortex. The neurons in this latter pathway have properties that are different from those in the lemniscal system, according to Poggio and Mountcastle (1960). Nearly 60 percent of the cells in the area of the posterior group nuclei responded only to noxious stimuli, but their receptive fields were very large, were not topographically organized, and often lacked specificity. It is suggested that medications such as narcotics exert their effects primarily on the spinal thalamic projection system, and thus produce their pain-alleviating effects. There are further experimental studies in animals, which support this concept, that the lemniscal and spinothalamic systems differ in their pharmacologic reactivity. Melzack and Haugen (1957) produced neural responses by stimulating the tooth pulp of cats; these neural responses appeared both in the lemniscal and in the spinothalamic systems. It was shown in these experiments that nitrous oxide abolished selectively the response from the lemniscal system only. These pharmacologic differences may relate to differences in the size of the fiber tracts.

Antidepressants of the tricyclic type have been employed in the management of chronic pain syndromes, especially headache. (Lance & Curran, 1964) These agents may decrease pain by altering central appreciation of the quality or intensity of pain, as it occurs in the depressed patient. As a consequence of his depression, the depressed patient may misinterpret afferent stimuli at the cortical level and appreciate pain when, in fact, he should not. The structural relationship of the tricyclic antidepressants to anticonvulsants such as carbamazepine is striking (See Figure 25.1). These agents may be of great aid in the management of various clinical pain states, where they provide a more satisfactory method of treatment than do the narcotics.

Thus we observe that pain is an integrated experience which is dependent on an intact and functioning central nervous system involving the peripheral nerves, the spinal cord, and the brain. Psychological factors such as past experience, attention, and emotion may influence pain response and perception greatly. It is to be emphasized that the quantitative measurement of pain is hazardous, that pain is an individual perception which the perceiver may communicate only poorly, and that laboratory models of experimental pain may be difficult to interpret, especially in terms of clinical situations wherein analgesia is sought.

THE NATURE OF HEADACHE

Headache is a unique symptom in medicine. It has been termed the most common complaint of civilized man. Since headache is not often caused by organic disease, we may infer that headache represents an inappropriate reaction on the part of the individual, either to a form of environmental stimulus, or to a mood disorder, in the great majority of instances. Nonetheless, headache may also be the presenting complaint of catastrophic illnesses such as brain tumor, cerebral hemorrhage, or meningitis, among others, and to ignore the symptoms in this context is to risk the life of the patient. Headache may be equally intense whether its source

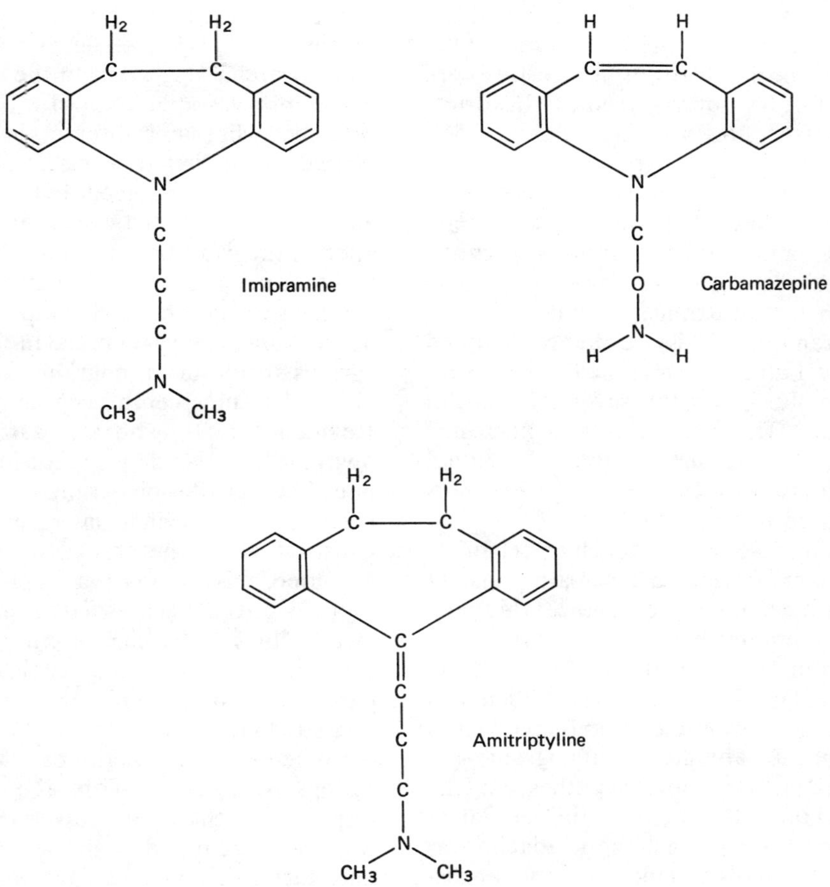

Figure 25.1 Tricyclic compounds useful as analgesics.

is benign or malignant. The problem is compounded further by the difficulties of studying the brain and its appendages which, encased in the bony fortress of the skull, resist the usual efforts of diagnosis and force one to rely on peripheral methods of investigation.

The history of headache is almost as old as medicine itself. In early times, especially before Christ, allusions to pain in the head and face were usually confused. This is not surprising, since concepts regarding the function of the brain itself were poorly developed. For example, Aristotle could find no better use for the brain than to cool the blood, "keeping the heart cool enough for optimal mental activity." (The brain itself was insensitive) . . . "and without mental activity."

By the end of the first century AD, however, a form of headache recognizable as migraine was reported by Aretaeus of Cappadocia. He described a unilateral and paroxysmal headache with associated nausea which occurred at regular intervals, and which he termed "heterocrania." The reader will find his description of this topic remarkably accurate; the English translation of this work is available in several medical historical libraries (see, for instance, Adams, 1856). Galen accepted this type of headache as constituting a clinical entity, terming it hemicrania about a half century later. Thereafter the name was altered through several different forms. The term was adopted by the Romans and translated into Latin as "hemicranium." This was later corrupted into low Latin ("hemigranea") and eventually evolved into the several European languages. The French term "migraine" gained ascendancy in the eighteenth century, although as late as 1873 some English authors still insisted on "megrim."

The chronology of headache mechanism or etiology provides a fascinating insight into the development of medical thinking. Aretaeus limited his clinical writing to a description of the headache only, and did not speculate on its etiology. Galen was concerned with etiology and evolved a theory of the pathogenesis of migraine that was based on the humoral hypothesis and the effects of black bile on the brain (see Galen, 1826). He believed that the headache was generated by disturbances in several disparate parts of the body, which then dispatched vapors containing harmful substances to the brain. Galen was much impressed with the nausea and vomiting that may often accompany the migraine attack. He postulated a sympathetic connecting system between the stomach and the brain.

Caelius Aurelianus (A.D. 400) attributed head pain to chills, exposure to the sun, or prolonged vigilance (see Aurelianus, 1547).

During the Dark Ages, little original research or interest in migraine evolved. The theories of the older writers were usually quoted without question, and occasionally they were embellished and elaborated to absurd degrees.

Charles Lepois (1714) published an autobiographical account of migraine that was notable primarily for its detailed description of his own headaches. They were frontoparietal in nature and often terminated with vomiting. Lepois proposed that his headaches were related to alterations in climate, especially the appearance of west winds and rainstorms.

Wepfer published his observations on headache in 1776. He suggested that head pain was related to stasis of the blood with associated vasodilatation. In 1783 Tissot produced what some observers have characterized as the first truly scientific study of migraine. Tissot believed that the stomach and the intestinal tract were of great importance in the causation of a migraine attack, and that nervous irritation passed from the stomach to the brain. He emphasized that neuronal factors were crucial in eliciting the various symptoms of migraine.

In the nineteenth century, DuBois-Reymond (1860) who also suffered from migraine, suggested that headache was produced by an irritation of the cervical sympathetic nerves, which in turn evoked a constriction of the cranial blood vessels. He termed this disorder a vasomotor neurosis. In 1873, Liveing published his monograph on the subject (still using the term "Megrim"). Liveing stressed the episodic and paroxysmal nature of the disorder, and related migraine to epilepsy.

In the early years of this century, investigations concerned with the abnormal responses of the blood vessels in migraine were prominent and, in this setting, ergotamine tartrate became available for study and therapy. Thus, in 1938, Graham and Wolff published their classic article on the mechanism of migraine headache and the action of ergotamine tartrate which showed that the administration of ergotamine reduced the amplitude of the pulsations of the temporal artery in patients with headache, and that this effect was associated with a decrease in head pain. With this paper, the modern era of headache research was initiated.

It is difficult to discuss headache mechanisms without attempting to separate headache into its many and varied types. There have been admirable headache classifications proposed before. The present effort attempts to separate headache into three main groups, rather than listing a series of disparate headache syndromes which may tax the memory. It is proposed that all headaches be classed as either vascular, or related to muscle contraction, or to traction and inflammatory forces (see Table 25.1).

It should be stated at the onset that much of the material to be presented was the work of Dr. Harold Wolff and his associates which was published in 1963. Indeed, a considerable part of the terminology of the classification that is used here represents Dr. Wolff's precision in medical observation and description.

In a series of anatomic studies, performed for the most part on patients prepared for neurological surgery, Ray and Wolff (1940) showed that the pain sensitive structures of the head include the skin of the scalp and its blood supply and appendages, the head and neck muscles, the great venous sinuses and their tributaries, parts of the dura at the base of the brain, the dural arteries, the intracerebral arteries, at least, the fifth, sixth, and seventh cranial nerves, and the cervical nerves. The cranium, the brain parenchyma, much of the dura and pia mater, the ependymal lining of the ventricles and the choroid plexuses were not sensitive to pain.

In general, pain pathways for structures above the tentorium cerebelli are contained in the trigeminal nerve, and pain that is referred from these structures is usually appreciated in the frontal, temporal, and parietal regions of the skull. Pain pathways for structures below the tentorium cerebelli are contained especially in the glossopharyngeal and vagus nerves, as well as the upper cervical spinal roots. Pain referred from these structures is usually appreciated in the occipital region of the head.

Vascular Headache—Classic Migraine

This is the most troublesome form of headache, which may be considered as a symptom complex, since vascular headache represents a whole spectrum of body alterations, of which headache is only a single part. Classic migraine is considered the prototype of this form of headache. Thus, in addition to headache which may last from a few hours to a few days, one may also note photophobia, nausea, vomiting, constipation, or diarrhea, weight gain and fluid retention followed by diuresis, scotomata or field defects, paresthesias or defects in motility, vertigo, and elevation of the blood pressure. Many of these alterations provide the basis for migraine equivalents. These equivalents are paroxysmal, recurrent symptom complexes, occurring in patients with a previous history or family history of migraine, an absence of symptoms between attacks, or a replacement of headaches by the equivalent syndrome; they may be relieved with appropriate therapy, often similar to that used to abort the headache attack itself. Migraine

Table 25.1 Classification of Headaches

Vascular Headache	Muscle Contraction Headache	Traction and Inflammatory Headaches
A. Classic migraine	A. Cervical osteoarthritis, chronic myositis	A. Mass lesions
B. Cluster (histamine)	B. Depressive equivalents, conversion reactions	B. Arteritis, infections
C. Hemiplegic migraine		C. Diseases of the eye, ear, nose, throat, and teeth
D. Opthaloplegic migraine		D. Cranial neuritis and neuralgias
E. Toxic vascular		

equivalents may take many forms, and involve the abdomen, chest, pelvis, eye, cerebral cortex (hemiplegic), and perhaps other organs. It has been estimated that migraine equivalents may occur in approximately 20 percent of subjects with migraine. This topic has recently been reviewed (Catino, 1965).

Our emphasis here will be on the headache phase of migraine, however. In classic migraine, preheadache and nonpainful sensory experiences precede the headache phase. Most often, they are expressed as scotomata or field defects. Rarely paresthesias and defects in motility may occur, usually unilateral. These phenomena are usually attributed to intracranial vasoconstriction. It has been demonstrated that the cranial arteries of patients with migraine are especially reactive; any one of a number of stimuli may set off a migraine attack, with the vasoconstrictor phase representing the initial vector of vascular activity (Ostfeld & Wolff, 1958). In some patients the prodromal symptoms may be of unusual intensity and complexity, especially in young women. In this situation, thought by Bickerstaff (1961) to be related to migraine involving the basilar-vertebral arterial system, visual loss and scotomata may involve both sides of the field of vision, with associated vertigo, dysarthria, loss of consciousness and bilateral peripheral symptoms and signs. In at least one episode of this sort, death following migraine has been reported (Wolff & Quest, 1964).

The initial phase of vasoconstriction is followed by vasodilatation, which provokes the headache phase of the migraine attack. The vessels so involved become painful, with the pain usually described as aching and throbbing, often coincident with the pulse beat, and sometimes relieved by extra arterial pressure. After a period of vasodilatation, a sterile inflammatory reaction begins about the vessel wall itself, so that edema and inflammation of the affected arterial wall and the surrounding tissues may occur. It has been demonstrated by Chapman and his colleagues (1960) that a polypeptide substance accumulates locally in the tissues at the site of headache and contributes to a sterile, local inflammatory reaction. Wolff and Chapman have termed this substance "neurokinin" to emphasize its neural origin and polypeptide structure. They suggest that it is formed within the neuron and extruded during nerve activity, thus, provoking true neurogenic inflammation (see previous discussion on pain.)

It is Sicuteri's (1963) opinion that the mast cells are involved in the microcirculatory changes that accompany migraine, and that activation of the mast cells by histamine liberators, such as 48/80, evokes reactions similar to the ones observed in classical migraine. In this respect it is of note that lysergic acid derivatives will interfere with the activation of mast cells by histamine liberators. Sicuteri believes that the headache prophylaxis provided by these agents is related to the effect. Futhermore, Sicuteri et al. (1961) have been able to demonstrate an increase in vanilmandelic acid and 5-hydroxy-tryptamine in the urine at the time of a migraine crisis. The significance of these observaions, which have not been consistently confirmed, is unknown at present.

Sicuteri (1966) provides the following hypothesis of migraine, which he also divides into two phases. The first step is termed adrenergic, and is characterized by vasoconstriction, excitation, and sensory manifestations, but is painless. The second stage is termed indolepeptide, and is attended by severe symptoms which include vasodilatation, pain, and nervous depression.

Sicuteri also finds a vasodilator polypeptide liberated at the capillary level, similar to the one described by Wolff. He believes this to be bradykinin, however.

Schayer (1963) and Zweifach (1964) have suggested that histamine is the substance responsible for much of the control of the microcirculation. Schayer states that this form of histamine, concerned with the intrinsic regulation of the microcirculation, should be termed "induced histamine," to distinguish it from histamine that is bound to the tissues. Induced histamine is believed to be newly synthesized in a pharmocodynamically active form in or near the vascular endothelial cells (Schayer 1962). Thus the amount of histamine formed is related to changing environmental conditions and large numbers of stimuli. Schayer postulates that the induced histamine is not a by-product of microcirculatory changes, but that it is in fact their direct mediator. The regulation of the small vessels may then be autonomous; furthermore, Schayer believes that the glucocorticoids produce their effects through moderating the microcirculatory actions of induced histamine. He posits that a number of major observations on migraine headache patients are shown to be clearly comprehensible when viewed in the light of the histamine glucocorticoids relationship.

It has recently been demonstrated that serotonin constricts the scalp arteries in man (Lance et al., 1967) and that the plasma level of serotonin falls suddenly at the onset of migraine (Curran et al., 1965; Anthony et al., 1967). These authors suggest that the sudden withdrawal of the tonic constriction provided by serotonin is one of the factors that permits the extracranial vasodilatation which is characteristic of migraine. They suggest that methysergide may be useful in migraine primarily because it simulates the vascular action of serotonin by maintaining tonic vasoconstriction when the serotonin levels fall. This proposition is supported by the observations of De la Lande and his co-workers (1966), who found that methysergide potentiated the vasoconstrictor effect of norepinephrine in the same manner as serotonin when tested on an isolated perfused artery of the rabbit's ear. This effect of methysergide confirms studies cited below (Dalessio, 1962).

Hanington and Harper (1968) have investigated the effects of tyramine, a pressor amine found in patients taking monoamine oxidase inhibitors, in the production of headache. They were able to provoke headache in susceptible subjects who were given tyramine by mouth in a blind trial. This finding is of interest since tyramine is contained in many foods that have been implicated in the production of migraine in the past. These foods include especially cheeses. The authors suggest that in some patients an excess of tyramine in the blood liberates norepinephrine from the tissues. This might give rise to a selective cerebral vasoconstriction and a generalized extracerebral vasoconstriction. When tissue stores of norepinephrine are exhausted, a rebound vasodilatation occurs, affecting primarily the extracerebral vessels, with the production of vascular headache.

If the size of the small vessels of the intracranial and extracranial circulation is, then, related to local hormonal control, what of the profound alterations of major arterial trunks which may occur during migraine? What is the nature of neurons and synapses by which this entire process is initiated and nurtured?

Recently, interest has been stimulated by the properties of methysergide (Sansert) which has been reported by many observers to be effective in the prophylaxis of migraine headache, although it is relatively ineffective in the therapy of an acute attack. In addition to its importance as a therapeutic agent, this medication afforded an opportunity to investigate further the pathophysiology of the syndrome from other aspects.

Initially, because of its structural similarity to the vasoconstrictor ergot alkaloids. and because of some intrinsic vasoconstrictor properties which became readily apparent, it was presumed that methysergide exerted its effects through the production of a permanent state of vasoconstriction. The demonstration that it would also potentiate blood vessel responses to catecholamines was further evidence in this regard. It became obvious, however, that although these properties were of importance in the prophylaxis of headache in some instances, there were many patients who experienced relief from headache, yet did not manifest significant vasoconstriction. Furthermore, reports in the literature of improvement in peripheral vascular disease obtained after treatment with methysergide were difficult to reconcile with this concept (see, for instance, Dalessio, 1962).

A series of experiments (Dalessio, 1963) were then designed to test the inference that unstable central vasomotor functions might play a role in the pathophysiology of migraine. Observations were made on the responses of the bulbar conjunctival blood vessels during a period of relative oliguria and diuresis, and on the cold pressor reflex, selected as examples of vasomotor phenomena that could be tested in man. In animals, the pressor reflex produced by unilateral carotid occlusion, the depressor reflex produced by stimulation of the central end of the vagus nerve, and direct stimulation with a sterotaxic instrument of the vasopressor area of the hypothalamus, were employed as models. Inhibition and alteration of the magnitude of all of these vasomotor reflexes was readily produced by the prior administration of methysergide, in man and in animals. Inhibition of vasomotor responses was especially notable in humans subjected to migraine, and was associated with a decrease in intensity and frequency of headaches. These observations suggested that unstable central vasomotor functions are a prime factor in migraine, and that the prophylactic action of methysergide is related, at least in part, to its property of modulating these unstable vasomotor centers.

Since it has been postulated that methysergide diminishes the reactivity of the central vasomotor centers, and in this way diminishes cranial vascular activity, we might properly infer that the central vasomotor centers do play a role in the regulation of the cerebral tone. The mechanism by which methysergide exerts its effects on the central vasomotor centers is unknown. Among its more interesting properties, however, is the capacity of methysergide to inhibit serotonin. This inhibition is competitive and presumably related to a similarity of structure.

Brodie and Shore (1957) by using the concepts of Hess (1954), have suggested that serotonin may function as a neural hormone of a parasympathetic subcortical system that integrates the autonomic nervous system with the remainder of the brain. These authors further suggest that norepinephine may be the hormone of a competitive adrenergic system of a similar sort. Furthermore, it has been demonstrated that the concentration of brain serotonin is intimately related to the functions of the central vasomotor centers in animals. It is at least worthy of speculation, then, to suggest that the antiserotonin action of methysergide may be associated with its ability to modify the functions of the central vasomotor centers.

Thus, concepts of migraine arise, as follows. Migraine is viewed as a form of relatively benign cerebral vasospasm, an episodic disorder of an integrative nature produced by the interaction of the central vasomotor centers, the extra and intracranial blood vessels, and the microcirculation. It involves both central and peripheral vasomotor mechanisms, as well as a sterile inflammatory reaction, evoked by activity of the nervous system, with the eventual production of the clinical-syndrome, as it is appreciated by the patient.

A type of headache similar to the one described above, save that the preheadache phenomena are not so evident, is termed common migraine. The headache may be more often bilateral than unilateral. This clinical distinction is appropriate, since this headache is often more obviously related to environmental stress or obligations, to the menses, or to one's occupation. Descriptive terms such as "weekend headache," "Saturday morning headache," or "premenstrual headache" are commonly included in this group. It has been postulated that the degree of vascular responsiveness of patients in this group is not as significant as the ones demonstrated by patients with classic migraine. Hence both the preheadache phenomena and the headache itself are usually less intense in common migraine.

Vascular Headache—Cluster Headache

This headache is delineated by virtue of its unique clinical characteristics. It is consistently periodic, of short duration, often nocturnal, with associated unilateral lacrimation and rhinorrhea. It more nearly resembles a paroxysmal disorder than any other form of migraine. Horton (1956) attributes this type of headache to a unique form of histamine sensitivity, and advises that desensitization with increasing doses of parenteral histamine be used in its therapy. Kunkle (1959) suggests that a parasympathetic discharge involving the seventh, and, more rarely, the tenth cranial nerves may evoke this form of headache. The detection of an acetylcholinelike substance in the cerebrospinal fluid during an attack supports this view.

The patholphysiology of vasodilation during cluster headache is similar to that occurring in classical migraine. Clinical evidence points strongly to a locally liberated vasodilator agent of some nature. Lovshin (1963) believes that this form of headache is particularly susceptible to prophylaxis with methysergide, suggesting again that both central and peripheral factors play a role here, as in classical migraine.

Vascular Headache—Hemiplegic Migraine and Ophthalmoplegic Migraine

Vascular reactions as described in the section on classical migraine are also operative here. In hemiplegic migraine the vascular reactions may be exaggerated to the point that long lasting ischemia of brain tissue occurs. It is of note that this form of migraine may be strikingly familial, suggesting again that an inherited instability of vascular control is present (see Goodell et al., 1954). Whether the sequelae of this form of migraine are related to the prolongation of the vasodilator or of the vasoconstrictor phases of migraine is unknown; possibly both factors are implicated.

In opthalmoplegic migraine, first described by Charcot, ocular palsy is associated with headache. Those structures served by the third cranial nerve are most often involved. This is considered as a result of the pressure on the nerve exerted by the dilated and edematous wall of the internal carotid artery and its branches (Friedman et al., 1961). Segmental narrowing of all or part of the intracranial portion of the internal carotid artery has been demonstrated by arteriography in patients in the midst of a migraine attack. It has also been suggested that brain edema produced by migraine may provoke herniation of the hippocampal gyrus to a degree significant to compress the third nerve, but this concept is speculative.

In patients with repeated attacks, ocular palsies are usually transitory. Rarely, however, these palsies may become persistent. It is important to differentiate between the mechanisms operative in ophthalmoplegic migraine, and the ones that produce similar symptoms but that are related to intracranial aneurysms.

Vascular Headaches—Toxic Vascular Headache

This category of headache includes all those medical diseases and conditions that produce headache of a vascular nature as a part of their overall symptomatic picture. The most common nonmigrainous vascular headache is the one produced by fever. Generalized vasodilation may occur as a consequence of any fever of significance, with the vasodilatation usually becoming more intense as the fever rises. Particularly intense vascular headaches may occur with pneumonia, tonsillitus, septicemia, typhoid fever, tularemia, influenza, measles, mumps, poliomyelitis, infectious mononucleosis, malaria, and trichinosis. The vasodilatation that occurs in these situations is often intracranial as well as extracranial. Pickering (1939) demonstrated that increasing the cerebrospinal fluid pressure by means of a manometer attached to a needle in the lumbar subarachoid space reduced fever headache, which evidence supports this view.

In addition, nonmigrainous headache may occur in a whole series of miscellaneous disorders which include diverse entities such as "hangover headache" and headache associated with hypoglycemia from whatever cause. In hypoxic states, headaches may be a persistent complaint, especially where an increased CO_2 tension in the blood exists concurrently. Exposure to carbon monoxide may provoke an extremely severe form of vascular headache. Headaches may be produced by the administration of nitrates, either as medicament or unintentionally, as in industry. Many poisons may evoke headache, including lead, benzene, carbon tetrachloride, and insecticides. Treatment with monamine oxidase inhibitors may evoke serious headache, especially when small amounts of catecholamines are ingested at the same time. The headache produced by this combination may be catastrophic, and death has been reported in these circumstances, as well as cerebrovascular accidents.

Withdrawal from many pharmacologic agents may provoke headache. This is especially liable to occur after prolonged therapy with ergot derivatives, but may also follow the discontinuation of caffeine, benzedrine, and many of the phenothiazines. Treatment of arthritis with indomethacin may evoke headache, presumably by producing a chemical vasodilatation.

Muscle Contraction Headache—Cervical Osteoarthritis and Chronic Myositis

This is perhaps the most common form of headache. It has been demonstrated that sustained contraction of the muscles of the scalp and neck occur in this form of headache, with the production thereafter of chronic, often dull but persistent pain. These headaches are often sustained, and may persist for weeks, months, or years. Examination of the patient with this form of headache will usually demonstrate one or many tender areas, especially in the posterior great muscles of the neck, as well as muscular contraction and limitation of motion. Excessive muscular contraction may also be demonstrated by electromyography. Onel and his associates (1961) have shown an increase in muscle blood flow during muscle contraction headache, by using a radioactive sodium tracer. They suggest, however, that this increased blood flow may be related to muscle contraction only, and do not infer that the increased blood flow evokes pain. Indeed, patients with this form of headache are not benefited by the use of vasoconstrictor agents. This form of pain is presumably related to prolonged contraction of muscles of the face, neck, and scalp; eventually this form of response may evoke localized areas of fibrositis or chronic myositis. These findings are more likely to occur in patients with associated osteoarthritis of the cervical spine.

Muscle Contraction Headache—Depressive Equivalents and Conversion Reactions

In this category are also included headaches that do not appear related to structural or organic disease. This is a broad category of headache in which unconsciously simulated chronic headache may serve to obscure a serious emotional disorder, most often a depression. The patients complain of specific and enduring headache for which no organic basis can be found. Anxiety and especially depressive symptoms are converted into acceptable (to the patient) physical symptoms. This form of headache may vary considerably depending on the structure and the stresses engendered by the culture in which it occurs. As the general level of education and sophistication rises, so also the complaints of patients with headaches of this sort become more complex. These patients are usually convinced of the somatic nature of their complaints. Many patients with post-traumatic headaches may fit into this category, especially when their complaints are prolonged and the initial injury was trivial. Walker (1965) makes this point in a review of patients with post-traumatic headache. These individuals were demonstrated to have elevations in their hysterical, depressive, and hypochrondriacal scales when psychologic testing was performed. Walker interprets their headaches as a manifestation of an inappropriate reaction to trauma that occurs in persons with an already vulnerable personality.

Traction and Inflammatory Headaches—Mass Lesions

Headache from intracranial sources is produced most often by inflammation, traction, displacement, or distension of the pain sensitive structures of the head, usually blood vessels. Most of this displacement is produced by traction, and hence the term "traction headache" is used to cover this group. This form of headache is evoked by hematomas of any sort, abscesses, nonspecific brain "edema" and, perhaps, after lumbar puncture. In particular, traction headache is produced by brain tumors. In the latter situation, local traction on adjacent pain-sensitive structures by the brain tumor may occur, as well as distant traction which is related to displacement of the brain. Thus, distant traction may be related to the tumor mass directly, or indirectly, when internal hydrocephalus and ventricular obstruction occur. For this reason, localization of a brain tumor by determining the site of headache can be unreliable. Nonetheless, several clinical maxims that relate to this situation are worthy of repetition. When a brain tumor is located in the posterior fossa, the headache is usually occipital. As Symonds (1956) has reported, in this situation the headache evoked by coughing may be a significant clue. When the tumor is located superior to the tentorium, the headache is most often appreciated in the anterior aspects of the skull. Finally, in the absence of papilledema, the headache is usually found on the same side as the brain tumor. It has been possible to demonstrate localized skull tenderness at the site of meningiomas, or in the mastoid area with a cerebello-pontine angle tumor, presumably because of local involvement and extension into the skull or its structures by these tumors.

Traction and Inflammatory Headache—Arteritis and Infections

This form of headache is related to inflammatory processes within or without the skull. In particular, headaches associated with meningitis, subarachnoid hemorrhage, intracranial arteritis, and phlebitis should be included in this group. The pain of the headache is evoked by an inflammatory response that includes the pain-sensitive structures of the head. The head pain is in most instances coincident with the course of the disease, is not recurrent or paroxysmal, and usually remits as the disease comes under control.

Extracranial inflammation may also produce headache. The mechanism operative here is inflammation of the extracranial arteries. This may be observed in a localized form, as it occurs in temporal arteritis, or in a more generalized disease as a part of a widespread collagen-vascular syndrome. The intracranial arteritis that may occur as a part of systemic lupus erythematosis or periarteritis nodosa can produce excruciating headache of a generalized nature.

The headache of temporal arteritis may occur in the absence of obvious clinical signs of that disease. Recently, interest in temporal arteritis has increased, with the observation that even this localized form of arteritis may be a manifestation of a more subtle, generalized disease, which has been termed the temporal arteritis-polymyalgia rheumatica complex (Alestig & Barr, 1963).

The etiology of the arteritis that generates the headache in these cases is unknown, although it has been suggested that this lesion represents another example of an auto-immune reaction in an immunologically defective individual.

Toxic and Inflammatory Headache—Disease of the Cranial or Neck Structures

Headache may be related to disease of the eyes, nose, teeth, or to pathology in any of the other structures of the head. Noxious stimuli can be evoked by localized pressure phenomena, muscle contraction, trauma, tumor, or inflammation. Generally, these headaches are well localized to the affected area, although on occasion, because of central spread of excitation, their effects may be appreciated in more distant regions of the skull. These persistent painful stimuli may lower pain threshold and so evoke other forms of headache of different types. For example, pain from ocular disease can be related to several different mechanisms and, thus, can present a diagnostic challenge to the clinician Eye pain may occur with increased ocular pressure, traction on ocular muscles, inflammation of the eye tissues, hyperopia or astigmatism, exposure to light, new growths, or trauma. In pseudotumor of the orbit, severe pain is felt along with the appearance of ophthalmoplegia, usually because of an inflammatory lesion of the cavernous sinus, or of the orbit itself.

The headache that is related to nasal disease is usually anterior in nature, and is often related to nasal vasomotor phenomena. The symptoms are accompanied by local pain and discomfort. The demonstration of a precise paranasal disease, such as sinusitis, or allergic rhinitis, usually removes the headache from this category. This form of headache is often associated with "vasomotor rhinitis" and is assumed to represent a localized vascular reaction to stress.

Traction and Inflammatory Headaches—Cranial Neuritis and Neuralgias

This category includes those forms of facial pain that are related to pain perceived by the cranial nerves, excluding the trigeminal and glossopharyngeal neuralgias. This group usually includes the atypical facial neuralgias, lower half headache, vidian neuralgias, carotidynia, buccal neuralgia, and the like. Some of these syndromes are poorly developed and may not deserve separate status. Some of them probably represent vascular pain, or a form of migraine that is perceived in an unusual location. This is particularly true of lower half headaches, which may respond to prophylaxis with lysergic acid derivatives such as methysergide.

The syndromes delineated as trigeminal neuralgia (tic douloureux) and glossopharyngeal neuralgia are better characterized.

In tic douloureux, the pain is experienced chiefly in the tissues supplied by the second and, to a lesser extent, the third and first divisions of the fifth cranial nerve. It may be felt in any part of the face, but never below the ramus of the jaw or in back of the ear, and rarely in the entire distribution of the fifth nerve at any one time. The pain is of an aching and burning quality, and may occur spontaneously, but is more often initiated by cold air or a light touch on the skin of the cheek, or by biting, chewing, laughing, swallowing, talking, yawning, sneezing, or similar movements. The pain is usually described as a high-intensity "jab" of 20 to 30 seconds' duration that is followed by a period of relative freedom from pain of a few seconds to a minute, to be followed again by another jab of high-intensity pain. The pains do not last longer than a minute. The attack, or series of these brief pains, usually lasts one or more hours.

Glossopharyngeal tic is a related phenomenon. Here, similar pain of a severe nature, as described above, is experienced in the tonsillar area and the ear. It is often initiated by eating, yawning, or swallowing. Syncope may occur during the painful episode, presumably because of asystole.

Treatment of Headache

It may be helpful to consider the possible treatment of an individual patient with recurrent headache. This presumes that a thorough medical workup has been done, and that those conditions that predispose the patient to traction and inflammatory headache have been ruled out. If this has been done successfully, and it may take no little effort, one may then assume that the headache is of a benign type, although this does not necessarily mean that it is any less painful or distressing to the patient. The headache in question is thus assumed to be either vascular or related to muscular contraction, or a combination of both.

Vascular headaches have been described in detail above. The cornerstone of treatment of vascular headache is ergot in one form or another. Ergot must be given early in the headache process, and in an adequate dose, if it is to be effective. Oral ergot is sometimes well tolerated. If nausea is a problem, however, some other form of ergot should be employed. Many of them exist, including sublingual, rectal and parenteral forms, as well as an ergot nebulizer. The author finds it helpful to add a sedative agent to the ergot prescription. A phenothiazine such as prochlorperazine is particularly useful in this regard, since it has antiemetic properties as well.

If vascular headache is recurrent, and occurs more often than twice weekly, thereby seriously interfering with the patient's happiness and productivity, some form of headache prophylaxis should be attempted. Methysergide is most effective in this regard, but should not be given for longer than three months consecutively, because of the side effects of significance that may occur with the chronic ingestion of this drug. Cyproheptadine is less effective than methysergide for this purpose, but it has the advantage of being considerably less toxic and may be employed for prolonged periods. The author has little experience with the use of histamine, given parenterally in an attempt to reduce individual response to its vasodilator properties. Others are convinced of its efficacy, particularly in cluster headaches. No specific diet is given to headache patients, except that they are advised to avoid alcohol and other vasodilators, as well as foods that contain large amounts of tyramine, such as cheese.

If it can be determined that the headache is nonvascular, and is associated with chronic muscular contraction, ergot will not be helpful. Here one relies on aspirin, often combined with a mild sedative such as phenobarbital or a related agent. Compounds that contain phenacetin should be avoided. It is not wise to allow the patient to use aspirin or any other analgesic in a continuous manner. Narcotics should never be provided. Patients with chronic tension headache are very often significantly depressed. Their headache will be relieved as their depression remits. This may be accomplished by using tricyclic antidepressants of the amitryptyline variety. These agents should be given over a prolonged period, usually 90 days, and possibly longer on a lower, maintenance dose. Environmental counseling and manipulation may be helpful. Behavioral therapy may be tried. The author has little experience with hypnosis. Referral for formal psychiatric counseling may be necessary.

Less often simple physical therapy to the neck and head may be helpful. This is indicated especially if significant cervical osteoarthritis is present. A local injection of trigger areas may be attempted. Operative section of the occipital nerves is unwise and should be avoided.

Anticonvulsants such as diphenylhydantoin and carbamazepine should not be used, unless typical tic douloureux is present.

The successful treatment of a patient with chronic headache may not be easily accomplished. The physician will often find that his therapeutic suggestions have not brought forth the desired result. Patience and perseverance on the part of both physician and patient may be necessary. The art of medical practice may be more important here than scientific pharmacology. The physician must first remember to do no harm (*Primum Non Nocere*), since headache complications associated with analgesic abuse are almost always more dangerous than the headaches themselves. Nonetheless, with careful attention to the whole patient, some resolution of the problem can be achieved in the majority of patients who complain of headache.

REFERENCES

Adams, F. *Extant works of Aretaeus the Cappadocian*, London: The Syndenham Society, 1856.

Alestig, K., and Barr, J. Giant-cell arteritis. *Lancet*, 1963, **1**, 1228.

Anthony, M., Hinterberger, H., & Lance, J. W. Plasma serotonin in migraine and stress. *Arch Neurol.*, 1967, **16**, 544.

Armstrong, D., Keele, A., Jepson, J. B., & Stewart, J. W. Pain producing substances in human inflammatory exudates and plasma. *J. Physiol.*, 1957, **135**, 350.

Aurelianus, Caelius: Liber 1. De Capitis Passione, Quam Graeci Cephalaean Nomiant. In: *Medici Antique Omnes Qui Latinis, etc. Venetiis* 1547, pp. 249–258, **4**.

Beecher, H. K, Pain in men wounded in battle. *Ann. Surg.*, 1946, **123**, 96.

Bickerstaff, E. R. Basilar artery migraine. *Lancet*, 1961, **1**, 15.

Brodie, B. B., & Shore, P. A. A concept for the role of serotonin and norepinephrine as chemical mediators in the brain. *Ann. N. Y. acad. Sci.*, 1957, **66**, 631.

Catino, D. Ten migraine equivalents. *Headache*, 1965, **5**, 1.

Chapman, L. F., Goodell, H., & Wolff, H. G. Augmentation of the central nervous system. *A. M. A. Archives of Neurology*, 1959, **1**, 557.

Chapman, L. F., Goodell, H., & Wolff, H. G. Changes in tissue vulnerability induced during hypnotic suggestion. *J. Psychosom Res.*, 1959, **4**, 99.

Chapman, L. F., Ramos, A. O., Goodell, H., & Wolff, H. G. Neurokinin: A polypeptide formed during neuronal activity in man. *Trans. Am. Neurol. Assn.*, 1960, **85**, 42.

Curran, D. A., Hinterberger, H., & Lance, J. W. Total plasma serotonin 5-hydroxyindoleacetic acid and p-hydroxy-m-methoxymandelic acid. Excretion in normal and migrainous subjects. *Brain*, 1965, **88**, 997.

Dalessio, D. J. On migraine headache: Serotonin and serotonin antagonism. *J.A.M.A.*, 1962, **181**, 318.

Dalessio, D. J Recent experimental studies on headache. *Neurology*, 1963, **13**, 7.

Dalessio, D. J. Medical treatment of tic douloureux. *J. Chron. Dis.*, 1966, **19**, 1043.

De la Lande, I. S., Cannell, V. A., & Waterson, J. G. The interaction of serotonin and noradrenaline on the perfused artery. *Brit. J. Pharmacol.*, 1966, **28**, 255.

DuBois-Reymond, E. Zur Kenntniss der Hemikrania. *Arch. F. Anat. Phys. U. wiss.*, ed., 1860, pp. 461–468.

Eccles, J. C. *The physiology of synapses.* New York: Academic Press Inc., 1964.

Friedman, A. P., Harter, H., & Merritt, H. H. Ophthalmoplegic migraine. *Trans. Am. Neurol. Assn.*, 1961, **86**, 169.

Galen. De Compositione Medicamentorum Secundum Locos. In: Opera Omnia. Ed. Kuhn. Lipsiae: C. Cnoblochii. Tomus XII, Liber II, Cap. III. (de Hemicrania), 1826, p. 591.

Goodell, H., Lewontin, R., & Wolff, H. G. The Familial occurrence of migraine headache: A study of heredity. *Arch. Neurol. and Psychiat.*, 1954, **72**, 325.

Graham, J. R., & Wolff, H. G. Mechanism of migraine headache and action of ergotamine tartrate. *Arch. Neurol. and Psychiat.*, 1938, **39**, 737.

Hagbarth, K. E., & Finer, B. L. The plasticity of human withdrawal reflexes to noxious skin stimuli in lower limbs, In Moruzzi, G., Fessard, A., & Jasper, H. H., Eds., *Progress in brain research*, Vol. 1, Amsterdam: Elsevier, 1963, p. 64.

Hanington, E., & Harper, A. M. The Role of tyramine in the etiology of migraine, and related studies on the cerebral and extracerebral circulations. *Headache*, 1968, **8**, 84.

Hess, W. R. Diencephalon, autonomic and extrapyramidal functions. *Monogr. Biol. Med.*, Vol. 3, Grune and Stratton, 1954.

Honde, R. W., Wikler, A., & Irwin, S. Comparative actions of analgesics, hypnotic and paralytic agents on hindlimb reflexes in chronic spinal dogs. *J. Pharmae. Exp. Ther.*, 1951, **103**, 243.

Horton, B. T. Histaminic cephalgia differential diagnosis and treatment *Proc. Mayo Clin.*, 1956, **31**, 325.

Iggo, A. Cutaneous mechanoreceptors with afferent C fibers. *J. Physiol.*, 1960, **152**, 337.

Kunkle, E. C. Acetylcholine in the mechanisms of headache of the migraine type. *Arch. Neurol. and Psychiat*. 1959, **81**, 135.

Lance, J. W., & Curran, D. A. Treatment of Chronic Tension headache. *Lancet* 1964, **1**, 1236.

Lance, J. W., Anthony, M., & Gonski, A. Serotonin the carotid body, and cranial vessels in migraine. *Arch. Neurol.*, 1967, **16**, 553.

Lasagna, L., & Werner, G. Conjoint clinic on pain and analgesia. *J. Chron. Dis.*, 1966, **19**, 695.

Lepois, C. Selectoirum observationum. Ludg. Batav. Boutestein, C., and Langerak, J. A. *De Hemicrania*, 1714, pp. 67–77.

Lim, R. K. S. Salicylate analgesia. In M. J. H. Smith (Ed.), *The salicylates*. New York: Wiley, 1966.

Lim, R. K. S. A revised concept of the mechanisms of analgesia and pain. *Henry Ford Hospital Int. Symposium on Pain*. Boston: Little Brown, 1966.

Liveing, E. *On megrim. Sick-headache and some allied disorders.* London: Chruchill, 1873.

Livingston, W. K. *Pain mechanisms*. New York: MacMillan, 1943.

Lovshin, L. L. Treatment of histaminic cephalalgia with methysergide. *Dis. Nerv. Sys.*, 1963, **24**, 3.

Melzack, R., & Haugen, F. P. Responses evoked at the cortex by tooth stimulation. *Am. J. Physiol.*, 1957, **190**, 570.

Melzack, R., & Wall, P. D. Pain mechanisms: A new theory. *Science*, 1965, **150**, 337.

Onel, Y., Friedman, A. P., & Crossman, J. Muscle blood flow studies in muscle-contraction headaches. *Neurology*, 1961, **11**, 935.

Ostfeld, A. M., & Wolff, H. G. Identification, mechanisms and management of the migraine syndrome. *Med. Clin. N. A.*, 1958, **42**, 1497.

Pavlov, I. P. *Conditioned reflexes*. Oxford: Milford, 1927.

Pickering, G. W. Experimental observations on headache. *Brit. Med. J.*, 1939, **1**, 4087.

Poggio, G. F., & Mountcastle, V. B. A study of functional contributions of the lemniscal and spinothalamic systems to somatic sensibility. *Bull. Johns. Hopkins Hosp.*, 1960, **106**, 266.

Ray, B. S., & Wolff, H. G. Experimental studies on headache. Pain sensitive structures of the head and their significance in headache. *Arch. Surg.*, 1940, **41**, 813.

Rocha e Silva, M., Beraldo, W. T., & Rosenfeld, G. Bradykinin. A hypotensive and smooth muscle stimulating factor released from plasma globulin by snake venom and by trypsin. *Am. J. Physiol.*, 1949, **156**, 261

Schayer, R. W. Evidence that induced histamine is an intrinsic regulator of the microcirculatory system. *Am. J. Physiol.*, 1962, **202**, 66.

Schayer, R. W. Significance of induced synthesis of histamine and its possible relationship to headache. *Headache*, 1963, **3**, 67.

Sicuteri, F., Testi, A., & Anselmi, B. Biochemical investigations in headache. *Int. Arch. Allergy and Applied Immunology*, 1961, **19**, 55.

Sicuteri, F. Mast cells and their active substances: Their role in the pathogenesis of migraine. *Headache*, 1963, **3**, 86.

Sicuteri, F. Vasoneuractive substances in migraine. *Headache*, 1966, **6**, 109.

Symonds, C. P. Cough headache. *Brain* 1956, **79**, 557.

Tissot, S. S. D. Traite des Nerfs et de Leurs Maladies. Paris. Ed., Lausanne, 1783.

Walker, A. E. Chronic post-traumatic headache. *Headache* 1965, **5**, 67.

Wepfer, J. J. Observations medico-practicae de affectibus capitis internis et extremis. Schaffhausen, J. A. Ziegler, 1927.

Wolff, H. G. *Headache and other head pain.* New York: Oxford University Press, 1963.

Wolff, A. L., & Quest, I. A. Fatal infarction of the brain in migraine. *Brit. Med. J.*, 1964, **1**, 225.

Zweifach, B. W. Microcirculatory aspects of tissue injury. *Ann. N. Y. Acad. Sci.*, 1964, **116**, 831.

Appendix

Werry-Weiss-Peters Activity Scale

	NO	YES-A LITTLE BIT	YES-VERY MUCH
During Meals			
Up and down at table	☐	☐	☐
Interrupts without regard	☐	☐	☐
Wriggling	☐	☐	☐
Fiddles with things	☐	☐	☐
Talks excessively	☐	☐	☐
Television			
Gets up and down during program	☐	☐	☐
Wriggles	☐	☐	☐
Manipulates objects or body	☐	☐	☐
Talks incessantly	☐	☐	☐
Interrupts	☐	☐	☐
Doing Home-work			
Gets up and down	☐	☐	☐
Wriggles	☐	☐	☐
Manipulates objects or body	☐	☐	☐
Talks incessantly	☐	☐	☐
Requires adult supervision or attendance	☐	☐	☐
Play			
Inability for quiet play	☐	☐	☐
Constantly changing activity	☐	☐	☐
Seeks parental attention	☐	☐	☐
Talks excessively	☐	☐	☐
Disrupts other's play	☐	☐	☐
Sleep			
Inability for quiet play	☐	☐	☐
Inadequate amount of sleep	☐	☐	☐
Restless during sleep	☐	☐	☐
Behavior away from home (except school)			
Restlessness during travel	☐	☐	☐
Restlessness during shopping (includes touching everything)	☐	☐	☐
Restlessness during church/movies	☐	☐	☐
Restlessness during visiting friends, relatives, etc.	☐	☐	☐
School Behavior			
Up and down	☐	☐	☐
Fidgets, wriggles, touches	☐	☐	☐
Interrupts teacher or other children excessively	☐	☐	☐
Constantly seeks teacher's attention	☐	☐	☐
Total score	____	____	____

Author Index

Subject Index